The **Rough**

Central
America
ON A BUDGET

this edition written and researched by
**Caroline Daly, Amber Dobrzensky, Huw Hennessy,
Neil McQuillian, Shafik Meghji, James Smart and Iain Stewart**

ROUGH
GUIDES

www.roughguides.com

Contents

◀◀ ROADSIDE STALL, PANAMA ◀ TREE FROG, COSTA RICA

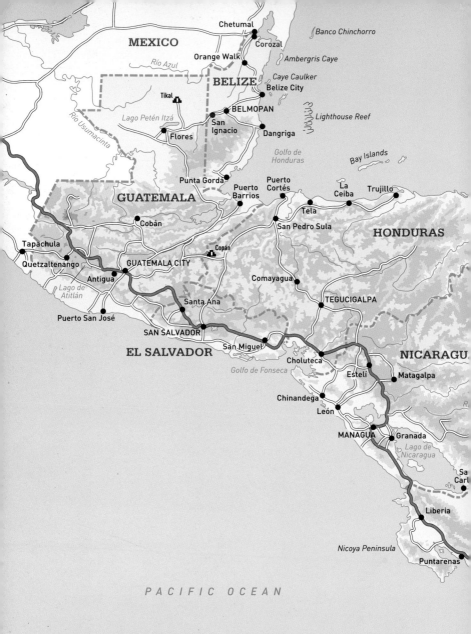

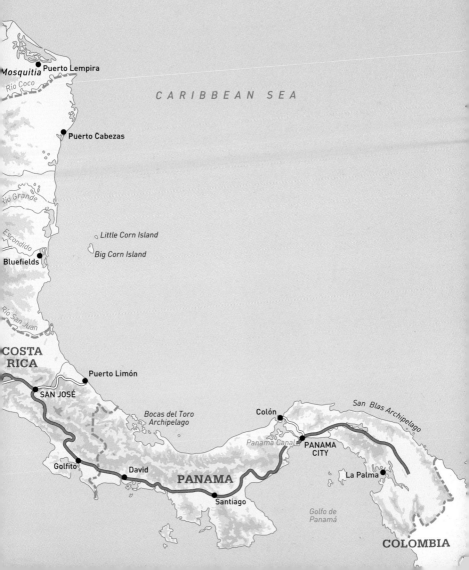

N

Metres
4000
3000
2000
1000
500
200
0

Mosquitia ● Puerto Lempira

Río Coco

CARIBBEAN SEA

● **Puerto Cabezas**

Río Grande

Escondido

○ *Little Corn Island*

○ *Big Corn Island*

Bluefields ●

Río San Juan

COSTA RICA

● **Puerto Limón**

● **SAN JOSÉ**

Bocas del Toro Archipelago

Colón ●

San Blas Archipelago

Panama Canal ● **PANAMA CITY**

● **Golfito**

● **David**

PANAMA

Santiago ●

Golfo de Panamá

● **La Palma**

COLOMBIA

Introduction to
Central America

Small in size but packed with an exotic mix of volcano-dotted landscapes, atmospheric colonial towns, jungle-shrouded relics and desert-island beaches, Central America is what travellers' dreams are made of. In contrast to its big brother further south, the region's diminutive area makes country-hopping both straightforward and cheap. In the space of a day you could be lazing on a white-sand beach, then wildlife-spotting in lush jungle, before spending your evening sampling the local rum and dancing the night away in one of the many laidback surf towns. The next day could be spent whitewater rafting and soothing your aches and pains in hot springs, followed by a dinner of home-cooked comida típica under the highland stars.

Unfairly overlooked in the past, in recent years this slender isthmus has really come into its own, and travellers are increasingly making Central America the sole focus of their trip. It may look insignificant on the map – at its narrowest point the isthmus is squeezed to a mere 65 kilometres across – but the region's unique topography ensures that there's enough here to fill months of travel. Crammed into this small area, coral-fringed beaches give way to dense jungle that, in turn, yields to brooding volcanic highlands, while towering Maya ruins find their modern-day counterpart in the skyscraper-stacked skylines of metropolises such as Panama City and Guatemala City. Travelling from place to place is easy and won't break the budget: a combination of the colourful local "chicken buses", border-crossing international coaches, and *lanchas* and ferries for sea trips will get you wherever the fancy takes you.

Relatively well set up for travellers, English-speaking **Belize** makes a good first stop; most travellers head to the cobalt blue waters of the

VOLCÁN CONCEPCIÓN, NICARAGUA

cayes and atolls to dive the longest barrier reef in the Americas, or you could spend a few nights on the lookout for big cats in a jaguar reserve. In **Guatemala**, trek through jungle to discover Maya ruins, kick back in colonial Antigua or head for the hills to haggle in vibrant indigenous markets. While its world-class Pacific surf beaches are no secret, much of **El Salvador** is off the tourist trail: if you're after peace and quiet head for the flower-filled villages and coffee plantations of the Ruta de las Flores, or the magnificent rainforest of Bosque El Imposible. The Bay Islands are **Honduras's** main draw: the archetypal Caribbean dream

Chicken buses

One authentic piece of Latin American culture that you'll soon become familiar with is the "chicken bus". Called "camionetas", "colectivos" or simply "buses" (pronounced "boo-ses") in Spanish, these contraptions are colourfully repainted and repurposed US school buses. In pastel or primary colours, with decorations both religious and profane dangling and jangling from every corner and destinations hand-lettered on the front windscreen, travelling by chicken bus is an economical and unforgettable experience. Passengers, goods and livestock jostle along bumpy roads, embarking and departing with great frequency in a boisterous and generally well-timed dance of old tyres, children, overstuffed luggage and boxes of peeping chicks (the buses' namesake). Though Guatemala is particularly known for its chicken buses, versions of this mode of transport can be found throughout Central America.

of swaying palms and powdery white sand, they also provide plenty of opportunities for watersports on a budget. At the other end of the tourism scale, the largely uninhabited Mosquitia offers an enormous variety of wildlife, as well as the possibility of trips to remote Garífuna villages. Billed by many as the up-and-coming travel destination of the Americas, **Nicaragua** boasts the lively colonial towns of León and Granada, volcano-strewn landscapes and idyllic, low-key islands such as Little Corn. No less beautiful, **Costa Rica** is one of the region's biggest draws and a well-established ecotourism destination, with its million-year-old rainforests and pristine beaches; learn to surf at Playa Tamarindo, admire the macaws in Parque Nacional Corcovado, or watch turtles lay their eggs on the Caribbean coast. **Panama**'s laidback Bocas del Toro archipelago is celebrated for its unmissable diving and chilled-out surf scene, or you could explore buzzing Panama City or the highlands around Boquete, home to hiking trails, hot springs and what many regard as the world's finest coffee.

See our **Ideas** section for more can't-miss destinations, events and activities throughout Central America, and check out our **Itineraries** to help chart the best adventures throughout the region. Whether you follow these routes or set out on your own, our **Basics** section gives you all the practical information you'll need. Each chapter within the **Guide** kicks off with a country profile covering key places not to miss, plus rough costs for food, accommodation and transport.

CHICHICASTENANGO MARKET, GUATEMALA

When to go

Subtropical Central America overflows with verdant landscapes, nourished by the semiannual rhythms of the wet and dry seasons. Tourism is at its peak during the **dry season** – or "summer" (*verano*) – that runs from roughly from December to April. The **rainy season**, often called "winter" (*invierno*), lasts from May until November. The different seasons are more distinctly felt on the Pacific side of the isthmus than they are on the Caribbean, and the major determining factor of climate here is altitude. Coming from sea level or the lowland plains to the interior highlands can grant welcome relief from high heat and humidity. Average **temperatures** here are a good 10°C (15–20°F) cooler than in low-lying areas, where humidity levels can be uncomfortable and temperatures hover in the mid-thirties (95°F) for much of the year. See the "When to visit" boxes in each chapter's Introduction for a country-specific overview.

Coming to Central America to escape the dreary winter days of chillier climes is always welcome, but it's worth considering a trip during the wet season, also known as the "green season", when tourism lulls and cut-price deals are to be found. Take extra care when planning a trip at this time of year, as **road conditions** can deteriorate significantly with heavy rains, making travel more difficult. However, rain showers are short-lived afternoon downpours, more often than not, and there's a good chance that changes in the weather will hardly interfere with your trip at all.

Ideas
Festivals and events

DAY OF THE DEAD, SANTIAGO SACATEPÉQUEZ, GUATEMALA
Massive, beautiful kites are flown in the cemetery to commemorate the dead. **See p.149**

SEMANA SANTA, ANTIGUA, GUATEMALA
Spectacular street processions to mark Holy Week. **See p.138**

GARÍFUNA SETTLEMENT DAY, BELIZE
Enthusiastic celebrations to mark the arrival of the Garífuna people in Belize. **See p.99**

CARNAVAL, PANAMA CITY Four days of raucous and vibrant celebrations. **See p.594**

TODOS SANTOS CUCHUMATÁN, GUATEMALA A massive stampede and inebriated riders characterize this outrageous all-day horse race. **See p.184**

Ideas History and culture

WAR MEMORIAL, EL MOZOTE, EL SALVADOR
A moving monument to the country's worst wartime massacre. **See p.289**

COPÁN, HONDURAS
Magnificent Maya site displaying impressive craftsmanship. **See p.357**

KUNA CULTURE, KUNA YALA, PANAMA Experience the fascinating island life of the San Blas archipelago. **See p.636**

TIKAL, GUATEMALA Six awe-inspiring pyramids tower above the rainforest. **See p.227**

IDEAS

COWBOY CULTURE, GUANACASTE, COSTA RICA A distinct region known for its *sabanero* (cowboy) culture. **See p.559**

COLONIAL ARCHITECTURE, LEÓN, NICARAGUA The energetic old capital is home to some beautiful colonial buildings. **See p.423**

Ideas Outdoor activities

SURFING, EL SALVADOR
The Pacific coast boasts some of Central America's best surfing beaches. **See p.266**

HIKING, NICARAGUA
The forested mountains surrounding Matagalpa provide fantastic hiking opportunities. **See p.435**

RAFTING, PANAMA
Exhilarating white water trips on the Chiriquí River. **See p.656**

JAGUAR-SPOTTING, BELIZE Explore the stunning Belizean rainforest in search of these beautiful creatures. **See p.103**

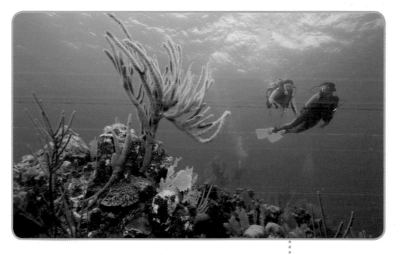

DIVING IN THE BAY ISLANDS, HONDURAS Abundant marine life, clear waters and a stunning coral reef. **See p.390**

VOLCANO-HOPPING, COSTA RICA Activities abound in this spectacular volcanic landscape. **See p.502 & p.564**

ITINERARIES

ITINERARIES

Central America itineraries

You can't expect to fit everything Central America has to offer into one trip and we don't suggest you try. On the following pages are a selection of itineraries that guide you through the different countries, picking out a few of the best places and major attractions along the way. Enjoy the region's startling natural beauty, from the cloudforests of Costa Rica to the coral-fringed islands of Panama's San Blas archipelago; explore the unique indigenous culture of the Maya; and discover remote beaches and world-class diving on the Caribbean coast.

INDIGENOUS CULTURES

❶ **HOPKINS, BELIZE** Stretching along a bay, this small Garifuna village comes alive with the enthusiastic celebrations of Settlement Day, and is a great place to sample the local cuisine. See p.101

❷ **IXIL TRIANGLE, GUATEMALA** Though remote, the three towns of the Ixil triangle are worth the effort for a glimpse of the traditional Ixil way of life, and for spectacular hikes into the surrounding hills. See p.169

❸ **TODOS SANTOS CUCHUMATÁN, GUATEMALA** The unique culture of the indigenous Maya, combined with the beautiful alpine scenery, makes this a favourite with travellers – especially for the experience of the Día de Todos Santos. See p.183

❹ **LA ESPERANZA, HONDURAS** Best visited for its colourful weekend market, when Lenca farmers from the

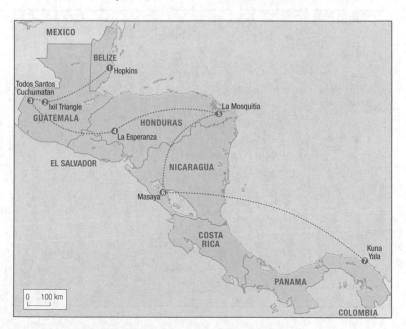

surrounding villages flock to town. In nearby San Juan Intibucá you can watch traditional handicrafts being made. **See p.348**

5 LA MOSQUITIA, HONDURAS
Indulge your spirit of adventure by getting right off the beaten track to explore the indigenous villages of the Caribbean coast in the country's wild southeastern corner. **See p.385**

6 MASAYA, NICARAGUA The centre of Nicaragua's *artesanía* production, this attractive town's walled market is a great place to pick up hammocks, traditional clothing and other handicrafts, while regular festivals bring its streets to vibrant life. **See p.437**

7 KUNA YALA, PANAMA
Encompassing the tropical islands of the San Blas archipelago, the autonomous territory of the Kula people offers a unique opportunity to learn about community life, with the added bonus of beautiful beaches. **See p.633**

ALONG CA-1

From Guatemala to Panama, Central America Highway 1 (part of the Pan-American Highway) runs for over a thousand kilometres past beaches, cities and jungles. The following sites are all en – or just off – route.

1 QUETZALTENANGO, GUATEMALA
This beautifully sited city is a popular spot for learning Spanish or volunteering, and is ideally placed for a leisurely tour of the highlands too. **See p.171**

2 SAN SALVADOR, EL SALVADOR
El Salvador's buzzing capital is occasionally intimidating and rarely peaceful. But with its slowly smartening Centro Histórico, surprisingly green outskirts and politicized museums, it repays a visit. **See p.250**

3 SAN VICENTE, EL SALVADOR
Climb El Salvador's second-highest volcano, eye the famous clock tower and relish the stunning drive to this relaxed city. **See p.281**

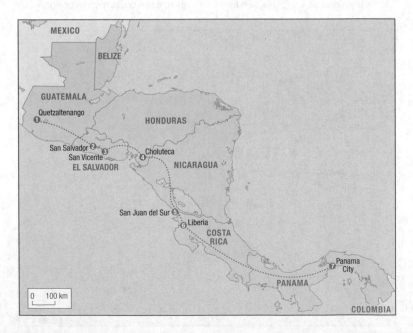

❹ CHOLUTECA, HONDURAS

Steamy, substantial city containing one of Honduras's finest old colonial quarters – the tranquil park and imposing cathedral are among the highlights. **See p.341**

❺ SAN JUAN DEL SUR, NICARAGUA

Located just off the highway in a gorgeous bay washed with rolling Pacific waves, this gringo-friendly beach town offers surfing, turtle-watching, fishing and plenty of nightlife. **See p.451**

❻ LIBERIA, COSTA RICA This beautiful

"White City" is home to a number of festivals and the sleepy colonial Calle Real district. **See p.559**

❼ PANAMA CITY, PANAMA Both

a base for visiting the nearby wildlife and famous canal and a sparkling, cosmopolitan city, this is one of the continent's must-visits. **See p.595**

THE CARIBBEAN COAST

❶ PLACENCIA, BELIZE Away from

the tourist hustle of the north, this relaxed fishing village has Belize's best beaches, inexpensive accommodation and a growing arts scene. **See p.104**

❷ LÍVINGSTON, GUATEMALA Carib

cuisine, punta rock and reggae make Lívingston a great place to party and an intriguing contrast to Guatemala's latino interior. **See p.198**

❸ BAY ISLANDS, HONDURAS

This 125-kilometre chain of islands off Honduras's Caribbean coast is a perfect destination for world-class (and affordable) diving, sailing and fishing. **See p.388**

❹ RÍO PLÁTANO BIOSPHERE

RESERVE, HONDURAS This UNESCO World Heritage Site on the remote Mosquito Coast preserves one of the finest remaining stretches of Central American rainforest. **See p.386**

❺ LITTLE CORN, NICARAGUA Once a

haven for pirates, this tiny, unspoilt island offers swaying palm trees, white-sand beaches and warm, clear water – the perfect place to recharge. **See p.472**

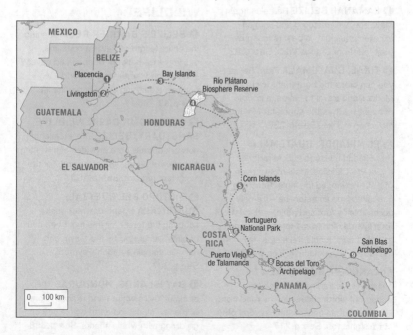

⑥ TORTUGUERO NATIONAL PARK, COSTA RICA
While turtle-watching is the big draw at this coastal national park, a trip along the Tortuguero Canal in a dugout canoe comes a close second. See p.516

⑦ PUERTO VIEJO DE TALAMANCA, COSTA RICA
One of the liveliest backpacker towns in Central America, Puerto Viejo also boasts one of the best surf breaks on the Caribbean coast. See p.524

⑧ BOCAS DEL TORO ARCHIPELAGO, PANAMA
Touted as "the Galapagos of the twenty-first century", this once-isolated region is growing in popularity as an ecotourism destination. See p.659

⑨ SAN BLAS ARCHIPELAGO, PANAMA
Part of the autonomous Kuna region, these idyllic offshore islands offer a mix of beach holiday and the chance to sample a unique culture. See p.633

MAYA RUINS

① LAMANAI, BELIZE
Belize's largest Maya site, well restored and with an excellent museum, is best reached by boat tour from Orange Walk. See p.82

② TIKAL, GUATEMALA
From Belize you can cross the border at Melchor de Mencos and travel to Flores, a couple of hours south of the superstar Maya attraction at Tikal. See p.227

③ EL MIRADOR, GUATEMALA
Remote and mysterious El Mirador is a vast Pre-Classical Mayan city, much of it still enveloped in jungle. Reaching it requires time and stamina – it's only accessible by foot and mule, and most opt for a five-day trip from Flores, including up to eight hours' jungle trekking a day – but the reward is spectacular. See p.233

④ CANCUÉN, GUATEMALA
This affluent Maya trading town is a little-visited but worthwhile site. The road from Flores to Cobán passes near several other Maya sights too. See p.217

⑤ TAZUMAL, EL SALVADOR
Smaller than its Guatemalan counterparts, but with a certain charm, the site features both Maya and Pipil constructions. See p.310

⑥ COPÁN, HONDURAS
One of the country's main tourist destinations, Copán is smaller than Tikal but features exquisite carvings and sculpture, both throughout the site and in its impressive museum. See p.352

WILDLIFE

① BELIZE'S BARRIER REEF
Running the entire length of Belize's coastline, this immense network of coral and cayes – the second largest in the world – is home to a dazzling array of marine life. See p.68

② COCKSCOMB BASIN WILDLIFE SANCTUARY, BELIZE
The excellent network of trails here provides exhilarating glimpses of tapirs, anteaters and, for the lucky few, jaguars. See p.103

③ BIOTOPO DEL QUETZAL, GUATEMALA
Spend dawn or dusk scouring the forest for this most beautiful of birds, venerated by the Maya, and now Guatemala's national symbol. See p.207

④ BAY ISLANDS, HONDURAS
This string of idyllic white-sand islands is one of the few places on earth where you can go diving with whale sharks. See p.388

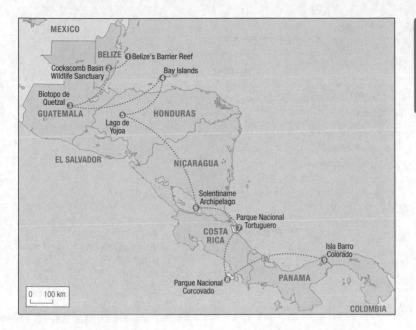

⑤ LAGO DE YOJOA, HONDURAS

Take an early-morning paddle in this picturesque lake, surrounded by mountains and home to over four hundred species of bird. See p.345

⑥ SOLENTINAME ARCHIPELAGO, NICARAGUA

Spot sloths, howler monkeys, parrots and macaws on this isolated scattering of islands, marooned in the middle of mighty Lago de Nicaragua. See p.461

⑦ PARQUE NACIONAL TORTUGUERO, COSTA RICA

The fantastic journey here – drifting through verdant jungle, past wooden houses on stilts – is only a sideshow to the main event: the *desove*, where hundreds of green, hawksbill and leatherback turtles haul themselves ashore each night to lay their eggs. See p.516

⑧ PARQUE NACIONAL CORCOVADO, COSTA RICA

The most biologically diverse area in Central America – akin to the Amazon in the eyes of some experts – Corcovado harbours everything from tapirs to tayras; you'll most likely stumble across them on one of the park's mammoth jungle treks. See p.578

⑨ ISLA BARRO COLORADO, PANAMA

Sitting plum in the middle of the Panama Canal, Barro Colorado is a living laboratory, six square miles of biodiversity. Hike through its rainforest with specialist guides from the Smithsonian Institute. See p.616

THE GRAND TOUR

① BELIZEAN CAYES & ATOLLS

Snorkel, scuba dive or fish off the hundreds of cayes which form part of Belize's spectacular Barrier Reef, and don't miss the Great Blue Hole, a collapsed cave. See p.68

② TIKAL, GUATEMALA

Arguably the most impressive Maya ruin in Central America, this ancient city is dominated by six temples and surrounded by thousands of other structures, all surrounded by jungle. See p.227

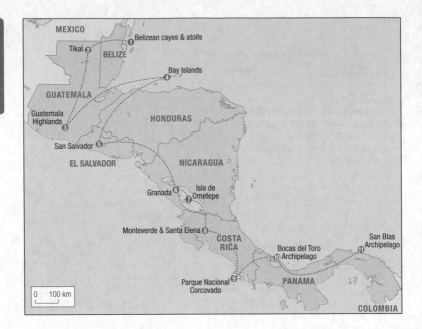

❸ GUATEMALA HIGHLANDS With its volcanoes, mountain ranges, lakes and valleys, this is one of Guatemala's most beautiful areas. **See p.161**

❹ BAY ISLANDS, HONDURAS To catch a glimpse of the elusive whale shark, head here in October or November – or simply spend days sailing or fishing on a remote island. **See p.388**

❺ SAN SALVADOR, EL SALVADOR Nestled at the foot of a volcano, El Salvador's buzzing capital is a heady mix of galleries, museums and nightclubs. **See p.250**

❻ GRANADA, NICARAGUA With its elegant colonial buildings, Granada is Nicaragua's architectural gem, and makes an ideal base for exploring nearby lakes and volcanoes. **See p.442**

❼ ISLA DE OMETEPE, NICARAGUA This magical island, formed by two volcanoes, sits in the middle of a freshwater lake. There's jungle rainforest teeming with monkeys as well as

beaches and mountains to explore. **See p.455**

❽ MONTEVERDE & SANTA ELENA, COSTA RICA These nature reserves are known as cloudforests because of their high altitude. Take a canopy tour to see lush vegetation and hundreds of wildlife species. **See p.529**

❾ PARQUE NACIONAL CORCOVADO, COSTA RICA Most people come to the park in search of rare animals like ocelot and tapir, and there are also deserted beaches, waterfalls and rainforests to explore. **See p.578**

❿ BOCAS DEL TORO ARCHIPELAGO, PANAMA One of the most remote and beautiful provinces in Panama, this diverse archipelago boasts tropical rainforests, beaches and mangroves. **See p.659**

⓫ SAN BLAS ARCHIPELAGO, PANAMA Strung out along the Caribbean coast, the vast majority of these islands are uninhabited. Come here to get away from it all. **See p.633**

BASICS

BASICS

Getting there

While you can get to Central America overland from Mexico or by sea from Colombia, your most likely point of entry to Central America is through one of the region's international airports. Of these, the most popular gateways are Guatemala City, San José and Panama City.

Prices for flights to the region with established carriers can vary hugely. For the best fares on scheduled flights, book well in advance of travel, as airlines only have a fixed number of seats at their lowest prices. Fully check conditions before making a booking, however, as these cheap fares are almost always heavily restricted; the one provision nearly all carriers attach to tickets is the required duration of trip – generally the best prices allow a maximum stay of one to three months, with prices rising for a six-month duration, and again for a year's validity. It is not always cheapest to book direct with the airline; some **travel agents** (see p.30) can negotiate discounted fares, in particular for students or those under 26. It may be worth considering a **one-way ticket** if you are planning a long trip (although you may have difficulties passing through immigration without an onward ticket – see "Entry requirements", p.45).

Another option for bargain-hunters is to look into routes operated by **charter airlines** to package-holiday destinations. For the most part these are available from the US to Belize, Costa Rica and Panama, although it is also possible to reach Cancún in Mexico's Yucatán Peninsula from the UK. These charter flights allow limited flexibility, usually for a fixed period of one or two weeks, but can be picked up last-minute at very reasonable prices.

If planning a substantial amount of overland travel in Central America consider purchasing an **open-jaw ticket** (for example, arriving in Guatemala City and returning from Panama City). Prices for open-jaw tickets are usually comparable to a straightforward return. Alternatively, **round-the-world (RTW)** itineraries can incorporate Central American destinations if you travel via the US and onward to Auckland, Sydney, etc (see p.29).

FROM THE UK AND IRELAND

There are **no direct flights** from the UK or Ireland to Central America. Most routes are offered by US carriers (namely, American, United, Continental and Delta) and involve connections in the States. Onward flights to Central America may be operated by regional airlines such as Copa, TACA and Lineas Aereas Costarricenses (LACSA).

> ## ESTA CLEARANCE
>
> Since 12 January 2009, the US government has required those travellers coming to or through the US on the Visa Waiver Program to apply for clearance via **ESTA** (Electronic System for Travel Authorization). This is not something to ignore – if you arrive at the airport without having done it, the airline won't allow you to check in. To apply for clearance visit ⓦhttp://esta.cbp.dhs.gov/esta/. Make sure you do this at least three days before travelling; you'll need your passport to hand and the admin fee at the time of publication is US$14. Clearance remains valid for two years. Companies advertising assistance with ESTA clearance should be ignored, as no officially recognized bodies provide this service.

SIX STEPS TO A BETTER KIND OF TRAVEL

At Rough Guides we are passionately committed to travel. We feel strongly that only through travelling do we truly come to understand the world we live in and the people we share it with – plus tourism has brought a great deal of **benefit** to developing economies around the world over the last few decades. But the extraordinary growth in tourism has also damaged some places irreparably, and of course **climate change** is exacerbated by most forms of transport, especially flying. This means that now more than ever it's important to **travel thoughtfully** and **responsibly**, with respect for the cultures you're visiting – not only to derive the most benefit from your trip but also to preserve the best bits of the planet for everyone to enjoy. At Rough Guides we feel there are six main areas in which you can make a difference:

* Consider what you're contributing to the **local economy**, and how much the services you use do the same, whether it's through employing local workers and guides or sourcing locally grown produce and local services.
* Consider the **environment** on holiday as well as at home. Water is scarce in many developing destinations, and the biodiversity of local flora and fauna can be adversely affected by tourism. Try to patronize businesses that take account of this.
* Travel with a purpose, not just to tick off experiences. Consider **spending longer** in a place, and getting to know it and its people.
* Give thought to how often you **fly**. Try to avoid short hops by air and more harmful night flights.
* Consider **alternatives to flying**, travelling instead by bus, train, boat and even by bike or on foot where possible.
* Make your trips "**climate neutral**" via a reputable carbon offset scheme. All Rough Guide flights are offset, and every year we donate money to a variety of charities devoted to combating the effects of climate change.

A few European airlines also offer flights through their hub cities to Guatemala City, San José or Panama City – these include Iberia, Air Comet or Air Europa (via Madrid) and KLM or Martinair (via Amsterdam). As clearing US immigration and customs can be a lengthy process, these European flights can frequently be faster. Alternatively – and less expensively – a wide network of carriers flies from Europe direct to Mexico, from where you can travel to Central America (see opposite).

Journey times from the UK and Ireland vary according to connection times, but it is possible to get door-to-door in a day. Published return **fares** from London to Central American capitals start at around £700.

FROM THE US AND CANADA

Several US carriers operate **direct flights** to all Central American capitals. The main US hubs, offering good connections with other North American cities, are Houston (Continental Airlines), Miami (Spirit Airlines), Dallas (American and United Airlines) and Atlanta (Delta), but there are also direct routes from New York and Los Angeles to Guatemala City, San Salvador, San José and Panama City. Flights are frequent and can take as little as two hours (Miami to Belize City, for example). Prices vary – advance fares start from as little as US$250 (including taxes), though a more realistic estimate would be in the region of US$400–600.

From **Canada** you can fly direct with Air Canada from Toronto to Costa Rica (San José; 7hr). There are also seasonal direct flights between Toronto and Montréal to Central American cities with Air Transat. Lineas Aereas Costarricenses (LACSA) and Air Transat connect flights from Montréal and Toronto to Central American cities, including to San José, Liberia and San Salvador. Return trips between Canada and Central America start at about US$700, although there are many travel companies offering seasonal packages with flights from US$400. Alternatively, there are many connections to all Central American capitals via the US.

FROM AUSTRALIA, NEW ZEALAND AND SOUTH AFRICA

There are **no direct flights** from Australasia or South Africa to Central America, but it's easy enough to connect with flights in the US or Europe. From **Australia** and **New Zealand**, the quickest route is through Los Angeles and then Dallas or Houston (approximately 20hr; Aus$2750/NZ$3300). From **South Africa** (Johannesburg) the options include Iberia via Madrid (from ZAR12,000) and Delta via Dakar and Atlanta (from ZAR14,700). Connections are not great: the journey takes at least 24 hours.

Round-the-world (RTW) flights

Round-the-world flights connect Sydney, Perth, Auckland and Johannesburg to Mexico City, Guatemala City, San José and Panama City, usually via Los Angeles or London using American Airlines or code-share partners. It is also possible to reach Australasia from both Santiago (Chile) and Buenos Aires (Argentina) as part of the same RTW tickets with BA/Qantas's Oneworld. British Airways/Qantas and United/Air New Zealand Star Alliance fares from London start at around £1500, and allow multiple stops in several continents within a certain mileage.

FROM MEXICO

It is fairly straightforward to travel overland **by bus** from Mexico to Guatemala or Belize. Several companies offer services with varying degrees of comfort (worth taking into consideration, given the length of most trips – Palenque to Flores is eight hours, Tulum to Belize City is nine). Popular **routes** include: Cancún/Tulum (via Chetumal/Corozal) to Belize City; Palenque (via Frontera Corozal/Bethel) to Flores, Guatemala; San Cristóbal de Las Casas (via Ciudad Cuauhtémoc/La Mesilla) to Huehuetenango; and the Mexican Pacific coast (via Ciudad Hidalgo/Ciudad Tecún Umán) to Quetzaltenango.

Unfortunately, one annoyance experienced by many travellers (particularly crossing into Guatemala) is the demand for unofficial "fees" at immigration; it's often easier to go with local services than one of the long-distance carriers – travelling with a busload of gringos can prove expensive. It is worth changing pesos at the border with moneychangers, as an opportunity may not arise later. Be sure to do your sums prior to agreeing to a transaction and check what you're given before handing over your cash.

It's possible, too, to **fly** from many of Mexico's airports to Central America's main cities with airlines such as TACA and Copa; tickets start at around US$200.

FROM SOUTH AMERICA

There is currently **no overland passage** between Central and South America due to lack of infrastructure and a guerrilla presence in the Darién jungle bordering Colombia and Panama. Known as the "Darién Gap", this break in the Interamericana Highway means that intercontinental travellers will need to cross this area either **by air** or **by sea**.

Unless part of an airpass or RTW ticket, **flights** from South to Central America are typically cheaper bought in the country of departure (agents there will have access to discounted fares). However, as always, booking at the last minute can mean settling for the highest prices, so ideally you should plan at least a few weeks in advance. One-way fares from Quito/Bogotá to Panama are in the region of US$500 (considerably cheaper with a student card).

There's a steady flow of **sea traffic** between Panama and Colombia via the Caribbean, and private sailboats often offer passage as crew for the three- to five-day journey between Colón and Cartagena (see box, p.621). While there are still no regularly scheduled "ferries", many boats frequently make the run – usually depending on demand.

AIRLINES, AGENTS AND OPERATORS

Airlines

Aeromexico ⓦ www.aeromexico.com.
Air Canada ⓦ www.aircanada.com.
Air Comet ⓦ www.aircomet.com.
Air Europa ⓦ www.aireuropa.com.
Air New Zealand ⓦ www.airnz.co.nz.
American Airlines ⓦ www.aa.com.
British Airways ⓦ www.ba.com.
Continental Airlines ⓦ www.continental.com.
Copa Airlines ⓦ www.copaair.com.
Delta ⓦ www.delta.com.
Iberia ⓦ www.iberia.com.
KLM (Royal Dutch Airlines) ⓦ www.klm.com.
Martinair ⓦ www.martinair.com.
Qantas Airways ⓦ www.qantas.com.
South African Airways ⓦ www.flysaa.com.
TACA ⓦ www.taca.com.
United Airlines ⓦ www.united.com.

Agents and operators

Coco Tours Honduras ☎ 504/3335-4599, ⓦ www .hondurascoco.com. Small, locally-based tour company leading a variety of Central American tours, including cultural Garífuna visits, with a portion of profits supporting Garífuna projects.
Gecko's Adventures Australia ☎ 613/8601 4444, ⓦ www.geckosadventures.com. Australian-based agency, with a number of tours led by local guides within Latin America.
Journey Latin America UK ☎ 020/8622 8469, ⓦ www.journeylatinamerica.co.uk. Long-established tour operator offering tailor-made itineraries as well as sound advice on travel in the region.
Keka's Travel Agency ☎ 1-800/593-5352, ⓦ www.kekastravel.com. Miami-based operators specializing in Latin American travel, offering low airfares and budget packages.
North South Travel UK ☎ 01245/608 291, ⓦ www.northsouthtravel.co.uk. Friendly, competitive travel agency, offering discounted fares worldwide. Profits are used to support projects in the developing world, especially the promotion of sustainable tourism.
Quetzaltrekkers Nicaragua ☎ 505/2311-6695, Guatemala ☎ 502/7765-5895; ⓦ www .quetzaltrekkers.com. Nonprofit organization providing trekking tours in Guatemala and Nicaragua, with profits directly funding children's educational and recreational projects.
STA Travel UK ☎ 0871/230 0040, US ☎ 1-800/781-4040, Australia ☎ 134 STA, New Zealand ☎ 0800/474 400, South Africa ☎ 0861/781 781; ⓦ www.statravel.com. Worldwide specialists in independent travel; also student IDs, travel insurance, car rental, rail passes, and more. Good discounts for students and under-26s.
Trailfinders UK ☎ 0845/058 5858, Republic of Ireland ☎ 01/677 7888, Australia ☎ 1300/780 212; ⓦ www.trailfinders.com. One of the best-informed and most efficient agents for independent travellers.
Tucan Travel UK ☎ 020/8896 1600, Australia ☎ 0293/266 633; ⓦ www.tucantravel.com. An independently owned agency offering a variety of worldwide tours, including comprehensive budget expeditions.
Yampu Tours UK ☎ 0800/011 2424, Australia ☎ 1800/224 201, US ☎ 1-888/YAMPU-01; ⓦ www .yampu.com. Another small indie outfit, offering a large number of tours within Latin America.

Getting around

If you're not in a hurry and are willing to travel on public transport, you can get around most of Central America on US$1 an hour (probably slightly more in Belize, Costa Rica and Panama). While public transport systems are sometimes slow – and almost always crowded and sweaty – they can often also be extremely efficient: in most places you will rarely have to wait long for onward transport. On major roads, especially, buses run with high frequency and can offer a great insight into the day-to-day life of the country. Flights are relatively expensive but shuttle long-distance between major cities and can help access remote areas, such as the region's many wonderful islands.

The following is a general guide to Central American transport. More specific information can be found in the "Getting around" section of each country's "Basics" section.

BY BUS

Travelling **by bus** in Central America is by far the most convenient and comprehensive way to get around. The **cost** of travel depends mainly on the quality of the transport – you can look forward to paying anywhere from approximately US$1 per hour for one of the region's infamous "chicken buses" (see box, p.7) to US$6 per hour for a guaranteed seat on a more comfortable "Pullman"-style coach.

Chicken buses generally serve as second-class, or local, services. They stop on demand, wherever passengers ask to get off or people flag down passing services. Sometimes it can seem like you're stopping every thirty metres, but these buses are handy for impromptu itineraries and each country's extensive network of routes allows you to get off the beaten path with relative

ease. In most places chicken buses tend to run **on demand** rather than to schedules, departing when full, though in Costa Rica and Panama schedules are a bit more regular – in those countries it is wise to check at bus terminals in advance of travel for current timetable information. **Tickets** are usually bought on board, once the journey is underway, either from the conductor or from his assistant. It is always worth checking the price before boarding to avoid rip-offs, which are not unknown. **Luggage** usually goes on the roof; always keep valuables on your person and an eye on your stuff as best you can, as theft on buses is unfortunately all too common – interior overhead luggage racks are particularly risky.

Pullman buses generally cover long-distance routes and operate to a schedule, making much quicker progress and so remaining economical when you wish to cover ground more rapidly. Seats should be reserved at the appropriate ticket office in advance. Several bus companies run services from one country to another as well

---

NAVIGATING CENTRAL AMERICAN CITIES

The majority of Central American cities are laid out on a **grid system**, making navigation fairly straightforward: usually numbered calles (streets) run east–west and numbered avenidas (avenues) run north–south, with a *parque* or plaza as the point zero. For more information on navigating specific cities, see the relevant chapter.

SMALL GROUP ADVENTURES

Voted Mexico and Central America's Leading Tour Operator in the 2010 World Travel Awards

www.grandamericanadventures.com
Or call 0844 576 1368

as within individual countries (see below for some of the major firms).

Regional bus contacts

Hedman Alas Ⓦ www.hedmanalas.com. Connecting major cities in Honduras and Guatemala.
King Quality Ⓦ www.king-qualityca.com. Buses from Tapachula, Mexico, depart for all Central American capitals down to San José, Costa Rica.
Tica Bus Ⓦ www.ticabus.com. Tica Bus covers the most ground, spanning the region from Panama City through to Chiapas, Mexico, and stopping at most major cities.
Transnica Ⓦ www.transnica.com. Routes from Managua (Nicaragua) to San Salvador (El Salvador), San José (Costa Rica) and Tegucigalpa (Honduras).
Transportes Galgos Ⓦ transgalgosinter.com.gt. For travel between Tapachula in Mexico and Quetzaltenango and Guatemala City in Guatemala.

BY AIR

Although Central America has a good **international flight network**, connecting the region's key points of interest with its capital cities, unless you are severely pushed for time few flights are worth the money, since distances are usually short and accessible by bus, and prices aren't particularly cheap (Guatemala City–San José is US$200/US$400 student/standard fare). Regional carriers TACA and Copa both offer youth fares; to be eligible you will need to have an ISIC card (see p.44). If you do plan to do a bit of flying, **airpasses** (allowing short hops within Central America, as well as routes to Mexico, the US and some South American destinations) can be bought in conjunction with your international ticket in your country of origin. However, these usually force you to specify your route in advance and rarely allow for trips to your preferred destinations (most travellers are not necessarily interested in visiting the region's chaotic capital cities).

Of greater interest to budget travellers are the **domestic flights** that connect the region's more populous areas to isolated tourist destinations – such as Nicaragua's Corn Islands, Panama's Bocas del Toro and Honduras's Bay Islands, all of which are more than a day's travel by bus from their respective capital cities. Internal flights can be reasonably priced, especially if bought in advance, although in general you will have to purchase them locally.

BY BOAT

You're likely to travel **by boat** at some point if you spend any time in Central America – in some places watercraft are the only way to get around, in others they can provide a welcome break from the monotony of bumpy bus rides. Vessels range from the canoe-like *lanchas* with outboard motor to chugging ferries to speedy catamarans. Watery journeys of note include: Placencia (Belize) to Lívingston (Guatemala) and onward to the Río Dulce area (see p.200); across Lago de Nicaragua to Isla de Ometepe (see p.457); down the Río San Juan to the Caribbean (see p.462); and through the banana plantations around Changuinola to the Caribbean cayes of Bocas del Toro (Panama; see p.659). Although passage through the world-famous Panama Canal costs vessels from US$17,000, there are a few budget-friendly options available (see box, p.615).

BY CAR

Considering the prevalence of public transport and the relative expense of **car rental**, hiring a vehicle is unlikely to have much appeal. If, however, you want to reach isolated spots, and can find a trusted group to share the costs and/or risks, renting a car (or 4WD) does give you some flexibility. **Prices** vary throughout the region (US$25–40 per day, depending on your location, for the cheapest vehicles). Always familiarize yourself with the conditions of hire before signing a contract and be aware that in the event of an accident, insurance excess levels are usually huge. If you do decide to rent a vehicle you will need a full driving licence and credit card and passport. Some agencies do not rent to under-25s, although others may have an age limit of 21. Always park securely, preferably in a car park with attendant, especially in cities. There are no breakdown services available, but petrol stations are plentiful; the price of fuel is slightly higher than in the US and considerably cheaper than in Europe.

Taxis

Travelling by **taxi** in Central America is something of a gamble, but a necessary one: drivers are either some of the friendliest, helpful folk you'll encounter or some of the biggest swindlers, but at night, especially in large cities, they provide the only safe mode of transport. Always settle on a **price** before getting in (even if there is a meter, try to get an estimate), clarifying that the price is for the journey, regardless of the number of passengers or amount of luggage; throughout the region most journeys are a minimum of US$2. In terms of safety, always use registered taxis. Costa Rica and Nicaragua in particular have seen a rise in taxi-jackings; as taxis are **colectivos**, picking up random passengers along the route, it has become all too frequent for drivers to pick up armed passengers who will forcibly ask you to hand over your cash (if you are lucky), or drive you around to drain your bank accounts with ATM withdrawals (see box, p.412). Ask at tourist information and local hotels for recommended drivers, and be alert. It also pays to keep an eye on the map as your journey progresses – a possible deterrent to drivers quite literally taking you for a ride.

BY BIKE

Despite the prevalence of bicycle use among locals, **bike rental** is not widely available in Central America. However, some countries, like Belize, are seeing increased bicycle tourism, and a number of travellers are also touring the region with their own bikes. Notwithstanding the dangers of Central America's anarchic road customs, cycling in the region is facilitated by the mostly flat terrain, relatively short distances between settlements and ease of transporting bicycles aboard buses.

Accommodation

Budget accommodation in Central America is plentiful, and often of excellent quality. The best places to stay are truly memorable for their warm atmosphere, great facilities and stunning location. Others, however, can promise cockroaches, poor sanitation and noisy neighbours. It's worth shopping around for a place you are comfortable with.

As a rule, you should ask to view rooms before agreeing to stay. Do not be afraid to walk away and look at alternatives – this may even precipitate a drop in prices. **Booking ahead** is generally not necessary, except during holiday periods in busy tourist centres – plan on arriving early or calling in advance.

HOTELS AND GUESTHOUSES

The mainstays of travellers' accommodation in Central America are **hotels** and **guesthouses** (and their regional equivalents: *posadas*, *pensiones*, cabinas, cabañas and *hospedajes*). Cabinas and cabañas, where accommodation is in individual structures and detached from other guests, are usually found at the beach or in the jungle.

The room rates given throughout this guide are for the **cheapest double room in high season**. A basic double room (around US$20) will have a bed, a light and probably a fan (*ventilador*). Most places offer the choice of private or shared **bathroom**; a private bath (*baño privado*) will cost a few dollars more than a shared one (*baño compartido*). **Hot water** is a rarity unless you're splurging on a swankier room; keep an eye out for

gas-fired hot water systems – the standard (and decidedly dodgy) electrical showerheads tend to produce tepid water at best and can also deliver electric shocks. Some hotels will provide you with towels and soap and most with toilet paper. By paying a few extra dollars you can also find rooms that come with cable TV, fridge, air conditioning, mosquito nets and/or balcony. Double rooms are often equivalent in price to two dorm beds (good news for couples and something for friends to consider). Private **single rooms**, on the other hand, are often only marginally discounted (if at all) from the standard price for a double.

HOSTELS

Hostels, while not particularly widespread, are increasingly common in Central America, often run by foreigners with a keen eye for backpackers' needs. These establishments offer some of the most sociable and comfortable lodgings in the region. A dorm bed should cost around US$5–10, but in capital cities (especially San José and Panama City) expect to pay around US$15. Most hostels have a few private rooms as well as dorms.

The best hostels may provide **facilities** such as a kitchen, internet access, lockers,

---

JUNGLE LODGES

Throughout Central America you will find an array of rural **jungle lodges** in some truly magical locations. While many lodges charge fairly exorbitant prices, not all are beyond a budget traveller's means. If you have the opportunity, staying at a lodge is usually well worth the splurge and/or detour. However, as lodges are usually isolated, you will be captive to spending all your cash in one place. Lodge owners are of course wise to this and lay on all sorts of tempting treats to help relieve you of your *dinero*.

bar and restaurant areas, TV and movies, as well as tours and activities. The lockers are a definite plus – theft does occur, so do not leave valuables lying around; you might consider travelling with your own padlock. Some hostels will even offer free board and lodging if you want to stay put and **work** for a period (see "Work and study", p.36).

Hostelling International cards are of little or no use in Central America.

CAMPING

Organized **campsites** are a rarity in Central America. However, some **national parks** do allow camping and have limited facilities such as drinking water, toilets and campfire provisions. Expect to pay around US$3–5 per person to pitch a tent (though Costa Rica can be pricier). Camping doesn't hold much appeal for locals, so don't expect to find gear on sale or for rent – you will have to carry what you need. It is also possible to pay to hang a **hammock** (your own or hired) in some areas. This may seem more appealing than an airless room, but the **mosquitoes** can be fierce – make sure you have a net.

Culture and etiquette

Despite a pervasive media image portraying Latin America as a scantily clad world of steamy salsa and sizzling-hot spirit, the reality is much more conservative. Throughout Central America the Church (both Catholic and Evangelical Protestant) retains a powerful influence on everyday life.

Traditional **family values** are prevalent throughout Central America: children are commonly considered to be a blessing – a sign of virility and in many cases an economic asset – and consequently families are often large in size. **Homosexual** relationships are publicly frowned upon if not actively condemned; gay and lesbian travellers should be discreet.

While undeniably friendly, local people can seem shy and unsure about the gringos squeezed into their chicken bus. You will seldom experience hostility, but it pays to greet fellow passengers with a simple "Buenas" and a smile to break the ice. **Politeness** is valued highly, so even if your Spanish is poor, take the trouble to learn key pleasantries and they'll serve you well.

Information about social customs specific to each country is given in the relevant chapter.

DRESS

Most locals **dress modestly** but smartly and visitors not wishing to draw unwelcome attention should do the same. You will make a better impression if you do – especially worthwhile with officials. Flashy exhibitions of wealth are not recommended (jewellery should be left at home). Shorts (for men and women) are not generally worn away from beaches, but low-cut tops for women are becoming more usual, especially among the young. If visiting places of worship, especially, dress modestly – skimpy shorts and flesh-revealing tops are not appropriate. Women will probably also want something to cover their heads.

MONEY MATTERS

Travellers to Central America, especially Westerners, are likely to experience the uncomfortable assumption by locals that you are in fact a multimillionaire (even if you are looking scruffy). Although you may be on a strict budget, the very fact that you have been able to travel abroad, coupled with your potential earning power back home, means you have an economic freedom unobtainable to many you will encounter. As a rule, however, you will ultimately be judged on your conduct and not your wealth: it isn't helpful, therefore, to be too liberal or too mean with your cash. Instead, show appreciation for good service by **tipping** (as part of your budget), pay what will satisfy both parties when haggling and exchange friendship and hospitality for free. **Haggling** is accepted in markets (both tourist and local). You can also haggle – gently – over room prices, tour prices and taxi fares. Prices in shops are generally fixed, although it's usually worth asking if there are discounts if you buy more than one item.

WOMEN TRAVELLERS

Machismo is an ingrained part of Central American culture – **female travellers** will frequently experience whistling, tssking and even blatant catcalls, though probably not anything more sinister than guys showing off to their friends. Ignoring such attention is the easiest way to deal with these situations, as retorts or put-downs are often seen as encouragement. No matter how modestly you behave, though, you will probably not counteract the view that foreign women are not only desirable, but also easily attainable.

Despite this, most female travellers report positive experiences in the region. Indeed, several will testify that they feel better treated by locals than their fellow male travellers. There are, however, still **precautions** to be taken. Golden rules when dealing with hopeful suitors include staying sober, and involving outside parties if you feel uncomfortable. At night, female travellers should try to move in groups.

Women travelling as part of a straight couple should be prepared to be invisible in many social interactions. Even if the woman is the only one to speak Spanish, for example, locals will often automatically address their reply to the man's perceived authority.

Work and study

A high unemployment rate and innumerable bureaucratic hurdles make the possibility of finding paid work in Central America very unlikely, although there are limited opportunities to teach English, especially in wealthier countries like Costa Rica. It's far easier to work as a volunteer – many NGOs operate in the region, relying mainly on volunteer staff. Opportunities for studying Spanish are plentiful and often fairly cheap, with a number of congenial Central American locations drawing students from all over the world.

TEACHING ENGLISH

There are two options for **teaching English** in Central America: find work before you go, or just wing it and see what you come up with after arriving; the latter is slightly less risky if you already have a degree and/or teaching experience. You can get a **CELTA** (Certificate in English Language Teaching to Adults), a **TEFL** (Teaching English as a Foreign

Language) or a **TESOL** (Teaching English to Speakers of Other Languages) qualification before you leave home or even while you're abroad. Courses are not cheap (about £1025/US$2250–2500/Aus$2550 for one month's full-time tuition) and you are unlikely to make this investment back very quickly on Central American wages. Once you have the necessary qualifications, check the **British Council**'s website (ⓦwww.britishcouncil.org) and the **TEFL** website (ⓦwww.tefl.com) for a list of English-teaching vacancies.

Places like Guatemala City and San José in Costa Rica are your best bet for teaching in Central America, although colonial, tourist-oriented towns like Antigua in Guatemala and Granada in Nicaragua are also likely spots.

VOLUNTEERING

There are **voluntary positions** available in Central America for everything from conservation work in Costa Rica to human-rights work in Guatemala. If you have a useful skill or specialization, you might have your room and board paid for and perhaps even earn a little pocket money, although more often than not you'll have to fund yourself. If you don't have any particular skills you'll almost definitely have to pay for the privilege of volunteering, and in many cases – particularly in conservation work – this doesn't come cheap. While many positions are organized prior to arrival, it's also possible to arrange something on the ground through word of mouth. Noticeboards in the more popular backpacker hostels are always good sources of information.

STUDYING SPANISH

Some people travel to Central America solely to **learn Spanish** and there are many cities and towns with highly respected schools. Antigua and Quetzaltenango in Guatemala, San José in Costa Rica and to a lesser extent, Granada and San Juan del Sur in Nicaragua are all noted centres for language instruction. **Prices** vary, but you can expect to pay around US$200 per week, to include room and board with a local family, a standard feature of many Spanish courses and great for full cultural immersion. Some schools will also include activities, allowing you to take your learning out of the classroom and providing an insight into the local area. Courses usually run Monday to Friday, but should include seven nights' homestay to include in the weekend. Cheaper courses are available if you are only interested in lessons without lodging or activities, although your learning curve is unlikely to be as steep. See the "Directory" sections of individual cities for language-school recommendations.

USEFUL CONTACTS

UK and Ireland

AFS UK ☎0113/242 6136, ⓦwww.afsuk.org. Six-month community volunteer placements for young people aged 18 to 34 in Costa Rica, Guatemala, Honduras and Panama.
British Council ☎020/7930 8466. The Council's Central Management of Direct Teaching (☎020/7389 4931) recruits TEFL teachers for posts worldwide (check ⓦwww.britishcouncil.org for current vacancies).
Global Vision International ☎017/2725 0250, ⓦwww.gvi.co.uk. Worldwide placements, many in Central America, including marine conservation and teaching work.
Volunteer Service Overseas ☎020/8780 7500, ⓦwww.vso.org.uk. UK-based charity organization, offering volunteer opportunities across the globe.

US and Canada

AFS Intercultural Programs US ☎1-800/AFS-INFO, Canada ☎1-800/361-7248 or 514/288-3282, ⓦwww.afs.org. Cultural immersion programmes for high-school students and graduates.
Aide Abroad ☎1-888/6-ABROAD or 512/904-1137, ⓦwww.aideabroad.com. Voluntary placements in Central America, lasting two weeks to one year. Intermediate Spanish ability required.
American Institute for Foreign Study US ☎1-866/906-2437, ⓦwww.aifs.com. Language study and cultural immersion in Costa Rica.
AmeriSpan ☎1-800/879-6640, ⓦwww.amerispan.com. Language programmes, volunteer/internship placements (English teaching, healthcare, environment, social work, etc) and academic study-abroad courses throughout Central America.
Amigos de las Américas ☎1-800/231-7796 or 713/782-5290, ⓦwww.amigoslink.org. Veteran nonprofit organization placing high-school and college-age students in child health promotion and other community projects in Central America.

Peace Corps ☎ 1-800/424-8580, ⊛ www.peace corps.gov. US institution which recruits volunteers of all ages (minimum 18) and from all walks of professional life for two-year postings throughout Central America. All applicants must be US citizens.
World Learning ☎ 1-800/336-1616, ⊛ www .worldlearning.org. Accredited college semesters abroad; the large Latin American studies programme includes an ecology/conservation course in Belize and a politics-themed course in Nicaragua.

Australia, New Zealand and South Africa

AFS Australia ☎ 1300/131 736 or 02/9215 0077, NZ ☎ 0800/600 300 or 04/494 6020, South Africa ☎ 11/447 2673; ⊛ www.afs.org.au. Cultural immersion programmes for high-school students and graduates.
Australian Volunteers International ☎ 03/9279 1788, ⊛ www.australianvolunteers.com. Postings of up to two years in Costa Rica, Guatemala, El Salvador and Nicaragua, as well as shorter-term, team-based assignments for younger volunteers.
Earthwatch Australia ☎ 03/9682 6828, ⊛ www .earthwatch.org/australia. Australian branch of this nonprofit organization that places prospective volunteers with an array of scientists from various fields in locations throughout Central America.

Worldwide

BUNAC UK ☎ 020/7251 3472, Republic of Ireland ☎ 1/477 3027, US ☎ 1-800/GO-BUNAC; ⊛ www .bunac.org. Organizes working holidays in Costa Rica for students.
Cactus Language ⊛ www.cactuslanguage.com. Language-holiday specialist with a wide range

of courses in Costa Rica, Guatemala, Honduras, Nicaragua and Panama. Prices are often lower than if applying directly to the schools.
Council on International Educational Exchange (CIEE) UK ☎ 020/8939 9057, US ☎ 1-800/40-STUDY or 1-207/533-7600; ⊛ www.ciee.org. Leading NGO offering study programmes and volunteer projects around the world.
Earthwatch Institute ⊛ www.earthwatch.org. International nonprofit organization dedicated to environmental sustainability. Voluntary positions assisting archeologists, biologists and even ethnomusicologists in Costa Rica, Nicaragua and Belize.
Gapyear.com ⊛ www.gapyear.com. Comprehensive resource with search engine providing links to volunteer and language teaching/ learning options worldwide.
Global Volunteer Network ⊛ www.global volunteernetwork.org. Voluntary placements on community projects worldwide.
Idealist ⊛ www.idealist.org. A comprehensive portal of global volunteering positions, connecting applicants with jobs and volunteer placements within the nonprofit sector.
Peace Brigades International ⊛ www.peace brigades.org. NGO dedicated to protecting human rights, with placements accompanying human-rights workers in Guatemala. Costs (including a small monthly stipend) are covered, although fundraising is encouraged. Applicants need to be age 25 or older and fluent in Spanish.
Raleigh International ☎ 020/7371 8585, ⊛ www.raleighinternational.org. Long-established youth-development charity working on community and environmental projects worldwide. Opportunities for both young volunteers (17–25) and older skilled staff (over 25). Central American projects in Costa Rica and Nicaragua.

Health

It's always easier to get ill in a country with a different climate, food and germs – still more so in a poor country with lower standards of sanitation than you might be accustomed to. Most visitors, however, get through Central America without experiencing anything more serious than an upset stomach as long as they observe basic precautions about hygiene, untreated water and insect bites.

Above all, it's important to get the best **advice** you can before you depart: visit your doctor or a travel clinic. You should also invest in **health insurance** (see p.48).

GENERAL PRECAUTIONS

There's no need to go overboard, but as you are packing consider putting together a **travel medical kit**. Components to include might be: painkillers and anti-inflammatory drugs, antiseptic cream, plasters (Band Aids) and gauze bandages, surgical tape, anti-diarrhoea medicine (Imodium or Lomotil) and rehydration salts, diarrhoea remedies (Pepto Bismol or similar), insect repellent, sun block, anti-fungal cream and sterile scissors and tweezers.

Once in Central America, basic hygiene will go a long way towards keeping you healthy. **Bathe** frequently, **wash your hands** before eating and avoid sharing water bottles or utensils. Make sure to eat a **balanced diet** – eating peeled fresh fruit helps keep up your vitamin and mineral intake (see p.40 for information about avoiding intestinal troubles); malnutrition can lower your resistance to germs and bacteria. Hepatitis B, HIV and AIDS – all transmitted through blood or sexual contact – are common in Central America. You should take all the usual, well-publicized precautions to avoid them. Two other causes of problems in the region are **altitude** and the **sun**. The answer in both cases is to take it easy; allow yourself time to acclimatize and build up exposure to the sun gradually. Avoid dehydration by drinking enough – water or fruit juice rather than beer or coffee (see opposite for information about water safety).

Overheating can cause heatstroke, which is potentially fatal. Lowering body temperature (by taking a tepid shower, for example) is the first step in treatment.

INOCULATIONS

If possible, all **inoculations** should be sorted out at least ten weeks before departure at your local health clinic. The only obligatory jab required to enter Central America is a **yellow fever** vaccination; however, this is only needed if you're arriving from a "high-risk" area – northern South America and much of central Africa – in which case you need to carry your vaccination certificate. A yellow fever shot is also highly recommended if travelling in Panama east of the canal. Long-term travellers should consider the combined hepatitis A and B and the rabies vaccines, and all travellers should check that they are up to date with the usual polio, diphtheria, tetanus, typhoid and hepatitis A jabs.

FOOD AND WATER SAFETY

People differ in their sensitivity to **food**. If you are worried or prone to digestive upsets then there are a few simple things to keep in mind: steer clear of raw shellfish and seafood when inland; only eat raw fruit and vegetables if they can be peeled; and avoid salads unless rinsed in purified water.

Contaminated water is a major cause of sickness in Central America, and even if it looks clean, drinking water should be regarded with caution (even when cleaning teeth and showering). That said, however, it's also essential to increase fluid intake to prevent dehydration. **Bottled water** is widely available, but always check that the seal is intact, since refilling empties with tap water for resale is not unknown. Many restaurants use purified water (*agua purificada*), but always ask.

There are various methods of **treating water** while you are travelling: boiling for a minimum of five minutes is the most effective method of sterilization, but it is not always practical, and will not remove unpleasant tastes. Water filters remove visible impurities and larger pathogenic organisms (most bacteria and parasites). To be really sure your filtered water is also purified, however, chemical sterilization – using either chlorine or iodine tablets, or a tincture of iodine liquid – is advisable; iodine is more effective in destroying amoebic cysts. Both chlorine and iodine unfortunately leave a nasty aftertaste (which can be masked with lime juice). Pregnant women or people with thyroid problems should consult their doctor before using iodine tablets or purifiers. Inexpensive iodine-removal filters are recommended if treated water is being used continuously for more than a month. Any good outdoor equipment shop will stock a range of water treatment products.

INTESTINAL TROUBLES

Diarrhoea is the stomach ailment you're most likely to encounter. Its main cause is simply the change in your diet: the food in Central America contains a whole new set of bacteria, as well as perhaps rather more of them than you're used to. Don't try anything too exotic in the first few days, but do try to find some local natural yoghurt, which is a good way to introduce friendly bacteria to your system. Powdered milk, however, can be troublesome, due to being an unfamiliar form of lactose.

If you're afflicted with a bout of diarrhoea, the best cure is the simplest one: take it easy for a day or two and make sure you rehydrate. It's a good idea to carry sachets of rehydration salts, although you can make up your own solution by dissolving five teaspoons of sugar or honey and half a teaspoon of salt in a litre of water. Reintroduce only bland foods at first

(rice, dry toast, etc) – papaya and coconut are also good. Diarrhoea remedies like Imodium and Lomotil should be saved for emergencies, like if you need to travel immediately. Only if the symptoms last more than four or five days do you need to worry. If you can't get to a doctor for an exact diagnosis, a last resort would be a course of Ciproxin (ciprofloxacin) – you may want to consider asking your doctor for a prescription and carrying some in your medical kit.

Cholera, an acute bacterial infection, is recognizable by watery diarrhoea and vomiting, though many victims may have only mild or even no symptoms. However, risk of infection is low: Central America was recently declared a cholera-free zone by the Pan American Health Organization.

If you're spending any time in rural areas you also run the risk of picking up various **parasitic infections**: protozoa – amoeba and giardia – and intestinal worms. These sound hideous, but they're easily treated once detected. If you suspect you have an infestation take a stool sample to a good pathology lab and go to a doctor or pharmacist with the test results (see "Getting medical help", p.42). More serious is amoebic dysentery, which is endemic in many parts of the region. The symptoms are more or less the same as a bad case of diarrhoea, but include bleeding. On the whole, a course of Flagyl (metronidazole or tinidozole) will cure it; if you plan to visit the isolated rural reaches of Central America then it's worth carrying these, just in case. If possible get some, and some advice on their usage, from a doctor before you go. To avoid contracting such parasites think carefully before swimming in rivers and lakes during or just after the rainy season, when waste washes down hillsides into the water.

MALARIA AND DENGUE FEVER

Malaria, caused by the transmission of a parasite in the saliva of an infected anopheles mosquito (active at night), is endemic in many parts of Central America, especially in the rural Caribbean lowlands. There are several different anti-malarial **prophylactics** available, all of which must be started in advance of travel, so make sure you leave plenty of time to visit your doctor. The recommended prophylactic for all of Central America, except for the area east of the Panama Canal, is chloroquine; east of the canal, including the San Blas Islands, it's Malarone, causing minimal side effects although its cost (around £20 per week) can be prohibitive. Consult your doctor about which drug will be best for you. It's extremely important to finish your course of anti-malarials, as there is a time lag between bite and infection. If you do become ill after returning home, let your doctor know that you've been in a malarial risk area.

In addition to malaria, mosquitoes can transmit **dengue fever**, a viral infection that is prevalent – and on the increase – throughout Central America (usually occurring in epidemic outbreaks). Thankfully, the more deadly strain of hemorrhagic dengue is less prevalent in Central America. Unlike malaria, the mosquitoes that pass dengue fever are active during the day, and there's no preventative vaccine or specific treatment, so you need to pay attention to avoiding bites (see below).

OTHER BITES AND STINGS

Taking steps to avoid getting bitten by insects, particularly **mosquitoes**, is essential. In general, sleep in screened rooms or under nets, burn mosquito coils containing permethrin (available everywhere), cover up arms and legs (though note that mosquitoes are attracted to dark-coloured clothing), especially around dawn and dusk when mosquitoes are most active, and use insect repellent containing over 35 percent DEET.

Sandflies, often present on beaches, are tiny and very difficult to see, and hence avoid – you will be made aware of their presence only when they bite, and by then it can be too late. The bites, usually found around the ankles, itch like hell and last for days. Don't give in to the temptation to scratch, as this causes the bites to get worse and last longer. Sandflies can spread cutaneous leishmaniasis, an extremely unpleasant disease characterized by skin lesions that can take months and even years to heal if left untreated.

Scorpions are common: mostly nocturnal, they hide during the heat of the day under rocks and in crevices. Their sting is painful (occasionally fatal) and can become infected, so you should seek medical treatment. You're less likely to be bitten by a spider, but the advice is the same as for scorpions and venomous insects – seek medical treatment if the pain persists or increases.

You're unlikely to see any **snakes**, but wearing boots and long trousers will go a long way towards preventing a bite in the event that you do – walk heavily and they will usually slither away. Most snakes are harmless – exceptions are the fer-de-lance (which lives in both wet and dry environments, in both forest and open country, but rarely emerges during the day) and the bushmaster (found in places with heavy rainfall, or near streams and rivers), both of which can be aggressive, and whose venom can be fatal. If you do get bitten remember what the snake looked like (kill it if it's safe to do so), wrap a lightly restrictive bandage above and below the bite area, but don't apply enough pressure to restrict blood flow and never use a tourniquet. Disinfect the bite area and apply hard pressure with a gauze pad, taped in place; then immobilize the bitten limb as far as possible. Seek medical help immediately.

Swimming and snorkelling might bring you into contact with potentially dangerous **sea creatures**. It's extremely unlikely you'll be a victim of shark attack, but jellyfish are common and all corals will sting. Some jellyfish, like the Portuguese man-o'-war, with its distinctive purple, bag-like sail, have very long tentacles with stinging cells, and an encounter will result in raw, red welts. Equally painful is a brush against fire coral: in each case clean the wound with vinegar or iodine and seek medical help if the pain persists or infection develops.

Rabies does exist in Central America. You'll see stray dogs everywhere; the best advice is to give them a wide berth. Bats can also carry the rabies virus; keep an eye out for them when entering caves. If you are bitten or scratched, wash the wound immediately with soap and running water for five minutes and apply alcohol or iodine. Seek treatment immediately – rabies is fatal once symptoms appear. If you're going to be working with animals or planning a long stay, especially in rural areas far from medical help, you may well want to consider a pre-exposure vaccination, despite the hefty cost. Although this won't give you complete immunity, it will give you a window of 24–48 hours to seek treatment and reduce the amount of post-exposure vaccine you'll need if bitten.

GETTING MEDICAL HELP

For minor medical problems, head for the local **pharmacy** (*farmacia*) – look for a green cross. Pharmacists are knowledgeable and helpful, and many speak some English. They can also sell drugs over the counter (if necessary) that are only available by prescription at home. Most large cities have doctors and dentists, many trained in the US, who are experienced in treating visitors and speak good English. Your embassy will have a list of recommended doctors and hospitals, and we've included some in the "Directory" sections of the main towns. Medical insurance (see p.48) is essential. If you suspect something is amiss with your insides, it might be worth heading straight for a **pathology lab** (*laboratorio médico*), found in all main towns, before seeing a doctor, as the doctor will probably send you there anyway. Many rural communities have a **health centre** (*centro de salud* or *puesto de salud*), where healthcare is free, although there may be only a nurse or health-worker available and you can't rely on finding an English-speaker.

Should you need an injection or transfusion, make sure that the equipment is sterile and ensure any blood you receive is screened.

MEDICAL RESOURCES FOR TRAVELLERS

UK and Ireland

Hospital for Tropical Diseases Travel Clinic ☎0845/155 5000 or 020/7388 9600, ⓦwww.thehtd.org.
MASTA (Medical Advisory Service for Travellers Abroad) ☎0870/606 2782 or ⓦwww.masta.org for the nearest clinic.
Travel Medicine Services ☎028/9031 5220.
Tropical Medical Bureau Republic of Ireland ☎1850/487 674, ⓦwww.tmb.ie.

US and Canada

Canadian Society for International Health ☎613/241-5785, ⓦwww.csih.org. Extensive list of travel health centres.
CDC ☎1-800/CDC-INFO, ⓦwwwnc.cdc.gov/travel. Official US government travel health site.
International Society of Travel Medicine ☎1-403/373-8282, ⓦwww.istm.org. Has a full list of travel health clinics.

Australia, New Zealand and South Africa

Travellers' Medical and Vaccination Centre ☎1300/658 844, ⓦwww.tmvc.com.au. Lists travel clinics in Australia, New Zealand and South Africa.

Travel essentials

COSTS

Your **daily expenses** are likely to include accommodation, food and drink and transport. You may wish to budget separately for activities, as one-off costs (for example, a day's snorkelling or diving) can be high

and would blow a daily budget. In general, the cheapest countries in the region are Honduras, Nicaragua, Guatemala and El Salvador, while Belize, Costa Rica and Panama are more expensive. However, even in these countries it is still possible to travel

BUDGET TIPS

- Slow down. Racing from place to place eats into your budget, as you'll be forking out for transport and tours every day.
- Eat and drink as the locals do. Local staples can be half the price of even the most reasonable tourist menu. Set lunches in traditional *comedores* are great value.
- Cut down your beer bill. When buying booze it's cheapest to get it from small *tiendas* (shops) and take back the bottles to claim the deposit. Litre bottles are more economical than the 330ml ones.
- Refill your water bottle. Many hostels/hotels offer water refills for free or a small fee. Alternatively, in some countries you can buy 500ml bags (*bolsitas*) of water. If you're not moving around, invest in larger gallon bottles.
- Use local transport. Tourist shuttles should be the exception, not the norm.
- Let your money work for you. Try to get a bank account that allows free withdrawals at ATMs. This also allows you to carry small amounts of cash, as ATMs are plentiful.
- Share costs with other travellers. The price of a private room for two is often cheaper than two dorm beds; a triple is even better value.
- Walk as much as possible. Taxis are often a disproportionately expensive method of transport.
- Shop in markets, bakeries and supermarkets. Self-catering is worthwhile if you're staying in one place and can eat your leftovers for breakfast.
- Learn to haggle – bargaining can be fun. Don't be afraid to confront taxi drivers or chancers who you suspect are trying to rip you off. However, don't be too ruthless – bargaining over a few cents is not cool.

on a budget of around US$35 per day, with the most significant difference being the cost of public transport and accommodation. By following the cost-saving tips above, it is possible to travel in Guatemala, for example, for as little as US$20 per day.

Generally speaking, the price quoted in restaurants and hotels is the price you pay. However, in some more upmarket establishments an additional **tax** will appear on your

bill; it's worth checking if tax is included from the outset. Service is almost never included, and while not expected, **tipping** for good service can make a huge impact on the basic wage. Prices for accommodation (as well as some airfares and organized tours) can be considerably cheaper in **low season** (generally Sept–Dec), when it's always worth negotiating to obtain the best price (prices quoted in this guide are based on high-season rates).

Tiered pricing (charging foreigners more than nationals) is becoming more common, in particular for entrance fees. This is based on the premise that tourists can afford to pay considerably more to visit attractions than those on local salaries.

PRICES IN THIS GUIDE

At the beginning of each chapter you'll find a guide to "rough costs", including food, accommodation and travel. Prices are quoted in US dollars for ease of comparison. Within the chapter itself prices are quoted mainly in local currency, though as US dollars are widely accepted prices are often quoted in that currency instead. Note that rates change all the time; we have done our best to make sure that all prices are accurate, but as tourism increases throughout the region it's likely that prices will rise incrementally.

CRIME AND PERSONAL SAFETY

While political violence has decreased over recent years, **crime rates** in Central America continue to rise, and tourists make handy targets. Though the majority of crime is **opportunistic theft** – bag snatching or pick pocketing – some criminals do operate in gangs and are prepared to use extreme violence. It is commonly accepted that Guatemala tops the list for crimes

YOUTH AND STUDENT DISCOUNTS

There are few youth or student discounts in the region. Indeed, often you will find yourself charged more than locals simply because you are a foreigner. It is always worth enquiring if discounts are available, however, as on occasion entrance fees may be tiered (and applicable to foreigners as well as nationals). If a discount is applicable you will need to show **ID**. Most useful is the International Student Identity Card (**ISIC**), which can also be used to obtain discounts on flight bookings. You can get these from STA Travel (see p.30) and affiliated agencies with current official ID issued by your school/university (enrolling at a Spanish language school is generally not sufficient to obtain official student ID).

committed against tourists, but it is possible to be the victim of crime anywhere in the region, especially if you let your guard down.

General precautions

As you're packing, keep the sentimental value of what you take with you to a minimum. Do not wear **jewellery**, and carry only a small amount of **cash** in your wallet. Larger volumes of cash and credit cards should be kept close to your body – in a money belt, hidden pocket or even in your shoes. Scan photocopies of any important **documents** (passport, insurance, etc) and email them to yourself, so you can access them even if you lose everything. It's worth carrying a paper copy too, so that you can leave the originals in a hotel safe. There is always a dilemma about whether to carry **electronic devices** (such as a camera or MP3 player) on your person or leave them in your hotel. If you choose to leave them, make sure they're not

GOVERNMENT TRAVEL ADVICE SITES

Australian Department of Foreign Affairs www.dfat.gov.au, www.smartraveller.gov.au.
British Foreign & Commonwealth Office www.fco.gov.uk.
Canadian Department of Foreign Affairs www.dfait-maeci.gc.ca.
Irish Department of Foreign Affairs www.foreignaffairs.gov.ie.
New Zealand Ministry of Foreign Affairs www.mft.govt.nz.
US State Department www.travel.state.gov.

accessible – you could always pack a small padlock and short length of chain (or cable lock), so that you can create a DIY safe in a wardrobe or under a bed.

It's very important in Central America to **keep an eye on your belongings** at all times. Never put anything down or let your possessions out of your sight unless you're confident they are in a safe place. The highest-risk areas for opportunistic theft are large urban centres, bus stations, at ATMs and at border crossings. **Buses** are also a focus for petty thievery. When travelling by bus you'll often be separated from your main bag – it will usually end up on the roof. This is generally safe enough (and you'll probably have little option in any case). Theft of the bag itself is unlikely, but opportunist thieves may dip into zips and outer pockets, so don't leave anything you'd miss accessible. Some travellers choose to put their pack into a sack to disguise it, prevent pilfering and also keep it clean and dry – not a bad idea. If you carry a day-pack, fill it wisely and keep it on your person (preferably strapped to you). Do not use overhead racks on buses. Needless to say, there is a greater risk of crime after dark, so try to arrive in new towns in daylight so that you're not wandering unlit streets with all your gear. Bear in mind, too, that the threat of petty crime does not exclusively come from the local population – unscrupulous fellow travellers have been known to help themselves to anything of value.

Violent crime does occur in Central America. Muggings at knifepoint, armed robbery (particularly of buses) and rape are all dangers to be aware of. If threatened with a weapon, do not resist. You can reduce your chances of falling victim to these crimes by staying in populated areas or around other travellers. However, it should be noted that tourist shuttles are actually more likely to be a target for hijackers, especially at night.

Drugs

Drugs of all kinds are available everywhere. Buying or using really isn't worth the risk: penalties are very strict. If you are arrested with drugs your embassy will probably send someone to visit you, and maybe find an English-speaking lawyer, but otherwise you're on your own. Practically every capital city has foreigners incarcerated for drug offences who'd never do it again if they knew what the punishment was like.

Reporting a crime

If you are unfortunate enough to suffer a crime, report the incident immediately to the **police** – if there is a tourist police force, try them first – if only to get a copy of the report (*denuncia*) which you'll need for insurance purposes. The police in Central America are poorly paid and, in the case of petty crime, you can't expect them to do much more than make out the report. If you can, also report the crime to your embassy – it helps the consular staff to build up a higher-level case for the better protection of tourists.

ELECTRICITY

All countries in the region use sockets accepting the flat two-pronged plug common to the majority of the Americas; ⓦwww .kropla.com is a useful website with information about adapters and converters. Standard **voltage** is 110–120v. Be wary of **electric showerheads**, often with protruding wires, in budget accommodation. If it isn't working (more than likely), do not touch the fitting. You may want to consider using a towel to turn off the conductive taps, too.

ENTRY REQUIREMENTS

Nationals of the UK, Ireland, Canada, the US, Australia and New Zealand do not need **visas** to visit any of the seven Central American countries. Visitors are eligible for stays of either thirty days (Belize, Panama) or ninety days (Costa Rica and the CA-4 countries – see box below). You should be able to **extend** this period by leaving the country and re-entering, or you can pay for a 30- or 90-day visa extension at immigration offices. You should have a valid **passport** with at least six months remaining and, officially, an onward ticket (these are seldom checked but may be a sticking point at border crossings or customs, especially entering Costa Rica).

All countries charge **entry fees** (sometimes referred to as a "tourist card") to certain nationalities, depending on relations between the countries. Investigate your destination's entry requirements before travelling, and arrive prepared with cash. For more information about specific countries and border crossings in Central America, see the relevant country's chapter, and always check with your embassy before travelling.

Embassies and consulates in Central America

Belize UK (High Commission), PO Box 91, Belmopan ☏(501) 822 2146, ⓦukinbelize.fco .gov.uk; US, Floral Park Rd, Belmopan ☏(501) 822 4011, ⓦbelize.usembassy.gov.

CENTRAL AMERICA BORDER CONTROL AGREEMENT

Guatemala, El Salvador, Honduras and Nicaragua are party to the **Central America Border Control Agreement (CA-4)**. Under the terms of this agreement, tourists may travel within any of these four countries for a period of up to ninety days without completing entry and exit formalities at border and immigration checkpoints, aside from paying entry fees. The ninety-day period begins at the first point of entry to any of the CA-4 countries. Fines are applied for travellers who exceed the ninety-day limit, although a request for an extension can be made for up to thirty additional days by paying a fee before the limit expires. You can get around this by travelling outside the CA-4 countries and then re-entering. If you are expelled from any of the four countries you are also excluded from the entire CA-4 region.

Costa Rica Canada, Oficentro Ejecutivo La Sabana, San José ☎ (506) 2242 4400, ✉ sjcra@international .gc.ca; UK, Apartado 815-1007, Edificio Centro Colón (piso/floor 11), San José ☎ (506) 2258 2025, ✉ britemb@racsa.co.cr; US, C 120/Av 0, Pavas, San José ☎ (506) 2519 2000, 🖳 costarica .usembassy.gov.

El Salvador Canada, Centro Financiero Gigante, 63 Av Sur y Alameda Roosevelt, Local 6, San Salvador ☎ (503) 2279 4655, ✉ ssal@international .gc.ca; UK (Honorary Consul), PO Box 242, San Salvador ☎ (503) 2281 555; US, Final Blvd Santa Elena, Antiguo Cuscatlán, La Libertad, San Salvador ☎ (503) 2501 2600, 🖳 sansalvador.usembassy.gov.

Guatemala Canada, 13 Calle 8–44, Zone 10, Edificio Edyma Plaza, Guatemala City ☎ (502) 2363-4348, ✉ gtmla@international.gc.ca; UK, Edificio Torre Internacional, Nivel 11, 16 Calle 0–55, Zona 10, Guatemala City ☎ (502) 2380 7300, ✉ embassy@intelnett.com; US, Av Reforma 7–01, Zona 10, Guatemala City, ☎ (502) 2326 4000, 🖳 guatemala.usembassy.gov.

Honduras Canada, Centro Financiero CITI Tercer Piso, Blvd San Juan Bosco, Colonia Payaquí, Tegucigalpa ☎ (504) 232 4551, ✉ tglpa @international.gc.ca; UK (Honorary Consulate), Colonia La Reforma, C Principal No. 2402, Tegucigalpa ☎ (504) 2237 6577; US, Av La Paz, Tegucigalpa M.D.C. ☎ (504) 236 9320/238 5114, 🖳 honduras.usembassy.gov.

Nicaragua Canada (Office), From "Los Pipitos" 2 cuadras abajo, 25 Calle Nogal, Managua ☎ (505) 2268-0433/3323, ✉ mngua@international .gc.ca; UK, Av Bolivar 1947, del hospital Militar 1 cuadra al Lago, Managua ☎ (505) 254 5454; US, Km5 1/2 (5.5) Carretera Sur, Managua ☎ (505) 2252-7100, ✉ consularmanagua@state.gov.

Panama Canada, Torres de las Americas, Piso 11, Punta Pacífica, Panama City ☎ (507) 264 2500, ✉ panam@international.gc.ca; UK, MMG Tower, Calle 53, Panama City ☎ (507) 269 0866, 🖳 ukinpanama.fco.gov.uk; US, Building 783, Demetrio Basilio Lakas Avenue, Clayton, Panama City ☎ (507) 207 7000, ✉ panamaweb@state.gov.

Central American embassies abroad

Belize Canada, High Commission, 250 Albert St, Suite 2120, Ottawa ☎ (613) 232 2826; El Salvador, C El Bosque Norte, Col La Lima IV, San Salvador ☎ (503) 2248 1423; Guatemala, 5 Av 5–55, Zona 14, Europlaza, Torre II, Oficina 1502, Guatemala City ☎ (502) 2367 3883, ✉ embelguat@yahoo.com; Honduras, Hotel de Honduras, R/do Hotel Honduras Maya, Tegucigalpa ☎ (504) 238 4614,

✉ consuladobelize@yahoo.com; Panama, Edificio Atalaya – Planta Baja, Oficina No. 3, Av Balboa y C 32 Este, Panama City ☎ (507) 227 0997; UK, Belize High Commission, 3rd Floor, 45 Crawford Place, London, W1H 4LP ☎ (020) 7723 3603, ✉ bzhc-lon @btconnect.com; US, 2535 Massachusetts Ave NW, Washington DC, 20008 ☎ (202) 332-9636, 🖳 www .embassyofbelize.org.

Costa Rica Canada, 325 Dalhousie St, Ottawa, ON K1N 7G2 ☎ (613) 562-2855, ✉ embcr@costarica embassy.com; Panama, Av Samuel Lewis, Edificio Omega Piso 3ro, a un costado del Santuario Nacional, Panama City ☎ (507) 264 2980, ✉ embarica@cwp .net.pa; UK, Flat 1, 14 Lancaster Gate, London, W2 3LH, ☎ (020) 7706 8844; US, 2114 S St, NW, Washington DC 20008 ☎ (202) 234-2945, ✉ embassy@costarica-embassy.org.

El Salvador Belize, 49 Nanche St, Belmopan ☎ (501) 235 162; Canada, 209 Kent St, Ottawa, K2P 1Z8 ☎ (613) 238-2939; Costa Rica, Paseo Colón, Av 1A C 30 No.53 "N", San José ☎ (506) 2256-0043; Guatemala, 5A Av 8–15, Zona 9, Guatemala City ☎ (502) 360 7660; Honduras, Colonia Rubén Darío, 2A Av y 5A C No.620, apartado Postal 1936, Tegucigalpa ☎ (504) 239 0901, ✉ embasalva@cablecolor.hn; Nicaragua, Km 9 1/2 Carretera a Masaya, Residential Las Colinas, Pasaje Los Cerros 142, Managua ☎ (505) 2276-0712, ✉ embelsa@cablenet.com.ni; Panama, Edificio Metropolis, C Manuel Espinoza Batista, Piso 4, Apt 4-A, Panama City ☎ (507) 223 6385, ✉ embasalva@cwpanama.net.

Guatemala Australia (Consulate), 41 Blarney Ave, Killarney Heights, NSW 2087 ☎ (02) 9551 3018; Belize, 8 A St, Belize City ☎ (501) 33314; Canada, 130 Albert St, Suite 1010, Ottawa, ON, K1P 5G4 ☎ (613) 233-7237, ✉ embguate@ottawa.net; Costa Rica, De Pops de Curridabat, 500 Sur, 30 Oeste, 2da Casa Izquierda, San José ☎ (506) 283-2555, ✉ embguat@sol.racsa.co.cr; El Salvador, 15 Av Nte, No.135, San Salvador ☎ (503) 271225; Honduras, C Principal, Col Loma Linda Norte, Tegucigalpa ☎ (504) 311596, ✉ embguat@david.intertel.hn; Nicaragua, Km 11, 1/2 Carretera a Masaya, Managua ☎ (505) 2279-9609; Panama, C Abel Bravo y Calle 57, Barrio Bella Vista, Edif. Torre Cancun, Apdo 14-A, Panama City ☎ (507) 269 3475; UK, 13 Fawcett St, London SW10 9HN ☎ (020) 7351 3042, ✉ embaguatelondon@btinternet.com; US, 2220 R Street NW, Washington DC 20008 ☎ (202) 745-4953.

Honduras Belize, 22 Gabourel Lane, PO Box 285, Belize City ☎ (501) 224-5889, ✉ embhonbe@btl .net; Canada, 151 Slater St, Suite 805-A, Ottawa, ON, K1P 5H3 ☎ (1-613) 233-8900, 🖳 www .embassyhonduras.ca; Costa Rica, Urbanización Trejos Montealegre, De Banca Promerica 100 al

Oeste, 100 Sur y 350 al Oeste, San Rafael de Escazu, San José ☎(506) 291 5147, ✉emhondcr@sol.racsa .co.cr; El Salvador, 89 Av Nte entre 7 y 9 C Pte, No.561 Colonia Escalón, San Salvador ☎(503) 263 2808; Guatemala, 19 Av "A", 20–19 Zona 10, Guatemala City 0101 ☎(502) 366 5640, ✉embhond @intelnet.net.gt; Nicaragua, Reparto San Juan, del Gimnasio Hércules 1 cuadra al Sur, 1 cuadra al Este, C San Juan, no. 312, Apartado Postal No.321 ☎(505) 2270-4133, ✉embhonduras@cablenet .com.ni; Panama, C 31, Av Justo Arosemena, Apdo Postal 8704, Zona 5, Panama City ☎(507) 264 5513, ✉ehpam@cableonda.net; UK, 115 Gloucester Place, London W1U 6JT ☎(020) 7486 4880; US, 3007 Tilden St NW, Suite 4M, Washington DC 20008 ☎(202) 966-7702, ✉embassy@hondurasemb.org. **Nicaragua** Costa Rica, Avenida Central #2540, Barrio La California, Frente al Pizza Hut, San José ☎(506) 223-1489, ✉embanic@racsa.co.cr; UK, Vicarage House, Suite 12, 58–60 Kensington Church St, London W8 4DB ☎(020) 7938 2373, ✉emb.ofnicaragua@virgin.net; US, 1627 New Hampshire Ave NW, Washington DC 20009 ☎(202) 939-6570, ✉agnesalvarado@embanic.org. **Panama** Canada, 130 Albert St, Suite 300, Ottawa, ON K1P 5G4 ☎(613) 236-7177, ✉embassyofpanama@gmail.com; Costa Rica, Barrio La Granja, del Antiguo Higueron de San Pedro 200 sur y 25 este, San Pedro, Apartado 103–2050 San Pedro de Montes de Oca, San José ☎(506) 280-1570, ✉panaembacr@racsa.co.cr; El Salvador, Av Bungamilias #21 Colonia San

Francisco, San Salvador ☎(503) 2298-0773; Guatemala, 12 C 2–65, Zona 14, Guatemala City ☎(502) 2366 3338, ✉panaguate@hotmail.com; Honduras, Colonia Palmira, Edificio Palmira Piso 2, Frente al Hotel Honduras, Maya Tegucigalpa ☎(504) 239 5508; Nicaragua, Reparto Mantica, del Cuartel General de Bomberos, 1c. abajo, Casa no. 93, Esquina Opuesta al Restaurante, Managua ☎(505) 2266-8633; UK, Panama House, 40 Hertford St, London W1Y 7TG ☎ (020) 7409 2255; US, 2862 McGill Terrace NW, Washington DC 20008 ☎(202) 483-1407, ⊕www.embassyofpanama.org.

Customs

All Central American countries allow the import and export of a small amount of **tobacco and alcohol**. The exact amounts vary, but at their minimum levels 80 cigarettes and 1.5 litres of alcohol are allowed. Belize and Panama do not allow the import or export of plants, fruit, vegetables, meat or animal products. In Belize you are restricted to bringing in and taking out up to 100 Belizean dollars, while in Guatemala the import/export of local currency (quetzales) is completely prohibited. At some border crossings (especially on the Interamericana Highway) you should expect to have your bags searched, often a lengthy process when travelling by long-distance bus.

BORDER CROSSINGS

Most travellers in Central America take advantage of the close proximity of the region's many distinct nations, crossing international borders regularly. While for the most part this is straightforward, "border days" can also be some of the most exhausting of your trip – follow the tips below to ease the strain.

• Always check specific entry requirements before heading for the border.
• Ensure that your passport is stamped on both entry and exit.
• Try to cross in the morning, when public transport links are more frequent and queues lighter.
• Research current exchange rates online at ⊕www.oanda.com or ⊕www.xe.com and be savvy when dealing with moneychangers.
• If asked for "processing fees" request a receipt (such as the stamp given by Panama). Without one, these fees are not legal.
• Do not engage in discussion of your business with strangers. Borders are notorious hangouts for petty criminals and con men. If you are confused about how to proceed, ask a uniformed official.
• At popular crossings avoid group transport, which will slow your progress considerably. Chicken buses operate these routes as frequently as any other (although not at night).
• If given a stamped entry document do not lose it – you will require it later for departure.

GAY AND LESBIAN TRAVELLERS

While there are no laws forbidding the practice of consensual homosexual acts, homosexuality is uncomfortably tolerated by conservative Central American society, and harassment does exist in certain areas. Gay and lesbian travellers are unlikely to experience problems, however, if they remain discreet. Unsurprisingly, there is little in the way of an open gay community or scene. In the more cosmopolitan capital cities a few gay clubs exist, although these are almost entirely geared towards men.

INSURANCE

You'd do well to take out an **insurance policy** before travelling to cover against theft, loss, illness or injury. Before paying for a new policy, however, it's worth checking whether you are already covered on any existing home or medical insurance policies that you may hold. A typical travel insurance policy usually provides cover for the loss of baggage, tickets and – up to a certain limit – cash or cheques, as well as cancellation or curtailment of your journey. Most of them exclude so-called dangerous sports unless an extra premium is paid: in Central America this can mean scuba diving, whitewater rafting, surfing and trekking. It is also useful to have a policy providing a 24-hour medical emergency number.

When securing baggage cover, make sure that the per-article limit – typically under £500/$1000 – will cover your most valuable possession. If you need to **make a claim**, you should keep receipts for medicines and medical treatment as well as any high-value items that are being insured. In the event that you have anything stolen, you must obtain a *denuncia* from the police.

Several companies now offer tailored "backpacker" insurance, which provides low-cost coverage for extended durations (beyond the standard 30-day holiday policies). These include Rough Guides' own recommended insurance (see box above).

INTERNET

Central America is increasingly well connected to the internet and you should have little difficulty getting online. Even smaller towns usually have at least one internet café, often populated by noisy gaming schoolkids. Many internet cafés are well equipped with webcams and headphones as well as the facility to download digital photos onto CD. On average you can expect to pay US$1 per hour. Many hostels also provide internet access, although they may be more restrictive on usage and marginally more expensive. Check ⓦwww.kropla.com for details of how to use your laptop when abroad.

MAIL

With the prevalence of email, the need to negotiate the idiosyncrasies of foreign mail systems is thankfully becoming less frequent. Should you wish to investigate, however, you will find that **stamps** are rarely available outside the post office (*correo*), although it can be worth asking if you are buying a postcard, for example, as occasionally souvenir shops and stationers do stock them. Sending mail from the main post office in any capital city is probably the best way to ensure speedy and efficient delivery. The cost and speed of mailing items varies from country to country, but is by far cheapest and quickest from Panama. To receive mail by **poste restante** you should address it to yourself at "Lista de Correos" at the "Correo Central" in the capital city of the appropriate country.

MAPS

The best overall map of Central America, covering the region at a scale of 1:1,100,000, is produced by Canada's International Travel Maps and Books (🕸www.itmb.com). They also publish individual country maps at various scales. Maps are generally hard to find once you get to Central America, so it's wise to bring them with you when possible.

MONEY

Cash payments are the norm in Central America, with the most convenient way to access money being via an **ATM** (*cajero automático*). Most machines accept Visa and MasterCard credit cards, as well as Visa debit cards, and are increasingly widespread throughout the region. However, it is always advisable to check specific destination listings in this guide in advance of travel to confirm that smaller settlements have an ATM, as not all do. If you are relying on ATMs, it's worth having a back-up card in case the first is lost or stolen. If you plan to be abroad for a significant period, it is worth thoroughly researching your bank's terms for cash withdrawals abroad – some make no charge at all, allowing you to make frequent withdrawals and carry only small amounts of cash around urban areas. As a possible alternative some banks will give **cash advances** over the counter (sometimes for a small fee). Try to hoard notes of small denominations; you will

constantly encounter problems obtaining change from local businesses, often stalling transactions as no one has anything smaller than a US$1 bill (or its equivalent). In general, budget-friendly hotels and restaurants do not take **credit cards**, though a few mid-range establishments and tourist handicraft shops may accept them. **Travellers' cheques** are increasingly difficult to change for the same reason, but are good to carry as a back-up.

Belize, Guatemala, Honduras, Nicaragua and Costa Rica each have their own **national currency** (see box below), while El Salvador and Panama both use the US dollar (in Panama the dollar is divided into 100 balboas – although US cents are also legal tender). However, **US dollars** are accepted throughout Central America and in many places prices for tourist services (eg, language school fees, plane tickets, tour fees) are quoted exclusively in them. Indeed, some ATMs (particularly those in Nicaragua) will actually dispense dollars on request. Local currency is always accepted at the current exchange rate, though, so there is no need to carry huge amounts of dollars in cash, though it is certainly useful to carry some to exchange at border crossings. Generally speaking, you should also get rid of any remaining unwanted local currency at border crossings, as it will be more difficult to exchange the further away from the border you are. Try to research the current exchange rates before dealing with moneychangers (🕸www.oanda.com or www.xe.com).

PHONES

It's easy enough to phone home from most cities and towns in Central America. Each country in the region has a national

EXCHANGE RATES

The following exchange rates were correct at the time of publication, though rates will inevitably vary over the course of the edition of the Guide in those countries whose currency is not pegged to the dollar; we've also given equivalents in British pounds and euros.

Belize (Belizean dollar; Bz$) US$1 = Bz$2 (fixed)/£1 = Bz$3/€1 = Bz$2.6
Costa Rica (colón; c) US$1 = 500c/£1 = 795.4c/€1 = 685.4c
Guatemala (quetzal; Q) US$1 = Q7.9/£1 = Q12.6/€1 = Q10.9
Honduras (lempira; L) US$1 = L18.9/£1 = L30.1/€1 = L25.9
Nicaragua (córdoba; C$) US$1 = C$21.9/£1 = C$34.9/€1 = C$30.1

telecommunications company with offices throughout the country. It's also worth keeping an eye out for internet cafés that offer **Skype**, for excellent-value international calls. **Mobile phones** are as prolific as they are in the developed world; despite living in relative poverty, the rural population can often be spotted checking their text messages. You may find that taking your own phone comes in useful in emergencies, but on the other hand, it does become one more item to keep secure. Also remember that rates to receive calls and messages while abroad are often extortionate. Alternatively, you may consider purchasing a phone locally, as packages that include call-time are reasonable. However, practically speaking, if you only anticipate making the odd call, forget the mobile and simply use local **payphones**, which are usually easy to come by. Country-specific details on phoning home are given in the "Basics" section of each chapter.

SHOPPING

If you're shopping for souvenirs of your trip, you'll often find that what's on offer is either significantly cheaper or significantly different to what's available back home – places like the Guatemalan highlands, where indigenous **craft markets** abound, and Panama City, where glitzy **shopping malls** offer cut-price designer clothing and shoes. Throughout the region you can also buy locally sourced **coffee**, thereby supporting local farmers.

In markets **haggling** is standard practice. Try not to get cornered by stallholders, who will try to pressure you into buying on the spot. It is always wise to research various sellers' best prices before agreeing to a sale. It's also worth scouting out official **tourist shops** (where prices are fixed) to get a ballpark figure to try and beat in markets. If you plan to buy several items you will get the best prices if you buy in bulk from the same seller. Haggling is not commonplace in shops. However, if you are unsure about whether or not prices are fixed, simply ask if discounts apply: "Hay descuentos?"

TIME

Panama is GMT -6, and all the other countries are seven hours behind GMT. In recent years, Central American governments have gone back and forth on the issue of whether or not to apply daylight savings as an energy-saving measure, and will no doubt continue to so in the future.

TOURIST INFORMATION

Official sources of tourist information in Central America are spotty at best. For the budget traveller, often the best way to obtain the latest advice is to talk to other backpackers about their experiences. Similarly, popular hostels usually have notice boards and the best have clued-up staff with local knowledge. All Central American countries do have their own official tourist offices, but the prevalence of these on the ground is not great. However, the following tourist-office websites provide a useful reference, especially for pre-trip planning. See also the "On the net" boxes in the individual chapters for further suggestions.

Central American tourist-office websites

Belize ⓦ www.travelbelize.org
Costa Rica ⓦ www.visitcostarica.com
El Salvador ⓦ www.elsalvador.travel
Guatemala ⓦ www.visitguatemala.com
Honduras ⓦ www.visithonduras.com
Nicaragua ⓦ www.visitanicaragua.com
Panama ⓦ www.panamatravel.com

TRAVELLERS WITH DISABILITIES

Central America is not the most accessible part of the world for travellers with disabilities. On the whole, it's the top-end hotels and services that may offer equipped facilities – out of the price range for most budget travellers. However, for the most part, Central American society is community-orientated and strangers take pleasure in helping and facilitating the passage of others. **Costa Rica** (where tourist facilities are well developed) and **Panama** (where there is a large expat community) have the best infrastructure, relative to the rest of the region.

The best course of action is to plan thoroughly in advance of travel. There are many specialist websites advising travellers with disabilities, including ⓦ www.able-travel.com, www.globalaccessnews.com and www.disabledtraveladvice.co.uk.

Belize

HIGHLIGHTS ✪

CAYE CAULKER:
admire the colourful
coral and dazzling
array of fish ✪

SAN IGNACIO:
excellent accommodation
and a fantastic choice of
adventure trips ✪

BLUE HOLE: ✪
dive deep into the
inky waters of this
coral-encrusted cavern

**COCKSCOMB BASIN
WILDLIFE SANCTUARY:**
hike the winding jungle
paths of the world's
first jaguar reserve ✪

CARACOL: ✪
explore Belize's
greatest and most
extensive Maya site

PLACENCIA:
relax on Belize's most
beautiful, white-sand
beaches

ROUGH COSTS

DAILY BUDGET Basic US$35/
occasional treat US$70

DRINK Beer US$2

FOOD Jerk chicken US$5

CAMPING/HOSTEL/BUDGET HOTEL
US$5/US$15/US$25

TRAVEL Belize City–Caye Caulker
(35km) by ferry: 45min, US$10;
Belize City–San Ignacio (120km)
by bus: 2hr 30min, US$4

FACT FILE

POPULATION 308,000

AREA 22,966 sq km

LANGUAGE English

CURRENCY Belize dollar (Bz$)

CAPITAL Belmopan (population:
20,000)

INTERNATIONAL PHONE CODE
☎501

TIME ZONE GMT -6hr

Introduction

With far less of a language barrier to overcome than elsewhere in Central America, Belize, perched on the isthmus's northeast corner, is the ideal first stop on a tour of the region. And, although it is the most expensive country in Central America, its reliable public transport and numerous hotels and restaurants make it an ideal place to travel independently.

Belize offers some of the most **breathtaking scenery** anywhere in the region: thick tropical forests envelop much of the country's southern and western regions, stretching up towards the misty heights of the sparsely populated Maya Mountains, while just offshore, dazzling turquoise shallows and cobalt depths surround the **Mesoamerican Barrier Reef**, the longest such reef in the Americas, as well as the jewels in Belize's natural crown: three of the four **coral atolls** in the Caribbean.

Scattered along the barrier reef, a chain of islands – known as **cayes** – protect the mainland from the ocean swell, and make wonderful bases for **snorkelling and diving**; the cayes are most travellers' top destination in the country. **Ambergris Caye** and **Caye Caulker** are the best known, though many of the less developed islands, including picture-perfect **Tobacco Caye**, are gaining in popularity. The **interior** has remained relatively untouched, thanks to a national emphasis on conservation:

in the west, the dramatic landscape – especially the tropical forests and cave systems – of the **Cayo District** provides numerous opportunities for adventure-seekers. Inexpensive **San Ignacio**, the region's transport hub, gives access to the heights of the **Mountain Pine Ridge Forest Reserve** and the rapids of the **Macal** and **Mopan rivers**. For those with an adventurous spirit of a different sort, hectic **Belize City** offers a fascinating – if nerve-wracking – opportunity to explore the country's energetic multicultural spirit. **Dangriga**, the main town of the south-central region, serves as a jumping-off point for the **Cockscomb Basin Wildlife Sanctuary**, while the **Placencia peninsula** has some of the country's best **beaches**. In the far south, Belize's most isolated region, the **Maya Mountains** rise to over 1100m and border some of the country's only **rainforest**. Throughout the country, the archeological treasures of the **ancient Maya** dot the landscape.

CHRONOLOGY

200–800 AD Classic period: Maya culture flourishes throughout Belize.

800–900 AD Maya cities across central and southern Belize decline, though Lamanai and other northern cities continue to thrive throughout the Postclassic period (900–1540 AD).

1530s The Spanish, led by Francisco de Montejo, engage in the first of numerous unsuccessful attempts to conquer the Maya of Belize.

1544 Gaspar Pacheco subdues Maya resistance and founds a town on Lake Balcar.

1570 Spanish mission is established at Lamanai.

1638 The Maya rebel, forcing the Spanish to abandon the areas they have settled.

WHEN TO VISIT

The country's climate is subtropical, with temperatures warm throughout the year, generally 20–27°C from January to May (the dry season) and 22–32°C from June to December (the wet season). The best time to visit the country is usually between January and March, when it's not (quite) as hot or humid. That said, these months are also Belize's peak tourist season, and prices tend to be higher.

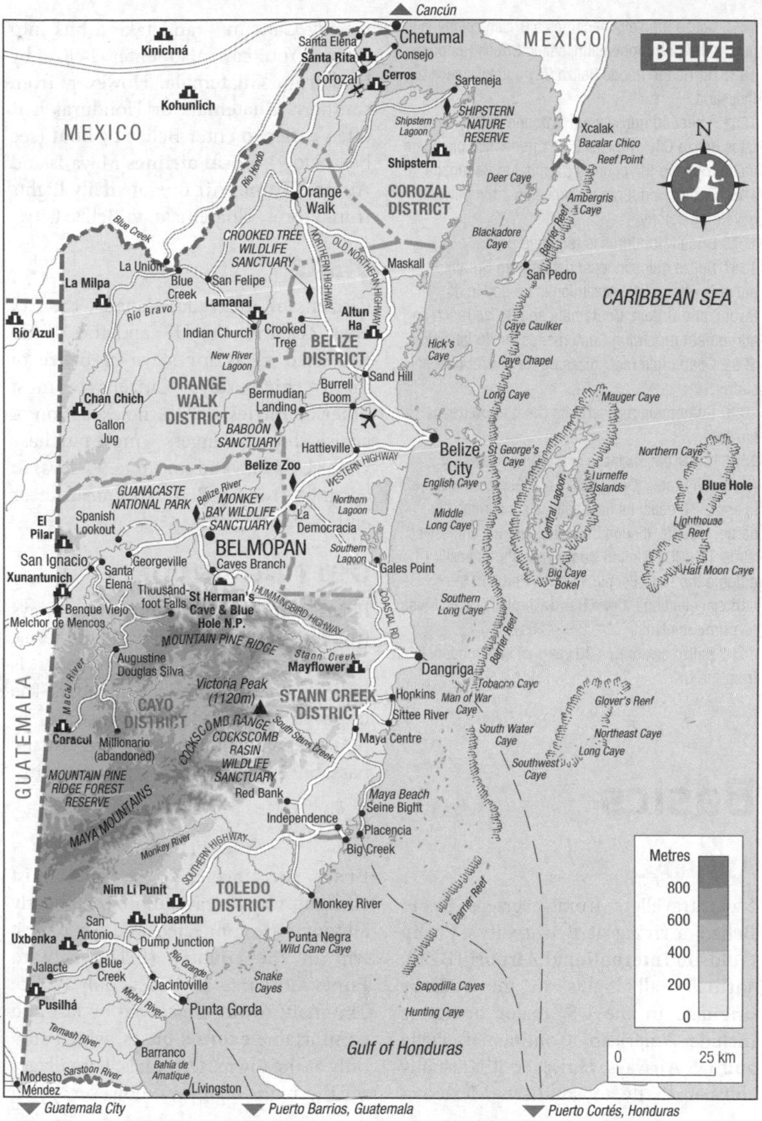
BELIZE
Cancún
MEXICO
Kinichná
Santa Elena
Santa Rita
Chetumal
Consejo
Corozal
Cerros
Sarteneja
Kohunlich
Shipstern Lagoon
SHIPSTERN NATURE RESERVE
Xcalak
Bacalar Chico
Reef Point
N
Shipstern
Rio Hondo
Orange Walk
COROZAL DISTRICT
Deer Caye
Ambergris Caye
Barrier Reef
Blue Creek
CROOKED TREE WILDLIFE SANCTUARY
NORTHERN HIGHWAY
OLD NORTHERN HIGHWAY
Blackadore Caye
La Union
Maskall
San Pedro
La Milpa
Blue Creek
San Felipe
CARIBBEAN SEA
Rio Bravo
Lamanai
Altun Ha
Río Azul
Indian Church
Crooked Tree
BELIZE DISTRICT
Caye Caulker
Hick's Caye
New River Lagoon
Caye Chapel
ORANGE WALK DISTRICT
Sand Hill
Burrell Boom
Bermudian Landing
Long Caye
Mauger Caye
Chan Chich
Gallon Jug
BABOON SANCTUARY
Hattieville
Belize City
St George's Caye
Northern Caye
English Caye
Turneffe Islands
Blue Hole
Belize Zoo
WESTERN HIGHWAY
GUANACASTE NATIONAL PARK
Belize River
MONKEY BAY WILDLIFE SANCTUARY
Northern Lagoon
Middle Long Caye
Central Lagoon
Lighthouse Reef
El Pilar
Spanish Lookout
La Democracia
BELMOPAN
Southern Lagoon
San Ignacio
Georgeville
Caves Branch
Gales Point
Big Caye Bokel
Half Moon Caye
Xunantunich
Santa Elena
Thousand-foot Falls
St Herman's Cave & Blue Hole N.P.
HUMMINGBIRD HIGHWAY
COASTAL RD
Southern Long Caye
Flores & Tikal
Benque Viejo
Melchor de Mencos
MOUNTAIN PINE RIDGE
Barrier Reef
Stann Creek
Mayflower
Dangriga
Augustine Douglas Silva
Tobacco Caye
Macal River
Victoria Peak (1120m)
Hopkins
Man of War Caye
Glover's Reef
STANN CREEK DISTRICT
Sittee River
CAYO DISTRICT
COCKSCOMB RANGE
South Stann Creek
Maya Centre
South Water Caye
Northeast Caye
GUATEMALA
Caracol
Millionario (abandoned)
COCKSCOMB BASIN WILDLIFE SANCTUARY
Long Caye
Southwest Caye
MOUNTAIN PINE RIDGE FOREST RESERVE
Red Bank
Maya Beach
Seine Bight
MAYA MOUNTAINS
Independence
Placencia
Monkey River
SOUTHERN HIGHWAY
Big Creek
Metres
800
600
400
200
0
Nim Li Punit
TOLEDO DISTRICT
Monkey River
Barrier Reef
San Antonio
Lubaantun
Uxbenka
Dump Junction
Punta Negra
Wild Cane Caye
Poptún & Flores
Rio Grande
Jalacte
Blue Creek
Snake Cayes
Jacintoville
Sapodilla Cayes
Pusilhá
Moho River
Punta Gorda
Hunting Caye
Temash River
Barranco
Gulf of Honduras
0
25 km
Bahía de Amatique
Sarstoon River
Modesto Méndez
Livingston
Guatemala City
Puerto Barrios, Guatemala
Puerto Cortés, Honduras

1630–1670 British buccaneers, later known as Baymen, plunder Spanish treasure ships along the Belizean coast, then begin to settle the coastline and harvest logwood, used for textile dyes in Europe. They rely heavily on slave labour from Africa.

1700s Spain and Britain clash over control of Belize. In 1763, Spain officially grants British settlers logging rights, but does not abandon territorial claims on the region.

1798 The British defeat the Spanish in the Battle of St George's Caye, gaining control of the region.

1838 Slavery is abolished.

1839 Citing Spanish territorial claims, newly independent Guatemala first asserts sovereign authority over Belize.

1847 Mexican refugees fleeing the Caste Wars in the Yucatán arrive in Belize.

1859 Britain and Guatemala sign a treaty that acknowledges British sovereignty over Belize.

1862 Belize officially becomes a British colony, and part of the Commonwealth, called British Honduras.
1931 Hurricane floods Belize City and kills several thousand.
1961 A second hurricane (Hurricane Hattie) devastates Belize City and kills 262, after which plans are made to move the country's capital to Belmopan.
1964 British Honduras becomes an internally self-governing colony.
1973 British Honduras is renamed Belize.
1981 Belize gains independence from Britain, but only after a UN Resolution is passed in its favour, and Britain, Guatemala and Belize reach an agreement regarding Guatemala's territorial claims.
1992 Guatemala recognizes Belize's independent status.
2000 Guatemala reasserts its claim to Belizean territory.
2005 Under the auspices of the Organization of American States (OAS), Belize and Guatemala agree to establish peaceful negotiations concerning the border dispute, though the issue remains unresolved.
2008 The UDP (United Democratic Party) easily defeats the PUP (People's United Party) in the national elections; Dean Barrow replaces Said Musa as prime minister.
2011 Belize celebrates 30 years of independence from the UK.

Basics

ARRIVAL

Most travellers from overseas **fly** to Belize, arriving at Belize City's **Philip Goldson International Airport (BZE)**. Virtually all flights to the country originate in the US; major operators include American, Continental, Delta and US Airways. However, it is usually cheaper to fly to southern Mexico –

usually Cancún – and take a **bus** into Belize. You can also enter Belize by land from Guatemala. However, from southern Guatemala or Honduras it is often easier to enter Belize by **boat** (see box below). **Local airlines** Maya Island Air and Tropic Air operate daily flights from Flores, Guatemala, to Belize City.

VISAS

Citizens of Australia, Canada, the EU, New Zealand, the UK and the US do not need **visas** for stays in Belize of up to **thirty days**. Citizens of most other countries – with the exception of cruise-ship passengers – must purchase visas (US$50; valid for up to 90 days) in advance from a Belizean consulate or embassy (see p.46).

GETTING AROUND

Belize only has three major highways (the Northern, Western and Southern), but the majority of the country is well served by **public transport**. The unpaved side roads are sometimes in poor repair, though they are usually passable except in the worst rainstorms.

By bus

Buses are the cheapest, and most efficient, way to travel in Belize – nearly all towns are connected, and the longest trip in the country (Belize City to Punta Gorda; 5–7hr) costs only Bz$25. The main towns are served by fast and comfortable **express buses**, which stop only at the towns' terminals. For villages off the main highways, however, you'll

LAND AND SEA ROUTES TO BELIZE

There are two land border crossings into Belize: one from Chetumal, Mexico, to Santa Elena (see box, p.84), and one from Melchor de Mencos, Guatemala, to Benque Viejo del Carmen (see box, p.95).

There are also sea routes to Belize from Guatemala and Honduras. Daily skiffs travel to and from Punta Gorda, in the far south, and Puerto Barrios, Guatemala. Dangriga (see p.97) and Placencia (see p.104), on the southern coast, are served by at least one weekly skiff from Puerto Cortés, Honduras.

have to rely on slower **local services**, often with just one bus a day running Monday to Saturday only. These buses are brightly painted, recycled North American school buses, which will pick up and drop off anywhere along the roadside. The most frequent services operate along the Western and Northern highways, usually from very early in the morning to mid-evening. The Hummingbird and Southern highways, to Dangriga, Placencia and Punta Gorda, are not quite so well provided for, though services are improving. **Tickets** are purchased from the conductor.

By car

In the most remote parts of Belize bus services will probably only operate once a day, if at all, and unless you have your own transport (which is expensive), **hitching** is the only option. Though common among locals, it is important to remember that this practice is never completely safe. Otherwise, the main drawback is the shortage of traffic; if cars do pass they'll usually offer you a lift, though you may be expected to offer the driver some money in return.

All **taxis** in Belize are licensed, and can be identified by their green plates. They operate from special ranks in the centre of all mainland towns. There are no meters, so establish your fare in advance; within towns a Bz$8–10 **fixed rate** should apply. It is also possible to negotiate taxi rides between cities, though this option can be quite expensive: usually at least US$60–100 per person for a three-hour ride.

By bike

Cycling can be a great way to reach Belize's more isolated ruins and towns. **Bikes** are increasingly available for rent (usually Bz$15–25 per day), especially in San Ignacio and Placencia. Though biking along major highways is

certainly possible, it is very uncommon, and drivers will not be watching for cyclists; it is therefore important to remain exceptionally alert during the day and to avoid cycling at night. You'll find repair shops in all towns. One thing to note, however, is that Belizean buses don't have roof racks, as they do in Guatemala; if there's room, the driver might let you take your bike onto the bus.

By boat

If you plan on visiting the cayes, you'll have to travel by **boat**, which will likely be a fast **skiff**, normally partially covered, though sometimes open to the elements (bring a raincoat). **Tickets** (usually Bz$25–45) cannot be purchased in advance for domestic routes, so it's worth showing up half an hour before your departure time, though there's usually plenty of room. Numerous skiffs run daily between Belize City, Caye Caulker and Ambergris Caye, and also connect Ambergris Caye with Corozal.

By air

Though quite expensive, some budget travellers do choose to travel by **air**, as flights are not only much faster than buses, but also connect destinations unreachable by road. Maya Island Air (☎223-1140, ⊛www.mayaregional.com) and Tropic Air (☎226-2012, ⊛www.tropicair.com) each operate numerous daily flights from both the Municipal and International airports in Belize City to San Pedro, Caye Caulker, Dangriga, Placencia and Punta Gorda. Flights also run from San Pedro to Corozal. Prices start at around Bz$70–90.

ACCOMMODATION

Belizean **accommodation** is expensive by Central American standards, but there are nonetheless plenty of budget hotels in all towns, and the most popular tourist destinations – Caye Caulker, San Ignacio, Placencia – have a great deal of choice and are often less expensive than the rest of the country. **Finding a room** is usually no problem, though at Christmas, New Year and Easter, booking ahead is advisable.

Hostels are uncommon in Belize, though some dormitory accommodation (usually US$10–15) is available in Belize City, Caye Caulker, Dangriga, Placencia, San Ignacio and San Pedro. Most budget travellers rely instead on **budget hotels**, which usually charge US$25–35 for a double, depending on the city. Check out Toucan Trail (Ⓦwww.toucantrail.com), which lists over 130 good-value places to stay for under US$60, for ideas.

There are also few proper **campsites** in the country, and those that do exist have only the most basic services. Some mid-priced hotels in smaller villages and on the coast will allow you to pitch a tent on their grounds, but this can be expensive. In order to camp in any protected area, you'll have to get permission from park authorities – except at the entrances to the Mountain Pine Ridge Forest Reserve and the Jaguar Reserve, where reservations are usually not necessary.

FOOD AND DRINK

Belizean food is a mix of Latin American and Caribbean, with Creole flavours dominating the scene in local restaurants, but with a number of international options as well – Indian and Chinese are the most prevalent. The basis of any Creole main meal is **rice and beans**, and this features heavily in smaller restaurants, where most meals run Bz$8–12. The white rice and red beans are cooked together in coconut oil and usually served with stewed chicken or beef, or fried fish; there's always a bottle of hot sauce on the table for extra spice. **Seafood** is almost always excellent. Red snapper or grouper is

invariably fantastic, and you might also try a barracuda steak, conch fritters or a plate of fresh shrimp. In San Pedro, Caye Caulker, San Ignacio and Placencia the food can be exceptional, and the only concern is that you might get bored with **lobster**, which is served in a vast array of dishes. The **closed season** for lobster (when it should not be served) is from mid-February to mid-June.

Breakfast (Bz$6–10) is usually served from 7am to 10am and generally includes eggs and flour tortillas. The **lunch hour** (noon–1pm) is observed with almost religious devotion – you will not be able to get anything else done. **Dinner** is usually eaten quite early, between 6 and 8pm; few restaurants stay open much later.

Vegetables are scarce in Creole food, but there's often a side dish of potato or coleslaw. There are few specifically **vegetarian** restaurants, but in touristy areas many places offer a couple of vegetarian dishes. Otherwise, you're likely to be offered chicken or ham even if you say you don't eat meat. Your best bet for a vegetarian meal outside the main tourist areas may well be one of Belize's many Chinese restaurants.

Drink

The most basic drinks to accompany food are water, beer and the usual soft drinks. **Tap water**, in the towns at least, is safe but highly chlorinated, and many villages (though not Caye Caulker) have a potable water system. Many travellers nonetheless choose to purchase filtered bottled water, which is sold everywhere for around Bz$2 per bottle. Belikin, Belize's main **beer**, comes in several varieties: regular, a lager-type bottled and draught beer; bottled stout; and Lighthouse and Premium, more expensive bottled brews. Cashew-nut and berry **wines** are bottled and sold in some villages, and you can also get hold of imported wine, though it's not cheap. Local **rum**, in both dark and clear varieties, is the best deal in Belizean alcohol. The legal drinking age for alcohol in Belize is 18.

Fruit juices are widely available, with fresh orange, lime and pineapple being the most popular options. **Coffee**, except in the best establishments, will almost certainly be instant, though decent **tea** is quite prevalent. One last drink that deserves a mention is **seaweed**, a strange blend of seaweed, milk, cinnamon, sugar and cream.

CULTURE AND ETIQUETTE

Belizeans are generally welcoming and accustomed to tourists, though it's important to remember that the country is, on the whole, quite **conservative**. Dress, except among professionals, is usually casual, though tourists – especially women – who wear revealing clothing will probably be looked down upon, particularly in Belize's many churches.

KRIOL WORDS AND PHRASES

Belizean Kriol, derived mainly from English, is the native language of the majority of the country's inhabitants. Some 70 percent of the population speak the language and it is not unusual to hear English and Kriol being used interchangeably in conversation.

Good morning Gud maanin.

What's up? Weh di go aan?

What's your name? Weh yu naym?

My name is … Mee naym …

How are you? Da how yu di du?

Fine Aarait.

What time is it? Weh taim yu gat?

How much does this cost? Humoch dis kaas?

I don't understand Mee noh andastan.

I don't know Mee noh know.

Where am I? Weh I deh?

It doesn't matter Ih noh mata.

The country's laidback attitude usually carries over into conversation; when approaching Belizeans, it's best to be friendly, relaxed and patient. **Women travellers** may receive advances from local men. Ignoring such attentions completely will sometimes only be met by greater persistence; walking away while flashing a quick smile and wave usually gets the message across, while remaining polite.

Belizeans are not particularly accepting of **homosexuality** and rarely open about sexual orientation. Though it is unlikely that locals will express disapproval, it is a good idea to avoid public displays of affection. There are no gay venues in the country.

Belizeans rarely **tip**, though foreigners are usually expected to give around ten percent in taxis and in restaurants. **Haggling** is also uncommon in Belize and will usually be considered rude, except at street markets.

SPORTS AND OUTDOOR ACTIVITIES

Football (soccer) and **basketball** are very popular in Belize, though the country's size and resources limit teams to the semiprofessional level, and visitors will find few spectator events.

However, Belize is a haven for a wide range of **outdoor activities**. Many travellers will participate in some form of **watersports**, including snorkelling, diving, windsurfing, kayaking and sailing. Companies in San Pedro, Caye Caulker and Placencia offer **diving courses** and lead multi-day kayaking and sailing trips to the cayes. See p.76, p.72 and p.106, respectively, for information about local operators. Inland, **canoeing** and **rafting** are popular, particularly out west in the Cayo district. Also in this region, operators organize **hiking** trips through the local jungle and Mountain Pine Ridge Forest, as well as **horseriding** to Maya ruins and natural sights. Stunning cave systems dot the south and west and **caving tours** are becoming more widespread and popular. See p.90 for operators in San Ignacio.

COMMUNICATIONS

Though more efficient (and expensive) than the rest of Central America, Belizean **postal services** can still be unreliable. Most towns have post offices, usually open Monday to Thursday 8am to 4pm and Friday 8am to 5pm. Sending letters, cards and parcels home is straightforward; prices start at Bz$0.75 for a letter and Bz$0.40 for a postcard.

Belize has a modern phone system, with **payphones** plentiful throughout the country. Payphones can only be used with **phonecards**, which are widely available from BTL (Belize Telecommunications Limited) offices, as well as hotels, shops and stations. Phonecards can be used for both local and international calls. There are **no area codes** in Belize, so you need to dial all seven digits. Making a reverse charge (collect) call home is easy using the Home Country Direct service, available at BTL offices, most payphones and larger hotels – dial the access code (printed on some payphones and in the phone book) to connect with an operator in your home country. **Mobile phones** are common in Belize, and almost all of the country receives excellent service. North Americans can usually connect to local systems with their regular service,

albeit at very high roaming charges. Alternatively, BTL sells SIM cards to visitors with compatible international phones and can usually help find rental mobile phones for around Bz$20 a day.

Belizeans are avid users of the **internet**, and web access is readily available in all the main towns and for guests at many hotels, though it can be expensive in tourist areas – up to Bz$12/hr.

CRIME AND SAFETY

Though Belize does have a relatively high **crime** rate, general crime against tourists is rare, especially in comparison to other Central American countries, and **violent crime** against tourists is seldom experienced, even in Belize City. It is important to note, however, that several attacks on tourist groups have occurred in recent years near the Guatemalan border, though most tour operators now take precautions to prevent this. Elsewhere in the country, theft does occur, the majority of cases involving **break-ins** at hotels: bear this in mind when you're searching for a room. Out and about there's always a slight danger of **pickpockets**, but with a bit of common sense you've nothing to fear. **Verbal abuse** is not uncommon, especially in Belize City. The vast majority of this harassment is harmless, though the situation can be more threatening for **women travelling alone**; most hecklers, however, will be satisfied with a smile and wave as you

---

BELIZE ON THE NET

Ⓦ **www.belizeaudubon.org** The latest information on Belize's growing number of reserves, national parks and associated visitor centres.

Ⓦ **www.belizebus.wordpress.com** Excellent guide to transport routes and timetables.

Ⓦ **www.belizefirst.com** Online magazine dedicated to Belize, featuring accurate reviews and articles about hotels, restaurants and destinations.

Ⓦ **www.spear.org.bz** In-depth information on social, cultural, political and economic matters concerning Belize.

Ⓦ **www.travelbelize.org** Belize's official tourism website offers excellent advice on travelling in Belize and can even help book accommodation and tours.

move quickly onwards. When making new acquaintances, women travellers should also keep in mind that there have been reports of incidences involving date-rape drugs in Belize, and should not accept food or drink from strangers. For general safety tips in Belize City, see the box on p.61. If you need to **report a crime**, your first stop should be the tourism police, ubiquitous in Belize City and becoming more common in many tourist hotspots, including Caye Caulker, Ambergris Caye and Placencia.

Many of the country's violent crimes are related to the **drug trade**, of which Belize is an important link in the chain between South and North America. Marijuana, cocaine and crack are all readily available, and whether you like it or not you'll receive regular offers. All such substances are **illegal**, and despite the fact that dope is smoked openly in the streets, the police do arrest people for possession of marijuana – they particularly enjoy catching tourists. If you are arrested you'll probably spend a couple of days in jail and pay a fine of several hundred US dollars; expect no sympathy from your embassy.

HEALTH

Health standards in Belize are quite high for the region, and Belize City has **hospitals** as well as a number of **private physicians** (see p.67). All other large towns have well-stocked **pharmacies and clinics**, which are usually free, though many will expect a donation for their services.

INFORMATION AND MAPS

Information on travelling in Belize is abundant, though often only available online, as even some major towns (except Belize City, Punta Gorda, Placencia and San Pedro) don't have a local tourist office. The office of the country's official source of tourist information, the **Belize Tourism Board** (BTB; ☎227-2420, ⊛www.travelbelize .org), is in Belize City and is not particularly helpful, though their website is excellent. The **Belize Tourism Industry Association** (BTIA; ⊛www.btia.org), which regulates many of the country's tourism businesses, has helpful representatives in touristed areas.

Local **maps** can be difficult to find and are often nonexistent in smaller towns and villages (where most streets don't have names), though the better hotels will usually be able to provide them to guests. The *Rough Guide Map to Guatemala and Belize* is a good, detailed resource.

MONEY AND BANKS

The national currency is the **Belize dollar**, which is divided into 100 cents and fixed at two to one with the US dollar (US$1=Bz$2); US dollars are also widely accepted, either in cash or travellers' cheques. On account of this dual-currency system, always check whether the price you are quoted is in Belizean or US dollars; we have noted prices in local currency unless an operation has specifically quoted their fees in US dollars.

Credit and debit cards are widely used in Belize and are increasingly accepted, even in smaller hotels and restaurants. Visa is the best option, though many establishments also accept MasterCard. Before you pay, check if there's a charge for using plastic, as you might have to pay an extra five or seven percent for the privilege. Any bank can give you a Visa/MasterCard **cash advance**, and most of them have **ATMs** that accept foreign-issued cards.

Taxes in Belize are quite high: sales tax is 12.5 percent and hotel tax is 9 percent. The hotel prices throughout this chapter are given inclusive of tax. Leaving Belize, you'll have to pay a US$15 **exit tax**, plus a PACT conservation fee of US$3.75; add US$15 if you are flying out of the country.

You'll find at least one **bank** in every town. Although the exchange rate is fixed, banks in Belize will give slightly less than Bz$2 for US$1 for both cash and travellers' cheques, so it can be a good idea simply to pay in US dollars if they are accepted and if you have them. Other than banks, only licensed *casas de cambio*, which can be difficult to find, are allowed to **exchange currency**, though there's usually a shop where locals go. To buy US dollars, you'll have to show an onward ticket.

OPENING HOURS AND HOLIDAYS

It's difficult to be specific about **opening hours** in Belize but in general **shops** are open 8am to noon and 1pm to 5pm.

The **lunch hour** (noon–1pm) is almost universally observed. Some shops and businesses work a half-day on Saturday, and everything is liable to close early on Friday. **Banks** (generally Mon–Thurs 8am–2pm, Fri 8am–4pm) and government offices are only open Monday to Friday. Watch out for **Sundays**, too, when shops and restaurants outside tourist areas are likely to be closed, and fewer bus services and internal flights operate. Archeological sites, however, are open every day. The main **public holidays**, when virtually everything will be closed, are listed in the box above, though note that if the holiday falls mid-week, it is observed on the following Monday.

FESTIVALS

Belize's calendar is full of **festivals**, ranging from the local to the national. The calendar below only includes a few highlights – you'll find plenty of entertainment at any given time.

February Carnaval is celebrated with dancing, parades, costumes and drinking.

March Celebrations throughout the country in honour of Baron Bliss Day (March 9); La Ruta Maya River Challenge in San Ignacio.

April Fiesta in San José Succotz honouring the village's patron saint.

May Cashew Festival in Crooked Tree; Toledo Cacao-Fest in Punta Gorda; Coconut Festival in Caye Caulker; National Agriculture and Trade Show in Belmopan.

June Caye Caulker Lobster Festival; three-day Día de San Pedro festival in San Pedro; Placencia Lobster Festival.

July Belize international film festival in Belize City.

August Week-long Deer Dance Festival in San Antonio; Costa Maya festival in San Pedro.

September Celebrations commemorating St George's Caye Day and Independence Day.

November Garífuna Settlement Day (Nov 19).

PUBLIC HOLIDAYS

January 1 New Year's Day

March 9 Baron Bliss Day

March/April (variable) Good Friday, Holy Saturday, Easter Monday

May 1 Labour Day

May 24 Commonwealth Day

September 10 St George's Caye Day/National Day

September 21 Independence Day

October 12 Columbus Day (Pan America Day)

November 19 Garífuna Settlement Day

December 25 Christmas Day

December 26 Boxing Day

Belize City

Even to the most hardened cosmopolite **BELIZE CITY** – the country's largest city, though not the capital – can be a daunting place. Dilapidated wooden buildings stand right on the edge of the road, offering pedestrians little refuge from the incessant traffic, and local attention ranges from simple curiosity and good-natured joking to outright heckling. Still, travellers who approach the city with an open mind – and those who are willing to spend more than a few hours here – may actually enjoy themselves. The streets, which certainly are chaotic, buzz with energy, the result of the diversity of the city's 76,000 citizens. And the city is, without a doubt, an experience; those who manage to feel comfortable here should have no problems anywhere else in the country.

What to see and do

Belize City is divided into northern and southern halves by **Haulover Creek**, a branch of the Belize River. The pivotal (literally) point of the city centre is the Liverpool-made **Swing Bridge**, the only manually operated swing bridge left in the Americas. Formerly opened twice a day, it is now only operated on special request due to the decrease in river traffic. **North** of the bridge is the slightly more upmarket part of town, home to the most expensive hotels. **South** of the Swing Bridge is the commercial zone, home to the city's banks and a couple of supermarkets. It's all compact enough that **walking** is the easiest way to get around.

Image Factory

The **Image Factory**, north of the Swing Bridge at 91 N Front St (Mon–Fri 9am–5pm; free, but donations welcome; ☏223-4093, ⊛www.imagefactorybelize .com), hosts displays by Belize's hottest contemporary artists. The gallery holds outstanding, frequently provocative exhibitions, and you often get a chance to chat with the artists themselves.

Tourism Village

Continuing east along North Front Street, you'll encounter an advance guard of trinket sellers, street musicians, hustlers and hair-braiders, announcing you're near **Tourism Village**, Belize's **cruise-ship terminal**. The Village itself is little more than a dock for the boats to disembark their passengers, and an attached shopping mall. Across the street, the **Fort Street Plaza** serves as an extension of the Village and includes a restaurant, bar and additional shops. A number of temporary vendors line the streets in this area, though the items tend to be overpriced; you're better off buying souvenirs in town (see p.67).

SAFETY IN BELIZE CITY

Walking in Belize City in daylight is perfectly safe if you use common sense: be civil, don't provoke trouble by arguing too forcefully and never show large sums of money on the street. Women should dress conservatively: female travellers, especially those wearing short shorts or skirts, are likely to attract mild verbal harassment from local men. However, the presence of a specially trained tourism police (☏227-6082), together with the legal requirement that all tour guides be licensed, generally prevents serious crime.

The chances of being mugged do increase after dark, but you'll find that you can walk – with others – around the centre in relative safety; you'll certainly encounter tourism police in this area. If you're venturing further afield, or if you've just arrived by bus at night, travel by taxi.

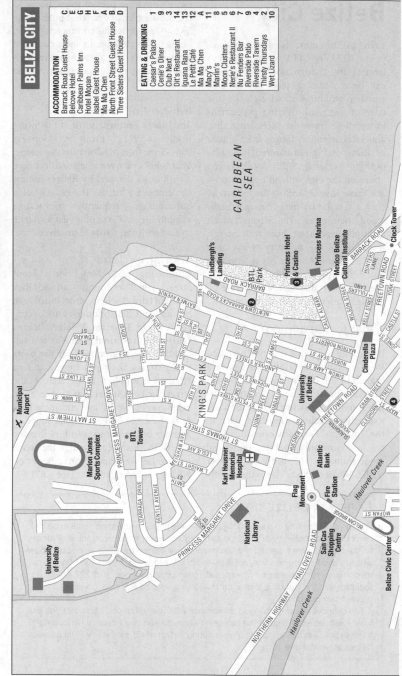

BELIZE CITY

ACCOMMODATION
Barrack Road Guest House	C
Belcove Hotel	E
Caribbean Palms Inn	G
Hotel Mopan	H
Isabel Guest House	F
Ma Ma Chen	A
North Front Street Guest House	B
Three Sisters Guest House	D

EATING & DRINKING
Caesar's Palace	1
Cenie's Diner	9
Club Next	3
Dit's Restaurant	14
Iguana Rana	13
Le Petit Café	12
Ma Ma Chen	A
Macy's	11
Marlin's	8
Moon Clusters	5
Nerie's Restaurant II	6
Nu Fenders Bar	7
Riverside Patio	9
Riverside Tavern	4
Thirsty Thursdays	2
Wet Lizard	10

CARIBBEAN SEA

Lindbergh's Landing

Princess Hotel & Casino

Princess Marina

Mexico Belize Cultural Institute

Clock Tower

BTL Park

NEWTOWN BARRACKS ROAD

BARRACK ROAD

BAYMEN AVENUE

HUNTERS LANE

FREETOWN ROAD

BARRACK ROAD

FULLERS LAND

WILSON STREET

KELLY STREET

YORK STREET

CASTLE ST

JONES

MATRON ROBERTS S

NURSE SEAY ST

SIMON LAMB ST

CALLE ALMAR

Cinderella Plaza

MAPP

ELEGHORN ST

STREET

CRAM STREET

SAN ANTONIO ROAD

HOUSE LANE

FREETOWN ROAD

University of Belize

Municipal Airport

Marion Jones Sports Complex

BTL Tower

PRINCESS MARGARET DRIVE

ST MATTHEW ST

ST MARK ST

ST LUKE ST

ST CHARLES ST

ST JOHN ST

ST EDWARD ST

KING'S PARK

18TH ST

17TH ST

16TH ST

15TH ST

14TH ST

13TH ST

12TH ST

11TH ST

9TH ST

7TH ST

1ST

2ND ST

3RD ST

4TH ST

5TH ST

6TH ST

B ST

C ST

ST JAMES ST

ST PETER STREET

HANDYSIDE STREET

HOPKINS STREET

GUADALUPE ST

DUNN STREET

K ST

1ST

19TH ST

ST THOMAS STREET

WILLIGHAM AVE

WRIGHT ST

LESLIE AVE

MIESSNER CR

University of Belize

Karl Heusner Memorial Hospital

SMITH ST

LIZARRAGA DRIVE

GENTLE AVENUE

PRINCESS MARGARET DRIVE

National Library

Atlantic Bank

Fire Station

Flag Monument

San Cas Shopping Centre

BELCAN BRIDGE

MOPAN ST

HAULOVER ROAD

NORTHERN HIGHWAY

Haulover Creek

Haulover Creek

Haulover Creek

Belize Civic Center

1

2

3

4

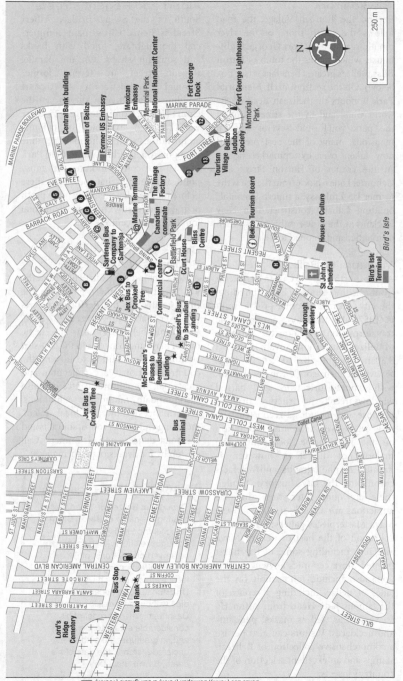

BELIZE

BELIZE CITY

250 m

MARINE PARADE BOULEVARD
Central Bank building
Museum of Belize
Former US Embassy
Mexican Embassy
Memorial Park
National Handicraft Center
Fort George Dock
Fort George Lighthouse
MARINE PARADE
Memorial Park
GAOL LANE
HUTSON STREET
FIRE STREET
QUEEN STREET
ST MARK'S ST
CORK STREET
SPARK ST
DRIDGE ST
FORT STREET
Belize Audubon Society
EVE STREET
HANDYSIDE ST
KEYHOLE ALLEY
NORTH FRONT STREET
BRIDES ALLEY
Marine Terminal
The Image Factory
Tourism Village
DALY ST
BARRACK ROAD
Sartenaja Bus Company to Sarteneja
Canadian consulate
SWING BRIDGE
FORESHORE
House of Culture
NEW ROAD
MERCURY LANE
FORD LANE
HYDE'S LANE
Battlefield Park
Bliss Centre
SOUTHERN FORESHORE
PALM LANE
Belize Tourism Board
LOVELY LANE
PETTY ALLEY
PROSPECT ST
Court House
REGENT STREET
RECTORY LANE
Jex Bus to Crooked Tree
Commercial centre
CHURCH ST
ALBERT ST
PRINCE ST
DEAN ST
SOUTH ST
COMMING ST
WAGNER'S LA
BERKLEY ST
St John's Cathedral
Bird's Isle Terminal
REGENT ST WEST
WATER LANE
VICTORIA STREET
PRINCESS
KING ST
BISHOP ST
BASRA STREET
WEST STREET
GEORGE ST
TIGRIS STREET
FORIES STREET
EUPHRATES AVENUE
AMARA AVENUE
ALLENBY ST
Yarborough Cemetery
ALBERT ST WEST
CEMETERY LANE
QUEEN CHARLOTTE STREET
DICKENSON
CAESAR RD
Russell's Bus to Bermudian Landing
McFadzean's Buses to Bermudian Landing
ORANGE ST
GUN ST
CAIRO ST
MOSUL ST
BAGDAD ST
ALEXANDRIA
RICHARD
LINDOS ALLEY
BECINA BRIDGE
DOUGLAS
Jex Bus to Crooked Tree
WOODS ST
JOHNSON ST
MAGAZINE ROAD
DOLPHIN ST
HICCATEE STREET
Bus Terminal
WELCH STREET
BOCATORA ST
VICTORIA ST
ARMADILLO
NORTH CREEK RD
SOUTH CREEK RD
Collet Canal
EAST COLLET CANAL STREET
WEST COLLET CANAL STREET
FAIRWEATHER ST
KUT AVE
MEX AVENUE
POUND RD
MYVETTE ST
RACCOON STREET
SEAGULL ST
PELICAN STREET
IGUANA STREET
ANTELOPE STREET
GIBNUT STREET
CURASSOW STREET
LAKEVIEW STREET
CEMETERY ROAD
VERNON STREET
SARSTOON STREET
COURTNEY'S CRES
CASSAVA STREET
MAHOGANY STREET
NARGUSTA STREET
EBONY STREET
PINE STREET
MAYFLOWER ST
GUMWOOD STREET
BANAK STREET
MAGISTA STREET
ST JUDE ST
CENTRAL AMERICAN BLVD
ZIRICOTE STREET
COFFIN ST
DAKERS ST
Bus Stop
Taxi Rank
WESTERN HIGHWAY
SANTA BARBARA STREET
PARTRIDGE STREET
Lord's Ridge Cemetery
CENTRAL AMERICAN BOULEVARD
HAYNES ST
BENBOW ST
NEALSPEN RD
RIVERO STREET
WAIGHT ST
FABERS ROAD
BARACAT ST
GILL STREET

N

0 · 250 m

The seafront

Beyond the Tourism Village, the road follows the north shore of the river mouth, reaching the **Fort George Lighthouse**, which marks the tomb of **Baron Bliss**, Belize's greatest benefactor (see box below). On the seafront itself, **Memorial Park** honours the Belizean dead of the world wars, and in the streets around the park you'll find several colonial mansions, many of the best preserved now taken over by upmarket hotels. At the corner of Hutson Street and Gabourel Lane a block from the sea is the former **US Embassy**: a superb "colonial" building actually constructed in New England in the nineteenth century, then dismantled and shipped to Belize.

Museum of Belize

At the north end of Queen Street, in front of the Central Bank building, the city's former colonial prison, built in 1857, has undergone a remarkable transformation to become the **Museum of Belize** (Mon–Thurs 8.30am–5pm, Fri 8.30am–4.30pm; Bz$10; ☎223-4524, Ⓦwww.nichbelize.org). The lower floor, with exposed brickwork and barred windows, recalls the structure's original purpose and includes a reconstruction of a cell as well as a small exhibition on the jail's former occupants. The majority of the floor, however, is devoted to photographs and artefacts chronicling the city's history. Though these are quite interesting, the star attractions are actually upstairs, in the Maya Masterpieces gallery: a first-class collection of the best of Belize's Maya artefacts, including some of the finest painted Maya ceramics anywhere. This floor also includes an exhibit on the jades of Belize, including a replica of the famous **Jade Head** from Altun Ha (see p.79), as well as masks, pendants and necklaces. Visitors can also peruse a comprehensive collection of Belizean stamps and an excellent selection of the country's insects.

Albert and Regent streets

South of the Swing Bridge, **Albert Street** is Belize City's main commercial thoroughfare, lined with banks and souvenir shops. On the parallel **Regent Street** are several former colonial administration and court buildings, collectively known as the **Court House**. Completed in 1926, these well-preserved examples of colonial architecture, with columns and fine wrought iron, overlook **Battlefield Park** (named to commemorate the noisy political meetings that took place here before independence), really just a patch of grass and trees with a dry ornamental fountain in the centre.

Bliss Centre for the Performing Arts

A block behind the Court House, on the waterfront at 2 Southern Foreshore, the **Bliss Centre for the Performing Arts** (Mon–Fri 8am–5pm; free; ☎227-2110, Ⓦwww.nichbelize.org) hosts an eclectic mix of plays and concerts in the 600-seat auditorium. In addition to hosting the country's national art collection and a café/bar, the cultural centre can also accommodate temporary exhibitions. Performances showcase local talent, including children's groups, solo acts and Garífuna dancers and drummers. Call or stop by for details of performances.

> ### BARON BLISS
>
> Throughout Belize you'll find places bearing the name of Baron Bliss, an eccentric Englishman with a Portuguese title. A keen fisherman, he arrived off the coast of Belize in 1926 after hearing that the local waters were rich with game. Unfortunately, he became ill and died without ever making it ashore. Despite this, he left most of his considerable estate to the colony and, in gratitude, the authorities declared March 9, the date of his death, Baron Bliss Day.

St John's Cathedral

At the end of Albert Street is **St John's Cathedral** (daily 6am–6pm; free), the oldest Anglican cathedral in Central America and one of the oldest remaining buildings in Belize. Begun in 1812, its red bricks were brought over as ballast in British ships – it does look more like a large English parish church than most of the other buildings here.

House of Culture

East of the cathedral, on the seafront, the renovated former Government House, now renamed the **House of Culture** (Mon–Thurs 8.30am–5pm, Fri 8.30am–4.30pm; Bz$10; ☏227-3050, ⓦwww.nichbelize.org), is one of the most beautiful spots in Belize City, with its manicured lawns and sea views. Built in 1814, the structure served as the British governor's residence until Belizean independence in 1981. The main room downstairs exhibits the possessions of former governors as well as colonial silverware, glasses and furniture; temporary historical and cultural exhibitions are also on this floor. Upstairs are rooms for painting, dance and drumming workshops, art exhibitions and musical performances.

Arrival and information

By air International flights land at Phillip Goldson International Airport, 17km northwest of the city. Taxis are the only way to get into town (with the exception of hitchhiking); they cost Bz$50. There's a branch of the Belize Bank (with ATM) in the terminal. Domestic flights come and go from the municipal airport, a few kilometres north of town on the edge of the sea; taxis from here to the city centre charge Bz$10.

By boat Boats to and from the cayes pull in at the Marine Terminal on the north side of the Swing Bridge or the terminal at Bird's Isle.

By bus Bus services terminate at various points throughout the city centre, but all buses will stop – at least briefly – at the main bus terminal at 19 West Collet Canal (☏227-2255), which is in a fairly run-down area on the western side of the city. It's only 1km or so from the centre, so you can walk to any of the recommended hotels, but take a taxi at night.

Tourist information The Belize Tourism Board is at 64 Regent St (Mon–Thurs 8am–5pm, Fri 8am–4pm; ☏227-2420, ⓦwww.travelbelize.org). The staff here are not particularly helpful, but the office does hand out city maps, hotel guides and brochures; they can also recommend tour guides for nearby sights. Inside the Marine Terminal, the Kaisa International shop has reliable information on bus and boat schedules, and sells tickets for the express buses to Chetumal, Flores and Guatemala City.

Tour operators A number of operators organize day-trips from Belize City, the most popular going to the Maya ruins at Altun Ha. Reliable options include S & L Travel, 91 N Front St (☏227-7593, ⓦwww.sltravelbelize.com), and Discovery Expeditions, 5916 Manatee Drive (☏223-0748, ⓦwww.discoverybelize.com).

City transport

Walking The best way to get around Belize City's compact centre is on foot; even going from one side to the other should only take around 15 minutes.

Taxis Identified by green numberplates, taxis charge Bz$7–9 for one or two passengers within the city limits.

Accommodation

Accommodation in Belize City is generally more expensive than elsewhere in the country, so prices for even budget rooms can come as quite a shock. There's usually no need to book in advance unless you're eager to stay in a particular hotel – you'll always be able to get something in the price range you're looking for. Keep in mind, however, that the further south and west you go, the more dangerous the area becomes; if you are travelling alone you may want to stay north of the river near Queen Street, the city's most populated area.

North of the river

Barrack Road Guest House 8 Barrack Rd ☏629-1624. Set back from the road down a winding alley, this basic guesthouse offers decent, if somewhat shabby, rooms with private baths and fans. US$20

Ma Ma Chen 7 Eve St, near the end of Queen St ☏223-4568. A Taiwanese couple runs this quiet, simple guesthouse/restaurant. Very basic rooms (some with a/c and private bath) line a hallway in the family home. US$30

North Front Street Guest House 124 North Front St, two blocks from Marine Terminal ☎ 227-7595, ✉ thoth@btl.net. Rooms in this budget travellers' favourite are small and very basic but clean; all share cold-water showers. US$10

Three Sisters Guest House 36 Queen St ☎ 203-5729. Large, clean rooms with private bath in a wooden building run by a friendly, mainly Spanish-speaking family. US$31

South of the river

Belcove Hotel 9 Regent St West ☎ 227-3054, ⊛ www.belcove.com. Basic, very clean rooms, some with a/c and private bath. Although it's on the edge of the dangerous part of town, the hotel itself is quite safe and enjoys great views of Swing Bridge from the balcony. US$33

Caribbean Palms Inn 26 Regent St, at the corner with King St ☎ 227-0472, ✉ cpalm@hotmail.com. Somewhat large hotel where a/c rooms all have private baths and some have TVs. Meals can be arranged, and there's internet access and laundry service. One shared budget room (US$18 per person). US$50

Hotel Mopan 55 Regent St ☎ 227-7351, ⊛ www.hotelmopan.com. Wood-fronted building with spacious rooms, all with private bath and some with a/c, TV and balcony. The restaurant serves good-value breakfasts and there's wi-fi and a bar too. US$45

Isabel Guest House 3 Albert St, 2nd floor ☎ 207-3139. Follow the signs from the Swing Bridge to this small guesthouse offering large rooms with private baths and small refrigerators. US$33

Eating

Belize City's selection of restaurants is quite varied, though simple Creole fare (rice and beans) still predominates at the lower end of the price scale. Be warned that many restaurants close early in the evening and on Sundays.

North of the river

Le Petit Café Cork St, at the *Radisson Hotel* ☎ 223-3333. Outdoor tables make *Le Petit* a great place to enjoy a genuine café atmosphere. Good coffee and baked treats, including croissants, for Bz$2–10.

Ma Ma Chen 7 Eve St ☎ 223-4568. Simple restaurant with tasty Taiwanese fare, including spring rolls for Bz$8 and other vegetarian dishes for Bz$10. See p.65 for the adjoining guesthouse.

Moon Clusters 36 Daly St. One of the only true coffee shops in Belize City. Relax in the bright and quirky interior with an excellent cup for Bz$7.

Nerie's Restaurant II At the corner of Queen and Daly sts ☎ 223-4028. Great Belizean food at reasonable prices: main dishes run from Bz$8 for rice and beans to Bz$15 for fish.

Thirsty Thursdays 164 Newtown Barracks Road ☎ 223-1677. The reincarnation of longtime favourite Jambel's Jerk Pit serves up Jamaican food at affordable prices. The cocktail list is expansive and the Bz$10 lunch special is particularly good value.

Wet Lizard Fort St, next to the Tourism Village ☎ 223-5973. Great views overlooking the sea make for a tourist-dominated clientele. The diverse menu includes tangy spring rolls, Thai and Mexican specialities and seafood. Main dishes Bz$10–20. Open only when cruise ships are in.

South of the river

Cenie's Diner Upstairs in the commercial building; follow the signs. Excellent Belizean dishes, with a daily lunch special (usually fish) for Bz$12, served cafeteria-style.

Dit's Restaurant 50 King St. A variety of Belizean and Mexican snacks (Bz$3–10) in a no-frills atmosphere. A great place for dessert, as well as a filling breakfast. The meat pies are a local favourite.

Macy's 18 Bishop St ☎ 207-3410. Long-established, reasonably priced Creole restaurant popular with locals and busy at lunchtime. The menu includes a variety of fish, including whole sea bass, and game dishes for Bz$12–20.

Marlin's 11 Regent St West, next to the *Belcove Hotel*. Great, inexpensive local food served in large portions on a veranda overlooking the river. Traditional rice and beans, soups or breakfasts for Bz$6–12.

Drinking and nightlife

Belize City's nightlife really comes into its own on Fridays and Saturdays; any other night of the week, you'll likely find the city deserted after 9pm, with only a few hard-drinking (and often rowdy) locals frequenting the bars that are open. On weekends, however, there are plenty of venues to choose from, playing everything from techno to Latin grooves to punta, soca and reggae, though even then don't arrive much before midnight, or you'll find many places empty. A relatively safe area of town with a variety of bars and clubs is the strip of Barracks Newtown Road from the *Princess Hotel* to *Caesar's Palace* bar.

Bars

Iguana Rana In the Tourism Village. Most of the time a relaxed bar frequented by tourists, but on

Friday nights locals take over to dance and drink next to the sea.

Nu Fenders Bar At the corner of Queen and Daly sts, opposite *Nerie's*. A relatively tame place to catch a drink with the locals almost any night of the week, though it's packed and rowdy at weekends.

Riverside Patio Regent St, next to the market building. Come here to have a beer with hard-drinking locals and watch the sun go down. Closes at 7pm.

Riverside Tavern 2 Mapp St. Owned by the Belikin brewery, this is one of the classier spots in town. Popular with locals and tourists alike, it has a spacious outdoor patio and an enviable cocktail menu.

Clubs

Caesar's Palace Newtown Barracks Rd, across from BTL Park. An energetic crowd comes here to dance to Latin, techno and reggae beats here after 10pm on Fri and Sat.

Club Next In the *Princess Hotel* ☎ 223-2670, ⓦ www.princessbelize.com. A lively local favourite. DJs play a variety of music and the dancefloor is packed late on Fri and Sat nights. Bz$20 cover.

Entertainment

Cinema At the *Princess Hotel*, on Newtown Barracks Rd. The only cinema in the city, it has one showing nightly of a recent Hollywood blockbuster. It is also the venue for Belize's annual Film Festival.

Performing arts The cultural centre of Belize is the Bliss Centre for the Performing Arts (see p.64), which stages a variety of events – everything from plays to concerts – in its large auditorium. The House of Culture (see p.65) also hosts exhibitions and events, including classical concerts, in its intimate upstairs rooms. Both venues are affordable (from free to Bz$30), but shows can be sporadic.

Shopping

Books The Angelus Press, 10 Queen St (Mon–Fri 7.30am–5.30pm, Sat 8am–noon; ☎ 223-5777), has a wide range of Belize-related books and maps.

Crafts and souvenirs For items like T-shirts, shells, wooden carvings and beaded jewellery, head to the Tourism Village (see p.61); Sing's, 35 Albert St; or the National Handicraft Center, 2 South Park St (Mon–Fri 8am–5pm, Sat 8am–4pm), which sells high-quality Belizean arts and crafts at fair prices.

Directory

Consulates Current addresses and phone numbers can be found under "Diplomatic Listings" in the green pages of the telephone directory. Canada ☎ 223-1060; Guatemala ☎ 223-3150; Honduras ☎ 224-5889; Mexico ☎ 223-0193. Most are normally open Mon–Fri mornings. The US embassy (☎ 822-4011) and British High Commission (☎ 822-2146) are in Belmopan (see p.88).

Exchange The main banks have branches on Albert St (usually Mon–Thurs 8am–2pm, Fri 8am–4.30pm). Most have ATMs that accept foreign-issued cards. For Guatemalan quetzales and Mexican pesos try Kaisa International in the Marine Terminal.

Health Karl Heusner Memorial Hospital, Princess Margaret Drive, near the junction with the Northern Highway (☎ 223-1548). There are a number of pharmacies on Albert St.

Immigration In the Government Complex on Mahogany St, near the junction of Central American Blvd and the Western Highway (Mon–Thurs 8.30am–4pm, Fri 8.30am–3.30pm; ☎ 222-4620). Thirty-day extensions of stay (the maximum allowed) cost US$30.

Internet Two centrally located establishments are Angelus Press (see above; Bz$4/hr) and Turton Library (North Front St; ☎ 227-3401; Bz$2.50/hr). Many hotels offer internet access to guests.

Laundry Belize Dry Cleaners & Laundromat, 3 Dolphin St (Mon–Sat 7am–6pm; reduced hours Sun).

Police The main police station is on Queen St, a block north of the Swing Bridge (☎ 227-2210). Alternatively, contact the Tourism Police (see box, p.61).

Post office North Front St, opposite the Marine Terminal (Mon–Thurs 8am–4.30pm, Fri 8am–5pm).

Supermarket Albert St, south of the Swing Bridge, is the city's central commercial district. A number of supermarkets line the street, including the city's largest, Brodie's, which is quite expensive, as most of the selection is imported.

Telephones There are payphones (operated using pre-paid cards) dotted all around the city, or visit the main BTL office, 1 Church St (Mon–Fri 8am–6pm), which also has fax and email services.

Moving on

Some travellers do leave Belize City via boat or plane, but buses are by far the most common and cheapest way to move around the country.

By bus

Belize's main bus company is **National Transport Services Limited (NTSL)**, although the company's original name – Novelo's – still appears on some signs. Other, smaller companies also serve specific destinations. Most buses depart from the terminal at 19 West Collet Canal (☎ 227-2255), but many companies maintain independent stops in the streets nearby. Services operate daily, though departure times may be erratic on Sundays.

Bus companies and stops

BBOC (BB) Departs for Northern and Western highways from the terminal.
James Bus (JA) ☎ 722-2049. Departs for Dangriga and Punta Gorda (via Belmopan) from the terminal.
Jex Bus (JX) ☎ 225-7017. Departs for Crooked Tree from Regent St West (Mon–Sat 10.55am) and Pound Yard, Collet Canal (Mon–Fri 4.30pm & 5.15pm).
McFadzean's Bus (MF) Departs for Bermudian Landing (via Burrell Boom) from Euphrates Ave, off Orange St, near the main bus depot.
NTSL ☎ 227-6372. All services depart from the terminal.
Russell's Bus (RU) Departs for Bermudian Landing from Cairo St, near the corner of Cemetery Rd and Euphrates Ave.
Sarteneja Bus Company (SC) Departs for Sarteneja from the south side of the Swing Bridge.

Bus destinations

Belmopan With NTSL, JA, BB. Departures hourly 5am–9pm (express); 1hr 15min.
Benque Viejo del Carmen With NTSL, BB. Departures hourly 5am–9pm (express); 3hr 30min (for the Guatemalan border).
Bermudian Landing With MF, RU. Departures Mon–Sat noon, 4.30pm & 5pm; 1hr 15min.
Chetumal, Mexico With NTSL. Departures hourly 5am–7pm (express); 3hr 30min.
Corozal With NTSL, BB. Departures hourly 5am–7pm (express); 2hr 30min.
Crooked Tree With JX. Departures Mon–Sat 10.55am & 4.30pm; 1hr 30min.
Dangriga With JA. Twelve departures daily 6am–5pm (express); 2hr via Coastal Rd, 3hr 30min via Belmopan.
Gales Point With NTSL. Two departures weekly; 1hr 40min.
Orange Walk With NTSL, BB. Departures hourly 5am–7pm (express); 1hr 30min.
Placencia With JA. Four departures daily, via Belmopan and Dangriga; 5–7hr.
Punta Gorda With JA. Twelve departures daily, all via Belmopan and Dangriga (express); 5–8hr.
San Ignacio With NTSL, BB. Departures hourly 5am–9pm, via Belmopan; 2hr 30min.
Sarteneja With SC. Four departures daily (10.30am, noon, 4pm, 5pm), Mon–Fri. Three buses on Saturday (10.30am, noon, 4pm).

Other transport

By air Domestic flights (see p.55) to all main towns leave from the Municipal or International airport.
By boat Skiffs to Caye Caulker (45min) and Ambergris Caye (1hr 15min) are operated by the Caye Caulker Water Taxi Association (☎ 223-5752, ⓦ www.cayecaulkerwatertaxi.com) and depart from the Marine Terminal at least every 1hr 30min from 8am to 4.30pm daily. San Pedro Water Jets Express, operating from a terminal at Bird's Isle, also provides several daily runs to the cayes (☎ 226-2194, ⓦ www.sanpedrowatertaxi.com).

The cayes and atolls

Belize's spectacular **Barrier Reef**, with its dazzling variety of underwater life, string of exquisite **cayes** (pronounced "keys") and extensive opportunities for all kinds of watersports, is the country's main attraction for most first-time visitors. The longest barrier reef in the western hemisphere, it runs the entire length of the coastline, usually 15 to 40km from the mainland, with most of the cayes lying in shallow water behind the shelter of the reef. **Caye Caulker** is the most popular destination for budget travellers. The town of **San Pedro** on **Ambergris Caye**, meanwhile, has transformed from a predominantly fishing community to one dominated by tourism. There are still some beautiful spots though, notably the protected sections of reef at either end of the caye: **Bacalar Chico National Park** and **Hol Chan Marine Reserve**.

Beyond the barrier reef are two of Belize's three **atolls**, the **Turneffe Islands** and **Lighthouse Reef**, regularly visited on day-trips from San Pedro and Caye Caulker. Lighthouse Reef encompasses two of the most spectacular diving and snorkelling sites in the country – **Half Moon Caye Natural Monument** and the **Great Blue Hole**, an enormous collapsed cave.

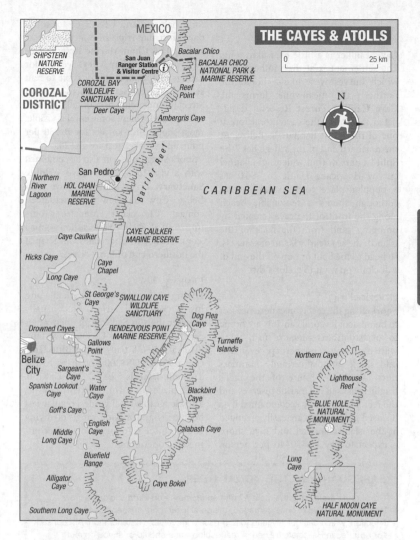

CAYE CAULKER

CAYE CAULKER, 35km northeast of Belize City, is relaxed, easy-going and more than merits its "Go Slow" motto. The **reef**, 1.5km offshore, is a **marine reserve**, offering unbelievable opportunities for any imaginable watersport. Even so, in general, the island is affordable, with an abundance of inexpensive accommodation and tour operators, though the number of expensive places is also increasing. The island is now a firm favourite on the backpacker trail, although up until about fifteen years ago, tourism existed almost as a sideline to the island's main source of income, **lobster fishing**. The money might be coming from tourists these days but there are still plenty of the spiny creatures around, most notably at the annual **Lobster Fest**, normally held in the third weekend of June to celebrate the opening of the season.

What to see and do

Caye Caulker is a little over 8km long. The settlement is at the southern end, which curves west like a hook; the northern tip, meanwhile, forms the **Caye Caulker Forest Reserve**, designated to protect the caye litoral forest, one of the rarest habitats in Belize. At the northern end of the village lies "**the Split**", a narrow (but widening) channel cut by Hurricane Hattie in 1961; it's a popular place to relax and swim. Although there's a reasonable beach along the front of the caye (created by pumping sand from the back of the island), the sea nearby is full of seagrass, so head to the Split or hop off the end of a dock if you want to go for a dip.

Snorkelling

Snorkelling the reef is an experience not to be missed; its coral canyons are home to an astonishing range of fish, along with eagle rays and perhaps even the odd shark (almost certainly harmless nurse sharks). Because of the reef's fragility, visits to the marine reserves and the reef itself must be accompanied by a licensed guide. **Trips** are easily arranged at the island's snorkel and dive shops – expect to pay US$30–40 per person for a half-day and US$45–65 for a full day. Most day-trips stop at the reef as well as **Hol Chan Marine Reserve** (see p.75) and **Shark-Ray Alley**. See p.75 for listings of operators. It's possible to rent **sea kayaks** from several places on Front Street for independent snorkelling closer to the island, where some coral is visible; most shops offer kayaks for Bz$30 per hour, and snorkel gear for Bz$20.

Snorkelling tours can also be combined with a visit to **Swallow Caye Wildlife Sanctuary**, on a mangrove caye near Belize City, to view the **manatees**; contact Chocolate's Manatee Tours (☎226-0151, ✉chocolateseashore@gmail.com; US$60), at Chocolate's Gift Shop at the northern end of Front Street.

Diving

Diving here is also excellent, and instruction and trips are usually cheaper than in San Pedro: open-water certification starts at US$300, two-tank dives at US$60, trips to the **Blue Hole** (see p.77) at US$200 and trips to the **Turneffe Islands** (see p.77) at US$150. Most places in town offer enthusiastic, knowledgeable local guides, regular fast boat trips and a wide range of diving courses – see p.76 for listings of recommended operators.

SAFEGUARDING THE CORAL REEF

Coral reefs are among the most fragile ecosystems on earth. Colonies grow less than 5cm a year; once damaged, the coral is far more susceptible to bacterial infection, which can quickly lead to large-scale irreversible deterioration. All licensed tour guides in Belize are trained in reef ecology, and should brief you on reef precautions. If exploring independently, keep the following points in mind:

- Never anchor boats on the reef – use the permanently secured buoys.
- Never touch or stand on the reef.
- Don't remove shells, sponges or other creatures, or buy reef products from souvenir shops.
- Avoid disturbing the seabed around corals – clouds of sand smother coral colonies.
- If you're a beginner or out-of-practice diver, practise away from the reef first.
- Don't use suntan lotion in reef areas – the oils remain on the water's surface; instead, wear a T-shirt to guard against sunburn.
- Don't feed or interfere with fish or marine life; this can harm not only sea creatures, but snorkellers and divers too – large fish may attack, trying to get their share.

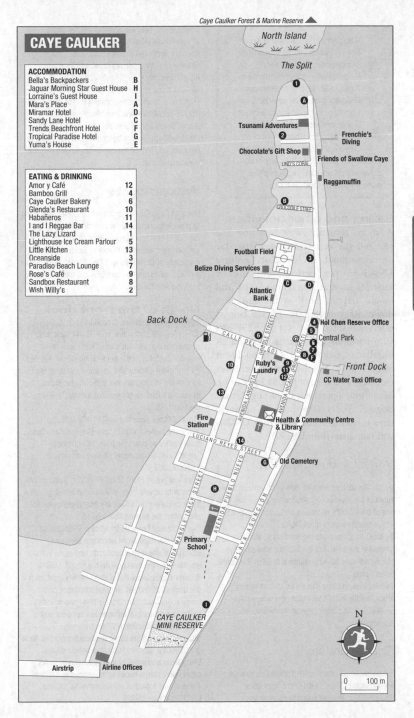

Caye Caulker Forest & Marine Reserve ▲

North Island

The Split

CAYE CAULKER

ACCOMMODATION
Bella's Backpackers	B
Jaguar Morning Star Guest House	H
Lorraine's Guest House	I
Mara's Place	A
Miramar Hotel	D
Sandy Lane Hotel	C
Trends Beachfront Hotel	F
Tropical Paradise Hotel	G
Yuma's House	E

EATING & DRINKING
Amor y Café	12
Bamboo Grill	4
Caye Caulker Bakery	6
Glenda's Restaurant	10
Habañeros	11
I and I Reggae Bar	14
The Lazy Lizard	1
Lighthouse Ice Cream Parlour	5
Little Kitchen	13
Oceanside	3
Paradiso Beach Lounge	7
Rose's Café	9
Sandbox Restaurant	8
Wish Willy's	2

Tsunami Adventures

Frenchie's Diving

Chocolate's Gift Shop

Friends of Swallow Caye

LIND'S CORAL

Raggamuffin

CROCODILE STREET

Football Field

Belize Diving Services

Atlantic Bank

Back Dock

CALLE DEL SOL

Hol Chan Reserve Office

Central Park

Ruby's Laundry

Front Dock

CC Water Taxi Office

AVENIDA LANGOSTA

AVENIDA HICACO (FRONT STREET)

Fire Station

Health & Community Centre & Library

LUCIANO REYES STREET

Old Cemetery

AVENIDA MANGLE (BACK STREET)

AVENIDA PUEBLO NUEVO

PLAYA ASUNCION

Primary School

CAYE CAULKER MINI RESERVE

N

Airstrip

Airline Offices

0   100 m

TREAT YOURSELF

Raggamuffin Camping Tour
For a unique island-hopping experience, sign up for Raggamuffin's three-day, two-night sailboat trip to Placencia. Passengers enjoy snorkelling and fishing by day, while nights are spent star-gazing around campfires on Rendezvous Caye and Tobacco Caye. The package costs US$300 per person, covering all snorkelling equipment, camping gear, food and drink.

Sailing and other activities

A more romantic way to enjoy the sea and the reef is to spend the day on a **sailboat**, which costs around US$45–55 per person, and usually includes several snorkelling stops and lunch, arriving back as the sun goes down. Raggamuffin Tours (see below) offers **sunset cruises** for US$25 with rum cocktails and *ceviche* included. A number of establishments along Front Street rent **kayaks**: Tsunami Adventures (see below) charge only US$5 per hour. Many tour operators, including Anwar Snorkel Tours (see below), organize trips inland to Altun Ha (from US$80) and Lamanai (from US$90).

Arrival and information

By air The airstrip is about 1km (a 15-minute walk) south of the town centre. Alternatively, you can take one of the island's numerous golf carts (Bz$6–8), which usually wait to meet flights.
By boat Boats pull into the front dock, which is located in the middle of the island's eastern edge and within easy walking distance of all of the hotels listed below.
Tourist information There's no official tourist office, but the town's websites (www.gocaye caulker.com and www.cayecaulkerbelize.net) are helpful.

Tour operators

For snorkelling, recommended operators include: Anwar Snorkel Tours, north of the front dock (226-0327, www.anwartours.page.tl);

Carlos Tours, near the *Sandbox* (226-0058, carlosayala@hotmail.com); Raggamuffin Tours, near the north end of Front St (226-0348, www.raggamuffintours.com); and Tsunami Adventures, near the Split (226-0462, www.tsunamiadventures.com). For diving, try: Frenchie's, towards the northern end of the village (226-0234, www.frenchiesdivingbelize .com); Belize Diving Services, on Back St (226-0143, www.belizedivingservices.net); or Big Fish, on Front St (226-0450, www.bigfish divecenter.com).

Accommodation

Some of Caye Caulker's hotels have been renovated to provide more upscale accommodation, but the island still has an abundance of simple, inexpensive, shared-bath rooms. Book in advance, especially at Christmas and New Year's. Even the furthest hotels are no more than ten minutes' walk from the front dock.

North of the front dock

Bella's Backpackers Crocodile St 226-0360, monkeybite38@yahoo.com. Dorm beds and private rooms, all with shared bath, in a clean, wooden building at the back of the island. There's a communal kitchen and common room, as well as canoes for guests' use. You can also camp in the yard (Bz$15 per person). Dorms US$10, doubles US$25
Mara's Place Near the Split 600-0080, maras_place@hotmail.com. Comfortable, clean, quiet cabins with private bath, TV and porch. There's also a communal kitchen and private sundeck. US$35
Miramar Hotel Front St 206-0357. Basic rooms, some with private bath, in a wooden building with a large balcony overlooking the sea; there's one hot shower on the second floor. US$15
Sandy Lane Hotel Middle St 226-0117. Basic, well-worn wooden rooms and cabañas, some with shared bath and some with en-suite, are the best deal on the island. US$13
Trends Beachfront Hotel Immediately right from the dock 226-0094, www.trendsbze.com. Large rooms with comfortable beds and private baths in a pastel-painted wooden building; some rooms have balconies. US$30
Yuma's House 75m along the beach from the dock 226-0019, www.yumashousebelize.com. Dorm beds and small, shared-bath rooms in an often noisy beach-house with communal kitchen. There's also a garden with hammocks. Dorms US$13, doubles US$29

South of the front dock

Jaguar Morning Star Guest House Across from the island's only school ☎626-4538, ◉www .jaguarmorningstar.com. Two large rooms in a house overlooking a beautiful garden and a cabaña. Rooms have private bath, coffee pot, fridge, cable TV and fan. Wi-fi Bz$8/day. US$45

Lorraine's Guest House At the southern end of the island, on the beach ☎206-0162. Wooden cabins with private baths are a very shabby but inexpensive option. US$15

Tropical Paradise Hotel At the southern end of Front St ☎226-0124, ◉www.tropicalparadise-caye caulker.com. A wide range of rooms, all with hot showers, private baths and fans, and some with a/c, in a series of brightly painted wooden buildings. The adjoining restaurant serves inexpensive meals. US$40

Eating and drinking

Restaurant prices in Caye Caulker are quite high compared to the rest of the country, and it can be difficult to find a meal for less than Bz$15. Still, lobster (in season) and seafood are delicious and generally good value. You can self-cater from several shops and supermarkets on the island, and children sell home-made banana bread, coconut cakes and other goodies. Note that the tap water is unfit to drink; rainwater and bottled water are widely available.

North of the front dock

Bamboo Grill On the beach. Good Belizean cuisine and seafood (Bz$17–40) served at high tables with wooden swings. The bar stays open late.

Caye Caulker Bakery Middle St. Delicious baked goods and desserts for Bz$1–4. Closed Sun.

Lighthouse Ice Cream Parlour Front St. Cool off with the second-best home-made ice cream in Belize (beaten only by *Tutti Frutti* in Placencia; see p.107). Ask for a scoop of soursop or coconut for a local taste experience.

Sandbox Restaurant Immediately north of the dock ☎226-0200. Great breakfasts, Belizean

cuisine and seafood are served both indoors and outside on the beach. The daily soup (Bz$8) is a great deal. Mains Bz$8–34.

Wish Willy's At the northern end of the island – follow the signs. Great, inexpensive seafood (Bz$10–20) in a sometimes frustratingly relaxed venue at the back of the island. The rum cocktails are not for the faint-hearted.

South of the front dock

Amor y Café Front St. This very popular restaurant serves excellent coffee and breakfasts (Bz$6–12) on a veranda overlooking the street. Daily 6.30am–noon.

Glenda's Restaurant Back St. Known for its cinnamon rolls, *Glenda's* dishes up breakfast and lunch for Bz$1–8.

🏃 **Little Kitchen** Back St. This tiny, out-of-the-way shack offers some of the cheapest and best food on Caye Caulker. Excellent seafood for Bz$10–25, and lobster starts at only Bz$20. The freshly squeezed fruit juices are also tasty.

Rose's Café Calle del Sol at Front St. Popular place for breakfast and simple Belizean and Mexican dishes. Mains Bz$7–20.

Drinking and nightlife

Many bars offer a happy hour from 3–7pm, with local spirits being the least expensive option.

I and I Reggae Bar Luciano Reyes St. An appealing option with strong cocktails and plenty of hammocks and swings on the rooftop terrace.

The Lazy Lizard On the Split. A typical night out on the island begins with a sunset drink here.

Oceanside Front St. Attracts a rowdy mix of locals and tourists. Open till late.

Paradiso Beach Lounge Along the beach from the dock. For alternative entertainment, this place runs a popular "movies under the stars" event several nights a week.

Directory

Exchange Atlantic Bank, just north of the centre, has a 24hr ATM.

Internet Cayeboard Connection, next to Anwar Tours, serves drinks and has a book exchange.

Laundry Drop-off services at Ruby's, on Calle del Sol.

Post office Front St.

Telephones The BTL office is on Back St.

Moving on

By boat Boats operated by the Caye Caulker Water Taxi Association (☎223-5752, ◉www.cayecaulker watertaxi.com) depart for Belize City (45min; Bz$20) at least every 1hr 30min from 8am to 4pm (5pm on weekends and holidays), and for San Pedro (30min; Bz$20) at least every 2hr from 8am to 5pm. San Pedro Water Jets Express (☏226-2194, ⓦwww.sanpedrowatertaxi.com) also provides a daily service to Chetumal (7.45am; 2hr; Bz$90), as well as several daily runs to Belize City and San Pedro.

AMBERGRIS CAYE AND SAN PEDRO

The most northerly and, at almost forty kilometres long, by far the largest of the cayes, is **AMBERGRIS CAYE**. The island's main attraction is the former fishing village of **SAN PEDRO**, facing the reef just a few kilometres from the caye's southern tip. San Pedro is a small town, but its population of over nine thousand makes it the biggest of any of the cayes. As the result of massive recent development, it has lost most, though certainly not all, of its Caribbean charm: it still retains a wonderfully relaxed atmosphere, despite the fact that some of the most exclusive hotels, restaurants and bars in Belize have been built here. The island's only budget places are in the

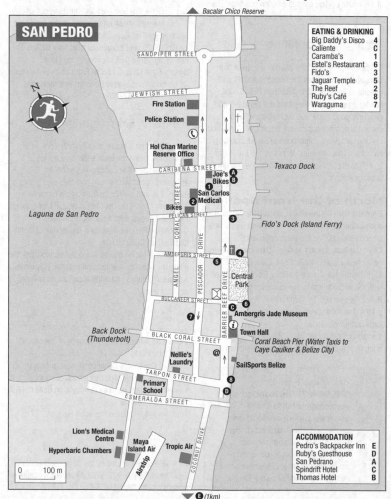

▲ Bacalar Chico Reserve

SAN PEDRO

EATING & DRINKING
Big Daddy's Disco 4
Caliente C
Caramba's 1
Estel's Restaurant 6
Fido's 3
Jaguar Temple 5
The Reef 2
Ruby's Café 8
Waraguma 7

SANDPIPER STREET

JEWFISH STREET
Fire Station
Police Station
Hol Chan Marine Reserve Office
CARIBENA STREET
Joe's Bikes
San Carlos Medical
Bikes
PELICAN STREET

Laguna de San Pedro

AMBERGRIS STREET

ANGEL STREET
PESCADOR DRIVE
CORAL STREET
BARRIER REEF DRIVE

Central Park

BUCCANEER STREET
Ambergris Jade Museum
Town Hall
Back Dock (Thunderbolt)
BLACK CORAL STREET
Coral Beach Pier (Water Taxis to Caye Caulker & Belize City)
Nellie's Laundry
SailSports Belize
TARPON STREET
Primary School
ESMERALDA STREET

Texaco Dock
Fido's Dock (Island Ferry)

Lion's Medical Centre
Maya Island Air
Tropic Air
Hyperbaric Chambers
Airstrip
COCONUT DRIVE

0   100 m

ACCOMMODATION
Pedro's Backpacker Inn E
Ruby's Guesthouse D
San Pedrano A
Spindrift Hotel C
Thomas Hotel B

▼ Ⓔ (1km)

original village of San Pedro, though even these are extremely expensive. To save money and still visit Ambergris, consider staying on Caye Caulker (see p.69) and doing a day-trip.

What to see and do

San Pedro's main streets are only half a dozen blocks long and the town does not boast any particular sights. The main focus of daytime entertainment is the **sea** and the **reef**, with activities from sunbathing to windsurfing, sailing, fishing, diving, snorkelling and glass-bottomed-boat rides. **Beaches** on the caye are narrow and the sea immediately offshore is shallow, with a lot of seagrass, so in town you'll usually need to walk to the end of a dock if you want to **swim**. Be careful, though: there have been accidents in San Pedro in which speeding boats have hit people swimming off docks. A line of buoys indicates the "safe area", but speedboat drivers can be a bit macho, so watch where you swim.

Diving and snorkelling

The most central snorkelling and diving spot on Ambergris is the **reef** opposite San Pedro, but it's also heavily used. You're better off heading north, to **Mexico Rocks**, or south, to Hol Chan (see p.75). For qualified divers, a two-tank local dive from Ambergris Caye costs around US$80. Open-water certification courses are around US$435, while a more basic, single-dive resort course ranges from US$140; both include equipment. All the dive shops in San Pedro also offer snorkelling trips, costing around US$25–35 for two to three hours and US$40–55 for four to five, and many will rent diving and snorkelling supplies; trips to the Blue Hole (see p.77) cost around US$250 and trips to the Turneffe Islands (see p.77) US$185. See p.76 for recommended dive shops.

Hol Chan Marine Reserve

The **Hol Chan Marine Reserve** (Bz$20), 8km south of San Pedro at the southern tip of the caye, takes its name from the Maya for "little channel" – it is this break in the reef that forms the focus of the reserve. Its three zones preserve a comprehensive cross-section of the marine environment, from the open sea through seagrass beds and mangroves. Tours to Hol Chan must be led by a licensed guide, and also stop at **Shark-Ray Alley**, another part of the reserve, where you can swim with three-metre **nurse sharks** and enormous **stingrays** – an extremely popular attraction. It's also somewhat controversial: biologists claim that the practice of feeding the fish to attract them alters their natural behaviour.

Other watersports

While most travellers come to the cayes to snorkel or dive, **windsurfing** and **sailing** are popular as well, though learning either sport can be quite expensive. The best rental and instruction for both is offered by SailSports Belize (☎226-4488, ⓦwww.sailsports belize.com), on the beach at *Caribbean Villas Hotel*. Sailboard rentals cost US$22–27 an hour, and from US$49 for a seven-hour day; sailboat rental is US$22–49 an hour, with discounts for multiple hours. They also offer **kite-surfing** lessons (US$165 for a 2hr 30min session) and sailing lessons (US$66/hr).

Guided day-trips

Day-trips from San Pedro to the ruins of **Altun Ha** (US$75–90; see p.79) or **Lamanai** (US$135–160; see p.82) are becoming increasingly popular, but can be done more cheaply from other parts of the country. However, with a good guide this is an excellent way to spot wildlife, including crocodiles and manatees, and the riverbank trees are often adorned with orchids. See p.76 for recommended guides.

It's also possible to visit some of the local ancient Maya sites on the northwest coast of Ambergris, many of which are just in the process of being excavated. On **San Juan** beach you'll be scrunching over literally thousands of pieces of Maya pottery, but perhaps the most appealing site is **Chac Balam**, a ceremonial and administrative centre with deep burial chambers.

Arrival and information

By air The airport is just south of the city centre, within easy walking distance of any of the recommended hotels, though golf buggies and taxis also line up to give you a ride for around Bz$8–10.

By boat Boats arriving from Belize City and/or Caye Caulker usually dock at the Coral Beach pier on the front (reef) side of the island at the eastern end of Black Coral St, though the *Thunderbolt* from Corozal (see opposite) pulls in at the back of the island at the western end of Black Coral St. Arriving at either dock, you're pretty much in the centre and within walking distance of most of the hotels listed below.

Tour operators For diving trips and courses, try: Belize Academy of Diving, based at Mexico Rocks, 11km north of San Pedro (☎ 226-2873, 🌐 www.belize-academy-of-diving.com); Belize Diving Adventures (☎ 226-3082, 🌐 www.belizedivingadventures.net); Ecologic Divers (☎ 226-4118, 🌐 www.ecologicdivers.com); and Seaduced by Belize (☎ 226-2254, 🌐 www.seaducedbybelize.com). Several of these operators also offer inland tours to Maya ruins, manatee tours and fishing trips.

Tourist information The official tourist information office is on Barrier Reef Drive at Black Coral St. Ambergris Caye has a good website (🌐 www.ambergriscaye.com) with links to most of the businesses on the island. For listings, pick up a copy of *The San Pedro Sun* or *Ambergris Today*, the island's tourist newspapers (Bz$1), available from the tourist office and at most hotels and restaurants.

Accommodation

Accommodation in San Pedro is some of the most expensive in the country – all but a few places cost at least US$70. Most of the year reservations are not necessary, though it's risky to turn up at Christmas, New Year or Easter unless you've booked a room.

Pedro's Backpacker Inn Coconut Drive, 1km south of town ☎ 226-3825, 🌐 www.backpackersbelize.com. A bit of a walk from town,

and the rooms are very basic (two single beds, lockers and shared showers) but they are clean and come at the cheapest rate on the island. There's also a 24hr pool, lively bar, wi-fi and bike hire, and the knowledgeable staff can organize a range of tours. US$23

Ruby's Guesthouse Barrier Reef Drive, just north of the airstrip ☎ 226-2063, 🌐 www.ambergriscaye.com/rubys. Family-run hotel on the seafront; rooms with a/c, with private baths and on the higher floors cost more, but all are good value, especially those in the annexe on the lagoon. US$20

San Pedrano Corner of Barrier Reef Drive and Caribeña St ☎ 226-2054, 📧 sanpedrano@btl.net. Family-run hotel in a wooden building set back slightly from the sea, with comfortable, private-bath rooms (some with a/c and all with TV) and breezy verandas. US$35

Spindrift Hotel Barrier Reef Drive ☎ 226-2174, 🌐 www.ambergriscaye.com/spindrift. Centrally located and well-decorated hotel with large garden and adjoining restaurant. All rooms have private bath and fans; more expensive rooms have a/c and balconies. US$54

Thomas Hotel Barrier Reef Drive, north of the centre ☎ 226-2061. Rooms here (some with a/c) are a good deal, with private baths, fridges and TVs. US$33

Eating

Restaurant prices in San Pedro are also generally higher than elsewhere in Belize. Seafood is prominent at most restaurants, and you can also rely on plenty of steak, shrimp, chicken, pizza and salads. In the evening, several inexpensive fast-food stands open for business along the front of Central Park. Self-catering isn't much of a bargain: there's no market and the supermarkets are stocked with expensive imported canned goods.

Caliente On the beach at *Spindrift Hotel* ☎ 226-2170. Enjoy Mexican cuisine on a patio overlooking the sea. Closed Mon.

Caramba's Near the north end of Pescador Drive ☎ 226-4321. A lively crowd comes to this large restaurant for a variety of dishes, including Mexican and Caribbean cuisine as well as seafood. Mains Bz$11–55.

Estel's Restaurant On the beach just south of the park ☎ 226-2019. This locally owned restaurant serves breakfast all day and Belizean food at lunch for Bz$5–22.

Fido's Barrier Reef Drive. A favourite of tourists and expats, who come to eat seafood and international cuisine and sip cocktails. There's a terrace overlooking the sea. Mains Bz$18–28.

The Reef Near the north end of Pescador Drive ☎226-4145. Good Belizean food, including delicious seafood, at relatively inexpensive prices for the island: most mains are Bz$10–22.

Ruby's Café Barrier Reef Drive, next to *Ruby's Guesthouse*. Delicious home-made cakes, pies and sandwiches, and freshly brewed coffee. Popular with locals. Opens at 5am.

Waraguma Towards the south end of Pescador Drive. The main restaurant serves great-quality but expensive seafood dishes, but across the street the same family runs a tiny, unnamed hole-in-the-wall featuring wonderful Belizean and Mexican cuisine starting at just Bz$2.

Drinking and nightlife

San Pedro is the tourist entertainment capital of Belize, and if you check locally, you'll find live music on somewhere every night of the week. Most of the hotels have bars, several of which offer happy hours, while back from the main street are a couple of small cantinas that serve both locals and tourists.

Big Daddy's Disco On the beach just south of the park. Locals flock to this beach bar and club for reggae and Latin beats on weekend nights. Drinks can be expensive so ask for a price list before making a choice.

Fido's Barrier Reef Drive. A restaurant by day, by night *Fido's* becomes one of the most popular evening spots in San Pedro, hosting a live band most evenings.

Jaguar Temple Barrier Reef Drive opposite the park. Tourists and locals pack this large, colourfully painted club on most nights.

Directory

Exchange Belize Bank near Central Park on Barrier Reef Drive has an ATM, and the other banks will give cash advances, but travellers' cheques and US dollars are accepted – even preferred – everywhere.

Internet Caribbean Connection, on Barrier Reef Drive, offers internet access for Bz$10/hr.

Laundry There are two laundries on Pescador Drive.

Post office In the Alijua building, opposite the Atlantic Bank on Barrier Reef Drive (Mon–Thurs 8am–noon and 1–4pm, Fri until 3.30pm).

Moving on

By boat Boats from San Pedro to Caye Caulker (30min; Bz$20) and Belize City (Bz$30; 1hr 20min) are operated by the Caye Caulker Water Taxi Association (☎223-5752, ⓦwww.cayecaulkerwatertaxi.com)

and leave from the front dock at least every 1hr 30min 7am–3.30pm (4.30pm on weekends and holidays). San Pedro Water Jets Express (☎226-2194, ⓦwww.sanpedrowatertaxi.com) provides a daily service to Chetumal (8am; Bz$70; 1hr 30min) as well as several daily runs to Belize City and Caye Caulker. The *Thunderbolt* (☎610-4475 or 601-7759) also operates from the back dock in San Pedro to Corozal and will stop in Sarteneja on request (daily 7am and 3pm; 1hr 45min).

TURNEFFE ISLANDS

Although Caye Caulker and San Pedro are the only villages on the reef, there are a couple of dozen other inhabited islands, as well as some excellent diving spots. The virtually uninhabited **TURNEFFE ISLANDS**, 40km from Belize City and south of cayes Caulker and Ambergris, comprise an oval archipelago of low-lying mangrove islands around a shallow lagoon 60km long. These are enclosed by a beautiful coral reef, which offers some of the best diving and snorkelling in Belize. The island boasts several resorts, all of which are out of the reach of the typical budget traveller, but you can still visit this incredible spot on a day-trip from San Pedro and Caye Caulker. See opposite and p.72 for tour operators.

LIGHTHOUSE REEF

About 80km east of Belize City is Belize's outermost atoll, **LIGHTHOUSE REEF**, home to the popular underwater attractions of the Blue Hole and Half Moon Caye Natural Monument.

The Blue Hole

The **Blue Hole**, technically a karst-eroded sinkhole, is over 300m in diameter and 135m deep, dropping through the bottom of the lagoon and opening out into a complex network of caves and crevices; its depth gives it an astonishing deep-blue colour that is, unfortunately, best appreciated from the air. Though visibility is generally limited, many divers still find the trip worthwhile for the drop-offs and underwater caves, which include stalactites and stalagmites. Unfortunately for budget travellers, trips to the Blue Hole – which must be led by a licensed guide or company – usually cost at least US$200.

Half Moon Caye Natural Monument

The **Half Moon Caye Natural Monument**, the first marine conservation area in Belize, was declared a national park in 1982 and became one of Belize's first World Heritage Sites in 1996. The 180,000-square-metre caye is divided into two distinct ecosystems. In the west, guano from sea birds fertilizes the soil, enabling the growth of dense vegetation, while the eastern half has mostly coconut palms. A total of 98 bird species has been recorded here, including frigate birds, ospreys and a resident population of four thousand red-footed boobies, one of only two such nesting colonies in the Caribbean. Upon arrival (most people come as part of a tour), visitors must pay the Bz$20 entrance fee at the visitors' centre; you can **camp** here (☎223-5004; US$10 per person), but you need to call ahead for permission.

The north

The level expanses of northern Belize are a mixture of farmland and rainforest, dotted with swamps, savannas and lagoons. Most visitors come to the region for its **Maya ruins** and **wildlife reserves**. The largest Maya site, **Lamanai**, served by regular boat tours along the New River Lagoon, features some of the most impressive pyramids and beautiful scenery in the country. The site of **Altun Ha**, meanwhile, is usually visited on a day-trip from Belize City. The northern reserves also host an astonishingly diverse array of wildlife. At the **Community Baboon Sanctuary**, a group of farmers

have combined agriculture with conservation to the benefit of the black howler monkey, and at the stunning **Crooked Tree Wildlife Sanctuary**, rivers and lagoons offer protection to a range of migratory birds.

Many of the original residents in this region were refugees from the nineteenth-century Caste Wars in Yucatán, and some of the northernmost towns are mainly Spanish-speaking. The largest settlement today is **Orange Walk**, the country's main centre for sugar production. Further north, near the border with Mexico, **Corozal** is a small Caribbean town, strongly influenced by Maya and mestizo culture.

COMMUNITY BABOON SANCTUARY

Heading north from Belize City, the **COMMUNITY BABOON SANCTUARY** (Bz$14; ⓦ www.howler monkeys.org), to the west off the Northern Highway, is one of the most interesting conservation projects in Belize. It was established in 1985 by Dr Rob Horwich and a group of local farmers (with help from the World Wide Fund for Nature), who developed a code of conduct of sustainable living and farming practices. A mixture of farmland and broad-leaved forest along the banks of the Belize River, the sanctuary coordinates seven villages, of which **Bermudian Landing** is the most convenient, and more than a hundred landowners, in a project of conservation, education and tourism.

The main focus of attention is the **black howler monkey** (known locally as a "baboon"). These primates generally live in groups of between four and eight, and spend the day wandering through the canopy, feasting on leaves, flowers and fruits. At dawn and dusk they let rip with their famous howl: a deep and rasping roar that carries for miles. The sanctuary is also home to over two hundred bird species, as well as iguanas, peccaries and coatis. You can find exhibits and information on the riverside habitats and animals you are likely to see in the **natural history museum** – Belize's first – at the reserve's visitors' centre in Bermudian Landing.

Arrival and information

By bus Buses arriving from Belize City circle the village of Bermudian Landing, and stop at the sanctuary's visitors' centre only a few minutes' walk from all recommended accommodation.
Tourist information The reserve's visitors' centre (daily 8am–5pm; ☎660-3545) is at the west end of Bermudian Landing. The Bz$14 entrance fee includes a guided nature walk and a tour of the small natural history museum. The reserve also organizes a range of inexpensive activities including horseriding, canoeing and night hikes.

Accommodation and eating

If you have your own tent, you can camp at the visitors' centre (US$5 per person). Alternatively, a number of local families offer rooms in B&Bs (US$45); enquire at the visitors' centre. Apart from the *Lodge*, there are extremely limited catering options so it is advisable to bring your own food if staying in other accommodation.
Howler Monkey Lodge On the river near the visitors' centre ☎220-2158, ⊛www.howlermonkeylodge .com. Cabins with private baths and fans (some with a/c); the price includes dinner and breakfast. US$100

Moving on

By bus to: Belize City (Mon–Sat 6.30am, 7am & 3.45pm). For Orange Walk and Corozal, take the Belize City bus to the Northern Highway junction and wait at the side of the road for a non-express northern-bound bus to pass.

ALTUN HA

Some 55km north of Belize City and just 9km from the sea is the remarkable Maya site of **ALTUN HA** (daily 8am–5pm; Bz$10), which was occupied for twelve hundred years until it was abandoned around 900 AD. Its position close to the Caribbean suggests that it was sustained as much by trade as by agriculture – a theory upheld by the discovery here of obsidian and jade, neither of which occurs naturally in Belize.

Altun Ha clusters around two Classic-period plazas. Entering from the road, you come first to **Plaza A**, enclosed by large temples on all sides. A magnificent tomb was discovered beneath Temple A-1, the **Temple of the Green Tomb**. Dating from 550 AD, this yielded jades, jewellery, stingray spines, skin, flints and the remains of a Maya book. The adjacent Plaza B is dominated by the site's largest temple, the **Temple of the Masonry Altars**. Several tombs have been uncovered within the main structure; in one, archeologists discovered a carved jade head of Kinich Ahau, the Maya sun god. Just under 15cm high, it is the largest carved jade found in the Maya world; a replica is on display in the Museum of Belize (see p.64).

Outside these two main plazas are several other areas of interest, though little else has yet been restored. A short trail leads south to **Rockstone Pond**, a reservoir in Maya times, at the eastern edge of which stands another mid-sized temple. Built in the second century AD, this contained offerings from the great city of Teotihuacán in the Valley of Mexico.

Arrival and information

By bus Altun Ha is difficult to reach independently. In theory there are buses from the Belize City terminal to the village of Maskall, passing the turn-off to the site at the village of Lucky Strike, but service is erratic.
Tours Travel agents in Belize City can arrange tours (US$45–60 per person) and increasing numbers of people visit on a day-trip from San Pedro and Caye Caulker (US$85–95 per person). Your best bet to save money is to find a group in Belize City and split the cost.

CROOKED TREE WILDLIFE SANCTUARY

Midway between Belize City and Orange Walk, a branch road heads west to **CROOKED TREE WILDLIFE**

SANCTUARY (daily 8am–4.30pm; Bz$8), a reserve that encompasses swamps, wetlands and four separate lagoons. Designated Belize's first Ramsar site (to protect wetlands of international importance), the sanctuary provides a resting place for thousands of migrating and resident birds, such as snail kites, tiger herons, snowy egrets, ospreys and black-collared hawks. The reserve's most famous visitor is the **jabiru stork**, the largest flying bird in the New World, with a wingspan of 2.5m. The **best months** for birdwatching are late February to June, when the lagoons shrink to a string of pools, forcing wildlife to congregate for food and water.

In the middle of the reserve, straggling around the shores of a lagoon, is the village of **Crooked Tree**, which is linked to the mainland by a **causeway**. One of the oldest inland villages in the country, Crooked Tree is also one of Belize's loveliest, with well-kept houses and lawns dotted along tree-lined lanes. Though guided tours to the lagoon are quite expensive (at least US$50–80), numerous trails, signposted from the roads, wind around the island and along the shoreline, where you'll see plenty of birds and wildlife even without a guide.

Arrival and information

By bus Buses from Belize City make a loop around the village of Crooked Tree before heading to the causeway. Hitching is a viable (and common) option; any non-express bus can drop you at the junction with the Northern Highway.

Tourist information The wildlife sanctuary visitors' centre (8am–4.30pm) is at the end of the causeway in Crooked Tree. Pay the reserve's Bz$8 entrance fee here.

Accommodation

Most of the accommodation in Crooked Tree is in mid-priced hotels, though some of these also have camping space.

Rhaburn's Rooms ☎225-7035. Turn left at the large Crooked Tree sign, then right through the field after the Church of the Nazarene. A friendly couple

manages four small, simple rooms with fans and a clean shared bathroom. **US$25**

Sam Tillet's Hotel In the centre of the village along the bus route ☎220-7026, ⓦwww.crookedtree belize.com. Good-value hotel set amid lovely gardens. Rooms have private baths and fans; most share a balcony. You can camp on the grounds, the restaurant serves delicious breakfasts and dinners, and tours can be arranged. Camping **US$10**, doubles **US$55**

Eating

3-J's In the centre, in a green building on the bus route. Friendly place serving Creole meals and international fare.

Bird's Eye View Restaurant In the hotel grounds. Worth the one-mile walk from the centre, with a patio overlooking the lagoon. Serves large breakfasts and light, fresh lunches for around Bz$24. Dinner (Bz$30) is usually a three-course affair, though you can also ask solely for the main course.

Moving on

By bus to: Belize City (Mon–Sat 6.30am & 7am). For transport to Orange Walk and Corozal, take the Belize City bus to the Northern Highway junction and wait at the side of the road for a non-express northern-bound bus to pass.

ORANGE WALK

Like many of Belize's northern cities, **ORANGE WALK**, the largest town in the region, was founded by mestizo refugees fleeing the Caste Wars in the Yucatán. Long before their arrival, however, the area around Orange Walk had been worked as some of the most productive arable farmland in Belize – aerial surveys have revealed evidence of raised fields and a network of irrigation canals dating from ancient Maya times. Today, Orange Walk is a thriving community by Belizean standards, and though there aren't any real attractions in the town itself, it's a pleasant, low-key base for those looking to explore one of the region's highlights: the nearby ruins at Lamanai.

What to see and do

At the centre of town is a distinctly Mexican-style formal plaza, and the town hall is referred to as the Palacio Municipal, reinforcing the town's strong historical links to Mexico. The only real sight in town, per se, is the **Banquitas House of Culture** (Mon–Thurs 8.30am–5pm, Fri 8.30am–4.30pm; free; ☎322-0517, Ⓦwww.nichbelize.org), on the riverbank near the bridge, which houses a permanent exhibition charting the history of Orange Walk District from Maya times to the present.

Arrival and information

By bus Hourly buses from Belize City and Corozal pull up on the main road in the centre of town, officially Queen Victoria Ave but always referred to as the Belize–Corozal Rd. Services to and from

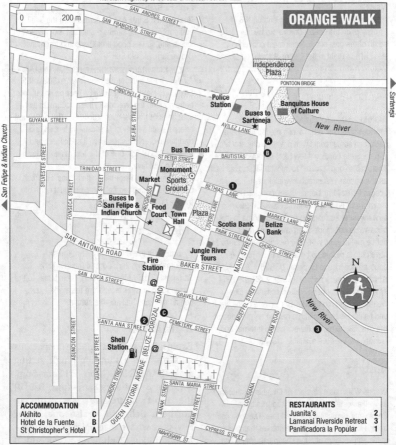

ORANGE WALK

ACCOMMODATION
Akihito — C
Hotel de la Fuente — B
St Christopher's Hotel — A

RESTAURANTS
Juanita's — 2
Lamanai Riverside Retreat — 3
Panificadora la Popular — 1

MENNONITES IN BELIZE

Members of Belize's **Mennonite** community, easily recognizable in their denim dungarees, can be seen trading produce and buying supplies every day in Orange Walk and Belize City. The Mennonites, a Protestant group often noted for their pacifist beliefs and rejection of modern advancements, arose from the radical Anabaptist movement of the sixteenth century and are named after Dutch priest Menno Simons. Recurring government restrictions on their lifestyle, especially regarding their objection to military service, have forced them to move repeatedly over time. Having emigrated to Switzerland, they then travelled to Prussia, and in 1663 a group moved to North America. After World War I they migrated from Canada to Mexico, eventually arriving in Belize in 1958. In recent years, farm-produced prosperity has caused drastic changes in their lives: the Mennonite Church in Belize is increasingly split between a modernist section – who use electricity and power tools, and drive trucks, tractors and even cars – and the traditionalists, who prefer a stricter interpretation of beliefs.

Sarteneja stop opposite *St Christopher's Hotel* on Main St.

Internet Access is cheap and plentiful; K & N Printshop, on the Belize–Corozal Rd two blocks south of the post office, is the most convenient.

Post office Right in the centre of town, on Queen Victoria Ave.

Accommodation

Akihito 22 Queen Victoria Ave ☎302-0185. Provides clean but basic accommodation – dorm beds, and some rooms with private baths and a/c – in a concrete building a few blocks from the centre. There's also one "deluxe" room with jacuzzi, as well as a Japanese restaurant downstairs and internet access for Bz$4/hr. Dorms US$8, doubles US$15

Hotel de la Fuente 14 Main St ☎322-2290, ⒲www.hoteldelafuente.com. Bright rooms in this good-value hotel include private baths, refrigerators, coffee makers and wi-fi. The owners can arrange to have guests picked up by Jungle River Tours (see opposite) for trips to Lamanai. US$35

St Christopher's Hotel 10 Main St ☎302-1064, ⒲www.stchristophershotelbze.com. Very clean, well-decorated rooms with TVs, private baths, wi-fi and balconies overlooking a garden on the edge of the river. Some rooms have a/c, and internet and laundry services are available. US$33

Eating

Orange Walk has a plethora of Chinese restaurants as well as establishments serving traditional Creole and Mexican-influenced fare. The food court behind the town hall, near the market, has a line of cafés and vendors offering cheap eats, including Mexican snacks for Bz$2–4 and good-sized breakfasts for Bz$6–8.

Juanita's 8 Santa Ana St, across from the Shell station. This small, simple restaurant is popular with locals and serves good breakfasts and traditional Creole fare. Closed Sun.

Lamanai Riverside Retreat Lamanai Alley, on the bank of the New River ☎302-3955. Enjoy breakfast, dinner or just a beer on an outdoor patio right on the riverbank where you might just spot one of the local river crocodiles. The restaurant offers a wide variety of Mexican-influenced and traditional Creole dishes as well as burgers and fries for Bz$10–25. One of the few places in town open on Sundays.

Panificadora la Popular Bethias Lane. For fresh bread and cakes, head to this place, just north of the Plaza.

Moving on

By bus to: Belize City (hourly; 1hr 30min); Chetumal (hourly; 2hr); Corozal (hourly; 1hr); Sarteneja (3 daily Mon–Sat; 2hr). Local buses to the surrounding villages leave from the market area, behind the town hall and fire station.

LAMANAI

Extensive restoration, a spacious museum and a stunning jungle setting make **LAMANAI** (Mon–Fri 8am–5pm, Sat, Sun & holidays 8am–4pm; Bz$10) the most impressive Maya site in northern Belize. It is also one of the few sites whose original Maya name – *Lama'an ayin* ("Submerged Crocodile")

– is known, hence the numerous representations of crocodiles on stucco carvings and artefacts found here. *Lamanai*, however, is a seventeenth-century mis-transliteration, which actually means "Drowned Insect". The site was continually occupied from around 1500 BC up until the sixteenth century, when Spanish missionaries built a church alongside to lure the Indians from their "heathen" ways.

Today the site is perched on a bank of the New River Lagoon inside a 950-acre archeological reserve, where the jungle surroundings give the site a feeling of tranquillity. Before heading to the ruins, visit the spacious new **archeological museum**, which houses an impressive collection of artefacts, eccentric flints and original stelae. Within the site itself, the most remarkable structure is the prosaically named N10-43 (informally the "High Temple"), a massive **Late Preclassic temple** over 37m tall and the largest from the period in the Maya region. The view across the surrounding forest and along the lagoon from the top of the temple is magnificent, and well worth the daunting climb. North from here is N9-56, a small **sixth-century pyramid** (often called the "Mask Temple", for its exceptionally well-preserved four-metre-high stucco mask of a ruler represented as a deity, probably Kinich Ahau, the sun god). At the southern end of the site, on a grand plaza, is another sixth-century pyramid, structure N10-9, known as the **Jaguar Temple** for the two large, stylized jaguar masks adorning its lowest level.

Arrival and information

By boat The easiest, most pleasant way to get to Lamanai is by river; the cheapest and most informative way to do this is as part of an organized tour.
Tour operators A number of operators organize day-trips from Orange Walk, departing around 9am; the price (US$40–50) will usually include lunch. The most informative is 🛶 Jungle River Tours, 20 Lover's Lane (☎302-2293, ✉lamanaimayatour @btl.net), run by the Novelos.

SARTENEJA AND SHIPSTERN NATURE RESERVE

Across Chetumal Bay from Corozal, the largely uninhabited **Sarteneja peninsula** is covered with dense forests and swamps that support an amazing array of wildlife. **SARTENEJA**, the peninsula's only settlement, is a peaceful, Spanish-speaking, lobster-fishing community that boasts several hotels and restaurants. Tourism is just beginning to take off in this quiet village but, unlike some parts of the country, the locals are keen to ensure that future development is carried out at a financially and environmentally sustainable level.

All buses to Sarteneja pass the entrance to **SHIPSTERN NATURE RESERVE** (daily 8am–4pm; Bz$15; ⓦwww.shipstern.org), 5km before the village, though you can also get here by renting a bike from *Fernando's* or *Backpackers Paradise* in Sarteneja (see p.84). The reserve encompasses an area of eighty square kilometres, including large areas of tropical moist forest, some wide belts of savanna, and most of the shallow Shipstern Lagoon, dotted with mangrove islands. The **visitors' centre** offers a variety of guided walks, though even if you choose the shortest, you'll encounter more named plant species here than on any other trail in Belize. Shipstern is also a birdwatcher's paradise: the lagoon system supports blue-winged teal, American coot and huge flocks of lesser scaup, while the forest is home to keel-billed toucans and at least five species of parrot. Other wildlife in the reserve includes crocodiles, jaguars, peccaries and an abundance of wonderful butterflies.

Arrival

By boat The *Thunderbolt* skiff, running between Corozal and Ambergris Caye, can call at Sarteneja if there's sufficient demand (☎610-4475/7759), pulling into the main dock on North Front St.

By bus Buses pull into Sarteneja at its southern end and make a loop around town; if you talk to the driver beforehand, they will usually drop you off wherever you like.

Accommodation

Backpackers Paradise La Bandera Rd ☎423-2016, ⊛www.backpackers.bluegreenbelize .com. Super-cheap cabañas and camping just a 5-minute drive out of town; ask the bus driver to drop you off at the Sarteneja Monument. There's also a superb restaurant (see below), bike rental (Bz$10/day) and free wi-fi. The owners, Nathalie and Ed, are extremely helpful and can arrange horseriding excursions and pick-up from the pier. Camping US$3, cabañas US$11

Fernando's Guesthouse North Front St, 100m along the shoreline from the main dock ☎423-2085, ⊛www.fernandosseaside.com. Four large, tiled rooms have private baths and share a veranda overlooking the sea. Snorkelling and nature tours can be arranged. Bike rental also available. US$35

Oasis Guesthouse One block south of North Front St, west of the main dock ☎423-2121, ⓔoasis @corozal.bz. Wooden building with four large rooms with private bath. US$30

Eating

🏃 **Backpackers Paradise Restaurant** Chef Nathalie serves excellent local, vegetarian and French dishes for Bz$6–18. Meals are available throughout the day and the traditional French crêpes are particularly recommended.

Estrella del Mar Tzatenaha St, just off North Front St. Local favourite serving inexpensive fried fish, *empanadas* and burritos for Bz$5–12.

Lily's At the eastern end of the village. Come here for traditional Belizean fare (Bz$6–12). Closed Sun.

Moving on

By boat The *Thunderbolt* skiff (☎610-4475/7759) departs for Corozal (8.20am & 4.20pm; 30min) and San Pedro (7.30am & 3.30pm; 1hr 20min) if there's sufficient demand.

By bus to: Belize City (5–6 Mon–Sat, 4–6.30am, Sun 6am; 3hr 30min); Chetumal (daily, usually at 6am; 3hr 30min). All buses to and from Sarteneja pass through Orange Walk.

COROZAL

South from the Mexican border, the road meets the sea at **COROZAL**, near the mouth of the New River. The **ancient Maya** prospered here by controlling river- and seaborne trade, and the impressive site of **Cerros** is nearby, if complicated to reach. Present-day Corozal was founded in 1849 by refugees from Mexico's Caste Wars, although today's grid-pattern town, a neat mix of Mexican and Caribbean, is largely due to reconstruction in the wake of Hurricane Janet in 1955.

What to see and do

There's little reason to spend time in Corozal unless you are trying to get to Cerros. However, it is an ideal place for a few days of quiet relaxation. The breezy shoreline **park** is good for a stroll, while on the tree-shaded main plaza, the **town hall** is worth a look inside for a mural by Manuel Villamar Reyes, which vividly describes local history. In the block west of the plaza you can see the remains of **Fort Barlee**, built to ward off Maya attacks in the 1870s.

Santa Rita

The small Maya site of **Santa Rita** (open 24hr; free) is within walking distance of the centre, about 15 minutes northwest

---

INTO MEXICO: SANTA ELENA

It's less than four hours by bus along the Northern Highway from Belize City to Chetumal, Mexico, via the border crossing at Santa Elena. Entering Belize, Mexican immigration and customs posts are on the northern bank of the Río Hondo, 12km from Chetumal; when you're finished there, the bus will pick you up again to take you to Belizean immigration. Leaving Belize, you'll have to pay an exit tax of Bz$30 and the PACT conservation fee of Bz$7.50. Moneychangers wait on the Belize side of the border; make sure to get rid of your Belize dollars before crossing into Mexico.

COROZAL

RESTAURANTS
Joe Mel In	2
Patty's Bistro	1
Venky's Kabab Corner	3

N

Shell Station
Bus Terminal
Police Station
Atlantic Bank
Market
Belize Bank
Taxis
Central Park
Town Hall
Library
Scotia Bank

Thunderbolt Dock

Corozal Bay

ACCOMMODATION
Bayside Guesthouse	A
Hok'ol K'ln Guesthouse	D
Maya World Guesthouse	B
Sea Breeze Hotel	C

Hotel Maya

0   200 m

BELIZE   THE NORTH

Copper Bank, Airstrip, Sarteneja, Orange Walk (48km) & Belize City (135km)

of town; follow the main road towards the border, bear right at the fork and turn left at the Super Santa Rita store. Though it is an interesting enough spot if you have time to kill, the site is no longer maintained and does not justify extending your stay in Corozal. Founded around 1500 BC, Santa Rita was in all probability the powerful Maya city later known as Chactemal. It was still a thriving settlement in 1531 AD, when the conquistador Alonso Davila entered the town, only to be driven out almost immediately by Na Chan Kan, the Maya chief, and his Spanish adviser Gonzalo Guerrero. The main remaining building is a small pyramid, and excavations here have uncovered the burial sites of an elaborately bejewelled elderly woman and a Classic-period warlord.

Arrival and information

By air Flights from San Pedro arrive at the airstrip 2km south of town. Taxis meet flights and charge Bz$8–10 for a trip to the centre.

By boat The *Thunderbolt* skiff arriving from San Pedro pulls into the main dock on 1st Ave, just two blocks southeast of the town centre.

By bus The Northern Transport depot is near the northern edge of town, opposite the Shell station. In addition to local services between Belize City and Corozal, express buses pass through Corozal en route to Chetumal, Mexico, roughly hourly in each direction.

Tour operators For organized tours to local nature reserves and archeological sites, contact Henry Menzies (☏422-2725, ⊛www.belizetransfers .com); he's also an expert on travel to Mexico.

Tourist information Corozal has no tourist office, but the city's website (⊛www.corozal.com) is a good place to find information.

Accommodation

Bayside Guesthouse 31 3rd Ave ☎625-7824, ⓦwww.baysideguesthouse.webplus.net. Four tastefully decorated rooms with private baths, fans and coffee makers; one has a/c. The friendly English owners provide off-road parking, evening meals in the terrace bar/restaurant and a complimentary continental breakfast. US$46

Hok'ol K'in Guesthouse 89 4th Ave ☎422-3329. Decent option right on the seafront. Large rooms include private baths, fans and balconies; some have a/c. The outdoor bar is open 24hr. US$52

Maya World Guesthouse 16 2nd St North ☎666-3577, ⓔbyronchuster@gmail.com. Very basic budget hotel with private baths and fans. There's a communal kitchen and pleasant veranda too. US$28

🏃 **Sea Breeze Hotel** 23 1st Ave ☎422-3051, ⓦwww.theseabreezehotel.com. The best budget choice in Belize with friendly staff, a wonderful bar and comfortable accommodation. Rooms include private baths, fans and cable TV; some have a/c. Guests can charter owner Gwyn's speedboat for trips to Cerros (see below) for US$30 per person. US$18

Eating

Joe Mel In 5th Ave and 2nd St South. Belizean and Mexican dishes (from Bz$7) in a large, open-air restaurant.

🏃 **Patty's Bistro** 7 2nd St North ☎402-0174. Recently relocated to a more spacious venue, *Patty's* continues to be deservedly popular with locals and tourists alike. Excellent Belizean, Mexican and American fare – cheeseburgers to fish soups – for Bz$7–22.

Venky's Kabab Corner 5th Ave and 5th St South ☎402-0536. Ignore the uninspiring interior and concentrate on *Venky's* unusually good quality Indian food. Expect to pay Bz$15 for generous portions, with both meat and vegetarian options available.

Directory

Exchange Belize Bank (with 24hr ATM), on the north side of the plaza.
Internet Easy to find; look for signs along 4th and 5th aves.
Post office On the west side of the plaza (Mon–Fri 8.30am–4.30pm).

Moving on

By boat The *Thunderbolt* (☎610-4475 or 601-7759) runs to San Pedro, on Ambergris Caye, from the dock southeast of the centre (daily 7am & 3pm; 1hr 45min; Bz$45).

By bus to: Belize City (hourly 4am–6pm; 2hr 30min); Chetumal (hourly 6am–9pm; 1hr); Orange Walk (hourly; 1hr). Buses for surrounding villages (including Copper Bank, see below) leave from the market area. If booked in advance, the Linea Dorada express bus to Flores, Guatemala, can pick you up from *Hotel Maya*, on 7th Ave, 2km south of the centre.

CERROS

Built in a strategic position at the mouth of the New River, the late Preclassic centre of **CERROS** (daily 8am–5pm; Bz$10) was one of the first places in the Maya world to adopt the rule of kings. Despite this initial success, however, Cerros was abandoned by the Classic period. The ruins of the site now include three large acropolis structures, ball courts and plazas flanked by pyramids. The largest building is a 22-metre-high temple, whose intricate stucco masks represent the rising and setting sun.

A sporadic bus service runs from Corozal to the nearby village of **Copper Bank**, and from there it is possible to rent a bike to access the ruins (20min). However, the most comfortable and reliable way to reach the ruins is by boat. Hotels in Corozal can give advice on arranging a charter (ask at the *Sea Breeze Hotel* or *Hok'ol K'in Guesthouse*), which operate either with (from US$75 per person) or without (from US$30 per person) a guided tour. If you wish to stay in the atmospheric surroundings of the ruins for a night or two, *Cerros Beach Resort* (☎623-9763, ⓦwww.cerros beachresort.com; US$40) offers four charming cabañas with private bath, TV and internet access, and also has a bar/restaurant serving local and international cuisine at Bz$8–20 to both guests and day-trippers. Lastly, visitors should note that mosquitoes around the site are particularly pesky – prepare accordingly.

The west

Heading west from Belize City towards the Guatemalan border, you'll traverse varied landscapes, from open grassland to dense tropical forest. A fast, paved road, the **Western Highway**, runs the entire way, moving from the heat and humidity of the coast to the cooler, lush foothills of the Maya Mountains.

Before reaching Belize's tiny capital, **Belmopan**, the road passes two excellent attractions: the **Belize Zoo** and the **Monkey Bay Wildlife Sanctuary**. West of Belmopan, following the Belize River valley, the road skirts the **Maya Mountains**. You're now in **Cayo District**, the largest of Belize's six districts and arguably the most beautiful. South of the road, the **Mountain Pine Ridge** is a pleasantly cool region of hills and pine woods. **San Ignacio**, on the Macal River, makes an ideal base for exploring the forests, rivers and ruins of western Belize, including **Caracol**, the largest Maya site in Belize, and the region's many dramatic **caves**, often filled with Maya artefacts.

BELIZE ZOO

The **BELIZE ZOO**, at Mile 29 on the Western Highway (daily 8am–5pm; Bz$20; ⓦwww.belizezoo.org), is easily visited on a half-day trip from Belize City or as a stop on the way west. Probably the finest zoo south of the US, and long recognized as a phenomenal conservation achievement, the zoo originally opened in 1983. Now organized around the theme of "a walk through Belize", the zoo offers the chance to see the country's native animals at close quarters. Residents include tapirs, a wide variety of birds and all the Belizean cats. To **get to the zoo** take any bus between Belize City and Belmopan and ask the driver to drop you at the signed turn-off, a 200-metre walk from the entrance; you can leave your luggage at the visitors'

centre. If you'd like to stay overnight in the area, the zoo's **Jungle Lodge** (☏220-8003, ⓔinfo@belizezoo.org), on the opposite side of the highway about 300m back towards Belize City, offers wooden dorms (US$30) with shared baths and hot showers. Guests can take a nocturnal tour of the zoo for Bz$30.

One kilometre past the zoo, the **Coastal Road** (served by only two weekly buses in each direction) provides an unpaved short cut to Gales Point (see p.100) and Dangriga. A kilometre or so past the junction is *Cheers*, a friendly **restaurant** with good food at reasonable prices, and reliable information.

MONKEY BAY WILDLIFE SANCTUARY

Half a kilometre past *Cheers* and 300m off the Western Highway, **MONKEY BAY WILDLIFE SANCTUARY** (☏820-3032, ⓦwww.monkeybaybelize.org), a 44-square-kilometre protected area extending to the Sibun River, offers birding and nature trails through five distinct types of vegetation and habitat. Adjoining the sanctuary is the **Monkey Bay National Park**, enclosing a biological corridor that runs south through karst limestone hills to connect with the Manatee Forest Reserve. Apart from being a relaxing place **to stay** in a private room (US$27) or to camp under thatched shelters (US$6), Monkey Bay is a viable experiment in sustainable living, using solar power, rainwater catchment and biogas fuel for cooking; the food (some of it grown in the station's organic gardens) is plentiful and delicious, and the staff arranges excursions. *Amigos Bar* next to Monkey Bay has great food and a daily happy hour.

GUANACASTE NATIONAL PARK

Just off the highway at the turn-off towards Belmopan is tiny **GUANACASTE NATIONAL PARK** (daily 8am–4.30pm; Bz$5), a 52-acre area of beautiful tropical forest. Several short, circular trails leave from the **visitors' centre**, winding through the forest and passing the Belize and Roaring rivers; there's even a spot for swimming. Although a visit here isn't necessary if you're planning on spending time in Belize's other forested areas, Guanacaste provides an excellent introduction to the country's flora and fauna and is exceptionally accessible; any bus heading west can drop you off at the visitors' centre, where you can leave your belongings while you explore.

BELMOPAN

At Guanacaste, the Hummingbird Highway (see p.97) splits from the Western Highway and heads south to **BELMOPAN** (and eventually, Dangriga). The city was founded in 1970, after Hurricane Hattie swept much of Belize City into the sea. The government decided to use the disaster as a chance to move to higher ground and, in a bid to focus development on the interior, chose a site at the geographical heart of the country. The name of the city combines the words "Belize" and "Mopan", the language spoken by the Maya of Cayo, and the layout of the main government buildings is modelled loosely on a Maya city, with buildings grouped around a central plaza. When built, Belmopan was meant to symbolize a new era, with tree-lined avenues, banks, embassies and communications worthy of a world centre. Few people, however, chose to move here, and Belmopan remains the smallest capital city in the world. And although the population is growing slowly, there's little reason to stay any longer than it takes your bus to leave.

Arrival

By bus Buses from Belize City to San Ignacio, Benque Viejo, Dangriga and Punta Gorda all pass through Belmopan, so there's at least one service in either direction every 30min. All buses stop at the terminal, which is located in the city centre and within walking distance of most of the city's hotels.

Accommodation and eating

Belmopan's accommodation is for the most part expensive and aimed at visiting dignitaries and professionals. Many restaurants here are closed on Sunday, so snacks from the bus terminal may be your only option if you're passing through, unless you are willing to wander quite a bit further afield.
Caladium Beside the bus terminal. Good Belizean food, with an inexpensive daily special, in a/c surroundings.
El Rey Inn 23 Moho St ☏822-3438, ⊛www .belmopanhotels.com. If you do have to stay here, this place has the cheapest rooms in town, all with private bath. It is, however, quite a long walk from the bus station (20–30min), so consider taking a taxi (Bz$5–6). US$23

Directory

Exchange Banks (with ATMs) are close to the bus terminal.
Immigration The office is in the main government building by the fire station.
Internet PC.Com, next to *Caladium*, across from the bus station.

Moving on

By bus to: Belize City (every 20min, until 7pm; 1hr 15min); Benque Viejo, for the Guatemalan border (every 30min; 1hr 30min); Dangriga (every 2hr, until 6pm; 1hr 40min); Punta Gorda (every 2hr; 6hr); San Ignacio (every 30min, until 10pm; 1hr 15min).

SAN IGNACIO

On the west bank of the Macal River, about 35km from Belmopan, **SAN IGNACIO** is a friendly, relaxed town that draws together the best of inland Belize. Surrounded by fast-flowing rivers and forested hills, it's an ideal base from which to explore the region, offering a pleasant climate, good food, inexpensive hotels and frequent bus connections. The town is usually referred to as **Cayo** by locals, the same word that the Spanish used to describe the offshore islands – an apt description of the area, which is set in a peninsula between two converging rivers. The early Spanish Conquest in

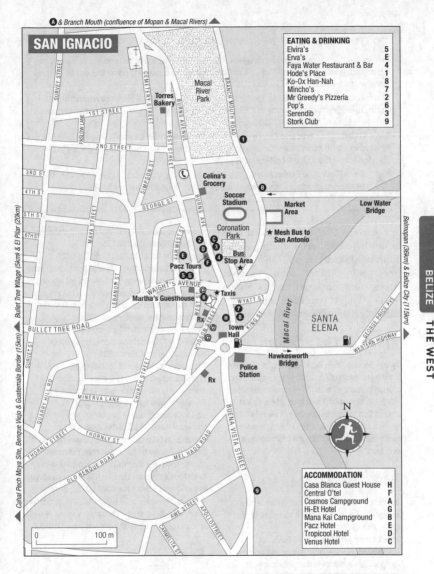

SAN IGNACIO

A & Branch Mouth (confluence of Mopan & Macal Rivers)

Macal River Park

Torres Bakery

Celina's Grocery

Soccer Stadium

Market Area

Low Water Bridge

Coronation Park

★ Mesh Bus to San Antonio

Bus Stop Area

Pacz Tours

Martha's Guesthouse

★ Taxis

Town Hall

Police Station

Hawkesworth Bridge

SANTA ELENA

Macal River

Belmopan (36km) & Belize City (115km)

Cahal Pech Maya Site, Benque Viejo & Guatemala Border (15km)

Bullet Tree Village (5km) & El Pilar (20km)

Western Highway

0 — 100 m

EATING & DRINKING

Elvira's	5
Erva's	E
Faya Water Restaurant & Bar	4
Hode's Place	1
Ko-Ox Han-Nah	8
Mincho's	7
Mr Greedy's Pizzeria	2
Pop's	6
Serendib	3
Stork Club	9

ACCOMMODATION

Casa Blanca Guest House	H
Central O'tel	F
Cosmos Campground	A
Hi-Et Hotel	G
Mana Kai Campground	B
Pacz Hotel	E
Tropicool Hotel	D
Venus Hotel	C

1544 made little impact here, and the area was a centre of rebellion in the following decades. **Spanish friars** arrived in 1618, but the population continued to practice "idolatry", and in 1641 Maya priests threw out some Spanish clerics. Tipu, the region's capital, retained a measure of independence until 1707, when the population was forcibly removed to Guatemala.

What to see and do

There's little to do in San Ignacio proper, though relative to other Belizean towns, you can spend many pleasant days here, as it's both relaxed and low-hassle and the streets of the centre are lined with bars and restaurants. Numerous independent local operators – see the

TOUR OPERATORS IN SAN IGNACIO

Belize Culture Tours *Casa Blanca Hotel* ☏824-2661, ⓦwww.belizeculturetours.com. Specializing in day-trips to Tikal, Elias Cambranes also leads trips to the caves and ruins at Xunantunich and Caracol (US$55–115).

Cayo Adventure Tours Based in Santa Elena ☏824-3246, ⓦwww.cayoadventures .com. In addition to customized tours to the caves and ruins, a daily shuttle service to Belize City is available (US$30–35).

Easy Rider In the Arts and Crafts store on Burns Ave under *Central O'tel* ☏824-3734, ©easyrider@btl.net. Charlie Collins organizes the best-value horseriding packages in San Ignacio (US$30 for a half-day, US$50 for a full day).

Pacz Tours 30 Burns Ave ☏824-0536, ⓦwww.pacztours.net. A wide variety of informative tours, including trips to Actun Tunichil Muknal (US$85), Caracol (US$80) and Tikal, in Guatemala (US$135).

box above – offer superb guided trips to nearby attractions, including Actun Tunichil Muknal (see p.92) and Caracol (see p.95). There's some turnover among tour operators, so it's always worth asking at your hotel about what's currently being offered.

Arrival and information

By bus Services from Belize City stop in the centre of town just south of Coronation Park, within easy walking distance of all of the recommended hotels.
Tourist information There is no official tourist office in San Ignacio but the town's website (ⓦwww.sanignaciotown.com) is helpful, and most hotels will be able to offer good information on local tours.

Accommodation

San Ignacio has some of the best-value budget accommodation in the country, and you'll almost always find space.
Casa Blanca Guest House 10 Burns Ave ☏824-2080, ⓦwww.casablancaguesthouse.com. Very popular hotel with immaculate rooms, all with private bath and cable TV (some with a/c) and a comfortable sitting area with fridge, coffee and tea. Booking advisable. US$30
Central O'tel 24 Burns Ave ☏824-3734, ©easyrider@btl.net. Simple, somewhat shabby rooms with shared baths at the cheapest rates in town; the balcony with hammocks is a great place from which to watch the street below. US$12
Cosmos Campground 1km along the Branch Mouth Rd ☏824-2116, ©cosmoscamping@btl.net. Campsite with showers, flush toilets and a kitchen,

plus simple cabins with shared hot-water showers. Camping US$5, cabins US$25
Hi-Et Hotel 12 West St ☏824-2828, ©thehiet@btl.net. Popular, comfortable hotel with shared-bath rooms in a beautiful old wooden building. Each room comes with a tiny balcony, and there are larger rooms with private bath in a new concrete building. Book ahead. US$13
Mana Kai Campground Branch Mouth Rd ☏824-2317. Centrally located campsite with hammocks and showers. US$4
Pacz Hotel 4 Far West St ☏604-4526, ©paczghouse@btl.net. Five clean, comfortable rooms (some with private bath) at bargain rates. The sitting room has a fridge and cable TV. Good for local information. US$18
Tropicool Hotel 30 Burns Ave ☏804-3052, ©tropicoolgift@gmail.com. Bright, clean rooms with shared hot-water baths, and wooden cabins with private showers and cable TV. The sitting room has a TV and a laundry area. Doubles US$18, cabins US$40
Venus Hotel 29 Burns Ave ☏824-3203, ©midas @btl.net. Two-storey hotel with a variety of accommodation, including shared-bath economy rooms as well as rooms with private baths, a/c and cable TV. US$33

Eating

San Ignacio has an abundance of good, inexpensive restaurants. The Saturday market is also the best in Belize, with local farmers bringing in fresh produce.
Elvira's 6 Far West St. Delicious Belizean cuisine at some of the cheapest prices in town – most dishes are Bz$10 or under but note that portions are small.
Erva's 4 Far West St, under *Pacz Hotel.* Traditional Belizean dishes for under Bz$20, as well as seafood and filling, topping-laden pizzas from Bz$18 served on a pleasant patio. Popular with both tourists and locals.

Ko-Ox Han-Nah 5 Burns Ave. Small restaurant with some of the most delicious food in the country – everything from Belizean to Burmese, accompanied by fresh salads – at great prices; get here early or you'll have to wait. Mains Bz$8–20.

Mincho's Southern end of Burns Ave. Locals crowd around this tiny food-stand for Mexican snacks, including tacos and burritos, for Bz$1–5.

Mr Greedy's Pizzeria 34 Burns Ave. A lively happy hour, free wi-fi and the closest thing to a real Italian pizza you're likely to get in Belize make *Greedy's* an appealing choice.

Pop's Far West St. Huge, inexpensive breakfasts and bottomless cups of coffee for Bz$10, as well as traditional Belizean dishes.

Serendib 27 Burns Ave. Excellent Sri Lankan cuisine for Bz$10–22. Closed Sun.

Drinking and nightlife

As tourism to San Ignacio increases, so does the number of bars, some of which can get quite rowdy later at night. The town is also a popular weekend spot for many Belizeans, and there's live music and dancing every Friday and Saturday night.

Faya Water Restaurant & Bar Burns Ave, across from *Central O'tel*. I aidback restaurant by day, *Faya* becomes a popular bar at night, open until late, with pool tables and dartboards.

Hode's Place Bullet Tree Rd. Popular with locals and travellers, this bar and grill has a patio and pool tables.

Mr Greedy's 34 Burns Ave. A great place to relax, sink your feet into the sandy floor and sip rum cocktails while watching the world go by.

Stork Club 18 Buena Vista St, in *San Ignacio Resort Hotel*. Relaxed and somewhat upscale bar most nights, with karaoke on Thurs and a DJ or band on Fri.

Directory

Exchange Belize, Scotia and Atlantic banks are on Burns Ave; all have 24hr ATMs. Moneychangers will approach anyone they think is heading west to exchange for Guatemalan quetzales; they also board buses bound for Benque before departure.

Internet Tradewinds, on West St at Waight's Ave, offers internet access for Bz$5/hr.

Laundry Drop-off laundry at *Martha's Guest House*, on West St.

Post office Next to Courts furniture store on Hudson St in the centre of town.

Travel agent For domestic and international air tickets head to Exodus Travel, 2 Burns Ave (☎824-4400).

Moving on

By bus to: Belize City via Belmopan (every 30min 4am–6pm; 3hr); Benque Viejo, for the Guatemalan border (every 30min; 15min).

By taxi It's more comfortable to get a shared taxi from San Ignacio to the Guatemalan border for Bz$20 than taking the bus.

AROUND SAN IGNACIO

San Ignacio makes a great base from which to explore the **Cayo District**'s impressive **Maya ruins** and stunning natural scenery. You'll be required to hire a local guide in order to visit several of the region's highlights, though this is often a good idea anyway, to get the best experience; see the box opposite for recommended tour operators.

Cahal Pech

The hilltop Maya site of **Cahal Pech** (daily 6am–6pm; Bz$12), twenty minutes' walk west of San Ignacio along the road to Benque Viejo, is well worth a visit. There's a good chance you'll have the forested ruins all to yourself, and although the structures are not particularly tall, the maze of restored corridors, stairways, plazas and temples is enchanting. Cahal Pech was the royal acropolis-palace of an elite Maya family during the Classic period, and there's evidence of monumental construction from at least as early as 400 BC, though most of the remaining structures date from the eighth century AD. The **visitors' centre and museum** has a scale model of the site, excellent displays and a variety of artefacts. Entering the site itself, you arrive at **Plaza B**, where your gaze is drawn to Structure 1, the **Audiencia**, the highest building at Cahal Pech. From the top, the ruins of Xunantunich (see p.96) are clearly visible to the southwest. Behind Structure 1, in **Plaza A**, is a restored three-storey temple, as well as other sacred buildings.

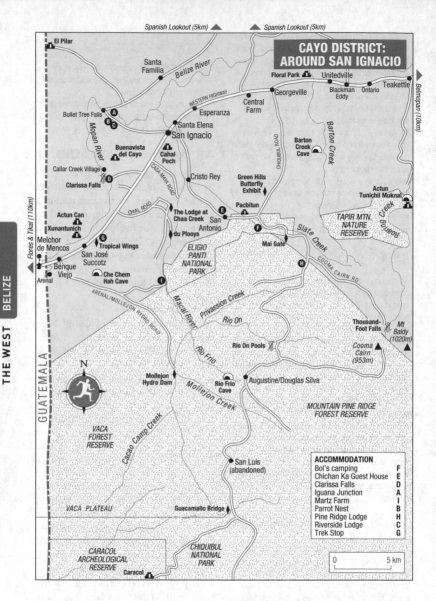

Spanish Lookout (5km) ▲ ▲ Spanish Lookout (5km)

CAYO DISTRICT: AROUND SAN IGNACIO

El Pilar

Santa Familia

Belize River

Floral Park 🏛 Unitedville

Georgeville   Blackman Ontario Teakettle
                Eddy

Bullet Tree Falls Ⓐ
                  Ⓑ
                  Ⓒ

WESTERN HIGHWAY

Esperanza   Central
              Farm

Santa Elena
San Ignacio

Mopan River

Buenavista
del Cayo   🏛 Cahal
               Pech

Callar Creek Village Ⓓ

Clarissa Falls   Cristo Rey

CHIAL ROAD

CASA MAYA ROAD

CHIQUIBUL ROAD

Barton
Creek
Cave

Barton Creek

Green Hills
Butterfly
Exhibit ◆

Pacbitun 🏛

Actun
Tunichil Muknal 🏛

Actun Can 🏛
Xunantunich 🏛

Tropical Wings Ⓖ

San José
Succotz

Benque
Viejo

Arenal

Che Chem
Hah Cave

The Lodge at
Chaa Creek ◆   Ⓔ San
du Plooys   Antonio

ELIGIO
PANTI
NATIONAL
PARK

Ⓕ
Mai Gate

Slate Creek

Roaring Creek

TAPIR MTN.
NATURE
RESERVE

COOMA CAIRN RD

Ⓗ

ARENAL/MOLLEJON HYDRO ROAD

Ⓘ

Macal River

Privassion Creek

Rio On

Rio Frio

Mollejon
Hydro Dam

Rio Frio
Cave

Rio On Pools

Augustine/Douglas Silva

Mollejon Creek

Thousand-
Foot Falls

Mt
Baldy
(1020m)

Cooma ▲
Cairn
(953m)

MOUNTAIN PINE RIDGE
FOREST RESERVE

GUATEMALA

N

VACA
FOREST
RESERVE

Cacao Camp Creek

San Luis
(abandoned)

VACA PLATEAU

Guacamallo Bridge

CHIQUIBUL
NATIONAL
PARK

CARACOL
ARCHEOLOGICAL
RESERVE

Caracol 🏛

Melchor
de Mencos

Flores & Tikal (110km) ◀

Belmopan (10km) ▶

ACCOMMODATION

Bol's camping	F
Chichan Ka Guest House	E
Clarissa Falls	D
Iguana Junction	A
Martz Farm	I
Parrot Nest	B
Pine Ridge Lodge	H
Riverside Lodge	C
Trek Stop	G

0 ——— 5 km

Actun Tunichil Muknal

Actun Tunichil Muknal (tours around US$85, including lunch, entry fee and transport from San Ignacio; you must be accompanied by a licensed guide to enter), in Roaring Creek valley, gets its name ("Cave of the Stone Sepulchre") for the astonishingly well preserved skeletons, fourteen in total, of Maya human sacrifices found here. As the cave has historically been inaccessible to looters, little has been touched since the Maya stopped using it over a millennium ago, and the artefacts are spellbinding. Perhaps the most dramatic sight is the skeleton of a young woman lying below a

THE WEST | BELIZE

rock wall – and nearby the stone axe that may have killed her. The cave is certainly worth the high price of a tour; note, though, that you'll need to be pretty fit and able to swim to do the trip; for much of the time you're wading knee- or even chest-deep in water.

Barton Creek Cave

Barton Creek Cave (tours around US$60, including Bz$20 entry fee; you must be accompanied by a licensed guide to enter) is also accessible only by river, though this time by canoe. Framed by jungle, the cave's entrance is at the far side of a pool, and inside the river is navigable for about 1600m before ending in a gallery blocked by a huge rockfall. If it's been raining, a subterranean waterfall cascades over the rocks – a truly unforgettable sight. The clear, slow-moving river fills most of the cave width, though the roof soars 100m above you in places. Several **Maya burial sites** and pottery vessels line the banks, the most awe-inspiring indicated by a skull set in a natural rock bridge used by the Maya to reach the sacred site.

Along the Macal River

Steep limestone cliffs and forested hills edge the lower **Macal River**, whose main tributaries rise in the Mountain Pine Ridge Forest Reserve and the Chiquibul Forest. In the upper reaches the water is sometimes suitable for whitewater kayaking, though you'll need a guide for this (see p.90). A guided canoe trip, however, is by far the best way to visit one of the river's top sights, the **Rainforest Medicine Trail** (daily 8am–5pm), in the grounds of *The Lodge at Chaa Creek*, 5km upriver from San Ignacio. The medical knowledge of the Maya was extensive, and the trail, dedicated to a Maya bush doctor (*curandero*), is fascinating: among the plants here you'll see the negrito tree, whose bark was once sold in Europe for its weight in gold as a cure for dysentery. The **Chaa Creek Natural History**

Centre, next to the Medicine Trail (daily 8am–5pm), offers a marvellous introduction to Cayo's history, geography and wildlife. A combined ticket for both the above is Bz$20. At *du Plooy's* resort, a few kilometres upstream from *Chaa Creek*, the ambitious **Belize Botanic Gardens** (daily 7am–5pm; Bz$20; ☎824-3101, ⓦwww.belizebotanic.org) aim to conserve many of Belize's native plant species in small areas representative of their habitats.

Most **accommodation** on the Macal River is in high-end resorts, though there is one less-expensive option (see box above).

Along the Mopan River

Rushing down from the Guatemalan border, the **Mopan River** offers some attractive and not too serious **whitewater rapids**. Though there's less **accommodation** along the Mopan branch of the Belize River than there is along the Macal, what's available is more within reach of the budget traveller. All of the places below can arrange river trips, as well as trips throughout Cayo.

Accommodation

Clarissa Falls 2km along a signed track, to the right off the Western Highway ☎824-3916, ⓦwww.clarissafalls.com. Restful place on the river with simple, clean cottages with private bathrooms, plus camping with shared hot-water showers. There's also a restaurant, and the staff can arrange a variety of tours. Camping US$8, cottages US$75

Iguana Junction Bullet Tree Falls village centre, 5km west of San Ignacio ☎ 824-2249, ⓦ www .iguanajunction.com. Two individual cabins and two cabin-style rooms, all with private bath, in a riverside setting. Excellent home-cooked meals. US$61

Parrot Nest Bullet Tree Falls, at the end of the track just before the bridge ☎ 669-6068, ⓦ www.parrot -nest.com. Six cabins (two up a tree and one with private bath) set in beautiful gardens on the riverbank, with shared, hot-water baths. Filling meals are available, and there's free tubing and a free daily shuttle to San Ignacio. US$49

Riverside Lodge Bullet Tree Falls ☎ 820-4007, ⓦ www.riversidelodgebelize.com. Simple cabins with private bath and fan are some of the cheapest in the area, and there's a restaurant serving good, home-made meals. US$39

MOUNTAIN PINE RIDGE FOREST RESERVE

South of San Ignacio, the **MOUNTAIN PINE RIDGE FOREST RESERVE** comprises a spectacular range of rolling hills, jagged peaks and gorges interspersed with areas of grassland and pine forest. In the warm river valleys the vegetation is gallery forest, giving way to rainforest south of the Guacamallo Bridge, which crosses the upper Macal River. One of the most scenic of the many small rivers in the Pine Ridge is the **Río On**, rushing over cataracts and into a gorge. On the northern side of the ridge are the **Thousand-Foot Falls**, actually over 1600ft (488m) and the highest in Central America. The reserve also includes limestone areas riddled with caves, the most accessible being the **Río Frio**. The area is virtually uninhabited but for a few tourist lodges and one small settlement, **Augustine/Douglas Silva**, site of the reserve headquarters.

What to see and do

It can be very difficult to get around the reserve, as there are not many roads. A mountain bike can be very helpful in this respect – the whole area is perfect for

hiking and **mountain biking**; hitching is another option.

San Antonio

Nestled in the Macal River valley, **San Antonio** is the southernmost settlement outside the reserve. It's a good place to learn about traditional Maya practices: the village was the home of famous Maya healer Don Eligio Panti, and there's a small, informal museum in the village, dedicated to his life and work. The García sisters, Don Eligio's nieces, run the inexpensive *Chichan Ka Guest House* (☎ 669-4023, ⓔ tanah_info @awrem.com; US$13) on the road approaching the village; buses from San Ignacio stop outside. The sisters also serve traditional meals, offer courses in the gathering and use of medicinal plants and are also renowned for their slate carvings – their **gift shop** has become a favourite tour-group stop. Nearby, the **Tanah Museum** has exhibits on village life.

The reserve

Not far beyond San Antonio, the two entrance roads meet and begin a steady climb to the **reserve**. One kilometre beyond the junction is a **campsite** (US$7.50) run by Fidencio and Petronila Bol, who operate Bol's Jungle Tours; Fidencio can guide you to several nearby caves. About 5km uphill from the campsite is the **Mai Gate**, a checkpoint with information about the reserve, toilets and drinking water. There are plans to levy an **entrance fee**, but for the moment all the guards do is write your name in the visitors' book (to ensure against illegal camping).

Once in the reserve, pine trees replace the dense, leafy forest. After 3km a road heads off to the left, running for 16km to a point overlooking the **Thousand-Foot Falls** (US$2). The setting is spectacular, with thickly forested slopes across the steep valley. The waterfall is about 1km from the viewpoint, but try to resist the temptation to climb around for a closer look, as the slope is a lot steeper than it first appears.

Around 11km further on from the junction to the falls lies one of the reserve's main attractions, the **Río On Pools** – a gorgeous spot for a swim. Another 8km from here and you reach the reserve headquarters at **Augustine/Douglas Silva**. You can **camp** here and the village store has a few basic supplies. The huge **Río Frio Cave** is a twenty-minute walk from Augustine/Douglas Silva, following the signposted track from the parking area through the forest to the main cave. Sandy beaches and rocky cliffs line the Río Frio on both sides as it flows through the cave.

Caracol

Beyond Augustine/Douglas Silva, the Maya Mountains rise up to the south, while to the west is the wild Vaca plateau. Here the ruins of **Caracol** (daily 8am–4pm; Bz$20), the most magnificent Maya site in Belize, and one of the largest in the Maya world, were lost for over a thousand years until their rediscovery in 1936. Two years later they were explored by A.H. Anderson, who named the site Caracol – Spanish for "snail" – because of the large numbers of snail shells found there. The first detailed, full-scale excavation of the site began in 1985, and research and restoration continues today.

Most arrive with a guided tour from San Ignacio (see p.90), as there is no public transport to, or even near, the site. If you manage to make it here on your own, you'll be guided around by one of the guards. The **visitors' centre** is one of the best at any Maya site in Belize and an essential first stop. Of the site itself, only the core of the city, comprising thirty-two large structures and twelve smaller ones grouped round five main plazas, is open to visitors – though even this is far more than you can effectively see in a day. The most massive structure, **Caana** ("Sky Place") is 42m high and still one of the tallest buildings in Belize. Hiero-glyphic inscriptions here have enabled epigraphers to piece together a virtually complete dynastic record of Caracol's rulers from 599 AD. One altar records a victory over Tikal in 562 AD – a triumph that sealed the city's rise to power.

Arrival and information

Arrival There are two entrance roads to the Mountain Pine Ridge Reserve, one from the village of Georgeville, on the Western Highway, and the other from Santa Elena, along the Cristo Rey road and through the village of San Antonio. If you're fit, a good way to get around is to rent a mountain bike in San Ignacio; you can take it on the bus to San Antonio. There are also four Mesh buses a day (Mon–Sat) from San Ignacio to San Antonio via Cristo Rey.

INTO GUATEMALA: BENQUE VIEJO DEL CARMEN

The westernmost town in Belize, 2km before the Guatemalan border, is **Benque Viejo del Carmen**. This quiet town is served by constant **buses** (which terminate here); to get to the border itself you'll need to take a **shared taxi** (Bz$10).

Leaving Belize you pay an exit tax of Bz$30, plus the PACT Conservation fee of Bz$7.50. There's no charge to enter Guatemala for North Americans or citizens of the EU, Australia and New Zealand; if you do require a visa (up to US$10), they can sometimes be issued here, though it's a good idea to check if you need one in advance. The Guatemalan border town of **Melchor de Mencos** has little to recommend it, so it is best to continue as soon as you're ready. **Moneychangers** will be waiting on either side of the border, though you might want to bargain with them to get the best rate.

Minibuses (US$10–15) to **Flores** or **Tikal** usually wait just over the border, and *colectivo* minibuses to Flores wait just over the bridge at the border; regular second-class buses pass the junction just beyond the bridge.

Pine Ridge Lodge ☎606-4557, ⓦwww.pineridgelodge.com. If you decide to splurge and stay in the reserve, this lodge, on the banks of Little Vaqueros Creek, is one of the cheapest options in the area and the most likely to be within the reach of budget travellers. The simple accommodation is in thatched or tiled-roof cabins set among grounds with trees full of orchids and trails leading to pristine waterfalls. Continental breakfast is included, and other meals are served at the lodge's excellent restaurant. US$100

Tours Tours can be arranged from San Ignacio (see box, p.90).

Accommodation

The resorts in Mountain Pine Ridge include some of the most luxurious and expensive accommodation in the interior of Belize. There are no budget options, and none of the resorts allow camping – the only options are Bol's Nature Tours (see p.94) and in Augustine/Douglas Silva (see p.94).

XUNANTUNICH

On the Western Highway, around 12km west of San Ignacio, the quiet village of **San José Succotz** is home to the ruins of **XUNANTUNICH** (pronounced Shun-an-tun-ich), "the Stone Maiden" (daily 8am–5pm; Bz$10). This impressive Maya site is also one of the most accessible in Belize; any bus heading west from San Ignacio can drop you at the old cable-winched ferry that crosses the river (daily 8am–5pm; free). From the other side, a steep road leads through the forest for about two kilometres to the site. Note that the river occasionally floods in the rainy season so check in advance that the site is open before making a trip.

Your first stop should be the **visitors' centre**, with a scale model of the ruins. The site itself, on an artificially flattened hilltop, includes five plazas, although the

surviving structures are grouped around just three. Recent investigations have found evidence of Xunantunich's role in the power politics of the Classic period, during which it probably joined Caracol and Calakmul in an alliance against Tikal. By the Terminal Classic period, Xunantunich was already in decline, though still apparently inhabited until around 1000 AD.

The track from the entrance brings you out into Plaza A-2, with large structures on three sides. Plaza A-1, to the left, is dominated by **El Castillo**, at 40m the city's tallest structure. The climb up can be daunting, but the views from the top are superb, with the forest stretching out all around and the rest of the ancient city beneath you.

Accommodation

The Trek Stop Signed on the left just before San José Succotz ☎823-2265, ⓦwww.thetrekstop.com. A wonderful budget place to stay, with clean cabins and a campsite. The restaurant serves large portions and has good vegetarian choices, and there's a shared kitchen, free wi-fi, and bikes, kayaks and tubes available for rent. Next door is the well-designed Tropical Wings Nature Centre (daily 8am–5pm; Bz$5) and the country's first Frisbee golf course. Camping US$5, doubles US$24

The south

South of Belmopan lies Belize's most rugged terrain. Population density in this part of Belize is low, with most of the towns and villages located on the water. **Dangriga**, the largest settlement, is home to the **Garífuna** people and is the transport hub for much of the region. Further south, the **Placencia peninsula** is the area's focus for coastal tourism, boasting some of Belize's only true beaches, and is also the departure point for the south's idyllic cayes. The Southern Highway comes to an end in

Punta Gorda, from where you can head to Guatemala or visit **ancient Maya sites** and present-day **Maya villages**.

Inland, the **Maya Mountains** form a solid barrier to land travel except on foot or horseback. The Belizean government, showing supreme foresight, has placed practically the whole massif under some form of protection. The most accessible area of rainforest is the **Cockscomb Basin Wildlife Sanctuary**, a reserve designed to protect the area's sizeable jaguar population.

THE HUMMINGBIRD HIGHWAY

Southeast from Belmopan, the **Hummingbird Highway** heads towards Dangriga, passing through magnificent scenery. On the right the eastern slopes of the **Maya Mountains** become visible, forming part of a ridge of limestone mountains riddled with underground rivers and **caves**, several of which are accessible.

St Herman's Cave

About 19km out of Belmopan the road crosses the **Caves Branch River**, a tributary of the Sibun River. Just beyond, by the roadside on the right, is **St Herman's Cave** (daily 8am–4.30pm; Bz$8; includes entrance to the Blue Hole National Park; see below). After

paying the entrance fee at the visitors' centre, a ten-minute walk on a marked trail leads to the cave entrance, located beneath a dripping rock face; you'll need a flashlight to enter, heading down steps that were originally cut by the Maya. Inside, clamber over the rocks and splash through the river for about 300m, admiring the stunning natural formations, before the section of the cave accessible without a guide ends. To go further, consider hiring a guide (see below). Behind the visitors' centre and cave, trails lead through the surrounding forest and, after 4km, to a **campsite**. All buses between Belmopan and Dangriga can drop you at St Herman's Cave or the Blue Hole.

Blue Hole National Park

Two kilometres past St Herman's Cave, accessible from the highway or via a marked trail from the visitors' centre, is **Blue Hole National Park**, centred on a beautiful pool whose cool turquoise waters are perfect for a refreshing dip. The "Hole" is actually a short stretch of underground river, whose course is revealed by a collapsed cavern. Other trails depart from here, including the Hummingbird Loop.

The **guided cave and rappelling trips** run by *Caves Branch Jungle Lodge* (see box above) aren't cheap (from US$85 per person), but well worth it for the experience. Many of the caves contain Maya artefacts – burials, ceramics and carvings. The best independent guide to the area is Marcos Cucul, based in Belmopan (☎600-3116, ⓦwww.mayaguide.bz).

DANGRIGA

From the junction of the Hummingbird and Southern highways, it's 10km to **DANGRIGA** (formerly known as Stann Creek), the district capital and the largest town in southern Belize. Dangriga is the cultural centre of the **Garífuna**, a people of mixed indigenous Caribbean and African descent, who overall make up

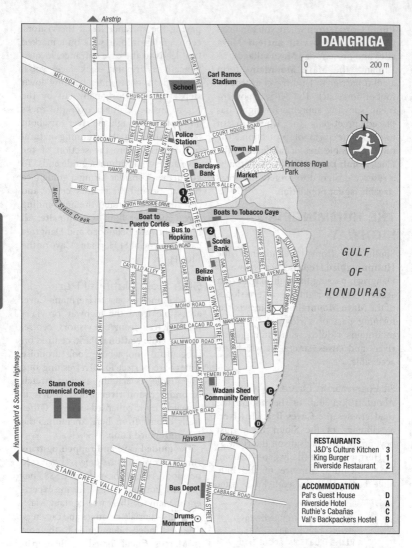

DANGRIGA

0   200 m

▲ Airstrip

PEN ROAD
MELINDA ROAD
CHURCH STREET
School
Carl Ramos Stadium
FRONT STREET
KUYLEN'S ALLEY
GRAPEFRUIT RD
COCONUT RD
CITRON STREET
GIBNUT ALLEY
LEMON STREET
PLUM STREET
ORANGE ST
COURT HOUSE ROAD
Police Station
RECTORY RD
Town Hall
Princess Royal Park
RAMOS ROAD
Barclays Bank
Market
WEST ST
DOCTOR'S ALLEY
North Stann Creek
NORTH RIVERSIDE DRIVE
1 A
Boats to Tobacco Caye
Boat to Puerto Cortés
★ Bus to Hopkins
2
Scotia Bank
BLUEFIELD ROAD
CASTILLO ALLEY
REAR PINE ST
PINE STREET
CANAL STREET
CEDAR STREET
Belize Bank
OAK STREET
ST VINCENT STREET
ALEJO BENI AVENUE
MAGOON ST
KNOPP'S STREET
CHA TUYE ST
SOUTHERN FORESHORE
HAVANA STREET
GULF OF HONDURAS
MOHO ROAD
ECUMENICAL DRIVE
MADRE CACAO RD
MAHOGANY ST
3
SALMWOOD ROAD
TUBROOSE STREET
SHARP STREET
GARV STREET
B
POLACK STREET
YEMERI ROAD
C
Stann Creek Ecumenical College
ZERICOTE STREET
Wadani Shed Community Center
MANGROVE ROAD
D
Havana Creek
ISLA ROAD
SAMSON'S ST
DANIEL S ST
UNITY STREET
STANN CREEK VALLEY ROAD
Bus Depot
HAVANA STREET
CABBAGE ROAD
Drums Monument

RESTAURANTS
J&D's Culture Kitchen   3
King Burger   1
Riverside Restaurant   2

ACCOMMODATION
Pal's Guest House   D
Riverside Hotel   A
Ruthie's Cabañas   C
Val's Backpackers Hostel   B

about eleven percent of the country's population. The town is also home to some of the country's most popular artists, including painters and drum-makers, and you may catch an exhibition or performance. Still, for most travellers the town is of little interest unless you're here during a festival, though it makes a very useful base for visiting **Tobacco Caye** offshore and the **Jaguar Reserve** near Hopkins (see p.103).

Arrival and information

By air Dangriga's airstrip, served by at least eight daily flights on the route from Belize City to Punta Gorda, is on the shore just north of the *Pelican Beach Hotel*, 2km north of town; taxis into town cost Bz$8–10.

By bus NTSL and James buses pull up at the terminal 1km south of the centre. Though taxis are usually available for Bz$5–7, all of the hotels we recommend are an easy 10–15min walk from the terminal.

THE GARÍFUNA

The Garífuna trace their history to the island of St Vincent, in the eastern Caribbean, where two Spanish ships carrying slaves from Nigeria to America were wrecked off the coast in 1635. The survivors took refuge on the island, which was inhabited by Caribs, themselves recent arrivals from South America. At first the Caribs and Africans fought, but the Caribs had been weakened by disease and wars against the native Kalipuna, and eventually the predominant race became black with some indigenous blood, known by the English as the Black Caribs, or Garífuna.

For most of the seventeenth and eighteenth centuries St Vincent fell nominally under British control, though in practice it belonged to the Garífuna, who fended off British attempts to gain full control until 1796. The British colonial authorities, however, would not allow a free black society, so the Carib population was hunted down and transported to Roatán, off the coast of Honduras (see p.394). The Spanish Commandante of Trujillo, on the Honduran mainland, took the surviving Black Caribs to Trujillo, where they became in demand as free labourers, fishermen and soldiers.

In the early nineteenth century small numbers of Garífuna moved up the coast to Belize. The largest single migration took place in 1832, when thousands fled from Honduras after they supported the wrong side in a failed revolution to overthrow the government. It is this arrival that is today celebrated as Garífuna Settlement Day (see p.60).

Tour operators Island Expeditions, on the Southern Foreshore, rents sea kayaks (singles Bz$70/day, doubles Bz$110/day), and will also shuttle you and your boat out to the nearby cayes.

Tourist information There's no tourist office in Dangriga, but the *Riverside Restaurant* (see below) can answer questions on transport and local information. The town's website (www.dangrigalive.com) is also very helpful and has a downloadable map.

Accommodation

Pal's Guest House 868 Magoon St ☎522-2365, www.palsbelize.com. Quiet hotel set right on the beach north of the creek. The basic, tiled rooms have private baths and TVs. US$35

Riverside Hotel 135 Commerce St, beside the bridge ☎660-1041. This very central hotel has clean rooms with shared bath and views over the river. US$15

Ruthie's Cabañas 31 Southern Foreshore ☎502-3184. Two bargain, thatched cabañas on the beach with private bath and porch. US$28

Val's Backpackers Hostel 1 Sharp St, near the beach ☎502-3324, www.valsbackpackerhostel.com. Though the dorms in this concrete building are not the most attractive, they are clean, and the hostel offers same-day laundry service, an internet café, a book exchange, ice cream for sale, bike hire and lovely views of the sea from its veranda. The friendly owner, Dana,

can arrange local tours and Garífuna language and culture classes. Dorms US$11

Eating and drinking

Despite Dangriga's central position in Garífuna culture, few restaurants specialize in Garífuna cuisine, though some serve a few dishes – it's generally more readily available in Hopkins (see p.101).

J&D's Culture Kitchen Canal St. Small, local restaurant serving Creole and Garífuna dishes, usually around Bz$10–12.

King Burger Commerce St. Takeaway and sit-down restaurant popular with locals. Serves fast food, Belizean cuisine and seafood for Bz$6–12.

Riverside Restaurant On the south bank of the river by the bridge. Tasty Creole cuisine, including great breakfasts and a daily special, for Bz$8–25. Also a great place to find tourist information.

Directory

Exchange Belize Bank and Scotia Bank are located close to the bridge on St Vincent St; both have 24hr ATMs.

Internet The internet café in *Val's Backpackers* charges Bz$4/hr.

Laundry *Val's Backpackers* has a same-day drop-off laundry service.

Post office Mahogany St at Ganey St.

Moving on

By boat Boats to Tobacco Caye (40min; Bz$35) leave from the bridge near the *Riverside Restaurant*, though there are no scheduled departures; ask in the restaurant for Captain Buck. For boats to Puerto Cortés, Honduras, see box below.

By bus to: Belize City, mostly via Belmopan (at least every 2hr; 2–3hr) with two weekly services via Gales Point; Placencia (3 daily, 11am, 2pm & 4.30pm; 1hr 45min); Punta Gorda (6–8 daily; 3hr). The 10.30am and 5.15pm Placencia buses also pass through Hopkins (Mon–Sat only; 30min) and continue south via the Sittee River.

AROUND DANGRIGA

Dangriga serves as the jumping-off point for two of the coast's most intriguing sights, including the small village of **Gales Point**, where visitors can learn the art of traditional drumming, and **Tobacco Caye**, a tiny, stunning island located right on the reef.

Gales Point

Some 14km along the Hummingbird Highway back towards Belmopan from Dangriga, a coastal road heads north to the small Creole village of **Gales Point**. The village straggles along a narrow peninsula that juts into the **Southern Lagoon**, a large, shallow body of water which – along with **Northern Lagoon**, to which it's connected – comprises **Gales Point Wildlife Sanctuary**, a breeding ground for rare wildlife, including jabiru storks, turtles, manatee and crocodiles. The area is bounded to the west by limestone hills, riddled with caves and cloaked with mangroves. Gales Point is also a centre of **traditional drum-making**; you can learn to make and play drums at the Maroon Creole

---

INTO HONDURAS

A fast **skiff** (☎522-0062) leaves Dangriga for **Puerto Cortés**, Honduras, every Friday morning (check-in at 8.30am; 3hr; US$55) from the north bank of the river.

Drum School (☎603-6051, ⒺImethos _drums@hotmail.com).

Gales Point is served by two weekly **buses** in each direction on the Coastal Road, usually leaving Belize City and Dangriga on Mondays and Fridays; other traffic passes the junction, 4km from the village, and hitching is relatively easy.

Accommodation

Ionie's In the first shop as you enter the village ☎220-8066. One of several houses in Gales Point offering simple rooms, *Ionie's* has five rooms with shared bath and fans. You can arrange meals here too. US$15

Metho's Coconut Camping In the northern part of the village. This campsite has space in a sandy spot. US$5

Tobacco Caye

About 20km offshore from Dangriga is **Columbus Reef**, a superb section of the Barrier Reef. **Tobacco Caye**, idyllically perched on its southern tip, is the easiest of the cayes in the area to visit and has a number of places to stay. The island is tiny: stand in the centre and you're only a couple of minutes from the shore in any direction, with the unbroken reef stretching north for miles. The reef is so close to shore that you won't need a boat to go **snorkelling** or **diving**, and several of the resorts, including *Reef's End Lodge*, have dive shops that rent gear even to those who are not guests; snorkelling gear costs US$7.50 and diving gear US$25.

Boats (40min; Bz$35) leave daily from near the bridge in Dangriga, though there are no scheduled departures; ask at the *Riverside Restaurant*.

Accommodation and eating

Though accommodation on the caye is simple, it remains quite expensive; however, all places to stay include three meals.

Gaviota Coral Reef Resort ☎509-5032. Private-bath cabins on the sand and less expensive rooms in the main building with shared bath. US$25

Tobacco Caye Paradise ☎520-5101, ⓔbluefield @btl.net. Simple, shared-bath rooms in a wooden house and cabañas overlooking the sea. US$40

HOPKINS

The small village of **HOPKINS**, south of Dangriga and stretching along a bay, is home to well over a thousand Garífuna. Garífuna Settlement Day (see box, p.99), on November 19, is celebrated enthusiastically here, and the friendly villagers are rightly proud of their rich heritage. Garífuna continues to be widely spoken here and the village is a great place to learn more about this unique culture. You can see **drumming** at the Lebeha Drumming Center (see p.102), and there are plenty of artists' workshops dotted throughout the village; visit Charlie Miller at his

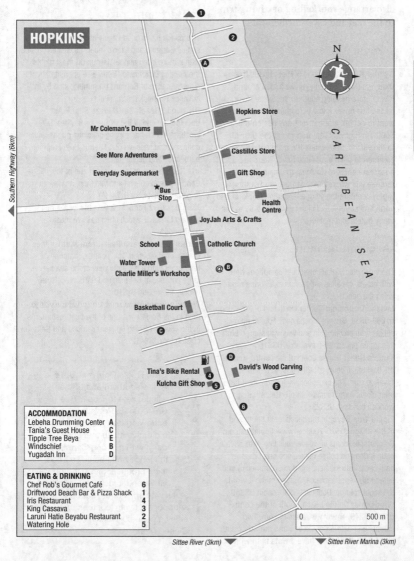

HOPKINS

N

Southern Highway (6km)

CARIBBEAN SEA

Hopkins Store

Mr Coleman's Drums

See More Adventures

Everyday Supermarket

Castillós Store

Gift Shop

★ Bus Stop

Health Centre

JoyJah Arts & Crafts

School

Catholic Church

Water Tower

Charlie Miller's Workshop

Basketball Court

Tina's Bike Rental

Kulcha Gift Shop

David's Wood Carving

ACCOMMODATION
Lebeha Drumming Center — A
Tania's Guest House — C
Tipple Tree Beya — E
Windschief — B
Yugadah Inn — D

EATING & DRINKING
Chef Rob's Gourmet Café — 6
Driftwood Beach Bar & Pizza Shack — 1
Iris Restaurant — 4
King Cassava — 3
Laruni Hatie Beyabu Restaurant — 2
Watering Hole — 5

0   500 m

Sittee River (3km) ▼   ▼ Sittee River Marina (3km)

workshop near the school for his excellent local knowledge and charming wooden handicrafts.

You can rent **kayaks** at *Tipple Tree Beya* – the lagoon just north of the village is a great place for kayaking; windsurfing equipment at *Windschief*; and **bicycles** (Bz$20/day) from Tina's Bike Rental, on the road toward the village's southern end. Many hotels can also arrange **snorkelling** or **diving** trips to the reef and cayes further out.

Arrival

By bus The 10.30am and 5.15pm buses from Dangriga (Mon–Sat only) make a loop around town before heading south to the Sittee River; let the bus driver know beforehand where you want to get off. Alternatively, any bus on the Southern Highway can drop you at the turn-off to the village, from where it's quite easy and common to hitch a ride into town. There are no street names in Hopkins; the main point of reference is where the road from the Southern Highway enters the village – dividing Hopkins into north and south – and signs point the way to the many hotels and restaurants.

Accommodation

There are plenty of accommodation options here, with hotels, cabañas and resorts at all price ranges lining the beach.

Lebeha Drumming Center North end of the village ☎666-6658, ⓦ www.lebeha.com. Four simple cabins with private bath and two with shared bath at bargain prices. Wi-fi available. US$15

Tania's Guest House South of the centre, just past the basketball court ☎523-7058, Ⓔs taniaprim @yahoo.com. The exceptionally friendly staff here offer clean, basic rooms with private bath in a wooden building. US$23

Tipple Tree Beya On the beach, near south end of the village ☎520-7006, ⓦ www.tippletree.com. Comfortable rooms in wooden building with private bath, fridge and coffee maker, and one private bath cabin with kitchen. The deck, hammocks and beautifully kept beachside location make it worth the slight splurge. Doubles US$30, cabin US$50

Windschief On the beach, south of the centre ☎523-7249, ⓦ www.windschief.com. Two cabins, one with a double bed and the other with two double beds. Both have private bath with cold-water showers, fridges, coffee makers and free wi-fi. Windsurfing lessons Bz$60/hr, rental Bz$60/day. US$25

🏃 **Yugadah Inn** On the beach at the southern end of the village ☎503-7089. The Nuñez sisters offer four compact rooms with shared bath at the cheapest rate in town. Bring a torch as rooms have poor-quality lighting. The adjoining restaurant serves excellent Garífuna food. US$10

Eating, drinking and entertainment

The village has a good variety of restaurants serving simple Garífuna and Creole meals as well as cuisine with a more international flavour. On most nights, the *Lebeha Drumming Center* (see opposite), hosts a performance of Garífuna drumming; stop by in advance to check the schedule.

Driftwood Beach Bar & Pizza Shack At the northern end of the village, on the beach. Laidback beach bar serving delicious pizzas and daily seafood specials (Bz$16–30). Holds regular barbecues and beach parties.

Iris Restaurant At the southern end of the village. Good Belizean cuisine and fast food, as well as large breakfasts, for Bz$4–20.

King Cassava For a drink with the locals, head to *King Cassava*, which often has live music at weekends.

Laruni Hatie Beyabu Restaurant North of the centre, on the beach. This popular, thatched restaurant with a beautiful view of the sea serves large portions of Belizean and Garífuna cuisine, usually for around Bz$10.

Watering Hole At the southern end of the village, next to *Iris Restaurant*. One of the best restaurants in the village, dishing up great seafood and Belizean cuisine for Bz$8–12.

TREAT YOURSELF

Chef Rob's Gourmet Café At the southern end of the village, next to *Tipple Tree* ☎670-0445. Rob's four-course extravanganza (Bz$55) features a creative menu that changes daily, with a strong Caribbean influence and freshly sourced, local produce. Sit on the open-air veranda, tuck into a rib-eye steak with spiced rum sauce or red snapper fillet with lobster sauce, and enjoy a peaceful Hopkins evening. Closed Mon.

Moving on

By bus to: Dangriga (Mon–Sat; 7am & 2pm). For transport south to Placencia or Punta Gorda, take the Dangriga bus to the Southern Highway junction and wait at the side of the road for the next southbound bus to pass.

GLOVER'S REEF

GLOVER'S REEF, the southernmost of Belize's three coral atolls, lies around 40km off the coast from Hopkins. Roughly oval in shape, it stretches 35km north to south, with a number of cayes in its southeastern section. Famous for its wall diving, which is thought to be among the best in the world, the atoll also hosts a stunning lagoon, which offers spectacular snorkelling and diving, as well as a staggering diversity of wildlife. The entire atoll is a **marine reserve** (Bz$20 entry fee, usually payable to your accommodation or tour guide), with a research station on Middle Caye.

Activities include sailing, sea kayaking, fishing, snorkelling and diving (including dive training), which is spectacular, thanks to a huge underwater cliff and some tremendous wall-diving.

Accommodation and eating

Glover's is something of an anomaly among the remote atolls: it offers accommodation within the reach of budget travellers.

Glover's Atoll Resort Northeast Caye ☎ 520-5016, ⓦ www.glovers.com.bz. Thatched cabins over the water or on the beach (US$287/week) overlook the reef, or there are dorm beds (US$229/week) in a wooden house and camping space (US$171/week); all rates include transport from the Sittee River in the resort's boat (leaves Sun 9am, returns following Sat; 3hr). Meals are not included, so you can either bring your own food or eat at the restaurant. The staff pretty much leave you to your own devices – you can choose to enjoy the simple desert-island experience or take part in activities (see above; paid for separately).

COCKSCOMB BASIN WILDLIFE SANCTUARY

Back on the mainland, the jagged peaks of the **Maya Mountains** rise to the west of the Southern Highway. The tallest summits are those of the Cockscomb range, which includes **Victoria Peak** (1120m), the second highest mountain in Belize. Beneath the ridges is a vast bowl of stunning rainforest, over four hundred square kilometres of which is protected by the **COCKSCOMB BASIN WILDLIFE SANCTUARY** – better known as the **Jaguar Reserve** (daily 7.30am–4.30pm; Bz$10). The basin could be home to as many as sixty of Belize's 800-strong **jaguar population**, and though you'll almost certainly come across their tracks, your chances of actually seeing one are very slim, as they are mainly active at night and avoid humans. Over 290 species of **bird** have also been recorded here, including the endangered scarlet macaw, the great curassow and the king vulture.

The sanctuary is at the end of a rough ten-kilometre road that branches off the main highway at the village of **Maya Centre**, runs through towering forest and fords a couple of streams before crossing the Cabbage Hall Gap and entering the Cockscomb Basin. Here, you'll find the sanctuary headquarters, where you can pick up maps of the reserve. Beyond the headquarters, a system of very well maintained trails of varying lengths winds through tropical moist forest, crossing streams and leading to a number of picturesque waterfalls and ridges. For those who have the time – and have made the necessary preparations – it's also possible to take the four- or five-day hike and climb to the summit of Victoria Peak. If you're looking for a more relaxing experience, however, you can float down South Stann Creek in an inner tube, available for rent (Bz$5 per day) at the headquarters.

BELIZE

THE SOUTH

Arrival and information

By bus All buses between Dangriga and Punta Gorda pass Maya Centre. If visiting the reserve, you need to sign in and pay the entrance fee at the craft centre at the junction of the road leading up to the Cockscomb. From the craft centre in Maya Centre, you can catch a ride with a taxi or truck to the reserve headquarters; this usually costs about Bz$30–40 each way for up to 5 people. The 10km walk to the reserve from this point, however, is relatively easy but will take several hours.
Internet Julio's Store, just beyond the intersection, sells basic supplies and cold drinks (there's no shop in the reserve), and it's also a bar with internet access. The owner runs Cockscomb Maya Tours (℡ 660-3903, ⓦ www.cockscombmayatours.com) and can arrange guides and transport into the reserve.

Accommodation and eating

The reserve headquarters offers a variety of accommodation, including private furnished cabins for four or six people (US$54), wooden dorm rooms with showers (US$20) and a more "rustic" cabin with dorm beds (US$10). Camping space (US$10) is available, though you can also camp for the same price at two other designated sites along the trails, for which you'll need to get a permit at the reserve headquarters. Note that there is no restaurant at the headquarters so you must come armed with supplies. Maya Centre also has several inexpensive places to stay (see below), all of which can arrange meals, tours, guides and transport.

Nu'uk Che'il Cottages Maya Centre, 500m up the track to the reserve ℡ 520-3033. Delightful rooms with private bath and a large wooden cabin with shared showers and dorm beds. The restaurant serves excellent Maya cuisine (Bz$5–15), and the owner has developed a medicinal plant trail out back. Dorms US$10, doubles US$23
Tutzil Nah Cottages On the highway just before the junction ℡ 520-3044, ⓦ www.mayacenter.com. Two clean cabins, one wood and one concrete, house four rooms with choice of shared or private bath. Run by the Chun brothers, excellent guides to the reserve. Out front, the family also runs a small grocery store. US$20

Moving on

By bus All buses bound for north and south pass through Maya Centre (about 12 daily in either direction).

PLACENCIA

Some 16km south of Maya Centre, a newly paved road cuts east from the Southern Highway, heading through pine forest and banana plantations before reaching the sea and snaking south down the narrow **Placencia peninsula**, immensely popular for its sandy beaches, which are among the best in Belize. Though accommodation throughout most of the peninsula, including the villages of Maya Beach and Seine Bight, is limited to upscale resorts and hotels, **PLACENCIA** village itself has an abundance of budget options. Shaded by palm trees and cooled by the sea breeze, the village is an ideal spot to relax. However, a recent and unrestrained boom in the property market has led to justified fears for local ecology, along with concerns that the peaceful atmosphere of the peninsula may soon be a thing of the past.

What to see and do

Apart from simply hanging out on the beach, Placencia is a good, if expensive, base for snorkelling and diving trips to the southern cayes and reef or a day-trip to the **Monkey River**.

Diving and snorkelling

Diving options from Placencia are excellent, but the distance to most dive sites (at least 30km) means that trips here can be more expensive than elsewhere. Trips usually cost around US$90 for a two-tank dive, and US$350 for open-water certification. You could visit uninhabited **Laughing Bird Caye National Park**, beyond which lie the exquisite **Silk Cayes**, where the Barrier Reef begins to break into several smaller reefs and cayes, or nearby **Gladden Spit**, now a marine reserve created to protect the enormous **whale shark**.

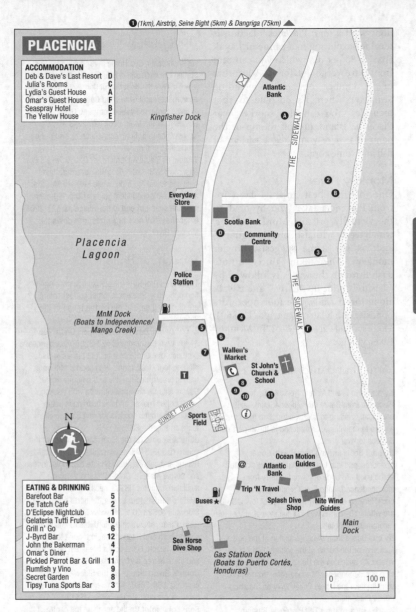

PLACENCIA

ACCOMMODATION
Deb & Dave's Last Resort	D
Julia's Rooms	C
Lydia's Guest House	A
Omar's Guest House	F
Seaspray Hotel	B
The Yellow House	E

Placencia Lagoon

Kingfisher Dock

Everyday Store

Scotia Bank

Community Centre

Police Station

MnM Dock
(Boats to Independence/
Mango Creek)

Wallen's Market

St John's Church & School

Sports Field

Atlantic Bank

THE SIDEWALK

THE SIDEWALK

Ocean Motion Guides

Atlantic Bank

Trip 'N Travel

Buses ★

Splash Dive Shop

Nite Wind Guides

Main Dock

SUNSET DRIVE

N

EATING & DRINKING
Barefoot Bar	5
De Tatch Café	2
D'Eclipse Nightclub	1
Gelateria Tutti Frutti	10
Grill n' Go	6
J-Byrd Bar	12
John the Bakerman	4
Omar's Diner	7
Pickled Parrot Bar & Grill	11
Rumfish y Vino	9
Secret Garden	8
Tipsy Tuna Sports Bar	3

Sea Horse Dive Shop

Gas Station Dock
(Boats to Puerto Cortés,
Honduras)

0   100 m

BELIZE

THE SOUTH

Other activities

Other trips from Placencia can include anything from an afternoon on the water to a week of camping, fishing and sailing. For excellent four- to six-day river and sea **kayaking tours**, head to Toadal Adventure (see p.106). For **day-trips inland**, including trips to Maya ruins, caves and the Cockscomb Basin Wildlife Sanctuary (see p.103), check with Sea Horse Dive Shop or Trip 'N Travel (for both, see p.106). If you

105

don't want a tour, Placencia's lagoon is ideal for exploring in a **canoe** or **kayak** (Bz$70–80 per day, which you can rent from Dave Vernon of Toadal Adventure or a number of hotels, including *Seaspray*), where it's possible to spot manatees. You can also snorkel near Placencia Island, just off the tip of the peninsula; here you'll see a variety of fish and some coral.

Monkey River

One of the best inland day-trips from Placencia takes you by boat to the virtually pristine **Monkey River**, which teems with fish, birdlife, iguanas and, as the name suggests, howler monkeys. The 20km, thirty-minute dash through the waves is followed by a leisurely glide up the river and a walk along forest trails. The tour operators opposite can all arrange trips (US$60). There's a restaurant, *Alice's*, in Monkey River village.

Arrival and information

By air Maya Island Air and Tropic Air fly to Placencia from Belize City (about 45min). Taxis are usually waiting to take you the 3km from the airstrip to the village, or someone in the airport can call one for you.

By boat Boats arriving from Puerto Cortés, Honduras, pull into the Gas Station Dock, located at the southern edge of town; the ferry from Independence/Mango Creek stops at the MnM dock, located on the northwest edge of town. Both are within 10–15min walking distance of any of the recommended hotels.

By bus Buses from Dangriga pull in at the petrol station near the beach at the southern end of the village. All buses on the Dangriga–Punta Gorda line stop at Independence/Mango Creek, from where you can take the Hokey Pokey ferry on the short ride to Placencia.

Tourist information The Placencia Tourism Centre, on the road, near *Gelateria Tutti Frutti* (Mon–Fri 9–11.30am & 1–5pm; ☎ 523-4045, ⓦ www.placencia.com), is probably Belize's best tourist office. It also distributes *Placencia Breeze*, a free local newspaper filled with transport schedules, local listings and a good map of the village and peninsula.

Tour operators

For snorkelling, Sea Horse Dive Shop, near Gas Station Dock (☎ 523-3166, ⓦ www.belizescuba .com), offers the best instruction, excursions and equipment rental. Nite Wind Guides (☎ 523-3847, ⓔ doylegardiner@yahoo.com) and Ocean Motion Guides near the Main Dock (☎ 523-3363, ⓦ www.oceanmotionplacencia.com) also put on snorkelling and manatee-watching trips. Dave Vernon, of Toadal Adventure, *at Deb & Dave's Last Resort* (☎ 523-3207, ⓔ toadaladventure.com), runs sea-kayaking trips; while Evaristo Muschamp, a very experienced local guide at Trip 'N Travel near the southern end of the village (☎ 523-3205, ⓔ lgodfrey@btl.net), organizes trips down the Monkey River.

Accommodation

There are numerous inexpensive accommodation options in Placencia. Most budget rooms are clustered around the northern end of the Sidewalk.

Deb & Dave's Last Resort On the road, near the centre ☎ 523-3207, ⓔ debanddave @btl.net. One of the best budget places in Belize, offering four clean rooms with shared hot-water bath in a secluded annexe to the family home. Guests share a common veranda with deckchairs and a coffee maker, and the building is set in beautiful gardens. Kayaks for rent and excellent tours arranged. US$25

Julia's Rooms On the Sidewalk just north of the centre ☎ 503-3478, ⓦ www.juliasrooms.com. Rooms and cabañas with private bath, TVs, fridges and coffee makers. Drop-off laundry service available. Doubles US$38, cabañas US$60

Lydia's Guest House Near the north end of the Sidewalk ☎ 523-3117, ⓦ www.lydiasguesthouse .com. Clean, secure and affordable rooms with shared bath and kitchen use, in a quiet location near the beach. Lydia cooks breakfast on request and there is free wi-fi access. US$25

Omar's Guest House On the Sidewalk in the centre ☎ 660-7686, ⓔ omarsguest@btl.net. Very basic rooms with shared baths. US$13

Seaspray Hotel On the beach, in the centre of the village ☎ 523-3148, ⓦ www.seasprayhotel.com. Popular, well-run hotel in a great location, with a variety of excellent accommodation, all with private bath and fridge, and some with TV, kitchenette and balcony. There are hammocks on the beach and kayaks for rent. US$20

The Yellow House In the centre of the village, between the road and the Sidewalk ☏ 523-3481, ⓦ www.ctbelize.com. Bargain rooms, all with private bath and some with fridge, in a bright-yellow wooden building with balcony. Deals on multiple-night stays. US$30

Eating

There are plenty of good restaurants in Placencia, but establishments change management fast, so ask locally for the latest recommendations. Most places close early and you'll certainly have more of a choice if you're at the table by 8pm.

🏃 **De Tatch Café** On the beach, just past *Seaspray Hotel*. Excellent international and Belizean cuisine and seafood, served in a quiet, open-air restaurant right by the sea. There's a lunch special for Bz$11 and a dinner special for Bz$26, as well as internet access. Other mains Bz$10–32.

🏃 **Gelateria Tutti Frutti** Near the southern end of the road. Without a doubt the best ice cream in Belize, available in literally dozens of flavours for Bz$4 and up. Closed Wed.

Grill n' Go On the road, near *Wallen's Market*. Bargain takeaway stand serving up filling burritos and fajitas for Bz$6–10.

John The Bakerman Near the centre of the Sidewalk. The place for fresh bread and pastries.

Omar's Diner On the road next to *Barefoot Bar*. Very inexpensive, small restaurant serving filling breakfasts, Mexican cuisine and seafood. Breakfast and lunch Bz$7–12, dinner Bz$16–30.

Pickled Parrot Bar & Grill Set back from the road near the centre. Popular, open-air restaurant and bar featuring fresh seafood, pizza and international dishes, as well as fantastic blended cocktails. Mains Bz$14–40. Closed Sun.

Secret Garden Opposite the sports field. Set back from the road in a quiet, secluded spot, this coffee-house and spa serves great breakfasts and fresh European and Belizean dishes. Closed Mon.

> **TREAT YOURSELF**
>
> **Rumfish y Vino** Opposite the sports field. The village's classiest restaurant: friendly staff, an inventive tapas menu (Bz$12–30) and an extensive wine list make this self-professed "gastro-bar" a welcome new addition to the Placencia dining scene. The candlelit surroundings and veranda are as enjoyable as the food.

Drinking and nightlife

Although most of the restaurants also serve drinks, there are a few places with live music and more of a bar atmosphere.

Barefoot Bar On the road near the MnM dock. Old favourite in a brightly decorated and prominent new location. Very popular bar serving great cocktails (happy hour 5–6pm). Open late most nights.

D'Eclipse Nightclub Near the airstrip. The peninsula's only true clubbing experience attracts a good mix of locals and travellers. Busy at weekends from midnight.

J-Byrd Bar Near Gas Station Dock. A great place to meet local characters and sometimes catch live music.

Tipsy Tuna Sports Bar On the beach. This lively bar and restaurant is often packed and sometimes hosts live music on weekends. Happy hour is 5–7pm daily and includes free banana chips. Wi-fi available.

Directory

Exchange Atlantic Bank and Scotia Bank can exchange currency and have 24hr ATMs.

Internet Placencia Office Supply, on the road south of the centre, has numerous computers and a reliable connection; there's also access at *De Tatch Café* and *Tipsy Tuna*.

Laundry *Julia's Rooms* has a drop-off laundry service.

Post office On the road, at the northern end of the village.

Moving on

By air Belize City (45min); Dangriga (20min).

By boat The *Hokey Pokey* ferry (6–7 daily; 20min; Bz$10) departs from the MnM Dock for Independence/Mango Creek, where buses on the Dangriga–Punta Gorda line are usually timed to meet the ferry. A fast skiff leaves Placencia for Puerto Cortés in Honduras (☏ 523-4045; US$55; 4hr) every Fri at 9.30am.

By bus to: Dangriga (3 daily, usually at 6:15am, 7am and 1pm; 2hr).

THE FAR SOUTH

Beyond Independence, the Southern Highway leaves the banana plantations, first twisting through pine forests, crossing numerous creeks and rivers, and arriving in the sparsely populated **Toledo District**, Belize's least developed region. Here, the Mopan and Kekchi, the country's two main Maya groups, comprise almost half the population. About 73km from the Placencia junction lies **Nim Li Punit** (daily 9am–5pm; Bz$10), a Late Classic Maya site, possibly allied to nearby Lubaantun and to Quiriguá in Guatemala (see p.195). The ruins stand on top of a ridge, surrounded by the fields of the nearby Maya village of **Indian Creek**. The **visitors' centre** has a good map of the site and explanations of some of the carved texts found here, which include eight stelae, among them **Stela 15**, at over 9m the tallest yet found in Belize. The site is only 1km off the highway, making it an easy day-trip from Punta Gorda.

Accommodation

If you're looking to be isolated in Toledo's wilderness, there are several good places to stay along the Southern Highway, located along the final 22 kilometres to Punta Gorda.

Casa Bonita Apartments Cattle Landing, 3km north of Punta Gorda ☎722-2270. A good range of furnished, private apartments in a concrete building facing the sea. Discounts for students, and meals can be arranged. US$45

Sun Creek Lodge Sun Creek, 3km south of the Dump junction ☎604-2124, ⓦwww.suncreek lodge.com. Five beautiful thatched cabañas, all with electricity, some with private bath. One of the owners knows the area exceptionally well and can organize tours. Internet access available and breakfast included. US$45

Tranquility Lodge Jacintoville, 10km south of the Dump junction ☎677-9921, ⓦwww.tranquility -lodge.com. Set in gardens on the bank of Jacinto Creek, the lodge offers a/c comfort in spacious en-suite rooms. The restaurant upstairs provides great views, and the creek is perfect for a dip. Breakfast included. US$100

PUNTA GORDA

The Southern Highway comes to an end in **PUNTA GORDA**, the heart of the still isolated Toledo District. The town is populated by a mixture of eight thousand Creoles, Garífuna and Maya – who make up more than half the population of the district – and is the focal point for a large number of villages and farming settlements. In recent years, the town has placed increasing emphasis on its burgeoning trade in cocoa production (see box below). Though there are few other attractions in Punta Gorda itself, it makes an excellent base from which to explore the nearby Maya villages and ruins.

Arrival and information

By air Maya Island Air and Tropic Air both operate 4–5 daily flights from Belize City (via Dangriga and Placencia), landing at the airstrip five blocks west of the main dock and a 5–10min walk from any of the recommended hotels.

By boat Skiffs from Puerto Barrios and Livingston, Guatemala, use the main dock, near the centre of the seafront.

By bus Buses from Belize City via Dangriga circle the town, usually stopping at the petrol station at the northeast edge of the centre, which is within easy walking distance of all the recommended hotels – though you usually can convince the bus driver to drop you anywhere within the centre.

Tourist information The staff at the excellent tourist information office, on Front St and run by the Belize Tourism Industry Association (☎722-2531), can help with transport schedules and assist in setting up tours of the outlying cayes and sites in Toledo District.

> ### THE HOME OF FAIRTRADE CHOCOLATE
>
> The Toledo Cacao Growers' Association, set up in conjunction with the British chocolate company *Green & Black's*, became the world's first fairtrade cacao producers in 1993, and the product of this partnership, Maya Gold chocolate, is now sold internationally. 2007 marked the first ever Cacao Festival (ⓦwww.toledo chocolate.com), which has quickly established itself as an annual fixture in the town's calendar. Local business has also profited, with several home-grown brands of chocolate springing up in the district. A great example is the Cotton Tree Chocolate Factory on Front St, which offers a complimentary tasting session and guided tour of their tiny workshop.

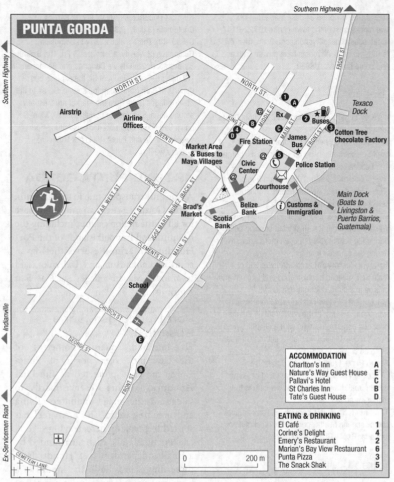

PUNTA GORDA

Southern Highway

Southern Highway

Airstrip

Airline Offices

NORTH ST

NORTH ST

QUEEN ST

KING ST

MIDDLE ST

FRONT ST

Texaco Dock

Rx

Buses

Cotton Tree Chocolate Factory

Fire Station

Market Area & Buses to Maya Villages

James Bus

Civic Center

Police Station

Courthouse

Main Dock (Boats to Livingston & Puerto Barrios, Guatemala)

PRINCE ST

FAR WEST ST

WEST ST

JOSE MARIA NUÑEZ BACK ST

MAIN ST

Brad's Market

Scotia Bank

Belize Bank

Customs & Immigration

CLEMENTS ST

School

CHURCH ST

GEORGE ST

FRONT ST

Indianville

Ex-Servicemen Road

CEMETERY LANE

0   200 m

N

ACCOMMODATION
Charlton's Inn   A
Nature's Way Guest House   E
Pallavi's Hotel   C
St Charles Inn   B
Tate's Guest House   D

EATING & DRINKING
El Café   1
Corine's Delight   4
Emery's Restaurant   2
Marian's Bay View Restaurant 6
Punta Pizza   3
The Snack Shak   5

BELIZE

THE SOUTH

Tour operators The local TIDE (Toledo Institute for Development and the Environment; 14 Front St ☎722-2129, ⓦwww.tidetours.org) is involved with many conservation projects and also offers mountain-bike and kayak tours and camping trips to Payne's Creek National Park.

Accommodation

Accommodation in Punta Gorda is generally inexpensive. For an alternative to staying in town, contact *Nature's Way Guest House* (see below), which operates a programme of guesthouse accommodation in surrounding villages in conjunction with the Toledo Ecotourism Association (TEA).

Charlton's Inn 9 Main St ☎722-2197, ⓦwww.charltonsinn.com. Rooms with private, hot-water showers and a/c in a two-storey concrete building. US$45

Nature's Way Guest House 65 Front St ☎702-2119. The best budget place in Punta Gorda and a good place to meet other travellers and get information. Clean rooms overlooking the sea have shared baths and cold showers. Serves breakfast and has a paperback exchange. US$13

Pallavi's Hotel 19 Main St ☎702-2414, ⒺGracemcp@hotmail.com. Clean, tiled rooms with private bath in the centre of town. US$28

St Charles Inn 23 King St ☎722-2149, Ⓔstcharlespg@btl.net. One of Punta Gorda's smartest options, with very friendly staff. All rooms have private bath, and most have TV and a/c. US$25

Tate's Guest House 34 José María Nuñez St, two blocks west of the town centre ☎722-0147, 📧 tatesguesthouse@yahoo.com. Quiet, friendly, family-run hotel. All rooms have private bath and TV and some have a/c. US$30

Eating

It's easy to get a good, filling meal in Punta Gorda for a reasonable price.

El Café North St, behind *Charlton's Inn*. Small, bright restaurant serving good breakfasts, burgers and Belizean cuisine for Bz$3–12.

🏃 **Corine's Delight** José María Nuñez St, beside *Tate's Guest House*. Wonderful selection of home-made cakes (Bz$1–4) to take away, sold from a hut in local schoolteacher Corine Westby's back garden. Restricted opening hours during the school year but open more extensively during the summer months.

Emery's Restaurant At the northern end of Main St. Excellent, fresh seafood and international cuisine in a large, open-air restaurant.

Marian's Bay View Restaurant Front St, across from *Nature's Way*. Large restaurant on the third floor of a concrete building with a beautiful view over the sea. Choose from a small menu of fresh Belizean cuisine (Bz$8–12).

Punta Pizza Front St, above Cotton Tree Chocolate Factory. Decent pizza and desserts, but the real draw of this sea-view café is the extensive coffee menu.

The Snack Shak BTL parking lot. Popular local choice serving healthy portions of breakfast and lunch for Bz$4–10. Convenient for the dock.

Directory

Exchange Belize Bank (with ATM) is on the main square across from the Civic Center. There will usually be a moneychanger outside the immigration office when international boats are travelling.

Internet V-Comp (Mon–Sat 8am–8pm), on Main St, charges Bz$6/hr.

Laundry PG Laundry, on Main St across from Belize Bank (Mon–Sat 8am–5pm).

Post office In the government buildings a block back from the ferry dock.

Moving on

By air Maya Island Air and Tropic Air operate 7–9 daily flights to Belize City via Dangriga and Placencia.

By boat Departures daily to: Puerto Barrios, Guatemala (3 daily, 9.30am, 2pm & 4pm; 1hr; Bz$35–40). There's also a ferry to Lívingston, Guatemala (2 weekly, 10am Tues & Fri; 1hr; Bz$40).

By bus to: Belize City via Dangriga and Belmopan (12 daily; 5–7hr) from Front St; the express bus departs at 6am from the petrol station. Buses to the Maya villages leave from the market area, usually around noon: San Antonio (2 daily, usually Mon–Sat only); San Pedro Columbia (for Labaantun; 4 per week); Jalacte and Pueblo Viejo (for Uxbenka; 4–8 per week).

AROUND PUNTA GORDA

As the only transport hub in the far south, Punta Gorda serves as an important base for all of the region's sights, including the beautiful and tranquil islands of the **Port Honduras Marine Reserve**, the Mayan ruins of **Labaantun** and **Uxbenka**, and traditional Mayan villages such as **San Antonio**.

Port Honduras Marine Reserve

Six hundred square kilometres of the bay and coast north of Punta Gorda are now protected as the **Port Honduras Marine Reserve**, partly to safeguard the many **manatees** living and breeding there. The main reef has started to break up here, leaving several clusters of islands, each surrounded by a small independent reef. Hundreds of these tiny islands lie in the mouth of a large bay, whose shoreline is a maze of mangrove swamps.

North of Punta Gorda are the **Snake Cayes**, idyllic and uninhabited Caribbean islands that draw a small number of visitors for their stunning beaches. Further out in the Gulf of Honduras are the **Sapodilla Cayes**, now a **marine reserve** (Bz$20 entrance fee), of which the largest caye, **Hunting Caye**, is frequented by Guatemalan as well as Belizean day-trippers; though most visitors simply choose to relax on the beach, the reef, located only a few hundred metres offshore, provides excellent opportunities for snorkellers.

Some of these islands already have accommodation, and more resorts are planned, though at present the cayes and reserve receive relatively few foreign visitors and are fascinating to explore on a day-trip from Punta Gorda; contact TIDE (see "Tour operators", p.109) for more information on how to visit the reserve and cayes.

San Antonio

Perched on a small hilltop, the Mopan Maya village of **San Antonio** is one of the only towns served by daily buses from Punta Gorda (usually Mon–Sat only). The founders of San Antonio came from the village of San Luis, just across the border in Guatemala, and they maintain many age-old traditions, including their patron saint, San Luis Rey, whose beautiful church stands in the centre of the village.

The area around San Antonio is rich in wildlife, dominated by jungle-clad hills and swift-flowing rivers. Though most visitors come to town to relax and to learn about Maya village life, this stunning region also provides excellent **hiking** opportunities. In town, *Bol's Hilltop Hotel* (community phone ☎702-2144; US$10) offers basic **rooms** with shared bath and superb views, and is a good place to get information on local natural history and archeology.

Blue Creek

About 4km back towards Punta Gorda, and down a branch road heading southwest, lies the village of **Blue Creek**, whose main attraction is a beautiful stretch of water running through magnificent rainforest. To get to the best swimming spot, a lovely turquoise pool, walk ten minutes upriver along the right-hand bank. Near the pool is *Blue Creek Rainforest Lodge* (☎523-7076, ⓦwww.ize2belize.com; US$45), which has bunk-bed accommodation in wooden cabins with porches overlooking the creek. The price includes three daily

meals and a range of outdoor activities is available at reasonable prices. Alternatively, you could try to rent a room in the village. The creek's source, **Hokeb Ha** cave, is another fifteen minutes' walk upriver through the privately owned **Blue Creek Rainforest Reserve**. A guide can take you to Maya altars deep in the cave. To get to Blue Creek, take the village bus from Punta Gorda to San Benito Poite.

Uxbenka

Some 7km west of San Antonio, towards the village of **Santa Cruz**, which is served by four weekly buses, the ruins of **Uxbenka**, a small Maya site, are superbly positioned on an exposed hilltop with great views towards the coast. As you climb the hill before the village you'll be able to make out the shape of two tree-covered mounds and a plaza, and there are several stelae protected by thatched shelters.

If you do make it out here you can enjoy some wonderful **waterfalls** within easy reach of the road. Between Santa Cruz and Santa Elena, the **Rio Blanco Falls** tumble over a rocky ledge into a deep pool, and at **Pueblo Viejo**, 7km further on, an impressive series of cascades provides a spectacular sight. Trucks and buses continue 13km further west to **Jalacte**, at the Guatemalan border, used regularly as a crossing point by nationals of both countries, though it's not currently a legal entry or exit point for tourists.

Lubaantun

The Maya site of **Lubaantun** (daily 8am–5pm; Bz$10) is an easy visit from Punta Gorda via the bus to **San Pedro Columbia**. To get to the ruins, head through the village and cross the Columbia River; just beyond you'll see the track to the ruins, a few hundred metres away on the left. Some of the finds made at the site are displayed in glass cases at the **visitors' centre**, including astonishing, eccentric flints and ceramics.

Lubaantun ("Place of the Fallen Stones") was a major Late Classic Maya centre, though it was occupied only briefly, likely from around 750 to 890 AD. The ruins stand on a series of ridges which Maya architects shaped and filled, building retaining walls up to 10m high. The whole site is essentially a single acropolis, with five main plazas, eleven major structures, three ball courts and some impressive pyramids surrounded by forest.

Lubaantun's most enigmatic discovery came in 1926, when the famous **Crystal Skull** was found beneath an altar by Anna Mitchell-Hedges, the daughter of the British Museum expedition's leader. The skull was given to the local Maya, who in turn presented it to Anna's father as a token of their gratitude for the help he had given them. Carved from pure rock crystal, the skull's origin and age remain unclear, though much contested.

Guatemala

HIGHLIGHTS ✪

TIKAL:
once a great
Maya metropolis, now
an incomparable site

SEMUC CHAMPEY & LANQUÍN:
chill in idyllic turquoise waters,
then explore nearby caves

LAGO DE ATITLÁN:
a breathtaking,
steep-sided crater lake

ANTIGUA:
the former capital, boasting
restored buildings and
ruined churches

HIGHLAND VILLAGES:
for an insight into Maya life,
spend some time in a
traditional Highland village

MONTERRICO:
a sweeping, almost undeveloped
Pacific beach visited by sea turtles

ROUGH COSTS

DAILY BUDGET Basic US$20/
occasional treat US$30

DRINK Beer (330ml) US$2, coffee
US$1

FOOD Burrito US$1.50

HOSTEL/BUDGET HOTEL US$6/
US$12

TRAVEL Antigua–Guatemala City
(45km) by chicken bus: 1hr, US$1;
Antigua–Cobán (258km) by shuttle
minibus: 5hr, US$14

FACT FILE

POPULATION 14 million

AREA 109,000 sq km

LANGUAGES Spanish (official), plus
23 indigenous languages

CAPITAL Guatemala City
(population: 3 million)

CURRENCY Quetzal (Q)

INTERNATIONAL PHONE CODE
☎502

TIME ZONE GMT -6hr

Introduction

Tourism is booming in Guatemala, and understandably so: the country simply overflows with natural, historical and cultural interest. In established destinations – Antigua, around Lago de Atitlán, Flores – you'll have your choice of Western comforts and convenient transport options. Get off the beaten track, though, and opportunities for activities like jungle trekking, exploring ancient Maya ruins and cooling off in crystalline pools and waterfalls abound. Whatever preconceived notions you have, throw them away – you'll doubtless be surprised by the variety of beguiling experiences the country has to offer.

Guatemala's landscape, defined by extremes, is dramatic and wildly beautiful. Rising steeply from the Pacific coast, and contributing to the country's status as the most mountainous Central American nation, is a chain of volcanoes (some still smoking). In many **highland villages** these behemoths are just a fact of life. Then there are the **lowlands** – on the flat, steamy Pacific side you'll find black-sand beaches, turtles and mangroves, while the tropical Caribbean coast is fringed with coconut palms. **El Petén**, the country's least populous yet largest department, fosters everything from savanna to rainforest, and is extraordinarily rich in both **Maya ruins** and wildlife. If cities are more your cup of tea, Guatemala has some gems: **Antigua** is home to irresistible colonial architecture, cobbled streets and a plethora of restaurants, cafés and Spanish schools while **Quetzaltenango** is the de facto capital of the highlands and another important study centre. Even **Guatemala City**, avoided by many, possesses its own gritty charm.

The country's landscape has had an undeniable effect on the history and lifestyle of its people. **Indigenous groups** (mostly Maya) are in the majority here, especially in the highlands; villages such as Todos Santos Cuchumatán, Chichicastenango and Nebaj display riotously coloured textiles and some of the most sense-assaulting markets in the world. Throughout the country you'll find that Guatemalans (or Chapines, as they call themselves), while perhaps more reserved than some of their neighbours, are polite, helpful and welcoming at every turn.

WHEN TO VISIT

As with all mountainous countries, Guatemala's climate is largely governed by altitude. Many places of interest (including Antigua, Lago de Atitlán, Cobán and the capital) are between 1300 and 1600m, where the climate is temperate: expect warm days and mild evenings. Low-lying Petén is a different world, with steamy conditions all year round, and the Pacific and Caribbean coasts are equally hot and humid.

The rainy season is roughly from May to October. Precipitation is usually confined to the late afternoon, and the rest of the day is often warm and pleasant. As a rule, it's only in remote areas that rain can affect travel plans. The busiest times for tourism are during July and August, between Christmas and the end of January, and around Easter, when Holy Week (Semana Santa) celebrations are quite a spectacle to behold.

CHRONOLOGY

c. 2500 BC Proto-Maya period. Agricultural communities are formed and an early Maya language spoken.

1800 BC Pre-Classic Maya culture emerges in the forests of Petén.

1000 BC Early settlement at sites including Nakbé and El Mirador.

300 BC Colossal temple construction at El Mirador and other cities.

150 AD Pre-Classic cities in the Mirador Basin are abandoned.

300–900 AD Classic Period of Maya culture sees astounding advances in architecture, astronomy and art, and development of political alliances.

378 AD Tikal defeats Uaxactún; Teotihuacán influence permeates the Petén.

682 AD Hasaw Chan K'awil begins 52-year reign at Tikal, which becomes a "superpower" of Maya world. Vast temple construction programmes commence.

750 AD Population peaks at around 10 million in Maya region.

780 AD Warring increases and Maya cities gradually decline.

1200s Toltecs invading from Mexico institute a militaristic society that fosters highland tribal rivalries.

1523 Conquistador Pedro de Alvarado arrives, and takes advantage of tribal rivalries to bring the Maya under Spanish control.

1540 The last of the highland tribes are subdued.

1541 Guatemala's capital (present-day Antigua) presides over the provinces of modern-day Costa Rica, Nicaragua, El Salvador, Honduras and Chiapas.

1773 Antigua is destroyed by an earthquake, resulting in the relocation of the capital to its present-day site.

1821 The Captain-General of Central America signs the Act of Independence and Guatemala briefly becomes a member of the Central American Federation.

1847 Guatemala declares itself an independent republic.

1871 Rufino Barrios arrives from Mexico to start a liberal revolution, which heralds sweeping social change but crushes dissent and marginalizes the rural poor.

1901 The United Fruit Company begins to grow bananas in Guatemala. It monopolizes railway and port facilities, and establishes a pervasive political presence.

1944 Guatemala embarks on a 10-year experiment with "spiritual socialism".

1952 Law redistributing United Fruit Company land is passed, to the benefit of 100,000 peasant families.

1954 The CIA sets up an invasion of Guatemala to overthrow its "communist-leaning" government.

1955–85 Military governments send the country into a spiral of violence, economic decline and corruption.

1976 Huge earthquake strikes, leaving 23,000 dead, 77,000 injured and a million homeless. Presence of guerrilla groups increases in the wake of the destruction.

1978 Lucas García takes over, escalating the civil war and massacring some 25,000 peasants, intellectuals, politicians, priests and protesters.

1982 Efraín Ríos Montt stages a successful coup. His Civil Defence Patrols polarize the country, trapping peasants between armed forces and guerrilla groups.

1985 The first legitimate elections in 30 years are won by Vinicio Cerezo, but the army is still clearly in control.

1992 Civil war rumbles on. Rigoberta Menchú is awarded the Nobel Peace Prize for campaigning on behalf of Guatemala's indigenous population.

1996 Peace accords are signed on December 29.

1998 Bishop Juan Gerardi is assassinated two days after publishing an investigation of wartime atrocities, exposing the military's continuing strength.

1999 Alfonso Portillo takes office. His reign is plagued by corruption, and the country is left virtually bankrupt.

2004 Newcomer Oscar Berger is inaugurated president; the economy makes some teetering progress.

2007 Guatemala's first left-leaning president in 50 years, Alvaro Colom, is elected.

2011 Security remains a pressing concern as drug traffickers and street gangs challenge the rule of law.

Basics

ARRIVAL

The vast majority of Guatemala's visitors arrive at **La Aurora International Airport** (GUA) in the southern suburbs of Guatemala City. Most long-haul flights arrive from the US: Delta flying from Atlanta/Los Angeles; Continental from Houston/Newark; and American Airlines from Dallas–Fort Worth/Miami. TACA also connects Cancún, Chicago, Los Angeles, Mexico City and

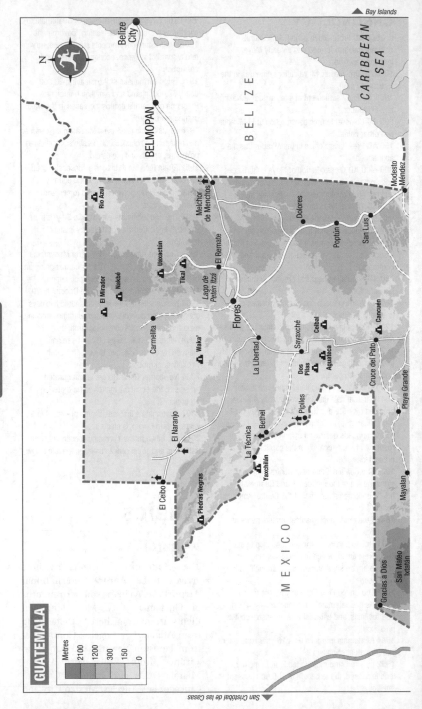

Bay Islands

CARIBBEAN SEA

BELIZE

BELMOPAN

Belize City

Modesto Méndez

Río Azul

Melchor de Menchos

Dolores

San Luis

Poptún

Uaxactún

Tikal

El Remate

El Mirador

Nakbé

Lago de Petén Itzá

Cancuén

Carmelita

Flores

Sayaxché

Ceibal

Waka'

La Libertad

Dos Pilas

Aguateca

Cruce del Pato

El Naranjo

Piipiles

Playa Grande

Bethel

La Técnica

Yaxchilán

El Ceibo

Piedras Negras

Mayalan

M E X I C O

Gracias a Dios

San Mateo Ixtatán

GUATEMALA

Metres
2100
1200
300
150
0

San Cristóbal de las Casas

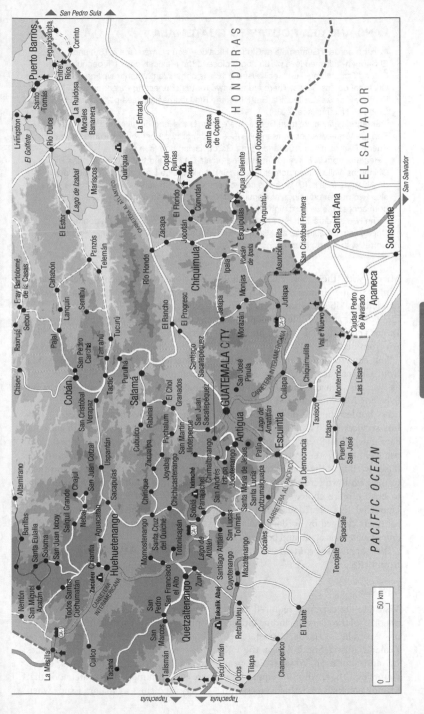

HONDURAS

EL SALVADOR

▲ San Salvador

PACIFIC OCEAN

Puerto Barrios

Livingston
El Golfete

Río Dulce

Lago de Izabal

Fray Bartolomé
de las Casas

Cobán

Salamá

Huehuetenango

Quetzaltenango

GUATEMALA CITY

Antigua

Lago de Atitlán

Lago de Amatitlán

Escuintla

Chiquimula

Copán
Ruinas

Copán

Santa Ana

Sonsonate

Apaneca

50 km

0

LAND AND SEA ROUTES TO GUATEMALA

Mexico borders Guatemala at Ciudad Hidalgo–Tecún Umán (see p.186) and
El Carmen–Talismán (see p.186), both close to the Mexican city of Tapachula.
Ciudad Cuauhtémoc–La Mesilla (see p.185) is convenient when travelling from San
Cristóbal de Las Casas. There are also two routes connecting Palenque and Flores:
Frontera Corozal–La Técnica/Bethel via the Río Usumacinta (see p.236) and El
Ceibo–El Naranjo (see p.236).

Entering Guatemala from Belize, there's either the land crossing in Petén at
Benque Viejo–Melchor de Menchos (see p.224) or two boat routes: Punta Gorda to
Puerto Barrios (see p.196) and Punta Gorda–Lívingston (see p.198).

Heading from El Salvador, most Guatemala City-bound traffic uses the Las
Chinamas–Valle Nuevo border (see p.194), while the La Hachadura–Ciudad Pedro
de Alvarado (see p.191) route is convenient for Guatemala's Pacific coast. There are
also two border crossings at Anguiatú and at San Cristóbal Frontera (see p.194);
both access the eastern highlands.

The two borders with Honduras are at El Florido (see p.192), which connects
Copán with Chiquimula, and Corinto–Entre Ríos (see p.198), which links Puerto
Cortés with Puerto Barrios.

Miami with the Guatemalan capital, while Spirit Airlines fly from Fort Lauderdale. Iberia also offers direct flights from Madrid. **Flores airport** in Petén is currently only served by Tropic Air from Belize City.

You can enter Guatemala by **land** from Chiapas and Tabasco in Mexico, as well as Belize, Honduras and El Salvador. Many travellers choose to take cross-border shuttles or long-distance **bus** services (such as the ever popular Tica Bus), though it's also possible to use local transport – you'll always find buses waiting at the border to take you to the next town (cross early in the day to ensure more choice of departures). Unofficial fees of a dollar or two are routinely charged by border officials to enter Guatemala at all land borders.

There are two **sea routes** to Guatemala from Belize.

VISAS

Visas are not currently required by the majority of travellers (including citizens of Australia, Canada, Israel, New Zealand, Russia, South Africa, the UK, US and almost all Western European countries). Those who do require visas include nationals of Serbia. Check with

the closest Guatemalan embassy well in advance of your trip, or consult ⓦ www
.minex.gob.gt.

Guatemala is part of the CA-4 Central America trade agreement (see box, p.45), which facilitates the smooth passage of goods and people between El Salvador, Honduras, Nicaragua and Guatemala. You will, therefore, not necessarily receive a stamp when you move between these countries. This means you are only entitled to a stay of ninety days in the CA-4 region. You qualify for another ninety days if you hop over to Belize or Mexico and then re-enter the CA-4 region. Alternatively, you can extend your stay by a further ninety days at the immigration office in Guatemala City (see p.136).

GETTING AROUND

Expect to get what you pay for when it comes to Guatemalan **transport**: the methods available range from the country's "chicken buses" (see box opposite) to luxury shuttles. If you're in a hurry, you can also expect to be frustrated – despite frequent services and an improved road network, delays are still common. Be aware, too, that safety remains a major issue when travelling in Guatemala; premium services are not necessarily more secure. Highway robberies do occur, and tourist vehicles are lucrative targets; keep your valuables close and your wits about you. Traffic accidents are also frighteningly common (you'll soon see why). If you're feeling uncomfortable with your driver, consider asking him to slow down (if a private shuttle), or if on public transport, get off and wait for the next bus.

By bus

Buses in Guatemala are incredibly crowded, but they're also cheap and the easiest way to get around. In urban and rural areas alike, **second-class buses** – known as *camionetas* to Guatemalans and "chicken buses" to foreigners – are numerous. Second-class buses generally start and stop at the local terminal (chaotically often in the same place as the local market), though you can get off or on at any point in between. They don't generally have schedules (except on more remote routes), instead leaving every thirty minutes or when full. Pay your **fare** (expect it to be about US$1 per hour of travel) to the *ayudante* (conductor) on the bus. It pays to be open to help from locals when trying to negotiate your passage – the *ayudantes* are invariably friendly, knowledgeable and for the most part honest.

In many areas **microbuses**, or *micros*, supplement (or have replaced) chicken buses. They cost roughly the same (around US$1 per hour of travel). Micro-buses can depart from a central bus station, private terminal or just a bus stop.

First-class, or **Pullman**, buses are more comfortable and make fewer stops. Each passenger has a seat, and tickets can be bought in advance (but drivers will usually stop for you en-route if they have space). Pullmans usually leave from the bus company's office rather than a town's main bus terminal. Expect to pay about US$1.50–2 per hour of travel.

All the main tourist routes are also served by **shuttle buses** that will whisk you around in a lot more comfort, for a price (Antigua–Panajachel is around US$10). Tickets are booked (best the day before) through a travel agent or your hotel. You'll be picked up from your accommodation and dropped off where you choose.

By car

Driving in Guatemala is not for the faint-hearted, though if you prepare yourself for some alarming local practices it can be a highly enjoyable way to get around. The main routes are paved, but minor roads are often extremely rough and landslides are common in rainy season. **Parking** and **security** are the main problems; in

GUATEMALA'S CHICKEN BUSES

Guatemala's "chicken buses" are legendary. They'll probably look familiar at first glance – that's because they're old school buses from North America, just with a few important modifications to get them ready for the rigours of travel: most likely some Jesus stickers, elongated seats for extra bums and a speaker system for the reggaeton soundtrack. Once you find the bus you need, get on and wait for it to fill up around you; luggage (livestock, bicycles, chickens, the kitchen sink, your backpack) goes wherever it will fit. Just when you think the bus couldn't possibly get any fuller, twenty snack vendors will jump aboard, screaming at you to buy various tempting goodies. Journeys are never dull. But besides entertainment, all the madness does provide one of the best opportunities to chat to local people. Even if your Spanish is shaky, a smile and a simple "Buenas" goes a long way. Once the ice is broken, your fellow passengers will undoubtedly help you to reach your destination with ease.

ADDRESSES IN GUATEMALA

Like the majority of towns and cities in Central America, Guatemala's streets generally follow a **grid system**, with the occasional diagonal thrown in for variety. In most towns, **avenidas** run north–south and are numbered from 1 Avenida (on either the west or east side of town), while **calles** run east–west (and will start at 1 Calle in the north). Even small towns will centre on a plaza (with the exception of waterside settlements such as Panajachel and Lívingston). In the capital and a few other cities (Cobán and Quetzaltenango, for example) the ever-expanding street network is divided into **zonas**, each of which may have its own separate set of numbered calles and avenidas (ie, 1 Calle may exist in more than one *zona*). **Addresses** in Guatemala (and in this guide) are given listing first the calle or avenida that the property is on, followed by a number signifying the calle/avenida that intersects to the north/west. The final number given is the property number. For example "6 Av 9–14, Zona 1" is in Zona 1, on 6 Avenida south of 9 Calle, house number 14.

the larger towns you should always get your car shut away in a guarded car park. **Petrol** costs around US$3.25 a gallon, **diesel** a little less. **Renting a car** costs from as little as US$25 a day for a small vehicle, but watch out for extra charges (excesses on any damage caused can be huge). All major rental firms have an office at the airport in Guatemala City (see p.136).

If you plan to visit the more remote parts of the country, then it's almost inevitable that you will **hitch a ride** with a pick-up or truck from time to time. You'll usually have to pay for your lift – around the same as the bus fare. This said, hitching is never entirely safe, and carries obvious risks.

Taxis are available in all the main towns. Rates are fairly low (around US$4 for a 3km trip), but except in Guatemala City, meters are nonexistent, so it's essential to **fix a price** before you set off (clarify that the price is for the journey, not per person). Local taxi drivers will almost always be prepared to negotiate a rate for a half-day or day's excursion to villages or sites.

By bike

Cycling is the most exhilarating way to see Guatemala, but the country's mountainous terrain makes it challenging. If you set out and it all gets too much, most buses will carry bikes on the roof. You can rent mountain bikes in Antigua and Panajachel (see p.138 & p.150), as well as several other cities. Repair shops are fairly widespread.

By boat

Small, speedy, motorized boats called **lanchas** are the main form of water transport, though there's still a slow ferry service between Puerto Barrios and Lívingston. The two definitive boat trips in Guatemala are through the Río Dulce gorge system, starting in either Lívingston or Río Dulce, and across Lago de Atitlán, usually beginning in Panajachel. The Monterrico and Lago de Petexbatún regions also offer the possibility of excellent boat excursions.

By air

The only internal **flight** most tourists are likely to take is from Guatemala City to Flores (from US$220 return), with two airlines, TACA and TAG, offering daily services. Virtually any travel agent in the country can book you a ticket.

ACCOMMODATION

Accommodation in Guatemala comes in different guises: *pensiones*, *posadas*, *hospedajes* and hotels. The names don't actually mean much, however, as they're approximately the same thing, although in general hotels are towards the top end of the price scale and most *hospedajes* and *pensiones* towards the bottom. Budget options are plentiful and even in tourist centres you can sleep for as little as US$4 in a dorm. **Hostels and lodges** tailored to backpackers are springing up across the country; most have dorms and camping facilities as well as private rooms. Wherever you stay, **room prices** are fixed by Inguat, the tourist board, and there should be a tariff posted by the door of your room. You should never pay more than the posted rate.

Rates rarely include breakfast; however, many moderately priced rooms (US$15–25) come with cable TV and the promise of hot-water showers. Actually getting a hot-water shower is a different story, as electric shower-head water heaters are notoriously ineffective (and dangerous). Keep your eyes open for gas-fired hot-water systems – much safer bets. Only on the coasts and in Petén will you need a **fan** or **air conditioning**, while you'll need heavy-duty blankets in the highlands. A **mosquito net** is sometimes provided in lowland areas, but if you plan to spend time in Petén or on either coast it's probably worth investing in one. They're essential if you plan to do any jungle trekking or camping.

Camping facilities are rare and a tent is not worth bringing along unless you're a complete canvas addict. Panajachel, Lanquín, Laguna Lachúa, Poptún, El Remate and Tikal have campgrounds.

FOOD AND DRINK

You can be well fed in Guatemala for only a few dollars a day. Cheap eats are abundant, from fresh produce at markets to street stalls selling tasty snacks. **Lunch** is the main meal for locals; you'll get a two-course lunch, with a drink, for US$3–4 in *comedores* throughout the country. These *menú del día* or *almuerzo* set menus are usually

served from noon to 3pm. **Breakfast** is also good value, if fattening, with traditional *desayunos* including a combination of eggs, beans, tortillas, cheese, fried plantains and cream. Most places in tourist centres also offer continental options for slightly more money. Alternatively, fresh fruit can be bought from street vendors, and muffins and breads from bakeries, cutting your breakfast bill considerably. **Evening meals** in restaurants are generally more expensive (from US$4).

Maya cuisine is at the heart of Guatemalan cooking. Maize is an essential ingredient, appearing most commonly as a **tortilla**, which is like a small, thick corn wrap. **Beans** (*frijoles*) are served either refried (*volteados*) or whole (*parados*). Chillis, usually in the form of a spicy sauce (*salsa picante*), are the final ingredient. Popular **market snacks** include *pupusas* (thick stuffed tortillas topped with crunchy, grated salad vegetables) and *tostadas* (corn crisps smeared with avocado, cheese and other toppings). On the Caribbean coast there is a distinct **Creole cuisine**, heavily based on fish, seafood, coconuts, plantains and banana. *Tapado* (a coconut-based fish or shellfish soup) is the signature dish in these parts. In small towns and rural areas across the country, you can expect your choice to be confined to rice, tortillas and beans, and fried chicken or grilled beef. Vegetarians receive a mixed bag; Guatemala City offers some gems (even for vegans) and tourist hubs such as Flores, Antigua and Lago de Atitlán present interesting veggie menus too. Elsewhere, options can be quite limited.

Drink

Guatemalan **coffee** is great – unfortunately, most of it is exported. In tourist centres espresso machines are becoming very common – expect to pay US$1–2 for a cappuccino – but off the gringo trail very weak or instant coffee is the norm. During the day locals drink water or **refrescos**, water-based drinks with some fruit flavour. **Fizzy drinks** like Coca-Cola or Fanta (all called *aguas* or *gaseosas*) are also popular. For a healthy treat, order a **licuado**: a thick, fruit-based drink with either water or milk (milk is safer). **Bottled water** (*agua pura*) is available almost everywhere and cheapest bought in 500ml plastic bags (*bolsitas*).

The national **beer** (*cerveza*) is Gallo, a medium-strength, bland lager that comes in 330ml or litre bottles (around US$2 and US$4 respectively in a bar; much less in a supermarket). Brahma, a Brazilian import, is also widely available while Moza, a dark brew with a slight caramel flavour, is worth trying, too. Better still, and served in traditional bars, is a *mixta* – a mix of draught clear (*clara*) and dark (*oscura*) beers. **Rum** (*ron*) and **aguardiente**, a clear and lethal sugar-cane spirit, are also popular and cheap; Ron Botran Añejo is an acceptable brand (around US$6 a bottle). Hard drinkers will soon get to know Quetzalteca, a local *aguardiente*. Chilean and Argentinean **wines** are popular in tourist centres: a glass costs from US$3 in a bar; bottles start at about US$10.

CULTURE AND ETIQUETTE

Perhaps more than in other Central American countries, **religious doctrine** – Catholic, Evangelical Protestant, indigenous spiritual beliefs – continues to influence cultural behaviour in Guatemala. Consequently, Guatemalans are fairly modest, reserved folk. This is particularly true of the Maya, who can be suspicious of outsiders; tradition rules in indigenous communities. The dominant Ladino (Latin American) culture is generally less rigid, thanks to the more immediate effects of globalization. Women show more skin, and the Latin American **machismo** is more obvious. Even this, though, is pretty

inoffensive – mostly whistles and catcalls from men trying to impress their friends – and can be ignored by female travellers. **Homosexuality** is not illegal, though it is generally frowned upon. There are small gay communities in Guatemala City, Antigua and Quetzaltenango, but few public meeting places.

It would be a mistake to take Guatemalan reserve for unfriendliness and you're likely to receive gracious hospitality from all levels of society. **Politeness** is valued highly by Ladino and Maya society alike, and there is a pleasantry for nearly every occasion – you will endear yourself to locals by returning these. "Buen provecho", for example, is usually exchanged among strangers in restaurants; it literally translates to "I hope your meal is of good benefit to you!" Be prepared, though, for the fact that **noise** and **personal space** are almost foreign concepts: it is quite usual to be woken by firecrackers at 5am, and even in rural areas Evangelical PA systems blare. Expect a good deal of pushing and shoving on buses and around markets.

Tipping in restaurants and *comedores* is not expected, but is certainly appreciated.

SPORTS AND OUTDOOR ACTIVITIES

Football is the country's top spectator sport, by a mile. The two big local teams, both from Guatemala City, are Municipal and Communications. Admission to games is inexpensive (starting at US$3). Football also provides for easy cross-cultural conversation, as most Guatemalan men are well versed on the topic and have a favourite team in Spanish Primera Liga. The website Ⓦ www.guatefutbol.com (Spanish only) details fixtures and results.

Guatemala is something of a paradise for outdoor activities. With a sturdy pair of shoes, you can **hike** volcanoes, jungles and national parks, and even "circumstroll" Lago de Atitlán. **Caving** is another popular activity, especially in the area north of Cobán (see p.208) where you can explore great caverns and float down underground rivers: Lanquín, Chisec, Candelaria and Finca Ixobel (see p.219) are the places to head for. Finca Ixobel also makes a good base for exploring the countryside on horseback. Wildlife- and **birdwatching** can be very rewarding in Guatemala, as the nation is home to ten percent of the world's registered species and encompasses 19 ecosystems and some 300 microclimates. National parks and reserves good for wildlife include Tikal (see p.227), Monterrico (see p.189), Cerro Cahuí (see p.226) and the Biotopo del Quetzal (see p.297). Other, more eclectic activities on offer include **cycling** in the highlands, **whitewater rafting** on the Río Cahabón (see p.214), **altitude diving** in Lago de Atitlán's volcanic lake (see p.150) and **surfing** on the Pacific coast. You can also **sail** from Río Dulce – one popular route takes you to Belize's more remote cayes.

COMMUNICATIONS

The cheapest way to make an **international phone call** is usually from an internet café or a privately-owned communications business, both of which are common throughout the country. Prices start at around US$0.15 per minute to the US or US$0.25 to Europe via web-phone facilities. **Local calls** are cheap, and can be made from either a communications office or a phone booth (buy a Ladatel phonecard). Guatemalan numbers are always eight digits, generally formatted in two groups of four.

Many North American and European **mobile phones**, if unlocked, will work in Guatemala; all you'll need is a local SIM card (Tigo and Claro are the most popular networks and have excellent coverage). Phones can also be bought locally from as little as US$20 (including around US$15 of calling credit). Keep an eye out for the "double" and "triple" offer days, when you can get two to three times the top-up credit you pay for.

Guatemalan **postal services** are fairly efficient by Latin American standards, and even the smallest of towns has a *correo* (post office); hours are generally Monday to Friday 8am to 5pm. Airmail letters generally take around a week to

> ## GUATEMALA ON THE NET
>
> Ⓦ **www.fhrg.org** The US-based Foundation for Human Rights in Guatemala site has news of current campaigns and news items.
>
> Ⓦ **www.guatemala-times.com** Good source for news, features and comment about Guatemala in English.
>
> Ⓦ **http://lanic.utexas.edu/la/ca /guatemala/** The University of Texas provides a comprehensive Guatemala portal offering access to news sources and academic resources.
>
> Ⓦ **www.revuemag.com** The *Revue*'s website has fully downloadable files of the monthly magazine, including back copies.
>
> Ⓦ **www.visitguatemala.com** Official Inguat site.

the US, and a couple of weeks or so to Europe. Post coming into Guatemala is fairly reliable too, though note that **poste restante** is no longer operational.

Guatemala is very well wired to the **internet**. Most small towns have atleast a couple of internet cafés, while the cities have dozens. Rates vary between US$0.50 and US$4 an hour. Many hotels and hostels also provide internet facilities. **Wi-fi** is becoming more popular and you'll find good coverage (normally free for customers) in cafés, restaurants and hotels in Guatemala City, Antigua and Quetzaltenango.

CRIME AND SAFETY

Personal safety is a valid concern for visitors to Guatemala. Recorded incidents of armed gangs actively targeting tourists, including groups on shuttle buses, have dropped in recent years but the risk remains. Ask first before taking **photographs** in indigenous areas, and be particularly careful not to take pictures of children without permission from their parents. (In remote regions wild rumours circulate that tourists steal children, or their organs.) **Muggings** and acts of **violent crime** are common in Guatemala City; there's not too much danger in the daylight hours, but use taxis at night. There have also been a few cases of armed robbery in Antigua and around Lago de Atitlán.

All this said, relatively few tourists actually have any trouble. However, it's essential that you minimize your chances of becoming a victim. **Petty theft** and **pickpocketing** are likely to be your biggest problems – as anywhere, theft is most common in bus stations and crowded markets. As a rule, ask for local advice on safety issues. If you do plan to be in a risky spot, don't take more than you can afford to lose – many travellers carry "decoy" wallets with just a small amount of cash to satisfy muggers. You could also consider buying pepper spray, which is available locally, including stores at Las Próceres mall in Guatemala City (see p.136).

If you are robbed you should file a report with the police – at the very least for insurance purposes – though Guatemala's civilian **police** force has a poor reputation. In Antigua, Panajachel and Tikal there are well-established **tourist police** forces. Also useful is the "Asistur" service, dedicated to assisting tourists. They have representatives across the country (see box below).

Drugs (particularly marijuana and cocaine) are quite widely available. Don't partake: **drug offences** are dealt with severely – even the possession of marijuana could land you in jail.

HEALTH

Guatemala's **pharmacies** can provide many over-the-counter medications, and some pharmacists can diagnose ailments and prescribe the appropriate pills. However, pharmacists are not qualified medics – so make sure your Spanish is correct.

Even in remote communities there are basic **health centres**, although you may find only a nurse or health worker available. In case of serious illness, head for a city and a private **hospital**. Guatemala's doctors often speak English, and many were trained in the US. You must travel with medical insurance (see p.48), as without it you'll need to pay for any hospital treatment up front.

MONEY AND BANKS

The Guatemalan currency is the **quetzal**; the exchange rate at the time of writing was Q7.96 to US$1. US dollars are also

EMERGENCY NUMBERS

Ambulance ☎128
Asistur (tourist assistance) ☎1500
Fire ☎122/123
Police ☎110/120
Red Cross ☎125

accepted in many of the main tourist centres; prices for tours are often quoted in dollars, and some ATMs in Antigua and Guatemala City will allow you to withdraw dollars as well as quetzals. In general, ATMs dispense Q100 bills. You will soon learn that some Guatemalan businesses would, seemingly, rather lose a sale than have to find change for one of these, so keep a stash of *sencillo* (change) about you.

ATMs are the easiest and most convenient way to get money, though note that most add a withdrawal fee of US$2–3. Virtually every town in the country has at least one ATM accepting both Visa/Plus and MasterCard/Cirrus cards. Most banks will also give cash advances with cards if there's no hole in the wall.

Travellers' cheques are a less useful alternative; US dollar cheques are accepted in a dwindling number of banks, so check before you queue up. Euros and other currencies can only be exchanged at a few (mainly European-owned) businesses. **Bank hours** are extremely convenient, with many opening until 7pm (and some as late as 8pm) from Monday to Friday and until 12.30pm or 1pm on Saturdays.

Student discounts are rare in Guatemala but some museums do offer reduced entry rates. You'll need an International Student Identity Card (ISIC), available from STA-affiliated travel agencies.

INFORMATION AND MAPS

The national tourist board, **Inguat** (ⓦ www.visitguatemala.com), with offices in Guatemala City, Panajachel, Antigua, Flores and Quetzaltenango, gives out glossy brochures and will try to help you with your trip, but don't expect too much independent travel advice. The main office in Guatemala City (see p.133) has a library of information about tourism in the country and can also provide you with a good map of the country.

PUBLIC HOLIDAYS

January 1 New Year's Day
Semana Santa Easter Week (March–April)
May 1 Labour Day
June 30 Army Day, anniversary of 1871 revolution
August 15 Guatemala City fiesta (capital only)
September 15 Independence Day
October 12 Discovery of America (only banks are closed)
October 20 Revolution Day
November 1 All Saints' Day
December 25 Christmas Day

OPENING HOURS AND HOLIDAYS

Most offices and shops are **open** between 8am and 5pm, though some take a break for lunch. **Archeological sites** are open every day, usually from 8am to 5pm (Tikal maintains longer hours), while most museums open Tuesday to Sunday from 9am to 4pm. **Sundays** remain distinguishable – many businesses close and transport is less frequent, though tourist centres such as Antigua keep buzzing. On **public holidays** (see box above) virtually the entire country shuts down, and though some buses do run it's not the best time to be travelling.

FESTIVALS

Traditional **fiestas** are one of the great excitements of a trip to Guatemala, and every town and village, however small, devotes at least one day a year to celebration. Many of the best fiestas include some specifically local element, such as the giant kites at **Santiago Sacatepéquez** (see p.148), the religious processions in Antigua and the wild horse race in **Todos Santos Cuchumatán** (see p.184). At certain times virtually the whole country erupts simultaneously. The following is only a selection of some of the most interesting regional and national festivals.

January The town fiesta in Rabinal, in Baja Verapaz, is renowned for pre-colonial dances (Jan 23–24).

March/April Semana Santa (Easter week) is celebrated nationwide. Particularly impressive processions take place in Antigua, Guatemala City, Santiago Atitlán & San Cristóbal Verapaz. Every Sunday of Lent sees massive street processions in Antigua, which culminate with the main event on Easter Sunday.

July Cubulco, Baja Verapaz, hosts the Palo Volador, a bungy-jump-style ritual (July 25); Cobán celebrates the national folklore festival (July 31–Aug 6).

August Guatemala City fiesta (Aug 15).

November The first of the month is All Saints' Day, with celebrations all over, but most dramatic in Todos Santos Cuchumatán and Santiago Sacatepéquez, where massive kites are flown.

December Bonfires (the Burning of the Devil) take place throughout the country on Dec 7; main fiesta in Chichicastenango (Dec 13 & 21). Christmas is celebrated countrywide.

Guatemala City

Spilling across a highland basin, surrounded on three sides by jagged hills and volcanic cones, **GUATEMALA CITY** is the largest city in Central America, home to over three million people. Characterized by an intensity and a vibrancy that simultaneously fascinate and horrify, Guatemala's capital is a shapeless and swelling metropolitan mass, and the undisputed centre of the country's politics, power and wealth. Not even a wild imagination will be able to make it out as a pleasant environment –

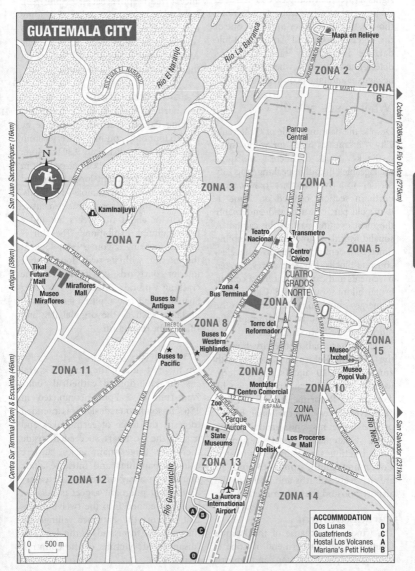

GUATEMALA CITY

ZONA 2

ZONA 6

Río La Barranca

Río El Naranjo

BULEVAR EL NARANJO

AVENIDA SIMÓN CAÑAS

Mapa en Relieve

CALLE MARTÍ

► Cobán (208km) & Río Dulce (275km)

Parque Central

ZONA 3

ZONA 1

ANILLO PERIFÉRICO

N

◄ San Juan Sacatepéquez (16km)

Kaminaljuyú

ZONA 7

AVENIDA ELENA

9A AVENIDA

7A AVENIDA

6A AVENIDA

Teatro Nacional

Transmetro

Centro Cívico

ZONA 5

◄ Antigua (38km)

CALZADA SAN JUAN

CALZADA ROOSEVELT

AVENIDA BOLÍVAR

Tikal Futura Mall

Miraflores Mall

Museo Miraflores

Buses to Antigua

TREBOL JUNCTION

CALZADA AGUILAR BATRES

Zona 4 Bus Terminal

CUATRO GRADOS NORTE

AVENIDA BARRANQUILLA

ZONA 4

Torre del Reformador

ZONA 8

Buses to Western Highlands

Buses to Pacific

BULEVAR LIBERACIÓN

Museo Ixchel

Museo Popol Vuh

ZONA 15

◄ Centro Sur Terminal (2km) & Escuintla (46km)

ZONA 11

ZONA 9

7A AVENIDA

AVENIDA REFORMA

Montúfar Centro Comercial

12 CALLE

PLAZA ESPAÑA

Zoo

Parque Aurora

State Museums

ZONA 10

ZONA VIVA

CALLE REAL DE PETAPA

CALZADA RAÚL AGUILAR BATRES

Río Negro

CALLE VILLA GUADALUPE

Los Próceres Mall

► San Salvador (231km)

ZONA 12

Río Guadronchito

ZONA 13

CALZADA ATANACIO TZUL

Obelisk

AVENIDA HINCAPIÉ

BULEVAR LOS PRÓCERES

CC 20

La Aurora International Airport

AVENIDA LAS AMÉRICAS

ZONA 14

A
B
C
D

0   500 m

ACCOMMODATION
Dos Lunas   D
Guatefriends   C
Hostal Los Volcanes   A
Mariana's Petit Hotel B

indeed, for many travellers time spent in the capital is an exercise in damage limitation, struggling through bus exhaust and swirling crowds. However, once you get used to the pace, Guatemala City can offer some surprises, including a satisfying variety of restaurants, authentic bars, a sprinkling of interesting sights as well as multiplex cinemas and shopping plazas. It is important to note, though, that the city's crime rate is one of the highest in Central America. While daytime is relatively safe, conditions deteriorate after dark, when you should be vigilant and take taxis to get around.

What to see and do

Despite the daunting scale of Guatemala City – it consists of 25 sprawling zones – the key areas of interest are quite manageable. Broadly speaking, the city divides into two distinct halves. The northern section, centred on **Zona 1**, is the old part of town, and undeniably the most exciting part of the capital. A squalid world of low-slung, crumbling nineteenth-century townhouses, faceless concrete blocks, low-rent stores, broken pavements and car parks, it has a certain brutal allure. South of 18 Calle, Zona 1 merges into **Zona 4**, home to the Municipalidad, tourist and immigration offices and the Teatro Nacional.

The southern half of the city, beyond the Torre del Reformador, begins with **zonas 9 and 10** and is the modern, wealthy part of town, split in two by **Avenida La Reforma**. Here you'll find exclusive offices, international hotels, private museums and, in the **Zona Viva**, Guatemala's most expensive clubs, boutiques, restaurants and cafés. Continuing south, **zonas 13 and 14** are rich leafy suburbs and home to the airport, zoo and the state museums.

Parque Central

The windswept expanse of the **Parque Central**, at the northern end of Zona 1, is a good place to stop and absorb the flavours of Guatemala City. This concrete plaza is full of life, especially on Sundays and public holidays as pigeons, shoe-shiners, herds of goats and raving Evangelicals jostle for space. On the west side of the square is a concrete bandstand, the Concha Acústica, where you'll find marimba and classical music performances (Wed 4–6pm & Sat 3.30–5pm; free). Most of the city's major sights – including the cathedral, Palacio Nacional and two semi-restored colonial arcades, the Pasaje Aycinena and Pasaje Rubio (leading off the park's south side) – lie nearby.

Palacio Nacional

Just north of the Parque Central is the striking **Palacio Nacional** (entrance by guided tour only, conducted every 30min in Spanish or English daily 9.30am–4pm; Q40), a lavish, pale-green palace built in the 1940s by president Jorge Ubico and nicknamed "El Guacamole" by locals. It housed the government's executive branch for about fifty years but today hosts cultural exhibitions. The thirty-minute tour gives you a brief look at the interior, with its two Moorish-style interior courtyards; you'll also see some cracking murals depicting warring Spaniards and Maya, plus a few items of nostalgia such as the original flag and rifles of the revolution.

Cathedral

On the east side of the Parque Central sits the blue-domed **cathedral** (daily 7am–1pm & 3–7pm), completed in 1868. Its solid, squat design was intended to resist the force of earthquakes and has, for the most part, succeeded. Inside there are three main aisles, austere colonial paintings and intricate altars housing an array of saints. The cathedral's most poignant aspect is outside, however: etched into the twelve pillars that support the entrance railings are the names of thousands of the dead and "disappeared" victims of the country's civil war.

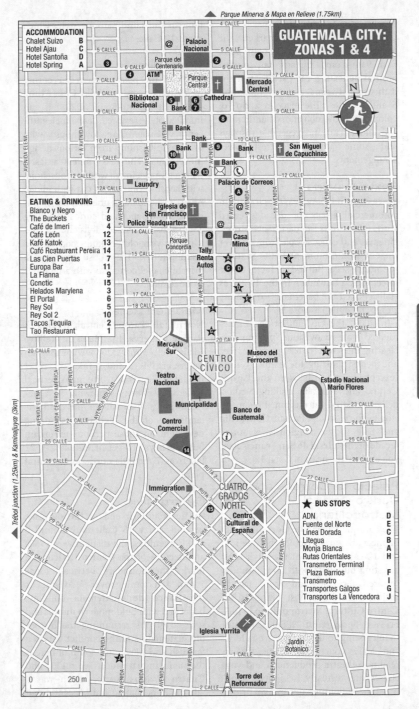

Parque Minerva & Mapa en Relieve (1.75km)

GUATEMALA CITY: ZONAS 1 & 4

ACCOMMODATION
Chalet Suizo   B
Hotel Ajau   C
Hotel Santoña   D
Hotel Spring   A

EATING & DRINKING
Blanco y Negro   7
The Buckets   8
Café de Imeri   4
Café León   12
Kafé Katok   13
Café Restaurant Pereira 14
Las Cien Puertas   7
Europa Bar   11
La Fianna   9
Genetic   15
Helados Marylena   3
El Portal   6
Rey Sol   5
Rey Sol 2   10
Tacos Tequila   2
Tao Restaurant   1

Palacio Nacional
Parque del Centenario
ATM
Parque Central
Biblioteca Nacional
Bank
Cathedral
Mercado Central
Bank
Bank
Bank
Bank
Bank
San Miguel de Capuchinas
Laundry
Palacio de Correos
Iglesia de San Francisco
Police Headquarters
Casa Mima
Parque Concordia
Tally Renta Autos
Mercado Sur
CENTRO CÍVICO
Museo del Ferrocarril
Teatro Nacional
Municipalidad
Banco de Guatemala
Estadio Nacional Mario Flores
Centro Comercial
Immigration
CUATRO GRADOS NORTE
Centro Cultural de España

★ BUS STOPS
ADN   D
Fuente del Norte   E
Línea Dorada   C
Litegua   B
Monja Blanca   A
Rutas Orientales   H
Transmetro Terminal
  Plaza Barrios   F
Transmetro   I
Transportes Galgos   G
Transportes La Vencedora   J

Iglesia Yurrita
Jardín Botánico
Torre del Reformador

Trébol junction (1.25km) & Kaminaljuyu (3km)

0   250 m

Mercado Central

Guatemala City's best market, the **Mercado Central** (Mon–Sat 6am–6pm, Sun 9am–1pm) spreads out underground beneath a car park east of the cathedral between 8 and 9 avenidas and 6 and 8 calles. The place is a riot of colour, with the obligatory handicrafts, souvenirs, fruit and vegetable displays and some impressive fresh-flower arrangements.

Sexta Avenida

Sexta Avenida (6 Av) was the city's main commercial artery for decades, lined with glamorous department stores, cinemas and cafés. People from all over the city would promenade the Sexta to see and be seen. But the character of the street took a downturn in the 1980s, as stalls choked the pavements, and many stores and cinemas closed.

In 2009, the city authorities implemented a renovation programme, clearing the street traders, planting trees and pedestrianizing the entire avenida (except for cycles) between the Parque Central and 18 Calle, making Sexta a delight to stroll once again. Be sure to stop by the well-kept **Parque Concordia** and take in the fabulously elaborate facade of the **Iglesia de San Francisco** as you explore the heart of Zona 1.

Palacio de Correos and Centro Cultural Metropolitano

The baroque **Palacio de Correos**, south of the park on 7 Avenida between 11 and 12 calles, is one of the city's most arresting buildings, with an elaborately restored terracotta-and-cream facade. Inside, behind the post office, is the **Centro Cultural Metropolitano** (Mon–Fri 9am–5pm; free; ☎2285 0075), home to interesting contemporary art galleries and leafy courtyards. Films, poetry readings, theatre productions and yoga classes are regularly held here. Don't miss the adjoining decorative bridge, built in the same baroque style, which spans 12 Calle.

Casa Mima

South of the post office, at the corner of 8 Avenida and 14 Calle, **Casa Mima** (Mon–Sat 10am–5pm; Q20) is an immaculately restored, late nineteenth-century Guatemalan townhouse with original furnishings from various design movements. The decor offers a fascinating glimpse into a wealthy household, with lavish rooms kitted out with gilded mirrors, chandeliers, oriental rugs, hand-painted wallpaper and curios including a gloriously detailed dolls' house and a ninety-year-old "talking machine" (a gramophone). The house even has a private chapel complete with a fabulous wooden altar.

Mapa en Relieve

North of the Parque Central, in Zona 2's Parque Minerva, the **Mapa en Relieve** (daily 9am–5pm; Q25; ⓦwww.mapaenrelieve.org) is a huge, open-air relief model of Guatemala. The map's vertical scale has been somewhat exaggerated, but still highlights the dramatic landscape of the highlands, shedding new light on those perilous mountain bus journeys. To get here, take a V-21 bus from 7 Avenida north of the central plaza.

Centro Cívico

At the southern end of the old city, beyond sleazy 18 Calle and around 6 and 7 avenidas, the distinctively 1960s architecture of the **Centro Cívico** area marks the boundary between zonas 1 and 4. Looming over 7 Avenida is the **Banco de Guatemala** building, bedecked with bold modern murals and stylized glyphs recounting the history of Guatemala and the conflict between Spanish and Maya. Just south of here is the main Inguat office (see p.133) and **Cuatro Grados Norte**, which was a vibrant boho barrio until recently, but is now very quiet, apart from a couple of cultural centres. On a small rise to the west of 6 Avenida is the futuristic **Teatro Nacional**, designed to resemble a ship (see p.136).

Jardín Botánico

The city's **Jardín Botánico** (Mon–Fri 8am–3pm, Sat 9am–noon; Q10), at the northern end of Avenida La Reforma, is part of San Carlos University. It's a beautiful evergreen space with quite a selection of species, all neatly labelled in Spanish or Latin. An anachronistic natural history museum, the **Museo de Historia Natural** (same hours), also sits within the grounds; the collection is pretty dull, mainly mangy stuffed animals.

Torre del Reformador

South of the Centro Cívico, at the junction of 7 Avenida and 2 Calle, in Zona 9, is the landmark **Torre del Reformador**, Guatemala's stunted version of the Eiffel Tower. The steel structure was built in honour of President Barrios, whose liberal reforms transformed the country between 1871 and 1885. Unfortunately, you can only admire it from below. Just to the north, at the junction with Ruta 6, is the **Iglesia Yurrita** (Tues–Sun 8am–noon & 3–6pm), built in a weird neo-Gothic style reminiscent of a horror-movie set.

Museo Ixchel and Museo Popol Vuh

The campus of the University Francisco Marroquín, reached by following 6 Calle Final off Avenida La Reforma, is home to two excellent privately-owned **museums**. The **Museo Ixchel** (Mon–Fri 9am–5pm, Sat 9am–1pm; Q35, students Q15; ⓦwww.museo ixchel.org) shouldn't be missed if you're

a fan of textiles, or just can't get enough of Guatemalan traditional dress: its collection is dedicated to Maya culture, with particular emphasis on traditional weaving. There's a number of stunning hand-woven fabrics, including some impressive examples of ceremonial costumes, with explanations in English, plus information about techniques, dyes, fibres and weaving tools and the ways in which costumes have changed over time.

The excellent **Museo Popol Vuh** (Mon–Fri 9am–5pm, Sat 9am–1pm; Q35, students Q20; ⓦwww.popolvuh .ufm.edu.gt), next door, is home to an outstanding collection of archeological artefacts collected from sites all over the country. The small museum is divided into Pre-Classic, Classic, Post-Classic and Colonial rooms, and all the exhibits are top quality. Particularly interesting is a copy of the Dresden Codex, one of very few surviving written and illustrated records of Maya history.

Parque Aurora

Further south, in Zona 13, **Parque Aurora** houses the city's **zoo** (Tues–Sun 9am–5pm; Q20; ❽www.aurorazoo .org.gt). Here you can see African lions, Bengal tigers, hippos, giraffes, elephants, monkeys and all the Central and South American big cats, including some well-fed jaguars. As zoos go, it's not bad and the grounds are a delight. It's also open on full-moon nights, the ideal time to see nocturnal animals.

Museo Nacional de Arqueología y Etnología

Opposite the Parque Aurora is a complex of three state-run museums, of which the **Museo Nacional de Arqueología y Etnología** (Tues–Fri 9am–4pm, Sat & Sun 9am–noon & 1.30–4pm; Q60) is the best. The collection includes a world-class selection of Maya treasures, though the layout and displays are somewhat confused. Noteworthy pieces include some spectacular jade masks from Abaj Takalik, a stunning wooden temple-top lintel from Tikal and artefacts from Piedras Negras, one of the remotest sites in Petén. Stela 12, dating from 672 AD, depicts a cowering captive king begging for mercy, and there's an enormous carved stone throne from the same site, richly engraved with glyphs and decorated with a two-faced head.

Museo Nacional de Arte Moderno

Opposite the archeological museum, the city's **Museo Nacional de Arte Moderno** (Tues–Fri 9am–4pm, Sat & Sun 9am–noon & 1.30–4pm; Q50) also suffers from poor presentation, but does boast some imaginative geometric paintings

by Dagoberto Vásquez, and a collection of startling exhibits by Efraín Recinos, including a colossal marimba-cum-tank sculpture. Both Vásquez and Recinos are twentieth-century Guatemalan artists particularly noted for their mural work, which can be seen on various public buildings throughout the city, including the Banco de Guatemala and the Biblioteca Nacional. There's also a permanent collection of Cubist art and massive murals by Carlos Mérida, Guatemala's most celebrated artist, in the museum.

Museo Nacional de Historia Natural

The third museum in the complex, the **Museo Nacional de Historia Natural** (Tues–Fri 9am–4pm, Sat & Sun 9am–noon & 1.30–4pm; Q50), is pretty dismal, featuring a range of miserable stuffed animals from Guatemala and elsewhere and a few mineral samples. Close by on 11 Avenida is the touristy **Mercado de Artesanías** (see p.136).

Kaminaljuyú

Way out on the western edge of the city lies Zona 7, which wraps around the ruins of pre-colonial **Kaminaljuyú** (daily 8am–4pm; Q50). Archeological digs have uncovered more than three hundred mounds and thirteen ball-courts here, though unlike the massive temples of the lowlands, these structures were built of adobe, and most of them have been lost to erosion and urban sprawl. Today the site (incorporating only a tiny fraction of the original city) is little more than a series of earth-covered mounds, and it's virtually impossible to get any impression of Kaminaljuyú's former scale and splendour. To **get to** the ruins, take bus #35 from 4 Av in Zona 1.

You can visit the **Museo Miraflores** (Tues–Sun 9am–7pm; Q40; ❽www .museomiraflores.org), a ten-minute walk south of the ruins on Calzada Roosevelt, to learn more about the ancient city; displays explain the history of Kaminaljuyú and its importance as a trading centre. To get there, take any bus headed to "Tikal Futura"; the museum is between the Miraflores shopping centre and the Tikal Futura mall.

Arrival and information

By air Aurora International Airport in Zona 13 has been recently renovated. Avoid all the official-looking exchange desks, which offer derisory rates (25 per cent lower than the banks') and represent something of a corporate scam. Seek out the Banrural bank (Mon–Fri 8am–7pm, Sat & Sun 9am–6pm) instead, where you can change US dollars and travellers' cheques. There is an ATM in the Arrivals area. Don't risk taking a city bus outside the terminal; taxis (Q50/Q60/Q80 to Zona 13/10/1) are available at all hours. There are regular shuttle bus services from the airport to Antigua (US$10/Q80) until about 9pm, though they don't have a fixed schedule and only leave when they have at least three passengers. A taxi to Antigua is around US$35.

By bus First-class (Pullman) buses arrive at the private terminal of whichever company you're using. Some of these are in Zona 10 (including Tica Bus, Hedman Alas and Pullmantur). Others are in Zona 1, some around 18 Calle, which is not the safest part of town, particularly at night. See the map on p.129 for locations of the main companies. Be sure to take a taxi to and from these Zona 1 terminals.

Most second-class buses from the coast use the new Centra Sur (also called Centro de Mayorío) terminal on the southwest side of the city; take a Transmetro bus to get to the centre. Buses from the highlands use a row of bus stops in Zona 8 close to Trébol junction.

Tourist information The main Inguat office (Mon–Fri 8am–4pm; ☎ 2421 2800, ⊛ www.visit guatemala.com) is at 7 Av 1–17, Zona 4. The information desk has plenty of material including maps, and there's always someone who speaks English. There are also information desks (daily 6am–9pm) on the Departures and Arrivals floors at the airport. **Travel agents** Viajes Tivoli 6 Av 8–41, Zona 9 (☎ 2386 4200, ⊛ www.viajestivoli.com), and at Edificio Herrera, 12 C 4–55, Zona 1 (☎ 2285 1050).

City transport

Buses Guatemala's excellent new bus network Transmetro operates on dedicated bus lanes that are closed to all other traffic. The articulated buses are modern, air-conditioned, wheelchair-friendly and only stop every kilometre or so along specific routes. Transport police provide security. The green line (#CC) runs north–south from Plaza Barrios, 18 Calle in Zona 1, along 6 Av through zonas 4 and 9 to Zona 13, returning along 7 Av. The orange line (#70) connects Plaza Barrios and the Centro Cívico with points to the southwest, along Av Bolívar via the Trébol junction and down to the Centra Sur bus terminal. It's useful for connecting chicken buses to/from the highlands with zonas 1 and 4.

Taxis There are both metered and non-metered taxis. Metered taxis are comfortable and fairly cheap; Amarillo (☎ 2470 1515) is highly recommended and will pick you up from anywhere in the city. The fare from Zona 1 to Zona 10 is about Q40, or a short hop within zones will be around Q20. With non-metered taxis, be sure to set a price before you get in. Always take taxis after dark.

Accommodation

The guesthouses in Zona 13 are very convenient for the airport, though this is a purely residential area and there are no restaurants or bars close by. Zona 1 has plenty of budget options, but it's not the best area to walk around at night, so take a taxi or order a takeaway. There are only a couple of budget places in Zona 10, but they're good choices as it's a lively, secure area.

Zona 1

Chalet Suizo 7 Av 14–34 ☎ 2251 8191. An excellent choice, this long-running place is a lot like a European youth hostel, with large, plain, spotless rooms (with or without private bathroom), all with quality beds and reading lights. The management are friendly and efficient, and there's always someone sweeping or cleaning up. Filling meals are available and there's wi-fi too. Q150

Hotel Ajau 8 Av 15–62 ☎2232 0488,
✉hotelajau@hotmail.com. Historic building with
an impressive lobby and an old-school ambience
– the corridors have lovely original floor tiles.
The 41 rooms are well scrubbed, all with TV,
and many have en-suite bathrooms. There's a
comedor for breakfast and evening meals, plus
internet (Q12/hr). US$15

Hotel Santoña 8 Av 15–13 ☎2232 6455. The
perfect option if you're using the Monja Blanca bus
terminal for Cobán (it's right opposite), this efficient
and welcoming modern hotel has spacious, light
rooms (though no singles), all with cable TV and
firm beds. Q210

Hotel Spring 8 Av 12–65 ☎2230 2858, ⓦwww
.hotelspring.com. A solid choice, this large rambling,
secure place has been hosting travellers and Peace
Corp workers for decades. Most of the 43 rooms
are spacious and many have private bathroom
and cable TV. The pretty central courtyard is a nice
focal point for meeting other guests. Breakfast is
available, plus laundry and internet. Q150

Zonas 9 & 10

Hostal Plaza Plaza Aeropuerto 13–92, off 6 Av A,
Zona 9 ☎5417 2143, ⓦwww.hostalplaza.page.tl.
A few blocks from the Zona Viva, this well-run new
place has helpful family owners. The attractive
singles and doubles boast bright bedspreads and
there's an attractive patio for drinks. US$30

Quetzalroo 6 Av 7–84 Zona 10 ☎5746 0830,
ⓦwww.quetzalroo.com. New Australian/
Guatemalan-owned backpackers just north of
the Zona Viva with good-quality accommodation,
helpful travel information and a communal vibe.
Prices are cheap considering the location and there
are some great freebies: a ride from the airport,
internet and light breakfast. City tours can be
arranged for US$5. Dorms US$15, doubles US$35

Xamanek Hostel 13 C 3–57, Zona 10 ☎2360
8345, ✉xamanek.guatemala@gmail.com. Well-
established hostel with friendly owners in the heart
of the Zona Viva, with myriad cafés, restaurants
and stores on your doorstep. The rate includes
breakfast, internet, wi-fi and the use of a DVD
library. There's also a kitchen, laundry, living room,
rear terrace and reliable hot water. All four dorms
are on the large side. Dorms US$15, doubles US$30

Zona 13

Dos Lunas 21 C 10–92 ☎2261 4248,
ⓦwww.hoteldoslunas.com. An exceptional
place to stay, this welcoming guesthouse is very
efficiently managed by fluent English speaker
Lorena Artola and her Dutch husband Hank, who
take great care of travellers. Free airport transfers,

internet and breakfast, and tasty evening meals
are offered. Transport and tourist advice is second
to none. Very popular, so book well ahead. Dorms
US$14, doubles US$28

Guatefriends 16 C 7–40 ☎4151 3866, ⓦwww
.guatemalahostel.com. A good option in this district,
with complimentary airport transfers and internet.
It's run by a young Guatemalan family who are
incredible cooks: they bake their own bread and
offer delicious, nutritious and creative cooking (try
a crêpe with spiced pear compote for breakfast).
Dorms US$18, doubles US$40

Hostal Los Volcanes 16 C 8–00 ☎2261 3040,
ⓦwww.hostallosvolcanes.com. Only 600m from
the airport, this B&B has clean rooms, a pleasant
sitting area and garden. All rooms have cable TV
and rates include breakfast, airport transfers and
internet use. Dorms US$15, doubles US$30

Mariana's Petit Hotel 20 C 10–17 ☎2261 4105,
ⓦwww.marianaspetithotel.com. A well-managed,
welcoming guesthouse very close to the airport
with inexpensive rates, a quiet location, free airport
transfers and wi-fi. US$35

Eating

Zona 1 has some great budget options, while in
the smarter parts of town, notably in the Zona Viva,
the emphasis is more on refined dining, but even
here you'll find some decent, less expensive places.
Wherever you are, you are never far away from a
market, street vendor or fast-food chain. Note that
most *comedores* and cafés tend to close fairly early
– usually around 7pm.

Zona 1

The Buckets 9 C 7–64. This bar/grill is conveniently
located across the road from some of Zona 1's
best bars. The building has a refined atmosphere,
although prices remain moderate (Q25–50). A
selection of daily combos (meat and two veg plus
drink Q15–35) are offered noon–3pm. The friendly
management speaks English. Closed Sun.

Café de Imeri 6 C 3–34. Popular European-style
café with alpine decor and filling breakfasts, pasta,
sandwiches, baguettes and an excellent *menú del
día* (Q28).

Café León 12 C 6–23. Guatemala's best café
operation now has a second branch – a highly
atmospheric historic place of high ceilings, art and
vintage photography that showcases occasional
exhibitions. Renowned for its coffee and pastries,
but also serves full breakfasts (Q22), sandwiches
and draught beer. Closed Sun.

La Fianna 10 C 7–24. Courtyard restaurant
serving economical buffet breakfasts, lunches and

dinners. Breakfasts are a real deal with coffee/tea, juice, granola, yoghurt, fresh fruit, eggs, sausages, plantain, hash browns, bread and, of course, beans, for around Q20.

Helados Marylena 6 C 2–49. Head here for an incredible selection of ice creams – there are around 150 flavours including *yuca* and pumpkin. Waffle cones start at Q10.

Kafé Katok 12 C 6–61. A very agreeable rustic-style place replete with huge wooden beams and chunky tables that specializes (appropriately enough) in hearty country cooking, especially grilled meats. Come hungry for the epic set lunch (Q55), or tuck into a sandwich (Q25) or a few tapas.

Rey Sol Old-school vegetarian café/restaurant/deli with filling food that's also good for a snack. There's a second branch at 11 C 5–51. Both closed Sun.

Tao Restaurant 5 C 9–70. There's no menu here – you just enjoy the meal of the day at tiny tables around a plant-filled courtyard. Three-course veggie lunch Q18. Open for lunch only, Mon–Fri noon–2.30pm.

Zona 4

Café Restaurant Pereira Inside the Centro Comercial mall (6 Av & 24 C). A no-nonsense *comedor*-cum-restaurant just a couple of blocks west of Inguat that makes a good lunch stop for *comida típica*.

Zona 10

Café de Jabes 14 C 4–12. Top-drawer *comedor* that offers Guatemalan breakfasts and the best-value lunch in Zona Viva. The menu changes daily, but there are always four dishes – including perhaps *carne a la plancha* or *pollo dorada* accompanied with vegetables. The price (Q22) includes soup, tortillas and a drink, and you eat in clean surrounds on gingham tablecloths. Daily 7am–3pm.

La Chapinita 1 Av 10–24. Popular with office workers, this bright, buzzing *comedor* does a set lunch (soup, main course and *refresco*) for Q25.

Shucos 3 Av & 12 C. For bargain-basement nosh in Zona 10, this simple place is perfect: *shucos* (hot dogs with avocado) and taco-style snacks start at Q10; a beer costs the same. Daily noon–3pm & 6pm–1am.

Sophos Fontabella Plaza, 12 C & 4 Av. In a new location inside an upmarket courtyard-style shopping mall, this bookstore/café is a delightfully civilized place to browse a book or magazine, sip a *café con leche* and snack on a sandwich or cake.

Tacontento 2 Av & 14 C. One of the more affordable places in Zona 10, come here to feast on tacos, wraps and Mexican dishes inside or on the streetside terrace. The lunch special (Q29) includes soup, three tacos and a drink.

Drinking and nightlife

Guatemala City isn't going to win any prizes for its nightlife. The once-buzzing enclave of Cuatro Grados Norte is now all but moribund. Essentially it comes down to two choices. First up is the gritty, edgy vibe of Zona 1, which has some terrific, highly atmospheric old bars and raucous student places. Small numbers of the left-wing elite and bohemians still drink here, as well as students, but the area is quite unsafe after dark, so take taxis to get around. Alternatively, Zona 10's Zona Viva, largely the domain of wealthy Guatemaltecos, offers expat- and US-style sports bars and a few upmarket clubs; it's safe enough to stroll around here at night. Guatemala City's small gay nightlife scene is mostly underground; the key venue is *Genetic* (see below).

Zona 1

Blanco y Negro Pasaje Aycinena, 9 C between 6 & 7 Av. This place really jumps on weekends when lovers of Afro-Caribbean music descend en masse to groove to the Jamaican dancehall, ska and punta sounds.

Las Cien Puertas Pasaje Aycinena, 9 C between 6 & 7 Av. Bohemian bar in a beautiful, shabby colonial arcade with graffiti-plastered walls. Popular with artists, students and political activists. Good Latin music and reasonable prices. Closed Sun.

Europa Bar 11 C 5–16. Classic, if slightly tired expat hangout set inauspiciously inside a multi-storey car park that serves comfort gringo grub. Also popular with English-speaking Guatemalans. Closed Sun.

El Portal Pasaje Rubio, 9 C between 6 & 7 Av. One of Che Guevara's old drinking haunts, and the decor (and clientele) is little changed since the revolutionary era. It's a fantastic place to share a *chibola* of *cerveza mixta*, munch on a few (complimentary) *boquitas* and soak up the scene: hard drinkers glued to bar stools and wandering trios of musicians prowl the tables, mariachi style.

Tacos Tequila 7 Av 5–47. A bohemian drinking den *par excellence*, it's plastered in tequila bottles, flags and murals of Bob Marley and Che Guevara. You should find the place buzzing shortly after opening time (5pm), making it a good spot for pre-dinner drinks. Closed Sun.

Zona 4

Genetic Via 3 & Ruta 3. Guatemala's best-established gay club is packed at weekends, when a young, fashionable crowd gathers to groove to trance, house and Latin anthems. There's a pleasant rooftop patio and a dark room. Fri & Sat 9pm–1am.

Zona 10

Rattle & Hum 4 Av 16–11. Upmarket but casual Australian-owned bar, popular with both expats and locals, with a lively atmosphere and rock music on the stereo.

Entertainment

For full listings of cultural events in the city, see W www.cultura.muniguate.com or consult supplements in the national press (best are *Prensa Libre* and *El Periódico*).

Cinema

There are plenty of cinemas in the city showing both Hollywood blockbusters and alternative art-house films. For English audio with Spanish subtitles, head for the shopping-mall multiplexes. For the best-quality audiovisuals Cinépolis, inside the Oakland Mall (Zona 10) is top of the pile, followed by Los Próceres (Zona 10) and Miraflores and Tikal Futura (both Zona 11). Check the listings at the Centro Cultural de España, Via 5 1–23, Zona 4 (W www.cceguatemala.org), and at the Centro Cultural Metropolitano (inside the post office, Zona 1) for art-house movies – often with free admission.

Live music

La Bodeguita del Centro 12 C 3–55, Zona 1 T 2230 2976. Guatemala City's bohemian heart, this barn-like place emblazoned with revolutionary art hosts live music (particularly *trova* – folk – and protest rock), poetry and all manner of left-field events. Free entry during the week, with cover around Q35 at weekends. Tues–Sun from 8pm.
Trovajazz Via 6 3–55, Zona 4 W www.trovajazz .com. Intimate venue that showcases quality jazz, blues, acoustic and *trova*. Entrance is around Q40 for most acts. Closed Mon.

Theatre

Teatro Nacional W www.teatronacional.com.gt. The national complex has several theatres, including an amphitheatre, and stages some diverse and prestigious events.

Shopping

Books Sopho's, Fontabella Plaza, 2 C & 4 Av, Zona 10. Includes English-language fiction and travel guides.
Malls Los Próceres in Zona 10 is a mid-range mall with a good selection of clothes and electrical stores. Oakland Mall, the latest and most upmarket mall in Zona 10, has stores including Diesel, Apple and Zara, a good food-court and free wi-fi. Way out on the western fringes of the city, along Calzada Roosevelt, are the malls of Tikal Futura and Miraflores.
Markets Best is the Mercado Central, in an underground warren between 8 & 9 Av and 6 & 8 C. The city's biggest market is at Centra Sur (the terminus of the Transmetro route). There is also the touristy Mercado de Artesanías opposite the zoo in Zona 13. However, traditional handicrafts will be cheaper, and the selection better, in local highland markets.

Directory

Car rental About a dozen companies have offices inside the airport, including Tally (T 2334 5925, W www.tallyrentaautos.com), which also has a branch in Zona 1 (7 Av 14–60; T 5900 4488).
Embassies Most embassies are in the southeastern quarter of the city, along Av La Reforma and Av Las Américas: Canada, 13 C 8–44, 8th floor, Edificio Edyma Plaza, Zona 10 T 2333 6102; Germany, 20 C 6–20, Zona 10 T 2364 6700; Netherlands, 16 C 0–55, 13th floor, Torre Internacional, Zona 10 T 2381 4300; UK, 16 C 0–55, 11th floor, Torre Internacional, Zona 10 T 2367 5425; US, Av La Reforma 7–01, Zona 10 T 2326 4000.
Exchange ATMs are widespread across the city; see p.133 for airport exchange. Many of the major banks will change travellers' cheques and give Visa/MasterCard cash advances, including Banco Industrial, 7 Av & 11 C, Zona 1. You can exchange euros at Banco Internacional, Av Las Américas 12–54, Zona 13.
Health The Centro Médico, 6 Av 3–47, Zona 10 (T 2332 3555), is a private hospital with 24hr cover and English-speaking staff. Central Dentist de Especialistas, 20 C 11–17, Zona 10 (T 2337 1773), is the best dental clinic in the country.
Immigration The main immigration office (*migración*) is at 6 Av & Ruta 3, Zona 4 (T 2411 2411). Visas can be extended here for another 90 days; you'll need copies of your passport, proof of funds (such as a credit card) and a passport-style colour photograph.
Internet There are plenty of internet cafés throughout the city, particularly in Zona 1. Expect to pay around Q6/hr, although it's possible to sniff out places asking only Q3/hr; hotels charge Q10/hr.
Laundry Lavandería el Siglo 2 C 3–42 Zona 1 (Mon–Sat 8am–6pm). Q40 for wash and dry.
Police The police headquarters are in the fortress building on 6 Av, Zona 1. However, if you actually need anything, go to the yellow and blue office on the corner of 11 Av and 4 C, Zona 1.
Post office The main post office is at 7 Av and 12 C, Zona 1 (Mon–Fri 8.30am–5.30pm, Sat 9am–noon).

Telephones There is a large Telgua office one block east of the post office (daily 7am–midnight).

Moving on

Travellers do leave Guatemala City via plane (mostly for international destinations), but buses are the most common way to other parts of the country.

By air

Flights depart La Aurora Airport for other Central American cities, a variety of US hubs and Spain (with Iberia). For connections to South America you'll usually have to change in San Salvador, San José or Panama City. There are three daily domestic flights to Flores (two operated by TACA and one by TAG). A Q20/US$3 airport security tax is payable by all passengers.

By bus

First-class buses depart from the offices of the relevant bus company (see below). Chicken buses (second-class) for the western highlands and Antigua depart from points scattered around the Trébol junction, those for the south coast from the Centra Sur terminal. Note that buses listed as having regular departures (hourly or more frequent) run from about 6am–6pm, unless otherwise stated.

Bus companies

ADN Mayan World (ADN) 8 Av 16–41, Zona 1 ☎2251 0610, ⊕www.adnautobusesdelnorte.com.
Fuente del Norte (FN) 17 C 8–46, Zona 1 ☎7447 7070, ⊕www.grupofuentedelnorte.com. Buses for Tecún Umán leave from a different terminal at Calzada Aguilar Batres 7–55, Zona 12.
Hedman Alas (HA) 2 Av 8–73, Zona 10 ☎2362 5072, ⊕www.hedmanalas.com.
King Quality (KQ) 18 Av 1–96, Zona 15 ☎2369 7070, ⊕www.king-qualityca.com.
Línea Dorada (LD) 10 Av and 16 C, Zona 1 ☎2415 8900, ⊕www.lineadorada.info.
Litegua (L) 15 C 10–40, Zona 1 ☎2220 8840, ⊕www.litegua.com.
Los Halcones (LH) Calzada Roosevelt 37–47, Zona 11 ☎2432 5364.
Monja Blanca (MB) 8 Av 15–16, Zona 1 ☎2238 1409, ⊕www.tmb.com.gt.
Pullmantur (P) Based at *Holiday Inn*, 1 Av 13–22, Zona 10 ☎2363 6240, ⊕www.pullmantur.com.
Rutas Orientales (RO) 21 C 11–60, Zona 1 ☎2253 7282, ⊕www.rutasorientales.com.
Tica Bus (TB) Blvd los Próceres 26–55, Zona 10 ☎2459 2848, ⊕www.ticabus.com.
Transportes Alamo (TA) 12 Av A 0–65, Zona 7 ☎2471 8626.

Transportes Galgos (TG) 7 Av 19–44, Zona 1 ☎2253 4868, ⊕www.transgalgosinter.com.gt.
Transportes La Vencedora (V) 3 Av 1–38, Zona 9.

Domestic destinations

Antigua (1hr) HA: 2 daily, 5am & 7pm; Litegua: 2 daily, 2pm & 6pm. Second-class services leave from Trébol every 10min until 6.30pm.
Chichicastenango (3hr 15min) Various second-class services from 41 C, Zona 8, every 30min.
Chiquimula (3hr 30min) RO: 2 hourly.
Cobán (5hr) MB: hourly.
Flores (8–9hr) FN: 18 daily 1am–10pm; LD: 3 daily, 10am, 9pm & 9.30pm; ADN: 2 daily, 9pm & 10pm; TR: 2 daily, 5pm & 8pm.
Huehuetenango (5hr) LD: 2 daily, 6.30am & 10.30pm; LH: 2 daily, noon & 4pm.
La Mesilla (7hr) LD: 3 daily, 6am, 7am & 10.30pm.
Monterrico (3hr) Various second-class services from Centra Sur terminal. Or travel via Puerto San José (every 15min from Centra Sur), from where there are connections to Monterrico, or via Iztapa (7 daily; 1hr 30min), from where there are (roughly hourly) onward connections until 4pm.
Nebaj Various second-class services from 41 C, Zona 8. Five daily departures, or travel via Santa Cruz del Quiché.
Panajachel Various second-class services from 41 C, Zona 8. Hourly until 4pm.
Poptún (6hr) LD: 3 daily, 10am, 9pm & 9.30pm; TR: 2 daily, 5pm & 8pm.
Puerto Barrios (5hr 30min–6hr 30min) L: 19 daily, including 12 *directos*.
Quetzaltenango (4hr) TA: 6 daily; LD: 2 daily, 7am & 3pm; TG: 3 daily, 8.30am, 2.30pm & 5pm; FD: 2 daily, 5am & 7.30pm.
Rio Dulce (4–5hr) L: 5 daily; or catch a Flores-bound bus.
San Pedro la Laguna (4hr) Various second-class services from 41 C, Zona 8.
Santa Cruz del Quiché (4hr) Various second-class services from 41 C, Zona 8. 1–2 hourly.
Tecún Umán (6hr) FN: 6 daily.

International destinations

Copán (Honduras) (5hr) HA: 2 daily, 5am & 9am; FN: 1 daily, 6am.
La Ceiba (Honduras) (12hr) HA: 2 daily, 5am & 9am; FN: 1 daily, 6am.
Managua (Nicaragua) TB: 2 daily.
San Pedro Sula (Honduras) (8–9hr) HA: 2 daily, 5am & 9am; RO: 2 daily, 5.30am & 1.30pm.
San Salvador (El Salvador) (5hr) V: hourly; TB: 2 daily, 5.30am & 1pm; P: 2–3 daily, 7am & 3pm (and Fri & Sun at 1.30pm); KQ: 2–3 daily, 8am, 2pm & 3.30pm.

Tapachula (Mexico) (6hr) LD: 1 daily, 6am; TB: 1 daily, noon; TG: 6 daily.

Tegucigalpa (Honduras) (12–13hr) HA: 2 daily, 5am & 9am. The following all involve a stopover in San Salvador (around 36hr in total): KQ: 2 daily, 7am & 3.30pm; P: 1 daily, 7am; TB: 1 daily, noon.

Antigua

A visit to the colonial city of **ANTIGUA** is a must for any traveller in Guatemala. Nestled in a valley between the Agua, Acatenango and Fuego volcanoes, the city was founded in 1541 and built on a grand grid pattern as befitting a capital. Antigua grew in importance over the next two hundred years, peaking in the mid-eighteenth century, before being largely destroyed by an earthquake in 1773. Since then, it's become something of an open-air architectural museum, with many of its major remaining structures and monuments preserved as ruins – the impressive churches and magnificent buildings on view today date back to the Spanish empire. Local conservation laws are strict, ensuring that the city will remain in its current atmospheric state, and continue to draw in thousands of visitors every year.

Long favoured by travellers as an antidote to hectic, nearby Guatemala City, in recent years Antigua has seen its population joined by both large numbers of *guatemaltecos* from "la capital" and many expats attracted by the city's sophisticated and relaxed atmosphere. Tourists of every nationality continue to permeate the town, along with numerous foreign students attending the city's language schools. With smart restaurants and wine bars catering to this international, cosmopolitan crowd, Antigua's civilized world can at first seem a bit too comfortable, but like most travellers, you will probably end up staying a lot longer than planned.

What to see and do

Antigua is laid out as a grid, with avenidas running north–south, and calles east–west. Each street is numbered and has two halves, either a north (*norte/nte*) and south (*sur*) or an east (*oriente/ote*) and west (*poniente/pte*) with the city's main plaza, the **Parque Central**, at their centre. Despite this apparent simplicity, most people get lost here at some stage. If you're confused, remember that Volcán Agua, the one closest to town, is almost directly south.

SEMANA SANTA IN ANTIGUA

Antigua's Semana Santa (Holy Week) celebrations are some of the most impressive and remarkable in all Latin America. The celebrations start on Palm Sunday with a procession representing Christ's entry into Jerusalem, and continue through to Good Friday, when processions re-enact the progress of Christ to the Cross. Setting out at about 8am from La Merced, Escuela de Cristo and the village of San Felipe, and accompanied by solemn dirges and clouds of incense, penitents carry images of Christ and the Cross on massive platforms. Initially garbed in either purple or white, after 3pm, the hour of the Crucifixion, the penitents change into black. Some of the images they carry date from the seventeenth century, and the procession itself is thought to have been introduced in the early years of the Conquest.

Check the exact details of events with the tourist office (see p.143). Remember that hotels fill up during Holy Week – reserve in advance if you want to stay in the city.

ANTIGUA

0   200 m

San Jerónimo

La Merced

Arch of Santa Catalina

Las Capuchinas

Mercado & Bus Terminal

El Carmen

Mercado de Artesanías

Handicraft Market

Ayuntamiento

Parque Central

Catedral de San José

Palacio de los Capitanes Generales

Museo de Arte Colonial

Casa Popenoe

San Pedro

Parque Unión

Santa Clara

San Francisco

San José El Viejo

see "Central Antigua" map for detail

N

Santa Cruz

Río Pensativo

El Calvario

ACCOMMODATION

Black Cat Hostel	K	El Hostal	L
La Casa de Don Ismael	J	Hotel Casa los Arcos	B
Casa Jacaranda	D	Kafka	F
Dionisio	I	Onvisa	M
Earth Lodge	A	Posada Juma Ocag	H
International Mochilero		Umma Gumma Hostal	G
Guesthouse	E	Yellow House	C

EATING & DRINKING

Café No Sé	2
Las Mañanitas	1
Sky Café	4
Y tu Piña Tambien	3

Parque Central

Antigua's focal point is its main plaza, the **Parque Central**. It's a popular hangout, with both visitors and locals congregating, chatting and relaxing on its many benches around the central **Fuente de Las Sirenas** fountain, built in 1739. For travellers, the square is not only an easy rendezvous point, but is also a good place to begin exploring the city, starting with the cathedral, which looks onto the square.

Catedral de San José

Of the structures surrounding the plaza, the **Catedral de San José**, on the east side, is the most arresting. Built in 1670, the cathedral was quite elaborate for its time

and location – it boasted an immense dome, five aisles, eighteen chapels and an altar inlaid with mother-of-pearl, ivory and silver – but the 1773 earthquake almost destroyed the building. Today only two of the original interior chapels remain; take a peek inside and you will find a gold cloister and several colonial images. To get some idea of the vast scale of the original building check out the ruins to the rear (enter from 5 C Ote; daily 9am–5pm; Q5) where you'll find a mass of fallen masonry and rotting beams, broken arches and hefty pillars. Buried beneath the floor are some of the great names of the Conquest, including Pedro de Alvarado and his wife, Bishop Marroquín and the historian Bernal

Díaz del Castillo. At the very rear of what was once the nave, steps lead down to a burial vault that's regularly used for Maya religious ceremonies – an example of the coexistence of pagan and Catholic beliefs that's so characteristic of Guatemala.

Palacio de los Capitanes Generales

One of the oldest buildings in Antigua, the **Palacio de los Capitanes Generales**, or the Palace of the Captains-General, takes up the entire south side of the Parque Central. Dating to 1558, it's been rebuilt more than once, and been through several incarnations, serving as the mint for all of Latin America, the home of the colonial rulers, dragoon barracks, stables, law courts, ballrooms and more. It's currently undergoing a lengthy renovation project, but will reopen in the future as the headquarters of

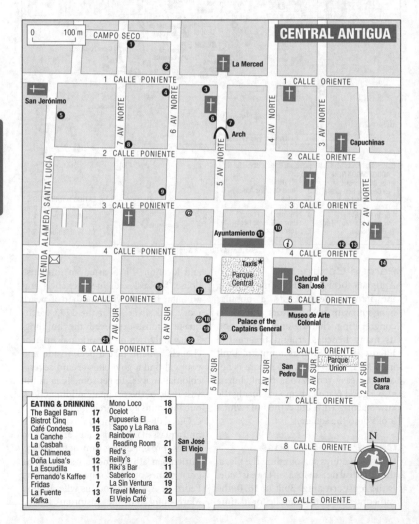

CENTRAL ANTIGUA

0   100 m

CAMPO SECO

La Merced

1 CALLE PONIENTE

1 CALLE ORIENTE

San Jerónimo

7 AV NORTE

6 AV NORTE

4 AV NORTE

3 AV NORTE

Arch

Capuchinas

2 CALLE PONIENTE

5 AV NORTE

2 CALLE ORIENTE

ALAMEDA SANTA LUCIA

3 CALLE PONIENTE

3 CALLE ORIENTE

2 AV NORTE

Ayuntamiento 11

AVENIDA

4 CALLE PONIENTE

4 CALLE ORIENTE

Taxis
Parque
Central

5 CALLE PONIENTE

Catedral de
San José

5 CALLE ORIENTE

7 AV SUR

6 AV SUR

Palace of the
Captains General

Museo de Arte
Colonial

6 CALLE PONIENTE

6 CALLE ORIENTE

5 AV SUR

4 AV SUR

3 AV SUR

2 AV SUR

San
Pedro

Parque
Union

Santa
Clara

7 CALLE ORIENTE

EATING & DRINKING		Mono Loco	18
The Bagel Barn	17	Ocelot	10
Bistrot Cinq	14	Pupusería El	
Café Condesa	15	Sapo y La Rana	5
La Canche	2	Rainbow	
La Casbah	6	Reading Room	21
La Chimenea	8	Red's	3
Doña Luisa's	12	Reilly's	16
La Escudilla	11	Riki's Bar	11
Fernando's Kaffee	1	Saberico	20
Fridas	7	La Sin Ventura	19
La Fuente	13	Travel Menu	22
Kafka	4	El Viejo Café	9

San José
El Viejo

8 CALLE ORIENTE

9 CALLE ORIENTE

N

local government, probably including Antigua's main tourist office.

Ayuntamiento

Directly across from the Palace of the Captains-General sits the **Ayuntamiento** (City Hall), which dates from 1740. It's so solidly built that even after three centuries of earthquakes little reconstruction has had to be undertaken: the walls, more than one metre thick, and the double arcaded facade are good examples of anti-seismic building techniques. When the capital moved to Guatemala City following the 1773 earthquake the Ayuntamiento was abandoned, but was later restored in 1853. Today it houses two museums, the **Museo de Santiago** (daily 9am–4pm; Q30), housed in the section of the building that was once the city jail and containing a collection of colonial artefacts, and the **Museo del Libro Antiguo** (same hours; Q30), in the rooms that held the first printing press in Central America. A replica of the press is on display, alongside some copies of the works produced on it. From the upper floor of the Ayuntamiento there's a wonderful **view** of the three volcanoes that surround the city – it's especially fine at sunset.

Museo de Arte Colonial

Across 5 Calle Oriente from the ruined cathedral is the **Museo de Arte Colonial** (Tues–Fri 9am–4pm, Sat & Sun 9am–noon & 2–4pm; Q50), located on the site of the former Universidad de San Carlos. The building's ornate Moorish-style arcades make it one of the finest architectural survivors in the city, and the collection inside is good, too: mostly dark and brooding religious art, sculpture, furniture and murals depicting life on the colonial university campus.

Casa Popenoe

Further down 5 Calle Oriente, at the corner with 1 Avenida Sur, is the **Casa Popenoe** (Mon–Sat 2–4pm; Q15), a restored seventeenth-century mansion that offers an interesting glimpse into the domestic life of the colonial elites. It was painstakingly refurbished in the 1930s by United Fruit Company scientist Dr Wilson Popenoe, who furnished the house with antiques – you can see the bread ovens, herb garden and pigeon loft, whose occupants would have provided the mansion's owners with their mail. There are also some interesting paintings, including portraits of Bishop Marroquín and a menacing-looking Pedro de Alvarado.

Church of San Francisco

South on 1 Avenida Sur from the Casa Popenoe is the colossal **Church of San Francisco** (daily 6am–6pm). One of the oldest churches in Antigua, dating from 1579, during the colonial period it served as a vast religious and cultural centre that included a school, a hospital, music rooms, a printing press and a monastery. All of this was lost, though, in the 1773 earthquake. Restoration of the chapel started in 1960 and today very little remains of what was once the original monument. However, the **ruins** of the monastery (daily 8am–5pm; Q5) are still visible, and among the city's most striking, including a large bell tower. The fallen arches, pillars and pleasant grassy verges make a good background for a picnic. Inside the church, meanwhile, is the tomb of **Hermano Pedro de Betancourt**, a Franciscan from the Canary Islands who founded the Hospital of Belén in Antigua, and is credited with powers of miraculous intervention. Pope John Paul II made him Central America's first saint in 2002 and his tomb is regularly visited by pilgrims.

Parque Unión

One block west and one block north of San Francisco is **Parque Unión**, flanked on each end by a church (both daily 8am–4.30pm). The one on the western side is **San Pedro**, dating from 1680, and the one to the east is **Santa Clara**, a former convent with a fine ornate facade. In colonial times the latter was a popular place for aristocratic ladies to take the veil – the hardships were not too extreme, and the nuns gained a reputation for their fine cooking. In front of Santa Clara is a large *pila* (washhouse) where women today gather to scrub, rinse and gossip.

Las Capuchinas

At the junction of 2 Calle Oriente and 2 Avenida Norte are the remains of **Las Capuchinas** (daily 9am–5pm; Q30), dating from 1726, once the largest and most beautiful of the city's convents. These ruins are among Antigua's best preserved, and yet least documented: the Capuchin nuns who lived here were not allowed any contact with the outside world, and vice versa. Food was passed to them by means of a turntable, and they could only speak to visitors through a grille. You should wander through the ruins – they are beautiful, with fountains, courtyards, massive pillars and a unique tower, or "retreat", which has eighteen tiny cells set into the walls on the top floor and a cellar that probably functioned as a meat storage room. The exterior of the tower is also interesting, ringed with small stone recesses representing the Stations of the Cross. The convent was damaged following the 1751 earthquake, and in 1773 the sisters left the premises. The building lay abandoned until 1813. Since 1972 it has been home to the National Council for the Protection of La Antigua Guatemala.

Santa Catalina and La Merced

A couple of blocks west of Las Capuchinas, spanning 5 Avenida Norte, the **arch of Santa Catalina** is all that remains of yet another convent, this one founded in 1609. The arch was built so that the nuns could walk between the two halves of the establishment without being exposed to the outside world. At the end of the street, just to the north, the church of **La Merced** boasts one of the most intricate facades in the entire city. Look closely and you'll see the outline of a corncob, a motif probably added by the original Maya labourers. The church is still in use, and the cloisters and gardens, including a monumental fountain, are open to the public (daily 8am–5pm; Q5).

VOLCÁN PACAYA

Volcán Pacaya, one of Guatemala's many cones, is a spectacular Strombolian volcano (characterized by low-level, intermittent explosions). Though technically closer to Guatemala City than Antigua, it's nonetheless more commonly reached from the latter – indeed, it is *the* trip to make in the area. Depending on Pacaya's activity level, you may be able to scale its slopes.

You can only visit the volcano with guided tours (prices start at Q50 for budget tours), which are offered daily (leaving at 2pm) by virtually all travel agents and tour operators in town. Tours entail an hour's climb up the volcano where you can, quite literally, poke at the lava with a stick (make sure you wear good shoes, as thin soles can melt). The views at sunset are breathtaking – remember to bring a torch, as it will be nearly dark when you walk down. The volcano sits inside Pacaya National Park, for which entry is an additional Q40. Note that sulphurous fumes and high winds can occasionally make the ascent impossible.

The budget tours described above can feel impersonal and rushed, as you're herded in a large group from packed minibus up the crater and back again. If you want to experience the volcano differently, contact the recommended tour operators (see opposite), who can organize bespoke trips.

Cerro de la Cruz

Northeast of Antigua, the **Cerro de la Cruz**, a hilltop with a giant cross, has commanding views of the city and Volcán Agua. It was something of a mugging hot spot for years but an increased police presence has meant it's now considered safe. Nevertheless it's wise to check the current situation in advance at the tourist office.

Arrival and information

By bus Antigua's second-class bus terminal is beside the market; the street opposite (4 C Pte) leads directly to the Parque Central. Shuttle buses will drop you off at your hotel.

Tourist information The Inguat office (Mon–Fri 8am–5pm, Sat & Sun 9am–5pm; ☎ 7832 5682, ✉ antigua@inguat.gob.gt) is presently at 2 C Ote 11, but should move back to its usual location on the south side of the Parque Central when renovations of the Palacio there are complete. The English-speaking staff are extremely helpful. Otherwise, check out the noticeboards in places including *Doña Luisa's* restaurant (see p.145) and the *Rainbow Reading Room* (see p.144) for everything from private language lessons to apartments for let.

Tour operators Maya Mountain Bike Tours, 1 Av Sur 15 (☎ 7832 3383, ✇ www.guatemalaventures .com), have a wide range of bike, hike and horseriding trips as well as bike rental; Old Town Outfitters, 6 C Pte 7 (☎ 7832 4171, ✇ www .adventureguatemala.com), run mountain-biking, rock-climbing, kayaking and hiking trips, and offer tent, sleeping bag and bike rental. Elizabeth Bell, 3 C Ote 28 (☎ 7832 2046, ✇ www.antiguatours .net), offers excellent twice-daily historical walking tours of Antigua (US$20).

Travel agents There are dozens of travel agents in Antigua, many of a low quality. Rainbow Travel Center, 7 Av Sur 8 (☎ 7832 4202, ✇ www .rainbowtravelcenter.com), is very efficient, and Viajes Tivoli, 4 C Ote 10 (☎ 7832 4274/4287, ✉ antigua@tivoli.com.gt), is a good all-rounder. A number of tourists have reported bad experiences with the following agents: Ruta Maya, Centroamérica and Universal.

City transport

By taxi Taxis wait on the east side of the cathedral, or you can call ☎ 7832 0479; a local journey is about Q25.

By tuk tuk Tuk tuks charge Q10 per trip.

Accommodation

There's a plentiful supply of excellent budget accommodation, including many good hostels, in Antigua. Be warned that rooms can get scarce (and prices increase) in July and August. During Semana Santa the whole town is fully booked, but you can usually find a room in a family home (locals with spare rooms approach travellers at the bus station).

Hostels

Black Cat Hostel 6 Av Nte 1A ☎ 7832 1229, ✇ www.blackcathostels.net. One of *the* key meeting points for young backpackers, this party-minded place is well set up for travellers on a roll. The dorms (some en-suite) are adequate, though not Swiss-clean, and there are colourful, cosy private rooms too. There's also a TV lounge, generous free breakfast, internet and wi-fi. Dorms Q60, doubles Q160

Casa Jacaranda 1 C Pte 37 ☎ 7832 5115, ✇ www.hostelcasajacaranda.com. Spread over a large plot, the roomy dorms, singles and doubles here are kept pretty tidy, some with a wardrobe. All bathrooms are shared, and there's a big garden at the rear, plus complimentary wi-fi and breakfast. Dorms Q50, doubles Q150

🎒 **Dionisio** 3 C Pte ☎ 5644 9486, ✇ www .hoteldionisioantigua.com. An excellent new option, the superb-value *Dionisio* offers spacious dorms and rooms with good mattresses and lockers in a quiet location. You'll find free wi-fi, a kitchen, friendly staff, a sunny terrace and a travel agency here too. Dorms Q45, doubles Q150

🎒 **Earth Lodge** ☎ 5664 0713, ✇ www .earthlodgeguatemala.com. High above Antigua in a remote, beautiful rural location, this Canadian/American-owned place offers volcano views, hiking trails, a lively communal atmosphere and fine home-cooked grub. Stay in a treehouse, dorm or cabin, or camp (Q20 per person). Getting here is tricky, so call for an inexpensive ride from Antigua. Dorms Q35, cabins Q150

🎒 **El Hostal** 1 Av Sur 8 ☎ 7832 0442, ✉ elhostal.antigua@gmail.com. A very well managed place, this hostel offers high-quality rooms and dorms that have space and style, all with lockers. The communal bathrooms (with superb hot-water showers) are spotless, and there's a great central courtyard for chilling. Rates include breakfast and it's right by one of the best bars in town: *Café No Sé*. Dorms Q75, doubles Q130

International Mochilero Guesthouse 1 C Pte 33 ☎ 7832 0520, ✇ www.internacionalmochilero.com. One of the first hostels in town, this place has cheap rates, especially for private rooms, as well as free wi-fi and a garden. Check out the old musical instruments in the hall, including a marimba. Dorms Q50, doubles Q135

Kafka 6 Av Nte 40 ☎5270 6865, ⓔkafkaantigua @gmail.com. Attractive, nicely designed place with neat little dorm rooms, all with solid wood beds and highland blankets, set off a slim patio with hammocks. Upstairs is a terrific open-air bar-restaurant with great views, popular happy hour and a sociable vibe. Q50

Onvisa 6 C Pte 40 ☎5909 0160, ⓔonvisatravel @hotmail.com. New hostel with very cheap, clean and fairly spacious dorms (most with three or four beds) set around a pretty patio. The private rooms, with antique floor tiles and cable TV, are great value too. A guests' kitchen and free internet completes the picture. Dorms Q40, doubles Q125

Umma Gumma Hostal 7 Av Nte 34 ☎7832 4413, ⓔummagumma@itelgua.com. It could do with a makeover, but this hostel still draws a few backpackers with its cheap rates, vaguely bohemian ambience, free internet and breakfast, kitchen and rooftop bar. Many rooms are dark, though upstairs rooms are brighter. Dorms Q40, doubles Q170

Yellow House 1 C Pte 24 ☎7832 6646, ⓔyellowhouseantigua@hotmail.com. The *Yellow House* boasts a lovely rustic-style roof terrace with hammocks, greenery and views. Rooms vary: the 3-bed dorms (Q60) are the best value, while the cabin-like upstairs rooms are lovely (no.10 has its own little private terrace). Rates include use of kitchen, internet and a good buffet breakfast. The hostel uses solar-powered hot water for its four bathrooms. Dorms Q50, doubles Q150

Hotels and guesthouses

La Casa de Don Ismael 3 C Pte 6 ☎7832 1932, ⓦwww.casadonismael.com. Cosy, long-running guesthouse on a quiet side-street that has real character, including a cute little garden. The seven rooms are kept neat and clean, communal bathrooms looked after well, and there's free wi-fi and breakfast. Q180

🏃 **Hotel Casa los Arcos** Callejón Camposeco (off 7 Av Nte) ☎7832 7813, ⓔcasa _losarcos@hotmail.com. With a Guatemalan family atmosphere, this guesthouse is excellent value. All eleven modern rooms (nine are en suite) in the compound are spotless, spacious and come with *típica* bedspreads and cable TV. It's a great deal for single travellers (rooms are Q100 per person) or couples who want some privacy. Q200

🏃 **Posada Juma Ocag** Alameda Santa Lucía Nte 13 ☎7832 3109, ⓦwww.posadajuma ocag.com. Representing exceptional value, this lovely little guesthouse has flashpacker written all over the neat, immaculately presented rooms decorated with local fabrics. The owners are very accommodating and security is good. Upstairs there's a little terrace, and you'll find laundry service and free wi-fi too. Q150

Eating

Antigua boasts a terrific array of cafés and restaurants, with most types of cuisine represented (though Asian cuisine can be disappointingly inauthentic). The only thing that seems hard to come by is authentic Guatemalan *comedor* food. Restaurants in Antigua stay open much later than in the rest of the country, making long (boozy) dinners possible.

Cafés

The Bagel Barn 5 C Pte 2. Does what it says on the tin. An intimate little place serving excellent bagels (from Q15) and other snacks. Free wi-fi, and films are also shown here twice daily.

Café Condesa West side of the Parque Central; enter through the Casa del Conde bookshop. Incredibly classy, if (just slightly) staid place, with a gorgeous cobbled patio, smart dining rooms and "proper" service. Great venue for a breakfast (from Q25) or evening meal, light lunch or simply a coffee.

Fernando's Kaffee 7 Av Nte 43 ⓦwww .fernandoskaffee.com. The very hospitable English-speaking Guatemalan owner here is a complete bean-ista who selects and roasts (on the premises) his own arabica coffee from small estates. He's also now turned his attention to gourmet chocolate. Breakfasts (from Q18), sandwiches (Q20), light lunches and wonderful juices, smoothies and cakes are also available.

La Fuente 4 C Ote 14. Attractive courtyard café with beautiful photographs and paintings of Guatemalan children available to buy. Great for a leisurely coffee and a snack.

🏃 **Rainbow Reading Room** 7 Av Sur 8 ☎7832 1919, ⓦwww.rainbowcafeantigua .com. Ever-popular courtyard café/restaurant that offers a tempting choice of imaginative salads, Mexican and vegetarian dishes. Prices have crept up recently but there's always a set lunch for Q32. Hosts live events (music, political and social lectures) most nights. Also home to one of Antigua's best travel agents and a good second-hand bookshop.

Saberíco 6 Av Sur 7. Fab deli/café/restaurant where can you munch in one of several dining rooms, or in the lovely walled garden at the rear, which has hammocks and plenty of shade. Menu-wise it's all about the pancakes, omelettes, pastas, salads and sandwiches, with most items Q30–50.

El Viejo Café 3 C & 6 Av Nte 12. A rustic dining room and pleasant little courtyard decorated with antique knick-knacks. Good coffee, and the baguettes and delicious croissants are baked fresh daily.

Y Tu Piña También 1 Av Sur 11. Antigua's hippest café is popular with a creative crowd who lap up the near-legendary blended fruit juices, filling wraps, baguettes and bagels, and tasty soups (Q26). Free wi-fi, and always an art or photography exhibition to take in on the walls.

Restaurants

La Canche 6 Av Nte 42. For a very local experience, chow down at one of the lino-topped tables inside this humble store-cum-*comedor*. Filling Guatemalan *comida típica* (Q12–18 a meal) is the order of the day – take your pick from the steaming pots. Tables are shared; if there's space someone will shout "*¡hay lugar!*"

Doña Luisa's 4 C Ote 12. The menu at this two-storey converted colonial mansion is pretty basic – sandwiches (from Q25), burgers (Q28) and salads – but the in-house bakery really is the best in town. Pastries, cakes and fresh bread can be purchased from the adjoining shop.

La Escudilla 4 Av Nte 4. Elegant courtyard restaurant offering a choice of breakfasts (try the "Kill Hangover" for Q30), Mexican and European dishes. The lunch deal (Q25) is a serious bargain given the colonial surrounds. Also home to *Riki's Bar* (see p.146).

Fridas 5 Av Nte 29. Upmarket Mexican restaurant festooned with 1950s Americana and Frida Kahlo memorabilia. Portions are very generous, with delicious tacos, flautas and enchiladas, though it's on the pricey side – budget Q80 a head.

Kafka 6 Av Nte 40. This casual rooftop place has a terrific terrace for alfresco dining, and the fire pit provides real ambience (when weather permits). It's slightly pricier than you'd expect (despite being above a hostel), though the delicious breakfasts (Q15–39), pastas (Q40), sandwiches (around Q40) and burgers (Q45) are filling and flavoursome.

Las Mañanitas 4 C Ote 28. Owned by a friendly Oaxacan couple, this excellent place is located on the edge of town, just past a petrol station. Cheap and highly authentic southern Mexican dishes, including some terrific *mole* and salsa sauces. You can snack on a few tacos, *tamales* or tostadas for around Q15, or get stuck into the mains (from Q30). Wine is available by the glass.

Pupusería El Sapo y La Rana Alameda Santa Lucía Nte 7. No frills at all, just a good honest *pupusería*, serving up chunky *pupusas* (Q25 with

Bistrot Cinq 4 C Ote 7 ☏7832 5510. There are plenty of upmarket restaurants in Antigua, but in many cases it's the furnishings and prices which are fancy, not the cooking. *Bistrot Cinq* delivers on every level, with highly accomplished, technically adept French cooking and sleek, modern decor. The menu is short and to the point, with classics (most around Q100) like *filet mignon au poivre* served with truffle and cheddar potatoes, fava beans and red wine sauce.

drink) as well as *churrascos* (Q28) and burgers. Vegetarians should go for *yuca* with salad.

Travel Menu 6 C Pte 14. This candlelit Dutch-owned place has real atmosphere and very fair prices; it makes a great escape from the backpacker crowds. The menu is geared to both veggies and *carne*-lovers: try a *plato típico* (Q32) or nachos with guacamole (Q20).

Drinking and nightlife

There are bars spread throughout Antigua. Two of the main areas are around the arch on 5 Avenida Norte and over on 1 Avenida Sur. The city's club scene is fairly small but lively, even drawing a crowd from Guatemala City. All places (including clubs) officially close at 1am. "After hours" parties (technically illegal), featuring local and visiting DJs, are held most weekends in private houses, publicized by flyers and word of mouth.

Bars

Café No Sé 1 Av Sur 11C. This near-legendary place has grown from a classic hard-drinking dive bar into the liveliest joint in town. Attracts a good mix of characters – Guatemalan artists, gringo wasters, travellers and boozy expats – plus the odd stray dog. There's live acoustic music virtually nightly, comfort food and a (semi-) secret mescal bar: order the house brand, Ilegal.

La Chimenea 7 Av Nte & 2 C Pte. This long-running bar has recently smartened up its act and now serves food too. It's a good bet for happy hour when there are cocktail specials. Closed Sun.

Kafka 6 Av Nte 40. The roof terrace here is a superb spot for a relaxed drink, with drinks specials (noon–7pm) including Gallo, vodka, wine and Cuba libres for Q10–12. It's a great spot at sundown.

Mono Loco 2 Av Nte 6B. A typical gringo sports bar/Tex-Mex place, which is always packed.

Ocelot 4 Av Nte 3. Tired of grungy backpacker places? Try this very stylish new bar, with classy colonial interior and a superb cocktail list (around Q30). There's patio seating out back for smokers.

Red's 1 C Pte 3. *The* place to watch English football and enjoy pub grub (Q40–60) like shepherd's pie or a good old curry. Pool table, darts and a big patio out back.

Reilly's 6 Av Nte 2. Now in new (larger) premises, this ever-popular Irish bar is still packing 'em in with its gregarious vibe, friendly staff and Sunday pub quiz.

Riki's Bar 4 Av Nte 4, inside *La Escudilla*. Intimate bar with a wildly popular and inexpensive happy hour and an eclectic jazz and lounge music policy.

Sky Café 1 Av Nte. The sunset views are unmatched here, with the city and its volcanic neighbours revealed to all. Not quite as popular as it once was, but still has a sociable vibe.

Clubs

La Casbah 5 Av Nte 30. The only real club in town, and a pretty decent one, with large, airy premises and views over the floodlit ruins of a Baroque church. Attracts a well-heeled crowd with DJs spinning Latin house, reggaeton and salsa via a powerful sound system. Cover Q30.

La Sin Ventura 5 Av Sur. More of a disco than a club. A bit cheesy around the edges, but popular with the salsa crowd and visitors from the capital.

Entertainment

Art galleries The upmarket hotel *Panza Verde*, 5 Av Sur 19 (@www.panzaverde.com), always has a quality art exhibition. La Antigua Galería de Arte, 4 C Ote 15 (T 7832 2124, @www.artintheamericas .com), is also recommended.

Cinemas The following places show Western and Latin American films daily: *The Bagel Barn* (see p.144); *La Sin Ventura* (see above); Cooperación Española, 6 Av Nte (T 7832 1276, @www.aecid-cf .org.gt); and El Sitio (see below), which is good for art-house movies. Weekly listings are posted on noticeboards all over town.

Cultural institutes @www.antiguacultural .com is a useful resource. El Sitio, 5 C Pte 15 (T 7832 3037, @www.elsitiocultural.org), has an active theatre, art gallery, café and regularly hosts exhibitions and concerts. Cooperación Española (see above) promotes all manner of cultural events: films, exhibitions, lectures and workshops, and its library is a terrific resource. Mosaico Cultural, 3 C Ote 28 (T 7820 1220,

@www.mosaicocultural.com), organizes events including concerts and painting exhibitions, often in the Parque, ruined churches or at the *Hotel Casa Santo Domingo*, 3 C Ote 28.

Shopping

Books Available at Casa del Conde and Un Poco de Todo, both on the west side of the plaza; Librería Pensativo, 5 Av Nte 29; Hamley and White, 4 C Ote 12. For secondhand titles check out Dyslexia Books, 1 Av Sur 11, and the *Rainbow Reading Room*, 7 Av Sur 8.

Crafts Nim Pot, 5 Av Nte 29 (T 7832 2681, @www.nimpot.com), is an astounding place, more of a museum than a store. This warehouse-sized place is stuffed with all manner of Guatemalan crafts: rare and everyday huipils and weavings from every corner of the nation, masks, ceremonial outfits, as well as books, souvenirs and even Maximón mannequins.

Markets The main mercado (daily 7am–5.30pm) by the bus terminal is a fascinating place. Browse the Latino CDs and Hollywood DVDs and shop for unusual tropical fruit. Just south of here, the Mercado de Artesanías is a tad touristy, so bargain hard. There's another handicraft market next to the El Carmen church on 3 Av Nte.

Supermarkets La Bodegona, 4 C Pte and Calzada Santa Lucía; La Despensa, Calzada Santa Lucía between 4 and 5 C.

Directory

Bike rental Maya Mountain Bike Tours and Old Town Outfitters (see p.143) rent mountain bikes from around Q125 a day. La Ceiba, 6 C Pte 6 (T 7832 4168, @www.ceibarent.com), rents out scooters for US$44/day and 250cc trail bikes for US$55/day.

Car rental La Ceiba (see above) offers small cars (like a Daihatsu Charade) for Q230/day, Q1350/week; 4WDs start at Q300/day, Q2160/week.

Exchange Banco Industrial, on 4 C Pte 14 just south of the plaza, is one of the biggest banks in town and has an ATM.

Health 24hr emergency service at the Hospital Privado Hermano Pedro (T 7832 1190). Dr Marco Antonio Bocaleti has a surgery on 3 Av Nte 1 (T 7832 4835) and speaks English and German. Ivory Pharmacy is at 6 Av Sur 11 (daily 7am–10pm; T 7832 5394).

Internet Dozens of internet cafés; rates are Q4–8 an hour. Funky Monkey, 5 Av Sur 6, is open daily till 12.30am and has quick connections, including Skype and netcalls.

Laundry Lavandería Detalles, 6 Av Nte 3B. A pound of washing costs Q5.

Police The headquarters are outside town. If you're a victim of a crime in Antigua, contact English-speaking Asistur, Rancho Nimajay, 6 C Pte Final (☎5978 3586), who will help you deal with the police and file a report.

Post office Alameda de Santa Lucía, opposite the bus terminal (Mon–Fri 8am–6pm).

Telephones You can netcall on good lines at Funky Monkey (see "Internet") for Q1/min to North America and Q3 to Europe, Australia, New Zealand and the rest of the world. Telgua, 5 Av Sur, is expensive and you'll have to queue.

Moving on

Few buses originate in Antigua. Shuttle buses provide convenient daily connections to Chichicastenango, Cobán, Monterrico, Panajachel, San Marcos La Laguna, San Pedro La Laguna and even San Cristóbal de Las Casas in Mexico. Promotional shuttle-bus deals are often available in Antigua offering a cheap ride (Q80) to *El Retiro* in Lanquín that includes a free night in a dorm there; these deals can be booked at many travel agents and hostels in town.

By bus to: Chimaltenango (every 30min 6am–6pm; 45min); Guatemala City (every 15min 5.30am–7pm; 1hr). For the following destinations you need to change in Chimaltenango: Chichicastenango, Nebaj, Panajachel, Quetzaltenango, Huehuetenango.

AROUND ANTIGUA

The countryside **around Antigua** is extremely beautiful. The valley is dotted with small villages, ranging from the *ladino* coffee centre of Jocotenango to the *indígena* village of Santa María de Jesús. For the more adventurous, Agua and Acatenango volcanoes offer strenuous but superb hiking, best done through a specialist agency (see p.143). Northwest of Antigua is **Santiago Sacatepéquez**, renowned for its annual Festival of the Day of the Dead, when beautiful, intricately decorated kites – some with a diameter of up to seven metres – soar through the skies. Further west are the ruins of **Iximché**, the "Place of the Maize Tree", where you can visit what remains of a pre-Columbian archeological site. All of these sites (except the latter) are less than an hour from Antigua.

Santa María de Jesús and Volcán Agua

Heading south from Antigua, a good paved road snakes through the coffee bushes and past the village of San Juan

---

LANGUAGE SCHOOLS IN ANTIGUA

Antigua is an extremely popular place to attend language school. Listed here are only a few of the many schools offering Spanish courses.

APPE 1 C Ote 15 ☎7882 4284, ⊛www.appeschool.com.

Centro Lingüístico Internacional Spanish School Av del Espíritu Santo 6 ☎7832 1039, ⊛www.spanishcontact.com.

Centro Lingüístico Maya 5 C Pte 20 ☎7832 0656, ⊛www.clmaya.com.

Christian Spanish Academy 6 Av Nte 15 ☎7832 3922, ⊛www.learncsa.com.

Guate Linda Language Center 7 Av Norte 76 ☎4360 5238, ⊛www.guatelinda center.com.

Instituto Antigüeño de Español 1 C Pte 10 ☎7832 7241, ⊛www.spanishacademy antiguena.com.

Ixchel Spanish School 7 C Pte 15 ☎7832 0364, ⊛www.ixchelschool.com.

Ixquic 7 Av Nte 74 ☎7832 2402, ⊛www.ixquic.edu.gt.

Probigua 6 Av Nte 41B ☎7832 2998, ⊛www.probigua.org.

San José El Viejo 5 Av Sur 34 ☎7832 3028, ⊛www.sanjoseelviejo.com.

Spanish Academy Sevilla 1 Av Sur 17 C ☎7832 5101, ⊛www.sevillantigua.com.

Tecún Umán Spanish School 6 C Pte 34A ☎7832 2792, ⊛www.tecunuman .centramerica.com.

Zamora Academia 9 C Pte 7 ☎7832 7670, ⊛www.learnspanish-guatemala.com.

del Obispo before arriving in **Santa María de Jesús**. Perched on the shoulder of **Volcán Agua**, the village is some 500m above the city, with brilliant views over the Panchoy valley and east towards smoking Volcán Pacaya. Though the women wear beautiful purple *huipiles*, the village itself is of minimal interest – most people come through here on their way up Agua, the easiest and most popular of Guatemala's major cones to climb.

The **trail** starts right in town: head straight across the plaza, between the two ageing pillars, and up the street opposite the church doors. Turn right just before the end, then continue past the cemetery and out of the village. From here it's a fairly simple climb on a decent path. The ascent takes around six hours, and the peak, at 3766m, is always cold at night. There is shelter (though not always room) close to the summit. If you're not up to the hike, you can rent horses at Ravenscroft Stables, 2 Av Sur 3, in the village of San Juan del Obispo (☎7830 6669). **Buses** run from Antigua to Santa María every 30 minutes or so from 6am to 6pm, and the trip takes thirty minutes.

Jocotenango

Despite being rather unattractive, the suburb of **Jocotenango**, just 3km north of Antigua, does boast a couple of interesting sights, both of which are grouped in the **Centro La Azotea** cultural centre (ⓦwww.centroazotea.com, Mon–Fri 9am–4pm, Sat 8.30am–2pm; Q50, students Q25, including tour in English). **Casa K'ojom**, which forms one half of the centre, is a purpose-built museum dedicated to Maya culture, especially music. Displays clearly present the history of indigenous musical traditions, beginning with its pre-Columbian origins and moving through sixteenth-century Spanish and African influences – which brought the marimba, bugles and drums – to today. Other rooms are dedicated to the village weavings of the Sacatepéquez department and the cult of Maximón (see opposite). Next door, the 34-hectare **Museo de Café** plantation dates from 1883, and offers the chance to look around a working organic coffee farm. All the technicalities of husking, sieving and roasting are explained, and you can sample a cup of the home-grown brew after the tour. A free hourly **shuttle bus** connects the Parque Central in Antigua with the centre.

San Andrés Itzapa

Past Jocotenango, the Antigua–Chimaltenango road ascends the Panchoy valley, past small farming villages, before a side road branches off to **San Andrés Itzapa**. San Andrés is known as the home of the cult of **San Simón** (or Maximón), the "evil saint" – a kind of combination of Judas Iscariot and Pedro de Alvarado – who is housed in his own pagan chapel (see box opposite).

There are direct **buses** from the Antigua terminal to San Andrés every two hours. Alternatively, catch a bus to Chimaltenango (every 30min) and ask to be dropped off at the entrance to the town.

Santiago Sacatepéquez

Santiago Sacatepéquez, almost directly east of Guatemala City on the Interamericana Highway, is renowned for its

---

CRIME AROUND ANTIGUA

Visitors to the areas around Antigua should be aware that crime against tourists – including violent robbery and rape – is not common but does occur. Keep informed by taking local advice, and try to avoid walking alone at night, or to isolated spots during the day. Asistur (see p.124) will accompany you free of charge, or even give you a ride to many sites.

THE CULT OF MAXIMÓN

Despite being just 18km from Antigua, few tourists visit the shrine of the "evil saint" of San Simón (or Maximón), and you may feel more welcome here than at his other places of abode, which include Zunil (see p.179) and Santiago Atitlán (see p.155). To reach the saint's "house" ("Casa de San Simón") – which is only open from sunrise to sunset – head for the central plaza, turn right when you reach the church, walk two blocks, then up a little hill, where you should spot street vendors selling charms, incense and candles.

Once you've tracked down the shrine, you'll find that Maximón lives in a fairly strange world, his image surrounded by drunken men, cigar-smoking women and hundreds of burning candles, each symbolizing a request. You may be offered a *limpia*, or soul cleansing, which, for a small fee, involves being beaten by one of the resident women with a bushel of herbs. A bottle of *aguardiente* is also demolished: some is offered to San Simón, some of it you drink yourself and the rest is consumed by the attendant, who may spray you with alcohol (from her mouth) for your sins.

fiesta honouring the **Day of the Dead** (Nov 1). On this day, colourful, massive paper kites with bamboo frames – some take months to create – are flown in the town's cemetery, symbolizing the release of the souls of the dead from agony. Teams of young men struggle to get the kites aloft while the crowd looks on with bated breath, rushing for cover if a kite comes crashing to the ground. At other times of the year, there's little to see or do here – if you find yourself passing through on a Tuesday or a Sunday you might visit the town market, but that's about it.

To reach Santiago Sacatepéquez, catch a **bus** to San Lucas Sacatepéquez (buses running between Antigua and Guatemala City pass through), and then change there – many buses shuttle back and forth between the two.

Chimaltenango

Founded by Pedro de Portocarrero in 1526 on the site of the Kaqchikel Maya centre of Bokoh, **Chimaltenango** looks to have made few strides in civic development since then. Frankly, it's a traffic-plagued hellhole on the Carretera Interamericana, the grossly polluted roadside littered with mechanics' workshops and sleazy bars. However, it's also a transport hub: buses from Chimaltenango run to all points along the Interamericana. Frequent **buses** arrive in town from both Guatemala City and Antigua; you can change here for buses to destinations in the highlands. Services to Antigua leave every fifteen minutes between 6am and 7pm from the turn-off on the highway.

Iximché

The Maya site of **Iximché** (daily 8am–5pm; Q50) sits on a beautiful exposed hillside about 5km south of the small town of **Tecpán**, an hour and a half east of Guatemala City. These are the ruins of the pre-Conquest capital of the Kaqchikel Maya, who allied themselves with the conquistadors in the early days of the Conquest. Time and weather have taken their toll, though, and the majority of the buildings – which once housed over ten thousand people – have disappeared, and only a few low pyramids, plazas and ball courts are left. Nevertheless, the site – protected on three sides by steep slopes and surrounded by pine forests – is quite peaceful; the grassy plazas make excellent picnic spots and you may have the place to yourself during the week. George W. Bush stopped here in 2007 on a visit to Guatemala to take in a Maya ceremony, though not all the locals were impressed; after he'd left, Maya shamen performed a cleansing ritual to rid the site of what they called "bad energy". The ruins are still used as a Maya worship site: ceremonies, sacrifices and offerings take place down a small trail behind the final plaza.

Take any **bus** travelling along the Carretera Interamericana between Chimaltenango and Los Encuentros and ask to be dropped at Tecpán. Regular buses shuttle back and forth from Tecpán's plaza to the ruins. Plan to be back on the Carretera Interamericana before 6pm to be sure of a bus. Tecpán itself is of no interest, but there are a number of restaurants and guesthouses, if you get stuck.

Lago de Atitlán

Lago de Atitlán, one of the most visited destinations in Guatemala's western highlands, was described by Aldous Huxley in 1934 as one of the most beautiful lakes in the world – and it really is exceptionally scenic. For travellers, Atitlán is of interest both for its majestic setting – it's hemmed

CRIME AROUND LAGO DE ATITLÁN

Though crime against tourists is rare, hikers have been sporadically attacked on paths around Lago de Atitlán and on the trails that climb the volcanoes. Take precautions: hire a local guide or walk in a large group. In the more remote areas, where foreigners are a much rarer sight, attacks are extremely uncommon.

in by three volcanoes and steep hills – and for its cultural appeal – the lake's shores are dotted with thirteen diverse yet traditional Maya settlements. With the exception of cosmopolitan **Panajachel** and **San Pedro La Laguna**, most of the villages are subsistence farming communities, and you can hike or take a boat between them; highlights include visits to **Santiago Atitlán**, where Maya men still wear traditional dress, and **Santa Cruz** and **San Marcos**, both of which give access to excellent hiking.

PANAJACHEL

Not too long ago **PANAJACHEL**, known locally as "Pana", was a quiet little village of Kaqchikel Maya, whose

GETTING AROUND LAGO DE ATITLÁN

There's no one road that circumnavigates Atitlán. To explore the lake it's usually easiest to catch a boat – mainly small *lanchas* – which connect the villages on the shore at regular intervals, generally every thirty minutes or so. Some sections of the shore are connected by road; it's easiest to travel this way from Panajachel to Santa Catarina Palopó and San Antonio Palopó, and also between San Pedro and San Marcos. **Panajachel** serves as a sort of hub for the lake, with two piers. The pier at the end of Calle del Embarcadero has departures for all villages on the north side of the lake: Santa Cruz (about 15min), Jaibalito (20min), Tzununá (30min) and San Marcos (40min). Direct (15min) and local (1hr) boats also depart from here for San Pedro, from where you can easily get to San Juan and San Pablo. The second pier, at the end of Calle Rancho Grande, is for Santiago Atitlán (1hr by scheduled ferries three times daily, or 20min by unscheduled *lancha*). The last boats on all these routes leave around 7pm. A semi-official fare system operates: tourists pay Q10 for a short trip, Q20 for a longer journey (locals pay less). Tours of the lake (Q100), visiting San Pedro, Santiago Atitlán, Santa Catarina, Panajachel and San Antonio Palopó, can be booked with travel agents in nearly every town; all leave around 9am and return by 4pm from the pier at Calle Rancho Grande.

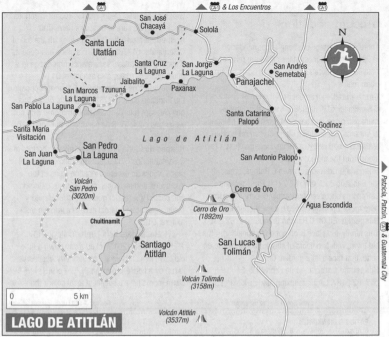

ancestors settled here centuries ago. These days, it's an established resort town, highly popular with foreigners and holidaying Guatemalans. Yet somehow Panajachel has retained a traditional feel in spite of its cosmopolitan nature: the river delta behind the town continues to be farmed, and the bustling Sunday market remains oblivious to the tourists who come in droves. For travellers, the town is something of an inevitable destination – with good travel connections and a lovely setting, it makes a comfortable base for exploring the lake. No one ever owns up to actually liking Panajachel, but most people stay for a while.

What to see and do

There are two main daytime activities in Pana: **shopping** and simply **hanging out**, enjoying the town's lakeside location. Weaving from all over Guatemala is sold here, mainly on Calle Santander. There is also a market at the top of Calle Principal, but it mainly deals with local produce. While the water looks inviting, it's probably best to swim elsewhere, as the lake is not very clean close to town. You could rent a kayak (available on the lakeshore between the piers) for a few hours – mornings are usually much calmer.

Arrival and information

By boat See box opposite.

By bus Buses drop you by the Banco Agromercantíl, at the top of the main drag, Calle Santander, which runs down to the lakeshore. Straight ahead, up Calle Principal, is the old village.

Tourist information The tourist office, on C Santander (daily 9am–5pm; ☎7762 1106), has English-speaking staff, some hotel information and boat and bus schedules.

Travel agents Adrenalina Tours, C Santander (☎7762 6236, ✆www.adrenalinatours.com), or Servicios Turísticos Atitlán, C Santander near C 14 de Febrero (☎7762 2075, ✉turisticosatitlan @yahoo.com).

Accommodation

There's no shortage of cheap accommodation in Pana, although most places take the form of *hospedajes* or hotels as opposed to hostels with dorm rooms.

Casa Linda Down an alley off the top of C Santander ☏7762 0386. A well-run, family-managed place that has neat rooms, with balcony or veranda, set around a stunning central garden. It's secure and enjoys a tranquil location just a few steps from the main drag. Q110

Hospedaje Contemporáneo C Ramos, opposite the Santiago dock ☏7762 2214. The spacious bathrooms and clean but simply decorated rooms here make *Contemporáneo* a decent option. Q195

Hospedaje Eli Off C Rancho Grande ☏7762 2466. This family-run place is an option to consider in the old town, with two floors of simple rooms, some en suite, that face a little garden. Q80

Hospedaje García C 14 de Febrero 2–24 ☏7762 2187. Large, rambling, garish-looking place with tons of basic, clean, spartan rooms in various blocks. There's sure to be space here. Q90

Hospedaje Montúfar Down an alley off the top of C Santander ☏7762 0406. This place has decent, if slightly featureless, secure accommodation in a quiet location. Triples also available. Q110

Hospedaje Nuevo Amanecer C Ramos, opposite the Santiago dock ☏7762 0636. This *hospedaje* has pleasant rooms, sparkling bathrooms with hot water and cable TV. Safe parking in the courtyard too. Q200

Hospedaje El Viajero Down an alley at bottom of C Santander ☏7762 0128. This relaxed, tranquil place enjoys an excellent location close to the lakeshore, and all rooms have en-suite bathroom and cable TV. A (basic) guests' kitchen, laundry facilities and free internet access complete the picture. Q125

Hospedaje Villa Lupita Callejón El Tino ☏7762 1201. Tucked away down a little old town lane, this excellent, very tidy *hospedaje* is run by a house-proud family. The pretty, very clean rooms have a splash of local colour thanks to

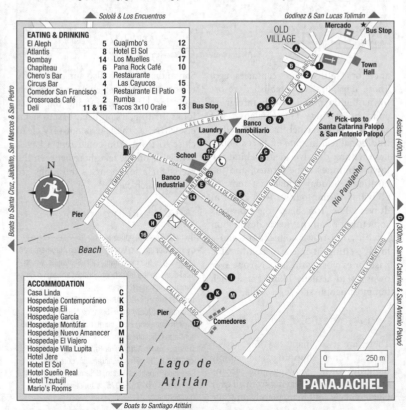

EATING & DRINKING

El Aleph	5	Guajimbo's	12
Atlantis	8	Hotel El Sol	G
Bombay	14	Los Muelles	17
Chapiteau	6	Pana Rock Café	10
Chero's Bar	3	Restaurante	
Circus Bar	4	Las Cayucos	15
Comedor San Francisco	1	Restaurante El Patio	9
Crossroads Café	2	Rumba	7
Deli	11 & 16	Tacos 3x10 Orale	13

ACCOMMODATION

Casa Linda	C
Hospedaje Contemporáneo	K
Hospedaje Eli	B
Hospedaje García	F
Hospedaje Montúfar	D
Hospedaje Nuevo Amanecer	M
Hospedaje El Viajero	H
Hospedaje Villa Lupita	A
Hotel Jere	J
Hotel El Sol	G
Hotel Sueño Real	L
Hotel Tzutujil	I
Mario's Rooms	E

Sololá & Los Encuentros

Godínez & San Lucas Tolimán

OLD VILLAGE

Mercado

Bus Stop

Town Hall

Bus Stop

Pick-ups to Santa Catarina Palopó & San Antonio Palopó

Banco Inmobiliario

Laundry

School

Banco Industrial

Asistur (400m)

G (300m), Santa Catarina & San Antonio Palopó

Pier

Beach

Pier

Comedores

Lago de Atitlán

0   250 m

PANAJACHEL

CALLE DE LOS ÁRBOLES

CALLE PRINCIPAL

CALLE REAL

CALLE EL CHALI

CALLE DEL EMBARCADERO

CALLE SANTANDER

CALLE 14 DE FEBRERO

CALLE RANCHO GRANDE

AVENIDA EL FRUTAL

Río Panajachel

CALLE 15 DE FEBRERO

CALLE LONDRES

CALLE BUENAS NUEVAS

CALLE DEL LAGO

CALLE DEL RIO

CALLE LOS SAPORES

CALLE DEL CEMENTERIO

N

Boats to Santiago Atitlán

the highland rugs and blankets; some have private bathrooms. There's parking and free water and coffee too. Q90

Hotel Jere C Rancho Grande ☎7762 2781, ⓦwww.hoteljere.com. The owners have made an effort to brighten up the clean, spacious rooms here with textiles, fabrics and photographs. It's towards the top of the budget range; all rooms are en suite. Q110

Hotel El Sol Ctra Santa Catarina Palopó ☎7762 6090. A great new Japanese-owned option, this place has super-clean digs: an eight-person dorm with lockers plus four immaculate rooms. There's delicious Japanese food available and the bathrooms have reliable hot showers. The only slight drawback is the location, 1km from the centre on the other side of the river. Dorms Q50, doubles Q200

Hotel Sueño Real C Ramos, opposite the Santiago dock ☎7762 0608. This hospitable Maya-owned place has beautifully decorated, immaculate rooms, most with private bathroom and some with lake views and private terrace. Q170

Hotel Tzutujil In a little alley off C Rancho Grande ☎7762 0102. Clean, simple rooms with cable TV and free drinking water. Q90

Mario's Rooms C Santander ☎7762 1313. This place maintains high standards and the accommodation has character, with attractive if smallish rooms (some with private bathroom) overlooking a slim, sunny courtyard. There's free wi-fi, breakfast and drinking water. Staff are very accommodating. Q120

Eating

Panajachel has an abundance of restaurants, most of them on Calle Santander, all catering to the cosmopolitan tastes of its visitors. For really cheap, authentic Guatemalan food, head to the *comedores* close to the market, while there are good local fish restaurants around the Santiago dock.

Bombay Halfway along C Santander. Interesting vegetarian options which, despite the name, have little to do with India, instead including a variety of international dishes such as Indonesian *gado-gado*, fried rice, falafel, lasagne (Q61) and organic coffee.

Chero's Bar At the beginning of C de los Árboles. Simple *pupusería* where the Salvador-style healthy snacks are made right in front of you. A good feed is around Q20.

Comedor San Francisco C del Campanario, Old Town. Come to this good, honest *comedor* for a filling Guatemalan lunch. Dishes might include *caldo de pollo* or *chuleta a la plancha*; all are priced at Q15–20 and include rice, salad and a drink.

Crossroads Café C del Campanario 0–27. Coffee fans look no further: this café is in a class of its own. The owner imports beans from as far away as Africa, roasts them on the premises and blends them with local varieties for the perfect cup. Herbal teas, real hot chocolate and freshly baked pastries are also available. Closed Sun, Mon & 1–3pm.

Deli Bottom of C Santander. The best café-restaurant in Pana by some distance. Come here for fresh, flavoursome and inventive salads, veggie dishes like falafel, huge sandwiches (made from home-made bread), chunky hand-cut fried potatoes and filling burgers. The garden location is a delight: you can eat your meal surrounded by fluttering butterflies and hovering hummingbirds. There's a second branch halfway up C Santander with the same menu.

Guajimbo's Halfway up C Santander. Bona fide South American-style *churrasco* restaurant, serving up huge portions of barbecued meat, along with live music in the evenings.

Hotel El Sol Ctra Santa Catarina Palopó. Need your fix of Asian flavours? The restaurant at this Japanese-run hotel serves authentic, delicious miso soup, soba and ramen, sushi and tempura for between Q40 and Q00 a meal. You can even sip some sake with your meal.

Los Muelles By the Santiago pier. Right above the water, with stunning views, this is one of the best of several lakeside choices. The menu features lake fish (including *mojarra*) and seafood. Reckon on paying Q50–80 a head unless you go for the lunchtime special.

Restaurante Las Cayucos Bottom end of C Santander. This large, Maya-owned upper-level restaurant has a good perspective over the main drag and scores highly for inexpensive local grub. You'll find very cheap breakfast deals (from Q15), lunches (Q25) and welcoming staff.

Restaurante El Patio Towards the top of C Santander. A lovely front patio, set just off the street, is the main appeal here, from where you can relax and watch Pana life go by. The menu is pretty standard Guatemalan fodder, but portions are massive and the *licuados* (shakes) are cheap (Q10).

Tacos 3x10 Orale Halfway up C Santander. This taco place, painted in bright yellow, offers three tacos for Q10 or fajitas for Q22.

Drinking and nightlife

Pana's mini Zona Viva (situated around the southern end of Calle de los Árboles) buzzes on weekend nights. Many places have happy hours, and either live music or a DJ.

Bars

Atlantis At the beginning of C Principal. Candlelit place with a number of Elvis posters and old-school ads decorating the walls. Also serves breakfast, lunch and dinner. Live music Fri & Sat evenings.

Circus Bar C de los Árboles. Highly atmospheric bar-restaurant decorated with circus memorabilia and posters, and the wooden bar is the perfect spot for a margarita. Good pizzas (from Q50) and live music (jazz, salsa, flamenco, bolero, *trova*) every day at 7.30pm. There's wi-fi too.

Pana Rock Café Towards the top of C Santander. A kind of *Hard Rock Café* theme bar with "Pana Rock Café" T-shirts for sale and an old American school bus converted into a sitting area with tables. It's a popular place to watch sports games, and there are numerous drinks specials.

Clubs

El Aleph Northern end of C Santander. Hosts some lively dancefloor action on weekends, with reggae, reggaeton and Latin sounds. Live acts some nights.

Chapiteau At the southern end of C de los Árboles. This club is also known for its reggaeton and occasional live music.

Rumba On C Principal. Flash disco where a young local crowd gathers to dance to Latin chart sounds.

Entertainment

Billiards The Billares de León pool hall is on C Principal.

Cinema The best place to watch a movie is at *Solomon's Porch*, C Principal & C de los Árboles. Take your pick from hundreds of DVDs, and book the big screen while you munch on some grub. Q18 per person.

Directory

Bike rental Emanuel, C 14 de Febrero, has mountain bikes for US$8/day and dirt motorbikes for US$32.

Books Librería Libros del Lago, C Santander 9, near the post office, has a good selection of books on Maya culture, Central American society and politics, maps and guidebooks. Bus Stop Bookshop, C Principal 00–99, has 4000 used titles; Get Guated Out, C de los Árboles, has some decent secondhand English titles.

Exchange Banco Industrial, C Santander (Mon–Fri 9am–6pm, Sat 9am–1pm), has an ATM, and there's a 5B ATM at the north end of this road too.

Health Dr Edgar Barreno speaks good English; his surgery is down the first street that branches to the right heading north off C de los Árboles

(☎7762 1008). There's a pharmacy, Farmacia La Unión, on C Santander.

Internet You'll find lots of internet cafés in Pana, including Mayanet, midway along C Santander. Rates are around Q6–8/hr.

Language schools Courses are cheaper in San Pedro, but these two schools are professional: Escuela Jabel Tinamit, Callejon las Armonias (☎7762 6056, ⊛www.jabeltinamit.com), and Jardín de América, off C El Chali (☎7762 2637, ⊛www.jardindeamerica.com).

Laundry Lavandería Santander, C Santander opposite *Pana Rock* (Mon–Sat 7am–8pm), charges Q5 for a pound of washing, drying and folding.

Police For emergencies, first contact Asistur, Av El Tzalá (☎5874 9450), who will help you deal with the police.

Post office C Santander & 15 de Febrero, or try Get Guated Out, C de los Árboles (☎7762 0595), for bigger shipments.

Telephones Get Guated Out (see "Post office") charges Q1/min for webcalls to all landlines worldwide and Q3.50 to all mobiles. Otherwise, the internet cafés on C Santander offer competitive international rates.

Moving on

By boat See box, p.150, for information on boat transport around Lago de Atitlán, including connections from Panajachel.

By bus The main bus stop is close to where Calle Santander and Calle Real meet. There are regular buses to Santa Cruz del Quiché via Chichicastenango (1hr 30min), Guatemala City (3hr 30min) and Quetzaltenango (2hr 30min). If there are no direct buses to your destination, catch a bus to Los Encuentros and change there. Shuttle buses serve most destinations, including Antigua, Guatemala City, Quetzaltenango and Chichicastenango (on market days), and can be organized with all travel agents.

AROUND PANAJACHEL

It's well worth taking the time to explore the area around Pana, the best connected of the lake towns. The landscape surrounding the different villages is so diverse that if you take the time to visit more than one or two it's easy to forget they all look over the same lake.

Sololá

Perched on a natural balcony overlooking Lago de Atitlán, **SOLOLÁ** is a fascinating settlement, largely ignored by the majority of travellers. It is probably the largest Maya town in the country, with the vast majority of the people still wearing traditional costume – the women covered in striped red cloth and the men in their outlandish "space cowboy" shirts, woollen aprons and wildly embroidered trousers. Although the town itself is nothing much to look at, its Friday **market** is one of Central America's finest, drawing traders from all over the highlands, as well as thousands of local Maya. There's also another, smaller market on Tuesdays. Another interesting time to visit Sololá is on Sunday, when the *cofrades*, the elders of the Maya religious hierarchy, parade through the streets in ceremonial costume to attend mid-morning Mass.

To **get to** Sololá, take a bus from Panajachel (every 30min 5am–7pm).

SANTIAGO ATITLÁN

SANTIAGO ATITLÁN, a microcosm of Guatemala's past, sits sheltered on the side of an inlet on the opposite side of the lake from Panajachel. The largest of the lakeside villages, it's one of the last bastions of traditional life here, serving as the main centre for the Tz'utujil-speaking Maya. Though during the day the town is a fairly commercial place, by mid-afternoon, when the boats have left, the village is much quieter and becomes a lot friendlier and more accessible. It's worth taking a few hours to wander around town – and if you want to get away from the foreign crowds that pervade other parts of the lake, consider staying for a night or two.

What to see and do

There's not much to do in Santiago other than stroll around and soak up the atmosphere. During the day the town's main street, which runs from the dock to the plaza, is lined with weaving shops and souvenir stands. **Market** day is Friday, with a smaller event on Sunday.

The one museum in town, the **Museo Cojolya** (Mon–Fri 9am–4pm, Sat 9am–1pm; free; ⓦwww.cojolya.org), about 100m up the main drag from the dock on the left, also takes weaving as its subject. Inside you'll find excellent displays about the tradition of backstrap weaving in Santiago. At 11am and 1pm guided tours (a donation is asked for) depart the museum to visit the homes of local weavers; the tours are conducted in English and Spanish.

The old whitewashed Baroque Catholic **church**, which dates from 1571, is an essential visit. The huge central altarpiece culminates in the shape of a mountain peak and a cross, which symbolizes the Maya world tree. On the right as you enter, there's a stone memorial commemorating **Father Stanley Rother**, who translated the New Testament into the Tz'utujil language and died here in 1981, defending his parishioners against the military and death squads.

Folk Catholicism plays an important role in the life of Santiago – the town is one of the few places where Maya still

---

TRADITIONAL DRESS IN SANTIAGO ATITLÁN

You're likely to see Maya men and women in Santiago dressed in traditional costume, which here is both striking and unusual. The men wear long shorts, which, like the *huipiles* worn by the women, are striped white and purple and embroidered with birds and flowers. Some women also wear a *xk'ap*, a band of red cloth approximately 10m long, wrapped around their heads. Sadly, though, this head cloth is going out of use – you'll probably only see it at fiestas and on market days, and then mainly on older women.

pay homage to **Maximón**, the "evil" saint (see p.149), known locally as Rilej Mam. Every May he changes residence – any child will take you to see him: just ask for the "Casa de Maximón". It costs Q2 to enter his current home and Q10 to take his picture.

Arrival and information

By boat The dock is a ten-minute walk from the centre – when you get off the boat, walk up the hill, which will lead you into town.
Internet and telephones There are a number of internet cafés with Skype on C del Turista.
Tourist information Santiago does not have a tourist office. Consult the excellent website ⓦ www.santiagoatitlan.com for history and information in English.

Accommodation

Few budget travellers stay in town, most visiting as a day-trip from elsewhere around the lake, though there are some adequate places.
Casa de las Buganvillas Opposite Clínica Rxiin Tnamet in Cantón Chechiboy, about 5min east of the church ☎ 7820 7055. A good choice, this place has spacious, spotless en-suite rooms and attractive wooden furniture. The rooftop restaurant serves a mean *pollo dorado*. Q160
Hospedaje Colonial Rosita Just south of the church ☎ 5397 7187. This simple, secure *hospedaje* has no-frills rooms, a vigilant owner and fairly clean communal bathrooms. Q100
Hotel Lago de Atitlán Uphill from the dock, on the left ☎ 7721 7174, ⓔ hotellagodeatitlan@hotmail .com. Functional concrete block with several storeys of clean, plain rooms, all with private bathrooms and cable TV. Q140

Eating

Comedor Brendy In the centre of town by the main square. A classic Guatemalan *comedor* with good set lunches (from Q15), including tasty *carne asada* and broths.
El Gran Sol One block up from the dock on the left. Family-run place with a palm roof, a little terrace and colourful tablecloths. Good for grilled meats (Q25) and soups (Q20).
El Horno 400m up from the dock, on the left. If you're after something more gringo-geared, this great bakery has delicious baguettes, wonderful cakes and pies and strong local coffee.

Wach'alal 400m up from the dock, on the right. A clean, good-value *comedor*, with an unpronounceable name but satisfying food.

Moving on

By boat to: Panajachel (3 daily ferries; 1hr); San Pedro La Laguna (5 daily 6am–5pm; 40min). The ferries are supplemented by much faster *lanchas*.
By bus to: Guatemala City, via Cocales (8 daily 3am–3pm). The village is also well connected by bus with most lakeside destinations, except Panajachel.

CHUITINAMIT

Opposite Santiago Atitlán, on the lower flanks of the San Pedro volcano, the Post-Classic Maya ruins of **Chuitinamit** are worth a visit. This modest site, originally called Chiya, was the fortified capital of the Tz'utujil before the conquistador Alvarado and his Kaqchikel allies laid waste to the place in 1524 – arriving in a flotilla of 300 canoes. Sadly, the site is in pretty poor shape today as locals have re-carved the stone monuments (and even added a Virgin Mary), creating Disneyesque figures. That said, Chuitinamit is still actively used by shamen for ceremonies and its position high above the lake affords panoramic views. The paths around the site are littered with Maya ceramic fragments and obsidian arrowheads and blades.

To get to Chuitinamit you'll need to hire a **boat** (around Q100 for a return trip of an hour) from the dock in Santiago; it's a steep ten-minute hike up to the ruins.

SAN PEDRO LA LAGUNA

Around to the west of Volcán San Pedro lies the village of **SAN PEDRO LA LAGUNA**, considered by many travellers as the place to be. It's *the* party destination of the lake, with happening bars playing everything from reggae to trance till the early hours of the morning. All this raving has spawned a pretty serious drug culture, and although the town has clamped down in recent years, tensions remain.

If you've no interest in the high life, you'll still find plenty to do in San Pedro, with yoga classes, some good language schools and plenty of hiking trails. It's the kind of place people love or hate – come and make your own mind up.

What to see and do

There's a decent little **beach** just southeast of town, below the road to San Juan (see p.158), and some **thermal pools** between the two boat docks offer another place to relax. As the lake water is quite polluted around San Pedro, the **swimming pool** (Tues–Sun 11am–dusk; Q20) by the Santiago dock is a popular place to hang out and cool off. **Volcán San Pedro**, which towers above the village at some 3020m, can be climbed in four to five hours. If you want to make the **hike**, hire a guide – the foliage is dense, the route very difficult to find and there have been occasional attacks on tourists on the slopes. Indian Nose is another great hike, with arguably an even better perspective of Atitlán. Guides can be organized via Excursion Big Foot (see "Tour operators", below). For something less strenuous, considering hiring a **kayak** (Q15/hr) from the lakeshore on the right of the Pana dock.

Arrival and information

By boat There are two docks in San Pedro. All boats from villages on the north side of the lake, including Panajachel, Santa Cruz and San Marcos, arrive and depart from the Panajachel dock on the north side of town, while boats from Santiago Atitlán use a separate dock to the southeast, a ten-minute walk away.

By bus The bus stop for all arrivals and departures is in front of the church.

Tourist information There's no tourist office in town. Juan at Excursion Big Foot (see below) can give you all the information you need.

Tour operators Excursion Big Foot (☎7721 8203), just left of the Panajachel dock, organizes hikes, horses for Q40/hr (guide included) and bicycles for Q50/day.

Accommodation

San Pedro has some of the cheapest accommodation in Latin America: many places charge as little as Q30 per person per night.

Hotel Gran Sueño Left of the Pana dock ☎7721 8110. Run by a welcoming local family, this mini-hotel has three storeys of spotless rooms, some on the small side, and free wi-fi. Q120

Hotel Nahual Maya Turn left after *Nick's Place* ☎7721 8158. This attractive whitewashed place has a Spanish colonial look, and the rooms are in excellent shape, all with private bathroom and balcony or veranda. Q110

Hotel Pinocchio Between the docks ☎5845 7018. Yes, it's a large concrete block, but the rooms are kept tidy, the huge garden is lovely, staff are very sweet and there's wi-fi and a guests' kitchen. Q60

Hotel Posada Manuel Ta Uphill from Santiago dock, first turning on the left ☎5976 5671. Very inexpensive *posada* owned by an elderly Maya lady, with two storeys of good, clean, basic rooms, each with twin beds. Q60

Hotel San Antonio Left of the Pana dock and towards the end of the road ☎5823 9190. A good mustard-coloured place where all the inviting rooms have TV and bathroom, and there's wi-fi and a café too. Q100

Jarachik Between the docks ☎5543 4111 or 5847 4857. With a sociable backpacker vibe, this place has two clean dorms (with shared bathrooms) and plain, spacious and well-kept en-suite rooms on the upper storey. There's wi-fi and a great café here. Dorms Q40, rooms Q90

Zoola Left off the Pana dock, and right up the hill ☎5543 4111 or 5847 4857, ☻www.zoolapeople.com. A popular travellers' retreat, this Israeli-owned place has pleasant, clean dorms and rooms (four have private bathroom), hammocks, chill-out and TV lounges and great Middle Eastern food. Minimum two-night stay. Q80

Eating

San Pedro's restaurants, most of which are excellent value for money, have a decidedly international flavour, and vegetarians are well catered for. There are also a few typical Guatemalan *comedores* in the centre of the village and by the Santiago dock.

D'Noz By Pana dock. Something of a San Pedro establishment, this recently refurbished bar-restaurant offers a global menu, friendly service, free films (8.30pm every night), wi-fi and a long happy hour (5–8pm). There's a health-food store on the lower level too.

Hummus-Ya Left at the Pana dock. Come to this big barn of a place for authentic Israeli and Middle Eastern food including *shakshuka* (Q30), falafel (Q25) and tasty kebabs. There are dockside and lakeview tables with stunning perspectives of Atitlán. Doubles as a bar.

Nick's Place By the Pana dock. A great spot to relax and watch the day go by. Big breakfasts available for Q20, plus pancakes, Guatemalan staples, pasta (Q25) and pizza (Q30).

🏃 **La Puerta** Between the docks. The best food in San Pedro, courtesy of an accomplished Guatemalan cook, and it offers a lovely garden setting, with tables under the trees. A lot of thought has gone into the healthy, creative menu, with dozens of delicious breakfast choices (Q18–38) including porridge with coconut, flax seed, nuts and fruit. The pasta and bread are home made, salads are wonderful and wine is available by the glass.

Zoola At *Zoola* hotel. The food here – Israeli, Western and Guatemalan – is very good, but service is extremely slow. Relax on the cushions and play backgammon as you wait.

Drinking and nightlife

San Pedro's vibrant bar action is concentrated on the trail between the docks, and around the Pana dock. There are some great boho bars, and most places have happy hours. After the 1am curfew "after parties" start up, often with DJs.

Alegre Pub Near the Pana dock, on the left. Pub showing English and Spanish football, NFL and NBA games, and serving comfort grub such as huge Sunday roasts (Q38), curries and burgers.

Buddha Bar Between the docks. This American-owned bar is looking a little run down these days, but it's still popular for its live music, films and party atmosphere.

Freedom Right at the Pana dock. Restaurant-bar-club with a pool table, great lake views and a dancefloor pumping to house, trance and techno. Wildly popular on the right night.

Directory

Cinema *Buddha Bar* and *D'Noz* both show films daily.
Exchange Banrural (Mon–Fri 8am–5pm, Sat 9am–12.30pm) will change travellers' cheques. There is an ATM by the Pana dock.
Internet *D'Noz* by the Pana dock is one of a dozen or so places with web access. You can also burn photos to disk here, Skype, and they also do laptop repairs.
Language schools Cooperativa Spanish School, uphill from the Santiago dock (☎5398 6448,

ⓦ www.cooperativeschoolsanpedro.com), is very well regarded. Casa Rosario, south of Santiago Atitlán dock (ⓦ www.casarosario.com); Corazón Maya, 1.5km south of Santiago dock (☎7721 8160, ⓦ www.corazonmaya.com); and San Pedro Spanish School, between the piers (☎5715 4604, ⓦ www .sanpedrospanishschool.com), are also good.
Market In the centre of town; mainly sells food.
Post office Behind the church in the town centre; erratic hours.

Moving on

By boat Boats leave every 30min for all villages on the north coast of the lake (first boat 6am, last boat 5pm). Direct *lanchas* leave for Panajachel and Santiago about every hour.
By bus Buses depart from opposite the church to Guatemala City (9 daily, last at 2pm; 4hr) and Quetzaltenango (7 daily; 2hr 45min). Casa Verde Tours, just up from the Pana dock (☎5837 9092), run shuttles to Chichicastenango, Quetzaltenango, Antigua, Cobán and Lanquín, Guatemala City, Huehuetenango and San Cristóbal de Las Casas in Mexico.

SAN JUAN LA LAGUNA

Two kilometres west of San Pedro, at the back of an inlet and surrounded by shallow beaches, is **SAN JUAN LA LAGUNA**. The village specializes in the weaving of *petates*, lake-reed mats; two large co-ops, Las Artesanías de San Juan, signposted on the left from the dock, and the Asociación de Mujeres de Color, on the right, have goods for sale. Next to the latter is the *Hospedaje Estrella del Lago* (Q60), with secure, simple rooms and a kitchen open to guests. Uphill, in the centre of the village, is a quiet *comedor, Restaurant Chi'nimaya*, and almost next door, a shrine to **Maximón** (see box, p.149), the "evil saint", dressed in local garb.

Regular **pick-ups** run between San Pedro and San Juan, or you can walk. Leaving the village by footpath, you'll pass below the Tz'utujil settlement of **San Pablo La Laguna**, perched high above the lake. It's a twenty-minute walk away, and connected to the Carretera Interamericana by a steep road.

SAN MARCOS LA LAGUNA

SAN MARCOS LA LAGUNA is the most bohemian place on the lake, and is home to legions of foreigners of an artistic and spiritual persuasion. If you're enticed by veggie cafés, holistic centres, yoga and rebirthing classes and all things esoteric, this is the place for you. The village has a decidedly tranquil feel – there's no real bar scene – so it's a perfect place to relax and read a book in your hammock and enjoy the natural beauty of the lake. The bulk of hotels and restaurants are closer to the water, while the Maya village sits on higher ground further away from the shore.

What to see and do

Apart from a huge stone **church**, built to replace the colonial original destroyed in the 1976 earthquake, there are no sights as such (though the sartorial tastes of some of the gringo residents are amusing). The main draws are of the spiritual variety. One of these is the *Las Pirámides* yoga and meditation retreat (see below), but there's a surplus of other practitioners and masseurs, plus the requisite organic bakery and a healing centre – **San Marcos Holistic Centre** (ⓦ www.sanmholisticcentre.com), which offers massage, reflexology, kinesiology and natural remedies. Many places offer **yoga**, including *La Paz* (see below) for Hatha and Vinyasa, and Soul Projects (ⓦ www.soulprojects.org) for classes and meditation sessions in dramatic locations, including the forests high above the lake.

The recent rise in Atitlán's lakewater means that you might struggle to find a good spot to **swim** from, but there are wooden jetties by the shore. On a clear day the views of Atitlán's three **volcanoes**, including double-coned Tolimán, are sublime, while in the distance you can glimpse the grey peak of Acatenango near Antigua.

Arrival and information

By boat *Lanchas* from other lakeside villages, including San Pedro (35min; last boat 5pm), Santa Cruz and Pana (25min; last boat 7.30pm), pull up at the dock, which is about a 5-minute walk from the centre of town.

Accommodation

San Marcos has some good accommodation options, though few with rock-bottom rates. To access most places, get off at the westernmost dock, by *Posada Schumann*: all accommodation is signposted from there.

Hospedaje Panabaj Up in the Maya village, behind the town hall ☎ 5483 1225. Two-storey block in a quiet location, with simple rooms that face a nice garden. The shared bathrooms are kept tidy. Q60

Hotel Quetzal In the Maya village ☎ 4146 6036, ⓦ www hotelquetzal-gt.com. A very well run Swiss–Guatemalan-owned place with high-quality rooms that are decorated with local textiles and have en-suite bathrooms. The owner is a baker, so be sure to try his delicious breads in the restaurant here. Q115

Hotel Silani Turn right off the dock and walk to the end of the path ☎ 2425 8088, ⓦ www.silani.net. Enjoys one of the best settings in town, right on the shore. Accommodation includes a treehouse and charming adobe rooms, and there's a restaurant and sauna. Q80

La Paz ☎ 5702 9168, ⓦ www.sanmarcoslapaz .com. Long-running place with very spacious, rustic cottages, a superior six-bed, two-storey dorm, good home-cooking and yoga classes. Guests get the run of a lovely leafy garden. Dorms Q60, doubles Q115

Las Pirámides ☎ 5205 7302/7151, ⓦ www .laspiramidesdelka.com. Meditation retreat set in leafy grounds. Courses (available for daily, weekly and monthly enrolment) include hatha yoga, healing and meditation techniques. Accommodation is in comfortable, though not huge, pyramid-shaped cabañas; rates include courses but not food (which is delicious and vegetarian). US$40

🏃 **Posada del Bosque Encantado** ☎5208 5334, ⓦwww.hotelposadaencantado.com. Managed by charming staff, this wonderful place has four huge, gorgeous adobe cottages that face a lovely garden. You'll find a *temascal* (sauna) and hammocks to lounge in; a *comedor* is planned. Q160

Eating

🏃 **Aaculaax** See p.159. For filling, nutritious food (most meals Q25–45) in a leafy, sunny setting, this charming terrace restaurant is hard to beat. Famous for its breakfasts.
Blue Lily Great new ramshackle-chic place owned by a friendly English traveller with tables scattered around a lush garden. Popular for breakfasts (from Q20) and lunch; try the *meze* (Q35) or just a bagel or sandwich. Closed Sun.
Comedor Mi Marquensita Susi In the Maya village. Simple, local place ideal for your fill of *comida típica* at very reasonable prices.
Moon Fish Shorefront, west of the dock. Café-resto with great lakeside views and organic food – salads, Guatemalan dishes, sandwiches. Veggies are grown in the little yard at the front.

Moving on

By boat Boats leave about every 30min from the dock, serving all villages east to Panajachel and around the shore to San Pedro (first boat 6.15am, last boat 5.15pm).
By bus If you're travelling to Quetzaltenango it's best to travel via San Pedro; to Guatemala City and Antigua it's quickest via Panajachel. Casa Verde (☎5837 9092, ⓦwww.casaverdetours.com), inland from the Posada Schumann dock, can organize shuttle-bus connections to all these destinations.

JAIBALITO

JAIBALITO, an isolated lakeside settlement nestling between soaring *milpa*-clad slopes, remains resolutely Kaqchikel – very little Spanish is spoken, and few women have ever journeyed much beyond Lago de Atitlán – though the opening of a few hotels means that outside influence is growing.

From Jaibalito it's a 30-minute walk to Santa Cruz along a glorious, easy-to-follow path that parallels the steep hillside.

Accommodation and eating

La Casa del Mundo ☎5218 5332, ⓦwww.lacasadelmundo.com. Superb, if pricey, lodge with stunning lake views from its cute cottages, and great food. US$34
🏃 **Posada Jaibalito** ☎5598 1957, ⓦwww.posada-jaibalito.com. For a budget base, you can't beat this excellent option, which has a superb-value six-bed dorm with its own en-suite bathroom, great private rooms, plus fine Guatemalan food (Q14–25) and cheap drinks – treat yourself to a shot of 23-year-old Ron Zacapa for just Q15. Dorms Q35, rooms Q90
Vulcano Lodge ☎5410 2237, ⓦwww.vulcanolodge.com. Inland from the shore, this lovely Norwegian-run place has great-value, immaculate rooms (though no lake views) and outstanding food (dinner is around US$12 a head). US$38

SANTA CRUZ LA LAGUNA

Set well back from the lake on a shelf 100m or so above the water, **SANTA CRUZ LA LAGUNA** is the largest of the lake's northwest villages, with a population of around four thousand. There isn't much to see in the village itself, apart from a fine sixteenth-century church, and most people spend their time by the bucolic lakeshore, which is fringed by mature trees, dotted with holiday homes and a handful of lovely hotels.

It's a fine base for swimming, chilling out with a book, or exploring the tough but spectacular inland **hiking** trails. Local Maya guide Pedro Juan Solis (☎5355 8849, ⦿www.tours-atitlan.com), who speaks fluent English, knows the area like the back of his hand and charges around Q50 per person (minimum four) for day-treks.

On the shore, you'll find the ⼂ *Iguana Perdida* (☎5706 4117, ⦿www.laiguana perdida.com), owned by a wonderful English–American couple, with one of the most convivial atmospheres in Lago de Atitlán. There are basic dorms (Q35) and budget rooms (US$10), as well as more luxurious options (US$40), but it's the gorgeous, peaceful site overlooking the lake that really makes this place. Dinner (Q50) is a wholesome, three-course communal affair. There are fancy-dress nights on Saturdays and the hotel also offers yoga classes, massage, internet, a TV lounge, book exchange and great travel advice. The *Iguana* is also home to a professional PADI **dive school**, ATI Divers, for fun dives (US$35) and courses.

Lanchas leave Panajachel about every 30 minutes from 6am to 7pm. The last one from San Pedro leaves at 5pm. There's a very rough road to Santa Cruz that's quite a challenge even in a 4WD or dirt bike; no buses serve the village.

The western highlands

Guatemala's **western highlands** are home to some of the most dramatic and breathtaking scenery in the entire country. The area also has the highest concentration of one of the Americas' largest indigenous groups, the Maya. Languages and traditional costume still remain largely intact – probably the most striking dress of all is that worn in **Todos Santos Cuchumatán**. From the wild and ragged mountains surrounding **Nebaj** to the bustling colourful market of **Chichicastenango**, you are bound to be captivated by the region's sublime scenery, culture and colour. The western highlands are also home to the country's second most populous city, **Quetzaltenango**, which draws numerous language students and voluntary workers. Travelling in remote parts of the highlands can be arduous, but the main highways are all paved.

CHICHICASTENANGO

CHICHICASTENANGO, Guatemala's "mecca del turismo", is known best for its twice-weekly markets, which are some of the most colourful in the country. It also offers an insight into indigenous Maya society in the highlands. Over the years, Maya culture and

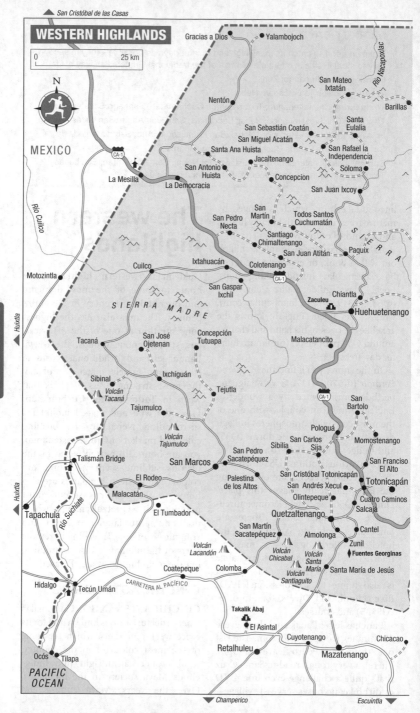

WESTERN HIGHLANDS

0   25 km

N

MEXICO

San Cristóbal de las Casas

Gracias a Dios   Yalambojoch

Río Nacapoxlac

Nentón

San Mateo Ixtatán

Barillas

San Sebastián Coatán

Santa Eulalia

San Miguel Acatán

San Rafael la Independencia

Santa Ana Huista

Jacaltenango

Soloma

San Antonio Huista

Concepcion

La Mesilla

La Democracia

San Juan Ixcoy

San Martín

Todos Santos Cuchumatán

San Pedro Necta

SIERRA

Santiago Chimaltenango

Motozintla

Cuilco

Ixtahuacán

Colotenango

San Juan Atitán

Paquix

Río Cuilco

San Gaspar Ixchil

CA-1

Chiantla

SIERRA MADRE

Zaculeu

Huehuetenango

Tacaná

San José Ojetenan

Concepción Tutuapa

Malacatancito

Sibinal

Ixchiguán

Volcán Tacana

Tejutla

Tajumulco

San Bartolo

Volcán Tajumulco

San Pedro Sacatepéquez

Pologuá

San Carlos Sija

Momostenango

Talismán Bridge

San Marcos

Sibilia

San Francisco El Alto

El Rodeo

Palestina de los Altos

San Cristóbal Totonicapán

Totonicapán

Malacatán

San Andrés Xecul

Cuatro Caminos

Tapachula

El Tumbador

Olintepeque

Salcajá

Río Suchiate

San Martín Sacatepéquez

Quetzaltenango

Almolonga

Cantel

Zunil

Hidalgo

Tecún Umán

Volcán Lacandón

Volcán Chicabal

Volcán Santa María

Fuentes Georginas

Santa María de Jesús

Coatepeque

Colomba

CARRETERA AL PACÍFICO

Volcán Santiaguito

Takalik Abaj

El Asintal

Cuyotenango

Chicacao

Ocós

Tilapa

PACIFIC OCEAN

Retalhuleu

Mazatenango

Champerico

Escuintla

GUATEMALA

THE WESTERN HIGHLANDS

Huixtla

Huixtla

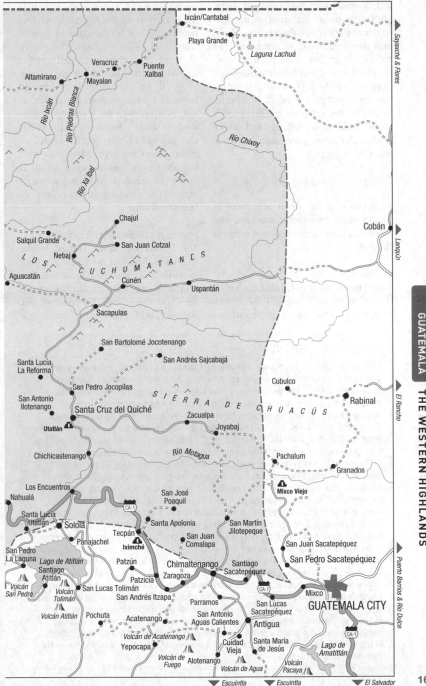

folk Catholicism have merged here, with indigenous rituals continuing often under the wings of the church. You'll also see traditional weaving adhered to, mostly by the women, who wear beautiful, heavily embroidered *huipiles*. For the town's fiesta (Dec 14–21), and on Sundays, though, a handful of *cofrades* (elders of the religious hierarchy) still wear traditional clothing and carry spectacular silver processional crosses and incense burners.

What to see and do

Although Chichi's main attraction is undoubtedly its vibrant markets, the town also offers other sights of cultural interest.

Markets

Most visitors come to Chichicastenango for its **markets**, which fill the town's central plaza and all surrounding streets on Sundays and Thursdays – Sunday is the busiest. Fruit and vegetable vendors congregate inside the covered Centro Comercial (which adjoins the plaza); most of the other stalls sell textiles and souvenirs. The crowds are eclectic – you'll be surrounded by myriad foreigners and commercial traders, as well as Maya weavers from throughout the highlands – but many of the goods are geared to the tourist trade, so initial prices are high. Make sure your bargaining abilities are up to snuff, as they'll be needed. The trading starts early in the morning, and goes on until late afternoon.

Iglesia de Santo Tomás

The **Iglesia de Santo Tomás**, in the southeast corner of the plaza, was built in 1540 and now is a local religious centre, home to a faith that blends pre-Columbian and Catholic rituals. For the faithful, the entire building is

---

HIGHLAND HISTORY

The Maya have lived in the Guatemalan highlands for some two thousand years. The Spanish arrived in the area in 1523, making their first permanent settlement at Iximché (see p.149), the capital of their Kaqchikel Maya allies. Not long after, conquistador Pedro de Alvarado moved his base to a site near modern-day Antigua, and gradually brought the highlands under a degree of Spanish control. Eventually, Antigua also served as the administrative centre for the whole of Central America and Chiapas (now in Mexico). In 1773, however, the city was destroyed by a massive earthquake and the capital was moved to its present site.

The arrival of the Spanish caused great hardship for the native Maya. Not only were their numbers decimated by Spanish weaponry, but waves of infectious diseases also swept through the population. Over time, indigenous labour became the backbone of the Spanish Empire, with its indigo and cacao plantations. The departure of the Spanish in 1821 and subsequent independence brought little change at village level. *Ladino* authority replaced that of the Spanish, but Maya were still required to work the coastal plantations and at times were press-ganged to work, often in horrific conditions.

In the mid-1960s, guerrilla movements began to develop in opposition to Guatemala's military rule, seeking support from the highland population and establishing themselves in the area. The Maya became the victims in this process, caught between the guerrillas and the army. A total of 440 villages were destroyed; around 200,000 people died and thousands more fled the country, seeking refuge in Mexico. Despite the harsh conditions and terrific adversity the Maya survived: traditional costume is still worn in many areas (particularly by women), a plethora of indigenous languages still spoken and some remote areas even still observe the 260-day Tzolkin calendar.

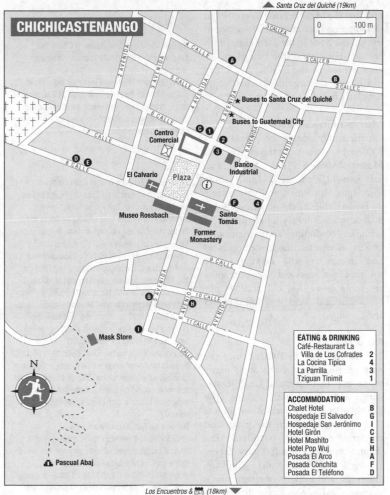

CHICHICASTENANGO

0   100 m

★ Buses to Santa Cruz del Quiché

★ Buses to Guatemala City

Centro Comercial

Banco Industrial

El Calvario   Plaza   ℹ

Museo Rossbach   Santo Tomás

Former Monastery

Mask Store

N

Pascual Abaj

EATING & DRINKING

Café-Restaurant La Villa de Los Cofrades	2
La Cocina Típica	4
La Parrilla	3
Tziguan Tinimit	1

ACCOMMODATION

Chalet Hotel	B
Hospedaje El Salvador	G
Hospedaje San Jerónimo	I
Hotel Girón	C
Hotel Mashito	E
Hotel Pop Wuj	H
Posada El Arco	A
Posada Conchita	F
Posada El Teléfono	D

Los Encuentros & 🚌 (18km) ▼

alive with the souls of the dead, each located in a specific part of the church. Before entering, it's customary to make offerings in a fire at the base of the steps or to burn incense in perforated cans. Don't enter the building by the front door, which is reserved for *cofrades* and senior church officials; use the side door instead and be warned that **taking photographs** inside the building is considered deeply offensive – don't even contemplate it. You are likely to find the devout here at all times of the day,

in particular on Sundays, when Maya swing censers and murmur prayers on the church steps. At the entrance there are candles scattered around the floor; these are put here by living Maya in honour of their ancestors, some of whom are buried beneath the church.

Beside the church is a former **monastery**, now used by the parish administration. It was here that a Spanish priest, Francisco Ximénez, became the first outsider to be shown the Popol Vuh, the Maya holy book; it is said that the Maya became interested in worshipping here after Ximénez began to read the book in the early eighteenth century. His copy of the manuscript is now housed in the Newberry Library in Chicago; the original was lost some time later in the eighteenth century.

Museo Rossbach

On the south side of the plaza, often hidden by stalls on market day, the **Museo Rossbach** (Tues, Wed, Fri & Sat 8am–12.30pm & 2–4pm, Thurs 8am–4pm, Sun 8am–2pm; Q5) houses a broad collection of pre-Columbian artefacts, mostly small pieces of ceramics (including some demonic-looking incense burners), jade necklaces and earrings, and stone carvings (some two thousand years old). Also on show are some interesting old photographs of Chichi and local weavings, masks and carvings.

Pascual Abaj

The Iglesia de Santo Tomás is not the only religious site in the area: many of the hills that surround Chichicastenango are topped with shrines. The closest of these, **Pascual Abaj**, is less than a kilometre from the plaza and regularly visited by outsiders. The shrine comprises small altars facing a stern pre-Columbian sculpture. Offerings are usually overseen by a shaman, and range from flowers to sacrificed chickens, always incorporating plenty of incense, alcohol and incantations. Remember that any ceremonies you may witness are deeply serious – keep your distance and be sensitive about taking photographs. To get to Pascual Abaj, walk down the hill beside Santo Tomás, take the first right, 9 Calle, and follow this as it winds its way out of town. You'll soon cross a stream and then a well-signposted route takes you past a mask workshop, continuing uphill for ten minutes through a pine forest.

Arrival and information

By bus There's no bus station in Chichi, but the corner of 5 C and 5 Av operates loosely as a terminal.

Tourist information and internet Inguat is at 7 C 5–43 (daily 8am–6pm; ☎7756 2022). Information is pretty limited and hours are irregular, but they will sell you a map of the town for Q5 and have ranks of computers for internet connections.

Accommodation

There are a few good budget hotels in town. These can be in short supply on Saturday nights before the Sunday market, but you shouldn't have a problem at any other time (except on fiesta days). Prices can also rise on market days, though at other times you can usually negotiate a good deal.

Chalet Hotel 3 C 7–44 ☎7756 1360, ⓦwww .chalethotelguatemala.com. A good highland inn, this little hotel has attractive, though smallish rooms decorated with Mayan *artesanías* and beds with woollen blankets from Momostenango; all are en suite. It's solar powered, there's free internet and you can eat your breakfast (Q20) on the roof terrace overlooking the town. Q200

Hospedaje El Salvador 5 Av 10–09 ☎7756 1329. Age-old travellers' lodge with a motley collection of bare but serviceable rooms, though the communal bathrooms could be better maintained. If you're struggling to find a bed, there's sure to be room here. Q75

Hospedaje San Jerónimo 5 Av & 12 C ☎7756 1838. A well-run, quiet *hospedaje* with clean if simple rooms, all with en-suite, hot-water baths, and some with balcony. Q100

Hotel Girón 6 C 4–52 ☎7756 1156. Spacious, pine-trimmed rooms with clean bathrooms and safe parking. The location could not be more central. Q140

Hotel Mashito 8 C 1–7 ☎7756 1343. Nothing at all fancy, but has very cheap rates, and you have a choice of clean rooms, some with cable TV and private bathroom, others with shared facilities. Q80

Hotel Pop Wuj 6 Av, between 10 & 11 C ☎7756 2014. Pleasantly decorated, spotless rooms, all en suite. The most expensive doubles have huge beds. There's also a restaurant downstairs. Q150

Posada Conchita 8 C 6–14 ☎7756 1258. On a lane just behind the church, this posada has real charm, with huge, colonial-style rooms, all en suite, that have fireplaces and decorative Mayan artefacts. Rates are charged per person, so it's a great deal for solo travellers. Q100

Posada El Arco 4 C 4–36
☎7756 1255. This very fine
guesthouse is run by a couple
of Guatemalan brothers who
lived in the USA for years and
look after travellers well. The
beautiful garden has stunning
countryside views. All the well-
furnished, attractive rooms
have wooden beds and reading
lights, and have been individually
decorated with local fabrics; rooms
6 and 7 even have access to a
pleasant terrace. US$20

Posada El Teléfono 8 C 1–64 ☎7756 1197.
The spartan rooms at this friendly guesthouse are
accessed via vertiginous, rickety stairways, though
many have fine highland views, and the communal
bathrooms are kept pretty tidy. Q60

Eating and drinking

There is plenty of good-value Guatemalan *comedor*
food available in Chichicastenango, especially in the
plaza on market day. Many restaurants are quite
pricey, however, as they're geared to day-tripping
westerners; on non-market days many of these
places close.

Café-Restaurant La Villa de Los Cofrades 6 C
& 5 Av, on the first storey. Observe local Chichi life
from the first-storey balcony while you enjoy great
churrascos and breakfasts (Q25). Real coffee and
wine are available.

La Cocina Típica 7 Av. Simple, decent *comedor* of
the plastic chairs and no-frills variety that has filling
set lunches for Q18.

La Parrilla 6 C & 5 Av. Set in a little courtyard, this
is a good place to get away from the market crowds.
Meat lovers should try the *especial la parrilla* (Q50).

Tziguan Tinimit 5 Av & 6 C. A large dining hall,
painted with images of the Mayan cosmos. Most
of the grilled meat, pasta and pizza dishes are in
the Q40–70 range but there's always a good daily
special (like *longaniza* sausages; Q28). They serve
espresso coffee here too.

Directory

Exchange Banco Industrial, 6 C (Mon, Wed &
Fri 10am–4pm, Thurs & Sun 9am–5pm, Sat
10am–3pm), has an ATM.

Post office North of the square on 4 Av (Mon–Fri
8.30am–5pm, Sat 9am–1pm).

Moving on

By bus Buses heading between Guatemala City
and Santa Cruz del Quiché pass through
Chichicastenango about every 20min, stopping in
town for a few minutes to load up with passengers.
Chichi Turkaj Tours (☎7742 1359, ⓔchichiturkaj
tours@yahoo.com) in the *Hotel Chuguila*, 5 Av
5–24, offers shuttle bus connections to Lago de
Atitlán, Antigua and Guatemala City.

SANTA CRUZ DEL QUICHÉ

SANTA CRUZ DEL QUICHÉ, known
locally as "Quiché", is capital of its
eponymous department, and half an
hour north of Chichicastenango. A good
paved road connects the two towns,
running through pine forests and ravines.
The town has a good street market but
few attractions except the minor ruins
of K'umarkaaj, and foreigners are a rare
sight. In the central **plaza** there's a large
colonial **church**, built by the Domini-
cans with stone from the Maya ruins of
K'umarkaaj. In the middle of the plaza,
a defiant **statue** of the K'iche' hero,
Tecún Umán, stands prepared for battle.
His position is undermined somewhat
by the ugly urban tangle of hardware
stores, bakeries and trash that surrounds
the square.

Arrival and information

By bus Buses pull into the bus terminal, which
is about four blocks south and a couple east of
the central plaza. The street directly north of the
terminal is 1 Av, which takes you into the heart of
the town.

Exchange Banco Industrial, on the northwest
corner of the plaza (Mon–Fri 8am–5pm, Sat
8am–noon), has an ATM and will change travellers'
cheques.

Internet Alex Cybernet is at 2 Av 8–36 (Q5/hr).

Accommodation

Hotel Luisito 10 C 00–27 ☎7755 2547. Good-
value place with simple rooms and spotless
bathrooms. Q100

Hotel Rey Kiche 8 C 0–39 ☎7755 0827,
ⓔhotelreykiche@gmail.com. This modern, brick-
faced hotel has spacious, plain rooms with firm

beds, TV, desk and wardrobe, and there's free tea, coffee and water. Singles, doubles and triples are available, and there's a *comedor* too (breakfast and dinner only). Q180

Hotel San Andrés 0 Av 9–04 ☏ 7755 3057, ⓔ hotelsan_andres@hotmail.com. A three-storey hotel with spacious, clean rooms, all with cable TV and private bathroom with tub. There's a restaurant and wi-fi. Q130

Eating

Café San Miguel Opposite the church. Old-fashioned café-restaurant with filling local food, including *empanadas* and sandwiches (from Q12). The pastries can be very dry though.

Loven Pastería South side of the Parque. Come here for espresso coffee (Q7), a burger, slab of cake or a sandwich.

Moving on

Microbuses supplement the chicken bus services listed below.

Buses to: Guatemala City (every 20min 3.30am–5pm; 3hr 30min) via Chichicastenango (30min) and Los Encuentros (1hr); Nebaj (7 daily 7am–5pm; 2hr 45min); Quetzaltenango (9 daily; 3hr); Totonicapán (4 daily 6am–3pm; 1hr 30min); Uspantán (7 daily 8am–4pm; 3hr 30min).

AROUND QUICHÉ

The Quiché countryside is mountainous and thickly forested. Although not much remains of the ruins of K'umarkaaj, the history of the area is fascinating and serves to highlight the region's rich Maya heritage. The site is still used for religious ceremonies.

K'umarkaaj (Utatlán)

Early in the fifteenth century, the K'iche' king Gucumatz (Feathered Serpent) founded a new capital, **K'umarkaaj**. A hundred years later, the Spanish arrived, renamed the city **Utatlán** and then destroyed it. Today you can visit the ruins, about 4km to the west of Santa Cruz del Quiché.

Once a substantial city, there has been little restoration at **the site** (8am–5pm; Q30), and only a few of the main structures are still recognizable, most

buried beneath grassy mounds, but it is impressive nonetheless. The one-room **museum** has a scale model of what the original city is thought to have looked like. You should be able to make out the main plaza, three temple buildings, the foundations of a circular tower and the remains of a ball court. Beneath the plaza is a long tunnel containing nine shrines. Perhaps the most interesting thing about the site today is that *costumbristas*, traditional Maya priests, still come to these shrines to perform **religious rituals**. If a ceremony is taking place you'll hear the murmurings of prayers and smell incense smoke as you enter the tunnel; don't disturb the proceedings by approaching too closely.

A **taxi** from Santa Cruz del Quiché's plaza with an hour at the ruins costs around Q80. If there's a bus heading to Totonicapán, jump aboard as the road passes the ruins. To **walk**, head south from the plaza along 2 Avenida, and then turn right down 10 Calle, which will take you all the way out to the site – it's a pleasant forty-minute stroll.

SACAPULAS

Just over an hour from Quiché, spectacularly situated on the Río Negro and beneath the foothills of the Cuchumatanes, lies the little town of **SACAPULAS**, with a small colonial church and a good market every Thursday and Sunday. The town is worth visiting for the journey itself, as the bus winds its way up and down the slopes of the ragged hills that form part of the dramatic Cuchumatanes mountain range. A two-minute walk outside of town, upriver, takes you to some small **salt flats**; several roadside stallholders will sell you bags of black salt (Q2), which is said to have medicinal purposes.

Getting to Sacapulas is easy – catch any **bus** from Santa Cruz del Quiché heading to Uspantán or Nebaj. Leaving can be a bit trickier (see "Moving on", opposite).

THE IXIL REGION

The three small towns of Nebaj, Chajul and Cotzal, high in the Cuchumatanes, form the hub of the Ixil-speaking region, a massive area of over 120,000 inhabitants whose language is not spoken anywhere else. For all its charm and relaxed atmosphere today, the region's history is a bitter one. After many setbacks, the Spanish finally managed to take Nebaj in 1530, but by then they were so enraged that not only did they burn the town to the ground, but they condemned the survivors to slavery. Independence didn't improve conditions – the Ixil people continued to be regarded as a source of cheap labour, and were forced to work on the coastal plantations. Over a century later, in the late 1970s and early 1980s, the area was hit by horrific violence when it became the main theatre of operation for the EGP (the Guerrilla Army of the Poor). Caught up in the conflict between the guerrillas and the military, the civilians suffered terribly. Despite this bloody legacy, the region's fresh green hills are some of the most beautiful in the country, and the three towns are friendly and accommodating.

Accommodation and eating

If you get stuck here, you'll find two simple places.
Comedor y Hospedaje Tujaal Riverside ☎5983 5698. A good bet for a meal, with sweeping views over the Río Negro. Q125
Hospedaje y Restaurante Río Negro Just south of the bridge ☎5385 7363. An ageing but cheap place with basic rooms and shared bathrooms. Q100

Moving on

By bus Buses to Quiché (every 30min; 1hr) run until around 4pm. There are also buses to Nebaj (7 daily; 1hr 45min), Huehuetenango (5 daily; 2hr) and Uspantán (7 daily; 2hr).

NEBAJ

NEBAJ is the centre of Ixil country, a bustling market town with a dwindling number of attractive old adobe houses and plenty of new concrete structures. Though the pretty central plaza is well kept, the surrounding streets are riddled with potholes and none too clean. Nebaj is remote, but it's well worth a visit for the glimpse it affords of the traditional Ixil way of life. The weaving, especially, is spectacular, with the women's *huipiles* an artistic tangle of complex geometrical designs in superb greens, yellows, reds and oranges. There are some wonderful **hikes** in the surrounding region too.

What to see and do

The **plaza** is the community's focal point, lined by its major shops, municipal buildings and police station. The **market area**, which sprawls southeast of the plaza, is worth investigating. On Thursdays and Sundays the town explodes, as out-of-town traders visit with secondhand clothing from the US, stereos from Taiwan and Korea and chickens, eggs and produce from across the highlands. The town **church** on the plaza is also worth a look – inside its door on the left are dozens of crosses, forming a memorial to those killed in the civil war. If you're here for the second week in August, you'll witness the **Nebaj fiesta**, which includes processions, dances, drinking, fireworks and a marimba-playing marathon.

There are several beautiful **hikes** in the hills around Nebaj, for which guides can be arranged at *El Descanso* (see p.170).

Arrival and information

By bus All buses pull into the bus terminal, two blocks southeast of the plaza.
Tourist information *El Descanso* restaurant (see p.170), an excellent community tourism initiative, can arrange numerous treks (from Q125/day). There's also an information office (daily 8am–5pm) inside the Mercado de Artesanías, two blocks southeast of the plaza, though it's frequently closed.

Accommodation

Grand Hotel Ixil 2 Av 9–15 ☎ 7756 0036. It's not actually very grand, but the owners, the Briz family, are hospitable and it's a comfortable, relaxed place to stay. All the rooms are spacious and well kept, have a private bathroom and TV, and overlook a central garden. Q122

Hospedaje Ilebal Tenam Calzada 15 de Septiembre ☎ 7755 8039. About 400m along the road to Cotzal/Chajul, this fine *hospedaje* has a profusion of humble, very cheap rooms, as well as some smarter options with TV and private bathroom in a separate block. Q60

Hostal Media Luna Medio Sol 3 C 6–15 ☎ 5847 4747. Clean, simple rooms and dorm beds, as well as cooking facilities, a ping-pong table and TV room. It's operated by the *El Descano* team. Dorms Q40, doubles Q110

Popi's 5 Av 3–35 ☎ 7756 0092. Two blocks north of the square, this place is run by an elderly, hospitable North American, and has two decent dorms (with six/eight beds) and a couple of private rooms. Popi is a fine cook, always baking or preparing fresh grub for his guests. There's free internet, and wi-fi should be available in the future. All profits fund the NGO Mayan Hope. Dorms Q30, doubles Q90

Eating

Asados el Pasabien On the road south to Sacapulas, this meat-feast restaurant excels at *churrascos* (from Q30).

Comedor Elsin East side of the Parque. A classic Guatemalan *comedor* with humble surrounds, a loyal clientele and filling portions of dishes like *pollo dorado*, chorizo and *longaniza* (sausage), all priced at Q20. No alcohol.

El Descanso Two blocks northwest of the plaza on 3 C. A key meeting-point for backpackers, voluntary and NGO workers and many locals, this place has sofas, rocking chairs, armchairs and a number of magazines to flick through as you wait for your food. There's a long menu, including bowls of granola, fruit and yoghurt for breakfast (Q25), while the mains – pasta, Mexican, sandwiches and grilled meats – are around Q30. There's also cold beer (Q13) and wine by the glass.

Popi's Restaurant Inside *Popi's* hostel. Popi serves up excellent-value food including bacon-and-egg breakfasts (Q28), sandwiches on home-baked bread, and dishes like stir-fried veggies with tofu (Q28). Everything is freshly cooked to order.

Directory

Exchange Banrural, on the north side of the plaza, has an ATM.

Internet *El Descanso* restaurant has a number of terminals.

Language schools The Nebaj Language School is in the same building as *El Descanso* restaurant.

Moving on

By bus to: Guatemala City (3 daily; 6hr); Santa Cruz del Quiché (7 daily; 2hr 30min). There's a daily microbus to Cobán at 5am (6hr), or you can take any bus to the Cunén junction and catch an onward connection there. For Huehuetenango change in Sacapulas. Buses for Acul (20min), Chajul (40min) and Cotzal (50min) leave regularly between 5.30am and 5pm.

By pick-up Pick-ups and trucks supplement the buses; the best place to hitch south is on the road out of town.

ACUL

One of the most interesting hikes from Nebaj takes you to the village of **Acul**, about a ninety-minute walk away. Starting from the church in Nebaj, cross the plaza and head along 5 C past *Hotel Turansa*. At the bottom of the dip, after *Tienda y Comedor El Oasis*, the road divides: take the right-hand fork and head out of town along a dirt track. This switchbacks up a very steep hillside, and heads over a narrow pass into the next valley, where it drops down into Acul. The village was one of the country's original so-called "model villages" into which people were herded after their homes had been destroyed by the army during the civil war. There's a charming little place in Acul, *Posada Doña Magdelena* (☎5782 0891; Q40), where the owner also serves tasty, inexpensive meals. On the outskirts of the village is the wonderful, alpine-lodge-like *Hacienda San Antonio* (☎5305 6240), run by an Italian–Guatemalan family who have lived here for more than sixty years. They make some of the country's best cheese, Chancol, which they sell at pretty reasonable prices, and they also rent out delightful **chalets** (Q168).

SAN JUAN COTZAL

SAN JUAN COTZAL, the second of the three Ixil towns, is about 40 minutes from Nebaj. The town sits in a gentle dip in the valley, which is sheltered somewhat beneath the Cuchumatanes and often wrapped in a damp blanket of mist. Cotzal attracts very few Western travellers, though there is some great hill-walking nearby. Intricate turquoise *huipiles* are worn by the Maya women here, who also weave bags and rope from the fibres of the maguey plant.

The **community tourism** project Tejidos Cotzal (T5428 8218, Wwww.tejidoscotzal.org), just behind the marketplace, can hook you up with a guide to show you around this lovely region, its waterfalls and hilltop Maya shrines, and introduce you to local weavers. Tours costs just US$15 for a two-day adventure well off the gringo trail. **Market days** (Wed & Sat) are a particularly good time to visit, when there's more transport and life in the town. You can **stay** at the basic but decent *El Maguey* (T7765 6199), where they also serve good meals.

Regular **buses** leave Cotzal for Nebaj between 5.30am and 5pm. It's possible to also visit Chajul the same day if you get an early start from Nebaj.

CHAJUL

CHAJUL, made up mainly of old adobe houses, with wooden beams and red-tiled roofs blackened by the smoke of cooking fires, is the most determinedly traditional and least bilingual of the Ixil towns. The women wear earrings made of old coins strung up on lengths of wool, and dress in bright reds and blues, while boys still use blowpipes to hunt small birds, a skill that dates from the earliest of times. The colonial church is home to the **Christ of Golgotha** and the focus of a large pilgrimage on the second Friday of Lent, a particularly good time to be here.

If you want to **stay**, local families rent out beds in their houses to the steady trickle of travellers who come to town, or head for the *Posada Vetz K'aol* (T7765 6114; Q50), which is well set up for travellers with bunk beds in dorms and has tasty, cheap grub (and even an espresso machine).

There are regular **bus**, microbus and pick-up connections between Nebaj and Chajul until 5pm; the journey takes 30 minutes. From Cotzal there's less transport but you shouldn't have to wait too long for a ride.

QUETZALTENANGO

QUETZALTENANGO, Guatemala's second city, sits in a beautiful mountain valley ringed by volcanoes. In pre-Columbian times the town belonged to the Mam Maya people, who named the town Xelajú, meaning "under the rule of the ten mountains" – hence the name, **Xela** (pronounced "Shay-La"), by which the city still goes; it was the Spaniards who dubbed the city Quetzaltenango, roughly translated as "the land of the quetzal". Xela went on to flourish during colonial times, thanks in large part to the area's abundant coffee crops, but a massive earthquake in 1902 destroyed nearly the entire city. Subsequently almost completely rebuilt (all the Neoclassical buildings that you can see today date to this time), Xela is once again one of the country's major centres. Nonetheless, it manages to preserve an air of subdued, dignified calm, and remains popular among travellers, especially language students looking for more of an authentic Guatemalan experience than their counterparts in Antigua.

What to see and do

There aren't many sights in the city itself, but if you have an hour or two to spare then it's worth wandering through the streets, soaking up the atmosphere and taking in a museum or a market. The city is divided into zones; you'll primarily be interested in zonas 1 and 3, home to the central plaza and the (second-class) bus terminal, respectively. Most places are within walking distance, except the bus terminal.

Parque Centro América

The **Parque Centro América**, with a mass of mock-Greek columns and imposing bank facades, is at the centre of Xela. There's none of the buzz of business that you'd expect, though, except on the first Sunday of the month when the plaza hosts a good artisan market with blankets, baskets and piles of weavings for sale. On the west side of the plaza is the impressive **Pasaje Enríquez**, planned as a sparkling arcade of upmarket shops. It was left derelict for many years, but it's now been restored and is home to a number of good bars and restaurants.

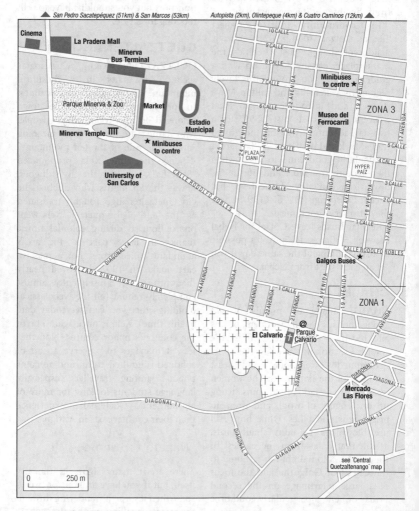

Casa de la Cultura

At the southern end of the plaza, next to the tourist office, is the **Casa de la Cultura** (Mon–Fri 8am–noon & 2–6pm, Sat & Sun 9am–5pm; Q6), the city's blatant architectural homage to ancient Greece. On the ground floor you'll find a display of sports trophies and a room dedicated to the marimba, along with assorted documents, photographs and pistols from the liberal revolution and the state of Los Altos, which declared itself the sixth state of the Federal Republic of Central America in the 1830s, with Xela as capital. Upstairs there are some modest Maya artefacts, historic photographs and a bizarre natural-history room. Among the dusty displays of stuffed bats, pickled snakes and animal skins are the macabre remains of assorted freaks of nature, including a sheep born with eight legs and a four-horned goat.

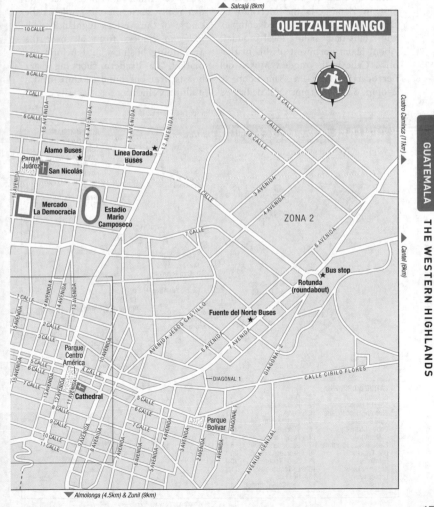

▲ *Salcajá (8km)*

QUETZALTENANGO

N

10 CALLE
9 CALLE
8 CALLE
7 CALLE
6 CALLE
15 AVENIDA
14 AVENIDA
13 AVENIDA
12 AVENIDA
13 CALLE
11 CALLE
10 CALLE

Álamo Buses
Línea Dorada Buses

Parque Juárez
San Nicolás

16 AVENIDA

Mercado La Democracia
Estadio Mario Camposeco

4 CALLE
3 AVENIDA
4 AVENIDA

ZONA 2

6 AVENIDA

7 CALLE

Bus stop
Rotunda (roundabout)

14 AVENIDA A
14 AVENIDA
13 AVENIDA
1 CALLE
15 AVENIDA
2 CALLE
3 CALLE

AVENIDA JESÚS CASTILLO

Fuente del Norte Buses

6 AVENIDA
7 AVENIDA

DIAGONAL 2

CALLE CIRILO FLORES

Parque Centro América
4 CALLE
5 CALLE
6 CALLE
13 AVENIDA
12 AVENIDA
11 AVENIDA

DIAGONAL 1

Cathedral

5 CALLE
6 CALLE
7 CALLE
9 CALLE
10 CALLE
11 CALLE
9 AVENIDA
7 AVENIDA
6 AVENIDA
5 AVENIDA
3 AVENIDA
2 AVENIDA
1 AVENIDA

DIAGONAL 2

Parque Bolívar

AVENIDA CENTRAL

▼ *Almolonga (4.5km) & Zunil (9km)*

14 Avenida

Away from the plaza, the city spreads out, a mixture of the old and new. The commercial heart is **14 Avenida**, complete with blaring neon signs. At the top of 14 Avenida, at the junction with 1 Calle, stands the **Teatro Municipal**, another grandiose Neoclassical building (see p.177).

Zona 3

Further afield, Xela's role as a regional centre of trade is in evidence. Out in Zona 3 is the **Mercado La Democracia**, a vast covered complex with stalls daily selling local produce. About 500m northwest of this market on 4 Calle is the modest **Museo del Ferrocarril** (Mon–Fri 8am–noon & 2–6pm, Sat 8am–1pm; Q6), dedicated

to the long-gone railway that once connected Xela to the Pacific coast.

The Minerva Temple and around

There's another Greek-style structure right out on the edge of town, the **Minerva Temple**, built to honour President Barrios's enthusiasm for education – it has no practical purpose. Below the temple are the sprawling daily produce **market** and the **Minerva Bus Terminal**. It's here that you can really sense the city's role as the centre of the western highlands, with *indígena* traders from all over the area doing business. Just behind the market, **La Pradera** shopping plaza boasts over one hundred stores and a multiplex cinema.

Minerva (2km)   Mercado La Democracia (300m)

CENTRAL QUETZALTENANGO

ACCOMMODATION

Black Cat Hostel	C
Casa Argentina	E
Casa Renaissance	G
Hostal Don Diego	D
Hostal Miguel	F
Hostal Siete Orejas	A
Hotel Horiani	B
Pensión Altense	H

Teatro Municipal

2 CALLE
3 CALLE
CALZADA SINFOROSO AGUILAR
4 CALLE
Microbuses to Minerva Terminal
5 CALLE
Pasaje Enríquez
6 CALLE
Parque Centro América
Municipalidad
Mercado Las Flores
DIAGONAL 11
Despensa Familiar
7 CALLE
Casa Noj
Cathedral
Casa de la Cultura
8 CALLE
9 CALLE
Hospital San Rafael
10 CALLE
Buses to Zunil
11 CALLE
Buses to Rotunda
Rotunda (1.25km)

0   100 m

EATING & DRINKING

Al Natur	19	Ojalá	4
Bajo La Luna	12	Pool and Beer	21
Blue Angel Video Café	16	Red	1
Café Baviera	8	Restaurante	
Coffee Company	6	Portofino	21
El Cuartito	17	Royal Paris	2
Discoteca La Parranda	7	Sabor de la India	5
Dos Tejanos	9	Sagrado Corazón	20
El Infinitivo	15	Salón Tecún	10
Kapeh Kakaaw	18	La Taquería	11
Leprechaun	13	Ut'z Hua	3
La Luna	12	Xela Café Gourmet	14

Almolongo (4.5km) & Zunil (9km)

TOURS FROM QUETZALTENANGO

Xela has several excellent tour operators offering some fascinating trips around the region.

Adrenalina Tours Inside Pasaje Enríquez, Plaza Central América ☎7761 4509, ⓦwww.adrenalinatours.com. A well-organized company with some excellent tours of the region, including trips to Zunil and Fuentes Georginas and San Andrés Xecul; prices depend on numbers taking the tour. They also run shuttle buses, offer volcano climbs (Chicabal and Volcán Santa María) and sell airline tickets.

Altiplano's 12 Av 3–35, Zona 1 ☎5247 2073, ⓦwww.altiplanos.com.gt. Another good, locally owned operator with trekking and tour programmes to villages around Xela and beyond; they buy and rent camping gear too.

Quetzaltrekkers Inside *Casa Argentina* (see below) ☎7765-5895, ⓦwww.quetzal trekkers.com. Offers some outstanding hikes, including a three-day trek from Xela to Atitlán (minimum donation Q600) and a two-day ascent of Tajumulco (Q400), plus rock climbing (Q300); all profits go to a charity for street children.

Arrival and information

By bus Unfortunately, most buses arrive and depart from nowhere near the centre of town. Second-class buses pull into the chaotic Minerva Bus Terminal on the city's northwestern edge; to get to the main plaza, walk 300m through the market stalls to 4 C and catch a microbus marked "Parque". There are four companies operating first-class buses to and from the capital, each with their own private terminal: Fuente del Norte, 7 Av 3–33, Zona 2 (☎7761 4587, ⓦwww.grupofuentedelnorte .com); Línea Dorada, 12 Av 5–13, Zona 3 (☎7767 5198, ⓦwww.lineadorada.info); Álamo, 14 Av 5–15, Zona 3 (☎7767 7117); and Galgos, C Rodolfo Robles 17–43, Zona 1 (☎7761 2248).
Tour operators See box above.
Tourist information The Inguat tourist office, on the south side of Parque Centro América (Mon–Fri 9am–5pm, Sat 9am–1pm; ☎7761 4931, ⓔinfo-xela@inguat.gob.gt), is not particularly helpful. You'll find the tour operators (see box above) a better source of local information. To find what's on in Xela, pick up a copy of *Xela Who* (ⓦwww.xelawho.com), available in many of the popular bars and cafés.

Accommodation

Once you've made it to the plaza, all the places listed here are within a ten-minute walk.
Black Cat Hostel 13 Av 3–33 ☎7761 2091, ⓦwww.blackcathostels.net. The grooviest-looking hostel in town. The best thing about this place is the sociable vibe and the lounge bar with retro sofas and lights. The dorms are fine for a night or two, but the private rooms are overpriced. Rates include internet and a massive breakfast. Dorms Q60, doubles Q160
Casa Argentina 12 Diagonal 8–37 ☎7761 2470/ 0010, ⓔcasargentina.xela@gmail.com. One of Xela's original budget places, this friendly place has dozens of simple rooms (with cable TV) and a huge dorm. There's also a kitchen, sun terrace and café. It's a ten-minute walk from the centre, and also the home of Quetzaltrekkers (see box above). Dorm Q25, doubles Q65
🏃 **Casa Renaissance** 9 C 11–26 ☎7761 8005, ⓦwww.casarenaissance .com. This relaxed guesthouse in a fine old townhouse has a lot going for it: five huge rooms, gorgeous original floor tiles, free tea/coffee/water, sunny patios, fast wi-fi, good bathrooms and a TV lounge stocked with over a thousand DVDs. It's owned by a Thys, a genial Dutchman. Q160
Hostal Don Diego 6 C 15–12 ☎5308 3616, ⓦwww.hostaldondiegoxela.com. This secure place has twenty simple, cheap rooms (none with private bathroom), a pleasant courtyard and guests' kitchen. There's free wi-fi and purified water. Dorms Q45, doubles Q110
Hostal Miguel 12 Av 8–31 ☎7765 5554, ⓦwww .learn2speakspanish.com. Very welcoming guesthouse within a Spanish language school. There are eight simple rooms in a slightly ramshackle old house, one with private bathroom, plus a living room with TV, cooking facilities and free wi-fi. Q48
Hostal Siete Orejas 2 C 16–92 ☎7768 3218, ⓦwww.7orejas.com. A fine new flashpacker place with very high quality, spacious rooms, each with hand-carved beds, good mattresses and a wooden chest of drawers. There's an upstairs bar – though few drinkers – as well as wi-fi, and your continental breakfast is gratis. Dorms Q65, rooms Q230

Hotel Horiani 12 Av 1–19 ☎5486 0164. Very basic and fairly stuffy small rooms, but dirt cheap and central. Q50

Pensión Altense 9 C 10–41 ☎7765 4648. It could do with a makeover, but the basic old-fashioned rooms do still have a flicker of charm, and there's safe parking. Q150

Eating

Quetzaltenango has a moderate choice of cafés and restaurants, suiting its modest, unpretentious character. Few places open before 8am.

Cafés

Al Natur 13 Av 8–34. Ideal for a snack, this café-deli has tasty dishes like *tortas de papas* with grated carrot, and shelves stocked with organic and co-op produce. Try the delicious home-made *limonada* or an espresso coffee.

Blue Angel Video Café 7 C 15–19. Chow down on a veggie meal while you watch one of the daily films here. Perfect for a rainy day. Free wi-fi.

Café Baviera 5 C 13–14. Anachronistic, pine-panelled coffeehouse with old photos of Xela on the walls. Fine for a coffee (from Q7), and they also offer cakes, snacks and sandwiches.

Coffee Company 14 Av A 3–16. This modern café opens early, so it's good for cereal or a hot muffin or perhaps a crêpe or salad later in the day. The coffee is great, the service excellent and there's a reading room upstairs with a few books to browse and free wi-fi. Daily 6am–7.30pm.

🏃 **El Cuartito** 13 Av 7–09. A mellow place to while away a few hours, this very stylish little place's decor is all crooked bookshelves, funky lights and interesting art and photography. It offers a fine selection of loose-leaf herbal teas (Q10), good coffee, great breakfasts and snacks including brochettas (Q25), bagels (Q22), crêpes (Q32) and salads. It's more of a bar in the evening. Free wi-fi.

🏃 **El Infinitivo** 7 C 15–18. The hippest place in town, *Infinitivo* is run by a gregarious, friendly crew who are mainstays of Xela's DJ and electronica scene; this is their HQ. There's a tempting menu of global dishes, including *tempe* fingers, miso soup, *gado gado* and sandwiches made with home-made bread. Check out the live music here on Tuesdays and Thursdays.

La Luna 8 Av 4–11. Crammed with curios including a collection of 1930s radios and antiques, *La Luna* has seven different varieties of wonderful drinking chocolate (Q6) and lots of interesting choc-coffee options.

Red 3 C 15A–20. One of Xela's creative hubs, this courtyard café has snacks including paninis and brochettas, and there's always some art or photography to take in. Service can be a tad slow, though, and there's no espresso machine. Tues–Sun 11am–7pm.

Xela Café Gourmet 6 C Av 9–26. Upmarket café just off the Parque with a long list of espresso-based coffees and a menu that takes in paninis and burgers.

Restaurants

Dos Tejanos Inside the Pasaje Enríquez. The best place in town for great Mexican-American food (meals from Q40); expect huge portions and big flavours.

Kapeh Kakaaw 12 Av 8–21. An elegant new restaurant set in a historic building, with rooms decorated with antiques and courtyard seating. The Q20 set lunch (12.30–3pm) is a steal, or go for some of the interesting Maya K'iche' dishes like *chok'a* or *pulique* (both Q48).

Restaurante Portofino 12 Av 10–21. The chef at this place really knows his Italian food, and his gnocchi and pasta (both around Q45) are superb. Doubles as a low-key bar with pool tables.

🏃 **Royal Paris** 14 Av A 3–06. Authentic, enjoyable French-owned restaurant with a diverse menu of really flavoursome dishes (meat dishes from Q55), plus snacks like *croque-monsieur* (Q26). Prices are moderate, given the quality of the cuisine.

Sabor de la India 15 Av 3–64. This Indian-owned place serves up filling and pretty authentic dishes like chicken biryani (Q65) and lots of vegetarian options including a good thali (Q60). The premises lack atmosphere though. Closed Mon.

Sagrado Corazón 9 C & 11–16. For a very local feed, this large, popular *comedor* has a long menu including Guatemalan-style breakfasts – the *completo* is just Q15 – set lunches (including a veggie special for Q20) and all sorts of *plátos típicos*.

La Taquería 8 Av & 5 C. Enjoyable Mexican food with good-value tacos (Q10), enchiladas and grilled meats (around Q40).

Ut'z Hua 12 Av & 3 C. A good choice for authentic, tasty Guatemalan cuisine, including *jocon* (chicken with sesame and pumpkin seeds, tomato and coriander) and *costilla adoboda* (pork ribs in a red chilli and vinegar sauce). Reckon on Q30–40 for a feed.

Drinking and nightlife

The main area for nightlife and dancing in central Xela is 14 Av A. Pasaje Enríquez, on the west side of the plaza, has several good bars too. *El Cuartito* and *El Infinitivo* (see "Cafés") are also key hangouts.

Bajo La Luna 8 Av 3–72. In an atmospheric cellar, this relaxed wine bar with background tunes is perfect for a quiet drink. You can nibble on a cheese platter (Q20–35) while you sip.

Discoteca La Parranda 14 Av 4–41. Strut your stuff here to salsa on Wednesdays (when there are free classes), while from Thursday to Saturday it's a mix of hip-hop, reggaeton and Latin electronica.

Leprechaun 10 Av 5–27. Small Irish bar kitted out with the requisite photos of U2 and the Emerald Isle. If you're missing Guinness they sell bottles at a steep Q40 a pop, alongside moderately priced Guatemalan beers. Live music some nights.

Ojalá 15 Av A 3–33. A kind of drinking centre for the cultural classes, or a cultural centre for the drinking classes, this lounge-bar-restaurant hosts live music (jazz, hip-hop, funk, *trova*) and art exhibitions, and serves up tasty international grub (Spanish, Lebanese and Latin American).

Pool and Beer 12 Av 10–21. Pool tables and table football are available in this spacious bar with dim lighting. A litre of beer will set you back Q25. 2-for-1 tequilas (Q15) at any time.

Salón Tecún Inside the Pasaje Enríquez. Xela's most dependable and popular bar, this pub-like institution is a favourite of both locals and travellers. There's a sociable interior and bench seating inside the arcade.

Entertainment

Cinema *Blue Angel* café has a daily video programme (Q10) at 8pm with a large selection of movies (mainly Hollywood blockbusters and cult films). *Royal Paris* restaurant shows French and European movies on Tues at 7pm. There's a multi-screen cinema by La Pradera mall, near the Minerva terminal.

Cultural institutes The Teatro Municipal, 14 Av A & 1 C (☏7761 2218), hosts recitals, dance and theatre performances, concerts and exhibitions. Casa N'oj (☏7768 3139, ⓦ casanoj.blogspot.com) hosts art exhibitions, films and lectures in a wonderful restored building on the Parque.

Directory

Bike rental The Bike House at 15 Av 5–22, Zona 1, has mountain bikes (40/24hr or 100Q/week); the Vrisa bookstore (see below) has similar rates.

Books Vrisa, 15 Av 3–64, has thousands of used titles. North & South, 15 Av & 8 C, Zona 1, has a good choice of political, social and anthropological books on Guatemala, as well as guidebooks and a café.

Exchange Both Banrural (Mon–Fri 9am–7pm, Sat 9am–1pm) and Banco Industrial (Mon–Fri 9am–6pm,

---

LANGUAGE SCHOOLS IN QUETZALTENANGO

Quetzaltenango has many excellent language schools, and if you're looking for a full-immersion experience it's ideal, as the city is not a prime tourist destination and few people speak English. There are several dozen good schools in town, including the following:

Casa de Español Xelajú Callejón 15, Diagonal 13–02, Zona 1 ☏7761 5954, ⓦwww.casaxelaju.com.

Celas Maya 6 C 14–55, Zona 1 ☏7761 4342, ⓦwww.celasmaya.com.

Centro Bilingüe Amerindía (CBA) 12 Av 10–27, Zona 1 ☏7761 8535, ⓦwww.cbaspanishschool.com.

Educación para Todos Av El Cenizal 0–58, Zona 5 ☏5935 3815, ⓦwww.spanishschools.biz.

Juan Sisay 15 Av 8–38, Zona 1 ☏7765 1318, ⓦwww.juansisay.com.

Inepas 15A Av 4–59, Zona 1 ☏7765 1308, ⓦwww.inepas.org.

Madre Tierra 13 Av 8–34, Zona 1 ☏7761 6105, ⓦwww.madre-tierra.org.

Miguel de Cevanates 12 Av 8–31, Zona 1 ☏7765 5554; ⓦwww.learn2speakspanish.com.

El Nahual 28 Av 9–54, Zona 1 ☏5606 1704, ⓦwww.languageselnahual.com.

La Paz 2 C Callejon 16 2–47, Zona 1 ☏4018 2180, ⓦwww.xelapages.com/lapaz.

Pop Wuj 1 C 17–72, Zona 1 ☏7761 8286, ⓦwww.pop-wuj.org.

Proyecto Lingüístico Quetzalteco de Español 5 C 2–40, Zona 1 ☏7765 2140, ⓦwww.hermandad.com.

Sakribal 6 C 7–42, Zona 1 ☏7763 0717, ⓦwww.sakribal.com.

Sat 9.30am–1.30pm) on the Parque Central have ATMs and will change travellers' cheques.

Health Hospital San Rafael is at 9 C 10–41, Zona 1 (☎7761 4414/2956).

Internet There are dozens of places in Xela for internet connections and wi-fi (*Xela Who* has a comprehensive list), including Xela Pages at 4 C 19–48, Zona 1. Rates are Q3–6/hr.

Laundry Lavandería Tikal, Diagonal 13 8–07; Q25 for a typical load, washed and dried in two hours.

Post office 15 Av & 4 C (Mon–Fri 8.30am–5.30pm, Sat 9am–1pm).

Supermarket Despensa Familiar, 3 Av & 7 C, in the centre of town.

Telephones Xela Pages (see "Internet") offers cheap netcalls all over the globe; Q1 to North America, Europe and Australia, Q3 to foreign mobile phones.

Moving on

By bus There are regular chicken buses (no fixed schedule – they usually leave when full, around every 30min) to most major destinations, including: Chichicastenango (3hr); Cuatro Caminos (30min); Guatemala City (4hr 30min); Huehuetenango (2hr); La Mesilla (4 daily; 4hr); Momostenango (1hr 30min); Panajachel (2hr 30min); Retalhuleu (1hr). There are also buses to Zunil and the Rotonda (both every 15min) from 10 C in the city centre, as well as the main terminal. For Antigua, take any Guatemala City-bound bus and change in Chimaltenango. There are 12 daily Pullman buses to Guatemala City (4hr), operated by four companies from private terminals (see "Arrival", p.175). For the latest schedule check out ⓦ www.xelawho.com or www.xelapages.com.

AROUND QUETZALTENANGO

Based in Quetzaltenango, you could easily spend a week or two exploring the highlands. There are numerous smaller towns and villages nearby, mostly indigenous agricultural communities and weaving centres with colourful weekly markets, as well as some lovely hot springs. The area also offers excellent **hiking**. The most obvious climbs are **Volcán Santa María**, towering above Quetzaltenango itself, and up **Volcán Chicabal** to its sublime crater lake. Straddling the coast road to the south is **Zunil** and the hot springs of **Fuentes Georginas**, overshadowed by more breathtaking volcanic peaks, while to the north are **Totonicapán**, capital of the department of the same name, and **San Francisco El Alto**, a small town perched on an outcrop overlooking the valley. Beyond that lies **Momostenango**, the country's principal wool-producing centre and a centre of Maya culture. For organized **tours** to all these places, see the box on p.175.

Volcán Santa María

Due south of Quetzaltenango rises **Volcán Santa María** (3772m). Though you can only see the peak from town, in the rest of the valley the cone seems to preside over everything around it. The view from the top is, as you might expect, truly spectacular, with nine other volcanoes visible on clear days, including the smoking summit of Santiaguito directly below. You can climb the volcano as a day-trip, but to really see it at its best you need to be on top at dawn, either sleeping on the freezing peak, or camping at the site below and climbing the final section in the dark by torchlight. Either way you need to bring enough food and water for the entire trip; and make sure you're acclimatized to the altitude for a few days before attempting the climb. It is highly recommended you go with a guide; they can be organized at most of the tour operators in Quetzaltenango (see box, p.175).

Laguna Chicabal

Another spectacular excursion in the area is to **Laguna Chicabal**, a crater lake set in the cone of the Chicabal volcano, about 25km southeast of Xela.

To visit the lake get a Coatepeque-bound bus (every 30min; 40min) from the Minerva terminal to the town of San Martín Sacatepéquez, from where it's a two-hour trek to the lake. The hike starts just before the village; your bus driver will drop you off at the right spot on the highway, where you'll see a sign to the lake. On the way you'll pass the entrance to the reserve (Q15), where there's a *comedor* and a shop selling snacks, juice and water.

Once you enter the reserve, a signposted route to the left shows you to a *mirador*, from where there are stunning views of the emerald lake, and the volcanoes of Santa María and Santiaguito, Tajumulco and Tacaná, or alternatively via precipitous steps straight down to the shore. Small sandy bays bear charred crosses and bunches of fresh-cut flowers, marking the site of ritual sacrifice. Every May 3 *costumbristas* gather here for ceremonies to mark the fiesta of the Holy Cross; never disturb any rituals that are taking place. You can **camp** at the shore, though you'll have to bring your own supplies.

Be back at the highway for your return bus to Xela by 5pm; there are later buses but it's best not to travel after dark.

Zunil
Some 10km south of Quetzaltenango is the village of **Zunil**, a vegetable-growing market town hemmed in by steep hills and a sleeping volcano. The main plaza is dominated by a beautiful white colonial church with a richly decorated facade; inside, an intricate silver altar is protected behind bars. The women of Zunil wear vivid purple *huipiles* and carry bright shawls – the plaza is awash with colour during the Monday market. Just below the plaza is a **textile co-operative**, where hundreds of women market these weavings. Zunil is also one of the few remaining places where **Maximón**, the "evil saint" (see box, p.149), is still worshipped. Here he also goes by the name Alvarado; his mannequin is usually paraded through the streets during Holy Week, dressed in Western clothes and smoking a cigar. Virtually any child in town will take you to his current abode for a quetzal.

Buses to Zunil run from Quetzaltenango's Minerva Bus Terminal every 30 minutes or so, though some also go from closer to the centre of town, stopping beside the Shell petrol station at 10 Calle and 9 Avenida in Zona 1. The last bus back from Zunil leaves at around 6.30pm. Shuttle-bus trips organized by Adrenalina Tours (see p.175) leave Xela for Zunil daily.

Fuentes Georginas
High in the hills, 8km from Zunil, are the **Fuentes Georginas** (daily 8am–5.30pm; Q25), a set of luxuriant hot springs. Surrounded by fresh green ferns, thick moss and lush forest, the baths are sublime, and to top it all there's a restaurant (meals around Q60, snacks Q30) and a well-stocked bar, with decent wine, beside the main pool. It's easy to spend quite some time here soaking it all in (literally). Rustic stone **bungalows** are available for the night (☏5904 5559; Q200), complete with bathtub, two double beds, fireplace and barbecue.

Pick-up trucks from the plaza in Zunil charge Q100 for the return trip, no matter how many passengers there are – it's an exhilarating journey up a smooth paved road which switchbacks through magnificent volcanic scenery. Most people visit as a package from Xela (see box, p.175); all the tour companies in town offer trips from Q100 upwards, the price depending on which other sights are combined.

Totonicapán
A one-hour bus journey from Xela will take you to the town of **Totonicapán**, an intensely farmed little region surrounded by rolling hills and pine forests. The valley has always held out against outside influence, and it's still a quiet place, disturbed only by the Tuesday and Saturday **markets**, which fill the two plazas. Recently, it has become one of the highlands' chief centres of commercial weaving. To take

a closer look at the work of local artisans, head for the town's visitor centre, the **Casa de la Cultura**, on 8 Av 2–17 (Mon–Sat 9am–5pm; ☎5630 0554), which organizes good guided tours (starting at Q250 per person, minimum four people; includes a guided tour of the town, visiting weaving, ceramics and wood-carving centres and a school). The tours are pricey, but fees funnel back into the community.

Totonicapán is best done as a day-trip from Xela; **buses** shuttle from the Minerva terminal and back every 15 minutes or so, via the Cuatro Caminos junction.

San Francisco El Alto

The small town of **San Francisco El Alto** overlooks the Quetzaltenango valley from a lovely hillside setting just north of Totonicapán. The view alone is worth a visit, with the great plateau stretching out below and Volcán Santa María on the horizon, but the main reason for a trip here is the **Friday market**, possibly the biggest in Central America and attended by traders from every corner of Guatemala – many arrive the night before, and some start selling by candlelight from as early as 4am. Throughout the morning a steady stream of buses and trucks fills the town to bursting; by noon the market is at its height, buzzing with activity; things start to thin out in the early afternoon.

The market is separated into a few distinct areas. At the very top of the hill is an open field used as an **animal market**, full of everything from pigs to parrots. Buyers inspect the animals' teeth and tongues, and at times the scene degenerates into a chaotic wrestling match, with livestock and men rolling in the dirt. Below this is the town's plaza, dominated by **textiles**. On the lower level, the streets are filled with produce, pottery, furniture, cheap *comedores* and more. Many of the stalls deal in imported denim, but under the

arches and in the covered area opposite the church is usually a nice selection of traditional cloth. For really good views of the market and the surrounding countryside, pay the church caretaker a quetzal and climb up to the church roof.

Buses go from Quetzaltenango to San Francisco, 16km away, leaving every twenty minutes or so from the Minerva terminal; the first is at 6am, and the last bus back leaves at about 5pm (45min).

Momostenango

Some 22km from San Francisco is **Momostenango**, a small, isolated town and the centre of wool production in the highlands. The main reason for visiting is to take in the town's **Sunday market**, which fills the town's two plazas. Momostecos travel throughout the country peddling their blankets, scarves and rugs – years of experience have made them experts in the hard sell and given them a sharp eye for tourists. The town is also famous for its unconventional folk-Catholicism, and there are many Maya **shamans** working here. While you're here you could also walk to the *riscos*, a set of bizarre pumice pillars, or beyond to the **hot springs** of Pala Chiquito, about 3km away to the north.

Visits are best done as day-trips from Quetzaltenango, or you could head on to Huehuetenango. **Buses** run from the Minerva terminal in Quetzaltenango, passing through Cuatro Caminos and (most) via San Francisco El Alto (every 30min 6am–5pm; 1hr 45min). Returning, they run from Momostenango between 6am and 4pm. There are additional services on Sundays, for the market.

HUEHUETENANGO

Bustling **HUEHUETENANGO**, capital of the department of the same name, lies at the foot of the Cuchumatanes mountain range. It's a small city, and not wildly exciting, but it does have a real Guatemalan feel to it. The majority

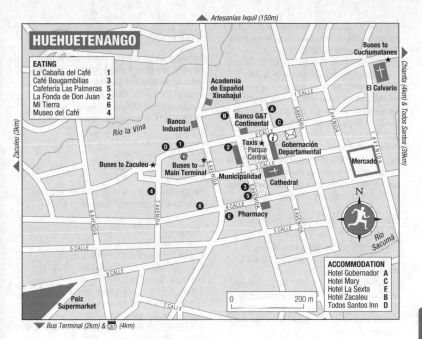

Artesanías Ixquil (150m)

HUEHUETENANGO

EATING
La Cabaña del Café	1
Café Bougambilias	3
Cafetería Las Palmeras	5
La Fonda de Don Juan	2
Mi Tierra	6
Museo del Café	4

Zaculeu (3km)

Buses to
Cuchumatanes

Chiantla (4km) & Todos Santos (39km)

El Calvario

Academia
de Español
Xinabajul

Río la Vina

Banco
Industrial

Banco G&T
Continental

Taxis
Parque
Central

Gobernación
Departamental

Mercado

Buses to Zaculeu

Buses to
Main Terminal

Municipalidad

Cathedral

N

Pharmacy

Río
Sacumá

5 CALLE

6 CALLE

Paiz
Supermarket

0   200 m

ACCOMMODATION
Hotel Gobernador	A
Hotel Mary	C
Hotel La Sexta	E
Hotel Zacaleu	B
Todos Santos Inn	D

Bus Terminal (2km) & (4km)

of the inhabitants are *ladino*, though there is also a sizeable *indígena* population as well. The attractive square at the centre of the *ladino* half of town is surrounded by shaded walkways and administrative offices, while a few blocks east around 1 Avenida the *indígena* part of town is always alive with activity, its streets packed with people attending the nearby market. Few travellers stay long in Huehue, but if you're heading to or from Mexico or Todos Santos Cuchumatán you'll probably find yourself here to change buses. While you're in town, it's easy to take in the minor ruins of **Zaculeu** on the outskirts of town (see p.182).

What to see and do

Huehue's main attraction is the *indígena* **market**, located in the hub of the Maya part of town, where every day the streets are crowded with traders from the surrounding areas. This is also pretty much the only part of town where you will be able to see traditional dress,

as most of the city's inhabitants wear western clothes.

Arrival and information

By bus The bus terminal is halfway between the Carretera Interamericana and the centre. Minibuses make constant trips between the town centre and the bus terminal at all hours of the day, though the frequency decreases after dark.
Tourist information There is no tourist office in Huehue. Mario Martínez (☎5762 1903) is a knowledgeable guide who runs tours in the region.

Accommodation

Huehuetenango's budget hotels are simple and basic, and mainly cater to Guatemalans on the road. There are no hostels here.
Hotel Gobernador 4 Av 1–45 ☎7764 1197. An ancient place with a warren of basic, bare rooms (some en suite), none of them fancy, but all of them cheap. The shared bathrooms are clean enough. Q65
Hotel La Sexta 6 Av 1–49 ☎7764 6612. Fairly clean rooms, though some need ventilation. The private bathrooms are spick and span, the communal ones less so. Q90
Hotel Mary 2 C 3–52 ☎7764 1618. This is a well-kept, friendly and secure place. The rooms, all

with private bath, are showing signs of age but will suffice for a night; some have a sofa or wardrobe. There's a *comedor* too. Q130

Hotel Zacaleu 5 Av 1–14 ☎7764 1086. This fine colonial-style inn has real class, with spacious if old-fashioned rooms set around a lovely leafy courtyard (and a newer section which is far less appealing). Don't miss the fantastic old bar, with piano and elegant chairs. Solo travellers get a great deal here. Q250

Todos Santos Inn 2 C 6–74 ☎5432 3421. Run by a hospitable lady, this budget place has clean if spartan rooms – smell that bleach. Those upstairs are fairly bright and cheery, those downstairs less so. The shared bathrooms are clean. Q100

Eating

You'll find plenty of budget options close to the plaza. There's no real bar scene, but 6 C has a couple of possibilities.

La Cabaña del Café 2 C 6–50. A tiny log-cabin-style place with wonderful coffees (from Q6); all beans are from the Huehue region. Sandwiches (there's even roast beef), snacks and cakes are also served.

Café Bougambilias Opposite the church. This four-storey pink and lurid green *comedor* is a good place for breakfast – try the highland-style *mosh*: porridge with cinnamon, wheat and sugar.

Cafetería Las Palmeras Opposite the church. This very popular, clean and efficiently run restaurant has been recently renovated, so the premises are quite smart. You can't go wrong with the set lunch deals (Q25), which all include soup and a *refresco* – try the *chiles rellenos*. Also offers lots of tasty meat dishes and *tamales* for Q5 (Sat only).

La Fonda de Don Juan 2 C 5–35. Large restaurant with gingham tablecloths. The menu includes good pizzas, pastas and burgers, though it's a little overpriced, with most dishes in the Q40 range. Open 24hr.

Mi Tierra 4 C 6–46. Intimate little restaurant, set in a covered patio with a welcoming atmosphere. There's plenty of choice on the menu, with popular Guatemalan dishes like *pollo dorado*, grilled meats and Mexican classics too, most Q20–40.

🏃 **Museo del Café** 7 Av 3–24. A huge and refined place dedicated to the coffee bean. You'll find coffee sacks on the walls, photographs of coffee *fincas* and lots of café curios. Great cappuccino, espresso and filter coffee served, and it's also a good choice for breakfast (from Q17), or lunch and dinner dishes including steamed vegetables (Q30), grilled beef (Q45) or the *menu del día* (Q22). And if you have a sweet tooth, don't miss the cakes.

Directory

Exchange G&T Continental on the main square (Mon–Fri 8am–7pm, Sat 8am–1pm) has an ATM and changes travellers' cheques and US dollars.
Internet Try Génesis, 2 C 6–37 (Q5/hr).
Language school Xinabajul, 4 Av 14–14, Zona 5 (☎7764 6631, 🌐www.spanishschoolinguatemala.com).
Pharmacy Farmacia El Cid, 4 C & 5 Av (daily 8am–1pm & 2pm–7.30pm).
Post office 2 C 3–51 (Mon–Fri 8am–5.30pm, Sat 9am–1pm).
Telephones The Telgua office (daily 8am–6pm) is in the Centro Comercial el Triángulo, 10 Av & 6 C.

Moving on

By bus There are regular chicken buses to Guatemala City (6hr), La Mesilla (2hr), Xela (2hr) and Todos Santos Cuchumatán (hourly 11.30am–4.30pm; 2hr 30min) – get there early to mark your seat and buy a ticket. If you'd rather travel in more comfort, Los Halcones, 10 Av 9–12, in Zona 1 next to the Paiz supermarket, runs four daily Pullmans to Guatemala City. For Antigua, get a Guatemala City bus and change at Chimaltenango. You'll find very regular connections to Aguacatán (40min), from where microbuses continue on to Sacapulas.

AROUND HUEHUETENANGO

Huehuetenango serves as a good base to explore the nearby ruins of Zaculeu, the setting of one of the most legendary confrontations in the country's history – the Mam fought the Spanish here in a battle that lasted over a month.

Zaculeu

A few kilometres west of Huehuetenango are the ruins of **Zaculeu** (daily 8am–5pm; Q50), once the capital of the **Mam**, who were one of the principal pre-Conquest highland Maya tribes. The site includes several large temples, plazas and a ball court, all restored pretty unfaithfully by the United Fruit Company in 1946–47: the walls were recoated with white plaster, a technique seldom used for restoring pre-Columbian buildings, as it leaves them lacking the roof-combs, carvings and stucco mouldings that would have adorned the structures. Nonetheless, Zaculeu has a unique atmosphere – surrounded by pines, and with fantastic views of the mountains, its grassy plazas make excellent picnic spots. There's a small **museum** at the site (same hours) with examples of some of the unusual burial techniques used and some ceramics found during excavation. To get to Zaculeu from Huehuetenango, take one of the **buses** that leave every thirty minutes from close to the school, at 7 Avenida between 2 and 3 calles – make sure it's heading for "Las Ruinas".

AGUACATÁN

It's 22km east from Huehue to **AGUACATÁN**, a small agricultural town strung out along a very long main street, and the only place in the country where the Akateko and Chalchitek languages are spoken. It is best done as a day-trip, preferably in time to see Aguacatán's huge Sunday **market**, which actually gets under way on Saturday afternoon, when traders arrive early to claim the best sites. On Sunday mornings, a steady stream of people pours into town, cramming into the market and plaza, and soon spilling out into the surrounding area. Around noon the tide turns as the crowds start to drift back to their villages, with donkeys leading their drunken drivers home.

Aguacatán's other attraction is the source of the **Río San Juan**, which emerges fresh and cool from beneath a nearby hill, making a good place for a

ALL SAINTS' DAY IN TODOS SANTOS

The **All Saints' Day** fiesta (Nov 1) in Todos Santos Cuchumatán is one of the most famous in the country. The all-day horse race on All Saints' Day attracts large crowds, and is characterized by a massive stampede as the inebriated riders tear up the course, thrashing their horses with live chickens. On the "Day of the Dead" (November 2), the action moves to the cemetery, with marimba bands and drink stalls set up among the graves – a day of intense ritual that combines grief and celebration. By the end of the fiesta, the streets are littered with drunken revellers and the jail packed with brawlers.

chilly dip. To get there, walk east along the main street out of the village for about a kilometre, until you see the sign. From the centre it takes about twenty minutes.

Buses and microbuses connect Huehuetenango to Aguacatán between 6am and about 5pm (roughly every 30min; 40min). Beyond Aguacatán the road runs out along a ridge, with fantastic views stretching out below, eventually dropping down to the riverside town of **Sacapulas** an hour and a half away (see p.168); very regular microbuses ply this route until 5pm.

TODOS SANTOS CUCHUMATÁN

TODOS SANTOS CUCHUMATÁN is many travellers' favourite place in Guatemala. The beauty of the alpine surroundings is a key attraction: the entire region is crisscrossed with excellent trails, offering fantastic **hiking**. The highland Maya culture here is all pervading: the vast majority of Todosanteros are indigenous and speak Mam as their first language, and the ancient 260-day Tzolkin calendar is still observed. Most houses have a low mud-brick structure outside, called a *chuj*, which is similar to a sauna, with a wood fire lit under the rocks; family members use the steam generated to cleanse themselves. The local costume is incredible: the men wear straw hats, red-and-white-striped trousers and pinstripe shirts decorated with pink and blue collars, while the women wear dark blue *cortes* and intricately woven purple *huipiles*.

What to see and do

The village itself is pretty – a modest main street with a few shops, a plaza and a church – but is totally overshadowed by the looming presence of the Cuchumatanes mountains. Todos Santos sits at an altitude of 2460m, and it can be very chilly up here when the mists set in. Though most of the fun of this place is in simply hanging out, it would be a shame not to indulge in a traditional *chuj* **sauna** while here; most of the guesthouses will prepare one for you. If you want to take a shirt, pair of trousers or *huipil* home with you, you'll find an excellent co-op selling quality weavings next to the *Casa Familiar*. The **Museo Balam** (Mon–Sat 7am–5am; Q5), on the left after the Hispanomaya language school, is definitely worth a visit, with such eclectic local objects as old pottery and statues, a sheep's head, a deer's legs, old traditional hats made of beeswax, a drum and a hundred-year-old marimba.

Above the village – follow the track that goes up behind the *Comedor Katy* – is the small Maya site of **Qman Txun** where you'll find a couple of mounds sprouting pine trees. The site is occasionally used by *costumbristas* for the ritual sacrifice of animals.

Arrival and information

By bus After a number of hair-raising bends through steep hills and dramatic, spectacular mountain scenery dotted with corn and potato crops, buses will drop you off in the town centre.

Tourist information The Hispanomaya Spanish School, 150m south of the plaza (☎5163 9293, ⓦwww.academiahispanomaya.org), is a good source of tourist information; they have a book exchange here, show videos and can also organize guided walks. Roman (☎5900 7795, ⓔromanstopp @yahoo.com), the Swiss owner of the *Casa Familiar*, is a font of knowledge about the village and region.

Accommodation and eating

Plenty of families rent out rooms very cheaply – ask at the Hispanomaya Spanish School (see above). All hotels listed below are clustered close together just above the plaza past *Comedor Katy*. *Comedores* are scattered around the market. Note that Todos Santos is now a dry town; no alcohol is served except to guests of the *Casa Familiar*.

Comedor Katy One block from the square. There's always something bubbling on the hearth at this simple *comedor* with excellent food (meals from Q15).

Hospedaje Casa Familiar ☎5580 9579, ⓔromanstopp@yahoo.com. This long-running travellers' mecca is undergoing a lengthy renovation project, with accommodation and facilities being steadily upgraded. Rooms have balconies with valley views, TV, woven bedspreads and private hot-water bathrooms. Warm up in the guests' lounge around the fireplace or enjoy a *chuj* on the roof terrace. The café here is excellent for Western or Guatemalan food, though quite pricey (meals Q20–40) compared to the local places. Wine and beer are available to guests. There's a store selling local weavings too. Q150

Hotel Mam ☎5523 4148. The bare, moderately clean rooms are cheap, at least; showers are shared. Q60

Hotelito Todos Santos ☎7783 0603 or 5327 9313. Popular place with small, plain but tidy tiled-floor rooms (some with bathroom) and a good *comedor* (meals Q20). Q95

Directory

Exchange On the square, Banrural (Mon–Fri 8.30am–5pm & Sat 7–11am) changes travellers' cheques and US dollars. There are no ATMs in town.
Internet You can access the net at Hispanomaya Spanish School (Q5/hr).
Language school Hispanomaya Spanish School (☎5163 9293, ⓦwww.academiahispanomaya.org), 150m south of the plaza.
Post office On the plaza (Mon–Fri 8am–5pm, Sat 8am–noon).

Moving on

By bus Nine daily buses pass through Todos Santos on the way to Huehuetenango from Jacaltenango (1hr 30min).

AROUND TODOS SANTOS

It would be a real shame to miss out on one of the many hikes that can be done around Todos Santos – make sure you spend some time exploring the surrounding areas, home to some of the country's most breathtaking and dramatic scenery.

San Juan Atitán

The village of **San Juan Atitán** is around five hours on foot from Todos Santos via a wildly beautiful, isolated highland trail. It's best to go with a guide: Hispanomaya Spanish School in Todos Santos (see "Tourist information", above) organizes hikes, or you can look for Roman at *Casa Familiar*. Follow the path that bears up behind the *Comedor Katy*, past the ruins and high above the village through endless muddy switchbacks until you get to the ridge overlooking the valley where, if the skies are clear, you'll be rewarded by an awesome view of the Tajumulco and Tacaná volcanoes. Take the easy-to-follow central track downhill from here

---

INTO MEXICO: LA MESILLA

From Huehuetenango the Carretera Interamericana runs for 79km to the Mexican border at La Mesilla. There are buses every thirty minutes between 5am and 6pm (2hr). The two sets of customs and *migración* are 3km apart, connected by shared (*colectivo*) taxis. At Ciudad Cuauhtémoc on the Mexican side you can pick up buses to Comitán (1hr 15min) and even direct to San Cristóbal de Las Casas (2hr 30min). Heading into Guatemala, the last bus leaves La Mesilla for Huehuetenango at around 6pm.

past some ancient cloudforest to San Juan Atitán. There are two *hospedajes* (both Q40) if you want to stay, and irregular **transport** heads to Huehue (around six daily pick-ups; 1hr). Market days are Mondays and Thursdays.

Alternatively, you can continue west along the valley from Todos Santos to **San Martín** and on to **Jacaltenango**, a route which also offers superb views. There's a basic accommodation and a Banrural bank (with ATM) in Jacaltenango, so you could stay the night and then catch a bus back to Huehuetenango in the morning. Some buses from Huehue also continue down this route.

The Pacific coast

The **Pacific coast**, a strip of two hundred and fifty kilometres of black volcanic beaches, is known in Guatemala as La Costa Sur. Once as rich in wildlife as the jungles of Petén, in recent years it's been ravaged by development, and is now the country's most intensely farmed region, with coffee grown on the volcanic slopes and entire villages effectively owned by vast cotton- and sugar-cane-growing *fincas* (ranches or plantations). A few protected areas try to preserve some of the area's natural heritage; the **Monterrico Reserve** is the most accessible of these, a swampy refuge for sea turtles, iguanas, crocodiles and an abundance of birdlife. It also harbours a beachside village with a near-endless stretch of clean, dark sand and is popular with visitors from Antigua and Guatemala City at weekends.

You can glimpse the impressive art of the Pipil around the town of **Santa Lucía Cotzumalguapa**, and the Maya site of **Takalik Abaj** is worth a detour on your way to or from Mexico, or as a day-trip from Quetzaltenango. Otherwise, the region's pre-Columbian history isn't as visible as that in other parts of the country.

The main route along the coast is the **Carretera al Pacífico**, which runs from the Mexican border at Tecún Umán into El Salvador at Ciudad Pedro de Alvarado. It's the country's swiftest highway and you'll never have to wait long for a bus. Venture off this road, however, and things slow down considerably.

RETALHULEU

RETALHULEU, usually referred to as **Reu** (pronounced "Ray-oo"), may be one of the largest towns in the area, but that doesn't mean it's exciting. There is nothing much to do in the town itself – the main reason to visit is to see the

---

INTO MEXICO: EL CARMEN AND TECÚN UMÁN

There are two border crossings with **Mexico** in the coastal region, both open 24hr. The northernmost is the **Talismán Bridge**, also referred to as **El Carmen**. On the Mexican side, a constant stream of minibuses and buses leaves for Tapachula (30min). Coming from Mexico, there are regular buses to Guatemala City until about 7pm; if heading towards Quetzaltenango or the western highlands, take the first minibus to Malacatán or Coatepeque and change there.

Further south and leading directly onto the Carretera al Pacífico, the **Tecún Umán–Ciudad Hidalgo** crossing is favoured by most Guatemalan and virtually all commercial traffic. If you're Mexico-bound, there are very frequent bus services to Tapachula (40min) over the border. There's a steady flow of buses to Guatemala City along the Carretera al Pacífico via Retalhuleu and also regular direct buses to Quetzaltenango until 3pm (3hr 30min).

ruins of Takalik Abaj, about 15km west (see below). However, it is something of a transport hub, with virtually all **buses** running along the coastal highway stopping at the Retalhuleu terminal on 7 Avenida and 10 Calle, a ten-minute walk from the plaza. If you find yourself waiting for a bus, the **Museo de Arqueología y Etnología**, in the plaza (Tues–Sat 8.30am–1pm & 2–5pm, Sun 9am–12.30pm; Q15), is home to an amazing collection of anthropomorphic figurines, mostly heads, and some photographs of the town dating back to the 1880s.

Also in the plaza are a number of **banks**, including a Banco Industrial with an ATM. Budget **hotels** are slim on the ground; *Hotel América* at 8 Av 9–32 (☎7771 1154; Q138) is the best bet and has a small pool. When it comes to **eating**, try the *Cafetería La Luna* on the plaza for good breakfasts (from Q16) and lunches (Q25).

From Reu there are **buses** to Guatemala City (3hr), the Mexican border (1hr 30min) and Quetzaltenango (1hr 15min) about every thirty minutes, plus regular buses to Champerico (1hr) and El Tulate (1hr 45min) until about 6.30pm.

TAKALIK ABAJ

TAKALIK ABAJ (daily 7am–5pm; Q50) is among the most important Mesoamerican sites in the country and one of the few that has both Olmec and Maya features. Though the remains of two large **temple platforms** have been cleared, it's the sculptures and stelae found carved around their base, including rare and unusual representations of frogs and toads (monument 68) and an alligator (monument 66), that make a trip here worthwhile. Among the finest carvings is stele 5, which features two standing figures separated by a hieroglyphic panel that has been dated to 126 AD. Look out for giant Olmec-style heads too, including one

with great chipmunk cheeks. In 2002, archeologists unearthed a royal tomb, complete with jade necklace and mask belt, below the observatory structure 7A, confirming that following the Olmec, the site was later occupied by the Maya; Maya rituals occasionally still take place here. You will be able to get water at the entrance, and there is also a little restaurant.

To get to Takalik Abaj, take a local **bus** from Reu 15km west to the village of El Asintal, from where you can take a pick-up (Q5) to the site 4km away.

CHAMPERICO

A fast highway runs the forty-odd kilometres south from Reu to the beach at **CHAMPERICO**, which, though it doesn't feel like it, is the country's third port, and best visited as a day-trip. The town enjoyed a brief period of prosperity many decades ago when it was connected to Quetzaltenango by rail, though there's little sign of this now apart from a rusting pier. The dark sand **beach** is impressive for its scale (though watch out for the dangerous undertow), but perhaps the best reason for visiting is **seafood**; there are rows of beachside *comedores*, all offering deep-fried prawns and fresh fish for around Q60 a head. Don't wander too far from the busiest part of the beach – muggings have occurred in isolated spots here. **Buses** run between Champerico and Quetzaltenango every hour or so until 6pm (2hr 15min), and there are also very regular connections to Retalhuleu.

SANTA LUCÍA COTZUMALGUAPA

SANTA LUCÍA COTZUMALGUAPA, a rather nondescript coastal town, functions as a good base to explore three mysterious Pipil **archeological sites** that are scattered around the surrounding cane fields. Bear in mind, though, that getting to them all isn't easy unless you have your own transport or hire a taxi. There are no decent budget places in the centre, but *Hotel Internacional* (☎7882 5504; Q140), just south of the main highway, has spacious, fan-cooled rooms which will suffice for a night. For **food**, *Taquería Palankiny*, one block north of the plaza on 4 Calle, does the job, with excellent tacos (three for Q10). Banco Industrial on 3 Avenida has an ATM. Pullman **buses** passing along the highway will drop you at the entrance road to town, ten minutes' walk from the centre, while second-class buses go straight into the terminal, a few blocks from the plaza. Buses to the capital leave the terminal every thirty minutes until 4pm, or you can catch a bus from the highway.

AROUND SANTA LUCÍA COTZUMALGUAPA

Three **archeological sites** around Santa Lucía are all that remains of the Pipil civilization, an indigenous non-Maya culture with close links to the Nahuatl tribes of Central Mexico. To this day, it is unclear as to how these people, now known for their intricate stone carvings, came to live in this area (possibly as early as 400 AD), as it was largely inhabited by the Maya. It is possible, although not advisable, to visit the sites on foot passing through cane fields – but beware that this can be dangerous, as muggers hide in the fields. It is much safer to hire a **taxi** in the plaza in Santa Lucía – to visit all three sites in a couple of hours reckon on Q100. You can also get to the Museo El Baúl by **bus** (every 30min); take one heading to Colonia Maya from either the bus terminal or the park in Santa Lucía.

Bilbao

Unearthed in 1860, the site of **Bilbao** has four sets of stones visible in situ, two of which perfectly illustrate the magnificent precision of the Pipil carving techniques, beautifully preserved in slabs of black volcanic rock hidden in sugar cane. A path leading left into the cane brings you to two large stones carved with bird-like patterns, with strange circular glyphs arranged in groups of three: the majority of the glyphs are recognizable as the names for days once used by the people of southern Mexico. In the same cane field, further along the same path, is another badly eroded stone, and a final set with a superbly preserved set of figures and interwoven motifs. If you get lost at any stage, ask for "las piedras", as they tend to be known locally.

Finca El Baúl

The second site, in the grounds of the **Finca El Baúl**, is about 5km further afield. The hilltop site has two stones, one a massive half-buried stone head with wrinkled brow and patterned headdress. In front of the stones is a set of small altars on which local people make animal sacrifices, burn incense and leave offerings of flowers. The next stones of interest are at the **finca** itself, in the **Museo El Baúl** (admission free), a few kilometres further away from town, where the carvings include some superb heads, stone skulls, a massive jaguar, the emblem of Santa Lucía and an extremely well preserved stele of two boxers (monument 27) dating from the Late Classic period. Alongside all this antiquity is the *finca*'s old steam engine, a miniature machine that used to haul the cane along a system of private tracks.

Finca Las Ilusiones

The third site is on the other side of town, at **Finca Las Ilusiones**. Here another collection of artefacts and some stone carvings has been assembled in the **Museo Cultura Cotzumalguapa** (Mon–Fri 8am–4pm, Sat 8am–noon; Q25). Two of the most striking figures within are the pot-bellied statue (monument 58), probably from the middle Pre-Classic era, and a copy of monument 21, which bears three figures, the central one depicting a ball player. There are several other original items, including a fantastic stele, plus some more replicas and thousands of small stone carvings and pottery fragments. To **get here**, head out of town east along the highway for about 1km, and follow the signs on the left.

LA DEMOCRACIA

The next town east along the highway is Siquinalá, a run-down place from where another branch road heads to the coast. Some 9km south along this road is **LA DEMOCRACIA**, worth a quick visit for its multiple collections of archeological relics taken from the site of **Monte Alto** to the east of town. Some of these are now displayed around the town plaza under a huge ceiba tree. Called "fat boys", these are massive stone heads with simple, almost childlike faces, carved in Olmec style and thought to date from the mid-Preclassic period, possibly from as far back as 500 BC. Some are attached to smaller rounded bodies and rolled over on their backs clutching their swollen stomachs like stricken Teletubbies. Also on the plaza, the town **museum** (Tues–Sat 9am–4pm; Q30) houses carvings, a wonderful jade mask, yokes worn by ball-game players, pottery, grinding stones and a few more carved heads.

There are regular **buses** here from both Santa Lucía and Escuintla. Buses leave from the plaza every thirty minutes heading to the capital (2hr), Escuintla (45min) and Santa Lucía (30min).

ESCUINTLA

Sitting at the junction of the two main coastal roads from the capital, **ESCUINTLA** is the largest of the Pacific towns, typified by relentless heat and traffic. Unfortunately, it's also the most dangerous, and the only reason you should find yourself in town is to change buses. If for some reason you're stuck here check into the *Hotel Costa Sur*, 12 C 4–13 (☎5295 9528; Q135), a clean, orderly place where the rooms are decent value for money.

Arrival

By bus Buses to Guatemala City leave from 8 Calle and 2 Avenida. For other destinations, there are two terminals: for places en route to the Mexican border, buses run through the north of town and stop by the Esso station opposite the Banco Uno (take a local bus up 3 Av); buses for the coast road and inland route to El Salvador are best caught at the main terminal on the south side of town, at the bottom of 4 Avenida (local bus down 4 Av). Buses leave every thirty minutes for the eastern border and hourly for Antigua.

MONTERRICO

The tiny beachside settlement of **MONTERRICO** enjoys one of the finest settings on the Pacific coast. Scenically, things are reduced to a strip of dead-straight sand, a line of powerful surf and an enormous curving horizon. The village is scruffy but friendly and relaxed, separated from the mainland by the waters of the Chiquimulilla canal, which weaves through a fantastic network of **mangrove swamps**. Mosquitoes can be an issue during the wet season, but Monterrico is still certainly the best place on the coast to spend time by the sea, though take care in the waves as there's a vicious **undertow**.

If you're looking for a really tranquil experience, try to avoid visiting on a weekend (when Monterrico is much busier with visitors from Guatemala City).

What to see and do

Monterrico's long stretch of **beach** is perfect for kicking back with a book and watching one of the many beautiful sunsets that tinge the sky pink.

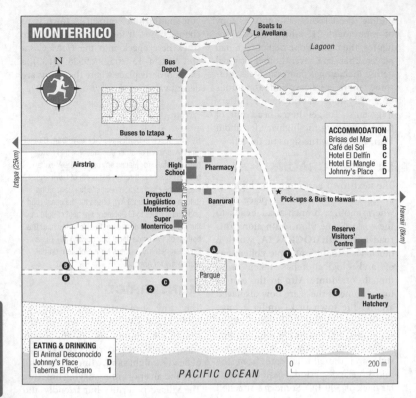

MONTERRICO

Boats to
La Avellana

Lagoon

N

Bus
Depot

Buses to Iztapa ★

Airstrip

High
School

➕ Pharmacy

ACCOMMODATION
Brisas del Mar   **A**
Café del Sol   **B**
Hotel El Delfín   **C**
Hotel El Mangle   **E**
Johnny's Place   **D**

Iztapa (25km)

Proyecto
Lingüístico
Monterrico

Banrural

★ Pick-ups & Bus to Hawaii

Super
Monterrico

A

Reserve
Visitors'
Centre

B

Hawaii (8km)

B

2

C

Parque

1

D

E ▪ Turtle
Hatchery

EATING & DRINKING
El Animal Desconocido   **2**
Johnny's Place   **D**
Taberna El Pelicano   **1**

0   200 m

PACIFIC OCEAN

Biotopo Monterrico-Hawaii nature reserve

Natural beauty aside, Monterrico's other attraction is the **Biotopo Monterrico-Hawaii nature reserve**, which embraces the village, the beach – an important **turtle** nesting ground – and a large slice of the mangrove swamps behind. The reserve is actually home to four distinct types of mangrove, which act as a kind of marine nursery, offering small fish protection from their natural predators, while above the surface live hundreds of species of bird and a handful of mammals, including racoons and armadillos, plus iguanas, caimans and alligators. The best way to explore the reserve is in a small *cayuco* (kayak); these are best organized via your guest-house or down at the dock itself. The reserve's **visitors' centre** (daily 8am–

noon & 2–5pm; Q30), just off the beach between *Hotel El Mangle* and the *Pez d'Oro* hotel, has plenty of information about the environment (Spanish only) and sections where endemic species including sea turtles, caimans, iguanas and other lizards are bred for release into the wild. There's a short interpretive **trail** through the grounds of the centre to explore too.

Arrival and information

By bus Buses from Guatemala City and Iztapa arrive at a bus stop just south of the dock, a five-minute walk from the beach.

By shuttle bus Most visitors arrive by the daily shuttle buses that link Antigua with Monterrico (Q60). Shuttle buses drop off at hotels.

Tourist information There is no tourist office. Check out the community website ⓦ www.monterrico -guatemala.com for up-to-date information. The

Proyecto Lingüístico Monterrico (see p.192) is by far the best source of information on the ground; they also provide maps.

Accommodation

Expect to pay a little more here than in many places in Guatemala. At weekends it's best to book ahead (and price rises of 20 percent are common). All places listed below are right on or just off the beach. Avoid the *Hotel Baule Beach*, as regular thefts have been reported.

Brisas del Mar Turn left just before the beach ☎5517 1142. Its soulless motel-style appearance is slightly off-putting and it's about 100m inland from the beach, but the 26 bungalows here (with fan or a/c) are in decent condition, have private bathroom and prices are affordable. All face a garden with two pools. Q130

Café del Sol Turn right at the beach and walk for 250m ☎5050 9173, ⓦwww.cafe-del-sol.com. Perhaps the best reason to stay here is the lovely beach-facing frontage, with sunbeds facing the ocean. It's a well-run place with accommodation divided between inland and beachside blocks (avoid rooms in the bar-restaurant which lack privacy). The food is tasty, though quite pricey, and there's a small pool. Q290

🏃 **Hotel El Delfin** 50m right at beachfront ☎5702 6701, ⓦwww.hotel-el-delfin.com. This once-grim place is being steadily renovated by an enthusiastic American–Guatemalan couple and now offers great value and fine service. All rooms have fans and mosquito nets, there's a good-sized pool, a popular bar and great food. In fact, the only thing that's not chilled about this place is the bad-tempered parrot. Q80

Hotel El Mangle Turn left at the beach ☎5514 6517. This is a relaxed lodge with charming, attractive fan-cooled rooms, all with mosquito nets, bathrooms and little terraces with hammocks. The a/c rooms are overpriced. The central garden area has a small pool. Q130

Johnny's Place Turn left at the beach ☎5812 0409, ⓦwww.johnnysplacehotel.com. For years this place has been the main backpacker watering-hole, and the prime beachside location and chillout zone (a *palapa* with hammocks) are enticing. However, the accommodation is rough and ready so it's best used just as a place to crash. Be warned (or be happy) that it's party central on weekend nights. Dorms Q50, doubles Q170

Eating and drinking

There are quite a few places to eat out in town, the cheapest being the *comedores* on the main drag. You'll find a row of traditional Guatemalan places on C Principal just before you hit the beach, all offering huge portions of fried prawns and fresh fish.

El Animal Desconocido Beachside. By far the liveliest bar (especially at weekends), this place blares out an eclectic selection of rock and dance music and serves mean cocktails.

Johnny's Place Turn left at the beach. Monterrico's main traveller hangout has wave-side seats for decent if unremarkable sandwiches, veggie dishes, fish and grilled meats. The juices and shakes are good.

🏃 **Taberna El Pelicano** Behind *Johnny's Place*. Hats off to the creative Swiss chef here who serves fine European food, including Italian dishes (from Q40), fresh seafood and grilled fish (around Q70). The attractive thatched premises have atmosphere and make up for the lack of sea views.

Moving on

By boat Boats leave eight times daily for La Avellana (30min; passengers Q5, cars Q85), from where there are connections to Taxisco (see box below) on the coastal highway.

By bus Shuttle buses leave from Proyecto Lingüístico Monterrico on the main drag for Antigua (Q60) at 4pm daily. Buses for Iztapa (hourly until 4pm) leave from a stop between the dock and the beach.

Directory

Exchange Banrural (Mon–Fri 8am–5pm, Sat 9am–1pm) changes US dollars. The only ATM in town is inside Super Monterrico on Calle Principal.

INTO EL SALVADOR: CIUDAD PEDRO DE ALVARADO

Very regular buses run along the coastal highway to the border with **El Salvador** at **Ciudad Pedro de Alvarado**. From Taxisco the border is just over an hour away. The border is a fairly quiet one, as most traffic uses the Valle Nuevo post to the north, but there are a few basic *hospedajes* and *comedores* on both sides of the border if you get stuck.

Language school The Proyecto Lingüístico Monterrico (☎5475 1265, ⓦwww.monterrico-guatemala.com/spanish-school), on the main drag, offers inexpensive one-on-one Spanish instruction (20 hours for US$90).

The eastern highlands

The **eastern highlands**, southeast of the capital, are probably the least-visited part of Guatemala. The landscape lacks the appeal of its western counterpart – the peaks are lower and the volcanoes lie higgledy-piggledy – and the towns, whose residents are almost entirely Latinized, are nearly universally featureless. You're unlikely to want to hang around for long. **Esquipulas** is worth a visit, though, for its colossal church, home to the Cristo Negro Milagroso (Miraculous Black Christ), and the most important pilgrimage site in Central America. It's conveniently positioned very close to the border with Honduras and El Salvador. However, if you're heading into Honduras, you're most likely to end up spending the night in **Chiquimula**, the gateway to the ruins of Copán, just over the border. Finally there's the idyllic crater lake on top of the **Volcán de Ipala** – its isolation adds to its appeal.

CHIQUIMULA

Perennially hot and dry, the town of **CHIQUIMULA** is an unattractive, bustling *ladino* stronghold. Few travellers spend the night here – if you've just arrived in Guatemala, things only get better from here. Although the city centre itself is nothing to boast about, the little **Parque Calvario** square, a couple of blocks south of the main plaza, is a pleasant spot with a number of cafés and restaurants.

Arrival and information

By bus The bus terminal is on 1 C between 10 & 11 Av, Zona 1.
Exchange Banco G&T Continental at 7 Av 4–75 (Mon–Fri 9am–6.30pm, Sat 9am–1pm) changes US dollars.
Internet Power Net, 3 C & 7 Av (daily 9am–10pm).
Telephones The Telgua office (daily 8am–6pm) is on the corner of the plaza.

Accommodation

Hotel Hernández 3 C 7–41 ☎7942 0708.
A dependable choice, this rambling hotel has friendly owners and dozens of inexpensive, if plain rooms, most with private bathroom. There's a small pool at the rear for cooling off, and safe parking. Q125
Posada Don Adán 8 Av 4–30 ☎7942 0549.
Another solid option, this pleasingly old-fashioned place is secure and clean, and if the temperature is soaring the rooms' a/c will come in handy. Q150

Eating and drinking

The nicest places to eat are on Parque Calvario, a trendy hangout for the young two blocks south of the main square. There are inexpensive *comedores* in and around the market just east of the main plaza.

Jalisco On Parque Calvario square. Pleasant little café with a couple of tables set outside; try the Mexican dishes (from Q20).
Parillada de Calero 7 Av 4–83. For sizzling *churrascos*, this enjoyable place excels at barbecued *lomito*, *pollo* and *carne de res*. From Q45 a meal.
Peccato Café 5 C & 6 Av. A half-trendy place that's popular for a cocktail or a chilled Gallo. Also serves up reasonable Guatemalan dishes, snacks and pastas (Q30). Closed Sun.

> ### INTO HONDURAS: EL FLORIDO
>
> Microbuses leave from the north side of the market for **El Florido**, and the **Honduran border** (every 30min 6am–6pm; 1hr 30min). Buses (every 30min) then leave the border for Copán.

By bus to: Guatemala City (every 30min
3.30am–6pm; 3hr 15min); Esquipulas
(every 15min 5am–7pm; 1hr); Jalapa, via Ipala
(8 daily 6am–4pm; 2hr 30min); Puerto Barrios
(hourly; 3–4hr).

VOLCÁN DE IPALA

Reached down a side road off the main highway between Chiquimula and Esquipulas, the **VOLCÁN DE IPALA** (1650m) may at first seem a little disappointing – it looks more like a hill than a grand volcano. However, the cone is filled by a beautiful little **crater lake** ringed by dense tropical forest – you can walk round the entire lake in a couple of hours. The easiest route to the top is via a trail from the village of **El Chagüitón**; it's a 2km climb to the visitors' centre where you pay a Q15 entrance fee. It's well worth heading here if you're looking for some peace; chances are that if you visit on a weekday it should be pretty quiet.

The village of **Ipala** is connected by bus with Jutiapa to the south, Jalapa in the west and Chiquimula to the north. It's a pretty forlorn place with a few **places to stay**, the best of which is the *Hospedaje Pinal* (Q65), which has good clean rooms with private bathroom. Buses run from Ipala towards the village of Agua Blanca hourly; get off at **El Sauce** at km 26.5, from where it's an hour and a half to the summit via El Chagüitón.

ESQUIPULAS

ESQUIPULAS is home to the most important Catholic shrine in Central America. For the past four hundred years pilgrims from all over the region have flocked here to pay their respects to the **Cristo Negro Milagroso** (Miraculous Black Christ), whose image is found in the town's magnificent basilica. The principal day of **pilgrimage** is January 15; if you're in town at this time make sure you book accommodation in advance (or commute from Chiquimula). The rest of the town is a messy sprawl of cheap hotels, souvenir stalls and restaurants which have sprung up to serve the pilgrims.

What to see and do

The **Black Christ** is the focus of the town, and is approached through the church's side entrance, past a little area full of candles which are lit upon exiting the building. Pilgrims stand reverently in line, slowly making their way towards the image. The walls are plastered with anything and everything – golden plaques with engraved messages to Christ, passport-sized photos that the pious slip into large picture frames, interwoven gold and silver necklaces that viewed from a distance form the image of Christ. Pilgrims mutter prayers as they approach the image: some kneel, while others briefly pause in front of it, before getting moved on by the crowds behind. As they leave, they do so walking backwards so as to show

---

THE BLACK CHRIST OF ESQUIPULAS

In 1595, following the indigenous population's conversion to Christianity, the town of Esquipulas commissioned famed colonial sculptor Quirio Cataño to carve an image of Christ. Sculpted in a dark wood, the image acquired the name **Cristo Negro** (Black Christ). Rumours of its miraculous capacities soon spread – according to the religious authorities, the first miracle took place in 1603, but it wasn't until 1737, when the archbishop Pardo de Figueroa was cured of an illness, that its healing properties were recognized. It has ever since been the object of the most important religious pilgrimage in Central America.

their respects to Christ by not turning their back on Him.

Arrival and information

By bus Buses from Guatemala City will drop you off at the Rutas Orientales bus station on 11 C & 1 Av, just outside the town centre.
Exchange Banco Industrial has a branch with an ATM at 9 C & 3 Av.

Accommodation

Most budget options are clustered together in the streets off the main road, 11 Calle. Avoid staying on Saturday nights, when rooms cost double.
La Favorita 2 Av 10–15 ☎7943 1175. Small, functional and inexpensive rooms, some en suite, a two-minute walk from the church. Q85
Hospedaje Esquipulas 1 Av & 11 C A ☎7943 2298. This place has neat, plain, though smallish rooms with private bathroom. Q135
Hotel Villa Edelmira 3 Av 8–58 ☎7943 1431. Pleasant, family-run hotel with excellent rates for single travellers. Q90

Eating and drinking

Many of the cheaper restaurants and *comedores* are on 11 Calle and the surrounding streets.
Pollo Campero On 11 C. Guatemala's most popular fast-food chain scores for fried chicken in clean surrounds. There's free wi-fi too.

Restaurante La Frontera Opposite the park. There's usually a bustle about this large place which has a good selection of local dishes, including fish and tasty *carne a la plancha*.

Moving on

By bus There are regular minibuses to the borders with El Salvador (every 30min 6am–5pm; 1hr) and Honduras at Agua Caliente (every 30min 6am–5.30pm; 30min). Rutas Orientales (11 C & 1 Av) runs a half-hourly bus service between Esquipulas and Guatemala City (4hr 30min). To get to the ruins of Copán, catch a bus to Chiquimula (every 15min; 45min) from the east side of 11 C, and change there for the El Florido border post (see p.192).

East to the Caribbean

Coming from Guatemala City, the Caribbean Highway passes through the upper Río Motagua valley before reaching the Río Hondo junction. Here the road divides, with one arm going south to Esquipulas and the main stretch heading east towards the

Caribbean. As you approach the coast, skirting the Maya ruins of **Quiriguá**, the landscape dramatically changes from dry, infertile terrain to lush, green vegetation. Although **Puerto Barrios** is nothing more than a port town, the relaxed town of **Lívingston**, home to the black Garífuna people, has a unique blend of black Caribbean and Guatemalan cultures.

QUIRIGUÁ

Sitting in an isolated pocket of rainforest, surrounded by a forest of banana trees, the small Maya site of **QUIRIGUÁ** is home to some of the finest Maya carvings anywhere. Only Copán, across the border in Honduras (see p.352), offers any competition to the site's magnificent stelae, altars and so-called "zoomorphs", covered in well-preserved and superbly intricate glyphs and portraits.

What to see and do

Entering the site (daily 8am–4.30pm; Q80), you emerge at the northern end of the **Great Plaza**. By the ticket office is a small **museum** (daily 7am–4pm; free), which explains the site's history (see box below) and discovery. Quiriguá is famous for the **stelae** scattered across the Large Plaza, seven (A, C, D, E, F,

H and J) of which were built during the reign of Cauac Sky and depict his image. The nine stelae are the tallest in the Maya world – the largest of all is Stele E, elevated 8m above ground and weighing 65 tonnes. Note the vast headdresses, which dwarf the faces, as well as the beards, an uncommon feature in Maya life. As you make your way towards the **acropolis**, you will be able to make out the remains of a **ball court** on your right, before reaching six blocks of stone carved with images representing animal and human figures: the **zoomorphs**. Have a look at the turtle, frog and jaguar.

The **ruins** are some 70km beyond the junction at Río Hondo, and 4km down a turn-off from the main road. All **buses** coming from Guatemala City on their way to Flores or Puerto Barrios, and going to Flores from Esquipulas and Chiquimula pass by. There's a fairly regular bus service from the highway to the site itself, plus assorted motorbikes and pick-ups. You shouldn't have to wait too long to get a ride back to the highway; it's probably best not to walk to the site as this is a pretty isolated region.

Quiriguá village, just south of the turn-off, has a few **places to stay** if you want to break your journey, including *Hotel y Restaurant Royal* (Q60), a classic budget place with clean, simple rooms.

THE HISTORY OF QUIRIGUÁ

Quiriguá's early history is still relatively unknown, but during the Late Pre-Classic period (250 BC–300 AD) migrants from the north established themselves as rulers here. In the Early Classic period (250–600 AD), the area was dominated by Copán, just 50km away, and doubtless valued for its position on the banks of the Río Motagua, an important trade route, and as a source of jade. It was during the rule of the great leader Cauac Sky that Quiriguá challenged Copán, capturing its leader 18 Rabbit in 738 AD and beheading him, probably with the backing of the "superpower" city of Calakmul. Quiriguá was then able to assert its independence and embark on a building boom: most of the great stelae date from this period. For a century Quiriguá dominated the lower Motaguá valley. Under Jade Sky, who took the throne in 790, Quiriguá reached its peak, with fifty years of extensive building work, including a radical reconstruction of the acropolis. Towards the end of Jade Sky's rule, in the middle of the ninth century, the historical record fades out, as does the period of prosperity and power.

The **Posada de Quiriguá**
(☎5349 5817) is a new,
Japanese-owned guesthouse,
beautifully run by Masuki,
with lovely, immaculately
clean rooms in a fertile garden
setting. The four "single"
rooms have a double bed and
can accommodate a couple
comfortably, while the two
doubles are much more spacious.
You'll find the food a real highlight,
with wonderful Guatemalan and
Japanese meals (dinner Q80), and
good vegetarian choices too. US$20

PUERTO BARRIOS

PUERTO BARRIOS is not somewhere you'll want to hang around for too long – probably just long enough to hop on a boat to your next destination. Named after President Rufino Barrios in the 1880s, the port fell into the hands of the United Fruit Company – the harbour was partly built by Theodore Roosevelt's Corps of Engineers in 1906–08 – and was used to ship UFC bananas to New York and New Orleans. The Guatemalan government, dissatisfied that the port had been built to satisfy foreign interests, built a state-owned port, Santo Tomás de Castilla, six kilometres away, and Puerto Barrios went into a long decline. A new container facility has revived Barrios's fortunes to a degree in recent years, but the place retains a seedy feel, with potholed streets, a clutch of strip bars and iffy characters.

Arrival and information

By boat Boats from Lívingston and Punta Gorda (Belize) arrive at the dock at the end of 12 C.
By bus There's no purpose-built bus station in Puerto Barrios. Litegua buses, which serve all destinations along the Caribbean Highway to Guatemala City, have their own terminal in the centre of town on 6 Av, between 9 & 10 C. All second-class buses arrive and depart from an unmarked stop directly opposite, beside the railway tracks. Microbuses

for the Entre Ríos Honduran border leave from the market, a block north of the second-class bus stop.
Tourist information There's no tourist office. You can get bus schedules at the Litegua terminal.

Accommodation

Barrios is not very backpacker-friendly: there are few decent cheap places.
Hotel La Caribeña 4 Av between 10 & 11 calles ☎7948 0384. Large, rambling place with a variety of reasonable, if ageing rooms (some with a/c). There's a good-quality seafood restaurant here. Q110
Hotel El Dorado 7 Av & 13 C ☎7948 1581. Family-run place with basic but spacious good-value rooms, some with private bath. Q85
Hotel Europa 2 3 Av & 12 C ☎7948 1292. The most popular travellers' hotel in Barrios is clean, secure and very close to the dock. Nearly all the rooms have an en-suite shower and are either fan-cooled or have a/c. Good rates for single travellers. Q150
Hotel del Norte 7 C & 1 Av. An astonishing landmark, this is a wonderful old Caribbean-style architectural monument – an elegant, green-and-white wooden building with a wrap-around balcony, mahogany bar and period-style restaurant. The rooms are actually pretty basic, but a night here is still a wonderfully evocative experience. There's a pool and ocean views; the restaurant's food is disappointing. Q170

Eating

There's an abundance of *comedores* and juice stands around the market.
El Cafecito 13 C 6–22. An intriguing little café that is one of the more civilized places in town for an espresso coffee, Portuguese-style meals like *adobado*, snacks, sandwiches and pastries.
La Caribeña 4 Av between 10 & 11 calles. Recommended for seafood, including delicious *sopa de mariscos* (Q90) and *tapado*.
Safari North of the centre on the seafront, at the end of 5 Av. A huge barn of a place with a *palapa* roof and bay-side seating. It's pricey but portions are enough for two: seafood platters (Q100), *ceviche* (Q75), *tapado* (Q90) and fried shrimps (Q80).

Drinking and nightlife

There are better places for a bar crawl, unless you're into strip clubs. Take care if venturing out

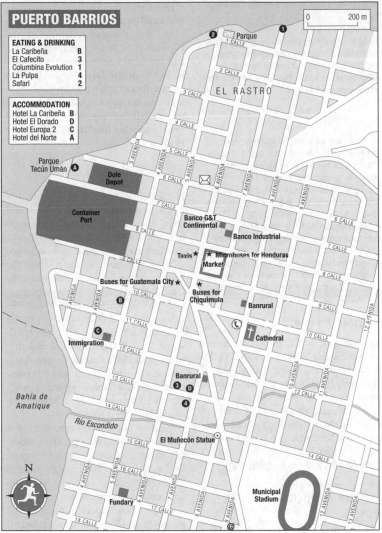

PUERTO BARRIOS

EATING & DRINKING
La Caribeña — B
El Cafecito — 3
Columbina Evolution — 1
La Pulpa — 4
Safari — 2

ACCOMMODATION
Hotel La Caribeña — B
Hotel El Dorado — D
Hotel Europa 2 — C
Hotel del Norte — A

0   200 m

Parque

1 CALLE

2 CALLE

EL RASTRO

3 CALLE

4 CALLE

Parque
Tecún Umán Ⓐ

5 CALLE

Dole
Depot

6 CALLE

Boats to Livingsson & Punta Gorda

Container
Port

7 CALLE

8 CALLE

Banco G&T
Continental

Banco Industrial

Taxis ★ ★ Microbuses for Honduras
Market

6 CALLE

7 CALLE

8 CALLE

Buses for Guatemala City ★

★
Buses for
Chiquimula

Ⓑ

10 CALLE

Banrural

Ⓒ

11 CALLE

Immigration

12 CALLE

Ⓒ

Cathedral

9 CALLE

10 CALLE

Bahía de
Amatique

13 CALLE

Banrural

3

Ⓓ

4

11 CALLE

12 CALLE

Río Escondido

14 CALLE

15 CALLE

El Muñecón Statue

N

16 CALLE

Fundary

17 CALLE

Municipal
Stadium

14 CALLE

18 CALLE

@

Carretera al Atlántico & Guatemala City (293km) ▼

to clubs late at night, and be sure to take a taxi. *El Cafecito* (see opposite) also has draught beer and is good for a relaxed drink.

Columbina Evolution North of the city centre at the end of 7 Av. The city's best club, with two dancefloors and huge sound systems pumping out reggaeton, punta rock and Latin dance. Also hosts concerts.

La Pulpa 7 Av & 13 C. This bar and grill gets quite lively at weekends; a good place to have a drink.

Directory

Exchange Banco Industrial, 7 Av & 7 C, and Banco G&T Continental, 7 C between 6 & 7 avs, both have ATMs and will change US dollars and travellers' cheques.

Immigration For Belize, clear *migración* before buying a ticket; the office is a block west of the dock on 12 C (open 24hr). You'll also need to pay a US$10 sea departure tax.

GUATEMALA   EAST TO THE CARIBBEAN

197

Internet Red Virtual, 17 C & 9 Av, offers access for Q6/hr.

Post office 6 C & 6 Av.

Taxis There are many taxis around town; available drivers honk for customers as they drive through the streets. There's also a rank by the market.

Telephones The Telgua office (daily 7am–6pm) is at the junction of 8 Av & 10 C.

Moving on

By boat There are scheduled *lancha* services to Lívingston at 6.30am, 7.30am, 9am & 11am (30min; Q35); buy your ticket early on the day of departure. Irregular *lanchas* supplement the former, leaving only when full, but you shouldn't have to wait longer than an hour. The daily *lancha* to Punta Gorda in Belize leaves at 10am (Q200).

By bus Litegua (6 Av & 9 C; www.litegua.com) runs comfortable a/c services to Guatemala City (18 daily; 5–6hr), though only three of these are speedy *directos*. There are also regular buses, roughly hourly, for both Chiquimula (4hr 30min) via Quiriguá (2hr), and Río Dulce (2hr), that leave from 6 Av & 9 C.

LÍVINGSTON

Lying at the mouth of the Río Dulce and only accessible by boat, **LÍVINGSTON** is unlike anywhere else in Guatemala – it's largely inhabited by the **Garífuna**, or black Carib people, whose communities are strung out along the Caribbean coast between southern Belize and northern Nicaragua (for a brief history of the Garífuna, see p.99). The town is a little scruffy, and has a slightly edgy vibe

INTO HONDURAS: ENTRE RÍOS

Microbuses (every 30min 6.30am–4.30pm; 1hr) for the border crossing to Honduras at Entre Ríos depart from the Puerto Barrios marketplace. Once there, you may be asked for an unofficial "exit tax" (US$1–2) on the Guatemalan side and an entry fee of a similar sum on the Honduran side. Buses leave the border post of Corinto for Puerto Cortés (hourly; 2hr) via Omoa. The border crossing is open 24hr.

at times, with resident hustlers peddling ganja and cocaine and assorted dubious tours. But the vast majority of the population is relaxed and welcoming, and the local culture is certainly fascinating: a unique fusion of Guatemalan and Caribbean life, with a lowland Maya influence for good measure. Be sure to try the delicious *tapado* (spicy seafood soup) and other local treats while you're in town.

What to see and do

Lívingston is a small place with not much to do other than kick back and relax. There is one interesting museum in town, the **Museo Garífuna** (take the first left from the dock; erratic hours; Q20), where you can learn about the town's cultural mix, including the Garífuna and Q'eqchi' Maya peoples.

The local **beaches**, though safe for swimming, are not the stuff of Caribbean dreams, with dark sand and greyish water. The sole exception is wonderful, white-sand **Playa Blanca**, though this is privately owned and can only be visited on a tour (see "Travel agents", below). Don't walk alone on the beaches at night; attacks have been reported.

The most popular trip around town is to **Las Siete Altares**, a group of waterfalls about 5km to the northwest, a good spot to take a dip and have a picnic. In the past there have been sporadic attacks on tourists walking out to the falls, but the police now supervise the area and it's now considered safe, particularly if you visit as part of a tour (see below).

Arrival and information

By boat The only way to get to Lívingston is by boat, either from Puerto Barrios, the Río Dulce or Belize; they arrive at the main dock on the south side of town.

Travel agents Exotic Travel (☎7947 0049, www.bluecaribbeanbay.com), in the same building as the *Bahía Azul* restaurant, and Happy Fish (☎7947 0661, www.happyfishtravel.com),

LÍVINGSTON

0   100 m

Siete Altares   **A** (1.5km)

Bahía de Amatique

ACCOMMODATION
Casa de la Iguana   E
Flowas   A
Garden Gate Guest House   D
Hotel California   C
Hotel Casa Rosada   F
Hotel Garífuna   B

EATING & DRINKING
Antojitos Gaby   9
Bahía Azul   6
Buga Mama   8
Happy Fish   7
Margoth   4
Tiburón Gato   5
Tilingo Lingo   3
Trópico La Playa   2
Ubafu   1

Nuestra Señora del Rosario

Banco Reformador

Banrural

Immigration

Museo Garífuna

Río Crique

Río Dulce

CALLE MARCOS SANCHEZ DIAZ

Boats for Río Dulce Town, Puerto Barrios & Punta Gorda (Belize)

just down the road, are the best travel agents in town. They can arrange trips (minimum six people) around the area, including visits to the Siete Altares (daily; Q80), Playa Blanca (Q120; minimum six people) and the Sapodilla Cayes off Belize for snorkelling (Q420; minimum six people). Several companies, including Exotic Travel, run morning boat trips up the Río Dulce (Q130 per person).

Accommodation

Make sure you book ahead during holidays; at other times you should easily be able to find a bed.
Casa de la Iguana Turn left at the dock and walk for 5min ☎ 7947 0064. If you're up for meeting other travellers (and a party), this fun hostel is ideal. Rusty, the friendly English owner, and his team will keep you entertained, and there is a fearsome happy hour. Dorms are well built, rooms are comfortable and bathrooms spick-and-span. Mosquito nets are provided. Guests eat together every evening, and you'll find cable TV and 400 DVDs. Spanish classes and day-trips can be organized too. Dorms Q40, doubles Q110

Flowas On the beach, about 2km west of the centre ☎ 7947 0376, @ infoflawas@gmail.com. A Spanish-owned place with solid wooden cabañas and a dorm set between coastal palms. The beachside location is excellent, swimming is enjoyable, and there's tasty home-cooking (including seafood). Taxis will drop you off close to the front gate for around Q12. Dorms Q75, rooms Q160
Garden Gate Guest House Northwest of the dock ☎ 7947 9272, Ⓦ www.gardengate-guesthouse .com. A fine place in a quiet hillside location, surrounded by greenery. The (no-smoking) rooms have sweeping views, screened windows, good-quality mattresses and en suites with reliable hot showers. Q160
Hotel California Turn left just before the *Bahía Azul* restaurant ☎ 7947 0176. Its unappealing concrete exterior is a bit off-putting but rooms are clean and functional, and most have private bath. Q125
Hotel Casa Rosada About 400m left of the dock ☎ 7947 0303, Ⓦ www.hotelcasa rosada.com. This lovely hotel has an unmatched location on the south side of the bay and a lovely garden to enjoy. The cute little wooden cabins, with

hand-painted details, are smallish but comfortable, though none have private bath. The cooking is excellent too, with daily specials and lots of choice for healthy eaters and vegetarians. Q170

Hotel Garífuna Turn left off the main street towards the *Ubafu* bar and walk 250m ☎7947 0183, ✉quiqueboss@hotmail.com. This is a clean, secure guesthouse with tidy, slightly old-fashioned rooms, managed by a hospitable Garífuna family. Q80

🏃 **Hotelito Perdido** In the rainforest by the Río Lampara, 20min from town by boat ☎5725 1576, ⓦwww.hotelitoperdido.com. Located in a tiny creek just off the Río Dulce, 12km inland from Lívingston, this is a blissfully tranquil travellers' hideaway run by Chris, an Englishman lost in the jungle. Lovely rustic bungalows, a warm atmosphere, home-cooking and kayaks are available for guests. Boat trips from Río Dulce Town or Lívingston will drop you off here, or call Chris for a ride. Dorms Q45, bungalows Q150

Eating

Prices tend to be higher than in most parts of Guatemala. Make sure you try *tapado* (seafood soup with coconut), the local speciality.

Antojitos Gaby Turn left at the dock and walk for 250m. A simple family-run *comedor* with a long menu of inexpensive dishes – try the *tapado* or *sopa caracol*.

Bahía Azul On the main street. You get a ringside view of Lívingston streetlife from the tables at this popular, efficient little café-restaurant. The menu takes in fish, seafood and cocoburgers.

Buga Mama Left at the dock. This café-restaurant, in a Caribbean-style wooden structure, is staffed by trainees from the local Ak' Tenamit development project. Offers tasty seafood, fried fish (Q70), pasta (from Q40) and strong Guatemalan coffee.

Happy Fish On the main street. Serves good Guatemalan breakfasts (Q25), seafood, salads, grilled meat and fish.

Margoth Turn left after *Tiburón Gato*. A good bet for Garífuna food, fried fish and jumbo shrimp.

Tiburón Gato 2min from the jetty, on the main drag. Other than local specialities, this place also serves pasta (Q22), *ceviche* (Q38) and fried fish (Q45), all at very reasonable prices.

Tilingo Lingo At the end of the main drag heading north towards the beach. María, the owner-chef, is a skilled cook who can turn her hand to good Mexican, Indian, Italian, Guatemalan and Garífuna dishes.

Drinking and nightlife

Lívingston has some groovy bars, most with African drum music and reggae beats playing in the background.

Trópico La Playa Bar-club where the dancefloor bounces to punta, reggae, Latin and reggaeton beats. Closed Mon & Tues.

Ubafu The best bar in town for live music, with Garífuna drummers working up a hypnotic rhythm most evenings.

Directory

Exchange Banrural on C Principal has an ATM and changes dollars.

Immigration About 200m up the main drag (daily 7am–7pm). Get your exit and entry stamps and pay your departure tax (US$10) here.

Internet Happy Fish, C Principal (Q10/hr).

Post office Walk up the main street and take the first right (Mon–Fri 8am–5.30pm, Sat 9am–1pm).

Taxis Can be grabbed from the dock; fares are Q12 to anywhere in town.

Telephones The Telgua office (Mon–Fri 8am–6pm, Sat 9am–1pm) is on the right, up the main street from the docks, next door to the post office. You cannot make international calls, but you can buy phonecards.

Moving on

By boat to: Puerto Barrios (*lanchas* Mon–Sat 5.30am, 6.30am, 8am, 10am and when full thereafter, roughly hourly; Sun only when full); Punta Gorda, Belize (Tues & Fri 7am; 1hr).

Lago de Izabal and the Río Dulce

The largest lake in the country, **Lago de Izabal** remains largely unexplored and is well worth a visit if you're looking for some tranquillity. **El Estor** serves as a good base to access the beautiful nature reserve to the west of the lake, which is home to numerous species of

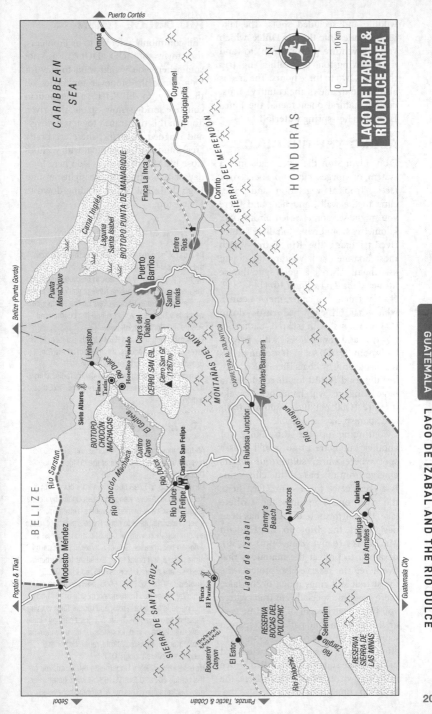

LAGO DE IZABAL & RÍO DULCE AREA

N

0   10 km

CARIBBEAN SEA

Puerto Cortés
Omoa
Cuyamel
Tegucigalpita
Corinto
SIERRA DEL MERENDÓN
HONDURAS

BIOTOPO PUNTA DE MANABIQUE
Canal Inglés
Laguna Santa Isabel
Punta Manabique
Finca La Inca
Entre Ríos
Puerto Barrios
Santo Tomás

Belize (Punta Gorda)

Livingston
Finca Tatín
Hotelito Fendido
Siete Altares
RÍO DULCE
Cayos del Diablo
CERRO SAN GIL
Cerro San Gil (1267m)
MONTAÑAS DEL MICO
Morales/Bananera
CARRETERA AL ATLÁNTICO

BIOTOPO CHOCÓN MACHACAS
El Golfete
Cuatro Cayos
Río Chocón Machaca
Río Dulce
Río Dulce
San Felipe
Castillo San Felipe
La Ruidosa Junction

BELIZE
Río Sarstún

Poptún & Tikal
Modesto Méndez

SIERRA DE SANTA CRUZ
Boquerón Canyon
El Estor

Denny's Beach
Mariscos
Los Amates
Quiriguá
Quiriguá
Río Motagua

Finca El Paraíso
Lago de Izabal

RESERVA BOCAS DEL POLOCHIC
Río Polochic
Selempim
Río Tinajo
RESERVA SIERRA DE LAS MINAS

Sebol
Panzós, Tactic & Cobán

Guatemala City

GUATEMALA   LAGO DE IZABAL AND THE RÍO DULCE

201

wildlife and secluded spots. The lake itself empties into the **Río Dulce**, which you can venture up (or down) to (and from) Lívingston, a breathtaking trip that takes two to three hours. The area is also home to one of the country's most curious natural phenomena, the Finca El Paraíso hot-spring **waterfall**.

ALONG THE RÍO DULCE

From Lívingston the river leads into a system of **gorges** cut into sheer rock faces. Tropical vegetation and vines cling to the walls, and here and there you might see some varied birdlife. Six kilometres from Lívingston there's a nice river tributary, the **Río Tatín**, which most boatmen will venture up if you ask them. There's a good guesthouse up here, the *Finca Tatín* (☎4148 3332, Ⓦ www.fincatatin.centramerica.com), which has an eight-bed rustic dorm (Q45), rooms with shared bathroom (Q110) and bungalows with private bathroom (Q160) set in dense jungle; it's reachable only by boat. There's also tasty, healthy food (Q110 for three meals), a large living area with hammocks, kayaks for hire (Q60 per day), walking trails and Spanish classes available.

Continuing up the Río Dulce for another kilometre or so, you'll pass a spot where warm sulphurous waters emerge from the base of the cliff – this is a great place for a swim. Past here, the river opens up into the **Golfete** lake, the north shore of which has been designated the **Biotopo de Chocón Machacas** (daily 8am–5pm; Q50), designed to protect the **manatees** that live here. The reserve also protects the forest that still rings much of the lake; there are some specially cut trails where you might catch sight of a bird or two, or, if you've time and patience to spare, a tapir or jaguar. The river closes in again after the lake, passing the marina and bridge at the squalid town of **Río Dulce** (also known as Fronteras), where the boat trip comes to an end.

RÍO DULCE TOWN

Still commonly referred to as Fronteras, the town of **RÍO DULCE** is not somewhere you would want to stay for long. Once the stopover for ferries on their way to El Petén, a gargantuan concrete bridge now spans the river. Though this tiny transit town is unlovely and plagued by traffic, there are pretty creeks and marinas popular with yachties close by. Many travellers stop here for a day or two exploring the sights around Lago de Izabal before heading down to Lívingston.

Arrival and information

By boat A side road leads down to the dock from the north side of the bridge.
By bus If arriving by bus, ask to be dropped off on the north side of the bridge (unless you're planning on staying at *Hotel Backpackers* on the south side), which is where you will also find the Litegua and Fuente del Norte bus offices.
Exchange Banrural and Banco Industrial have ATMs.
Internet You can access the internet at the *Río Bravo* restaurant north of the bridge.
Tourist information Ⓦ www.mayaparadise.com has good links and listings covering the Río Dulce region.

Accommodation

All the following places will come and pick you up by boat from the north side of the bridge in Río Dulce Town.
Casa Perico ☎7790 5666. In a little cove 1km from town. In a lovely position surrounded by dense jungle, this Swiss-owned travellers' retreat makes a very relaxing place to stay. There's plenty of rustic accommodation, with well-built dorms reached via wooden boardwalks. Expect a lively (if not a party) atmosphere and great food. Excellent trips around the lake are offered. Dorms Q45, doubles Q125
Hacienda Tijax ☎7930 5505, Ⓦ www.tijax.com. 2min by water-taxi from the north side of the bridge, this place is a working teak and rubber farm with a pleasant lakeside plot. There's a great canopy jungle walk, hiking trails and horseriding, plus a swimming pool. Prices are geared at mid-range rather than budget travellers though. Q37
Hotel Backpackers Underneath the south side of the bridge ☎7930 5480/5168, Ⓦ www.hotelbackpackers.com. This huge, slightly disheveled

LAGO DE IZABAL AND THE RÍO DULCE | GUATEMALA

wooden structure has huge dorms and some mediocre doubles. Unfortunately it lacks atmosphere (and guests – you're likely to have a dorm to yourself), which is a shame as it's owned by the nearby Casa Guatemala children's home, and many of the young staff are former residents. Dorms Q40, doubles Q115

Hotel Kangaroo ☎ 4513 9602, ⓦ www.hotel kangaroo.com. On a creek opposite the Castillo. This sociable Aussie-owned place has a six-person dorm with lake views and attractive wooden rooms, some with private bathrooms. There's a jacuzzi, a fully stocked bar, and filling local and Aussie tucker (though meals might be a tad pricey for backpackers). Dorms Q60, doubles Q150

Eating

There's a strip of pretty undistinguished *comedores* on the main road close to the bus stop.
Río Bravo On the north side of the bridge. A good place to meet other travellers, eat pizza or pasta (meals around Q50) and drink the night away – you can also surf the internet and make radio contact with most places around the river and lake from here.

🏃 **Sun Dog Café** On the north side of the bridge. An excellent Dutch-owned café, with delicious sandwiches and baguettes, snacks and creative European and Guatemalan grub. The coffee and juices are superb, the beer is cold, and they serve wine by the glass.

Moving on

By boat If you're heading for Lívingston via the Río Dulce gorge, the *lancha* boat captains will ambush you as soon as you step off a bus; boats (Q125 per person) leave when they have enough passengers until about 5pm. There are also scheduled departures at 9am and 1.30pm, which pause briefly at the Castillo, bird islets and hot springs on the way.
By bus to: Guatemala City (every 30min until around 6pm; 5–6hr); Flores (every 30min until around 6pm; 3hr) via Poptún (1hr 30min); some late-night departures too. Minibuses go to Puerto Barrios, roughly hourly (2hr). Heading to El Estor, there are buses around the lakeshore, running about every hour between 6am and 5pm (1hr 45min).

CASTILLO DE SAN FELIPE

Looking like a miniature medieval castle, the **CASTILLO DE SAN FELIPE** (daily 8am–5pm; Q20), 1km upstream from the Río Dulce bridge, marks the entrance to Lago de Izabal, and

is a tribute to the audacity of English pirates, who used to sail up the Río Dulce to raid supplies and harass mule trains. The Spanish were so infuriated by this that they built the fortress to seal off the entrance to the lake, and a chain was strung across the river. Inside there's a maze of tiny rooms and staircases, plenty of cannons and panoramic views of the lake.

LAGO DE IZABAL

Guatemala's largest lake, the **LAGO DE IZABAL**, is most definitely worth a visit – not only does it boast great views of the highlands beyond its shores, but the west of the lake on the Bocas del Polochic is also home to untouched forests and bountiful wildlife. Most hotels in Río Dulce Town will organize a lake cruise taking in the main sights, or you can explore the north shore by bus along the road to El Estor. The **hot-spring waterfall** (daily 7am–5pm; Q10) near the *Finca El Paraíso* (see below), 25km from Río Dulce and 300m north of the road, is a truly remarkable phenomenon, with near-boiling water cascading into cooled pools, creating a steam-room environment in the midst of the jungle. There is also a series of caves above the waterfall, their interior of different shapes and colours (remember to bring a torch) – one of the employees at the ticket office can show you there. Buses and pick-ups travel in both directions until about 6pm.

Some 7km further west is the hidden **Boquerón canyon**, with near-vertical cliffs rising more than 250m; villagers (including Hugo, a *campesino*-cum-boatman) will paddle you upstream in a canoe for a small fee. Hiking trips into the canyon can be organized too; speak to *Casa Perico, Hotel Kangaroo* or *Sun Dog* (see opposite).

EL ESTOR

Supposedly given its name because of the English pirates who came up the Río

Dulce to buy supplies at "the store", the tranquil lakeside town of **EL ESTOR** lies six kilometres further west of El Boquerón. Few tourists make it to this corner of the lake, so it's a great place to escape the gringo trail. The town is ideally positioned to capitalize on the vast **ecotourism** possibilities of the lake and its surrounding areas, but the recent resumption of nickel mining on the western fringes of El Estor has raised the threat of pollution.

Arrival and information

By bus Buses arrive and depart from the Parque Central.
Bike rental You can rent bikes at 6 Av 4–26.
Exchange Banrural on Calle Principal has an ATM and will change travellers' cheques and dollars.
Tour operators *Café El Portal* (☎ 4181 6361), on the east side of the plaza, organizes tours, as does Hugo at *Hotel Ecológico* and Oscar Paz at *Hotel Vista del Lago*. All can arrange boats and guides to explore the surrounding countryside, plus fishing trips on the lake.

Accommodation and eating

Café El Portal On the main square. For genuine Guatemalan food, this busy little place is ideal.
Hotel Ecológico Cabañas del Lago 1km east of the centre ☎ 4037 6235. In a lovely, tranquil lakeside setting, these wooden bungalows are spacious and attractive. There's a guests' kitchen and a restaurant with sweeping views. Hugo will give you a lift here from the centre. Q180
Hotel Vista del Lago In a historic building facing the lake ☎ 7949 7205. The rooms, with bathroom, are clean but perfunctory – ask for one on the upper storey. The owner claims this was the original "store" that gave the town its name, and also that Che Guevara once stayed here. Q150
Posada Don Juan On the main square ☎ 7949 7296. A good budget choice, this concrete hotel has clean, plain rooms with fan, some with private bathroom. Great value. Q75
Restaurant Chaabil On the lakeside, east of the plaza. Right by the water, these attractive wooden rooms enjoy a blissfully quiet location and have hand-made beds and private bathrooms. Meals here are a treat, with seafood (Q80), grilled meat (from Q45) and fresh lake fish

(from Q60), and you can swim off your meal from the private dock afterwards. Q160

Moving on

By boat There are no public boats to other destinations along the lake.
By bus to: Río Dulce (hourly 6am–5pm; 1hr 45min). There are six daily buses to Cobán (7hr) via Tactic. You can get to Lanquín via Cahabón by pick-up and possibly bus, though this route is very mountainous and may not be possible during heavy rains. *Café El Portal* will have the latest schedule.

RESERVA BOCAS DEL POLOCHIC

The **RESERVA BOCAS DEL POLOCHIC** is one of the richest wetland habitats in Guatemala, and shelters around 300 species of bird and a large number of mammals, reptiles, amphibians and fish. The ecosystem is one of the few places in the country where you can find manatees and tapirs, and you're bound to spot (or certainly hear) howler monkeys.

Arrival and information

By boat To get to Selempím, on the edge of the reserve, catch a public *lancha* from El Estor (Mon, Wed & Sat; Q35 one way) or hire a private *lancha* (around Q380).
Tour operators Locals organize treks into the foothills of the Sierra de las Minas or can take you kayaking around the river delta. Defensores de la Naturaleza, 5 Av y 2 C, El Estor (☎ 7949 7130, Ⓦ www.defensores.org.gt), who manage the reserve, organize excellent tours deep into the heart of the refuge. Contact Hugo or Oscar in El Estor (see "Tour operators", opposite) for day-trips (around US$60 per boat) to the zone nearest to El Estor.

Accommodation and eating

A good place to stay is the village of Selempím, which is right on the edge of the reserve. Accommodation is in a large, screened wooden house with bunk beds (US$10), organized through Defensores de la Naturaleza (see above). Remember to bring bottled water as they do not sell any in the village. Simple meals can be arranged too.

The Verapaces

The twin departments of the **Verapaces** harbour some of the most spectacular mountain scenery in the country, yet attract only a trickle of tourists. **Alta Verapaz**, in particular, is astonishingly beautiful, with fertile limestone landscapes and mist-soaked hills. The mountains here are the wettest and greenest in Guatemala – ideal for the production of the cash crops of coffee, cardamom, flowers and ferns. To the south, **Baja Verapaz** could hardly be more different: a low-lying, sparsely populated area that gets very little rainfall.

Many travellers completely bypass Baja Verapaz, whizzing through on Carretera 14 from Guatemala City to Cobán and the rest of Alta Verapaz. There are, however, a few sights worth stopping off for en-route. Clustered around the village of Purulhá are **sacred caves**, **waterfalls** and the **Biotopo del Quetzal**. To the west of the highway the **Salamá valley** drops dramatically away, leading to the sleepy department capital and beyond.

MARKET DAYS IN THE VERAPACES

Monday Salamá, Senahú, Tucurú
Tuesday Chisec, Cubulco, Lanquín, Purulhá, Rabinal, San Cristóbal Verapaz
Friday Salamá
Sunday Chisec, Cubulco, Lanquín, Purulhá, Rabinal, San Jerónimo, Santa Cruz, Tactic

North of the La Cumbre junction for Salamá and the quetzal reserve is the departmental border with Alta Verapaz, and shortly thereafter the city of **Cobán**, where you'll find great cafés and restaurants and a good range of budget accommodation. Heading further towards Petén, take time to check out some of the interesting community tourism projects that showcase Alta Verapaz's limestone landscape, as well as its living Maya heritage. The star attraction in the area, however, has to be the natural wonder of **Semuc Champey**, just outside the village of **Lanquín**.

SALAMÁ

From the La Cumbre junction on Carretera 14, a paved road drops steeply towards the secluded Salamá valley. **SALAMÁ** itself, capital of the department, is a quiet town, where you are unlikely to bump into other tourists. There isn't a great deal to see, but it does have a lively twice-weekly market and makes a handy base for visiting the Chilascó waterfall and Achi Maya town of Rabinal to the west.

Arrival and information

By bus Buses coming from CA-14 enter Salamá from the north. The town is strung out for some way before the central plaza. Stay on the bus until after it crosses the old bridge, from where it climbs a couple of blocks to the plaza. For orientation purposes, the church is on the eastern side of the plaza. Minibuses terminate and depart from the dusty car park off Av 6 one block west of the plaza.

Accommodation

Hotel Real Legendario 8 Av 3–57 ☎ 7940 0501. A modern-ish, efficiently run hotel with comfortable beds, private hot-water bathrooms and cable TV. There's a good little *comedor* here for breakfast. Q160

Posada Don Maco 3 C 8–26 ☎ 7940 0083. A hospitable family-run place where the well-scrubbed, neat rooms have private bath, cable TV and nice decorative touches. Rather off-puttingly, however, they keep squirrels in cages in the courtyard. Q145

Eating

Antojítos Zacapanecos 6 C & 8 Av. A popular, friendly snack-bar with filling tortillas stuffed with shredded meat, salsa and salad (Q20).

🏃 **Deli Donas** 5 C 6–61, just off the west side of the plaza. The town's best café is ideal for coffee and a slice of home-made cake (15Q). Also good for breakfasts (around Q20) or a sandwich – try a *bocadillo de jamón y queso*.

Moving on

By bus to: Chilascó (4 daily at 6.30am, 10.30am, noon & 5.30pm; 1hr 45min), from the northeast side of the plaza; Guatemala City (hourly 6am–4pm; 3hr 30min), from the southeast side of the plaza; La Cumbre (for connections with Pullman buses to Cobán and Guatemala City; every 15min 6am–6pm; 30min), from the car park on 6 Av one block west of the plaza.

SALTO DE CHILASCÓ

Just north of the La Cumbre junction, at km 144.5, a track leads east from the highway, towards the dramatic scenery of the **Sierra de las Minas**. After 12km you reach the village of **Chilascó**, where the community administer the impressive **SALTO DE CHILASCÓ** (last entry 1pm; US$5; ⓦ www.chilasco .net.ms), one of the highest **waterfalls** in Guatemala. Most transport will drop you at the information centre in Chilascó village, where you pay your entrance fee. From here it's a 3km walk, continuing along the track road past village houses and plantations, to the beginning of the trail that leads down to the foot of the falls. This trail begins as a steep, muddy mule-path heading down to a ridge flanked by broccoli plantations. Take the footpath to the left for much easier passage. After 1km the path plunges down into the forested valley. The well-maintained trail offers viewpoint picnic sites with views towards the Chilascó falls, information on local flora and fauna, as well as a campsite with eco-toilet midway down.

Don't miss the **Saltito**, a delightful smaller waterfall halfway down, where you can bathe in the plunge pool and admire the stunning views. At the base of the main falls, water cascades onto huge boulders and seemingly disappears into the cavernous valley beyond the trail's end. The walk back up to Chilascó village requires a moderate level of fitness (allow at least 2hr).

Microbuses from Salamá to Chilascó village pass the Chilascó junction of CA-14 at 7am, 11am, 12.30pm and 6pm. Occasional pick-ups also cover this route. Otherwise, from the Chilascó junction, walk 200m back towards La Cumbre, and you'll find the *Río Escondido Lodge*, where you may be able to arrange a lift for a fee (US$10). Basic **accommodation** (Q35) and food are available in Chilascó village. The last bus back to the highway leaves the village at 3pm.

BIOTOPO DEL QUETZAL

Back on CA-14 towards Alta Verapaz and Cobán, the road sweeps around endless tight curves below forested hillsides. Just before the village of **Purulhá** (km 161) is the **BIOTOPO DEL QUETZAL** (daily 7am–4pm; US$4.50), an 11.5-square-kilometre nature reserve designed to protect the habitat of the endangered bird. The reserve comprises steep and dense rain- and cloudforest, pierced by waterfalls, natural pools and the Río Colorado. There are two **hiking** trails, one an easy one-hour circuit, and the other a half-day Stairmaster. Trail maps are sold at the information centre at the park

---

THE RESPLENDENT QUETZAL

The quetzal, Guatemala's national symbol, has a distinguished past but an uncertain future. From the earliest of times, the bird's feathers have been sacred: to the Maya the quetzal was so revered that killing one was a capital offence, and the bird is also thought to have been the *nahual*, or spiritual protector, of the Maya chiefs. When Tecún Umán was slain by conquistador Alvarado, the quetzal is said to have landed on his chest, and consequently obtained its red breast from the Maya's blood.

Today the quetzal's image permeates the entire country: as well as lending its name to the nation's currency, citizens honoured by the president are awarded the Order of the Quetzal, and the bird is also considered a symbol of freedom, since caged quetzals die in confinement. Despite all this, the sweeping tide of deforestation threatens the existence of the bird.

The heads of males are crowned with a plume of brilliant green, while the chest and lower belly are a rich crimson and trailing behind are the unmistakeable oversized, golden-green tail feathers, though these are only really evident in the mating season. The females, on the other hand, are an unremarkable brownish colour. Quetzals can also be quite easily identified by their strangely jerky, undulating flight.

entrance. There are picnic areas, but no food is allowed on the trails.

The best time to catch a glimpse of the quetzal is March–April at either dawn or dusk. Since the reserve is not open during these hours it's definitely worth spending the night to increase your viewing opportunities. You can stay near the reserve at the *Ranchitos del Quetzal* (☎5191 0042; Q90), 100m north of the entrance. The owner here was cunning enough to nurture the habitat of the quetzal's favoured foods and nesting places, so it's now one of the prime places to view the plumed legend. There is also a simple *comedor* with meals in the Q20–30 range.

Buses from Cobán pass the reserve entrance every thirty minutes. To the north of the Biotopo, just past Purulhá at km 167 on the highway, are the sacred **Chicoy Caves** (daily 9am–5pm; US$3), where there are towering stalagmites of up to 20m. Maya religious rituals are still regularly performed here.

INTO ALTA VERAPAZ

Beyond the quetzal sanctuary, Carretera 14 crosses into the department of Alta Verapaz. The first place of any size is **Tactic** – a small, mainly Poqomchi'-speaking town adjacent to the main road, which most buses bypass. The colonial **church** in the centre of the village, boasting a Baroque facade decorated with mermaids and jaguars, is worth a look, as is the Chi-Ixim chapel high above the town.

About 10km past Tactic is the turn-off for **San Cristóbal Verapaz**, a pretty town almost engulfed by fields of coffee and sugar cane, set on the banks of the Lago de Cristóbal. From here a mostly paved road continues to **Uspantán** in the western highlands.

COBÁN

Though not as visually impressive as other Guatemalan colonial cities, once you get to know the welcoming mountain town of **COBÁN**, you may find yourself sticking around and making a few friends. When the weather is dry, Cobán has a perfect alpine climate, allowing for fantastic day-trips to surrounding forests, rivers, caves and natural swimming pools. It's thanks to this fresh mountain air (and a good deal of rain) that the town became an important coffee-growing centre; now the local *fincas* offer tours and provide beans to the town's many excellent cafés. Ecotourism and cultural tourism are also increasingly bringing business here.

What to see and do

Probably the nicest thing to do in Cobán is to simply slow down and enjoy the world-class coffee and local hospitality. However, there are also several interesting attractions. The town is centred on an elevated **plaza**, with the **Cathedral** gracing its eastern side. To the north and south the streets fall away steeply, while the main thoroughfare, **1 Calle**, stretches westwards to the mall of Plaza Magdalena, on the town's outskirts. The town's central area is divided into four zones, which are separated north–south by 1 Calle and east–west by 1 Avenida.

Finca Santa Margarita

For a closer look at Cobán's principal crop, take the guided tour offered by the **Finca Santa Margarita**, 3 C 4–12, Zona 2 (Mon–Fri 8am–12.30pm & 1.30–5pm, Sat 8am–noon; US$4), a coffee plantation just south of the centre of town. The interesting tour (in English or Spanish) covers the history of the *finca*, examining all the stages of cultivation and production. You also get a chance to sample the crop and, of course, purchase some beans.

Museo El Príncipe Maya

Several blocks southeast of the central plaza you'll find an excellent collection of Maya artefacts and carvings

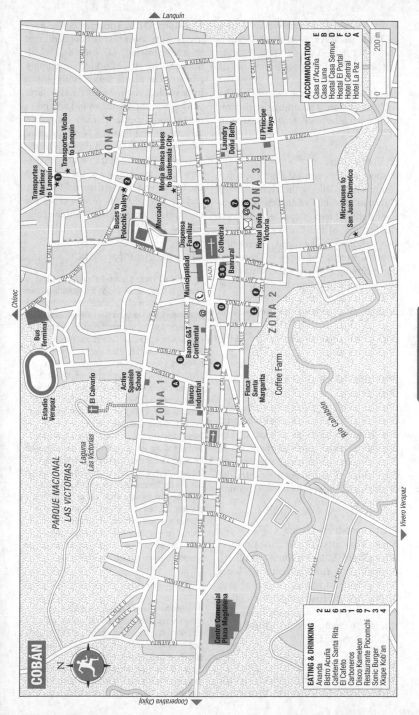

COBÁN

ZONA 4
ZONA 3
ZONA 2
ZONA 1

PARQUE NACIONAL
LAS VICTORIAS

Laguna
Las Victorias

Estadio
Verapaz

Bus
Terminal

El Calvario

Active
Spanish
School

Banco
Industrial

Banco G&T
Continental

Municipalidad

Dispensa
Familiar

Mercado

Buses to
Polochic Valley

Transportes Viciba
to Lanquín

Transportes
Martínez
to Lanquín

Cathedral

Bahrural

Monja Blanca buses
to Guatemala City

Laundry
Doña Betty

El Príncipe
Maya

Hostal Doña
Victoria

Microbuses to
San Juan Chamelco

Finca
Santa
Margarita

Coffee Farm

Río Cahabón

▲ Lanquín

◄ Chisec

▼ Vivero Verapaz

◄ Cooperativa Chijol

GUATEMALA   THE VERAPACES

ACCOMMODATION

Casa d'Acuña	E
Casa Luna	B
Hostal Casa Semuc	D
Hostal El Portal	F
Hotel Central	C
Hotel La Paz	A

EATING & DRINKING

Ananda	2
Bistro Acuña	6
Cafetería Santa Rita	5
El Cafeto	1
Carboneros	8
Disco Kameleon	7
Restaurante Pocomchi	3
Sonic Burger	4
Xkape Kob'an	

0   200 m

N

inside the small, privately run **Museo El Príncipe Maya**, 6 Av 4–26, Zona 3 (Mon–Sat 9am–5.45pm; Q15), including shell necklaces, polychrome bowls and human figurines. Don't miss the eccentric flints, incense burners or the main attraction: a stunning panel from a Cancuén altarpiece, embellished with 160 glyphs.

El Calvario

A short stroll northwest from the town centre on 3 Calle is the church of **El Calvario**, one of Cobán's most attractive sights. Steep steps lead up via the Stations of the Cross – blackened by candle smoke and decorated with scattered offerings. There's a commanding view over the town from the whitewashed church, which has a distinctly pagan aura, often filled with candles, incense and corn cobs. The Calvario attracts many Maya worshippers, and the Sunday services are in the Q'eqchi language.

Parque Nacional Las Victorias

On the northwest edge of town, just past El Calvario, is the **Parque Nacional Las Victorias** (daily 8am–5pm; US$1), a well-managed forested park, with barbecue areas and grassy verges good for picnics. If you've got your running shoes, you'll find excellent trails through the pines.

Cooperativa Chijoj

Some 7km west of Cobán is the **Cooperativa Chijoj** (Mon–Fri 8am–4pm; Q50), a community-run coffee farm. Tours here include zip-lining across a river and a full explanation of the coffee-production process. To get here, take a micro heading west to **Chijoj** from 3 Calle, Zona 2 (Q2).

Vivero Verapaz

Another place worth a look is the **Vivero Verapaz** (Mon–Sat 9am–noon & 2–4pm; Q10), a former coffee *finca* just outside town that is now dedicated to the growing of **orchids**, which flourish in the sodden mountain climate. The plants are carefully grown in a shaded environment, and a farm worker will show you around and point out the most spectacular blooms, which are at their best between November and January. It's a forty-minute walk to the nursery: leave the plaza on Diagonal 4, turn left at the bottom of the hill, cross the bridge and follow the road for 3km; taxis charge US$2.50, or you can jump on a micro heading for **Tontem** from 3 Calle, Zona 2.

Arrival and information

By bus Unfortunately, almost all public transport arriving in Cobán drops you on the outskirts of town (with the exception of Monja Blanca buses from Guatemala City). The main bus terminal, also known as Campo Dos, has services to Chisec, Sayaxché, Flores, Uspantán, Nebaj, Salamá and Playa Grande. Buses for Lanquín use a bus stop on 3 Av, on the northeast side of town. From Campo Dos it's a 20min walk or Q15 taxi ride to the central plaza.

Tour operators Aventuras Turísticas, inside *Hostal Doña Victoria*, 3 C 2–38, Zona 3, ⊛www.aventuras turisticas.com, offers trips all over the Verapaces including Semuc Champey and Laguna Lachúa. Proyecto EcoQuetzal, 2 C 14–36, Zona 1, ⊛www .ecoquetzal.org, arranges off-the-beaten-path treks to the Chicacnab cloudforest and boat trips along the Río Ik' Bolay; you stay with Q'eqchi communities and the income helps provide a sustainable living for villagers, who also serve as guides. Many of Cobán's hotels also provide tour services, with shuttles and trips to nearby attractions.

Tourist information There is no tourist office in town. Staff at the *Casa Luna* and *Casa D'Acuña* (see opposite) are very helpful, however.

City transport

By microbus For excursions just outside town (where many of the interesting attractions are), it's cheapest to flag down a microbus. Many run east–west along calles 2 and 3 in Zona 2; fares cost Q1–3 depending on the distance.

By taxi There is a constant pack of hopeful *taxistas* hanging out at the plaza. Agree fares before departure – within town these shouldn't exceed Q20.

Accommodation

There's some great budget accommodation in town, with many places very close to the plaza. Note that the once-popular *Hostel Casa Blanca* has gone downhill.

Casa d'Acuña 4 C 3–11, Zona 2 ☎7951 0482, ✉casadeacuna@yahoo.com. A long-running travellers' lodge, this fine place has good four-bed dorms and a couple of private doubles (all with shared bathroom) set to one side of a simply gorgeous colonial courtyard restaurant. As your bed for the night is cheap, make sure you indulge in a meal while you're here. Tours can be booked too. Dorms Q50, doubles Q100

Casa Luna 5 Av 2–28, Zona 1 ☎7951 3528, ✉cobantravels.com. This backpacker haunt is well run by Lionel, a fluent English-speaker, and his family. There are spacious rooms and a dorm (none with private bath) around a pleasant courtyard garden with hammocks, as well as a TV lounge stocked with DVDs and magazines. Tours and shuttle buses can be booked, information provided is reliable and there's a free breakfast too. Dorms Q60, doubles Q150

Hostal Casa Semuc 3 Av 2–12, Zona 2 ☎7951 4505. Just below the plaza, this excellent new place offers secure, high-quality budget accommodation in a lovely old house. There's a good dorm, plus eleven smallish, very clean private rooms with good mattresses. An airy guests' living room with sofas and internet access (Q5) completes the picture. Dorms Q50, doubles Q100

Hostal El Portal 4 C & 3 Av, Zona 2 ☎7952 1487. New place with plain, clean rooms (some with bathroom) that lack natural light downstairs so go for one on the upper storey. It's cheap and secure. Q80

Hotel Central 1 C 1–79, Zona 4 ☎7952 1442, ✉hotelcentraldecoban@yahoo.com. An ageing hotel with decent if plain rooms around a central courtyard. The rooms are a tad on the dark side but have cable TV and private bathroom with gas-fired hot water. There's wi-fi too. Q170

Hotel La Paz 6 Av 2–19, Zona 1 ☎7952 1358. This safe, pleasant budget hotel, run by a very vigilant *señora*, is a good deal. Rooms are basic but clean and face onto open corridor/courtyard sitting areas. There is parking and a small *comedor* downstairs. Q85

Eating

Eating in Cobán comes down to a choice of some excellent European-style restaurants and cafés and very basic, cheap *comedores*. In the latter, look out for *kaq' ik*, a terrific turkey soup. You'll find the cheapest food around the market, but as it's closed by dusk, head to the street stalls set up around the plaza.

Cafetería Santa Rita 2 C, on the plaza. An archetypal *comedor* with friendly service and filling *comida típica*. Great prices – almost everything is under Q20.

El Cafeto 2 C 1–36, Zona 2. Right on the plaza, this cosy little place serves coffee (from the local Chijoj *finca*), including capuccino. It's a good bet for an early breakfast (from 7.30am): take your pick from pancakes (Q16), cereal (Q17), fruit salad (Q19) or a full-on Guatemalan fry-up (from Q22). Sandwiches, burgers, hot dogs and pastas are also served.

Carboneros 6 C 3–40, Zona 4. A ten-minute walk north of the centre, this suburban "*Casa de Carne y Más*" serves up delicious grilled meats cooked over charcoal at very moderate prices: plates of chicken, beef or pork are just Q18.

Restaurante Pocomchi 3 C 2–36, Zona 3. A humble canteen full of bubbling pots, toasting tortillas and friendly staff. They serve Maya specialities, including *kaq' ik*.

Sonic Burger 1 C 3–50, Zona 3. Burgers, nachos, sandwiches, salads and set meals (around Q18) are all good value here.

Xkape Kob'an Diagonal 4 5–13, Zona 2. This community-oriented place in a grand old house and garden features local produce and recipes. Tuck into snacks and meals (Q20–60), sip a Verapaz coffee or try the *kakaw-ik* (milky chocolate drink with vanilla, chilli and honey). Walls are decorated with fine textiles and local artefacts, and there's a large handicraft store here too. Closed Sun.

> **TREAT YOURSELF**
>
> **Bistro Acuña** 4 C 3–17, Zona 2. One of Guatemala's most enjoyable restaurants, this is an incredibly classy place to blow your budget, and enjoy spending every quetzal. It's fantastic for breakfast (a bowl of granola and fruit, or a *pláto típico*), lunch or dinner – try the *pinchos de camarón* (Q70). Waiters in starched white uniforms bring out little complimentary appetizers in the evening and the wine list (bottles from Q110) is great. There's an enticing dessert cabinet, as well as freshly baked cake to take away. The setting is just superb, an Antigua-style courtyard shaded by trees, as well as several elegant dining rooms.

Drinking and nightlife

Ananda 4 C 3–24, Zona 4. Alternative bar, popular with groups of students, with regular drink promotions and always something interesting on the music front. They have sheeshas for languid tobacco-smoking and lots of cushioned seating.
Disco Kameleon 3 C & 4 Av, Zona 3. Perhaps the most happening place in town, this raucous club draws a lively, hedonistic crowd with DJs spinning techno, trance and Latin house.

Directory

Cinema Inside Plaza Magdalena (at the western end of C 1) is a three-screen cinema.
Exchange Cobán has plenty of banks in the central area, including G&T Continental and Banco Industrial on 1 C west of the plaza; both will change dollars and have ATMs.
Internet There's a good internet café inside the *Hostal Doña Victoria*, 3 C 2–38, Zona 3.
Language schools Cobán is a popular place to learn Spanish. Oxford Language Center, 4 Av 2–16, Zona 3 (W www.olcenglish.com), is well regarded and has attractive premises.
Laundry Doña Betty's Laundry, 2 C 6–10, Zona 3 (daily until late). They provide wash and dry service in 2hr for Q30.
Post office 2 C & 2 Av (Mon–Fri 8am–5.30pm, Sat 9am–1pm).
Shopping The lively daily market is centred on the junction of 3 C & 1 Av at the meeting of zonas 1 & 3, and extends uphill to the streets behind the cathedral, where you can find cheap street-food. For supermarket shopping head to Dispensa Familiar just north of the cathedral, or Plaza Magdalena on the town's western outskirts, where you can also find a small selection of clothing stores. For souvenirs, Casa d'Acuña and Xkape Kob'an (see p.211) sell an excellent range of local crafts and produce, including several single-estate coffees.
Telephones Telgua has its main office on the plaza. There are plenty of payphones here too.

Moving on

Note that the highway west to Uspantán suffered serious damage in a landslide a few years ago. Micros still ply the road regularly, but it involves a scary descent down an unstable mountainside; services may not run during heavy rains.
By bus to: El Estor (5 daily; 7hr), from 3 C A & 3 Av, Zona 4; Guatemala City (roughly hourly 2am–4pm;

4hr 30min), with Monja Blanca, 2 C 3–77, Zona 4 (take these buses for the Biotopo del Quetzal, Chilascó and Salamá – change at La Cumbre); Lanquín (hourly 6am–6pm; 2hr 15min; some buses continue on to Semuc Champey).
By micro All the following buses depart from the main Dos Campos terminal: Chisec (every 30min; 1hr 30min); Flores (1 daily at 1pm or change in Sayaxché; 6hr); Fray Bartolomé de las Casas (hourly; 3hr); Nebaj (1 daily at 5am or travel via Uspantán; 6hr); Playa Grande (every 30min; 4hr); Raxrujá (every 30min; 2hr 30min); Sayaxché (hourly; 4hr); Uspantán (hourly, though see above; 3hr). For San Juan Chalmeco (10min) there are micros every 10min from the bridge at the bottom of 1 Av A, Zona 3.

AROUND COBÁN

The area surrounding Cobán is both craggy and lush, with limestone bedrock and a surface of patchwork fields. There are still some areas of forest, mainly to the southeast, but the Maya population of Alta Verapaz have turned most of the land over to the production of maize, coffee, cardamom and ferns. It's worth venturing into this rural heartland of Guatemala to explore traditional market towns and their surrounding villages, as well as fresh-water swimming pools and stalactite caves.

San Juan Chamelco

A few kilometres southeast of Cobán, easily reached by regular micros, **San Juan Chamelco** is the most important Q'eqchi' settlement in the area. It is claimed, in fact, that the village was never conquered by the Spanish, and certainly the community here remains largely indigenous. However, Chamelco's focal point is its hilltop **church**, a huge, open-plan space with timber-frame roof and several Jesus effigies with bloody stigmata. The best time to visit the village is the week preceding its annual **fiesta** (June 23), when celebrations include folk dancing in traditional dress and the arrival of numerous saints from neighbouring San Pedro Carchá, brought to greet the holy effigies from Chamelco's own church.

Just outside Chamelco are the **Grutas del Rey Marcos**, an extensive cave network (daily 7am–5pm; US$5, including the services of a guide, plus hard hat and boot rental). You can take a tour that explores up to 100m into the caverns, which are full of stalagmites that uncannily resemble various familiar objects. To reach the caves, catch a micro from the church in Chamelco headed for Santa Cecilia.

Microbuses congregate behind the church on the hilltop and head to Cobán and the surrounding Maya villages.

Swimming pools
On the road to Chiscc, half an hour outside Cobán, is the **Ecocentro Sataña** (daily 9am–5pm; Q20), a bathing complex that includes both natural and man-made swimming pools in a jungle setting, with gardens and picnic areas as well as a restaurant at weekends. Take any micro headed to Chisec.

At the town of San Pedro Carchá, 5km east of Cobán, is the **Balneario las Islas**, another natural pool with a river tumbling into it. To get to Carchá there are regular departures from the car park opposite the Monja Blanca terminal in Cobán. The Balneario is about 15 minutes east of town – locals should be able to direct you.

LANQUÍN

From Cobán a paved road heads east, almost as far as the village of **LANQUÍN** (the last 11km are painfully slow and bumpy). The journey is a stunningly beautiful one, in spite of the evident deforestation – sit on the right side of the bus for the best views. The nearby natural wonder of Semuc Champey is now well and truly on the backpacker trail, and consequently some excellent accommodation and activity options have sprung up. Most visitors stay at least two nights (either in Lanquín or around Semuc), with weekends and holidays being especially busy.

What to see and do

The town of Lanquín itself is a sleepy, Q'eqchi' village superbly sheltered beneath towering green hills.

The Grutas de Lanquín
As you enter the village from Cobán you pass the **Grutas de Lanquín** (daily 8am–6pm; Q30), from where the Río Lanquín emerges. The river is fairly feisty, but if you're up for it locals will rent you inner tubes and pick you up downstream. To view the caves you can enter without a guide, but for a closer look take a guided tour (all the hostels organize trips). You should refrain from using flash photography in the cave as it unsettles the bats. At dusk every day thousands of bats fly out of the cave to feed – you can watch them for free from the entrance car park or anywhere along the river bank, but the tour also allows you the opportunity to stand in the cave entrance as they zip past you.

Arrival and information

By bus If your bus terminates in Lanquín, you'll be dropped at the junction where the road splits east for Cahabón (and *El Retiro* lodge) and south for Semuc Champey (and the village centre, just up the hill). If heading for *El Retiro*, it's a 15min walk from the junction, so if your bus goes to Cahabón, stay aboard.

Exchange Banrural, just south of the parque, changes dollars and has an ATM. Many lodges will give you a cash advance (for a hefty commission of around 7 percent).

Tour operators Most of the lodges offer tours, including zip-lining and tubing down the Río Lanquín; rates are very similar. *Zephyr Lodge* charges Q165 for day-trips to Semuc (including entrance), Q40 for tubing on the Río Lanquín, and Q65 for a Grutas de Lanquín cave tour. Guatemala Rafting is currently inactive in Lanquín, but may return to the area and run trips from the *Zephyr Lodge*.

Tourist information There's no official information outlet in town. *El Retiro*, *Zephyr Lodge*, *Las Marías* and *El Portal* all offer good practical information.

Accommodation

Posada Ilobal Past the market and bank in the village centre ☎ 7983 0014. Locally owned, with five simple, clean and airy rooms with shared bathroom, some with valley views, this is a good option if you'd rather not be surrounded by gangs of gap-year students. There's a nice garden too. Q90

El Retiro On the banks of the Río Lanquín ☎ 4513 6396, ⊛ www.elretirolanquin.com. The place that put Lanquín and Semuc on the map, this near-legendary riverside lodge has recently undergone a change of ownership and it remains to be seen if standards will be maintained. The setting is lovely, and accommodation is well designed, consisting of four-bed dorms, cabins and rooms, some with private bath, as well as camping. If you're up for partying with a young crowd it's ideal, with drinks specials most nights and a gregarious vibe. Buffet-style dinners are served. Lockers, internet and book swap are available and good tours are offered. Dorms Q35, doubles Q170

🏃 **Zephyr Lodge** Down a little dirt lane, just north of village centre ☎ 5168 2441, ☎ zephyrlodgelanquin@gmail.com. A wonderful new lodge, set on a little spur of land that offers stunning views over the Lanquín river valley. A lot of thought has gone into the design, and the bar-restaurant and fine accommodation – dorms, doubles and two-storey cabañas – enjoys a great perspective of the evergreen Verapaz hills. Staff could not be more helpful, the food is great with plenty of veggie choices, cocktails are the best in town, fine tours are offered, and there's free wi-fi and purified water. A hot tub and swimming pool are planned too. The British/Dutch owners are very switched on to travellers' needs. Reserve ahead – it's usually full. Dorms Q35, cabañas Q130, doubles Q160

Eating

Most people eat dinner at their lodge, but there are some good local options in the village too.

Cafetería Champey Halfway between *El Retiro* and the village. This large restaurant offers an interesting range of international dishes, including *shakshuka* (Q18–50) and local options like *carne asada*.

Comedor Shalom In the village. An excellent local place with three or four set-meal deals (Q22) that change daily, friendly local staff and clean surrounds.

Moving on

By bus Buses for Cobán (2hr) depart from the central junction (but also tour the village picking up potential passengers) hourly from 5am, then in the afternoon at 2pm, 4pm & 5pm. Buses arriving from Cobán pass the central junction of Lanquín and continue to Semuc Champey (45min) or Cahabón (1hr 15min). If you're heading for El Estor and the Río Dulce, check the latest schedule as times changes frequently on this route and the steep mountain road is sometimes not passable. Get an early start, around 6am. Five daily buses leave Lanquín for Cahabón, from where you'll have to change; there are usually three or four daily connections down to El Estor (5hr 30min). Shuttle-bus tickets to Antigua (8hr) are sold by all the lodges.

PARQUE NACIONAL SEMUC CHAMPEY AND THE KAN'BA CAVES

The big draw in Alta Verapaz are the extraordinary natural pools of **SEMUC CHAMPEY** (daily 6am–6pm; Q50), 10km southeast of Lanquín. Here the bulk of the Río Cahabón cuts underground, leaving a suspended limestone bridge. The top of the bridge is graced with a series of idyllic **pools** that descend in a natural staircase of turquoise waters, bordered by steep jungle gorge walls, while below the bridge is a raging torrent. You could wallow for hours in the sublime pools, which are perfect for swimming. For an eagle's-eye perspective of Semuc, hike up the vertiginous signposted **trail** (it's about a twenty-minute trek and very slippery in the wet) to the *mirador*, which overlooks this natural extravaganza.

While you can visit on your own, most travellers choose to visit Semuc as part of a **tour**, which avoids having to wait for infrequent public transport. In addition, coming with a tour (see p.213 for operators in Lanquín) can offer additional opportunities to explore: some allow you to descend underneath the bridge to see the raging river below. This is not for the faint of heart (it involves a rope ladder), but it does give a complete perspective on this outstanding geological feature.

There are security guards at the site, but it's best not to leave your belongings unattended. You'll find a small café (reasonable meals are around Q40) and there are vendors selling drinks and snacks at the entrance.

Another worthwhile adventure in the area is a visit to the privately owned **KAN'BA CAVES** (entrance by guided tour only 8am, 10am, 1pm & 3pm; Q50), on the riverbank directly opposite the entrance to Semuc. Best for adrenaline junkies, tours here are run without hard hats and torches and instead feature stubby candles – you need to swim one-handed while holding them aloft. Sharp rocks and slippery surfaces add to this treacherous assault-course, which will leave you shivering and happy to emerge into the daylight. Some tubing is usually included at the end of the tour.

Arrival

By pick-up To get to Semuc Champey without a tour you'll need to catch a pick-up or truck from Lanquín (roughly hourly until 4pm; 45min). There were direct Cobán–Semuc micro services until recently but these have been suspended, as the Semuc access road is in such poor condition.

Accommodation

El Portal ☏ 7983 0046. A few steps from the entrance to Semuc, this is another riverside option, with pretty thatched cabins, dorms and a clean communal bathroom-block dotted around a meadow that drops down to the Río Cahabón. Staff are helpful, tours are offered and there's a small restaurant and well-stocked bar. Dorms Q40, doubles Q100

Moving on

By bus Irregular trucks to Lanquín leave in the morning and early afternoon (45min), the last at 5pm, though always check the latest schedule. Pick-ups also pass by and charge Q5 for the ride to Lanquín.

CAHABÓN

Beyond Lanquín the road continues 24km to the settlement of **CAHABÓN**. From here, a rough road plunges down towards the village of **Panzós**, cutting high over the mountains through some of the finest, most verdant scenery in Guatemala. Public transport (buses, trucks and pick-ups) leaves Cahabón for the four- to five-hour trip to El Estor in the Polochic valley. Exact schedules are tricky as the road is extremely steep and in very wet weather micros don't attempt it, but there are normally four daily services. Check at *Zephyr Lodge* in Lanquín (see opposite) for the latest information. There are basic *hospedajes* (US$10) and places to eat in town if you get stuck here.

CHISEC

CHISEC is a small town, bisected from north to south by CA-14. There's not much here – in fact, the huge plaza seems to account for half the town. However it makes a convenient base for visiting nearby attractions and has several hotels.

What to see and do

Just outside Chisec are a couple of wonderful natural attractions.

B'omb'il Pek

2km north of town, with an office on the highway, is the entrance to the **B'omb'il Pek** caves. Tours (daily 8am–3pm; US$9) are community run, and last around two hours. The first "cave" is actually a sink hole, with vertical sides clad in jungle. You can rappel down (for an extra US$3), or use a slippery wooden staircase. Maya ceremonies are performed here. The second cave is only accessed via a tiny entrance, which you'll have to squeeze through horizontally; those with a larger physique will not be able to make it. Inside there's an ancient painting of two monkeys, thought to represent the hero twins of the Popul Vuh (see p.131). A pleasant addition to the tour involves inner tubing for thirty minutes (US$4) on the nearby **Río San Simón**, which cuts a tiny gorge through the rock. Very regular micros pass the tour office on the highway, shuttling between Chisec and Raxrujá.

Lagunas Sepalau

Some 10km east of Chisec are the beautiful **Lagunas Sepalau** (daily 7am–5pm; US$8 including guide). Set among a protected forest reserve, these three lovely lagoons are ringed by towering rainforest. Guides escort you along a trail, pointing out wildlife (iguanas and monkeys are sometimes seen) and medicinal plants, and can provide you with canoes for paddling across the lakes. The pristine lake waters are perfect for swimming. Camping (Q30) is permitted at the lakesides, as well as at the entrance, where there are showers and cooking facilities. To get here from Chisec there is a 10am microbus and a few infrequent pick-ups you can hitch a ride with (Q5). Stand on the track road heading east from the Municipalidad (on the plaza) to flag one down. Returning, most transport passes the lakes in the afternoon; there is a 1pm micro and later pick-ups too. Alternatively, a taxi should cost Q50 each way.

Arrival and information

By micro From Cobán, micros run right past the plaza, then continue northwards past *La Estancia* en route to Chisec.

Accommodation and eating

Café La Huella On the main road, just off the north side of the plaza. A decent *comedor* of the filling meals and cheap snack persuasion. Reckon on Q20 for lunch or dinner; breakfast is Q15.
Don Miguel About 300m north of the plaza. This place styles itself as a "mini-restaurant", with tasty snacks and Guatemalan staples for Q18–40.

Hotel La Estancia On the road north out of town ☎ 5514 7444. There are dozens of rooms at this multistorey concrete hotel, from basic options with shared facilities to slightly more comfortable ones with cable TV, private shower and a/c. You'll also find a *comedor* for your breakfast or evening meal and a small swimming pool. Q85
Hotel Nopales On the plaza ☎ 5514 0624. This small hotel has basic, ageing rooms with bathroom, TV and fan. There is also a small *comedor*. Q80

Directory

Exchange There are two banks on the plaza; the Agromercantíl has an ATM.
Internet You'll find several places on the main road heading north out of town; one is right next door to *Don Miguel*.
Post office One block up from the eastern side of the plaza.

Moving on

By micro to: Cobán (1hr 30min), from the south side of the plaza; Raxrujá (1hr) and Playa Grande (2hr 30min), from one block north of the plaza. Some northbound micros also continue on to Sayaxché or Fray Bartolomé de las Casas. Micros depart approximately every 30min.

RAXRUJÁ

The small town of **RAXRUJÁ** provides a handy base for visiting the nearby **Candelaria cave network** and the Maya ruins of **Cancuén**. The town itself, however, is no beauty: little more than a sprawl of buildings along the roadside, centred at the junction where the paved road ends and rough tracks lead to La Unión and **Fray Bartolomé de las Casas.**

Accommodation and eating

Hotel Cancuén Towards the western end of town ☎ 5764 0478. Getting everything right, this expanding hotel has 48 excellent-value, clean, neat rooms around a large car park. There are some very smart options available for very moderate rates with cable TV and a/c, but even the basic rooms are perfectly comfortable and have cold-water bathrooms. Dr César, the friendly owner, also offers great tours to the Cuevas de los Nacimientos and to Cancuén ruins. There's a small *comedor* on site, plus internet access (Q10). Q5

Doña Reyna Just north of the main junction in the centre. This *comedor* looks a tad dark, but it's busy and the food (meals from Q18) is fresh, tasty and filling.

Moving on

The direct road south to the Pajal junction (for Lanquín and Semuc Champey) is in terrible condition and only covered by the odd hard-core pick-up. It's quicker to use the long detour via Cobán.

By micro to: Cobán (2hr 15min) via Chisec (45min), Fray Bartolomé de las Casas (40min) and Sayaxché (2hr 30min), from the central junction every 30min 6am–5pm.

AROUND RAXRUJÁ

The limestone hills around Raxrujá are riddled with cave networks and subterranean rivers. Also nearby is the rarely visited Maya ruin of Cancuén.

The Candelaria caves

Forming a core section of 22km, the spectacular **Candelaria cave system** is the longest underground complex in Latin America. (If subsidiary streams, galleries and systems are included then it measures more than 80km.) It's quite straightforward to visit part of this cave network, but rather confusingly, there are four possible entrances. Two are community run (**Candelaria Camposanto** and **Mucbilha'**) and two are privately owned (**Cuevas de Candelaria** and **Cuevas de los Nacimientos**); the two most impressive sections are the latter two options.

Hotel Cancuén in Raxrujá (see opposite) offers a full-day tour (Q125; minimum four people) to Los Nacimientos, where you can visit the crystalline Cueva Blanca, as well as float for several hours through creepy bat-filled caverns on a tube. Consult ⓦ www.cuevaslosnacimientos .com for more information.

The Cuevas de Candelaria contain some truly monumental caverns, including the 200m-long Tzul Tacca cave. To reach this cave complex, hop on a micro heading west from Raxrujá.

At the large "Cuevas de Candelaria" sign, about 5km from town, a path leads south towards a resort complex containing some overpriced rustic bungalows. You don't have to be a guest to visit the caves. A one-hour group tour on foot is US$4 per person, or by inner tube US$13.50. Usually you can tag onto a group if they have one visiting and simply pay per head. Otherwise, you need a minimum of three to obtain the above rates.

Cancuén

North of Raxrujá is the large Maya site of **Cancuén** (daily 8am–4pm; US$6), where a huge Classic-era palace, which had 170 rooms, has been unearthed. You can also see the remains of an impressive bathing pool (which was used for ritual purification). Uniquely, Cancuén seems to have lacked the usual religious and defensive structures characteristic of Maya cities, instead existing as an essentially secular trading city. The vast amounts of jade, pyrite, obsidian and fine ceramics found recently indicate that this was actually one of the greatest trading centres of the Maya world, with a paved plaza (which may have been a marketplace) covering two square kilometres. Cancuén is thought to have flourished because of its strategic position between the great cities of the lowlands, like Tikal and Calakmul, and the mineral-rich highlands of southern Guatemala. There's a trail with good information panels (in English), and a visitors' centre.

To **get to** Cancuén, pick-ups (approximately hourly) leave Raxrujá for the *aldea* of La Unión, 12km to the north, where boatmen will take you by *lancha* for the thirty-minute ride along the Río Pasión to the site. Unfortunately it's an expensive trip – around Q300 – but the boat can accommodate up to sixteen people. It's also possible to travel via the village of La Isla, but connections here are not as good.

Fray Bartolomé de las Casas

One hour east of Raxrujá is the isolated settlement of **Fray Bartolomé de las Casas**, referred to as simply Fray (pronounced "Fry") by locals. The town has some basic accommodation and *comedores*, as well as ATMs and a thriving market. Otherwise, there isn't much of interest here. However, it is a main **transport** link between Alta Verapaz and other popular areas to the east and north.

Moving on

Regular transport leaves the marketplace bus terminal for Sebol, Raxrujá, Cobán and the village of Chahal (1hr 30min), from where there are further micros heading east towards the highway junction of Modesto Méndez/Cadenas (2hr 30min), where you can connect with passing transport to Poptún or Río Dulce. There's one daily bus to Poptún via San Luís (3am), though this is a painfully slow road, making the route via Chahal potentially quicker and certainly more convenient.

Chahal and around

In between Chahal and Modesto Méndez are the **natural pools** of Las Conchas and the nearby backpackers' hideaway of *Oasis Chiyu* (☎5839 4473, ☜www .naturetoursguatemala.com), where you can sleep in rustic rooms (Q130) or dorms (Q50) and there are hiking trails and caves to explore. Note that it's a very remote spot, there's no electricity, and guests are rare.

PARQUE NACIONAL LAGUNA LACHUÁ

In the far northwest corner of Alta Verapaz is the frontier town of Playa Grande and the nearby natural attraction of **PARQUE NACIONAL LAGUNA LACHUÁ** (daily 7am–4pm; US$5.50; ☎7861 0086), a great place to get off the beaten track for a day or two of tranquillity and swimming in pristine water. The lake is a near-perfect circle of crystal water, ringed by a tropical forest reserve that's home to a host of wildlife, including jaguars, ocelots, otters and tapirs. The scrupulously maintained national park provides **camping** facilities (Q25) as well as a lodge with mosquito-netted bunks (Q50). There are good cooking facilities and drinking water, but you need to bring your own food.

Lachuá is a sublime spot and it's well worth the effort **getting here**. From Cobán, take a micro bound for Playa Grande (every 30min); these pass the San Luís junction (4hr), from where you'll need to catch another micro or pick-up to the park entrance about 6km to the west. Coming from Chisec or Raxrujá get to the Xuctzul junction and catch an onward micro from there; micros and pick-ups run roughly hourly until 3pm. You pay your entrance fee and accommodation costs at the **visitors' centre** on the road. It is also possible to leave your backpack here and take just a smaller bag on the sweaty 4km walk through the jungle to the lakeside lodge.

Petén

The low-lying northern department of **Petén**, once the Maya heartland, occupies about a third of Guatemala's territory but is home to just three percent of its population. In the last thirty years there has been a wave of immigration to the area, initially encouraged by the government in an attempt to cultivate this wild land. Vast swathes of rainforest have been cleared for ranching and commercial logging, despite the fact that forty percent of the department is officially protected by the **Maya Biosphere Reserve**. However, most sights of note are at least still shrouded in jungle, and you will doubtless witness some of Petén's remarkably vibrant wildlife.

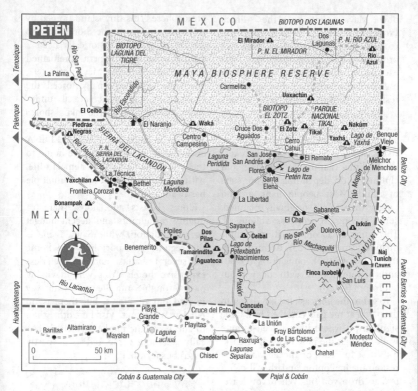

The map labels include:

MEXICO — BIOTOPO DOS LAGUNAS — PETÉN — BIOTOPO LAGUNA DEL TIGRE — El Mirador — Dos Lagunas — P. N. RÍO AZUL — Río San Pedro — La Palma — P. N. EL MIRADOR — Río Azul — MAYA BIOSPHERE RESERVE — Río Escondido — Carmelita — Uaxactún — El Ceibo — BIOTOPO EL ZOTZ — PARQUE NACIONAL TIKAL — Piedras Negras — El Naranjo — Waká — Cruce Dos Aguados — El Zotz — Tikal — Nakúm — Benque Viejo — Centro Campesino — Cerro Cahuí — Yaxhá — Lago de Yaxhá — SIERRA DEL LACANDÓN — Río Usumacinta — P. N. SIERRA DEL LACANDÓN — San José — El Remate — Melchor de Menchos — La Técnica — San Andrés — Flores — Lago de Petén Itzá — Yaxchilán — Bethel — Santa Elena — Frontera Corozal — Laguna Mendosa — Laguna Peridida — La Libertad — Sabaneta — Bonampak — MEXICO — N — Pipiles — Sayaxché — El Chal — Dolores — Ixkún — Dos Pilas — Ceibal — Río San Juan — MAYA MOUNTAINS — Benemerito — Tamarindito — Aguateca — Lago de Petexbatún — Nacimientos — Río Machaquilá — Naj Tunich Caves — Río Lacantún — Río Pasión — Poptún — Finca Ixobel — San Luis — BELIZE — Playa Grande — Cruce del Pato — Cancuén — La Unión — Barillas — Altamirano — Mayalan — Playitas — Fray Bártolomó de Las Casas — Modesto Méndez — Laguna Lachuá — Candelaria — Raxrujá — Chisec — Lagunas Sepalau — Sebol — Chahal — 0 50 km — Cobán & Guatemala City — Pajal & Cobán

Tenosique — Palenque — Huehuetenango — Belize City — Puerto Barrios & Guatemala City

Pctén also boasts an incredible number of **Maya sites** – several hundred ruined cities have been mapped in the region, though most are still buried beneath the jungle. The superstar attraction is **Tikal**, but other, less-visited highlights include atmospheric **Yaxhá** and the immense **El Mirador**. Of modern towns, lakeside **Flores** and **Santa Elena** form the hub of the department, and you'll find hotels and restaurants to suit all tastes. Halfway between Flores and Tikal is the tranquil alternative base of **El Remate**. The caves and scenery around **Poptún**, on the main highway south, also justify exploration, while down the other road south, **Sayaxché** is surrounded by yet more Maya sites.

POPTÚN AND AROUND

Heading north from the Río Dulce the smooth paved highway to Flores cuts through a degraded landscape of small *milpa* farms and cattle ranches that was jungle a few decades ago. Many travellers choose to stop along the way at the sublime *Finca Ixobel* (see below) outside the small town of **POPTÚN**. There's no particular reason to stay in the town itself, but you may well pause to use an internet café (try Servicio de Internet, next to the Fuente del Norte bus office) or banks (there are several ATMs). The area around Poptún also offers excellent opportunities to visit little-known attractions, including the Naj Tunich caves, the delightful swimming pool of Las Cataratas waterfalls near the village of Mopán and the minor archeological sites of El Chal, Ixcún and Ixtontón.

Finca Ixobel

About 4km south of Poptún, surrounded by fragrant pine forests in the foothills of the Maya mountains, is the 🏕 **Finca Ixobel** (☎5892 3188, ⓦwww.finca ixobel.com), a working farm that also provides guest accommodation, local excursions, a swimming pond and memorable home-style cooking in the restaurant (dinner is Q30–60). There's a really sociable atmosphere with guests sharing stories at meal times, and either so much (tours to caves, rivers, Maya ruins, horseriding, hikes) or so little (hammock-swinging and chilling) to do, depending on your state of mind. Most people hang around longer than they'd originally planned, some staying to work as volunteers. The range of accommodation options includes camping (Q25), dorms (Q40), treehouses (Q100), bungalows (Q300) and private rooms with or without bathroom (Q120).

To **get to** the *finca* ask the bus driver to drop you at the gate (marked by a large sign), from where it's a fifteen-minute walk through the pine trees; after dark, it's safest to head for the *Fonda Ixobel* restaurant in Poptún and they'll call a taxi to drop you off. When you leave, there are direct shuttle services to Flores and Río Dulce, or alternatively, back on the main road, flag down a passing micro to Poptún town and arrange onward public transport.

Moving on

By bus to: Guatemala City (every 30min; 7hr), including deluxe services operated by Línea Dorada and Maya de Oro (Fuente del Norte's luxury buses), all via Río Dulce; chicken bus to Fray Bartolomé de las Casas (1 daily at 10.30am; 6–7hr).
By microbus to: Santa Elena (very frequent; 1hr 30min).

FLORES AND SANTA ELENA

Despite the legions of tourists that pass through **FLORES**, the gateway to the Mundo Maya and the capital of Petén, it has nonetheless retained an easy pace and a sedate, old-world atmosphere. This tiny island (joined by a 500m causeway to the shore) on Lago de Petén Itzá has historically been a natural point of settlement. It remained the capital of the Itzá Maya until 1697, when the Spanish finally forced the town (then known as Tayasal) under their control. Today the lake's shores host a more cosmopolitan crowd. Across the causeway, **SANTA ELENA** and adjoining San Benito are home to the gritty business of Guatemalan life, with sprawling markets and multiple hardware stores.

Flores boasts the lion's share of quality restaurants and decent budget accommodation, while Santa Elena is the region's transport hub and home to several banks and characterless expensive hotels. You will inevitably pass through Santa Elena on your way in and out of Flores, but there is no particular reason to visit here other than to check out the market, which chaotically surrounds the old (still partly used) bus terminal.

Arrival and information

By air The airport is in Santa Elena, 3km east of the causeway (a Q5 tuk-tuk or Q15 taxi ride into town). Returning to the airport, local buses leave from the Flores end of the causeway every 20min or so.
By bus All buses stop in Santa Elena. There is a new bus terminal on the southern outskirts, where Pullman buses and many micros and chicken buses terminate. From here a tuk-tuk to anywhere in Flores or Santa Elena costs Q5, and a taxi should be Q15. Some buses (notably the international services from Palenque, Chetumal and Belize City) drop you just a block up from the causeway, from where it's a short walk to Flores' accommodation. There is also a chaotic second (old) bus terminal, the Terminal Viejo, still in use for regional departures and arrivals. From here, you'll need to navigate your way through the market stalls onto 4 Calle, from where it's a 10min walk to Flores (or Q5 in a tuk-tuk).
Tour operators Flores has dozens of tour operators, many of them pretty average. Two of the best are Martsam Travel, C 30 Junio (☎7867 5093, ⓦwww.martsam.com), who offer trips to sites including Waka' (El Perú), Yaxhá and Aguateca; and Turismo Aventura, 6 Av & 4 C, Santa Elena

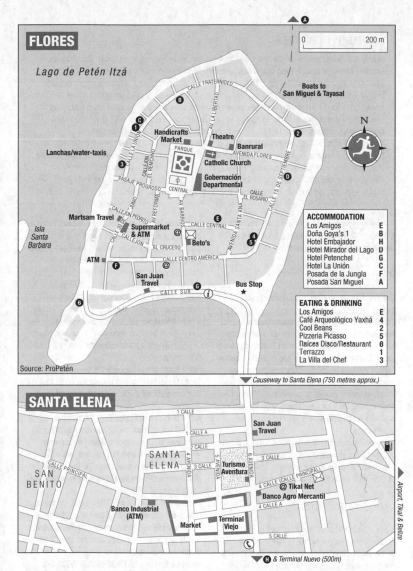

FLORES

0   200 m

Lago de Petén Itzá

N

Boats to
San Miguel & Tayasal

CALLE FRATERNIDED

AV. LA LIBERTAD

Handicrafts
Market

Theatre

Banrural

AVENIDA FLORES

Catholic Church

Lanchas/water-taxis

PARQUE

CALLE 15 DE SEPTIEMBRE

CALLE LA UNION

CALLEJON EL REMCHO

PASAJE PROGRESO

CENTRAL

Gobernación
Departmental

CALLE
EL ROSARIO

CALLE
CENTRAL

Isla
Santa
Barbara

CALLEJON PEDRITO

Martsam Travel

AV REFORMA

AV BARRIOS

AVENIDA SANTA ANA

CALLE 30

CALLEJON

Supermarket
& ATM

Beto's

EL CRUCERO

CALLE CENTRO AMÉRICA

ATM

San Juan
Travel

CALLE SUR

Bus Stop

CALLE SUR

ACCOMMODATION

Los Amigos	E
Doña Goya's 1	B
Hotel Embajador	H
Hotel Mirador del Lago	D
Hotel Petenchel	G
Hotel La Unión	C
Posada de la Jungla	F
Posada San Miguel	A

EATING & DRINKING

Los Amigos	E
Café Arqueológico Yaxhá	4
Cool Beans	2
Pizzeria Picasso	5
Raíces Disco/Restaurant	6
Terrazzo	1
La Villa del Chef	3

Source: ProPetén

Causeway to Santa Elena (750 metres approx.)

SANTA ELENA

1 CALLE

San Juan
Travel

SANTA
ELENA

1 CALLE A

2 CALLE

4 AVENIDA

5 AVENIDA

6 AVENIDA

3 CALLE

Turismo
Aventura

3 CALLE

CALLE PRINCIPAL

SAN
BENITO

4 CALLE (CALLE PRINCIPAL)

@ Tikal Net

Banco Agro Mercantil

4 CALLE A

Banco Industrial
(ATM)

Market

Terminal
Viejo

5 CALLE

H & Terminal Nuevo (500m)

Airport, Tikal & Belize

(☎ 7926 0398, ⓦ www.toursguatemala.com), a
good all-rounder with trips to many Maya ruins in
Petén and also cheap airline tickets. It's also worth
dropping by *Café Yaxhá* to see if Dieter is running
any trips to Maya sites. For Tikal, it's easiest to
book your bus via your hotel, as no matter who
you book with you're likely to end up on a shuttle
operated by San Juan Travel (☎ 5847 4729), on
the Calle Sur (Flores) or 6 Av (Santa Elena). For
years this company had a (justifiably) poor reputation for overcharging foreigners. They've recently

cleaned up their act somewhat, but it's best to just
use them for shuttle services to Tikal (Q60 return),
Palenque and Belize City, not other trips.

Tourist information There's no shortage of information sources in Flores, but be careful who you
listen to as there are *coyotes* about (see box, p.222).
Los Amigos Hostel is probably the best source of
advice for budget travellers. Otherwise Inguat, the
official tourist board, has an office at Av Santa Ana
(daily 8am–4.30pm; ☎ 7867 5334), and two booths:
one on Calle Sur in Flores (daily 7.30am–noon &

FLORES' COYOTES

Many travellers experience the hard sell on arrival in Flores from local ticket touts, known as **coyotes**. These guys know every trick in the book to persuade you to spend your money with them. Be especially aware on tourist shuttles arriving from Belize and Mexico, when you are likely to be travel-weary and green (ie, new to the country). Most *coyotes* speak excellent English and will bamboozle you with their seemingly exhaustive knowledge of your future travel options. Many susceptible backpackers are persuaded to book hotel rooms, tours and onward travel arrangements before even setting foot on Flores Island. In some cases *coyotes* have been found selling completely fake tickets; even if you do receive the service you've paid for, you will almost certainly have paid over the odds, as *coyotes* take a cut. Always buy tickets from a legitimate tour operator or hotel staff, and don't hurry – if you shop around you're likely to get the best price and service.

2–6pm) and another at the airport (daily 7am–11am & 3–6pm). There is also an Asistur booth on the causeway if you have any problems.

Getting around

Canoes *La Villa del Chef* (see opposite) rents canoes for Q20 per hour.

Lanchas You can hop across to the Tayasal Peninsula by *lancha* for Q5. They run on a regular basis until 11pm from the dock on Flores' northeast shore. Boatmen also offer day and half-day trips to explore the lake by *lancha*. They tend to hang out around the southwest corner of the island, close to *Hotel Petenchel*, as well as beside the *Villa del Chef* and near the dock for San Miguel. Look for Miguel, who was born in Flores in 1925 and has some great stories.

Taxis and tuk-tuks For short hops, tuk-tuk drivers charge Q5 for anywhere in the Flores/Santa Elena/San Benito area. For longer journeys, taxi fares start at Q15. To reach other lakeside villages, see p.224.

Accommodation

There are several good budget places in Flores itself, making it unnecessary to stay in noisier and dirtier Santa Elena. Many tour groups pass through, using the mid- to top-range accommodation, but there are also plenty of businesses tailored to the backpacker market. Unless otherwise marked, all places listed below are in Flores.

Los Amigos C Central ☎7867 5975, ⓦwww .amigoshostel.com. If you're into dorm-sharing and hostel culture look no further. Plus points are the courtyard garden, inexpensive rates, filling food, sociable vibe, DVD selection and unmatched travel advice. Not so great are the dorms (some are on the large side), cleanliness (ashtrays are rarely emptied), rising food prices and the 4am Tikal tour exodus

every morning (which means that you can forget all thoughts of a peaceful lie-in). You'll also find lockers, secure charge-points for mobiles and iPods, a book swap and wi-fi. Dorms Q35, doubles Q90

Doña Goya's 1 C La Unión ☎7867 5513, ⓔhospedajedonagoya@yahoo.com. Popular alternative to *Los Amigos* with dorm beds and reasonable, spacious doubles. The rooftop terrace is a huge bonus and you'll find a small breakfast room and internet facilities downstairs. A second branch of *Doña Goya's* is 20m around the corner. Dorms Q35, doubles Q90

Hotel Embajador Opposite the bus terminal in Santa Elena. No phone. A secure, no-frills place that's very handy if you've got an early-morning departure. Q80

Hotel Mirador del Lago C 15 Septiembre ☎7867 5409. You'll find cheap rates and friendly staff here. The basic rooms have fan, screened windows and bathroom but no view, while those facing the lake also have cable TV. There's inexpensive water refills, internet, a laundry service and a small restaurant. Q80

Hotel Petenchel C Sur ☎7867 5450. On the south side of the island facing the lake, this little place has a row of good, clean, freshly-painted double rooms with hot-water bathroom, fan and TV. There's a little café here too. Q120

Hotel La Unión C La Unión ☎7867 5531. For smart private rooms this place is excellent value – rooms are clean, bright and come with bathroom and fan. Those with direct lake views cost a bit extra. Downstairs is an internet café. Q90

Posada de la Jungla C Centroamérica ☎7867 5185, ⓔinfo@travelpeten.com. The double rooms at this hotel are smallish but neat, all with bathroom and cable TV and either a fan or a/c. Q160

Posada San Miguel Across the lake in San Miguel village ☎7867 5312, ⓔposadasanmiguel1 @gmail.com. A delightful family-run posada that represents great value, though it's over the lake in sleepy San Miguel. Large lakeside rooms have attractive furnishings, private bathroom, TV and stunning views. There is a small beach directly out front and a simple *comedor* downstairs. *Lanchas* (Q5) connect San Miguel with Flores every few minutes. Q125

Eating and drinking

You'll find a good selection of restaurants in Flores, though prices are high compared to the rest of Guatemala. For economical eats, head for the stalls on the plaza (7am–10pm). Santa Elena has numerous *comedores* where you can find a feed for less than US$2. Be aware that some local restaurants still serve wild game (such as *venado*, *pavo silvestre*, *coche de monte* or *tepesquintle*) – this is best avoided, as it is most likely to be poached from reserves. All restaurants and bars listed below are in Flores.

Los Amigos C Central. This backpackers' stronghold has a shady courtyard in which to enjoy Western favourites, though it's a tad pricey and service can be slow. Strong on veggie food, including excellent salads (Q40), and the *licuados* are almost a meal in themselves. Happy hour (7–8pm) means 2-for-1 beers and discounted cocktails.

Café Arqueológico Yaxhá C 15 Septiembre ☎ 5830 2060. An interesting choice, the menu here boasts many pre-Hispanic dishes of Maya origin using ingredients like *yuca* and squash. Most meals are in the Q40–60 range. The walls of the café are covered with posters and photos relating to local Maya sites, to which Dieter, the German owner, runs excellent tours. Evening slide-shows about the Maya are well worth attending too.

Cool Beans C 15 Septiembre. This is an atmospheric place to eat and drink, with a thatch-shaded seating area that runs down to a lakeshore garden where there are hammocks. The extensive menu features such favourites as pancakes (Q22), sandwiches (from Q20) and pasta, as well as dishes such as fried aubergine with rice and salad. They also sell draught beer, fine espresso coffee and cocktails. Mon & Wed–Sun 7am–9pm.

Pizzeria Picasso C 15 Septiembre. Deep-pan bases and generous toppings mean a regular pizza can feed two (unless your appetite is fuelled by a day's temple-climbing). Pizzas are mostly in the Q40–70 range; pastas and burgers cost less. Closed Mon.

Raíces Disco/Restaurant Western end of C Sur. The restaurant is a pricey affair that packs in the tour groups but the bar-disco is the only game in town for dancefloor action. Closed Mon.

La Villa del Chef C La Unión. One of the most attractive restaurants in Flores, this elegant place has a lovely lookout over the lake from its huge windows and terrace seating. You'll find lots of vegetarian choices, including Mediterraneo salad (Q29) and burritos (Q39), while the beef burgers (Q44) are wonderfully flavoursome. However, watch out for annoying sting-in-the-tail extra charges, including bread and water.

Directory

Exchange In Flores, there's a Banco Industrial ATM inside the supermarket on C 30 de Junio. You'll find many more banks in Santa Elena, including a Banco G&T and Banco Agromercantíl at the main junction on 6 Av and 4 C, both with ATMs. There's also an ATM inside the Terminal Nuevo bus station.

Internet and telephone There are several internet cafés along C Centroamérica. The best are Petén Net and Tikal Net, which have fast connections and discounted international phone calls.

Language schools Academia de Español Dos Mundos (c/o *Café Yaxhá*; ☎ 5830 2060, ⊛ www.flores-spanish.com) has one-on-one, group and crash courses in Spanish. On the other side of the lake, the villages of San José and San Andrés (see p.225) also have schools.

Laundry Cheapest is Beto's on Av Barrios (wash and dry Q25). Since he runs sunrise tours to Tikal, the shop is often closed until noon.

Post offices In Flores, on Av Barrios (Mon–Fri 8.30am–1pm); in Santa Elena, on C Principal, two blocks east of the Banco Agromercantíl (Mon–Fri 8am–4.30pm, Sat 9am–1pm).

Shopping As well as the plethora of tourist shops, there is a friendly handicraft market on the Parque Central (9am–9pm).

Moving on

By air to: Guatemala City (3 daily; 50min; from US$240 return), with TACA (℡ 2470 8222, ⊕ www .taca.com) and TAG (℡ 2380 9400); demand is heavy for these flights in peak periods, and over-booking is common. Reserve well in advance and arrive promptly for check-in; Belize City (2 daily; 45min; US$220 return), with Tropic Air (⊕ www .tropicair.com). At the time of research there were no direct flights to Cancún. A Q25 security tax is charged on all flights, and there's also a US$30 international departure tax (normally included in the price of your ticket).

By bus and micro from Terminal Nuevo to: Belize City (1 daily at 7am with Línea Dorada; 5hr); Chetumal (1 daily at 7am with Línea Dorada; 8hr); El Ceibo/La Palma (12 daily; 4hr); El Remate (every 30min; 30min); Guatemala City (2 daily at 9pm & 11pm with ADN; 2 daily at 10am & 10pm with Línea Dorada; 15 daily with Fuente del Norte; 8–9hr); La Técnica via Bethel (five daily; 4hr 30min); Melchor de Menchos (micros every 30min; 1 bus daily at 2.30am with Fuente del Norte; 1 bus daily at 7am with Línea Dorada; 2hr 15min); Poptún (hourly; 2hr); San Pedro Sula, Honduras (1 daily at 5.45am, with Fuente del Norte; 12hr); San Salvador (1 daily at 5.45am, with Fuente del Norte; 12hr); Sayaxché (every 20min; 2hr); Tikal (4 daily at 5am, 7am, 9am & 1pm); Uaxactún (1 daily at 1pm; 2hr 30min). Most buses to Guatemala City stop in both Poptún and Río Dulce en route. For Copán in Honduras catch a bus heading for San Pedro Sula.

By bus and micro from Terminal Viejo to: Carmelita (2 daily at 5am & 1pm; 3hr). There are also buses to destinations across Petén, including Poptún and Sayaxché, from here.

By shuttle bus Destinations include Belize City (1 daily at 5am with San Juan Travel; 5hr; US$18);

Chetumal (1 daily at 5am with San Juan Travel; 8hr; US$28); Cobán (4hr 30min; Q125); Lanquín (1 daily at 9am; 8hr; Q100); Palenque (1 daily at 5am; 8hr; Q230). You can book all the above through most hotels and guesthouses.

LAGO DE PETÉN ITZÁ

While the majority of visitors to Flores rightly prioritize a visit to Tikal, there are a string of other worthwhile day-trip excursions in the region surrounding **LAGO DE PETÉN ITZÁ**.

From Flores it's possible to visit a number of nearby attractions by *lancha*. These include: the tiny **Museo Santa Barbara** (8am–5pm; Q10), on an island just off Flores' western shores, which houses a collection of Maya pottery and a very old gramophone; **ARCAS**, an animal rescue NGO 5km east of San Miguel village (9am–4pm; Q50), where you can volunteer (US$130 per week) and learn about wildlife protection in Petén, walk an interpretive trail and view animals that cannot be released into the wild. Beyond ARCAS, the **Petencito Zoo** (8am–5pm; Q25), which is home to (among others), crocodiles, tigers and some zippy – though dodgy – waterslides. For the best *lancha* prices you'll need to get a group together and haggle fairly fiercely. Estimate about US$10 per hour.

Peninsula Tayasal

Incredibly, this attractive peninsula, just a five-minute *lancha* ride across the lake from Flores, is largely overlooked by the tourist dollars flooding into that town.

INTO BELIZE: MELCHOR DE MENCOS

There is regular transport from Santa Elena to the Belize border at Melchor de Mencos (every 30min; 2hr 15min) from the Terminal Nuevo; most buses make a stop in the market area on their way west. It is also possible to take direct services to Belize City and beyond (see "Moving on", above). The border is fairly straightforward, although you'll probably be charged a Q10 unofficial exit tax. Moneychangers should give you a fair rate. Once in Belize you'll need to take a taxi (US$3) for the short journey to Benque Viejo del Carmen, from where it's a half-hour bus journey to the pleasant town of San Ignacio, or three hours to Belize City (last bus leaves at 6pm).

The village of **San Miguel** and nearby **El Mirador** and **Playita El Chechenal** make for an easy excursion. Regular *lanchas* leave from the northeast shores of Flores to San Miguel. To reach the *mirador* it's a twenty-minute, fairly isolated walk. Follow the lakeshore west past the village, turn uphill after the last buildings, then follow the track up until it evens out to a shaded trail and take the left branch (keeping the lake to your left). Eventually you'll reach a clearing from where concrete steps lead up to the wooden lookout tower. There are fantastic views of the lake and its settlements. Back down at the clearing you can follow another trail for ten minutes around the northern side of the peninsula (keeping the lake to your left), until you reach a signposted left turn for La Playita. You can see the turquoise water beckoning you and there is a quiet beach area with picnic benches and toilets. To return to San Miguel village, simply turn left at the end of the beach road and follow the track for fifteen minutes to complete your circuit.

Ak'tun-Kan caves

Just north of Santa Elena, past the bus terminal, is the entrance to the **Grutas Ak'tun-Kan**, or serpent caves

(8am–5pm; Q20). Bring your own torch and decent shoes, as the interior is dark and pretty slippery. The cave comprises a series of small passageways and some stalactites apparently resembling well-known people and objects. There are, however, no snakes. A tuk-tuk to the caves is Q5.

San Andrés and San José

Across the lake from Santa Elena and Flores are the quiet villages of **San Andrés** and **San José**. There is no longer a public boat service here as the road has been paved and regular micros now whiz past. The villages' roads slope steeply up from the shore, lined with colourful buildings. San José, in particular, has an impressive array of facilities (including a water park and music stadium). There is also a lovely public beach, a bank with ATM and several *comedores* serving *comida rápida*. The village is undergoing something of a cultural revival: Itzá, the pre-Conquest Maya tongue, is being taught in the large school.

Most visitors come this way to study or volunteer at one of the local **language schools**. You'll pay around US$180–200 per week for twenty hours of one-to-one lessons, food and lodging and a homestay with a local family. Very few locals here speak English so you can progress quite quickly. Good schools include: Eco Escuela de Español (☎5940 1235, ⓦwww.eco escuelaespanol.org), a community-run, long-established school in San Andrés; Escuela Nueva Juventud (☎5711 0040, ⓦwww.volunteerpeten.com), located just outside San Andrés; and Escuela Bio Itzá (☎7928 8056, ⓔescuelabioitza @hotmail.com), in San José, part of a project for the conservation of the Itzá biosphere and culture. Activities include volunteer work in the botanical garden and preparing natural medicines and cosmetics.

EL REMATE

The tranquil village of **EL REMATE** lies midway between Flores and Tikal on the northeastern corner of Lago de Petén Itzá. The lake is a beautiful turquoise blue here and many of the budget hotels offer swimming access – an extremely welcome idea after a sweaty morning climbing Tikal's jungle temples. It's a lovely place to take a break from the rigours of the road, with little traffic and a lot of nature to enjoy.

What to see and do

On the north shore of the lake, fifteen minutes' walk from the centre of El Remate, the **Biotopo Cerro Cahuí** (daily 7am–4pm; US$5) is a 6.5-square-kilometre wildlife conservation area comprising lakeshore, ponds and some of the best examples of undisturbed tropical forest in Petén. There are hiking trails (4km and 6km), a couple of small ruins and two thatched *miradores* on the hill above the lake; pick up maps and information at the gate where you sign in. It's recommended to visit the park in the early morning as wildlife is most active and it is cooler at this time.

Arrival and information

By bus and microbus El Remate lies just north (15min walk) of the Puente Ixlú (sometimes known

as El Cruce) junction. Buses/micros taking the main road between Santa Elena and the Belize border will drop you here. There's also regular transport to the village itself. The main bus stop is located in the village centre at the point where a minor road branches west (around the northern lakeshore) off the main Tikal road. However, you can ask your driver to drop you anywhere between the Puente Ixlú junction and the bus stop. For accommodation on the northern lakeshore road you will need to walk.

Exchange There are no banks, but you can change dollars (US and Belize) and travellers' cheques at *La Casa de Don David* in the village centre.

Tourist information There is an information booth on the left as you enter the village, but don't bank on it being open. Several hotels provide good information, including *La Casa de Don David* and *Mon Ami*.

Accommodation

El Remate has plenty of budget deals and a few mid-range options, too. You'll pay slightly more for lake views or access, but the setting is so idyllic it's probably worth it. The following are listed in the order you reach them from Puente Ixlú.

Hostal Hermano Pedro Down off the main road opposite the football pitch ☎5719 7394, ⓦwww .hhpedro.com. On a quiet side-road, this large

TREAT YOURSELF

La Casa de Don David ☎7928 8469, ⓦwww.lacasadedondavid .com. The genial American owner of this lodge has lived in Petén for over 30 years and was the original *gringo perdido*. His guesthouse, which he runs with his Guatemalan wife and daughter, is a beautifully maintained place, with spotless rooms (most with a/c), all facing a huge grassy garden that extends down towards the lakeshore. Guatemalan and Western meals are served on a deck that makes the most of the views, and there's a full bar, as well as excellent independent travel advice and copies of *National Geographic* to browse. It's geared at mid-range travellers, but if you've been roughing it in the jungle for days, it could be the perfect retreat. Breakfast is included, and rates include lunch or dinner. US$61 wooden house has a profusion of good-quality rooms (most with private bath) that open onto a communal decked balcony. There's wi-fi and a *comedor*. Q150

Hotel Sun Breeze Lakeside, in the centre of the village ☎7928 8044, ✆sunbreezehotel@gmail .com. A good choice as many of the well-scrubbed, screened rooms (some with private bath) have a lovely perspective over the lake. It's great value, and the friendly owners offer tours. Q70

Casa Roja 500m down the road to Cerro Cahuí on the right ☎5173 2593. This very cheap place has simple, well-constructed, stick-and-thatch cabañas. They rent beds dorm-style, and there is also one large two-bed room that makes a particularly good deal for a couple. There's also an inexpensive vegetarian restaurant and kayaks for rent. Dorms Q35, doubles Q90

Casa de Doña Tonita 800m down the road to Cerro Cahuí on the right ☎5701 7114. One of the most popular gringo hangouts, this is one of the cheapest deals in town. Four basic clapboard rooms, built above the lake, with great views, plus a reasonable six-bed dorm. There's tasty budget-friendly food in the *comedor* and the owners look after their guests well. Dorms Q30, doubles Q60

🏃 **Mon Ami** 300m past *Dona Tonita's* ☎7928 8413, ⓦwww.hotelmonami.com. A wonderful place to stay, this French-owned guesthouse is run by Santiago Billy, a likeable and knowledgeable long-term resident of Petén. This is quite a place, with gorgeous rooms and bungalows scattered around a tranquil, forested plot of land. All the accommodation has style and character, enhanced by the use of local textiles and artistic flourishes, while the dorm is probably the most attractive in Guatemala. There's excellent swimming from the dock, and be sure to treat yourself to a meal here too. Dorms Q50, doubles Q150

Eating

Most places to eat are on the main road, though many hotels also have their own restaurants. *Casa Don David*, in the village centre, features a specials board tailored towards the palates of their inter-national guests.

Mon Ami The best food in town is served in this charming hotel's lake-facing *palapa*. French and Italian dishes including magnificent shrimps with garlic and butter, pasta with pesto (Q30) and crêpes are all very flavoursome. There's a good set lunch for Q35 and wine by the bottle and glass.

Restaurant Cahuí Opposite *Hostal Hermano Pedro*. It's all about the great lake-facing deck at the rear of this restaurant, which has breakfasts (Q20),

comida típica, burgers and pasta (meals from Q30). There's a well-stocked bar too, and it makes a great place for a sundowner.

Restaurant El Muelle Past the football pitch, south of *Restaurant Cahuí*. This smart restaurant's menu is not cheap, though there are snacks (sandwiches, burgers and nachos) below Q30, and you get free use of the fantastic lakeside swimming pool if you eat here.

Moving on

By bus All of El Remate's hotels offer door-to-door return shuttles to Tikal for Q50 (30min). A few local buses and a swarm of minibuses ply the route to Flores (every 30min; 30–45min). For Belize (2hr), catch a ride or walk to Puente Ixlú for micros to Melchor de Menchos (every 30min). Alternatively, any hotel can book you a shuttle bus.

TIKAL

Towering above the rainforest, **TIKAL** is possibly the most renowned of all Maya ruins (daily 6am–6pm; Q150; ⓦwww.parque-tikal.com). The site is dominated by six giant temples, steep-sided pyramids that rise up to 64m from the forest floor. In addition, literally thousands of other structures, many half-strangled by giant roots and still hidden beneath mounds of earth, demand exploration. The site itself is deep in the jungle of the **Parque Nacional Tikal**, and the forest is home to all sorts of wildlife, including howler and spider monkeys, toucans and parakeets, coatis and big cats. Perhaps early explorer Sylvanus Morley coined the most fitting description of Tikal: "Place Where the Gods Speak". The sheer scale of the place is astounding and its jungle location spellbinding. Whether you can spare as little as an hour or as long as a week, it's always worth the trip.

What to see and do

Tikal is vast. The **central area**, with its five main temples, forms by far the most impressive section; if you start to explore beyond this you can wander seemingly endlessly in the maze of

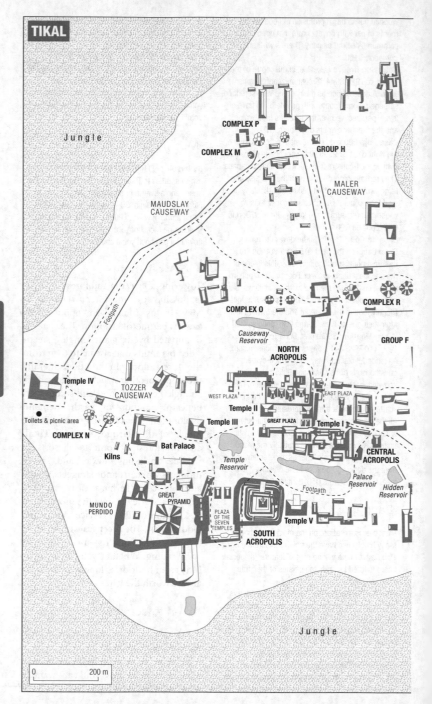

TIKAL

Jungle

COMPLEX P
COMPLEX M
GROUP H
MALER CAUSEWAY

MAUDSLAY CAUSEWAY

Footpath

COMPLEX O

COMPLEX R

Causeway Reservoir

GROUP F

NORTH ACROPOLIS

Temple IV

TOZZER CAUSEWAY

WEST PLAZA

Temple II

EAST PLAZA

GREAT PLAZA

Temple I

Toilets & picnic area

COMPLEX N

Temple III

Kilns

Bat Palace

CENTRAL ACROPOLIS

Temple Reservoir

Palace Reservoir

Hidden Reservoir

Footpath

MUNDO PERDIDO

GREAT PYRAMID

PLAZA OF THE SEVEN TEMPLES

Temple V

SOUTH ACROPOLIS

Jungle

0   200 m

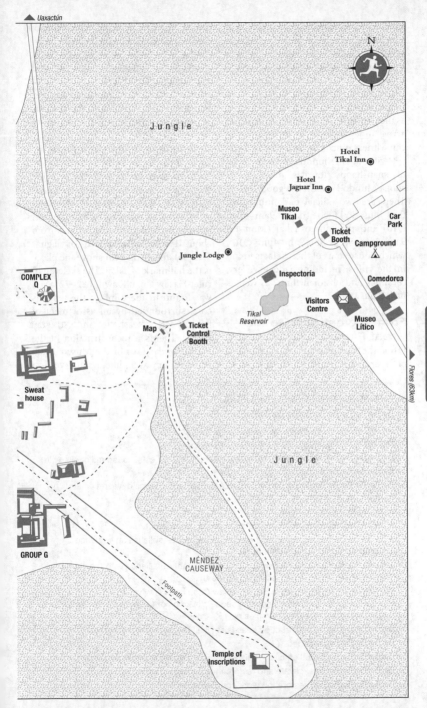

smaller, unrestored structures and complexes. Whatever you do, Tikal is certain to exhaust you before you exhaust it. Rather too many visitors congregate to witness the sunrise from Temple IV when the forest canopy bursts into a frenzy of sound and activity. However, as the park officially opens at 6am, if you arrive independently at this hour you can witness much the same atmosphere, yet without the hundred-strong crowd of snap-happy tourists, from other spots; Mundo Perdido is a good choice. There are two official park **museums**, the Museo Lítico (daily 9am–4pm; Q10) and the Museo Tikal (Mon–Fri 9am–5pm, Sat & Sun 9am–4pm; Q10), which house some of the artefacts found in the ruins, including jade jewellery, ceramics and obsidian flints, as well as numerous stelae.

From the entrance to the Great Plaza

From the site map at the entrance, a path branches right to **complexes Q**

and R. The first pyramid, with a line of eight stelae in front of it, is also known as the Temple of Nine Mayan Gods. Bearing left after Complex R, you approach the **East Plaza**; in its southeast corner stands an imposing temple, beneath which were found the remains of several severed heads, the victims of human sacrifice. From here a few short steps bring you to the **Great Plaza**, the heart of the ancient city. Surrounded by four massive structures, this was the focus of ceremonial and religious activity at Tikal for around a thousand years. Beneath the grass lie four layers of paving, the oldest of which dates from about 150 BC. **Temple I** (or Jaguar Temple), towering 44m above the plaza, is the hallmark of Tikal. The skeleton of ruler Hasaw Chan K'awil (682–721 AD) was found in the tomb at the temple's core, surrounded by an assortment of jade, pearls, seashells and stingray spines. There's a reconstruction of the tomb (*tumba* 116) in the Museo Tikal. Standing opposite, like a squat version

---

THE RISE AND FALL OF TIKAL

900 BC First known settlement at Tikal.

500 BC Evidence of early stone buildings at the site.

250 BC Early pyramid built in the Mundo Perdido.

c.10 AD Great Plaza begins to take shape and Tikal is an established major site with a large permanent population.

c.250 AD Continuous eruption of the Ilopango volcano causes devastation and disrupts trade routes.

292 AD First recorded date on stelae at Tikal.

378 AD Tikal, aligned with Teotihuacán, defeats rival Uaxactún.

550 AD Tikal conquers neighbouring city-states and establishes an influence reaching as far as Copán in Honduras.

562 AD Caracol defeats Tikal in a "star war", probably in alliance with the city of Calakmul, a formidable new power to the north.

700–800 AD Tikal's legendary leader Hasaw Chan K'awil revives the city with a series of incredible victories deposing sequential kings of Calakmul. The Great Plaza is remodelled and five great temples built.

869 AD Ceremonial construction ceases at Tikal; the population dwindles.

1000 AD Tikal abandoned.

1848 AD Ruins of Tikal officially rediscovered by a government expedition.

1956 AD Project to excavate and restore the buildings started.

1984 AD Most major restoration work completed.

of Temple I, is **Temple II**, known as the Temple of the Masks for the two grotesque masks, now heavily eroded, which flank the central stairway. The **North Acropolis**, which fills the whole north side of the Great Plaza, is one of the most complex structures in the entire Maya world. In true Maya style it was built and rebuilt on top of itself, and beneath the twelve temples that can be seen today are the remains of about a hundred other structures.

Central Acropolis
On the other side of the plaza is the **Central Acropolis**, a maze of tiny interconnecting rooms and stairways. The buildings here are usually referred to as palaces rather than temples, although their precise use remains a mystery. Behind the acropolis is the palace reservoir, which was fed with rainwater by a series of channels from all over the city.

From the West Plaza to Temple IV
Behind Temple II is the **West Plaza**, dominated by a large Late Classic temple on the north side, and scattered with various altars and stelae. From here the Tozzer Causeway leads west to **Temple III** (60m), still covered in jungle vegetation. Around the back of the temple is a huge palace complex, of which only the **Bat Palace** has been restored.

At the end of the Tozzer Causeway is **Temple IV**, at 64m the tallest of all the Tikal structures, built in 741 AD. Twin ladders, one for the ascent, the other for the descent, are attached to the sides of the temple. Its summit, with stupendous views over an ocean of rainforest, is unmatched, with the roof combs of the great temples piercing the canopy and intermittent roars of howler monkeys resonating across the jungle. However, it's become such a popular place for sunrise you may want to opt for a less obvious location.

Mundo Perdido and Plaza of the Seven Temples
Southeast of Temple IV, a trail passes some Maya kilns before winding round down to the **Mundo Perdido**, or Lost World. This magical and very distinct section of the site has its own atmosphere and architecture, its building designed as an astronomical observatory. The main feature is the **Great Pyramid**, a 32-metre-high structure whose surface hides four earlier versions, the first dating from perhaps as early as 500 BC. After accidents on the steep stone staircase, it is no longer possible to climb this temple. Just to the east is the **Plaza of the Seven Temples**, which forms part of a complex dating back to before Christ. There's an unusual triple ball-court on the north side of the plaza and a lot of archeology work ongoing here.

Temple V and the Temple of the Inscriptions
Continuing east you pass the unexcavated South Acropolis before you reach the 58-metre-high Temple V, constructed between 600 AD and 700 AD (archeologists are still debating the exact date). It's possible that it was dedicated to the rain god Chaac, due to the six large masks found on the roof comb. Climb the ladder at the side of the temple for a sublime, but vertigo-inducing vista from a viewing platform.

Finally, there's the **Temple of the Inscriptions**, also known as Temple VI, reached via a ten-minute hike through the forest along the Méndez Causeway. The temple (only discovered in 1951) is famous for its twelve-metre roof comb, at the back of which is a huge but rather faint hieroglyphic text.

Arrival and information

Arrival It's easy to get to Tikal from Flores and El Remate (see p.224 & p.227). You can usually hitch a ride home with one of the many shuttles, even if you don't have a pre-booked ticket.

Tour guides Ask at the ticket booth for services; many guides speak excellent English. Tours cost US$12 per person, or US$60 for a group of up to eight for a 4hr tour – a very worthwhile investment if you can afford it.

Visitors' centre Before the ticket booth and parking lot is a large visitors' centre. It houses toilets, souvenir stalls, an over-priced restaurant, a post office, a museum and, of greatest interest, a scale model of the site (a good place to orient yourself and overhear knowledgeable private guides).

Accommodation and eating

Most backpackers choose to visit Tikal as a day-trip. There are three hotels at the ruins but all of them are expensive and not especially good value. However you'll find decent, secure camping facilities, and hammock rental is also possible. If you do decide to stay overnight, buy your park entrance ticket after 3pm and it will be valid for the following day as well. There's nowhere cheap to eat inside the Tikal National Park. Your best bet are the *comedores* opposite the visitors' centre; try the *Comedor Imperio Maya* for tasty local-style eggs, beans, grilled meat and chicken dishes (from Q30). Cold soft drinks and snacks are sold around the ruins. If arriving before 9am, you should bring your own snacks and plenty of water.

Camping Between the car park and the *comedores*, a well-maintained campground has toilets, showers and campfire facilities. There are also thatched shelters from which to hang your own hammock (Q35). You can also rent good hammocks for Q35 that have mosquito nets attached.

Jaguar Inn ☎ 7783 3647, ⊛ jaguartikal.com. It's possible to rent a hammock with net here for Q50 a night, and they also have a dorm and camping, but space is very limited for all these budget options, so book ahead. Their bungalows are quite decent, though pricey, and have a hot-water bathroom, fan and porch. Camping Q40, dorms Q80, bungalows Q350

AROUND TIKAL

Dotted throughout the Petén jungle are literally thousands of Maya ruins. With tourism booming in the region many of these are becoming more accessible via a selection of trips offered by Flores- and El Remate-based operators. To see these more remote sites independently you will need plenty of time to account for sporadic transport schedules. In addition, some larger, still unexcavated sites require a local guide simply to navigate the ruins themselves.

Uaxactún

Some 23km north of Tikal, strung out by the side of a disused airstrip, are the village and ruins of **Uaxactún** (pronounced "Wash-ak-toon"). The overall impact of the place may be a little disappointing after the grandeur of Tikal, but you'll probably have the site to yourself. The most interesting buildings are in **Group E**, east of the airstrip, where three low reconstructed temples, built side-by-side, are arranged to function as an observatory. Viewed from the top of a fourth temple, the sun rises behind the north temple on the longest day of the year and behind the southern one on the shortest day. On the other side of the airstrip is **Group A**, a series of larger temples and residential compounds, some of them reconstructed, a ball court and some impressive stelae.

Arrival

By bus A bus leaves Flores at 1pm and passes through Tikal en route to Uaxactún. The return bus leaves Uaxactún at 7am.

By shuttle bus The alternative is to arrange a shuttle – done most cheaply from El Remate.

Accommodation and eating

If you end up staying overnight in Uaxactún you have two options.

Aldana's The bare-bones option, which has simple wooden rooms and space for camping. Camping Q18, doubles Q40

Campamento Ecológico El Chiclero ☎ 7926 1095. This welcoming place offers clean, functional rooms without bath, or you can camp or sling up a hammock. Owner Antonio Baldizón also organizes 4WD trips, and his wife Neria prepares excellent food. Camping Q25, doubles Q115

Yaxhá

Midway between El Remate and Melchor de Menchos, some 12km off the highway, is the restored site of **Yaxhá**

(6am–5pm; US$10). The site is rarely visited, but is very well managed with an impressive collection of restored/reconstructed temples and palaces and numerous stelae. Yaxhá's greatest attraction is its stunning location on the northern shores of the tranquil **Yaxhá lagoon** (no doubt the site was originally chosen with this in mind). Many of the remains are from the Pre-Classic period and there's a terrific example of triadic temple arrangement at the North Acropolis where you'll probably have a 2000-year-old ceremonial centre to yourself. Views over the lake from the top of **Temple 216**, the site's largest structure, are unforgettable, with 360-degree vistas over an intact rainforest. You ought to be lucky enough to see plenty of monkeys too.

Arrival and information

By pick-up There is no public transport to the park entrance. However, on the main road, in the village of La Máquina, it should be possible to negotiate a price for a pick-up (approx US$10). Ask at the *tienda* opposite the school.

Tours Some El Remate hotels arrange return transport, or you can take the excellent tour with *Café Yaxhá* in Flores (see p.223), which also takes in the remote, nearby site of La Blanca and stops with a local village family for lunch (US$35 per person, minimum four).

El Zotz

Thirty kilometres southwest of Uaxactún, along a rough track passable by 4WD, is **El Zotz**, a large Maya site set in its own nature reserve. A royal tomb, dating from around 400 AD, was discovered here in 2010 beneath the El Diablo pyramid, containing the king buried with the tiny corpses of six infants (possibly sacrificial victims). Totally unrestored and smothered by vegetation, El Zotz had been systematically looted, although there are guards on duty today. Zotz means "bat" in Maya and each evening at dusk you'll see tens, perhaps hundreds of thousands of **bats** of several species emerge from a cave near the campsite – one of the most remarkable natural sights in Petén. From the tops of El Zotz's jungle-shrouded temples it's also possible to see the roof combs of Tikal.

To **get here** you can rent vehicles, supplies and equipment in Uaxactún, or take a three-day tour from Flores (ask at *Los Amigos* to form a group). The tour involves approximately six hours of walking per day and two nights camping in the jungle, and finishes at the ruins of Tikal.

Waka' (El Perú)

It's possible to reach the Maya ruins of **Waka'** (previously known as El Perú) independently but you'll need a tent, a good grasp of Spanish and plenty of initiative. A chicken bus leaves Santa Elena's market terminal at 10am for **Paso Caballos** (4hr), from where you can hike or take a boat to the site. The ruins are largely unreconstructed but mainly date from the Classic period when the city was allied to Calakmul. A royal tomb unearthed here in 2004 contained the remains of a queen, who was buried along with stingray spines (used for ritual bloodletting). Tour companies based in Flores (see p.220) offer tours of Waka', often dubbed the "Scarlet Macaw Trail" on account of the large concentrations of the critically endangered birds that live in the forests around the site. Local guides may also be hired in Paso Caballos.

El Mirador

Only accessible on foot or by mule, beyond the village of **Carmelita** is the colossal Pre-Classic site of **El Mirador**, perhaps the most exotic and mysterious of all Petén's Maya sites. Still buried in the forest, this massive city matches Tikal's scale, and may even surpass it. By 1000 BC a settlement was thriving here, and by 450 BC impressive temple construction had begun, the city peaking in influence between 350 BC and 100 AD when it was unquestionably the superpower of Mesoamerica, eclipsing the Olmecs in Mexico and lording it over the entire Maya region. Fittingly, Mirador's name in Pre-Classic Maya times is thought to have been Te Tun ("The Birthplace of the Gods").

The core of the site covers some sixteen square kilometres, stretching between two massive pyramids that face each other across the forest. One of these, **La Danta**, sits on a vast stone base platform measuring 600m by 300m, the pyramid itself reaching 79m above the forest floor – the tallest pre-Columbian structure in the Americas.

The area around El Mirador is riddled with smaller Maya sites, and as you look out across the forest from the top of either of the main temples you can see others rising above the canopy on all sides – including giant Calakmul in Mexico. Although much of the site is still buried, archeologists are currently excavating and have already uncovered fantastic Maya artwork inside some temples. It is likely that in the coming decades El Mirador will be opened up to mass tourism – there's even talk of a monorail through the jungle.

SAYAXCHÉ

The small town of **SAYAXCHÉ**, on the banks of the Río Pasión, is a handy base for visiting the nearby archeological sites of Ceibal, Aguateca and Dos Pilas. The complex network of rivers and swamps that cuts through the surrounding area has been an important trade route since Maya times and there are several ruins in the area. There's no bridge, so all road transport has to use a ferry to shuttle across the river.

What to see and do

The Maya sites of Ceibal, Aguateca and Dos Pilas are in an isolated pocket of the country and are seldom visited. If you only have the time (or finances) for one ruin, Aguateca is the most impressive. Whether you choose to arrive by boat or by trekking, the journey through the jungle gives all these ruins a special *Heart of Darkness* aura. Trips can be organized via Flores tour operators (see p.220) or the friendly *Restaurant Yaxkín* (see p.236) also offers useful advice.

Ceibal

Surrounded by forest and shaded by huge ceiba trees, and reachable either by land or river, the ruins of **Ceibal** (daily 6am–5pm; free) are a mixture of cleared open plazas and untamed jungle. Though many of the largest temples lie buried under mounds, Ceibal does have some outstanding and well-preserved carving: the two main plazas are dotted with lovely **stelae**, centred around two low platforms. During the Classic period Ceibal was unimportant, but it grew rapidly between 830 and 930 AD, apparently after falling under the control of colonists from what is now Mexico. This is evident in the fantastic Mexican-influenced carving displayed here.

It's easy enough to make it here and back to Sayaxché in an afternoon **by boat**; haggle with the boatmen at the waterfront and you can expect to pay around US$60 (for up to five people). The boat trip is followed by a short walk through towering rainforest. **By road**, Ceibal is just 17km from Sayaxché. Any transport heading south out of town passes the turn-off, from where an 8km track leads to the site through the jungle. Alternatively hire a pick-up for the full journey for around US$25 return (ask at *Restaurant Yaxkín*; see p.236).

You can **camp** at the site, but there are no toilets or drinking water.

Lago de Petexbatún: Aguateca and Dos Pilas

To the south of Sayaxché is **Lago de Petexbatún**, a spectacular expanse of water ringed by dense forest and containing plentiful supplies of snook, bass, alligator and freshwater turtle. The shores of the lake abound with birdlife and animals (including howler monkeys) and there are a number of Maya ruins.

Aguateca (daily 7am–5pm; Q40), perched on a high outcrop at the southern tip of the lake, is the furthest away from Sayaxché but the most accessible. Extensive restoration work is still ongoing at this intriguing site, which is split in two by a natural chasm. The atmosphere is magical, surrounded by dense tropical forest and with superb views of the lake from two *miradores*. Throughout the Late Classic period, Aguateca was closely aligned with (or controlled by) nearby Dos Pilas, and military victories were celebrated at both sites with remarkably similar stelae – look out for Stele 3 here which shows Dos Pilas ruler Master Sun Jaguar in full battle regalia. In the late eighth century, these Petexbatún cities began to lose regional control, and despite the construction of 5km of walls around the citadel (the remains are still visible today) Aguateca was overrun in 790 AD.

The resident guards will provide you with stout walking sticks – essential as the slippery paths here can be treacherous – before escorting you around the site's steep trails, past palisade defences, stelae, temples and palaces (including the residence of Aguateca's last ruler, Tante K'inich) and a barracks.

A beautiful two- to three-hour **boat-ride** (US$50) can get you to within twenty minutes' walk of the ruins. Alternatively it's usually possible to access the site via the village of **Nacimientos** (no facilities apart from *tiendas*), from where it's an hour or so's walk; the trail may not be passable in rainy season however. A micro leaves Sayaxché at 2pm directly to Nacimientos, and from the highway junction of Las Pozas, south of Sayaxché, there's more transport.

Dos Pilas, where restoration is ongoing, is buried in jungle west of the Lago de Petexbatún. Once the centre of a formidable empire in the early part of the eighth century, with a population of around ten thousand, it has some tremendous stelae, altars and four short **hieroglyphic stairways** decorated with glyphs and figures around its central plaza. To get to Dos Pilas from the lakeshore you have to trek 12km on foot (or by horse).

Arrival and information

By boat and bus All transport arriving in Sayaxché will arrive at the dock (on either bank of the Río Pasión). From Flores you'll arrive on the north bank and will need to catch a *lancha* (Q2) to the other side, where the bulk of Sayaxché stretches uphill and westwards along the riverbank. From the dock, the plaza is three blocks up and one to the left.

Internet and exchange There is an ATM and an internet café in the plaza.

Tourist information There is no official tourist information but the friendly owner at *Restaurant Yaxkín* (see p.236) offers excellent free advice and has a big map of the area painted on the wall. Better still, if you're staying for a few days, head to the hotel *Yaxkín Chel*, where Don Rosendo Girón is an authority on the region.

INTO MEXICO

There are two possible routes into **Mexico** from Petén.

Via Bethel/La Técnica

The crossing via **Bethel/La Técnica** to **Frontera Corozal** is the most popular route and offers the chance of seeing the first-class Maya ruins of Yaxchilán on the way (booking a tour is the best way to do this unless you break the journey with a night in Frontera Corozal). If you just want to get direct to **Palenque**, there's a daily 5am shuttle from Flores (8hr; US$30) that uses this route. It's also not hard to do this journey independently: first you need to catch a bus from the main Santa Elena terminal to La Técnica (4hr 30min; Q30), via immigration in the village of Bethel where you're also asked for an unofficial exit (or entry) tax of around Q10. The bus continues to **La Técnica** from where *lanchas* zip across to Frontera Corozal (Q15/M$20).

    Lanchas leave regularly from the Mexican side to **Yaxchilán**, a stunning 45-minute journey along the Usumacinta river; it's normally possible to join a group to save costs (around US$20 per person return). Back in Frontera Corozal, there are simple *hospedajes* and places to eat. If you're travelling independently from here you'll find a flow of minibuses (roughly hourly) to Palenque from the highway, 18km west of Corozal. *Colectivo* taxis (US$3 per person) run between the town and the highway bus stop. (If you're on a shuttle-bus package to Palenque all this is taken care of for you, and the taxi price included in the ticket.)

Via El Ceibo

A second, northern route to Mexico has recently become popular as road connections have improved. It's now the fastest and cheapest way to get to Palenque from Flores, though note the warning below. From the main bus terminal in Santa Elena catch a bus for **El Ceibo** (12 daily; 4hr; Q32), where you'll find a Guatemalan immigration shack. Get your stamp, pay the unofficial exit tax (Q10–20) and walk across the border to Mexico, where there is an impressive new immigration and customs building. Minibuses leave here for Tenosique (1hr 15min; US$3), where you change and catch another minibus for Palenque (1hr 45min; US$5). If you choose this route note that it is used by Central American migrants heading to *El Norte* and there's plenty of military in evidence. Get an early start and avoid getting stuck for the night in El Naranjo (the nearest town in Guatemala to El Ceibo), which is a rough place with little to recommend it.

Accommodation and eating

Hotel La Pasión 50m up from the dock ☎4056 5044. Occupying the upper storeys of this red-brick building, rooms are spacious, comfortable and have cable TV, bathroom and fan. There's free coffee in the pleasant lounge area. Q90

Oasis 1km west of town. A slightly bizarre combo, this is part-hardware store, part-civilized, air-conditioned café that serves snacks like hot dogs and nachos. It has the only espresso machine in town. Closed Sun.

Restaurant Yaxkín One block up from the dock, on the left. Friendly place that serves up tasty meals and snacks, including good burgers (Q25) and sandwiches. Offers impartial tourist information too. Closes 8pm.

Yaxkín Chel Paraíso In Barrio Esperanza, six blocks up and five across (southeast) from the dock ☎4053 3484. Rustic bungalows and a restaurant in a verdant garden, where the family grow cocoa, pepper and tropical flowers. Owner Chendo can arrange tours and transport. Q90

Moving on

By boat to: Mexico (see box above).
By bus/micro to: Cobán (hourly until 5pm; 4hr); Flores (every 20min; 2hr); Raxrujá (every 30min; 2hr).

El Salvador

go to El tunco (handwritten)

HIGHLIGHTS ✪

SANTA ANA:
El Salvador's second city,
home to the finest Parque
Central in the county ✪

PERQUÍN:
see the horrors of the civil war
in the haunting Museo de la
Revolución Salvadoreña ✪

BOSQUE
✪ **EL IMPOSIBLE:**
this pristine mountain
forest is a haven
for native wildlife

✪ **SUCHITOTO:**
widely considered the finest
colonial town in El Salvador

✪

PACIFIC BEACHES:
try out the surf or
just bum around

✪

**ISLANDS OF THE
GOLFO DE FONSECA:**
spend a quiet night on these tiny islands
sandwiched between El Salvador and Honduras

ROUGH COSTS

DAILY BUDGET Basic US$25/
occasional treat US$35

DRINK Coffee US$0.50, Pilsener
beer US$1.50

FOOD *Pupusa* US$0.50

CAMPING/HOSTEL/BUDGET HOTEL
US$4/US$10/US$18

TRAVEL San Salvador–Santa Ana
by bus (63km): 1hr 15min, US$1

FACT FILE

POPULATION 6.3 million

AREA 21,040 sq km

LANGUAGE Spanish

CURRENCY US dollar (US$)

CAPITAL San Salvador (population:
1,570,000)

INTERNATIONAL PHONE CODE
☎ 503

TIME ZONE GMT -6hr

Introduction

The smallest and most densely populated country in Central America, El Salvador is also the region's least visited nation. Known less for its world-class surf and stunning forest reserves than the vicious civil war it suffered through in the 1980s and gang violence that occurred in the 1990s, the country has long struggled to gain tourists' trust. Those who do make it here, however, are well rewarded by the hospitality of its proud inhabitants and the sheer physical beauty of the place. Almost every journey in El Salvador yields photogenic vistas: majestic cones of towering volcanoes, lush lowlands sweeping up through fertile hills, coffee plantations, rugged mountain chains – you'll see them all.

Pivotal **San Salvador** is one of Central America's most appealing cities, boasting an emerging bohemian scene and student-rich nightlife. Within easy reach is the glorious sweep of the **Pacific coast**, including surfers' favourite **Costa del Bálsamo**, dark beauties like **Playa El Espino**, and white-sand fishing communities such as **Los Cóbanos**. Some of these beaches offer true seclusion, while others receive the best waves in all of Central America.

Further east are the undervisited mangrove swamps of the **Bahía de Jiquilisco** and the idyllic islands of the **Golfo de Fonseca**, while further inland the small city of **San Vicente** gives access to delightful artistic villages like floral **Alegría** and larger **San Miguel**, which hosts one of the biggest carnivals in Central America. The **Ruta de Paz** climbs poor and rugged Morazán towards the moving war museum at **Perquín** and the town of **El Mozote**, the site of one of the civil war's worst atrocities – unmissable for anyone interested in El Salvador's recent history.

In the west, the laidback grandeur of **Santa Ana** lies between the exquisite **cloudforests** of Montecristo and El Imposible. For climbers, the nearby

volcanic peaks of Izalco and Cerro Verde provide good hiking, while at their base is the spectacle of the deep-blue crater lake of **Coatepeque**; for gastronomes, the **Ruta de las Flores** features **Juayúa**'s famous food festival, as well as other charming towns.

The north, though rough and wild, hosts the still unspoiled colonial gem of **Suchitoto**, above the glorious crater lake of Suchitlán, while **La Palma** is famous for its naïf crafts, producing wooden handicrafts, pottery and hammocks.

CHRONOLOGY

Pre-8000 BC Paleo-Indian cave dwellers around Corinto are the first known inhabitants.

Pre-1200 BC Maya arrive from Guatemala.

900 AD Maya culture mysteriously collapses.

900–1400 AD Waves of Nahuat-speaking settlers, later dubbed "Pipils", migrate from Mexico, establishing seats of power at Cihuatán, Tehuacán and Cuscatlán.

1524 Pedro de Alvarado crosses the Río Paz to conquer the area; he names the region "El Salvador".

1600–1800 Hacienda feudalism creates a rich ruling elite and indentured labour force.

1811 Father José Delgado leads an unsuccessful revolution against the Spanish.

1821 Central American provinces, including El Salvador, break with Spain, but are annexed by Mexico.

1823 Central American countries win independence from Mexico under Salvadoreño Manuel

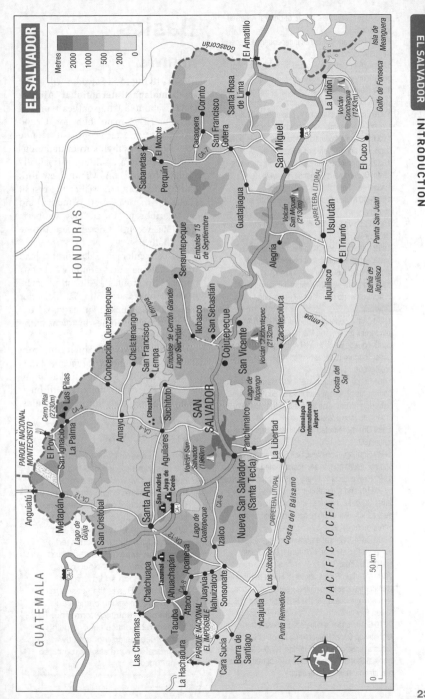

EL SALVADOR

Metres
2000
1000
500
200
0

GUATEMALA

HONDURAS

Las Chinamas

Anguiatú

Metapán

Lago de Güija

San Cristóbal

PARQUE NACIONAL MONTECRISTO

Cerro Pital (2730m)

El Poy

Las Pilas

San Ignacio

La Palma

CA-4

Amayo

CA-4

Concepción Quezaltepeque

Chalatenango

San Francisco Lempa

Lempa

Suchitoto

Cihuatán

Aguilares

San Andrés
Joya de Cerén

Santa Ana

Chalchuapa

Tazumal

Ahuachapán

Apaneca

Ataco

Tacuba

PARQUE NACIONAL EL IMPOSIBLE

CA-8

Juayúa

Nahuizalco

Sonsonate

Acajutla

Punta Remedios

Cara Sucia

Barra de Santiago

La Hachadura

CA-2

Izalco

Lago de Coatepeque

Volcán San Salvador (1960m)

SAN SALVADOR

Nueva San Salvador (Santa Tecla)

Panchimalco

Lago de Ilopango

La Libertad

CARRETERA LITORAL

Costa del Bálsamo

PACIFIC OCEAN

50 km

0

Sensuntepeque

Embalse 15 de Septiembre

Ilobasco

San Sebastián

Embalse de Cerrón Grande/ Lago Suchitlán

Lempa

Cojutepeque

San Vicente

Volcán Chinchontepec (2132m)

Zacatecoluca

Lempa

Costa del Sol

Comalapa International Airport

Guatajiagua

Alegría

Jiquilisco

Bahía de Jiquilisco

El Triunfo

Usulután

CARRETERA LITORAL

Punta San Juan

Volcán San Miguel (2130m)

San Miguel

San Francisco Gotera

Cacaopera

Corinto

Santa Rosa de Lima

El Amatillo

Goascorán

Sabanetas

El Mozote

Perquín

CA-1

CA-1

La Unión

Volcán Conchagua (1243m)

Golfo de Fonseca

Isla de Meanguera

El Cuco

N

0

PACIFIC OCEAN

239

José Arce; Federal Republic of Central America is created.

1841 El Salvador declares independence; Federal Republic is dissolved.

1840–1931 Coffee becomes main export crop; private interests dominate government.

1927 Liberal Pío Romero Bosque is elected, takes steps to dismantle oligarchies.

1929 Economy collapses in response to Wall Street crash; Liberal plans for democracy derailed.

1931 General Maximiliano Martínez seizes power in coup, starting 50 years of military rule.

1932 Communist-led rebellion sees thousands killed. Government response is a week-long massacre, "La Matanza".

1932–80 Military and oligarchies jointly rule country.

1969 El Salvador attacks Honduras in the six-day "Soccer War".

1972 Reformist José Napoleon Duarte wins presidential elections; but he is immediately deposed and exiled by the military.

1977 As many as 300 unarmed civilians shot in front of world media while protesting in San Salvador.

1980 Leftist opposition parties and guerrilla groups join forces to form the FMLN–FDR, while right-wing death squads wage terror campaigns. Archbishop Oscar Romero is assassinated; full-scale civil war breaks out.

1981 US pumps aid to military to stem "spread of Communism", despite its links to death squads. Salvadoreño battalion massacres the village of El Mozote (see p.289).

1984 Duarte "elected" first civilian president since 1932.

1989 Fighting intensifies; San Salvador is occupied, and six Jesuit priests are assassinated.

1992 Peace accords finally signed, presided over by the UN and the Catholic Church.

2001 US dollar replaces the colón. Two earthquakes kill over 1000 people and destroy infrastructure.

2005 CA-4 free-trade agreement signed between El Salvador, Honduras, Guatemala and Nicaragua.

2009 Mauricio Funes, leader of FMLN party, wins presidential elections. Full diplomatic relations with Cuba restored, for the first time since 1959 Cuban Revolution.

2010 Government apologizes for assassination of Archbishop Oscar Romero and for other human rights abuses committed during 1980–92 civil war. Tropical Storm Agatha causes widespread flooding, resulting in at least 13 deaths.

Basics

ARRIVAL

Visitors **flying** to El Salvador will arrive at **Comalapa International Airport (SAL)**, about 50km southeast of San Salvador. The main hub for Grupo TACA (Ⓦwww.taca.com), it's quite busy, with daily flights from numerous North American cities (principally Dallas, Houston, LA, Miami, New York and Mexico City) as well as the rest of Central America, South America and the Caribbean. Iberia (Ⓦwww.iberia.com) has recently started a direct route from Madrid.

You can enter El Salvador by land from Guatemala and Honduras (see box opposite for routes). Almost all international **buses** arrive in San Salvador (see p.250). Chicken buses run from border crossings to nearby towns in the daylight hours.

The only international **boat** runs from the Honduran and Nicaraguan islands in the Golfa de Fonseca to La Unión (see p.277). You must go through customs before travelling to the islands.

WHEN TO VISIT

The **dry season** (Nov–March) is the best time to visit El Salvador: northeasterly winds make for less humid air, more accessible dirt roads, sandier beaches and less daunting waves. Humidity builds throughout late March and April into the **wet season** (May–Oct), which is fed by Pacific low-pressure systems and sees clear mornings cloud over to late afternoon and overnight downpours. This is the season for big waves, flowering orchids and spectacular lightning storms, but travel can be difficult and flooding and hurricanes are not unknown. **Temperatures** are always regulated by altitude.

LAND ROUTES TO EL SALVADOR

The main border crossings with **Honduras** are in the east at El Amatillo (see p.292), convenient for connections to Tegucigalpa, and at El Poy (see p.301) in the northwest.

The main border with **Guatemala** is at La Hachadura (see p.304) in the southwest, best for the Pacific beaches and used by international buses from Mexico. Another Guatemala crossing is at Las Chinamas (see p.309), just outside Ahuachapán, with regular connections from Guatemala City. The crossing at Anguiatú (see p.318), in the north near Metapán, is used by buses from Esquipulas. A smaller crossing at San Cristóbal (see p.314) is close to the city of Santa Ana.

VISAS

Visas for El Salvador are not currently required for citizens of the US, Canada, Argentina, Australia, Brazil, Chile, Israel, New Zealand, Paraguay, Singapore, South Africa, most European countries, all Central American nations and many Caribbean islands; citizens of other countries need authorization from the immigration authorities. Under the CA-4 agreement, there is one tourist card for El Salvador, Guatemala, Honduras and Nicaragua (see box, p.45). Make sure you get a 90-day allowance rather than a 30-day one. Stays can be extended once by contacting the Dirección General de Migración y Extranjería, in the Galerías Escalón, Paseo Gen Escalón (☎2202-9650), in San Salvador, though you must be sponsored by a CA-4 national. A US$10 border **entry fee** is levied at the airport, but only for nationals of Canada, China, Greece, Malaysia, Mexico, Portugal, Singapore and the US. See ⓦhttp://www.rree.gob.sv/ for details.

GETTING AROUND

El Salvador's **bus** network is without doubt the best, and cheapest, way to travel. The size of the country, and the efficient road layout around the Carretera Interamericana, mean that budget travellers can get from one point to another within the country in less than a day. Most long-distance journeys route through San Salvador, often requiring at least one change of bus if travelling to smaller towns. A new road, the Longitudinal del Norte, is being built, which will run from La Unión on the Pacific coast up to Metapán in the northwest, via San Miguel and Chalatenango, bypassing the capital and saving several hours' travel time. The road is due to be completed by the end of 2011, though some think this is unlikely.

By bus

Buses are subsidized and extremely cheap: a trip from San Salvador to Sonsonate (1hr 30min) costs just US$1.30. Centrally placed San Salvador, with its three busy bus terminals (see p.258), is the hub of all bus travel in the country. All other towns of any significant size have at least one bus terminal; in smaller towns the corner of a block near the central square or market gets stacked up with buses picking up or dropping off. Services run in daylight hours, with rare exceptions going just after dusk, so plan your overnight stops carefully.

All routes are covered by the same "**chicken buses**" you'll see in other Central American countries – recycled and decorated US school buses. Occasionally you'll be issued a **ticket** when you pay as you board the bus: it may be inspected, so keep hold of it. Otherwise, have change ready for your fare; you pay the driver if there is a turnstile, and the guy yelling instructions and jumping on and off the bus if not. Most drivers will stop if hailed, and you can bang on the side of the bus or whistle to get off mid-trip. Big bags go in overhead racks or in a heap at the back; theft is rare, but you should keep an eye on your bags just in case. There are only three routes in the whole country served by the more comfortable, air-conditioned, **coach-style buses**; these go to and from San Miguel, Santa Rosa de Lima and La Unión, cost US$3–4 and knock about an hour off the standard journey.

By car and taxi

Licensed **taxis** in El Salvador are yellow and black. They can be hailed or found in large towns and cities around the main squares, shopping centres or bus stations. There are no meters, so **fares** should be agreed before you set off. Expect to pay US$5–6 for most trips within San Salvador and US$3–5 in other cities, but you can bargain a bit if you are polite. Avoid people offering lifts in other types of car.

It can be helpful to have a **car** if you want to explore some of the country's more remote areas, especially stretches of the Pacific coast (see box, p.266). Western companies **rent** at Western prices; local garages often charge a quarter of those rates (don't pay more than US$20). Recommended local rental companies include: Sandoval Rent Cars (☎2225 0379), Auto Lote Marvin (☎2278 8702) and Margarita de Diaz (✉maggie@quick rentacar.com.sv).

When driving, look out for abrupt coned-off lanes on the motorway – these are **police stops**, where you will be asked to present your passport, driving licence and car documents. If you need assistance, petrol stations and mechanics are widespread along the road. At night, **cows** often wander onto main roads, including the Interamericana, so keep the speed down. Also, dirt roads can become impassable during the rainy season, even with a 4WD; ask locally about conditions before you set off. Armed hold-ups of private cars are extremely rare now, but keep US$20 or so aside just in case, and offer no resistance. It's good to rent an old-looking car, so as not to draw attention to yourself. In cities, thefts of cars, or items left in them, do occur, so it's wise to leave your car in a guarded or locked car-park overnight.

Hitching is common off the highways. This said, it carries obvious risks, and we don't recommend it. If you do hitch, it's polite to offer payment – about the same as the bus fare – for the journey.

By bike

Bikes offer great freedom in rural areas, and you can take them on buses if you get tired. There are no formal rental places, but it is possible to do deals with locals, tour operators and at hotels; rates are around US$5/hr or US$15/day. Otherwise, a cheap mountain bike shouldn't cost more than US$50 to buy from a general store in any of the bigger towns.

By boat

Although only the islands of the Golfo de Fonseca and the islands of the Bahía de Jiquilisco require **boat** access, there are plenty of other opportunities to get out on the water. Scheduled services are always much cheaper (US$1–5), but *lancha* owners and fishermen need little persuasion to provide private lifts and tours of the country's lakes and mangrove swamps. This is usually done as a set fee for the boat (usually about US$30, depending on duration), so getting into a sizeable group reduces the cost.

ACCOMMODATION

El Salvador's **accommodation** industry – long stagnant – is finally beginning to wake up to the traveller market: new places are appearing, and very few destinations have nowhere at all to stay. However, the number of **hostels** with dorm rooms is still less than ten nationwide, with none in the east at all, so it's best to budget for cheap **hotels**. Unfortunately, thanks to dollarization, prices are pretty high: in San Salvador a clean, secure, double room comes to at least US$30, often more, while outside the capital you can expect to pay at least US$15–20, or US$25–30 for air conditioning. Lots of hotels rent multi-bed rooms (intended for Salvadoran families), where you can pack in like sardines – these can be a good way to cut costs if you're with a group. Discounts on longer stays are also often available. Rooms vary within an establishment, so look around. Hot water is rare in the cheaper places.

The Ministerio de Trabajo, C Nuevo Dos #19 in San Salvador (☎2298-8739), run four centres providing **free accommodation** around the country (see box, p.264).

Camping possibilities are also expanding countrywide, with campsites now available at most lakes, national parks and several towns and beaches. Salvadoreños with spare land may be willing to let you pitch a tent – offer around US$4. Hammock-slinging is possible on some beaches (though steer clear of the sketchier beaches around La Libertad, for safety reasons) and at some beach hotels (also for about US$4). The hotels will usually put your bag somewhere safe, if you ask.

Accommodation fills up around Santa Semana (the week before Easter), Christmas, the Fiestas Agostinas (the last week of July and first week of August) and/or at the time of local festivals; at these times it's worth **reserving** in advance.

FOOD AND DRINK

Eating well in El Salvador is far more about fresh ingredients than refined cooking. The main meal of the day is **lunch**, which most locals eat in a *comedor*, where *típicos* (local dishes of meat or fish, rice, vegetable or salad) and coffee go for around US$3, or a *pupusería*, where you can get **pupusas** – small tortillas served piping hot and filled with cheese (*queso*), beans (*frijoles*), pork crackling (*chicharrón*), or all three – for around US$0.50. *Pupusas* are normally made from cornmeal, and are served with hot sauce, tomato juice and/or *curtido*, a jar of pickled cabbage, beetroot and carrots. Many *comedores* serve evening *pupusas*, though most close early, between 7 and 8pm. The cleanliness and quality of establishments vary, but are usually OK, though with no frills; if doubtful, choose one that's busy and cooks unfrozen meat.

A standard **breakfast** is composed of *frijoles*, *queso* and *huevos* (eggs, either fried or scrambled), along with coffee. This combination is tasty and energy-packed, which is lucky, as it is generally the only option. Although San Salvador's Western suburbs are the only place to find the full gamut of international cuisine, most towns have a handful of **restaurants**. Chinese, Italian and Tex-Mex, and Argentine meat-grilling restaurants are the most widespread, though their authenticity varies. **Vegetarians** will find dedicated restaurants only in the biggest cities, and should be prepared to eat a lot of beans and cheese. There are also US-style **fast-food chains** – set meals for about US$5 – throughout the country, usually clustered along the Panamerican Highway or in the increasingly ubiquitous malls. Fried chicken is the *plat du jour*; the *Pollo Campero* chain is best. El Salvador had the dubious honour in late 2010 of opening Central America's first branch of *Starbucks*, in Plaza Santa Elena on the outskirts of the capital.

In addition to *pupusas*, other Salvadoreño **specialities** include *mariscada* (huge bowls filled with fish and crustaceans in a creamy soup), *tamales* (meat or chicken wrapped in maize dough and boiled in a leaf), *ceviche* (raw, marinated fish) and *sopa de frijoles* (black or red bean soup). On the coast, *conchas* (cockles or any other shellfish) are served raw with lemon juice, tomato, coriander and Worcester-shire sauce. Try the *ostras* (oysters), especially in popular eateries by the sea; they are fresher here than in most Western restaurants.

Drink

Local **coffee** is very good, usually drunk black and strong at breakfast and mid-afternoon with *tamales*. In small villages it will be boiled up with sugar cane and called *lista*. El Salvador's tropical fruits make delicious **juices**. *Jugos* are pure juices – most commonly orange, papaya, pineapple and melon – mixed with ice. *Licuados* (sometimes called *batidos*) blend juice with sugar, ice and sometimes milk, while *frescos* are fruit-based sweet drinks made up in bulk and served with lunch or dinner. Unless you ask otherwise, sugar will be added to *jugos* and *licuados*. *Horchata* is a dense milk drink with a base of rice, sweetened with sugar and cinnamon.

The usual brands of **soft drinks** are available. **Water** is safe to drink in San Salvador only; elsewhere check that the water and ice used in drinks is purified. Bottled mineral water and bags of pure spring water are available almost everywhere, while most hotels provide drinking water. El Salvador produces five good **beers** – the most important decision you will have to make is between Pilsener and Golden Light. True lager followers will go for the excellent and textured former. Also well worth trying are Regia and the crisp Bahía; the costliest and worst is Suprema. **Aguardiente** is a sugar cane-based liquor, fiery but quite smooth, produced under government control and sold through outlets called *expendios*; Tic-Tac is a favourite label.

CULTURE AND ETIQUETTE

Salvadoreños are generally confident, principled, hardworking and keen to laugh; they will often vie to help travellers. This said, not many Westerners pass through the country, especially rural areas, so you may be regarded as something of a novelty and children especially may stare and touch your

SALVADORAN EXPRESSIONS AND PHRASES

The Salvadoran slang, called Caliche, is formed from Nahuat and English roots. While you may just hear it spoken by others, particularly kids and *campesinos*, usage will never fail to raise a smile.

ahuevo/cabal (that's) right
ba! yes/sure/fine!
bayunco rowdy, immature, crazy
birria/polarizado beer
brosa/chero/chera friend/friend (m)/ friend (f)
cachimbo/vergo loads of ...
Ceviche It's alright
chavo/chava boy/girl (informal)
chele a "white" person with blond hair
chivo/chivisimo cool/very cool
chucho/chucha male dog/female dog
chuco/chuca dirty
cora a quarter of a dollar
guanaco a person from El Salvador (nickname)

huevón/huevonazo/huevonada lazy/ very lazy/lazy thing
mara gang or group of friends
marero gang member
paloma a penis, or something cool
palomísima/vergonísimo very cool
Púchica Wow!
salú goodbye
talega drunk
vacilar chill out, have fun
vergón cool or amazing (from "verga", penis)
yuca (literally, a root plant) something difficult

hair. Over eighty percent of the population is **Catholic**, though Evangelism is on the rise.

You should be confident and **polite**: say "Buenos" (morning) or "Buenas" (evening) when you catch someone's eye or enter a room, shake hands when meeting and do not offend by being paranoid about your safety or belongings. Women should not react to macho male posturing, as this is seen as flirtatious; understand that if you dress to be noticed, you will be. Remember to wear sleeves and trousers and to remove hats when entering a church (women should cover their heads). It is also considered rude to point at anything or anyone inside a church. Always ask permission before taking **photos** of people in indigenous areas, though you will generally find lots of eager posers.

Tipping at restaurants is not expected at the cheaper places, and may not be received well. More Western-style eateries may add around a ten-percent service charge, and you can increase this should you want to; tipping in bars in the capital goes down well too. Free guides should also be tipped. There is no need to tip anyone else, but if you are not awkward about it then they won't be offended. Gentle **bartering** is acceptable – sometimes it works, sometimes it doesn't.

SPORTS AND OUTDOOR ACTIVITIES

Fútbol (football, soccer) is by far the biggest spectator sport in El Salvador. There are two domestic seasons every year, the first (the *clausura*) runs every weekend from February to mid-May, the second (called *apertura*) goes from September to mid-December; both are followed by play-offs and finals. The big **teams** of the last few years are FAS from Santa Ana, Firpo from Usulután and Metapán. The quality of football is mixed but the crowds are awesome; don't bring anything valuable, and always sit with and cheer for the home side. See Ⓦhttp://www.laprensagrafica.com /deportes/futbol-nacional for fixtures and information. Great attention is paid to the international scene, too: the whole country has arranged itself behind two Spanish clubs, FC Barcelona and Real Madrid. **Baseball** is popular as well; San Salvador has a stadium, opposite the Artesan Market on Alameda M.E. Araujo, with games on Sundays. Football, baseball and basketball games take place on widespread municipal facilities, in parks and on beaches across the country. If it is not a training session you will be more than welcome to join in.

In terms of outdoor activities, El Salvador's 320km of coastline is widely accepted to have the best **surfing** in Central America and is known for several world-famous breaks. The best areas are on the Costa del Bálsamo (see p.270) and the eastern beaches around El Cuco (see p.275). See Ⓦwww.surfing elsalvador.com for surf reports, beach reviews and general information. The best **hiking** is in the national parks. For good challenges try the Montecristo–El Trifinio Cloudforest (see p.317), up the volcanoes of the Cerro Verde (see p.315) and through the dramatic, dry rainforest of Bosque El Imposible (see p.303). **Diving** here is not as good as in the Bay Islands or Belize, but there is the opportunity to see underwater thermal vents in a crater dive on Lago de Ilopango (see p.165), and the only Pacific coral diving in Central America is off Los Cóbanos (see p.302), along with a couple of good wreck dives. See Ⓦwww.elsalvadordivers.com for more information.

COMMUNICATIONS

Mail (letters) from San Salvador generally take about one week to the US and nine or so days to Europe; there are parcel services available, but you should use a courier service if sending anything of value. **Post offices** across the country are generally open Monday to Friday 8am to 5pm and Saturday 8am to noon.

Telecom has offices in every town (daily 7am–6pm), from where you can make local, long-distance and international calls. All in-country numbers have eight digits; mobile numbers begin with a 7, land lines with a 2. Some signs and printed materials still list seven-digit numbers – just add a 2 to the start and you'll probably have the new one. **Public phones** – both the yellow Telecom booths (with instructions in Spanish and English) or the lime-green Telefónica booths (instructions in Spanish only) are **cardphones**, requiring pre-paid cards, which can be purchased everywhere. You can make international calls from both types of cardphone (approximately US$1.50/min to Europe), but it's cheaper to go to a Telecom office. By far the cheapest

EL SALVADOR ON THE NET

Ⓦ**www.buscaniguas.com.sv** Long-standing portal – in Spanish only – with masses of useful listings, including hotels, restaurants and entertainment, plus interesting blog pages.

Ⓦ**www.elsalvador.travel** The newest official tourist site, with good information and a directory of businesses, hotels, restaurants and a calendar of events (most details in Spanish only).

Ⓦ**www.fotosdeelsalvador.com** An appetite-whetting archive holding thousands of photos from across the country (info in Spanish only).

Ⓦ**www.laprensagrafica.com** & **www.elsalvador.com** The websites for the two big conservative daily papers (the latter in Spanish only).

Ⓦ**www.raices.com.sv** A feisty and intelligent online magazine publishing excellent photography, news, features and opinion polls (Spanish only).

Ⓦ**http://luterano.blogspot.com** An excellent English-language blog, updated almost daily, summarizing current affairs and adding well-informed commentary.

option, however, is web-based calls; almost all internet places are now equipped with headsets. Alternatively, a pay-as-you-go **mobile phone** costs around US$15 and can make and receive international calls. There are two networks, Tigo and Claro; Tigo currently has better coverage but Claro has the cheapest rates: US$1.47/min to Europe and US$0.14/min to the US. The telephone code for the whole of El Salvador is ☎503.

Internet of varying speeds is now available everywhere except a handful of beach communities. Rates range from US$0.70–1/hr, often higher in hotels. In most large towns the government-funded **Infocentros** (daily 9am–6pm) have the fastest connections.

CRIME AND SAFETY

El Salvador has a reputation for guns, gangs and danger, which, while not unfounded, is no longer a problem in areas frequented by most tourists. *Maras* (**gangs**) exist across the country, but really dangerous characters generally concern themselves with the more profitable fields of drugs, extortion and human trafficking; they don't look for tourists, nor will they be found in any of the neighbourhoods you are likely to visit.

Generally, you should be fine if you stay confident (say "Buenos" to people), stay in groups and in busy areas – particularly **women travellers**. Ignore the usual cat-calls and loud blown kisses, as attempts to scold will be seen as flirtatious; the less attention you pay, the less attention you will receive. Male or female, if you are being pestered don't show animosity and head for a busy café or restaurant. Although muggings are extremely rare, you should avoid wearing expensive clothing and flashing valuables and, if you are mugged, never fight back. It's worth keeping US$10–20 in a pocket while travelling, as this will be enough for most *banditos*. Be

especially careful after nightfall in Sonsonate and San Salvador's *centro*; La Unión and San Miguel can also be dodgy.

In the event of difficulties, the **National Civilian Police** (PCN) is one of the best forces in Central America, with little corruption and a good presence in cities, at least until nightfall. Additionally, an often English-speaking **tourist police** operates nationwide to guide treks, assist and advise, and can be reached on ☎2245-5448.

Statistically, the biggest threats to tourists in El Salvador are the **riptides** on its beaches. It is best not to go out too far on your own and ask locally about the conditions. If you are unable to swim back, try not to panic, swim parallel to the shoreline and wait for the rip to die down. There is no coastguard, so call the police in an emergency, or better still find the nearest surfer.

HEALTH

Pharmacies are widespread, though stock varies; generally the Brasil Pharmacy chain is the best stocked. If you have stomach troubles and are not anti-medicine, almost every pharmacy has a wide range of antibiotics.

Two private **hospitals** in San Salvador – Hospital de Diagnóstico (C 21 Pte at 2A Diagonal; ☎2226-8878) and Hospital Diagnóstico Escalón (C 3 Pte at 99A Av Norte; ☎2264-4422) – provide the best medical services in the country. If you are in the east, San Miguel's Hospital Clínica Laboratorio San Francisco (Av Roosevelt Norte #408 ☎2661-1991) is another good private hospital; otherwise, it's best to head to the capital. All three of these hospitals have 24hr emergency rooms.

> **EMERGENCY NUMBERS**
>
> Cruz Roja (ambulance) ☎2222-5155
> Fire ☎2271-2227/1244
> Police ☎911

247

Make sure you have comprehensive medical cover in your **insurance policy**; any kind of medical treatment is likely to be expensive, and you will probably be asked to pay up front whether or not you are insured. Have insurance documents or cash at the ready if you need treatment.

MONEY AND BANKS

El Salvador has officially used the **US dollar** (US$) since 2001. All US dollar notes and coins are currently in free circulation, but try to stockpile US$1 and US$5 bills, as anything over US$10 is likely to send the shopkeeper running down the street in search of change.

ATMs (*cajeros*) are becoming increasingly widespread, particularly in tourist destinations. Keep a stash of cash, however, for Perquín, Tacuba, every beach outside of La Libertad, some parts of the Ruta de las Flores and the eastern craft towns. Elsewhere, the main **banks** – Banco Agrícola, HSBC, Scotiabank and Banco Cuscatlán – have ATMs, which charge a handling fee of around US$1.70. Occasionally, they will inexplicably refuse your card (HSBC is the worst offender). Payment by **credit card** is unheard of at the budget level, but if you do encounter an establish-ment that will take your card there will be a charge of five percent. **Travellers' cheques** are less widely recognized, and at present can only be changed in banks, which are open Monday to Friday, 8.30 or 9am until 4 or 5pm, though some of them close from 1 to 2pm. Some banks in the larger cities also open between 9am and midday on Saturday. There are **casas de cambio** (generally daily 9am–5pm) along Alameda Juan Pablo II in San Salvador, in Santa Ana and San Miguel and at the borders. There are Western Union and Moneygram outlets in almost every mid-size town, in case you get stuck.

INFORMATION AND MAPS

The national tourist board, **Corsatur** (Ⓦwww.elsalvador.travel), produces an annual bilingual travellers' guide, *Guía de Viajero* – distributed only in the country, it's short on practicalities but a great travel teaser, with glossy photos of the highlights – as well as country-wide maps. Corsatur has its main office in San Salvador at Alameda Manuel Araujo, Pasaje y Edificio Carbonel #2, Colonia Roma (Mon–Fri 8am–12.30pm & 1.30–5.30pm; ☏2243-7835). The staff (who do not speak English) will help

---

NATIONAL PARK INFORMATION

Officially, there is a permission-granting ritual that must be performed before you enter any of El Salvador's national parks, though if you go with a guide on an organized visit, wardens will usually waive this. Confusingly, parks are administered by three different agencies. All three also allow entry to, and have information about, other preserved areas as well.

Instituto Salvadoreño de Turismo (ISTU) C Ruben Darío, 9–11A Av Sur, San Salvador (Mon–Fri 8am–4pm, Sat 8am–noon; ☏2222-8000, Ⓔistu@mh.gob.sv). Manages Parque Nacional Walter T. Deininger, and has information about all the country's national parks.

Ministerio de Medio Ambiente y Recursos Naturales C Las Mercedes, km 5.5 Carretera a Santa Tecla (Mon–Fri 7.30am–12.30pm & 1.30–3.30pm; ☏2267-6276, Ⓕ2267-6259, Ⓦwww.marn.gob.sv). Issues permits to the Bosque Montecristo in person or by fax.

SalvaNatura 33A Av Sur #640, Colonia Flor Blanca (Mon–Fri; 8am–12.30pm & 2–5.30pm; ☏2279-1515, Ⓦwww.salvanatura.org). Covers the Bosque El Imposible and Parque Nacional Los Volcanes, with books and useful maps for sale, and some free leaflets.

with enquiries if you persist. Three other, less helpful, outposts exist in Nahuizalco, Suchitoto and Puerto La Libertad, and there's a seldom-manned desk at the airport. Small towns like Apaneca and Perquín have kiosks that issue little more than pamphlets in Spanish, but often the best tips come directly from the hostel and hotel owners that have pioneered El Salvador's backpacker industry.

Maps of El Salvador are rare and generally terrible, except for those produced on the second floor of the Centro Nacional de Registros, 1A C Pte and 43 Av Nte #2310, San Salvador (Mon–Fri 8am–noon & 1–4pm; ☎2261-8400, ⓦwww.cnr.gob.sv). ITMB's 1: 250,000 *El Salvador* map is also a useful resource.

OPENING HOURS AND HOLIDAYS

Opening hours throughout the country vary. The big cities and major towns generally get going quite early in the morning, with government offices working from 8am to 4pm and most businesses from 8.30/9am to 5/5.30pm, with some closing for an hour at lunch. Hotels in smaller places lock up for the night between 9 and 10pm, and you may be banging on the door for a while and paying extra if you don't warn them of your late arrival. On **public holidays** everything will be shut, with some businesses also closing on the day of local fiestas. Museums and archeological sites all close on Mondays.

PUBLIC HOLIDAYS

Jan 1 New Year's Day
March/April Easter (Thursday–Easter Sunday)
May 1 Labour Day
Aug 1–6 El Salvador del Mundo
Sept 15 Independence Day
Oct 12 Columbus Day
Nov 1 Day of the Dead
Nov 2 All Saints' Day
Dec 24–25 Christmas
Dec 31 New Year's Eve

FESTIVALS

Ferías (festivals) in El Salvador, like the rest of the continent, are very important events in the calendar. Almost every town will have its own annual celebration, honouring the saint most connected to the place in question.

January Cristo Negro and Feria Gastronómica Internacional in Juayúa (Jan 8–15). Street fiesta with the best range and quality of food.
February Festival Internacional de Arte y Cultura in Suchitoto. A month-long celebration of classical music, opera, art and theatre.
March/April Santa Semana in Izalco. Popularly known as the best place for the Easter processions and street paintings.
May Las Flores y Las Palmas in Panchimalco (second Sun). Celebrates flower and palm-tree cultivation with music, dancing and fireworks.
July Fiesta al Divino Salvador del Mundo in San Salvador (July 25–Aug 6). Street party that shuts down the capital.
August Festival del Invierno in Perquín (Aug 1–6). Exciting, young and bohemian music and arts festival in this mountain town.
November Carnaval celebrated in San Miguel (Nov 14–30). One of the biggest fiestas in Central America, with processions and multiple music floats, dancing and drinking.

San Salvador and around

Sprawling across the Valle de las Hamacas at the foot of the mighty Volcán San Salvador is the urban melee of **SAN SALVADOR**, El Salvador's mercurial capital. Founded in 1545, it remained a pretty minor place until 1785, when it was named the first *intendencia* within the Reino de Guatemala. Father José Delgado first made the call for independence here, and the city was the only capital of the Central American Federation, before being named capital of El Salvador when the federation dissolved in 1840. Not much remains of this illustrious history today, though: a series of earthquakes throughout the nineteenth and twentieth centuries, and bombings when the FMLN seized portions of the city in 1989, have levelled most of the centre. Little you can see predates the nineteenth century.

Nowadays, the atmosphere of the place is forward-looking and vibrant; after two progressive mayorships and a more proactive chief of police, the city is going through something of a renaissance. Pleasant suburbs, peaceful little parks, genuinely interesting museums, a bustling centre and thriving commercial zone make for an exciting place to explore, while a bohemian arts scene, good bars and safe clubs provide fun night-time distractions.

Northwest of the city, **Volcán San Salvador** looms over the valley, while to the south the extensive **Parque Balboa** offers vistas the length of the coast. Tucked beneath the park, the village of **Panchimalco**'s splendid colonial church belies its predominantly indigenous populace. Some 15km east of San Salvador sits the country's largest crater lake, beautiful **Lago de Ilopango**, with views on a clear day across to the peaks of Volcán Chichontepec (see p.282). To the west are the natural gorge and pools of **Los Chorros**, a favourite weekend retreat for Salvadoreños from the city, and for those with an interest in archeology, the ruins of **Joya de Cerén**, which are of international importance for their remarkable state of preservation. The ruins at **San Andrés** nearby have been partially reconstructed, with pyramids and temples.

What to see and do

San Salvador's social and geographical landscape is fantastically linear. The eastern part of the city – industrial, poor, dangerous and not recommended for visitors – morphs into the crowded and pungent Centro Histórico, or **El Centro**, around the Terminal de Oriente bus station. The historic centre's churches and theatre are some of the country's best, though surrounded by chattering stall traders and street *comedores*. West of here the road creeps uphill to the more relaxed shops and services around the green acres of **Parque Cuscatlán**, and the heady commercialism of the Metrocentro. Continuing west, the climb continues to the trimmed hedges, fancy bars and cultural monoliths of the **Zona Rosa**, before finishing at the fine restaurants, exclusive nightclubs and guarded castles of **Colonia Escalón**. Floating above this east-to-west progression are the arty, studenty, liberal, traveller-friendly cafés, hostels and late-night bars north of **Boulevard los Héroes**.

Plaza Barrios

Though the heart of the raging *centro*, the rejuvenated **Plaza Barrios** is a good spot for a rest, with shaded benches and a good sampling of the local population present at any one time. Plaques on the central island commemorate the six Jesuit priests murdered at La UCA in 1989 (see p.256). On the plaza's western edge stands the **Palacio Nacional**, seat of government until the devastating earthquake of 1986. The Renaissance-style palace dates back to 1905, having

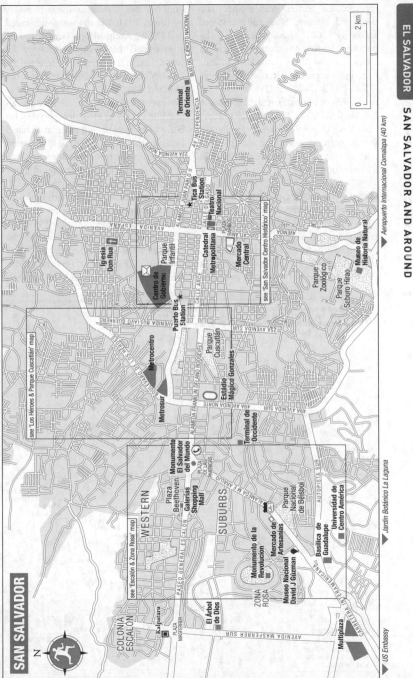

SAN SALVADOR

N

COLONIA ESCALÓN

Kalpataru ■
PLAZA MASFERRER

see 'Escalón & Zona Rosa' map

El Árbol de Dios ■

WESTERN

Plaza Beethoven
Galerías Shopping Mall

Monumento El Salvador del Mundo

PLAZA DE LAS AMÉRICAS

PASEO GENERAL ESCALÓN

SUBURBS

Monumento de la Revolución ◆
Mercado de Artesanías ◆
Museo Nacional David J Guzman ■

ZONA ROSA

AVENIDA MASFERRER SUR

Parque Nacional de Béisbol

Basílica de Guadalupe ■
Universidad de Centro América ■

AUTOPISTA SUR

CA-1

ALAMEDA M E ARAUJO

Terminal de Occidente ■

49A AVENIDA SUR
49A AVENIDA NORTE

ALAMEDA FRANKLIN DE ANO ROOSEVELT

Estadio Mágica Gonzales

Parque Cuscatlán

Metrosur

Metrocentro

see 'Los Héroes & Parque Cuscatlán' map

BOULEVARD DE LOS HÉROES

AVENIDA GUSTAVO GUERRERO

Puerto Bus Station

Centro de Gobierno ✉ ★

Iglesia Don Rua ■ ✝

AVENIDA ESPAÑA

Parque Infantil

CALLE ARCE

see 'San Salvador Centro Histórico' map

Catedral Metropolitana ■
Mercado Central

ALAMEDA JUAN PABLO II

CALLE DELGADO

Tica Bus Station ★
Teatro Nacional ■

AVENIDA CUSCATLÁN

BARRIOS

29A AVENIDA SUR

AVENIDA

Parque Zoológico
Parque Schuro Hirao

Museo de Historia Natural ■

24A AVENIDA NORTE

AV INDEPENDENCIA

Terminal de Oriente ■

BLVD DEL EJÉRCITO NACIONAL

0   2 km

▶ Aeropuerto Internacional Comalapa (40 km)

▶ Jardín Botánico La Laguna

CARRETERA PANAMERICANA

Multiplaza ■

▶ US Embassy

replaced an earlier edifice that was destroyed by fire. Now fully restored following 2001 quake damage, the building houses the national archives and a national history museum, in four beautifully restored formal chambers (Mon–Fri 8am–3pm; US$3). On the south side of the plaza is the **Biblioteca Nacional** (Mon–Fri 8am–4pm, Sat 8am–noon), which houses Salvadoran literary works on the second floor, along with a portrait mapping all the presidents of El Salvador until 1994.

Catedral Metropolitana

The square's most imposing and notorious structure is the **Catedral Metropolitana** (Mon–Fri & Sun 6am–6pm, Sat 6am–1pm & 4–6pm; donations optional), on its north side. The building dates back to 1888, but has been severely damaged

on a number of occasions, most notably by fire in 1951. Repairs were suspended in 1977 by **Archbishop Oscar Romero**, who argued that funds laid out for the work should be diverted to feeding the country's hungry. It was Romero's murder in March 1980 that is widely perceived as the event that sent the country spiralling into civil war: mourners carrying his body to its final resting place in a chapel beneath the cathedral were fired upon by government troops stationed on top of the surrounding buildings, and many were slaughtered as they tried to reach sanctuary inside the cathedral. Work on the building resumed after the civil war, and was finally completed in 1999. The colourful naïf murals around the outside of the main doors, by El Salvador's most famous artist, Fernando Llort, are worth admiring, and you can visit

▲ Iglesia Don Rua (2 blocks)

SAN SALVADOR CENTRO HISTÓRICO

0 — 500 m

◀ Parque Cuscatlán

Centro de Gobierno

Buses to Lago Ilopango

Parque Infantil

Puertobus Terminal

Iglesia Sagrado Corazón

Parque Bolívar

Catedral Metropolitana

Teatro Nacional

Tica Bus Terminal

Mercado Ex Cuartel

Palacio Nacional

PLAZA BARRIOS

Parque Libertad

Biblioteca Nacional

Iglesia El Rosario

Iglesia La Merced

Iglesia Calvario

Mercado Central

Terminal de Oriente ▶

Police Station

ACCOMMODATION	
American Guest House	B
Internacional Custodio	D
Nuevo Panamericano	C
Villa Floréncia	A

EATING & DRINKING	
Café Maquilishuat	3
Koradi	2
Pan Salvador	1

▼ Parque Zoológico Nacional & Museo de Historia Natural

Romero's tomb in the eerie and expansive chapel below (Mon–Sat 9.30–11.30am & 2.30–4.30pm, Sun 8.30am–5pm; free guide, in Spanish only; donations optional). Confession in the early-Christian, open confessionals of the side altars takes place late morning and late afternoon every day.

Iglesia Calvario

One block south and two blocks west of the plaza, and in the jaws of the street market, is the dark, neo-Gothic and slightly derelict **Iglesia Calvario** (7am–5pm; donations optional), whose pretty blue-and-yellow roof is worth a look – the colours are the result of light passing through stained glass rather than paint.

Iglesia el Rosario

Two blocks east of Plaza Barrios is the wide and busy **Parque Libertad**, where the central statue of feather-winged Liberty stands watch over crowds that gather in the square. Dominating the east side, the smog-stained, ugly concrete facade of the **Iglesia el Rosario** (Mon–Sat 6.30am–noon & 2–6.30pm; Sun 8.30am–noon & 2–6.30pm; donations optional) looks like an industrial turbine. Do not, whatever you do, let this put you off, as the interior is the most spectacular and original in the country. Sunlight passing through stained glass set in the arc of the roof casts acid-bright colour dispersions across the brick walls, the contorted metal sculptures, the doll-like shrines and the chequered floor. The tomb of Father José Delgado, father of independence and the man who ended slavery in all of Central America, is beneath the church.

Plaza Morazán and the Teatro Nacional

One block north of El Rosario is the compact **Plaza Morazán**, bounded on its southern edge by the Renaissance-style **Teatro Nacional**. Built with the

profits of the country's coffee plantations and reflecting the global vogue for French culture in the early twentieth century, the restored interior – all red plush, marble and decorative plaster-work – harks back to grander times. The magnificent modern ceiling frieze by Salvadoran artist Carlos Cañas depicts Rubenesque maidens cavorting in the clouds. Regular musical and theatrical events are held here, including perform-ances by the national orchestra most fortnights; tickets are heavily subsidized and sometimes free. Upcoming events can be found in the Friday edition or website of the national newspaper *Diario del Hoy* (Ⓦ www.elsalvador.com).

Parque Infantíl

Several blocks north of the Centro Histórico, near the intersection of Avenida España and Alameda Juan Pablo II, is the forested **Parque Infantíl** (Parque Campo Marte; daily 9am–5pm; US$0.57). Despite being a busy departure and arrival point for city buses, it is also popular with lunching workers from the nearby Centro de Gobierno and with local families, who picnic here at weekends. There's a children's playground, forested tracks planted with native and medicinal species of trees, and an open-air theatre.

Iglesia Don Rua

Continue north past the eastern edge of the Parque Infantíl for five blocks and you come to perhaps the most commanding church in the city – and its largest functioning one – the **Iglesia Don Rua**. Built in the nineteenth century, the white bulk of the church towers above the surrounding houses and is particularly notable for its stunning stained-glass windows.

Parque Zoológico and Museo de Historia Natural

A kilometre or so south of Plaza Barrios along Avenida Cuscatlán is the

Parque Zoológico Nacional (Wed–Sun 9am–4pm; US$0.60), with shaded paths, a good range of local birds and a great monkey island. In the park just south of the zoo, on the appropriately named Calle los Viveros ("plant/animal nurseries road"), the **Museo de Historia Natural** (Wed–Sun 9am–4.30pm; US$0.60) has some interesting exhibits on animals, plants and the country's geological development, as well as a little botanical garden.

Parque Bolívar and Iglesia Sagrado Corazón

West along Calle Rubén Darío from Plaza Barrios is the recently refurbished **Parque Bolívar**, of little interest save for a horseback statue of the liberator himself. One block north, on Calle Arce, is the nineteenth-century **Iglesia Sagrado Corazón**, with impressive stained-glass windows and a wooden interior.

Parque Cuscatlán

Parque Cuscatlán, west of Parque Bolívar along Calle Rubén Darío, is a large expanse of shady walkways and grass lawns that not only offers respite from the heat and noise, but also is home to several interesting sights. The **Monumento a la Memoria y la Verdad** (Tues–Sun 6am–6pm; free) lists the names of the thousands upon thousands who died or "disappeared" leading up to and during the civil conflict of 1980–92. Nearby, the **Sala Nacional de Exposiciones** (daily 9am–noon & 2–5pm; free) has interesting and high-quality rotating art exhibitions, while at the eastern end of the park, the **Tin Marín Children's Museum** (Tues–Fri 9am–1pm & 2–5pm, Sat & Sun 10am–1pm & 2–6pm; US$2; ⓦwww.tinmarin.org) may well be the best kids' museum ever, with hands-on attractions like painting a VW Beetle, sitting in a cockpit of a 727 and playing in a sloping house. A favourite is the grumpy little General

Fintan who points and shakes his head when you get near him. The only catch is that if you are not a child, you will have to find one to accompany you in.

Boulevard de los Héroes

Eight blocks west of Parque Cuscatlán, Alameda Roosevelt crosses 49 Avenida Norte by **Estádio Mágico Gonzalez**, where international football matches are played. Three blocks north the avenida curls eastward and becomes **Boulevard de los Héroes**, dripping in American fast-food chains. Beyond these, at 27 Av Norte #1140, is the **Museo de la Palabra y la Imagen** (Mon–Fri & Sun 8am–noon & 2–5pm, Sat 8am–noon; US$1; ⓦwww.museo.com.sv), nominally a museum of literature, but dominated by graphic displays on the civil war (from a leftist viewpoint). The war photography regularly on display is moving, shocking and excellent. There's also a re-creation of **Radio Venceremos**, the clandestine guerrilla radio station that counterbalanced government media propaganda during the civil war, hidden at the back, with push-button sound recordings.

Colonia Centroamérica

Heading northwest of Boulevard los Héroes on Calle Centroamérica takes you into the arty and pleasant **Colonia Centroamérica**, the most traveller-friendly area of town. Straight up the hill on the calle, the **Parque Colonia Centroamérica** has two free floodlit basketball courts, as well as benches and gnarled trees to sit in; it's the only park you should consider being in after dark. At the northern end of the park, the **Museo de Arte Popular** (Tues–Fri 10am–5pm, Sat 10am–6pm; US$1; ☎2274-5154; ⓦwww.artepopular.org) has an interesting collection of folk art, in particular some fine examples of the miniature clay people made around Ilobasco and known as *sorpresas* (surprises) – see p.280 for more. Call ahead for a free guide, but only if you can speak Spanish, as their English is

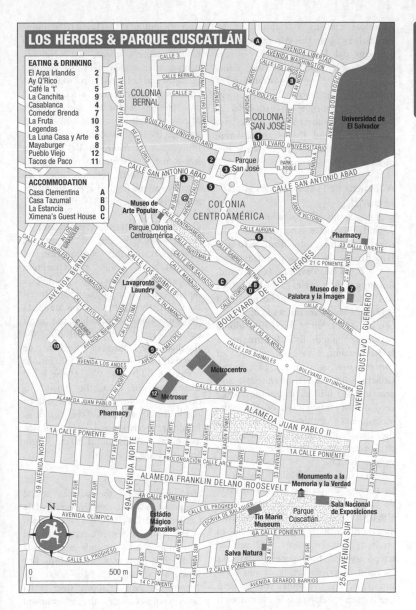

not good. The tiny tableaux of everyday life, ceremonies and special events are fascinating – children will love them – and there are even miniature figures of rock band Aerosmith and the Miami Dolphins football team.

Plaza de las Américas

Alameda Roosevelt continues west past Boulevard de los Héroes up to the rich but sight-less suburbs of **Colonia Escalón**, on the slopes of Volcán San Salvador. Halfway along, the **Plaza de las**

Américas contains a sculpture of the national symbol, the **Monumento El Salvador del Mundo**, which portrays Jesus standing on top of the globe. Curiously situated on the central island of a four-lane roundabout, the monument was given a makeover in 2010. If you're not daunted by the roaring traffic, you can stroll around the gleaming-white paved plaza fringed with clipped lawns, monkey puzzle trees and stone benches.

Avenida la Revolución and around

Running south off Alameda Roosevelt, Avenida Manuel e Araujo crosses the river and turns into **Boulevard del Hipódromo**, the pumping central artery of the **Zona Rosa** evening playground. Running at right angles to the boulevard is **Avenida la Revolución**, home to San Salvador's best monument and two best museums. Up in the leafy Colonia San Benito stands the **Monumento a la Revolución**, a vast, curved slab of concrete bearing a mosaic of a naked Goliath with head thrown back and arms uplifted. Built to commemorate the revolutionary movement of 1948, the monument's location – overlooking the bars and boutiques where the city's rich fritter their money away – is supremely ironic.

Behind the weeping Goliath, inside the Complejo Cultural, the **Museo de Arte de El Salvador** (Tues–Sun 10am–6pm; US$1.50, free Sun; ☎2243-6099 ⓦwww .marte.org.sv) offers a great overview of modern Salvadoran art as well as temporary exhibitions, generally of works by Latin American artists. If you book two to four days in advance you can get a free English-speaking guide. Next door is the modern **Teatro Presidente**, less impressive architecturally than the Teatro Nacional but nonetheless featuring a packed schedule of opera, ballet, classical concerts and musicals.

The southern end of Avenida la Revolución holds the **Museo Nacional**

de Antropología "Dr David J. Guzmán" (Tues–Sun 9am–5pm; US$3, or US$5 to use camera inside; ☎2243-3927), named after an eminent Salvadoreño biologist and home to the nation's largest collection of cultural artefacts and anthropological displays, plus exhibits of modern Salvadoran life and science. Perhaps the most important piece in the museum is the **Monolito del Jaguar**, a five-tonne representation of a jaguar's head. It is worth phoning ahead to organize a free English-speaking guide, as the plaques are all in Spanish.

Carretera Interamericana

At the southern end of Avenida la Revolución is the continuation of Alameda M.E. Araujo, the **Carretera Interamericana**, which runs from Plaza de las Américas through the southwest quarters of the city to meet the Autopista del Sur. Here is possibly the most beautiful church in San Salvador, the **Basílica de Nuestra Señora de Guadalupe** (daily 7am–5pm; donations optional). Built after World War I and consecrated in 1953, the basilica is dedicated to the Virgen Morena, or Black Virgin, patroness of the Americas. Inside are lovely stained-glass windows, as well as a 1950s mural of the Virgin and angels over the altar.

La UCA

Stretching behind the basilica is the campus of the fee-paying **Universidad de Centro América** ("La UCA"; also known as the Jesuit University), pleasantly laid out amid shady grounds and sports fields. The moving **Centro Monseñor Romero** (Mon–Fri 8am–noon & 2–6pm, Sat 8am–11.30pm; free) at La UCA commemorates the assassinated Archbishop Romero, along with the six Jesuit priests, their housekeeper and her daughter, who were murdered here by the security forces in November 1989. Volunteer students, usually including English speakers, act as guides to the small museum, which houses clothing,

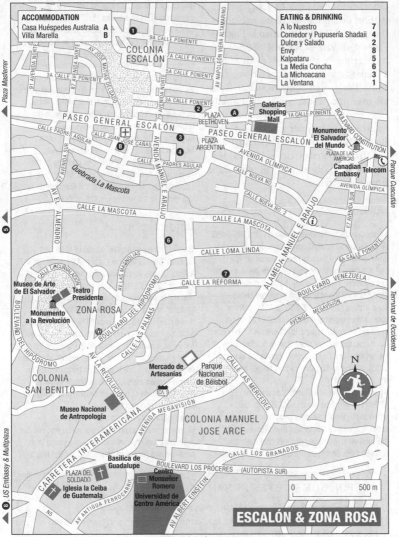

ACCOMMODATION
Casa Huéspedes Australia **A**
Villa Marella **B**

EATING & DRINKING
A lo Nuestro 7
Comedor y Pupusería Shadaii 4
Dulce y Salado 2
Envy 8
Kalpataru 5
La Media Concha 6
La Michoacana 3
La Ventana 1

ESCALÓN & ZONA ROSA

Jardín Botánico La Laguna

photographs and personal effects of Romero and the priests, along with those of other human-rights workers killed during the years of conflict. Among the more chilling exhibits is a display of glass jars containing the ashes of six victims, arranged in the shape of a cross. There are diagrams and explanations of the campus massacre, as well as eyewitness descriptions of other atrocities during the war, such as the massacres at Río Sumpul (May 1980) and El Mozote (Dec 1981). Outside, a small rose garden has been planted in tribute; the circle of six bushes is for the six priests, while the white rose in the centre is for Monseñor Romero. In the middle of the campus, the student cafeteria serves cheap meals and drinks.

Jardín Botánico la Laguna

A short distance south of the university, the tranquil **Jardín Botánico la Laguna** (Tues–Sun 9am–5.30pm; US$0.50) sits incongruously at the edge of an industrial park and at the foot of old volcanic cliffs. The garden contains plants from all over the world, set among shady trees and streams, and is a good place to escape the city for an hour or two. Buses #101D (from Plaza Barrios) and #44 (from Boulevard de los Héroes) will drop you off about five minutes' walk from the entrance.

Arrival

By air Comalapa International Airport (☎ 2366-9455, ⓦ www.aeropuertoelsalvador.gob.sv) is a 45-minute drive southeast of the city centre. Buses (#14, #15 and #29, among others) stop by the highway turn-off to the airport; #29 then stops in the city centre. After 7pm, taxis are the only way to get to the centre. Taxis Acacya (☎ 2271-4937/2222-1202) have a booth at the airport and charge US$25–28 day or night to the capital, regardless of numbers. They also run a *colectivo* service (9am, 1pm & 5.30pm from the airport; 6am, 7am, 10am & 2pm to the airport; US$3), leaving and arriving at their offices at 19A Av Nte & C 3 Pte #1107.

By international bus Puerto Bus services (☎ 2271-1361) from Guatemala and Honduras arrive at the terminal by the Centro de Gobierno or at the Terminal de Occidente, Blvd Venezuela, in the southwest of the city (from Guatemala); take bus #52 from Centro de Gobierno to the city centre, and bus #34 from Terminal de Occidente to the city centre. Tica Bus buses (☎ 2222-4808) from Costa Rica, Nicaragua and Guatemala have their own terminal at C Concepción #121 in the Centro Histórico. Both companies' buses coming from Guatemala also stop at a terminal in San Benito – handy for Zona Rosa and Colonia Escalón.

By domestic bus Buses from the north and east arrive at Terminal de Oriente, east of the centre, from where city buses #9, #29 or #34 go to the centre and #29 and #54 go to Blvd los Héroes. Buses from the west and beaches west of La Libertad arrive at the Terminal de Occidente; bus #44 goes to Blvd los Héroes and #34 to the Terminal de Oriente via the Centro. Buses from the eastern coastal highway go to the Terminal de Sur, connected to the centre via #26 or #11B.

Information

Tourist information The offices of Mitur and Corsatur, both at Edificio Carbonell #1, Alameda M.E. Araujo, Colonia Roma (Mon–Fri 9am–5pm; ☎ 2243-7835 or 2241-3200, ⓦ www.elsalvador.travel), give out basic maps and advertisement-laden "guides". If you are persistent they can answer queries. ISTU, C Rubén Darío #619 (☎ 2222-8000), provides information on national parks and *parques recreativos familiares* (see p.264). For event listings, keep a lookout for *Ke Pasa*, a free weekly entertainment guide available in bars and restaurants. *The Revue*, Guatemala's English-language magazine, also includes an El Salvador section and is widely available throughout the city.

Tour operators Akwaterra (☎ 7888-8642, ⓦ www.akwaterra.com) speak great English and run active ecotours on land and sea – everything from kayaking and surfing to horseriding, paragliding and

---

USEFUL BUS ROUTES IN SAN SALVADOR

#29 From Terminal de Oriente to Metrocentro via Centro Histórico.

#30B Along Boulevard de los Héroes, up Alameda Roosevelt and part of Paseo Escalón, then turning west to run past the Zona Rosa.

#34 From Terminal de Oriente through Centro Histórico to Terminal de Occidente and out along the Carretera Interamericana, past the Mercado de Artesanías.

#44 Along Boulevard de los Héroes, onto 49A Av Sur close to the Terminal de Occidente, past the Universidad de Centroamérica and out past the US Embassy to Santa Elena.

#52 Along Alameda Juan Pablo I, past Metrosur and on to El Salvador del Mundo (opposite the Telecom office), then up Paseo Escalón past the Galerías shopping mall.

#101A/B/C/D From Centro Histórico up Alameda Roosevelt to Plaza de las Américas, then on to Santa Tecla.

mountain biking. El Salvador Divers, C 3 Pte 5020-A at 99A Av Nte (℡ 2264-0961, ⓦ www.elsalvador divers.com), offers diving trips along the Los Cóbanos/ Los Remedios stretch of the Pacific coast and crater diving at Lake Coatepeque, plus PADI courses and equipment rental. Ríos Aventuras (℡ 2298-0335, ⓔ grupotropic@navegante.com.sv) organizes rafting on the ríos Paz and Lempa for groups of at least four people. At most places tours start at around US$30 per person, more if the group is smaller.

Travel agents The offices of most airlines with service to the country, as well as many other travel agents, can be found along the Alameda Roosevelt/ Paseo Escalón, with TACA and AA offices in the Metrocentro (see p.262).

City transport

Buses The city bus network (schoolbuses and minibuses) runs from 6am until around 8pm and is comprehensive, frequent and cheap – it's US$0.25 to anywhere in the city. Pay the driver if there is a gate, or the roaming, shouting driver's assistant if not. Most stops are not marked, so look for large public buildings, shopping centres or groups of people waiting by the road; usually you can also hop on or off if they stop in traffic.

Taxis Yellow city taxis ply the streets and wait around bus terminals, markets and major hotels and shopping areas. They cost US$5–6, which you should agree on before getting in. Take taxis after dark.

Accommodation

The Centro Histórico is not generally conducive to peace of mind or a pleasant stay, and there is very little to do there at night but wait for a morning bus. The western suburbs are safe and there's plenty to see and do, but there are few genuinely budget options. North of Boulevard de los Héroes is the middle ground, and much better for travellers: it's safe and with a good amount of nightlife and eating options.

Centro Histórico

American Guest House 17A Av Nte 119, between C Arce & C 1 Pte ℡ 2222-8789, ⓔ americanguest house@hotmail.com. Dimly lit and rather gloomy decor, but the service is friendly. Rooms come with a choice of private or shared bath, plus hot water and cable TV. International phone calls available and meals served at on-site café. US$15

International Custodio 10A Av Sur 109 ℡ 2502-0678, ⓔ peraltavictor62@hotmail.com. One of the centre's best options, with friendly service, great views from the roof, clean sheets and decent fans.

Credit cards are accepted and the manager, who speaks good English, can give advice on the area. Reductions available on extended stays. US$12

Nuevo Panamericano 8A Av Sur, by the Mercado Ex-Cuartel ℡ 2221-1199 or 2222-2959, ⓔ hayderiveracere@yahoo.es. Firm beds with ornate bedsteads, a choice of humming a/c or silent ceiling fans, and en-suite showers all serve to make this a great choice in the centre. US$10

Villa Floréncia C 1 Pte 1023, between 17 & 19 Av Nte ℡ 2221-1706. One of several similar hotels in the area behind the Puerto Bus terminal. With large, bright, airy en-suite rooms, cable TV and communal seating areas, this is the best of the bunch. US$20

North of Blvd de los Héroes

Casa Clementina Av Morazán 34 at C Washington, Col Libertad ℡ 2225-5962. Friendly, peaceful and secure with communal garden, TV and outdoor seating. Simply furnished but attractive en-suite rooms with cold water and fan. Rates include breakfast. US$30

Casa Tazumal 35A Av Nte 3 ℡ 2235-0156, ⓦ www.hoteltazumalhouse.com. A good, homely hotel with plenty of perks – free internet access, airport or bus terminal pick-up, good food and laundry service (US$5) – in addition to clean rooms with cable TV and firm beds. US$44

La Estancia Av Cortés 216 ℡ 2275-3381. A relaxed travellers' hostel on a quiet residential street just off Boulevard de los Héroes, with a large cable-TV area, free kitchen use and coffee. The dorm bunks spill out into the corridor and the clean en-suite rooms are small, but great value, especially the room with a private terrace. Breakfast included. Dorms US$10, doubles US$30

Ximena's Guest House C San Salvador 202, Col Centro América ℡ 2260-2481, ⓔ ximenas .guesthouse@gmail.com. The original San Salvador hostel is not necessarily still the best. Beds are lumpy or saggy and the electric hot water (which you pay extra for) is shockingly inconsistent. It

TREAT YOURSELF

Villa Marella C Juan José Cañas and 83A Av Sur ℡ 2263-4931. The best deal of the upmarket Escalón hotels, with giant beds, powerful hot showers, complimentary mineral water, free internet, an indigo-coloured splash pool with accompanying loungers, great service and tasty, if equally costly, food. US$65 remains a travellers' favourite though, not least for the wide range of breakfasts, helpful English-speaking owner and sociable evening atmosphere. Dorms US$6, doubles US$30

Colonia Escalón

Casa Huéspedes Australia 1A C Pte 3852 ☏2298-6035. Lacks the atmosphere of the Blvd de los Héroes hostels, but is certainly cleaner and more comfortable, offers free breakfast and internet and the showers are big and hot. It's incredible value for Escalón, but choose the cheapest rooms, as there is no massive difference in the more expensive – rates are per person. US$20

Eating

The best restaurants are concentrated in the western suburbs, catering to those with the money and time to indulge. There are *comedores* and *pupuserías* everywhere and, if they look hygienic or locals are eating at them you shouldn't be afraid to. The Boulevard de los Héroes itself is dominated by fast-food chains, but there are good options off the main drag.

Centro Histórico

Café Maquilishuat C 4 Pte & 9A Av Sur. Sodas, great juices (US$1), and *típicos* (US$3–5) with a Mexican and American influence dished out on plastic trays in lively a/c surroundings.
Koradi 9A Av Sur 225, at C 4 Pte. One of the few places catering to vegetarians, with soya burgers (US$3), wholewheat pizzas and great juices. Open in the daytime only; closed Sun.
Pan Salvador C Arce, between 7A & 9A Av Sur. Popular with local workers, this busy *comedor* and bakery serves meat dishes for around US$1, with combo deals for US$2 and coffee for US$0.50. The whole place is redolent of the scent of baking cakes.

Around Boulevard de los Héroes

Ay Q'Rico Blvd Universitario 217. Popular among the local students for its cheap daily menus (US$2–3), served with free beer. Also a wide selection of seafood and poultry dishes with a touch of Mexican flavour.
Casablanca C San Antonio Abad & Av San José. A well-prepared canteen menu (US$3–5), with large soup portions, is served in a cool and open room shielded from the traffic by climbing plants.
Comedor Brenda Next to the Museo de Palabra y Imagen. An outstanding *comedor* with *a la vista* (canteen) lunches for around US$2 and great snacks in the afternoon, including the best *yuca frita* (US$0.50) around. Daily noon–6pm.

La Fruta Av Maracaibo 519 ☏2260-1253. Come here for more than 200 juice combinations, as well as breakfasts and lunches made from all-natural ingredients. Evening meals available if you call in advance. Mon–Sat 9am–6pm.
Mayaburger Behind the Esso station on C G. Cortés. This trustworthy burger van outstrips the big franchises both on price (a two-burger sandwich, onions and salad are US$2) and taste – plus, it's open 24/7.
Tacos de Paco C Andes 2931. Tasty Mexican tacos (US$4–5) with a twist – they are served in a room that has original art on the walls and hosts poetry readings on Wed evenings. Daily noon–3pm & 5–10pm.

Colonia Escalón and the Zona Rosa

Comedor y Pupusería Shadaii 77A Av Sur, behind Super Selectos. The *comedor* and *pupusería* of choice for the area's workers, with *típicos* breakfasts (US$2) and lunches (US$2–3) that are the cheapest around.
Dulce y Salado 3 C Pte, by Plaza Beethoven. Although decorated like a little girl's bedroom, this little restaurant has good pancake, juice and coffee breakfasts (US$4) and great quiche (US$6).
Kalpataru Plaza Kalpataru, Calle La Mascota ☏2263-1204. Imaginative vegetarian fare: try the *pupusas* (US$4) with unusual fillings like stir-fried broccoli and curried vegetables. There's also a natural medicine counter and bookshop on site.
La Michoacana Local 3, Paseo General Escalón & 75 Av Norte. Delicious Mexican-style fresh-fruit ice cream (US$1–2); more than 60 flavours, including tamarind and chile, beer, tequila and *mojito cubano*. The perfect relief for mad-dog gringos out on the sun-baked streets.

Drinking and nightlife

San Salvador's clubs and bars are found mainly in the western suburbs, but there are also small pockets of expat and tourist nightlife, particularly in and around around *Ximena's Guesthouse* and *La Estancia* in Colonia Centroamérica, behind

Boulevard de los Héroes. If you fancy mingling with the city's jet set, there's a cluster of swanky clubs and bars in the shadow of the towering *Hilton Hotel* off Boulevard del Hipódromo in Colonia San Benito, including *Bar Republika*, *Zanzibar* and *Basilea* (☎2279-0833).

Around Blvd de los Héroes

El Arpa Irlandés Av A, on the west side of Parque San José. This shiny and laidback bar is the place to come for a Guinness (US$3) or a Pilsener (US$1). There's a pool table, and it livens up on Sat nights with rock bands, which draw a young crowd.

Café la 't' C San Antonio Abad 2233. Owner Anna has turned this into a great little arty café and bar offering once-monthly live music and art exhibitions. The *tiramisù* (US$3) is rumoured to be the best in the country and the lemon, honey and vodka-filled "Café Ivanovic" cocktail (US$2.50) is excellent. Evenings only, until 11pm or midnight on Fri–Sun.

La Canchita C Lamatepec, by C los Andes. This fun and feisty bar, which offers buckets of six bottles of beer for US$6 and has the best full-sized pool tables in town (US$1 per 30min), is the pick of several places in the area.

Legendas On the south side of Parque San José. This orange-walled late-night spot has darts, table-football, music that gets people dancing, and neither charges entry nor inflates its beer prices. Rum & coke US$2.

La Luna Casa y Arte C Berlin 228 ⊛www .lalunacasayarte.com. Hands down the best bar in San Salvador, with a film, live music and exhibition programme every night. The furnishings are eclectic but tasteful, and the walls are decked with paintings. Brilliant cocktails (US$3) include ice cream and Baileys, and White Russians. Check out the schedule online or nailed to the tree outside. Wed–Sun 7pm–2am. US$3–6 entry after 9pm.

Pueblo Viejo In the Metrosur on Blvd de los Héroes ☎2260-3551. The popular *Pueblo* has salsa dancing in a welcoming atmosphere Thurs–Sat 9pm–midnight. US$3 Fri & Sat.

Colonia Escalón and the Zona Rosa

Envy 2nd floor, Multiplaza shopping mall, Antiguo Cuscatlán ☎2243-2576. A favourite of the rich San Salvador set, who all get dressed up, and you have to too (trousers, shirt, shoes). Music is dance, R&B and hip-hop. US$5.

La Media Concha 79A Av Sur, by C La Mascota. Unlike the majority of Zona Rosa restaurant-cum-dancehalls, this bar, selling barbecue and beer

giraffes (four-pint towers of beer; US$8.60) is brimming with personality and boasts a terrace to cool off on when you become overwhelmed by the young Salvadoreños busting moves on the dancefloor.

La Ventana Plaza Palestina, Col Escalón between 9A C Pte & 83 Av Nte. European-run restaurant and bar with an interesting selection of dishes (US$5–9) inspired by cuisines from around the world. Very popular at the weekends with expats, tourists and moneyed Salvadoreños. Daily until 1am.

Entertainment

Cinema There are a couple of multi-screen complexes – a Cinemark at the Metrocentro (☎2261-2001) and an 11-screen Cinépolis at Galerías Escalón (⊛www.cinepolis.com.sv/). Both show some original-language films and some dubbed (tickets US$2–3). Independent cinema can be found at *La Luna* (see opposite) on Wed–Sun, starting at around 7pm, or *Café la 't'* (see opposite) on Wed & Thurs around 8pm.

Theatre The Teatro Presidente (see p.256) and the magnificently restored Teatro Nacional (see p.253) host everything from ballet to musicals to opera, at anything from free to US$30, while the Teatro Luis Poma, just inside the main arched entrance to the Metrocentro, shows locally produced plays (US$5). Information can be found in the Friday edition and on the website of *El Diario de Hoy* (⊛www.elsalvador.com).

CRAFTS IN SAN SALVADOR

Artisan work is still highly valued in El Salvador, and many communities have defined themselves by a chosen craft. The most well-known types are the brightly painted, naïf-style wood and ceramics from La Palma, the hammocks from Concepción Quezaltepeque and the interesting ceramics at Ilobasco. These are far cheaper in their place of manufacture, but the Mercado Ex Cuartel and the Mercado de Artesanías in San Salvador both have an extensive selection of goods from across the country at reasonable prices; a number of more expensive shops around town also carry smaller selections. Hammocks can usually be found for sale in the Parque Central in San Salvador.

Shopping

Art The El Árbol de Dios art gallery, on Av Masferrer y C la Mascota (Mon–Sat 9am–6pm; free), is the shop of El Salvador's emblematic painter Fernando Llort. Everything from prints to cooking aprons in his naïf style can be purchased; most items are produced in the workshop in the back. Originals go for about half a million dollars.

Books and newspapers The bookshop on the second level of the Metrocentro has English-language titles and US magazines. La Ceiba is the biggest chain of bookstores, branches of which you'll find in Galerías Escalón and other malls, with a reasonable range, including some books in English (average US$10 for a paperback). Punto Literario, Blvd del Hipódromo 326, has English, French, German and Spanish literature.

Malls Reputedly the largest mall in Central America, the Metrocentro/Metrosur complex at the southern end of Blvd de los Héroes holds three storeys of expensive boutiques, sporting-goods outlets, pricey souvenir shops, a supermarket and a food court. Galerías Escalón, at Paseo Gen Escalón 3700, is the same but classier. Multiplaza, on the Carretera Panamericana to Santa Elena, with its flashy bars and restaurants, is the most upmarket.

Markets There are two good markets for artisan handicrafts: the central Mercado Ex Cuartel, three blocks east from the Teatro Nacional, and the higher-quality Mercado de Artesanías, opposite the baseball stadium on Alameda M.E. Araujo; see box, p.261, for more details. Southwest of Plaza Barrios are the ever-expanding street stalls of the Mercado Central, where anything and everything can be bought for about a dollar, even on Sundays.

Directory

Embassies Most embassies are located in or around the Paseo Escalón and Zona Rosa districts. The US embassy, the second most heavily fortified in the world, is on Blvd Santa Elena, Antiguo Cuscatlán ☎2501-2999/2004 (bus #44). Canada is at Alameda Roosevelt y 63A Av Sur (☎2279-4655). British citizens should call the honorary consul on ☎2281-5555. Australians can contact the Canadian embassy.

Exchange Most banks ask for the original receipt when cashing travellers' cheques and give over-the-counter cash advances on Visa and MasterCard. Banco Hipotecario, at Av Cuscatlán between C 4 & 6 Ote, and other branches around the city, do not require the receipt. American Express issues travellers' cheques from their office at 55 Av Sur, Edificio Credomatic, between Alameda Roosevelt & Av Olímpica (☎2245-3774). Banks and ATMs are ubiquitous around the western suburbs and Blvd de los Héroes.

Health There's a 24hr pharmacy at Farmacia Internacional, Edificio Kent, Local 6, Alameda Juan Pablo II at Blvd de los Héroes. The Medicentro at 27A Av Nte and C 21 Pte has a number of doctors specializing in different fields (☎2225-1312). A consultation will cost around US$30.

Immigration Ministerio del Interior in the Centro de Gobierno, on Alameda Juan Pablo II between 13 Calle Poniente and 3A Av Norte (Mon–Fri 8am–4pm; ☎2221-2111), is the place to get stamps, tourist cards and visas extended.

Internet The Metrosur has two fast internet cafés; and Cyber Café Genus, on Av Izalco by the church, is also very friendly. Cyber Snack, on the east side of Plaza Barrios, is fast enough. There are Infocentros on C Arce between 19A and 21A Av Sur, and in the Zona Rosa where Blvd del Hipódromo meets Av la Revolución. Expect to pay US$0.60–1/hr.

Laundry Lavandería Lavapronto, C Los Sismiles 2944 (Mon–Sat 7am–7pm; average load US$2–3).

Libraries La UCA has a very good library and the Biblioteca Nacional (see p.252) is open to the public, but you have to show ID.

Police The main station is in the Scottish-castle-like building which occupies an entire block on 10A Av Sur at C 6 Ote (☎2271-4422).

Post office Behind the Centro de Gobierno on Blvd Centro de Gobierno; look for the large building with "UPAE" on the side. There are smaller offices in the lower level of the Metrocentro mall.

Telephones Telecom, the French-owned former state phone company, has an enormous glass office at La Campaña on Plaza de las Américas.

Moving on

San Salvador is El Salvador's bus hub, with the best land transport connections in the country. There are also flights, both domestic and international, out of the city's airport.

By air

You can get flights out of Comalapa airport with: TACA Airlines (⊛www.taca.com), to North, South and Central Americas and the Caribbean; American Airlines (⊛www.aa.com) and Continental Airlines (⊛www.continental.com), for the US; and Air Transat (⊛www.airtransat.com) to Canada.

By bus

San Salvador has three domestic terminals and two international terminals. Despite this, leaving the city is a remarkably easy exercise. Most international buses can also be caught on Blvd del Hipódromo as they leave the city, but these departures are very early in the morning, so check the day before and get a taxi. Bus route information is available in Spanish only from the Association of Salvadoran Bus Owners (AEAS; ☎ 2225-2661) at C 27 Pte 1132, Colonia Layco, or the tourist office.

Domestic bus departures

Terminal de Occidente On Blvd Venezuela (reached by buses #4, #27, #34 and #7C). Serves the south and west of the country, including: Ahuachapán (#202; frequent; 3hr 30min); Desvío Opico, via Joya de Cerén (#108; frequent; 1hr); La Libertad (#102; very frequent; 1hr); Metapán (#201A; every 30min; 3hr 30min); Santa Ana, via San Andrés (#201; frequent; 1hr 20min–2hr); Sonsonate (#205; very frequent; 1hr 30 min).
Terminal de Oriente On Blvd del Ejército (reached by buses #3, #5, #7, #8, #9, #28, #29, #34 and #42). Serves the east and north of the country, including: Chalatenango (#125; frequent; 2hr 30min); Ilobasco (#111; every 15min; 1hr 20min); La Palma/El Poy (#119; every 30min; 4hr 30min); La Unión (#304; every 30min; 3–4hr); San Francisco Gotera (#305; direct; 3 daily; 3–4hr); San Miguel (#301; frequent; 3–4hr); San Vicente (#116; frequent; 1hr 30min); Suchitoto (#129; every 20min; 1hr 30min); Usulután (#302; 2 daily; 2hr 30min). Luxury services to San Miguel (every 40min; 2hr) and San Vicente (8 daily; 1hr) also depart from this terminal.
Terminal del Sur On the Autopista a Comalapa (reached by buses #11B, #21 and #26). The stop for buses along the eastern Carretera Litoral to Zacatecoluca and Usulután, including: Costa del Sol (#495; every 30min; 2hr 30min); Puerto El Triunfo (#185; 6 daily; 2hr); Usulután (#302; frequent; 2hr 30min); Zacatecoluca (#133; frequent; 1hr 30min).

International bus departures

Terminal King Quality Bus On Alameda Juan Pablo II & 19 Av Norte ☎ 2271-1361 (reached by bus #52). Departures to: Guatemala City (daily; 5hr); Tegucigalpa, Honduras (2 daily; 6hr 30min).
Terminal Puerto Bus On Alameda Juan Pablo II ☎ 2271-1361 (reached by bus #52). Departures to: Guatemala City (18 daily Mon–Sat, 4 daily Sun; 5hr); Managua, Nicaragua (daily; 11hr); San José, Costa Rica (daily; 18hr); San Pedro Sula, Honduras (2 daily; 6hr); Tapachula, Mexico (daily; 10hr); Tegucigalpa, Honduras (3 daily; 6hr 30min).
Terminal Tica Bus By the *Hotel San Carlos* on C Concepción ☎ 2222-0848 (reached by buses #29 and #34). Departures to: Tapachula, Mexico, via Guatemala City (daily; 10hr/5hr); Panama City via San José, Costa Rica, and Managua, Nicaragua (daily; 36hr/18hr/11hr).

AROUND SAN SALVADOR

San Salvador is an excellent transport hub, and within easy reach of the city are a number of destinations offering immediate relief from the heat and crowds. Head in any direction and in well under an hour you'll find lush, rolling countryside.

Los Chorros

West along the Carretera Interamericana from San Salvador light industrial and residential districts blend indiscernibly

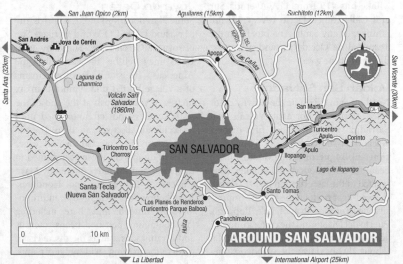

AROUND SAN SALVADOR

PARQUES RECREATIVOS FAMILIARES

Most large, urban settlements in El Salvador are within a stone's throw of one of the country's fourteen **parques recreativos familiares**, government-subsidized holiday centres designed to give city dwellers the opportunity to enjoy nature in comfortable surroundings. There are three in the vicinity of San Salvador – Los Chorros (see p.263), Apulo (p.265) and Parque Balboa (p.266) – but whichever city you're in, one is never far away. Most involve some kind of water-based diversion – swimming pools or natural lakes – along with ample provision of food and cabañas to escape the sun. Opening hours are generally between 9am and 5pm and there is an entry charge of US$1. Contact ISTU (see p.248) for more information.

For those who want full accommodation on the government, there are also four **centros obrajo**, or workers' centres, at El Tamarindo beach, Lago de Coatepeque, La Palma and Puerto La Libertad. Recently constructed and nicer than they sound, they are free of charge, provided you contact and visit the Ministerio de Trabajo (see p.243) with your passport beforehand. They are closed on Mondays and Tuesdays and, like the *parques recreativos*, get very busy on weekends and holidays.

into **Santa Tecla**, briefly the capital in 1854 but now only of minor interest. Six kilometres further along the highway, El Salvador's most popular *parque recreativo familiar*, **Los Chorros** (daily 7am–5pm; US$1), is a great spot for a swim. Small waterfalls cascade through mossy jungle slopes into a series of landscaped pools; there are public changing rooms and showers – don't bring valuables – and a couple of *comedores* provide meals. If you're in a group and feel brave enough to ignore the warnings about robbers, the surrounding hills provide pleasant walks.

Take **bus #79** from 11A Avenida Sur and Calle Rubén Darío (every 15min; 30min), or any Santa Ana bus from the Terminal de Occidente, and ask to be dropped at the gate.

Volcán San Salvador

North of Santa Tecla lie the heavily cultivated slopes of dormant **Volcán San Salvador** (1960m), the fifth-highest volcano in the country. Its 540m-deep crater **El Boquerón** ("Big Mouth") has a beautiful floral floor and a smaller cone created in the last eruption in 1917. From the well-kept **park** on the rim are impressive views of San Salvador, Lake Ilopango, Puerto del Diablo and the crater's interior; adventurers can tackle the walk around it (about 2hr) or down the wooded slopes

inside (1hr 30min). Early morning is the best time to go, when the views from the summit are clearest. You can also walk up to the crater, though robberies have been reported; the police at the entrance may be willing to provide an escort for groups.

Bus #103 (hourly) and pick-ups run from 4A Avenida Sur and Calle Hernández in Santa Tecla (reached via the La Libertad, Santa Ana and Sonsonate buses from Terminal de Occidente), to Pueblo del Boquerón, 1km from the rim; the last bus down leaves mid afternoon.

Joya de Cerén

Some 9km northwest of Los Chorros, the Maya and UNESCO World Heritage Site of **Joya de Cerén** (Tues–Sun 8am–4pm; US$3) may well be "the Pompeii of the Americas". The site houses the remains of a village buried under more than six metres of volcanic ash at the end of the sixth century and left untouched until its accidental discovery in 1976. The site itself is small, protected behind cages and will disappoint those accustomed to the photo opportunities offered by Maya edifices of Guatemala and Honduras. It will, however, delight the anthropologically minded: finds here, including jars containing petrified beans, utensils and ceramics, as well as the discovery of gardens for growing a wide range of plants, have helped confirm a picture of a well-organized and stable pre-colonial society, with trade links throughout Central America. As yet, no human remains have been uncovered, which concurs with the hasty departure suggested by the number of artefacts discovered. A small, Spanish-language museum at the site details the development of the Maya culture and the excavation project itself.

Bus #108 from San Salvador's Terminal de Occidente runs right by the site – get off just after crossing the Río Sucio. If you want to go to San Andrés (see below) in the same trip, start here and take #108 back towards San Salvador as far as the highway, where you can intercept a #201 (towards Santa Ana from the Terminal de Occidente) to San Andrés.

San Andrés

A few kilometres southwest of Joya de Cérén over lush undulations of agricultural land lies the Maya ceremonial centre of **San Andrés** (Tues–Sun 8am–4pm; US$3). One of the largest pre-Columbian sites in El Salvador, originally supporting a population of about twelve thousand, the site reached its peak as the regional capital around 650–900 AD. Only sections of the ceremonial centre have been excavated – seven major structures including a temple, altar and indigo works – and sadly, they've been preserved using rather too liberal amounts of concrete. You can climb freely around the site, which is also a popular picnic spot at the weekends. A small, well-curated museum (Spanish only) includes a good model of what the site would have looked like in the late first millenium.

The #201 **bus** between Terminal de Occidente and Santa Ana will drop you by a black ruin on the highway a couple of hundred metres from the site – you will need to tell the driver to stop. It's possible to walk to Joya de Cerén in the same trip. A path leads across the fields behind San Andrés, coming out about 4km northeast at an abandoned railway station. From here take a left towards San Juan Opico; it is another 3km or so to Joya de Cerén. It is preferable to travel in a group.

Lago de Ilopango

Heading east from San Salvador, the Carretera Interamericana passes the city's dismal eastern slums and bends northwards. A few kilometres past the airport at Ilopango, a dirt road branches south and winds down through scrubby hillsides, offering stunning views across **Lago de Ilopango** to the peaks of Volcán San Vicente. The country's largest and deepest crater lake, resulting from one of the biggest eruptions in history in around 250 AD, Ilopango is a contrast of blue waters and tumbling, thickly vegetated cliffs. Further along the road, in the dusty hamlet of Apulo, the decent (but busy at weekends) **parque recreativo familiar** (daily 8am–5pm; US$1) has a beach, swimming pools and fine *comedores*. Small boats tout for custom here (US$12/hr; reductions for groups), and drifting around the Isla de Amor or touring the rich lakeside communities is a pleasant way to spend a hot afternoon. The best **volcano diving** in the country also takes place under the surface of the lake, on the underwater volcanic cone La Caldera. This should be organized with El Salvador Divers (see p.259) in the capital beforehand.

Bus #15 runs from the corner of Calle 9 Pte and 1A Avenida Nte in San Salvador every 30 minutes or so.

Los Planes de Renderos

Overlooking the Valle de Hamacas from the brim of the valley's southern watershed, **Los Planes de Renderos** offers fresh air, good food and great views. The best panoramas of San Salvador are from the *Casa de Piedra* (km 8.5; ☎2280-8822), an open-fronted bar/restaurant serving seafood and *típicos* with weekend music or karaoke. Cheaper, though, is the *mirador* lookout point off the road just before the restaurant as you come up the hill. Another

PACIFIC COAST ROAD TRIP

Along with Ruta de las Flores (see p.305) and the climb to Perquín (see p.289), the Carretera Litoral, running the length of El Salvador's Pacific coast, is one of the country's best road trips. Public transport runs regularly to many places along the route. However, it's still worth renting a car for a few days to reach some of the more remote and beautiful beaches (see p.242 for recommended rental companies, or contact Alex Novoa at *Esencia Nativa*, in Playa El Zonte, who has many useful local contacts – see p.271).

great restaurant is the barn-like *Pupusería Paty* (km 10), which serves some of the best and biggest *pupusas* in the country. The best views of the coast are from the **Puerta del Diablo**, a split rock formation at the summit of the Cerro Chulo, a 40-minute walk from the road through the somewhat grubby Turicentro **Parque Balboa** (km 12; daily 8am–6pm; US$1). The rock's legendary origins – split by a bolt of lightning over three hundred years ago – have been eclipsed by its very real role in the civil war as a place of death-squad interrogations, executions and body-dumping.

Bus #12 runs up the Carretera Los Planes, along which all kilometre markers are given, from Avenida 29 de Agosto. If you don't fancy walking to the Puerta del Diablo, you can take the bus to the last stop, at km 14.

Panchimalco

Further south, the largely indigenous town of **Panchimalco** lies sleepily beneath the Puerta del Diablo. The area was once widely inhabited by the Panchos, descendants of the Pipils, and although a number still remain, traditional dress is rarely seen nowadays. The town's colonial **church**, built in 1725, is the oldest surviving church in the country and is also remarkable for its statue of a dark-skinned, indigenous Jesus. There are indigenous **crafts** for sale too, including pre-Hispanic musical instruments, at the Casa de la Cultura. Usually a quiet place, things become livelier during the town's annual **festivals** (see p.249). **Bus** #17 runs regularly to the town from Avenida 29 de Agosto in San Salvador (30min).

The Pacific coast

El Salvador's **Pacific coast** is a 300-kilometre sweep of sandy tropical beaches, dramatic cliffs, mangrove swamps and romantic islands. While the tourist potential of many of the beaches is now being developed, most stretches of sand are still, blissfully, a far cry from international resorts. Indeed, the beauty of this part of the country lies in relaxing on clean, wide beaches, catching world-class waves or spending time in relatively untouched fishing villages.

Coming from San Salvador, the most accessible stretch of coast is the **Costa del Bálsamo**, extending around the small fishing town of **La Libertad**. This stretch boasts some of Central America's best surfing beaches, and El Salvador's biggest gringo community. Further down the coast are the green waterways and islands of the mangrove swamps of the **Bahía de Jiquilisco**, as well as what many consider to be the finest beach in the country, **Playa El Espino**. In the extreme east of the region you can catch early-morning *lanchas* to the tranquil islands of the **Golfo de Fonseca**, and away from sweltering **La Unión**.

The beaches near Acajutla (Los Cóbanos and Los Remedios) and to the west are best accessed via Sonsonate rather than along the coastal road, and are thus covered in the section beginning on p.302.

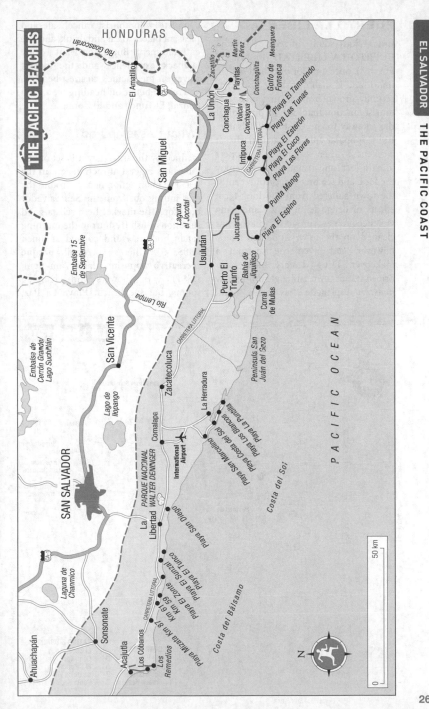

PUERTO LA LIBERTAD

Just 34km south of San Salvador, **PUERTO LA LIBERTAD** (or just "El Puerto"), once a major port and still an important, if shabby, fishing town, has recently grown from surfing mecca to tourist junction thanks to its position at the gateway to the Costa del Bálsamo. It's a popular place, particularly at weekends, when capital day-trippers join the local and gringo surfers to enjoy the food and sea breezes. Until recently, the town suffered from the long-term effects of drug, delinquency and gang violence. A new, proactive mayor has cleaned up the town in recent years, however, and given the seafront a makeover. Drug dealers have been driven out of town and a gleaming new *malecón* esplanade has been built,

complete with tourist office, safe and pleasant places to eat and drink, and live entertainment. But if you want a truly laidback experience and the biggest waves on the Pacific's cleanest beaches, you're still better off heading west to El Sunzal, El Tunco and El Zonte.

What to see and do

Defined by the small bay it is set on, La Libertad's biggest attractions are in the sea. The main action occurs around the pier jutting out from the San Salvador bus stop. The **market** here sells a good selection of fish fresh from the morning catch, both raw and cooked at lunch (US$3–5). There's a small **parque recreativo** opposite (daily 7am–5pm; US$1), with showers and changing rooms, but the beach, **Playa La Paz**,

LA LIBERTAD

N

Buses from Sonsonate

1A CALLE PONIENTE

Bank

CALLE BARRIOS

Supermarket

Pharmacy

CALLE EL CALVARIO

Buses from
Eastern Beaches

2A CALLE ORIENTE

Buses from
San Salvador

2A CALLE PONIENTE

4A CALLE ORIENTE

Hospital de Surf

Market

4A CALLE PONIENTE

Playa El Sunzal

Playa Las Flores, Playa San Dreya & Parque Walter T. Deninger

PACIFIC OCEAN

0   100 m

ACCOMMODATION	
Hotel Rick	D
Hotel Surf Club Inn	A
Mango's Lounge	B
La Posada Familiar	C

EATING & DRINKING	
El Buen Asado	1
Comedor Paty	2
El Delphin	5
La Dulce Vita	3
Punta Roca	4

Punta Roca Surf Break

FISHY PRICING

Restaurant **prices** on El Salvador's Pacific coast may seem inflated, but this is often due to the value of the ingredients. The unmissable coastal speciality, a creamy seafood soup called **mariscada**, contains crab, whole fish, langoustine and shrimp, is also one of the most expensive dishes – a good one is hard to find for under US$10, and will probably be closer to US$12. Oysters should cost around US$7, and a whole langoustine is likely to set you back US$12. It may seem like you're being overcharged, but the seafood is generally very fresh, and you get what you pay for.

is quite dirty, and becomes rocky and prone to riptides in the rainy season.

The town's heartbeat, however, is the world-famous **Punta Roca** surf break, which tubes perfectly around the point a couple of hundred metres to the west of the pier. This is not a beginner's wave, and localism (local hostility to you sharing their great surf spot) does exist – confrontations are best avoided by hiring a local guide: ask at your hotel or at the tourist office. Even if you don't surf, it is exciting just to go and watch experts take on the wave in the morning and evening, or at any of the regular surf events held here. **Surfboards** can be bought, sold, rented and repaired at the Hospital de Tablas, on 3 Avenida Sur between 2A & 4A Calle Pte (7am–4pm; US$12/day). If you need to work on your surf skills before hopping on a board, there are better beaches along the coast to the west (see p.270). For sunbathers, the small and busy **Playa Las Flores** is a kilometre and a half east, reachable by bus #82.

Arrival and information

By bus Services from San Salvador arrive at 2A C Ote, one block inland from the pier. Buses to and from the eastern beaches go from 4 Av Norte, on the other side of the *parque recreativo*. Further up that road on the corner with 1A C Pte is the stop for Sonsonate and the western beaches.

Tourist information The tourist office is upstairs in the white seafront centre opposite the pier (Mon–Fri 8am–4pm, Sat & Sun 9am–1pm; ☎2346-1634), with clean public toilets opposite the entrance.

Internet Infocentro, 1A C Pte & 4 Av Nte (Mon–Sat 8am–6pm; US$1/hr), also has internet call capabilities.

Accommodation

As a rule, the hotels on 5 Av Sur, on the west side of the bay, are in the safest part of town, but also the most expensive. You are perfectly safe in other areas, but it is riskier to go out at night. If you're hoping to get a room on a holiday weekend, it's best to book in advance.

Hotel Rick 5A Av Sur 30 ☎2335-3033. This traditional surfers' favourite is ideally located opposite Punta Roca. Rooms are all en suite, with cable TV and room for boards. There's a/c in some, but a slightly musty smell in others. US$20

Hotel Surf Club Inn C 2 Pte #22 ☎2346-1104. Spacious en-suite rooms, with a/c options (US$8 more), cable TV, kitchenette, refrigerator and internet, and laundry available in the building. It's probably the best budget deal in town. US$15

Mango's Lounge 4A C Pte between 1 & 3 Av Nte ☎2346-1626. A great budget option. The basic rooms have TV, surf racks and optional a/c, and there are sofas and internet in the good communal lounge. They also provide competitive board rental, tours and lessons. US$18

La Posada Familiar 3A Av Sur at C 4 Pte ☎2335-3252. Very friendly and popular place with basic rooms, some with bath, all with outdoor hammocks. They are just about the cheapest in town, but certainly not the cleanest. A small *comedor* serves meals and you can see the sea from the roof veranda. US$10

Eating and drinking

The dining-out scene in La Libertad is quite pricey but varied, with an inevitable emphasis on seafood (see box above). The more expensive restaurants are gathered at the new seafront esplanade at the western end of town, with live music at weekends, while savings can be made buying fresh fish and *ceviche* from the pier, and supermarket lunches.

La Dulce Vita Playa Las Flores, 200m past the Shell station ☎2335-3592. If you are going to shell out for seafood, this is the best place in town to do it, with giant platters and expertly cooked langoustines (US$18). There are also large pasta dishes for the energy-drained surfer, all served to great sea views.

El Buen Asado 3 Av Nte, by C El Calvario. The pick of the *pupuserías*, also serving good and sizeable bean, cheese and egg breakfasts (US$2).

Comedor Paty 2 Av Sur, by 2A C Ote. For huge juices (US$0.50) and *típicos*, this is your best choice in town.

El Delfin 5 Av Sur, opposite *Hotel Rick*. A good seafood joint closer to town, serving heaps of paella (US$9) for dinner and shrimp omelettes (US$4) for breakfast in nice surroundings on the western point.

Punta Roca 5 Av Sur ☎2335-4342, 🌐www .puntaroca.com.sv. A local institution, after which the break itself is named. There is hearty food with a Western nod (gringo fry US$7), and it is downright the best place for a Pilsener (US$1.25) in town.

Directory

Exchange C Barrios, between 4 & 6 Av Nte. This is the only ATM along the Costa del Bálsamo, so stock up.

Pharmacy Centro Médico Moises, C Barrios (Mon–Fri 7am–6pm, Sat 7am–noon; ☎2335-3531).

Post office 4A C Ote, between 2 & 4 Av Nte (Mon–Fri 8am–noon & 12.45–4pm, Sat 9am–noon).

Supermarket Supermercado de Todos, C Barrios, opposite the bank. It's the only supermarket along the Costa del Bálsamo, so stock up if you're camping.

Telephones Telecom (4A C Ote at 2 Av Sur) also has internet access.

Moving on

By bus to: La Perla, via all beaches including El Zonte and Km 59 (#192; every 30min; 1hr 30min); Playa San Diego, via Playa Las Flores and Parque Walter Deininger (#80; every 30min; 15min); Playa El Sunzal, via El Tunco (#80A/B; every 30min; 40min); San Salvador, Terminal de Occidente (#102; very frequent; 1hr); Sonsonate, via all beaches to the west (#287; 7 daily; 2hr 30min); Zacatecoluca

(#540; 7 daily; 1hr 20min) – change at Comalapa for the Costa del Sol.

COSTA DEL BÁLSAMO

Strung out on either side of Puerto La Libertad is the **COSTA DEL BÁLSAMO**, a favourite destination for surfers and day-trippers from the capital. The coast takes its name from the now-defunct trade in medicinal balsam that was once centred here, before tourism took over as the main source of income. More and more expensive beach clubs are now popping up, as international tourists gain confidence in El Salvador, but reasonable accommodation and surfing communities still dominate. **West** of La Libertad, the Carretera Litoral runs through thickly wooded hills and tunnels to palm-fringed black beaches. To the **east** the beaches are more disappointing, infringed upon by the expansion of the town; the sole exception is the surfer-free **Playa San Diego**, a quick escape from the intensity of La Libertad. All kilometre distances given are for the Carretera Litoral, along which there are markers to help you out. La Libertad is the transport hub for the area – see above for details of moving on from that town.

Playa El Tunco

The beaches just west of La Libertad are crowded with people and resorts. Beyond these, at km 42, **Playa El Tunco** has a much better atmosphere and the liveliest nightlife on the stretch. The beach here is pebble-strewn, but the waves draw plenty of surfers and it is a good spot for the inexperienced to learn the sport. A single road leads down from the Carretera through the village to a fork; a right here leads to the beachfront, with an array of surf shops (expect to pay US$10 for a day's board rental and US$10 for an hour's lesson; bodyboards are also available for US$4/hr and US$8/day), and a left takes you parallel to the beach.

Accommodation

Lining the estuary is a smattering of good accommodation.

Mangle ☎2389-6126. If *Papayas* is full, *Mangle* is similar in character though slightly more expensive. Spare a thought for the monkey on a chain in the back, however, and don't use the internet: it is fifty cents cheaper just across the road. US$19

Papayas ☎2389-6027, ⊛www.papayalodge.com. The best-value accommodation, with good communal space, including a treehouse-like roof terrace, a kitchen, DVDs and books. US$17

Roots Along the road parallel to the beach. *Roots* has its own tents to lend out and hosts renowned Saturday-night beach parties. Remember not to stray too far from the party at these events, as muggings have occurred on the beach. US$5

Tunco Lodge ☎2389-6318, ⊛www.tuncolodge .com/playa_el_tunco.html. For brand-new, spotless rooms, a pool and huge showers, check out this place, opposite *Mangle*. US$40

Eating and drinking

Hotel Roca Sunzal ☎2389-6126, ⊛www.roca sunzal.com. Go to this ritzy place on the beach, next to *Restaurante La Bocana*, only to eat *mariscada* (US$10); eating a meal here will allow you a few hours on their luxury poolside loungers.

Restaurante La Bocana On the beach. Serves huge seafood platters and ice-cold beers, accompanied by sporadic live music. The next-door *comedor* has similar fare, and also shows DVDs.

Playa El Sunzal

Wading across an ankle-deep estuary from El Tunco takes you to the long and wide black-sands of **Playa El Sunzal** (road access at km 44.5). For surfing, this is the best learners' beach in the country, with long, uncrowded breaks. It's also good for sunbathing, swimming and playing on the beach. While this is all easily accessible from Tunco (and Tunco's surf shops are accessible from here), staying here offers the benefit of a distinctly more laidback atmosphere.

Information

Internet Across the road from *Surfer's Inn*, Ciber Fox (8am–8pm; US$1/hr) has the fastest internet around.

Accommodation and eating

There is a string of *comedores* by the roadside.

Rancho Gladymar Right on the beach. Does a filling US$3 chicken, onion and tortilla meal and has US$1 beers.

San Patricio On the coast road, 250m from the beach ☎2389-6107, ⊛www.ranchosanpatricio .es.tl. More comfortable rooms than *Surfer's Inn*, with a splash pool. US$12

El Sunzalito Good breakfasts for US$1.25.

Surfer's Inn Just off the Carretera on the beach ☎2389-6266. This place has well-shaded camping and basic, concrete en-suite rooms with access to a kitchen and fridge. Camping US$6, doubles US$10

Playa El Zonte

Down a track just beyond the bridge at km 53, the small, surfer-dominated **Playa El Zonte** is a real gem, set apart by its stunning location between two high headlands and its friendly community vibe. Sparkling grey volcanic sands cover the beach in the dry season, but recede as the waves grow from March to October. The surf here is harder going for beginners than Sunzal and Tunco, better suiting those who are intermediate and above. However, this is no reason for non-surfers to avoid it, as anyone can enjoy the surroundings, swim and join evening games of football.

Accommodation and eating

Opposite *Esencia Nativa* on the beach, the nameless *comedor* does good, cheap burgers (US$2).

Costa Brava High on the cliffs at the western end of the beach. For great food, head to *Costa Brava*. Spanish owner Manel is a cable-TV chef and local celebrity, in view of which his big breakfasts (US$3) and excellent seafood dishes (US$6–10) are great value, though he is only usually there at weekends. He will also organize trips to his turtle sanctuary in the dry season.

Esencia Nativa On the right as you reach the beach ☎7337-8879. Pleasant rooms and dorms around a yard containing a pool, bar and pizza restaurant, as well as hammocks, airy upstairs terrace, plenty of reading material and table football. The owner, Alex Novoa, really knows his surfing and will organize rental (US$10/day) and

El Dorado Surf Resort
Playa El Zonte ☎7226-6166,
Ⓦwww.surfeldorado.com.
There is a great atmosphere
running through this top-notch
surfer haven with spotless,
comfortable rooms (ranging
from US$19 to US$90), starting
with welcoming Quebecois
owners Olly and Ben. Surfers
(and non-surfers) will find everything
they need – board hire, lessons,
longboard skateboards, even a
training pool – and the staff will even
help guests plan the rest of their
travels in the country. One of the
country's best treats. US$19

surf lessons (US$10/hr). He's also helping to revive
the local turtle population by setting up a protected
nursery (*vivero*) in the village. Dorms US$8,
doubles US$20

Playa San Diego

Some 5km east from La Libertad, the
beautiful **Playa San Diego**, with its
clean, light and seemingly endless
stretch of sand, is deserted during the
week except for a few fishermen. A
turtle-nesting reserve has recently been
set up here to help protect these endangered species. Views to the sea from the
road behind the beach are blocked by
ranks of private homes behind locked
gates, but if you get off the bus outside
the *San Diego Beach* restaurant, there's
a path just to the left of the nearby
Hotel Villa del Pacífico that leads down
to the sand.

Accommodation and eating

The cheap accommodation options are pretty poor,
but there are some good budget places to eat.
Costa Brava has similar prices and fare to *La
Fincita*, and two swimming pools as well.
La Fincita de Don Juan 1A C Pasaje #16. Serves
good-value chicken and steaks (US$3–5) as well as
the obligatory fish dishes.
Hotel Villa del Pacífico Right by the beach
☎2345-5681. If you are set on staying the
night, this is the place: a/c rooms with bath,

plus a restaurant and a pool set in manicured
gardens. US$50
El Pijon At the eastern end of the beach road. A
good spot for a beer.

Parque Nacional Walter Deininger

A little further east along the Carretera
Litoral, the **Parque Nacional Walter
Deininger** makes a welcome alternative
to beach pursuits. An extensive stretch
of **dry forest**, it is home to a range of
flora and fauna, including deer, falcons,
racoons and the torogoz, the national
bird. There's an 18km **trail** through the
park, though shorter routes can be
taken. Entry is US$0.80, but a guide
must accompany you at a fee of
US$11.50, so try to go in a group to
reduce costs. Technically, you should
also get permission from ISTU in San
Salvador (see p.248) before coming out
here, but pleading ignorance has been
known to work.

EL SALVADOR'S BEST HIDDEN BREAKS

Going **west** beyond El Zonte along
the Carretera Litoral are three more
great and often empty **surfing spots**.
Km 59, a right-hand beach and
point break, tubing when big (though
poor at low tide), is often compared
to Punta Roca, but without the
crowds. Around the corner, **Km 61**
has equally empty long breaks for
longboarders. Further along, **Playa
Mizata** at km 87 is a wave machine,
with point and beach breaks going
right and left. All three can be
reached on the #197 or #287 buses
from La Libertad.

In the **east** of the country, **Playa
Las Flores** (not to be confused
with the Las Flores right next to
La Libertad) has sandy right-hand
point breaks, but far more special is
Punta Mango, unreachable by car;
boat trips here can be organized at
Mango's Lounge in La Libertad
(see p.269).

ZACATECOLUCA

East of Playa San Diego, the Carretera Litoral swings inland to the small pre-Columbian, Nonualco city of **ZACATECOLUCA**, or Zacate, as it is known. Though it peacefully endured Spanish rule, it played a key role in 1833 in the indigenous revolt against El Salvador's newly independent rule, led by Anastasio Aquino. Today it is a pleasant place to lazily pass the time, though there is little to occupy go-getters here.

What to see and do

Apart from its big daily **market**, there's little of interest in Zacatecoluca except its proximity to the nearby beaches. The impressive, whitewashed Moorish **Catedral Santa Lucía** has good roof frescoes along with the usual doll-like statues. In front of the church stands a monument to the city's most famous son, **José Simeon Cañas**, the man responsible for the abolition of slavery across Central America. The cathedral is somewhat strangled by the jumble of market stalls around it, but if a priest is around he may let you climb the tower to see the marvellous **views** over the town and its volcano.

Arrival

By bus Buses arrive and depart from the bus station four blocks south of the Parque Central on Av J.V. Villacorte, except the Usulután bus, which stops only on the Carretera Litoral, two blocks further south.

Accommodation

Hotel Brolyn Av J.V. Villacorta #24 ☎ 2334-1084. A cheap option all round – the owner may proudly show you the switch that turns your cable into fuzzy pornography – but it's clean, en suite, has new mattresses and offers a/c. US$8
Primavera Av J.V. Villacorta #20 ☎ 2334-1346. Tidy rooms with good mattresses, bath, hammock and internet, plus a small pool, jacuzzi and table tennis are all available here. US$26

Eating

Golden Gate 5A C Ote between Av J.M. Delgado & Av J.V. Villacorta. A decent and cheap Chinese restaurant by the bus station. Noodles US$1.50.
Sorbetería Estrella Polar Av N Monterrey and 5A C Ote. Home-made ice cream draws young Zacatecolucans here on dates, but there's also decent vegetarian cooking on offer. *Caramel boule* US$0.50.
Verona's Pizza Off C Dr Molina. Freshly made crusty pizzas (US$5) in a very clean, white restaurant in an alley off the park. They're open 9am–8pm, so you can have pizza for breakfast.

Moving on

By bus to: Costa del Sol, via all beaches to La Puntilla (#193; twice hourly; 1hr 30min); La Libertad (#540; 7 daily; 2hr); San Salvador, Terminal del Sur (#133; every 15min; 1hr); San Vicente (#177; every 15min; 1hr); Usulután (#302; twice hourly; 1hr 30min).

COSTA DEL SOL

Due south of Zacatecoluca lies El Salvador's premier beach playground, the **COSTA DEL SOL**, a fifteen-kilometre peninsula with a strip of palm-fringed beaches on the southern side. The clean expanses of sand here are good for swimming, but guarded by a wall of development built seemingly to force you through a pay-to-enter beach resort to gain access. This and the widespread artificial price inflation might lead you to believe that this is an area that does not wish to accommodate travellers on a budget, but there are some exceptions.

San Marcelino to Playa Los Blancos

Behind **Playa San Marcelino**, the first beach along the strip, the rather plush *Costa del Sol Club* has swimming pools, sports facilities and a restaurant – try negotiating at the gate to be allowed in for the day. For an easier route to the water, continue some 3km east to **Playa Costa del Sol**, where a *parque recreativo* (daily 7am–6pm; US$0.90) rents

BOAT TRIPS AROUND THE ESTERO

A **boat trip** around the Estero is really the highlight of this section of coast. *Lancha* owners run trips from La Puntilla across to the **Isla de Tasajera**, around the mangrove swamps of the Estero and up the Río Lempa. You'll be approached by touts as soon as you step off the bus, but don't let yourself be led to a boat or you'll pay the "agent's" commission. It's better to go hunt a boat down yourself; it should cost about US$20, so try to get a group together to reduce costs.

cabañas for the day. A few kilometres further on, at km 64, is **Playa Los Blancos**.

Accommodation and eating

There are also a couple of small restaurants in Playa Costa del Sol.

Comedor Just past *Hotel Mila* (fifth along the row of eateries in the middle of the road). This nameless *comedor* does good burgers and stays open until late for fair-priced beers.

Haydee Mar About 50m before the *Hotel Mila* ☎2338-2046. This hotel has two pools, but is haunted by a deadly sense of kitsch. US$28

Mini Hotel y Restaurante Mila Playa Los Blancos ☎2338-2074. The area's best deal, with small but comfortable rooms, a swimming pool and beach access. US$28

La Puntilla

At the far eastern tip of the Costa del Sol, **La Puntilla** is an attractive array of thatch-and-bamboo beach settlements with a great view across the mouth of the **Estero de Jaltepeque**.

Accommodation and eating

There is cheap lodging here, but it is largely shockingly bad.

Rafael Antonio Right on the seashore by the entrance to the narrow spit. While at La Puntilla, it's well worth having seafood or oysters (US$5–8) while enjoying the views from the raised platform of *Rafael Antonio*, but check that they are in season. You can't miss the restaurant: it's the only two-storey platform there.

Rancho Playa Dorada At the end of the road ☎7141-8784. The best of the options available: the good *comida* (US$4 *coctel*), kind service and new pool compensate for the prison-like rooms and seatless toilet. US$15

USULUTÁN

East of Zacatecoluca, the Carretera Litoral crosses the Río Lempa at San Marcos Lempa before running through lush, green coffee country to the city of **USULUTÁN**, on the southern slopes of the volcano of the same name. Much like Zacatecoluca, it holds little interest except as a transit point en route to the **Bahía de Jiquilisco**, or a stepping stone on the journey further east; even the Carretera Litoral seems to bypass it, branching off through the centre and reforming again at its extremities. At the eastern fork, market stalls invade the tarmac; buses arrive and depart from here. The westbound lane then takes the name Calle Grimaldi as it heads to the centre of town, passing through the neatly pruned Parque Central six blocks west.

Accommodation and eating

La Posada del Viajero Calle 6 Ote between 2A and 4A Avenida Nte ☎2662-0217. Close to the centre, clean and friendly, with decent mattresses. US$12

Tortas Lito's Calle Dr F. Penado by 1 Avenida Nte. A good selection of big Mexican tacos and enchiladas. Open until 8pm.

Moving on

By bus to: Playa El Espino (#351; 7 daily; 1hr 30min); Puerto El Triunfo (#363; frequent; 1hr); San Miguel (#373; frequent; 1hr 40min); San Salvador (#302; frequent; 2hr 30min); San Vicente (#417; 6 daily; 2hr); Santiago de María, for transfers to Alegría (#392C, #35, #348 or #349; very frequent; 45min).

THE EASTERN BEACHES

Wider and wilder than their western counterparts, the eastern beaches seem to be over-visited by Salvadoreños at the weekend but under-visited by travellers during the week. The exception is El Cuco, where the busy beachside community is supplemented by large annual doses of surfers during the wet season. The whole stretch, however, offers you the chance to stay in beautiful surroundings where you are unlikely to see another traveller for days on end.

Puerto El Triunfo

About 20km southwest of Usulután, down a road lined with sugar-cane fields, is **Puerto El Triunfo**, a sketchy port set on the north shore of the **Bahía de Jiquilisco**, separated from the ocean by the San Juan del Gozo peninsula. Formed by coastal mangrove swamps, the beautiful bay features 12km of waterways and a number of islands. A long, fine sandy beach forms the ocean side of the peninsula, while floating platforms can be swum to from the bay-side beach.

Passenger boats (US$2) cross to El Icaco on **Corral de Mulas** on the peninsula, leaving when full, which happens much more regularly in the early morning; if you miss these, renting a boat can be costly – expect to pay up to US$35. Other than the Islas de Golfo de Fonseca, Corral de Mulas offers the best opportunity to engage in real Salvadoran life – it's a great place to walk and chat to locals, and as well as camping you can ask to stay with a family when here. In both cases ask at the *alcaldía* and they will help you out. Otherwise, the small, grubby *El Jardín* (T 2663-6089; US$12) between the pier and the bus station in Puerto El Triunfo, is a decent Plan B.

Moving on

By bus to: San Miguel (#377; every 40min; 3hr); San Salvador (#185; 6 daily; 2hr); Usulután (#363; every 10min; 1hr).

Playa El Espino

At the far eastern end of the Bahía de Jiquilisco is one of El Salvador's finest beaches, **Playa El Espino**. The once-remote beach has been developed, with a 26km paved road from the Carretera Litoral opening it up to visitors. Sadly, some of this redevelopment has taken a distinctly garish aspect. The beach itself remains a singular beauty, however, and the water is bathtub-warm.

Accommodation and eating

It is best to be in a group of four or five to stay cheaply on Espino. Book the hotels ahead at weekends. A whole host of *comedores* and basic restaurants sell similar fare, though prices for seafood are high and the quality is mixed.

Arcos del Espino At the entrance to the area next to the beach T 2608-0785. Has a/c, en-suite, spotless rooms and toilets, around a crystal-clear pool for four people. US$50

Natali To the right as you reach the beach. Takes five in their a/c and en-suite rooms – with use of a kitchen – including one in an indoor hammock. US$65

El Pacífico On the eastern side of the beach. Good for fried fish (US$4–10) and a beer on their relaxed and elevated terrace.

Rancho de Don Francisco On the other side of the beach. Good for solo travellers, this place rents out hammocks to sleep under the stars. US$5

Restaurant y Bar Bambú On the western side of the beach. This wicker barn has cheaper food than *El Pacífico*, and karaoke too, though it is only open Fridays to Sundays.

Moving on

By bus to: Usulután (#351 & #358B, changing at Jucurán to #358; 7 daily, last one back at 4pm; 1hr 45min).

Playa El Cuco

Some 30km east of Usulután the Carretera Litoral turns south, winding up through glorious mountain views before descending again towards the east's most famous beach community, **Playa El Cuco**. The village itself is rather ugly and manic, with a beach-front crowded by tourism opportunists.

The beaches to either side, however, are fantastic: the 300m breaks at **Las Flores** to the west, and the wide and empty peace of **El Esterón** to the east.

Information

Internet There is internet in the Centro de Internet on the main plaza in El Cuco village (US$1/hr).

Accommodation

Accommodation in the town is terrible, but there are good options to the east. A mini US-expat enclave has opened several good backpacker hostels in El Esterón recently, including *La Tortuga Verde* (see below). For longer stays, there two flats for rent, at the end of the road behind the beach. The smaller sleeps two in a simple room with bed, fan, window and bathroom next door (US$13), but the spacious larger flat (US$20), intended for four, has a fully equipped kitchen and roof terrace with hammocks and chairs overlooking the beach. Reserve them with local surf godmother Joan (☎7789-6312), who has spare mattresses if needed.

Cucolindo Closer to town along the road ☎2619-9012. This beach-fronted place is a decent budget option, with clean rooms. US$30

La Tortuga Verde ☎7774-4855, ✉latortugarest @yahoo.com. This is a funky little place, run by Tom from California. Right on the seafront, it has sand floors, arty hidden lighting and a restaurant overlooking the beach. They also have *lanchas* that will take you to Las Flores and other nearby surfing beaches. Dorms sleeping up to 10 US$10, doubles with a/c US$50

Eating

Fresh fish should be bought from the El Cuco co-operative, in El Cuco village.

Comedor At the end of the beach road and down the right-hand cul-de-sac. This unnamed *comedor* has a tradition of excellent fish.

La Gimelos The stall on the left as you approach the end of the beach road. The best local fish is sold at this fried-fish stall (US$3), known as *La Gimelos*.

Rasta Pasta ☎7789-6312. Joan – American owner of nearby *Rancho Amor del Mar* – feeds weary surfers in a restaurant run from a summer house in her plant nursery in Esterón. The sign outside says *Federicos*, but it's known as *Rasta Pasta*, as she serves lasagna, canelloni and pasta (US$8) to the sound of reggae (Fri–Sun only).

Moving on

By bus to: San Miguel (#320; twice hourly; for La Unión transfer at El Delirio; 1hr 30min). The ride is one of the finest bus journeys in the country, with spectacular views of the valleys and the ineffable Volcán San Miguel; sit on the right side of the bus on the way to El Cuco for the best view.

Intipucá

Beyond El Cuco, the highway runs parallel to the coastline, passing a turn-off for the spotless little town of **Intipucá**. More Intipucans live in Washington, DC, than in Intipucá, and remittances per head here are more than any other place in the country. This is evident: relaxed, safe and entirely paved, with phonebooths and money-wire companies encircling the plush Parque Central, it would be a perfect place to stay – if there was a hotel. It's worth having a look nonetheless, as the town is starting to awaken to tourism. There is a good Italian (spaghetti Bolognese US$6) and *típicos* **restaurant**, *Torentinos*, overlooking the *parque* on the south-western corner.

Buses run direct to La Unión (#339; 8 daily; 1hr 30min), passing beaches further east, and from the highway to San Miguel (#385; twice hourly; 1hr 30min), passing the turning to El Cuco. Buses and pick-ups also go direct to El Esterón (10min) or the highway (5min).

Playa Las Tunas and Playa El Tamarindo

Further east along the Carretera, past the featureless Playa El Icacal, another turn-off heads along a tooth-like peninsula pointing out across the mouth of the Golfo de Fonseca. **Playa Las Tunas** is the first beach that you encounter, with a fine dark-sand beach and tides that wash right up into the village. It has a friendly atmosphere to it, and, budget-wise, it is your best option for accommodation on a beach between Cuco and La Unión. There's a small village here with several restaurants.

The final beach on the peninsula, **Playa El Tamarindo**, is a panorama-lover's dream. The huge golden arc of sand, backed by uninterrupted palm trees, curves around the mountainous bay; sitting beneath the Volcán de Conchagua, the islands of the Golfo de Fonseca loom large, and in the distance the mountainsides of Honduras are clearly visible.

Arrival

By bus Buses to La Unión run along the peninsula, passing through Las Tunas as well (#383; three hourly); the last one back leaves at 5pm.
By boat For a much more interesting shortcut to El Tamarindo, take a boat from the pier at El Embarcadero (US$0.25) on the Carretera Litoral.

Accommodation and eating

Hotel Restaurant Buenos Aires At the bend in the road a few yards past the entrance to the village of Playa La Tunas ☎2681-5581. Basic, air-conditioned rooms and good grilled fish (US$3–5) served in the restaurant. US$45
Rancho Las Tunas Playa La Tunas ☎2526-5542. The highlight of the restaurants, not only perched on a rock with water rushing around it at high tide, but also the best place for oysters (US$5) in the area. They also have two overpriced rooms on the beach side. US$35
Tropitamarindo Playa El Tamarindo ☎2649-5082. The only accommodation on the beach is too pricey for what are little more than standard mid-range rooms, but they will let you use the pool and loungers if you spend US$10, so it's a good spot for beers and food. US$80

LA UNIÓN

The port town of **LA UNIÓN** sits in a stunning location on a bay on the edge of the Golfo de Fonseca. Faded since its glory days of colonial naval trade, La Unión's web of low white houses crumble a little further every day in the ferocious heat. There are no particular attractions here to detain most visitors, but the town is a useful jumping-off point for trips around the bay and to the beautiful islands of the Golfo de Fonseca. Shops are scarce on the islands, and prices high, so it's worth stocking up before you go. The town has several banks, supermarkets and of course the ubiquitous fast-food takeaways. The Parque Central has benefitted from a recent facelift, with a new lick of paint on its tin-roofed bandstand, and shady trees offer a little shelter from the sun. A new stone jetty saves *lancha* passengers the inconvenience of wading out to the boats in knee-deep gloopy sludge at low tide. The new deep-sea port at **Puerto Cutuco**, the largest Pacific port in Central America, virtually contiguous with La Unión, has yet to bring the industry and prosperity it promises. Until it does – though there are no guarantees – the atmosphere around the town is muted but not unfriendly.

Arrival

By boat *Lanchas* from the islands of the Golfo de Fonseca arrive on the pier jutting out from the northern end of 3A Av Nte.
By bus The main bus terminal is on C 3 Pte, 4–6A Av Nte, two blocks west and one north of the Parque Central. If you're travelling from the coastal highway, you will need the Terminal Los Cantones, two blocks south and one block west of the main terminal, on C San Carlos.

Accommodation

El Dorado C San Carlos & 2A Av Nte ☎2604-4724. The price and the pleasant, mango tree-filled courtyard will easily compensate for the soft mattresses and tatty en-suite bathrooms. There are fans and hammocks in the rooms and you can ask for extra beds to cram in economically. US$10
Portobello 4A Av Nte at C 1 Pte ☎2604-4115. The best-value a/c rooms in a very hot town are here, right in the thick of it. Large, clean rooms with partitioned baths in the rooms and good beds. US$25

Eating and drinking

Captain John's 3A Av Sur & C 4 Ote. The captain is proprietor of a pleasant outdoor terrace, where a wide choice of fish steaks, including marlin, sailfish and wahoo, are served in huge portions. Try the *tazón de sopa de pescado* (US$5).
Maurita's C 3 Pte at Av Cabañas. The closest you'll come to a pavement café, with a large covered veranda from which to watch the street activity. The

local favourite serves marinated seafood, *ceviche* (US$4) and your typical *típicos*.

El Viajero C Menéndez, just off the Parque. A cavernous *comedor* next to the Despensa Familiar supermarket. Best for its cooked breakfasts of coffee, egg, cheese, fried plantains and beans (US$2).

Directory

Exchange Banco Agrícola, C 1 Pte & Av General Cabañas, or Scotiabank, 1A Av Nte, one block downhill from the *parque*; both change money and have 24hr ATMs.

Immigration At Av Cabañas at 7 C Pte (℡2604-4375). Ask here about the party boat to Honduras (see box below) and the planned ferry service to Nicaragua from the new port (see "Moving on", below).

Internet Meg@byte, C 1 Pte between 2A & 4A Av Nte, is the cheapest and latest opening of the bunch (US$1/hr).

Supermarket The large Despensa Familiar, on the southeast corner of the *parque*, is open daily until 6 or 7pm.

Telephone Telecom is on C 1 Ote at 5A Av Nte, two blocks east of the *parque*.

Moving on

By boat to: Isla Meanguera (1 daily, departs after 9.30am, when full; 45min; US$3); Isla Zacatillo (1 daily; 30min; US$3).

By bus and boat to: Nicaragua. A new combined bus and boat service goes to León, Nicaragua, and Suchitoto and San Miguel, including a stop at the *Hotel Joya del Golfo* (see opposite) on Isla Meanguera. Departs on Sat; US$90. See ⓦwww .crucedelgolfo.com for details and reservations.

By bus There are plenty of buses from here to the beaches to the south – El Cuco in particular is developing a thriving US expat community, with several backpacker hostels – and to the north. Buses from the Terminal los Cantones to:

Conchagua (#382; 4 daily; 30min); El Tamarindo, via El Embarcada and Las Tunas (#383; every 20min; 1hr 30min); Intipucá (#339; 8 daily; 1hr 15min). Buses from main bus terminal to: San Miguel (#324; very frequent; 1hr); San Salvador (#304; twice hourly; 2hr 30min); Santa Rosa de Lima (#342; every 15min; 1hr 30min) – change here for the Honduran border at El Amatillo. There are also luxury buses to: San Miguel (#304 and others, frequent departures all day; 40min); San Salvador (#304);3 daily at 4am, 6am & 12.30pm; 2hr).

AROUND LA UNIÓN

La Unión's surrounding attractions – namely, the islands of the **Golfo de Fonseca** – put its heat into quite some relief. If you visit the tranquil and rustic Isla Meanguera you will have to spend the night in one of its good hotels because of ferry times, but you will doubtless want to do that anyway.

Islas del Golfo de Fonseca

Four delightfully secluded **islands** – Conchagüita, Martín Pérez, Meanguera and Zacatillo – sit out in the **Golfo de Fonseca** under the stewardship of El Salvador. **Conchagüita** was sacked by English pirates in 1682 and the island remained deserted until the 1920s, when settlers finally began moving back. In its centre, on the Cerro del Pueblo Viejo, are the remains of a tiny pre-Columbian settlement; a path to the north of the ruins leads up to a large rock bearing engravings that some believe is a map of the gulf. Even now you can see fairer, blue-eyed, pirate descendants among the islands' inhabitants, and rumour has it

---

LA UNIÓN'S PARTY BOAT

A **party boat** (℡2604-2222) leaves La Unión at 10am on Saturdays and Sundays for a cruise of the bay, with plenty of beer, a karaoke machine and a fairly lame pool. It rarely stops at the islands, but you can enjoy the breathless gulf views and the devil-may-care atmosphere aboard.

One Saturday a month the boat sets off at 8.30am on a longer tour that stops at Amapala, on the Honduran island of El Tigre. From here, regular ferries make the trip back to Coyolitos on the Honduran mainland. To use this route, phone ahead (℡2604-2222), and visit the immigration office in La Unión on Av Cabañas at 7 C Pte (℡2604-4375).

that Sir Francis Drake buried a stash of Spanish silver while at anchor on **Meanguera**. There are still plenty of secluded coves to explore, as well as good swimming and boundless scope for hiking. For fantastic views of the surroundings, climb Cerro de Evaristo, the highest peak on Meanguera. The best **beach** on the islands, El Majahual, is also on Meanguera. Wide, secluded and black sand, it can be reached on foot in 45 minutes by the road south of town and the track it turns into, or by boat in ten minutes if you can persuade a *lancha* owner. For bird lovers, the small, outlying **Isla Meanguerita** can only be reached by *lancha*. **Isla Zacatillo**, the nearest island to La Unión, has a small fishing settlement and a few unremarkable beaches; tiny **Martín Pérez**, just beyond, has some sandy coves, but no facilities for visitors.

Arrival

By ferry Morning ferries leave from La Unión for Meanguera (US$3) and Zacatillo (US$2.50) between 9 and 10am. The only ferry back from Meanguera departs at 6am, so unless you plan to charter a private boat you will have to stay overnight.
By lancha Local boatmen will rent out a *lancha* for the day at a non-negotiable US$80 per boatload, though you can commandeer one on the islands for a little less.

Accommodation and eating

The smaller islands – Conchagüita, Zacatillo and Martín Pérez – have no accommodation, but Meanguera is a terrific getaway spot. There are two good backpacker hostels here, with little difference

TREAT YOURSELF

Hotel Joya del Golfo ☎2648-0072, ⊛www.hotellajoyadelgolfo .com. Reservations are essential for this place, ten minutes' walk up the hill from Meanguera's harbour. It has four wonderful rooms (a/c, cable TV) and an excellent restaurant, plus kayaks, a *lancha* to beaches (US$10) and extremely friendly US–Salvadoran owners. US$80

between them, and both have great seafood restaurants with shellfish under US$4; they're close enough together to compare. Otherwise, *comedores* in the village serve fresh seafood, delivered daily by a colourful fishing fleet that floats in the bay.
El Mirador Meanguera ☎2648-0072. This pretty hostel has spotless rooms with hard mattresses, en-suite baths, cable TV and perhaps a fractionally better view than *El Paraíso*. US$21
El Paraíso Meanguera ☎2648-0145. Older rooms, cable TV and en-suite baths with the elusive hot-water shower. US$23

Conchagua

Looming to the south of La Unión is **Volcán Conchagua** (1243m), with beautiful views across the gulf to Nicaragua and Honduras. The friendly village of **Conchagua**, sitting on its northern slopes, was founded by the inhabitants of Conchagüita at the end of the seventeenth century. The climate is fresher here, a pleasant relief from the heat of La Unión, and walks around the village let you enjoy the scenery and possibly get chatting to the townsfolk. From Conchagua pick-ups will take you to the lookout point up the volcano, where there are short and long walking routes, camping (US$5) and simple accommodation with shared bathrooms (US$13) at a spectacular spot near the summit of the volcano. Take **bus** #382A from the Terminal los Cantones in La Unión (5 daily; 15min).

The east

The rough and wild terrain of **eastern El Salvador** remained relatively unexplored territory for the pre-Columbian Pipils, who did not venture far beyond the natural frontier of the Río Lempa into this land of lofty volcanoes, hot plains and mountain ranges. As a result, its Lenca inhabitants developed their society in isolation from the west, and it was only with some difficulty that the Spanish conquered this frontier. Today, coffee production around the region's major cities, the earthquake-damaged **San Vicente** and bustling **San Miguel** create a wealth that contrasts cruelly with the rural poverty found further north. Along the **Ruta de Paz**, refugees from communities devastated by the civil war – this region saw the worst of the fighting – have in the last two decades returned to try and pick up the pieces in this wild and beautiful area. Some, particularly in Perquín and El Mozote, have turned to "war tourism" as a viable new occupation, but their ongoing struggle with poverty is often still painfully apparent.

Around San Vicente are several delightful villages, including the flower-filled mountain town of **Alegría** and the brilliant pottery centre of **Guatajiagua**. Buses head north along the mountainous Ruta de Paz to the former guerrilla stronghold of **Perquín**, with its terrific war museum, and the haunting and unmissably sad village of **El Mozote**, scene of the conflict's most horrific massacre.

COJUTEPEQUE

Past Lago de Ilopango to the east, the Carretera Interamericana flies past the up-and-coming Sunday retreat of **COJUTEPEQUE**. There's little to see in the actual town, but half-an-hour's walk up the Cerro de las Pavas to the south is the shrine of the **Virgen de Fátima** of Portugal, a statue brought here in 1949 that attracts worshippers from across the region. For those who also worship food, a Sunday **food festival** to rival Juayúa's weekend festival (see p.305) has successfully been set up on the Cerro, with the imperious summit as a backdrop. **Bus** #113 goes to San Salvador (frequent; 2hr) – get off on the highway for #301 to San Miguel or other services to towns further east.

ILOBASCO

Some 6km beyond Cojutepeque, a road branches north off the highway through beautiful rolling countryside to the small town of **ILOBASCO**, noted for its brightly painted earthenware decorated with animals and everyday scenes. The town's hallmark pieces are known as *sorpresas* (surprises) – detailed scenes of village life contained in small, clay shells like humble Fabergé eggs. The government arts organization **Cedart**, on Avenida Bonilla, has a small exhibition on the evolution of ceramic art in the town, and a collection of products in its shop; they'll direct you to a potter you like, or you can just stroll around and look in. Further down the avenida, *Italyan Pizza* cooks much better than it spells, with good Mexican fare as well as pizzas (US$5). If you have to stay, *Hotel Ilobasco*, 4A C Pte (☎2332-2563; US$20) is friendly, though tatty and overpriced. **Bus** #111 (frequent; 1hr 30min) is the nominal service to San Salvador, but from the highway you can catch the quicker #301 to destinations along it in either direction.

SAN SEBASTIÁN

Between Ilobasco and San Vicente, a paved road leads off the Interamericana to the small village of **SAN SEBASTIÁN**, famous for its hammocks, patterned cloth sheets and bedspreads. The first place to start learning about the traditions and mind-bending patience involved in the town's chosen craft is the **Casa de la Cultura** on Calle Molina (Mon–Fri 8am–4pm). Several **weaving shops** around town will let you watch the goods being produced on simple wooden looms, though you will be pressured into buying. One of the oldest and best shops is Casa Durán, just off C Molina on 12A Av Nte (Mon–Fri 9.30am–5.30pm). Soft **hammocks** are the prize item; compare prices and materials, then bargain before handing over any money. **Bus** #110 goes to San Salvador twice hourly and #176 goes to San Vicente four times a day.

SAN VICENTE

SAN VICENTE was founded in 1635 by fifty local Spanish families in accordance with the 1600 Law of the Indies, which prohibited the Spanish from living among the indigenous people. This division brought violence to the city in 1833, when the forces of Anastasio Aquino, leader of a Nonualco indigenous uprising, stormed the city. "Inebriated with alcohol and success", the rebels removed the crown from the statue of San José in the Iglesia El Pilar and crowned Aquino "Emperor of the Nonualcos". The rebels then returned to Santiago Nonualco, some 30km away; here, Aquino was captured by government forces on April 23 and later sent back to San Vicente and hanged. Nowadays San Vicente is a calm, low-slung city with a rich agricultural area producing sugar cane, cotton and coffee. The town still has a conspicuous military presence – the barracks are at the southwestern corner of the Parque Central – rivalled only by the number of American Peace Corps trainees, who come here to prepare for forthcoming missions.

What to see and do

The centrepiece of the Parque Central is the **Torre Kiosko**, an eye-catching open-fronted clock tower. Resembling a miniature Eiffel Tower, it was actually inspired by the Parisian monument. Although climbing it is no longer permitted (the 2001 earthquake rendered it rather lame), it is still ticking.

Two blocks south of the *parque* on Avenida María de los Angeles is the **Iglesia El Pilar**, built in 1769 on the site where a miraculous shaking statue of the Virgin Mary persuaded one Manuela Arce not to stab her husband, or so it's told. Now restored after the earthquake damage, you can enter the building. The statue of San José, complete with crown, stands in a glass case behind the altar as you walk in.

An extensive **market** stretches over several streets to the west of the big green army barracks. In most respects pretty much like any other market, this one also sells the famous hammocks made in nearby towns such as San Sebastián, adding a notable splash of colour to the town.

Arrival

By bus The station is on C 8 Pte and 15A Av Sur, a long walk southwest of the centre, but all buses pass the Parque Central going in or out, so watch out for the tower of the Torre Kiosko and get off there.

Accommodation

As well as the places below, there are also some basic guesthouses in the centre of town.
Casa de Huéspedes El Turista C 4 Pte 15 ☎2393-0323. The best option in town has simple rooms with fans around a leafy courtyard, with a good roof terrace. It's worth paying US$2 more for a private bathroom and cable TV, as the shared toilets aren't up to the same standard. US$15
Hotel Central Park On the west side of the Parque Central ☎2393-0383. Rooms are not tasteful, and en suites are a bit garish, though most have a/c and firm beds. There's a bar with pleasant communal balcony offering views of the *parque*, and the restaurant serves well-priced *típicos* until 10pm. US$13

Eating and drinking

There are a number of bars around the park as well as good eating options around town.
Casa Blanca 2 C Ote. Meat and fish dishes including *codorniz* (quail; US$7) served in a lovely shaded garden that doubles as a good place for an evening drink.
Dany's 4A C Pte just off Av C Miranda. Serves big portions of your typical Americanized cuisine (hamburgers, tacos, pizzas; US$5) in a nice venue with wooden tables.
Pupusería Av C Miranda. This nameless *pupusería* does a range of good *pupusas* every night and also sells US$1 beers.
Pupusería Thea 1A Av Sur #68. A pretty place, with fairies on the walls. The best treats, though expensive, are worth it for their eccentricity: "golden nuggets" (US$9), and a steaming home-made brew, known as "gloín" (US$4).

Rivoly's On 1A Av Sur. A real treat of a *comedor a la vista* with big, fresh and tasty meat meals such as *pollo con arroz* (chicken with rice; US$3) on spick-and-span orange tables. It also does good breakfasts.

Directory

Exchange Banco Agrícola on the Parque Central, and a Scotiabank on the corner of 1A Av Nte and C Quiñonez de Osorio.

Internet Matrix on C 2 Ote by 2A Av Sur is fast, with web-based call equipment (US$0.75/hr).

Pharmacy Santa Fé II, 4 C Ote (℡2393-6726), serves after 9pm if you ring the bell.

Post office The office, with regular opening times, is on C 1 de Julio, one block south of the *parque*.

Telephones Telecom office is just off the corner of the *parque* opposite the De Todo supermarket.

Moving on

By bus to: Carretera Interamericana, for #301 between San Salvador and San Miguel (#157; frequent; 10min); Costa del Sol (#193E; 4 daily; 2hr 30min); Ilobasco (#530; 3 daily; 1hr); San Salvador (#116; frequent; 1hr 30min); Usulután (#417; 6 daily; 2hr); Zacatecoluca (#177; every 15min; 50min).

AROUND SAN VICENTE

Near San Vicente is one of the most memorable-looking volcanoes in the country, the **Volcán Chichontepec**, which rises up into twin craters, while on the other side of town is the peaceful picnic spot of the **Laguna de Apastepeque**.

Volcán Chichontepec

San Vicente is dominated by the towering bulk of **Volcán Chichontepec** (also known as Volcán San Vicente) to the southwest. Meaning "Hill of Two Breasts" in Nahuatl, the twin peaks rise to 2182m, making it the second-highest volcano in the country. It's considered dormant, with cultivated lower slopes and the steep summit left to scrub and soil. A number of paths lead up the slopes from both the village of **San Antonio** on the east side and from **Guadelupe** on the northwest flank.

It's a stiff walk of around three hours to the top from any of the trails, and good walking shoes, sun protection and lots of water are essential. From the summit there are panoramic views north across the Jiboa valley, with San Vicente nestled at the bottom, and west across to Lago de Ilopango. **Buses** to San Antonio and Guadelupe leave every hour or so until mid afternoon from San Vicente's market.

Laguna de Apastepeque

Laguna de Apastepeque, 3km northeast of the city (bus #156), is a small, well-maintained *parque recreativo* (daily 8am–6pm; US$0.90) set around a crater lake with clean blue water and shady banks. It's a great place to relax in the hammock you just bought, read and swim, though the good swimming makes this an extremely popular spot among families at weekends. If you don't bring a picnic there are unremarkable *comedores* around, and the *parque recreativo* has toilets and changing facilities.

ALEGRÍA

At El Triunfo on the Carretera Interamericana a road leads south to Usulután, passing the pleasant town of Santiago de María, from where a steep road leads up the slopes of Volcán Tecapa to the floral haven of **ALEGRÍA**. The highest town in El Salvador, it offers predictably great views, and is also home to an extraordinary number of flower nurseries – it simply erupts with blossoms during orchid season. Paths lead up the volcano from town to the sulphurous **Laguna de Alegría**, a crater lake whose hot and cold waters will strip you of your dead skin if you can take the smell. It is an energetic walk of about one hour – try to get there at 4pm when the water is at its highest. The surrounding area is predominantly coffee-growing country, and occasionally beans can be seen drying on the streets.

Arrival and information

By bus Buses stop on C Masferrer, a hundred metres or so to the west of the Parque Central.
Internet *Café Casa Vieja*, on 1 Av Nte at C Masferrer, is a quaint little café on the *parque* that has fast internet for US$0.80/hr.
Tourist information Alegriá has a real, live tourist kiosk at the southwestern corner of the Parque Central, offering maps, accommodation, tours and flower information.

Accommodation

Casa Alegre Av C Campos ☎ 7201-8641. The coolest place to stay, with firm beds in clean rooms with a shared bathroom below the studio of the artists that own it. US$14
Casa del Huésped la Palma On the east side of the Parque Central ☎ 2628-1012. The friendly old owners here have lovingly maintained the original old-fashioned decor. Bed sizes and firmness (in shared rooms) varies. A better deal for solo travellers, as rates are per person. US$8
Hostal Tecupa 3 C Ote ☎ 2628-1093. The rooms are quite chabby, but there's good *comida* served in the flowery courtyard, a very clean toilet and shower. US$8

Eating and drinking

Café Expresso Southeast corner of the *parque*. A classy place for a coffee (US$0.75). Nice breakfasts served until late morning.
Casa de Mi Abuelo 4A Av Nte & C M. Aranjo. This streetside *comedor* and *tienda* serves ice cream, milkshakes and beers (US$1). Cool off or chill out on the shaded seating.
Christina's 4A Av Sur & Pasaje Grimaldi. The best *pupusería* in town, with a *chicharrón*-filled option (US$0.50) that is well above average.
Merendero Mi Pueblito Opposite the *alcaldía* on C A. Masferrer. The town's vogue restaurant, possibly because of the jaw-dropping views all the way to the northern border from its own *mirador*, but also perhaps for its big portions (*pollo dorado* US$4) and veg options.

Moving on

By bus to: Santiago de María (#348; every 30min; 15min); change here for Usulután (#362; frequent; 45min) and the Carretera Interamericana (#362; frequent; 10min).

SAN MIGUEL

Some 135km from San Salvador, the bustling, hot and flat city of **SAN MIGUEL** is the country's main trade centre. Initially the least important of the Spanish cities, it grew wealthy, firstly through the profits of gold, and then on the coffee, cotton and *henequén* grown on the surrounding fertile land, leading to the nickname "The Pearl of the East". More recently it was a centre of arms trading during the civil war, though today the city's grimy streets hum and rattle with more mundane forms of commerce and travellers will find the sort of facilities offered in the capital, albeit on a smaller scale. But despite being the birthplace of several national heroes, the city is surprisingly short on sights and attractions. The best time to visit is during the November **Carnaval**, a huge and free event, supposedly the biggest in Central America. In any case it is the pivot of the east: a base for the beaches to the south or a stopover on journeys to Perquín and the Honduran border.

What to see and do

The city is laid out in the usual quasi-grid system, with the main avenida (Av Gerardo Barrios/Av José Simeón Cañas) and the main calle (C Chaparrastique/C Sirama) intersecting at **Parque Gerardo Barrios**, the Parque Central.

Parque David J. Guzmán

Although Parque Barrios is technically the central plaza, the heart of San Miguel – and a much better place to sit – is the shady **Parque David J. Guzmán**, a block away to the northeast. It was named after the eminent nineteenth-century Migueleño biologist and member of the French Academy of Science, though his former residence on C 4 Pte lays derelict.

On the east side of the Parque Guzmán sits the **cathedral**, built in the 1880s. Despite a modern makeover, it

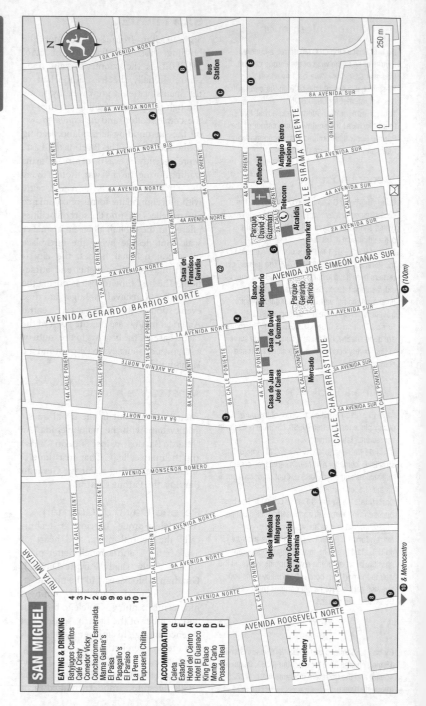

SAN MIGUEL

EATING & DRINKING

Batyjugos Carlitos	4
Café Cristy	3
Comedor Vicky	7
Conchadromo Esmeralda	2
Mama Gallina's	6
El Paisa	9
Papagallo's	8
El Paraiso	5
La Pema	10
Pupuseria Chilita	1

ACCOMMODATION

Caleta	G
Estadio	E
Hotel del Centro	A
Hotel El Guanaco	C
King Palace	B
Monte Carlo	D
Posada Real	F

NUESTRA SEÑORA DE LA PAZ

San Miguel's imposing cathedral, while rather disappointing inside, holds the cherished statue of Nuestra Señora de la Paz, the city's patroness. Though accounts differ as to how and when the statue arrived in the city, it is generally held that her true moment of glory came during the eruption of Volcán Chaparrastique on September 21, 1787. On seeing a glowing river of lava advancing on San Miguel, the terrified citizens, praying to the Virgin to save them, took the statue to the door of the cathedral and presented her to the volcano. The lava changed course and the city was saved. In honour of these events, San Miguel holds two months of fiesta, beginning with the Virgin "descending" the volcano on September 21 and culminating in a procession through the streets, attended by thousands, on November 21. A more recent coda to the fiesta is the annual Carnaval held on the last Saturday in November, when free live music, fireworks and street dancing dominate the whole town. Instituted in 1958, it has quickly grown to be the largest carnival in Central America (or so locals like to claim). If you're around during the festival look out for people wandering around holding large plastic iguanas aloft – the locals are nicknamed *garroberos* (iguana eaters) due to their penchant for the lizard's meat.

is still an impressive building, with a cast-iron statue of Christ bearing his crown of thorns standing between two red-roofed bell towers. Inside it is rather bare, but offers a blissfully cool refuge from the grimy heat outside, with the famed statue of **Nuestra Señora de la Paz** (see box above) above the altar.

Just south of the cathedral is the **Antiguo Teatro Nacional**, a honey-coloured Renaissance-style building completed in 1909. It's closed during the day but evening performances occasionally take place here, particularly during fiesta time; check the *Prensa Gráfica* at weekends. On the south side of the square, the colonnaded **Alcaldía** (town hall), dating from 1935, is in serious need of renovation.

Iglesia Capilla Medalla Milagrosa

Of the few other minor sights within town, the most appealing is the Gothic **Iglesia Capilla Medalla Milagrosa**, located at the western end of Calle 4 Pte where it joins 7A Avenida Sur. The church was built by French nuns working in the hospital that once stood next door, and is known for its beautiful stained-glass windows, best seen on a clear evening. Its pretty gardens have become overgrown and neglected, but hopefully will be restored along with the church (refurbishment ongoing at the time of writing).

Arrival and information

By bus Buses arrive at the well-ordered main terminal on C 6 Ote between 8A & 10A Av Nte, four blocks (or a 10-minute walk) east of the centre.
Tourist information There is no official tourist office, but staff at the Alcaldía (town hall) on the south side of Parque David J. Guzmán will help you with quick questions. During Carnaval, contact the Comite de Festejos de San Miguel for programme details (☎2660-1326 or 2661-9100, ⊛www .sanmiguelencarnaval.com.sv).
Internet Access is available at the Euro Cyber Café, part of the Academía Europea at Av Roosevelt 300 Sur (US$1/hr) or Infocentros, 6 C Pte, in town, for the same price.

Accommodation

The majority of accommodation clusters around the bus terminal, inevitably a rather sleazy area. There are posher hotels away from the city centre, mostly along Av Roosevelt Sur, but you'll have to pay a bit more.
Caleta 3A Av Sur 601 between C 9 & 11 Pte ☎2661-3233. Clean and quiet hotel, popular with business travellers during the week. There's a small courtyard with hammocks, and some rooms have private bath. Staff can also help arrange surf trips to secluded beaches. US$13

Estadio 4 C Ote ☎2660-2734. A clean and friendly place behind the bus terminal (not as noisy as hotels by the bus station entrance) named after the football stadium 100m further up the road, offering dark but clean little rooms with TV and either a/c or fan. US$8

Hotel del Centro C 8 Av 505 at 8A Av Nte ☎&℉2661-5473. This very friendly, helpful and spotlessly clean hotel is the best of the cheaper options around the bus terminal. The rooms are smallish but well arranged, with cushions on beds and bedside lights; all rooms have bath and TV. There's free internet for guests and US$0.40 laundry washes. US$13

Hotel El Guanaco 8A Av Nte Pje Madrid ☎2661-8026, ℉2660-6403. A giant hotel with gaudy green paintwork and kitsch cowboy decor. It has big, airy and clean en-suite rooms all with a/c and cable TV, and is a better deal for groups, with an equally oversized three double-bed room for US$40. Meals are served in the restaurant opposite. US$20

King Palace C 6 Ote ☎2661-1086. Good-value and professional hotel opposite the bus terminal, with a glitzy mirrored-window facade. The clean rooms are en suite, some with balcony, cable TV, a/c and telephone. Secure parking, restaurant, fast internet, laundry, swimming pool and rooftop gym and pool also available. US$30

Monte Carlo 4 C Ote 610 ☎2660-2737. Another near-terminal budget option, this one has very firm beds (some with Doric bedsteads), with mattresses that are quite thin in the rooms without a/c but better in the a/c rooms. Basic, and staff can be offhand, but just about acceptable. US$13

🏃 **Posada Real** 7A Av Nte at 2 C Pte ☎2661-7174/5/7/8/9. A few blocks from the hectic city centre, and close to the restaurants and nightlife along Av Roosevelt, this spotless two-storey hotel has big rooms with great beds, clear cable TV and access to a patio on the second storey. Off-road parking available. They'll wash and iron clothes for US$0.30/item. US$30

Eating

There are plenty of established places to eat in San Miguel, and new ones are popping up all the time, particularly on Av Roosevelt Sur, so it's worth gambling on unknowns. Local bakeries also sell *tustacos*, a local speciality resembling a sweet tortilla.

Batyjugos Carlitos 1A Av Nte & C 4 Pte. Carlito serves excellent snacks and lunches in an intimate, colourful downstairs and roomier first floor. His speciality is a wide range of big *licuados* (US$0.70).

Café Cristy 5A Av Nte at 6 C Pte. This classy-looking canteen has an airy feel and bustles with

patrons. The menu is standard *típicos*, but good at the price (*pollo con arosa* US$2).

Comedor Vicky 7A Av Nte. A small, friendly *comedor* that does an ice-cold, freshly squeezed orange juice (US$1.50) and cooked breakfast. The *sopa Gallina India* (US$2.50) is fine for lunch too.

Conchadromo Esmerelda 6A Av Nte between C 4 & 6 Ote. Good, basic breakfasts and *comidas a la vista*. One of a clutch of similar places in a former car park. Closed Sun.

El Paraíso Parque Guzmán. Well-prepared *pupusas* and *comidas a la vista* (US$3) are dished out in an attractive colonial building in a conveniently central location. Prices are low and quality is good. Steer clear of the juices though; they are surprisingly horrible.

Pupusería Chilita C 8 Ote at 6A Av Nte. A barn of a neighbourhood *pupusería*, particularly popular at weekends. The *pupusas* are good, but there's also a decent selection of *comidas a la vista*. Seating is available on a breezy terrace at the back. Closed Sun.

Drinking and nightlife

By night the focus shifts to the *comedores* and fast-food chains along Av Roosevelt. Think about ordering taxis, not least because the action is quite far out of town. Return journeys can be arranged with the barmen. No journey should be over US$3.

Mama Gallina's Av Roosevelt Sur ☎2661-2123. The most renowned of a clutch of bar/restaurants on the town side on Roosevelt is ostensibly a big dark room, but company is everything and it fills up. Drink rather than eat unless you really want to spend; on top of beer there's sangría (US$4), shots (US$7 double) and wine by the bottle (US$20).

El Paisa Av Roosevelt Sur opposite the *Hotel Trópico Inn*. Popular Mexican food spot that also does steaks for US$8, though the large tacos are cheaper at US$4. It's used more as an outdoors booze hall with a big screen and a stage for live musicians at weekends. Daily 10am–2am.

Papagallo's Plaza Chaparrastique, Av Roosevelt
Sur ☎2661-0400. The town's big venue has big
Mexican dishes starting at US$3, but most come
to drink and dance under the a/c. On certain
nights they have live music and comedy for a
US$5 entry fee, redeemable in drink. Thurs–Sun
noon–2am.

Shopping

Centro Comercial de Artesanías Alameda
Roosevelt between C 4 & 6 Pte. It is less artisan
than souvenir, but there are some pockets of
genuine produce to be found.
Mercado Central Parque Barrios. A sprawling
affair lined with narrow warrens filled with stalls
selling all manner of food, clothes and other goods.
Metrocentro Av Roosevelt Sur. Situated at the
edge of town, this consumer vortex includes stores,
banks, bookshop, supermarket, fast-food restaurants and a cinema; any bus heading south down
Av Roosevelt will drop you outside.

Directory

Exchange BanCo, Banco Cuscatlán and Banco
Salvadoreño (which gives Visa cash advances)
cluster around the west side of the *parque* and
along C 4 Ote.
Health Hospital Clínica Laboratorio San Francisco,
on Av Roosevelt Norte #408 (☎2661-1991), is
a private hospital with 24hr emergency care.
Farmacia El Progresso, 4 C Ote & 6A Av Nte
(☎2661-1098), is open weekdays until 6pm and
Saturdays until noon.
Laundry Lava Rápido (6A Av Nte, just past 8 C Ote)
is a rare laundry service at US$3/load. It also sells
the detergent. Daily 8am until 7pm.
Post office 4A Av Sur at C 3 Ote, south from the
cathedral.

Supermarket There's a Super Selectos super-
market on Av Roosevelt at C 11 Pte, a Despensa
Don Juan in the Metro Centro and a Despensa
Familiar in town on 4A Av Sur at C Sirama Oriente.
Telephones On the corner of Parque Guzmán next
to the Alcaldía.

Moving on

By bus to: Corinto (#327; twice hourly; 2hr); El
Amatillo, via Santa Rosa de Lima (#330; frequent;
1hr 30min); El Tamarindo, via Las Tunas (#385;
hourly; 1hr 30min); La Unión (#324; frequent;
1hr); Perquín (#332; 6 daily; 3hr); Playa El Cuco
(#320; twice hourly; 1hr); Puerto El Triunfo (#377;
every 40min; 1hr); San Francisco Gotera (#328;
frequent; 1hr); San Salvador (#301; every 15min;
3hr); Usulután (#373; frequent; 1hr 15min). Luxury
services go to San Salvador (10 daily; 2hr).

SAN FRANCISCO GOTERA

North of San Miguel, Highway CA-7
runs 25km to **SAN FRANCISCO
GOTERA** (usually called "Gotera"). It's
the least exciting of the towns along
the Ruta de Paz, but is a pivotal transport
point for the more interesting destinations beyond. There's no real reason
to stay here, as onward bus connections
are good, but if you have some time to
kill, check out the panoramic view from
the Parque Concordia.

Buses stop just after the dusty and ugly
main square. Buses run regularly north
to Perquín from the same place, and
pick-ups do the route from the northern

THE RUTA DE PAZ

North of San Miguel, the beautiful and sparsely populated mountainous department
of **Morazán** experienced some of the civil war's worst atrocities, with massacres
and bombing raids a regular occurrence. Much of the region is now encompassed
by the conversely named **Ruta de Paz**, part of a major project to rebuild much-
needed housing, schools and infrastructure, as well as to develop tourism in the
region. The locals here all have a story to tell, though some are more willing to share
their experiences than others. The main interest lies in the village of **Perquín**, with
its war museum, and the nearby town of **El Mozote**, scene of a horrific massacre
that wiped out the village population of some 800 people, including women,
children and babies. Some former guerrillas now operate as guides; ask helpful
US owner Ronald at *Hotel Perkin Lenka* (see p.291). Undervalued **Guatajiagua** is a
charming town with arguably El Salvador's best artisan output.

end of Avenida Morazán between 5am and 5.30pm.

Accommodation and eating

Cocina de Chinchilla C Los Almendros. Good for pastas (US$4), vegetarian dishes (US$3.50) and burgers.
Comedor Vanessa Barrio la Soledad #1. Where everyone in the know goes, with full meals costing US$2.25.
San Francisco Av Morazán at C 3 Pte ☎2654-0066. A block away from the bus stop, this is the best hotel in town, with a good range of rooms including en-suite doubles with cable TV and a/c. US$13

Moving on

By bus to: Cacaopera (#337; hourly; 1hr); Perquín (#332A & #328; every 30min; 1hr 30min); San Miguel (#328; every 10min; 1hr).

GUATAJIAGUA

Lying in the basin of an open valley between Gotera and the Interamericana, peaceful **GUATAJIAGUA** is a highlight of Salvadoran small-town life. Like many other towns, Guatajiagua has a unified creative output – black clay pottery and sculpture – but the products are of far higher quality than the usual souvenirs. Moreover, the town is very approachable, and as yet untainted by tourism.

Calle Principal, running west of the *parque*, is the town's unofficial centre and the location of **Cedart** (Mon–Fri 8am–5pm, Sat 8am–noon), which provides a useful introduction to and an exhibition of local crafts (ask for directions to workshops if you see a piece you like). There are many **workshops** here, including that of Sarbelio Vásquez García, whose sculptures of a kneeling man you'll see imitated throughout town.

Arrival and information

By bus Buses from San Francisco Gotera stop by the market, as does the San Miguel bus (#326; hourly; 1hr 20min), which you can pick up at Chapeltique on the highway if you're coming from the west.

Internet Across the road from Cedart, an unnamed internet café provides connections for US$0.01/min.

Accommodation and eating

Canales C Cementerio ☎2634-5003. This four-storey hotel has spotless, light and airy rooms, with towels provided in the bathrooms and fans and TVs in the rooms. The best part is the views from the roof – you can see far past San Miguel in the next valley. US$20
Merendero de la Vista Head right out of the hotel and left at the end of the road until you get to the Art Nouveau cross. You'll feel like you're in someone's living room as soon as you enter this excellent bar and restaurant: there is a sofa and armchair and a little garden out back where you can play checkers with bottle caps. The owners offer good *hamburgesas* (US$1), *pupusas* (US$0.50) and cold beers for under a dollar (if you buy enough).

Moving on

By bus to: San Francisco Gotera (#410; hourly; 1hr); San Miguel (#326; hourly; 1hr 20min).

CACAOPERA

The small village of **CACAOPERA**, north of Gotera, takes its name from the Ulúa language, and refers to the heavy cultivation of cacao in the area during colonial times. Indigenous culture and religion is still strongly adhered to in this region, and an excellent place to learn about it is the **Centro Maya Kakawira** (Mon–Fri 9am–3pm; US$1), about half a mile from the town, which has fine exhibits on indigenous tradition and culture, as well as photos, arts and crafts; it also organizes hikes to nearby petroglyphs. You can stay overnight here, putting into practice what you have just learned, as the bunk dorms (US$5) have no electricity or water, and have buckets for toilets; you can self-cater on the fire. Another worthy stop is the colonial **church** dating back to 1660 (though heavily restored), with walls up to five metres thick. Adjacent is a bell tower with three huge bronze bells dating from 1772. The church is the focus of festivities on January 15–17, when the villagers dance in memory of the eight *caciques* (priests) and the indigenous warrior deities Tupaica and Tumaica. There are hourly **buses** (#337) here from Gotera.

CORINTO

From Cacaopera, a road heads a little further northeast to the town of **CORINTO**, an important commercial hub and home to a **market** on Wednesday and Sunday that attracts vendors from neighbouring Honduras. All the usual tat is on sale, but look for hand-rolled cigars and locally grown foods. The town's main claim to fame is the **Grutas del Espíritu Santo** (Tues–Sun 9am–4.30pm; US$2), a series of caves bearing pre-Columbian wall art located about a fifteen-minute walk north of the village. Though faint, the art is said to date back some ten thousand years, and the whole area makes a very pleasant stroll.

Corinto can be reached as a day-trip from San Miguel (bus #327 from the main terminal), or #782 (hourly; 1hr) comes from Cacaopera.

Eating

Café la Casona On the *parque*. Does tasty pastries.
Pollo Silvestre 1 Calle Pte. Good *pollo dorado* (US$3.50).

EL MOZOTE

A few kilometres further on sits **EL MOZOTE**, the scene of the country's most atrocious wartime massacre (see box, p.290). Ruined El Mozote is still deeply rooted in its recent past, a situation that ensures a high volume of war tourism but obviously hinders the recovery progress. Families are slowly moving back, however, and a **mural** by Argentinian artist Claudia Bernard on the left side of the church describes the village's old agricultural life and hopes for the future. On the other side, colourful mosaics of children playing form the backdrop to a heart-rending memorial garden to all the young lives lost.

Although the massacre's one survivor, Rufina Amaya, passed away in 2007, newer inhabitants are continuing the guide work she did (no charge, but tipping is expected), and are vital to understanding the scars left from the war: you can see a bomb crater, the massacre's mass graves and the hole that the survivor hid in for five days. A moving **monument** to the victims features an iron sculpture of the silhouette of a family and a wall bearing the names of those killed. Opposite the church is a small handicrafts shop run by a women's co-operative; volunteers will show you around the church displays and monuments (free but tips welcome). For a small fee (around US$4), local children will take you to the caves where the guerrillas were hiding out, a pleasant walk of four or five kilometres through forest and brush, where wildlife abounds. The caves themselves are not overly spectacular, but it was from here that **Radio Venceremos** ("We Will Overcome") was first broadcast, and as you look out over the surrounding, densely forested countryside it is easy to see why the army never discovered the guerrillas' hiding place.

Arrival

By bus You can take a pick-up to Arambala, 3km down the CA-7, where you change to a Joateca bus that leaves at 8am every morning (the return bus leaves El Mozote at 12.45pm).
On foot El Mozote can be reached on foot from Perquín.

PERQUÍN

At the Desvío de Arambala, the main paved section of road begins its final climb to **PERQUÍN**, a small and, given its history, surprisingly friendly mountain town set in the middle of glorious walking country. During the war the town was the FMLN headquarters, and in later years Radio

Venceremos was broadcast to the nation from here. Attempts by the army to dislodge the guerrillas mostly failed, leaving the town badly damaged and deserted. Today, the "town that refused to die" has repaired most of its buildings, although the scars of war are still evident and nearly everyone has a horrendous tale to tell. Recently community action has been moving away from the retrospective outlook that war tourism has created, and instituted new schools, coffee production and a young and hip annual festival, the Festival del Invierno, which hosts live music and events in August.

What to see and do

The town itself is clumped around its pentagonal Parque Central, where there is a municipal basketball court. One block uphill is Calle de los Héroes, containing most of the town's attractions.

Museo de la Revolución

Perquín's main draw is the moving **Museo de la Revolución Salvadoreña** (Tues–Sun 8am–4.30pm; US$1.20), set up by former guerrillas in the wake of the 1992 Peace Accords. The curators travelled throughout the country collecting photographs and personal effects of "disappeared" guerrillas, a collection that is still growing and displayed in the first room. There is a succinct summary (in Spanish) of the escalation to the armed struggle, weaponry and examples of international propaganda aimed at bringing the events in El Salvador to the world's attention, but the most moving exhibits are the anonymous transcripts of witnesses of the El Mozote massacre, and drawings by refugee schoolchildren, depicting the war's events as they saw them. A separate room contains the transmitting equipment and studio used by Radio Venceremos, whose clandestine broadcasts every afternoon throughout the war transmitted the guerrillas' view of events, as well as interviews and music. After the peace accords, the station received an FM licence, and is now a commercial music station based in San Salvador, a status viewed by some as a bit of a sell-out.

Outside the museum is the crater left by a 500lb bomb dropped on the village – next to which a disarmed one is on display, with "Made in the USA" stencilled on the side – and a mock-up of a guerrilla camp. Behind the museum lie the remains of the helicopter that was carrying Domingo Monterrosa (architect of the El Mozote massacre) when it was shot down by the FMLN in 1984.

LOS INOCENTES

In December 1981, the elite, US-trained Atlacatl army battalion entered the village of El Mozote and rounded up its inhabitants on the suspicion that they had been harbouring FMLN guerrillas. Earlier, the villagers had been warned by guerrillas of the army's intent, but the mayor had been assured by the government that they would be safe staying put. This was not to be: under orders to set an example and obtain information, for three days the soldiers tortured and raped the inhabitants, before executing them all, including the children, who were shot in front of their parents. In all, some thousand people were killed, and their bodies subsequently burnt or buried in mass graves. The eyewitness testimonies to the events were ignored for years, and the bodies of the victims did not begin to be exhumed until 1992. Foreign groups are still working to uncover these mass-burial sites today; in some graves upwards of 85 percent of the bodies belong to children. On the right side of the church, a small garden for "the innocent ones" commemorates the tragedy of their lost lives.

Cerro de Perquín

Opposite the museum, a track leads up from a parking lot to the panoramic views from the peak of the **Cerro de Perquín**. It's an easy 1km stroll to the top, where climbers can picnic and have their picture taken next to a sign marking the summit.

Arrival and information

By bus Buses arrive on the south and west sides of the Parque Central, though it's easier to jump off before town for many of the accommodation options. Pick-ups from San Francisco Gotera stop one block south of the park on C San Sebastián.
Tourist information There's a small but enthusiastic tourist office (Mon–Sat 8am–4pm; ☎2680-4086) on the outskirts of town, beyond *Posada Don Manuel*. Co-owners Perkin Tours also run a wide range of tours, locally and around the country. You can pick up a basic map of the town (US$0.25) at the war museum, though like most maps in El Salvador it's hopelessly inaccurate.
Internet Access can be found on Calle de los Héroes for US$1/hr.

Accommodation

There are quite a few places to camp in the hills around Perquín – ask at the tourist office for recommendations.

🏃 **Hotel Perkin Lenca** 1.5km south of town on CA-7 ☎2680-4046, ⓦwww.perkinlenca.com. The owner here, a former aid-worker called Ronald, built the entire site himself, including the huge barn where excellent meals are served (US$5–10) – worth a visit even if you don't stay here. Spotless, spacious rooms in log cabins, hot-water en suites, firm beds, hammocks and chairs on the porches, great views, table tennis, free internet and a laundry service are worth every penny. Breakfast is included, and advance booking is recommended; Ronald offers a 20 percent discount during the week if enough rooms are available. He also sets up tours to El Mozote with ex-guerrilla guides, and runs a local educational charity. US$40

Hotel y Restaurante La Posada Signed at km 206 on CA-7, 500m south of town ☎2680-4037. This hotel used to be a sawmill, evidenced by the lofty reception area, where simple *típicos* are served. The beds are firm and good, though the rooms are quite dark, and the shared bathroom has toilet paper and seats. It stands out for its pool table, in great condition, and gym facilities. US$13

El Ocotal Km 201 on CA-7 ☎2634-4083. The cabins with private bath, set in a pine forest, are a paler version of *Perkin Lenca*, but the restaurant is worth a trip. US$30
Parque Recreativo Salto El Perol 4km east of town on the road to Marcala ☎2680-6071. These camping pitches, situated in one of three contiguous *parques recreativos* on the Río Guaco, have the best waterfall and fresh-water swimming pools, as well as *comedores*. The walk to town takes two hours. US$5
Perquín Real At the southern end of town on CA-7 ☎2680-4158, Ⓔxiomvarela@yahoo.com. The best budget option in town has a row of spacious rooms with at least two double beds in each. The bathroom situation is a little sketchy (it's shared with the restaurant in the courtyard, and still uses a bucket shower – quite abrasive in the cooler climate). US$5

Eating

Blanquita's Av los Próceres. This is the best *comedor* in town, with a small selection but popular *a la vista* and cakes. Breakfast US$1.50.
Marisol Av los Próceres. If you fancy a drink or two, and good burgers and fries (US$3), this is your place, though its decor resembles that of a hospital. Open late (until 10pm at weekends).
La Muralla C de los Héroes, at the foot of the climb to the museum. The evening *pupusa* spot, frying on demand out front while the townsfolk watch dubbed US soaps on the cable TV inside. It costs around US$2.50 for five *pupusas*. Open until 9pm.
El Ocotal Km 201 on CA-7. Good *sopas* (US$3) and a mean fried *yuca* on weekends. It's set in a pine forest, which curiously suits the 80s power ballads they favour on the stereo. Bring your swimsuit – you can use the pool once you've paid for something.

Directory

Pharmacy Next to the post office on the west side of the *parque*.
Police Politur – tourist police – opposite the church just off the *parque*, are very helpful and friendly and will take you to the tourist office on the edge of town if you ask nicely.
Post office The post office is on the west side of the *parque* (Mon, Tues, Thurs & Fri 8am–5pm).

Moving on

By bus to: San Miguel, via San Francisco Gotera (#332; 4 daily; 2hr); El Mozote (#426; 2 daily; 20min).
By pick-up to: San Francisco Gotera (twice hourly; 1hr).

AROUND PERQUÍN

The area around Perquín offers very enjoyable **hiking**, the highlights of which are the route over **Cerro el Pericón** to El Mozote, taking around three hours with a stop to swim in the middle, and a two-hour loop around **Cerro Gigante**. The tourist office (see p.291) can organize guides a day in advance, some of whom have reasonable English. Paying for a guide (around US$15 per group) is tremendously worthwhile, as they are mostly ex-guerrillas who will bring the history of the landscape to life.

SANTA ROSA DE LIMA

East of San Francisco Gotera, a road continues through hot, low hills to **SANTA ROSA DE LIMA**, a messy but thriving place with a large weekly market, a cheese industry and a well-maintained church. Besides the Wednesday **market** there's not much to do here, but it's a convenient stopover if you're crossing late from Honduras.

Accommodation and eating

Comedor Chayito At the corner of C Giron and C 1 Ote. A very clean place which does a good, cheap *comida a la vista*.

INTO HONDURAS: EL AMATILLO

Beyond Santa Rosa, the road connects with the Carretera Interamericana to run to the border over the Río Goascora at El Amatillo. The border crossing is easy and free but busy, and teeming with moneychangers – who generally do slightly better rates than the bank here – and beggars. On the Honduran side, buses leave regularly until late afternoon for Tegucigalpa and Jícaro Galán, and there are also direct buses to Choluteca, for onward connection to the Nicaraguan border along the Carretera Interamericana.

El Recreo 4A Av Nte between C Giron and C 1 Ote ☎ 2664-2126. The best of the few places to stay, whose clean rooms come with bath, though it does get a little noisy. US$15

El Tejano C Giron between 6A and 8A Av Nte ☎ 2664-2459. A basic but adequate place with a 7am check-out. US$9

Taquería Tex Mex Av G Arias between C 1 and 3 Ote. If you fancy something with a bit more kick, this is the place.

Moving on

Buses stop at the western end of 6 C Pte.
By bus to: the border at El Amatillo (#346; every 20min; 1hr 30min); La Unión (#304 or #342; frequent; 1hr 30min); San Miguel (#330; frequent; 1hr); San Salvador (#306; twice hourly; 4hr).

The north

North of San Salvador, hilly pastures and agricultural land give way to the remote, rugged and sparsely populated Chalatenango and Cuscatlán provinces, a region of poverty and pride all but closed to outsiders until recently. The Spanish found few natural riches to attract them this far north, and successive generations of *campesinos* have vainly struggled to make a living. This harsh terrain created fertile ground for dissent and support for the FMLN, who controlled large parts of the department of Chalatenango for significant periods during the 1980s. Both army and guerrillas struggled to take control, leaving devastated communities in their wake and refugees fleeing across the border to Honduras. The legacy of the region's wartime status was not exclusively detrimental, however, and the effect of the subsequent repopulation has been the reinvention and modernization of its big towns. Each now has a very singular character: colonial **Suchitoto** is the darling of culture and tourism; **La Palma** is a mountainous escape with a legion of artisans; and bustling **Chalatenango** is a centre of rural commerce.

SUCHITOTO

Cobbled and colonial **SUCHITOTO** perches like a crown on the ridge above the southern edge of Lago de Suchitlán. The left-leaning, but increasingly gentrified town was made a site of National Cultural Heritage in 1997, and culture is indeed the order of the day. There are food and arts festivals every weekend, and the month-long festival of culture in February draws the country's best painters, orchestras, performers and poets.

During the 1980s, the area was the scene of bitter fighting as the army struggled to dislodge FMLN guerrillas from their nearby mountain strongholds. Upwards of ninety percent of the inhabitants left the town, which was largely resettled by ex-guerrillas after the war. Today life here is generally quiet. The town offers great restaurants, bars and luxury hotels, and as such presents an antidote to rough travelling.

What to see and do

Suchitoto has some of the finest examples of colonial architecture in the country, so before getting stuck into the cafés and shops it's worth taking a stroll to admire the low red-tiled adobe houses lining the town's streets and around its peaceful plazas.

The centre

Overlooking the Parque Central, the post-colonial **Iglesia Santa Lucía** has an impressive Neoclassical front and a particularly fine wooden altar and strange, hollow wooden columns inside. The **Casa de Cultura** (Mon–Fri 9am–5pm; free), a block north of the church, has displays on local history and information on local walks, while the shaded **Parque San Martín**, a couple of blocks northwest of the church, commands stunning views across the blue waters of the lake. Group tours of the town centre's architecture can be organized at the tourist office.

SUCHITOTO

Lago de Suchitlán, Museo de Alejandro Cotto & ❶

ACCOMMODATION

2 Gardenias	A
Blanca Luna	E
Casa de Niña Rubia	F
El Cerrito	D
Villa Balanza	C
Vista del Lago	B

EATING & DRINKING

Artex Café	11
Casa del Escultor	5
La Fonda	1
Lupita del Portal	10
El Necio	6
Noe's Disco	7
La Piedra	9
La Posada	4
Rinconcito del Gringo	8
El Tejado	2
Villa Balanza	C
Vistaconga	3

❶, Cerro Guazapa & Los Tercios Waterfall

Museo de Alejandro Cotto

From the northeast of town, Avenida 15 de Septiembre leads down to the lakeshore, passing the **Museo de Alejandro Cotto** (Sat & Sun 2–6pm; US$4), a beautifully restored colonial house replete with a fine collection of local paintings, sculpture, indigenous artefacts and musical instruments. The owner, Cotto himself, is a famous Salvadoran writer and filmmaker, and is often here. The entrance price, while relatively steep, goes towards funding the February arts and culture festival.

Lago de Suchitlán

It's a couple of kilometres to **Lago de Suchitlán**, but it's worth the trip as you can swim in the clear but cool waters, and a couple of small lakeside bars are good for a relaxing drink. A small boat sometimes runs around the lake, or local fishermen may be persuaded to take you out onto the water. Also known as Embalse Cerrón, the lake is actually a reservoir, created in 1973. Several lakeside villages on the north shore were inundated as a result, with residents moved to new housing estates – *ubicaciones* – outside Chalatenango. Boat trips (US$10–15) to **Isla de los Pájaros** in the middle of the lake, the home of a range of fish-eating bird life, take about forty minutes. To get to the lake, walk north on Avenida 15 de Septiembre from the Parque Central and keep going, or take a mini-bus from the corner of that road and 4A Calle Pte (10min; US$0.30).

Los Tercios

You can also be dropped off on the lakeshore by a trail that leads to a waterfall, the **Cascada Los Tercios** (boat US$4–6), or walk to it by following the signposts south out of town (30min). The waterfall has unusual hexagonal basaltic columns over which the water flows, but note that the water level gets low in the dry season.

Salto El Cubo

A better waterfall to swim in is **Salto El Cubo**, with its chilly twin pools. It is a pleasant one-hour walk west of town – go to the western end of Calle Morazán, then follow the sign down the track at the signpost.

Cerro Guazapa

A former guerrilla stronghold, the roads up and around **Cerro Guazapa**, to the south of the town, still bear witness to the crumbling remains of the trenches and dugouts used by both sides, now quietly submerged beneath green vegetation. Horseriding is popular in this area and hacks across the volcano can be organized through the tourist office (US$35 per person; 6hr). Check the condition of the horses before you go, as some aren't in great shape.

Arrival and information

By boat Ferries from San Francisco Lempa, across Lago de Suchitlán, arrive at the boat dock, 1.5km north of town along C al Lago, with shops, cafés and toilets in the new visitors' centre. A frequent microbus runs to the Parque Central for US$0.30.
By bus Buses stop at 1 C Pte.
Tourist information Possibly the best tourist office in the country is on C V. Morazán & 2A Av Nte (Wed–Sun 8am–noon & 1–4pm; ☎2335-1782, ⊛www .suchitoto-el-salvador.com), with information on tours, sights and cultural events, also available through the website. The MITUR office on the corner of the main square, with same opening hours, is also very helpful, as are the tour operators below.
Tour operators Suchitoto Adventure Outfitters (☎2335-1429, ⊛www.suchitotooutfitters.com), based in the *Lupita del Portal* café on the main square, organize waterfall treks (US$6; 4hr), as well as mountain-biking trips around the hills (US$7), kayakking, horseriding and excellent tours of guerrilla battlefields. Owner René Borbón speaks good English and is a mine of information. The town's other main source of advice is Robert Broz at *Café El Gringo*, who also organizes tours further afield.

Accommodation

More and more accommodation options are springing up as Suchitoto responds to increasing numbers of visitors. You can find information on most hotels and restaurants at ⓦwww.gaesuchitoto.com. Book ahead at weekends, and for all of February.

2 Gardenias 3A Av Nte 48 ☎2335-1868, ⓔhostal2gardenias@hotmail.com. The rooms at the oldest backpacker spot in town have become rather shabby, but it has a great mango-filled communal space. There's internet access and a bar that serves reasonably priced food and drinks. US$12

Blanca Luna One block south of the *parque* ☎2335-1661, ⓔposadablancalunasuchitoto @hotmail.com. The most central of the cheap hotels in town has two or three double beds in the basic rooms, as well as fan, cable TV and en suites. None too clean but not bad value, and an airy roof terrace makes up for the scruffy rooms, with hammocks and climbing bougainvillea. The artist manager's paintings decorate the walls. US$8

Casa de Niña Rubia Av 5 de Noviembre 29 ☎2335-1833. If the tourist-centric atmosphere is getting to you, come here, where you literally stay with Ruby's family in her house. Two clean, basic rooms. US$8

El Cerrito On the track between 6 & 4 C Pte ①2517-1665, ⓔvmlc81@hotmail.com. It has just one room, with three hard double beds in it, although this leads to a sitting room with cable TV and a clean bathroom. Priced by person, the room is rented like a dorm. US$6

Villa Balanza Parque San Martín ☎2335-1408, ⓦwww.villabalanzarestaurante.com. Two very good, wood-finished rooms down the hill behind the restaurant of the same name on the edge of town. The en-suite rooms have a splendid view of the lake. US$22

Vista del Lago At the end of 2A Av Nte ☎2335-1357. The rooms here are small and cubicle-esque, with passable beds and a shared bathroom, but the owners are relaxed, the cosy courtyard has a bar and serves food, and the bench overlooking the lake is possibly the best spot in town for an evening drink. US$7

Eating

There's a very good selection of restaurants in Suchitoto, so it's worth staying somewhere cheap and splashing out on a nice meal.

Artex Café Plaza Central. Not only does this place have the best coffee in town (they'll sell you bags for US$4.50) but also fast internet (US$1/hr), excellent cultural information (the café is run by a nonprofit organization promoting the arts) and nice outdoor tables for a beer (Pilsener US$1).

Casa del Escultor 6 C Ote & 3A Av Nte ☎2335-1711 or 7820-5092, ⓦwww.miguelmartino.com. Not so much a restaurant as the art-filled house of an Argentine sculptor who cooks his country's famous giant grills every Sunday lunch for a lucky few. Reserve ahead, or if you have a group of four or more, call to arrange a day and time and he'll cook especially for you. It's worth it even at US$7–14.

La Piedra Opposite the church on Parque Central ☎2335-1173. It looks like a tourist trap, but there is good variety in the menu, including rabbit (US$7) and chorizo (US$4), and it does a great rum and coffee to pick you up mid afternoon (US$1.50).

Rinconcito del Gringo C V. Morazán 27 ☎2327-2351. From the same gringo, Roberto Broz, who runs the internet *Café El Gringo* and local tours, this largely Mexican restaurant offers big, spicy portions that really should cost more (*quesadillas* US$4, half-litre of orange juice US$2). There's a good atmosphere when busy and occasionally it stays open later for drinkers. Closed Thurs.

El Tejado 3A Av Nte ☎2335-1769. Big meat and chicken dishes (US$6) are served in a pleasant garden with an unrivalled lake view. The best thing about this place is that it gives you access to the giant and clean swimming pool to cool off on hot days; you may be asked for a US$3 supplement for this, but not always.

Villa Balanza At the *Villa Balanza* hotel ☎2335-1408. This open-sided barn restaurant has impressive antique-ranch decor, with romantic tables in a corner alcove overlooking the lake. The food is good, with breakfasts and lunches (chicken *suprema* US$6.50) served by waitresses in "traditional" milk-maid outfits.

Vistaconga Final Cielito Lindo 8 ☎2335-1676. A friendly place with great lake views, live music or dance on Sat nights and tours arranged to surrounding attractions. There's a Mexican-inspired menu, and reasonable cocktails (US$4). Closed Mon & Tues.

TREAT YOURSELF

La Posada C 4 Pte ☎2335-1064, ⓦwww.laposada.com.sv. Not just a very expensive hotel in a beautiful 200-year-old colonial house full of eclectic Moroccan and Indian crafts: out back you'll find the best restaurant in town, with quality food and professional service for far less than you pay at home (salmon lasagne US$10.85). Be sure to visit the parrots before you leave.

Drinking

Suchitoto is a good place to go out, both in terms of choice and safety, so take advantage. Nonetheless, if you're female and on your own in *El Necio* or *Noe's* you should expect the all-too-usual attention.

La Fonda Northern end of Av 15 de Septiembre ☎2335-1126. The largely expensive menu has some cheap and filling treats (seafood salad US$4), but it really comes into its own as a spot for evening drinks with great views of the lake.

Lupita del Portal Parque Central. Laidback café and bar with outdoor tables, specializing in some interesting *pupusas* (spinach US$0.60), tasty sweet pasties and a potent *chaparro* (*aguardiente, or cane liquor*). Owner René Barbón runs Suchitoto Adventure Outfitters (see p.294) from here, one of the best tour operators in the country.

El Necio 4 C Pte 9. The only out-and-out bar in town is a local favourite, serving regular priced beers (US$1) and spirits, amid guerrilla decor. Good for a pre-*Noe's* warm up.

Noe's Disco 4 C Ote. Also known as *Disco Mowy*, this is the only place to dance in town and is cheap, cheeky and cheerful. The music is pop, with an obvious Latino influence, and the beers are reasonably priced. Open weekends 8pm–2am.

Shopping and entertainment

Arts and cultural venues are dotted around all Suchitoto's streets, so it's well worth wandering around to check out all of the options.

Centro Arte para la Paz 4 C Pte & 6A Av Nte. A venue for a range of arts events, including film, theatre, concerts and art. Ask at the *Artex Café* to find out what's going on.

La Galería de Pascal Av 15 de Septiembre. A large exhibition space that sells original paintings, which are naturally very expensive, as well as local artisanal work.

Directory

Exchange There is, surprisingly, no bank here, so bring plenty of cash if you want to stay a while.

Internet Rinconcito del Gringo, C Morazán, beyond 6 Av Nte, is a great internet café, not least because the gringo in question, Californian Robert Broz, is an authority on the town and area.

Laundry *Hotel El Obraje* on 2 C Ote, though dull accommodation, does loads for US$4–6.

Pharmacy Santa Lucía, on the corner of C V. Morazán and Av 5 de Noviembre, is well stocked but closes noon–2pm, and at 6pm.

Police The tourist police have a good presence in town and are open 24hr on the corner of Av 15 de Septiembre and 4 C Pte (☎2335-1141).

Moving on

By boat to: San Francisco Lempa (20min; 10 daily), from where buses travel to Chalatenango. Car ferries are cheaper than passenger ferries.

By bus to: Aguilares (#163; every 40min; 1hr) for transfer to Chalatenango (#125) & La Palma (#119); San Martín (#129; 10 daily; 1hr) for Cojutepeque (#119) or San Miguel (#301); San Salvador, Terminal de Oriente (#129; every 15min; 1hr 30min).

AGUILARES AND CIHUATÁN

Some 35km north of the capital on the border-bound CA-4, or the Troncal del Norte, lies the pleasant workaday town of **AGUILARES**, with nothing more to offer than a relaxing snack in

---

VILLAGE COLONIALISM

Twenty minutes north of Aguilares, at km 46.5 on the Troncal del Norte, is **La Hacienda Colima** (☎2309-3335), an ageing hacienda set in stunning surroundings. Run by the local village *cooperativa*, there is a choice of private (US$20) and dorm (US$10) accommodation, with shared bath set around a pristine courtyard. There is good camping space, too (US$5). The views of Embalse Cerrón Grande and the nearby volcanoes are magnificent, but it is the **activity** possibilities here that are the best: canoeing, fishing, horseriding and swimming in the lake or a swimming pool. The *cooperativa* will set you up with local guides. Birdwatchers will also be delighted by the thousands of **waterbirds** in their nature reserve, including seven species of heron, white pelicans, and vast flocks of ducks and waders. To get here, take any bus running between Aguilares and La Palma or Chalatenango and ask the driver to let you off at the entrance. Ask at the Suchitoto tourist office (see p.294) for more information.

the garden at *Río Bravo* on the *parque*. Archeology buffs might want to pass through, however, as 4km to the north sit the ruins of **CIHUATÁN** (Tues–Sun 9am–4pm; US$3; ⓦ www.cihuatan.org), the most important Post-Classic site in the country. Originally covering an area of around four square kilometres, Cihuatán (meaning "Place of Women" in Nahaut) was founded sometime after the first waves of Pipils (or Toltecs) began arriving in El Salvador in the tenth century and destroyed for reasons unknown around 1200 AD. The excavations, which include stepped pyramids and a pelota court bearing a clear Mexican influence, were officially opened in 2007, along with a very informative bilingual museum. To really get into it, it's worth reading the information on the website before going.

Take any **bus** from Aguilares or the capital to Chalatenango or La Palma and ask to be dropped at the gates they're right on the highway.

CHALATENANGO

Further north along the Troncal del Norte is a major crossroads at the scrubby town of **Amayo**, the east branch of which leads through agricultural and pasture lands along the fringes of the lake to **CHALATENANGO**. An important centre of rural trade, Chalatenango has the rough-and-ready feel of a frontier settlement, an atmosphere enhanced by the fortress-like army barracks on the main square. During the early 1980s it was under FMLN control, and though much of the town's physical damage has been repaired, the barracks still has bullet holes in its walls. Nowadays, though, Chalatenango is a bustling and very friendly place.

What to see and do

Chalatenango lies in a beautiful setting – southeast of the La Peña mountains, overlooking the distant Cerro Grande

to the west and Lago de Suchitlán to the south – and much of its attraction lies in day-trips to what surrounds it (see p.298). However, the daily **market** that seals off Calle San Martín every morning from 5am to 1pm is full of fresh, locally-grown produce and cowboy attire, which is even more prevalent when the Friday horse fairs come to town. Twenty minutes from the centre to the east is the **Parque Recreativo Agua Fría** (daily 8am–5pm; US$0.90), with artificial pools, a water slide and a café in a pleasant park.

Arrival and information

By bus All buses arrive and depart from along 3A Av Sur. From here it's only a couple of blocks north to the Parque Central.
Exchange There are several banks with ATMs along 3A Av Sur, including HSBC and Western Union.

Accommodation

Hotel La Ceiba Behind the garrison building and down the hill on 1 C Pte ☎2301-1080. Standard features for the price (cable, en suite, a/c), though a bit run-down. US$20
Hotelito San José 3 C Pte ☎2301-0148. The thrifty choice, with firm beds, fans and toilets (some with seats) in its rooms around a pleasant yard, but they aren't spotless. It's wise to arrive early and air out the mildewy smell. US$10
La Posada del Jefe C el Instituto ☎2335-2450. The furthest option from the centre is just about adequately clean, though rooms are dark and poky, and – despite its enviable hilltop location – there are no views over the town. At the price and at ten blocks' slog uphill beyond the church to the east of the centre, it's a bit steep. US$25

Eating and drinking

If you fancy an evening drink, the nameless stall on the south side of the church on Calle San Martín does cheap beer as well as burgers, and stays open until 11pm. There are plenty of open-air pizzerias among the craft stalls on the square, with eat-in tables or takeaway (US$4–5).
Blanquita's on the corner of C Morazán & Av Libertad. The other good *comedor* in town, with the usual *comida típica*, as well as good burgers and chips (US$2.80), though going to the toilet might put you off your food.

Columbia Café 4 C Pte. Its average sandwiches (US$1.50) lack good ingredients, but not so their Irish coffee, which is topped with Chantilly cream; they have an odd phone-charger collection should you need more battery life.

Comedor Carmary 3A Av Sur on the other side of *Pollo Campero*. A popular *comedor* around lunch time, serving the locally favoured *a la vista* (US$3–4), with vegetarian options too.

Don Mario's 3A Av Sur. No need to patronize the *Pollo Campero* next door – this Mexican-style grill does good, big burritos for under US$5.

Otto's 6 C Pte at 1A Av Sur. Pizzas as big as a car tyre (*especial gigante* US$12) to feed more than one hungry traveller, with smaller options starting at US$3.

Sarita 1A Av Sur. The countrywide ice-cream chain has a branch here, with plenty of different flavours to satisfy your needs on a hot day, or try a Giga, their cheaper but just as delectable version of a Magnum (US$1).

Moving on

By bus to: Concepción Quetzaltepeque (#300B; every 30min; 20min); La Palma – take the San Salvador bus and change at Amayo (#119; every 30min; 3hr); San Francisco Lempa (#542; 5 daily; 45min); San Salvador, Terminal de Oriente (#125; frequent; 2hr).

AROUND CHALATENANGO

The villages north of Chalatenango are spread across forested mountains and rarely visited. More adventurous travellers may want to explore beyond the artisan town of Concepción Quetzaltepeque; find out more beforehand by asking at the tourist office or local experts in Suchitoto (see p.294). By the lake, San Francisco Lempa is a great little stop before crossing the lake to Suchitoto.

Concepción Quetzaltepeque

Some 12km northwest of Chalatenango, the village of **Concepción Quetzaltepeque** is notable for its **hammock** industry. Workshops lining the village's main street and homes around the village turn out colourful items in nylon and, less commonly, cotton and *mezcal* fibres for prices at about half those in San Salvador. Most producers sell in the market at Chalatenango at roughly the same bargain rate as in the workshops here. The annual hammock festival takes place November 10–12.

San Francisco Lempa

The little lakeside town of **San Francisco Lempa** is home to the pier for ferries to and from Suchitoto. The town itself is very pleasant for a dock community, but holds no real interest. In the vicinity, however, are an excellent restaurant and a great camping spot. *Tao Tao*, right next to the pier, is worth a visit even if you're not getting a ferry. It serves tasty, big, predominantly seafood dishes (*camerones* soup US$4) on its lakeside veranda and will sort out boats or any kind of tourist information. Its best feature, though, is its booming jukebox; bring plenty of quarters. The owners will tell you how to walk to, or organize a boat to, *Hacienda Grande*, 3km west along the shore (☎2375-1447). Probably the nicest camping in the country is here (US$5; they have five tents available for those that need to borrow), next to their swimming pool and restaurant (*pollo dorado* US$4). They also have horses you can take out on your own around the surrounding countryside for US$4 per hour. Boats from San Francisco Lempa cost US$10, from Suchitoto US$20.

LA PALMA

Beyond Amayo, the Troncal del Norte winds up the Cordillera Metapán Alotepeque to the Honduran border through an abundance of vertiginous, pine-clad mountain vistas (for the best views sit on the left-hand side of the bus on the way up). Some 8km short of the border lies the calm village of **LA PALMA**, supposedly named after the indigenous custom of building houses out of palms. The climate is cooler here and the peace is only broken during the annual fiesta of **Dulce Nombre de María**, in the third week of February. But under the surface the village's

LA PALMA

N

Honduran Border

Semilla de Dios

Museo
Fernando
Llort

Pharmacy

Alfredo
Linares
Gallery

Supermarket

5A CALLE ORIENTE
5A CALLE PONIENTE
3A CALLE ORIENTE
3A CALLE PONIENTE
2A AVENIDA NORTE
AVENIDA DE CARDO
1A CALLE PONIENTE
1A CALLE ORIENTE
CALLE INDEPENDENCIA
1 CALLE PONIENTE
1 AVENIDA NORTE
1 AVENIDA SUR
CALLE BARRIOS
CALLE LIBERTAD
2A AVENIDA SUR

E & San Salvador

EATING & DRINKING		ACCOMMODATION	
Antijoles Rincon Mexicano	5	Casa Hotel	D
Cartagenas Pizza	1	Centro Obrero Dr Rivas	E
Del Pueblo	3	Hotel La Palma	C
La Estancia	4	Piedra del Bosque	A
Pupusería La Palma	2	Quechelàh	B

0   100 m

plentiful *artesanías* are hives of industry, reproducing the brightly painted, naïf-style representations of people, villages and farming life and religion made famous by Salvadoreño artist Fernando Llort in the 1970s on wooden and ceramic handicrafts and toys, which are now sold all over the world. The **Museo Fernando Llort**, at the far end of town, displays a selection of his colourful paintings (Mon–Fri 9am–5pm, Sat 10am–4pm; US$4).

What to see and do

The **crafts industry** is the economic mainstay of the village, with **workshops** lining the main road. Most sell their goods on the spot and are pretty relaxed about visitors turning up to watch; prices are somewhat cheaper than in San Salvador and the items are hard to beat as presents for family and friends.

North of La Palma are several fine **hiking trails**, including El Salvador's highest mountain, **Cerro Pital** (2730m), 10km away on the Honduran border. A rough road branches east just before La Palma to run to Las Pilas on the lower slopes of the mountain; a dirt road also leads up from the village of **San Ignacio** (see p.301). Hiking to the summit is an adventure of two or three days, for which you will need to be fully equipped – the owners of the *Hotel La Palma* are a good source of information on shorter walks and guides, and run their own excursions around the hillsides.

Arrival and information

By bus There is no bus station as such. You can ask to get off at either end of town or in the centre; the bus goes along 2A Av Nte on the way up to the border, and calles Delgado and Barrios on the way back down.

Tourist information The MITUR office, 2A Av Norte & 1A C Oriente (Mon–Sat 9am–5pm; ☎2335-9076), produces a good booklet on the area, with maps and hotel and restaurant listings.

Accommodation

There is plenty of good accommodation in La Palma at all price ranges – even free.

Casa Hotel Opposite *Hotel La Palma* ☎2335-9129. Cosy rooms with firm beds and good furnishings that include welcome bedside lights. The toilets have no seats. The owner offers a great one-month deal for US$35. **US$11**

Centro Obrero Dr Rivas 5km south of town on the Troncal del Norte. One of the four national workers' centres with free accommodation, this place offers simple but surprisingly clean cabins in a forested area with swimming pools. Contact the Ministerio de Trabajo in San Salvador for reservations (see p.243).

🏃 **Hotel La Palma** Barrio el Tránsito ☎2335-9012, ⓦwww.hotellapalma.com.sv. Supposedly the oldest functioning hotel in El Salvador, this friendly and good-value place at the entrance to town has clean and bright rooms, with hot-water en suites, nicely decorated with huge Llortist murals. There's a reasonably priced restaurant, plus a pool and hammock area, and a special deal of US$35 half-board per double room. **US$20**

Piedra del Bosque Across the river from C Independencia ☎2335-9067, ⓦwww.piedradelbosque.com. Charming owner Oscar built this entire eco-complex, with wooden cabins up the hill, a swimming pool fed by the river, restaurant, hammocks, space for camping, collection of archeological finds, craft shop, and bonfires in the evening. Oscar will talk you through everything stone by stone, but the cabins are extremely basic and overpriced. Camping US$10, doubles **US$25**

TREAT YOURSELF

Quecheláh 500m west of town by 1 C Pte ☎2305-9328, ⓔquechela@hotmail.com. This arty B&B is a 15-minute walk uphill from town, but the tasteful bedrooms with amazing beds and hot-water baths, not to mention the bar, lovely artwork, mountain views and friendly owners, make it a real treat. Only three rooms, so advance booking advisable. **US$40**

Eating

Antijoles Rincón Mexicano Next to *Casa Hotel*. American and Salvadoreño food with no pretence served right on the street. It's cheap and hits the spot (hot dog US$1.50).

Cartagenas Pizza Av Delgado & 5A C Ote. Hearty grub like tacos and enchiladas as well as pizzas (US$2–12). They do excellent banana and vanilla *licuados* too (US$1).

Del Pueblo 2A Av Sur. A family-run establishment with bags of character, and carved wooden chairs and candles, *Del Pueblo* serves a good-value menu featuring mostly meats and one of the best *típico* breakfasts around (US$3.75).

La Estancia C Barrios ☎2335-9049. Very popular with the locals, the menu here may seem pricey but portions are generous; the US$4 Caesar salad is lighter and cheaper. Colourful murals of rural life provide the backdrop to the small-town bustle inside.

Pupusería La Palma C Barrios. The best *pupusería* in town is small and always busy with locals, and serves soft and flavoursome *pupusas* (US$0.50), as well as *típicos* all day.

Shopping

Alfredo Linares Gallery C Barrios. A small gallery where the internationally established naïf artist exhibits with other local artists. The fine watercolour and pen-and-ink originals are a little steep, but there are also poster prints for US$10 and postcards for US$1.50.

Semilla de Dios 3 C Pte at 5A Av Nte ⓦwww.cooperativasemilladedios.com. An artistic production line built around Llort's iconic, colourful naïf style. It is mostly exported, so there isn't a huge amount of hand-painted stuff for sale, but you can see how the work is done in the workshop.

Directory

Exchange Citibank on C Delgado exchanges currencies and has an ATM.

Internet Palma City Online, next to the supermarket on 2A Av Sur, has a fast connection, plus web calls for US$0.65/hr.

Pharmacy Farmacia San Rafael (Mon–Fri 8am–12.30pm & 1.30–6pm) on C Barrios & 1A C Pte.

Post office On 1 C Pte, with usual daytime opening hours.

Supermarket Super La Palma, on 2A Av Sur, is open until 8pm every night.

Crossing the border to Honduras at El Poy is straightforward and quick: the #119 bus drops you within sight of the gate; there is a US$2 entrance charge for Honduras, but no exit charges for El Salvador. Many trucks use this route, but private traffic is light; crossing early in the day is advisable. The last bus from the border for La Palma and San Salvador leaves at 4.15pm. On the Honduran side, buses run the 10km to Nueva Ocotepeque (see p.352) every forty minutes or so until 5pm, departing from just the other side of the gate that marks the beginning of Honduras.

Moving on

By bus to: the junction at Amayo, for onward connections to Chalatenango (#119; every 30min; 1hr); El Poy (#119; every 30min; 30min); San Ignacio (#119; every 30min; 15min); San Salvador, Terminal de Oriente (#119; every 30min; 3hr 30min).

SAN IGNACIO AND AROUND

The highway continues past La Palma to the Honduran border at El Poy, 11km away, a thirty-minute journey by bus. The village of **SAN IGNACIO**, 6km from La Palma and much quieter, also has a few craft workshops and two places to stay. In town, *La Posada de San Ignacio*, on the square (T2352-9419; US$13), has simple log cabins with shared bath, or rather better standard rooms with modern ceramic bathrooms. If you are a group of four to seven people, one of the three self-catering log cabins of *Cabañas Prashanti* (no phone; US$13), 500m north of town off the Troncal del Norte, will fit you all while providing a sitting room and great views from the porch. You can also camp at the *Parador de Compostela* (no phone; US$5), where there are good hikes and tours on horseback (US$12/hr). To get there you need to take an El Poy bus; look out for the big sign where the road to El Rosario turns off. Just short of El Poy, a road branching to the left crosses the Río Lempa and runs to the village of **Citalá**. From here a daily bus (5am) runs west through rugged wilderness on the scenic mountain road to **Metapán** (see p.316), over three to four hours. There's a basic *posada* (no phone; US$5) close to the centre of the village if you don't fancy the early-morning walk.

The west

The rich landscape of western El Salvador in many ways offers a perfect advertisement for the country. Soft mountain chains edge back from valleys dominated by vibrant green expanses of coffee plantations. Spared from the most violent hardships of the conflict of the 1980s, the friendly towns and cities here have a relatively well-developed tourist infrastructure that makes travelling here easier than in other regions.

The joy of visiting this part of the country consists largely of soaking up the atmosphere. The Carretera Interamericana runs between San Salvador and the main city of the west, **Santa Ana**, but the main access route leads through the sweaty town of **Sonsonate**, 65km west of the capital. From here, buses head off in several directions: down to the coast for the untouched beaches of **Los Cóbanos**, **Los Remedios** and **Barra de Santiago**; to the tranquil forest reserve at **Bosque El Imposible**; and northwest into the mountains. The mountain towns of

Apaneca and Juayúa, and the nearby city of Ahuachapán are perfect for a few days' relaxation, and are conveniently situated near the border with Guatemala. The larger, centrally located Santa Ana is a mellow contrast to the capital, while the peaks of Cerro Verde, Volcán Santa Ana and Volcán Izalco, the sublime crater lake of Lago de Coatepeque, and the pre-Columbian site of Tazumal are all close by. In the north of the region, near the Guatemalan border, the accommodating little town of Metapán gives access to the Bosque Montecristo, where hiking trails weave through unspoilt cloud-forest amid some of the most remote and perfectly preserved mountain scenery in this part of the world.

SONSONATE

SONSONATE, set in tobacco and cattle-ranching country, prickles with heat in the day and menace at night. It has a history of gang problems, and since there is nothing here to see, its best feature is the bus terminal, with connections to Los Cóbanos and Barra de Santiago to the south, and the Ruta de las Flores to the north. There are good times to visit Sonsonate, chiefly the Verbena de Sonsonate festival at the end of January, when there's a host of music and drama performances, and the town puts on a good Semana Santa celebration at Easter, when crowds flock to join the street processions and intricate pictures are drawn in coloured sawdust on the pavements.

With such good accommodation on the coast and up the Ruta de las Flores, and plentiful bus connections until nightfall, you would have to be either stupid or unlucky to get stuck here, but if it happens, the ageing *Hotel Orbe* on Av F. Mucci Sur and C 4 Ote (☎2451-1517; US$11), two blocks east of the *parque*, has large, clean rooms with private bath, and cable TV and a/c for double that. If you want something nicer than the

terminal *comedores*, *La Casona* on 3 C Pte is famed for its meaty *comida a la vista* for around US$3. The bus terminal is 1.5km east of the centre – take bus #53C if you don't fancy walking.

Moving on

By bus to: Ahuachapán, via all towns on the Ruta de las Flores (#249; every 15min; 2hr); Barra de Santiago (#285 direct/#259 getting off at the turning off the Carretera Litoral; 2 daily/ frequent; 1hr 20min/1hr); Bosque El Imposible main entrance (#259; frequent; 1hr 20min); Los Cóbanos (#257; every 30min; 40min); La Libertad, via the Costa del Bálsamo (#287; 2 daily; 2hr 45min); San Salvador (#205; every 15–20min from 4.30am–5pm; 1hr 30min); Santa Ana (#216 via Los Naranjos/#209B via El Congo; every 20min/hourly; 1hr 15min/1hr 45min).

LOS CÓBANOS AND LOS REMEDIOS

The idyllic white-sand beach of LOS CÓBANOS, caressed by warm and gentle waves, is the place for sedate beach activities such as sunbathing and paddling, though it's also the only reef-diving spot in the country. Just 25km due south of Sonsonate, via a fast highway, it is a favourite beach among Salvadoreños at weekends, when it is better to round the headland at the west end of the small bay to the quieter beach of LOS REMEDIOS. Although rather rocky, the pretty, gently curved beaches make a nice contrast to the dark palm-fringed expanses further down the coast.

Bus #257 leaves Sonsonate twice every hour for Los Cóbanos until early evening, and there are also occasional direct buses from San Salvador (#207); the last bus leaves the beach at 5pm.

Accommodation and eating

There are two outstanding accommodation options at Los Remedios. The best places to eat are the fishermen's restaurants that line the shore. The delicious fish is all caught in the morning and cooked at lunch; the menu depends on what they caught. Pick any busy one – the one to the left of Tienda Angelito is excellent.

Los Cóbanos Village Lodge Los Remedios ☎2420-5248, ⓦwww.loscobanos.com.sv. The older of the two accommodation options has clean thatched rooms with balconies onto the beach, fridges and coffee makers. They also provide breakfast, use of the pool, and rent out snorkel gear and kayaks. US$65

Hostal Kalindgio Right by the headland, backing right onto the beach. This beachhouse offers two big and spotless rooms with private bathroom, as well as dorms and plenty of hammocks, plus a little pool and a kitchen in which to cook the morning catch. Dorms US$10, doubles US$30

BARRA DE SANTIAGO

West of the rough and decaying port of Acajutla, the Carretera Litoral heads to the Guatemalan border at La Hachadura (see box, p.304), with the slopes of the Cordillera Apaneca rising to the north and rolling pasturelands to the south. After 35km an unmarked track leads south to **PLAYA BARRA DE SANTIAGO**, a sandy strip of land separating the ocean from a protected estuary and mangrove reserve inland. The peninsula is inhabited by a largely fishing community, but the expanse of beach is delightfully empty and the locals still seem a little surprised to see visitors.

Julio Cesar (☎7783-4765) runs excellent birdwatching boat trips around the mangroves and to a small archeological site, **Isla del Cajete**, where obsidian arrowheads and other remains have been found; he is also very knowledgeable on local flora and fauna. *Capricho Beach House* can organize canoe trips into the nature reserve, and probably the cheapest deep-sea fishing around (US$27/hr).

Bus #259 from Sonsonate passes the turning from the Carretera, where pick-ups go to the village; or Lena of *Capricho Beach House* can organize a lift. You can also wait for direct buses (#285) that go twice a day from Sonsonate.

Accommodation and eating

Julio César (see above) has a dorm and hammock space at the back of his house, close to the village (US$10). There are *tiendas* and *comedores* within walking distance of *Capricho Beach House*.

Capricho Beach House On the left at the end of the road ☎7932-2318. The place to stay here is a side project from Lena at *Ximena's* in San Salvador. The rooms are nicer here, though there are some reports of dodgy beds. The choice is between firmer metal beds in the dorms, and doubles with fan or a/c and en suite; the outdoor kitchen is for public use. Dorms US$10, doubles US$35

BOSQUE EL IMPOSIBLE

Near the border along the Carretera Litoral is the steamy and uninteresting town of **Cara Sucia**, from whose crossroads a road leads up to one of El Salvador's greatest hidden glories, the forest reserve of **BOSQUE EL IMPOSIBLE**, so called because of the early hazards in transporting coffee by mule pack down from its sheer heights and steep gorges to the coastal port. Covering more than 31 square kilometres and rising through three climatic zones across the Cordillera de Apaneca, the reserve contains more than four hundred species of tree and 1600 species of plant, some unique to the area. It is the largest and most biodiverse protected area in El Salvador. Birdwatchers may glimpse some of the more than three hundred species, including the emerald toucanet, trogons, hummingbirds and eagles, while the park provides a secure habitat for a diverse range of animals, including anteaters, the white-tailed deer and ocelot, plus over five hundred different species of butterfly, including the dazzling blue morpho.

There are clearly marked **trails** starting from the park's visitors' centre (daily 7am–5pm): from two hours to whole-day hikes. It is not advisable, however, to try to explore deeper within the densely forested park without a guide; for a US$10-a-day recommended tip, they are worth every cent, and without them you will get lost within minutes.

Arrival and information

Exploring El Imposible can be time-consuming and expensive; there are no cheap options near the main entrance and most of the San Salvador operators listed on p.258 run expensive tours here. It is actually easier to approach from Tacuba in the north (see p.309).

By bus Bus #259 stops at the crossroads in Cara Sucia on its way to the Guatemalan border – get off here and catch the 11am bus or 2pm pick-up to the park gate. The main entrance to the park is at the Desvío Ahuachapío turn-off from the Carretera Litoral, halfway between the Sonsonate–Acajutla road and Cara Sucia, and about 13.5km from the park itself.

Entry There's a US$6 entry fee to enter the reserve, managed by a nongovernmental organization, SalvaNatura (33 Av Sur 640, Col Flor Blanca, San Salvador; ☏ 2279-1515, ⊛ www.salvanatura.org) – you're meant to visit their office to pay and arrange a guide beforehand, but you can usually do it by phone or just turn up and plead ignorance.

Information Inside the park is a solar-powered visitors' centre (daily 7am–5pm) with information boards about the park's wildlife, and a small souvenir store.

Accommodation and eating

There are *comedores* inside the park. SalvaNatura allows camping on three pitches, small campfires and rinsing (but not washing) in the river.

Hostal El Imposible Inside the park ☏ 2411-5484. A good, eco-neutral hostel with five comfortable cabañas, a springwater pool and a very decent restaurant. US$30

INTO GUATEMALA: LA HACHADURA

From Cara Sucia the highway continues the last few kilometres to **La Hachadura**, a 24hr border crossing used by international buses heading for Mexico and reached via bus #259 from Sonsonate. There's a small *hospedaje* on the Guatemalan side, and buses to Guatemala City (4hr; last bus 3pm), stopping at Esquintla along the way, leave from a kilometre down the road.

NAHUIZALCO

The population of the village of **NAHUIZALCO**, on the southern edge of the range about 10km north of Sonsonate, is mostly descended from the region's indigenous peoples, although few wear traditional dress any longer. The town thrives on the manufacture of **wicker**, with workshops lining the main street. Some of the pieces are small enough to take home, and gentle bargaining is acceptable. As always, the Cedart on 3 C Pte is a helpful place to start and has a shop; there's also a night market, with food stalls. There are no hotels here, but *La Cocina de Doris* on 5A Av Nte is a large canteen serving tasty *típicos* (bean soup US$3). **Bus** #249, which runs the length of the Ruta de las Flores from Sonsonate to Ahuachapán every fifteen minutes, stops at the highway turn-off, which is a 500m walk downhill to the centre.

JUAYÚA

Beyond Nahuizalco, the air freshens as the road winds its way up to the colourful and colonial **JUAYÚA** (pronounced "hwai-**oo**-a"). The settlement was traditionally a coffee-producing town, but when coffee prices slumped in the early 1990s, Juayúans started the food festivals (*ferias gastronómicas*) that dominate the centre every weekend. The town itself is safe at night, clean and attractive (new projects include colourful murals by local painters in one block of C Mercedes), and the coffee-growing countryside around it offers plenty of activities to work off the weekend's indulgences.

What to see and do

On the west side of the main square stands the magnificent **Templo del Señor de Juayúa**. It was built in colonial style in 1957, and houses the Black Christ of Juayúa, carved by Quiro

RUTA DE LAS FLORES

Beginning at the northern edge of the Bosque El Imposible and stretching east for more than 70km from the Guatemalan border, the glorious mountains of the Cordillera Apaneca are covered in a patchwork of coffee plantations and acres of pine forest. The so-called "Ruta de las Flores", covering the area between Concepción de Ataco and Nahuizalco, is named after the abundant white coffee flowers visible during May and the wild flowers that colour the hills and valleys from October to February. This stretch is one of the country's biggest attractions, home to a string of cool and pleasant towns with good accommodation, restaurants and sights, the highlights of which are Juayúa's now-famous *ferias gastronómicas*, the high Laguna Verde and the strongly artistic community of Ataco.

Cataño, sculptor of the Black Christ of Esquipulas in Guatemala (see p.193). Consequently, the town is something of a pilgrimage site, particularly during the January 8–15 festival.

On Saturdays and Sundays the main square and roads leading onto it are replete with the **feria gastronómica**'s food stalls; look out for iguana, paella, snake, Chinese and Mexican dishes, frogs, excellent seafood and chocolate-covered frozen fruit on sticks (US$1). Motorized miniature trains (15min; US$0.50; commentary in Spanish) leave from in front of the church for a short tour of the town. The open-topped double-decker Conga Bus (several daily; 1hr 30min; US$3) leaves from the same place and tours the sights of the Ruta, while a party atmosphere takes off on board, disco music pounding out from giant speakers strapped to the top deck.

Just 2km out of town, **Los Chorros de la Calera** is the town's local swimming spot, with two pools artificially created, the top one deep enough to jump in. You can walk there, or take a tuk-tuk at weekends. There are also trekking, horse-riding, geysers and further coffee tours to be enjoyed locally – organize trips with one of the tour operators listed below.

Arrival and information

By bus On weekdays, the Sonsonate-to-Ahuachapán buses stop on the east side of the Parque Central, but at weekends they are pushed out to Pasaje San Juan, three bocks west along 4 C Pte.

Exchange Scotiabank, by the weekend bus stop on 4 C Pte, has an ATM.

Internet There is a café on 1A Av Nte, open until late, with internet access for US$0.75/hr.

Tour operators Juayúatur (☎ 2469-2387) can provide guides to local attractions, including several nearby waterfalls. César at *Hotel Anáhuac* (see below) does similar tours, and speaks very good English; take a look at the website. Expect to pay up to US$6 per person for during the week, more at weekends.

Accommodation

The town is largely quiet during the week, but at weekends you should book ahead.

Doña Mercedes 2 Av Sur & C 6 Ote ☎ 2452-2287. A cheerful place with comfortable rooms, hot water and cable TV. The shared bathrooms are very clean, or there are en suites for just US$2 more. US$30

Hostal Casa Mazeta 2A Av Nte & C 1 Ote ☎ 2406-3403. A friendly and popular new addition to Juayúa's backpacker scene, two blocks from the main plaza; French run, with clean rooms, dorms and cheap hammock space under cover. The accommodation is arranged around a leafy little garden, plus there's a lounge area, DVD, wi-fi, laundry and kitchen. Dorms US$7, doubles US$20

Hotel Anáhuac 1 C Pte & 5A Av Nte ☎ 2469-2401, ⓦ www.hotelanahuac.com. The clear choice in town and probably the best hostel in the country, run by young and friendly couple César and Janne. Immaculately clean rooms, comfortable beds, powerful hot-water showers, a lovely courtyard with hammocks, vibrant modern art on the walls, free internet, a good DVD collection, book exchange and tours organized. Dorms US$47, doubles US$25

El Mirador 4 C Pte ☎ 2452-2432. A large hotel with hard mattresses in clean but gloomy en-suite rooms around a two-storey atrium. Internet and laundry are available. US$32

Restaurant R & R C Mercedes, one block east of the church. One of the best restaurants around, *R & R* reinvents Central American cuisine with a Western twist (red bean pasta US$8). A main course will cost around US$10, with vegetarian options slightly less.

Eating and drinking

Café Cadejo A couple of blocks down from *Hotel Anáhuac* on Av Nte. Owned by César of *Hotel Anáhuac*, this is a cosy, lively little bar/restaurant spilling out onto the street, and hosting great live music at weekends. Their mojitos are a speciality (US$2.50) – after a couple the day-glo paintings will be dancing before your eyes. They also serve pizzas, burgers and excellent local dishes (US$5–10). Thurs–Sun 5.30pm till late.

Café Festival On the south side of the *parque*. This old *pastelería* serves good coffee, traditional Spanish cakes and fine breakfasts.

El Mirador 4 C Pte. Come here for breakfast on the third floor. They have pancakes (US$1.50) and fruit salads as well as the *típicos*, and the panoramic views – only slightly marred by the glass – are a good morning eye-opener.

Taquería Guadalupana 2 C Ote. Big portions of really good-value Mexican food on the menu here – daily deals for US$2.50. *Tacos al pastor* (US$2) are a favourite.

Moving on

By bus to: Ahuachapán, stopping at Apaneca and Ataco (#249; every 30min; 1hr 15min); Sonsonate, stopping at Nahuizalco (#249; every 30min; 1hr).

APANECA

A short leg further along the road from Juayúa stands another quiet and charming mountain town – **APANECA**, founded by Pedro de Alvarado in the mid-sixteenth century. The town retains an air of friendly tranquillity, decorated with painted lampposts and tidy trimmed hedges, despite being both popular with weekend visitors and home to some fine-dining establishments and expensive accommodation. During the week, you're likely to have the place – and the wonderful surrounding mountain scenery – all to yourself.

What to see and do

There's little to do in Apaneca itself, but it's an enjoyable and not too strenuous walk through woods and *fincas* to the **Laguna Verde**, a small green crater-lake 4km northeast of town. Fringed by reeds and surrounded by mist-clad pine slopes, the lake is a popular destination, and at weekends you're likely to share the path with numerous families and groups of walkers. From the highway on the southern edge of town, follow the well-signed dirt road to the right of the garden centre, and keep going straight up. The hamlet just above the lake, reached after about ninety minutes, has sweeping views from Ahuachapán to Cerro Artillería on the Guatemalan border. The grassy slopes around the lake make a good spot for a picnic.

Closer to town to the north, the smaller and less impressive **Laguna Las Ninfas** is an easy forest walk of about 45 minutes. Other outdoor options include horseriding tours; prospective guides usually gather at 1A Av Nte at 4 Calle Ote, charging around US$5 per person. The town is also known for its *viveros*, or plant nurseries, and the staff at **Vivero Alexandro**, by the track to Laguna Verde on the main road, will show you around, after which you can eat their strawberries in the cheaply priced café.

Arrival and information

Exchange There is an ATM next to the police station, two blocks north and one block east of the Parque Central.

Internet Turbonet, on the far side of the *parque* from the tourist office (US$0.70/hr), lets you drink beers while you check your emails.

Tourist office It is literally an office, on the Parque Central (Sat & Sun 9am–5pm, in theory), with some leaflets and a very helpful man at his desk. A kiosk, opposite, is manned at weekends.

Accommodation

Hostal Rural Las Orquídeas 4 C Pte between 1 Av Sur and Av Central ☎2433-0061. A well-signposted hostel at the north end of town with four clean, simple rooms and hot water. US$15

Hotel Colonia 1A Av Sur by 6 C Pte ☎2433-0662. This pretty hotel does indeed have a colonial-looking courtyard. It's furnished with sofas and hammocks, and the rooms are good, with sturdy mattresses and en-suite bathrooms. US$20

🏃 **Laguna Verde Guest House** To the left of the school in the hamlet by Laguna Verde ☎7859-2865. In a magnificent position on the edge of the El Cuajusto crater and a short walk from Laguna Verde, the "guest house" is in fact two delightfully remote structures: the white igloo with four bunks and a kitchenette is a good, if a little damp-smelling, novelty, but the cabin is a better pick, with views down to Ahuachapán which are beautiful at night. No one lives on site, so calling ahead is essential. Dorms US$12, doubles US$25

Eating

Comedor Next to the *tienda* on 1A C Pte. This nameless *comedor* is the place to come for cheap *típicos*. They do full cooked meals in the evening too.

🏃 **El Jardín de Celeste** Km 92.5 on the road to Ataco ☎2450-5647. Don't believe the hype: Ataco's renowned *La Cocina de mi Abuela* on 1A Av Nte is not what it once was and most now rate this hotel's restaurant to be the best around. It's not as expensive either, serving very well prepared *típicos* like *pollo con arosa* as well as international dishes for under US$10, and with its own plant nursery on site, the surroundings are pretty good too.

Típicos Texizal 1 Av Nte. A brightly coloured and amiable restaurant, which has good daily meal deals for US$2 or full meals for US$6–8, with tasty fried bananas for dessert.

Moving on

By bus to: Ahuachapán, stopping at Ataco (#249; every 30min; 45min); Sonsonate, stopping at Nahuizalco (#249; every 30min; 1hr 15min).

ATACO

Unlike its quiet neighbour, **ATACO** (full name Concepción de Ataco) is full of vibrant life. Children play in the municipal basketball court on the square (they'll let you join in), older generations chat in the square and you'll see artisans at work throughout the town. Some good, cheap accommodation and restaurants have emerged here recently, giving it the feel of an up-and-coming destination.

What to see and do

Ataco is home to the artist known as "Axul", whose boldly coloured, manga-influenced **paintings** of cats, moons and fish cover several buildings both here and in San Salvador. Her shop on the corner of 1A Avenida Nte and 1 Calle Pte sells stylish canvases, masks, wooden figures and boxes for surprisingly little. She is also involved in the Diconte Axul, on the corner of 2A Av Sur and C Central, which pools together the work of many local artists, along with general bric-a-brac. At the back of the shop, the *Café del Sitio* (daily 8am–8pm) serves drinks and snacks in a lovely little garden.

On the opposite street corner is Artesanías Madre Tierra, its exterior walls painted in similar day-glo designs and selling a similar mix of local and Guatemalan handicrafts, souvenirs and weavings. **Tours** of the surrounding area are available from the tourist booth at the entrance to town (see below) – the guides can take you to the swimming spots of the 50-metre Salto de Chacala as well as the upwelling of Chorros del Limo, the opposite of a waterfall, for around US$6 per person.

Arrival and information

By bus Buses come and go from beside the market on the corner of 2 C Pte & 4A Av Nte.

Tourist information There is a tourist kiosk (Sat & Sun 7am–7pm) at the entrance to town by the road out to Ahuachapán.

Accommodation

Posada Don Oli 1A Av Sur ☎2450-5155. This family-run hotel has swings in its pretty courtyard, hot water, and breakfast included. It's a better deal for four people, who can all fit into one of the two rooms for US$48.

Segen Hostel A block north of the main square ☎2450-5832, ✉segenhostel@hotmail.com. The rooms are small but neat and tidy; the dorms come with bunk beds. The best deal in town for backpackers. Dorms US$10, doubles US$25

Eating

Doña Mercedes 2A Av Sur. A large, newly finished food hall with smart wooden tables that does an excellent range of *pupusas* for US$0.30 each, as well as good *tortas* along with foreign beers.

Fonda y Vivero 1A Av Sur. A friendly and leafy restaurant that does good *típicos* in their open courtyard, including a great sausage and beans for US$3.

El Portal Opposite the church. The ornate wooden doors and Maya artefacts may jar with the table-top cooker, but these are good-quality *típicos* – the *yuca* fried in cinnamon is particularly tasty.

AHUACHAPÁN

From Apaneca the road tumbles down 13km or so to the city of **AHUACH-APÁN**. This area, and the lands further north, are some of the oldest inhabited regions of El Salvador, due in large part to the extremely fertile soil. Artefacts found in the region date back to 1200 BC and the early Maya. Ahuachapán is also one of the oldest Spanish settlements in the country, made a city in 1862, and like most towns in the area, its wealth grew from the coffee trade.

Today the city retains an air of peaceful charm, with tight streets and a quiet Parque Central. The main industry is geothermal electricity generation, at one time supplying seventy percent of the country's power, but the generator stations cannot be visited and like many of El Salvador's bigger cities, it is principally a springboard for surrounding attractions.

What to see and do

Confusingly, the **Parque Central** is not at the exact centre of town, but two blocks east of the intersection of the two main streets, Calle Gerardo Barrios and Avenida Francisco Menéndez. The latter and 2A Avenida Nte run parallel to each other from the bus terminal to the cathedral on the *parque*.

The imposing white edifice of the **Iglesia Parroquia de Nuestra Señora de la Asunción**, on the Plaza Concordia, with attractive stained glass and a wooden ceiling, dominates the centre of the city and acts as the focus for the annual fiesta in the first week of February.

Some 5km east of town, near the hamlet of El Barro, are the **ausoles** (geysers) that form the basis of the local geothermal industry. The plumes of steam hang impressively over the lush green vegetation and red soil – particularly photogenic in the early morning light. Access to the area is via the turn-off signed "Planta Geotérmica" on the road to Apaneca – get a pick-up or take the yellow school bus which leaves twice daily from the market. The plant itself is off-limits, but locals will allow you access to their land for a small fee, from where you can get a better view.

Arrival and information

By bus The terminal, a chaotic affair, is on Av Comercial, between C 10 and 12 Pte, eight blocks from the Plaza Concordia.

Internet Infocentros (US$1/hr), on C 3 Pte at 1A Av Nte, has a fast connection and headphones for web calls.

Tourist information There is no tourist office, but Tours & Aventuras (☎2422-0016) will tell you about things to do in the area while trying to sell you a tour.

Accommodation

Las Brisas del Mar On Laguna Espino ☎2443-0775. The local *discoteca* owner offers camping by the lake, with use of pool and hammocks. It's a pretty spot, and there's a restaurant on site too. US$5

La Casa Blanca 2A Av Nte at C Barrios ☎2443-1505, A good-value option, housed in a well-decorated colonial building with large,

Tayúa Av Nte at C Fray Pania ☎7233-6508. A wonderful and atmospheric place, two blocks uphill from the plaza, spearheading Ataco's burgeoning gourmet scene. Owner-chef Veronica (trained in Bournemouth, UK) serves up excellent local cuisine, using organic vegetables and herbs grown in the patio garden (mains around US$6). The decor is arty and tasteful, with background jazz music – a rarity around here – and the bakery out front sells the best bread and pastries for miles around. It's worth phoning in advance as they are often only open at weekends and in high season.

clean rooms, all with bath and TV. The restaurant is slightly overpriced, but set around a relaxing courtyard. US$40

Eating and drinking

Las Brisas del Mar On Laguna Espino ☎2443-0775. The best disco in these parts, which blares corny pop out over the lake, is actually 5km out of town, but call them and they will give you a free lift here and back, from your hotel. It's very popular with the locals.
Casa Grande 4A Av Nte 2. There's plenty of character in this restaurant, with loud music blaring and a standard menu featuring some game specialities including venison (*venado*) and rabbit (*conejo*) for under US$6.
La Estancia 1A Av Sur at C Barrios. Housed in a rather run-down former coffee mansion, this *comedor* has well-prepared *comida a la vista* at standard prices.
Mixta "S" 2A Av Sur by the *parque*. A "mixta" is a flatbread stuffed with meat, cheese or vegetables, and that is what they do here for under US$2, as well as some fast food and a big selection of fruit juices.

Directory

Exchange Scotiabank is on the corner of C 4 Pte & Av Francisco Menéndez, with money exchange, travellers' cheque-cashing and an ATM.
Pharmacy Farmacia Central, 2A Av Sur & C Barrios (☎2443-0158).

Post office C 1 Ote & 1A Av Sur (Mon–Fri 8am–5pm, Sat 8am–noon).
Supermarkets De Todo and Despensa Familiar are by the bus terminal.
Telephones Telecom is at C 3 Pte & 2A Av Sur by the Parque.

Moving on

By bus to: Chalchuapa, for Tazumal (#210; frequent; 30min); Las Chinamas (#263; every 15min; 45min); Santa Ana (#202/#210; frequent; 1hr); San Salvador (#202; frequent; 3hr 30min); Sonsonate (#249; every 15min; 2hr 30min); Tacuba (#264/#15; every 20min; 40min).

AROUND AHUACHAPÁN

While the Ruta de las Flores heads off to the east, there are also two great spots to the north and south. Tacuba, to the south, is now the best point of entry to the dramatic Bosque El Imposible, while Tazumal, a short trip north, is one of the best Pipil sites in the country.

Tacuba

Some 15km west of Ahuachapán lies the quiet mountain village of **Tacuba**, reached via a winding and scenic road with grand views of coffee plantations and the Bosque El Imposible (see p.303). An important settlement existed here long before the Spaniards arrived,

see p.303

> ### INTO GUATEMALA: LAS CHINAMAS
>
> From Ahuachapán, a reasonably good and very scenic road runs the 20km or so to the Guatemalan border, just past **Las Chinamas**. Local bus #11AH leaves for the border every fifteen minutes, taking about an hour. International buses from Santa Ana also pass through at about 5.30am. There is no ticket office – stand on C 6 Pte more or less opposite the *Hotel San José* and flag them down. Buses run to Guatemala City from Valle Nuevo on the Guatemalan side.

and the village retains strong folkloric traditions, although you'll only really notice these at fiesta time.

The town is small and welcoming, but the only thing to see is the ruins of the colonial **church**, which was much less ruined before the 2001 earthquake. Either the guard or Manolo of Imposible Tours (see box below) will let you in to walk through and climb up the remaining structure. The real draw of Tacuba is, however, its back route into Bosque El Imposible and the outdoor activities it offers.

Tacuba can be reached by **bus** (#264) or minibus (#15) every fifteen minutes from Ahuachapán, a journey of forty-five minutes.

Accommodation and eating

There is a good place to eat and drink opposite the *Miraflores* as well as a few unextravagant *comedores* in town.

Hostal Mamá y Papá 1A C 1 ☎2417-4268. The mama and papa in question are Mr and Mrs González, parents of Manolo (see box below) and very good hosts. Hot showers, clean and comfortable rooms, coffee every morning and shady hammocks add to the appeal, and the roof terrace is a nice place to watch the sunset with a beer. Dorms US$8, doubles US$13

Miraflores 2A Av Nte ☎2417-4746. If *Mamá y Papá* is full, this place is bright and breezy, and birds sing in the flower-filled courtyard. Try to get an en-suite room – they are brighter and with two windows on the first storey. Rates include two meals. US$20

Tazumal

Northeast from Ahuachapán, the road winds down onto a broad and scenic plain, and the town of **Chalchuapa**, whose main draw is the archeological site of **Tazumal** (Tues–Sun 9am–5pm; US$3) on the edge of town. The ruins cover a period of 750 years, mostly the Late Classic period (600–900 AD) and are – by comparison with sites in Honduras and Guatemala – rather small, although they do have their own, impressive, beauty. The central and largest structure is a fourteen-stepped ceremonial pyramid, influenced by the style of Teotihuacán in Mexico, though sadly rather sloppily restored. Earlier remains, dating back to 100–200 AD, have been found beneath the pyramid. The Maya abandoned the city around the end of the ninth century, during the collapse of the Classic Maya culture, and, unusually, Pipils moved in and occupied the site, building a pyramid dating back to the Early Post-Classic (900–1200 AD) and another pelota court, to the northwest corner of the site. Tazumal was finally abandoned around 1200 AD. A very decent **museum** (same hours; Spanish only) displays artefacts discovered during excavations. The nearby ruins of El Trapiche and Casa Blanca are currently being excavated and aren't yet open to the public.

Bus #218 from Ahuachapán drops passengers off at a small plaza a few blocks from the centre of town; from here, walk uphill for about four blocks and follow the sign.

IMPOSIBLE TOURS

Based in Tacuba, Imposible Tours (ⓦwww.imposibletours.com) is one of the best tour operators in the country, due in most part to good-humoured and charismatic leader Manolo González, whose ceaseless enthusiasm comes from a genuine desire to get to know everyone he guides. The company's hallmark tour takes you along the back route through Bosque El Imposible along a series of occasionally staggering waterfalls and sheer-walled canyons, though the setup is flexible. Other ideas include mountain biking along ridges to the coast, several day-treks and wallowing in hot volcanic springs with a beer or two. Tours start from US$20 per person.

SANTA ANA

Self-possessed **SANTA ANA**, El Salvador's second city, lies in a superb location in the Cihautehuacán valley. Surrounded by green peaks, with the slope of Volcán Santa Ana rising to the southwest, the gently decaying colonial streets exude a certain bourgeois complacency and restrained, provincial calm that is generally only ruptured during the July fiesta, when a host of events bring the streets to life. It's a good place to relax, see the classiest Parque Central around and enjoy a couple of nights out, though the natural attractions of Lago de Coatepeque, the forest reserve of Cerro Verde, and the Santa Ana and Izalco volcanoes all beckon.

What to see and do

Santa Ana's **town centre** possesses arguably the finest main square in the country: the Parque Libertad is neatly laid out with a small bandstand, where people gather to sit and chat in the early evening, surrounded by eye-catching architecture.

Catedral de Santa Ana

On the eastern edge of the *parque* is the magnificent **Catedral de Santa Ana**, an imposing neo-Gothic edifice completed in 1905. It's the second cathedral to occupy this site: a Spanish settlement was initially founded here in July 1569, when Bishop Bernardino de Villapando

SANTA ANA

EATING & DRINKING
Ban Ban — 3
Café Expresión — 7
Cafetería Central — 5
Cuatro Estaciones — 11
Drive Inn Molina — 12
Los Horcones — 2
Jam Rock — 9
Lovers' Steak House — 8
Parrilla Texana — 1
Paulina's — 6
El Pelicano — 10
El Sin Rival — 4

ACCOMMODATION
Casa Frolaz — E
Casa Verde — B
El Faro — C
Libertad — A
Tazumal — D

Buses to Metapán

Bus Station

Mercado

2nd Bridge Military Barracks

4A CALLE PONIENTE
El Calvario
Parque Menéndez
2A CALLE PONIENTE
CALLE LIBERTAD PONIENTE
1A CALLE PONIENTE
Mercado Central
3A CALLE PONIENTE
5A CALLE PONIENTE
7A CALLE PONIENTE
9A CALLE PONIENTE
11A CALLE PONIENTE
CALLE MÉNDEZ
13A CALLE PONIENTE
15A CALLE PONIENTE
17A CALLE PONIENTE

4A CALLE ORIENTE
Teatro Nacional
Cathedral
Parque Libertad
Alcaldía
Supermarket
Telecom
Museo Regional del Occidente
Mercado de Artesanías
CALLE LIBERTAD ORIENTE
1A CALLE ORIENTE
Pharmacy
3A CALLE ORIENTE
Parroquia Nuestra Sra del Carmen
5A CALLE ORIENTE
7A CALLE ORIENTE
9A CALLE ORIENTE
11A CALLE ORIENTE
15A CALLE ORIENTE

10A AV NORTE
2A AVENIDA NORTE
1A AVENIDA NORTE
3A AVENIDA NORTE
5A AVENIDA SUR
7A AVENIDA SUR
14A AVENIDA SUR
AV JOSE MATIAS DELGADO
10A AVENIDA SUR
8A AVENIDA SUR
6A AVENIDA SUR
4A AVENIDA SUR
2A AVENIDA INDEPENDENCIA
3A AVENIDA SUR

0 — 200 m

N

E, 9, 10, 11, @ & Buses to Guatemala   12 & Metrocentro

arrived en route from Guatemala. Commenting on the beauty and fertility of the area, he ordered work to begin on a church dedicated to Nuestra Señora de Santa Ana, the saint of the day of his arrival. Completed seven years later, this occupied the site of the present cathedral until it was destroyed in the early twentieth century to make way for the new building.

Inside the cathedral, the high naves, rather unsympathetically painted in pink and grey, soar upwards, and images – some dating back four hundred years – line the walls to the altar. Inset into the walls are plaques from local worshippers giving thanks to various saints for miracles performed.

Teatro Nacional

On the northern edge of the plaza, the **Teatro Nacional**, completed in Renaissance style in 1910, was funded by taxes on local dignitaries. Once the proud home of the country's leading theatre companies, the building became a cinema before falling into disuse. Now restored to something resembling its former glories, it once again hosts recitals and concerts, as well as exhibitions and plays (see opposite).

Alcaldía

Facing the cathedral on the western edge of the plaza is the **Alcaldía**, another fine Renaissance-style piece of cream-coloured architecture – for writer Paul Theroux its facade possessed the "colonnaded opulence of a ducal palace." Although there is nothing to do in it, and for that matter nothing inherently ducal about it, the building is quite easy on the eye.

Museo Regional del Occidente

On the second block down Avenida Independencia from the *parque*, the **Museo Regional del Occidente** (Tues–Sun 9am–noon & 1–5pm; US$0.35) provides a comprehensive introduction to the region's history and archeological sites, though the best bit is the room dedicated to the various evolving forms of legal tender in the country, right up to the dollar – a strangely appealing exhibit.

Arrival and information

By bus The main terminal is on 10A Av Sur between C 13 & 15 Pte. Buses for Metapán (#325) arrive and depart two blocks west of the main terminal, in front of the Despensa Familiar supermarket, and international buses to and from Guatemala arrive and depart from C 25 Pte between 6A & 8A Av Sur, just north of *Casa Frolaz*.

City transport

Buses Bus #51 runs between the centre and the bus terminal, and you can take any bus going up and down Av Independencia to get between the centre and the Metrocentro.
Taxis There are stands on the *parque*, outside the Metrocentro and on 10A Av Sur, by the market, or you can just hail one on the street. They should cost US$3–4, which you should politely agree beforehand.

Accommodation

The area around 8A and 10A Av Sur has the highest concentration of cheap and basic places to stay, co-dependent on the vice industry operating on the streets at night. Book ahead to get a spot in *Casa Frolaz* or *Casa Verde*.

Casa Frolaz 29 C Pte No 42B ☎2440-5302. One of the country's finest accommodation options is in the house of Javier Díaz, who is a descendant of one of the oldest families, a painter of international repute and a perfect host. With a private kitchen, laundry, hot water and a fruit-filled garden, a stay here could be three times the price. Camping US$5, dorms US$8, doubles US$20
Casa Verde 7 C Pte between 8A & 10A Av Sur ☎7860-7180. A very good option close to the centre, and quite different from the standard of neighbouring hotels. Spotless rooms on an open courtyard and very well equipped kitchen. There are board games and a laundry machine, and the young owners are keen and helpful. Dorms US$7, doubles US$25
El Faro 14A Av Sur ☎2447-7787. Packets of sweet and savoury snacks await in these fairly clean rooms covered in bold murals. There is one good

room with three double beds upstairs, hot water and a stained-glass balcony. The hotel is safe and secure, but you should not go out at night alone in this area. US$15

Libertad C 4 Ote at 1A Av Nte ☎ 2441-2358, ⓔ javal@navegante.com.sv. Great location right by the cathedral with gigantic, quite clean and basic rooms with TV, some with bathroom. Free internet for guests. Bring your own padlock for the doors. US$20

Tazumal C 25 Pte & 10A Av Sur ☎ 2440-2830. Large rooms in an ageing building around a courtyard. Service is amiable and all rooms are en suite, some with cable TV, some with a/c. If both the *casas* are full, this is the next most pleasant option in town. US$5

Eating

Santa Ana has a reasonable number of moderately priced places to eat. There's fast food along Av Independencia and in the Metrocentro.

Ban Ban Av Independencia Sur. The best bakery in town, with a second outlet in the Metrocentro, has sandwiches for lunch, and cake, pastries and coffee all day.

Café Expresión C 11 Pte between 6A and 8A Av Sur. An arts and cultural centre, bookshop and internet café in bohemian surroundings. They do especially good sandwiches, as well as full meals (US$7–8) and desserts (US$3–4). Closed Sun.

Cafetería Central 2A Av Sur between C 1 & 3 Pte. A good *comedor* for breakfast and cheap lunches. There's basic *comida a la vista* available, as well as excellent *pupusas* (US$1.50).

Lovers' Steak House 4A Av Sur & 17 C Pte ☎ 2440-5717. A meat grill and Santa Ana institution that serves huge portions of meat and seafood, accompanied by a *bocadillo* (appetizer), as well as wine or beer. Mains cost around US$10, but you will definitely be full when you leave.

Parrilla Texana C Libertad between 4A & 2A Av Sur. Meats served from the grill in a variety of combinations and forms amid American diner-style

decor. Though around the US$10 mark for a main course, the portions are large and the food good.

El Sin Rival C Libertad Ote. A cool place to chill out in the centre, this *sorbetería* serves original flavours of sorbet (US$0.70–1); blueberry is the best.

Drinking and nightlife

Much of Santa Ana's pretty decent nightlife is outside of the centre to the south, so take a taxi (US$3–4). Heading out of town, taxis are easily found on Av Independencia; on the way back, get the barman to arrange one.

Drive Inn Molina 25A Av Sur at Carretera Antigua ☎ 2447-5290. A little out of town and best accessed by taxi, this big and well-known club has pool tables, live music and dancing. The best night is Thurs, but it's lively all weekend. Open from 11pm until the early morning.

Los Horcones Next to the cathedral on Parque Libertad ☎ 2484-7511. The best views in the city, with seats on a rickety terrace facing the cathedral and plaza. There are drinks promotions on Saturdays, and there's often dancing too.

Jam Rock Off the bypass south of town. This young and cool bar with regular and good live bands is the current favourite place to go after dark in Santa Ana. Beers are just US$1 and the atmosphere is very friendly.

Paulina's Av Independencia at C 7 Pte. Bar and restaurant with international meals for less than US$5 and a background of blaring music videos. Nicely furnished with log tables and chairs as well as a jukebox.

El Pelicano Av Moraga, 1km south of town ☎ 2449-0386. A small bar with good food, including over sixty appetizers (US$2–3) – you'll only need three to fill you up. They play pop music and regularly host karaoke.

Entertainment

Cinema Cinemark, in the Metrocentro, shows dubbed or subtitled Hollywood blockbusters.

Theatre The beautifully restored Teatro Nacional (see opposite; ☎ 2447-6268) has a calendar of classical music, theatre and performance arts. Look out in the Friday *Prensa Gráfica* or stop by to find out times. Tickets should be under US$4 a show.

Directory

Exchange There is a clump of four or five banks around 2A Av Nte behind the Alcaldía, while Banco Cuscatlán is on the corner of C 3 Pte & Av Independencia.

TREAT YOURSELF

Cuatro Estaciones 23 C Pte & 8A Av Sur ☎ 2440-3168. This smart local favourite distinguishes itself from the pricier options nearby by its fine cooking rather than the size of its portions. It has an Italian influence, with good bruschetta and spaghetti dishes, as well as a fine wine menu and coffee selection. US$18–20 per head.

Internet Time Out (open until 7 or 9pm; US$1/1hr 30min) is on 10A Av Sur & 29A C Pte, while Infocentros, on Av Independencia between C 9 & 11 Ote, is near the centre (until 7pm; US$1/hr).

Market The Mercado Central is on 8A Av Sur between C 1 & 3 Pte, and the Mercado de Artesanías, with a range of national crafts, is on 1A Av Sur.

Post office Av Independencia between 7 & 9 C Pte (Mon–Fri 7.30am–5pm).

Supermarket La Despensa de Don Juan (8am–8pm), on the southeast corner of the park, has a good selection; there is also a bigger super-market at the Metrocentro.

Telephones Telecom is on C Libertad at 5A Av Sur.

Moving on

By bus to: Ahuachapán (#210; frequent; 1hr); Chalchuapa (#218; frequent; 30min); Guatemala City, Guatemala (standard/first class; hourly/2 daily; 4hr/3hr 30min); Juayúa (#238; 6 daily; 1hr 30min); Lago de Coatepeque (#220; every 30min; 1hr 30min); Metapán (#235; every 20min; 1hr 15min); Parque Nacional Los Volcanes (#248; 6 daily; 1hr 30min); San Cristóbal (#248; every 20min; 1hr); San Salvador (#201; frequent; 1hr 30min); Santa Elena, Belize, via Flores, Guatemala (daily; 9hr); Sonsonate (#216/209; frequent; 1hr 15min/1hr 45min).

AROUND SANTA ANA

One of the best advantages to Santa Ana is its access to the volcano and a crater lake as picturesque as you are ever likely to see to the southeast. As neither has particularly good accommodation, it's worth making separate day-trips to each one.

Lago de Coatepeque

From El Congo junction, 14km south-east of Santa Ana, a winding branch road descends to the truly stunning crater-lake of **Lago de Coatepeque**. The views are so lovely that it's worth getting off the bus at the *mirador*, 4km from the water's edge, to take your time soaking them in, and then walking down the rest of the way. As much of the shore is bounded by private houses, access to the water itself is difficult. **Boat rides** are available at *Parque Recreativo Rancho Alegre* (in reality little more than a pier and a *comedor*), costing from US$3 per person for a thirty-minute trip to US$15 per person for a full circuit of the lake, with prices based on a group of four.

Buses #220 and #240 leave Santa Ana every thirty minutes for the lake, taking an hour and passing all points of interest mentioned. If you're heading back to San Salvador, take the Santa Ana bus as far as El Congo then walk down the slip road to the main highway and catch any bus running from Santa Ana to the capital.

Accomodation and eating

Accommodation on the lake is limited. The *comedor* on the pier is pretty good, and cheap; otherwise the restaurant in *Torremolinos* is the best around, and getting a meal could earn you the right to jump in the pool if you're not staying.

Centro de Obreros Km 55 by the lakeshore. If on a budget, this free place might appeal, though you need a permit from the Ministeros de Trabajo (see p.243). Bring a sleeping bag or sheets and mosquito repellent.

Torremolinos Calle Principal, 200m on the right down the road alongside the lake ☎2441-6037, ⓦwww.torremolinoslagocoatepeque.com. The road leads on from the *Centro de Obreros* to this more comfortable hotel, with large, clean rooms, two pools and a small private beach. They also arrange boat trips, but rates are much higher than at Rancho Alegre. US$40

INTO GUATEMALA: SAN CRISTÓBAL

Crossing to Guatemala at San Cristóbal is quick and easy: it's open 24hr, and there are frequent buses from Santa Ana (#36; 1hr) to the crossing. There are no official exchange facilities, but the touting moneychangers can offer reasonable rates. On the Guatemalan side, buses run to Asunción Mita, with connections to Guatemala City.

PARQUE NACIONAL LOS VOLCANES

Around 14km southeast of Santa Ana on the Interamericana, a narrow road winds up from the El Congo junction through coffee plantations, maize fields and pine woods to the **PARQUE NACIONAL LOS VOLCANES** (daily 7am–5.30pm; US$1). Here the three volcanic peaks of Cerro Verde, Santa Ana and Izalco form a living example of geological evolution and offer great climbing and ecotourism opportunities.

What to see and do

The oldest volcano in the park, **Cerro Verde**, is now a softened, densely vegetated mountain harbouring a wealth of wildlife. **Santa Ana**, the highest volcano in the country at 2365m, has erupted out of its dormant state, while **Izalco**, one of the youngest volcanoes in the world, is an almost perfect, bare lava cone of unsurpassed natural beauty, and a very novel climb.

Volcán Cerro Verde

Dense forest fills the crater of the long-extinct **Volcán Cerro Verde**, inside of which a now-rare mix of Salvadoran flora and fauna combine, like a big bowl of nature soup. The numerous species of **plants**, including pinabetes and more than fifty species of orchid, are best viewed in season (for most species, between November and March), while armadillos and white-tailed deer are shy and hard to see year-round. Agoutis, which look like long-legged guinea pigs, can be found rummaging in the forest floor, but it's the **birds** that are most regularly spotted. Humming-birds and toucans are commonly seen, as is the turquoise-browed motmot (*torogoz* – El Salvador's national bird), identifiable by its pendulous, racketed tail. *Miradores* along the way overlook Volcán Santa Ana and, far below, Lago de Coatepeque.

From the car park (see p.316), go clockwise along the main trail, the *sendero natural*, for an enjoyable walk of around 45 minutes through the green calm of the forest. Smaller trails branch off through the trees if you want to explore. The trails are clear and very well managed, but can get busy at weekends.

Volcán Santa Ana

A path branches left from a signed turn ten minutes into the *sendero natural*, and leads eventually to the summit of **Volcán Santa Ana**, known also as "Ilamatepec" (Nahuat for "old lady mountain"). In October 2005 the old lady turned out to be a bit more vigorous than her name suggests, erupting violently, killing two people in a boiling mudslide that broke off down its side and spitting rocks, some the size of cars, in a one-mile radius. A second eruption was predicted, though has never materialized, and evacuated communities have long since moved back. The trail to the summit was closed for several years, but has recently reopened; guided climbs follow the same format as Volcán Izalco (see below), but check with Corsatur (☎2243-7835) for an update in case of further eruptions. Some guides may offer to take you up through the woodlands and lava formation to the top, but as this involves hiding from the police, it is inadvisable.

Volcán Izalco

Sitting in contrast to the green slopes around it, the bleak, black volcanic pile of majestic **Volcán Izalco** began as a small hole in the ground in 1770. The volcano formed rapidly over the next two centuries, during which time its lava plume, known as the "lighthouse of the Pacific", was used by sailors to navigate. Then in 1966, just as a new hotel was built at its base, the plume dried up. Now guided tours leave daily at 11am from the car park for the steep climb to the top (3–4hr; US$1); be there at 10.30am for the tour briefing. There are two separate tours up Izalco and Santa Ana, both leaving here at the same time. The guides are compulsory, for your safety, set up in response to muggings. A marked trail leads from the lookout down for about thirty minutes to a saddle between Volcán Santa Ana and Volcán Izalco. From here it takes at least an hour to climb the barren moonscape of volcanic scree to the summit. Bring water and good shoes.

Arrival

By bus Sonsonate-bound bus #248 runs directly to the car park (6 daily; 1hr 30min) from the Vencedora terminal in Santa Ana; catch the 8.30am departure if you want to catch the guides.

Accommodation

If you have your own tent, you can camp for free around the visitors' centre in the car park, though there are no dedicated facilities, so bring food and water; ask a warden to tell you where to set up.

Moving on

The last bus from the car park leaves at 5pm and runs to El Congo only, from where you can pick up services to either Santa Ana or San Salvador.

METAPÁN

Some 40km north of Santa Ana, the small, friendly town of **METAPÁN** is scenically situated on the edge of the mountains of the Cordillera Metapán–Alotepeque, which run east along the border with Honduras. Metapán was one of only four communities that supported Delgado's first call for independence in 1811. With low-set, gently whitewashed buildings, it is one of the more pleasant of Salvadoran provincial towns, the market less unsightly than most and confined to the outskirts well away from the centre. The main reason for staying in Metapán, however, is for access to the international reserve of **Bosque Montecristo**, jointly administered by the governments of El Salvador, Honduras and Guatemala.

What to see and do

At the Parque Central, the **Iglesia de la Parroquia**, completed in 1743, is one of El Salvador's finest colonial churches, with a beautifully preserved facade. Inside, the main altar is flanked by small pieces worked in silver from a local mine while the ornately decorated cupola features paintings of San Gregorio, San Augustín, San Ambrosio and San Gerónimo. On the south side of the plaza, the colonnaded **Alcaldía** is an attractive building in its own right, watched over by two statues of teeth-baring jaguars symbolizing the strength and suffering of the indigenous people of the department. The west side, rather bizarrely, forms one of the stands of the town's football stadium, though it's cunningly disguised with a neo-colonial colonnaded facade and balcony restaurant, which also offers a good people-watching perch over the square.

Arrival and information

By bus Buses arrive at the main terminal on the Carretera Internacional, five or six blocks from the centre down C 15 de Septiembre, which heads past the market and most of the hotels towards the centre.

Accommodation

California Carretera Internacional at 9 C Ote ☎ 2442-0561. Fans of new hotels will prefer to stay a little further from the centre for these spotless en-suite rooms – arguably the best in town. US$13
Central Av Isero Menéndez ☎ 7535-6112. More basic, and cheaper, slightly creaky rooms are available here. Not a bad choice, though, as it's clean and the beds are fine, but some may begrudge the lack of toilet seats. US$10
Christina 4A Av Sur & C 15 de Septiembre ☎ 2442-0044. A nice hotel by the market which offers hot water, a/c and balconies over the street, supplies towels and has some lovely old furniture, although the beds are a little soft. US$15

Eating

Antojitos La Nueva Esperanza Off the *parque* on Av Benjamin Valiente. This lofty food hall in a colonial building is excellent, with seven dishes of *comida a la vista* a day (US$2–3). Open until 10pm.

Casa de Teja Just off the north side of the *parque* on Av 1A Nte. A bar and restaurant with a collection of antique knick-knacks and well-prepared dishes like *mariscada* (US$8) and tacos (US$4). It's a good spot for a relaxed evening drink too.

Pastelería La Exquisita C 15 de Septiembre near *Hospedaje Central.* Breakfast, cakes and sweets as well as lunch, all served by Osh-Kosh-wearing staff. Try the "Jennifer" – a cupcake that's so pretty you won't want to bite into it (US$1.80).

Directory

Exchange If you need to change money, there's a Banco Salvadoreño on the park and a Scotiabank at Av Ignacio Gomez and C 15 de Septiembre.

Internet Cyber Net, on the northeast corner of the park, has a sofa and PlayStation as well as internet for US$0.60/hr.

Supermarket Supermercado de Todo (7am–7pm) is near the bus terminal on Carretera Internacional.

Moving on

By bus to: Anguiatú and the Guatemalan border (#211A/#235; every 30min; 30min); San Salvador (#201A; 6 daily; 2hr); Santa Ana (#235; every 20min; 1hr 30min).

AROUND METAPÁN

If you are not crossing the border yet, there is only one thing to see around Metapán: the beautiful Bosque Montecristo straddling the three countries of El Salvador, Honduras and Guatemala.

Parque Nacional Montecristo

The brilliant **Parque Nacional Montecristo** reserve (daily 7am–3pm) rises through two climatic zones to the **Punto Trifinio**, the summit of Cerro Montecristo (2418m), where the borders of Honduras, Guatemala and El Salvador converge. The higher reaches of Montecristo, beginning at around 2100m, are home to an expanse of virgin **cloudforest**, with an annual rainfall of two metres and one hundred percent humidity. Orchids and pinabetes thrive in these climatic conditions, while huge oaks, pines and cypresses, some towering to over 20m, swathed in creepers, lichens and mosses, form a dense canopy preventing sunlight from reaching the forest

---

VISITING THE PARQUE NACIONAL MONTECRISTO

Getting to the park can be expensive, so try to get into a group of four and organize a taxi from around the Parque Central in Metapán (US$45 return). Alternatively, have a tour operator take you from San Salvador (US$30–50 per person; see p.258). Occasional pick-ups make the journey up for a negotiable fee; the best place to catch them is at the turning to the Bosque, by *Hotel San José* on the Carretera Internacional. In theory, you need permission to enter the park from the Ministerio de Medio Ambiente in San Salvador (☎2223-0444), but if you're on an organized tour your guide will take care of this. Note that you're not allowed to enter on foot, and that the upper reaches of cloudforest are closed to visitors from May to October.

The park entrance is 5km from Metapán. Pay the entrance fee (US$6 per person, US$1.50 per vehicle) here. After another 2km you come to the Casco Colonial, formerly Hacienda San José, where the wardens are based and where you have to register; it has an interesting collection of natural history and archeological exhibits, as well as a small orchid garden. From here the road continues for another 14km before reaching Los Planes (1890m), where there is a small restaurant serving *típicos* (US$2), as well as camping areas (with toilets and picnic tables; free, but no equipment, so bring food and water), and two simple cabañas sleeping up to eight each (US$35 per cabin).

INTO GUATEMALA: ANGUIATÚ

Another usually smooth border crossing to Guatemala lies 13km further north from Metapán at Anguiatú. It is open day and night and is the most convenient crossing if you're heading for Esquipulas in Guatemala or the Copán ruins in Honduras. Regular buses run from the Guatemalan side to Chiquimula until 5.30pm. If you're coming in the other direction note that the last bus to Metapán leaves at 6.30pm.

floor. **Wildlife** abounds, with howler and spider monkeys the most visible mammals, and jaguars and other large mammals hiding out. **Birds**, including hummingbirds, quetzals, toucans and the regional endemic bushy-crested jay, are more easily seen. Walking straight to the summit is a truly rewarding climb of around four hours; the path from Los Planes leads through the cloudforest, however, and you can branch off in any direction – bring warm clothing and good footwear. Trails also lead from just below Los Planes to the peaks of Cerro el Brujo and Cerro Miramundo.

Honduras

[handwritten annotation] basically you only need to go to Utila!

BAY ISLANDS:
with a unique personality and world-famous diving, these islands are the country's top destination ✪

LA MOSQUITIA:
an isolated and undisturbed land, where nature still rules ✪

COPÁN:
step back in time at these spectacular Mayan ruins ✪

OLANCHO:
tackle Honduras's most stunning and challenging terrain ✪

LAGO DE YOJOA:
hide in caves, fly over waterfalls, or just enjoy the beautiful scenery ✪

GRACIAS:
one of the country's oldest towns and the gateway to the Parque Nacional Celaque ✪

ROUGH COSTS

DAILY BUDGET Basic US$30/ occasional treat US$45

DRINK Nacional beer US$1, coffee US$0.90

FOOD *Almuerzo típico* US$3.50

CAMPING/HOSTEL/BUDGET HOTEL US$4/US$9/US$15

TRAVEL Copán–San Pedro Sula (140km) by bus: 3hr, US$6

FACT FILE

POPULATION 7.3 million

AREA 112,090 sq km

LANGUAGES Spanish, English in the Bay Islands

CURRENCY Honduras lempira (L)

CAPITAL Tegucigalpa (population: 1.7 million)

INTERNATIONAL PHONE CODE ☏504

TIME ZONE GMT -6hr

Introduction

All too often, Honduras receives short shrift on travellers' Central American itineraries: most visitors either race to see the Maya ruins at Copán or to the palm-fringed beaches of the Bay Islands, and skip the rest of the country entirely. And while these are two beautiful, worthy sights, there's much more to Honduras – from the wetlands of La Mosquitia to the subtropical shore of the Golfo de Fonseca, this is a land of inspiring, often untouched natural beauty – and a longer visit will pay ample rewards.

The capital, **Tegucigalpa**, is somewhat underwhelming, but is home to the best facilities and services in the country; while 100km south of the city lies the volcanic **Isla El Tigre**, a little-visited but worthwhile getaway. An essential detour on the way north to the energetic city of **San Pedro Sula** is the **Lago de Yojoa** region, which offers birdwatching, caves and a 43-metre waterfall. To the west, colonial towns like **Santa Rosa de Copán** and **Gracias** offer fantastic restaurants, hot springs and access to indigenous villages, while the sparsely populated region of **Olancho** – Honduras's "Wild East" – and the **Sierra de Agalta** national park has the most extensive stretch of virgin cloudforest in Central America. On the Caribbean coast, **Tela** and **Trujillo** are good-sized towns with great beaches, while **La Ceiba**, larger and with thriving nightlife, is the departure point for the **Bay Islands**, home to world-class diving and a rich cultural mix.

Gradually, Honduras is waking up to its potential as an **ecotourism** destination – its network of national parks and preserves is extensive – as well as the likely benefits of an increased tourist infrastructure for the country's struggling economy (it's the second poorest country in Central America, with over half of Hondurans living below the poverty line). The jewel in the crown of Honduras's natural resources is the biosphere reserve of the **Río Plátano** in **La Mosquitia**. Encompassing one of the finest remaining stretches of virgin tropical rainforest in Central America, the region is largely uninhabited and a trip here really does get you off the beaten track.

CHRONOLOGY

1000 BC Maya settlers move into the Río Copán valley.

100 AD Construction of the city of Copán begins.

426 AD Maya royal dynasty is founded. Copán, the civilization's centre for artistic and scientific

WHEN TO VISIT

The climate in Honduras is generally dictated by altitude. In the central highlands, the weather is pleasantly warm in the daytime and cool at night. The hot Pacific and Caribbean coasts offer the relief of breezes and cooling rain showers, while San Pedro Sula and other lowland towns can be positively scorching in summer.

Honduras's rainy season, "winter" (*invierno*), runs from May to November (most markedly June and July). In much of the country it rains for only a few hours in the afternoon, though along the northern coast and in Mosquitia rain is possible year-round. October and November are the only months you might want to avoid in these parts: in the middle of the hurricane season (generally said to begin in August), this is when you're most likely to be affected by storms.

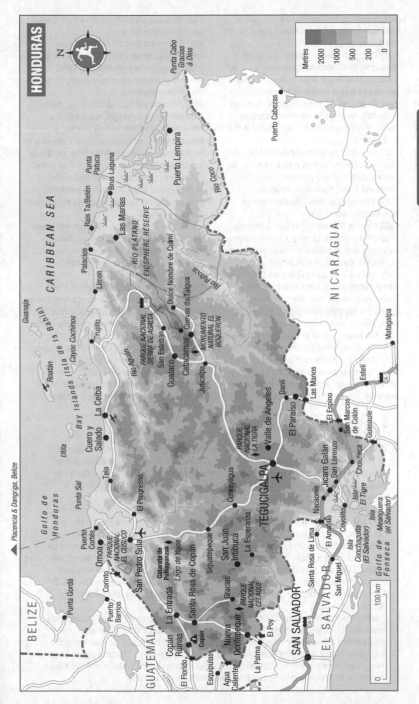

HONDURAS

N

Placencia & Dangriga, Belize

CARIBBEAN SEA

Golfo de Honduras

BELIZE

GUATEMALA

EL SALVADOR

NICARAGUA

Punta Cabo
Gracias á Dios

Puerto Cabezas

Punta Patuca

Puerto Lempira

Rio Coco

Rais Ta/Belén

Brus Laguna

Las Marías

Palacios

RIO PLÁTANO
BIOSPHERE RESERVE

Linon

Dulce Nombre de Culmí

Rio Paluca

Guanaja

Bay Islands (Isla de la Bahía)

Roatán   *Cayos Cochinos*

Utila

La Ceiba

Cuero y
Salado

Trujillo

Rio Aguán

San Esteban

PARQUE NACIONAL
SIERRA DE AGALTA

Gualaco

Catacamas   Cuevas de Talgua

Juticalpa

MONUMENTO
NATURAL EL
BOQUERÓN

Matagalpa

Estelí

CA-1

Las Manos

El Espino

San Marcos
de Colón

Guasaule

Danlí

El Paraíso

Valle de Ángeles

PARQUE
NACIONAL
LA TIGRA

Punta Sal

Tela

El Progresso

Comayagua

TEGUCIGALPA

San Lorenzo

Choluteca

Nacaome

Jícaro Galán

*Golfo de
Fonseca*

Isla
Conchagüita
(El Salvador)

Isla
El Tigre

Coyolito

Isla
Meanguera
(el Salvador)

El Amatillo

El Poy

San Miguel

Santa Rosa de Lima

SAN SALVADOR

CA-1

La Palma

Agua
Caliente

Nueva
Ocotepeque

Esquipulas

El Florido

Copán Ruinas

Copán

La Entrada

Santa Rosa de Copán

PARQUE NACIONAL
CELAQUE

Gracias

Siguatepeque

Intibucá

San Juan

La Esperanza

Cataratas de
Pulhapanzak

Lago de Yojoa

San Pedro Sula

Puerto
Cortés

Omoa

PARQUE
NACIONAL
EL CUSUCO

Corinto

Puerto
Barrios

Punta Gordá

Metres
2000
1000
500
200
0

0   100 km

321

development, controls area north to the Valle de Sula, east to Lago de Yojoa and west into present-day Guatemala.

900 AD Maya civilization collapses, and Copán is abandoned. Lenca becomes the predominant indigenous group, settling in small, scattered communities and absorbing other indigenous cultures.

1502 Christopher Columbus arrives on the island of Guanaja, naming it "Isla de Pinos" (Island of Pines). First Catholic Mass in Latin America is held on August 14.

1524 Hernán Cortés sends Cristóbal de Olid from Mexico to claim the isthmus in Cortés's name; the man arrives himself one year later, founds Puerto Cortés and Trujillo, then returns to Mexico.

1524–71 Indigenous population declines from 400,000 to around 15,000.

1536 Pedro de Alvarado arrives from Guatemala to govern the territory. Lempira, a Lenca chieftain, amasses a 30,000-man force, which rebels against the Spanish. Comayagua is destroyed.

1539 Lempira is assassinated and the Spanish hold on Honduras is assured. Gold and silver are discovered in the country's interior and mining begins. The *encomienda* labour system is put in place, assuring social stratification.

1573 Comayagua, rebuilt, is designated the capital.

1800 With mines failing and droughts destroying agricultural harvests, the economy enters a crisis period. Society is deeply divided, and the country still has no national printing press, newspapers or university.

1821 Honduras gains independence from Spain, but is annexed by Mexico.

1823 Provinces of Central America declare themselves an independent republic. Civil war begins.

1830 Honduran Francisco Morazán elected president of the Republic after defeating Conservative forces in Guatemala.

1839 Honduras and Nicaragua go to war against El Salvador. Morazán resigns, and the Central American Republic is essentially finished.

Independence is not kind to Honduras's economy or infrastructure, and intense rivalry between Liberals and Conservatives keeps the country in an almost permanent state of political and military conflict.

1876 Liberal Dr Marco Aurelio Soto is elected president. Improves infrastructure and encourages foreign investment.

Late 1800s Banana industry develops with arrival of US fruit companies, which gain control of national infrastructure; private interests dominate government. Tegucigalpa becomes national capital in 1880.

1956 A coup introduces the military as a new element in the country's hierarchy of power. Civilian government is reinstated in 1957, but a new constitution that year gives the military the right to disregard presidential orders.

1963 Another coup brings Colonel Oswaldo López Arellano to power as provisional president; he remains in power for twelve years.

1969 So-called "Football War" breaks out on the Honduras–El Salvador border (see box below).

THE FOOTBALL WAR

In one of the more bizarre conflicts in modern Latin American history, on July 14, 1969, war broke out on the Honduras–El Salvador border. Ostensibly caused by a disputed result in a soccer match between the two countries, the conflict also stemmed from tensions generated by a steady rise in illegal migration of *campesinos* from El Salvador into Honduras in search of land.

In April 1969 the Honduran government had given settlers thirty days to return to El Salvador, and then begun forced expulsions – the result was the breakout of sporadic violence. In June, the two countries began a series of qualifying matches for the 1970 World Cup. The first game, held in Tegucigalpa, was won by Honduras, with a score of 1–0. At the second game (won 3–0 by El Salvador), held in San Salvador, spectators booed the Honduran national anthem and attacked visiting Honduran fans. The third, deciding match was then pre-empted by the El Salvadoran army bombing targets in Honduras, and advancing up to 40km into Honduran territory.

After three days, around 2000 deaths and a complete breakdown of diplomatic relations, the Organization of American States (OAS) negotiated a ceasefire, establishing a three-kilometre-wide demilitarized zone along the border. Tensions and minor skirmishes continued, however, until 1980, when a US-brokered peace treaty was signed. Only in 1992 did both sides finally accept an International Court of Justice ruling demarcating the border in its current location.

1975 The "Bananagate" scandal (the payment of over US$1 million to government officials by United Brand in return for reductions on export taxes) forces López to resign. Under his successors – all high-ranking military officials – the country becomes even more stratified.

1981 Honduras becomes focus for US-backed Contra war in Nicaragua; relationship between military and government grows closer; human-rights violations rise.

1989–98 Following US withdrawal, the economy collapses completely, but power is slowly wrested back from the military.

1998 Hurricane Mitch hits Honduras, killing over 7000. President Carlos Flores declares Honduras has been set back fifty years.

2005 Manuel Zelaya of the Liberal Party of Honduras is elected.

2006 Honduras signs the Central America Border Control Agreement (see box, p.45).

2009 Manuel Zelaya is ousted from government in a move seen by many as a coup and by others as a legitimate action. Porfirio Lobo of the conservative National Party is elected president in November. Honduras is suspended from the Organization of American States (OAS).

2011 Zelaya and Lobo sign an agreement that allows the former to come out of exile and return to the country. The move is likely to lead to Honduras's re-entry into the OAS.

Basics

ARRIVAL

Visitors **flying** to Honduras have their choice of airports. The three most commonly used are: **Toncontín International (TGU)**, outside Tegucigalpa (allegedly one of the most dangerous airports in the world, for its difficult runway); **Ramón Villeda Morales International (SAP)**, southeast of San Pedro Sula; and **Juan Manuel Gálvez International (RTB)**, on Roatán. All three are served by direct flights from other Central American capitals, as well as North American (namely Miami, Houston and Atlanta) and South American destinations. There's a departure tax of US$37 for international flights.

LAND CROSSINGS AND SEA ROUTES TO BELIZE

Honduras has land borders with Guatemala, El Salvador and Nicaragua, and sea crossings with Belize.

From **Guatemala**, there are three crossings. The most frequently used is at El Florido for Copán Ruinas (see p.362); there is also a crossing at Agua Caliente (see p.352) used by buses from Esquipulas and one at Corinto–Entre Ríos (see p.371), which connects Puerto Barrios and Puerto Cortés.

El Salvador has two crossings: El Amatillo (p.341) in eastern El Salvador, and El Poy in western El Salvador (p.352).

There are three crossings from **Nicaragua**. The easiest is Las Manos (see p.339), for Tegucigalpa; the others are at El Espino (see p.343) and Guasaule (see p.342).

From **Belize**, there are weekly skiffs from both Placencia and Dangriga to Puerto Cortés (see p.370).

You can enter Honduras by **land** from Guatemala, El Salvador and Nicaragua (see box above). International services such as Tica Bus (Ⓦwww.ticabus.com) offer long-haul trips from other Central American cities, but you can also travel via slower, cheaper local transport. If you do come by local bus, you'll have to disembark, cross the border on foot and change buses on the other side. The only **sea routes** to Honduras are from Belize.

VISAS

Citizens of Australia, Canada, Japan, New Zealand, the UK, the US and most European countries do not need visas for stays in Honduras of up to ninety days. **Tourist cards**, given on entry, are good for stays of between thirty and ninety days. The card is a yellow slip of paper that needs to be returned when you leave, or stamped if you extend your stay.

Honduras is part of the **CA-4 border control agreement**, which means you can move freely within Honduras, Guatemala, El Salvador and Nicaragua for up to ninety days (see box, p.45).

GETTING AROUND

The primary means of transport for budget travellers in Honduras is buses, though to reach the popular Bay Islands you will need to invest in a flight or take a boat.

By bus

Bus services in Honduras are fairly well organized, with frequent departures from the main transport hubs of Tegucigalpa, San Pedro Sula and La Ceiba, as well as a network of local services. These local, or **"chicken" buses** (refurbished old American school buses) are the cheapest, but also get packed and stop frequently, so can be quite slow. **Rapiditos** also serve local routes. Usually minibuses, they are much quicker but a little more expensive than chicken buses. On the longer intercity routes there's usually a choice of services, with an increasing number of luxurious air-conditioned **express buses** (*ejecutivos* or *lujos*), plus comfortable services with a few scheduled stops (*directos*). **Fares** are extremely low on most routes, at around US$1 an hour or less, though they can triple on some of the really smart services – travelling between Tegucigalpa and La Ceiba can cost as much as US$22. For the express buses (for example, Hedman Alas and El Rey), you should buy tickets in advance when possible; if you are getting on at smaller destinations the conductor will come through and collect the fare. The frequency of buses slows down considerably after lunch, so you should try to be at your final destination by 4pm to avoid getting stranded.

By car

If your budget will stretch, **renting a car** can open up the country's more isolated areas. Including insurance and emergency assistance, **rates** start at around US$35 a day for a small car, and US$80 for larger models and 4WDs. The highways connecting the main cities are well looked after, but the numerous dirt roads in the highlands can be impassable at certain times of the year, so always seek local advice on conditions before starting out. Rental agencies can be found at the airports in San Pedro Sula, Tegucigalpa and Roatán as well as in San Pedro Sula and Tegucigalpa towns (see p.376 & p.330).

Taxis operate in all the main towns, tooting when they are available. Meters are nonexistent, so always agree on a price before getting in. Expect to pay US$1.75–2.25 for a city ride in Tegucigalpa or San Pedro, while in smaller towns the standard fare is around US$0.80. For safety, use taxis at night in the bigger towns.

ADDRESSES IN HONDURAS

Honduras's major cities are mainly laid out in a grid, with a park or plaza at the centre. Here calles run east–west, and avenidas north–south. In some towns, such as Santa Rosa de Copán, street names are followed by the designation "NO", "NE", "SO" or "SE" (northwest, northeast, southwest and southeast respectively), depending on their location around the central park. Note that smaller towns (including Copán) don't have street names, so addresses tend to be given in terms of landmarks. Exact street numbers tend not to exist anywhere; a city address written in the Guide as "C 16, Av 1–3", for example, means the place you're looking for is on Calle 16, between avenidas 1 and 3, while "Av 1, C 11–13" means it's on Avenida 1, between calles 11 and 13.

Hitching is very common in rural areas, and generally safe. Keep an eye out for pick-up trucks with lots of people in the back, and stick out your thumb. You're expected to offer payment at the end of the ride, usually the same as the bus fare. Don't hitch if alone.

By air

Internal flights in Honduras are fairly affordable. A small number of domestic airlines offer competitive fares, with frequent departures between Tegucigalpa and San Pedro Sula, La Ceiba and the Bay Islands. A one-way ticket between Tegucigalpa and San Pedro costs around US$110, while La Ceiba to Utila or Roatán is US$58 and La Ceiba–Puerto Lempira around US$115. There's a departure tax of US$3 for internal flights.

By boat

Boats are the most budget-friendly option when it comes to reaching the Bay Islands. The *MV Galaxy 11* runs between La Ceiba and Roatán (1hr 30min; US$27–32), while the *Utila Princess* runs to Utila (1hr 30min; US$27).

ACCOMMODATION

That Honduras is slowly waking up to tourism is reflected in the country's accommodation options. The larger cities – Tegucigalpa, San Pedro Sula – offer the widest range of places to stay, with something to suit all budgets. Hostels are beginning to spring up across the country, generally representing excellent value for money; Copán has some of the best budget hostels on the mainland. Of the Bay Islands, Utila is the cheapest and Roatán has a few places catering to backpackers, while Guanaja is aimed more at luxury tourists. On the mainland, US$9–18 gets you a basic room; US$19 and above will secure a well-furnished room, with extras such as TV, air conditioning and hot water. A twelve percent tax is occasionally added to the bill. Usually the only time you need to reserve in advance is at Semana Santa or during a big local festival, such as the May Carnaval in La Ceiba.

The only formal provisions for camping are at Omoa, Copán Ruinas and in some of the national parks. Elsewhere, pitching a tent is very much an ad hoc affair. If you intend to camp, make sure you ask permission from the landowner. Tempting though they may seem, the North Coast beaches are not safe after dark and camping here is highly inadvisable.

FOOD AND DRINK

Budget travellers can eat very well in Honduras. The best way to start the day is with a *licuado*, a sort of fruit smoothie. Many places mix them with bananas and cornflakes, so they're very filling. Most towns have markets where you can pick up a huge amount of fresh produce. With an eye on your budget, you'll find that eating a big lunch is a better option than waiting for dinner. Market areas tend to be where you will find the cheapest *comedores*, where typical *almuerzos* of rice, beans, tortillas and meat can be had for around L60–80. The larger cities have a decent range of restaurants, including an increasing number of fast-food chains. On the whole, you'll pay L100 for a good-sized lunch at a restaurant. The ever-popular Chinese restaurants routinely have portions big enough for two, making them a reliable budget option. Note that most shops and facilities close from noon to 2pm so that families can eat lunch together.

Honduran specialities to try include anafre, a fondue-like dish of cheese, beans or meat, or a mixture of all three, sometimes served as a bar snack, and tapado, a rich vegetable stew, often with meat or fish added. The north coast has a strong Caribbean influence, with lots of seafood. **Guisado** (spicy chicken stew) and **sopa de caracol** (conch stew with coconut milk, spices, potatoes and vegetables) should both be tried at least once. Probably the most common street snack, sold all over the country, is the **baleada**, a white-flour tortilla filled with beans, cheese and cream; two or three of these constitute a reasonable meal.

Drink

Licuados or **batidos** are a mix of fruit juice and milk. **Tap water** is unsafe to drink; bottled, purified water is sold everywhere and many hotels have water machines. The usual brands of **fizzy drink** are ubiquitous.

In terms of alcohol, Honduras produces five brands of **beer**: Salvavida and Imperial are heavier lagers, Port Royal slightly lighter and Nacional and Polar very light and quite tasteless. **Rum** (*ron*) is also distilled in the country, as is the Latin American rotgut, **aguardiente**. Adventurous connoisseurs of alcohol might wish to try **guifiti**, an elixir of various plants soaked in rum, found in the Garífuna villages of the north coast.

CULTURE AND ETIQUETTE

Catholicism is the main **religion** in Honduras – though American Evangelical missionary groups are having an impact – and with it comes traditional values and roles. Family is very important, and children tend to grow up and settle close to their parents, though increasingly Honduran youngsters are going to the US in order to send back some money. Anti-gay attitudes are prevalent, and while not illegal, public displays of affection are frowned upon.

Hondurans are very friendly, and, on the whole, are glad to have visitors in their country and keen to tell you about where they come from. Greeting shop

> ### HONDURAN EXPRESSIONS AND PHRASES
>
> bola a dollar
> jalón a pick-up
> birria a beer
> macizo cool
> ando hule I'm broke
> la riata something/someone useless

assistants is polite, and in smaller towns a simple "buenos días" can win you new friends in no time. Of Honduras's population, 85–90 percent are *ladino* (a mix of Spanish and indigenous people). The rest of the country is a mixture of **ethnic minorities**. Prominent groups include the Maya Chorti in the department of Copán; the Lenca, with their traditional clothing, found along the Ruta Lenca in the area around Santa Rosa de Copán; and the Miskitos in La Mosquitia.

A ten percent **tip** is the norm for waiters and tour guides, but is not expected in taxis.

SPORTS AND OUTDOOR ACTIVITIES

The largest spectator sport in Honduras is **football**, and the Honduran national league (ⓦ www.lina.hn) and the major European leagues are all keenly followed. Olimpia and Motagua from Tegucigalpa, Marathón and Real España from San Pedro Sula, and Victoria from La Ceiba are the biggest teams and usually pull in a fairly decent crowd. David Suazo, currently at Inter Milan, is one of the nation's favourite sons. **Tickets** don't need to be bought in advance, as most games don't sell out.

With a number of **national parks** – most of which have accommodation and/or camping and well-marked trails – Honduras is a fantastic place to **hike**. Parque Nacional Celaque, with the highest peak in the country, is a great place to start. For water lovers, the Bay

Islands offer some of the cheapest places in the world to take PADI **diving** certification courses; both the diving and the **snorkelling** are excellent. For more sedentary types, Lago de Yojoa (see p.345) has **fishing** and **birdwatching** trips.

COMMUNICATIONS

There are **post offices** in every town; letters generally take a week to the US and up to two weeks to Europe. Opening hours are usually Monday to Friday 8am to noon and 2pm to 5pm, Saturday 8am to 1pm.

International **phone** calls can be made from Hondutel offices (there's a branch in every town), but are very expensive to Europe (around 44L/min) – you are much better off visiting an internet café with web-phone capabilities. Many public telephones are out of use or damaged so for local calls (eight-digit numbers), it's better to buy a cheap **mobile phone** (US$20–30) and periodically top up the credit (*recarga*), which can be done in most small shops. Alternatively, you could visit an office

of mobile-phone provider Claro (the largest provider in Latin America) to see if your phone will accept a foreign SIM card. All landline numbers start with a 2, while mobile numbers start with different digits (3, 8 or 9) according to the provider.

Internet cafés can be found in most towns, and some hotels have internet available for guests; the average rate is L22 per hour.

CRIME AND SAFETY

On the whole, Honduras is a safe place for tourists. Government crackdowns on "mara" (gang) culture have drastically reduced the amount of gang-related crime in recent years, and the installation of tourist police in towns like Tela has had a positive effect on crimes against tourists.

Travel in rural areas is generally an exercise in mutual trust and respect; in urban areas, however, **street crime** is a concern. Take the usual precautions, and try to avoid walking around alone at night. The Comayagüela district in Tegucigalpa, particularly around the market, and the streets south of the old railway line in San Pedro Sula are both considered dangerous. Along the north coast it's not advisable to walk alone on the beach at night. If you are the victim of a crime the **police** are unlikely to be of much help, but any incidents of theft should be reported for insurance purposes (see box, p.48).

HEALTH

The Honduras Medical Centre, Av Juan Lindo in Tegucigalpa, is considered one of the best **hospitals** in the country; in San Pedro Sula head for the Hospital Centro Médico Betesda, Av 11A NO between C 11A & 12A NO. Facilities in rural areas tend to be much more limited, though most towns have at least one **pharmacy**, and staff tend to be very helpful. In general, it's worth trying to learn a little emergency Spanish, as

> ### HONDURAS ON THE NET
>
> ⓦ www.honduras.com The country's official website and one of the best.
>
> ⓦ www.hondurastips.hn The definitive guide to the country, also published as an indispensable monthly magazine (available free in hotels) detailing all the sights and latest developments of interest to tourists.
>
> ⓦ www.letsgohonduras.com The website of the Instituto de Turismo offers a good introduction to the main attractions and numerous organized tour packages.
>
> ⓦ www.travel-to-honduras.com General site covering a range of subjects – everything from business and tourism to Spanish schools and volunteer work.

English is not widely spoken. Pharmacists can issue prescriptions.

Honduras has one of the highest rates of AIDS in Central America, so it is especially important to take all the usual precautions when it comes to sex. Make sure, too, if you seek medical help that all instruments are sterilized.

MONEY AND BANKS

Honduras's currency is the **lempira** (L), which consists of 100 centavos; at the time of writing, the exchange rate was 18.92L to US$1. Coins come as 1, 2, 5, 10, 20 and 50 centavos and notes as 1, 2, 5, 10, 20, 50, 100 and 500 lempiras. In heavily touristed areas – Copán, the Bay Islands – US dollars are widely accepted, but on the whole lempiras are the standard currency.

You will need **cash** for day-to-day expenses. Acceptance of foreign **debit cards** in ATMs can be a hit-and-miss affair. Make sure before you leave home that your PIN is four digits or less; your card will be rejected if it is longer. As a rule Visa is more widely accepted than other cards. Visa cardholders can also get cash advances in several banks, including Banco Atlántida; MasterCard is sometimes accepted but not to be relied upon.

Honduras has a number of national **banks**, of which the biggest are Banco Atlántida, Banco de Occidente and BAC/Credomatic. Many banks change **travellers' cheques** – American Express is the most widely accepted brand. When cashing travellers' cheques you will often be asked to show proof of purchase receipts and your passport. Banks in larger towns are generally open 8.30am to 4.30pm and until noon

on Saturdays, while those in smaller towns shut for an hour at lunch.

INFORMATION AND MAPS

The national tourist office, the **Instituto Hondureño de Turismo** (🌐 www.lets gohonduras.com), is fairly helpful. The main office, in the Edificio Europa in Tegucigalpa (see p.333), can provide general **information** about where to go and what to see in the country. They also have booths at the Tegucigalpa and San Pedro Sula airports, and a free information service in the US (☎ 800/ 410-9608). Most towns you'll visit will have a municipality-run tourist office. These vary in helpfulness; the better ones sell maps, can arrange homestays and can tell you the cheapest places to stay. **National parks** and reserves are overseen by the government forestry agency, **ICF** (🌐 www.icf.gob.hn). If you intend to spend much time in any of the parks, it's worth visiting one of their offices for detailed information on flora and fauna.

Honduras Tips, a free magazine found in the better hotels and tourist offices, has fairly up-to-date information on hotel listings and bus routes – it is updated every few months. The magazine also has maps of most towns in the country.

The best **map** of Honduras is published by Reise Know-How (🌐 www .reise-know-how.de), and can be bought in bookshops or online; unfortunately, the chance of finding it in Honduras is unlikely.

OPENING HOURS AND PUBLIC HOLIDAYS

Business hours for **shops** are generally Monday to Friday 9am to noon and 2pm to 4.30 or 5pm, and Saturday from 9am to noon. **Museums** often stay open at lunch, but close at least one day each week. On public holidays (see box opposite), almost everything closes.

PUBLIC HOLIDAYS

Jan 1 New Year's Day

March/April Semana Santa: Thursday, Friday and Saturday before Easter Sunday

April 14 Day of the Americas

May 1 Labour Day

Sept 15 Independence Day

Oct 3 Birth of Francisco Morazán

Oct 12 Discovery of America

Oct 21 Armed Forces Day

Dec 25 Christmas Day

FESTIVALS

Honduras's calendar is full of **festivals**, everything from small local events to major national parties. The following are just a few highlights.

February Pilgrims flock to Tegucigalpa to worship and celebrate the Virgen de Suyapa.

April Punta Gorda celebrates the arrival of the Garífuna (April 6–12).

May La Feria de San Isidro or Carnaval in La Ceiba, during the week leading up to the third Saturday. Festivities culminate in a street parade through the city centre, followed by live music until the early morning.

June San Pedro Sula holiday (June 29).

Tegucigalpa and around

Situated 1000m above sea level, deep in a mountain valley, the Honduran capital of **TEGUCIGALPA** is not, at least on first impression, the most welcoming city. The winding, narrow streets are thick with motorized traffic, and the sidewalks full to the gills with shoppers and loafers. This said, unlike other capital cities in the region, Tegucigalpa isn't totally without charm, and its colonial feel and cool climate actually make it an ideal starting point, to allow you to get to grips with the Honduran pace of life.

Tegucigalpa's first mention in records is in the 1560s, when silver deposits ("tegucigalpa" means "silver mountain" in the Nahuatl language) were found in the hills to the east. It was given town status in 1768, and named a city in 1807. With wealth from the country's mines pouring in, the city's location at the centre of key trade routes became highly advantageous, and Tegucigalpa soon rivalled the then capital, Comayagua. In 1880, the Liberal President Soto officially shifted power to Tegucigalpa, and in 1932 Comayagüela became a part of the capital. Since then, the nation's economic focus has shifted to San Pedro Sula, but Tegucigalpa continues to function as the nation's political and governmental centre.

Surrounded by reminders of its past – crumbling colonial buildings and decaying nineteenth-century mansions – the city today is a vibrant, noisy place. A handful of churches and a fantastic history museum will easily keep you entertained for a day or two.

What to see and do

The heart of Tegucigalpa's **old city** is the pleasant **Plaza Morazán**; a number of interesting churches and museums, plus many hotels, lie within easy walking distance of the square. East from the centre, two major roads, Avenida Jeréz (which becomes Avenida Juan Gutemberg and then Avenida La Paz) and Avenida Miguel Cervantes (changing its name to Avenida República de Chile), skirt the edges of upmarket **Colonia Palmira**.

Running west from Plaza Morazán, the pedestrian-only **Calle Peatonal** is lined with shops, cafés and the fabulous Museo para la Identidad Nacional (see below). Further west of the old centre, the character of the city rapidly becomes more menacing as you approach the banks of the Río Choluteca.

Plaza Morazán

Plaza Morazán is the centre of life for most people who live and work in the capital. Shaded by a canopy of trees, and populated with shoe-shiners and other vendors, it's an atmospheric, if not particularly peaceful, place. A **statue** at the centre of the square commemorates national hero Francisco Morazán, a soldier, Liberal and reformer who was elected president of the Central American Republic in 1830. On the eastern edge of the plaza, the recently refurbished facade of the **Catedral San Miguel** (daily 8am–6pm), completed in 1782, is one of the best preserved in Central America. Inside, look out for the magnificent Baroque-style gilded altar and the baptismal font, carved in 1643 from a single block of stone by indigenous artisans.

Museo para la Identidad Nacional

The permanent exhibition at the excellent **Museo para la Identidad Nacional**, on Calle Peatonal (Mon–Sat 9am–5pm, Sun 10am–4pm; L60; ☎2238 7412, ⑩www.min.hn), focuses on the history of Honduras. Starting with the geographical formation of Central America, the displays move

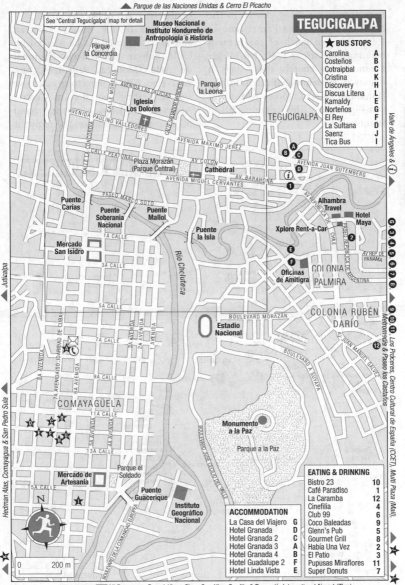

Parque de las Naciones Unidas & Cerro El Picacho

See 'Central Tegucigalpa' map for detail

Museo Nacional e Instituto Hondureño de Antropología e Historia

TEGUCIGALPA

★ **BUS STOPS**

Carolina	A
Costeños	B
Cotraipbal	C
Cristina	K
Discovery	H
Discua Litena	L
Kamaldy	E
Norteños	G
El Rey	F
La Sultana	D
Saenz	J
Tica Bus	I

Parque la Concordia

Parque la Leona

TEGUCIGALPA

Valle de Ángeles & ⓘ

AVENIDA LAS DELICIAS

Iglesia Los Dolores

AVENIDA PAULINO VALLEDORES

CALLE MORELOS

CALLE SALVADOR MENDIETA

CALLE LA CONCORDIA

CALLE PEATONAL

AVENIDA MÁXIMO JEREZ

AV COLÓN

AVENIDA JUAN GUTEMBERG

Plaza Morazán (Parque Central)

Cathédral

AV. BARAHONA

AVENIDA MIGUEL CERVANTES

ⓘ

Puente Carías

PASEO MARCO SOTO

Puente Soberanía Nacional

Puente Mallol

Puente la Isla

Alhambra Travel

Hotel Maya

PSE REPÚBLICA DE CHILE

Xplore Rent-a-Car

AV REP DE PANAMÁ

1A CALLE

Mercado San Isidro

Río Choluteca

3A CALLE

E

F

Oficinas de Amitigra

COLONIA PALMIRA

AV REP DE ARGENTINA

5A CALLE

Juticalpa

BOULEVARD MORAZÁN

COLONIA RUBÉN DARÍO

Estadio Nacional

AV JUAN MANUEL GÁLVEZ

12

7A CALLE

9A CALLE

AVENIDA IDARRAYDO DE CUBA

8A AVENIDA

7A AVENIDA

6A AVENIDA

2A AVENIDA

1A AVENIDA

BOULEVARD SUYAPA

Los Próceres, Centro Cultural de España (CCET), Multi Plaza (Mall),

Metromedia & Paseo los Castaños

Hedman Alas, Comayagua & San Pedro Sula

COMAYAGÜELA

11A CALLE

5A AVENIDA

4A AVENIDA

13A CALLE

Monumento a la Paz

Parque a la Paz

BOULEVARD JOSÉ CECILIO DEL VALLE

Mercado de Artesanía

5A CALLE

Parque el Soldado

Puente Guacerique

BOULEVARD DE LA COMUNIDAD EUROPEA

Instituto Geográfico Nacional

N

0   200 m

ACCOMMODATION

La Casa del Viajero	G
Hotel Granada	D
Hotel Granada 2	C
Hotel Granada 3	A
Hotel Granada 4	B
Hotel Guadalupe 2	F
Hotel Linda Vista	E

EATING & DRINKING

Bistro 23	10
Café Paradíso	1
La Caramba	12
Cinefilia	4
Club 99	6
Coco Baleadas	9
Glenn's Pub	5
Gourmet Grill	8
Había Una Vez	2
El Patio	3
Pupusas Miraflores	11
Super Donuts	7

Mi Esperanza, Royeri, Viana Clase Oro, King Quality & Toncontín International Airport (7km)

---

chronologically through the Maya civilization and colonial era to the various post-colonial presidents and their influence on the country. The museum's highlight is a 3D tour of Copán (four showings daily Tues–Sun) that re-creates how the Maya kingdom would have looked at the height of its power.

Iglesia San Francisco

Three blocks east of the museum, on Avenida Paz Barahona, the **Iglesia San**

Francisco is the oldest church in the city, first built by the Franciscans in 1592, although much of the present building dates from 1740. No longer a functioning church, these days it houses a **museum** dedicated to the Honduran armed forces (Mon–Fri 8am–4pm; free). The signage is all in Spanish.

Galería Nacional de Arte

Just south of the Parque Morazán and next to the Iglesia La Merced on Calle Bolívar, the **Galería Nacional de Arte** (Mon–Sat 9am–4pm, Sun 9am–1pm; L30) is home to an extensive and interesting collection of Central American art. Displays on the ground floor range from prehistoric petroglyphs

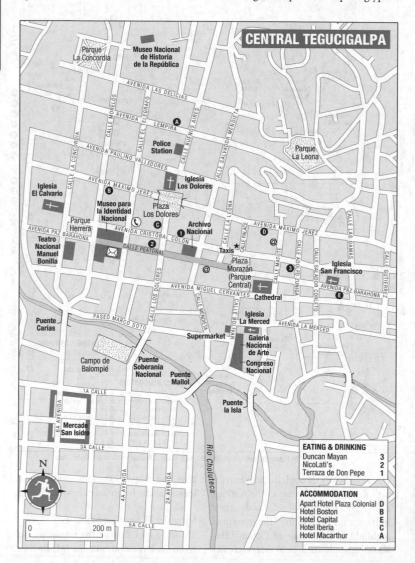

CENTRAL TEGUCIGALPA

Parque La Concordia

Museo Nacional de História de la República

AVENIDA LAS DELICIAS

CALLE MORELOS

AVENIDA EL TELEGRAFO

AVENIDA LEMPIRA

CALLE BUENOS AIRES

CALLE SALVADOR MENDIETA

Parque La Leona

A

Police Station

AVENIDA PAULINO VALLEDORES

CALLE LA CONCORDIA

AVENIDA MÁXIMO JEREZ

Iglesia Los Dolores

Iglesia El Calvario

B

Museo para la Identidad Nacional

Plaza Los Dolores

CALLE LA LEONA

CALLE PALACE

AVENIDA MÁXIMO JEREZ

Parque Herrera

C

Archivo Nacional **1**

AVENIDA CRISTÓBAL COLÓN

CALLE PEATONAL

@

2

Taxis ★

AVENIDA PAZ BARAHONA

Teatro Nacional Manuel Bonilla

@

Plaza Morazán (Parque Central)

CALLE MATUTE

CALLE ADOLFO ZUNIGA

CALLE SALVADOR CORLETO

Iglesia San Francisco

CALLE LAS DAMAS

CALLE GUTIÉRREZ

D

3

E

AVENIDA MIGUEL CERVANTES

CALLE LOS DOLORES

Cathedral

AVENIDA PAZ BARAHONA

Puente Carías

PASEO MARCO SOTO

CALLE MENDIETA

CALLE BOLÍVAR

Iglesia La Merced

AVENIDA LA MERCED

Supermarket

Galería Nacional de Arte

Campo de Balompié

Puente Soberanía Nacional

Puente Mallol

Congreso Nacional

1A CALLE

Puente la Isla

6A AVENIDA

Mercado San Isidro

3A CALLE

Río Choluteca

N

4A AVENIDA

2A AVENIDA

5A CALLE

0   200 m

EATING & DRINKING	
Duncan Mayan	3
NicoLati's	2
Terraza de Don Pepe	1

ACCOMMODATION	
Apart Hotel Plaza Colonial	D
Hotel Boston	B
Hotel Capital	E
Hotel Iberia	C
Hotel Macarthur	A

and Maya stone carvings to religious art, while rooms upstairs house an ambitious selection of modern and contemporary Honduran art, including some works by Pablo Zelaya Sierra, one of the country's leading twentieth-century artists. Originally serving as a convent during the seventeenth century, and later as the national university, the building's Neoclassical facade sits rather uncomfortably alongside the stained concrete bulk of the **Congreso Nacional**, the country's seat of government next door.

Iglesia Los Dolores
A couple of blocks northwest from the central plaza, the pleasant, white, domed **Iglesia Los Dolores** (daily 8am–6pm), completed in 1732, sits next to the small **Plaza Los Dolores**. Its Baroque facade is decorated with a representation of the Passion of Christ, featuring a crowing cock and the rising sun; inside, the elaborate gold altar dates from 1742. A choir usually sings at 6pm on Saturdays and Sundays. The plaza itself is crowded with cheap, shabby stalls.

Colonia Palmira and around
Upscale **Colonia Palmira** is home to most of the capital's foreign embassies, luxury hotels, restaurants and wealthy residences. A particular landmark, the modern **Hotel Honduras Maya**, is on the Avenida República de Chile, just south of Colonia Palmira, fifteen minutes' walk east from the centre. A kilometre beyond the hotel, an overpass gives access to eastward-bound **Boulevard Morazán**, Tegucigalpa's major commercial and entertainment artery. No city buses run along here, so you'll have to walk or take a taxi. On Calle 1, the **Centro Cultural de España Tegucigalpa (CCET)** (Tues–Sun 10am–8pm, Sun 9am–3pm; ☎2238 2013, ⊛www.ccet-aecid.com) is housed in an attractive modern building and puts on a stimulating programme of music, art exhibitions and talks.

Cerro El Picacho
To the north of Plaza Morazán, older suburbs – previously home to the wealthy middle-classes and rich immigrants, now long gone – edge up the lower slopes of **Cerro El Picacho**. Grab a picnic and escape to the **Parque Naciones Unidas El Picacho** for fantastic views over the city. At the top stands the open-armed **Cristo del Picacho**, illuminated at night in a dazzle of coloured lights. Take a bus from in front of *Hotel Granada 2*; it's a twenty-minute ride or L150 taxi fare.

Comayagüela
The brown waters of the polluted Río Choluteca form the border of Tegucigalpa's twin, **Comayagüela**, which sprawls away through down at heel business districts into industrial areas and poor barrios. Such is its dangerous reputation that tourists are not advised to spend any more time there than it takes to change buses.

Arrival

By air Toncontín International Airport is 7km south of the city. Taxis wait outside the terminal, but hailing one 50m down the highway will save you a couple of dollars. Bus #24 also passes the airport, running through Comayagüela and Tegucigalpa.
By bus There is no main bus station, with the result that each international or intercity bus line has its own terminal, most of them scattered around Comayagüela (see above). Take a taxi to your drop-off point.

Information

Tourist information The main tourist office is in Edificio Europa, Av Ramón Ernesto Cruz, Colonia San Carlos (☎2222 2124). Another, which focuses on the city centre's historic buildings, can be found at the Alcaldía Municipal del Distrito Central (AMDC) building, Barrio la Plazuela, C Los Horcones (☎2238 0708).
Travel agent Alhambra Travel (Mon–Fri 8am–noon & 1–5pm, Sat 9am–noon; ☎2220 1700), in the "area comercial" close to *Hotel Honduras Maya*, Av República de Perú and C 3, is quick, friendly and efficient.

City transport

Buses Chicken buses run the urban routes, usually 6am–9pm. Route names and numbers are painted on the front and fares are L5 anywhere within the city. Pay your fare on the bus. No buses pass close to Plaza Morazán or Boulevard Morazán.

Taxis Taxis are usually white with numbers painted on the side. A short ride within the city costs about L50 during the day, a little more at night. *Colectivo* taxis gather at predetermined stops (*puntos*); the most central one is on C Palace just north of Plaza Morazán. They generally leave when full with passengers going to a similar area of the city. Though you may have to wait a bit, they are cheaper than standard taxis: around L15 per person.

Accommodation

As the national capital, Tegucigalpa's accommodation is pricier than other areas of Honduras.

Apart Hotel Plaza Colonial Av Máximo Jeréz, behind Plaza Morazán ☎2222 7727 or 2237 9159. Truly a haven of calm away from the capital's busy streets, with nice details like a fountain on the ground floor and carved wooden bedframes. Rates include breakfast, and all rooms are en suite. Ten percent discount for cash payments. L958

🏃 **Hotel Boston** Av Máximo Jeréz 321, between C El Telégrafo and C Morelos ☎2237 9411. Spotlessly clean and atmospheric en-suite rooms in a good location near Iglesia Los Dolores. The large, old rooms at the front are nicer. L400

Hotel Capital Av Miguel Cervantes ☎2220 0156. Clean and family-run. Rooms have big windows which let in plenty of light. L350

Hotel Granada Av Juan Gutemberg at Av Cristóbal Colón ☎2237 2381, ℮hotelgranadategus@yahoo .com. Consistently popular budget option with basic but clean rooms, some with bath, plus hot water and a communal TV area. The better rooms have TV and en-suite bathroom. L480

Hotel Granada 2 & Hotel Granada 3 Opposite each other on Subida Casa Martín, just off Av Juan Gutemberg. *Granada 2* ☎2238 4438, *Granada 3* ☎2237 8066. Similar to and just round the corner from the original *Hotel Granada*. All rooms, including triples and quadruples, have private bath. L550

Hotel Granada 4 Facing *Granada 3* ☎2237 4004. The newest and nicest of all the *Granada* hotels. All rooms have TV and private bath, and

internet is available in the entrance area (L20/hr). L517

Hotel Guadalupe 2 Av Juan Manuel Galvez 324 ☎2238 5009/2958, ℮hotelguadalupe@cablecolor .hn. In a safe, residential area, this hotel has 14 rooms, all with private hot-water baths. Communal areas have comfy sofas, and wi-fi is available, as well as a/c, at a price. L440

Hotel Iberia Plaza Los Dolores ☎2237 9267. Rooms are basic but very clean. There's little natural light, no a/c and hot water is only available 6–8am, but sharing a bathroom makes things very cheap. L220

Hotel Linda Vista C Las Acacias 1438, just beyond the Edificio Italia on the opposite side of the road, in an unmarked yellow building with a red garden wall ☎2238 2099/0188, Colonia Palmira ⊛www .lindavistahotel.net. It's a little worn but gives such a wonderful view of the city that it's as if it were built for that very purpose. *Típico* breakfast included. US$65

Hotel MacArthur Av Lempira 454 ☎2237 9839/5906, ⊛www.hotelmacarthur.com. A nice pool area and plenty of rooms. Choose a fan over a/c to keep the price down. Breakfast included. L760

Eating

The centre has all the usual fast-food chains and cheap and cheerful cafés, as well as a few good-value restaurants with meals under L100; nicer restaurants are to be found in Colonia Palmira and along Blvd Morazán.

Cafés

Bistro 23 Second floor of the Nova Centro mall on the Los Próceres site. Three or four options daily, such as fish chowder (L115) and Greek moussaka (L140). Mon–Wed & Sun 11am–8pm, Thurs–Sat 11am–2am.

Café Paradiso Av Paz Barahona 1351. Great place with decent art on the walls and a nice outdoor seating area dominated by hanging baskets. It's gay friendly, and there's a cine club every Tues (6.30pm). Coffees from L16, beers from L22, yoghurt with granola and honey L32, pastas L80–120.

Coco Baleadas Los Próceres. A Honduran take on the classic sandwich bar, the basic *coco baleada* (dough made using coconut) is L16, then add various fillings, from avocado to bbq beef, for L9–22.

Gourmet Grill At the back of The Bakery Center on Paseo República de Argentina in Colonia Palmira. This place is cheerfully decorated with primary colours, padded banquettes and zebra print throughout. Three doorstep slices of French toast with sausage, bacon and maple syrup may be pricey at L140, but you won't need lunch.

NicoLati's C Peatonal. A chain-like atmosphere but pleasant nonetheless, with good coffee, wireless access and sandwiches from L27. There's another branch in Plaza Miraflores.

Super Donuts Blvd Morazán. In spite of the name they are locally revered for their varied breakfast menu, from the basic eggs (L21) and ham (L23) to beer-stewed *frijoles borrachos* (L23), and banana-leaf-wrapped corn, meat and rice, known as *nacatamales* (L36).

Restaurants

Duncan Mayan Av Cristóbal Colón. In a new location but as popular as ever. The central of the three large rooms would be a pleasant courtyard but for the covering of corrugated plastic. Soup of the day L65, mains from L100. Open till 10pm.

El Patio Far eastern end of Blvd Morazán. Meat may not be Honduras's strong point but they make a good stab at it in this cavernous banqueting hall. Try the *pincho olanchano* of beef, chorizo and pork (L325) – the cowboys from Honduras's own Wild East would be proud.

Pupusas Miraflores 2 Blvd Suyapa. Good, cheap restaurant crammed with locals, specializing in tacos, *pupusas* (L15) and *flautas* ("flute" tacos). Try the *loroco* flower-filled *pupusa* when it's in season. Take a taxi here – drivers should know it.

La Terraza de Don Pepe Av Cristóbal Colón. On two floors above a fried-chicken shop, this restaurant is a characterful place with once-grand rooms and a slip of a balcony. *Desayuno latino* L60, dish of the day L80.

Drinking and nightlife

Most bars in the centre are fiercely local hangouts, so you're best off heading to Colonia Palmira and Boulevard Morazán. Head also to Paseo Los Próceres (closed Sun), a peculiar strip of bars at the large Los Próceres site, in units that were originally intended for clothing boutiques. Try *La Vinacoteca*, *Tanino*, *La Partenza* and *Sopra* at the far end of the *paseo* above *Napoli* restaurant. Use taxis when going out at night.

Bars

Café Paradiso Av Paz Barahona 1351. Popular with local artists, this is a great place to kick off the evening (it's only open until 10pm), with film and literary events midweek.

Cinefilia C 3A, Colonia Palmira. Planning to change name to *Tierra Libre*, *Cinefilia* shows (non-Hollywood) movies every Tuesday and bands at weekends. Local beers L30, but also Leffe and Franziskaner among others (L55). Mon–Sat 5pm–midnight.

Glenn's Pub Av 1A, Colonia Palmira. Better than its bland name might suggest, this is a tiny, satisfyingly grungy place. It's not easy to spot – look out for it just past the triangular traffic island with trees. Opens at 6pm.

Había Una Vez Near *Hotel Maya*. An artsy bar/café with original work on the brightly painted walls (and colanders for lampshades). Beer L35–69, fresh juice/coffee L28, croque monsieur L151, pork chop with walnuts and Gorgonzola L240.

Clubs

La Caramba Col Rubén Darío, opposite Cybex gym. Live music specialists, with Beatles-themed nights, "salsa Saturdays", jazz, reggae and popular Honduran acts such as Requiem. Drinks from L25. Thurs–Sat 7pm–2am; entrance around L50.

Club 99 Blvd Morazán, behind a *Subway* and just after an enormous *KFC*. Formerly *Bambu*, this place attracts tourists, students and volunteers. Wed, Fri & Sat from 9pm; entrance L150.

Entertainment

The website ⓦ www.agendartehonduras.com is a helpful up-to-the-minute resource for cultural events listings.

Cinema The modern Multi Plaza complex (see p.336) has an eight-screen cinema, Cinemark, showing subtitled Hollywood blockbusters for L65, 3D for L100, and L40 on Tuesdays.

Football The Estadio Nacional, at the western end of Blvd Morazán, hosts international and domestic football games. Buy tickets at the stadium. Depending on the teams playing and whether you are in a sunny or shady spot, tickets range from L80 to L300.

Theatre The Teatro Nacional Manuel Bonilla (☎2222 4366) is 15min west of Parque Morazán along Calle Peatonal; ask at the box office inside for details of current shows.

Shopping

Books Metromedia, on Av San Carlos after C República de Mexico, has a wide range of English-language fiction, nonfiction and travel titles, as well as used books and US newspapers and magazines. There's a café inside. There's a smaller branch in Multi Plaza.

Food and drink La Colonia, south of the Plaza on C Bolívar, and Paiz in Multi Plaza, stock everything you need to make lunch, as well as toiletries and alcohol.

Malls Multi Plaza, Av Juan Pablo II, has international shops like Diesel, Paul Frank and Mango; a huge food court with the usual fast-food chains; and a cinema. Tigo and Claro stores here sell SIM cards and mobile phones.

Directory

Car rental Advance Rent A Car (☎2235 9531/ 9528, ⓦwww.advancerentacar.com) on C República de México and at the airport; Maya Rent A Car (☎2232 0682), Av República de Chile 202, Colonia Palmira; X Plore Rent A Car (☎2239 0134), near *Hotel Maya*.

Embassies Belize, ground floor of *Hotel Honduras Maya*, Av República de Perú and C 3 (Mon–Fri 9am–1pm; ☎2238 4616); Canada, Edificio Financiero Banexpo 3, Col Payaqui, Blvd San Juan Bosco (Mon–Fri 9am–3pm; ☎2232 4551); Costa Rica, Residencial El Triángulo, 1A Calle, Casa 3451 (Mon–Fri 8am–3pm; ☎2232 1768); El Salvador, Colonia Altos de Miramontes, Casa 2952, Diagonal Aguan (Mon–Fri 8.30am–noon & 1–3pm; ☎2232 4947); Guatemala, Colonia Lomas de Guijarro (Mon–Fri 8.30am–3pm; ☎231 1543); Mexico, Colonia Lomas del Guijarro, Av Eucalipto (Mon–Fri 8–11am; ☎2232 0141); Nicaragua, C 11, Block M1, Colonia Lomas del Tepeyac (Mon–Fri 8.30am–1pm; ☎2232 1966); Panama, Edificio Palmira 200, Colonia Palmira (Mon–Fri 8am–1pm; ☎2239 5508); UK, Centro Financiero Banexpo 3 piso, Colonia Payaqui (Mon–Thurs 8am–noon & 1–4pm, Fri 8am–3pm;

☎2232 0612); US, Av La Paz (Mon–Fri 8am–5pm; ☎2236 9320).

Exchange Virtually all banks will change dollars and travellers' cheques. Banco Atlántida, on Plaza Morazán (with 24hr ATM) and elsewhere, gives advances on Visa cards, while Credomatic, C Mendieta at Av Cervantes, offers both Visa and MasterCard advances.

Immigration Dirección General de Migracíon, on Av La Paz, near the US Embassy (Mon–Fri 8.30am–4.30pm).

Internet Multinet, east end of C Peatonal (Mon–Fri 8.15am–7.45pm, Sat 8.30am–7.30pm, Sun 9am–5.45pm; L24/hr; calls L2/min to the US and L3–6 to Europe, L8 to mobile phones). In Paseo Los Castaños, Accessnet is 30L/hr. Cybercafé Colonial on Calle Matute is L18/hr.

Laundry Super Jet, Av Juan Gutemberg after Parque Finlay (Mon–Sat 8am–5pm).

Medical care Emergency departments (24hr) are at Hospital Escuela, Blvd Suyapa (☎2232 6234), and Hospital General San Felipe, C La Paz by the Bolívar monument.

Police Go to the FSP office on C Buenos Aires, behind Los Dolores church, with any problems.

Post office C Peatonal at C El Telégrafo, 3 blocks west of the main plaza (Mon–Fri 8am–7pm, Sat 8am–1pm).

Supermarket Supermarket La Colonia, just south of the Parque.

Moving on

Travellers do leave Tegucigalpa via plane (mostly for international destinations and the Bay Islands), but buses are the most common way to reach other parts of the country.

By air
All flights leave from Toncontín International Airport, 7km south of the centre.

Flights to: La Ceiba (1 daily with Isleña; 1hr); Roatán (1 daily with Isleña via La Ceiba, 2hr; 1 daily with Isleña via San Pedro Sula, 4hr 25min); San Pedro Sula (2 daily with Isleña; 40min); Utila (1 daily Mon, Wed & Fri with SOSA; 1hr 30min).

By bus

Domestic bus destinations
Choluteca With direct B (7 daily 6.30am–4.30pm); with luxury ME (4 daily at 6am, 10am, 2pm & 6pm); with normal ME (hourly 4am–6pm); with R (1–2 hourly 4am–5.45pm); 3hr 30min.

BUS COMPANIES AND STOPS

Tegucigalpa does not have a central bus terminal. Instead, each bus company has its own office and bus stop – most are in Comayagüela. Take a taxi when travelling to and from this area.

Blanquito Express (B) Direct to Choluteca from stop in Barrio Villa Adela.

Carolina (CA) To La Esperanza from Av 7 (Solidaridad de Cuba), C 7–8.

Costeños (CN) Normal services to San Pedro Sula from Av 7, C 11–12.

Cotraipbal (C) ☎2237 1666. Direct to Trujillo from Av 7, C 11–12.

Cristina (CR) ☎2220 0117 or 2225 0233. Direct services to La Ceiba depart from Blvd Fuerzas Armadas.

Discovery (D) ☎2222 4256. Normal services to Juticalpa depart from Av 7, C 12–13.

Discua Litena (DL) ☎2230 2939/0470. Direct services to El Paraíso (for Nicaragua) depart from Col Kennedy, near Mercado Jacaleapa.

El Rey (ER) ☎2237 1462. Normal services to Comayagua, La Guama and San Pedro Sula depart from C 12, Av 7–8.

El Rey Express (RE) ☎2237 8561. Direct services to San Pedro Sula depart from the same spot as El Rey.

Hedman Alas HA) ☎2237 7143. Direct and luxury services to La Ceiba and San Pedro Sula depart from Av 11, C 13–14.

Kamaldy (K) ☎2220 0117. Services to La Ceiba depart from the corner of Av 8 and C 12.

King Quality (KQ) ☎2225 5415. Luxury services to Guatemala City (Guatemala), Managua (Nicaragua) and San Salvador (El Salvador) depart from Blvd Comunidad Económica Europea, Barrio La Granja.

La Sultana (LS) ☎2237 8101. Normal services to Santa Rosa de Copán depart from Av 8, C 11–12.

Mi Esperanza (ME) ☎2225 1502. Luxury and normal services to Choluteca depart from C 23–24, Barrio Villa Adela.

Norteños (N) ☎2237 0706. Normal services to Comayagua, La Guama and San Pedro Sula depart from C 12, Av 6–7.

Royeri (R) ☎2225 2863. Normal services to Choluteca depart from C 23–24, Barrio Villa Adela.

Saenz ☎2213 9200 or 2231 3112. First-class services to Choluteca depart from the small Centro Comercial Centroamerica on Blvd Centroamerica.

Tica Bus (TB) ☎2220 0579. Luxury services to Guatemala City (Guatemala), Managua (Nicaragua), Panama City (Panama), San José (Costa Rica) and San Salvador (El Salvador) depart from C 16, Av 5–6.

Viana Clase Oro (V) ☎2239 8288. Luxury services to La Ceiba and San Pedro Sula depart from Las Cascadas mall on Blvd Fuerzas Armadas.

Comayagua With N (every 30min 6am–2.30pm); with ER (every 30min 3am–7pm); 2hr.

Copán Ruinas Buses go via San Pedro Sula (see opposite; 8hr).

Juticalpa With direct D (hourly 6.15am–4.15pm; 2hr); with normal D (hourly 6.45am–5pm; 3hr).

La Ceiba With CR (7 daily 5.45am–3.30pm); with HA (3 daily at 5.45am, 10am & 1.30pm); with K (3 daily at 7am, 11am & 3.15pm); with V (2 daily at 6.45am & 2.30pm); 5hr 30min–7hr.

La Esperanza With CA (hourly 5am–4.50pm); 4hr.

La Guama (for Lago de Yojoa) With N or ER (2hr 30min); as per departures for San Pedro Sula.

San Pedro Sula With CN (hourly 8.45am–4.15pm); with ER (4 daily at 7.30am, 9.30am, noon & 2pm); with HA (hourly 6.30am–5.30pm); with N (1–2 hourly 6am–2.30pm); with RE (1–2 hourly 6.30am–6.30pm); with V (4 daily: Mon–Fri & Sun at 6.30am, 1.30pm, 3.30pm & 6.15pm, Sat at 6.30am, 9.30am, 1.30pm & 3.30pm); 3hr 30min. Take San Pedro Sula-bound buses for Lago de Yojoa (ask for La Guama), Copán Ruinas and Tela.

Santa Rosa de Copán With LS (4 daily at 6am, 7.30am, 8.30am & 10am; 7hr).

Siguatepeque With N or ER; as per departures for San Pedro Sula; 2hr.

Tela Take a La Ceiba-bound bus (see p.337; 5hr).

Trujillo With C (2 daily at 6.30am & 8.30am; 5hr 30min).

International bus destinations

Guatemala City (Guatemala) With HA (3 daily at 5.45am, 10am & 11am); with KQ (2 daily at 6am & 1pm); with TB (1 daily at 6am, with overnight in El Salvador); all 12–14hr.

Managua (Nicaragua) With KQ (2 daily at 6am & 1pm); with TB (1 daily at 9.15am); 8hr.

Panama City (Panama) With TB (1 daily at 9.15am with overnights in Nicaragua and Costa Rica; 2 days).

San José (Costa Rica) With TB (1 daily at 9.15am with overnight in Managua; 1 day).

San Salvador (El Salvador) With KQ (2 daily at 6am & 1pm); with TB (1 daily at 5.30pm); 7hr.

AROUND TEGUCIGALPA

Though Tegucigalpa isn't so bad, chances are you'll want to escape the city pretty quickly. Luckily, there are several places a short bus ride away where you can while away an afternoon, or even a day or two. The famous Basílica de Suyapa takes only twenty minutes to reach, or for a really adventurous couple of days you could take yourself off to Valle de Ángeles for a morning before going on to the Parque Nacional La Tigra to hike.

Basílica de Suyapa

Some 6km east of Tegucigalpa's centre, the monolithic white bulk of the **Basílica de Suyapa** (daily 9am–5pm) rises from the flat plains. Built in the 1950s, it is home to the **Virgen de Suyapa**, patron saint of Honduras. The statue of the Virgin was discovered by two *campesinos* in 1743. The story goes that after bedding down for the night, one of them noticed he was lying on something, but without looking to see what the offending object was, threw it to one side. Within a few minutes,

however, the object had returned. The next day, the two carried the little statue down to Suyapa where, placed on a simple table adorned with flowers, the Virgin began to attract worshippers.

Today you can see the tiny statue (it's only 6cm tall) behind the wooden altar in **La Pequeña Iglesia**, the original eighteenth-century chapel behind the Basílica. According to legend, each time she is placed in the larger Basílica, the Virgin mysteriously returns to the simple chapel, built by Captain José de Zelaya y Midence in thanks for the recovery of his health.

City **buses** to Suyapa run regularly from the Mercado San Isidro in Comayagüela (20min).

Valle de Ángeles

Continuing east, the road rises gently amid magnificent scenery, winding through forests of slender pine trees. Some 22km from the capital is **Valle de Ángeles**, a former mining town now reincarnated as a handicraft centre and scenic getaway for *capitalanos*. Surrounded by forested mountains, the small town slumbers during the week, then explodes with activity at weekends. The town is chiefly noted for its quality carved wooden goods, and it's a nice place to while away a couple of hours. For **food**, *Restaurante Manolo* on the main square is your best bet, where the meat from the outside grill is freshly cooked and tender. *Anafre* – a kind of Honduran fondu with beans and cheese –will set you back L70–75, a plate of steak or chorizo L90.

Buses leave Tegucigalpa for Valle de Ángeles from a car park near the San Felipe Hospital (every 45min until 6pm; 45min–1hr) and terminate a couple of blocks from the town's Parque Central. The last return bus leaves at 5.30pm.

Parque Nacional La Tigra

The oldest reserve in Honduras, **Parque Nacional La Tigra** (daily 8am–2pm;

INTO NICARAGUA: LAS MANOS

The **Las Manos** border crossing, some 120km from Tegucigalpa, is the most convenient place to enter **Nicaragua** from the capital. Buses run to the town of El Paraíso (Discua Litena; hourly 6am–6pm; 2hr 15min), 12km from the border, from where minibuses and pick-ups shuttle to the border every thirty minutes or so. With an early enough start, it's possible to reach Managua (see p.412) the same day. Taxi drivers hawking for business may well tell you that no buses run to the border from El Paraíso, but this is not true. However, if you don't want to wait around for one of the buses, a taxi will cost you about US$4.

The border post itself is a collection of huts housing the immigration and customs officials. Both sides are open daily until 5pm and crossing is generally straightforward. There are no banks, but eager moneychangers accept dollars, lempiras and Nicaraguan córdobas. There's a US$0.50 exit tax to leave Honduras. On the Nicaraguan side, trucks leave every hour for Ocotal, from where you can pick up buses to Estelí and Managua.

US$10) was designated a national park in 1980. Only 22km from Tegucigalpa, its accessibility and good system of trails make it a popular destination; however, much of the original cloudforest has been destroyed through heavy logging, so what you see is generally secondary growth. Parts of the park still shelter oak trees, bromeliads, ferns, orchids and other typical cloudforest flora, along with **wildlife** such as deer, white-faced monkeys and ocelots – though they tend to stick to parts of the park that are out of bounds to visitors. You can visit the park as a day-trip but it's worth staying a couple of nights.

The park has two entrances. The western side is reached via the village of **Jutiapa**, 17km east of Tegucigalpa. Though slightly easier to reach from the capital, this entrance has few facilities. Take the El Hatillo bus from the corner of Calle Finlay and Calle Cristóbal; it's a fifty-minute ride. The second entrance is best reached via the village of **San Juancito**, to which direct buses run from Mercado San Pablo, Barrio El Manchen (3 daily; 2hr) or from Valle de Ángeles (3 daily at 7am, 11am and 3pm; pick-ups are also available). From San Juancito it is a steep 5km hike up the mountain to the visitors' centre; pick-ups are sometimes available for around L250. The visitors'

centre has **accommodation** (US$15) and the friendly warden is usually around to provide information and trail maps. **Guides** (US$10 per day) are also available, though they only speak Spanish. The **trails** are well laid out, and provide some easy hiking, either on a circular route from the visitors' centre or across the park between the two entrances.

Southern Honduras

Stark, sun-baked coastal plains stretch **south** from Tegucigalpa all the way to the Pacific Ocean. Though a world away from the clean air and gentle climate of the highlands, this region is nonetheless beautiful in its own right, defined by a dazzling light and ferociously high temperatures. Traditionally a poor region, it's also a little-visited one, with the foreigners who do pass through usually in transit to Nicaragua or El Salvador. If you're really looking to get off the gringo trail, this is the place to do it.

The chief attraction in the area – and well worth a visit – is **Isla El Tigre**, a volcanic island set in the calm waters of the **Golfo de Fonseca**, while the colonial city of **Choluteca** offers a change of pace from the frenzy of the capital and makes a convenient stopover en route to Nicaragua.

The main transport junction in this part of the country is the village of **Jícaro Galán**, at the intersection of Highway CA-5 and the Carretera Interamericana, some 70km south of Tegucigalpa. Buses stop here to exchange passengers before continuing west to the border with El Salvador at El Amatillo, 42km away (see box opposite), or east to Nicaragua.

ISLA EL TIGRE

Boats depart the fishing village of **Coyolito**, on the coast of the Golfo de Fonseca, southwest of Jícaro Galán, for the volcanic **ISLA EL TIGRE**, whose conical peak rises sharply against the sky across the sparkling water. With good beaches, calm waters and constant sunshine, it's an ideal spot to hide away for a couple of days.

What to see and do

The island's only town is **Amapala**, once the country's major Pacific port and now a decaying relic of the nineteenth century. Looking up from the dock, ageing wooden houses cluster along the hillside, while the newly restored church in the **Parque Central** shows signs of the island's desire to get on the tourist map. Nonetheless, during the week there's every chance you'll be the only visitors on the island.

An 18-kilometre road runs all the way around the island, giving access to some glorious deserted **beaches**; it takes four or more hours to walk the whole thing, or you can take one of the *mototaxis* that hang around the end of the dock in Amapala (around L300 for a one-way trip around the island).

A 45-minute walk, or L10 *mototaxi* ride (avoid the car taxis that may be

waiting at the end of the pier – find a red *mototaxi* near the square) east from the Parque Central takes you to **Playa El Burro**, where you can while away the afternoon people-watching – children and taxi drivers play football on the beach before cooling off in the sea. Popular **Playa Grande**, a L10 ride west of the plaza, is backed by rows of *comedores* serving freshly barbecued fish at the weekend. A further ten minutes west lies **Playa Negra**, a pretty volcanic sand beach.

From the southern side of the island there are stunning **views** across the gulf to Volcán Cosiguina in Nicaragua, and in some places to Isla Meanguera and mainland El Salvador. The island's peak can be climbed in a steep and very hot two- to three-hour **walk**; ask for directions to the start of the trail, opposite the naval base, about fifteen minutes' walk southwest of Amapala.

Arrival

By bus and boat Mi Esperanza runs a service to Choluteca from Tegucigalpa, dropping you off at Jícaro Galán on the Carretera Interamericana, marked by a Dippsa fuel station. From here local buses wait on the highway to take the slow but beautiful road to Coyolito; the last stop is a few steps away from the dock. From Coyolito regular taxi boats (1am–6pm; 15min) run to Amapala's dock. You can also sometimes be dropped off at Playa El Burro.

Information

Exchange The nearest ATM is in San Lorenzo, between Coyolito and Choluteca.
Tourist information The tourist office is on the pier (Mon–Fri 8am–noon & 2–5pm, Sat 8am–noon), with a hand-drawn map of the island on the wall that you can copy or photograph. There is currently no internet on the island.

Accommodation and eating

A good option is to contact the tourist office to arrange a homestay (from L200 a night). Staying with a local family is a great way to experience island life.

INTO NICARAGUA OR EL SALVADOR: EL ESPINO, GUASAULE AND EL AMATILLO

Choluteca is a transport hub for most of the country's border crossings with Nicaragua and El Salvador.

For **Nicaragua's El Espino** border, buses run the 110km from Choluteca to San Marcos de Colón with El Rey Express (3 daily at 9am, 3pm & 7pm). From there frequent *colectivo* taxis (US$0.75) go to El Espino and the border, 10km away. The border post itself (daily 8am–5pm) is quiet and straightforward, with moneychangers on both sides. On the Nicaraguan side, regular buses run to Somoto, 20km from the border. White *rapiditos* leave Choluteca for **Guasaule** (every 30min 6am–5pm; 40min). There's regular transport from Guasaule on to Chinandega, León and Managua.

For **El Salvador**, local buses run from Choluteca to **El Amatillo** (hourly 3.15am–5.45pm; 2hr 15min). This point of entry (open 6am–10pm) teems with border traffic, moneychangers and opportunistic beggars. Crossing, however, is straightforward. A bank on the El Salvadoran side changes dollars and lempiras, but you'll get slightly better rates from the moneychangers as long as you're careful. If coming **from Tegucigalpa** you don't need to go all the way to Choluteca – just change at Jícaro Galán onto the Choluteca–El Amatillo service. Over the border in El Salvador, buses leave for Santa Rosa de Lima – 18km away, and the closest place offering accommodation (see p.292) – and San Miguel (58km; see p.283) every ten minutes until around 6.30pm.

Aquatours Marbella Playa El Burro ☏ 2795 8075. Owned by Juan Gonzales, this is a nice little hotel, albeit a little overpriced. Juan can also arrange accommodation at the home of a family friend in the nearby community. Owned by Wendy Guadalupe (☏ 2795 8053), it's a peaceful house very close to the beach (L400). Call Wendy directly or go to Aquatours Marbella and speak to Juan. L700.

El Faro Victoria At the end of the Amapala dock. Atmospheric place seemingly staffed entirely by under-18s with a terrace that sits over the water. There's good food, including fried fish (L100–150) and *curiles* cocktail (local clams marinated in their own blood, lime juice and *chismol*; L75). Excellent lemonade too (L25).

Veleros Casa de Huéspedes Playa El Burro ☏ 2795 8040 or 9898 2285. A friendly place with simple, immaculately kept rooms (L600). The attached palapa-roofed beach café is a great place to watch the locals coming and going on the launches. Shrimp *ceviche* L115; fried fish L95; breakfast L55.

Moving on

By boat *Lanchas* (2am–6pm; 15min) leave regularly for Coyolito from Amapala's dock and from Playa El Burro.

By bus From the Coyolito dock buses leave for the Jícaro Galán/Coyolito turn-off (every 15min; 1hr) for connections to Tegucigalpa or Choluteca.

CHOLUTECA

Honduras's fourth-largest city, with a population of around a hundred thousand, **CHOLUTECA**'s main attraction is its old colonial centre, one of the finest in the country. Most places of interest are grouped around the **Parque Central**, itself a pleasant place to enjoy the evening air. Dominating the square, the imposing seventeenth-century **cathedral** is worth a look for its elaborately constructed wooden ceiling. On the southwest corner of the square is the birthplace of **José Cecilio del Valle**, one of the authors of the Central American Act of Independence in 1821. The town's authorities have started to turn the building into a municipal museum, but the project is as yet incomplete. It is Valle's statue that stands in the middle of the square. Once you've seen the centre, there's not much reason to hang out in the heat, and most people move on fairly quickly.

Arrival and information

By bus The main terminal is ten blocks northeast of the Parque Central, a twenty-minute walk or L15 taxi ride. Mi Esperanza also has a stop down the street from the main terminal.

Information

Exchange Banco Occidente, one block south of the *parque* (Mon–Fri 8am–4pm, Sat 8am–noon), has a 24hr ATM, as does Banco Atlántida, on Av J.C. del Valle at the corner with Calle F.D. Roosevelt.
Internet Global Cyber in Pasaje Sarita, near *Espresso Americano*, charges L18/hour.

Accommodation

Bonsai Av Valle ☎ 2782 2648. The most basic rooms here are little more than a bed with fan and shared bathroom, but there are also a/c rooms with private bath. The grassy courtyard which most rooms open onto saves the place from drabness. L350
Hotel Mi Esperanza C 2 NO ☎ 2782 0885. A bland motel-style place with similar rooms to *Bonsai*, though this is cheaper. Rooms are available with a/c, or more cheaply with fan. L190
Santa Rosa On Av La Rosa between C Williams and C Paz Barahona ☎ 2782 0355/0884.
The simple rooms – all with private bath and fan, and some with a/c and TV – are hardly full of character, but they're kept clean, and you can always relax out on the hammocks by the patio. L170

Eating

Comedor Mi Esperanza A homely *comedor* with an army of ceiling fans battling the heat. Breakfasts and dinners L50, lunch L55.
El Paraíso de los Jugos Long, handsome café/restaurant with a wooden ceiling and lush garden. A good *típico* breakfast costs L50 (same price for lunch and dinner); juices are L30. No alcohol served. Open until 9pm daily.

Moving on

By bus to: Tegucigalpa (with Mi Esperanza 18 daily, 3hr 30min normal or 2hr 30min luxury; with Saenz 3 daily, 2hr 30min; with El Rey Express 3 daily, 3hr). For buses to Nicaragua and El Salvador, see the box on p.341.

The central highlands

With gritty San Pedro Sula to the north and the sprawl of Tegucigalpa to the south, the appeal of Honduras's central highlands lies in their relative serenity. Whether it's an early-morning birding trip on **Lago de Yojoa** or a twilight stroll around former capital **Comayagua**, this is a region for relaxation. The one exception is the **Catarata de Pulhapanzak**, a 43-metre waterfall that you can clamber behind and explore, or simply admire the crashing white water from the comfort of a picnic spot.

COMAYAGUA

Once the capital of Honduras, faded **COMAYAGUA** lies just 85km north of Tegucigalpa. Santa María de Comayagua, as it was first known, was built in 1539, and quickly gained prominence thanks to the discovery of **silver** nearby, becoming the administrative centre for the whole of Honduras. Following independence, however, the city's fortunes began to decline, particularly after Tegucigalpa was designated alternate capital of the new republic in 1824, and especially when President Soto permanently transferred the capital to Tegucigalpa in 1880. Although Comayagua is today a relatively rich and important provincial centre, its rivalry with Tegucigalpa has hardly waned over the centuries. The main reason to visit is the architectural legacy of the colonial period, in particular the dramatic cathedral overlooking the Parque Central.

What to see and do

Most sights of interest are within a few blocks of the large, tree-lined **Parque Central**, which is graced by a fountain and a pretty bandstand.

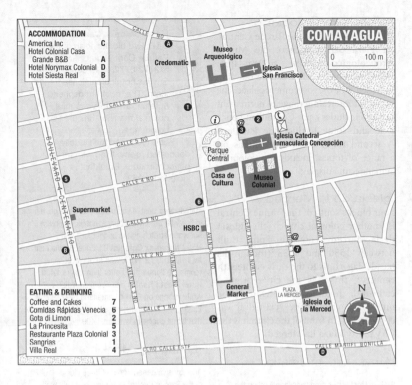

It's a great place to watch city life, especially in the evenings, when music plays out of speakers. Few of the city streets are numbered, but the centre is relatively compact and orientation straightforward.

Iglesia de la Inmaculada Concepción

On the southeast corner of the *parque* is the recently renovated **cathedral** (daily 7am–8pm), whose intricate facade consists of tiers of niches containing statues of the saints. More properly known as **Iglesia de la Inmaculada Concepción**, it was the largest church of its kind in the country during the colonial period, housing sixteen altars, though only four of these survive today. The cathedral's bell tower, built between 1580 and 1708, is considered one of the outstanding examples of colonial Baroque architecture in Central America, and is home to the twelfth-century **Reloj Arabe**, one of the oldest clocks in the world. Originally made for the Alhambra in Granada, Spain, the timepiece was presented to the city in 1582 by King Philip II.

Museo Colonial

The small **Museo Colonial de Arte Religioso**, a block southeast of the Parque Central is currently under reconstruction, with no date set for reopening as the work is dependent on donations and fundraising.

Casa de Cultura

The **Casa de Cultura**, on the south side of the Parque Central (Mon–Fri 9am–5pm, Sat & Sun 9am–12pm; free; ⓦwww .municomayagua.com) hosts changing exhibitions, usually related to the city's history. Its location makes it a nice place to hide from the sun for a while.

343

Museo Arqueológico

Two blocks north of the Parque Central, on Plaza San Francisco, the **Museo Arqueológico** (daily 8.30am–4pm; US$4) occupies a single-storey building that used to be the government palace. The small but interesting range of permanent exhibits includes a pre-Columbian Lenca stele and some terrific jade jewellery. A second room houses exhibitions on a range of topics, including a colourful Semana Santa display.

Iglesia de la Merced

Four blocks south of the Parque Central is another colonial church, the **Iglesia de la Merced** (daily 7am–8pm). Built between 1550 and 1558 (though its facade dates only to the early eighteenth century), this was the city's original cathedral, holding the Reloj Arabe until 1715, when the new cathedral was consecrated. In front of the church is the very pretty **Plaza La Merced**.

Arrival and information

By bus Most buses drop passengers off on the highway at the top of "the Boulevard", which connects CA-5 to the centre; the stop is about 1km from the Parque Central – either a L15 taxi ride or 20-minute walk. Some buses come directly to the town centre with various stops in the streets south of the Parque.

Exchange HSBC (Mon–Fri 8.30am–3.30pm, Sat 8.30–11.30am) and Banco Atlántida (1A Av NO between C 2 and C 3) have 24hr ATMs and change travellers' cheques.

Internet La Red, on the Parque (Mon–Sat 8am–9pm, Sun 9am–8pm), charges L25/hr; computers have Skype. There is another internet place by *Coffee and Cakes* (L20/hr).

Tourist information Tourist information and a map (L20) in Spanish is available at the Casa Cultura or at the *municipalidad*. There is an interesting map on the side of the small souvenir cabin in front of La Red internet café (see above), with photographs depicting noteworthy buildings in town.

Accommodation

America Inc Av 1 NO after C 1 NO ☎2772 0360, ⓦwww.hotelamericainc.com. A big, faded hotel but

TREAT YOURSELF

Hotel Colonial Casa Grande B&B Two blocks north of the Parque Central on C 7 NO ☎2772 0772/0845/0853, ⓦwww.hotelcolonialcasagrande .com. The most atmospheric hotel in town, this beautiful colonial mansion has a colonnaded, flower-filled courtyard and individually decorated rooms filled with tasteful period furniture. Breakfast is included. L952

staff do their best. If you barter you might get a price in line with the town's budget hotels, otherwise it's not worth stretching the budget for. L804

Hotel Norymax Colonial C Manuel Bonilla near Av 1 NE ☎2772 1703. Well-kept place; some rooms are lighter and better than others. L400

Hotel Siesta Real In a dark pink building with white railings on Blvd 4 Centenario ☎2772 3690/2383/2329. A friendly, clean, family-run place; note that latest check-in is 10pm. L400

Eating and drinking

An extensive general market three blocks south of the Parque Central sells meat and fish, while stalls around the main building have fresh fruit and vegetables. You can easily pick up an *almuerzo* for under L50 in the surrounding *comedores*.

Coffee and Cakes Av 1, C 2 NE. Not as New York as it may sound – coffee comes either black or white – but it's a pleasant place which doubles as a bakery. Lunch L40/60 for a half/full portion; coffee and cookie L18. Closed Sat & Sun.

Comidas Rápidas Venecia Av 1 NO, one block south of the Parque Central. A simple café, but clean and friendly. The menu is priced by item: pancakes L10, beans L12, egg L12, meats L30, veg L15. Closed evenings & Sun.

Gota de Limón There's a vibrant, clubby feel to this bar, but be aware that sex workers are said to frequent the place, perhaps because of the presence of American military from the local base. Beers L30.

La Princesita Blvd 4 Centenario, C 4–5 NO. Decorated with a princess-themed wallpaper border, but their *baleadas* are definitely for grown-ups. Try the "super" (L30) with beans, cheese, egg, chorizo, shredded chicken and *encurtido* (pickles).

Restaurante Plaza Colonial Next to the cathedral, on the eastern side of the Parque Central. You couldn't ask for a better spot, right on the square – grab an outside table. Inside is also nice, with film posters and flamenco imagery. Few mains cost less than L150.

Sangrías Just north of the Parque Central on Av 1 NO. Housed in a 150-year-old building with a pleasant outside terrace and giant handmade barrels serving as tables, the music at this bar ranges from traditional Honduran to electronic. Beers L30.

Villa Real A block southeast of the Parque Central on Av 1 NE @ www.villarealcolonial.com. The food is unreliable but this atmospheric place is definitely worth a visit for a drink (local beers L25). It's set in a beautifully restored colonial home with a large garden courtyard; note the Barcelona FC shrine in a display cabinet. Closed Mon.

Moving on

By bus to: San Pedro Sula (with El Rey 15 daily until 8.30pm, 2hr 30min; with Sultana 3 daily until 1pm, 2hr 30min; with Rivera 10 daily until 5pm, 3hr 15min); Tegucigalpa (with Carolina 10 daily until 5pm, 1hr 30min; with El Rey 16 daily until 9.30pm, 1hr 30min; with Sultana 5 daily until 5pm,

1hr 30min). For Lago de Yojoa, catch any San Pedro Sula-bound bus and ask for La Guama.

LAGO DE YOJOA

Beyond Comayagua, the highway descends from the mountains and the air becomes appreciably warmer. Some 67km north of Comayagua sits the spectacular, sparkling blue **LAGO DE YOJOA**, a natural lake approximately 17km long and 9km wide. Its reed-fringed waters, sloping away to a gentle patchwork of woods, pastures and coffee plantations, are overlooked by the mountains of **Cerro Azul Meámbar** to the east and **Santa Bárbara** to the north and west. Both of these contain small but pristine stretches of **cloudforest** and are protected as national parks. The bowl of the lake is a microclimate and attracts over four hundred species of **bird**, one of the highest concentrations in the country.

During the week, the waters – and surrounding hotels – are virtually empty, making this a supremely relaxing place for a couple of days of rowing, birdwatching and general outdoor exploring. However, at weekends the lake is a favourite with middle-class *hondureños*, and the peace can be shattered by the crowds and the buzz of jet skis.

What to see and do

The area around Lago de Yojoa offers some of the most adventurous activities of the region: you can hike through the cloudforests of the national parks, get wet crawling behind a 43-metre waterfall, explore some dark and mysterious caves or get up close to the local wildlife (see box below).

Las Cuevas de Taulabé
The **Taulabé caves** (8am–4pm; L40) make an easy and interesting stop off the CA-5 at km 140. Over 12km of tunnels and caverns have so far been explored, but only four hundred metres have paths and lighting. You can walk through the caves on your own, but local guides also hang around (negotiate a price beforehand – generally L50–70).

NATURE TOURS OF LAGO DE YOJOA

If it's nature you're after, the very knowledgeable Malcolm (ⓔ malcolmbirdwatch@hotmail.com), resident bird expert at *D&D Brewery* (see opposite), runs fantastic early-morning **tours** on the lake (L250 per person). With so many species of bird – including herons, kingfishers and hawks – as well as bats, iguanas and otters, this is a great introduction to the lake. He also offers guided walks up Santa Bárbara mountain (L500), exploring the dense cloudforest at 1400–2000m, with the possibility of spotting quetzals.

The caves can be slippery, so make sure you have suitable shoes. All local **buses** running along the CA-5 will drop you off here; it's also easy to catch a bus on to La Guama (L20 in a *rapidito*) for the lake or back to the junction at Siguatepeque (L15 in a *rapidito*) for connections to the west.

Parque Nacional Cerro Azul Meámbar
Continuing north, the highway divides at the small town of **La Guama**, from where a dirt road runs east for another 7km to the entrance to **Parque Nacional Cerro Azul Meámbar** (daily 7am–5pm; L40; ☎9865 9082 or 2608 5506, ⓦwww .paghonduras.org). Named after its highest peak, the blue-hued Cerro Azul Meámbar (2047m), this is one of the smaller and most accessible national parks, with a core of untouched cloudforest. The **visitors' centre** at the park's entrance has information on a number of short walking trails. Anyone planning to hike should be prepared for precipitously steep gradients in the upper reaches of the reserve, with dense vegetation and tumbling waterfalls. The excellent marked **trails** – you don't really need a guide – are suitable for day-trips, though it is worth staying overnight so that you can see the forest in the early morning.

Taxi fares to the park from La Guama vary wildly, with L200 the cheapest you can hope for. **Buses** that ply the route to Santa Elena may take you on to the entrance to the lodge for around L200. It's money well spent due to the steep one-hour walk from Santa Elena, and there have been occasional assaults along this route.

Peña Blanca
The village of **Peña Blanca**, north of the lake, is the commercial focus for the area. Approaching from the south on CA-5, ask for the *desvío* (turn off) to Peña Blanca, just after La Guama; from

here you can catch one of the frequent *rapiditos* (L20) or local buses (L10) to Peña Blanca itself. The El Mochito bus from San Pedro Sula also passes through Peña Blanca.

There are various useful services here: Internet Exploradores (L12/hr) is on a small dirt road that runs down the side of Minisuper Surticasa; Banco Occidente changes dollars and travellers' cheques, though there is no ATM; and if you're hungry, the pizza served above Mercado El Mexicano is good quality.

Catarata de Pulhapanzak

The absolute highlight of this region is the **Catarata de Pulhapanzak** (daily 8am–6.30pm; L50), a stunning, 43-metre-high cascade of churning white waters on the Río Lindo. Probably the prettiest waterfall in the country, the cascade is at its most dazzling in the early mornings, when rainbows form in the rising sun. It's easy enough to explore on your own, but to really get the most out of your visit take advantage of the **guided tours** run by the staff (L100; wear sturdy shoes), which are fantastic but not for the faint-hearted. They'll take you jumping or diving in and out of pools, ducking behind the falls and climbing in and out of the caves behind the curtain of water. The canopy tour (L300) is also recommended: a network of five ziplines work their way down the river until you are flying through rainbows above the waterfall. Do not be tempted to swim in the area of water immediately above the falls as there have been fatalities.

The falls are an easy, partly uphill, fifteen-minute walk from the village of **San Buenaventura**, 8km north of Peña Blanca; **buses** between El Mochito and San Pedro Sula run hourly, passing through both Peña Blanca and San Buenaventura en route. A football field inside the waterfall site entrance fills with locals at the weekend and a restaurant offers cheap fish or fried chicken.

Accommodation and eating

Agua Azul On the road between La Guama and Peña Blanca ☎ 9992 8928, ✉ aboesch87@hotmail .com. Rustic cabins – all with hot water – enjoy a lovely setting among wooded grounds sloping down to the waterside. The restaurant (breaded bass fillet L130) has a veranda with fabulous views across the lake; there's also a pool, and the hotel rents kayaks (L150/hr). Buses between La Guama and Peña Blanca can drop you on the main road, from where it's a 5-minute walk to the hotel. Cabins L480

El Cortijo del Lago On the road to Peña Blanca, 2km from La Guama ☎ 2608 5527 or 2521 0830, ⊛ www.elcortijodellago.com. Up to thirty people can be accommodated in a variety of simple rooms and cabins. One popular room right on the lake feels like a birdwatching hut with twin beds. In the attractive restaurant try tilapia fillet (L180) with *chismol*, rice and sweet vegetables from the garden. Dorms L150, doubles L200

D&D Brewery A little way outside Peña Blanca on the road to San Pedro Sula ☎ 9994 9719 or 9830 8600, ⊛ www.dd-brewery .org. This marvellous brewery/restaurant/hostelry, set in a thickly wooded area near the lake, is a real treat. The garden is teeming with bird and plant life and the home-brewed beer packs a tangy punch, best soaked up with a plateful of the restaurant's fabulous fries. In the morning, tackle a face-sized blueberry pancake (L85). Accommodation ranges from basic but well-maintained rooms to atmospheric cabins. Be sure to book in advance. Take the El Mochito bus from San Pedro Sula until you see the *D&D Brewery* sign. Dorm L100, doubles L300

Panacam Lodge 7km from the highway between San Pedro Sula and Tegucigalpa, La Guama turn-off ☎ 2608 5506/9865 9082, ✉ panacam@paghonduras .org. The park has some fantastic accommodation, from simple dorms to wood cabins with hot-water bathrooms, and is well signposted from La Guama. Bring your own equipment if you want to camp. Camping L100, dorms L160, doubles L800

The western highlands

The **western highlands** of Honduras are a picturesque landscape of pine forests, sparsely inhabited mountains and remote villages. The departments of **Lempira** and **Intibucá** contain the highest concentration of indigenous peoples in the country, and many of the towns in the region make up the so-called **Ruta Lenca**. Around the village of **La Esperanza** particularly, look out for Lenca women wearing traditional coloured headdresses while working in the fields.

Cobbled, colonial **Gracias** makes a relaxing base for hikes in the pristine cloudforest reserve of the **Parque Nacional Celaque**. An easy bus ride away is **Santa Rosa de Copán**, which is also a relaxing place to stay and still unspoilt, despite its growing popularity with tourists and its proximity to the **Copán ruins**.

LA ESPERANZA

Just north of the town of Siguatepeque, a good paved road heads west from CA-5 to the village of **LA ESPERANZA**, the centre of commerce for western Honduras and the capital of the department of Intibucá. During the week there's nothing much of interest here, but the town livens up considerably during the colourful **weekend market** (Sat & Sun), when Lenca farmers from surrounding villages pour into town. It's likely that if you're heading to Gracias you'll need to **stay overnight** in La Esperanza due to the lack of buses.

Arrival and information

By bus Buses running between Tegucigalpa and San Pedro Sula can drop you off at the *desvío* (turn-off) to La Esperanza, just north of Siguatepeque. From the *desvío*, buses run to the town until mid-afternoon (every 2hr; 2hr).
Banks La Esperanza has one ATM that takes Visa cards.
Internet Available at Communicaciones Vasquez opposite *Opalaca* restaurant.

Accommodation and eating

Hotel La Esperanza Four blocks southeast of the Parque ☎ 2783 0068 or 3351 8322,

✉ luispalencia04@yahoo.com. Rooms verging on the luxurious, with hot water, cable TV and plush bedding, at fair prices. L280
Hotel Mina Four blocks east of the Parque ☎ 2783 1071. A cheaper option, also with hot water, whose smart outward appearance is not reflected in the pokey rooms. L300
Mi Jardín In the daytime, this does indeed feel like a charming little garden and offers a *plato del día* for L50, coffee (including decaffeinated) for L12–18 and a cake of the day for L14.
Opalaca This restaurant has decent food, with meat dishes for L140–195 and burgers for L85.

SAN JUAN INTIBUCÁ

A bumpy 52km north of La Esperanza, the village of **SAN JUAN INTIBUCÁ** is slowly finding its way onto the tourist map thanks to a local *cooperativa* promoting the area's Lenca traditions. Information about tours and demonstrations is available from *Hotel Guancascos* in Gracias (see opposite) or from Gladys Nolasco (☎ 2754 7150 or 9786 1012, ✉ glaisra7@yahoo.com), who can be found at a building marked *Docucentro Israel copias y mas*, five minutes' walk from the main square, opposite a small fruit and veg market. Options include participating in the roasting of coffee beans, hikes to nearby waterfalls and cloudforests, and observing the production of traditional handicrafts. Three daily **pick-ups** from La Esperanza (10am–4pm; 2hr) run to the town. If you're lucky, you can grab a *rapidito* back from San Juan to Gracias (until 5pm; 45min–1hr).

GRACIAS

Founded in 1536 by Spanish conquistador Juan de Chávez, **GRACIAS** lies in the shadow of the nearby **Parque Nacional Celaque**. It's a hot and dusty cobbled town, but well located for day-trips to surrounding natural attractions, including the park and some natural **hot springs** (daily 7am–11pm; L50), about an hour's walk south or L60 each way in a *mototaxi* – you can arrange for one to come and collect you for the return leg. These are small pools purpose-built for bathing in the 36–39°C waters; an on-site *comedor* serves basic meals. Another, more pleasant area of hot pools, a further minute's walk into the complex, is overseen by Frenchman Jean-Claude Mayer (☎9738 4777, Ⓔpandih@hotmail.fr), who offers very basic *cabaña* accommodation on the site for L350.

Arrival and information

By bus Buses from Santa Rosa de Copán, La Esperanza and San Juan arrive at the terminal three blocks west of the Parque Central.

Exchange Banco Occidente, one block west of the Parque (Mon–Fri 8am–4pm, Sat 8–11.30am), changes dollars, cash and travellers' cheques, but doesn't have an ATM.

Internet Ecolem, in front of *Guancascos* hotel, charges L20/hr.

Shopping Lorendiana, which sells beautifully bottled pickles, preserves and other food delicacies, is well worth a look.

Tourist information The office in the centre of the Parque (daily 8am–noon & 1–4.30pm) sells maps (L15) and offers good information.

Accommodation

Erick allows you to leave bags if hiking at the national park.

Erick One block north of the Parque ☎2656 1066. Rooms are clean but basic, with pipes for showers. Some bathrooms are separated by a half-wall, so not completely private. L280

Hotel Guancascos East side of Castillo San Cristóbal ☎2656 1219, Ⓦwww.guancascos.com. Owner Fronica (Frony) Miedema takes pains to make sure *Guancascos* is a "green hotel". Sixteen good-quality rooms, with hot water throughout. Tours and information are offered too. L540

Eating and drinking

Guancascos Three blocks west and two blocks south of the Parque Central. Diners enjoy a superb view from the terrace, especially if you make it for an early breakfast. Breakfast L60, soup from L55, set lunches and dinners L100.

Kandil Kafe y Bar Three blocks from the park. An unexpectedly fashionable place, given the town's sleepy, traditional feel. It's crisply painted, with minimal furnishings, and the pizzas with *loroco* (L80) or prosciutto (L85) are recommended. Beers from L25, cocktails L60–80.

Riconcito Graciano Two blocks west and south of the Parque. The menu features dishes made solely from local ingredients (mains from L80), served in an atmosphere about as rustic as can be. You might find yourself drinking fresh *noni* juice, eating meat with a *loroco* flower sauce, or sampling *pinol* (L20) – described as Lenca chocolate.

El Señor de la Sierra The name of this café in the centre of the Parque Central refers to Lempira, whose image graces their drinks menu. There's wi-fi, the coffee's good (L10) and there are usually one or two cake options (*quesadilla, torta, semitas, empanadas,* doughnuts) for L7.

Moving on

By bus to: San Pedro Sula (with Gracianos 1 daily direct; with Congolón 5 daily; 4hr); Santa Rosa de Copán (various buses from main terminal until 5pm; 1hr 15min). For Copán, take any San Pedro Sula-bound bus and change at La Entrada.

PARQUE NACIONAL CELAQUE

PARQUE NACIONAL CELAQUE (L100) protects one of the largest and most impressive expanses of virgin cloudforest in Honduras. Thousands of years of geographical isolation has resulted in several endemic species of flora. Locals also claim that the park is home to more quetzals than all of Guatemala, though you'll still have to keep a sharp eye out to see one. The focus of the park is the nation's highest peak, **Cerro Las Minas** (2849m).

What to see and do

Pay your entrance fee at the *Comedor Villa Verde* opposite the school. Inside the park, there are rambles and hikes of all experience levels to choose from. The most exciting and scenic option is the six-kilometre marked **trail** up to the summit of Cerro Las Minas. In the upper reaches of the park much of the main trail consists of forty-degree slopes, so this is not a hike for the unfit.

If the peak is your aim, you'll need to **camp** at one of the two designated spots along the way (see below). The cloudforest proper doesn't begin until after *Campamento El Naranjo*, so try to make it this far. **Guides** aren't necessary for the main trail, but you'll need one if planning to undertake the more difficult treks on the southern slopes; these can be arranged through *Hotel Guancascos* in Gracias (see "Information", below).

Arrival and information

On foot The park is best approached from Gracias; the entrance is an 8km walk from town. Take the dirt road through the village of Mejicapa, from where a marked track leads uphill to the entrance.
By pick-up Pick-ups from Gracias are sometimes available.
Information *Guancascos* in Gracias (see p.349) functions as an unofficial information centre for the park. As well as selling maps, they can arrange lifts up to the lodge, gear, guide and entrance (US$20–25 per person per day).

Accommodation and eating

Sleeping bags, decent boots and a change of warm clothing are essential. There are two designated camping spots on the way to the peak, *Campamento Don Tomás* and *Campamento El Naranjo* (L60).
Doña Alejandra Just outside the lodge entrance. If you haven't brought your own supplies, head here for dinner (until 7pm; L50).
Lodge 2km from the entrance. A track leads through the pine forest to the basic lodge, where there are bunkrooms and showers. L150

SANTA ROSA DE COPÁN

It's an easy ninety-minute bus ride 45km northwest from Gracias to **SANTA ROSA DE COPÁN**, a colourful colonial relic built on the proceeds of the tobacco industry. Unusual for a town of this size, the majority of its streets are still cobbled, preserving an authentic feel. While fresh in the mornings and evenings, Santa Rosa de Copán heats up during the day.

Bus Terminal (2km), Flor de Copán Cigar Company (2km) & Colonia San Martin • Boulevard Jorge Bueso Arias, Copán, Gracias & San Pedro Sula

EATING & DRINKING

Casa Típica	7
Cristy	6
Cuates	9
Doña Toya	1
Flamingos	5
El Rodeo	8
La Taza	3
Ten Napel Café	2
Weekends Pizza	4

ACCOMMODATION

Alondra's	C
Blanca Nieves	A
Hotel Escalon	D
El Rosario	B

SANTA ROSA DE COPÁN

0   100 m

What to see and do

Chosen in 1765 as the headquarters of the Royal Tobacco Factory, the golden weed continues to play a role in the local economy. The **Flor de Copán Cigar Company** maintains offices in the town centre – in the original Royal Tobacco building on Calle Centenario – but their **factory** is located 2km northwest of the town centre, about 300m after turning right out of the bus station. Around thirty thousand hand-rolled cigars are produced daily, and **tours** in Spanish and English are available at 10am and 2pm (US$2). **Colonia San Martín**, a short taxi ride away, is home to another mainstay in the local economy, the **Beneficio Maya** (@www .cafecopan.com) coffee *finca*. A family-run business, they offer tours (US$2) during the coffee season (Nov–Feb) but welcome visitors year-round. Tours at both factories should be organized through the tourist office a day ahead.

Back in the centre of town is the delightful, shady **Parque Contreras**, also called the Parque Central, with a beautiful cathedral on its eastern side. **Calle Centenario**, lined with shops and restaurants, runs along the southern edge of the Parque, past the town's central **market** a couple of blocks east.

Arrival and information

By bus Buses arrive at a terminal just off the highway, 2km northwest of the centre. Taxis (L15) and the yellow buses marked *urbanos* (city buses; L5) run regularly to the Parque Contreras.
Internet The cheapest rates are available at the tourist office (L15/hr), but access is also available at Zona Digital (L18/hr) on Av 3 NE and Bonsay Cyber Café (L18/hr) on C Real Centenario.
Tourist information The tourist office in the centre of the Parque (Mon–Sat 8am–noon & 1.30pm–6pm; @www.visitesantarosadecopan.org) has city maps (L20) and helpful staff.
Tour operators Max Elvir of Lenca Land Trails (@2662 1128 or 9997 5340, @max@lenca -honduras.com), a local guide, offers a number of excellent tours, including trips to Parque Nacional

Celaque, indigenous villages and hot springs, all for around US$40.

Accommodation

A great option in Santa Rosa de Copán is to organize a homestay through the tourist office (from around L160 per night).
Alondra's Av 2 SO @2662 1194/3583. Opt for one of the upstairs bedrooms for a bit more light. The open communal area has lots of seating, there's hot water and cable TV, and coffee, juice and pastries are available at breakfast. L600
Blanca Nieves Av 3 NE @2662 1312. A decent budget option with friendly owners. En-suite rooms are larger and better value than those with shared bathrooms. L300
Hotel Escalon Av 2 and C 3 SO @2662 0652 or 9636 8304, @carlosescalon@yahoo.es or molinasrc@yahoo.es. Clean and new with a family atmosphere, and hot water and TVs in the bedrooms. Look around before choosing as some rooms (all doubles) are brighter than others. L350
El Rosario Av 3 NE @2662 0211. Rooms are clean, though some are a little dark and cell-like, with bathrooms separated from bedrooms by a shower curtain. L300

Eating

Santa Rosa's popularity has resulted in something of a glut of eating establishments. Cheap *comedores* line the bus station and upstairs in the Mercado Central, where filling *almuerzos* can be had for L40–50. In the evenings street vendors sell *tamales* and tortillas around the Mercado Central and Parque.
Casa Típica C 2 Av 2–3 SO. The walls of this locally popular place are decorated with various odds and ends. Open from 6pm, though snacks such as *pupusas* (L20) are sometimes offered earlier in the day.
Cristy C Centenario. This canteen-style café is great for a quick lunch, with different meats, potatoes, salad, rice, mash, noodles and vegetables on the menu. Lunch with three sides L80, breakfast L55. Closes 2.30pm.
Doña Toya Av 4 C1–2 NO. The walls are flaking, the floor is chipped and yet this place has a charming, friendly feel. The nourishing, tangy *atol chuco* (L10–15) – a savoury corn-based drink – is served in carved bowls, and fried or boiled *yuca* with *chicharrón* will set you back L40. Daily 8am–10.30pm.
El Rodeo Av 1 SE. The best meat in town: a mixed grill that will feed four, comprising steak (including *puyaso*), chorizo, pork chop, chicken and sides, is L395.

La Taza C Centenario Av 3–4 NO. Their certification of good coffee practice ("high grown") is proudly on display at the counter in this small, homely café. Very good coffee and cake L30. Wi-fi is available too.

Ten Napel Café C 1 Av 2–3 NO. A lovely place with a fantastic garden, wi-fi, and bags of coffee, cigars and maps of the town for sale. *Tiramisù* L48, *licuados* L30, panini L59.

Weekends Pizza Av 4 NO & C 2 SO. Run by English-speaking sisters Ana and Claudia, this is a popular, vibrant place. Pizzas start at L150. Wed–Sun 9am–9pm.

Drinking

Cuates C 1 SE, Av 4–5 SE. A Mexican bar and restaurant with happy-hour offers on food and drink 7–9pm and karaoke on Thursdays. Beer L24–30. The kitchen is open until 11pm, and the bar until 2am.

Flamingos Av 1 SE, half a block south of the Parque. From Wed to Fri they offer two-for-one *boquitas* (snacks), and happy hour is 8–10pm daily (beer L25).

Directory

Exchange Banco Occidente, south of the Parque, has a 24hr Visa/Plus ATM and also changes cash dollars and travellers' cheques. A second ATM (Mon–Fri 9am–4pm, Sat 9am–noon) is opposite Manzanitas supermarket.

Pharmacy Farmacia Cruz Roja on the corner of C 1 and Av 3 NE (daily 8am–6pm).

Post office On the west side of the Parque (Mon–Fri 8am–noon & 2pm–5pm, Sat 8am–noon).

Shopping Supermarket Manzanitas (in an unmarked, large yellow building), C Real Centenario and Av 2 (Mon–Sat 8am–7.30pm, Sun 8am–2pm). The Mercado Santa Teresa (in Barrio Santa Teresa) has fresh fruit and vegetables.

Telephones Hondutel, on the west side of the Parque (daily 7am–9pm).

Moving on

By bus to: Copán (take any San Pedro Sula-bound bus and change at La Entrada; 4 daily until 4pm; 2–3hr); Gracias (every 30min until 6pm; 1hr 30min); La Entrada (local services every 30min; 45min); Nueva Ocotepeque (with La Sultana de Occidente, hourly 8.45am–6.30pm; 2hr); San Pedro Sula (with La Sultana de Occidente direct, hourly 6am–1.30pm, 2hr 30min; local services every 30min, 3hr 30min); Tegucigalpa (with La Sultana de Occidente direct, hourly 4am–1.30pm; 7hr 30min).

COPÁN RUINAS

A charming town of steep cobbled streets and red-tiled roofs set among green hills, **COPÁN RUINAS** has more to offer than just its proximity to the

---

INTO EL SALVADOR AND GUATEMALA: EL POY AND AGUA CALIENTE

Buses to both El Salvador and Guatemala pass through Nueva Ocotepeque (hourly from Santa Rosa de Copán with Sultana; 2hr). It's a dirty, busy town, and most people change buses and move on quickly, but if you get stuck, the *Hotel Turístico*, up from the bus stop (☏2653 3639; L400), is a good option. The Banco de Occidente, near the bus stop, changes currencies and travellers' cheques, but you'll get better rates for Guatemalan quetzales at the border.

For El Poy (El Salvador), *rapiditos* run the 7km from Nueva Ocotepeque every 15min 6am–6pm (10min). El Poy itself is drab and dusty, but the crossing is straightforward, as the immigration windows are next to each other in the same building just a short walk from where the bus drops you. Banpaís (Mon–Fri 8am–noon & 1pm–5pm) will change currencies. For most nationalities, there's no fee to enter El Salvador, though residents of Canada, Greece, Portugal and the US will be charged US$10 for a tourist card. Buses to La Palma, the nearest town over the border, and San Salvador leave every thirty minutes until 4.30pm.

For Agua Caliente (Guatemala), yellow local buses make the thirty-minute trip from Nueva Ocotepeque every thirty minutes until 6.30pm (L25). There are no banking or accommodation facilities on the Honduran side. Over in Guatemala, minibuses leave every twenty minutes for Esquipulas (see p.193) until 6pm.

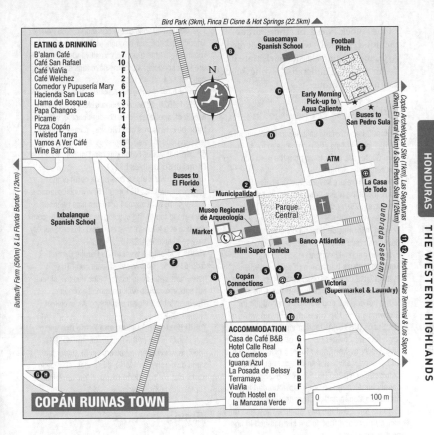

EATING & DRINKING

B'alam Café	7
Café San Rafael	10
Café ViaVia	F
Café Welchez	2
Comedor y Pupusería Mary	6
Hacienda San Lucas	11
Llama del Bosque	3
Papa Changos	12
Picame	1
Pizza Copán	4
Twisted Tanya	8
Vamos A Ver Café	5
Wine Bar Cito	9

ACCOMMODATION

Casa de Café B&B	G
Hotel Calle Real	A
Los Gemelos	E
Iguana Azul	H
La Posada de Belssy	D
Terramaya	B
ViaVia	F
Youth Hostel en la Manzana Verde	C

COPÁN RUINAS TOWN

infamous archeological site of Copán. Despite the weekly influx of visitors, Copán Ruinas has managed to remain largely unspoilt. Many travellers are seduced by the relaxed atmosphere, clean air and rural setting, and end up spending longer than planned, studying Spanish, eating and drinking well or exploring the region's other minor sites, hot springs and beautiful countryside.

What to see and do

Half a day is enough to take in virtually all the in-town attractions. The **Parque Central** is lined with banks, municipal structures and a simple, whitewashed Baroque-style church. On the west side of the plaza is the **Museo Regional de Arqueología** (daily 9am–5pm; US$3), housing some impressive Maya carvings from the Copán region, including glyph-covered altars T and U and **Stela 7**, discovered just 100m from the Parque Central. There are also two remarkable **tombs**, one of which contains the remains of a female shaman, complete with jade jewellery, an entire puma skeleton, the skull of a deer, and two human sacrificial victims.

In the **municipalidad** on the Parque Central is a fantastic photography exhibition (Mon–Fri 8am–4pm; free) donated by Harvard University's Peabody Museum, detailing, in beautifully reproduced prints, the first archeological expeditions to Copán at the turn of the twentieth century.

One block west of the Parque is the food market, while the Mercado Artesanal, selling classic tourist fare like T-shirts and handicrafts, is one block south of the Parque.

Arrival and information

By bus Buses from the east generally terminate by a small football field at the entrance to town. Buses from Guatemala enter town from the west and stop just before the Parque.

Internet There are several internet cafés in town, including Maya Connections, just south of the plaza (L25/hr), and La Casa de Todo (daily 7am–9pm; L20/hr).

Tourist information Copán Connections and Basecamp (see below) are excellent sources of local and national information.

Tour operators Basecamp (T 2651 4695), in the *ViaVia* café (see opposite), offers tours to a local coffee plantation, horseriding trips, visits to the hot springs and transport to Antigua in Guatemala (US$13). The 8am mountain walk to Los Sapos (US$10) is recommended, as is the town tour that owner Gerardo offers. He'll explain what really makes Copán Ruinas tick, politically and economically – it's an eye-opener. Copán Connections (T 2651 4182, W www.copan connections.com) is a one-stop source of information on Copán and popular destinations like Lago de Yojoa and the Bay Islands. They also offer canopy tours and trips to hot springs and indigenous villages.

Accommodation

Some of the best hostels in this region are in Copán. Beware of unofficial hotel representatives trying to shepherd you into hotels upon arrival.

Casa de Café B&B At the southwest edge of town, overlooking the Río Copán valley T 2651 4620 or 9917 1484, W www .casadecafecopan.com. A charming place with ten comfortable and airy rooms, all with nice individual touches, and private, hot-water bathrooms. There's a fabulous garden where you can lie in a hammock and enjoy the views. An excellent breakfast is included. US$55

Hotel Calle Real Two and a half blocks north of the Parque T 2651 4230, E hotelcallereal@yahoo.com. Well-kept rooms with hot water set within shady surroundings; rooms come with fan or a/c. The garden and hammock-slung area make this even better value. US$20

Los Gemelos Close to the bus stop T 2651 4077. Friendly backpacker stronghold. The very basic rooms are a little tired with small windows but they are kept spotless. All rooms have fans and shared bath. US$14

Iguana Azul Next to the *Casa de Café B&B* T 2651 4620, W www.iguanaazulcopan.com. An excellent, spotlessly-clean budget choice, with three private rooms and two very pleasant dorms (eleven beds in total). Amenities include a pretty garden, hot-water bathrooms and laundry facilities. Dorms US$6, doubles US$14

La Posada de Belssy One block north of the Parque Central T 2651 4680, W www.laposadade belssy.com. With a small pool and nice hangout area at the top of the building, hot-water bathrooms and use of a kitchen, this is a solid choice. Laundry service available. US$16

ViaVia Two blocks west of the Parque Central T 2651 4652, W www.viaviacafe.com. This hotel-cum-café-cum-tourist office has five simple but spotless rooms with en-suite bathrooms. The hospitable Belgian owners speak excellent English. US$16

Youth Hostel en la Manzana Verde One and a half blocks north of the Parque Central T 2651 4652, W www.lamanzanaverde.com. Under the same ownership as *ViaVia*, this impeccably clean hostel has six-bed dorm rooms, a kitchen (closes at 10pm) and laundry facilities. US$6

Eating

Copán's wide range of places to eat generally maintain high standards. Most stop serving at 10pm.

Terramaya Two and a half blocks north of the Parque T 2651 4623, W www.terramaya copan.com. From the outside, the whitewashed walls, terracotta roof and wrought-iron metalwork have a reassuring solidity, while from the moment you step through the heavy wooden doors, it's all about comfort and relaxation (there's even a pillow menu). There's a massage pavilion outside in the beautiful garden, and some of the six rooms have balconies overlooking the Copán River valley and archeological park. Breakfast is included. US$85

Cafés

B'alam Café One block south of the Parque. An intimate café with a tiled floor and tiny terrace. It serves coffee (L16) and *quesadilla* cake (L25), as well as snacks such as bagel with cream cheese and jalapeño jelly (L42) and pitta with chicken, cheese, tomatoes and *papalinas* (potato chips) for L95. Wi-fi. Daily 7am–7pm.

Café San Rafael Two blocks south of Parque Central. Owner Carlos Guerra studied cheese-making in California and this café is the result. Sandwiches are good value, such as the grilled mozzarella and gouda served with plantain chips (L50). Coffees start at L12 all the way up to the "San Rafael Forest", adorned with cherry and chocolate syrup, whipped cream and chocolates (L45).

Café ViaVia Two blocks west of the Parque. Belgian-owned establishment with a streetside terrace and leafy garden. In addition to an array of sandwiches and good breakfasts – including pancakes and omelettes – there is a very reasonably priced fixed menu with vegetarian options. Mains around L100.

Café Welchez Northwest corner of Parque Central. Boasts some of the world's smallest balconies, with great views of the square. Inside, there's a distinguished feel with wood panelling. Coffee and desserts are the focus (coffees from L15, German chocolate cake L45).

Picame One block northeast of the Parque. A friendly café perfect for breakfast, from *típico* (L85) to pancakes with fruit salad and honey (L75). Take on their legendarily huge burritos (L110) if you dare. Daily 7am–9pm.

Vamos a Ver Café One block south of the Parque. Busy garden café, popular with travellers thanks to affordable and delicious home-made soups, sandwiches and snacks. Sandwiches under L100, mains under L110.

Restaurants

Comedor y Pupusería Mary One block southwest of the Parque, though planning to move to a site near the football field. This great local restaurant specializes in *pupusas* served with pickles made from everything from cauliflower to chilli. All *pupusas* are L10 on Wednesdays.

Llama del Bosque Two blocks west of the Parque. Slightly old-fashioned restaurant with a reasonably priced menu including local breakfasts, meat and chicken dishes, *baleadas* and snacks (most dishes L60–120).

Pizza Copán (Jim's Pizza) Half a block south of the Parque. Both locals and tourists come here to

indulge in delicious, generously-sized pizza and pasta (L140–250). Takeaway available.

🏃 **Twisted Tanya** One block south of the plaza ⓦwww.twistedtanya.com. Perhaps the best food in the town, with mains such as chicken curry and papaya chutney, roast pork with sherry gravy and home-made seafood linguine. Mains US$16, or US$22 for three courses. The "backpackers' special" (3–6pm) has offerings such as home-made beef ravioli with vegetables followed by carrot cake (US$8). Mon–Sat 3–10pm.

Drinking

Café ViaVia Two blocks west of the Parque. This is the town's social hub, and runs themed nights from salsa to movies. Closes at midnight.

Papa Changos Ten minutes' walk south of the Parque Central. Things don't really get going much before 10pm, when they start playing a mix of merengue and other latin beats. Its safety record is not impeccable, so take advice in town. Currently only open Fri & Sat.

Wine Bar Cito One block south of the Parque. Cushioned bottle-crates for seats and low lighting make this a cosy spot for a drink. Head chef Hans describes their tapas as "Maya flavours, European technique". Daily 5pm–midnight; happy hour 5–7pm.

Shopping

Books Exchange available at La Casa de Todo (daily 7am–9pm), on the next corner from *Los Gemelos*.

Crafts and souvenirs La Casa de Todo has every souvenir imaginable. There is a *mercado de artesanías* opposite *Yat B'alam* (C La Independencia, one block south of the Parque).
Supermarket Mini Super Daniela on the Parque, or Victoria one block south.

Directory

Exchange Banco de Occidente (Mon–Fri 8.30am–4.30pm, Sat 8.30–11.30am & 1–4pm) and Banco Atlántida (Mon–Fri 9am–5pm, Sat 9am–noon) have 24hr ATMs.
Language schools Guacamaya (☎2651 4360, ⓦwww.guacamaya.com), two blocks north of the plaza, offers a week-long course for US$235 which includes 20 hours of one-on-one tuition, homestay, a day-trip and university credits. Without the homestay it is US$135. Ixbalanque (☎2651 4432, ⓦwww.Ixbalanque.com) is also worth considering.
Laundry La Casa de Todo has a one-day service (L12/pound, minimum charge L50), or try the service at the back of Victoria supermarket.
Post office Behind the Museo Regional de Arqueología (Mon–Fri 8am–4pm, Sat 8am–noon).
Telephones There's a Hondutel office next to the post office (daily 7am–9pm; L2/min to the US, L44/min to Europe).

Moving on

By bus to: Agua Caliente (regular buses 5am–4pm; last return to Copán at 4pm; 1hr); Antigua (with Hedman 2 daily at 2.20pm & 6pm; via Guatemala City; 6hr); La Entrada, for connections to Santa Rosa de Copán and Gracias (local buses every 45min until 5pm; 1hr); San Pedro Sula (with Hedman Alas 2 daily at 10.30am & 2.30pm, 2hr 45min; with Casasola 5 daily at 4am, 5am, 6am, 7am & 2pm, 3hr). For Tegucigalpa, Tela and La Ceiba, you have to go via San Pedro Sula.

AROUND COPÁN RUINAS

While the main draw for travellers to Copán is the nearby ruins, there's a lot more on offer to help you while away a few days. Nature parks give visitors the chance to walk among beautiful butterflies and exotic birds, while lesser-known archeological sites like Las Sepulturas can be void of fellow tourists and a local family-run farm can show

you how your morning cup of coffee came into existence.

Enchanted Wings Butterfly House

A twenty-minute walk west from the plaza, along the road to Guatemala, stands the **Enchanted Wings Butterfly House and Nature Centre** (daily 8am–4.30pm; L115), owned by an American enthusiast and his Honduran wife. You will be shown any butterflies they are currently breeding before entering a large enclosure where you're surrounded by fluttering wings. Types to look out for include the speckled brown "giant owl" and the scarlet-and-yellow "helicopter". Butterflies hatch in the morning hours, so time your visit accordingly. For your best chance to see orchids flowering in the adjacent enclosure visit between February and April or July and August.

Macaw Mountain Bird Park

On the other side of town, 3km north of the plaza (L20 each way in a *mototaxi*), the **Macaw Mountain Bird Park** (daily 9am–5pm; US$10; ☎2651 4245 or 9986 0804, ⓦwww.macawmountain.com) is home to parrots, macaws and toucans rescued from captivity. Your ticket gives you entrance for three days – with walk-through aviaries, a stunning forest location and a natural pool for swimming, it's worth the entrance fee. The riverside *Jungle Bistro* is in the safe hands of the people behind *Twisted Tanya* (see p.355; daily 8am–4pm), and offers mains from L80.

Las Sepulturas

Some 2km east of Copán along the highway is the smaller archeological site of **Las Sepulturas** (daily 8am–4pm; entrance with the same ticket as for Copán, see opposite), the focus of much interest in recent years because of the information it provides on daily domestic life in Maya times. Eighteen of the forty-odd residential compounds at the site have been excavated, yielding a hundred buildings that would have been inhabited. Smaller compounds on the edge of the site are thought to have housed young princes, as well as concubines and servants. It was customary to bury the nobility close to their residences, and more than 250 tombs have been excavated around the compounds. One of the most interesting finds – the tomb of a priest or shaman, dating from around 450 AD – is on display in the museum in Copán Ruinas Town.

Luna Jaguar hot springs

Some 22km north of Copán, set in lush highland scenery dotted with coffee *fincas* and tracts of pine, the **Luna Jaguar spa resort** is a great place to relax. Here thermal waters pour into the cold-water river, creating natural pools and showers. L40 will get you into the man-made pools, but across the river, with another L200 entrance fee, you enter a world fit for a Maya king, with pools and footbaths all around.

COPÁN

Set in serene, rolling hills 45km (as the crow flies) from Santa Rosa de Copán, **COPÁN** (daily 8am–4pm; ruins US$15, includes entrance to Las Sepulturas, see opposite, Museo de Arqueología US$3, tunnels US$15) is one of the most impressive of all Maya sites. Its pre-eminence is not due to size – in scale it's far less impressive than sites such as Tikal or Chichén Itza – but to the overwhelming legacy of artistic craftsmanship that has survived over so many centuries. Copán now ranks as the second most visited spot in the country after the Bay Islands.

Museum of Maya Sculpture

Opposite the visitors' centre at the ruins (see above) is the terrific **Museum of Maya Sculpture** (daily 8am–4pm; US$7), arguably the finest in the entire Maya region, with a tremendous collection of stelae, altars, panels and well-labelled explanations in English. Entrance is through an impressive doorway made to look like the jaws of a serpent; you then pass through a tunnel signifying the passage into *xibalba*, or the underworld.

Once out of the tunnel you are greeted by a full-scale, flamboyantly painted replica of the magnificent **Rosalila Temple**, built by Moon Jaguar in 571 AD and discovered intact under Temple 16. A vast crimson-and-jade-coloured mask of the Sun God, depicted with wings outstretched, forms the main facade. Other exhibits concentrate on aspects of Maya beliefs and cosmology, while the upper storey houses many of the finest original sculptures from the Copán valley, comprehensively displaying the skill of the Maya craftsmen.

TREAT YOURSELF

If you want to get a real insight into the local way of life, take a day-trip or stay overnight at **Finca El Cisne** (☏2651 4695 or 9920 4836, ⊛www.fincaelcisne .com), 23km north of Copán. Owner Carlos Castejón's family has worked the land here since 1885, and they now invite guests to explore their working farm, which is involved in the production of cardamom, coffee and cattle. Day-long tours (from US$70) include transport to and from the *finca*, fantastic scenic horseriding, swimming in the Río Blanco and a trip (entrance included) to the Luna Jaguar hot springs. Tours of more than one day (from US$90) include accommodation, breakfasts and dinners. Visits can be arranged through the Basecamp office in Copán Ruinas (see "Arrival and information", p.354).

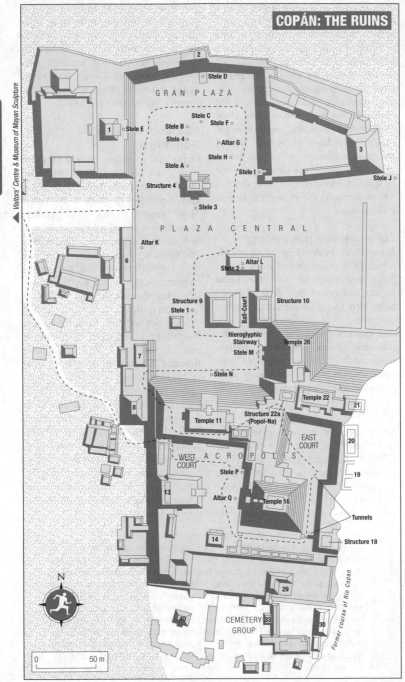

COPÁN: THE RUINS

Visitors' Centre & Museum of Mayan Sculpture

2

Stele D

GRAN PLAZA

1   Stele E

Stele C
Stele B   Stele F
Stele 4   Altar G

3

Stele H

Stele A   Stele I

Stele J

Structure 4

Stele 3

PLAZA CENTRAL

Altar K

6

Altar L
Stele 2

Structure 9   Ball-Court   Structure 10

Stele 1

7

Hieroglyphic
Stairway   Temple 26

Stele M

8

Stele N

Temple 22
21

Temple 11

Structure 22a
(Popol-Na)

20

WEST ACROPOLIS
COURT   EAST COURT

19

13

Stele P

Altar Q   Temple 16

Tunnels

14

Structure 18

29

N

40

CEMETERY
GROUP

33

30

Former course of Río Copán

0   50 m

Plaza Central and Gran Plaza

Straight through the avenue of trees from the warden's gate lie the **Plaza Central** and **Gran Plaza**, large, rectangular arenas strewn with the magnificently carved and exceptionally well preserved stelae that are Copán's outstanding features. The northern end of the Gran Plaza was once a public place, the stepped sides bordered by a densely populated residential area. **Structure 4** in the centre of the two plazas is a modestly sized pyramid-temple.

Dotted all around are Copán's famed **stelae** and altars, made from local andesite. Most of the stelae represent **Eighteen Rabbit**, Copán's "King of the Arts" (stelae A, B, C, D, F, H and 4). Stele A (731 AD) has 52 glyphs along its sides including the emblem glyphs of the four great cities of Copán, Palenque, Tikal and Calakmul – a text designed to show that Eighteen Rabbit saw his city as a pivotal power in the Maya world. The original is now in the museum. **Stele B** (731 AD) depicts Eighteen Rabbit bearing a turban-like headdress intertwined with twin macaws, while his hands support a bar motif, a symbol designed to show the ruler holding up the sky. **Stele C** (730 AD) is one of the earliest stones to have faces on both sides. Two rulers are represented here: facing the turtle-shaped altar (a symbol of longevity) is Eighteen Rabbit's father Smoke Jaguar, while on the other side is Eighteen Rabbit himself. **Stele H** (730 AD), perhaps the most impressively executed of all the sculptures, shows Eighteen Rabbit wearing the latticed skirt of the Maize God, his wrists weighed down with jewellery, while his face is crowned with a stunning headdress.

Ball-court

South of Structure 4, towards the Acropolis, is the I-shaped **ball-court** (738 AD), one of the largest and most elaborate of the Classic period, and one of the few Maya courts still to have a paved floor. Dedicated to the great macaw deity, both sloping sides of the court are lined with three sculptured macaw heads. The rooms overlooking the playing area are thought to be where priests and the elite watched the game.

Hieroglyphic Stairway

Protected by a vast canvas cover just south of the ball-court is the famed **Hieroglyphic Stairway**, perhaps Copán's most astonishing monument. The stairway comprises the entire western face of the Temple 26 pyramid, and is made up of some 72 stone steps; every block forms part of the glyphic sequence – around 2200 glyph blocks in all, forming the longest-known Maya hieroglyphic text. Since their discovery at the end of the nineteenth century and a well-meaning reconstruction in the 1930s, the blocks have become so jumbled their true meaning is unlikely ever to be revealed. It is known that the stairway was initiated to record the dynastic history of the city; some of the lower steps were placed by Eighteen Rabbit in 710 AD, while Smoke Shell rearranged and completed most of the sequences in an effort to reassert the city's dignity and strength in 755 AD. At the base of the stairway the badly weathered **Stele M** depicts Smoke Shell and records a solar eclipse in 756 AD.

Temple 11

Adjacent to the Hieroglyphic Stairway, and towering over the extreme southern end of the plaza, are the vertiginous steps of **Temple 11** (Temple of the Inscriptions). At its base, **Stele N** (761 AD) represents Smoke Shell. The depth of the relief has protected the nooks and crannies, and in some of these you can still see flakes of paint – originally the carvings and buildings would have been painted in a whole range of bright colours, but only the red has survived.

THE HISTORY OF COPÁN RUINS

Once the most important city-state on the southern fringes of the Maya world, Copán was largely cut off from all other Maya cities except Quiriguá, 64km to the north in Guatemala (see p.195). Archeologists now believe that settlers began moving into the Río Copán valley from around 1400 BC, taking advantage of the area's rich agricultural potential, although construction of the city is not thought to have begun until around 100 AD. For those interested in finding out more, *Vision del Pasado Maya* by Fash and Fasquelle, available from the museums, is an excellent historical account of the site's history in Spanish.

426 AD Yax K'uk Mo' (Great Sun First Quetzal Macaw), a warrior-shaman, establishes the basic layout of the city. Yax K'uk Mo's son Popol Hol creates a cult of veneration for Yax K'uk Mo' which continues for over fifteen generations.

553 AD Golden era of Copán begins with the accession of Moon Jaguar, and the construction of his magnificent Rosalila Temple.

578–628 AD Reign of Smoke Serpent.

628–695 AD Reign of Smoke Jaguar.

695–738 AD Eighteen Rabbit reigns and oversees the construction of the Gran Plaza, the final version of the ball-court and Temple 22 in the East Court, creating much of the stonework for which Copán is now famous.

Following Eighteen Rabbit's capture and decapitation by Quiriguá's Cauac Sky, construction at Copán comes to a halt for seventeen years.

749–763 AD Smoke Shell reigns and completes the construction of the Hieroglyphic Stairway.

760 AD Copán's population booms at around 28,000, the highest urban density in the entire Maya region.

763–820 AD Yax Pasaj, Smoke Shell's son, commissions Altar Q, which illustrates the entire dynasty from its beginning.

776 AD Yax Pasaj completes the final version of Temple 16.

822 AD Ukit Took' assumes the throne; the only monument to his reign, Altar L, was never completed. Skeletal remains indicate that the decline of the city was provoked by inadequate food resources created by population pressures.

1576 Don Diego de Palacios, a Spanish court official, mentions the ruins of a magnificent city "constructed with such skill that it seems that they could never have been made by people as coarse as the inhabitants of this province" in a letter.

1834 Explorer Juan Galindo writes an account of the ruins.

1839 John Stephens, the US ambassador to Honduras, buys the ruins. Accompanied by Frederick Catherwood, a British architect and artist, they clear the site and map the buildings. *Incidents of Travel in Central America, Chiapas and Yucatán* is published by Stephens and Catherwood, and Copán becomes a magnet for archeologists.

1891 British archeologist Alfred Maudsley begins a full-scale mapping, excavation and reconstruction of the site sponsored by Harvard University's Peabody Museum.

1935 Washington's Carnegie Institution diverts the Río Copán to prevent it carving into the site.

1959–60 Archeologists Heinrich Berlin and Tatiana Proskouriakoff begin to decipher the site's hieroglyphs, leading to the realization that they record the history of the cities and the dynasties.

1977 Instituto Hondureño de Antropología e Historia starts running a series of projects, including tunnelling, with the help of archeologists from around the world.

1989 Rosalila Temple, buried beneath Temple 16, is discovered.

1993 Papagayo Temple, built by Popol Hol and dedicated to his father Yax K'uk Mo', is discovered.

1998 Yax K'uk Mo's tomb is discovered.

Acropolis

South of the Hieroglyphic Stairway monumental temples rise to form the **Acropolis**. This lofty inner sanctum was the reserve of royalty, nobles and priests where religious rituals were enacted, sacrifices performed and rulers entombed. For over four hundred years, the temples grew higher and higher as new structures were built over the remains of earlier buildings. A warren of excavated tunnels, some open to the public, bore through the vast bulk of the Acropolis to the Rosalila Temple and several tombs.

Popol-Na

A few metres east of Temple 11 are the **Popol-Na** (Structure 22A), a governmental building with interlocking weave-like brick patterns, and **Temple 22**, which boasts some superbly intricate stonework around the door frames and was the site of religious blood-letting ceremonies. The decoration here is unique in the southern Maya region, with only the Yucatán sites such as Kabáh and Chicanna having carvings of comparable quality.

East Court

Below Temple 22 are the stepped sides of the **East Court**, a graceful plaza with life-sized jaguar heads – the hollow eyes would have once held jade or polished obsidian. Dominating the Acropolis, **Temple 16** built on top of the **Rosalila Temple** is the tallest structure in Copán, a thirty-metre pyramid completed by the city's sixteenth ruler, Yax Pasaj, in 776 AD. It was Maya custom to ritually deface or destroy obsolete temples and stelae. Yax Pasaj's extraordinary care to preserve the Rosalila Temple beneath illustrates the importance of the previous centre of worship during a period that marked the apogee of the city's political, social and artistic growth. The discovery of the Rosalila Temple has been one of the most exciting finds of recent years.

You can now view the brilliant original facade of the buried temple by entering through a short **tunnel** – an unforgettable, if costly (US$15), experience. The admission price also includes access to two further tunnels, which extend below the East Court and past some early cosmological stucco carvings – including a huge macaw mask – along with more buried temple facades and crypts including the Galindo tomb.

At the southern end of the East Court is **Structure 18**, a small, square building with four carved panels, and the burial place of Yax Pasaj, who died in 821 AD. The diminutive scale of the structure reveals how quickly decline set in. The tomb, empty when excavated by archeologists, is thought to have been looted on a number of occasions. South of Structure 18, the **Cemetery Group** was formerly thought of as a burial site, though it's now known to have been a residential complex for the ruling elite.

West Court

The second plaza of the Acropolis, the **West Court**, is confined by the south side of Temple 11 and Temple 16. At the base of Temple 16 and carved in 776 AD, **Altar Q** celebrates Yax Pasaj's accession to the throne on July 2, 763 AD. Six hieroglyphic blocks decorate the top of the altar, while the sides are embellished with sixteen cross-legged figures representing previous rulers of Copán. All point towards a portrait of Yax Pasaj, which shows him receiving a ceremonial staff from the city's first ruler, Yax K'uk Mo', thereby endorsing Yax Pasaj's right to rule.

Arrival and information

On foot From Copán Ruinas centre the ruins are an easy 15-minute walk along a shaded pavement following the highway.
By mototaxi You can grab a *mototaxi* from the Parque Central to take you to the ruins (5min; L20).
Tourist information On entering, the visitors' centre is to your left, where you pay your entrance

The **Guatemalan border** is just 12km west of Copán, and crossing at the **El Florido** border post – usually busy with travellers coming to and from the ruins – is pretty easy, though it can be slow. Minibuses and pick-ups leave for El Florido from just west of the Parque about every thirty minutes until around 4pm. Copán Connections and Basecamp in Copán Ruinas (see p.354) have direct shuttles to Antigua and Guatemala City (2 daily at 6am & noon; US$12–15), with connections to Río Dulce. The ever-present moneychangers at the border handle dollars, lempiras and quetzales at fairly good rates.

From the border, buses leave every thirty minutes (the last is at 4pm) for Chiquimula (1hr 15min; see p.192), 57km away down a smooth, newly paved road.

fee. From here it's a 200m walk east to the warden's gate, where your ticket will be checked and you'll be greeted by squabbling macaws.

Tour guides Guides are available and are well worth the fee – they do an excellent job of bringing the ruins to life; get together with other visitors to spread the cost (around US$25/2hr).

LA ENTRADA

Northeast from Copán the CA-11 winds its scenic way through lightly wooded mountains and fertile pasture to **LA ENTRADA**, an unpleasant junction town 55km from Copán, useful only for its bus connections to San Pedro Sula, Santa Rosa and Copán Ruinas. If you get stuck here, *Hotel San Carlos* (☎2898 5228; L300), at the junction of CA-11 and CA-4, is the best of the available accommodation, where rooms are at least comfortable and secure with en-suite bathroom.

Olancho

Stretching east of Tegucigalpa to the Nicaraguan border and north into the emptiness of La Mosquitia, the sparsely populated uplands of **Olancho** are widely regarded as the "Wild East" of Honduras: an untamed frontier region with a not entirely undeserved reputation for lawlessness. Over time, everyone from the first Spanish settlers to the Honduran government has had trouble imposing

law and order here, and in many respects today is no different: the region's profitable cattle-ranching industry (which has encroached into national parks and other protected areas) and the logging of its massive forests (much of which is done illegally) have led to the creation of a powerful local oligarchy supported by military and police connivance. As a result, environmental issues have been sidelined, and activists have been threatened and even killed.

Despite Olancho's size – it makes up a fifth of Honduras's total territory – tourist attractions in this region are few, and its high, forested mountain ranges interspersed with broad valleys make getting from place to place difficult and slow. However, these same ranges harbour some of the country's last untouched expanses of tropical and **cloudforest**: the national parks of **El Boquerón** and **Sierra de Agalta** are awe inspiring. Along the valleys, now given over to pastureland for cattle, are scattered villages and towns. Both **Juticalpa**, the department capital, and **Catacamas**, at the eastern end of the paved road, are good bases for exploring the region.

Olancho's **climate** is generally pleasant, with the towns at lower altitudes hot during the day and comfortably cool at night; up in the mountains it can get extremely cold after dark. Once off the main highway, **travelling** becomes arduous, with the dirt roads connecting villages served by infrequent and invariably slow public transport.

JUTICALPA

Situated towards the southern end of the Valle de Catacamas, about 170km from Tegucigalpa, **JUTICALPA** is a pleasant little provincial city, where the streets are busy night and day with bustle and commerce, and it can be a refreshing place to spend a few days. The city's focal point is the leafy **Parque Banderas**, which includes a small pool of rather disgruntled looking turtles. The majority of facilities are on the streets around here. The general **market** stretches for a few blocks to the west, along Calle Perulapan. When the town's attractions have worn thin, the **cinema** at C 1, Av 2–3 shows subtitled US releases.

Arrival and information

By bus Juticalpa's two bus terminals are just off the highway on 1 Av SE, which leads straight to the centre, a 15min walk north. Local buses run from the terminal on the right side of the road (facing town); while direct buses to Tegucigalpa and the north coast use the other side.
Exchange Several banks dot the perimeter of Parque Banderas.
Internet Brothers Internet on Av 5 has access at L18/hr.
Tourist information ICF (formerly COHDEFOR) is set back from the road on Av 7 near C 14 (☎2785 2253). Boss Daniel Cerma is very helpful (Spanish only).

Accommodation

Don't expect too much in the way of cosseted luxury in town, or indeed anywhere in Olancho.
Hotel El Paso Blvd Los Poetas ☎2785 2311/4642/4155. A decent budget choice, with a choice of fans and a/c in the rooms. L308
Hotel Honduras Walk up Calle 2 from the square, turn left down Av 7 and it's on the left between C 2 and C 3 ☎2785 1580. Very clean and well looked after; rooms come with fan or a/c. L400

Eating

Juticalpa's range of restaurants is pretty modest, though there's a healthy profusion of inexpensive *comedores* and street-food stalls around Parque Banderas.

Oregano's C 2, beyond Av 7. There are just five stools at a granite-like table inset with coloured glass in this cosy little café. Pizzas from L75, *curry caribeño* with coconut, rum and white wine L150.
Rancho Restaurant Av 4 SE near C 2. The meat here is surprisingly good quality. Try the *pincho al rancho* (L130) or the grilled steak, beans, *tajadas* and *chismol* (L160).

Moving on

By bus to: Catacamas (23 daily; 40min); La Ceiba (2 daily; 9hr); Tegucigalpa (20 daily; 2–3hr); Trujillo (1 daily at 4am; 7hr).

MONUMENTO NACIONAL EL BOQUERÓN

Some 20km east of Juticalpa, **MONUMENTO NACIONAL EL BOQUERÓN**, one of the last remaining tracks of **dry tropical forest** in Honduras, is home to a wide variety of wildlife, including more than 250 species of bird.

What to see and do

To see the forest properly, you'll want to hike the moderately strenuous main **trail** through the reserve. The trail runs from where the bus drops you off near the Puente Boquerón bridge to a point a few kilometres west of the main entrance; the walk is manageable in one day if you get an early start.

Follow the track starting on the left-hand side of the Río Olancho – though it crosses over several times, so be prepared to wade – and after about a kilometre the path enters the gorge, eventually emerging onto the flood-plain at the other side. From here it is around two more easy hours through level pastureland to the village of **La Avispa**. Beyond the village, the path loops steeply uphill and through the cloudforest section of the park; you have a pretty good chance of seeing some of the country's elusive bird and animal life here, including mixed flocks of brightly coloured trogons and quetzals that feed together at fruit trees. The reserve is also the only known Honduran location of the white-eared ground sparrow, fairly easily seen in the undergrowth. Beyond the cloudforest the walk is downhill all the way, with the path finally emerging a few kilometres later on the highway at Tempisque, west of the main entrance.

Arrival and information

Arrival Monumento Nacional El Boquerón is about halfway between Juticalpa and Catacamas. Any bus going between the two towns can drop you near the start of the main trail, by the Boquerón bridge. After you're done trekking, you can easily flag down buses to either place on the main highway.
Tourist information The reserve is easily accessible as a day-trip from Juticalpa, though there are facilities should you want to camp (free). It is advisable to visit the ICF (formerly COHDEFOR) office in Juticalpa before setting out (see p.363), as the trail can be hard to follow, especially after heavy rainfall, and there are no rangers or information facilities once you reach the park. Bring your own food and water.

CATACAMAS

CATACAMAS, midway along the Valle de Catacamas beneath the southern flanks of the Sierra de Agalta, is a smaller version of Juticalpa. The fact that it's at the end of one of the paved roads through the region contributes to the affable, small-town charm of the place. It certainly has a more spectacular setting than its larger neighbour: a short walk up to the **Mirador de la Cruz**, fifteen minutes from the centre on the northern side of town, gives superb views over the town and valley.

What to see and do

The main reason for coming out this far is to visit the **Cuevas de Talgua** (daily 9am–5pm; US$6; Ⓦwww.ihah.hn). Located 8km northeast of town on the banks of the Río Talgua, the caves are one of the country's foremost historical sites, thanks to the discovery made here of a **prehistoric burial ground** featuring hundreds of skeletons arranged in chambers deep underground. Though the burial ground itself is out of bounds to visitors, the rest of the site has been developed for tourists, with a **museum** telling the tale of the finds and trails leading through the caves. To get here, take the local **bus** from Catacamas to Talgua (3 daily, at 7am, 11am and 3pm). The last return departs Talgua at 4pm. Taxis may quote L200–250, but it should be no more than L150.

Arrival and information

By bus Buses terminate four blocks south of Catacamas's Parque Central; the Parque itself, dominated by a giant ceiba tree, is a short walk away up a slight hill.
Exchange There are a few banks situated around the park and in the streets just to the north.
Internet Access is available at a few places in town, the best being the one right on the Parque Central.
Tourist information Jorge Yanes at the IHAH office (Instituto Hondureño de Antropología e Historia; ☏2799 3090, Ⓔtalguaihah@yahoo.es), opposite the *municipalidad* on Av Piedra Blanca, is very knowledgeable about all things Olancho and La Mosquitia. He can arrange tours in either region. Maps of town can be bought for L20 at *Hotel Plaza María*.
Tour operators Suyapa De Takeshita runs Olancho Tours (☏9811 7451, Ⓔolanchotours@yahoo.com), offering excursions throughout the region.

Accommodation

La Colina Av SW, just off the corner of the Parque ☏2799 4488. This is the best budget hotel in town, with reasonably comfortable rooms set round a courtyard, all with bath, TV and fan. L300
Hotel Plaza Maria Av 3 between C 3 and C 4 ☏2799 4828/4832, Ⓦwww.plazamaria.com. A new addition, with a pool, wi-fi and hot water throughout. The manager is helpful and English-speaking. Breakfast included. L1040
Oriental Close to *Colina*, just off the southwest corner of the Parque ☏2799 4038. *Oriental* has a selection of basic but orderly rooms, some with private bath. L250

Eating

As de Oro Three blocks south of *Hotel Plaza María* on Av 3. Described as a *restaurante típico* *olanchano*, and highly recommended locally. Breakfasts and lunches L45–65, *pincho* L120–190, or go all "Wild East" and try the euphemistically named *huevos de toro a la plancha* (L190) or *sopa de testiculo* (L135).

Francel Av 3 between C 3 and C 4. The buffet restaurant at *Hotel Plaza María* offers an array of items such as breaded fish fillet, rice, chorizo and various other meats. A plateful can be had for around L100. Clean, friendly and particularly good for breakfast. Daily 7am–9.30pm.

Moving on

By bus to: Catacamas (23 daily; 30–45min); Tegucigalpa (22 daily; 3–4hr).

PARQUE NACIONAL SIERRA DE AGALTA

Draped across the sweeping ranges of the Sierra de Agalta, the vast **PARQUE NACIONAL SIERRA DE AGALTA** shelters the most extensive stretch of **virgin cloudforest** remaining in Central America. Though the area has been designated a protected area since 1987, large stands of pine and oak in the lower parts of the park have nonetheless still been logged, and much of the land cleared for cattle pasture. The higher reaches of the mountains, however (including Honduras's fourth highest peak, La Picucha), are so remote that both vegetation and wildlife have remained virtually untouched. Here a typical cloudforest of oaks, liquidambar and cedar, draped in vines and ferns, cover the slopes up to about 2000m, where they give way to a dwarf forest.

In addition to the flora, the park's isolation ensures a protected, secure environment for a biologically diverse range of **mammals** and **birds**, many of them extremely rare. Tapirs, jaguars, ocelots, opossums and three types of monkey are among the species of mammal recorded. More evident are the birds, of which more than four hundred species have been sighted.

Note that there's no accommodation in the park other than official **camping** spots, for which you'll need to bring all equipment and supplies.

Arrival and information

By bus The easiest points of entry for the park are along the northern edge of the Sierra, via the small towns of Gualaco and San Esteban, which you can reach off Highway C-39 between Juticalpa and Trujillo. The daily bus from Juticalpa (1 daily at 4am; 1hr 30min to Gualaco; 3hr 30min to San Esteban; 8hr to Trujillo) passes by both towns – just ask the driver to stop so you can hop off. Accessing the park trails from either town requires a significant hike.

By pick-up Pick-ups from the market in Juticalpa also make the trip to the park.

Tour operators Hiring a guide is highly recommended, and pretty much essential for hiking the difficult trails: ask at the IHAH offices in Gualaco, San Esteban or Juticalpa (see p.363). In Gualaco ask for Francisco Urbina (☎9901 3400, ✉chicourbina @yahoo.com) at the *municipalidad*; he charges around US$26 per person. From the Catacamas side, Calixto Ordoñez (☎9783 8259, ✉calixtoo77 @yahoo.com) offers tours, including a hike up La Picucha, for a negotiable L500 per person.

The north coast

Honduras's **north coast** stretches for some 300km along the azure fringes of the Caribbean. A magnet for Hondurans and foreign tourists alike, the region provides sun, sea and entertainment in abundance, especially in the coastal towns of **Tela**, **La Ceiba** and **Trujillo**, with their broad expanses of beach, clean warm waters, plentiful restaurants and buzzing nightlife. **San Pedro Sula**, the region's major inland city and transport hub, provides amenities of a strictly urban kind. Dotted along the north coast between these main towns are a number of laidback **villages** blessed with unspoilt **beaches**. Populated by the **Garífuna** people (decendants of African slaves and Carib people; see p.99), these villages are often very much removed from the rest of Honduran culture and society, and can feel like visiting an entirely different country.

When beach life loses its appeal, there are several **natural reserves** to visit in the region. The national parks of **Cusuco**, **Pico Bonito** and **Capiro y Calentura**, whose virgin cloudforest shelters rare wildlife, offer hiking for all levels; the wetland and mangrove swamps at **Punta Sal** and **Cuero y Salado** require less exertion to explore.

The region's rainy season generally runs from November to January, while the hurricane season is August to October. Obviously, it's best to visit the region outside of these times but you won't necessarily be battered incessantly by rain or winds if you do visit during this period. Temperatures rarely drop below 25–28°C, but the heat is usually

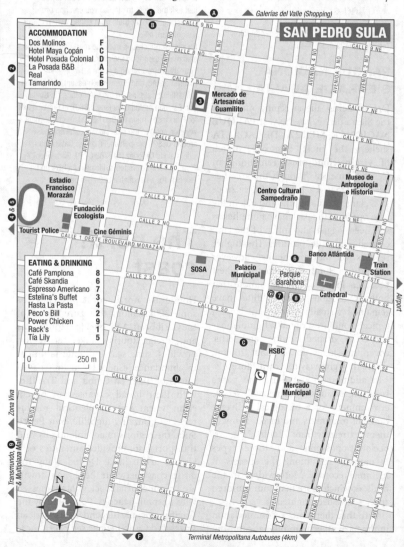

SAN PEDRO SULA

ACCOMMODATION

Dos Molinos	F
Hotel Maya Copán	C
Hotel Posada Colonial	D
La Posada B&B	A
Real	E
Tamarindo	B

EATING & DRINKING

Café Pamplona	8
Café Skandia	6
Espresso Americano	7
Estelina's Buffet	3
Hasta La Pasta	4
Peco's Bill	2
Power Chicken	9
Rack's	1
Tía Lily	5

0   250 m

Galerías del Valle (Shopping)

Mercado de Artesanías Guamilito

Estadio Francisco Morazán

Fundación Ecologista

Tourist Police

Cine Géminis

CALLE 1 OESTE (BOULEVARD MORAZÁN)

Museo de Antropología e Historia

Centro Cultural Sampedraño

Banco Atlántida

SOSA

Palacio Municipal

Parque Barahona

Train Station

Cathedral

HSBC

Mercado Municipal

Zona Viva

Transmundo, & Multiplaza Mall

Airport

N

tempered by ocean breezes. **Transport** is reasonably good, with frequent buses along the fast, paved highway that links the main coastal towns; as usual, reaching the remoter villages and national parks requires some forward planning.

SAN PEDRO SULA

The country's second city and driving economic force, **SAN PEDRO SULA** sprawls across the fertile Valle de Sula ("Valley of the Birds" in Usula dialect) at the foot of the Merendón mountain chain, just an hour from the coast. Flat and uninspiring to look at, and for most of the year uncomfortably hot and humid, this is a city for getting business done, rather than sightseeing. It's also the **transport hub** for northern and western Honduras, meaning a visit here is usually unavoidable, even if only to pass through. On a more positive note, San Pedro's **facilities** rate alongside Tegucigalpa, with an international airport, foreign consulates and a wide range of hotels, restaurants and shopping outlets – indeed, thanks to its practical location and better transport links, travellers who stick to the north of the country (as so many do) rarely need to make a visit south to the capital.

What to see and do

San Pedro's reputation – it is more dangerous than the rest of the country, and its attractions are few – generally precedes it, causing most tourists to get in and out as quickly as possible. Those who do stick around often shed their preconceptions, provided they use a bit of common sense when taking in the few sights to hand.

San Pedro's centre is in the southwest sector of the city. Running west from the **Parque Barahona**, Calle 1 is also known as Boulevard Morazán for the twelve blocks before it meets the **Avenida Circunvalación** ring road, which separates the city centre from San Pedro's wealthier residential districts. Most of what you'll want to see in the city is within walking distance of the centre, and the city's main general **market** is towards the southeastern edge of this area. The streets south of the market and over the old railway track can get rough and are not places to be wandering around after dark.

Parque Barahona

San Pedro's central plaza, the large **Parque Barahona**, is the city centre's focus, teeming with vendors, shoeshine boys and moneychangers. The Parque's centrepiece is a large fountain with bridges and bronze statues of washerwomen beating their clothes on the rocks. On its eastern edge, the colonial-style **Catedral Municipal**, completed in the mid-1950s, is open to the public, but there's nothing of particular interest inside. Facing it across the Parque is the unremarkable **Palacio Municipal**, home to the city administration.

Museo de Antropología e Historia

The **Museo de Antropología e Historia** (Mon & Wed–Sat 9am–4.30pm, Sun 9am–3pm; L38; ☎2557 1496), a few blocks north of the Parque at Av 3, C 4 NO, is worth a visit. The museum's fine collection of pre-Columbian sculptures, ceramics and other artefacts, the majority recovered from the Sula valley, outlines the development of civilization in the region from 1500 BC onwards; weaponry and paintings from the colonial period continue the theme.

Arrival and information

By air Aeropuerto Internacional Ramón Villeda Morales, the north coast's point of arrival for both domestic and international flights, lies 12km southeast of the city. There is no public transport into the city from the airport itself. Taxis cost around L200 from the airport into town.

TOURS FROM SAN PEDRO SULA

There are numerous **tour agencies** in San Pedro Sula.

Eli Gonzalez ⓔnaturalhonduras@yahoo.com. An independent tour guide with 20 years' experience.

Jungle Expedition Based in the *Banana Inn* hotel, near the airport ⓣ3392 5329 or 9762 6620, ⓦwww.junglexpedition.org. A reliable outfit who offer excellent hikes into Parque Nacional El Cusuco starting at US$35 per person, plus a range of other tours.

Mesoamérica Travel Col Juan Lindo, Casa 709, C 8 Av 32 NO ⓣ2558 6447/6258, ⓦwww.mesoamerica-travel.com. A ten- to fifteen-minute taxi ride from the centre (L60), this company offers tours throughout the country, including La Mosquitia, and responds promptly to enquiries.

Sula Tours In the *Gran Hotel Sula* on the northern side of the Parque ⓣ2545 2660 or 9618 1305, ⓔreservaciones@hotelsula.hn. Offers a number of different tours far and wide with prices starting at US$35.

By bus The majority of intercity and international buses to San Pedro Sula arrive at the Terminal Metropolitana de Autobuses, 5km south of the town centre. The city buses are dangerous (see "City transport", below), so take taxis from the terminal to the centre; they should cost no more than L80.

Tourist information In theory, the *policía turística* office (Blvd Morazán & Av 12 NO) should be able to offer information, but the nearby Fundación Ecologista (Av 12 NO) is more helpful.

Travel agent Transmundo (ⓣ2553 5072/5513, ⓦwww.transmundohn.com) is at Edificio Plaza del Carmen, Bo Suyapa, C 6, Av 16–17 SO.

City transport

Buses City buses (L5) can be dangerous and are not recommended. It's quicker and safer to get a taxi. If you do decide to chance it, check at the Metropolitana de Autobuses for bus routes and stops.

Taxis The plentiful taxis are licensed but none have meters, so make sure you settle on a price before setting off. It should be about L50–70 for travel within the centre, and around L110 to go from the centre to the edge of town.

Accommodation

San Pedro is the second-largest city in Honduras and one of the fastest-growing in Latin America. As a result, there is a good array of safe budget options, most of which are towards the southern side of town along Avenida 6. Don't be tempted by any of the super-cheap hotels – most aren't secure and can be dangerous.

Dos Molinos Bo Paz Barahona C 13, Av 8–9 SO 34 ⓣ2510 0335 or 9960 0857, ⓔlos2molinos@yahoo .com. In an unmarked green house, the principal appeal here is the friendly, homely atmosphere. The six rooms have high ceilings and big TVs, and wi-fi and breakfast are included. L500

Hotel Maya Copán C 4, Av 5–6 ⓣ2553 2049, ⓦwww.hotelmayacopanhn.com. A warm, characterful place, hung with traditional blankets on the walls and old photos of Honduras (as well as London's Big Ben). Internet, wi-fi, a/c, hot water and *típico* breakfast included. L600

Hotel Posada Colonial Bo El Benque C 6, Av 7–8 SO ⓣ2550 2763, ⓔposadacolonial@hotmail.com. A very friendly, well-kept little hotel with hot-water private bathrooms. L450

La Posada B & B Col Universidad C 21, Av 9 Casa 172 ⓣ2566 3312, ⓦwww.hirners.com/hotel /LaPosada. This spacious place feels like a modern suburban home. Currently there are five rooms, though four more and a communal area are under construction, plus a cool and pleasant dorm with a balcony. Wi-fi, internet and breakfast are included, and owner Alex speaks good English. Dorm L285, doubles L760

Real Av 6, C 6–7 ⓣ2550 7929, ⓦwww.hotel realhn.com. One of the city's best-value options. The communal courtyard is beautifully decorated with local crafts and climbing plants, and the en-suite rooms are large (if a touch dark). L300

Tamarindo Bo Los Andes C9, Av 10–11 NO ⓣ2520 0642 or 9959 0599, ⓦwww.tamarindo hostel.com. This popular hostel, about a 5-minute drive from the centre, has slightly stuffy dorms, clean bathrooms, a kitchen and a swimming pool. The private rooms are nice, but rather overpriced. Service can be a little sloppy. Dorms US$12, rooms US$32

Eating

Café Pamplona On the Parque Barahona. This place feels like the San Pedro institution it is, with decor of wood, brick and tiles. There's a menu, but also plenty of items canteen-style. *Baleadas* around L20, *desayuno campesino* L112. Mon–Fri 7am–7pm, Sun 8am–2pm.

Café Skandia In the *Gran Hotel Sula* on the northern side of the Parque Central. A/c and open 24hr, the *Skandia* feels like a Scandinavian diner, with everything in white and cool blues, and a sign depicting a Viking ship. Outside there's a terrace with palm trees and a pool. Breakfast from L65, cheeseburger L90.

Espresso Americano On the western corner of the Parque Central on C 2 SO. Modern *Starbucks*-style coffee house with good mochas, cappuccinos and even frappuccinos to recharge your batteries. Coffee L20.

Estelina's Buffet Mercado Guamilito. It has been said that if you don't eat here when you go to San Pedro, then you haven't been to San Pedro. These are *baleadas* (from L20) made by the experts.

Hasta La Pasta Col Moderna, C 2 Av 22, no. 200 ☎2550 3048/5494. An Italian restaurant with a homely, neighbourhood feel in a pleasant setting on the edge of the Zona Viva. The white tablecloths are classy, the stuffed cuddly lion less so. Lasagne L170, seafood soup L150.

Peco's Bill Av 15 C 6 NO. This rambling, open-sided place feels like an overgrown tree house, and is as popular with drinkers as it is with diners. 8oz *churrasco* from the grill with baked potato and beans L170, *chuleta a la parrilla* (pork chop) L95.

Power Chicken Near the junction of Av 15 and Av Circunvalación on the southern edge of the Zona Viva. You may scoff at the name but residents of the city will not hear a bad word said about this place, and they're right: this is fast food at its finest. Spicy chicken, ribs, steak, fried plantain, *yuca* – it's all here, with mains around L100. Daily until 10pm.

Drinking and nightlife

All of San Pedro Sula's action is, in theory, out in the so-called "Zona Viva", which is how the area around the southern half of avenidas 15 and 16 is known. It can often feel about as *viva* as a ghost town, however. In general, the clubs in this area are safer than the bars, which can get very dangerous. Take taxis out to the Zona Viva.

Racks Bo Los Andes, C11, Av 11 NO, near Parque Benito Juárez. A foreigner-friendly sports bar with pool tables and a decking area out front. Bands sometimes play at weekends. Buffalo wings L140, rice and shrimp L169. Beers from L25.

Tía Lily C 2A, round the corner from *Hasta La Pasta*. An open-sided bar hidden behind dense greenery, this is on the edge of the Zona Viva but feels rather cosy, and the food's good too. Try the chorizo with beans, *chismol* and *tajadas* (L108) – perfect beer food.

Entertainment

Centro Cultural Sampedrano C 3, Av 3–4 NO ☎2553 3911, ⓦwww.centrocultural-sps.com. This cultural centre regularly hosts concerts and plays; the building also houses the public library.

Cinema Near the Zona Viva is the four-screen Cine Géminis, at C 1 & Av 12 NO; there's another cinema with lots of screens at Multiplaza mall (L60 per person). Both show subtitled movies.

Shopping

Books Metro Nova on the first floor of Galerías del Valle (north of the town centre on C 25) has English-language books for less than L100.

Markets The Mercado Guamilito, Av 9, C 6–7 NO, is an indoor market with numerous stalls selling hammocks, ceramics, leatherwork and wooden goods. A couple of shops on the Calle Peatonal, just off the Parque Central, sell similar stuff, though prices are higher. The Mercado Municipal, between Av 4–5 SO and C 5–6 SO and along the old rail track, has stalls spilling onto the streets for several blocks; you can find a bit of everything here. Numerous malls are dotted around the city centre.

Directory

Airlines Isleña/TACA, at the airport (☎2545 2325/2339) and on Av Circunvalación, Edificio Taragon (☎2552 9910/9951); SOSA, at C 1, Av 7–8 SO (☎2550 6545) or at the airport (☎2668 3223). American (☎2553 3526 or 2668 3243), Continental (☎2557 4141 or 2668 3208) and Delta (☎2550 8188 or 2668 0233) are all at the airport.

Car rental Molinari, in the *Gran Hotel Sula* on the northern side of the Parque Central (☎2533 2639); Omega, Av 3, C 3–4 NO (☎2552 7626).

Consulates Belize, on the road to Puerto Cortés (☎2551 6247); El Salvador, Av 11, 5–6 NO (☎2557 5591); Germany, C 1, 8–9 SO (☎2553 1244); Mexico, C 2, Av 20–21 SO (☎2552 3672); Netherlands, Av 15, C 7–8 (☎2557 1815);

Nicaragua, Av 5, Av 4–5 SO (☎2550 0813); Spain, Av 2, C 3–4 NE (☎2553 2480); UK, C 2, Av 18–19 NO (☎2550 2337); US, in the Banco Atlántida building on the northern side of the Parque (☎2236 9320 or 2238 5114).

Exchange Banco Atlántida has a number of branches downtown, including one on the Parque Central with an ATM; there are several other banks along C 2 between Av 5 and 6. HSBC is at C 4 and Av 4 SO.

Health The Hospital Centro Médico Betesda is at Av 11, C 11–12 NO.

Internet Just off the Parque in a little arcade next to *Espresso Americano* is Diosita.net (L25/hr). Cyber Café Pro (L25/hr) on the first floor of Galerías del Valle, north of the town centre, has good computers and quick connection.

Post office C 9, Av 3 SO (Mon–Fri 7.30am–5pm, Sat 8am–noon).

Telephones Hondutel, on the corner of C 5 and Av 5, is open 24hr. Diosita.net (see "Internet", above) also offers decent international phone rates.

Tourist Police Bvd Morazán & Av 12 NO.

Moving on

By air to: Belize City (with TACA 1–2 daily via San Salvador or San Jose; 2–3hr); Guanaja (with SOSA 1 daily Mon–Sat; 2hr 50min); Guatemala City (with Taca 1 direct daily; 1hr 10min); La Ceiba (with SOSA 1 daily, with Isleña 2 daily; 30min); Managua, Nicaragua (with TACA 3 daily via San Salvador; 2hr 25min); Panama City (with TACA 1 daily via San Salvador; 5hr); Roatán (with SOSA 1 daily, with Isleña 1 daily; 2hr 35min); San José (with TACA 1 direct daily; 2hr 15min); San Salvador (with TACA 3 direct daily; 50min); Tegucigalpa (with Isleña 2 daily; 45min); Utila (with SOSA 4 weekly on Mon, Wed, Fri & Sat; 2hr 15min).

By bus to: Comayagüela (14 daily; 3–4hr); Copán Ruinas (11 daily; 3hr); Gracias (1 daily; 5hr); Guatemala City (2 daily; 8hr); La Ceiba (22 daily; 3hr); La Entrada (25 daily; 1–2hr); Managua, Nicaragua (1 daily; 12hr); Ocotepeque (5 daily; 5hr); Puerto Cortés (every 20min; 1hr); Pulhapanzak and Lago de Yojoa (14 daily; 1hr 30min); San Salvador (2 daily; 6hr); Santa Rosa de Copán (6 daily; 3hr); Siguatepeque (14 daily; 3hr); Tegucigalpa (every 40min; 4hr); Tela (18 daily; 1hr 30min); Trujillo (18 daily; 5–6hr). All services listed here leave from the main Terminal Metropolitana Autobuses, south of town.

PUERTO CORTÉS

North of San Pedro Sula, Highway CA-5 runs through the flat agricultural lands and lush tropical scenery of the Sula valley. After 60km the four-lane highway reaches the coast at **PUERTO CORTÉS**, Honduras's main port. There's nothing here to entice, and you'll likely pass through only to change buses en route to Omoa or to hop aboard a boat for Belize.

Arrival

By bus Three companies run buses between San Pedro Sula and Puerto Cortés, including the reliable Citul, who run the hour-long trip every 30min between 6am and 6pm. The Citul terminal in Puerto Cortés is a block north of the main plaza at Av 4 and C 4. Other buses arrive at the nearby Transportes Citral terminal.

Accommodation and eating

Budget accommodation is hard to come by, and there is also little choice in terms of places to eat.

Hotel El Centro Av 3, C 2–3 ☎2665 1160. Twenty-six small but clean rooms with en-suite bathrooms makes this your best bet. L450

Repostería Plata Av 3 and C 2. Popular with locals for their buffet meals, this place has the added advantage of being open on Sundays, when all other restaurants are closed. Mains from L60.

INTO BELIZE BY FERRY

In theory, two companies run **boats** between **Belize** and Honduras, although in reality the timetables are inconsistent and boats rarely leave on time. The Nesymein Neydy service (☎2223 1200, @mundomayatravels@yahoo.com) to Dangriga leaves from Puerto Cortés's Laguna de Pescadería (3km southeast of the town under the bridge close to the fish market) every Monday at 11am (US$60), but you should be at the dock at 9am. The "D" express (☎2665 0726, ⓦwww.belizeferry.com), leaving from the same spot, runs every Monday at 11.30am to Independence and Placencia – it's best to get there in plenty of time. The return journey is on a Friday.

Moving on

By boat There are ferries to Independence and Placencia in Belize (see box opposite).
By bus to: Corinto, for Guatemala (every 45min; 4hr); Omoa (every 30min; 1hr). Buses leave from the Transportes Citral terminal, which is on C 4 around the corner from the Citul terminal.

OMOA

Spreading inland from a deep bay at the point where the mountains of the Sierra de Omoa meet the Caribbean, **OMOA** was once a strategically important location in the defence of the Spanish colonies against marauding British pirates. Its popularity with travellers has waned in recent years, thanks to a gas company's decision to construct jetties here to protect their tanks. This has altered the current of Omoa bay, causing the beach to shrink – it is estimated that sixty percent has disappeared over the course of four years. The best beach now is to be found behind the fort.

What to see and do

Omoa's one outstanding sight, the restored **Fortaleza de San Fernando de Omoa** (Mon–Fri 8am–4pm, Sat & Sun 9am–5pm; US$4), stands amid tropical greenery in mute witness to the village's colourful history. Now isolated a kilometre from the coast, having been beached as the sea has receded over the centuries, the triangular fort was originally intended to protect the port of Puerto Barrios in Guatemala. Work began in 1759 but was never fully completed due to a combination of inefficiency and a labour shortage. The steadily weakening Spanish authorities then suffered the ignominy of witnessing the fortress be temporarily occupied by British and Miskito military forces in October 1779. A small museum on site tells the story of the fort and displays a selection of military paraphernalia including cannons and period weaponry.

Arrival and information

By bus Buses between Puerto Cortés and Corinto pass the southern end of the village at a crossroads, though some go all the way to the beach, where you'll find most of the action. *Mototaxis* ply the 2km stretch from the crossroads to the beach.
Exchange Banco de Occidente can advance cash on your cards but has no ATM.
Internet Omoa Surf charges L19/hr.

Accommodation

Fisherman Along the beach road ☎ 2658 9224. A good budget option with some of its eleven rooms right on the beach, but make sure you view a few before deciding. All have cold-water private bathroom. L300
Roli's Place Along the main road about 200m from the sea ☎ 2658 9082 or 3396 0156, ⓦ www .omoa.net. An excellent budget place with comfortable rooms as well as camping, hammocks and dorms; they also have kayaks, bikes and laundry facilities. Hammocks and camping L60, dorms L100, doubles L300

Eating and drinking

La Champa de Monchin Beside the pier. As cheap as can be: chicken tacos L39, *baleadas* from L10, conch or shrimp soup L160, coffee L15, local beer L25.
Eddy's Grill Asados On the main road between the beach and the highway. A friendly, family place, where you can sit on the tiled terrace outside the

> ### INTO GUATEMALA: CORINTO
>
> Moving on from Omoa to Guatemala is an excruciatingly slow journey along the notoriously bumpy road leading southwest to Corinto, 2km from the border (buses every 20min 8am–4pm). Corinto has its own *migración* (daily 8am–5.30pm). Pickups shuttle to and from the border, from where you can catch a minibus (every 30min) into Guatemala; there's usually an exit fee of US$1–2 charged. Minibuses pass through the village of Entre Ríos, for Guatemalan *migración*, to Puerto Barrios, an hour from the Honduran border.

house or on plastic garden chairs in the garden. The meat may be chewy, but it's flavoursome. *Pinchos* L80–120, soups L70–120.

Sueños de Mar At the western end of the beach road (turn right at the beach). Hearty, home-cooked food, Canadian style. Breakfast includes imported Virginia ham (L120), while "smokies" in a bun cost L70. Breakfast and lunch served 8am–5pm, bar open until 8pm.

Moving on

By bus to: Corinto, for Guatemala (every 20min 8am–4pm; 1hr); Puerto Cortés (every 30min; 1hr).

TELA

Sitting midway around the Bahía de Tela, surrounded by sweeping beaches, **TELA** has a near-perfect setting. In the past, the town has suffered from a reputation for violence, but a pilot force of tourist police is substantially cleaning up the town's image. Whether you choose to partake in the nightlife or not, the wealth of fantastic **natural reserves** – including Punta Sal – within minutes of the town makes Tela well worth a visit. The town is also one of the main destinations for Hondurans during **Semana Santa** (Easter Holy Week):

booking several weeks or months ahead is advisable for that period.

What to see and do

Today's Tela is a product of the banana industry. In the late nineteenth century United Fruit built a company town – **Tela Nueva** – here, on the west bank of the Río Tela; the old town became known as **Tela Vieja**. These distinctions still stand. The old town, which lies about 2km north of the highway and two blocks from the beach on the east bank of the river, encompasses the **Parque Central** and main shopping area. Five blocks west from the Parque Central is the Río Tela, and on the other side of the river, Tela Nueva. A fifteen-minute stroll covers practically everything there is to see. However, it's the **beaches** that most people come for; those in Tela Vieja, though wide, are more crowded than the stretch of pale sand in front of the hotel *Villas Telamar* in Tela Nueva. Even better beaches can be found along the bay outside town – if you walk far enough in either direction you should be able to have one entirely to yourself.

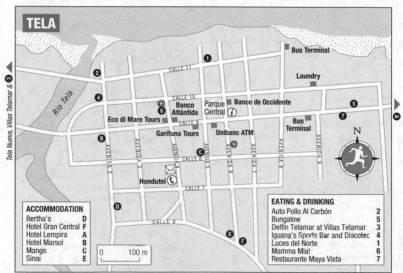

TELA

Tela Nueva, Villas Telamar & ③

Río Tela

Bus Terminal

Laundry

CALLE 11

CALLE 10

Banco Atlántida

Parque Central (i)

Banco de Occidente

Eco di Mare Tours

CALLE 9

Garífuna Tours

Unibanc ATM

Bus Terminal

N

Hondutel

CALLE 8

CALLE 7

CALLE 6

0   100 m

ACCOMMODATION	
Bertha's	D
Hotel Gran Central	F
Hotel Lempira	A
Hotel Marsol	B
Mango	C
Sinai	E

EATING & DRINKING	
Auto Pollo Al Carbón	2
Bungalow	5
Delfin Telamar at Villas Telamar	3
Iguana's Sports Bar and Discotec	4
Luces del Norte	1
Mamma Mia!	6
Restaurante Maya Vista	7

Highway to San Pedro Sula

Arrival and information

By bus Most local bus services, including the half-hourly buses to and from La Ceiba, use the terminal on the corner of Av 9 and C 9 NE. Buses to the surrounding villages use the terminal two blocks north at C 11 and Av 8 NE.

Tourist information The tourist office is in the municipal building off the southeast corner of the Parque Central (Mon–Fri 8am–6pm, Sat 8am–noon; ⓦ www.tela-honduras.com).

Tour operators Garífuna Tours, Parque Central (☏ 2448 1069, ⓦ www.garifunatours.com), run trips to Punta Sal (US$29) and Punta Izopo (US$26), as well as the "EcoPass" tour, which includes visits to both places plus Pico Bonito for US$75. Run by the English-speaking Ferdinand Florentino, Eco di Mare (☏ 2439 0110, 9932 3552 or 9855 8311, ⓦ www.ecodimaretours.com) offer tours to Punta Sal (US$29), Laguna Los Micos (US$35) and Punta Izopo (US$26). Their office is next to *Mamma Mia!*, opposite the parking lot for Banco Atlántida, Av 4, C 10 NE (daily 8am–6pm).

Accommodation

Many of Tela's older hotels are quite run-down. There are, however, a number of newer, better-value places opening up as the town becomes more of a fixture on the backpacker trail. Many of these tend to get busy at weekends, when it pays to book ahead.

Bertha's Av 2, C 6–7 ☏ 2448 3020. Seventeen rooms, all passably clean, with those upstairs a little brighter. Cold-water bathrooms. L350

Hotel Gran Central At the southern end of Av 6 ☏ 2448 1099, ⓦ www.hotelgrancentral.com. You'll receive a very friendly Gallic welcome here from Luc and Véronique. Four of the rooms have a nice big terrace, shuttered windows and high ceilings. US$50

Hotel Lempira Second road on the left past *Bungalow*, moving east from the Parque Central ☏ 2448 1229, ⓔ hotellempira@yahoo.com. One of Tela's newcomers, this place has a nice garden and terrace, as well as spacious, fresh-feeling rooms, quality bedding and hot water throughout. The hotel was for sale at the time of writing, and construction of a dorm is planned (US$10). Doubles L500

Hotel Marsol Av 2 near C 9 ☏ 2448 1781/1782, ⓦ www.hotelmarsoltela.com. The orange curtains on the windows cast a strange light but it's at least clean and spacious, with a/c. Breakfast L150. L600

Mango On the corner of C 8 and Av 5 ☏ 2448 0338, ⓦ www.mangocafe.net. A travellers' favourite, the

cheaper rooms here come with fan, while those a notch better have a/c and TV. Rooms are clean and there's a small communal terrace, but overall prices are a bit high. Bike rental L95/day. L406

Sinai At the southern end of Av 6 ☏ 2448 1486. A good, friendly option, though some way from the beach. The "showers" in the private bathrooms are just a tube. L400

Eating

Tela has an interesting mix of places to eat, with foreign-run restaurants that cater to the steady flow of European and North American visitors competing with locally owned seafood places. One staple that shouldn't be missed is the delicious *pan de coco* (coconut bread) sold by Garífuna women and children on the beach and around town.

Auto Pollo Al Carbón At the western end of C 11, by the bridge. Informal place on the doorstep of the Caribbean Sea with a grimy sort of beachside view, serving chicken and not much else (from L40).

Bungalow C 9, three and a half blocks east of the Parque Central. An eight-sided wooden affair decorated with American memorabilia, perhaps because owner and chef Norman Taylor grew up in New Orleans. Barbecue ribs L80, spaghetti with shrimp L125, plus fantastic beans and *tajadas* on the side. Thurs–Tues 11am–midnight.

Luces del Norte On the corner of C 11 and Av 5. Popular with tourists and locals alike, *Luces del Norte* offers a good range of seafood dishes, including an array of conch-based meals. Mains from L80.

Mamma Mia! Av 4, C 9–10, a block west of the Parque Central. Very friendly Italian-owned pasta spot with some seafood and meat dishes as well as a wide range of breakfast options. Small pizzas L79–129, pasta dishes L79–179.

Restaurante Maya Vista C 8 NE, Av 9–10 NE. Attached to a hotel on a hillside, so you can enjoy great ocean views as you dine. Lasagne L125, fish dishes from L160, *filet mignon* with mushroom sauce L195. Daily 7am–9pm.

Drinking and nightlife

Tela has a thriving nightlife, at weekends at least, when the bars along Calle 11 behind the beach host crowds listening to salsa, reggae and mainstream dance music.

Delfín Telamar at Villas Telamar 1km west of town, in Tela Nueva. This is the place to go for a tranquil drink while enjoying the sea breezes. It's also home to the *Guarumas Lounge Bar*, a lively spot open most nights till 11pm.

Iguana's Sports Bar & Discotec Av 2, C 10–11, up by the bridge in the northwest of town. This lively disco really gets going at weekends and is a popular hangout for both locals and travellers. Opens 8pm.

Directory

Exchange There is a Unibanc ATM on the southern side of the park. Banco de Occidente, on the eastern side of the Parque, has an ATM and does cash advances, while Banco Atlántida, on the corner of Av 4 and C 9, has an ATM and can change travellers' cheques.

Internet The unnamed bright-red building on Av 6 just south of *Espresso Americano* offers access for L15/hr; the place next door to *Mamma Mia!* charges the same rate.

Laundry Lavandería San Jose is at the eastern end of C 10.

Post office Av 4, C 7–8 SO, two blocks south of the Parque Central.

Telephones The Hondutel office is next to the post office; the internet place next door to *Mamma Mia!* also offers fairly cheap international calls.

Moving on

By bus to: La Ceiba (every 30min; 2hr 30min); San Pedro Sula (8 daily; 2hr). To get to San Pedro Sula you can also get a taxi out to the highway south of town and flag down one of the buses coming from La Ceiba.

AROUND TELA

Even if you're quickly bored with Tela itself, there is an abundance of places to visit in the nearby area. These include the **Garífuna villages** along the bay on pristine beaches on either side of town, the **Punta Sal** wildlife reserve, and **Lancetilla**, 5km south of town and probably the finest botanical reserve in Latin America. To get to any of these places, you can take taxis or rely on local buses, but renting a bike is probably the most enjoyable way to get around; ask at Garífuna Tours (see p.373) for rental information.

Garífuna villages

The **Garífuna communities** of the north coast have an entirely different history and culture from the Mestizo people who represent the majority of Hondurans. The villages, located on quiet and expansive stretches of beach, are an interesting getaway for a few hours. Weekends are the best time to visit them, when people congregate to perform the traditional, haunting and melodic drum-driven rhythms of Garífuna music.

Heading west from Tela, a dirt road edges the bay between the seafront and the **Laguna de los Micos**, which forms the eastern edge of Punta Sal (see below). Some 7km along this road is the sleepy village of **Tornabé**, and, beyond that, **Miami**, which is set on a fabulous stretch of beach at the mouth of the lagoon. Though Tornabé has a few brick-built houses, Miami consists of nothing but traditional palm-thatched huts.

Buses run to Tornabé from the eastern end of Calle 10 in Tela every hour on the hour, from 6am to 5pm. From Tornabé pick-ups run to Miami at 6.30am and 12.30pm from Monday to Saturday, with returns at 8am and 2pm. **Accommodation** in both towns is limited, though local families may rent out basic rooms if you ask around.

Parque Nacional Jeanette Kawas (Punta Sal)

The **Parque Nacional Jeanette Kawas** (daily 6am–4pm; US$5), commonly known as **Punta Sal**, is a wonderfully diverse **reserve** encompassing mangrove swamps, coastal lagoons, wetlands, coral reef and tropical forest, which together provide habitats for an extraordinary range of flora and fauna. Jeanette Kawas, for whom the reserve is named, was instrumental in obtaining protected status for the land, in the face of intense local opposition; her murder, in 1995, has never been solved.

Lying to the west of Tela, curving along the bay to the headland of Punta Sal (176m), the reserve covers three lagoons: **Laguna de los Micos**, on the park's eastern side; **Laguna Tisnachí**, in the centre; and the oceanfront **Laguna El Diamante**, on the western side of the headland. More than one hundred species of bird are present, including herons and storks, with seasonal migratory visitors bumping up the numbers; animals found in the reserve include howler and white-faced monkeys, wild pigs, jaguars and, in the marine sections, manatees and marine turtles. Boat trips along the Río Ulúa and the canals running through the reserve offer a superb opportunity to view the wildlife at close quarters. Where the headland curves up to the north, the land rises slightly to Punta Sal; a **trail** over the point leads to small, pristine **beaches** at either side

It's possible to visit parts of Punta Sal independently – you can rent a **boat** in Miami (see opposite) to explore the Laguna de los Micos and surrounding area – though most people opt to join an organized **tour** (see p.373). You could also **hike** the scenic eight kilometres from Miami to the headland along the beach, but it's best not to go it alone.

Jardín Botánico de Lancetilla

The extensive grounds of the **Jardín Botánico de Lancetilla** (Mon–Fri 7.30am–3pm, Sat & Sun 8am–3pm; US$6), 5km south of Tela, started life in 1925 as a United Fruit species research and testing station, and over time has grown into one of the largest collections of fruit and flowering trees, palms, hardwoods and tropical plants in the world. There are also 365 recorded species of bird. Guided **tours** of the arboretum and birdwatching tours are available, and visitors are also free to wander along the marked **trails**; maps are available at the **visitors' centre** at the entrance to the park. A small, refreshing swimming hole in the Lancetilla River is at the end of one of the trails.

To get to Lancetilla, take a San Pedro Sula-bound **bus** from Tela for a couple of kilometres to the signposted turn-off; ask the driver to drop you. From here, the park is a further 3km. A taxi from Tela costs L60–80 each way or you could rent a bike from *Mango* (L95). There's a *comedor* and a small **hostel** (L400) at the visitors' centre; beds should be reserved on ☎2448 1740.

LA CEIBA

Some 190km east along the coast from San Pedro Sula, steamy **LA CEIBA**, the lively capital of the department of Atlántida, is the gateway to the Bay Islands. Though the town is completely bereft of architectural interest and its sandy beaches are strewn with rubbish, it does enjoy a remarkable setting at the steep slopes of the Cordillera Nombre de Dios. La Ceiba is home to a cosmopolitan mix of inhabitants, including a large Garífuna community, and really comes into its own at night, with visitors and locals gathering to take part in the city's vibrant **dance scene**.

Ceiba, as it's generally known, owes its existence to the banana industry: the Vaccaro Brothers (later Standard Fruit and now Dole) first laid plantations in the area in 1899 and set up their company headquarters in town in 1905. Although fruit is no longer shipped out through La Ceiba, the plantations are still important to the local economy, with crops of pineapple and African palm now as significant as bananas.

What to see and do

Most things of interest to visitors lie within a relatively small area of the city, around the shady and pleasant **Parque Central**, with its busts of Honduran historical heroes. The unremarkable whitewashed and powder-blue **cathedral** sits on the Parque's southeast corner. Running north from the Parque almost to the seafront, Avenida San

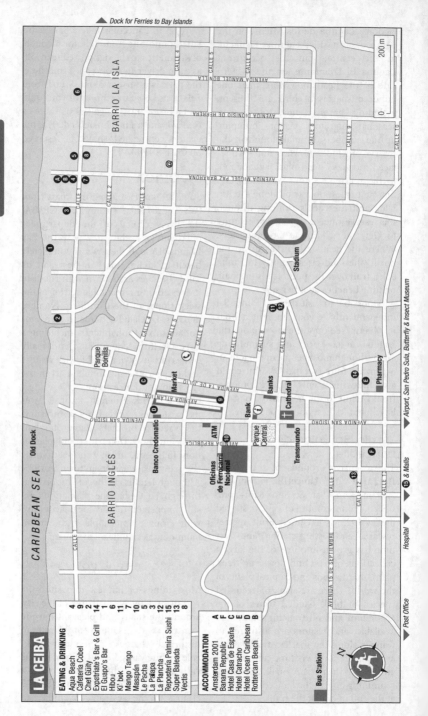

Dock for Ferries to Bay Islands

LA CEIBA

EATING & DRINKING

Aqua Beach	4
Cafetería Cobel	9
Chef Güity	14
Expatriate's Bar & Grill	2
El Guapo's Bar	1
Hibou	6
Ki' bok	11
Mango Tango	7
Masapán	10
Le Pacha	5
La Palapa	3
La Plancha	12
Repostería Palmira Sushi	15
Super Baleada	13
Vectis	8

ACCOMMODATION

Amsterdam 2001	A
Banana Republic	F
Hotel Casa de España	C
Hotel Catracho	E
Hotel Ocean Caribbean	D
Rottercam Beach	B

CARIBBEAN SEA

Old Dock

BARRIO INGLÉS

BARRIO LA ISLA

Parque Bonilla

Market

Parque Central

Stadium

Banco Credomatic

Oficinas de Ferrocarril Nacional

ATM

Bank

Banks

Cathedral

Transmundo

Pharmacy

Airport, San Pedro Sula, Butterfly & Insect Museum

& Malls

Hospital

Post Office

Bus Station

AVENIDA SAN ISIDRO

AVENIDA LA REPÚBLICA

AVENIDA ATLÁNTIDA

AVENIDA 14 DE JULIO

AVENIDA SAN ISIDRO

AVENIDA 15 DE SEPTIEMBRE

AVENIDA MIGUEL PAZ BARAHONA

AVENIDA PEDRO NUÑO

AVENIDA DIONISIO DE HERRERA

AVENIDA MANUEL BONILLA

200 m

0

N

Isidro, Avenida Atlántida and Avenida 14 de Julio frame the main commercial district, with shops, banks, a couple of supermarkets and the main municipal market. Stroll a block west of the Parque and you'll find the **Oficinas del Ferrocarril Nacional**, which is planted with tropical vegetation and dotted with museum-piece train carriages, many dating from the days of the peak of the banana trade.

All the **beaches** within the city limits are too polluted and dirty, even for the most desperate. It's better to head east to the much cleaner beaches a few kilometres out of town (see p.380). Calle 1, at the northern end of town near the seafront, extends east from the old dock and over the river estuary into **Barrio La Isla**, a quieter residential district, mainly home to Garífuna.

Museum of Butterflies and Insects

About a kilometre south of the plaza is the private **Museum of Butterflies and Insects**, Etapa 2, Casa G-12, Colonia El Sauce (Mon–Sat 8am–noon & 1–4pm; L60; ⓦ www.hondurasbutterfly.com), where over twelve thousand specimens from 68 countries are on view, though almost three-quarters are native species. Displays explain trapping techniques, and there are videos in English and Spanish.

Arrival

By air Aeropuerto Internacional Golosón is 9km from the centre, off the main highway west to San Pedro Sula. There's no local transport into town from the airport; a taxi to the centre will cost L100–200. To get to the airport you can take a bus marked El Confite or Primero de Maio from the central park (every 15min; 30min). *Colectivo* taxis at the Parque should charge L20, or L45–80 if you're the only passenger.
By boat Ferries to and from Roatán and Utila in the Bay Islands use the Muelle de Cabotaje municipal dock, about 5km east of the city. A shared taxi to the pier should cost L100–200 total (*Banana Republic* guesthouse can book one for L50 per person). Buses to the dock (every 30min; 20–40min) leave from outside *Banana Republic*.
By bus Long-distance and local buses arrive at the main terminal, 2km west of the centre; taxis to downtown, usually shared, charge L20–30 per person. Local buses also run into town and cost about L5.

Information

Tourist information There is a tourist office on C 8, one block east of the Parque Central, where some of the staff speak English.
Travel agent Transmundo, at Av San Isidro, C 9–10.

Getting around

Taxis Expect to pay L20 for a taxi ride in town during the day, rising to L30–40 after 8pm.

Accommodation

Given La Ceiba's status as both a provincial and a party centre, it's no surprise that there's a range of

---

LA CEIBA TOUR OPERATORS

Several companies offer tours to the surrounding area and further afield.
Jungle River Tours *Banana Republic*, Av República, C 12–13 ☏2440 1268, ⓦwww.jungleriverlodge.com. All tours include a night's accommodation at their *Jungle River Lodge*. Rafting, canopy and hiking tours start at US$40.
La Moskitia Ecoaventuras ☏2441 3279 or 9929 7532, ⓦwww.lamoskitia.hn. Jorge Salaverri is an expert on La Mosquitia and the Río Plátano, and his company also offers tours to Pico Bonito (from US$35), Cuero y Salado and Cayos Cochinos (both from US$53). Their office is located in Colonia Toronjal 2 close to Megaplaza mall: turn right at *Pollitos La Cumbre*, continue for two blocks then turn right again.
Omega Tours Río Cangrejal valley, 12 miles from La Ceiba ☏2440 0334 or 9631 0295, ⓦwww.omegatours.info. All tours start at their lodge, which borders both Pico Bonito and Nombre de Dios parks, and prices (from US$40) include a night's stay.

CARNAVAL IN LA CEIBA

The most exciting time to be in La Ceiba is during **Carnaval**, a week-long bash held every May to celebrate the city's patron saint, **San Isidro**. Dances and street events in various barrios around town culminate in an afternoon parade on the third Saturday. The 200,000 or so partygoers who attend Carnaval every year flock between the street events and the clubs on Calle 1 in the Zona Viva, where the dancing continues until dawn.

budget places to stay. The only problem is deciding whether you want to be near the centre or closer to the nightlife along Calle 1. Prices inevitably tend to rise around Carnaval time in May, when reserving ahead becomes essential.

Amsterdam 2001 1 C, Av Barahona, Barrio La Isla ☎2443 2311, ✉zaal_xx_12@hotmail .com. Dorms are dilapidated but the five private rooms with fans are adequate, some with bathroom. The 12-bed dorm is up a perilous metal staircase (go easy on the beer). Dorms L100, doubles L200

Banana Republic Av República, C 12–13 ☎2441 9404. Once the heart of the backpacker scene in La Ceiba, *Banana Republic* is now starting to show its age – and some of the dorm bunks are out in a corridor – but is still a decent option. Wi-fi, internet access, kitchen and very helpful staff. Dorms L150, doubles L285

🏃 **Hotel Casa de España** Av 14 de Julio, C 4–5 ☎2454 0210 or 9725 8973, ⊛www .hotelcasadespana.com. This 16-room hotel is impeccably clean, with plants and other homely elements dotted around throughout. A bargain if you are prepared to haggle a bit. Opt out of breakfast, though, which adds over L100 to the room price. Wi-fi-enabled. L400

Hotel Catracho Barrio Solares Nuevos, C 12 ☎2440 2312/2313, ⊛www.hotelcatracho.com. A clean, modern hotel at a good price, this place is saved from blandness by the pool and decking area. Only a minute's walk from *Expatriates* bar, too. Rooms from L400

Hotel Ocean Caribean C 5, between Av San Isidro and Av Atlántida ☎2443 1857 or 2454 0330. From the outside you might be expecting a string vest and a toothpick, but it's a surprisingly friendly family affair. The 32 rooms come with TV, fan and cold-water bathrooms. L400

Rotterdam Beach C 1, Av Barahona, Barrio La Isla ☎2440 0321. Next door to *Amsterdam 2001*, with eight clean and neat rooms with fan and private bathroom. L500

Eating

Be aware that tax and tip are often added to bills.

Cafetería Cobel C 7. This Ceiba institution features a simple, meat-heavy menu offering the usual *chuleta* and *res*. Soups include *mondongo*, *tapado*, meatballs and *nacatamales*. Lunches around L55, cake around L30. Mon–Sat 7am–6pm, though Sunday opening is planned.

Chef Güity C 1. With looks like this – mismatched tablecloths, rickety chairs, faded soccer photos – the food at this Garifuna *palapa* restaurant has got to be good, and it generally is, particularly the king fish (L130) and the *tapado garifuna* (a typical soup) for L190.

Expatriate's Bar and Grill C 12, two blocks east of Av San Isidro. A huge, thatched bar-restaurant slickly run by Frenchman Jérome Marchand. Food ranges from healthy organic (salads from L99) to the tastily stodgy (German sausage on a bun with fries L99). Local beers from L25, cocktails from L65. Wi-fi. Daily from 11am till late.

🏃 **Ki' bok** Next door to *La Plancha*. A friendly, good-value little café with original art on the walls and a homely feel. Pancakes with bacon and eggs L75, burger, salsa and fries L80, spaghetti with shrimp L90.

Mango Tango On the corner of C 1 & Av Barahona. Tropical-style bar with a covered decking and garden area. The open kitchen sends out good food and there's an impressive salad bar (L110–140). Chicken wings L110, fried *yuca* L60, fried fish L150–195, meat dishes with salad from L210.

Masapán C 7, Av La República–Av San Isidro. Consistently popular self-service cafeteria with a cheap buffet of Honduran and American-style food. Dish of the day L49, *baleadas* L12–24. Mon–Sat 7am–7pm, Sun 7am–3pm.

La Plancha Two blocks east of the Parque between C 9 and C 8 ☎2443 2304. A classy joint with green tablecloths and framed cowhides on the walls. They're proud of their meat here, and rightly so: it has a tenderness rare in Honduras and will be cooked just as you want it. *Filete a la plancha* with salad, bread and mash L230. Daily 11am–2pm & 5–11pm.

Repostería Palmira Sushi C del Hospital D'Antoni, Casa no. 4, opposite Uniplaza mall ☎2442 0312 or 9643 6936. In this unlikely merging of traditional Honduran bakery and sushi restaurant, owner-chef Jaime incorporates ingredients from manchego to plantain in his Japanese cuisine. Start with edamame (L45) or gyoza (L80), then try the San Pedro Sula roll (L180) with a fried tempura and sesame coating, filled with crispy breaded shrimp and spicy avocado salsa. Sushi and sashimi L40 per piece. Mon–Sat noon–9pm; Sun takeaway only, 4–8pm.

Super Baleada On the corner of Av Colón and C 12. The cheapest meal you're likely to have in La Ceiba and surely one of the best. *Baleadas* L9–70, coffee L6.

Drinking and nightlife

Not for nothing does La Ceiba have a reputation as the place to party. A hedonistic local crowd, plus a steady trickle of tourists and a growing number of resident expats, have helped to create a buoyant atmosphere. The action takes place along C 1, which runs parallel to the seafront. Nicknamed the Zona Viva due to its preponderance of bars and clubs, the area hums most nights of the week, though weekends are really explosive, with a profusion of places to drink and dance. Just stroll down the street to see what's going on and where the crowds are. Outside of the Zona Viva, *Expatriate's Bar and Grill* (see opposite) is a good place for an evening drink.

Aqua Beach On the same road as *Amsterdam 2001* and *Rotterdam Beach* hotels @ www.aquabeach -bar.com. Sit upstairs and watch city life go by while listening to the waves lap onto the beach and munching on Honduran and Mexican dishes (from L100). Mon–Thurs 11.30am–4am, Fri & Sat 11.30am–5am, Sun 4pm–4am.

El Guapo's Bar C 1. This is right next door to the sprawling *Snake* bar and shares the same *palapa* feel. Hugely popular on Fri and Sat nights, it has a fantastic atmosphere, especially when the karaoke takes over. The food is pricey, though. Beer L32.

Hibou C 1. This dance club is currently the place that has teenagers and twentysomethings patiently queueing for entry. L100 entrance.

Le Pacha Opposite *Vectis* on C 1. A huge space covered in massive stretched awnings, right on the beach. The music is a mix of reggaeton, merengue and bachata. Beer from L35, spirits from L30. Wed–Sun 10am–10pm; open much later on Saturdays.

La Palapa Just off C 1. Very popular spot in the Zona Viva, known for its large dancefloor. Sat nights are especially exciting: live bands perform a mix of merengue, reggae and rock cover songs. Tues–Sun from 6pm.

Vectis C 1. A small-ish, popular place, open to the street, that plays loud reggae and rock and hosts cover bands.

Directory

Airlines Isleña/TACA (℡ 2441 3190, @ www.taca .com, @ www.flyislena.com), at the Megaplaza mall (Mon–Fri 9am–6pm, Sat 9am–1pm) and at the airport (℡ 2442 1967); Aerolínea SOSA (℡ 2443 2519/2078, @ www.aerolineasosahn.com), at the Plaza Premier mall opposite Megaplaza mall (Mon–Fri 7am–5pm, Sat 7am–noon); LANHSA (℡ 2442 1283 or 9486 2127), at the airport.

Car rental Avis (℡ 2441 2802), one block east of Megaplaza mall by the San Miguel Plus terminal.

Cinema Cines Premiere, in Plaza Premier on the opposite side of the road from Megaplaza, shows subtitled movies Mon–Fri 5pm, 7pm & 9pm, Sat & Sun 3pm, 5pm, 7pm & 9pm; L50–60. Cines Millenium in Megaplaza mall has two screens showing different movies at the times above.

Exchange Most of the banks are on C 8 and Av 14 de Julio one block east of the Parque. The Megaplaza mall also has several banks.

Health Hospital D'Antoni (℡ 2443 2264) is at the southern end of Av Morazán. Two good pharmacies are Auto Farmacia Zaz (24hr) and Farmacia Mary Ann (daily 8am–11pm), both on C 13, near Av 14 de Julio.

Immigration Immigration is between C 17 and 18 on Av 14 de Julio.

Internet Café Internet in the Megaplaza food court charges L28/hr; or try Servi Office Internet at Barrio La Isla, C 4 (Mon–Sat 9am–7pm).

Language school Centro Internacional de Idiomas (Col Toronjal II, Etapa 5, Block 15, Casa L–13; ℡ 2441 1715 or 9984 2008, @ www.honduras spanish.com) is a good Spanish school. Rates are US$230 weekly for twenty hours of one-to-one tuition and homestay, including all meals (US$140 without the homestay).

Post office Av Morazán, C 13–14.

Shopping The main general market is on Av Atlántida, C 5–7. The Megaplaza mall is in the southern outskirts of town past the hospital.

Telephones Hondutel is at Av Ramón Rosa, C 5–6 (7.30am–5.50pm). Café Internet in the Megaplaza food court offers international calls to the US for L1/min (cell or landline) and to Europe for L8/min. Servi Office Internet at Barrio La Isla, C 4 (Mon–Sat 9am–7pm), offers international calls for L1/min to the US, L4–8/min to Europe.

Moving on

By air to: Roatán (with Isleña/TACA, SOSA; 4 daily; 30min); Guanaja (with SOSA; 1 daily; 30min); Tegucigalpa (with SOSA, Isleña/TACA; 4 daily;

40min); Utila (with SOSA; 2 daily; 15min); San Pedro Sula (with SOSA, Isleña/TACA; 5 daily; 30min).
Aero Caribe flies to Brus Laguna, Ahuas and Puerto Lempira (1 daily Mon–Sat; journey time varies).
By boat to: Roatán (on the MV *Galaxy II*; 2 daily; 1hr 30min; US$27–32); Utila (on the *Utila Princess*; 2 daily; 1hr 30min; US$27).
By bus to: Copán Ruinas (6 daily; 5hr); Guatemala City (2 daily; 11hr); Olanchito (for Juticalpa; 12 daily; 3hr); San Pedro Sula (25 daily with Mirna, Cotuc, Cotraipbal, Diana, 3hr 30min; 4 daily with Hedman Alas, 2hr 30min); Tegucigalpa (15 daily with Kamaldy and Cristina, 7hr; 3 daily with San Miguel, 6hr); Tela (27 daily; 2hr); Trujillo (22 daily; 3hr–4hr 30min).

AROUND LA CEIBA

The broad sandy beaches and clean water at **Playa de Perú** and the village of **Sambo Creek** are easy day-trip destinations east of La Ceiba. A trip to explore the cloudforest within the **Parque Nacional Pico Bonito** requires more planning, although the eastern edge of the reserve, formed by the **Río Cangrejal**, is still easily accessible, and also offers opportunities for swimming and whitewater rafting. Finally, a trip to the serene islands of the **Cayos Cochinos** is thoroughly worthwhile.

Playa de Perú

Some 10km east of the city, **Playa de Perú** is a wide sweep of clean sand that's popular at weekends. Any local **bus** running east up the coast will drop you at the highway-side turn-off, from where it's a fifteen-minute walk to the beach. About 2km past the turning for Playa de Perú, on the Río María, there's a series of **waterfalls** and **natural pools** set in lush, shady forest. A path leads from Río María village on the highway, winding through the hills along the left bank of the river; it takes around thirty minutes to walk to the first cascade and pool, with some muddy sections and a bit of scrambling during the wet season.

Sambo Creek

There are further deserted expanses of white sand at the friendly Garífuna village of **Sambo Creek**, 8km beyond Río María.

An excellent accommodation option in this area is *Paradise Found* (☎9861 1335 or 9552 3238, ⓦwww.paradisefoundlaceiba.com; US$55) at Playa Helen. The food is great too: try the ribs smoked with fruitwood (US$12). Olanchito or Juticalpa **buses** from La Ceiba will drop you at the turn-off to Sambo Creek on the highway, a couple of kilometres from the village; slower buses run all the way to the village centre from La Ceiba's terminal every 45 minutes.

Parque Nacional Pico Bonito

Directly south of La Ceiba, the Cordillera Nombre de Dios shelters the **Parque Nacional Pico Bonito** (daily 6am–4pm; US$6), a remote expanse of tropical broadleaf forest, cloudforest and – in its southern reaches, above the Río Aguan valley – pine forest. Taking its name from the awe-inspiring bulk of Pico Bonito (2435m), the park is the source of twenty **rivers**, including the Zacate, Bonito and Cangrejal, which cascade majestically down the mountains' steep, thickly tree-covered slopes. The park also provides sanctuary for an abundance of wildlife, including armadillos, howler and spider monkeys, pumas and ocelots. The lower fringes are the most easily accessible, with a few **trails** laid out through the dense greenery. The easiest way to get into the park is to enter via the *Lodge at Pico Bonito* (☎2440 0389, ⓦwww.picobonito.com), a world-class **jungle lodge** with bungalow accommodation, gourmet cuisine, a pool and a sublime setting in the foothills of the forest reserve. Trails from the lodge snake up through the tree cover to a lookout from where Utila is visible, and down to beautiful river bathing pools. You don't have to be a guest at the lodge to access the park and trails, but you will have to pay a US$33 fee, which includes lunch and a guide. To get there head for the village of **El Pino**, 12km from La Ceiba on the Tela highway, from where the hotel is signposted, 3km away up a dirt side-road. Alternatively, tour companies in La Ceiba (see box, p.377) operate day- and overnight trips to Pico Bonito from around US$35 per person.

Río Cangrejal

The **Río Cangrejal**, which forms the eastern boundary of the Parque Nacional Pico Bonita, boasts some of the best class III and IV rapids in Central America; **whitewater rafting** and **kayaking** trips are organized by some of the tour companies listed in the box on p.377. There are also some magnificent swimming spots, backed by gorgeous mountain scenery, along the river valley. It's tricky to get to the river under your own steam, but *Jungle River Lodge* (T2440 1268, Wwww.jungleriverlodge .com), managed by the same people as the *Banana Republic* guesthouse (see p.378) offers an array of packages from US$35. They can arrange your transport, and also have a river lodge in the park with a bar, a restaurant and a choice of private and dorm accommodation (dorms US$12, doubles US$40).

Refugio de Vida Silvestre Cuero y Salado

Some 30km west from La Ceiba, the **Refugio de Vida Silvestre Cuero y Salado** (daily 7am–4pm; US$10; T2440 1990) is one of the last substantial remnants of wetlands and mangrove swamps along the north coast. The reserve is home to a large number of endangered animals and bird species, including manatees, jaguars, howler and white-faced monkeys, sea turtles and hawks, along with seasonal influxes of migratory birds.

To get to the reserve independently (a journey of around 1hr 15min), catch an hourly **bus** (6.20am–3.30pm; 30min) from La Ceiba's terminal to the village of **La Unión**, 20km or so west. From here, take a *mototaxi* (10min; L15) to the El Bambú Estación del Motocarro then

take a *motocarro* (a very rudimentary train – a little like a tuk-tuk on rails; 30min; L40) to the visitors' centre; canoe tours can be arranged here, and there is also some accommodation, in the form of a small dorm (US$7). The Fundación Cuero y Salado (FUCSA) can be visited in La Ceiba (Barrio La Merced, C 15, Av Ramón Rosa, Edificio Daytona; T2443 0329 or 2440 1990, Efucsa @televicab.net, cuero_salado@yahoo .com or canp82@yahoo.es).

Cayos Cochinos

Lying 30km offshore, the **Cayos Cochinos** (**Hog Islands**) comprise thirteen privately owned cayes and two thickly wooded islands – **Cochino Mayor** and **Cochino Menor**. Fringed by a reef, the whole area has been designated a **marine reserve**, with anchoring on the reef and commercial fishing both strictly prohibited. The small amount of effort it takes to get to the islands is well worth it for a few days' utter tranquillity.

Organized **accommodation** on the two islands is limited to overpriced resort-style places. However, villagers in the traditional Garífuna fishing village of **Chachauate** on **Lower Monitor Caye** have allocated a hut for visitors to sling their hammocks in and they will also cook meals for you. There's no fixed cost, but a stay never costs that much. Basic groceries are available in the

---

DIVING IN THE CAYOS COCHINOS

Pirate Island Divers (T3228 0009 or 9563 9172, Wwww.pirateislands divers.com), based in Sambo Creek, is run by PADI Master Instructor Tony Marquez and offers introductory day courses (US$65), open-water courses (US$235), snorkelling trips (US$35 with lunch or US$65 with an overnight on the islands in very simple twin-bed rooms), plus two-tank diving trips (US$75) or a package of five dives (US$205 with room and meals).

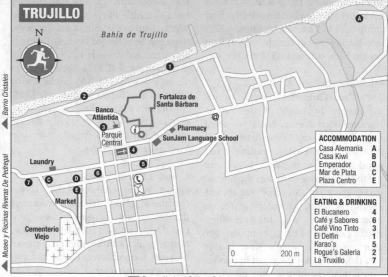

TRUJILLO

N

Bahía de Trujillo

Barrio Cristales

Museo y Piscinas Riveras De Pedregal

Bus Terminal & Laguna de Guaimoreto

Fortaleza de Santa Bárbara

Banco Atlántida

Parque Central

Pharmacy

SunJam Language School

Laundry

Market

Cementerio Viejo

ACCOMMODATION	
Casa Alemania	A
Casa Kiwi	B
Emperador	D
Mar de Plata	C
Plaza Centro	E

EATING & DRINKING	
El Bucanero	4
Café y Sabores	6
Café Vino Tinto	3
El Delfin	1
Karao's	5
Rogue's Galeria	2
La Truxillo	7

0   200 m

▼ *Parque Nacional Capiro y Calentura*

village, but there is no running water or electricity and toilets are latrines.

You will have to shell out a bit to travel to the islands, especially if you're on your own. The only feasible way to get there is with the fishermen who sail from the Garífuna villages of **Sambo Creek** or **Nueva Armenia** (40min; around US$25 per person return).

Buses from La Ceiba run every 35 minutes to Sambo Creek (45min), and six daily buses make the trip to Nueva Armenia (2hr). Alternatively, several tour companies in La Ceiba offer day-trips and overnight stays, starting from around US$35 per person (see p.377). There is a US$10 fee for visiting the Cayos Cochinos independently, and a US$5 fee if you are with a tour group. If arranging a tour, ask whether the price quoted includes the entrance fee.

TRUJILLO

Perched above the sparkling waters of the palm-fringed Bahía de Trujillo, backed by the beautiful green Cordillera Nombre de Dios, **TRUJILLO** immediately seduces the small number of

tourists who make the 90km trip from La Ceiba. The city has a very different feel from its big north-coast neighbours, La Ceiba and Tela – it's beautifully relaxed.

The area around present-day Trujillo was populated by a mixture of Pech and Tolupan groups when Columbus first disembarked here on August 14, 1502; the city itself was founded by Cortés's lieutenant, Juan de Medina, in 1525, though it was frequently abandoned due to attacks by European pirates. Not until the late eighteenth century did repopulation begin in earnest, aided by the arrival, via Roatán, of several hundred Garífuna. In 1860, a new threat appeared in the shape of US filibusterer and adventurer William Walker, who briefly took control of the town. Executed by firing squad three months later by the Honduran authorities, he is buried in Trujillo's cemetery.

What to see and do

Much of Trujillo's charm lies in meandering through its rather crumbly streets. The town proper stretches back five or so blocks south of the **Parque Central**, which is just fifty metres from cliffs overlooking the sea. On the north side of the square is a bust of Juan de Medina, the town founder. Southwest from the centre, a couple of blocks past the market, is the **Cementerio Viejo**, where Walker's grave lies overgrown with weeds – collect the key to the gate from the office in the fort.

The town's most outstanding attractions by far are its **beaches**, which have long stretches of almost pristine sand. The glorious sweep of the **Bahía de Trujillo** is as yet unaffected by excessive tourist development, and its calm, blue waters are perfect for effortless swimming. The beaches below town, lined with *champas*, are clean enough, but the stretches to the east, beyond the disused airstrip, are emptier. It's also possible to walk east along the beach to the reserve of **Laguna de Guaimoreto** or west to the Garífuna village of **Santa Fe**.

Fortaleza de Santa Bárbara

Just along from the Parque is the town's main attraction, the sixteenth-century **Fortaleza de Santa Bárbara** (daily 9am–5pm; US$3; ⑩www.ihah.hn), site of William Walker's execution. The low-lying fort hangs gloomily on the edge of the bluffs, overlooking the coastline that it singularly failed to protect against pirates. The museum charts the town's often-colourful history, and has an exhibition room on Garífuna culture.

Museo y Piscinas Riveras del Pedregal

Turn right past the Cementerio Viejo and a ten-minute stroll brings you to the privately run **Museo y Piscinas Riveras del Pedregal** (daily 7am–5pm; L50), an eccentric collection of rusty junk. Almost all of the original pre-Columbian ceramics once held by the museum have been sold off, though the replacement replicas are pretty convincing. Outside,

the wheels of an American jumbo jet that crashed in the area in 1985 can be seen. Behind the building are a couple of small, naturally fed swimming pools.

Parque Nacional Capiro y Calentura

Directly above the town lies the dark-green swathe of the **Parque Nacional Capiro y Calentura** (daily 6am–5pm; free). The reserve's huge cedars and pines tower amid a thick canopy of ferns, flowering plants and vines. As a result of the devastation wrought by Hurricane Fifi in 1974, much of the cover is secondary growth, but it still provides a secure habitat for howler monkeys, reptiles and colourful birdlife and butterflies. You can walk into the reserve by following the dirt road past the *Villas Brinkley* – it winds, increasingly steeply, up the slope of Cerro Calentura to the radio towers just below its summit; a ten-kilometre walk, this is best done in the relative cool of early morning. Alternatively, you could negotiate with a taxi driver to take you to the top and then walk down. Unfortunately there aren't any trail maps, so you'll have to do a bit of exploring.

Arrival and information

By boat The *Guanaja Express* from Guanaja runs Mon, Wed & Fri (see p.384) arriving at the old pier in central Trujillo at 10.30am and leaving again for Guanaja at 1pm (L800 each way; 1hr 30min).
By bus The bus terminal is to the east of town, at the bottom of the hill leading into the centre. From here infrequent urban buses head up the hill to the Parque Central, or you can take a taxi (L20).
Tourist information There's a small tourist office (sporadic opening hours) on the eastern side of the Parque, next door to the Fortaleza de Santa Bárbara office.

Accommodation

There's not much in the way of budget accommodation in town, but there are a couple of excellent places in glorious settings just outside the centre.

Casa Alemania 1km east of town ☎2434 4466. An extraordinary range of head-laying options are on offer here, from tiny backpacker rooms and camping all the way up to a penthouse. There's also a book exchange, housed in an attractive library-like room. L250

Casa Kiwi 7km east of town ☎2434 3050, ⓦwww.casakiwi.com. Undoubtedly one of the best hostels on the north coast, right on the beach. Dorms are clean and include a hot-water shower; there's a restaurant on site and the bar will stay open as long as you like. The staff are knowledgeable about travel to La Mosquitia. Dorms L100, doubles L250

Emperador By the market ☎2434 4446. The town's best budget hotel, run by an extremely friendly family. Rooms are clean – albeit rather small – and have en-suite bathroom, TV and fan. L450

Mar de Plata 5min west of the Parque. Avoid this place at weekends when the noise from the nearby *La Truxillo* may keep you awake. Otherwise, a solid budget choice. L400.

Plaza Centro By the market, opposite *Emperador* ☎2434 3006. The fresh white linen is the most eye-catching aspect of these 24 drab rooms, but they're kept in decent order and are fairly spacious. L450

Eating

El Bucanero In the *Hotel Colonial*, just off the Parque Central. The decent menu here includes some good, cheap seafood options. At night the place morphs into a bar with happy-hour drink offers. Mains from L80.

Café y Sabores One block south of the Parque. Doors and windows are propped wide open in this diner-like place, allowing for nice, breezy breakfasts. *Licuados* from L15, lunches L60, breakfasts L45. Mon–Sat 7am–8pm, Sun 7am–1pm.

Café Vino Tinto Behind the *municipalidad*. This sweet place has an open-sided seating area overlooking the bay, hung partly with white drapes. Try the delicious *tostones rellenos* (L80) – slices of fried plantain with various toppings – or the "Aztec chicken" (L130). Tues–Sun 9am–11pm.

El Delfin On the strip fronting the beach. More impressive than the other *champas* along this stretch, you can choose between the tiled, indoor dining area, or sand between your toes outside. The service is efficient and the king crab *a la ojo* (L180) superb.

Rogue's Galería On the beach below town. Commonly referred to as "*Jerry's*", this engaging American-owned bar/restaurant features superb seafood and has plenty of hammocks for daytime chilling. Mains from L80.

Drinking and nightlife

Karao's Southeast of the Parque. This well-worn disco charges around L30 for entry.

La Truxillo Up the hill towards the western side of town. Certainly the most popular place at weekends, when it heaves to Latin American rhythms and the bar fills up with a young crowd. Entrance at least L50.

Directory

Exchange Banco Atlántida, on the Parque, gives Visa cash advances and has a 24hr ATM.

Internet Try Ciber Café, on the eastern end of the main road running through town (9am–10pm; L20).

Language school Local teacher Vicente Lopez (☎2434 4944) is recommended. He can also be contacted through *Casa Kiwi*.

Laundry A block northwest of the market.

Pharmacy Two blocks south of the Parque.

Post office Three blocks south of the southeast corner of the Parque.

Telephones The Hondutel office is next to the post office.

Moving on

By bus to: La Ceiba (18 daily; 3hr); Puerto Castilla (7 daily, last one 6pm; 45min); San Pedro Sula (15 daily; 5–6hr); Tegucigalpa, via La Ceiba (2 daily at 12.30am & 4.45am; 10hr); Tocoa (24 daily; 2hr 30min).

By boat The Guanaja Express runs Mon, Wed & Fri from Trujillo, leaving at 1pm (L800 each way; 1hr 30min). For information call Captain Roy on ☎9962 6163 or 9600 2235.

AROUND TRUJILLO

Expanses of white-sand **beach** stretch for miles around the bay from Trujillo. All beaches are clean, wide and perfect for swimming; don't take anything valuable with you, though, and don't venture onto them after dark.

Aguas Calientes

Taking a hot bath in the heat of the Caribbean may not strike everyone as an appealing thought, but a soak in the clean and very hot mineral waters of the **Aguas Calientes** springs (L50), 7km inland from Trujillo, feels delightfully decadent. It's closed most of the time, but ask the caretaker of the hotel *Aguas Calientes* (where the pools are located) if you can use them. Any **bus** heading to Tocoa will drop you off at the entrance; the last return bus leaves at around 5.30pm.

La Mosquitia

Occupying the northeast corner of Honduras is the remote and undeveloped expanse of **La Mosquitia** (often spelt "Moskitia"). Bounded to the west by the mountain ranges of the Río Plátano and Colón, with the Río Coco forming the border with Nicaragua to the south, this vast region comprises almost a fifth of Honduras's territory. With just two peripheral roads and a tiny population divided among a few far-flung towns and villages, entering La Mosquitia really does mean leaving the beaten track. There are few phones in the region, and all accommodation is extremely basic, often without electricity and with latrine-style toilets. Food is usually limited to rice, beans and the catch of the day, so if you're making an independent trek, bring enough food with you for your party and guides. Getting around requires a spirit of adventure, but the effort is well rewarded.

To the surprise of many who come here expecting to have to hack their way through jungle, much of La Mosquitia is composed of marshy coastal wetlands and flat savanna. The small communities of **Palacios** and **Brus Laguna** are access points for the **Río Plátano Biosphere Reserve**, the most famous of five separate reserves in the area, set up to protect one of the finest remaining stretches of virgin tropical rainforest in Central America. **Puerto Lempira**, to the east, is the regional capital.

The largest ethnic group inhabiting La Mosquitia are the **Miskitos**, numbering around thirty thousand, who spoke a unique form of English until as recently as a few generations ago. There are much smaller communities of **Pech**, who

LA MOSQUITIA HISTORY AND POLITICS

Before the Spanish arrived, La Mosquitia belonged to the Pech and Sumu. Initial contact with Europeans was comparatively benign, as the Spanish preferred to concentrate instead on the mineral-rich lands of the interior. Relations with Europeans intensified when the British began seeking a foothold on the mainland in the seventeenth century, establishing settlements on the coast at Black River (now Palacios) and Brewer's Lagoon (Brus Laguna), whose inhabitants – the so-called "shoremen" – engaged in logging, trading, smuggling and fighting the Spanish.

Britain's claim to La Mosquitia, made nominally to protect the shoremen, though really intended to ensure a transit route from the Atlantic to the Pacific, supposedly ended in 1786, when all Central American territories except Belize were ceded to the Spanish. In the 1820s, however, taking advantage of post-independence chaos, Britain again encouraged settlement on the Mosquito Coast and by 1844 had all but formally announced a protectorate in the area. Not until 1859 and the British–American Treaty of Cruz Wyke did Britain formally end all claims to the region.

The initial impact of mestizo Honduran culture on La Mosquitia was slight. Since the creation of the administrative department of Gracias a Dios in 1959, however, indigenous cultures have become gradually diluted: Spanish is now the main language, and the government encourages mestizo settlers to migrate here in search of land. Pech, Miskito and Garífuna communities have become more vocal in recent years in demanding respect for their cultural differences and in calling for an expansion of health, education and transport infrastructures.

number around 2500, and **Tawahka** (Sumu), of whom there are under a thousand, living around the Río Patuca.

PALACIOS

Sited on what was once the British settlement of Black River, **PALACIOS** lies just west of one of the Río Plátano Biosphere Reserve's three coastal lagoons, Laguna Ibans. This is frequently the starting point for organized trips to the Río Plátano Biosphere Reserve, and, for independent travellers, a logical place from which to begin exploration of the region.

What to see and do

Dotted along the Caribbean shoreline around Palacios is a cluster of interesting **Garífuna villages**, including **Batalla**, just to the west of town across the Palacios lagoon, and **Plaplaya**, about 8km to the east, where a **turtle project** has been established. Highly endangered giant leatherbacks, the largest species in the world (reaching up to 3m in length and 900kg in weight), nest in the beaches around the village between April and June. There's a resident Peace Corps worker stationed here to oversee the project, and volunteers are welcome. **Rais Ta** and **Belén** are also worth visiting.

Accommodation

Hotel Moskitia ☎ 9996 5648/9659, ⊛ www .hotelmoskitia.com. This is the most modern and comfortable hotel in town, complete with a bar and restaurant on site. L450

Río Tinto You'll find adequate rooms at this hotel run by local Don Felix Marmol. L200

RÍO PLÁTANO BIOSPHERE RESERVE

The **RÍO PLÁTANO BIOSPHERE RESERVE** is the most significant nature reserve in Honduras, sheltering an estimated eighty percent of all the country's animal species. Visitors usually come to experience the rare tropical rainforest, but the reserve's boundaries – which stretch from the Caribbean in the north to the Montañas de Punta Piedra in the west and the Río Patuca in the south – also encompass huge expanses of coastal wetlands and flat savanna grasslands. Sadly, even its World Heritage status hasn't prevented extensive destruction at the hands of settlers: up to sixty percent of forest cover on the outer edges of the reserve has disappeared in the last three decades.

To get the most out of the park you should head for **Las Marías**, where plenty of prospective **guides** are available to help you explore the river and surrounding jungle for US$10–12 a day. One pleasant, if rather wet, trip you can make is by *pipante* (pole-propelled canoe), five hours upstream to rock **petroglyphs** at Walpaulban Sirpi, carved by an unknown people – these are more or less at the heart of the reserve. The journey itself is the main attraction, along channels too shallow for motorized boats to pass; in sections you'll be required to leave the boat and make your way through the undergrowth. *Pipantes* require three guides each, but carry only two passengers and cost US$25 (not including guides).

There are some basic *hospedajes* in the village – try *Hospedaje Doña Justa* or *Hospedaje Ovidio*, both of which serve meals. They'll charge around L200 for lodging.

Arrival and information

Arrival Getting to the heart of the Río Plátano reserve requires travelling up the Río Plátano to the small Pech and Miskito village of Las Marías. See box opposite, for prices.

Tourist information For general information about the reserve contact the tour operators who work within the region (see box opposite).

BRUS LAGUNA

Some 30km east along the coast from Palacios, on the southeastern edge of the

GETTING AROUND LA MOSQUITIA

A number of companies in La Ceiba, San Pedro and Tegucigalpa offer **tours** to La Mosquitia. Travelling **independently** is by no means impossible, as long as you're prepared to go with the flow.

Tour operators

La Moskitia Ecoaventuras in La Ceiba (see box, p.377) offer tours starting from around US$230 (not including transport to the region). Mesoamérica Travel (see box, p.368), based in San Pedro Sula, offer a relatively "budget" five-day tour including flights and three nights in Las Marias for US$524–675 per person. Another option is La Ceiba's Omega Tours (see box, p.377), whose all-inclusive tours start at US$500. La Ruta Moskitia (ⓦwww.larutamoskitia.com) offers excellent advice on visiting the region, as well as tour packages.

Transport

Transport to and within La Mosquitia is mainly by **air** or **water**: Puerto Lempira, Belén and Brus Laguna are currently connected to La Ceiba by regular flights, while *lanchas* ply the waterways connecting the scattered villages. Bear in mind that all schedules, especially those of the boats, are subject to change and delay; transport on the rivers and channels is determined by how much rain has fallen.

Boat travel is pricey, with *expreso* boats much more expensive than multiple-stop *colectivo* boats. Direct services from Palacios to Rais Ta/Belén are currently around L800 per boat and can hold up to ten people (1hr 30min); Rais Ta/Belén to Las Marías L3000 (4–5 person boat; 5hr) or to Brus Laguna L1500 per boat (2hr); Brus Laguna to Las Marías costs L3500 (4–5 person boat; 6hr). Prices to Las Marías include the charge for the driver spending two nights with you there. For *colectivo* services, the per-person rates are: Palacios to Rais Ta/Belén L150 (2–3hr); Rais Ta/Belén to Río Plátano L50 (overland; 45min); Río Plátano to Brus Laguna L200 (1hr 30min). There are no *colectivo* services to Las Marías.

Flights to La Mosquitia depart from La Ceiba only (see p.379). AeroCaribe (ⓣ2442 1097/1085/1088/2569, ⓔaerocaribehn@yahoo.com), based at La Ceiba's airport, currently run the only service into the region, flying to Brus Laguna, Ahuas and Puerto Lempira (Mon–Sat). Timetables are not strictly observed; take local advice as to their reliability at the time of your visit. SOSA (ⓦwww.aerolineasosahn .com) have offered travel into the region in the past and it's worth checking their website for developments. Central American Airlines is a new company which has already suffered one serious crash and cannot be recommended.

Ground transport to the region – the cheapest option – does exist, but progress is extremely slow. Take the bus from Trujillo to Tocoa, then a pick-up to Batalla (hourly 7am–noon; 4–5hr; L400). From Batalla, *colectivo* boats leave for destinations within La Mosquitia, such as the sister communities of Rais Ta/Belén (1–2hr; L150). If heading for Las Marías (see above) you will need to spend the night in one of these communities. Returning, you should spend the night in Batalla, from where early morning trucks depart for Tocoa, or in Rais Ta/Belén before taking the 4am *colectivo* boat to Batalla (L150). The *Casa Kiwi* hostel in Trujillo (see p.384) is a good place for information on entering by road and meeting others who are preparing to make the trip. Note that during the rainy season this trip becomes much more difficult. Some Spanish makes negotiating the various connections and inevitable delays much easier.

Laguna de Brus, is the friendly Miskito town of **BRUS LAGUNA**. *Laguna Paradise*, in the centre (ⓣ2433 8039 or 2898 7952; L300), has five acceptable rooms, while *La Estancia*, on the main street near the water (ⓣ2433 8043 or 2898 7959; L300), has twelve basic rooms with en-suite bathroom. The town is mostly seen by visitors as they are coming or going – regular **flights** connect the town with La Ceiba, and guides and boats can be hired for multi-day trips, travelling up the Río Sigre into the southern reaches of the Río Plátano reserve.

PUERTO LEMPIRA

Capital of the department of Gracias a Dios, **PUERTO LEMPIRA** is the largest town in La Mosquitia, with a population of eleven thousand. Set on the southeastern edge of the biggest of the coastal lagoons, Laguna de Caratasca, some 110km east of Brus Laguna, the town survives on government administration and small-scale fishing and shrimping. Like Brus Laguna, Puerto Lempira is mostly used by travellers as a transit hub – flights connect it with the rest of Honduras, and it's close to the border with Nicaragua. The best of the **accommodation** is at the *Gran Hotel Flores* (☎2433 6421; L350) in the centre of town, where the small rooms all have air conditioning and bathroom; the *Hospedaje Santa Teresita*, opposite (☎2433 6008; L250), is clean but basic. Banco Atlántida, next to *Hotel Flores*, changes travellers' cheques and gives Visa cash advances. Mopawi (☎2433 6022, ©mopawi@mopawi.org), the

Mosquitia development organization, has its headquarters in the town, three blocks south of the main dock.

The Bay Islands

Strung in a gentle curve 60km off the north coast, the **Islas de la Bahía**, with their clear waters and abundant marine life, are the country's main tourist attraction. Fringed by a coral reef, the islands are the perfect destination for cheap, water-based activities – diving, sailing and fishing top the list – or just relaxing. Composed of three main islands and some 65 smaller cayes, the chain lies on the **Bonacca Ridge**, an underwater extension of the Sierra de Omoa mountain range. **Roatán** is the largest and most developed of the islands, while **Guanaja**, to the east, is a bit more upmarket. **Utila**, the closest to the mainland, is a target for budget travellers from all over the world.

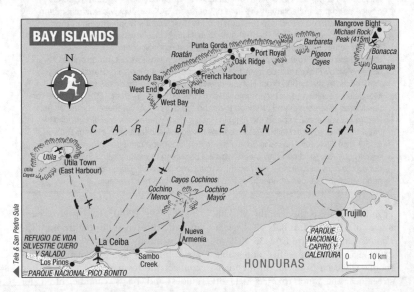

The Bay Islands' history of conquest, pirate raids and constant immigration has resulted in an unusual society. The original inhabitants were recorded by Columbus in 1502, but the indigenous population declined rapidly as a result of enslavement and forced labour. Following a series of pirate attacks, the Spanish evacuated the islands in 1650. Roatán was left deserted until the arrival of the Garífuna in 1797. These three hundred people, forcibly expelled from the British-controlled island of St Vincent following a rebellion, were persuaded by the Spanish to settle in Trujillo on the mainland, leaving a small settlement at Punta Gorda on Roatán's north coast. Further waves of settlers arrived after the abolition of slavery in 1830, when white Cayman Islanders and freed slaves arrived first on Utila, later spreading to Roatán and Guanaja.

Today, the islands retain their **cultural separation** from the mainland, although the presence of Spanish-speaking Hondurans and North American and European expats, who are settling in growing numbers, means the reshaping of the culture continues. A distinctive form of Creole English is still spoken on the streets of Utila and Guanaja, but Spanish has taken over as the dominant language in Roatán. The huge growth in visitors since the early 1990s – a trend that shows no signs of abating – has been controversial, as the islanders' income, which traditionally came from fishing or working on cargo ships or oil rigs, now relies heavily on tourism. Concern is also growing about the environmental impact of tourism.

GETTING TO THE BAY ISLANDS

All three islands – Utila, Roatán and Guanaja – are served by several daily flights from the mainland. Utila and Roatán have boat connections with La Ceiba, and Guanaja is linked with Trujillo by boat. Utila and Roatán are connected by one daily catamaran, which leaves Utila in the morning and returns from Roatán in the afternoon.

By air

Flying to the islands is straightforward; ticket prices are cheap and standardized by the Honduran government. Timetables, however, change frequently. Currently, Isleña/TACA fly to Roatán (1 daily; 30min; US$55); SOSA fly to Guanaja (1 daily; 30min; US$73), Roatán (3 daily; 30min; US$48) and Utila (2 daily; 15min; US$56).

You can buy your tickets on the spot at the airport, though you should book ahead in the peak holiday seasons (Christmas, Easter and August). All internal flights from San Pedro Sula (1hr) and Tegucigalpa (1hr) stop over briefly in La Ceiba. Bear in mind that schedules change at short notice and flights are sometimes cancelled altogether. Isleña/TACA, and SOSA have offices in La Ceiba (see p.379).

There are also several direct international flights serving Roatán: Continental have direct flights from Houston daily and Delta have one direct flight per week from Atlanta.

By boat

Most travellers use the excellent scheduled ferry services, leaving La Ceiba daily for Utila on the *Utila Princess* (2 daily at 9.30am & 4pm, return at 6.20am & 2pm; 1hr 30min; one way US$27) and for Roatán on the MV *Galaxy II* (2 daily at 9.30am & 4.00pm, return at 6.20am & 2pm; 1hr 30min; one way US$27–32). For the latest ferry information call the offices in Roatán (☎2445 1795) or Utila (☎2425 3390/3190 or 2440 7877). There are also three boats weekly from Trujillo to Guanaja (see p.400). Captain Vern's catamaran service (3–4hr; US$55; ☎3346 2600 or 9910 8040, ⓔvfine@hotmail.com) travels daily between Utila and Roatán, leaving Utila at 6.30am from behind Bush's supermarket, returning at 1pm. Call to book at least a day in advance.

UTILA

The smallest of the three main Bay Islands, **UTILA** is also the cheapest and one of the best places in the world to learn to dive (and even if you don't want to don tanks, the superb waters around the island offer great swimming and snorkelling possibilities), factors which combine to make it one of Central America's best destinations for budget travellers.

What to see and do

The island's principal **main road**, a twenty-minute walk end to end, runs along the seafront from **The Point** in the east to **Sandy Bay** in the west. **Utila Town** (also known as East Harbour) is the island's only settlement and home to the majority of its two thousand-strong population.

Diving

Most visitors come to Utila specifically for the **diving**, attracted by the low prices, clear water and abundant marine life. Even in winter, the water is generally calm and common sightings include nurse and hammerhead sharks, turtles, parrotfish, stingrays, porcupine fish and an increasing number of dolphins. **Whale sharks** also continue to be a major attraction – the island is one of the few places in the world where they frequently pass close to shore.

On the north coast of the island, **Blackish Point** and **Duppy Waters** are both good sites; on the south coast the best spot is **Airport Caves**. The schools (see box, p.393) will be happy to spend time talking to you about the merits of the various sites.

It's worth spending a morning walking around checking out all the schools. You want to feel comfortable with your decision, as diving can be dangerous – it is imperative that you get along with your instructor (see box opposite). The dozen or so dive shops all charge around US$260–290 for a three- to five-day

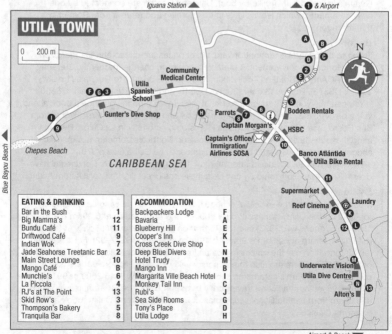

UTILA TOWN

0   200 m

Iguana Station ▲   ▲ ❶ & Airport

N

Community Medical Center

Utila Spanish School

Gunter's Dive Shop

Chepes Beach

Blue Bayou Beach ◄

CARIBBEAN SEA

Parrots

Captain Morgan's

Bodden Rentals

Captain's Office/ Immigration/ Airlines SOSA

HSBC

Banco Atlántida
Utila Bike Rental

Supermarket

Reef Cinema

Laundry

Underwater Vision
Utila Dive Centre

Alton's

Airport & Beach ▼

EATING & DRINKING	
Bar in the Bush	1
Big Mamma's	12
Bundu Café	11
Driftwood Café	9
Indian Wok	7
Jade Seahorse Treetanic Bar	2
Main Street Lounge	10
Mango Café	B
Munchie's	6
La Piccola	4
RJ's at The Point	13
Skid Row's	3
Thompson's Bakery	5
Tranquila Bar	8

ACCOMMODATION	
Backpackers Lodge	F
Bavaria	A
Blueberry Hill	E
Cooper's Inn	K
Cross Creek Dive Shop	L
Deep Blue Divers	N
Hotel Trudy	M
Mango Inn	B
Margarita Ville Beach Hotel	I
Monkey Tail Inn	C
Rubi's	J
Sea Side Rooms	G
Tony's Place	D
Utila Lodge	H

DIVING SAFETY IN THE BAY ISLANDS

Diving safety is an issue that is taken seriously by all professional dive schools in the Bay Islands. Make sure that you understand – and get along with – your instructors. Before signing up, check that classes have no more than six people, that the equipment is well maintained and that all boats have working oxygen and a first-aid kit. Anyone with asthma or ear problems should not be allowed to dive. Be aware that schools advertising discount rates may be cutting corners.

PADI course; Advanced and Divemaster courses are also on offer, as are fun dives, from US$25.

Swimming and snorkelling

The best **swimming** near town is at the **Blue Bayou**, a twenty-minute walk west of the centre. You can also snorkel further out; there's a US$1.50 charge to use the area, which also boasts a small sandy beach. Closer to town, where the road ends beyond *Driftwood*, **Chepes Beach** offers a narrow strip of sand, shallow water and a bar. East of town, **Bando Beach** (or **Airport Beach**) offers good snorkelling just offshore, as does the little reef beyond the **lighthouse**. The path from the end of the airstrip up the east coast of the island leads to a couple of small coves – the second is good for swimming and sunbathing.

Utila Iguana Station

The **Utila Iguana Station** (Mon, Wed & Fri 2–5pm; L40; ☎2425 3946, ⊛www .utila-iguana.de), signposted from the road five minutes west of the dock, is a breeding centre for the endangered Utila spiny-tailed iguana, found only on the island and facing extinction. Guided tours explain the life cycle of the species. It's worth a visit, especially if you need a break from all the diving.

Utila Cayes

The **Utila Cayes** – eleven tiny outcrops strung along the southwestern edge of the island – were designated a wildlife refuge in 1992. **Suc Suc** (or **Jewel**) **Caye** and **Pigeon Caye**, connected by a narrow causeway, are both inhabited, and the pace of life is even slower than on Utila. Small *lanchas* regularly shuttle between Suc Suc and Utila (US$8), or can be rented to take you across for a day's snorkelling (US$20). Ask at the *Bundu Café* (see p.393) or call Steve Christiensen (☎2425 3988).

Water Caye, a blissful stretch of white sand, coconut palms and a small coral reef, is even more idyllic. Camping is allowed and a caretaker turns up every day to collect the US$2 fee. To stay you'll need a tent, food, equipment for a fire and water. Captain Hal charges US$43 for return trips to Water Cay (ask for him at Parrots; see box, p.393). Water Caye is also the venue for the SunJam festival (see p.394).

Arrival and information

By air The airport is 3km north of Utila Town at the end of the island's second main road, Cola de Mico Road, which heads inland from the dock. Taxis wait for arriving flights.
By boat All boats dock in the centre of Utila Town.
Tourist information Captain Morgan's dive shop is often used as an unofficial information point.

Getting around

Quad bikes and scooters Motorized transport can be rented at Bodden (☎2425 3245, ⊛www .boddenrentals.com), by the dock. Golf cart US$40–60/day, scooters US$35, bicycles US$5.
Bikes Utila Bike Rental (Sun–Fri 8am–6pm) offers bikes for L25/hr, L100/day.

Accommodation

Utila has more than enough affordable lodgings. With the exception of Semana Santa and parts of the high season, there's always somewhere available. Most of the dive schools (see box opposite) have affiliated lodgings, and enrolling in a course invariably gets you a few free or discounted nights' accommodation. There are no designated places to camp except on the cayes. Electricity is very expensive on the island so opting out of a/c will make things cheaper.

East of the dock

Cooper's Inn 5min from the dock ☎ 2425 3184. One of the best budget places on the island, with orderly rooms (all with fans), some with private bathroom. US$12

Cross Creek Dive Shop See box opposite. The on-site accommodation is also available to non-divers. The cabañas, privates and dorms are all very nice and there's a clean, spacious kitchen and lounge area. Dorms US$6, doubles US$10, cabañas US$30

Deep Blue Divers See box opposite. The dorms are clean and airy, with typical hostel-style murals. Four private rooms share two bathrooms. Dorms US$8, doubles US$10

Hotel Trudy South end of the main road ☎ 2425 3103, ⓦ underwatervision.net Owned by Underwater Vision dive shop, this place has nine smart four-bed dorms, eight private rooms and seven suites. The bar area is one of Utila's social hubs. Dorms US$8, doubles US$35 (US$25 if diving)

Rubi's Next door to the Reef cinema ☎ 2425 3240, ⓦ www.rubisinn.com. This is one of the most popular mid-range places on the island. There's a communal kitchen, a pleasant beach and lots of trees dotted around the grounds. Rooms 6 and 12 have ocean views. US$25

Cola de Mico Road

Bavaria Up on the hill, just past the *Mango Inn* ☎ 2425 3809, ⓔ petrawhitefield3@hotmail.com. A nice wooden porch runs around the outside of the building and all but one of the rooms have a cold-water bathroom (L50 extra for hot water). Recommended. L350

Blueberry Hill On the left side of the road, right before the *Jade Seahorse* ☎ 2425 2199. Locally owned, no-frills hotel renting out rooms and apartments. The family who own it are usually at church on Saturdays, so it can be difficult to get a room then. L300

Mango Inn 5min from the dock ☎ 2425 3335, ⓦ www.mango-inn.com. A beautiful, well-run place, timber-built and set in shady gardens. The range of rooms stretches from thatched, a/c bungalows to pleasant dorms (only available to divers from Utila Dive Centre, who get three nights free; see box opposite). Doubles US$50, cabins US$85

Utila Lodge 3min from the dock ⓦ www.utilalodge.com. How often do you get to stay at a joint with its own helipad? Here's your chance. But it's the beautifully rustic rooms with private balconies and big, hot-water bathrooms that are worth splashing out on, not to mention the hot tub and bar lounge with billiards table. US$58

Monkey Tail Inn Opposite Gunter's Dive Shop ☎ 2425 2781. Owned and run by the affable Tonya, these twelve rooms share two bathrooms and a kitchen. The small grocery shop on site which functions as a reception is open Mon–Sat 7am–noon & 2–7pm. L200

Tony's Place Opposite *Mango Inn* ☎ 425 3376. The eight rooms here feel a little barren but are incredibly cheap, and the two shared bathrooms and kitchen are clean. L200

West of the dock

Backpackers Lodge Down an alley opposite Gunter's Dive Shop ☎ 2425 3350. Ten passable rooms (eight private rooms and two dorms) with shared bathrooms. Enquire at Gunter's Dive Shop. Dorms L90, doubles L190

Margarita Ville Beach Hotel Opposite *Driftwood* ☎ 2425 3366, ⓔ margaritavillehotel@yahoo.com. Very pleasant, big rooms, a wide terrace all around the house and hot water throughout. Recommended. US$20

Sea Side Rooms 8min from the dock, opposite Gunter's Dive Shop ☎ 2425 3150, ⓔ hotelseaside@yahoo.com. The best budget accommodation on the island: the shared rooms fit three people, each with a spotlessly clean bathroom. There's a communal kitchen and a nice balcony upstairs, where you can take in the Caribbean sunsets. US$13

Utila Cayes

Lone Star Hotel Jewel Caye ☎ 9925 1093. Four nicely-kept rooms with hot-water bathrooms. L350

Eating

Lobster and fish are excellent on the islands (though enquire as to reef-friendliness and sustainability), and then there's the usual rice, beans, chicken, and US and European fare. Prices are higher than on the mainland: main courses

DIVE SCHOOLS IN UTILA

Open-water courses cost around US$270; prices are supposed to be fixed but in reality some schools charge more and some less. The price normally includes accommodation for at least part of the course, and discounted accommodation afterwards.

Alton's 2min west of the airstrip ☎2425 3704, ⓦ www.altonsdiveshop.com. Accommodation on site (discounted following course), and use of kitchen. They have a conch nursery and a stringent ecological policy.

Bay Islands College of Diving 5min west of the dock ☎2425 3291, ⓦ www.dive -utila.com. Training pool on site for confined dives.

Captain Morgan's On the corner opposite the dock ☎2425 3349, ⓦ www.diving utila.com. Free accommodation at *Hotel Kayla* on Jewel Caye.

Cross Creek 5min east of the dock ☎2425 3397, ⓦ www.crosscreekutila.com. Pleasant accommodation set back from the road.

Deep Blue Divers 10min west of the dock ☎2425 3511, ⓦ www.deepbluedivers utila.com. Accommodation on site with use of kitchen.

Gunter's 8min west of the dock ☎2425 3350, ⓦ www.ecomarineutila.com. A small, relaxed operation that offers a "lazy boat" for late risers. Their dock is a favourite haunt of seahorses.

Paradise Behind Henderson's Market, 100m west of the dock ☎2425 3148, ⓦ www.todomundo.com/paradisedivers. Often undercuts the other shops' prices.

Parrots 2min west of the dock ☎2425 3772, ⓦ www.diveparrotsutila.com. Free accommodation and a dynamic environment.

Underwater Vision ☎2425 3103, ⓦ www.underwatervision.net. Good accommodation at *Hotel Trudy*.

Utila Dive Centre Near the end of the road west of the dock, close to the bridge ☎2425 3326, ⓦ www.utiladivecentre.com. Perhaps the best reputation for quality and safety, and courses are a bit pricier as a result. Free dorm accommodation at *Mango Inn*.

start at around US$4, and beers cost at least L25. For eating on the cheap, head for the evening stalls on the road by the dock, which do a thriving trade in *baleadas*. Many restaurants stop serving at around 9.30pm.

East of the dock

Big Mamma's 5min from the dock. Clean, cheap and popular with the nearby dive shops, with some dishes on display at the counter. Slice of pizza L25, mains from L110.

Bundu Café 2min from the dock. This place has a barn-like quality, with wooden "windows" propped open all round. The two sofas at the book exchange are great on rainy afternoons. Try the French toast stuffed with apple and cinnamon (L80); lunches and dinners will set you back L65–115. Open till 10pm.

Main Street Lounge Above *El Casino*. Located in what feels like an old wooden American house, with a porch that's a great spot to keep an eye on comings and goings. Tuna fillet, pork chop or chicken breast with choice of sauce served with generous sides L115. Beer from L30. Sporadic opening hours.

RJ's at The Point Beside the bridge. You can have anything you want – snapper, marlin, wahoo, king fish, steak, burgers – as long as it's grilled. Get there early as it fills up quickly. Mains from US$5. Wed, Fri & Sun 5.30–10pm.

Cola de Mico Road

Thompson's Bakery 3min from the dock. A great place for breakfast – try the delicious johnnycakes filled with cheese, ham and egg (US$2), though they won't do your buoyancy any favours. Open from 6am.

West of the dock

Driftwood Café A 10–15min walk west of the dock, right at the end of the path. The food here is excellent, and they have one of the most peaceful jetties on the island. The baja fish tacos (L150) are, frankly, addictive. Cheeseburger and fries L140, St Louis bbq ribs L265. Kitchen open until 9pm, bar until 10pm. Closed Mon.

Indian Wok 3min from the dock. They vow not to use fish from the reef, which means their sushi on Tuesdays is guilt-free as well as tasty (ten pieces

SUNJAM FESTIVAL

The **SunJam Festival** (Ⓦ www
.sunjamutila.com), held every year
in the first week of August, is a two-
day rave, with European house and
techno DJs. Founded by the owner
of Parrots Dive Shop, it takes place
on Water Caye, the largest and most
picturesque of the tiny cayes to the
southwest of the island. Information
is released usually just a few weeks
before it's due to take place, so if
you're going to be in the area, keep
your ear to the ground.

L120). *Rajma* (kidney bean curry) L125, red Thai
chicken L145. Mon, Tues & Sun from 6pm.
Munchies 1min from the dock. In an 1864 house
with an iguana garden out back, and a nice porch.
Burgers and *quesadillas* from L50, meat or fish
dishes from L110.
La Piccola 1min from the dock. The island's only
Italian restaurant serves excellent bruschetta
(L65) and mains such as gorgonzola and walnut
ravioli (L130) or the excellent 8oz *filet mignon*
with mushroom sauce (L200). One of the latest-opening
kitchens on the island.

Drinking and nightlife

Despite its tiny population, Utila is a hedonistic
party island.
Bar in the Bush Along the Cola de Mico Rd towards
the new airport. This huge open-air bar is the only
late-night venue on the island, open until 3am, and
often with live DJs. Currently Wed & Fri only.

🏃 **Jade Seahorse Treetanic Bar** A short
walk up the Cola de Mico Road. The most
eccentric place on the island. Run by an American
artist, this hotel/restaurant/bar is a maze of colour
and reflection that really comes alive by night. Open
until around 1am.
Mango Café At the *Mango Inn*. A popular spot for
cheap beer and a quiet drink. Pizzas from L78,
spaghetti dishes L75–220.
Skid Row's Next door but one to *Sea Side Rooms*.
Though it feels a little like somewhere they repair
boat parts, this is a small, friendly place full of expat
seadogs boozing throughout the day. Home-made
beef jerky (L100), good pizza (from L105) and the
cheapest beers on the island.
Tranquila Bar 2min east of the dock. This low-lit
bar over the water is a lively venue, packed with
locals and tourists most nights.

Directory

Airlines Tickets for SOSA can be purchased in the
captain's office by the dock.
Books The *Bundu Café* has a large book exchange
with titles in a variety of languages.
Cinema Reef Cinema just before Bush supermarket
has one screening daily at 7.30pm (L45).
Exchange Banco Atlántida and HSBC, both close to
the dock, have ATMs.
Health The Community Medical Center is 2min
west of the dock (Mon–Fri 10.30am–3.30pm).
Immigration At the captain's office (Mon–Fri
9am–noon & 2–4.30pm).
Internet Annie's Internet at the dock is L30/hour,
while Caye Caulker Cyber Café east of the dock is
L45/hour.
Language School Utila Spanish School
(Ⓔ utilaspanish@ymail.com) charges US$9/hr,
twenty hours over one week for US$100, or ten
hours for US$60.
Laundry Mrs Maralya's laundry, opposite *Rubi's*,
is closed on Sat. There is also a lady who does
laundry in a house behind *Sea Side Rooms*.
Post office At the main dock (Mon–Fri 8am–4pm,
Sat 8am–noon).
Telephones Some of the internet cafés, including
Caye Caulker Cyber Café, offer web calls at good
rates. Avoid the Hondutel office as the rates are
extortionate.

ROATÁN

Some 50km from La Ceiba, **ROATÁN**
is the largest of the Bay Islands, a
curving ridged hump almost 50km
long and 5km across at its widest point.
Unfortunately, Roatán can be a hard
place to enjoy if you're on a budget
– you should expect your spending
to go way above average. The island's
accommodation mostly comes in the
form of all-inclusive luxury resort
packages, although there are a few
good deals to be found in **West End**.
Like Utila, Roatán is a superb **diving**
destination, and also offers some great
hiking, as well as the chance to do
nothing except laze on a beach. **Coxen
Hole** is the island's commercial centre.
Note that credit-card transactions are
subject to a 16 percent fee in all establishments below.

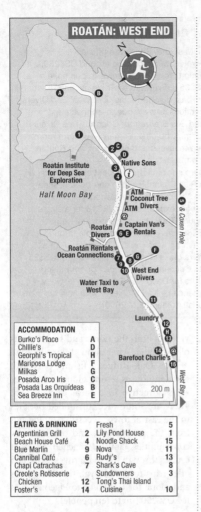

Roatán Institute
for Deep Sea
Exploration

Native Sons

Half Moon Bay

ATM
Coconut Tree
Divers
ATM
@
Roatán   Captain Van's
Divers   Rentals

Roatán Rentals
Ocean Connections

West End
Divers

Water Taxi to
West Bay

Laundry

Barefoot Charlie's

& Coxen Hole

West Bay

0   200 m

ACCOMMODATION

Burke's Place	A
Chillie's	D
Georphi's Tropical	H
Mariposa Lodge	F
Milkas	G
Posada Arco Iris	C
Posada Las Orquídeas	B
Sea Breeze Inn	E

EATING & DRINKING

Argentinian Grill	2	Fresh	5
Beach House Café	4	Lily Pond House	1
Blue Marlin	9	Noodle Shack	15
Cannibal Café	6	Nova	11
Chapi Catrachas	7	Rudy's	13
Creole's Rotisserie		Shark's Cave	8
Chicken	12	Sundowners	3
Foster's	14	Tong's Thai Island	
		Cuisine	10

What to see and do

Roatán's abundance of great diving and superb beaches often takes away from the charm of the island's smaller towns and villages, which are worth exploring to get a sense of what it would have been like before the tourists arrived.

Coxen Hole

Coxen Hole (also known as Roatán Town) is uninteresting and run down; most visitors come here only to change money or shop. All of the town's practical facilities and most of its shops are on **Main Street**, near where the buses stop.

Sandy Bay

Midway between Coxen Hole and West End, **Sandy Bay** is an unassuming community with a number of attractions. The **Institute for Marine Sciences** (Mon–Fri 7am–5pm, Sat & Sun 8am–5pm; L20; ☎2445 3049/3009), based at *Antony's Key Resort*, has exhibitions on the marine life and geology of the islands and a museum with useful information on local history and archeology. There are also **bottle-nosed dolphin shows** (Fri–Sun 10.30am; free), or you can enjoy "encounters" in waist-deep water (US$62 for 30min). Across the road, several short nature trails weave through the jungle at the **Carambola Botanical Gardens** (daily 8am–5pm; US$8; ⓦwww.carambolagardens.com), a riot of beautiful flowers, lush ferns and tropical trees. A 30-minute hike to the summit of Carambola Mountain gives a view of the coral in the ocean beyond.

West End

With its calm waters and incredible sandy beaches, **West End**, 14km from Coxen Hole, makes the most of its ideal setting at the southwest corner of the island. From the beautifully sheltered **Half Moon Bay** at the northern end of town, a sandy track runs a kilometre or so along the water's edge, past guesthouses, bars and restaurants geared towards independent travellers of all budgets. The year-round community of sun-worshippers and dive shops gives the village a laidback charm during the day and a vibrant, party feel after dark.

West Bay

Some 2km southwest of West End, towards the extreme western tip of Roatán, is the stunning white-sand beach of **West Bay**, fringed by coconut

WATERSPORTS AROUND WEST END

Dive courses for all levels are available in West End. Prices are officially standardized, with a four-day PADI Open-water course costing around US$280, with some schools including basic accommodation. You will also have to purchase a manual for US$35. Fun dives are set at US$35 a dive, with ten-dive packages set at around US$250. Recommended West End-based schools include: West End Divers (Ⓦwww.westenddivers.info); Ocean Connections (Ⓦwww.ocean-connections.com), who organize accommodation at *Milkas* and *Sea Breeze Inn*; Coconut Tree Divers (Ⓣ2445 4081, Ⓦwww.coconuttreedivers.com), who offer a smart new dorm room for US$5; Native Sons (Ⓣ2445 4003, Ⓦwww.nativesonsroatan.com); and Roatán Divers (Ⓣ8836 8414, Ⓦwww.roatandiver.com).

The reef lying just offshore provides superb snorkelling, the best spots being at the mouth of Half Moon Bay and at the Blue Channel, which can be accessed from the beach 100m south of *Foster's* bar. You can also rent sea kayaks from the *Sea Breeze Inn*, close to the entrance road; expect to pay US$18 for a single kayak and US$21 for a double, for eight hours. They also offer snorkelling gear (US$5 for half a day) and waterskiing (US$85/hr). Alfredo (contactable through *Sea Breeze Inn* or on Ⓣ9866 4582) offers fishing trips for US$70 per hour for a minimum of two hours. Captain Danillo offers glass-bottomed-boat tours (US$25 per person), leaving from the jetty opposite Coconut Tree Divers. For something completely different, visit the Roatán Institute for Deep Sea Exploration (Ⓦwww.stanleysubmarines.com). It's run by an American – Karl Stanley – who built his own submarine, in which he takes intrepid tourists to depths of 2000ft.

palms and washed by crystal-clear waters. There's decent snorkelling at the southern end of the beach, though the once-pristine reef has suffered in recent years from increasing river run-off and the close attentions of unsupervised day-trippers.

From West End, it's a pleasant 45-minute stroll south along the beach and over a few rock outcrops; alternatively you can take one of the small *lanchas* that leave regularly from the jetty near West End Divers (US$3/50L each way; three person minimum).

French Harbour

Leaving Coxen Hole, the paved road runs northeast past the small secluded cove of Brick Bay to **French Harbour**, a busy fishing port and the island's second largest town. Less run down than Coxen Hole, it's a lively and interesting place to spend the day.

Oak Ridge

From French Harbour the road cuts inland along a central ridge to give superb views of both the north and south coasts of the island. After about 14km the road reaches **Oak Ridge**, a fishing port with wooden houses strung along its harbour – it's attractive in a bleak sort of way. There are some nice, unspoiled beaches to the east of town, accessible by *lanchas* from the main dock, and other nearby communities can be reached by boat cruises through the mangroves. Boatmen offer trips to Port Royal, the mangroves and Morat for US$50 or to Pigeon Cayes for US$200 (up to ten people).

Punta Gorda

About 5km from Oak Ridge on the northern coast of the island is the village of **Punta Gorda**, the oldest Garífuna community in Honduras. The best time to visit is for the anniversary of the founding of the settlement on April 12, when Garífuna from all over the country attend the celebrations. At other times it's a quiet and slightly dilapidated little port with no buildings of note, though the black, white and yellow of the Garífuna flags brighten things up.

Port Royal

The road ends at the village of **Port Royal**, on the southern edge of the island, where the faint remains of a fort built by the English can be seen on a caye offshore. The village lies in the **Port Royal Park and Wildlife Reserve**, the largest refuge on the island, set up in 1978 in an attempt to protect endangered species such as the yellow-naped parrot.

The eastern tip of Roatán is made up of mangrove swamps, with a small island, **Morat**, just offshore. Beyond is **Barbareta Caye**, which has retained much of its virgin forest cover.

Arrival and information

By air Regular domestic and international flights land at Roatán's only international airport, on the road to French Harbour, 3km east of Coxen Hole – the main town on the south side of the island. There are information and hotel reservation desks, car rental agencies (Avis ☎2445 0122) and a bank at the airport. A *colectivo* taxi from the airport to Coxen Hole should cost L20, or around L60 to West End.

By boat Roatán's harbour, known as Brick Bay, sits directly between the towns of Coxen Hole and French Harbour. Captain Vern, who offers catamaran transport between Utila and Roatán, can usually drop you off at West End, though in rougher seas he will dock at Flying Fish harbour in Coxen Hole.

Tourist information There is a small information booth opposite *Beach House Café* in West End.

Getting around

Bikes and cars Captain Van's (daily 9am–4pm; ☎2445 4076, ✉info@captainvans.com), at the southern end of Half Moon Bay, rents out bicycles (US$9/day) and mopeds (US$24–39/day), with taxes charged on top. Opposite, you can rent cars (US$50–87/day) and scooters (US$30/day) from Roatán Rentals.

Minibuses There are two minibus routes covering all of the island's main settlements. Bus #1 (every 30min) goes from Coxen Hole to French Harbour, stopping in Oak Ridge; the last bus from Oak Ridge leaves between 4.30pm and 6pm. Buses from Oak Ridge pass through Punta Gorda. Bus #2 (every 15min) goes from Coxen Hole to Sandy Bay, stopping in West End. The price depends on how far you're going, and journey times depend largely on the driver. As a guide, Oak Ridge to Coxen Hole costs L44, Coxen Hole to West End L30.

Taxis It's never hard to find a taxi in Roatán, though as with everything else, it is often a lot more expensive than on the mainland. Be sure to establish that the ride is on a *colectivo* basis. A *colectivo* taxi from West End to Sandy Bay should be 20L, the same amount from Sandy Bay to Coxen Hole and from Coxen Hole to the airport. From Coxen Hole to French Harbour ought to be 40L, from there to the Oak Ridge *punta* 50L, or to Oak Ridge proper 60–70L. A regular water-taxi runs from West End to West Bay, leaving from the jetty near West End Divers (US$3 each way; three people minimum).

Accommodation

Discounts are available during low season (April–July & Sept to mid-Dec), particularly for longer stays.

West End

Burkes's Place At the northern end of the main beach road ☎2445 4146. One of West End's best deals, *Burke's* has three apartments on offer, with hot water, for US$25 per day.

Chillies Half Moon Bay ☎445 4062, ✪www .nativesonsroatan.com/chillies A well setup backpackers' choice. There's a choice of rooms with shared bath or private cabins, and a communal kitchen. Book in advance. The dorm beds are discounted for divers. Dorm beds US$10, doubles US$20

Georphi's Tropical Towards the southern end of the main beach road ☎2445 4205, ✪www .georphi.com. One of the better deals on the island, this is a sort of rustic resort, with dorm, cabaña and chalet lodgings. Dorms US$10, shared cabaña US$25, chalet US$100

Mariposa Lodge On a side street halfway down the main beach road ☎2445 4460, ✪www .mariposa-lodge.com. A good-value, quiet place with two apartments – complete with sundecks,

TREAT YOURSELF

Posada Arco Iris Half Moon Bay ☎2445 4264, ✪www .roatanposada.com. Set in attractive gardens just off the beach, with excellent, imaginatively furnished and spacious rooms, studios and tastefully decorated apartments, all with fridge and hammocks, and some with a/c. Doubles US$46, apartments US$60 kitchen and cable TV – and a small cabin with three private rooms, all sharing a large kitchen and bathroom. Shared facilities US$26, private bathroom and kitchen US$40

Milkas Set back off the main beach road ☎ 2445 4241 or 9781 3733. Very basic but kept impeccably clean, this is a reliable budget option. Choose between three-bed dorms or newer, more spacious private rooms. Dorms US$10, doubles US$25

Posada Las Orquídeas At the northern end of the main beach road ☎ 2445 4387/4386, ⓦ www .posadalasorquideas.com. With its secluded location there's a serene feel to this rather upmarket hotel. Rooms have ocean views, with room 14 the pick of the bunch. Doubles US$42, apartments US$60

Sea Breeze Inn Just south of Half Moon Bay, behind the *Cannibal Café* ☎ 2445 4026, ⓦ www .seabreezeroatan.com. A mix of (rather small) rooms, studios and apartments. The studios come with a large kitchen and represent the best value. Doubles US$25, studios US$45

Coxen Hole

Unless you've got an early ferry or flight, it's unlikely you'll have to stay in town.

Hotel Cay View About 10min north from the dock, on the main street further along from the HSBC ☎ 2445 0269. Fairly decent rooms with TV and hot showers. US$25

Eating

There's a more than adequate range of places to eat in West End, with fish and seafood featuring heavily on many menus – take advice from the dive shops as to the most reef-friendly choices. Prices are on the high side. In most cases 10 percent service tax and 12 percent government sales tax will be added to your bill.

West End

Argentinian Grill Half Moon Bay. Argentinian-style starters include grilled onions (L105) and the excellent chorizo with chimichurri L115. Catch of the day (such as wahoo steak) with sides L295.

Beach House Café Half Moon Bay. Open for breakfast and lunch, you can't get much better than one of their big mugs of coffee (L20) on the veranda in the morning. French toast L100, lunch such as blackened wahoo with pineapple salsa L200.

Cannibal Café Just south of Half Moon Bay, in front of the *Sea Breeze Inn*. This place serves typical Mexican fare at very reasonable prices. They host a "burritos challenge": eat three large burritos and get them for free. Mains from L95.

Chapi Catrachas A roadside shack with a few stools serving cheap Honduran food. Breakfast L70, chicken with *tajadas* L65, lunch and dinner L70–90.

Creole's Rotisserie Chicken Towards the southern end of the main beach road. If you're looking for value for money, this is the place. The *quesadillas* are particularly good. Half-chicken meal with two sides costs L140, while sides (potato salad, coleslaw, yellow rice, coconut rice and beans) all cost L40.

Fresh At Alba Plaza, around twenty minutes' walk from West End in Gibson Bight, just before Sandy Bay. This place sells excellent coffee and home-made cakes and pastries. Mon–Sat 7am–2pm.

Lily Pond House North section of Half Moon Bay. A sweet, almost romantic little restaurant in a secluded position with charming management. Starters from L120, "fisherman plate" with lobster, shrimp and fish L500, pork chops L200, fresh catch of the day with island spices L240.

Noodle Shack South end of the beach road. Sushi rolls L95–162, veggie noodle bowl L114, with shrimp, chicken or tofu L133–171, with a choice of sauces (sesame and ginger, Thai peanut) and noodles (from udon to rice stick). Tues–Sat noon–8pm.

Rudy's Towards the southern end of the main beach road. Legendary breakfasts, from US$3.65 to US$4/L70–80 for Rudy's signature banana pancakes. Sun–Fri 6am–5pm.

Shark's Cave Just south of Half Moon Bay. The pizzas are hardly authentic but they're slathered in cheese and tasty, and represent good value. Ham and cheese baguette 80L, pizza slices 40–60L, beer 30L.

Drinking and nightlife

Drinking can drain your pocket fast, so seek out half-price happy hour deals, some of which last until 10pm.

TREAT YOURSELF

Tong's Thai Island Cuisine Just south of Half Moon Bay. The truly hot *phat bai ka prao* with chicken and Thai basil is superb at L300; *pad Thai* costs L280 with chicken or L320 with beef, or go for green chicken curry at L300. Take a table out on the sliver of a jetty – with these flavours and the candlelight playing on the water you won't regret the expense.

West End

Blue Marlin Also a restaurant (try their meatballs), but very popular as a drinking spot, sometimes serving as the first stop after *Sundowners* closes and the crowds start heading down the beach. L130, chicken fried rice L190. Mon–Thurs noon–midnight, Fri & Sat noon–2am.

Foster's At the second of the big piers to the south of town. A West End institution. Friday nights get rowdy, when *Foster's* hosts a weekly reggae jump-up.

Nova 5min south of Half Moon Bay. With fluorescent strings dangling from the ceiling and swinging chairs around the bar, this atmospheric place sees DJs play electro breakbeat and drum'n'bass, but also Latin and 80s. Mon–Thurs until midnight, Fri & Sat until 2am.

Sundowners Half Moon Bay. This tiny bar often kicks the night off with happy hour from 4–7pm. Open until around 10pm.

Directory

Exchange In Coxen Hole, Banco Atlántida and the HSBC near the small square have ATMs. In West End there is an ATM outside *Shark's Cave* and another at the Coconut Tree Minisuper, right by the mini roundabout triangle.

Immigration The *migración* is near the small square on Main Street in Coxen Hole, in a green building.

Internet Barefoot Charlie's towards the southern end of West End charges L2/min and has a book exchange (daily 9am–3pm). In Half Moon Bay, Paradise Computers charge L2/min for internet. In Coxen Hole, Internet Cyber Planet down the side of the HSBC charge L40/hr.

Laundry Bamboo Hut Laundry, at the southern end of West End (Mon–Sat 8am–4pm), will wash and dry for 15L per pound.

Post office In a blue building near the *migración* and the small square on Main Street in Coxen Hole (Mon–Fri 8am–4pm).

Supermarket HB Warren, near the small square in Coxen Hole, is the largest supermarket on the island, plus there's a small and not too impressive general market just behind Main Street.

Telephones Paradise Computers in Half Moon Bay offer international calls (currently only to the US and Canada). In Coxen Hole, Internet Cyber Planet down the side of the HSBC charge L10–15/min to Europe, L1/min to the US and Canada.

GUANAJA

GUANAJA, some 25km long and only 4km wide at its largest point, is divided

into two unequal parts by a narrow canal – the only way to get between the two sections of the island is by water-taxi, which adds both to the atmosphere and to the cost of living. The island is very thinly populated – most of Guanaja's twelve thousand inhabitants live in **Bonacca** (also known as **Guanaja Town**), a crowded settlement on a small caye a few hundred metres offshore. It's here that you'll find the island's shops, as well as the bulk of the less unreasonably priced accommodation. The only other settlements of any substance are **Savannah Bight** (on the east coast) and **Mangrove Bight** (on the north coast). Note that sandflies and mosquitoes are endemic throughout the island, so arrive prepared to deal with them.

What to see and do

Wandering around Bonacca's warren of tight streets, walkways and canal bridges makes for an interesting half-hour or so – though government plans to eliminate the town's tiny waterways for new roads means the town may not be the Honduran Venice for much longer.

Virtually all the houses in town are built on stilts – vestiges of early settlement by Cayman islanders – with the main causeway running for about 500m east–west along the caye.

Though Guanaja's Caribbean pine forests were flattened by Hurricane Mitch in 1998, there's still some decent hiking to be found. A wonderful trail leads from Mangrove Bight up to **Michael Rock Peak**, the highest point in the Bay Islands (412m) and down to Sandy Bay on the south coast, affording stunning views of Guanaja, Bonacca and the surrounding reef. Fit walkers can do the trail in a day, or you can camp on the summit, provided you bring your own provisions.

Some of the island's finest white-sand beaches lie around the rocky headland of **Michael's Rock**, near the *Island House Resort* on the north coast, with good snorkelling close to the shore. **Diving** is excellent all around the main island, but particularly off the small cayes to the east, and at **Black Rocks**, off the northern tip of the main island, where there's an underwater coral canyon. The **Mestizo Dive Site** was opened in 2002 to mark the 500th anniversary of Christopher Columbus's visit, with sunken statues of the explorer and national hero Lempira on a reef surrounded by genuine Spanish colonial artefacts, including a cannon.

Arrival and information

By air The Guanaja airstrip is on the larger, northern section of the island, next to the canal. Aside from a couple of dirt tracks there are no roads, and the main form of transport is small *lanchas*. You can hire a water-taxi, though fares are high. If you have pre-booked a resort on the island you will be met at the airport.

By boat The *Guanaja Express* (see "Moving on", below) serves Bonacca and Mangrove Bight.
Tour operators To get to some of the underwater sites you'll have to contact one of the hotel-based dive schools: the *Island House Resort* (☏ 9991 0391) usually has the best rates, at around US$70 for two dives including equipment.

Accommodation

Miller Halfway along the main causeway, Bonacca ☏ 2453 4327. Housed in a slightly run down building, though the rooms are in reasonable condition; most have hot water and, for a little extra, a/c and cable TV. L1200
Rosario In a green building opposite the main causeway, Bonacca ☏ 2453 4240. Clean, well-ventilated rooms, all with hot-water bathrooms. A good option if *Miller* is full. L1100

Eating and drinking

Mexi-Treats Just past *Pirate's Den*, Bonacca. This Mexican restaurant is the best in town, serving up some surprisingly tasty dishes. Mains from L80.
Pirate's Den Towards the western end of the main causeway, Bonacca. Good for fresh seafood, daily lunch specials and Friday barbecues. Mains from L100.

Directory

Airlines In Bonacca, SOSA has an office opposite the bank and Isleña/TACA has an office at the main dock.
Exchange You can change dollars and get cash advances at Banco Atlántida, to the right of the dock in Bonacca.
Internet On the main causeway in Bonacca; access costs under L25/hr.

Moving on

By boat The *Guanaja Express* to Trujillo runs Mon, Wed & Fri to Trujillo (L800 each way). It leaves Mangrove Bight at 7am, Bonacca at 9am, and returns in the afternoon. Call Captain Roy on ☏ 9962 6163 or 9600 2235 for information.

Nicaragua

HIGHLIGHTS ✪

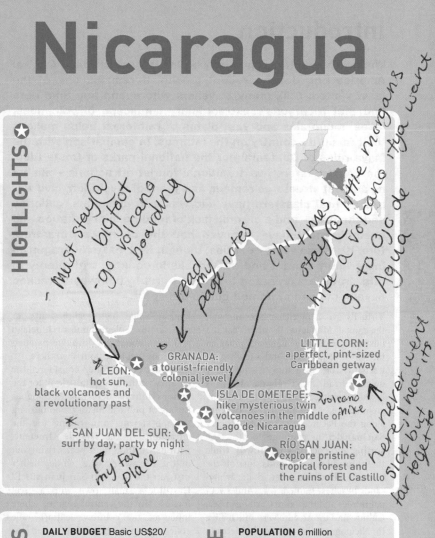

LEÓN: hot sun, black volcanoes and a revolutionary past

GRANADA: a tourist-friendly colonial jewel

SAN JUAN DEL SUR: surf by day, party by night

ISLA DE OMETEPE: hike mysterious twin volcanoes in the middle of Lago de Nicaragua

LITTLE CORN: a perfect, pint-sized Caribbean getway

RÍO SAN JUAN: explore pristine tropical forest and the ruins of El Castillo

ROUGH COSTS

DAILY BUDGET Basic US$20/ occasional treat US$50

DRINK Beer US$1, coffee US$0.50

FOOD *Comida corriente* US$3

HOSTEL/BUDGET HOTEL US$7/ US$16

TRAVEL Managua–Chinandega by bus (130km): 2hr, US$3

FACT FILE

POPULATION 6 million

AREA 130,000 sq km

LANGUAGES Spanish, plus Creole and indigenous languages on the Atlantic Coast

CURRENCY Nicaraguan córdoba (C$)

CAPITAL Managua (population: 1.8 million)

INTERNATIONAL PHONE CODE ☏505

TIME ZONE GMT -6hr

Introduction

Wedge-shaped Nicaragua may be the largest nation in Central America but, despite recent growth, it remains one of the least visited. Still, many travellers who spend any time here find that Nicaragua's extraordinary landscape of volcanoes, lakes, mountains and vast plains of rainforest helps make it their favourite country on the isthmus. In comparison with the Maya ruins of Guatemala or the national parks of Costa Rica, the country offers few traditional tourist attractions – almost no ancient structures remain, and years of revolution, civil war and natural disasters have laid waste to museums, galleries and theatres – and a chronic lack of funding, high inflation and unemployment have impoverished the country's infrastructure. It's these same qualities, though, that make Nicaragua an incorrigibly vibrant and individualistic country, with plenty to offer travellers prepared to brave its grubby highways, cracked pavements and crammed public transport.

Virtually every traveller passes through the capital, **Managua**, if only to catch a bus straight out – while the city has an intriguing atmosphere and a few sights, it's hard work as a tourist, and many quickly head for **Granada**, with its lakeside setting and wonderful colonial architecture. A smattering of **beaches** along the Pacific coast, notably cheery **San Juan del Sur**, continues to attract the **surfing** and backpacking crowds, while the beautiful **Corn Islands**, just off the coast of **Bluefields**, offer idyllic white-sand beaches framed by wind-swept palm trees and the azure Caribbean Sea. Culture and the arts are very much alive in Nicaragua; visit **Masaya**'s Mercado Nacional de Artesanía to find some fantastic-value high-quality crafts, or stay on the **Solentiname archipelago** and learn about the primitive painting traditions that have flourished there.

Buzzing **León** is often considered the country's cultural capital – look for the famous **murals** depicting Nicaragua's turbulent political history. Ecotourism, volcano-viewing and hiking are the attractions of the **Isla de Ometepe**, with its thrilling twin peaks rising out of the freshwater lake, while further east, up the lush Río San Juan sits **El Castillo**, a small town with a great fortress. In the central region, where much of the country's export-grade coffee is grown, the climate is refreshingly cool; hiking and birdwatching are

WHEN TO GO

Nicaragua has two distinct seasons, the dry summer (*verano*) and the wet winter (*invierno*). Summer (Dec–April) can be extremely hot and often uncomfortably dry. Fewer travellers come in the rainy season (May–Nov) – which alone could be a reason for choosing to put up with the daily downpour. On the Pacific coast, rain often falls in the afternoons from May to November, although the mornings are dry. The central mountain region has a cooler climate with sporadic rainfall all year, while the Atlantic coast is wet, hot and humid year-round, with September and October the height of the tropical storm season.

the main activities near the mountain town of **Matagalpa**.

Stepping off Nicaragua's beaten track is appealingly easy – the peaceful waters of the **Pearl Lagoon** and lush highlands of **Miraflor** reserve are fine spots for exploration, but really are just the tip of the iceberg. More than anything, the pleasures and rewards of travelling in Nicaragua come from interacting with its inhabitants – who tend to be engagingly witty and very hospitable. This is a country where a bus journey can turn into a conversational epic and a light meal into a rum-soaked carnival, a stroll round the street can be interrupted by a costumed giant and a marching band, and a short boat ride can seem like a trip into another world.

CHRONOLOGY

1000 AD Aztec migrate south after the fall of Teotihuacán (Mexico), following a prophecy that they would settle where they found a lake with two volcanoes rising from it – Isla de Ometepe.

1522 The Spanish arrive and name the region "Nicaragua", after the indigenous groups living there.

1524 Spanish establish the settlements of Granada and León.

1821 Nicaragua gains independence from Spain as part of the Central American Federation.

1838 Nicaragua becomes an independent nation (save the Atlantic coast, which is claimed as British territory).

1855 American adventurer William Walker takes control of the government.

1857 Walker is overthrown by joint efforts of Nicaragua, Costa Rica, Guatemala and the US. He is later executed in Honduras.

1857–93 "The Thirty Years": a period of relative prosperity. US companies come to dominate the Nicaraguan government.

1893 General José Zelaya seizes control, establishing a dictatorship.

1909 Civil war breaks out. Four hundred US marines land on the Caribbean coast. Zelaya resigns.

1912–25 US military bases are established.

403

1927 Augusto Sandino leads a guerrilla campaign in protest at the US military presence. US takes over Nicaraguan military and develops Nicaraguan National Guard.

1934 Under orders of National Guard commander General Anastasio Somoza, Sandino is assassinated.

1937 Somoza "elected" president, commencing forty-year dictatorship.

1956 Somoza is assassinated by Rigoberto López Pérez. One of Somoza's sons, Luís, becomes interim president, and another, Anastasio, head of the National Guard.

1961 Frente Sandinista Liberación Nacional (FSLN), or Sandinista National Liberation Front, is founded.

1967 Luis Somoza dies; his brother Anastasio becomes president.

1972 Massive earthquake flattens Managua, killing some 10,000.

1978 Opposition leader Pedro Chamorro is assassinated by National Guard; demonstrations and fighting spread across the country.

1979 Sandinistas gain control of the country, and Somoza is forced to flee. Revolution is officially won on July 19. Liberal Sandinistas are in control of government.

1981 Unhappy with Nicaragua's left-wing policies and communist ties, the US funds Contra troops in an anti-Sandinista campaign.

1984 FSLN's Daniel Ortega wins presidential election.

1988 FSLN and Contras sign a ceasefire.

1990 Violeta Chamorro defeats Daniel Ortega to become Latin America's first female president. US cuts off aid to Contras.

1996 Right-wing ex-lawyer Arnoldo Alemán, former mayor of Managua, becomes president.

1998 Hurricane Mitch devastates region.

2001 Alemán's vice president, Enrique Bolaños, is elected.

2002–03 Alemán is jailed on charges of embezzlement and money laundering.

2004–05 The World Bank and Russia clear much of the country's debts, as part of the Heavily Indebted Poor Countries Initiative.

2006 Former president Ortega wins the November elections and returns to power.

2009 Ortega announces he will run for president in late 2011, after the Supreme Court lifts the constitutional ban on back-to-back electoral terms.

2010 Periodic tensions over the disputed Río San Juan flare after Nicaraguan dredging of the river. Troops are mobilized but no shots fired; the UN ruling orders both Nicaragua and Costa Rica to keep their distance.

Basics

ARRIVAL

If arriving on an international flight, you'll land at **Augusto C. Sandino International Airport (MGA)** in Managua. As well as flights from neighbouring capitals such as San José and San Salvador (served mainly by COPA and TACA), Managua receives direct flights from major US hubs Atlanta, Miami and Houston through Spirit Airlines, Continental, American Airlines and Delta.

You can enter Nicaragua by land from Honduras and Costa Rica (see box below). International **buses** all pull into Managua, often via Granada and Rivas (if coming from the south); it's also possible to take local services to and from the border. There is a **water** crossing from the border at Los Chiles, Costa Rica (see box below), to San Carlos; from here it is a 10–12hr bus ride or 1hr plane ride on to Managua.

VISAS

Australian, British, Canadian, US and most EU nationals do not currently require **visas**. There is a US$10 **entry fee**, which you pay upon arrival. You

---

LAND AND SEA ROUTES TO NICARAGUA

Nicaragua shares borders with Costa Rica and Honduras. The busiest Nicaraguan land entry/exit point is at Peñas Blancas (see box, p.454), on the southern border with Costa Rica. Los Chiles in Costa Rica provides a water crossing further east, to San Carlos on the Río San Juan. The two main border crossings with Honduras in the north, meanwhile, are at Guasaule and El Espino (see p.430) and Las Manos (see p.434), with the latter providing the quickest access to Tegucigalpa.

ADDRESSES IN NICARAGUA

Nicaraguan towns are usually set up in a vague grid system, with a commercial build-up around the *parque central* and main streets, and residential neighbourhoods sprawling outwards from the centre. Only main streets are labelled with signs, and smaller towns do not have any street names at all, depending instead on their direction from the main square: calles go east–west and avenidas north–south, with a central calle and avenida acting as the grid's axis. Calles and avenidas northeast of the main park are generally designated *noreste* (NE), those northwest are *noroeste* (NO), southeast are *sureste* (SE) and southwest *suroeste* (SO). There is no set numbering system for streets in Nicaraguan towns, and this, combined with the lack of street names, result in addresses that refer to locations' proximity to local landmarks, such as churches, rotundas or traffic circles, malls, banks, restaurants and petrol stations. For advice on navigating Managua, see the box on p.415.

will also receive a **tourist card** at this time, which allows for stays of thirty to ninety days depending on your nationality. The permitted length of your visit will be hand-written on the entry stamp in your passport. While all tourist cards allow for thirty days entry, it is only the number written in your passport that counts. As part of the **CA-4 agreement** (see box, p.45), visitors are granted ninety days of travel within Nicaragua, Honduras, Guatemala and El Salvador.

GETTING AROUND

Finding your way around Nicaragua is half the fun of travelling in the country. Public transport, especially buses, is geared toward the domestic population, and is very cheap but quite uncomfortable.

By bus

The standard local **buses** in Nicaragua are the usual old North American school buses, though an increasing number of express minibuses and coaches also serve the more popular routes – only a few córdobas more, they are less crowded, stop less frequently and occasionally even have air conditioning. Most **intercity buses** begin running between 4am and 7am, departing about every thirty minutes,

or when the bus is full, with last buses leaving by 5 or 6pm. **Bus stops** are usually at the local market – only Estelí and Managua have anything approximating a modern terminal – and fares are very cheap, generally US$1–4. You can usually keep your **luggage** with you, although especially on busy services it may end up on the roof or in a pile at the back of the bus. It should be safe, but it's worth keeping valuables on your person or putting them deep in your bag. Most buses have a conductor (*ayudante*) as well as a driver – in most instances, you'll pay the conductor once the bus is moving. They're almost always honest – if in doubt, ask the person next to you what the fare should be.

SHUTTLE BUSES

Nicaragua's buses are cheap and safe, but if you're in a group, in a rush or want to travel later in the day you may want to consider a shuttle – cars or minibuses that head between the tourist hotspots. The trip from Managua airport to San Juan del Sur, for example, will set you back around US$65 between two or US$130 among six. Most tour companies can arrange this, or try ⓦ adelanteexpress.com or paxeos.com.

Timetables for key routes can be viewed on @vianica.com/busschedule.php, although the information isn't always up to date – your accommodation should be able to fill you in.

By car

Taxis – many on their last legs – are most often seen in cities, but they also make long-distance journeys; a good deal, especially if in a group, since drivers charge by the distance travelled. In Managua, most taxi fares are C$10–50 during the day, and C$20–80 at night. Outside the capital, in-town fares vary, but are usually around C$10–20. Always agree on the fare before getting into the cab, and don't be afraid to haggle if the rate seems high – at Managua's bus terminals, overcharging foreigners is the norm not the exception.

Renting a car is probably the best way to explore the country's many beaches. Rental is most reliable in Managua – Alamo, Avis, Hertz and Thrifty all have offices at the airport. You need a valid licence, passport and a credit card. Make sure you take out full-cover insurance. Throughout the country road signage is quite poor, and you'll need to ask directions frequently. As with other Central American countries, don't drive at night – it's less a question of crime than the lack of lighting disguising potholes, sudden deviations in the road or even the road disappearing altogether, as well as cattle straying onto the highway. Rates average US$40 a day for the cheapest models. Outside Managua and the main west-coast highway, you'll want something robust and preferably 4WD.

Nicaraguans are a little surprised to see foreigners hitching, although it's common for locals to do so. Women only hitch when accompanied by men, and it's wise to follow this rule as a traveller. You will be expected to at least attempt to pay for your lift, but usually no more than US$1.50–2, even for trips of a couple of hours.

By boat

Boats provide vital links around Nicaragua's numerous waterways and two large lakes. On the Atlantic Coast, they are the main means of transport. Travellers most commonly take boats between El Rama and Bluefields; Bluefields and Pearl Lagoon; Rivas or Granada and Ometepe; and Granada or Ometepe and San Carlos. San Carlos can also be accessed by boat from the border crossing at Los Chiles.

By air

Nicaragua's domestic airline, La Costeña (℡2263-2142, @lacostena.com.ni) operates fairly reliable flights around the country, with Managua the inevitable hub. Routes run from the capital to locations including San Carlos, Bluefields, the Corn Islands and Puerto Cabezas (the latter two are hard to reach without flying), and also run from Bluefields to the Corn Islands and Puerto Cabezas. A return will set you back US$80–180, and can be purchased by phone or online, as well as at the airport.

If the flight is full, there's a chance you'll be bumped off – a rare occurrence but not inconceivable, especially if you're travelling to or from the Corn Islands around Christmas or Easter. To be safe, call the airport you're departing from (numbers are given throughout the Guide) the day before you fly to confirm your booking. If you are bumped, your reservation will be valid for the next flight. Luggage occasionally gets left behind, especially on the smallest planes, but is almost always on the next scheduled arrival.

ACCOMMODATION

Most budget travellers to Nicaragua at some point find themselves in a Nicaraguan **hospedaje** – a small and usually pretty basic pension-type hotel, most often family owned and run. Simple *hospedajes* charge around US$5–15 for a double. This covers a bed and fan; in many places you'll have to share a bathroom, and breakfast is not normally included in the price. **Hostels** (US$3–10 for a dorm bed) are common in backpacker hotspots like León and Granada but rarely seen elsewhere. **Hotels** (US$20 and up) tend to be more "luxurious", with air conditioning, cable TV and services like tours and car rental; you are less likely to see these in very small towns. **Camping** is pretty rare thanks to the low cost of accommodation. If you're determined to camp, the most promising areas are beach spots around San Juan del Sur, Isla Ometepe and the Corn Islands.

FOOD AND DRINK

Central markets in Nicaraguan towns are guaranteed to have snack spots, with at least several small **comedores** or **cafetines** offering cheap **comida corriente** ("running"/fast food), a set plate of meat, rice and salad, for around US$3. Throughout Nicaragua, **streetside kiosks** sell hot meals, usually at lunch time. You'll soon become familiar with their plastic tablecloths, paper plates and huge bowls of cabbage salad; the food is cheap, generally well prepared and safe to eat. **Restaurants** are more expensive, and generally open for lunch and dinner. As in the rest of Central America, **lunch** is the main meal.

Nicaraguan **food** is based around the ubiquitous **beans**, **rice** and **meat**. Everything is cooked with oil – even the rice is fried. Meals usually include **chicken**, **beef** or **pork**, most deliciously cooked *a la plancha*, on a grill or griddle, and served with **gallo pinto** (beans and rice), plantain and shredded cabbage salad. There's little difference between breakfast, lunch and dinner, though breakfast will most likely involve an egg instead of meat. Roast chicken, pizza and Chinese restaurants also crop up in most towns. On the Atlantic Coast the cuisine becomes markedly more **Caribbean**. Here rice is often cooked in mild coconut milk, and the staple fresh **coconut bread** is delicious. **Ron don** ("run down"; in local parlance "to cook") is a stew of *yuca*, *chayote* and other vegetables, usually with fish added, which is traditionally eaten at weekends. Weekends are also the time to eat **nacatamales**, parcels of corn dough filled with either vegetables, pork, beef or chicken, which are wrapped in a banana leaf and boiled for a couple of hours.

On the sweeter side, tropical **fruit** is abundant, cheap and delicious. Throughout the country you'll see **ice-cream** sellers pushing their Eskimo carts. The quality isn't great, but the company produces an extraordinary range of flavours, including many local fruits and nuts.

Drink

Given Nicaragua's heat, it's just as well that there's a huge range of cold drinks, or **refrescos** (usually shortened to *frescos*), available. These are made from grains, seeds and fruits, which are liquidized with milk, water and ice. Some unusual ones to look for include *cebada en grano*, a combination of ground barley and barley grains mixed with milk, coloured pink and flavoured with cinnamon and lots of sugar; *pinolillo*, a spiced maize and cacao drink; and *semilla de jicaroa* (or "hickory seed"), which looks and tastes like chocolate. Just about every fruit imaginable is made into a *fresco*, including watermelon, granadilla (a variety of passion fruit), papaya, *pitaya* (dragon fruit) and rock melon.

Refrescos rarely cause stomach upsets, but **tap water** is generally worth avoiding. Alongside a fairly standard mix of soft drinks, bottled water is found everywhere – you'll also see it, and other liquids, served in economical plastic pouches; bite off the corner, and you're off. Nicaragua has two local brands of **beer**, Victoria and Toña, both bland but refreshing lagers. For spirits, local Flor de Caña **rum** comes in dark and white, gold, old, dry and light, and is an excellent buy at just US$5–10 per bottle. It's usually brought to the table with a large bucket of ice and some lemons, but you can mix it with soft drinks for something a little less potent.

CULTURE AND ETIQUETTE

Nicaraguans are generally courteous and appreciate this trait in visitors, and it is considered polite to address strangers with "Usted" or its local form "Vos" rather than "Tú". You will often hear the term *Adiós* (literally, "to God") used as a greeting – hardly surprising in a country where ninety percent of the population follows a Christian denomination. The older generations in particular are often religiously conservative in appearance and manner, and wandering about town with your top off won't impress anyone.

NICARAGUAN EXPRESSIONS AND PHRASES

Adiós Used as a greeting in passing, as well as the standard "goodbye"

Chele/a (pronounced che-le/che-la) White, or pale-skinned person (from *leche*: milk)

Dale pues (pronounced dah-lay pway) Literally, "give it, then", it's used to say "ok", "go on", "fine", "it's on", etc

Naksa/Aisabi "Hello"/"Goodbye" in the Miskito langauge

Por fa A shortening of *por favor* (please)

Machista attitudes are still prevalent, and female travellers may be harassed by cat-calls from local (usually young) men; this is best ignored, and occurs much less frequently if moving around within a group or when accompanied by a man.

With regard to **tipping**, posher restaurants, especially the tourist dens of Granada and León, will add a ten- to fifteen-percent service charge to the bill – you don't have to pay it. If someone carries your bag, they'll probably expect C$5–10 for their trouble. Most Nicaraguans don't tip, but most Nicaraguans are poor; you might want to leave a few coins on the table.

SPORTS AND OUTDOOR ACTIVITIES

Rather surprisingly for a Latin American country, Nicaragua's national sport is **baseball**, and every town has a field and numerous, active leagues. Ask your local taxi driver about league games, for which most of the town will turn out in support. **Football** is played by children in the street, but lacks the popularity here that it has in other Latin countries.

Visiting **surfers** are drawn to the country's Pacific coast, where there seems to be an endless run of deserted beaches with great breaks; the most popular area (with good tourist amenities) is around **San Juan del Sur**, near the Costa Rican border (see p.451) – you'll find the most surf camps, teachers, and board sales or rentals in this area. The country's landscape also provides a good selection of areas for **hiking**, from stunning volcanoes (like those on **Isla de Ometepe**; see p.455) to the mountains around Estelí (see p.431) and Matagalpa (see p.435). On the Atlantic coast, **diving** and **snorkelling** are a must, particularly on the **Corn Islands** (see p.470), where you can reach wrecks and reefs from right off the beach. Much of the coral is in good condition, and the abundance of undersea wildlife makes for spectacular viewing. Nicaragua is also the only country in the world currently offering **volcano-boarding** – using a customized plank to ride the ashes on the Cerro Negro volcano near León (see p.427).

COMMUNICATIONS

You'll find **internet cafés** in even the smallest towns. Rates – generally C$10–15 – often rise in smaller or more remote towns, where connections can be also painfully slow. Wi-fi is increasingly common too, even in cheaper accommodation. If you do bring a laptop, you're best off buying a **surge protector**, as power surges are common.

Most towns in Nicaragua have post offices (generally Mon–Fri 8am–5pm), although they are underrepresented on the Atlantic Coast. A postcard to the US is C$15, C$20 to Europe.

There are virtually no coin-operated **phones** in Nicaragua, and you're best off using phones in internet cafés or *pulperías* (small neighbourhood shops). **Mobile phones** can be bought for as little as US$15, and Movistar (ⓦwww .movistar.com) and Claro (ⓦwww.claro .com.ni) have pay-as-you-go packages.

Phone numbers within Nicaragua changed from seven to eight digits a few years back, but you'll still see some in the old format – just add a "2" (landline) or "8" (mobile) to the number. Calling Nicaragua from abroad, the **country code** is ☏505.

CRIME AND SAFETY

Nicaragua is one of the poorest nations in the Americas, and unemployment is rife. You'll almost certainly encounter street kids, tell-tale bottles of glue clasped beneath their t-shirts. But you're far more likely to be greeted with courtesy than aggression, and Nicaragua remains safer than many of its neighbours.

Petty theft can be a problem – keep an eye on your bags and pockets, especially on buses. **Muggings** have occurred in tourist stretches like the beaches of San Juan del Sur and at day-trip destinations around Granada – your accommodation should be able to advise you, and cabs are plentiful (although see p.412). Larger hotels will have safes where you can leave valuables. Wherever you are, **women** should be wary of going out alone at night, though the chief threat is being harassed by groups of drunken men.

The **police** in Nicaragua are generally reliable, but watch out for the traffic police (*policia de tránsito*), who are infamous for targeting foreigners and who will take any chance to give you a fine (*multa*). To **report a crime** you must go to the nearest police station. If you need a police report for an insurance claim, the police will ask you to fill out a *denuncia* – a full report of the incident. If the police station does not have the *denuncia* forms, ask for a *constancia*, a simpler form, signed and stamped by the police. This should be sufficient for an insurance claim.

Visitors to Nicaragua should in theory carry their **passports** on them at all times, though checks are rare and a photocopy is acceptable.

HEALTH

Serious medical situations should be attended to at a **hospital**; most towns and cities have one. Failing this, find a Red Cross (Cruz Roja) post, medical centre or pharmacy for advice on treatment. Head for the capital in the case of a serious medical emergency. **Pharmacies** are generally open daily between 8am and 5pm, although many stay open later.

MONEY AND BANKS

Nicaragua's **currency** is the **córdoba** (C$), which is divided into 100 centavos; at the time of writing, the exchange rate was C$22 to US$1. Notes come in denominations of 10, 20, 50, 100, 200 and 500 córdobas; coins come in denominations of 1, 5 and 10 córdobas, and 25 and 50 centavos. Get rid of C$200 and 500 notes when you can – in many places they're about as welcome as a stack of Russian rubles. Small US dollar bills are accepted for most transactions, and accommodation and tour prices are usually quoted in dollars – although US$100 bills can usually only be changed at a bank.

Banks are usually open Monday to Friday from 8am to 4pm and may close for an hour or so over lunch (12.30–1.30pm); many are also open on Saturday mornings until noon. Most will change US dollars, but no other currency. **Moneychangers** (*coyotes*) operate in the street, usually at the town market, and

are generally reliable – though it helps to have an idea of what you expect to get back before approaching them.

Travellers' cheques are only changed by the Banco de América Central (**BAC**) – even here you'll struggle with anything but US-dollar cheques – and they're probably not worth bothering with. **Credit cards** such as Visa and MasterCard are generally accepted in more expensive hotels and restaurants and can also be used to pay for car rental, flights and tours. BAC, Bancentro, Banco ProCredit and Banpro's **ATM** machines all accept foreign-issue cards, and in most reasonable-sized towns you will find at least one of these, distributing cash in dollars or córdobas. That said, you can't rely on ATMs alone and, especially out of the major centres, you'll have little alternative but to carry a decent amount of cash. There are currently no ATMs on Little Corn Island or Solentiname, or in Pearl Lagoon.

INFORMATION AND MAPS

The national tourist board, **INTUR** (ⓦintur.gob.ni), has **information** offices throughout the country, with the largest in Managua, and although the staff are usually friendly, they generally only speak Spanish and can't offer much besides colourful leaflets. They may stock *Anda Ya!*, a free quarterly booklet that's packed with advertorial, but also has some useful maps and details of travel frequencies.

OPENING HOURS AND PUBLIC HOLIDAYS

Shops and **services** in Nicaragua still observe Sunday closing: otherwise you'll find most places open from 8am to 4pm. Many **businesses**, **museums** and **sites** close for lunch, normally shutting their doors between noon and 2pm, before reopening again until 4 or 5pm. Supermarkets, smaller grocery shops and the small neighbourhood shops called

---

EMERGENCY NUMBERS

Police ☎118
Fire ☎115 (or ☎911 from mobile phones)
Red Cross ☎128
Traffic police ☎119

PUBLIC HOLIDAYS

January 1 New Year's Day

Easter week Semana Santa

May 1 Labour Day

May 30 Mother's Day

July 19 Anniversary of the Revolution

September 14 Battle of San Jacinto

September 15 Independence Day

November 2 All Souls' Day (Día de los Muertos)

December 7 & 8 Inmaculada Concepción

December 25 Christmas Day

pulperías or *ventas* generally stay open until 8pm. **Bars** and **restaurants** tend to close around 11pm or midnight, except for nightclubs – most of which are in Managua – which stay open until 2am or later. Public holidays (see box above) see almost everything shut down, so don't plan on visiting tourist attractions over those dates.

FESTIVALS

Nicaragua's calendar includes plenty of festivals, from local events to national fiestas and raucous *hípicas* (horse parades). In addition, each town in Nicaragua has its own patron saint whose saint's day is observed with processions and celebrations called **Toro Guaco**, during which you might catch a glimpse of old customs inherited from the Aztecs mixed with mestizo figures like the masked *viejitos* ("old ones" – masks of old men and women worn by young and old alike). In all cases, Nicaraguans love to dance, and you will probably see folkloric dances in the streets, usually performed by children. The calendar below only lists a few highlights.

March–April At Easter the whole country packs up and goes to the beach: buses are rammed, hotel rooms are at a premium, and flights to the Corn Islands are fully booked. Semana Santa (Holy Week) processions, in which crowds follow *pasos* (depictions of Christ and the Virgin), are the biggest in Granada.

May The Atlantic coastal town of Bluefields celebrates Palo de Mayo, an adapted May Day fiesta flavoured with the Caribbean rhythms of reggae and soca – a fusion of dance and folklore.

July 19 The holiday marking the Revolution is still celebrated ardently by Sandinistas and is usually accompanied by parades and marches. In Managua, the Plaza de la Revolución fills with Sandinista supporters, who gather in memory of the historical events.

December 31 Throughout much of the country, New Year's Eve is mainly celebrated in the home, although San Juan del Sur is known for drawing a crowd of young revellers. Bear in mind you'll find most things closed on January 1.

Managua and around

Hotter than sin and crisscrossed by anonymous highways, there can't be a more visitor-unfriendly capital than **MANAGUA**. Less a city in the conventional sense than a conglomeration of neighbourhoods and commercial districts, Managua offers few sights and cultural experiences – in fact, most visitors are so disturbed by the lack of street names and any real centre that they get out as fast as they can.

Not even the city's setting on the southern shore of **Lago de Managua** is particularly pleasant: the area is low lying, swampy and flat, relieved only by a few eroded volcanoes. It also, unfortunately, sits on top of an astounding eleven **seismic faults**, which have shaken the city severely over time. The result has been a cycle of ruin and rebuilding, which has created a bizarre and postmodern mixture of crumbling ruins inhabited by squatters, hastily constructed concrete structures and gleaming new shopping malls and hotels. The old city centre, damaged further in the **Revolution** of 1978–79 and never thoroughly repaired, remains eerily abandoned.

All this said, there *are* things to enjoy here, although being a tourist in Managua does require a good degree of tenacity. As Nicaragua's largest city and home to a quarter of its population, the city occupies a key position in the nation's economy and psyche, and offers more practical services than anywhere else in the country.

What to see and do

For the visitor, sprawling Managua can thankfully be divided into a few distinct areas. The **old ruined centre** on the lakeshore, finally undergoing redevelopment, is the site of the city's tourist attractions, including the few impressive colonial-style buildings that have survived all the earthquakes. **Lago de Managua**, which forms such a pretty backdrop to this part of the city, is unfortunately severely **polluted** from sewage and regular dumpings of waste.

Just to the south is the city's main landmark, the **Crowne Plaza**, formerly the **Hotel InterContinental**, whose white form, reminiscent of a Maya

---

SAFETY IN MANAGUA

Managua has its problems with poverty, theft and violence. The areas around the Carretera a Masaya are cleaner and safer, and many locals will warn you away from hostel-packed Barrio Martha Quezada. Like most of the city, however, it's safe enough to walk around in the daytime, if sketchy in the evening. Cabs are a good idea anyway, given Managua's perplexing layout and their low prices, and are worth investing in at night, especially if you're on your own.

Unfortunately, cab-based express muggings are on the increase. The common scam sees a tourist befriended on the buses coming into Managua (often by a woman) and helped into a cab at the terminal with several other passengers, before being threatened with a knife, driven around ATMs until their money runs out and dropped on the city fringes. In the unlikely event this happens to you, don't resist and report the crime at INTUR, in Managua if possible (see p.417). If in doubt, don't get in a packed cab or one without a numberplate, try to sit in the front seat and don't be afraid to find another vehicle – the vast majority of drivers want nothing more than to overcharge you slightly, and seeking one out around the corner is a better bet than letting yourself be directed into one. Away from the main terminals you're on safer ground catching a cab, and if they open the door to let another passenger in, don't panic – shared rides are the norm.

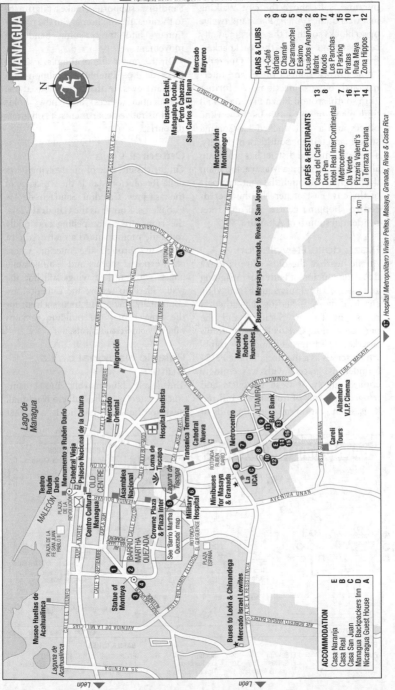

Tipitapa, Estelí & Augusto C. Sandino International Airport

MANAGUA

N

BARS & CLUBS

Art-Café	3
Bárbaro	9
El Chamán	6
El Caramanchel	5
El Eskimo	4
Licuados Ananda	2
Matrix	8
Moods	17
Los Panchas	4
El Parking	15
Piratas	10
Ruta Maya	1
Zona Hippos	12

CAFÉS & RESTURANTS

Casa del Cafe	13
Don Pan	8
Hotel Real InterContinental	7
Metrocentro	16
Ola Verde	11
Pizzeria Valenti's	14
La Terraza Peruana	

0   1 km

Hospital Metropolitaro Vivian Peñas, Masaya, Granada, Rivas & Costa Rica

Buses to Estelí, Matagalpa, Ocotal, Porto Cabezas, San Carlos & El Rama

Mercado Mayoreo

Mercado Iván Montenegro

Buses to Meysaya, Granada, Rivas & San Jorge

Lago de Managua

NORTHERN ACCESS VIA CA-1

PISTA DE LA SOLIDARIDAD

PISTA SABANA GRANDE

ROTONDA LA VIRGEN

PISTA SABANA GRANDE

Mercado Roberto Huembes

CARRETERA NORTE

PISTA LA ARGENTINA

PISTA 14 DE SEPTIEMBRE

CALLE 14 DE SEPTIEMBRE

Migración

Mercado Oriental

Teatro Rubén Darío

Monumento a Rubén Darío

Catedral Vieja

Palacio Nacional de la Cultura

OLD CENTRE

Centro Cultural Managua

Asamblea Nacional

Hospital Bautista

Transnica Terminal

Catedral Nueva

Loma de Tiscapa

Laguna de Tiscapa

Metrocentro

ALTAMIRA

ST. SANTO DOMINGO

BAC Bank

Alhambra V.I.P. Cinema

Careli Tours

ROTONDA RUBÉN DARÍO

La UCA

AVENIDA BOLÍVAR

CALLE COLÓN

Crowne Plaza & Plaza Inter

Military Hospital

Minibuses for Masaya & Granada

BARRIO MARTHA QUEZADA

See 'Barrio Martha Quezada' map

PLAZA ESPAÑA

ROTONDA EL GÜEGÜENSE

AVENIDA UNAN

PISTA SUBURBANA

CARRETERA A MASAYA

PLAZA DE LA FE SAN JUAN PABLO II

PLAZA DE LA REVOLUCIÓN

MALECÓN

Statue of Montoya

Museo Huellas de Acahualinca

Laguna de Acahualinca

CALLE EL TRIUNFO

AVENIDA DE LA MILICIAS

35 AVENIDA

Buses to León & Chinandega

Mercado Israel Lewites

PISTA PEDRO ARAUZ PALACIOS

AVE ROBERTO VARGAS BATRES

PISTA LA RESISTENCIA

León

León

ACCOMMODATION

Casa Naranja	E
Casa Real	B
Casa San Juan	C
Managua Backpackers Inn	D
Nicaragua Guest House	A

pyramid, sails above the city. Walking just west of the *Crowne Plaza* and twelve or so blocks south of the old ruined city centre brings you to the backpacker-frequented **Barrio Martha Quezada**, home to rock-bottom prices and international bus connections. A further 2km south, around **Plaza España**, you'll find many of the city's banks, airline offices and a well-stocked La Colonia supermarket. In the southeast of the city, a new commercial district has grown up along the **Carretera a Masaya**, the main thoroughfare through the southern part of the city. East of here lie the **Metrocentro** shopping centre and upmarket residential suburb of **Altamira**.

Plaza de la Revolución

At the heart of the old centre is **Plaza de la Revolución**, a battered, intriguing and often eerily empty square flanked by city landmarks, including the cathedral ruins, the Palacio Nacional and the park containing **Carlos Fonseca's tomb** (marked by an eternal flame). The tomb, which serves as a memorial to the FSLN founder, is graced with a seemingly endless supply of fresh bouquets and fringed by a row of huge black-and-red flags. Each year on July 19 thousands of Sandinista supporters make a pilgrimage to the area, paying homage to the revolutionary and the ensuing Sandinista movement.

On the north side of the plaza sits **La Casa de Los Pueblos**, a salmon-and-mustard eyesore that once housed the presidential offices and now holds administrative departments; it's off limits to tourists.

Catedral Vieja

On the eastern side of the evolving Plaza de la Revolución stands the wreckage of the ash-grey Catedral Santiago de los Caballeros. Known as the **Catedral Vieja**, the ruins are a compelling and oddly romantic monument to a destroyed city. Birds fly through the interior, where semi-exposed murals and leaning stone angels with cracked wings still line the walls. Plans to restore the cathedral are continually made and then shelved; for the time being, the building remains officially closed to visitors.

Palacio Nacional de La Cultura

The lovely blue-marble and cream-stucco exterior of the **Palacio Nacional**, next to the cathedral, holds a darker

▲ Old Centre

BARRIO MARTHA QUEZADA

CALLE COLON

N

ACCOMMODATION
Apartamentos Los Cisneros	C
Casa Castillo	A
Casa Gabrinma	G
Hostal Palmerita	D
Los Felipe	E
Casa de Huespedes Santos	B
Hostal Dulce Sueño	F

CALLE 27 DE MAYO

CALLE 8A

CALLE 9A

CALLE 10A

King Quality Terminal

Cine Dorado (closed)

AVENIDA WILLIAMS ROMERO
AVENIDA 10A
AVENIDA 9A
AVENIDA 8A
AVENIDA 7A
AVENIDA 5A
AVENIDA 4A
AVENIDA 3A
AVENIDA 2A
AVENIDA BOLIVAR

Tica Bus Terminal

Crowne Plaza Hotel

(i)

Monumento Roosevelt

0   300 m

1, 2, 3 & Montoya Statue ◄

▼ Plaza España

▼ Loma ▼ de Tiscapa

EATING						**BARS & CLUBS**			
Buffet La Vista	7	El Eskimo	2	Norma	6	El Caramanchel	13	Q	4
Café Tonallí	12	El Grillito	10	Los Ranchos	3	La Casa de Los		El Viajero	8
Café Mirna	11	Licuados Ananda	1	Típico Doña Pilar	5	Mejía Godoy	9		

NAVIGATING MANAGUA

In a city where nobody uses **street names** (if they actually exist) or addresses, it's helpful to have your destination given to you in terms of neighbourhood and distance from a **landmark** – taxi drivers will most easily find places in relation to a well-known city fixture. For destinations around Barrio Martha Quezada, use the *Crowne Plaza*, Tica Bus terminal or Montoya statue as a reference point; the Metrocentro shopping centre and La Union supermarket are useful landmarks around Zona Hippos and Los Robles.

Distances are measured in metres as much as in blocks – in local parlance, 100m is a city block, or **cuadra**. Sometimes an archaic measure, the **vara**, is also used: one *vara* (a yard) is interpreted as roughly equivalent to a metre. To confuse the issue still further, many Managuans do not use the cardinal points in their usual form: north becomes *al lago* – towards the lake; *al sur* is south; *arriba* – literally, "up", is to the east; and *abajo*, "down", is to the west. So, "del Hotel InterContinental (now the *Crowne Plaza*, although many people still use its old name) una cuadra arriba y dos cuadras al lago" means one block east and two blocks north of the *Crowne Plaza*.

history. During the long years of Somoza rule the columned building was the seat of government power: Colombian writer Gabriel García Márquez called it *"el partenón bananero"* – the banana parthenon. Then, on August 22, 1978, Sandinista commandos disguised as National Guard soldiers ran through its corridors to capture the deputies of the National Assembly, a cinematic coup d'état that effectively brought down the Somoza dictatorship.

Today, the Palacio, still a functioning government building, also houses the national library and archives, while the ground floor intersperses small, relaxing gardens with a **museum and art gallery** (Mon–Sat 8am–4pm, Sun 9am–4pm; US$4). There's a good display of Nicaraguan handicrafts, colourful murals and large sculptures, plus a few pre-Columbian artefacts. The museum frequently holds cultural and artistic events of dance, poetry and *artesanía*; ask at reception about upcoming events.

Centro Cultural Managua

Immediately southwest of the Palacio National is a distinctive green building housing the **Centro Cultural Managua**. The former home of the *Gran Hotel*, the exterior of the low-slung, mock-colonial structure gives you some idea of how pre-earthquake Managua looked. Inside, the downstairs area hosts sporadic exhibitions, seminars and concerts. The centre's upper storeys house many of the country's arts organizations. Upstairs, **historic photographs** line the corridors. Some show Managua before the 1972 earthquake as an attractive city of palm trees and some colonial architecture while others, taken immediately afterwards, show crumpled buildings, crushed cars and gaping holes in the road.

Teatro Nacional Rubén Darío

Perched like a huge white futurist bird north of the Plaza de la Revolución is the **Teatro Nacional Rubén Darío** (Mon–Fri 9am–6pm, Sat 10am–3pm; ☏2222-7426, ⓦwww.tnrubendario.gob .ni), Managua's main cultural venue. Foreign and Nicaraguan theatre, dance and opera groups all visit. It's worth going inside the building just to see the massive chandeliers, marble floors and stirring view out to the lake from the enormous windows upstairs. There are often small exhibitions (free), and theatre buffs might be interested in a tour (US$5, best booked in advance), which takes you around otherwise closed parts of the building. South of the theatre is the **Monumento a Rubén Darío**, a striking sculpted memorial to the iconic poet (see p.425).

Malecón

North of the theatre, an attempt has been made to spruce up the previously seedy lakeshore boardwalk, or **malecón**, with bars and food kiosks, plus a couple of fairground rides. A statue of Latin American liberator **Simón Bolívar** sits in the middle of the nearby roundabout, guarding the shorefront's entrance. The area gets quite lively at weekends, though it's fairly deserted during the week except for ambling teenage couples. There are pleasant views to the north from the *malecón*, where **Volcán Mombotombo** and little **Mombotombito** sit side by side against the horizon on the far shore of the lake, 50km away.

Plaza de la Fe San Juan Pablo II

Just south of the *malecón* is the vast **Plaza de la Fe San Juan Pablo II**, a square whose central obelisk commemorates Pope John Paul II's two visits to Nicaragua. At its lake end sits the Concha Acústica or "acoustic shell" statue (resembling a large white wave), which serves as a stage for concerts and shows. The plaza is rarely busy and is one of the fiercest suntraps in the city, though it looks better at night when floodlighting adds some definition to its vast expanse.

Museo Huellas de Acahualinca

Volcán Mombotombo's capacity for destruction is evoked in the **Museo Huellas de Acahualinca** (daily 9am–4pm; US$4), just west of the *malecón* in Barrio Acahualinca (take a taxi or bus #112). It's a rudimentary affair that still offers a fascinating glimpse into the area's history – though you'll need some

Spanish to make sense of the explanations. Alongside fragments of pottery and boards on fauna and geology, a series of great pits reveals animal and human footprints from prehistoric nomads – preserved in volcanic ash, the footprints date back between 6000 and 10,000 years.

Loma de Tiscapa

Directly behind the landmark *Crowne Plaza*, you can get some perspective on both Managua's dramatic history and its weird, battered cityscape in the **Loma de Tiscapa**, or Tiscapa Historical National Park (Mon–Fri & Sun 8am–9pm, Sat 1–9pm; C$20). The fifteen-minute walk up the hill takes you past the elegant white pillars of the Monumento Roosevelt and a decapitated statue of Justice on your right before the road winds round and up to a silhouetted statue of **Sandino**, marking the spot of the revolutionary leader's assassination; nearby lie a tank and statue donated to Somoza by Mussolini, relics of the former regime. Displays detail the disastrous earthquakes of 1931 and 1972, while a small **museum** (which closes at 5pm) has more on Sandino's life.

The **views** of the city from here are excellent, stretching north to Lago de Nicaragua and the distant volcanoes and south beyond the new cathedral towards Masaya. They can be enjoyed by **canopy tour**, if you're feeling adventurous (Tues–Sun 9am–5.30pm; US$15; ☎2886-2836). Three cables cover over a kilometre, allowing you to glide high above the city and the picturesque – but polluted – **Laguna Tiscapa**, which sits below the summit.

Carretera a Masaya and the Metrocentro

About 1km south of the laguna lies Managua's biggest concentration of residential and commercial neighbourhoods and most of its westernized nightlife. The main thoroughfare through this part of the city is the **Carretera a Masaya**, hemmed in to the east by the embassy neighbourhood of Altamira and to the west by La UCA, or the Universidad Centroamericana. It's on this road, just south of Pista Juan Pablo II, where you'll find the bland but blissfully cool **Metrocentro** shopping centre, which boasts shops, ATMs, a food court, banks, a cinema and the *InterContinental Metrocentro* hotel.

Catedral Nueva

A short walk from the Metrocentro shopping centre, in the middle of a field, is the Catedral Metropolitana de la Purísima Concepción, known simply as the **Catedral Nueva** (usually daily 6am–10pm), a striking and brutal piece of architecture whose roof resembles a collection of large concrete hand grenades. Inside there's a bleeding figure of Christ encased in glass, but the milling worshippers are more compelling than the cavernous interior.

Arrival

By air The Augusto C. Sandino International Airport is 11km east of Managua; on arrival, you'll have to pay a US$10 entry fee. Designated airport taxis wait just outside the terminal doors; reportedly safer and always air-conditioned, these cost US$15–20 for journeys to most parts of the city. If you cross the street from the airport you can catch a normal taxi, which shouldn't cost more than C$150. There are several ATMs here, and the Banco de la Producción has a window where you can change dollars,

but not travellers' cheques. You'll find car rental agencies in the arrivals hall. The domestic terminal sits at the main terminal's western end.

By bus Most international services come into Barrio Martha Quezada in central Managua. Domestic buses arrive at one of the several crowded, noisy and generally chaotic urban marketplaces that also serve as bus terminals: from Masaya, Granada, Rivas or other southern destinations, you'll come into the Mercado Huembes near the Carretera a Masaya on the southeastern edge of the city; buses from the north and east – including Estelí, Matagalpa, Ocotal, San Carlos and El Rama – arrive at the terminal in the Mercado Mayoreo in Barrio Concepción, near the airport; buses from the northwest towns of León and Chinandega use the busy Mercado Israel Lewites in the southwest of the capital. Regular express minivans from Masaya and Granada pull into a small unmarked terminal on the highway opposite La UCA, near the Metrocentro. Taxis crowd the arriving buses, so moving on from the markets should not be a problem, although see the box on p.412.

Information

Tourist information There is an under-stocked INTUR desk at the airport. The INTUR headquarters (Mon–Fri 8am–1pm; ☎2254-5191, @intur.gob.ni) are in central Managua, one block west of the *Crowne Plaza*. The staff are well intentioned and some speak English, but don't have much in the way of hand-outs or information on accommodation or tours. It's worth buying the detailed city map of Managua (US$5) from them, if available – for everything else, your hotel will probably be of far more assistance.

City transport

Buses Buses, generally labelled with a route number, cover the main city routes. The fares are dirt cheap (around C$5), but pick pocketing

---

TOUR OPERATORS IN MANAGUA

Organized tours are generally best arranged locally – we've listed operators throughout the Guide. If you've only got a short spell in the country and don't fancy the rigours of Nicaragua's clamorous bus terminals and ramshackle taxis, though, various places can arrange trips from Managua. These are usually pricey, but can get you to remote areas fast and will pick you up from your hotel or the airport. **Careli Tours**, opposite Colegio La Salle, Planes de Altamira (☎2278-6919, @www.carelitours.com), are good for expensive best-of-Nicaragua-type packages (US$200–1200), lasting up to a fortnight, as well as trips combining Nicaragua and Costa Rica. Otherwise, operators in León and Granada can help – try the likes of Green Pathways and Va Pues (see box, p.427) or Tierra Tour and Nicaragua Adventures (see box, p.445).

is common, so be alert. Fares are paid in cash, on board – use coins and smaller bills whenever possible. If unsure of your destination, ask the driver to point out stops, which are unmarked. Services start at 5am and continue until 10pm, becoming less frequent from about 6pm onwards. Useful buses include #109 (running from the *malecón* to Mercado Huembes), #110 (Mercado Israel Lewites, La UCA and Mercado Iván Montenegro) and #112 (Mercado Israel Lewites to the *malecón*).

Taxis Taxis are cheap and plentiful in Managua and will probably form your main mode of transport, with most trips costing around C$20–60 and the journey from Barrio Martha Quezada to the airport around C$150 (agree on a price before setting off and do your best to haggle, especially with taxis waiting at bus terminals). Drivers always like to have more than one passenger at a time, and will stop to pick up and drop off people en route (if travelling alone, it's safest to sit up front next to the driver – see box, p.412 for tips on safety). Legitimate taxis have red licence plates and are officially registered. Generally cheap, and with friendly, talkative drivers, they are always in good supply – as a tourist, taxis will honk at you as a matter of course, whether you want one or not.

Accommodation

Barrio Martha Quezada, where most international buses arrive, is the place for backpacker-friendly *hospedaje*-type accommodation; most places are scattered in the quiet streets on either side of the Tica Bus terminal. Elsewhere in the city, you'll find more secure and modern districts than Martha Quezada, notably in the relatively swish area around the Metrocentro, although taxis and buses will probably be necessary for transport.

Barrio Martha Quezada and around

Apartamentos Los Cisneros One block north and one and a half blocks west of the Tica Bus terminal ☎ 2222-3535, 🌐 hotelloscisneros.com. The sole upmarket option in the heart of Martha Quezada, offering bright standard rooms and chalet-style apartments with hot water, fridge, cooker and optional fan or a/c. Doubles US$30, two-person apartment US$40

Casa Castillo One block west and one and a half blocks north of Tica Bus ☎ 2222-2265. Hospitable, family-run *hospedaje* with seven basic, rather dowdy red-tiled rooms with private bath; the ones right at the back and upstairs are larger and quieter. US$14

Casa Gabrinma One block south and half a block east of Tica Bus ☎ 2222-6650. Welcoming guesthouse with a chatty owner whose cute, vaguely monastic rooms – all with ceiling fans – are set around a series of leafy inner courtyards. US$20

Casa de Huespedes Santos One block north and one and a half blocks west of Tica Bus ☎ 2222-3713, 🌐 casadehuespedessantos.com.ni. Big, ramshackle *hospedaje* that feels like a youth club when it's full and a shed when it's empty, with hammocks, easy chairs, funky art on the walls and an indoor patio with cable TV. Some of the 28 scruffy rooms are on the gloomy side – try to get one upstairs, where ventilation is better. All have ceiling fan, and some come with private bath. US$7

Los Felipe One and a half blocks west of Tica Bus ☎ 2222-6501, 🌐 hotellosfelipe.com.ni. This clean, peaceful hotel has 27 clean and compact rooms nestled amid an urban jungle of foliage. All come with private bath and TV, and there's wi-fi and laundry available alongside optional a/c and a sporadically open swimming pool. US$20

Hostal Dulce Sueño One and a half blocks east of Tica Bus ☎ 2228-4125, 📧 hospedajedulcesueno @yahoo.es. Helpful budget place in a secure courtyard. Try to get one of the two brighter upstairs rooms, which sit alongside a rooftop area with hammocks where you can squint over Martha Quezada's tin roofs and ponder your next excursion. There's a kitchen and fridge too. US$16

Hostal Palmerita One block west and half a block north of Tica Bus ☎ 2222-5956. Simple, faded hostel that draws a fairly Nica clientele. Nothing special, but the seven rooms are a reasonable deal. Private bathrooms cost an extra US$1. US$12

Elsewhere in the city

Casa San Juan C Esperanza 560, behind La UCA ☎ 2278-3220, 📧 sanjuan@cablenet.com.ni. Welcoming mid-range guesthouse in a quiet neighbourhood. The spotless rooms come with a/c, cable TV and well-equipped modern, private bathrooms. Breakfast is included and other meals are available with advance notice. The hotel is popular, so reserve in advance. US$45

Managua Backpackers Inn 100m south of the old *Chamán* nightclub, Los Robles ☎ 2267-0006, 🌐 managuahostel.com. A well-located, friendly hostel with tidy dorms and private rooms, some with en-suite bathroom. The courtyard garden with a pool, shaded by a mango tree and surrounded by deck chairs and hammocks, is tranquil, although the nearby nightlife can be noisy. There's a large communal kitchen and TV room, free internet and laundry services. Dorms US$8, doubles US$20

Casa Naranja Planes de Altamira ☎2277-3403, ⊕hotel casanaranja.com. Smart, quiet and charming upmarket option, its cool corridors dotted with furniture and musical instruments. Rooms have hot water and TVs, and some come with nice little outdoor areas too. Breakfast is included. US$100

Casa Real Two blocks west and two blocks south of the Rotunda Rubén Darío ☎2278-3838, ⊕casareal.com. Spotless, family-run hotel with spacious, clean rooms (with TV, a/c and private bath) grouped around a leafy inner lounge with huge hammocks; the upstairs rooms are brighter, with balconies. Breakfast is included. US$75

Nicaragua Guest House Two blocks south and two and a half blocks west of Rotonda La Virgen ☎2249-8963, ⊕3dp.ch/nicaragua. A small guest-house in a good location for the airport and most buses, with basic rooms, all en suite with TV and a fan or a/c, and a cool courtyard garden. US$20

Eating

Wherever you walk in Managua – on the street, at the bus stop or even under a shady tree – you will find someone selling a drink or *comida corriente*. Good, cheap food on the hoof is also easy to get in any of Managua's major markets – look out for *pupusas*, actually a Salvadoran concoction of cheese, tortillas, sauce and meat. Managua also has a surprisingly cosmopolitan selection of restaurants: Chinese, Spanish, Mexican, Japanese, Italian, Peruvian, North American – even vegetarian. Americanized fast food is virtually everywhere, but cafés are thin on the ground and tend to be frequented by expats and wealthier Managuans.

Barrio Martha Quezada and around

Buffet La Vista Two blocks west of the Tica Bus station. Definitive lunch-only buffet joint – the only thing bigger than the huge plates of satisfying *comida típica* (around C$80 with a drink) is the queue, which can sprawl from the busy counter through the restaurant hall and out into the street. If the buzz of the main room isn't to your taste, try the pleasant area upstairs.

Café Mirna One block west and south of the Tica Bus terminal. This compact, likeable, family-run place has become something of an institution over its thirty-year history, though the service can be uneven. They're open from 6.30am (7am on Sun) for decent *típica* or gringo breakfasts and you can tuck into the *comida casera* buffet (C$70) from noon until 3pm.

Café Tonallí Two blocks east and half a block south of Tica Bus. Principally a bakery selling specialist breads (from C$30), there are also a few tables in a leafy garden where you can enjoy good breakfasts – muesli, fruit and yoghurt (C$25), fresh coffee (C$6) and croissants baked on the premises – and healthy lunches like veggie lasagne and pesto.

El Eskimo 11A Calle Sud-Oest, just off the Paseo Salvador Allende. Fast food with pretensions: the tasty burgers and *quesadillas* will set you back around C$80, the air con is icy and the staff uniformed and attentive. Popular with moneyed Managuans and a decent spot for an undemanding meal.

El Grillito Just north of the INTUR office. There aren't too many spots in Martha Quezada that might tempt you in for both a meal and a drink: *El Grillito* won't win any prizes, but with bright murals, reasonably priced beers (C$25) and seafood and grilled meat (from C$70) served on its open terrace, it's a reasonable place to while away one of Managua's hot nights.

Licuados Ananda Next to the Montoya statue. This restaurant and juice bar, set around a covered patio and garden, is a veritable oasis in Managua's concrete chaos. The varied veggie menu includes a good-value *plato del día*, nice bread and superb milkshakes (C$20) – try the papaya. A meal plus drink will cost C$70–80.

Norma Just north of *Buffet La Vista*. A simple branch of a bakery chain, where you can pick up a coffee and cake for C$30.

Los Ranchos Opposite *El Eskimo*. Managua's classic steakhouse has been attracting reverent notices for years: sit by the gurgling water-features and chomp your way through *churrasco* (C$270) and oysters (C$70 for six).

Típico Doña Pilar One block east of *Casa de Huespedes Santos*. Simple plastic chairs and a large grill set up on the sidewalk every evening, offering *quesadillas*, enchiladas and lip-smacking grilled chicken for a mere C$50 (drink included).

Metrocentro and around

Casa del Cafe One block north of Carretera a Masaya, by the Mexican Embassy. This branch of a local chain serves reasonable coffee (from C$30) and snacks (cheese croissant C$70); the draw is the foliage-shaded balcony, a rare bit of tranquillity in this achingly modern stretch of town.

Don Pan One and a half blocks south of Monte de Los Olivos. This pleasant bakery, part of a small Nica chain, offers a mouth watering selection of croissants, pastries and other gooey treats as well as fresh coffee (C$17–50), sandwiches and more substantial meals like a burger (C$80) or chicken salad (C$90) to take away or savour in the modern café out front. There's also a branch at km 4 Carretera Norte.

Ola Verde Planes de Altamira, 2 blocks west and half a block north of Pharaoh's Casino ☎ 2270-3048, ⊛ olaverdesa.com. Quality vegetarian-friendly restaurant that marries good food with an evangelistic enthusiasm for ethical local food production. Both a breakfast and coffee and a main course like veggie lasagne or tomato and spinach fettucine will set you back around C$160. Try the sumptuous cakes and desserts too.

Pizzeria Valenti's One block east of *Domino's Pizza*, house no. 6 ☎ 2278-7474. The outside patio is a decent place to enjoy a thin-crust pizza – they're filling and good value considering the area. A meal and a beer will cost about C$150.

La Terraza Peruana Planes de Altamira No. 14, 150m south of *Ola Verde* ☎ 2278-0013. Upmarket, faintly Peruvian restaurant with a relaxing shaded terrace. The tasty and substantial dishes range from *mondongo* (tripe) soup (C$69) to Chinese chicken (C$115) and rice with seafood (C$269).

Drinking and nightlife

Managua's nightlife has been given a shot in the arm in the last decade or so with the return of some of the "Miami Boys" – wealthy families who fled revolutionary Nicaragua – who have helped drive

the demand for upmarket bars and discos. As well as the plusher options, the city offers a reasonable choice of venues for drinking and dancing for those on a budget, as most places only charge a few dollars cover and drinks are either included in the cover charge, or cost around C$20–60. Musically, you can expect to hear merengue, salsa, reggaeton, pop, house and even Nica *rancho* music (not unlike American country). Most bars shut between midnight and 2pm, and clubs start filling up from 10pm – Saturday is the busiest evening of the week.

Bars

Art-Café Opposite the Las Palmas park ☎ 2607-5104. A café/bar/cultural space, with a yummy Mexican menu on Sun (around C$68), as well as live music shows where you'll hear everything from folk to reggae. Cover US$40–80.

Bárbaro One block north, half a block west of Monte de Los Olivos. Rock and metal venue with an attached (and mostly open-air) bar with two pool tables and a friendly crowd. Beers cost from C$15, greasy but tasty finger-food from C$40. The bar is free, gig entry C$40–150 and there's a karaoke place next door. Closed Mon.

El Caramanchel Three blocks south and half a block west of Plaza Intern ☎ 8931-4199. Frequented by a lively international crowd, this "cultural bar" is decorated with Mexican tapestries, old beer ads and odd artworks. It hosts several live gigs a month as well as occasional poetry readings, theatre performances and photography exhibitions, but is worth a visit even when there's nothing on for a drink or for the tasty local dishes (from C$40). Entry free, beer from C$25. Wed–Sun 6pm–3am.

La Casa de Los Mejía Godoy Colonia Los Robles, opposite the *Crowne Plaza* ☎ 2222-6610, ⊛ losmejiagodoy.zonaxp.com. The brainchild of Nicaraguan guitar-playing and song-writing brothers Luís Enrique and Carlos Mejía Godoy, this is a cultural centre and bar rolled into one. There's an art gallery, CD and bookstore to browse as well as a café/bar selling *comida típica*. Thurs sees young local musicians jam here, and if the brothers aren't performing on Fri & Sat, there's likely to be a quality replacement. Cover from C$200.

El Parking Half a block north of *La Terraza Peruana*, Planes de Altamira. Massively busy on the weekends (when it stays open till 6am), this loud bar has a large outdoor patio and great cocktails (around C$70).

Piratas Half a block south of *Hotel Seminole*, Residencial Los Robles. Sit by the twee ships and televised sports indoors or perch on the buzzy outdoor terrace and watch as kids risk life and limb to hustle cash from drivers on the busy main road. Choose from beer (C$25), tapas, fishy mains and cocktails and tap your foot to a soundtrack of everything from reggaeton to grunge.

Ruta Maya 150m east from the Montoya statue ☎2268-0698, ☻rutamaya.com.ni. Long-standing cultural centre/bar which plays host to a diverse cross-section of the city's musical and artistic talent (Thurs, Fri & Sat) and tends to attract an older, more sophisticated crowd. Seating is outdoors under a big marquee and traditional Nica food is also available (from C$60). Gig tickets are usually C$60–120.

El Viajero Calle 9A, a block west of the Tica Bus terminal. Your best bet for an unfussy beer or four (C$40 for a litre) in Barrio Martha Quezada. Expect cheesy Nica pop and some uproariously drunk locals.

Zona Hippos Avenida Gabriel Cardenal, a block west of the *Hilton Princess* hotel. Not one bar but a collection of Americanized joints, including *Woody's*, *Lounge One* and *Hippos*: booze and groove till late, or arrive early for the daily 5–7pm happy hour.

Clubs

El Chamán 200m south of the *Tiscapa* restaurant, off Avenida Simón Bolívar ☻chamanbar.net. One of the biggest clubs in town, and arguably the most iconic: it's built in the shape of a Maya pyramid. Caters to a younger crowd, with Latin, hip-hop and pop playing on the three nicely decorated floors. There's regular live music and the occasional rock-centric talent contests are worth a look. Entry C$20–150, depending on the night. Wed–Sat 8pm–4am.

Matrix On the Carretera a Masaya, opposite the *Hilton Princess* hotel. It might not be terribly sophisticated, but *Matrix* is often packed with a young local crowd having a fairly boozy and very vocal good time. The music is pop and Latin, with the odd bit of dance music thrown in. Entry C$40–150, beers from C$15. Thurs is Ladies' Night.

Moods Second storey of the Galerías Santo Domingo. Exclusive and swanky *Moods* has quality DJs spinning dance music, a vast range of drinks and a hip crowd (dress up or getting in may be a hassle). The shopping mall location means there's no outdoor space, so it's not the best option on hot nights. Entry around C$200. Wed–Sat 9pm–6am.

Q Calle 27 de Mayo. Friendly, relaxed gay club playing mainstream US and Latin pop that can get pretty heaving come the weekend. It's one of only three gay clubs in town: nearby *Lollipop* and *Tabú* have a similar vibe. Entry around C$100. Thurs–Sun from 9pm.

Entertainment

Cinema Alhambra V.I.P. (see box opposite), Cinemark Metrocentro (☎2271-9037), Cinemas

Inter in Plaza Inter (☎2222-5122), Cinemas Galerías in Galerías Santo Domingo (☎2276-5065). American blockbusters (usually with subtitles) dominate the programming.

Theatre Teatro Nacional Rubén Darío (see p.415) is one of the best theatres in Central America, with a main auditorium seating 1200 people, an exhibition space and occasional experimental theatre in the basement. Events are scheduled there most weekends and it's easy to get to, with bus #109 stopping right in front. Check ☻www.tnrubendario .gob.ni or listings in *La Prensa* for details of performances.

Shopping

Books Hispamer (from UCA: one block east, one block south and then one block east again; ☎2278-1210) has the largest selection of academic, fiction and nonfiction books (in Spanish) in Nicaragua. There's a small shelf of classic and modern English-language fiction too.

Food and drink Well-stocked chains La Colonia and La Unión sell a large selection of local and imported food including organic produce. You can also buy a lot of the basics at local *pulperías*, small shops set up in people's houses. Fruit and vegetables are cheapest at the weekend markets, when the growers come into town to sell their produce.

Markets Mercado Oriental, a few blocks southeast of the old centre, is a small, lawless city-within-a-city where you can buy just about anything, but need to keep a close eye on your pockets and an even closer eye on your back – Nicaraguans will tell you that this is one of the most dangerous places in the country. If you must go, take someone with

Alhambra V.I.P. Centro Commercial, Camino de Oriente (☎2270-3842, ☻cinesalhambra .com). The tickets at this mall-set cinema might seem steep (C$135–180 a show), but once you're inside you'll see what the fuss is all about. Each person gets a leather seat, which reclines completely and comes equipped with a call button for summoning a waiter and ordering food and drinks, which will be discreetly delivered to your side through the darkness. The overly powerful a/c is perhaps the only downside; bring a sweater.

TREAT YOURSELF

you and leave your valuables in your hotel. In the streets around the entrance to the market are many shops selling furniture – including beautiful rocking chairs – and electrical goods. Mercado Huembes, near the Carretera a Masaya in the south of the city, is safer to wander around and has an excellent crafts section. There's a huge range of hammocks – everything from a simple net one (C$140) to a luxury, two-person, woven cotton one with wooden separators and beautiful tassels (from C$800). Products made of leather and skins are in abundance, but choose carefully as many of the species used are endangered. Paintings in the style of the artists' colony on the Solentiname islands are available here, along with many fine pen-and-ink drawings and abstract works. You can buy Nicaraguan cigars as well as pottery and wicker products (*mimbre*) such as baskets, mats, chairs and wall-hangings.

Directory

Embassies and consulates Canada, C El Nogal, no. 25, Bolonia (☎ 2268-0433, ✉ managua @international.gc.ca); UK, one block north of the Military Hospital (☎ 2254-5454); US, km 5.5, Carretera Sur (☎ 2252-7100, ⦿ nicaragua .usembassy.gov).

Exchange Central banks that exchange foreign currency include Banpro and Bancentro, both on the Carretera a Masaya near the *Hotel Princess*, and BAC (Banco de América Central), Plaza España. ATMs accepting foreign cards (Visa, MasterCard and Cirrus) can be found at these banks and in most malls, as well as in many Shell and Texaco garages and at the airport.

Health Hospital Bautista, in Barrio Largaespada (☎ 2249-7070, ⦿ www.hospitalbautistanicaragua .com) is your main option; Hospital Metropolitano Vivian Pellas, km 9 ¾, Carretera a Masaya, 250m west (☎ 2255-6900, ⦿ metropolitano.com.ni), is more sophisticated and more expensive. Both are private, with 24hr emergency departments. Medco is one of the larger pharmacy chains, with branches at Bello Horizonte or Plaza España. Alternatively, try the 24hr pharmacy at the Hospital Bautista.

Immigration The main office is two blocks north of Los Semáforos de la Colonia Tenderí (Mon–Fri 8am–noon, 2–4.30pm; ☎ 2244-3989) and there's another in the Metrocentro (Mon–Fri 10am–6pm, Sat & Sun 10am–1pm; ☎ 2244-3989). Both can renew visas (US$10 for thirty days).

Internet There are plenty of internet cafés around town – in Barrio Martha Quezada, try Cyber@Center, Av Williams Romero, one block north of Cine Dorado (C$15/hr), or Kafe@Internet a few metres away (C$15/hr).

Post office Palacio de Correos (Mon–Fri 8am–5pm, Sat 8am–noon), Plaza de la Revolución.

Moving on

As the transport hub of the country, Managua is virtually impossible to avoid. From here you can get almost anywhere by bus, while flights put the otherwise inaccessible parts of the country on the map.

By air

Flights depart from Managua's Augusto C. Sandino Airport. Copa (⦿ www.copaair.com) and Taca (⦿ www.taca.com) between them have international flights to San José, Panama City, Guatemala, San Salvador and Tegucigalpa. Domestic airline La Costeña (☎ 2263-2142, ⦿ www.lacostena.com.ni) runs one or more flights a day to San Carlos, Bluefields, Puerto Cabezas and the Corn Islands. Advance reservations are essential; the airline has an office at the airport and agencies across the city. Tickets can be reserved by phone or online – it's often worth confirming your flight over the phone before you fly too – see p.406.

By bus

The busiest domestic bus routes are those between the capital and the provincial cities, particularly León in the northwest and Granada in the south. Other main routes run to Matagalpa, Estelí, Masaya and Rivas, the last for connections to the Costa Rican border and the beach town of San Juan del Sur.

Domestic bus destinations

Domestic buses depart from one of several markets in Managua (see "Arrival", p.417), with the exception of Granada and Masaya minibuses, which can be hailed at La UCA. Note that buses listed as having regular departures (hourly or more frequent) run from 5am–6pm, unless otherwise stated. Buses to the Atlantic Coast can be grievously affected by the weather – in the rainy season in particular, times are elastic and journeys can be decidedly wearing.

Bluefields Express departure daily at 9pm, arriving in Rama around 3am for the early-morning *panga* to Bluefields; 10hr. From Mercado Iván Montenegro.

Chinandega Standard departures every 30min; 2hr 30min. Express departures every 30min; 1hr 40min. Both from Mercado Israel Lewites.

El Rama Five daily second-class departures; 8hr. From Mercado Mayoreo.

Estelí Standard departures every 30min; 3hr. Express departures hourly; 2hr. Both from Mercado Mayoreo.

Granada Second-class departures from Mercado Huembes every 15min; 1hr 20min. Express departures from La UCA every 15–20min; 1hr.

León Second-class departures every 15–30min; 2hr. Express departures every 15–20min; 1hr 30min. Both from Mercado Israel Lewites.

Masaya Second-class departures from Mercado Huembes every 20min; 1hr. Express services from La UCA every 15–20min; 40min.

Matagalpa Second-class departures every 30min; 3hr. Express services hourly; 2hr. Both from Mercado Mayoreo.

Ocotal Second-class departures hourly; 3hr 30min. From Mercado Mayoreo.

Puerto Cabezas Second-class departures at noon & 5pm; 24hr. It's a notoriously tough trip, and damn-near impossible after heavy rains – consider flying. From Mercado Mayoreo.

Rivas Second-class departures every 25min; 2hr 25min. Express services every 30min; 2hr. Both from Mercado Huembes.

San Carlos Five daily second-class departures; 10–12hr. From Mercado Mayoreo.

San Jorge Express departures every 30min; 2hr. From Mercado Huembes.

International bus destinations

Three major companies serve the international bus routes between Central America's capitals. The Tica Bus station (☎2222-6094, ☜www.ticabus.com) sits two blocks east and one block south of the old Cine Dorado, while the King Quality station (☎2228-1454, ☜kingqualityca.com) is nearby on Calle 27 de Mayo, opposite Plaza Inter. Transnica buses (☎2277-2104, ☜transnica.com) depart from 300m north and 50m east of the Rotonda Metrocentro.

Guatemala City With King Quality (2 daily at 2.30am & 3.30am; 17hr); with Tica Bus (1 daily at 5am, with overnight in San Salvador; 31hr).

Panama City With Tica Bus (1 daily at noon, with overnight in San José; 32hr).

San José With King Quality (1 daily at 2.30am; 9hr); with Tica Bus (3 daily at 6am, 7am & noon; 10hr); with Transnica (4 daily at 5am, 7am, 10am & 1pm; 9hr).

San Salvador With King Quality (2 daily at 3.30am & 11.30am; 11hr); with Tica Bus (1 daily at 4.45am; 11hr); with Transnica (2 daily at 3.30am & 11.30pm; 10hr).

Tegucigalpa With King Quality (2 daily at 3.30am & 11.30am; 9hr); with Tica Bus (1 daily at 5am; 8hr); Transnica (3 daily at 3.30am, 5am & 11.30am; 8hr).

The northwest

Nicaragua's Pacific **northwest** is hot and dry, with grassy plains punctuated by dramatic volcanoes. The largest city in the northwest, and once the capital of Nicaragua, is **León**, the birthplace of the Sandinistas and a lively town with a dynamic tourist scene. The northwest's sweeping **coastline** is just as appealing, with surf beaches and breezes that relieve the sometimes vicious heat. **Chinandega** offers no such relief, but is a convenient base near the Honduran border.

LEÓN

The capital of Nicaragua until 1857, **LEÓN**, 90km northwest of Managua, is now a provincial city, albeit an energetic, architecturally arresting one. A significant element in the city's healthy buzz is the presence of the **National University** (the country's premier academic institution) and its large student population, swelled by the ranks of young people studying at León's various other colleges. León's colonial architecture is arguably as impressive as Granada's; visitors are also attracted by an impressive range of tours, an entertaining backpacker scene and the best art gallery in the country.

Yet for all its buzz, León has a violent history. The original León was founded by Hernández de Córdoba in 1524 at the foot of Volcán Momotombo, where its ruins – now known as **León Viejo** (see p.429) – still lie. The city was moved northwest to its present-day location after León Viejo's destruction by an earthquake and volcanic eruption in 1609. In 1956, the first President Somoza was gunned down in León by the martyr-poet Rigoberto López Pérez. During the Revolution in the 1970s, the town's streets were the scene of several decisive battles between the Sandinistas and Somoza's

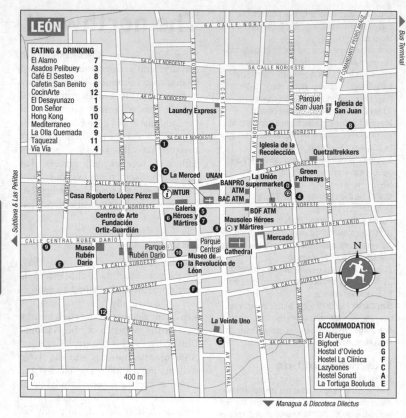

Managua & Discoteca Dilectus

forces, and many key figures in the Revolution either came from León or had their political start here. Although many years have passed since then, and most of the Sandinista graffiti has been painted over, the city continues to wear its FSLN heart on its sleeve: the street signs read "León: ciudad heroica – primera capital de la revolución", and a few fine examples of the city's famous murals remain.

What to see and do

León's heartbeat is the **Parque Central**, which is shadowed by the largest cathedral in Central America. **Calle Central Rubén Darío** runs along the Parque's northern edge, cutting the city in two from east to west, while **Avenida Central** runs between the Parque and Cathedral north to south. Splendidly and unusually, León has street signs, though people will usually still give you directions in relation to a landmark.

Parque Central

The **Parque Central**, at the intersection of Calle Central Rubén Darío and Avenida Central, is centred on a statue of General Máximo Jeréz guarded by four lions. It's a good place to take the city's pulse, visited as it is by a constant stream of locals, street vendors and tourists. If you value your hearing, avoid the square at 7am and noon, when a ludicrously loud air-raid siren wails across the city – a throwback to the days when workers flocked in to León's booming cotton factories.

Cathedral

The city's most obvious attraction is its colossal **Cathedral** (open from sunrise to late evening), a gorgeous, battered, cream-coloured structure whose volcano-blackened turrets tower over the heart of León. Begun in 1747, it took nearly a hundred years to complete. Despite its lofty exterior, the only items of interest inside are the statues of the Twelve Apostles and the tomb of local hero **Rubén Darío**, Nicaragua's most famous writer and poet, which is guarded by a statue of a mournful lion. Mass is held daily at about 5pm and is worth attending, if only to people-watch.

Museo de la Revolución de León

On the western side of the park is one of the city's Sandinista strong-holds, the **Museo de la Revolución de León** (daily 8am–5pm; C$30). You'll be shown around the airy, decaying building by an FSLN combat veteran, who'll talk you through the extensive collection of photos, articles and news clippings documenting the Revolution, its historical antecedents and its aftermath. It's an affecting tour, though you'll need some Spanish to make sense of things. You may be allowed onto the roof, which has cracking views of León.

Mausoleo Héroes y Mártires

The northeast corner of the Parque is home to the **Mausoleo Héroes y Mártires**, a star-shaped monument dedicated to those who died fighting for freedom during the civil war, surrounded by a large mural colourfully detailing Nicaragua's history from pre-Columbian times to the ending of the civil war.

La Recolección

Two blocks northeast of the Parque is one of Nicaragua's finest colonial churches, **La Recolección**, with a beautiful Mexican Baroque facade dating from 1786, and some fine mahogany woodwork inside.

Parque Rubén Darío

Followers of Nicaragua's other religion, poetry, might want to head for the **Parque Rubén Darío**, a block west of the Parque Central, which is home to a statue of the rather sombre-looking poet dressed in suit and bow tie.

Centro de Arte Fundación Ortiz-Guardián

Sitting on Calle Central Rubén Darío a little to the west of Parque Rubén Darío is the **Centro de Arte Fundación Ortiz-Guardián** (Tues–Sat 10.30am–6.30pm, Sun 11am–5pm; C$20), an expansive art gallery in two renovated colonial houses. The collection features an engrossing cross-section of Latin American art, including pre-Hispanic and modern ceramics and some impressive modern art.

Museo Archivo Rubén Darío

A few blocks further west is the **Museo Archivo Rubén Darío** (Mon–Sat 8am–noon & 2–5pm, Sun 8am–noon; donations requested), housed in a substantial León residence that was the home of the poet's aunt, Bernarda. Inside, the lovingly kept rooms and courtyard garden are home to wonderfully frank plaques detailing Darío's

---

RUBÉN DARÍO

Born in 1867 in a village outside Matagalpa, the writer Rubén Darío is little known beyond Latin America, but is one of Nicaragua's most famous sons. *Azul ...*, published in 1888, became particularly influential and is often cited as a cornerstone for the birth of Spanish-language modernism. Nearly a century after his death in 1916, he remains one of the region's most influential poets.

THE GIGANTONA OF SUBTIAVA

In November and December, the one sight in León not to be missed is that of posses of young boys hammering away at snare drums while a huge **Gigantona** (a papier-mâché, Rio Carnaval-style figure of an elegant colonial-era lady, directed from underneath by a slightly older teenager) weaves among them. Traditionally, the boys are given a few córdobas for a recital of poetry, typically that of national bard Rubén Darío. The *gigantonas* are judged during the festivities of La Purísima (a festival celebrating the Virgin Mary's conception) on December 7, with the best winning a prize.

tempestuous personal life and diplomatic and poetic careers, along with personal possessions and commemorative items, such as Rubén Darío lottery tickets.

Galería Héroes y Mártires

Continuing in a revolutionary vein, the **Galería Héroes y Mártires** (Mon–Fri 8am–5pm, Sat 8am–noon; C$20), a block north and half a block west of the Parque Central, houses wall after wall of simple, moving black-and-white photos of Nicaraguans (men and women, young and old) killed fighting for the Sandinista cause during the civil war.

La Veinte Uno

Three blocks south of the cathedral lie the ruins of **La Veinte Uno**, the National Guard's 21st garrison and scene of heavy fighting in April 1979. The garrison now houses two very different museums, which together go by the long-winded title of **Museo de Leyendas y Tradiciones Coronel Joaquín de Arrechada Antigua Cárcel de La Veinte Uno** (Tues–Sat 8am–noon & 2–5pm, Sun 8am–3pm; C$20). One half of the building houses a collection of ghoulish figures from Nicaraguan folklore, including a chariot-riding grim reaper and a giant crab, while the other focuses on the garrison's ugly past, with a small collection of revealing black-and-white photos taken during and after the Somoza era. Captions in Spanish document the torture that went on inside.

Subtiava

Four kilometres west of the city centre is the barrio of **Subtiava**, which long predates León and is still home to much of the city's indigenous population. It is also the site of one of the oldest **churches** in the country. Recently renovated, the small adobe building is not always open, but worth a visit if you're catching a bus to or from the beach at Las Peñitas (see p.429).

Arrival and information

By bus Buses arrive at the anarchic, traffic-clogged terminal northeast of the centre, from where you can hop in a taxi (standard fare anywhere in town is C$20) or walk the eight blocks west into town.
Tourist information INTUR, on 2A Av Noroeste, C 2–3 NO (Mon–Fri 8am–1pm), has a few leaflets and maps and general tour information – the hostels and tour companies are usually more helpful.

Accommodation

Budget accommodation in León has really taken off in the last few years, and there is now an abundance of good-value hostels.
El Albergue 3 C NE, Av 3–4 ☎ 2478-6497. Peaceful, good-value place set around a narrow courtyard with high walls that drown out much of the street noise. The dorms are clean and secure, and the private rooms large but basic. There's also a small kitchen and bar, plus free coffee. Dorms US$4, doubles US$14
Bigfoot Av 2 NE ☎ 8917-8832, ⦿ bigfootnicaragua .com. Located right opposite *Vía Vía*, this sociable place is popular with a younger backpacker crowd. The huge dorms are kept fairly clean, a large kitchen is available and there's a small foot-shaped pool. The pleasant veggie café has breakfasts at C$60. Dorms US$6, doubles US$13

* go volcano boarding

Hostal d'Oviedo Av Central ☎2311-3766. Small, quiet hostel downhill from the town centre with friendly Nica owners and a homely front room with easy chairs. There's internet, a kitchen and a fridge too. Dorms US$7, doubles US$15

Hostel La Clínica Av 1 SO, C 2–3 ☎2311-2031. Possibly the only hostel-cum-dental-clinic in existence, this friendly, family-run place offers decent rooms (some with private bath and a/c) around a tiny courtyard, including a small dorm room. The upstairs rooms (with foliage-shaded balcony) are the most desirable, but negotiating the precipitous staircase after a few beers might present a problem. Dorm US$5, doubles US$15

Hostel Sonati 3A C NE ☎2311-4251, ⓦsonati .info. Nonprofit hostel linked to the tour operator of the same name with animal-themed rooms and dorms, a flower-filled courtyard, a kitchen and a quieter atmosphere than some places in town. Dorms US$5, doubles US$15

Lazybones Av 2 NO ☎2311-3472, ⓦlazybonesleon.com. The clean and comfortable dorms at this large hostel are arranged around an airy courtyard with hammocks and a pool table, while the mellow back-courtyard boasts a swimming pool. The doubles and triples are pretty good too – try to get one of the upstairs rooms with a balcony. There's free coffee and tea, plus internet and wi-fi. Dorms US$8, doubles US$20

La Tortuga Booluda 1A C SO ☎2311-4653, ⓦtortugabooluda.com. Great little hostel that's a lovely place to relax during the day as well as lay your head down at night. Set only a few blocks from the centre, it still feels set apart, and the free pancake breakfasts, kitchen facilities, internet and pool table complete the package. Dorms US$7, doubles US$24

Vía Vía Av 2 NE ☎2311-6142, ⓦviaviacafe.com. Opposite *Bigfoot*, and just as popular. The on-site bar and restaurant are probably the biggest draws of this Belgian-owned branch of the hostel chain,

TOURS IN LEÓN

As you might expect from a backpacker-friendly city with volcanoes, beaches and mangroves within striking distance, León is packed with tour operators. The headline activity is volcano-boarding, in which you'll truck off to the ash-covered slopes of Cerro Negro early in the morning, spend a good hour slogging up its alien, gas-belching curves and then skid down on a board that generally moves at a fairly gentle pace despite the fierce gradient, although some boards are faster – and damp days can be especially quick. Almost every operator offers it – Quetzaltrekkers give you two runs (most operators only offer one), Bigfoot are allegedly the fastest and Va Pues offer some proper (if battered) snowboards.

Trips from León can also take in the wet ride through the canyon at Somoto, near the Honduran border, treks up the San Cristóbal and El Hoyo volcanoes, the ruins of León Viejo (see p.429) and more, and Spanish lessons can be arranged. Rates for excursions are a fairly standard US$30 per day, and are given on companies' websites, though you may be able to haggle, especially with a larger group. The companies below are all established and reliable.

Bigfoot Tours Av 2 NE ☎8917-8832, ⓦwww.bigfootnicaragua.com. Fun firm mostly focusing on volcano-boarding and surf trips to Isla Los Brasile, though other trips can be arranged.

Green Pathways Av 2 NE ☎2315-0964, ⓦgreenpathways.com. Country-wide adventures, including turtle-watching and volcano-scaling.

Quetzaltrekkers 2A C NE ☎2311-6695, ⓦquetzaltrekkers.com. Reliable bunch offering volcano treks around the country, including a full-moon lava hike up Volcán Telica. All profits go towards supporting street children in León.

Sonati 3A C NE ☎2311 4251, ⓦsonati.info. Relatively inexpensive non-profit-making company, operating from the hostel of the same name, whose volcano trips are supplemented by visits to the swamps of Isla Juan Verano and various birdwatching trips.

Va Pues On the corner of Av 4 SO and C 4 ☎2315-4099, ⓦvapues.com. From their office in the *CocinArte* restaurant, this moderately upmarket operator has countrywide tours, trips to local *fincas* and – of course – volcano-boarding.

but the tiled colonial corridors also hold two reasonable dorms and some pleasant private rooms. Dorms US$6, doubles US$17.50

Eating

León boasts a cosmopolitan and ever-increasing range of places to eat and drink, from pizza joints and seafood restaurants to chic café-bars and bohemian hangouts. Most of the restaurants close around 10pm, while the trendier places stay open until the small hours, especially at weekends.

Asados Pelibuey 2A Av NO. You'll find a handful of tables and platefuls of delicious chicken, beef and other *comida corriente* from C$45 at this excellent little place, run by a women's co-operative.

Café El Sesteo C Central Rubén Darío, on the corner of the Parque Central. The town's smartest café has a spacious and civilized interior and tables looking out over the Parque Central, making it a great place to people-watch and take in the atmosphere. Food isn't cheap (breakfast C$90, red snapper C$230), but it's a good pit-stop for a coffee (C$25).

Cafetin San Benito 2A Av NE. Tasty juices and a solid buffet will set you back a paltry C$30 in the café out front or courtyard out back. There's Chinese food (from C$25) too. Closed Sun.

CocinArte On the corner of 4 Av SO and C 4. Colourful restaurant towards the southern end of town serving a large vegetarian menu as well as local specialities. Mains from C$80.

El Desayunazo 2A Av NO. This green-tabled front room, half colonial elegance, half greasy spoon, serves decent grub to gringos from 6am – Nica breakfast C$40, *ranchero* breakfast C$55.

Hong Kong 1A C SO. Choose between reasonably priced Nica grub (chicken and pork plates will set you back C$50–70) and salty-but-filling Chinese dishes (chop suey C$55).

Mediterraneo 2A Av NO. One of León's classier joints, with smart staff, soft lighting and a starlit back room. The food's good too, and a change from *comida corriente* – try the fish curry (C$160) or carbonara (C$120).

Taquezal 1A C SO. Rustic but stylish café-bar with candle-lit tables and a good menu featuring decent vegetarian pasta dishes, Chinese food, wonderful iced tea with lemon and a fine selection of espresso drinks. Mains from C$100. It gets dancier later in the evening, when you may have to pay a C$50 cover charge. Closed Sun.

Drinking and nightlife

León is second only to Managua in the party stakes, thanks in large part to its many students, and Fridays and Saturdays are usually fairly happening. Most of the restaurants are good for a beer too.

El Alamo 1A Av NO. There's a sports bar downstairs and salads and steak on the menu (around C$100), but the draw here is the balcony up top, where you can sip a beer (C$21), look out over skateboarders and football games in the square below, and watch the sun ease its way over the surrounding buildings.

Don Señor 1A Av NO. With tables downstairs overlooking La Merced church and a dancefloor upstairs, this compact setting is ever popular with locals and tourists.

La Olla Quemada C Central Rubén Darío. You'll find big speakers and a lively, mostly local crowd at this scruffily funky bar, which is busiest on Wed (live music), Fri (karaoke) and Sun (films).

Vía Vía 2A Av NE. The bar-restaurant at this popular hostel is regularly full, especially when there's live music (every Fri) or a quiz night (fortnightly Mon). Its selling point is its lively atmosphere (complete with pool table) but they also do decent Mexican and European food. Mains from C$70, breakfast from C$45.

Directory

Exchange There's a cluster of banks on the corner of C1 NE and Av 1, all with ATMs.

Internet There are scores of internet cafés: CyberFlash.com, opposite *Vía Vía*, has a quick connection (C$10/hr) and can also burn pictures from your camera to disk.

Language schools Most of the hostels and tour companies, including Va Pues (see p.427) offer lessons and homestays, while Nicaragua Spanish Language Schools (W nicaraguaspanishschools.org) are an established institution.

Laundry Most hostels will wash clothes, or try the friendly Laundry Express (Av Central & 4A C NO; C$120/large load).

Post office Av 3 NO, C 3–4.

Moving on

By bus to: Chinandega (every 15min; 1hr 30min); Estelí (3 daily; 2hr 30min); Guasaule (1 daily at 6am; 3hr 30min); Las Peñitas (14 daily; 45min); Managua (every 15min; 1hr 15min–2hr); Matagalpa (3 daily; 3hr); San Isidro (for more frequent Matagalpa and Estelí connections; 24 daily; 2hr).

AROUND LEÓN

Worthwhile day-trip destinations from León include the Pacific beach of **Las**

Peñitas, west of the city and easily accessible by bus, and more out-of-the-way UNESCO World Heritage Site of **León Viejo**.

Las Peñitas and Poneloya

Surfers come to **Las Peñitas**, 20km west of León, for reliable Pacific waves, although the village's relaxed vibe is enjoyable whether you're bound for board or hammock. The water here is fairly rough, due to a combination of powerful waves and riptides, but you can swim here reasonably safely. **Poneloya**, 2km north, is a different story: ask locals about riptides (*corrientes peligrosos*) before venturing into the water here, and never swim alone. Nearby **Isla Juan Venado** is a nature reserve and turtle-nesting site.

Most travellers come to Las Peñitas as a day-trip from León. **Buses** leave León from the Terminal Poneloya on C Darío, near the Subtiava church (see p.426) every 55 minutes (until 6pm; 45min). The last bus back to León leaves at 6.45pm. A taxi will cost around US$12.

Accommodation

Accommodation in town is limited, but there are several simple places right on the black-sand beach. Both places offer surfboard hire and can help arrange fishing trips and excursions to Isla Juan Venado.

Barco de Oro On the beach ☎2317-0275, ⓦwww.barcadeoro.com. Formerly a nightclub frequented by Somoza, this place is now a tranquil travellers' haven. The basic rooms have rustic wooden beds, en-suite bathrooms and a lovely upstairs balcony for sunset-watching. There's quality seafood on offer in the restaurant. US$20

Beach Hostal Oasis On the beach ☎8839-5344, ⓦoasislaspenitas.com. Even more relaxed, with a thatched bar, bungalows and dorm beds. Dorms US$6, doubles US$20

León Viejo

Founded in 1524, **León Viejo** (Mon–Fri 9am–5pm, Sat & Sun 9am–4pm; C$45), 32km east of the modern city and now designated a UNESCO World Heritage Site, was the original site of **León**, before it was destroyed by an earthquake and volcanic eruption on December 31, 1609. Among the ruins excavated since the site's discovery in 1967 are a cathedral, monastery and church; the graves of Nicaragua's first three bishops and of the country's founder, **Francisco Fernández de Córdoba** were also uncovered. It's a modest site, although a wander around the half-restored buildings and accompanying plaques gives you a good idea of just how bloody Nicaragua's colonial history was. The surroundings are almost as fun: for much of the year the woods are rich with birds and butterflies, and the old fort, located just east of the main ruins, offers tremendous views of Lago de Managua and brooding Volcán Momotombo.

Unless you visit with a tour, getting to the site is half the fun. You'll first need to head to **La Paz Centro**, a village about 60km north of Managua – buses leave León every half-hour or so. Some will drop you off on the motorway just outside town: get a motorized rickshaw to La Paz Centro's bus terminal for a few córdobas. From here, buses run about hourly through small villages to the site itself, which sits a few hundred metres from the route's terminus, Puerto Momotombo. The total journey there can take anything from ninety minutes to double that – set off early.

CHINANDEGA

CHINANDEGA, 35km northwest of León, is primarily a working city and forms one of the many cogs in the Nicaraguan economy. Set on a plain behind looming Volcán San Cristóbal, the area's dry, kiln-like climate is ideal for growing cotton, the area's main economic activity, along with Flor de Caña **rum**, Nicaragua's export-grade tipple, produced in a distillery on the outskirts of town. Chinandega is generally visited on the way to the Honduran border and,

INTO HONDURAS

Crossing into **Honduras** via **Guasaule** can be chaotic. You'll get a fair bit of attention from touts – you can usually get better rates closer to the border, so if you are changing cash, it's worth waiting. You can get buses here from Chinandega and there may be a direct service from Managua – ask your accommodation in the city. The exit tax is currently US$2 (US$4 in the evenings, at weekends and during festivals), and the border post is open 24 hours. There is a US$10 fee to enter Nicaragua.

It's just under 1km between the Nicaraguan border post and the Honduran side, across an impressive bridge, and it's easily walkable, though you'll be repeatedly offered bicycle taxis (C$20) from Guasaule bus station. From the border there's a direct bus to Tegucigalpa every two hours.

There's another crossing at **El Espino**, which is connected to the small town of Somoto by frequent buses. Somoto, home to a smattering of accommodation and a canyon (which you can visit on tours from León and Estelí), is served by regular buses from Estelí and hourly departures from Managua's Mercado Mayoreo. Border fees are standard and the crossing relatively quiet.

with wildlife-rich volcanoes nearby and a decidedly untouristed vibe, it's not a bad place to stop off. Most action centres on the Parque Central, which has an odd miniature fort at its centre, and Parroquia Santa Ana, a faded but peaceful church opposite its northern end.

The coast west of here is truly beautiful and unspoilt, with great surfing and kayaking. If you're keen to explore, there is some laidback accommodation in the village of **Jiquilillo** – check out ⓦrancho-esperanza.com.

Arrival and information

By bus Buses arrive at the market southeast of the centre.
Exchange There are several ATMs, including a BAC a block east and half a block south of the Parque Central.
Tourist information There's an INTUR office (Mon–Fri 8am–1pm) opposite the BAC, where you can get info on climbing volcanoes and visiting the area's quiet beaches. Don Alvaro at *Hotel Casa Grande* can organize walking trips to San Cristóbal (US$25 per person) and a stay in his family farm on its slopes. Ibis Kayaking (☎8961-8548, ⓦibiskayaking.com) offer trips for a day or more to the spectacular mangrove estuaries of the Padre Ramos reserve, on the coast to the west of Chinandega.

Accommodation

Don Mario Two blocks north and one block east of the Parque Central ☎2341-4054. This lovely, relaxing little place is the best option in town, with welcoming rooms, neat en suites and a shared kitchen. Doubles US$18
Hotel Casa Grande A block and a half east of the Parque Central ☎2340-4283. Basic, cheap rooms (some without locks) above a friendly family home. Owner Don Alvaro is a good bet for tours (see "Tourist information", above). Doubles US$15

Eating and drinking

The competing sound systems of a series of bars at the northeast end of the Parque Central play everything from folk laments to Euro pop, and are your best bet for an evening drink.
Fritanga La Parrillada One block south of the Parque Central. Classic *comida corriente* café, its deliciously smoky meats cooked on a barbecue on the pavement. Meal and drink C$65.
Pizza Hot Two blocks south of the Parque Central. Fill your belly with reasonable pizzas (from C$145) and chicken (from C$85).

Moving on

By bus to: Guasaule (roughly every 30min; 1hr 30min); Jiquilillo (5 daily from the El Mercadito terminal – get a taxi from the main terminal; 1hr 30min); León (every 15min; 1hr 30min); Managua (every 20min; 1hr 40min–2hr 30min).

The central highlands

North of Managua, the **central highlands** sweep up from sea level in a lush procession of mountainous hillsides, bright-green coffee plantations and cattle-flecked alpine pastures, stretching north to the Honduran border and east to the jungles and mines of the interior. The climate here is fairly temperate and the soil productive, with plenty of tobacco plantations and an economy based on coffee, grains, vegetables, fruit and dairy farming. The 150km journey north from Managua to **Estelí**, the northeast's largest city, is one of the most inspiring in the country, as the Carretera Interamericana winds through the grassy Pacific plains,

skirting the southern edge of Lago de Managua before climbing slowly into a ribbon of blue mountains. East of here is **Matagalpa**, a town of steep slopes and coffee shops, while around the two sit *fincas* and reserves that merit deeper exploration.

ESTELÍ

Though the largest town in the north, at first sight **ESTELÍ** can seem downtrodden. But this low-key city is an engaging place and a hotbed of political activity. Notorious for its staunchly leftist character, Estelí saw heavy fighting and serious bloodshed during the Revolution. Somoza bore a particular grudge against the town's inhabitants, and waged brutal offensives on the city. The scars have not really healed, either on the bombed-out buildings that still dot the streets or in

ESTELÍ

Texaco Star Mart

UCA Miraflor

ACCOMMODATION
Los Arcos	A
Hospedaje Chepito	G
Hospedaje Luna	B
Hospedaje San Ramón	E
Hostal Tomabú	F
Miraflor	C
Sacuanjoche	D

Parque Central
Cathedral
Centro Recreativo Las Segovias
Galería de Héroes y Mártires
Artesanía Nicaragüense
Banco de América Central
Casa de Cultura

N

EATING & DRINKING
Café Luz	2
La Casita	8
Coffe Café	4
Don Pollo	1
Fuji Hipa Rincón Chino	7
Licuados Ananda	3
Pullaso's Olé	5
El Rincón Pinareño	6
Vuela Vuela	A

0   100 m

8, El Salto de la Estnzuela & Bus Terminals

people's minds, and the region remains a centre of Sandinista support.

Estelí's relatively rural setting makes it a good base for trips. **El Salto de la Estanzuela** – a secluded waterfall within walking distance of the centre – makes for a great day out, while the wonderful **Miraflor nature reserve** is just under 30km away.

What to see and do

Although Estelí lacks the stunning mountain views of Matagalpa, the centre of town is a nice place to wander, and the climate is refreshingly cool. Much of the pleasure lies in soaking up the atmosphere, particularly along **Avenida Central**, whose southern end sees shops' wares spill out onto the street, including cowboy boots and the local farmers' favourite, Western-style hats.

The town's **Parque Central** isn't as nice as some others in the country, but is nonetheless busy from dawn until dusk. The **cathedral** on the eastern side of the Parque has a rather austere facade but an interesting interior, with bright windows and red drapes. The south side of the Parque is dominated by the **Centro Recreativo Las Segovias**, which puts on regular music and sporting events, particularly basketball games. The **Casa de Cultura**, another cultural venue a block to the south, hosts local art exhibitions, dancing and music events. Across the street, the **Artesanía Nicaragüense** has a reasonable selection of crafts, pottery and cigars.

Galería de Héroes y Mártires

Just south of the Parque Central is the tiny **Galería de Héroes y Mártires** (daily 9am–5pm; C$20), a simple yet moving museum devoted to the Revolution and to the many residents of Estelí who died fighting in it. The women who work at the Galería are, for the most part, mothers and widows of soldiers who were killed.

Arrival and information

By bus Estelí has two bus terminals: Cotran Sur, at the southern entrance to town, serves all destinations south of Estelí, while Cotran Norte, 100m north, serves all destinations north of Estelí, plus most express buses to León and one daily Managua bus. Some buses may also drop you at the Shell Estelí or the Shell Esquipulas, on the southern edges of town. A taxi into town from any of these places should only be around C$10 per person.

Tour operators UCA Miraflor, Av 4 NE, C 2–3 (☎2713-2971, ⊛miraflor.org), can arrange accommodation in the reserve and give you general information on getting there independently, and sells coffee by the bag. The friendly TreeHuggers, based in *Hospedaje Luna* (see below), offer general advice, bike hire, information on Spanish classes and cigar tours and can also help organize trips to Miraflor and the canyon at Somoto, near the Honduran border.

Tourist information INTUR, C1 NE (Mon–Fri 8am–1pm; ☎2713-2468, ⊜esteli@intur.gob.ni), has some information on transport links and tours.

Accommodation

Budget accommodation is mostly on the simple side, with a few decent options around the Parque Central and the real cheapies clustered around the scruffy shopping streets to the south.

Hospedaje Chepito Av Central ☎2713-3784. Small, family-run *hospedaje* with decent camp beds and clean concrete floors. The rooms are a bit cell-like, but this is the best cheapie in town. US$5

🏃 **Hospedaje Luna** Av 2 NE ☎8441-8466, ⊛cafeluzyluna.com. Estelí's main backpacker hostel is a likeable place with a social conscience and what is probably the town's most useful information office ("TreeHuggers") within its walls. The dorms and private rooms are clean if basic, there's a good book exchange and wi-fi and the associated *Café Luz*, opposite, is a decent hangout too. Dorms US$8, doubles US$18

Hospedaje San Ramón Av Central ☎2714-0970. Family-run place behind a general store. Rooms are fairly basic and allow for very little ventilation, but the owners are friendly and the shared bathroom is clean. US$7

Hostal Tomabú Av Central ☎2713-3783, Ⓔhostaltomabu.esteli@gmail.com. With its bright courtyard, towel-toting rooms and pot plants, this feels a cut above its nearby rivals. US$18

Miraflor Av Central ☎2713-2003. Small hotel with homely, terracotta-coloured rooms, overhead fan and decent bathroom. There's also a restaurant and bar on site. It's a good deal, especially if you're travelling in a group (five-bed room US$30). US$18

Sacuanjoche Av 1 SE ☎2713-2482. Bright rooms with comfy beds, tiled floors, clean bathroom and varnished wooden ceilings, all set around a pretty patio just south of the centre. US$12

Eating and drinking

Estelí's restaurants depend little on tourists, and as a result most are fairly low-key.

Café Luz Av 2 NE. Civilized tourist den, and a good place to socialize. Most produce is organic and grown by local co-operatives, and everything from good black coffee (C$10), yoghurt (C$18) and *nacatamales* (C$45) to juices and beer is on offer.

La Casita 5min walk past the hospital on the right. Right on the southern edge of town, and a convenient stop if you're visiting El Salto, this charming café has beautifully carved tables, a botanic garden out back and some fairly slow service. Sit by the tinkling stream (surprisingly tranquil despite the nearby motorway), snack on small loaves of bread with honey (C$21) and drink lassis (C$16), pots of chai (C$20) and the like.

Coffe Café C Transversal. Simple coffee shop serving up omelettes, waffles, sandwiches and other light snacks. One of the best places in town for breakfast (plate of fresh fruit C$50).

Don Pollo C 3 NE. A big blue room with cheap and tasty chicken – you can eat well for C$50, if you don't mind a spot of grease. The atmosphere gets a bit boozier come the evening.

Fuji Hipa Rincón Chino Av Central. This restaurant serves up good-value Chinese food as well as some local dishes in its dark interior and plastic-chaired patio. An average meal will set you back C$100.

Licuados Ananda C Transversal. Arranged, rather surreally, around a disused swimming pool, this relaxing outdoor café has mostly veggie mains

(C$80), a reasonable range of smoothies and filling breakfasts. Closed Sun.

El Rincón Pinareño Av 1 SE. Popular restaurant with broad Caribbean and Italian influences but a Nica backbone. The service is slow but the dishes (C$70–150) are tasty. Closed Mon.

Pullaso's Olé C Transversal. The local branch of this small Nica chain offers attentive, uniformed service and succulent meat dishes (around C$150) in its a/c restaurant and restful front garden. A good bet if you fancy a minor splurge.

Vuela Vuela On the corner of C 3 NE and Av 1. This bright café-bar and separate restaurant is an NGO initiative, with profits going to help disadvantaged youths back into the job market. The menu veers from Spanish (seafood paella C$320) to American (cheeseburger C$70), and the coffee (C$20) is pretty decent.

Directory

Exchange There's a bank on every corner of C Transversal and Av 1 SO.

Internet There are plenty of places in town; try Cyber on Av 1 SE, which charges C$10/hr.

Moving on

By bus to: León (3 daily from Cotran Norte; 1 daily at 6.45am from Cotran Sur; 2hr 30min; alternatively, get on any bus to Matagalpa and get off at the San Isidro junction); Managua (15 daily from Cotran Sur; 2–3hr); Masaya (2 daily at 2pm & 3pm from Cotran Norte; 2hr 30min); Matagalpa (every 30min from Cotran Sur; 1hr 45min); Ocotal (12 daily from Cotran Norte; 2hr).

AROUND ESTELÍ

Estelí is blessed with beautiful natural surroundings, some – like the appealing waterfall of **El Salto de la Estanzuela** – an easy day-trip. The gorgeous **Miraflor** reserve to the north is worth staying in for a night or more.

El Salto de la Estanzuela

El Salto de la Estanzuela is one of the few waterfalls in Nicaragua easily accessible on foot from a major centre of population. Located in the **Reserva Natural Tisey-Estanzuela**, it's a lovely two-hour walk through green, rolling hills – although it's also possible to drive right to the foot of the falls. The path begins just past the hospital at the southern edge of town – it's a fairly dull 40min walk to get here, and you may want to get a bus (C$3) from the eastern end of the Parque Central. Turn right at the *Kiosko Europeo* and follow the path around to the left for 4km or so until you see a sign for "Comunidad Estanzuela"; go through the gate on the right-hand side and follow the path for another 1km (you can cut off early if you want to explore the lovely but litter-strewn stretch above). The falls themselves – 35m or so in height – are located at the bottom of a steep flight of steps and cascade spectacularly into a deep pool perfect for swimming in. Don't go directly underneath the falling water as rocks do occasionally fall down, especially after heavy rainfall. Nearby is **El Mirador**, one of the most spectacular viewpoints in all Nicaragua; on a clear day it's possible to see volcanoes as far away as El Salvador.

Miraflor nature reserve

The wonderful **Miraflor nature reserve**, 28km northeast of Estelí, is one of the country's most worthwhile attractions. It covers 206 square kilometres of forest, part of which is farmed by a group of agricultural co-ops – over five thousand locals currently produce coffee, potatoes, milk, cheese and exotic flowers in and around the protected area. One of the project's main aims is to find sustainable ways in which farming and environmental protection can coexist; the emphasis is firmly upon community-centred tourism.

The reserve itself comprises several different **ecosystems**, ranging from savanna to tropical dry forest and humid cloudforest. To best appreciate this diversity it's advisable to stay for at least two or three days, either walking or horseriding between the zones and staying with different families each night – a very satisfying back-to-basics experience. Guides can take you to waterfalls, swimming spots, viewpoints, flower gardens and caves once inhabited by the ancient Yeluca and Cebollal mountain peoples. In terms of flora and fauna, Miraflor is one of the richest reserves in the country, with over three hundred species of bird including quetzal, *guardabarranco* (the national bird of Nicaragua) and *urraca*, a local type of magpie, as well as howler monkeys and reclusive mountain lions. There are also over two hundred species of orchid.

To get to the reserve take a **bus** from Estelí. For El Coyolito, La Pita and El Cebollal, head to the Texaco Star Mart (on the Interamericana just north of the centre – any taxi can take you) at 6am or 1pm; for Yalí, La Rampla or Puertas Azules, head to Cotran Norte at 6am, noon or 3pm. UCA Miraflor and *Hospedaje Luna* in Estelí (for both, see p.432) can **arrange your trip** and advise you on different areas' strengths. Both are helpful (though more English is spoken at *Hospedaje Luna*), booking good, Spanish-speaking local guides (C$15 per group) and accommodation (C$15 for three starchy but delicious meals a day, plus a bed in a farmhouse).

INTO HONDURAS: LAS MANOS

The Las Manos border crossing for Honduras is less busy and less hassle-prone than the trip via Guasaule. The exit fee is US$2 (US$4 evenings, weekends and public holidays). There is a US$10 fee to enter Nicaragua. The post is open 24 hours, but vehicles can only cross between 8am and 5pm. To get here, take one of the regular buses from Managua or Estelí to the small town of Ocotal, then one of the hourly buses to Las Manos (1hr). Continuing on, there are regular buses from Las Manos to the nearest town, El Paraíso, while two direct buses a day leave for Tegucigalpa (usually at about 9am and 2pm).

MATAGALPA

Known as "La Perla del Septentrión" – "Pearl of the North" – **MATAGALPA** is spoken well of by most Nicaraguans, principally, perhaps, because of its relatively cool climate: at about 21–25°C, it's considered *tierra fría* in this land of 30°C-plus temperatures. Located 130km northeast of the capital on the Carretera Interamericana, this small, quiet town is a gateway to the blue-green mountains and coffee plantations that surround it, whether you fancy a short hike into the hills or a longer trip to *fincas* like the famous **Selva Negra** to the north.

What to see and do

Matagalpa's services, hotels and restaurants are spread out between the seven blocks that divide the town's two principal squares: **Parque Morazán** to the north and the smaller **Parque Darío** seven blocks to the south. The town's main thoroughfares, **Avenida José Benito Escobar** and **Avenida Central**, link the two.

At the northern end of town, sunny **Parque Morazán** fronts the **Catedral de San Pedro**, dating from 1874. Unusually, the cathedral was constructed side-on, with its bell towers and entrance facing away from the Parque. A large **Sandinista monument**, consisting of three men firing guns, stands on the eastern side.

One and a half blocks south, the **Museo del Café** (Mon–Fri 8am–12.30pm & 2–5.30pm; free) houses some old photos of Matagalpa life and explanations of the coffee-growing process. The museum sells quality coffee and is also behind Matagalpa's new **Feria Nacional del Café** (held in November), a festival celebrating the town's coffee expertise with talks and traditional music and dance.

The **Casa Museo Comandante Carlos Fonseca** (Mon–Fri 8am–5.30pm; donations welcomed), 100m southeast of the Parque Darío, documents the life

of martyred local hero Carlos Fonseca (co-founder of the Sandinista National Liberation Front), who was gunned down by Somoza's National Guard in 1976.

Cerro Apante

Matagalpa is not a city of intoxicating beauty, but several day-hikes take you out into the inspiring scenery that surrounds it, the most accessible exploring **Cerro Apante**. From Parque Darío head south up the hill for half an hour, following the road into the reserve itself. Turn left at the rangers' cottage, where you'll probably have to pay the C$40 entry fee, and climb the (at times steep) path through pleasant woodland to a *mirador* offering cracking views of the town and the crown of mountains that surrounds it. You can continue along the ridge, but the summit proper is private property – signs warn you off the final climb up some wooden stairs. The walk should take less than three hours in total.

Arrival and information

By bus Matagalpa's bus terminal is southwest of the city centre; it's about a 10min walk from the terminal to Parque Darío.

Tour operators Helpful Matagalpa Tours, one block southeast of Parque Morazán (T 2772-0108, W matagalpatours.com), offers excursions to the surrounding area, including tours of local coffee and chocolate farms and treks in the hills. Newer Nativos, based in *La Buena Onda* hostel (E nativotour@hotmail.com), can organize city tours (US$13), walks up Cerro Apante (US$15) and trips to waterfalls and *fincas*.

Tourist information INTUR (Mon–Fri 8am–1pm & 2–5pm) on Av Central can offer a few fliers and maps.

Accommodation

The choice of accommodation In Matagalpa isn't great, but has improved significantly in recent years.

Alvarado Just north of Parque Darío on Av José Benito Escobar T 2772-2830, E hotel alvarado@gmail.com. This charming, family-run hotel above a pharmacy has wood-panelled rooms, some on the small side (and two without windows). All rooms have en-suite bathroom, TV and fan. US$15

Apante On the east side of Parque Darío T 7272-6890. Offers tasteful rooms with TV, colourfully tiled, hot-water bathroom and modern beds. Some rooms are a lot bigger than others, so ask to see a few before choosing. US$12

La Buena Onda One block north and two blocks east of the cathedral T 2772-2135, W www.hostel matagalpa.com. Smart, welcoming hostel with solid facilities – wi-fi, book exchange, hot water, free coffee and a good in-house restaurant. Nativos tours are based here too. Dorms US$7, doubles US$20

Hospedaje Vic-Pal Three blocks north of the cathedral T 2772-6735. Up a steep street north of the cathedral, these simple rooms could do with soundproofing and a lick of paint, but they're clean and perfectly adequate if you're watching the pennies, and the large courtyard has tremendous views of the hills around. US$6

Eating

Artesanos Next to Matagalpa Tours. Appealing café-bar with a relaxed daytime vibe and a nice buzz come night-time, when it's pretty much *the* place to come. The food is reasonable and the coffee excellent.

Café Picoteo Opposite the Museo del Café. The mostly American-style food (breakfast C$50, fajitas C$110) is fairly average, but this central spot is a decent place for a beer.

Cafetería don Chaco Two blocks south of Parque Morazán on Av José Benito Escobar. Intimate little restaurant serving up a range of Honduran and Nicaraguan dishes. The breakfasts (C$45) will set you up nicely for a day's walking and there are good juices (C$20) and mains (around C$100) too.

Madre Tierra Half a block south of Parque Darío. Groovy little place whose TV-dotted walls don't destroy its alternative atmosphere. The food is unfussy and filling (fajita C$100, chicken with cheese and ham C$130) and it's good for a beer (C$20) in the evening.

Pique's A block and a half east of Parque Morazán. Mexican/Nica joint whose vague stab of sophistication is rather undercut by its cartoony mural of ninjas and conqistadors. The food is tasty, though (try the burrito, C$85, or the C$220 pork chops), and it's a cool place for a drink or two.

Directory

Exchange You'll find a couple of banks with ATMs on Av Central just south of Parque Morazán.
Internet G-Net Cyber Café (C$12/hr), on Av José Benito Escobar, is one of the quicker options.

Moving on

By bus to: Estelí (every 30min; 1hr 45min); León (3 daily; 3hr; alternatively get on any bus to Estelí and get off at the San Isidro junction); Managua (every 20min; 2–3hr); Masaya (2 daily; 3hr).

AROUND MATAGALPA

Although Matagalpa has an exceptional natural setting, most of the area is inaccessible to the independent traveller – see opposite for information on tours. You can get a good feel for it in the grounds of the Selva Negra, where footpaths weave through the thick tropical forest.

Selva Negra

North of Matagalpa, the **Selva Negra** (entry US$2.50, US$5 if staying overnight) is a stretch of dark blue, pine-clad mountains named by the area's German immigrants in the nineteenth century after their homeland's Black Forest, thanks to the physical resemblance and its spring-like climate. An amazing variety of **wildlife** flourishes in these pristine tropical forests, including over eighty varieties of orchid, many birds, sloths, ocelots, margay, deer, snakes, mountain lions and howler monkeys.

Because it offers an accessible route to the forest and mountains, many visitors to the area stay in the **hotel** *Selva Negra* (☎ 2772-5713, ◐ selvanegra.com), 10km north of Matagalpa. The faded but prestigious hotel has good-sized doubles (US$45), individually designed cabañas (US$85) and perfectly adequate dorms (US$15). There's a pricey restaurant on site (though your entry fee doubles as a voucher for food and drink), serving good coffee and traditional German fare as well as local options – avoid the disappointing Sunday buffet.

The **trails** range from short strolls around the central lake to the thigh-burning La Mosquitia, which ascends to 1570m. It's perfectly feasible to come up from Matagalpa early in the morning and pack most of them into a day's hiking. The hotel's owners have grown **coffee** here since 1891, and the *finca* still produces some of the best export-grade coffee in the country; the estate employs 250 workers, most of whom live nearby. Worthwhile **tours** of the operation are run daily at 9am and 3pm (US$5 for guests, US$7 for visitors), including horseback treks (US$10/hr), and there's a small museum too.

To get here, hop on one of the half-hourly **buses** to Jinotega and ask to be let off at Selva Negra. The hotel and office is twenty minutes' walk away – head 100m uphill, turn right at the tank and continue up the track.

The southwest

The majority of Nicaragua's population lives in the fertile **southwest** of the country. Bordered by Lago de Nicaragua to the east and the Pacific to the west, and

studded with volcanoes – Volcán Masaya, Volcán Mombacho and the twin cones of Ometepe's Concepción and Maderas – the southwest is otherwise a flat, low, grassy plain, home to what is left of Nicaragua's beef industry, while coffee plantations can be found at higher altitudes.

Masaya, 29km south of Managua, and **Granada**, 26km further south, are the region's key cities; Masaya's excellent crafts market attracts virtually everyone who comes to Nicaragua, while the nearby **Parque Nacional Volcán Masaya** offers the most accessible volcano-viewing in the country. The picturesque **"Pueblos Blancos"**, or White Towns, lie on the road connecting Managua, Masaya and Granada; the latter, with its fading classical-colonial architecture and lakeside setting, is Nicaragua's most beautiful and touristy city, and makes a good base for exploring nearby attractions such as the **Isletas de Granada** and **Volcán Mombacho**. Some 75km south of Granada, **Rivas**, the gateway to Costa Rica, is of little interest in itself, though many travellers pass through on their way to Isla de Ometepe (see p.455) and the popular beach town of **San Juan del Sur**.

MASAYA

Set midway between Managua and Granada and shadowed by the hulking form of Volcán Masaya, **MASAYA**'s stirring geography and regular festivals would make it an enjoyable stop even if it weren't also the centre of Nicaragua's **artesanía production**. During the Sandinista years, Masaya developed its crafts tradition into a marketable commodity, and the city is now the best place in the country to buy hammocks, rocking chairs, traditional clothing, shoes and other souvenirs. Most visitors come here on day-trips from Managua or Granada, easily manageable on the bus, but Masaya is a pleasant place to overnight too.

MASAYA

N

ACCOMMODATION	
Hostal Santamaria	E
Hotel Central	B
Hotel Ivanias	D
Hotel Regis	C
Madera's Inn	A

EATING & DRINKING	
Cafetin La Criolla	6
Coco Jambo	8
El Esfuerzo	5
La Jarochita	1
Panaderia y	
Reposteria Norma	3
Restaurante Che-Gris	7
Ritmo de la Noche	4
La Ronda	9
Tele Pizza	2
El Toro Loco	10

CALLE PALO BLANCO

San Jerónimo

CALLE EL POCHOTILLO

AVENIDA SAN JERONIMO

AVENIDA SERGIO DELGADILLO

AVENIDA EL PROGRESO

CALLE EL CALVARIO

Estadio

CALLE EL ESTADIO

MALECON

CALLE CENTRAL

CALLE SIMPSON

Parroquia La Asunción

Citibank

BAC & ATM

Police

Bancentro

Parque Central

Mercado Nacional de Artesanía

CALLE SAN MIGUEL

CALLE LA REFORMA

Banpro & ATM

Minibuses to/from Managua

Iglesia San Miguel

Red Cross

0   300 m

Mercado Ernesto Fernández & Bus Terminal ▲

THE SOUTHWEST   NICARAGUA

Volcán Masaya ▲

Laguna de Masaya

What to see and do

Masaya is an attractive place to explore on foot: there's not too much traffic in the streets and all the sights are within walking distance of each other.

Parque Central

What little action there is in downtown Masaya takes place in the local hangout, the **Parque Central**, where – with the help of Spanish finance – **La Parroquia de La Asunción** church (daily 6am–7pm) has been renovated. Its cool interior boasts a lovely wooden ceiling and images of various Central American saints, swathed in coloured satin and wilting gold lamé.

Iglesia de San Jerónimo

The ramshackle **Iglesia de San Jerónimo**, 600m north (opening hours vary but there should be someone to let you in) is the best example of colonial architecture in Masaya. The statue of San Jerónimo on the altar depicts an old man wearing a loincloth and a straw hat, with a rock in his hand and blood on his chest, evidence of self-mortification. Head up the stairs into the tower for great views, volcanoes rearing grandly from the plains.

Mercado Nacional de Artesanía

Two blocks east of the Parque Central sits the Mercado Viejo (daily 8am–6.30pm), which has been converted into the grandly named **Centro Cultural (Antiguo Mercado de Masaya) – Mercado Nacional de Artesanía**. Behind the large, fortress-style walls lies a complex network of stalls selling paintings, many in the naïf-art tradition of the Solentiname archipelago, as well as large, excellent-quality hammocks, carved wooden bowls, utensils and animals, simple wood-and-bead jewellery, cotton shirts, straw hats and leather bags and purses. It's a fun place for a potter even if you're not going to buy anything – safe, not too hustly and dotted with drinks stalls and restaurants. The weekly **Jueves de Verbena** party night (see box below) takes place here too. Check out the giant wall map of the country, which shows the places in Nicaragua where crafts are produced. If your Spanish is up to it, ask about visiting artisans at work in their homes and workshops. Many of the crafts on sale come from designs that originated in the indigenous barrio of **Monimbó**, fifteen minutes' walk south of the market, where you'll find more produce on sale around Iglesia de San Sebastián.

Laguna de Masaya

The **Laguna de Masaya** beckons on the western side of town, seven blocks from the Parque Central. Despite its crystal-line appearance and appealing, forested slopes the laguna is heavily polluted with sewage effluent from the town. It's still worth the walk, though, as the waterfront **malecón** has stunning views of the smoking cone of Volcán Masaya (see p.440) and most of the town's late-night bars and clubs.

Arrival and information

By bus Buses from Managua and Granada arrive at the dusty, chaotic terminal next to Masaya's main market, to the east of town; it's a 15min walk to the centre from here, so ask to be let off earlier, at the Iglesia San Jerónimo. Minibuses from Managua (every 15min) arrive at and depart from the street in front of the small Parque San Miguel, three blocks east of the Parque Central.

Tourist information The INTUR office (Mon–Fri 9am–noon; ☎2522-7615), half a block south of the police station and the Mercado Nacional, can provide some information on local hotels and volcano tours.

Accommodation

There are several reasonable budget options, most clustered a few blocks north of the Mercado Nacional. **Hostal Santamaría** Half a block southeast of the Mercado Nacional ☎2522-2411. The 22 small, tidy rooms here, all en suite with cable TV, are quiet and cool and just a stone's throw from the old market. Popular with Nica travellers. US$20

Hotel Central Av Sergio Delgadillo ☎2522-2867, ✉berperez86@hotmail.com. There's not much difference in ambience between the cheap and simple *Central* and the nearby *Regis*, but the rooms are marginally brighter here. US$8

Hotel Regis Two doors north of *Hotel Central* ☎2522-2300, ✉hotelregismasaya@hotmail.com. A spotlessly clean bargain, despite cell-like, wood-panelled rooms with thin partition walls, with a neat little courtyard. They shut their doors early – check the curfew time before hitting the town. US$8.50

FESTIVITIES IN MASAYA

You may see processions and hear music in festival-loving Masaya at any time of year, but the most exciting time to visit is on Sundays between mid-September and mid-December, when the town indulges in a ninety-day period of revelry known as the Fiesta de San Jerónimo. The beginning of the fiesta sees the Torovenado, a fascinating costumed procession of cross-dressing dancers, mythical creatures and grotesque caricatures. In late January, the Fiesta de San Sebastián features a large-scale mock battle followed by a peace ceremony. A more recent invention is the popular Jueves de Verbena, held every Thursday evening throughout the year in the renovated Mercado Nacional de Artesanía, which offers stalls, food and traditional music.

Hotel Ivania's Two blocks north and one and a half blocks east of the Mercado Nacional ☎2522-7632, ⓦ www.hotel ivanias.com. Smart, modern option a short walk from the centre, with a clientele of foreign travellers and local business folk. It offers bright furnishings, hot water, parking, air conditioning, cable TV and a bar, set around a mellow courtyard. Breakfast is included. US$45

Madera's Inn One block north of *Hotel Central* ☎ 2522-5825, ⓦ hotelmaderasinn .com. Probably the best of the lot in Masaya, with 13 bright and cosy rooms, including a dorm, spread over a tidy and welcoming family house with interesting nooks and knick-knacks and a nice dining area. Rooms come with shared or private bath and either fan or a/c, and breakfast is included. Dorms US$5, doubles US$15

Eating and drinking

Masaya's social scene is fairly low-key. If you fancy a boogie later on, three clubs, *Coco Jambo, Ritmo de la Noche* and *El Toro Loco* get going on the *malecón*, playing pop, reggaeton and salsa until around 3am Thurs–Sat. You'll pay a cover change of C$50 or so at the weekend; get a taxi there and back at night.
Cafetín La Criolla Southwest corner of the Mercado Nacional. Hearty, popular market cheapie – stuff yourself on chicken, plantain, rice and a drink for C$80 and watch tourists and locals browse and haggle.
El Esfuerzo Half a block east of the Parque Central. Small diner-style place that's a good spot to fill up at breakfast or lunch: the gigantic cheese pasties (C$20), burger and chips (C$50) or sandwiches (C$30) should see you right.
La Jarochita On Av Sergio Delgadillo, north of La Asunción ☎ 2522-0450. A charming Mexican restaurant where the waitresses are kitted out in traditional dress, and you can dine on authentic fajitas, burritos and *quesadillas* (C$90–120) and wash it down with tequila or a cold beer (C$20). Head upstairs to the pleasant balcony.
Panadería y Repostería Norma Across from the police station, just north of the Mercado Nacional. A branch of the cheap and delicious bakery, offering croissants (C$10) and various snacks and pastries; a coffee and a cake will set you back C$50.

Restaurante Che-Gris Southeast corner of the Mercado Nacional. The smartest option in the market, this place is renowned for its delicious *brochettas* (C$100–180), and offers seafood (C$150) too.
La Ronda Overlooking La Asunción and the Parque Central. An airy bar and restaurant, *La Ronda* draws a local crowd with cheap beer (C$20, or C$36 for a litre) and televised sport. The food (steak with jalapeños C$130, substantial salad C$100) is pretty decent too.
Tele Pizza Half a block north of La Asunción. This place offers tasty, decent-sized pizzas for C$95–140, as well as pastas (C$80) and salads (C$60–100) from its pink front room and restful courtyard.

Directory

Exchange Banks and ATMs are plentiful in Masaya; there's a handy Banpro machine by the old market, and a branch of BAC opposite the police station where you can change dollars and travellers' cheques.
Internet There are various spots around town: try Cyber Jet, opposite *Hotel Regis* (C$12/hr).
Post office There's a tiny office one block north of the Mercado Nacional next to the BAC (Mon–Fri 8am–noon & 1–4.30pm, Sat 8–11.30am).

Moving on

By bus Regular services run from the main market four blocks east of the artisans' market to: Estelí (2 daily – early; 2hr 30min); Granada (every 20min; 45min); Managua (every 20min; 1hr); Matagalpa (2 daily at 6am & 6.45am; 3hr). Express minibuses run from just east of the artisans' market to Managua (every 15–20min; 40min).

AROUND MASAYA

Attractions around Masaya include the natural sites of Masaya's namesake **volcano** and a crater lake, **Laguna de Apoyo**, which can be explored on foot and with a guide. The nearby **Pueblos Blancos** are famous for various forms of artisanal crafts, including pottery, which is made in the small workshops throughout the villages. The historical site of **Coyotepe**, meanwhile, is a must for anyone interested in the nation's political history.

Coyotepe

Three kilometres out of town on the road to Managua is the old fort of **Coyotepe** (daily 9am–6pm; C$20). Built on a hilltop by the Somoza regime to house political prisoners, the abandoned structure commands stunning views of Masaya and the volcanoes of Masaya and Mombacho, and also offers an eerie reminder of the atrocities carried out here by Somoza's National Guard: when Sandinistas stormed the fort during the Revolution, the National Guard responded by slaughtering all those inside. It's now administered by Nicaragua's Boy Scouts, who will illuminate the tunnels on a torchlit tour and tell you grim tales about Nicaragua's recent past.

From Masaya, take any Managua-bound **bus** and ask to be let off at the entrance, from where a winding path leads up to the fort. On your return, simply flag any Masaya-bound bus down from the roadside (some stop on the highway just outside Masaya – a cab back to town will cost C$20 or so).

Parque Nacional Volcán Masaya

Just outside Masaya, the **Parque Nacional Volcán Masaya** (daily 9am–4.45pm; C$75; ☎2528 1444) offers you the chance to peer into the smoking cone of a volcano, as well as some stunning long-distance views. Gazing warily over the smoke-blackened rim into the crater's sulphurous depths, you can well imagine why the Spaniards considered this to be the mouth of hell itself – the large white cross above the crater marks the spot where a Spanish friar placed a cross in the sixteenth century to exorcise the volcano's demonic presence. This is still one of the most active volcanoes in the world; the last eruption occurred in 2001, but plumes have been spotted since then, and signs advise drivers to park their cars facing downhill in case a quick getaway is required.

The **park entrance** lies between km 22 and km 23 on the Managua–Granada highway, about 4km north of Masaya. You can get off any **bus** (except the express) between Managua and Masaya or Granada at the entrance – you'll pass Coyotepe (see above) on the way. Alternatively, you could hire a taxi from Masaya (about C$200 return). From the entrance, it's a 1.5km walk up the road to the **Centro de Interpretación Ambiental** (daily 9am–4pm), home to an exhibition outlining the area's geology, agriculture and pre-Columbian history, along with an interesting 3D display of the country's chain of volcanoes.

From the centre you're best off hitching or getting a spot in one of the regular minibuses going up to the crater (C$50 up, C$100 return – they are less frequent in the afternoon so arrive early if you can), as it's a fairly steep 5km hike up a paved road. Walking down is more pleasant, although in theory (and despite the lack of any kind of danger) you must be accompanied by a guide along this stretch – if you're not, a ranger will probably follow you down, at a discreet distance, on a bike. The ranger service also offers guided **tours** on two other trails, Sendero Los Coyotes and Sendero de Las Pencas, as well as occasional night-hikes and short trips to the extinct cone of Comelito and the subterranean Cueva Tzinancanostoc, where you'll see bizarre lava formations and a bat colony. Look out for the stunted bromeliads common to high-altitude volcanic areas, and the famous *chocoyos del cráter*, small green parrots that have thrived in an atmosphere that should be poisonous. The rangers at the crater can point out a few short walks around the area that you can take unaccompanied.

Pueblos Blancos

Scattered within 15km of Masaya are the "**Pueblos Blancos**" or White Towns:

Nindiri, **Niquinohomo**, **Masatepe**, **Catarina**, **Diria** and **Diriomo**. The name comes from the traditional whitewash used on the villages' houses – called *carburo*, it is made from water, lime and salt – as well as a past tradition of practising white magic in the area. The white buildings are pretty, but there's not much more to see: although each town has its own specific artisan traditions and fiestas, and local identity is fiercely asserted, they seem remarkably similar, sleepy towns with a few hangers-out around nearly identical central squares. **Catarina** is the prettiest, the main draw being **El Mirador** (C$20), a lookout at the top of the village that stares right down into the blue waters of the collapsed crater lake of Laguna de Apoyo, with Volcán Masaya looming behind it. Restaurants, cafés and *artesanía* stalls have sprung up around the viewpoint.

A regular local **bus** runs roughly every thirty minutes from Masaya's main bus terminal to Catarina. From Granada, buses to Niquinohomo pass through the town, or alternatively you can take any Masaya or Managua bus and ask to be let off at the Catarina turning, from where you'll need to take another short bus ride to the edge of the village.

Laguna de Apoyo
fun for a day trip

The volcanic **Laguna de Apoyo** draws tourists with its mineral-rich waters, tropical rainforest and stunning views. Nature-lovers will be entranced by the rare **flora and fauna**, including howler monkeys, armadillos and toucans, and divers can check out the lake's unique fish, but it's a pleasant place just to relax and sip a few beers too. Its popularity means stretches get a bit party-centric on busy days, and others are under threat from developers despite its natural reserve status, but it remains a stunning place.

Masaya has direct **buses** to the laguna departing at around 10am and 3pm.

But more tourists visit from Granada, whether on a tour (see p.445), or using the *Bearded Monkey* or *Hostel Oasis* shuttles (C$40–60 return).

Accommodation

Apoyo Lodge ☎ 8837-3990, ⊛ apoyolodge.com. A bit swisher than the other options, and it gets good reports. It also offers yoga and breakfast is included. Dorms US$8, doubles US$35

Estación Biológica ☎ 8882-3992, ⊛ gaianicaragua .org. You can stay at this research centre, which also offers PADI courses and voluntary work. Dorms US$10, doubles US$21

Monkey Hut ☎ 8887-3546, ⊛ thebeardedmonkey .com. Many backpackers head to this place for day-trips, paying US$6 to use the hammocks, kayaks, kitchen and buzzing bar, which means the accommodation can feel like an afterthought. Dorms US$10, doubles US$25

GRANADA *1 or 2 nights*

Set on the western shore of Lago de Nicaragua, some 50km southeast of Managua, **GRANADA** was once the jewel of Central America. The oldest Spanish-built city in the isthmus, it was founded in 1524 by Francisco Fernández de Córdoba, who named it after his home town in Spain. During the colonial period Granada became fabulously rich, its wealth built upon exploitation: sited only 20km from the Pacific, the city was a transit point for shipments of gold and other minerals mined throughout the Spanish empire. In the mid-nineteenth century Granada fell to American adventurer William Walker, who briefly gained control of the city – and, by default, the entire country. Granada paid dearly for the eventual overthrow of Walker; as he retreated in the face of international resistance, he burned the city practically to the ground.

Today Granada is central to the Nicaraguan government's tourism ambitions. Its popularity with foreign visitors has led to a large-scale restoration of the stunning old **colonial buildings**, many of them newly repainted in pastel

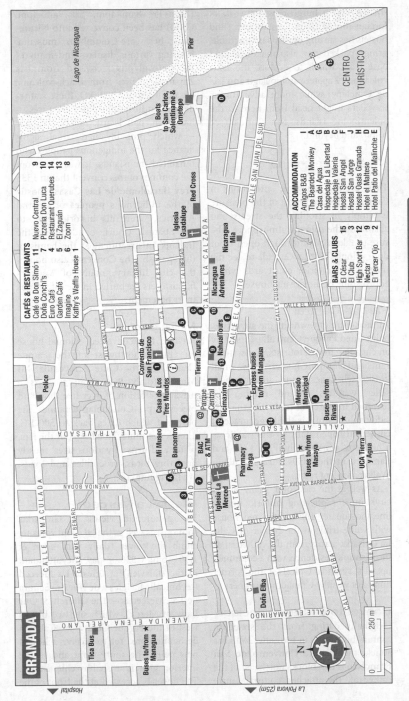

GRANADA

CAFÉS & RESTAURANTS
Café de Don Simón	11
Doña Conchi's	7
Euro Café	4
Garden Café	5
Imagine	6
Kathy's Waffle House	1
Nuevo Central	9
Pizzeria Don Luca	10
Restaurant Querubes	14
El Zaguán	13
Zoom	8

ACCOMMODATION
Amigos B&B	I
The Bearded Monkey	A
Casa del Agua	G
Hospedaje La Libertad	B
Hospedaje Valeria	C
Hostal San Angel	F
Hostal San Jorge	J
Hotel Oasis Granada	H
Hotel el Maltese	D
Hotel Patio del Malinche	E

BARS & CLUBS
El César	15
El Club	3
High S;port Bar	12
Nectar	9
El Tercer Ojo	2

Lago de Nicaragua

Pier

Boats to San Carlos, Solentiname & Ometepe

CENTRO TURÍSTICO

Iglesia Guadalupe

Red Cross

Nicaragua Mia

Nicaragua Adventures

Tierra Tours

NahualTours

Convento de San Francisco

Casa de Los Tres Mundos

Mi Museo

Bancentro

BAC & ATM

Parque Central

Bicimaximo

Express buses to/from Managua

Mercado Municipal

Buses to/from Rivas

Pharmacy Praga

Iglesia La Merced

Buses to/from Masaya

UCA Tierra y Agua

Doña Elba

Police

Tica Bus

Buses to/from Managua

Hospital

La Pólvora (25m)

CALLE LA CALZADA
CALLE SAN JUAN DEL SUR
CALLE EL CAIMITO
CALLE CUISCOMA
CALLE EL MARTIRIO
CALLE VEGA
CALLE ATRAVESADA
CALLE LA CONCEPCIÓN
CALLE LA CONSULADO
CALLE ESTRADA
CALLE LA HOYADA
AVENIDA BARRICADA
CALLE OBISPO ULLOA
CALLE EL REAL XALTEVA
CALLE EL TAMARINDO
CALLE LA CEIBA
CALLE NILFA
CALLE 4 DE SEPTIEMBRE
CALLE LA LIBERTAD
CALLE LA ATRAVESADA
CALLE SANTA LUCIA
CALLE EL CISNE
CALLE XALTEVA
CALLE EL ARSENAL
CALLE CORRAL
AVENIDA GUZMÁN
AVENIDA BODAN
AVENIDA AMELIA BENARD
CALLE INMACULADA
AVENIDA ELENA ARELLANO

250 m

N

443

shades, and a burgeoning network of foreign-owned bars, restaurants and hostels has sprung up. This manageable, gringo-packed city also makes a good base from which to explore the lake, volcanoes, Zapatera archipelago and Isla de Ometepe, while more adventurous travellers might head from here to the Solentiname islands, San Carlos (see p.460) and beyond.

What to see and do

There are few "must see" attractions in Granada itself, but most of the pleasure is simply in strolling the streets and absorbing the colonial atmosphere – be sure to take a peek through open front doors along Calle La Calzada to see the magnificent interior courtyards which adorn some of the private houses.

Parque Central

At the centre of town sits the attractive, palm-lined **Parque Central**, peopled by an engaging mix of tourists, stalls, itinerants and clumping horses. A few small kiosks sell snacks, and an ice-cream seller wanders around ringing his handbell in search of trade. On the east side of the Parque is the large, graceful **cathedral** (open daily to the public as a house of worship), built in 1712 and damaged in the 1850s during William Walker's violent reign.

As well as the cathedral, many of the city's most captivating historic houses line the square. The palatial red house with white trim on the corner of Calle La Calzada, across from the cathedral, is the **Bishop's Residence**, with a columned upstairs veranda typical of the former homes of wealthy Granadino burghers.

Convento de San Francisco

Originally dating from the sixteenth century but rebuilt in 1867 after Walker's attack, the historic **Convento de San Francisco** is two blocks northeast of the cathedral. The attached cultural centre (Mon–Fri 8am–4pm, Sat 9am–4pm; C\$40) has been converted into Nicaragua's best pre-Columbian museum, housing various displays and many of the **petroglyphs** recovered from Isla Zapatera. Hewn from black volcanic basalt in about 1000 AD, these statues depict anthropomorphic creatures – half man, half lizard, turtle or jaguar – which probably had ritual significance for the indigenous peoples who inhabited the islands. It was also from the confines of this convent that in 1535 **Frey Bartolomé de Las Casas**, apostle of the indigenous peoples of Central America, wrote his historic letter to the Spanish Court, condemning the Indians' mistreatment at the hands of the Spanish. The Convento also houses the city **library**: many of Walker's filibusterers are buried in the catacombs in its basement.

Mi Museo

Set in a fine converted colonial house one block northwest of the Parque Central on the Calle Atravesada, **Mi Museo** (daily 8am–5pm; free) is a private collection of over five thousand pieces of pre-Columbian ceramics, the oldest of which dates back to 500 BC. There's not much labelling, but the jars, plates and urns of various sizes, mostly depicting birds, crocodiles and toads, are intriguing.

Iglesia La Merced

For panoramic views of Granada's rooftops, as well as the lake and volcano, climb the tower (daily 9am–noon & 1.30–6pm; C\$20 – pay the attendant in the stairwell) at **Iglesia La Merced** (technically La Iglesia de Nuestra Señora de Las Mercedes – The Church of Our Lady of Mercy), which sits two blocks west of the Parque Central on Calle 14 de Septiembre. Yet to receive a lick of new paint, the sooty front and serene interior give it a shabby-chic charm. The tower is accessed at the front of the church on the left. If you suffer from vertigo, you may be put off by the tiny winding staircase with low railings that leads you upstairs. Once up top, there's a wraparound balcony for taking photos or simply soaking up the view.

West to La Pólvora

A pleasant fifteen-minute stroll west of La Merced takes you past a few smart churches to the old fort of **La Pólvora** (officially daily 8am–5pm, though it's not always open), which has a grand gate and good views. On the way you'll pass the small **Doña Elba** cigar factory (Mon–Thurs 8am–5pm), where you can have a go at rolling the product and take the result home – tip the worker who shows you around.

Lago de Nicaragua

The shoreline of **Lago de Nicaragua** is about 1km east of the Parque Central. Heading down the wide boulevard of Calle La Calzada, past churches and baseball diamonds, the stretch gets more and more dilapidated until you arrive at the shore, which has a huge vista of the lake, but feels eerliy empty unless you happen to arrive as the boat from San Carlos or Ometepe is docking. To the south a small park lines the lake, a few hundred metres beyond which is the entrance to the **Centro Turístico** (C$10 entry occasionally imposed), a group of lakeside bars and cheap restaurants that's ironically far more popular with locals than visitors. It's deserted on weekdays but popular at weekends, especially in the evenings, when the nightlife gets going. If heading here after dark, get a taxi back into town.

Arrival and information

By boat The twice-weekly boat from San Carlos and Altagracia docks at the pier at the bottom of C La Calzada.

By bus Buses from Managua come into the terminal west of town, 700m from the Parque Central, from where you can walk or grab a taxi into the centre (expect to pay around C$20). Services from Rivas and points south pull up at the market,

TOUR OPERATORS IN GRANADA

Guides hang around the larger hostels, and can be a reasonable bet as long as you ensure you know what you're getting for the price. The established operators below offer greater experience and professionalism, though.

NahualTours Next to *Nuevo Central*, C La Calzada ☎8988 2461, ✆nahualtours .com. A friendly, Nica-run operator offering half-day city tours (US$20), a costly but intriguing Zapatera day-trip (US$80) and a day's kayaking at Laguna Apoyo (US$25). There's also a small souvenir shop at the office selling handmade jewellery, postcards and T-shirts.

Nicaragua Adventures C La Calzada, half a block west of Iglesia Guadelupe ☎2552-5566, ✆nica-adventures.com. Long-standing, reliable company owned by European expats that offers trip-planning and shuttles and tours across Nicaragua, as well as Granada-specific activities like half-day kayak tours of Las Isletas, day-trips to Masaya and city tours.

Tierra Tour On C La Calzada two blocks east of the cathedral ☎2552-8723, ✆tierratour.com. Professional, well-run company (with offices in León too) offering shuttles, kayak tours of the Isletas (US$25 per person), as well as city and volcano tours, and diving in Laguna de Apoyo (US$65), as well as longer trips like a five-day Pacific-coast fishing trip (from US$700 per person).

UCA Tierra y Agua ☎2552-0238, ✆turismo@ucatierrayagua.org. This government-run co-operative can help organize homestays around Granada, notably around the Charco Muerto region, taking in crafts, horseriding and walking trails (bed and breakfast from US$5, guided tours from US$5).

a short walk southwest of the centre. Buses from Masaya pull up a block west of the market. Express minivans from Managua arrive at the small terminal half a block south of the Parque Central, though most will let you off at the plaza. If you're travelling from Costa Rica, the Tica Bus for Managua will stop and let you off at its Granada office on Avenida Elena Arellano, 1km northwest of the centre.

Tourist information Granada's better-than-average (in the sense that it might actually prove useful) INTUR office (Mon–Fri 8am–1pm & 2–5pm; ☎ 2552-6858, ✉ granada@intur.gob.ni) is on C El Arsenal, diagonal to the Convento San Francisco, and stocks information on climbing local volcanoes and other attractions.

Accommodation

The range of places to stay in Granada has improved immeasurably over the past five years and renovation work continues apace.

Amigos B&B C Estrada ☎ 2552-2085, ✉ hostalamigosgranada@yahoo.com. A sweet family-run B&B with dorms and private rooms. Guests have use of the communal kitchen and internet, and laundry services are also available (US$4–6). Dorms US$6, doubles US$20

The Bearded Monkey C 14 de Septiembre ☎ 2552-4028, ⊛ thebeardedmonkey.com. Granada's best-known backpacker hostel is worth visiting for its cool, verdant courtyard bar even if you don't stay here. The large dorms are perfectly decent, and there are private rooms and hammocks too. It's a big, busy place – watch your valuables and expect some noise. Dorms US$6, doubles US$14

🏃 **Casa del Agua** Av Guzmán ✉ gerry @casadelaguagranada.com, ⊛ casadelagua granada.com. Dinky but smart place with a handful of rooms and a kitchen encircling a cool little pool. It's small enough that you'll end up talking to everyone and offers a thoroughly mellow experience given its just-off-the-square location. Discounts for longer stays. US$24

Hospedaje La Libertad C 14 de Septiembre ☎ 8408-0003, ⊛ la-libertad.net. Another pleasant set of dorms, this one distinguished by some nice old *baños*, free use of the kitchen and a vaguely irritating philosophy about a "global family". Still, it's Nica-owned and the tours offered here include trips to a few remote beaches. Dorms US$7, doubles US$15

Hospedaje Valeria C El Martirio ☎ 8454-1325, ✉ hospedajevaleria@gmail.com. Friendly guest-house in a colonial house with large rooms boasting TV, en-suite bath and hot water. Free bike and internet use for guests. Triples are a good deal (US$45). US$35

Hostal San Angel Av Guzmán ☎ 2552-4591, ✉ mariacampos118@hotmail.com. This welcoming, family-run hostel, which stretches either side of *Casa del Agua*, offers quiet and tidy, if slightly dark rooms, all en suite with good mattresses and fans. Breakfast included. US$24

Hostal San Jorge South side of the market ☎ 2552-2613, ✉ hospedaje.sanjorge@yahoo.com. Its market location isn't terribly salubrious at night, but you'll get few better prices or better views in Granada. There's free ice, drinking water, fridge and internet, a pleasant terrace overlooking town, and the rooms are clean enough. A/c costs an extra US$10. US$15

Hostel Oasis Granada C Estrada, 100m north of Masaya bus terminal ☎ 2552-8006, ⊛ nicaragua hostel.com. A self-proclaimed "backpackers' paradise", this imaginatively conceived hostel offers comfortable dorm beds and private rooms in a restored colonial house. There's also free internet, plus DVDs, tours, a bar and even a tiny swimming pool. Dorms US$9, doubles US$20

Hotel El Maltese Malecón, 50m south of C La Calzada ☎ 2552-7641, ⊛ nicatour.net/en/elmaltese. The only accommodation option on Granada's battered lakeside is a pleasant place with clean rooms and a great courtyard and terrace. You'll be a 15-minute walk from the centre (get a taxi at night), but only moments away from the boats to Ometepe and beyond. Breakfast US$6; the on-site restaurant also offers lunch and dinner. US$30

Poste Rojo Pozo del Oro ☎ 8903-4563, ⊛ posterojo.com. Located 10km out of Granada near Volcán Mombacho, this funky collection of treehouses offers hammocks, dorms and doubles on the edge of the rainforest, with some great views. They also run yoga classes (Tues) and full-moon parties, and can organize tours to nearby Mombacho and beyond. Take a bus from Granada's market to Rivas, Nandaime or Diriomo, or get the daily noon shuttle from *Hospedaje La Libertad*. Hammocks US$4, dorms US$8, doubles US$20

Eating

Granada offers an increasingly cosmopolitan variety of places to eat, with Italian and Spanish food featured prominently. Budget travellers can grab a quick but basic bite at the town market, and in the early evening a couple of small food stands open up on the Parque Central, selling cheap and filling meat and rice dishes. Most of the gringo-orientated places sit at the western end of Calle La Calzada, where prices are higher, but there's a nice buzz most evenings.

Café de Don Simón Parque Central. Smart little coffee shop with a smashing location and prices to match. Sit at the rustic alfresco tables and work your way through an endless choice of coffees (from C$18) and perfectly passable breakfasts (granola C$45, eggs and bacon C$70). Daily from 6.30am.

Doña Conchi's 50m east of *El Club*. Colourful, half-tented, evenings-only bar-restaurant down a cool alley-like corridor. Chow down on a decent carbonara (C$150) or beef with red wine (C$180), or come on Thurs–Sun when the vibe is more bar-like (beer C$25): live salsa and meringue acts often play on the handsome wooden stage come late evening.

Euro Café Northwest corner of Parque Central. Pleasant, central café with pink-uniformed waitresses, plus decent coffees (from C$20), smoothies (C$45) and meals (soy burger C$55, salad C$60). The front room is a bit anonymous, but the back courtyard is fun, with free ping-pong for customers, a bookstore/exchange and Seeing Hands, a nonprofit which trains blind people as masseurs (massage from C$60).

🏃 **Garden Café** East of Enitel on C La Libertad and C El Cisne. This cool haven from the bustling streets is tucked inside yet another colonial conversion. There's an extensive breakfast menu (*huevos rancheros* C$80) as well as tasty and imaginative smoothies (C$40), salads and sandwiches (around C$80), and free wi-fi, and the leafy courtyard comes complete with tinkling fountain. Closed Sun.

Kathy's Waffle House Opposite the San Francisco convent on C El Arsenal. A breakfast institution in Granada offering good coffee and tasty grub, although service can be slow. The waffles (C$90), eggs, *gallo pinto* and toast (C$75) and filling lunches (burger C$100) are served on a beautifully shaded terrace looking across to the convent.

Nuevo Central C La Calzada. The interior, dominated by a long bar, is nice enough, but like most people on La Calzada you'll probably be on the paved street breathing in the night air and ignoring the hawkers. The food and drink –

omelettes (C$50), burgers (C$65) and lovely, juicy burritos (C$90) – is decent and relatively cheap for the location.

Pizzeria Don Luca C La Calzada, opposite *Zoom*. Popular and unpretentious, with pleasingly authentic Italian food. Be warned, though: the *pequeña* size is just that. Pizza from C$70, pastas from C$90. Closed Mon.

🏃 **Restaurant Querubes** Half a block north of the market on C Atravesada. A *buffet típica*, where hefty portions of rice, beans, plantain, salad and *churrasco* or grilled chicken come to C$65. The lunch menu has fewer options than the evening one; both offer food comparable in quality to La Calzada's offerings for half the price.

Zoom C La Calzada. Classic, decade-old gringo spot, with NFL on the TV, bets on the whiteboard, eggs Benedict (C$98), burgers (C$80) and assorted weekly specials. Nicaragua it ain't, but it's a decent place to shoot the breeze.

Drinking and nightlife

Most travellers in search of alcohol and company tend to head either to C La Calzada or the buzzing bar at *The Bearded Monkey*. There are also some great venues for a night out in Granada, with music ranging from acoustic Nicaraguan folk to the ever-present strains of reggaeton. The Centro Turístico (see p.445) is the place to head late on – take a taxi.

El César On the lakefront in the Centro Turístico. Granada's largest club has a party setting, under an open-air *rancho*. Latin and disco rhythms dominate, and it's open Fri–Sun (cover charge C$50–70). When it shuts at 3am the party usually heads to *Inuit* just down the road, which is open virtually 24hr at the weekend.

El Club Corner of C de La Libertad and Av Barricada at *El Club* hotel. Open for food and drink daily (*huevos rancheros* C$60, pasta C$125), and turns into bar and club Thurs–Sun, when the slightly over-the-top DJ booth oversees some serious boogying (one reason you might not want to stay in the otherwise reasonable hotel).

High Sport Bar On the corner of C Atravesada and C Real Xalteva. An upstairs balcony-bar with booming speakers, usually crammed with a merry crowd of hipswinging locals. Below the bar several places are open late for post-boozing munchies. Beer C$20.

Nectar C La Calzada. Small cocktail bar with groovy art, a nice back-room, decent juices during the day and everything from cold beer (C$20) to top-grade tequila (C$100). Closed Mon.

El Tercer Ojo C El Arsenal, opposite the Convento de San Francisco. Tapas bar and deli with a funky, cushion-strewn interior set in a lovely colonial building. The global food gets mixed reports, and you might prefer to stick to the booze – beer is C$30 but happy hour (5–7pm) offers good deals on rum, sangría and wine.

Directory

Bike rental Bicimaximo, next door to the cathedral (ⓦbicimaximo.com; US$6/US$3 day/half-day), are your best bet, and several hostels and tour agencies also rent out bikes.

Exchange All banks in town change dollars. The Banco de América Central (BAC), on the corner of C La Calzada and La Libertad, will change travellers' cheques, and also has one of many ATMs in the city.

Health The Praga pharmacy on C Real Xalteva is well stocked (daily 7am–10pm), while the Hospital Privado Cocibolca (ⓣ2552-2907) is just outside town on the highway to Managua.

Internet Cafés have sprung up all over town; the Alhambra on C La Libertad (daily 8am–10pm; C$20/hr) is central and pleasant enough.

Language schools There are plenty of places to learn Spanish in Granada – UCA Tierra y Agua (see box, p.445) can set you up with a rural homestay for the full cultural experience. Ask at tour offices or your accommodation for options in the city, or try Nicaragua Mia (Calle el Caimito ⓣ2252-0347, ⓦnicaraguamiaspanish.com), who offer one-on-one and group lessons, and come highly recommended.

Laundry Several spots offer services for dirty travellers; try Mapache on the corner of C La Calzada and C El Cisne (ⓣ2522-6711) or La Lavandería (ⓣ2252-0018) just north on C El Cisne. Both also offer pick-up and delivery.

Post office On C El Arsenal (Mon–Sat 8am–noon & 1–5pm).

Taxis Taxis line up in the northwest corner of the Parque Central. Any trip in Granada should cost C$10–20.

Moving on

By boat The ferry (Mon & Thurs at 2pm) to Ometepe (4hr) and San Carlos (14hr) departs from Granada's main dock. A/c first-class tickets – the only ones that can officially be sold to foreigners – are C$80 to Ometepe, C$160 to San Carlos. They're available on the day of travel from the dock office at the bottom of C La Calzada – arrive by midday to be safe.

By bus Express minibuses to Managua (every 15–20min; 40min) leave from a terminal a block south of the Parque Central, while normal buses (every 20min; 1hr) leave from Av Elena Arellano. Buses for Rivas (every 45min; 1hr 30min) use the small terminal in the market at the southern end of C Atravesada. Masaya-bound buses (frequent; 45min) depart from the even smaller terminal next to the Palí on C 14 de Septiembre.

AROUND GRANADA

Although Granada is a jumping-off point for trips to Ometepe and Solentiname (see p.461), there are a couple of worthwhile day-trips closer to hand.

Isla Zapatera

About 20km south of Granada, in Lago de Nicaragua, **Isla Zapatera** is one of over three hundred and fifty islands scattered about the lake, all believed to have been formed from the exploded top of Volcán Mombacho. At 52 square kilometres, Zapatera is the largest of the islands, skirted by attractive bays and topped by a much-eroded extinct volcano. Many of the pre-Columbian artefacts and treasures you find in museums throughout the country came from this group of islands, which must have been of religious significance for the Chorotega-descended people who flourished here before the Conquest. Guides should be able to show you **El Muerto** (The Dead), a site full of the remains of tombs, several **petroglyphs** and the scant remains – a few grassy mounds and stones – of **Sozafe**, a site sacred to the Chorotegas. These remains apart, there's really very little to see, bar lovely views of the lake. The easiest way to visit is with a **travel agency**, such as Nahual or Tierra Tour in Granada (see box, p.445), which offer informed but costly archeological excursions to the island, although you may be able to get a boat from the docks in the Centro Turístico.

Isletas de Granada
The alternative to a tour of Isla Zapatera is a *lancha* ride round the **Isletas de Granada**. Every tour operator in Granada (see box, p.445) runs half-day boat tours from US$25 per person – some can also arrange more tranquil kayak trips. Boats depart from Puerto Cabaña Amarilla and Puerto Asese, both at the southern end of the Centro Turístico, a fifteen-minute walk beyond the entrance – unless you're on the waterfront anyway it's easiest to get a cab down here. Take a hat and plenty of sunscreen – the sun out on the water is punishing.

Volcán Mombacho
The slopes of the rather lovely **Reserva Nacional Volcán Mombacho** (Tues–Sun 8am–5pm, although transport is scarce Tues & Wed; US$12.50) are home to one of only two **cloudforests** in Nicaragua's Pacific region (the other is at Volcán Maderas on Isla Ometepe). The reserve is run by the **Fundación Cocibolca** (Ⓦmombacho .org), whose interesting **research station and visitors' centre** at the volcano's summit acts as the centre for the study and protection of the reserve's flora and fauna – which includes three species of monkey, 22 species of reptile, 87 species of orchid, 175 species of bird and some fifty thousand species

of insect. There's also an "eco-albergue" with simple **rooms** where you can bunk down (☎2248-8234; US$40 per person, dinner, breakfast & transport included). The air is noticeably cooler up here, the views of the lakes and volcanoes around are tremendous, and several **trails** skirt the four craters at the top of the volcano.

To get to the volcano take any **bus** from Granada bound for Rivas or Nandaime and ask to be let off at the turn-off for the park (at Intersection El Guanacaste). From the turn-off it's a 2.5km walk to the entrance, from where it takes two hours to walk to the top. Alternatively, you can take the "Eco-truck" to the summit from the reserve entrance (Thurs–Sun 8.30am, 10am, 1pm & 3pm; included in the ticket price). Most visitors, however, choose the easier option of a tour from Granada (see box, p.445), which start from around US$35 per person and typically include a visit to a *coffee finca* and a canopy tour: Miravalle (near the bottom of the volcano; Ⓔcanopymiravealle@yahoo .com) is your best bet at present.

RIVAS

Most travellers experience **RIVAS** as a dusty bus-stop on the way to or from Costa Rica, San Juan del Sur or Ometepe, unaware of the pivotal role it played in Nicaraguan history. Founded in 1736, it became an important stop on the route of Cornelius Vanderbilt's Accessory Transit Company, which ferried goods and passengers between the Caribbean and the Pacific via Lago de Nicaragua – the town's heyday came during the California Gold Rush, when its streets were full of prospectors travelling with the Transit Company on their way to the goldfields of the western US. Modern-day Rivas isn't anything special, and can seem scarily deserted at night, but it's not a bad place to get stuck, especially if you fancy a taste of the real Nicaragua between gringo-tastic Granada and San Juan del Sur.

What to see and do

The colonial church near the Parque Central, **La Parroquia San Pedro**, is worth a visit, primarily for a fresco featuring a maritime-themed depiction of Catholicism triumphing over the godless communists. The desperately underfunded **Museo de Antropología e Historia de Rivas** (Mon–Fri 8am–noon & 2–5pm, Sat 8am–noon; C$40) sits four blocks west and two north of the Parque, with fine views of the rest of the town. Inside you'll find artefacts of the local Nahua Nicarao people dating from the fourteenth to sixteenth centuries, prehistoric bones (thought to be from a mammoth), some frightening stuffed animals and a few dusty 78rpm records from the early twentieth century.

Arrival

By bus Buses pull into the station in the market, a few blocks northwest of the town centre. You can walk easily enough; a taxi anywhere in town will set you back C$20 or less.

Accommodation

Hospedaje Lidia One block north and two and a half blocks east of Parque Central ☎2563-3477. Rooms housing up to five guests (some with private baths) spin off two pleasant courtyards at this decent family-owned option that's convenient for the Tica Bus, if further from the market than most. Traditional breakfast US$3. US$18

Hotel Gauri One block north of the market ☎2600-7292. A clean, family-run hotel where the en-suite rooms all have a fan and TV; there's also an on-site budget restaurant and secure parking provided. US$20

Principe No. 4 Next to *Hotel Gauri* ☎8937-1022. Clean, good-sized, if slightly impersonal motel-style rooms with en-suite bathroom, TV and fan. The attached restaurant has traditional breakfasts (C$45) and an assortment of mains (spaghetti C$65). US$20

Eating and drinking

A quick, cheap meal can be picked up at any of the *comedores* in the market, where you'll find good chicken, pork or beef and rice dishes for around C$50.

El Mesón Four blocks south of the market, behind Iglesia San Francisco. Classic lunch-only buffet joint. A fine, filling plate of meat and carbs with a drink goes for around C$80.

Repostería Don Marcos 100m east of the Parque Central's northern edge. Excellent for breakfast or stocking up for a long bus ride; a coffee and a piping-hot pastry will set you back C$20.

El Retorno Opposite *Hotel Gauri*. Feast on cheap beer (C$27/litre) and cheesy Spanish-language rock at this classic market-side booze-pit.

Vila's Rosti-Pizza On the southwest corner of the Parque Central. Probably your best bet for an evening, with a giant kids' playgound inside and great people-watching tables outside. Chow down on *pollo a la plancha* (C$135) or the delicious, garlicky *churrasco* (C$150).

Directory

Exchange There are a handful of banks in town: BAC (Mon–Fri 8.30am–4.30pm, Sat 8.30am–noon), two blocks west of the square, will change travellers' cheques and dollars and there are several ATMs around the Parque Central.

Health Clínica María Inmaculada, on the north side of the Parque, is open daily.

Internet Cafés are all over Rivas; try Cyber.Com (C$10/hr) past *Repostería Don Marcos*, a block east of Parque Central.

ONWARD TRAVEL: ISLA DE OMETEPE

The quickest route out to **Isla de Ometepe**, in Lago de Nicaragua, is via **San Jorge**, which is just east of Rivas on the lakeshore. San Jorge is best reached by shared taxi from Rivas (see opposite), although there are direct buses (every 30min) from Managua's Mercado Huembes; you can get boats from here out to the island. There's not much to the town, although it does have a small beach; *Hotel Hamacas* (☎2363-0048; US$32 including breakfast), a short walk from the ferry terminal, is a pleasant place to lay your head. See the box on p.457 for more on travel to Ometepe.

Moving on

By bus to: Granada (every 45min; 1hr 30min); Managua (every 20min; 2hr); Peñas Blancas (every 40min; 45min; see box, p.454); San Juan del Sur (every 30min; 45min–1hr – a shared taxi should only cost you C$40 per person). All these services depart from the ragged market and bus terminal three blocks north and two blocks west of the Parque Central. Both Transnica and Tica Bus pass through Rivas (by the Texaco station) en route to San José, Managua and beyond.

By taxi A shared taxi from the market to San Jorge should be about C$10 per person.

SAN JUAN DEL SUR

You would never suspect it, but in the mid-1800s the sleepy fishing village of **SAN JUAN DEL SUR** was a crucial transit point on Cornelius Vanderbilt's trans-isthmian steamboat line, on which people and goods were transported to Gold Rush-era California. The town is enjoying a second wave of prosperity, thanks to its popularity with wave-hunting Westerners, and you'll find few places in Nicaragua more geared up to backpackers.

Located in a lush valley with a river running down to the town's beach, the setting is beautiful; the beach itself is a long wide stretch of fine dark sand running between two cliffs. With excellent seafood restaurants, gringo-packed bars and an increasing number of good places to stay, San Juan is the kind of place where a two-day stay can turn into a two-week reverie. The locals are mostly happy with the attention, but there are occasional reports of muggings on the quieter beaches – get local advice before heading off on your own.

What to see and do

The lack of conventional sights in San Juan del Sur means that most people are engaged either in sunning themselves on the beach or undertaking something more energetic in the surrounding azure seas. While the waters around

ACCOMMODATION	
Casa 28	A
La Casa Feliz	C
Casa Oro	E
Hospedaje Eleanora	B
Hostel Esperanza	H
Hostel PachaMama	G
Hotel Estrella	D
Rebecca's Inn	F

EATING & DRINKING	
Arribas	3
Big Wave Dave's	5
The Black Whale	2
Chicken Lady	7
Crazy Crab Beach Club	1
El Gato Negro	4
Iguana Bar	6
Pelican Eyes	9
San Juan Pizzeria	10
Soda Mariel	8

Bancentro · Arena Caliente · Mercado · Farmacia Santa Ana · Bus stop · Cyber Call · Banco Pro Credit & ATM · Neptune Watersports · Andrea's Laundry · BDF Bank · Parque Central

0   100 m

SAN JUAN DEL SUR

TOUR OPERATORS IN SAN JUAN DEL SUR

There's plenty of competition in San Juan del Sur, and most operators offer similar deals at similar prices. It's easy to organize trips via accommodation – if in doubt, try *Casa Oro*, *Hostel PachaMama*, *Casa 28* or *La Casa Feliz* – but several other tour and rental companies are worth considering.

Arena Caliente Next to the market ☏ 8815-3427, ⊛ arenacaliente.com. Friendly place offering surf lessons, hire and transport, plus fishing trips (US$30). Lodging and packages can also be arranged.

Neptune Watersports Half a block south of the market ☏ 2568-2752, ⊛ www.neptune nicadiving.com. San Juan's diving specialists can take you below the waves (US$85 for a two-tank dive) and also run fishing trips (US$45/hr for a group of up to eight).

San Juan del Sur Surf and Sport Half a block west of the market ☏ 2568-2022, ⊛ sanjuandelsursurf.com. This long-standing local operator offers fishing trips (a boat of your own from US$250/day), tours to Refugio La Flor (US$30), ATV rentals and a nearby canopy tour (US$30) plus – of course – surf hire and lessons.

town aren't the cleanest, the stunning cliffs, reserves and beaches just along the coast are easily accessible.

Watersports

Surfing is the most popular sport in town, and you can easily rent boards and arrange transport – the town beach is surfable but not spectacular, and the good beaches are too far to walk to. Head for Remanso (to the south, and good for beginners), Maderas (to the north, popular with experienced surfers) or a number of further-flung options. Almost anywhere in town can arrange this – transport should set you back around US$5 and board hire about US$10. Water-taxis to playas Maderas and Majagual (12km to the north) leave from the area in front of *Hotel Estrella* at 10 or 11am daily, returning at 4 or 5pm (40min; US$10 return) – a taxi will cost about the same.

The beaches, inlets and bays of the coast are ripe for exploration, and **sailing** and **fishing** trips are almost as popular as surfing – *Casa Oro* arrange backpacker-oriented fishing tours, and local tour companies (see box above) all have trips of their own. San Juan isn't quite the Corn Islands, but there's still plenty of diving here: try Neptune Watersports.

Other activities

If you fancy Frisbee golf, Marsella Valley Nature Center (near Marsella Beach; ☏ 8805-6951, ⊛ marsellavalley.com) has a twelve-"hole" course surrounded by

REFUGIO DE VIDA SILVESTRE LA FLOR

The **Refugio de Vida Silvestre La Flor**, 19km south of San Juan del Sur (C$200 entrance fee; if travelling direct contact the national environment agency, MARENA ☏ 2563 4264), is a guarded reserve dedicated to protecting the sea turtles, primarily the Olive Ridley species, that nest here in large numbers between July and February. The night-time nestings themselves are an amazing spectacle, and the reserve also has good surf, a beautiful white sandy beach and a stand of shady trees, plus more great empty beaches within walking distance. Most hostels and operators can organize a trip here from San Juan – getting here independently (either via one of the water-taxis opposite *Hostel Estrella*, or by bus from the main stop) can be tricky and you're best asking in town for frequencies. Mosquitoes and sandflies are abundant – take repellent. Camping overnight (there are a few tents here to hire) is an expensive C$600 per tent.

nature trails, and offers accommodation. ATV hire can be arranged through a few hostels, including *Casa 28* (see below).

Arrival and information

By bus Buses from Rivas and Managua pull up outside the market. The direct express bus from Mercado Huembes in Managua (1 daily at 4pm, arriving 6.30–7pm) arrives at the same place.
Tourist information The INTUR office (Mon–Fri 9am–1pm) sits on the western corner of the Parque Central. Various websites offer news and information – Ⓦ www.sanjuansurf.com is the pick of the bunch.

Accommodation

Like Granada, San Juan del Sur is witnessing a major expansion of tourist accommodation, with big, sociable places bunched on the waterfront and mellower, smaller establishments tending to sit a few streets back. Bear in mind that many places raise their prices in high season (around Christmas and Easter), when it might be worth reserving in advance.
Casa 28 Half a block south of *El Gato Negro* ☎2568-2441, Ⓔmarvincalde@hotmail.es. A reasonable, chilled-out budget option offering fifteen basic rooms with a fan, shared bath and optional a/c. Quad-bike tours can be arranged at the in-house "Beach Fun" – US$60 gets you a day-trip around the nearby sights and beaches, US$90 throws in a nearby canopy tour too. US$16
🏃 **La Casa Feliz** Just southeast of the market ☎2689-7906, Ⓔlahappyhouse@gmail .com. Surfer haven with cosy TV room, kitchen and outdoor bamboo shower, as well as groovy low-rider bikes for rent. The rooms are small but the vibe is friendly. Surf rentals, trips and lessons can be arranged here. Dorms US$7
Casa Oro One block west of the Parque Central ☎2568-2415, Ⓦcasaeloro.com. Sprawling backpacker den offering everything the homesick surfer might require, from pizza delivery and DVD nights to wave reports, board rental and a funky rooftop terrace. There's a kitchen, and beach, sailing and surf trips can be arranged here. Decent dorms US$7.50, doubles US$20
Hospedaje Eleanora Just east of the market ☎2568-2191. Likeable family-owned cheapie offering six rooms, all with private bathrooms, and a small hammocked balcony. More mellow than the big beachside hostels too. US$12
Hostel Esperanza Three blocks west and half a block south of the Parque Central ☎8760-4343, Ⓦhostelesperanza.com. Relaxed, somewhat chaotic hostel with unexceptional rooms but a tremendous beachfront location. There's a barbecue, hammocks and wi-fi too. Dorms US$7, doubles US$15
Hostel PachaMama Two blocks west of the Parque Central ☎2568-2043, Ⓦhostelpachamama .com. This funky contemporary building hosts a lively hostel with ping-pong, free bike hire and a bar out back. Surf hire, fishing and snorkelling trips can be arranged. Dorms US$8, doubles US$20
Hotel Estrella On the beachfront, two blocks west of the market ☎2568-2210, Ⓔhotelestrella1929 @hotmail.com. With a plum location, reasonable prices and a downstairs area devoted to selling on secondhand ovens and fridges, this institution is one of the better beachfront options. The rooms at the back are nothing special and bathrooms are shared, but snag yourself a front balcony and you're sorted. Numerous tours are run from here too, including fishing trips for US$40/hr. US$16
Rebecca's Inn Just off the northwestern edge of the Parque ☎8675-1048. A pink-fronted family-run inn with colourful, clean, wood-panelled rooms (fan and shared bath) and friendly service. US$20

Eating

Seafood is king in San Juan del Sur – a whole baked fish costs about C$140, while fresh lobster starts at around C$200. There are plenty of bars and restaurants along the beachfront, though the same dishes are considerably cheaper and often equally tasty at the *comedores* inside the market (C$50 for a big plate).
Big Wave Dave's Half a block east of *Iguana Bar*. Chilled expat joint with a tasty menu featuring North American dishes such as hearty burgers (C$130),

TREAT YOURSELF

Pelican Eyes A block and a half east of the Parque Central Ⓦwww.pelicaneyesresort.com. *Pelican Eyes* is one of the plushest hotels in the area, but you don't have to shell out for the rooms (US$180–339) to get an eyeful of its greatest asset: the magical sunset views into the bay. Tramp up the stone steps – the second bar up offers better views – sip the pricey but mighty fine cocktails (from US$4), or slip into one of the three infinity pools (US$5). Happy hour (Wed 5–8pm) offers two-for-one drinks.

good salads (C$50–120), plus pancakes (C$80) and other breakfast delights.

The Black Whale 150m north of *Iguana Bar*. Nice German-owned hangout with bad pool tables, nice hammocks, tasty grub (grilled fish C$130, monster burger C$100) and Brahva beer for only C$15. DJs and live music keep things moving after dark.

"Chicken Lady" *Asados Juanita*, at the central market. A word-of-mouth traveller's favourite, this street-side BBQ serves lipsmacking chicken plates to eat in or take away from C$50. Evenings only.

El Gato Negro 50m east of *Iguana Bar*. A colourful, mellow café and bookshop with a reasonable menu (muffins C$25, sandwiches C$75) and splendid coffee (C$30 with refills).

San Juan Pizzeria Decent pizza, rather more authentic than usual (from C$80), alongside pasta dishes – bag one of the handful of tables outside and watch the world and its longboard swing by.

Soda Mariel A block west of the market. Unfussy café offering breakfasts, burgers (C$60), veggie plates (C$30–60) and yummy *refrescos* (C$15).

Drinking and nightlife

The seafront bars are perfectly located for soaking up the sunset with a cold beer. As well as *Crazy Crab*, several clubs and bars are open as late as 3 or 4 in the morning – all cater to a lively mix of locals, tourists and resident surfers.

Arribas 100m north of *Iguana Bar*. Buzzy beachside place where you can sip your beer (C$25) on the sands.

Crazy Crab Beach Club 500m north of *Iguana Bar*. Has salsa classes from 9pm, but only really gets busy after 1am, when everyone who hasn't gone to bed yet shakes their stuff to a merry mix of salsa and pop. Entry C$20 on Sat; beer C$15. Open Thurs–Sun.

Iguana Bar On the beachfront square, a block north of *Hotel Estrella*. This place is booming at night, when the huge bamboo balcony overlooking the beach and bay fills with flirting locals and foreign beach-bums. There's reasonable food during the day (clams C$90, fish C$90), while a beer is C$25.

Directory

Bike rental Bikes can be rented at many hotels, including *La Casa Feliz* and *Hospedaje Elizabeth* (opposite the bus stop) for US$6–8/day.

Exchange Banks have popped up all over town, and there are several ATMs. Bancentro, next to *Big Wave Dave's*, and Banco Pro Credit, one block east of *Hotel Estrella* (both Mon–Fri 8am–noon & 1–4.30pm, Sat 8am–noon), will change US dollars but not travellers' cheques.

Health Farmacia Santa Ana, half a block south of the market, is open daily.

Internet Connexion Cyber (opposite *Casa 28*) and Cyber Manfred (by *El Gato Negro*) charge C$20/hr and have phones.

Laundry Several hostels have DIY facilities (washboards, not machines) and there are several independent laundries charging about US$3–5 per load; try Andrea's, just south of *Casa Oro*.

Moving on

By bus to: Rivas (every 30min; 45min–1hr).
By taxi A shared taxi to Rivas should only cost you C$40 per person.

INTO COSTA RICA: PEÑAS BLANCAS

Crossing the border at **Peñas Blancas** can be a time-consuming process when countless migrant workers head back to see their families; don't be surprised if it takes up two hours – you'll be there most of the day if you try to do it around Christmas or Semana Santa. Local buses from Rivas go all the way to the border; if you're leaving from San Juan del Sur, take the Rivas bus only as far as the highway at La Virgen and then catch a connecting bus – there's no need to go all the way back to Rivas. If you're travelling on to a Central American capital, you can also head back to Rivas and catch a Transnica or Tica Bus as it passes through (see "Moving on", p.451).

The crossing is open daily 6am to 8pm, and packed with touts offering money-changing and to fill out your forms for you. You'll be charged an exit tax of US$2–4 (it's usually higher in the evenings and at weekends). There is a US$10 fee to enter Nicaragua. It's a fairly easy 1km walk (a *moto* will charge around C$20, a taxi a bit more) to the Costa Rican *migración* where you'll have to pay a US$3 municipal tax before hopping on the regular onward transport to San José.

Lago de Nicaragua

Standing on the shore and looking out onto vast **Lago de Nicaragua**, it's not hard to imagine the surprise of the Spanish navigators who, in 1522, nearly certain they were heading towards the Pacific, found the lake's expanse instead. They weren't too far off – merely a few thousand years – as both it and Lago de Managua were probably once part of the Pacific, until seismic activity created the plain that now separates the lake from the ocean. Several millennia later, by the time the Spanish had arrived, the Lago de Nicaragua was the largest **freshwater sea** in the Americas after the Great Lakes: fed by freshwater rivers, the lake water gradually lost its salinity, while the fish trapped in it evolved into some of the most unusual types of fish found anywhere on earth, including freshwater shark and swordfish. Locally, the lake is still known by its indigenous name, Cocibolca ("sweet sea").

It's easy to be captivated by the natural beauty and unique cultures of the **islands** that dot the southwest sector of the lake, including twin-volcanoed **Isla de Ometepe** and the scattering of small islands that make up the **Solentiname archipelago**. On its eastern edge the lake is fed by the 170km **Río San Juan**, which you can boat down to the remote **El Castillo**, an old Spanish fort surrounded on all sides by pristine jungle. The Río San Juan and El Castillo are reached via the largest town on the east side of the lake, **San Carlos**, a bug-ridden settlement mainly used by travellers as a transit point.

Making your way around the lake can be quite an undertaking: Lago de Nicaragua is affected by what locals call a "short-wave phenomenon" – short, high, choppy waves – caused by the meeting of the Papagayo wind from the west and the Caribbean-generated trade winds from the east. Crossing can be hell for those prone to seasickness. You'll need to be prepared for the conditions and patient with erratic boat schedules.

ISLA DE OMETEPE

Almost everyone who travels through Nicaragua comes to **ISLA DE OMETEPE**, Lago de Nicaragua's largest

LAGO DE NICARAGUA

0   30 km

N

▲ El Rama

Juigalpa

Granada

Managua ◄

Isla Zapatera

Lago de Nicaragua

Altagracia Moyogalpa

Rivas

San Jorge

Isla de Ometepe

San Miguelito

Sapoá

Peñas Blancas

San Juan del Sur

Solentiname Archipelago

Isla Mancarrón   Isla San Fernando

Isla Mancarroncito

Isla La Venada

Isla Chichicaste

Isla El Zapote

San Carlos

Sabalos

El Castillo

Río San Juan

RESERVA NATURAL LOS GUATUZOS

COSTA RICA

▼ San José

San Juan del Norte ▼

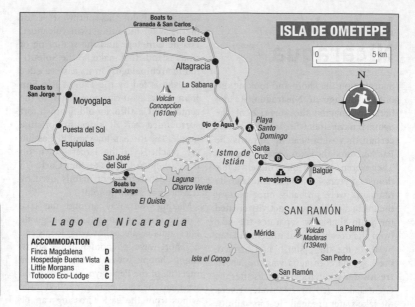

ISLA DE OMETEPE

0   5 km

Boats to
Granada & San Carlos

Puerto de Gracia

Altagracia

La Sabana

Boats to
San Jorge

Moyogalpa

Volcán
Concepción
(1610m)

Puesta del Sol

Ojo de Agua   **A**

Playa
Santo
Domingo

Esquipulas

Istmo de
Istián

Santa
Cruz   **B**

San José
del Sur

Balgüe

Boats to
San Jorge

Laguna
Charco Verde

Petroglyphs **C** **D**

El Quiste

SAN RAMÓN

Lago de Nicaragua

Mérida

Volcán
Maderas
(1394m)

La Palma

ACCOMMODATION
Finca Magdalena   **D**
Hospedaje Buena Vista **A**
Little Morgans   **B**
Totooco Eco-Lodge   **C**

Isla el Congo

San Pedro

San Ramón

N

---

island, to experience its lush scenery and tranquil atmosphere. Ometepe's name comes from the Nahuatl language of the Chorotegans, the original inhabitants of Nicaragua, who called it Ome Tepetl – "the place of two hills" – for its two volcanoes. The island has probably been inhabited since the first migration of indigenous groups from Mexico arrived in this area, and a few stone sculptures and **petroglyphs** attest to their presence on the island. Even from the mainland, taking in the sight of its two cones, you can tell it's a special place.

The higher and more symmetrical of the two is **Volcán Concepción** (1610m), Nicaragua's second highest volcano. Much of the island's 40,000-strong population live around the foot of Volcán Concepción, where you'll find the main towns of **Moyogalpa** and **Altagracia**. Smaller, extinct **Volcán Maderas** (1394m) is less perfectly conical in shape, but clothed with precious **cloudforest**, where you're likely to spot such **wildlife** as white-faced (*carablanca*) and howler (*mono congo*) monkeys, green parrots (*loro verde*) and

blue-tailed birds called *urracas*. Almost all activities on the island are based in the outdoors: **walking**, **hiking**, **volcano-viewing**, **volunteering** and **horseriding** are among the most popular.

What to see and do

Most people are here to visit Ometepe's iconic twin volcanoes, but there's plenty to do elsewhere, from chilling at lodges and stretching out on beaches – notably **Playa Santo Domingo** – to exploring waterfalls and pre-Columbian remains.

Moyogalpa

Moyogalpa, the largest town on the island, sits on the northwest side of Volcán Concepción. It's convenient for the ferry and has a few decent bars and restaurants, while its popularity with backpackers means it's not a bad place to arrange a tour or shoot the breeze for an evening. After you've walked up the hill and looked at the dock, there's not much sightseeing to do – the **museum** (daylight hours; C$40), on the right just before the church at the top end of town,

NICARAGUA

LAGO DE NICARAGUA

456

houses a few artefacts and petroglyphs. If you're looking for a properly tranquil base, tiny Playa Santo Domingo or *fincas* such as *Magdalena* and *Merída* are more inviting options.

Altagracia

While there's also little to detain travellers in **Altagracia**, a sleepy town set slightly inland on Ometepe's northeastern side, it is quieter and less touristed than Moyogalpa. The **Parque Central** is ringed by several pre-Columbian statues found on the island, while the **Museo de Ometepe** (daily 8am–noon & 2–5pm; C$30), off the west side of the park, houses a few more local archeological finds.

Volcán Concepción

The main **hike** (8–10hr return) up **Volcán Concepción** starts from just outside Altagracia. Much of the climb is extremely steep and it's compulsory to hire a **guide** for the upper sections – see p.458 for suggestions. Several **trails** wind up, and all are quite an exercise – start early and bring plenty of water – with an exposed and rocky stretch towards the summit that gets very windy. The cloudforests of the lower slopes are gorgeous (keep an ear out for howler monkeys) and the dramatic views from the top, encompassing neighbouring Volcán Maderas and the expanse of surrounding Lake Nicaragua, are genuinely breathtaking.

Playa Santo Domingo

Stretching for more than a kilometre on the east side of the narrow isthmus separating the two volcanoes is the grey-sand **Playa Santo Domingo**. This is the most swimming-friendly beach on the island, and many volcano-climbers and hikers spend a day soaking up some sun here. The beach is accessed from the main road circling Concepción, although the first kilometre or so of the road that forks off to Santo Domingo is in bad condition (4WD recommended).

Volcán Maderas

The **hike** (7–8hr return) up the verdant slopes of dormant **Volcán Maderas** is less arduous than the steep climb up and down Concepción, though it can nonetheless be a muddy and slippery walk – see "Tourist operators", p.458, for information on the mandatory guides. The final stretch down into the crater is not for the faint of heart; the rocks are almost sheer and you'll have to use a rope. Birds and monkeys can be heard (if not seen) all the way up, and the summit gives stunning views of Concepción and the lake. The crater itself is eerily silent and still, its lip covered by a mixture of

---

TRAVEL TO AND FROM ISLA DE OMETEPE

The only way to travel between Isla de Ometepe and the mainland is by a fairly bumpy boat trip. Moyogalpa's dock is at the bottom of the town's steep and narrow main street and Altagracia's is 2km out of town – minivans charge C$10 per person. The third port, at the village of San José del Sur, is less convenient – you'll probably have to get a taxi.

The majority of travellers arrive by ferry (C$40–60) or less comfortable *lancha* (C$30–40) via San Jorge, northeast of Rivas (see box, p.450). There are roughly hourly departures between San Jorge and Moyogalpa and a twice-daily ferry to San José del Sur, though itineraries change regularly – check at the INTUR office in Granada (see "Tourist information", p.446) or on ⓦ www.epn.com.ni.

There are also currently two boats a week from Granada (Mon & Thurs at 2pm; 4hr; C$80) and San Carlos (Tues & Fri at 2pm, arriving at midnight; C$140). These, and the return trips (Granada Wed & Sat at 12.30am; San Carlos Mon & Thurs at 7.30pm) use the docks at Altagracia.

SAN DIEGO DE ALCALÁ

Every year during the third week of November, Altagracia celebrates the week-long **fiesta of San Diego de Alcalá**, in honour of the village's patron saint. If you're passing through on November 17 you may be lucky enough to see one of the highlights of the festival, the **Baile del Zompopo** ("dance of the leaf-cutter ant"). The locals set out from the church in a traditional procession through the streets, parading aloft an image of San Diego. Participants act out the distinctive dance with tree branches held aloft – representing the indigenous leaf-cutter ant – while moving to traditional drum rhythms.

dense, rainforest-like vegetation and a few bromeliad-encrusted conifers. Make sure you take plenty of water, sunscreen and perhaps a swimming costume; the crater lagoon is swimmable, if pretty mucky.

The rest of the island

If you have time, it's worth exploring the quiet villages dotted around the lower slopes of Maderas. **Petroglyphs** are scattered over this part of the island, with one group clustered between the hamlets of Santa Cruz and La Palma – ask at *Finca Magdalena* for a guide (US$6). A two- or three-hour hike from the *Finca Magdalena* will take you to the pleasant, but extremely cold, **San Ramón waterfalls**. The naturally fed pools at **Ojo de Agua**, or "eye of the water", a twenty-minute hike from Villa Paraíso near Playa Santo Domingo, also merit a visit. If you've just hiked a volcano, there's nothing more refreshing than climbing on the rope swing and diving in to one of the rainforest-shaded pools.

Information

Tour operators There's no INTUR office on the island but you won't be short of advice – all accommodation will be able to point you towards a tour and in some you'll be approached by informal guides. These can be a reasonable bet for a simple trip – but in all cases, check exactly what you're getting. For something more substantial it's worth speaking to UGO (a block uphill from the dock at Moyogalpa, next to *The American*; ☏ 2827-7714, ⊛ ugometepe.com), a confederation of guides who can take you all over the island – trips cost

US$10–40 per person, depending on how large your group is and what you're after.

Island transport

A dirt and gravel road circles Volcán Concepción, though in the rainy season one stretch between Moyogalpa and Altagracia can become impassable, while another very rough road (4WD only) goes around Volcán Maderas. Navigating the island's roads is an adventure in itself.

Bikes and motorcycles Ometepe is one of the best places in Nicaragua to do some cycling, even if the state of the roads takes a little bit of getting used to. Ask at your accommodation or UGO (see "Tour operators", above) for the best place to hire bicycles or motorbikes and check the condition of your bike carefully before you get on it – some operators have been known to claim you've wrecked their machines and refuse to give you back your deposit.

Buses Somewhat erratic buses bump along the circuit that connects Moyogalpa and Altagracia (roughly hourly until 6pm; 1hr–1hr 30min), taking in Playa Santo Domingo. A handful of services connect the two towns with Mérida and Balgüe (2 daily) and San Ramón (1 daily) – check with your accommodation, as schedules fluctuate.

Taxis Minibus taxis are mostly found in Moyogalpa, and charge about C$600 for a trip to Mérida – a good option if travelling in a group. You can also hire these drivers/minibuses for the day; beware, however, of drivers telling you that the last bus has already left in order to get your custom.

Accommodation

Ometepe's accommodation is pretty basic, with plenty of budget options. In Moyogalpa and Altagracia, most rooms are simple, concrete and dry-wall cubicles, while those at the various *fincas* and haciendas can be charmingly rustic, with lots of polished wood and hammocked balconies. Many of the latter are splendidly located – but bear in mind you'll usually have to rely on their catering, as most are pretty isolated.

In Moyogalpa

The American A block east (uphill) from the dock ☎ 8645-7193. Spacious rooms – spotless to the point of seeming clinical – behind the café of the same name, with reliable hot water and an emergency power supply. The helpful owners supply breakfast and can help arrange tours. US$30

Hospedaje Central Three blocks east (uphill) and one south of the dock ☎ 8459-4262, ⓦ hostelometepe.com. Likeable, creaky hostel with a lively on-site bar and restaurant, *El Indio Viejo* (see p.460). There are reasonable doubles (a/c and bath US$3 extra), as well as rather gloomy dorms and a relaxing, hammock-bedecked courtyard. Most work is done by volunteers and there are links to ecological and spiritual projects which the grizzled owner will fill you in on if you ask. Hammocks US$2.50, dorms US$3.50, doubles US$12

The Landing Hotel 50m east (uphill) from the dock ☎ 2569-4113, ⓔ hbsaussy@gmail.com. Smart hotel with a decent downstairs bar and restaurant (pasta C$100, fillet of fish C$120), helpful staff and some splendid views from the upstairs terrace. The comfortable rooms – both en-suite and with shared bath – are a stone's throw from the dock, and good value too. Dorms US$5, doubles US$24

In Altagracia

Most of Altagracia's limited accommodation is situated just south of the centre, on the road in from Moyogalpa.

Hotel Castillo 100m south and 50m west of the Parque Central ☎ 2552-8744. Basic but spotlessly clean rooms, some with private bath, as well as a good restaurant, large hammocks, the only internet café in town (C$25/hr) and a bar showing sports. The latter gets busy when there's sport on, but the hammock- and rocking-chair-boasting courtyards remain mellow enough. You pay US$5 extra for private bath, a further US$15 for a/c. US$10

Hotel Central Two blocks south of the Parque Central ☎ 2552-8770. Probably the best choice in town, with excellent-value rooms, some with a balcony and private bath (extra US$16), and sweet little cabañitas. There's also a restaurant and bicycle rental (C$120/day). Doubles US$14, cabañas US$20

Posada Cabrera On the south side of the Parque Central ☎ 8664-2788, ⓔ anamariacabrera@yahoo.com. Nine simple, tidy rooms – with rather saggy mattresses and thin walls – set in the overgrown garden of a friendly family home. You'll also find a basic cafeteria and pharmacy on site. US$20

The rest of the island

Finca Magdalena Take the bus from Altagracia to Balgüe, from where it's a 20min walk up a signposted path ☎ 8498-1683, ⓦ fincamagdalena.com. This welcoming old hacienda, converted by the Sandinistas into an organic coffee co-operative (and still going strong), has stunning views across the lake. The no-frills accommodation consists of hammocks or camping, large dorm rooms, partitioned private rooms, and a private en-suite hut. A restaurant serves hearty meals and organic coffee, while tours take you round the plantations and to nearby waterfalls and petroglyphs. Hammocks US$3, camping US$3.50, dorms US$4, doubles US$6, hut US$10

Hospedaje Buena Vista At Playa Domingo ☎ 8690-0984. Probably the best budget bet near lovely Playa Domingo, with simple rooms, a cheap and cheerful *comedor* next door and a more tranquil vibe than the boozier options elsewhere on the island. US$20

Little Morgans On the outskirts of Balgüe ☎ 8611-7973, ⓦ www.littlemorgans.com. Groovy lodge by the lakeside that combines cool views and a good base for volcano hikes with a fairly party-tastic vibe come evening – the simple cabañas are quieter than the dorm beds. Infrequent buses run to Balgüe from Altagracia and Moyogalpa; otherwise you'll need to get a cab (US$30 per group). Dorms US$8, cabañas US$30

[handwritten annotations: "Stay here if you can!" "you must bike to the swimming hole!"]

PUESTA DEL SOL HOMESTAY

For an authentic Ometepe experience, consider arranging a homestay with a local family. For US$20 per night, one of ten families in the **Puesta del Sol** collective will take you in and share their home with you. The group (☎ 8619-0219, infrequently-updated website ⓦ puestadelsol.org) has small plots of land growing organic herbs, fruits and other plants from its base 2km from Moyogalpa, and makes wine and tea from hibiscus. Visitors can learn about cultivation, experience life with a typical Nica family and arrange visits to Ometepe's sights – bike and canoe hire can also be arranged.

Totoco Eco-Lodge Balgüe, near Volcán Maderas ☎ 8425-2027, ⓦ totoco.com.ni. This relaxing place isn't particularly cheap, but it does have fine views, a genuinely ecofriendly policy and plenty of tours, as well as a new swimming pool. They can arrange transport (US$35) or taxis are the same price per group. Most rates are half-board – see the website. Dorms US$22, lodges US$85

Eating and drinking

Moyogalpa has the largest number of places to dine on the island; Altagracia has a handful of others, while the shack on the north side of its Parque Central does classic, hearty fodder for around C$50. If you're staying out of town, most of the *fincas* and haciendas have excellent on-site restaurants. There's not a huge party scene on Ometepe; Moyogalpa has the busiest bars and "nightlife" on the island.

The American A block east (uphill) from the main dock in Moyogalpa. Bright café serving gringo-style food like hot dogs (C$45), chili con carne (C$100) and clam chowder (C$80), plus breakfasts, smoothies and coffee (C$20). It's open from 6am for breakfast.

Flor de Angel A block and a half up from the dock in Moyogalpa. Dead during the week, but rammed with carousing young locals on Saturday night, this place plays reggaeton, merengue and funk, and serves beers for C$20. Entrance C$20 at weekends.

Hotel Kencho Just south of the Parque Central, Altagracia. Reasonable, airy restaurant below the adequate hotel of the same name, where you can chomp down on chicken (C$70), grilled fish (C$120) or *desayuno típico* (C$50).

El Indio Viejo At *Hospedaje Central*, Moyogalpa. This bar and restaurant is the most sociable joint on the island, and the main backpacker hangout, offering breakfast for C$70, mains for C$40–120 and beer for C$20.

🚶 **Restaurante Ranchitos** Opposite *Casa Familiar* in Moyogalpa. This long, narrow bamboo-clad *rancho* offers a cracking Nica-style menu of meat and seafood plates (C$100–150), with decent sides, plus pizza (from C$90). The tilapia's so good you'll be slurping its bones till they bring the bill.

Sol de Ometepe 40m uphill (east) from Moyogalpa docks. Simple, tasty *comida corriente* from C$60 – the punchy breakfasts will get you in volcano-scaling mood.

Timbo al Tambo 100m uphill (east) from Moyogalpa docks. A funky little café-bar with a cool half-raised dancefloor playing Latin rhythms to a lively local crowd. Beer C$20, mojito C$30.

Yogi's Bar Three blocks east and one and a half blocks south of the main dock in Moyogalpa. Bar and restaurant with televised sports and films and a garden with hummingbirds outside. It's owned by a genial, dog-loving American and offers cold, cheap beer (C$15), breakfasts (C$55–100), sandwiches (C$50–70) and burgers (C$70).

Directory

Moyogalpa is home to most of Ometepe's services.
Exchange Banco ProCredit, three blocks east (uphill) of the dock on the main street has a Visa-only ATM, which is occasionally shut – bring enough cash to last you.
Health Emergencies can be attended to at the Héroes y Mártires Hospital, just outside Moyogalpa on the road to Altagracia.
Internet In Moyogalpa, try Ciber Café, one block uphill (east) from the dock on the left (C$10/hr), or Cyber Ometepe, opposite the bank (C$15/hr). Altagracia's only option is Cyber Vajoma, in the *Hotel Castillo* (C$25/hr). Most of the *fincas* and haciendas also offer (often slow) internet access.
Laundry Services are provided by many hotels on the island; alternatively, *Yogi's Bar* does a big load for C$120, which they can turn around in 2hr.

SAN CARLOS

Sleepy, bedraggled **SAN CARLOS**, at the southern end of the lake and the head of the Río San Juan, has to be one of the most unprepossessing towns in the whole country. Despite its position as one of the main transit towns for the lake area, and the odd bit of renovation work around the dockfront, an air of apathy pervades its ramshackle buildings and battered streets. The people are friendly enough, but few visitors spend the night here – travellers are generally in transit to the **Solentiname archipelago**, to **El Castillo** and points further south along the **Río San Juan** or to Costa Rica via Los Chiles, although San Carlos itself is an access point to the wild and relatively untouched Los Guatuzos reserve.

Arrival and information

By air La Costeña flies from Managua to San Carlos (40min), landing at the tiny, muddy field of an airstrip just north of town. It's not walking distance, but a taxi (5min) should cost about C$20.

By boat Boats depart Granada for San Carlos on Mon and Thurs at 2pm, stopping off at Altagracia on Ometepe at around 6pm, and arriving in San Carlos around 4am the next day at the eastern dock by the Petronic station; from here it's a 10min walk or 2min taxi ride to any of the town's accommodation. You can either strike out to find a hotel, or wait around (for about an hour) for boats on to El Castillo – they use the same dock. The ferry from Solentiname arrives at the *muelle municipal*, on the town's main waterfront strip.

By bus The bus station for services via Managua and Rama is by the eastern dock, opposite a cluster of *comedores*.

Tourist information There's a small INTUR office in San Carlos, one block east of the main square (Mon–Fri 8am–noon & 2–5pm, Sat 8am–noon; ☎2853-0301), where you can get up-to-date information on Solentiname and points south on the Río San Juan. The CANTUR office (Mon–Fri 8am–5pm), situated at the main dock in a small hectagonal building, also provides tourist information, along with a free map of town.

Tour operators *Hotel Cabinas Leyko* can organize wildlife trips, or try Ryo Big Tours (☎8828-8558, Ⓔ ryobigtours@hotmail.com), on the waterfront just west of the *muelle municipal*, for excursions to the Los Guatuzos reserve or further up the river.

Accommodation

San Carlos has a lot of transient traffic, which is reflected in its spartan hotels. There's little to choose between the few vaguely acceptable and not overly bug-ridden, sinister or noisy places in town.

Hospedaje Peña Just north of *Restaurante Kaoma* ☎2283-0298. Cramped and run down, with skimpy mattresses and slightly grotty bathrooms, though at least there are good views of the lake from the upstairs rooms and terrace. US$6

Hotel Cabinas Leyko Two blocks west of the Parque ☎2583-0354, Ⓔ leykou7@yahoo.es. The best budget rooms in town, which isn't saying too much. The decent, if slightly damp, wooden rooms come with wall fan or a/c (for an extra US$32), screened windows and shared or private bath. There's also a balcony with rocking chairs and lake views. US$13

Eating

Comedor Alondra Opposite the market, by the bus terminal. One of a string of perfectly decent and cheerfully cheap *comedores*, convenient for filling your belly with *gallo pinto*, plantains, fried chicken and the like for around C$70 before you travel onwards.

Restaurante El Granadino One block uphill from the *muelle municipal*. Probably the best restaurant in town, set on a huge wooden balcony overlooking the main square and dock. Steaks, fish and chicken are all on offer from C$100.

Restaurante Kaoma On the waterfront, a block up from the *muelle municipal*. Dishes up good, filling seafood and vegetarian (on request) plates for C$100–250 and gets a bit of a buzz come the evening.

Directory

Exchange There's a Bancentro with an ATM two blocks up from the waterfront.

Internet A couple of internet cafés sit near the Parque Central, two blocks up from the waterfront.

Moving on

By air Regular flights run from the tiny airport (☎2583-0167) to Managua.

By boat Boats departing for Solentiname leave from the main dock in San Carlos, while those for Granada, El Castillo, Sabalos, San Juan del Norte, Ometepe and Los Chiles leave from the dock on the east side, by the Petronic station – pay your US$2 exit fee at *migración*, just west of the municipal dock. The current return schedule for Altagracia/Granada is Tues and Fri at 2pm (10hr/14hr) – arrive early to pick up tickets.

By bus The gruelling buses (erratic in the rainy season) to Managua (5 daily; 10–12hr) and Rama (1 daily at 8am; 8hr) depart from opposite the Petronic station by the docks.

SOLENTINAME ARCHIPELAGO

Lying in the southeast corner of Lago de Nicaragua, the **SOLENTINAME ARCHIPELAGO** is made up of 36 islands of varying size. For a long time it was the islands' colony of naïf-art **painters** that brought it fame – priest and poet Ernesto Cardenal lived here for many years before becoming the Sandinistas' Minister of the Interior in the 1980s, and it was his promotion of the archipelago's primitive art and artisan skills that led to the government declaring Solentiname a national monument in 1990 – but today the islands are better known for their unspoilt natural beauty and remarkable wildlife. The archipelago's **isolation** keeps all but the most determined travellers away, so it's a nice departure from the backpacker trail.

What to see and do

The archipelago's largest islands are also the most densely inhabited: **Mancarrón**, **La Venada**, **San Fernando** (also referred to as Isla Elvis Chavarría) and **Mancarroncito**. Most people stay on Mancarrón, home to a simple church whose interior holds vibrant paintings of birds, trees and houses, and make trips to San Fernando and other nearby islands. It's worth paying a visit to the small MUSAS **museum** on San Fernando (Mon–Sat 7.30am–12.30pm & 2.30–5.30pm; C$40), where you'll find information on the local wildlife, petroglyphs, medicinal plants and, of course, the local artisanal process – you'll also have the opportunity to purchase artwork here. Make sure you bring plenty of córdobas with you – there's nowhere to change money on the islands. Other than that, you're best off interspersing long periods of relaxation with the odd hike along the many trails – where you'll see plenty of birdlife – and a few spots of fishing.

Arrival

By boat A "ferry" goes to Mancarrón (also calling at La Venada and San Fernando) from San Carlos twice a week (Tues & Fri at 1pm; 2hr; C$80), although it's best to check departure times at the dock. Unless you come on a tour, this is currently the only way to get here by scheduled transport, although unscheduled private *pangas* make the same trip for around US$100 per group – ask around at the San Carlos docks.

Accommodation and eating

Almost all accommodation offers inclusive meals; failing that, owners will point you to the nearest hotel that has a dining room – there are no dedicated restaurants on the islands.

On Mancarrón

Buen Amigo ☎ 8869-6619. A clean, basic and friendly *hospedaje* located up the hill just out of town. Traditional food is on offer too, from C$60. US$12
Cabañas Villa Esperanza Opposite *Buen Amigo* ☎ 2583-9020. Three sweet little cabinitas, all painted green. Rates include three meals per day. US$50

On San Fernando

Celentiname A 15min walk left of the main dock ☎ 8893-1977. The pretty but basic wooden cabinas here are set in a luscious garden and have superb views. Three decent meals included. US$50
Mire Estrellas Beside the lake ☎ 8894-7331. Cheap, simple rooms with a hammocked balcony on the lake. You can eat at the restaurant of the pricey *Hotel Cabañas Paraíso*, opposite. US$20

Moving on

By boat Returning to San Carlos, boats depart from Mancarrón at 4.30am on Tues and Fri.

RÍO SAN JUAN

The mighty 170km-long **RÍO SAN JUAN** is one of the most important rivers in Central America. In colonial times it was the route by which the cities of Granada and León were supplied by Spain and emptied of their treasure by pirates, and optimists still claim it could one day form the basis of a canal to rival Panama's. It's the site of regular squabbles between Nicaragua and Costa Rica (see p.404), although you wouldn't know it while drifting down its sinuous and gloriously verdant length: the only settlements nearby are remote and sleepy villages whose inhabitants make their living by fishing and farming. **Ecotourism** offers one of the few sources of income: pack a waterproof, insect repellent and a stout pair of boots, and get ready for grand castles, intriguing tours and giant grilled river shrimp.

What to see and do

Most travellers see the Río San Juan from a boat between **San Carlos** on the eastern shore of Lago de Nicaragua and the old Spanish fort and town of **El Castillo**, the only real tourist attraction in the area. **Wildlife** is abundant along the river, and travellers who venture up- or downstream will certainly spot sloths, howler monkeys, parrots and macaws, bats, storks, caimans and perhaps even a tapir.

El Castillo

The full name of the Río San Juan's historic fort is La Fortaleza de la Inmaculada Concepción de María, though everyone refers to it simply as **El Castillo**. Lying on a hillock beside a narrow stretch of the Río San Juan, the fort was built by the Spanish as a defensive measure against the pirates who continually sacked Granada in the seventeenth century. It was more or less effective for a hundred years, until a British force led by a young Horatio Nelson finally took it in 1780, after which it was abandoned for nearly two centuries. The neatly restored structure boasts an interesting small **museum** (daily 8am–noon & 1–4pm; C$40, plus C$25 to take photos) with dusty armaments of the period, information on the area's history and a few random artefacts found during the restoration of the castle, and a **library** (closed at weekends) with over a thousand books on the history of the castle and the Río San Juan area.

There's a small **tourist office** just up from the dock (Mon–Sat 8am–noon & 2–5pm; ☎8422-1959), run by the Asociación Municipal de Ecoturismo El Castillo. They offer canoe trips (US$70 for up to five people; 3–4hr) and walking tours in the nearby biological reserve, and atmospheric sunset caiman-spotting trips (US$40 for four people). **Nena Tours** (☎8821-2135, ⓦwww .nenalodge.com), operating from the lodge of the same name (see p.464), offer an English-speaking alternative, with tours of the reserve (see below; from US$64 for four people), *finca* tours including a fishing trip (US$102 for four people) and caiman-spotting (US$40 for four).

Reserva Biológica Indio Maíz

Downstream from El Castillo, heading out towards the Caribbean, the northern bank of the Río San Juan forms part of the 3000-square-kilometre **Reserva Biológica Indio Maíz**, the largest nature reserve in Nicaragua. The climate here is very wet and hot, with the vast expanses of dense rainforest sheltering many species, including the elusive manatee, jaguars, tapirs, scarlet macaws, parrots and toucans. The pristine Indio Maíz vegetation stands in sharp contrast with the Costa Rican side, where agriculture and logging have eroded the forest. The only place to stay is is **Refugio Bartola** (☎8880-8754), a scientific research station offering eleven rudimentary but comfortable wooden rooms (US$100, including breakfast). You'll have to hire a private boat from El Castillo (around US$50 one way) to get to the research station.

San Juan del Norte

It is possible to travel all the way from San Carlos down to **San Juan del Norte** on the Caribbean coast by cheap scheduled boats (Tues & Fri at 6am, Thurs at 7am; 9hr; C$277), where there are some tours and budget accommodation. A boat theoretically runs from here to Bluefields (4–6hr) two or three times a week. It's sporadic, weather-dependent, and a rough trip.

River transport

Boats Boats travel between San Carlos (from next to the Petronic station) and El Castillo (in both directions) at 6.30am, 8am, 10.30am, 1pm & 2pm (2–3hr; C$77–120), stopping off at Sábalos en route. Lodges can also organize transport. During the week there may be several more daytime departures, while on Sunday afternoon departures are unreliable – check at the docks.

Accommodation

The trip to and from El Castillo can be completed in a day, but the small and friendly village around the fort offers several accommodation options and is a charming place to rest up for a couple of days, especially if you've been travelling hard and fast via San Carlos. Just over halfway between San Carlos and El Castillo, the small riverside town of Sábalos offers several rather wonderful lodges – the only drawback is that you'll be dependent on their food and tours, which are more expensive than El Castillo's equivalents.

El Castillo

Albergue El Castillo On the hill by the entrance to the ruins ☎8924-5608. Simple but comfortable rooms with mosquito nets and fans in a huge, wooden cabin-style hotel with balcony and great river views – get a room upstairs. Breakfast is included, as is internet – C$20/hr for nonguests. US$30
Hospedaje Melany 5min from the dock, bearing right ☎2621-7298. A pretty, riverside house with a fantastic upstairs balcony set just beyond what passes for the bustle of town. The rates for the large, comfortable rooms (mostly en suite) include breakfast. Tours (including kayaking) can be arranged here. US$30
Hospedaje Universal Just left of the dock ☎2666-3264. This family-run hostel has small, clean wood-partitioned rooms and shared showers, along with a wooden balcony with hammocks right on the river. US$10
Nena Lodge 5min from the dock, on the left ☎8821-2135, ⊛nenalodge.com. Neat, tidy rooms in a friendly, family-run hostel that also offers tours. US$14

Sábalos

Hotel Sábalos ☎2271-7424, ⊛hotelsabalos.com.ni. A great hotel just up the river from *Sábalos*

The **Monte Cristo River Resort** (☎8649-9012, ⊛montecristoriverlodge.com), 6km west of El Castillo (the boat from San Carlos to El Castillo stops here), has luxury wooden cabins with TV, fridge and kitchen. Trips on offer include hiking, birding, kayaking and fishing trips – it's a great way to see the wealth of local wildlife. US$75 per person including meals and tours.

Lodge. The en-suite rooms are rather plain, but immaculately tidy, set over the river and accessed from a large, wooden porch. A wide variety of tours can be arranged here too. US$36
Sábalos Lodge 45km from San Carlos ☎8850-7623, ⊛sabaloslodge.com. A rustic-chic "eco-lodge" with en-suite cabinas in wild jungle grounds inhabited by howler monkeys and hummingbirds; stay in one of the larger, riverfront thatched huts for a real Tarzan experience. The (costly) tours include kayak trips down the river, birdwatching and treks. Breakfast is included; lunch and dinner are available on request from the restaurant (US$12). US$35

Eating

If you're staying in Sábalos you'll be eating at your accommodation, but El Castillo has a few decent spots.

El Castillo

Borders Coffee Right on the dock. The tables are upstairs on a lovely wooden open-air deck alongside easy chairs and an incongruous cross-trainer. Sip beer (C$25), great milkshakes and

INTO COSTA RICA: LOS CHILES

There are currently three boats per day (usually 10.30am, 1.30pm, 4pm; C$300) leaving from the east *muelle* (dock) in San Carlos for the scenic hour-plus chug to Los Chiles in Costa Rica. You might want to aim for one of the earlier boats to ensure transport doesn't dry up while you're en route. It's easiest to get your exit stamp from the customs office at the dock before departure – you'll pay US$2–4 depending on the time of day. Coming the other way the charge is US$10. The actual border post is just outside Los Chiles; you'll need to walk a few hundred metres down to the immigration office to get an entry stamp to Costa Rica at the Los Chiles *muelle*, then either hop in a taxi or walk a further kilometre to the bus stop. It's one of Nicaragua's more mellow borders, not that that's saying much.

proper coffee (C$20), and dine on reasonable food ("American" breakfast C$80, mixed grill C$150).

Restaurante Vanessa A few hundred metres along from the dock on the left. Mellow and faintly classy (for El Castillo) riverside spot offering fried fish (C$110) and river shrimp (C$270), plus a reasonable drinks range.

Soda La Orquidea 30m on the right from the dock. Has a sweet little upstairs balcony for typical breakfasts (C$35), tasty chicken (C$60) and fish (C$150).

The Atlantic Coast

Nicaragua's low-lying **Atlantic Coast** makes up more than half the country's total landmass. It's mostly made up of impenetrable mangrove swamps and jungle, and as such only a few places in the region attract visitors in any number: **Bluefields**, a raffish port town, the idyllic **Pearl Lagoon** just to the north, and the **Corn Islands**, which boast sandy beaches, swaying palm trees and a distinctly Caribbean atmosphere. Outside these areas, the coast remains an untouristed tangle of waterways and rainforests, and should be approached with caution and negotiated only with the aid of experienced locals and good supplies of food, water and insect repellent. Indeed, there is only one actual town in the northern half of the coast – **Puerto Cabezas**. Few travellers make the trip (flying is the only real transport option), but the impoverished town has a unique feel and is the best access point for the Miskito-speaking wildernesses of the northeast.

The possibilities for ecotourism in this vast, isolated coastal region are obvious, though a scarcity of resources and a lack of cooperation between central and local government have so far stymied all progress, while the long-discussed highway linking Managua and Bluefields has failed to leave the drawing board.

EL RAMA

Downtrodden **EL RAMA** is a major transit point to the Atlantic Coast – beyond here roads are limited, and you'll mostly travel by boat or plane. Most travellers only stop long enough to change from the Managua bus to a boat for Bluefields, or vice versa. The bus station sits in the town's low-key centre, and *pangas* leave from the small jetty two blocks south and one block west of here. The river curves northeast towards the Atlantic from the dock, enclosing the rest of El Rama – if you fancy a wander, Año Santo church is pleasant enough, set two blocks east from the bus station. Continue north from here to the crossroads and you'll spot a Bancentro bank to your left and an internet café down the road to your right.

Accommodation and eating

The market, right by the bus station, has a decent *comedor*, and there are a couple of other options if you're here overnight.

Eco-Hotel El Vivero A couple of kilometres outside of town on the road from Managua ☎8617-6001. The best option if you're intending to spend any time in Rama, with nice a/c rooms in a large wooden building set in the jungle. Ask the bus to drop you off or get a cab (C$20). US$30

El Expresso One block west and three blocks north of the bus station. A cool and somewhat clinical refuge from grubby Rama, this big-windowed restaurant offers tender chicken (C$140) and decent shrimp (C$210).

Hospedaje Garcia A block south from the bus station on the way to the *panga* dock ☎2517-0318. This convenient place offers passable singles and doubles, although some are on the dark side. US$10

Kingstown Ranch Opposite *El Expresso*. There's a cool balcony upstairs where you can eat for around C$120 or sip beer (C$15) come the evening, when music and karaoke liven things up, and a highly rated *comedor* downstairs during the day.

HISTORY AND POLITICS ON THE ATLANTIC COAST

The Atlantic coast never appealed to the Spanish conquistadors, and repelled by disease, endless jungle, dangerous snakes and persistent biting insects, they quickly made tracks for the more hospitable Pacific zone. As a result, Spanish influence was never as great along this seaboard as elsewhere. English, French and Dutch buccaneers had been plying the coast since the late 1500s, and it was they who first made contact with the Miskito, Sumu and Rama peoples who populated the area. Today the ethnicity of the region is complex, and the east can feel like another country. The indigenous peoples mixed with slaves brought from Africa and Jamaica to work in the region's fruit plantations, and while many inhabitants are Afro-American in appearance, others have Amerindian features, and some combine both with European traits. Creole English is still widely spoken.

During the years of the Revolution and the Sandinista government, the FSLN met with suspicion on the Atlantic Coast, which had never really trusted the government in Managua. The region was hit hard by conflict, and half the Miskito population went into exile in Honduras, while a much smaller number made their way to Costa Rica. In 1985 the Sandinistas tried to repair relations by granting the region political and administrative autonomy, creating the territories RAAN (Región Autonomista Atlántico Norte) and RAAS (Región Autonomista Atlántico Sur), though this only served to stir up further discontent, being widely seen as an attempt to split the Atlantic Coast as a political force. Improvements to infrastructure (notably the resurfacing of the road to Rama and the extension of the route right the way to Pearl Lagoon) show that the government has not forgotten the east coast, and tourism offers a route out, of sorts, but its profits remain focused on a handful of accessible destinations. As the jungles of the northeast are sacrificed for farmland and more Spanish-speakers from the west move to the Atlantic, this damp, diverse region is losing some of the qualities that make it so distinctive and appealing – for now, this great, troubled region remains a land apart.

Moving on

By boat A sporadic and very slow ferry service (5–7hr; C$140) runs along the Río Escondido between El Rama and Bluefields. Opt instead for the high-speed *pangas* (2hr; C$200) that run daily from 5.30am, with several departures in the early morning and a couple more heading downstream until around 1pm, although with sufficient demand another may leave later in the afternoon.
By bus to: Managua (5 daily; 8hr); Pearl Lagoon (1 daily at 4pm; 5hr); San Carlos (1 daily at 4.10am; 8hr).

BLUEFIELDS

There are no fields, blue or otherwise, near steamy **BLUEFIELDS**, the only town of any size on the country's southern Atlantic Coast. It acquired its name from a Dutch pirate, Abraham Blaauwveld, who holed up here regularly in the seventeenth century, and still has something of the fugitive charm of a pirate town, perched on the side of a lagoon at the mouth of the Río Escondido, though this is about the only allure it holds. Indeed, listen to some travellers' tales of constant rainfall, murderous mozzies and menacing streets, and you might never come here at all.

But despite being undoubtedly poor, frequently wet and utterly beachless, Bluefields can be an intriguing place to stop over on your travels around the area. Fine river views and a hospitable, partly Creole-speaking population reward those who do visit. Avoid the portside "hotels" and hustlers and get a taxi if you head out of the small central area, and you should be just fine – indeed, Bluefields' karaoke-country- and reggae-based nightlife can be pretty engaging if you keep half an eye out.

The few streets in Bluefields are named, though locals resort to the usual method of directing from landmarks: the Moravian church, the *mercado* at the end of Avenida Aberdeen and the *parque* to the west of town are the most popular ones.

Arrival and information

By air Flights from Managua, the Corn Islands and Puerto Cabezas land at the airstrip 3km south of the town centre. Taxis will take you into town for about C$20 – if you just fancy a bite to eat between flights, try the *Hotel Aeropuerto* (see opposite).

By boat Boats arrive at the dock about 150m north of the town's Moravian church, although you may be dropped at the market too. From the docks you can walk to all accommodation in Bluefields' centre – a three-block-by-three-block area where all the hotels, restaurants and services are concentrated.

Tourist information The small INTUR office, in a pink building south of the centre (Mon–Fri 8am–1pm; ☎ 2572-0221), has a few brochures but isn't much help.

Accommodation

Lodging in Bluefields is underwhelming, with gloomy, noisy, overpriced rooms the norm. The cheaper, more basic establishments attract a raffish local clientele – one reason why some places have a curfew.

Bluefields Bay Hotel In Barrio Pointeen ☎ 2572-2143. Probably the best choice in town if you don't mind shelling out a bit, with a few nice balconies looking over the bay and comfortable rooms boasting private bath, optional a/c and hot water. US$40

Hotel Aeropuerto Right by the airport ☎ 2572-2862. Perfectly located for travellers flying out the next day, the rooms here are all large. However, some are dark and musty, while others have wood panelling and windows leading onto a balcony with great views of the lagoon, so ask to see a selection. There's a fair range of food on offer at the downstairs restaurant too. US$14

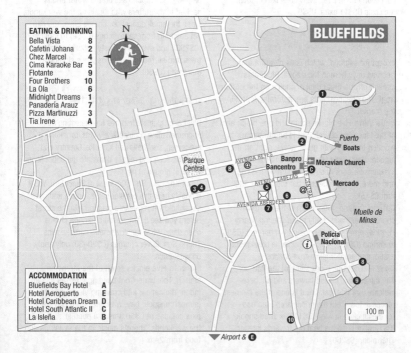

EATING & DRINKING
Bella Vista	8
Cafetin Johana	2
Chez Marcel	4
Cima Karaoke Bar	5
Flotante	9
Four Brothers	10
La Ola	6
Midnight Dreams	1
Panadería Arauz	7
Pizza Martinuzzi	3
Tia Irene	A

BLUEFIELDS

N

Puerto Boats

Parque Central

AVENIDA REYES

Banpro Bancentro

Moravian Church

AVENIDA CABEZAS

Mercado

AVENIDA ABERDEEN

Muelle de Minsa

Policia Nacional

ACCOMMODATION
Bluefields Bay Hotel	A
Hotel Aeropuerto	E
Hotel Caribbean Dream	D
Hotel South Atlantic II	C
La Isleña	B

0   100 m

Airport & **E**

¡MAYO YA! FESTIVAL

During the month of May, particularly in the last week, the streets of Bluefields are taken over by ¡Mayo Ya! or Palo de Mayo, one of the most exciting fiestas in the country. Derived from the traditional May Day celebrations of the British Isles and celebrating the arrival of spring, ¡Mayo Ya! features a mixture of reggae, folklore and indigenous dance that young Blufileños pair ingeniously with the latest moves from Jamaica. The celebrations wrap up with the election of the Mayaya Goddess, the queen of the festivities.

Hotel Caribbean Dream Calle Central ☎ 2572-0107, ✉ reyzapata1@yahoo.com. The snazziest option in the centre, not that that's saying a huge amount: all rooms are en suite, with TVs and a/c. Bag one of the brighter rooms upstairs, which lead onto a pleasant balcony. US$25

Hotel South Atlantic II Adjacent to the Moravian church ☎ 2572-1022. Friendly, central hotel and restaurant spread over three floors, with fairly clean, en-suite rooms with TVs, optional a/c, reasonable food (*comida típica* will set you back around C$60) and a spacious sports-bar upstairs with a terrace. US$18

La Isleña A block east of the Parque Central ☎ 2257-2070. These simple rooms are set off a cool courtyard in a relatively quiet part of town. A/c costs US$11 extra. US$9

Eating

Except for seafood, which is as plentiful and fresh as anywhere in Nicaragua, Bluefields doesn't offer a great deal of choice on the eating front. The cheapest eats are, naturally, found in the market.

Bella Vista Five blocks south and one block east of the Moravian church. Set in an atmospheric wooden building with great views, right on the lagoon, *Bella Vista* serves tasty and relatively inexpensive pork ribs (C$90), shrimp (C$165) and more, and is a decent bar too (beer C$18, rum C$15).

Cafetin Johana 100m north of the Moravian church. Cheap and chatty place offering hearty *comida corriente* – everything from burgers (C$50) to shrimp (C$130) – as well as large breakfasts (C$60) and great tropical-fruit *batidos*.

Chez Marcel One block south of the Parque. The tablecloths, plastic flowers and a/c here indicate that this restaurant is one of the fanciest places in town, but the prices aren't too bad – try the chicken in wine (C$110) or fried snook (C$125), or push the boat out towards lobster Thermidor (C$260).

La Ola A block west of the market. Munch on tasty *ceviche* (C$80), chicken and chips (C$100) and *pescado a la plancha* (C$120) on the breezy balcony or the functional downstairs space, which comes complete with "no hay credito" signs and groggy-looking men sipping beer (C$20).

Panadería Arauz Get a lovely squidgy snack and a coffee from this neat bakery and café for around C$20.

Pizza Martinuzzi Next to *Chez Marcel*. Local families love the cheese-drenched pizzas (C$100), a/c interior and background pop, and this is a pleasant enough place if you fancy a break from fried plantain.

Tia Irene Follow the stairs to the right past the *Bluefields Bay Hotel*. This tropical, bamboo-clad *rancho* sits on the water and is packed to the rafters with locals on the weekends, when the small dancefloor comes alive. You can eat anything from sandwiches (C$50) to lobster (C$250), and eye up the rusty hulks and palm trees that surround Bluefields while sipping a margarita (C$50).

Drinking and nightlife

Bluefields' nightlife features an interesting mix of promenading couples, likely lads, drunken policemen, pool halls and karaoke. Country and western, soca and reggae dominate the dancefloors. Travel in groups at night.

Cima Karaoke Bar 50m west of Bancentro. You'll probably hear this popular bar, a reggae and soca stronghold with speakers blasting into the street, before you see it. The upstairs bar and club is open daily, while the downstairs karaoke runs Thurs–Sun. Cover charges (C$20–30) only apply on weekends.

Flotante Five blocks south of the Moravian church. This waterfront building on stilts has an indoor dancefloor and cracking views into the (almost) unspoilt bay. With beer from C$15 and piña coladas at C$50, this is a popular spot on the weekends. There's music in the evenings and food from 2pm.

🏃 **Four Brothers** On the southern side of town (a short taxi ride). This big, groovy shed is the granddaddy of the Caribbean music scene in Bluefields, and commands a loyal, largely Creole crowd Thurs–Sun.

Midnight Dreams Three blocks north of the Moravian church. A waterfront watering-hole with a big wooden veranda, a beer-bottle-speckled entrance and a dancefloor swaying to country, soca, reggae and Latin rhythms. Beer C$20, seafood and *comida típica* from C$100.

Directory

Exchange There are several ATMs in town, with a Banpro opposite the Moravian church and a Bancentro just around the corner.

Internet Access is available for C$10/hr at Atlantic Cyber, 50m south of the Moravian church, and Cyberzone, a block and a half east of the park.

Moving on

By air There are several daily flights to Managua and Big Corn, and several flights a week to Puerto Cabezas. The small airport (☎ 2572-2500) is about 3km south of town – take a taxi (around C$30).

By boat *Pangas* head to Rama (daily from 5.30am, with several departures in the early morning and a few more heading upstream until around 1pm, with occasional afternoon departures; C$200) and Pearl Lagoon (7am, with sporadic departures until around 3pm; 1hr). There's a C$10 port fee on top of the ticket price. Several ferries head to Big Corn – the Bluefields Express (Wed at 9am; 5–7hr; C$210) is your best bet as the rest leave from El Bluff, outside Bluefields, making connections tricky.

PEARL LAGOON

Mellow, manageable and just a short hop from Bluefields, **PEARL LAGOON** (Laguna de Perlas), is a slowly growing spot on Nicaragua's tourist map. It's now connected to El Rama and thence Managua by road, but most visitors arrive on a bouncy but magical boat ride that takes you through tangled mangroves into a vast, shallow lagoon. In its southern corner, the village of Pearl Lagoon has sandy streets, quality seafood and a friendly Creole populace who make their living from fishing

and tourism. Once you've seen the big gun that looks out over Pearl Lagoon's small wharf, you've seen the sights, but it makes a fine base for fishing trips, longer excursions and sitting happily on your backside, sinking beer and lobster and watching the sun set.

Those who fancy exploring can head out to the remote Pearl Cays where the water really is crystal clear (for all its charms, Pearl Lagoon is a little more silty), or walk inland to **Awas**, a Miskito village half an hour west with a small beach and a decent restaurant.

Arrival and information

By boat The *panga* from Bluefields (1hr) leaves at around 7am, with occasional departures later in the day.

By bus The bus from El Rama (5hr) leaves at 4pm daily.

Internet Silmas's Cyber, 100m south of the wharf, offers a surprisingly quick connection.

Tour operators Fishermen at the dock offer trips, and most accommodation can point you in the right direction, but there are a couple of established players too. The friendly *Queen Lobster* restaurant (contact Pedro on ☎ 8499-4403) offers fun combined fishing and cooking classes (US$25), trips to the Pearl Cays (US$50 per person) and sports fishing in Top Lock Lagoon. George Fox (head right from the dock towards *Casa Ulrich* and his house is on the left) has trips to Orinoco and the Wawashang Reserve, and out to the Pearl Cays – a group of six will pay around US$200 for the day.

Accommodation

Casa Ulrich 300m north (right) of the wharf ☎ 2572-5009, ✉ casaulrich@hotmail.com. The smartest place on the waterfront, this bright hotel offers en-suite, a/c rooms, internet access and tremendous views from its terrace. US$35

🏃 **Green Lodge** 100m south of the wharf ☎ 2572-0507. Perhaps the village's best pick offers creaking rooms in the main house and newer lodgings in a modern annexe in an overgrown garden. Rooms have TV, and there are fine hammocks for chilling outside. US$14

Hospedaje Ingrid Two blocks west and three blocks south of *Green Lodge*, near the municipal stadium ☎ 2572-5007. Several small but pleasant cabins alongside a family home. Not the most convenient location, but it's reasonable and cheap for the town. US$15

Eating and drinking

Spices and seafood make Pearl Lagoon a fine place to chow down. Most restaurants are also decent options for a sundowner, and there are a couple of proper bars, soundtracked by the Atlantic Coast's traditional, surreal mix of country and reggae, too.

Bar Relax A block west (inland) from *Green Lodge*. This groove-ridden bar is a decent place to see the locals shake their stuff on the dancefloor and guzzle beer (C$17) in the covered outdoor area.

Casa Ulrich 300m north of the dock. The *filet mignon* (C$150), grilled fish (C$150) and other main meals get regular plaudits, but the elevated deck at this hostel/restaurant is a fine place to sink a few beers (C$20) too.

Coconut Delights Just south of the dock. Simple bakery offering delicious soda cake, ginger bread, rolls and cheese pasties from C$5.

Queen Lobster 200m north of the wharf ⓦqueenlobster.com. This charming round hut over the water offers excellent Creole cuisine, from *ron don* (C$140), a traditional mix of meat, seafood, cassava, coconut milk and peppers, to lobster (C$180), with spicy chicken (C$80) for those who want to stay on dry land. Tours and cooking classes are on offer, and there are plans to add accommodation too.

Moving on

By boat *Pangas* (1hr) head to Bluefields' municipal dock at around 6.30am – arrive early to reserve your seat – with sporadic departures later in the day.

By bus A bus leaves for Rama at 5am (5hr).

THE CORN ISLANDS

Lying 70km off the country's Atlantic coast, the **CORN ISLANDS** (Las Islas de Maíz) offer white beaches, warm, clear water and a Caribbean vibe. The islands are the epitome of relaxation – the kind of place you come to intending to stay for a couple of days and end up hanging around for a week or more.

Like many parts of the Caribbean coast, during the nineteenth century both larger **Corn Island** and tiny **Little Corn** were a haven for **buccaneers**, who used them as a base for raiding other ships in the area or attacking the inland towns on Lago de Nicaragua. These days it's drug-runners who use the islands, unfortunately, as part of the transportation route for US- and Europe-bound cocaine.

What to see and do

Big Corn is home to virtually all the islands' services, has a reasonable selection of hotels and restaurants, and is large enough to ensure that – if you're prepared to head far enough – you can get your own patch of beach. More backpackers head straight to idyllic Little Corn, though if you have time you might want to try them both out. Reached by a quick but bouncy *panga* from the bigger island, "La Islita" is extremely quiet, with **rustic** tourist amenities – bring sunscreen, mosquito repellent, a torch, money and an emergency roll of toilet paper. Set on just three largely undeveloped square kilometres, with a population of just over a thousand, the island boasts lush palm trees and beautiful **white-sand beaches**, great snorkelling and diving, good swimming, and above all, plenty of peace and quiet – with no cars on the island, traffic consists of bikes, dogs and wheelbarrows.

Big Corn

It's possible to walk round the entire island in about three hours. **Brig Bay** (just south of the fish-processing plant) stretches south from the dock and main town past shacks and perfectly serviceable sands. **Long Bay**, across the airstrip heading east, is quieter and less populated and there are plenty of places to swim in either direction. The southwest bay, **Picnic Center**, is a fine stretch of sand near a loading dock – it's the site of a huge party

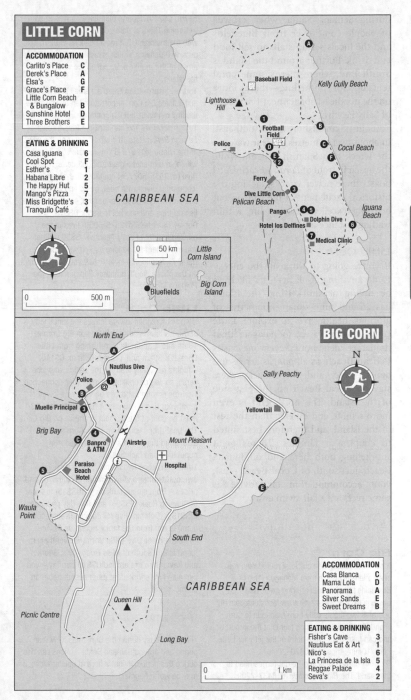

LITTLE CORN

ACCOMMODATION
Carlito's Place	C
Derek's Place	A
Elsa's	G
Grace's Place	F
Little Corn Beach & Bungalow	B
Sunshine Hotel	D
Three Brothers	E

EATING & DRINKING
Casa Iguana	6
Cool Spot	F
Esther's	1
Habana Libre	2
The Happy Hut	5
Mango's Pizza	7
Miss Bridgette's	3
Tranquilo Café	4

Baseball Field

Kelly Gully Beach

Lighthouse Hill

Football Field

Police

Cocal Beach

CARIBBEAN SEA

Ferry

Dive Little Corn
Pelican Beach

Panga

Dolphin Dive

Iguana Beach

Hotel los Delfines

Medical Clinic

N

0   500 m

0   50 km

Little Corn Island

Bluefields

Big Corn Island

BIG CORN

North End

Nautilus Dive

Police

@

Muelle Principal

Brig Bay

Banpro & ATM

Airstrip

Mount Pleasant

Hospital

Paraiso Beach Hotel

Waula Point

Sally Peachy

Yellowtail

N

Picnic Centre

Queen Hill

Long Bay

South End

CARIBBEAN SEA

ACCOMMODATION
Casa Blanca	C
Mama Lola	D
Panorama	A
Silver Sands	E
Sweet Dreams	B

EATING & DRINKING
Fisher's Cave	3
Nautilus Eat & Art	1
Nico's	6
La Princesa de la Isla	5
Reggae Palace	4
Seva's	2

0   1 km

during Semana Santa, when crowds of people come over from Bluefields and the locals set up stalls to sell food and drink. Further around the island is **South End**, where there's some coral reef good for snorkelling – there's more on the northeast corner near the village of Sally Peachy.

About 1.5km offshore to the southeast, in about twenty metres of clear water, is the wreck of a Spanish galleon, while the beach in front of *Paraíso Beach Hotel* boasts three newer wrecks, lacking the historical excitement of the galleon but boasting excellent marine life within wading distance of the shore.

Little Corn

If you're going to work up the energy to do anything at all here, it's likely to be **diving** or **snorkelling**; the island has around nine square kilometres of glorious, healthy reef to explore. Little Corn is even easier to navigate than its larger neighbour; everyone visits **Pelican Beach**, as all *pangas* arrive and depart here, and most backpackers stay on **Cocal Beach** on the east side of the island. The north end is even more remote and quieter than the rest of the island, and therefore best suited to couples or families. There's great snorkelling both here and off Iguana Beach, just south of Cocal Beach – ask your accommodation for advice as some reefs are a fair swim away.

Arrival and information

Big Corn

By air The easiest and quickest route takes you in an often-tiny plane from Managua (1hr) or Bluefields (30min), both offering great views. La Costeña (☎2263-2142, ⊛www.lacostena.com.ni) operates two flights daily from Managua to Corn Island. Taxis await incoming flights at the airport and can take you to your hotel or the jetty for Little Corn (10min); trips cost C$20–30.
By boat Cargo boats and freight ferries head to the island. The *Río Escondido* (☎8437-7209;

5–7hr; C$210) departs Bluefields on Wed at 9am (returning Thurs at 9am). Other ferries also connect with the mainland, but most head via El Bluff, just outside Bluefields, which is less convenient. Boats arrive at the *muelle principal* on the west side of the island.
Tourist information There's a small INTUR desk just outside Big Corn airport (turn left as you leave the tiny terminal), but it's not much use.
Tour operators You can arrange trips through *Paraíso Beach Hotel*, the small resort on the west of the island (☎2575-5111, ⊛paraisoclub.com), who also rent scuba gear and golf carts. Nautilus Dive (☎2575-5077, ⊛nautilus-dive-nicaragua .com) offer dives with boat, guide and complete equipment for US$35 per person, as well as fishing trips and snorkel tours for US$15.
Dorsey Campbell (☎2575-5059) lives in the relaxed hamlet of Sally Peachy; US$20 will get you equipment for as long as you want, plus Dorsey's formidable expertise. If you can't get him on the phone, you'll probably find him near the *Pulpería Victoria*.

Little Corn

By boat A regular *panga* leaves the small jetty at the northern end of Brig Bay on Big Corn at 10am and 4.30pm daily, returning from Little Corn at 6.30am and 1.30pm (30min; C$110) – flights generally wait for the *panga*, and vice versa, so you're unlikely to miss your connection. The ride is rough and can be very wet – water-proof your bag if you can. A harbour tax of C$3 must be paid at the harbour entrance on Big Corn. The boat drops you off on Little Corn's western side, amid the island's only real cluster of population and facilities.
Tour operators Two friendly, PADI-certified dive outfits offer a similar range of activities and prices – from single-tank dives (US$35) to trips to Blowing Rock (US$95) and five-day packages (US$150). Dolphin Dive (⊛dolphindivelittlecorn .com) is run from the fancy *Hotel Los Delfines*, while the older Dive Little Corn (⊛divelittlecorn .com) is just south of *Miss Bridgette's*. Snorkel and kayak hire are around US$10 per day – you can also hire snorkels at most accommodation on the island.

Accommodation

Things get busy during the Christmas/New Year period and around Semana Santa – prices can rise during this period. If you're here at quieter times, it may be worth haggling.

Big Corn

Much of Big Corn's accommodation is on the anonymous side, with options spread between built-up Brig Bay and the quieter beaches that sprawl around the island – you'll need taxis to access these.

Casa Blanca 100m south along the rough beach track skirting Brig Bay. A windswept *hospedaje* that feels fairly isolated (despite only being 10min walk from town) with inexpensive but tiny wooden rooms. Fans and mosquito nets supplied. There are also pleasant verandas with hammocks. US$15

Mama Lola Just past Silver Sands ☎8356-4615, ✉mamalolacon1@yahoo.com. It looks like a squat postmodern lighthouse, and this beach-set hotel has cracking views across the island and out to sea. The doubles are clean enough, and the upstairs bar (beer C$25) is a great place to contemplate the Caribbean. US$30

Panorama 20m north of the Nautilus Dive shop ☎2575-5065. Fairly anonymous block housing several spotless rooms, as well as a sweet veranda. The pricier rooms with a/c also come with hammocked porches and wicker rocking-chairs. US$15

Silver Sands Near *Casa Canada* and the baseball diamond on the east side of the island ☎8948-1436. Three rustic wooden cabinas, just off an empty beach, share a field with some space for tents. Food is on offer in high season (Jan–April – the whole place is pretty dead at other times of year) at the nearby bar-restaurant, and snorkel hire (US$10/day) and fishing tours (US$100/group) are available. Camping US$8, cabinas US$20

Sweet Dreams Right by the harbour ☎2575-5195. The location makes this orange-hued hotel a good bet for those heading off to Little Corn. The first-floor rooms are smallish but tidy, mostly en suite and all with TV, and there's a restaurant attached. En-suite rooms cost US$15 extra. US$20

Little Corn

Head to the east and north sides of Little Corn if you want tranquility and great snorkelling on your doorstep, although you'll have a 20min walk to get to the main village, where a couple of inexpensive options vie for your custom. Many places only have electricity in the evenings and at night.

Carlito's Place On Cocal Beach ⊕carlitosplace littlecorn.com. A friendly beachfront backpacker hangout with individual en-suite cabinas. Meals are served in a cheery pink space from around C$100, and there's a pool table (C$10). US$25

Elsa's Just up from *Carlito's Place* on Cocal Beach ☎2575-5014. An island institution, with simple, clean double cabañas and smaller rooms in thatched huts on the beach. Doubles US$20, cabañas US$25

Grace's Place Wedged between *Carlito's Place* and *Elsa's* ✉coolspotlittlecorn@hotmail.com. The most popular of the three budget-cabaña spots along this pleasantly breezy stretch of beach are these Rasta-coloured bamboo huts. They aren't particularly distinctive, but the attached *Cool Spot* bar-restaurant is fun. US$25

Sunshine Hotel 200m north of the ferry ☎8495-6223. Hostel-style accommodation in a rather grand building (in Little Corn terms), offering ten rooms (with two double beds in each), pool and ping-pong tables, internet access, a kitchen for guests, a cool shared balcony and among the cheapest snorkel hire on the island (US$3/day). Rooms US$20

Three Brothers 150m north of the ferry on the right ☎8927-0721. This simple guesthouse set around a tiny gym is a decent budget option if you don't mind being a short walk from the idyllic stuff. The rooms are small but clean and secure, and you can use the kitchen for US$2. US$12

TREAT YOURSELF

Derek's Place North Little Corn ⊕dereksplacelittlecorn.com. A handful of rustic-chic, wood-and-bamboo cabinas on stilts, complete with solar panels, ingenious fold-out tables and walls built from bright glass bottles, set among palms overlooking the beach. A treat for anyone after relaxed privacy, though all bathrooms are shared. Hearty communal meals cost US$6 (lunch) or US$12 (dinner). US$45

Little Corn Beach & Bungalow Cocal Beach, Little Corn ⊕www.littlecornbb .com. This neat place, set at the mellow north end of Cocal Beach, offers neat shipwreck-themed bungalows with nice touches (from the recycled rainwater to the little foot-baths by the door), and a friendly and professional restaurant (breakfast US$3.50, dinner US$9–15) that's a fine place to chill, with coffee and free wi-fi. Bunkhouse US$35, bungalows US$64

Eating and drinking

It's easy to get a good feed of fish, prawns or lobster for reasonable prices (C$100–200), although service can be slow. For inexpensive meals, there are several nameless *comedores* in Big Corn by the dock, which serve large plates of *comida típica* for C$50 (drink included). On Little Corn, *Elsa's, Cool Spot* (at *Grace's Place*) and *Carlito's Place*, on the east side, all serve up cold beers and dishes for C$120–180.

Big Corn

Fisher's Cave Beside the harbour entrance, and also known as *Lidia's Place*. Seafood specialists right in the thick of Big Corn's action. Perch in the courtyard dining area and go for classic Caribbean *ron don* (C$520 for four), lobster in tomato sauce (C$215) or the land-lubbing likes of chicken breast (C$125).

Nautilus Eat & Art 5min north of the harbour. This rickety terrace restaurant (affiliated with the diving shop next door) offers hearty food, including curried fish (C$230), pizza (C$130) and breakfasts and salads.

Nico's On the east side of the island – get a cab. Popular beachside nightspot, with a small waterfront balcony and heaving dancefloor where you join locals in "sexy dancing" to reggaeton and Caribbean rhythms, or swaying to country music. Beer C$20. Open Thurs, Sat & Sun.

Reggae Palace Tucked at the back of town past *Sweet Dreams*. The biggest disco in town,

centrally located and spinning reggae, soca and Garífuna music on weekends. Sat is usually the biggest night.

Seva's Sally Peachy. Locally renowned restaurant with a veranda facing the azure sea, serving tasty grilled fish (C$160), beef chow mein (C$150) and a big and tender plate of fish, chicken and lobster (C$220), as well as standard breakfasts (C$60).

Little Corn

Casa Iguana On the lower east side of the island ⓦcasaiguana.net. A busy little bar-restaurant offering US$6 breakfasts, snacks and hot food during the day, as well as sophisticated US$15

THE RAAN: NORTHERN NICARAGUA

The northern reaches of Nicaraguan Mosquitia – the famous **Mosquito Coast** – is one of the most impenetrable and underdeveloped areas of the Americas. No roads connect the area with the rest of the country, and the many snaking, difficult-to-navigate rivers and lagoons, separated by thick slabs of jungle, prevent the casual traveller – or any non-local, for that matter – from visiting the area. Bordered at its northern extent by the **Río Coco**, Nicaragua's frontier with Honduras, La Mosquitia is dotted by small settlements of the indigenous – mainly Miskito – peoples. The area was highly sensitive during the war years of the 1980s, when Contra bases in Honduras sent guerrilla parties over the long river border to attack Sandinista army posts and civilian communities in La Mosquitia and beyond. The Sandinistas forcibly evacuated many Miskitos from their homes, ostensibly to protect them from Contra attacks, but also to prevent them from going over to the other side.

Few travellers come to **Puerto Cabezas**, the only town of any size and importance in the area. Heading out beyond Cabezas is difficult, but with determination, a good guide, a water purification kit and a good mozzie net, you can use it as a springboard to get even further from the tourist routes and into isolated Miskito communities – Waspám, near the Honduran border, is the biggest.

three-course dinners (which need to be reserved in advance). Most food comes from their farm and garden – which also provides the mint for their mojitos (US$3.50). A range of cabinas (US$35) is also available.

Cool Spot Right next to *Grace's Place*. On the beach at the heart of the east side's backpacker accommodation, *Cool Spot* serves up chicken with pasta (C$130), chilli prawns (C$200) and more, and has more buzz and more tables than anywhere else on the east side of the island.

Esther's The small pink house on the path from the school to the baseball field. *Pan de coco*, or coco bread, is famous on the island and comes out of the oven here at about 2.15pm.

Habana Libre At the dock. This is the most touristy spot on the island – mainly due to the prices (from C$180 for mains – you'll have to order seafood specials in advance). It's a decent bet for cocktails too. Closed Sun.

The Happy Hut In the "village" behind *Tranuilo Café*. The name pretty much nails it – this simple club is the place to dance to reggae at weekends.

Mango's Pizza Just south of Dolphin Dive. A (possibly welcome) change from rice, beans and all things coconut: the cheesy pizzas (C$150 medium, C$200 large) are also available for takeaway.

Miss Bridgette's Opposite the dock. Renowned for having good seafood at the best prices on the island, *Miss Bridgette's* is always busy; lobster and *ron don* go for C$180 (the latter requires advance notice), while big breakfasts are C$90.

Tranquilo Café Just north of Dolphin Dive. This likeable (if not cheap) place is one of the island's main hangouts. There's wi-fi (US$2/20min), reasonable food of the diner variety, tasty organic coffee and a range of beers (C$30) and cocktails. There's a gift shop and book exchange too. Things can get busy in the evenings (especially on bonfire nights – usually Wed and Sat), when the music gets turned up and wide-eyed divers knock back mojitos.

Directory

Exchange On Big Corn, the Banpro, south of the centre on the road from the airport, has an ATM. It's best to come armed with plenty of dollars or córdobas – there's no bank at all on Little Corn.
Health Assistance can be found at the hospital on Big Corn, or the medical clinic just south of Dolphin Dive on Little Corn.
Internet Access on Big Corn is provided by Cyber USA just beyond *Nautilus Eat & Art* (C$15/hr). On Little Corn, *Hotel Los Delphines* charges a whacking C$60/hr. Higher-end places to stay and *Tranquilo Café* also offer wi-fi.

Moving on

By air There are regular flights to Bluefields and Managua from Big Corn's airport (☏2575-5131).
By boat The *Río Escondido* departs for Bluefields on Thurs at 9am – ask at Big Corn docks for more information on other services.

PUERTO CABEZAS

Small and scruffy **PUERTO CABEZAS** or **BILWI**, as it's been officially named in defiance of central governmental control (the name means "snake leaf" in the Mayangna-Sumo indigenous tongue), is the most important town north of Bluefields and south of La Ceiba in Honduras. Everyone seems to have come to this town of thirty thousand people in order to do some kind of business, whether it be a Miskito fisherman walking the streets with a day's catch of fish dangling from his hand, a lumber merchant selling planks to foreign mills, or the government surveyors working on the all-season paved road through the jungle that may one day link the town with Managua. Nevertheless, there is real potential for tourism here and there's at least one organization (**AMICA**) in town organizing trips to the isolated communities and beauty spots located largely to the south. The people are mostly welcoming, and more used to foreigners than you might expect, thanks to a relatively heavy NGO presence.

What to see and do

The town's amenities are all scattered within a few blocks of the Parque Central, a few hundred metres west of the seafront. The water at the local **beach** below the hotels can be clear and blue if the wind is blowing from the northeast, although the townspeople usually head

PUERTO CABEZAS

ACCOMMODATION
Hotel Casa Museo	A
Hotel Cortijo 1	D
Hotel Cortijo 2	C
Hotel Liwa Mair	F
Hotel Perez	B
Hotel Tangney	E

EATING & DRINKING
Aqui Me Quedo	2
Comedor Abril	4
Kabu Payaska	1
Restaurante Malecón	5
Rosti Pollo	3

to Bocana beach a few kilometres north of town; taxis can take you here for about C\$15. Watch your belongings as there are often a few dodgy characters around.

The southern horizon is broken by the atmospheric outline of the **muelle viejo** (old pier), a twenty-minute walk through the barrios (take a taxi after dark), where you'll find fishermen and rusting ships. It was built in 1924 and saw guns delivered for civil war and trussed-up turtles pulled in for their meat; now access is limited by a wire fence.

As well as being the base for AMICA's trips to nearby communities, Puerto Cabezas also serves as the headquarters for **YATAMA** (Yapti Tasba Masraka Nanih Aslatakanka, which translates roughly as "Children of the Mother Earth"), a political party which fights for the rights of the indigenous Atlantic Coast peoples, and which is fiercely opposed to central government, whether Conservative, Liberal or Sandinista.

Arrival and information

By air Flights from Managua (1hr 30min) and Bluefields (50min) touch down at the airstrip (☎2792-2282) 2km north of the town centre. Taxis will cost no more than C\$15 per person. Drivers wait at the airport when flights are due to arrive.

By bus The terminal is a taxi ride (C$15) west of town.

Tourist information The INTUR office (Mon–Fri 8am–1pm) behind the market can provide information about local hotels and restaurants.

Tour operators AMICA (Mon–Fri 8am–noon & 2–5.30pm; ☏ 2792-2219, ✉ asociacionamica @yahoo.es), four blocks south of the main square, focus their energies on improving the lives of the region's indigenous women. They're your best bet for local trips, heading to the lagoon-side fishing village of Haulover, the long black-sand beach at Wawa Bar and the small community of Karata, most of whose members were displaced in Honduras and Costa Rica during the war but many of whom have now returned.

Accommodation

There are a handful of cheaper options, but Puerto Cabezas is one place it's worth spending a bit more – there's a real jump in quality and it's nice to have comfortable digs in this dusty town.

Hotel Casa Museo 400m north of the INTUR office ☏ 2792-2225, ✉ casamuseojudithkain @hotmail.com. One of the prettier options in town, offering bright rooms with high ceilings, folksy bedspreads, hot water, internet and a choice of fan or a/c. There's a free museum, too, with stuffed figures, old canoes and mementos of the civil war. US$27

Hotel Cortijo 1 100m north of the Parque ☏ 2792-2659, ✉ cortijoaa@yahoo.com.mx. Cool and comfortable wooden rooms (all with fan or a/c and private bath) strung along a delightful balcony, itself wrapped around a lush garden. They also have a laundry service and do decent breakfasts with real coffee. Triples are a good deal at US$25. US$20

🏃 **Hotel Cortijo 2** On the street behind the main street (running parallel to the sea) ☏ 2792-2223, ✉ cortijoaa@yahoo.com.mx. The charming sister hotel to *Hotel Cortijo 1* isn't cheap but it's still great value, with seductive wooden rooms (try to get one of the ones at the back), a lovely back garden and balconies and hammocks should you wish to lounge. There's also a convenient wooden jetty running right down to the beach. US$27

Hotel Perez 100m north of *Cortijo 1* ☏ 2792-2362. This ageing place boasts the novelty of carpeted floors, European-style glass windows and a quirky reception. The best rooms, which you'll pay more for, are out back around the old wooden balcony. Meals (C$60 and up) are also available. US$25

Hotel Tangney A block and a half east of the Banpro ☏ 8338-9590. Ramshackle guesthouse with slightly shabby rooms, a cool balcony and fans but no mozzie nets – if you want cheap prices, it's adequate. US$11

Eating and drinking

Aqui Me Quedo Opposite the Parque Central. Classic beef, chicken and *gallo pinto* fare done well, in this simple pitstop that's well set for gazing over the market.

Comedor Abril Opposite Banpro. Cheap, home-style restaurant with decent, filling *comida corriente* from C$60 and some decent juices.

🏃 **Kabu Payaska** On a bluff 2km north of town. This great sweep of a terrace over the beach is a cracking place to enjoy delicious, oily lobster *a la plancha*, as well as fresh fish (C$180) and the ever-present chicken (C$150), or just sit back and glug a drink or two. Get a taxi here and back, especially at night.

Restaurante Malecón 300m south of *Liwa Mair*. Appealing beach-front restaurant and bar specializing in seafood; lobster and shrimp dishes are a reasonable C$170–180, while the cold beers are a good deal at C$17. Things get funkier at night, when there are sometimes DJs and karaoke.

Rosti Pollo Just southeast of the Parque. The place to eat chicken in town, be it fried (C$70) or grilled (C$95), its skin deliciously crackly. Meals include a *refresco* or soft drink.

Directory

Exchange The Banpro a block south of the Parque Central has an ATM, and there are

Bancentros at the airport and just east of the market.

Health Assistance can be sought at the Clinica y Farmacia Sukia, 100m south of Banpro (Mon–Fri 1.30–6.30pm, Sat 8am–noon).

Internet Access is available at several cafés; try Servinet y Comunicaciones Saballes just south of Banpro (C$15/hr).

Moving on

By air La Costeña flights head to Managua and Bluefields, crossing great swathes of forest on their way.

By bus The bus journey to Managua (2 daily; 24hr) is notoriously hellish, and impossible after heavy rain.

Costa Rica

LIBERIA:
this welcoming cowboy city
cranks up during its fiestas,
with rodeos, bullfights
and roving marimba bands

TORTUGUERO:
see green sea turtles tumble ashore
at this important nesting site

MONTEVERDE:
walk the trails of these
ancient, brooding cloudforests

**PUERTO VIEJO
DE TALAMANCA:**
surf the Salsa Brava and sway
to reggae in this lively little surf town

PARQUE NACIONAL CORCOVADO:
Costa Rica's last great wilderness –
steamy rainforest teeming with wildlife
and ringed by pristine beaches

stay @ fun party rodeos Js

Jungle zip lines

to panama

ROUGH COSTS

DAILY BUDGET Basic US$30/
occasional treat US$75

DRINK Beer US$2, coffee US$1.25

FOOD *CASADO* US$4

CAMPING/HOSTEL/BUDGET HOTEL
US$5/US$12/US$30

TRAVEL San José–Puerto Viejo
(210km) by bus: 4hr 30min, US$9

FACT FILE

POPULATION 4.6 million

AREA 51,000 sq km

LANGUAGES Spanish (official),
Creole (Mekatelyu) on the
Caribbean coast

CURRENCY Costa Rica colón (CRC; c)

CAPITAL San José (population:
365,000)

INTERNATIONAL PHONE CODE
☏506

TIME ZONE GMT -6hr

Introduction

Costa Rica can appear almost unfairly blessed with natural attractions. Within its boundaries lie lush rain- and cloud-forests, smouldering volcanos, long sandy beaches, and a simply stunning biological diversity, as well as tranquil colonial towns and chilled-out coastal resorts. In sharp contrast to the turbulence experienced by many of its neighbours, the country has become synonymous with stability and prosperity – Costa Ricans, or Ticos, enjoy the highest rate of literacy, health care, education and life expectancy in the isthmus. The country has a long democratic tradition of free and open elections, no standing army (it was abolished in 1948) and even a Nobel Peace Prize to its name, won by former president Oscar Arias. Indeed, Costa Rica's past and present are so quiet, comparatively, that it's often said that the nation lacks a history or identity. This is far from the truth: Costa Rica's character is rooted in its distinct local cultures, from the Afro-Caribbean province of Limón, with its Creole cuisine and Caribbean English, to the traditional ladino values embodied by the sabanero (cowboy) of Guanacaste.

For travellers, Costa Rica is the prime **ecotourism** destination in Central America. Every year many thousands of visitors come to experience the extreme biodiversity offered by its 161 parks and reserves, from **Monteverde** to **Corcovado** to **Tortuguero**; hiking, rafting and zip-line canopy tours are the most popular activities for exploring the enormous array of exotic flora and fauna. There's also the country's incredibly varied landscape: active volcanoes, such as **Arenal** and **Rincón de la Vieja**, punctuate its mountainous spine, while the beaches on both coasts – **Jacó**, **Tamarindo** and **Puerto Viejo de Talamanca**, among others – provide excellent surfing. The potent combination of sights and activities, accessibility and the country's relative safety mean Costa Rica can sometimes be expensive and crowded, but no trip to Central America would be complete without a trip here.

CHRONOLOGY

1000 BC Several autonomous tribes inhabit Costa Rica, the Chorotegas being the most numerous. Foundations are laid at the Guayabo settlement, which is later abandoned around 1400 AD.

WHEN TO VISIT

Costa Rican weather is unpredictable – and varied – but you can count on some general trends. The main rainy season runs from May to November, peaking in September and October (on the Caribbean coast, rain falls April to August and November to December). These months are less crowded and generally cheaper, as hotels, tours and activities lower their prices to attract the smaller numbers of tourists. Peak season (December, January and Easter) is the most expensive time to visit – accommodation and transport require advanced bookings during these times.

1502 AD Christopher Columbus lands on the Caribbean coast.

1506 Diego de Nicuesa is dispatched by Spain's King Fernando to govern the region; expedition fails.

1522 A third Spanish expedition sails from Panama to settle the region, which they name Costa Rica (Rich Coast). The indigenous people begin a campaign of resistance.

1540 The land is named part of the area of New Spain. Settlement is slow, mainly taking place in the centre of the country. After it's discovered that there is no gold in the region, Spain largely ignores its colony for the next several hundred years.

1723 Volcán Irazú erupts, nearly destroying the capital at Cartago.

1821 Costa Rica wins independence from Spain.

1823 Civil war breaks out, resulting in San José being named the federal capital. Costa Rica becomes a state in the Federal Republic of Central America.

1824 Juan Mora Fernández becomes the nation's first elected head of state. He encourages coffee cultivation with land grants, thereby creating an elite class of coffee barons.

1838 Costa Rica withdraws from the Federal Republic, and declares sovereignty.

1843 Coffee becomes the nation's major export crop after British merchant William Le Lacheur establishes a direct trade route between Costa Rica and England.

1856 American adventurer William Walker invades Costa Rica with dreams of annexing Central America to the US, but is defeated by Costa Rican troops, including national hero Juan Santamaría.

1870 General Tom Guardia seizes power, ruling as dictator for 12 years. In contrast to his ascent, his policies include curbing military power and taxation on coffee earnings to fund public works.

1948 President Rafael Calderón Guardia refuses to relinquish power after losing election to Otilio Ulate. Civil war erupts; "Don Pepe" Figueres defeats Calderón, becomes interim president, then returns power to Ulate. Later elected to two terms as president, Figueres abolishes the armed forces, establishes citizenship rights for black people and institutes the female vote.

1981 Economic crisis – Costa Rica defaults on loan interest payments, accruing one of the world's highest per capita debts – and instability, caused by civil war in Nicaragua.

1987 Costa Rican President Oscar Arias Sánchez is awarded the Nobel Peace Prize for his efforts in ending the Nicaraguan civil war.

2007 Costa Rica signs controversial CAFTA (a free-trade agreement with the US and Central American neighbours) after several years of fiery debate.

2010 Laura Chinchilla succeeds her political mentor Oscar Arias Sánchez to become the country's first female president.

Basics

ARRIVAL

Visitors flying to Costa Rica usually arrive at **Juan Santamaría International Airport (SJO)** in Alajuela (30min from San José). Iberia is currently the only airline offering direct flights from Europe (Madrid), but connecting flights can be taken from numerous North American cities, including Chicago, Houston, Los Angeles, New York and Toronto, as well as Panama City. Flights from North America also arrive at **Liberia International Airport** in Guanacaste, as do some charter flights from Europe during the high season.

Most travellers entering by **land** arrive with Tica Bus (☎2221-0006, ⓦwww.ticabus.com), which provides services from neighbouring Central American countries. There are overland border crossings with Nicaragua in the west, and Panama in the east (see box below).

VISAS

North American and European nationals do not require a **visa** for visits of less than thirty days (and most can stay for ninety days), though Irish, Australian and Bulgarian citizens require visas for stays of thirty to ninety days. A passport valid

> ### LAND ROUTES TO COSTA RICA
>
> Costa Rica has several land borders with neighbours Nicaragua and Panama. The main border crossing with Nicaragua is at Peñas Blancas (see p.563). Further east, there is another crossing at Los Chiles (see p.568), though it also involves a boat trip.
>
> The main crossing for Panama is at Paso Canoas (see p.579). Sixaola (see p.529), on the Caribbean coast, is a smaller crossing, as is Río Sereno in the southern highlands.

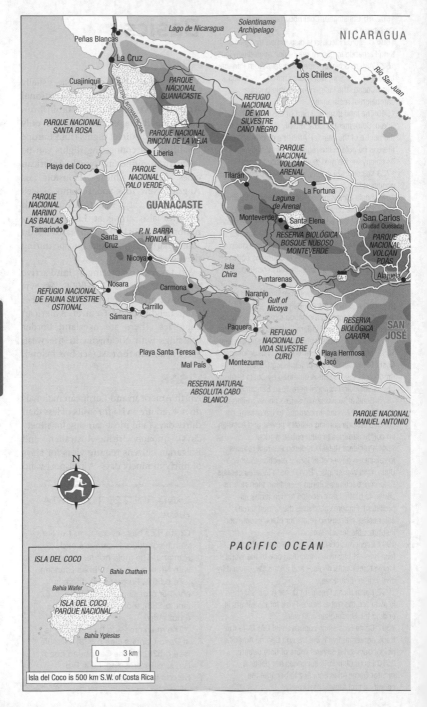

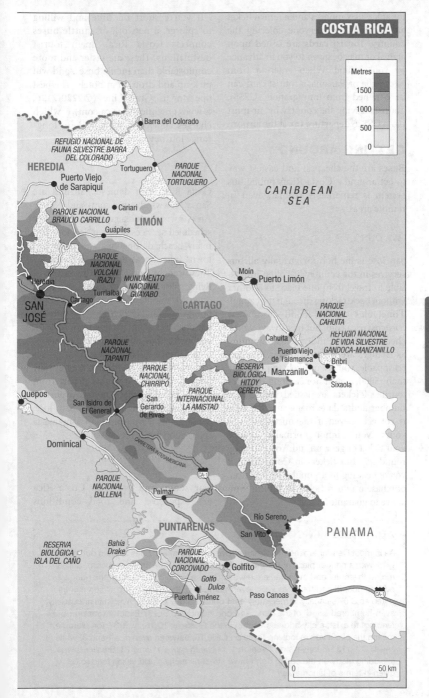

COSTA RICA

Metres
1500
1000
500
0

Barra del Colorado

REFUGIO NACIONAL DE
FAUNA SILVESTRE BARRA
DEL COLORADO

HEREDIA

Puerto Viejo
de Sarapiquí

Tortuguero

PARQUE
NACIONAL
TORTUGUERO

CARIBBEAN
SEA

Cariari

PARQUE NACIONAL
BRAULIO CARRILLO

LIMÓN

Guápiles

PARQUE
NACIONAL
VOLCÁN
IRAZÚ

MONUMENTO
NACIONAL
GUAYABO

Moín

Puerto Limón

Heredia

Cartago

Turrialba

SAN
JOSÉ

CARTAGO

PARQUE
NACIONAL
CAHUITA

PARQUE
NACIONAL
TAPANTÍ

Cahuita

REFUGIO NACIONAL
DE VIDA SILVESTRE
GANDOCA-MANZANILLO

Puerto Viejo
de Talamanca

PARQUE
NACIONAL
CHIRRIPÓ

RESERVA
BIOLÓGICA
HITOY
CERERE

Manzanillo

Bribri

PARQUE
INTERNACIONAL
LA AMISTAD

Sixaola

Quepos

San Isidro de
El General

San
Gerardo
de Rivas

Dominical

CARRETERA INTERAMERICANA

PARQUE
NACIONAL
BALLENA

Palmar

CA-1

Río Sereno

RESERVA
BIOLÓGICA
ISLA DEL CAÑO

Bahía
Drake

PUNTARENAS

San Vito

PANAMA

PARQUE
NACIONAL
CORCOVADO

Golfito

Golfo
Dulce

Puerto Jiménez

Paso Canoas

CA-1

0   50 km

COSTA RICA

BASICS

for at least six months and a return ticket are required for everyone entering the country. **Tourist cards** are issued upon arrival or may be given to you in advance by your airline. When entering from Nicaragua or Panama, a tourist card can be obtained from immigration (US$5). Tourists leaving the country by air must pay a US$26 **departure tax** at the airport.

GETTING AROUND

Buses are the cheapest and easiest way to get around – Costa Rica's public bus system is remarkably regular, even in remote areas.

By bus

San José is the hub for virtually all **bus** services in the country; it's often impossible to travel from one place to another without backtracking through the capital. **Timetables** can be found on Ⓦwww .visitcostarica.com, but it is always worth checking with the individual companies, as changes are frequent. **Fares** are very reasonable: you are unlikely to pay more than 5000c, even for a long-distance journey. **Tickets** are issued with a seat number and a date; make sure the date is correct – even if the mistake is not yours, you cannot normally change your ticket or get a refund. You can't buy round-trip bus tickets in Costa Rica; if you're heading to a popular destination, purchase a return ticket as soon as you arrive to guarantee a seat.

If you're short on time and willing to splurge, a network of **shuttle buses** connects Costa Rica's main tourist destinations. These are faster and more comfortable than public buses, and will pick up and drop off at hotels. The best operator is Gray Line (☎2220-2126, Ⓦwww.graylinecostarica.com), which charges US$40–75 for a mid- to long-range journey.

By air

Costa Rica's two domestic **airlines** are Sansa (Ⓦwww.flysansa.com) and Nature Air (Ⓦwww.natureair.com). They offer scheduled services between San José and many beach destinations and provincial towns (plus Bocas del Toro in Panama). These can be very handy time-savers – flying from San José to Tortuguero takes only 30 minutes, as opposed to eight hours of bus and ferry rides – and rates are reasonable (usually starting from US$50). Nature Air, though slightly more expensive than Sansa at full fare, offers "*loco*" prices (from US$25) for flights that are not fully booked. Nature Air flights depart from Tobias Bolaños International Airport in Pavas, 6km from downtown San José; Sansa flights leave from Juan Santamaría International Airport in Alajuela.

By car

Car rental and petrol in Costa Rica are expensive, and road conditions

---

ADDRESSES IN COSTA RICA

As in most Central American countries, Costa Rica's major cities are laid out in a grid, with a park or plaza at the centre (Puerto Limón is the only exception). Calles run north–south, and avenidas east–west. Generally the calles east of the park are odd-numbered and the ones west even-numbered; the Calle Central (sometimes noted as C 0) is usually immediately east of the Parque Central. Avenidas are usually even-numbered south of the park, and odd-numbered north. Exact street numbers tend not to exist; a city address written in the Guide as "C 16, Av 1/3", for example, means the place you're looking for is on Calle 16, between avenidas 1 and 3, while "Av 1, C 11/13" means it's on Avenida 1, between calles 11 and 13. Smaller towns (including many on the coast) don't have street names, so addresses tend to be given in terms of landmarks.

often poor, especially in rural areas. However, having your own transport is useful for visiting some of the country's more exciting sights, such as the Central Valley's volcanoes and the Osa Peninsula; few buses serve these routes, and the timetables of those that do often leave you with little time for exploration. In peak season, rentals vary from around US$250 per week for a regular vehicle, and from US$390 for a 4WD (both including insurance), and you can expect to pay roughly US$70 a tank on a mid-sized vehicle. To rent, you need a credit card with sufficient credit for a security deposit or the entire cost of the rental. Exercise caution in choosing a rental company – some have been known to claim for "damage" they insist you inflicted on their vehicle. Full insurance should cover you, and is recommended. While the majority of companies are based in San José, many also have offices in Liberia, Tamarindo and Jacó. Try Alamo (☎2243-7733, ⓦwww.alamo costarica.com) or Avanti (☎2430-4647, ⓦwww.avantirentacar.com).

Taxis are plentiful in urban areas – look for maroon-coloured vehicles with yellow triangles containing the license number marked on the front passenger door, and a taxi sign on the roof. Intra-city trips should set you back about US$2–6, while long-distance, inter-city trips cost upwards of US$40 – much more expensive than a regular bus, but often comparable with a shuttle bus.

By bicycle

Cycling is an inexpensive and popular way to get around. The poor condition of the country's roads is really the only deterrent – helmets are a must. Most beach towns have at least one bicycle rental outlet, with prices from US$4–15 a day. The quality of the bikes varies greatly, so check the equipment before you pay.

ACCOMMODATION

Although Costa Rica is one of the most expensive countries in Central America, there is still a fair amount of affordable lodging. Most towns have a range of places to stay, and even the smallest settlements have a basic **pensión** or **hospedaje**. US$8–15 (3900–7400c) a night covers a dorm or basic room in a hostel, while for around US$25–40 (12,600–20,200c) a night you'll get a more comfortable en-suite room, with a fan and possibly even a TV and phone, in a B&B environment. There are three HI hostels in Costa Rica (see ⓦwww.hihostels.com); card-holders save about US$2 a night. When looking at prices, be sure to ask if the national **hotel tax** (which stands at 16.39 percent, including a three percent "tourist tax") has been added to the published price. Most hostels and hotels price their rooms in US dollars, though you can pay in dollars or colones. Reservations are recommended year-round and are a necessity in high season (Dec–April).

Camping is fairly widespread. In the beach towns especially, you will usually find at least one well-equipped private campsite. Alternatively, you may be able to find a hotelier (usually in an establishment at the lower end of the price scale) willing to let you pitch your tent in the grounds. Although not all national parks have campsites, those that do are generally good, with at least some basic facilities, and cost around US$5 per person per day. You may also be able to bunk at some ranger stations.

FOOD AND DRINK

The cheapest places to eat are **sodas**, which are a sort of cross between North American diners and British greasy spoons. Serving breakfast and lunch options, *sodas* offer set *platos del día* (daily specials) for about US$4. **Restaurants**, particularly those serving international fare, can be pricey – expect to pay from US$10 for a main course in the capital, and almost double that in some coastal towns. A town's central **market** is usually a safe bet for a quick feed, and if you tire of rice and beans or roast chicken, most towns have a budget-friendly pizza place or Chinese restaurant. Generally, restaurants **open** early, around 7am, and most are empty or closed by 10 or 10.30pm.

Tican cuisine is economical and filling, with staples such as **gallo pinto** ("painted rooster"), a breakfast dish of rice and beans, often served with meat or eggs, and **casados** ("married"), combinations of rice, beans, salad, plantain and meat or fish that are frequently large enough for two to share. Fried/roast chicken is another national favourite. **Bocas** ("mouth" snacks) are great for keeping hunger at bay, and are commonly offered at bars where there's no formal menu. Fresh **fruit** is cheap and plentiful – try some less familiar fruits, like *mamones chinos* (a kind of lychee), *maracuya* (passion fruit) and *marañón*, whose seed is the cashew nut. With so much fresh produce, vegetarians generally do quite well in Costa Rica; most menus will have a meat-free option. You will also find excellent fresh **fish** here, including *pargo* (red snapper) and *corvina* (sea bass), with Tican-style *ceviche* a speciality.

Drink

Costa Rica is famous for its **coffee**, and it is not hard to locate a decent *café negro*. Another highlight of Costa Rica is its **juices** or *refrescos naturales*, combining fresh tropical fruit, ice and either milk (*leche*) or water (*agua*). You'll find **herbal teas** throughout the country; those served in Limón are especially good. In Guanacaste you can get the distinctive corn-based drinks **horchata** and **pinolillo**.

Costa Rica has several local brands of lager **beer** (all brewed by the same company). Most popular, and cheapest, is Imperial, but Bavaria Gold is the best of the bunch. Pilsen and Rock Ice (beer with lemon flavour) are also worth a try. Imported beers are available in bars, restaurants and hotels as pricier options.

For an after-dinner drink, try creamy, Baileys-style coffee **liqueurs** such as the famous Café Rica. For those with a stronger stomach, there is an indigenous sugarcane-based spirit, **guaro**, of which Cacique is the most popular brand. The **drinking age** in Costa Rica is 18, and many clubs and bars will only admit those with ID, so carry a photocopy of your passport.

CULTURE AND ETIQUETTE

Costa Rica is a friendly country. Although many Ticos speak English, an effort to **communicate** in Spanish is much appreciated; a greeting – usually "Buenas", a shortening of "good day/afternoon/evening" – is always well received. Though officially a **Catholic** nation, the degrees of orthodoxy are hugely varied and many denominations of Christianity are present.

Macho attitudes still exist. **Gay and lesbian** travellers should be discreet, but an increasing number of gay-friendly hotels and nightclubs, particularly in the capital, tells of a gradual shift in mentality; Ⓦwww.costaricagaymap.com is a useful website. Solo **women** can travel alone with relative confidence. While gringa-enticement is a rather competitive and popular way to pass the time – particularly in beach towns – and such focused attention can be intimidating, it is usually harmless and can be easily ignored. Women wanting to visit a church should make sure their shoulders are covered and that they have something to cover their heads.

Friendly **bartering** is worth a try at craft markets, but you are unlikely to get discounts anywhere else. In regard to **tipping**, most restaurants include a ten percent service charge in the bill. In fancier establishments, a small tip is expected. It is also polite to offer a token amount when photographing locals or performers (especially in a touristy setting).

SPORTS AND OUTDOOR ACTIVITIES

With a national team that has qualified for several World Cups, **fútbol** (or soccer; ⓦ www.futboldecostarica.com) is Costa Rica's most popular spectator sport. There's a fiercely competitive national league, and you'll find some kind of pitch in every town.

The nation's **surf** – some of the best in Central America – is one of its biggest draws. Over fifty well-known breaks dot the Pacific and southern Caribbean coasts, and all beach communities offer a selection of teachers and board rental companies; Jacó, Mal País and Puerto Viejo are among the most popular beach locations. The teeming oceans (and rivers) also bring in masses of sport-fishing and scuba-diving fanatics, although prices are generally steep. **Snorkelling** is the most economical way to get up close to the marine life. The best areas for exploring brilliant corals are Cahuita and Manzanillo, where equipment rental is available from local tour offices and some hotels. **Kayaking** is growing in popularity as a good, green way to explore the country's many lagoons, rivers and beaches; **whitewater rafting** is a more exciting way to do the same.

There's also a vast array of land-based activities and sights on offer. Zip-line **canopy tours** make the most of the country's ancient rainforests, while **hiking** is the best way to visit the nation's many volcanic sites; **horseriding** is also frequently offered for volcano tours but check the condition of the horses before you pay, as animal neglect or mistreatment is not unknown.

COMMUNICATIONS

The most reliable place from which to send **mail** is San José's Correo Central, or main post office (see p.500). **Opening hours** for most post offices are Monday to Friday from 7.30am to 6pm. Those in San José and Liberia also have limited Saturday hours (8am–noon).

Public **phones** require phonecards (*tarjetas telefónica*), which are available from most grocery stores, street kiosks and pharmacies. The cards can be used at any public payphone, or (with permission) on hotel and residential phone lines. ☎199 cards are for international calls, ☎197 cards for domestic/local calls. International cards come in three denominations: 3000c (17min talk time to the US, 12min to Europe), US$10 and US$20. Many payphones also accept credit cards. Dial ☎09 or 116 to get an English-speaking operator and make

---

COSTA RICA ON THE NET

ⓦ www.costarica-nationalparks .com A thorough guide to the country's parks and reserves.

ⓦ www.costaricaguide.info Excellent free maps (also available at ICT desks and many hostel-type accommodations), with useful directories, bus schedules and transport information, and plenty of budget listings.

ⓦ www.ticotimes.net Central America's leading English-language newspaper.

ⓦ www.visitcostarica.com The official tourist site for Costa Rica, with bus schedules, hotels, maps and useful contact numbers.

a collect call overseas; dial ☎110 for internal collect calls. There are no area codes and all phone numbers have eight digits. ☎2 precedes all landline numbers; mobile numbers are prefixed with ☎8.

In 2010, pay-as-you-go **mobile phones** were introduced; SIM cards with varying amounts of credit cost 2500–10,000c. Though you may have to get your mobile unlocked to use them, the SIMs generally work out cheaper than paying the high European or US roaming charges. Alternatively, a basic mobile phone in Costa Rica costs from 30,000c. To buy either a SIM card or a mobile phone you'll need to take two photocopies of your passport with you.

Internet rates are low in major towns – usually US$1–1.50 per hour – and rise up to US$4 per hour in smaller towns and more remote areas; you'll find an internet café in almost every town in Costa Rica. Most hostels and hotels, particularly in the capital, provide free internet and/or wi-fi.

CRIME AND SAFETY

Costa Rica is relatively safe and the crime that does exist tends to be **opportunistic** rather than violent. Pickpocketing and luggage theft are the greatest threats; it is never safe to leave possessions unattended, especially on the beach. If you have anything stolen you will need to file a report immediately at the nearest police station (*estación de policía*, or *guardia rural* in rural areas). For tourist-related crime, such as overcharging, contact the ICT in San José (see opposite).

EMERGENCY NUMBERS

All emergencies ☎911
Police ☎117
Fire ☎118
Red Cross ☎128
Traffic police ☎2222-9330/9245
Private ambulance Emergencias 2000, Guanacaste and Puntarenas ☎2380-4125

Car-related crime, particularly that which involves rental vehicles, is on the rise, so park securely (never on the street), especially at night. A common scam is to pre-puncture rental-car tyres, follow the car and pull over to "offer assistance"; beware of Good Samaritans on the roadside. Drivers with a puncture should keep driving to the nearest service station or public area to change tyres.

HEALTH

The **medical care** in the Valle Central (where ☎911 is fully functional) is the best in the country. The coastal areas and more remote corners of the country, however, lack doctors and facilities. **Pharmacies**, found in most towns and generally open from 8am to 4.30pm, may be able to suggest a local with medical experience in case of emergency; otherwise, head to a hospital in the nearest large city.

INFORMATION AND MAPS

The best source of **information** about Costa Rica is the Instituto Costarricense de Turismo, or ICT (ⓦwww.visitcosta rica.com). The main office (☎2299-5800) is in San José, inconveniently located out of town on the east side of Juan Pablo II bridge along the General Cañas highway. Staff can provide maps, museum details and bus schedules. There are a handful of regional ICT offices, but generally you'll have to rely on local initiatives, hotels and tourist agencies for information.

ⓦwww.maptak.com has download-able **maps** of the provinces and their capitals, as does the Costa Rica Guide (see box, p.487). Many places will have an informative town map on a billboard; these are usually centrally located.

MONEY AND BANKS

The official currency of Costa Rica is the **colón** ("c"; plural *colones*), collo-quially referred to as "pesos". There are two types of **coin** in circulation: the old silver ones (denominations of 5, 10 and 20) and newer gold ones (denominations of 5, 10, 25, 50, 100 and 500). There are also four bank **notes** (1000, 2000, 5000 and 10,000 colones). Many places will not accept torn notes; these can be exchanged at banks. US dollars (US$) are accepted at hotels and tourist sights across the nation (and many services, particularly those aimed at tourists, are priced in them), but *colones* are generally necessary for local transport and food.

Banking hours tend to be Monday to Friday, 9am to 4pm. Banco Nacional de Costa Rica is the country's most popular bank, with branches nationwide. **Debit cards** are extremely useful: most cities and towns have at least one ATM, or *cajero automático* (though there are none in Tortuguero). ATMs often dispense US dollars as well as colones. **Credit cards** are handy for making deposits or even obtaining cash advances; Visa is more widely accepted than MasterCard. **Travellers' cheques** should only be bought in US dollars,

but are not widely accepted outside the bigger cities. Bring plenty of cash when visiting smaller towns and beaches, as banking facilities can be scarce.

OPENING HOURS AND PUBLIC HOLIDAYS

Shops and businesses are usually open weekdays from 9am to 6pm (**malls** open about 10am–9pm), with shorter hours on Saturdays. Most businesses are closed on Sundays, while many museums shut on Mondays. The main public holidays, when all banks, post offices, museums and government offices close, are listed in the box below.

FESTIVALS

Costa Rica celebrates many festivals, or *feriados*, throughout the calendar year. The dates below only touch on the highlights – Ticos love a party and find many excuses for celebration.

January Palmares Civic Fiesta is celebrated over two weeks with concerts, carnival rides and bullfights.

March Celebrations held throughout the country in honour of San José Day (March 19).

April Fiesta honouring Juan Santamaría on April 11 marks the death of Costa Rica's national hero.

August The nation's patron saint, La Negrita, is honoured with a pilgrimage to Cartago (Aug 2).

October The whole country, but particularly Limón Province, where there are Carnaval festivities, celebrates its day of discovery, Columbus Day (Oct 12).

December The last week is a nonstop street party in Zapote, with music, bullfights, rides and games.

San José

Smack in the middle of the fertile Valle Central, sprawling **SAN JOSÉ** has a spectacular setting, ringed by soaring mountains and volcanoes on all sides. That's where the compliments generally end, however, and you'll be hard pressed to find anyone, even a native *Josefino*, who has much good to say about the city's potholed streets and car-dealership architecture – not to mention the choking diesel fumes, kamikaze drivers and chaotically unplanned expansion. In general, travellers talk about San José as they do about bank lines and immigration offices: a pain, but unavoidable. This said, if you've been travelling through the region, you'll find that compared to, say, Managua or Guatemala City, San José has some vibrant and cosmopolitan offerings. Most people end up spending a few days here – the city is a major transport hub, and many journeys across the country involve backtracking through the capital – and find they can enjoy it.

What to see and do

Few travellers come to San José for the sights, and it is certainly not a place that exudes immediate appeal. It does have its diversions, however, including some interesting museums and galleries. It's also a manageable city, with all the attractions close together. The **Parque Central** lies at the centre of the city, but the **Plaza de la Cultura** is considered

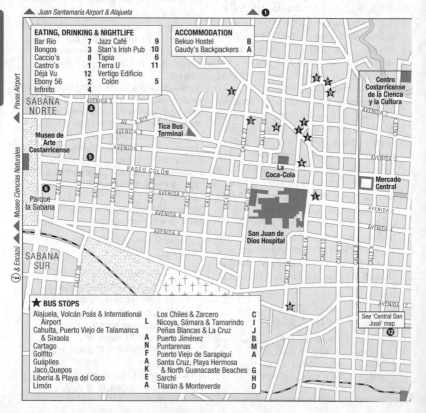

EATING, DRINKING & NIGHTLIFE
Bar Río	7	Jazz Café	9
Bongos	3	Stan's Irish Pub	10
Caccio's	8	Tapia	6
Castro's	1	Terra U	11
Déjà Vu	12	Vertigo Edificio	
Ebony 56	2	Colón	5
Infinito	4		

ACCOMMODATION
Bekuo Hostel	B
Gaudy's Backpackers	A

★ BUS STOPS

Alajuela, Volcán Poás & International Airport	L	Los Chiles & Zarcero	C
Cahuita, Puerto Viejo de Talamanca & Sixaola	A	Nicoya, Sámara & Tamarindo	I
Cartago	N	Peñas Blancas & La Cruz	J
Golfito	F	Puerto Jiménez	B
Guápiles	A	Puntarenas	M
Jacó, Quepos	K	Puerto Viejo de Sarapiquí	A
Liberia & Playa del Coco	E	Santa Cruz, Playa Hermosa & North Guanacaste Beaches	G
Limón	A	Sarchí	H
		Tilarán & Monteverde	D

Juan Santamaría Airport & Alajuela

SABANA NORTE

Museo de Arte Costarricense

Parque la Sabana

SABANA SUR

Tica Bus Terminal

PASEO COLÓN

AVENIDA 5
AV 3 BIS
AVENIDA 3
AVENIDA 1
AVENIDA 2
AVENIDA 4
AVENIDA 6

La Coca-Cola

San Juan de Dios Hospital

Centro Costarricense de la Cienca y la Cultura

Mercado Central

AVENIDA 7
AVENIDA 3
AVENIDA 1
AVENIDA 2

AVENIDA 2

See 'Central San José' map

Pavas Airport
Museo Ciencias Naturales
& Escazú

San José's social core. The area around it is subdivided into little neighbourhoods (**barrios**) that flow seamlessly into one another. Barrios Amón and Otoya, in the north, are the prettiest, while those to the east – La California, Escalante and Los Yoses – are home to comfortable houses and the odd embassy. Further east is the student municipality of **San Pedro**, home to the University of Costa Rica (UCR).

Museo de Oro Precolombino

The Plaza de la Cultura cleverly conceals one of San José's treasures, the **Museo de Oro Precolombino**, or Pre-Columbian Gold Museum (daily 9.30am–4.30pm; 5000c; ☎2243-4216, Ⓦwww.museos delbancocentral.org). The bunker-like underground space is a touch gloomy, but the gold on display is truly impressive and includes the largest array of animal-shaped gold ornaments and figurines in Central America. There is also a numismatic museum charting the history of Costa Rica's currency over the last 500 years, plus frequently changing temporary exhibitions.

Teatro Nacional

San José's heavily columned, grey-brown **Teatro Nacional** (Mon–Sat 9am–4pm, with free tours every hour; US$7; ☎2221-5341, Ⓦwww.teatro nacional.go.cr) sits on the corner of C 5 and Av 2, behind the Plaza de la Cultura. The theatre's marbled stairways, gilt cherubs and red-velvet carpets would look more at home in Old Europe than

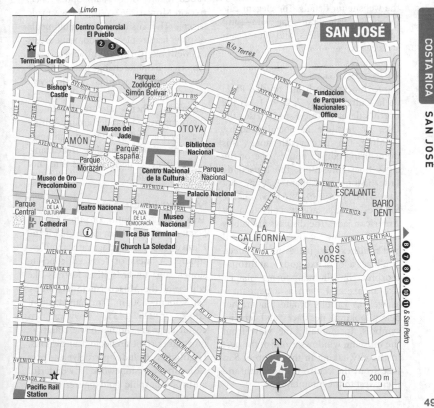

in Central America, and remain in remarkably good condition, despite the onslaught of the climate and a succession of earthquakes. During the day you can wander around the post-Baroque splendour, even if you're not coming to see a performance (see p.499). In the gallery (Mon–Sat 9am–4pm), changing exhibits are open to the public; check the website for details. The elegant café (Mon–Fri 9am–5pm, Sat 9am–4pm) serves pricey coffees and European-style cakes.

Museo de Jade

Three blocks northeast of the Plaza de la Cultura, at Av 7, C 9/11, on the north side of Parque España, rises the INS, or Institute of Social Security, building. On its eleventh storey, this uninspiring edifice houses one of the city's finest museums, the **Museo de Jade** (Mon–Fri 8.30am–3.30pm, Sat 9am–1pm; US$8; ☎2287-6034), home to the world's largest collection of American jade. The displays are subtly backlit to show off the multicoloured and multitextured pieces to full effect. You'll see a lot of **axe-gods** – anthropomorphic bird/human forms shaped like an axe and worn as a pendant – as well as various ornate (and rather heavy-looking) necklaces and fertility symbols. Incidentally, the **view** from the museum windows is one of the best in the city, taking in the sweep of San José from the centre to the south and then west to the mountains.

Museo de Arte y Diseño Contemporáneo

Sprawling across the entire eastern border of the Parque España, the former National Liquor Factory, dating from 1887, houses the Centro Nacional de la Cultura, home to the cutting-edge **Museo de Arte y Diseño Contemporáneo** (Mon–Sat 10.30am–5pm; 1500c, free on Mon; ☎2257-7202, ⊛www.madc .ac.cr). The cosmopolitan, multimedia displays feature pieces by domestic artists as well as works from across Latin America. Exhibits change frequently, but the museum is definitely worth a visit to see what's going on in the arts in the Americas. There's also a theatre in the complex – a wander around during the day may offer interesting glimpses of dancers and musicians rehearsing. Unfortunately, performances are not open to the public.

Museo Nacional

Two blocks south of the Centro Nacional de la Cultura along C 11 is the Plaza de la Democracia, a rather soulless square. A mess of terraced concrete slopes up towards the fortress-like edifice of the **Museo Nacional** (Tues–Sat 8.30am–4.30pm, Sun 9am–4.30pm; US$7; ☎2257-1433, ⊛www.museo costarica.go.cr), home to the country's most important archeological exhibits. Highlights include petroglyphs, pre-Columbian stonework, wonderful anthropomorphic gold figures and an

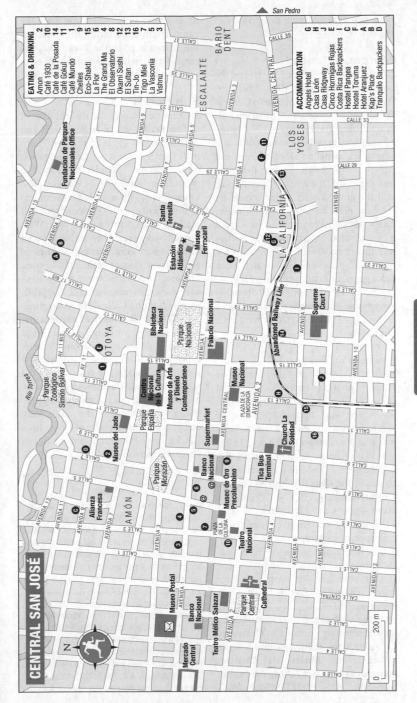

CENTRAL SAN JOSÉ

EATING & DRINKING

Amon	2
Café 1930	10
Café de la Posada	14
Café Gokul	11
Café Mundo	1
Chelles	9
Eco-Shakti	15
La Flor	6
The Grand Ma	4
El Observatorio	8
Okami Sushi	12
El Sultan	13
Tin-Jo	16
Trigo Miel	7
La Vasconia	5
Vishnu	3

ACCOMMODATION

Angels Hotel	G
Casa León	H
Casa Ridgway	J
Cinco Hormigas Rojas	E
Costa Rica Backpackers	C
Hostel Pangea	I
Hostel Toruma	F
Hotel Aranjuez	A
Kap's Place	B
Tranquilo Backpackers	D

open courtyard offering great views of the city.

Mercado Central

Northwest of the Parque Central and the commercial centre in the block between Av 0/1 and C 6/8 is the **Mercado Central** (Mon–Sat 6am–6pm). Entering its labyrinthine interior you're confronted by colourful arrangements of fruits and vegetables, dangling sides of beef and silvery ranks of fish. Shopping here is less expensive than in a supermarket, and the glut of *sodas* inside means it's the best place in town to get a cheap bite – not only that, but the view from a counter stool is fascinating, as traders and their customers jostle for *chayotes*, *mamones*, *piñas* and *cas*. Watch your belongings, or better yet bring nothing, as the bustling crowds and diverting sounds and sights make this a great spot for you to be pickpocketed or have your bag stolen.

Parque La Sabana

Stretching west from the market is Paseo Colón, a wide boulevard of shops, restaurants and car dealerships. At its very end, the solid expanse of green known as **Parque La Sabana** was San José's airport until the 1940s, and is now home to the country's key art museum. Housed in a converted air terminal, the attractive **Museo de Arte Costarricense**, Av 0, C 42 (Tues–Sun 10am–4pm; US$5, free Sun; ☎2222-7155, ⓦwww.musarco.go.cr), has a good collection of contemporary Costa Rican art, as well as the Jardín de Esculturas (sculpture garden) and Salón Dorado (golden room), which contains a huge mural painted by French artist Louis Ferón in 1940.

On the southwest corner of Parque La Sabana, forming part of the University La Salle, is the quirky natural science museum, the **Museo de Ciencias Naturales** (Mon–Sat 7.30am–4pm, Sun 9am 5pm; 825c; ☎2232-1306). Walk

in, and after about 400m you'll see the painted wall announcing the museum; the entrance is at the back. Displays range from pickled fish and snakes to some rather forlorn taxidermy exhibits.

San Pedro

First impressions of the student district of **San Pedro**, which begins when you pass the traffic circle at the San Pedro mall (you'll know it for its Flintstones-style jutting boulders), can be off-putting: Avenida Central (also known here as Paseo de los Estudiantes) is lined with petrol stations and dull malls as it passes through the area. Walk just a block away, however, and you'll find a lively combination of student ghettos and elegant residential houses. The area also claims some of the city's best bars, restaurants and nightlife, especially along **Calle de la Amargura**.

You'll most likely arrive here in a taxi or bus from downtown San José. Buses stop opposite the small **Parque Central**, centred on a monument to John F. Kennedy. Walking north from the square, through three blocks of *sodas*, bars, restaurants and abandoned railway tracks, you come to the cool, leafy campus of the **University of Costa Rica (UCR)**, one of the finest universities in Central America.

Arrival

By air Costa Rica's main airport, Juan Santamaría International (☎2443-0840), is 17km northwest of San José and 3km southeast of Alajuela. Taxis line up just beyond the airport exit and cost US$25–35 to the city centre. Buses to downtown San José depart from the airport bus stop just outside the terminal. Many hostels and hotels offer pick-up services (US$20). Nature Air uses Tobias Bolaños airport (popularly known as Pavas, the district where it is located), around 7km northwest of the city centre. A taxi into the centre costs US$10–15, or there are regular buses into San José.

By bus Most international buses from Nicaragua, Honduras, Guatemala and Panama pull into the Tica Bus station, C 3, Av 26 (☎2221-0006). The city has no central domestic bus terminal; the

TOUR OPERATORS IN SAN JOSÉ

San José is home to scores of **tour and activity operators**. Those listed here are experienced and reliable, and are all licensed (and regulated) by the ICT. Be wary of fly-by-night operations, of which there are plenty. You often see, for instance, posters advertising "packages" to Tortuguero or Monteverde for US$80–100 – half the price of a regular package. These are not really packages at all, and never worth the price: you may find yourself responsible for your own transport or accommodation, and no tours, orientation or guidance will be given.

Costa Rica Expeditions C 0, Av 3 ☎2257-0766, ⓦwww.costaricaexpeditions.com. This US-based firm is the most established and experienced of the major tour operators, with an extensive range of tours catering to most budgets.

Ecole Travel C 7, Av 0/1 ☎2234-1669, ⓦwww.ecoletravel.com. Small agency popular with backpackers offering two-night tours to Tortuguero (from US$189), full-day rafting (US$85) and three-day Corcovado (US$340) tours, as well as day-trips for US$70–90.

Expediciones Tropicales C 3B, Av 11/13 ☎2257-4171, ⓦwww.costaricainfo.com. Another backpacker favourite with knowledgeable guides, running the popular "combo" full-day tour of Volcán Poás, the La Paz waterfall and the Doka Coffee Estate (US$89), as well as a host of other trips.

Specops ☎+1/941/346-2603, ⓦwww.specops.com. Adventure education group, comprising US Special Forces veterans and expert Costa Rican guides, specializing in white-knuckle thrills, jungle-survival courses and adventure film and photography.

nearest thing to it is La Coca-Cola (named after an old bottling plant that used to stand on the site), five blocks west of the Mercado Central at Av 1/3, C 16/18 (the main entrance is on C 16); most buses from the Pacific coast arrive here. There are also a multitude of independent bus company stops in the blocks around La Coca-Cola. The Terminal del Caribe, Av 15, C Central, deals with transport to and from Limón. Arrivals from Monteverde and La Fortuna pull into the Terminal Atlántico Norte at C 12, Av 7/9, and buses travelling between Golfito, Nosara, Tamarindo and San José use the Alfaro-Tracopa Terminal at C 14/16, Av 5. The quickest (and, in the case of those leaving from Coca-Cola area, safest) way to get to and from the bus stations is by taxi, which should cost 1500–3000c.

Information

Tourist information San José's tourist office (also known as the ICT office; Mon–Fri 9am–5pm; ☎2299-5800, ⓦwww.visitcostarica.com), inconveniently located west of the city centre near the *Crowne Plaza* hotel on the east side of the Juan Pablo II bridge, over the General Cañas highway, has free maps and booklets detailing the (ever-changing) national bus schedule. They also hand out *San José Volando* (ⓦwww.sanjose volando.com), a free monthly culture guide.

City transport

Buses The bus network, connecting central San José with virtually all of the city's suburbs, generally runs daily 5am–10pm. Bus stops in the city centre seem to change every year; currently, most buses to San Pedro, Tres Ríos and other points east leave from Av Central, C 9/15, and those for Paseo Colón and Parque La Sabana (labelled "Sabana–Cementerio") from the bus shelters on Av 2, C 5/7. All buses have their routes clearly marked on their windshields, and usually the fare, too. Fares are payable either to the driver or conductor when you board and are usually 150–250c, though the faster, more comfortable *busetas de lujo* (luxury buses) to the suburbs cost upwards of 300c. Bus drivers or conductors always have plenty of change.

Cars You won't want – or need – a car in the city, but one can be useful for heading out on day-trips within the Valle Central, where public transport can be inconveniently scheduled. See p.499 for agency listings.

Taxis Cheap and plentiful, even at odd hours of the night and early morning. Licensed vehicles are red with a yellow triangle on the side, and have "SJP" ("San José Público") license plates. A ride anywhere within the city costs 1000–2500c, and about double that out to the suburbs. The starter fare (450c) is shown on the red digital display;

make sure the meter is on before you start (ask the driver to *toca la maría, por favor*) or agree on the fare in advance. Taxis usually line up along the Parque Central, but licensed vehicles are also safe to hail on the street.

Accommodation

The budget-to-moderate accommodation choices in San José are pretty good value, with plenty of hostels, guesthouses and family-run hotels. The very cheapest rooms are in the insalubrious neighbourhoods around La Coca-Cola, an area that's best avoided. Reserve in advance in high season (Dec–May) and on holidays. All places include breakfast and free internet access, unless stated otherwise.

Hostels

Bekuo Hostel Av 8, C 41/43 ☎2234-1091, Ⓦwww.hostelbekuo.com. Swish hostel with spotless dorms and private rooms, most of which have private baths, plus free wi-fi and a kitchen. It's in Los Yoses, a 10min walk from downtown and bordering San Pedro. Dorms US$13, doubles US$32
Casa Ridgway C 15, Av 6 bis (Av 6/8) ☎2233-2693 or 2222-1400, Ⓦwww.amigosparalapaz.org. Quaker-run guesthouse with super-clean, single-sex dorms, plus a few private rooms. Photos of prominent peaceful protestors cover the walls and there's a library of books on pacifism and human rights. Alcohol is banned and "quiet time" is from 10pm. Dorms US$14, doubles US$30
Costa Rica Backpackers Av 6, C 21/23 ☎2221-6191 or 2223-2406, Ⓦwww.costaricabackpackers.com. Lively hostel with simple dorms and facilities including a restaurant and bar (happy hour 5–7pm), and a garden with outdoor kitchen, hammocks and a pool. It also operates a guesthouse across the road with more comfortable private doubles. Dorms US$13, doubles US$32
Gaudy's Backpackers Av 5, C 36/38 ☎2258-2937 or 2248-0086, Ⓦwww.backpacker.co.cr. A cheap and cheerful hostel near Parque La Sabana: while the rooms are a bit cramped (particularly the larger dorms), the house has a cosy atmosphere, friendly staff, pool table and free wi-fi. Dorms US$12, doubles US$28
Hostel Pangea Av 7, C 3/3B ☎2221-1992, Ⓦwww.hostelpangea.com. San José's party hostel boasts a pool, rooftop restaurant, bar and dance-floor. As well as simple dorms, there are rooms with private or shared facilities and brand-new posh "suites" with plasma-screen TVs and king-sized beds. Dorms US$13, doubles US$32

Hostel Toruma Av Central, C 29/31 ☎2234-8186, Ⓦwww.hosteltoruma.com. In a colonial building once home to a former Costa Rican president, this hostel is smarter (and pricier) than most, with high ceilings, tiled floors and a pool. The dorms are clean and the doubles have safes; it's around US$20 extra for a room with private bath, sofa and cable TV. No kitchen, and breakfast costs extra. Dorms US$13, doubles US$36
Tranquilo Backpackers C 7, Av 9/11 ☎2223-3189, Ⓦwww.tranquilobackpackers.com. Despite the name, *Tranquilo* is a buzzing, sociable and – at times – noisy hostel (reception provides earplugs). With inexpensive though basic rooms (those upstairs are larger and quieter), funky painted walls, DIY pancake breakfasts and friendly staff, it's a great choice. Dorms US$10, doubles US$28

Hotels and B&Bs

Angels Hotel C 25, Av 0/2 ☎2258-8273. Family-run *casa de huéspedes* of seven large and clean rooms, with a choice of shared or private baths. There's also a laundry service, garden and a great little *soda* on site, and staff can organize travel and tours. US$30
Casa León Av 6 bis, C 13/15 ☎2221-1651, Ⓦwww.hotelcasaleon.com. Along the city's abandoned railroad tracks, this small, quiet lodge has simple rooms with shared or private baths, plus a kitchen, library, help with tours and car rental, and a patio garden with two pet ducks. No breakfast. It can be hard to find: tell your taxi driver it's a *calle sin salida* (dead-end road). US$30
Cinco Hormigas Rojas C 15, Av 9/11 ☎2255-3412, Ⓦwww.cincohormigasrojas.com. Billed as a retreat for travellers and artists, the "Five Red Ants" is a quirky guesthouse filled with modern art (even the toilet seats are decorated), offering cosy private rooms and a flower garden much loved by the local bird population. US$40
Hotel Aranjuez C 19, Av 11/13 ☎2256-1825, Ⓦwww.hotelaranjuez.com. This great-value hotel has tropical gardens, a lovely terrace and tasteful private rooms, most with (tiny) bathrooms, cable TV and safes: the colonial-style "superior" ones are well worth the extra couple of dollars. Rates include an excellent breakfast. US$27
Kap's Place C 19, Av 11/13 ☎2221-1169, Ⓦwww.kapsplace.com. Run by Karla Arias (a bottomless source of information), this welcoming hotel has a range of colourful rooms of varying size and price, plus a kitchen, terrace and living room to relax in. Tours, table football, yoga and dance classes are available. Quiet time is 8pm–8am. US$35

Eating

For a Central American city of its size, San José has a surprising variety of restaurants, though the 23 percent tax on restaurant food can easily wreck a budget; it's cheapest to eat in the centre, at the *sodas* and snack bars, where the tax doesn't apply. A sit-down breakfast or lunch at a *soda* will rarely set you back more than 3000c. Cafés and bakeries also abound: some have old-world European aspirations; others are resolutely Costa Rican, with *Josefinos* piling in to order birthday cakes or grab a coffee.

Cafés and bakeries

Café 1930 In *Gran Hotel Costa Rica*, Av 2, C 3/5. The closest thing in San José to a European street café, with great coffee (800–1400c). While the food isn't cheap (upwards of 3600c), this is a good place to sit and watch the buskers and street performers in the Plaza de la Cultura. Open 24hr.

Café de la Posada C 17, Av 2/4. This Argentine café (attached to the pretty *Posada del Museo Hotel*) serves continental breakfasts (2950c), *empanadas* (1550c) and *alfajores* (sweet Argentine biscuits) on its shady terrace.

Trigo Miel C 3, Av 0/1. The best-stocked branch of the national bakery chain, with a front window filled with cream cakes. Slices of these, plus sandwiches, pastries and savoury snacks (350–850c) can be eaten in or taken away.

Sodas

Amon C 7, Av 7/9. A tiny neighbourhood *soda* with inexpensive breakfasts (from 1350c) and lunches (*casado* 1950c); the few tables are always packed so you may have to wait for a seat.

Tapia C 24, Av 2. A bright retro-style diner with a huge menu featuring everything from burgers and sandwiches (from 1600c upwards) to main meals and ice-cream sundaes. Fri & Sat open 24hr.

The Grand Ma Av 1, C 3/5. Images of palm leaves and the eponymous Grand Ma herself cover the windows outside, while inside you find tastes of the Caribbean coast (often elusive in the capital): the chicken, rice and peas (from 2600c) and seafood soup (3150c) are both good.

La Vasconia Av 1, C 3/5. Dimly-lit place plastered with photos of the national football team (some dating back to 1905) and featuring economical dishes including *gallo pinto* (1100–1700c), *casados* (1925–2475c) and hearty main meals (3500–4500c). Save a few colones by eating at the bar, rather than at a table.

Vishnu Av 1, C 1/3. Cheery vegetarian *soda* serving healthy *platos del día*, soya burgers, salads,

sandwiches and breakfast options; you can have a good feed for 1700–3100c.

Restaurants

Café Gokul Av Central, C 9/11 ☎8853-9889. Inside Teatro Giratables, this restaurant offers good vegetarian Indian cuisine, including tasty samosas, spicy *paneer* curries and creamy lassis. Mains around 3500c.

Café Mundo Av 9, C 15 ☎2222-6190. This classy Italian-influenced restaurant may seem like a splurge, but the half-size portions of pasta (from 2800c) are a bargain, as is the daily lunch special (3300c). There's also a busy bar (attracting a largely gay clientele).

Eco-Shakti Av 8, C 13. Peaceful diner with a health-conscious slant: granola for breakfast, veg and fruit juices, herbal teas and numerous veggie options, as well as a good-value lunch menu (3500–4500c), featuring a soup, salad, main meal and drink.

La Flor Av 1, C 5/7. Lacking in atmosphere but popular with working class *Josefinos*, this downtown eatery offers good-value breakfasts (from 2000c), burgers and sandwiches (around 2000c).

Okami Sushi Av 0, C 23/25 ☎2221-0725. A slightly pricier alternative to the surrounding *sodas*, *Okami* has a decent Japanese menu; the *katsu* and teriyaki plates come with rice, vegetables and miso soup for 4400–6000c. Rolls 2270–4700c.

Drinking and nightlife

San José's nightlife is varied, with scores of bars. Stay away from the centre of town (see box, p.492), and head instead to Los Yoses, where Av Central features a trail of sports and soft-rock bars, or San Pedro, which is geared towards the university population. Bars often change character at weekends, when they host live music acts. If you want to dance, check out one of the city's many discos, but don't confuse these with the erotically associated "nightclubs" (see box below). Cover charges average around 3000c and often include a free drink; some establishments allow women to enter for free if business is slow. The Centro Comercial El Pueblo, just north of the city centre, is home to a maze of discos and bars, and provides an expensive but easy night out; expect to spend upwards of 6000c on drinks. Taxis back to the centre from El Pueblo charge around 2000c. With the exception of the university bars in San Pedro, most places close by 2 or 3am, earlier on Sun.

Bars

Bar Río On Blvd Los Yoses, the continuation of Av Central. A busy sports bar with a terrace out front and a large dancefloor (occasionally staging live music) at the back. Beer 1200c.

Caccio's C de la Amargura, San Pedro. Insanely popular student hangout with cheap pizza and cold beer (around 1000c).

Chelles Corner Av Central, C 9. Dating back more than 100 years, *Chelles* features wood-panelled walls, red leather seats and plenty of local colour. Beers from 900c, *casados* from 2700c. Open 24hr.

Jazz Café Av Central, San Pedro ☎ 2253-8933, ⓦ www.jazzcafecostarica .com. The best place in San José to hear live jazz, blues and Latin rhythms, with an intimate atmosphere and consistently good acts. Doors open at 9pm, music 10pm–2am. Cover charges 2000–5000c. It also stages regular art exhibitions, and has a sister venue in Escazú (☎ 2288-4740).

El Observatorio C 23, Av 0/1 ⓦ www.elo bservatorio.tv. A funky, warehouse-style bar that often showcases independent films, stand-up comedy (in Spanish) and music (reggae, rock and Latin). Beer around 1000c, cocktails 2500c.

Stan's Irish Pub 150m west of the Casa Presidential, Zapote, just south of San Pedro. The owners have made a reasonable stab at creating a pub-style atmosphere (there's even a darts board), but the real draw is the range of more than 60 beers (around 1200c) including – of course – Guinness.

El Sultan Av 0, C 29. Middle Eastern-themed pub, with good falafel (2200c), cheap beer (750c) and hookahs (waterpipes) pulling in a young crowd. Tues & Thurs are busiest.

Discos

Bongos El Pueblo. A small club offering numerous drink promotions. The packed dancefloor is dominated by Latin beats and live music most weekends. Check out the reggae/hip-hop night on Thursdays. Ladies free before 10pm.

Castro's C 22, Av 13. This stalwart attracts locals of all ages; you can have a bite and watch the crowds, or hit the dancefloor to salsa, cumbia, merengue and reggaeton.

Déjà Vu C 2, Av 14/16. One of the hottest gay clubs (drag night on Sat) in town, housing two large dancefloors of banging electronic music, as well as the more intimate *Sinners* bar. The neighbourhood is pretty scary, so take a taxi. *La Avispa*, C1, Av 8/10, is a popular alternative.

Ebony 56 El Pueblo. A young crowd fills *Ebony 56* to dance to salsa, pop and reggaeton; Ladies' Night on Thurs is buzzing.

Infinito El Pueblo. One of the busiest clubs in town, with three large dancefloors and a mix of inter-national music.

Terra U C de la Amargura, San Pedro ⓦ www.terrau.com. Hugely popular student disco, with three open-air levels and a heaving dancefloor where Latin and tropical rhythms predominate.

Vertigo Edificio Colón Paseo Colón, Av 38/40 ⓦ www.vertigocr.com. Swanky European-style club with house, electro and techno – from local and international DJs – on the main floor and a hip-hop/chill-out lounge upstairs.

PROSTITUTION AND SEX TOURISM IN SAN JOSÉ

Prostitution is legal in Costa Rica and, in San José, very mainstream, giving parts of the city a sleazy air. Sex tourism can be a problem, and many "bars" downtown – especially in the *zona roja* (red light district) between La Coca-Cola and Calle Central – are, in reality, little more than pick-up joints for professional transactions. The term **"nightclub"** generally implies some form of erotic enter-tainment, while a **discoteca** will be somewhere to dance (with your clothes on) – be aware of the distinction.

Entertainment

Josefinos love the theatre, and there's a healthy range of affordable venues, although you often need a strong grasp of Spanish to follow the rapid, colloquial dialogue. Performances are listed in the *Cartelera* section of the *Tiempo Libre* supplement in *La Nación* on Thurs, and the *Tico Times*. Going to the cinema in San José is a bargain, with tickets costing around 1500–3000c. Cinemas generally show subtitled versions of the latest American movies; the few that are dubbed will have the phrase "hablado en Español" in the newspaper listings or on the posters. Most of the large, multi-screen cinemas are in suburban malls, including the Multiplaza Escazú and Real Cariari, and require a taxi ride.

Cinema CCM in Mall San Pedro (see below; ☎2283-5716) is a huge complex screening international films. The a/c can get pretty chilly, so bring a sweater. Cine Magaly at C 23, Av 0/1 (☎2223-0085) is across the road from some of the city's hottest bars, and plays new releases, mostly in English. Sala Garbo, Av 2, C 28 (☎2222-1034), is a small venue with two screens showing foreign-language art-house movies.

Theatre Méllco Salazar, Av 2, C 0 (☎2221-4925), draws great musical talents from Costa Rica and further abroad; tickets cost from 1000c. Teatro Laurence Olivier, Av 2, C 28 (☎2223-1960), is a small venue favouring experimental performances, with a gallery and popular *Shakespeare* bar downstairs. Shows cost around 3000c per ticket. Finally, the Teatro Nacional, Av 2, C 3/5 (☎2221-1329, ⊛www.teatronacional.go.cr), is the most important theatre in the country, with productions ranging from Shakespeare to Chinese acrobatics. Ticket prices start at about 3000c.

Shopping

Avenida Central (C 3/6) is good for fairly inexpensive shoes and clothing, although you'll also find some more expensive shops. San José's souvenir and crafts shops are well stocked and in general pretty pricey; it's best to buy from shops run by regulated crafts co-operatives as more of the money filters back to the artisans. There are several markets that are good for browsing. Malls are very popular, springing up all over the capital's suburbs.

Books 7th Street Books, C 7, Av 0/1 (Mon–Sat 9am–6pm, Sun 10am–5pm), has both new and used books, is good on English literature and also has books and maps on Costa Rica. Librería

Internacional has branches at Av 0, C 0/1 and in the Multiplaza Escazú (Mon–Sat 9am–7pm), with the biggest selection in town of Spanish, English and German books.

Malls Mall San Pedro, Av 0, C 47, at the Fuente de La Hispanidad, is a large complex with a multitude of clothing stores, a multi-screen cinema, nightclub and food court with a breezy, outdoor balcony. Multiplaza Escazú, on the highway outside the city, is another enormous complex with international chains, bars and restaurants, and a huge cinema.

Markets La Casona, C 0, Av 0/1 (Mon–Sat 9.30am–6.30pm, Sun 9.30am–5.30pm), is a two-storey marketplace with stalls selling Latin American products such as Guatemalan knapsacks and bedspreads and Panamanian *molas*. Quality at some stalls is pretty poor. On C 22, Av 2 bis in the Plaza de la Democracia (daily 8am–6pm), the Mercado Nacional de Artesanía y Pintura is a touristy street market featuring hats, T-shirts, Sarchí ox-carts, jewellery, woodwork, hammocks and fabrics. In Pavas, in the city suburbs, is Plaza Esmerelda (closed Sun), a huge craft co-operative where you can watch cigars being rolled, necklaces set and Sarchí ox-carts painted.

Supermarkets The cheapest is Mas x Menos (Av 0, C 9/11; daily 8am–9pm), which stocks mainly Costa Rican brands of just about everything. There are several branches in San José and one in San Pedro on Av 0, 300m north of the church. Branches of the Automercado, Perimercado and the Am-Pm supermarkets are springing up all over town.

Directory

Car rental Alamo, Paseo Colón ☎2242-7733, ⊛www.alamocostarica.com; Avanti, at the airport and Paseo Colón, C 30/32 ☎2430-4647, ⊛www.avantirentacar.com.

Embassies and consulates Canada, Calle del Golf and Autopista 7 ☎2242-4400; UK, 11th floor, Edificio Centro Colón, Paseo Colón, C 38/40 ☎2258-2025; US, opposite the Centro Comercial in Pavas, or Av 0, C 120 (☎2519-2000) – take the bus to Pavas from Av 1, C 18.

Exchange All currency exchange in San José is done at banks. Try Banco de Costa Rica, Av 0/2, C 4/6 (Mon–Fri 8.30am–5pm); Banco Nacional, Av 1/3, C 4 (Mon–Fri 8.30am–3.30pm); or ScotiaBank, C 5, Av 0/2 (Mon–Fri 8.30am–6.30pm, Sat 9am–1pm). There's an American Express office in the Oficentro (Edificio 1), Sabana Sur (Mon–Fri 8.30am–5pm; ☎2242-8585).

Health The public hospital is San Juan de Dios, Paseo Colón, C 14–16 (☎2257-6282). The private hospital is Clínica Biblica, Av 14/16, C 0/1 (☎2522-1000, emergencies ☎2522-1030), which also has a pharmacy, open 24hr. Basic consultation and treatment starts at about US$100. Farmacia Fischel has branches at Av 3, C 2 (Mon–Sat 7am–7pm, Sun 9am–5pm) and Av 2, C 5/7 (Mon–Fri 7am–8pm, Sat 8am–7pm, Sun 8am–6pm).

Immigration *Migración* (Mon–Fri 8am–4pm; ☎2299-8100) is in Uruca, on the airport highway opposite the Hospital México; take an Alajuela bus and get off at the stop underneath the overhead walkway. Get there early if you want visa extensions or exit visas. The larger travel agencies listed in the box on p.495 can take care of the paperwork for you for a fee (roughly US$10–30).

Internet Free at most hostels and guesthouses, but there are also plenty of cafés; expect to pay around 400–600/hr. Try Café Digital, Av 0, C 5/7, or Centro de Copiado, C 5, Av 0/1.

Laundry Offered by many hotels and guesthouses. Otherwise, try Lava Sol, C 5, Av 9/11, or Sixaola (one of a chain), Av 2, C 7/9.

Post office The Correo Central (Mon–Fri 7 8am–5pm, Sat 8am–noon) is at C 2, Av 1/3.

Moving on

By air

Domestic airlines Sansa and Nature Air have daily flights to destinations across the country from Juan Santamaría and Tobias Bolaños/Pavas airports.

By bus

San José is the transport hub of Costa Rica, and eventually, all roads lead to it. A bewildering number of bus companies use the city as their base; although many services depart from the Coca-Cola terminal (C 16, Av 1/3), many others leave from independent stops in the streets around, or from the Terminal Caribe (C 0, Av 15).

Domestic bus destinations

Alajuela With Station Wagon or Tuasa (every 10min 4.30am–11pm, then every 30min; 35min).

Cahuita With Mepe (4 daily at 6am, 10am, 2pm & 4pm; 4hr).

Cariari (From the Terminal del Caribe, for Tortuguero: 9 daily; 1hr 30min–2hr).

Cartago With Lumaca (every 10min 5.05am–midnight; 45min).

Dominical With Transportes Morales (2 daily at 6am & 3pm; 7hr).

Golfito With Tracopa (2 daily at 7am & 3.30pm, Fri also 10.15pm; 8hr).

Heredia With MRA (every 10min 5am–3am; 30min).

Jacó With Transportes Morales (8 daily; 2hr 30min).

La Fortuna/Arénal With ATC (3 daily at 6.15am, 8.40am & 11.30am; 4hr–4hr 30min).

Liberia With Pulmitan (hourly 6am–10pm; 4hr 30min).

Mal País With Hermanos Rodriguez (2 daily at 7am & 3.30pm; 5hr 15min).

Manzanillo With Mepe (1 daily at noon; 4hr 30min).

Monteverde/Santa Elena With Tilarán (2 daily at 6.30am & 2.30pm; 5hr).

Montezuma (From La Coca-Cola; ☎2642-0219; 2 daily at 6am & 2pm; 5hr).

Nicoya With Empresa Alfaro (8 daily; 5hr).

Nosara With Empresa Alfaro (1 daily at 5.30am; 6hr).

Paso Canoas With Tracopa (4 daily at 5am, 1pm, 4.30pm & 6.30pm, Sun also 10pm; 6hr).

Peñas Blancas With Deldú (hourly 3am–7pm; 6hr).

Playa del Coco With Pulmitan (3 daily at 8am, 2pm & 4pm; 5hr).

Playa Sámara With Empresa Alfaro (2 daily at noon & 6.30pm; 5hr).

Puerto Jiménez With Transportes Blancos (1 daily at noon; 8hr).

Puerto Limón With Transportes Caribeños (hourly 5am–7pm; 2hr 30min).

Puerto Viejo de Sarapiquí (From Terminal del Caribe; ☎2222-0610: 10 daily; 2hr).

Puerto Viejo de Talamanca With Mepe (4 daily at 6am, 10am, 2pm & 4pm; 4hr 30min).

Puntarenas With Empresarios Unidos (hourly 6am–7pm; 2hr 20min).

Quepos/Manuel Antonio With Transportes Morales (express: 4 daily at 6am, noon, 6pm & 7.30pm, also Mon–Sat 9am & 2.30pm; local departures 5 daily at 7am, 10am, 2pm, 3pm & 4pm, also Mon–Fri 5pm; 3hr 45min–4hr 30min).

Sarchí (From C 18, Av 5/7; ☎2258-2004: 1 daily: Mon–Fri 12.15pm, Sat noon; 1hr 30min).

Sixaola With Mepe (4 daily at 6am, 10am, 2pm & 4pm; 6hr).

Tamarindo With Empresa Alfaro (2 daily at 11.30am & 3.30pm via Liberia); with Empresa Tralapa (1 daily at 4pm; 5hr 30min).

Volcán Irazú With Metropoli (1 daily at 8am, returning 12.30pm; 2hr).

Volcán Poás With Tuasa (1 daily at 8.30am, returning 2pm; 2hr).

BUS COMPANIES AND STOPS

ATC ☎2255-0567/4318/4300. Departs for La Fortuna/Arénal from C 12, Av 7/9.

Deldú ☎2256-9072 or 2677-0091. Departs for Peñas Blancas from C 14, Av 3/5.

Empresa Alfaro ☎2222-2666. Departs for Nicoya, Nosara, Playa Sámara & Tamarindo from Av 5, C 14/16.

Empresarios Unidos ☎2222-8231, 2222-9840 or 2661-3138. Departs for Puntarenas from C 16, Av 12.

Hermanos Rodriguez ☎2642-0219. Departs for Mal País from La Coca-Cola.

King Quality ☎2258-8834. Departs for El Salvador and Nicaragua from C 12, Av 3/5.

Lumaca ☎2537-2320. Departs for Cartago from C 5, Av 10.

Mepe ☎2257-8129. Departs for Cahuita, Manzanillo, Puerto Viejo de Talamanca and Sixaola from Terminal Caribe.

Metropoli ☎2536-6052. Departs for Volcán Irazú from Av 2, C 1/3.

Microbuses Rapiditos Heredianos (MRA) ☎2233-8392. Departs for Heredia from C 1, Av 7/9.

Nica Expreso ☎2256-3191. Departs for Managua from C 16, Av 3/5.

Panaline ☎2256-8721. Departs for Panama City from C 16, Av 3/5.

Pulmitan de Liberia ☎2222-1650 or 2666-3818. Departs for Liberia and Playa del Coco from C 24, Av 5/7.

Station Wagon ☎2441-1181. Departs for Alajuela from Av 2, north of Iglesia de la Merced.

Tica Bus ☎2221-0006, ⓦwww.ticabus.com. Departs for Guatemala, Nicaragua, Panama, El Salvador and Honduras from C 26, Av 3.

Tilarán ☎2222-3854. Departs for Santa Elena/Monteverde from C 12, Av 7/9.

Tracopa (domestic) ☎2771-4214. Departs for Paso Canoas and Golfito from Av 5, C 18/20.

Tracopa (international) ☎2222-2666 or 2223-7685. Departs for Panama from Av 5, C 14/16.

Transnica ☎2223-4242 ext 101, ⓦwww.transnica.com. Departs for Nicaragua from C 22, Av 3/5.

Transportes Blancos ☎2257-4121 or 2735-5189. Departs for Puerto Jiménez from C 14, Av 9/11.

Transportes Caribeños ☎2221-2596 or 2222-0610. Departs for Puerto Limón from Terminal Caribe.

Transportes Morales ☎2223-5567. Departs for Dominical, Jacó and Quepos/ Manuel Antonio from La Coca-Cola.

Tuasa ☎2222-5325. Departs for Alajuela and Volcán Poás from Av 2, C 12/14.

International bus destinations

El Salvador (San Salvador) With King Quality (1 daily; 19hr); with Tica Bus (3 daily; 19hr).

Guatemala (Guatemala City) With Tica Bus (3 daily; 60hr).

Honduras (Tegucigalpa) With Tica Bus (3 daily; 48hr).

Nicaragua (Managua) With King Quality (1 daily; 11hr); with Nica Expreso (1 daily; 11hr); with Tica Bus (4 daily; 11hr); with Transnica (4 daily; 11hr).

Panama (Panama City) With Panaline (1 daily; 16hr); with Tica Bus (2 daily; 16hr).

By train

A train service (30–45min) runs from several stations in San José to Heredia, but as it currently only operates Monday to Friday during the morning and afternoon rush hours, it's of limited use to travellers. A convenient central station in San José is the Estación del Atlántico on Av 7, near C 19.

The Valle Central and the Highlands

Despite its name – literally "Central Valley" – Costa Rica's **Valle Central** is actually an intermontane plateau poised at an elevation of between 3000 and 4000m. The area supports roughly two thirds of Costa Rica's population, as well as its four most important cities – San José and the provincial capitals of **Alajuela**, **Heredia** and **Cartago**. Other than that, it's a largely agricultural region, with green coffee terraces shadowed by the surrounding mountains, many of which are volcanoes. These volcanoes, especially **Irazú** and **Poás** and the national parks around them, are the chief attractions for visitors, but there's also good **white-**water rafting, and the **Monumento Nacional Guayabo**, the country's most important archeological site.

Most people use San José as a base for forays into the Valle Central: with the exception of Alajuela the provincial capitals have little to entice you to linger. If you do want to get out of the city and stay in the Valle Central, the nicest places are the lodges scattered throughout the countryside.

ALAJUELA

With a population of just over 46,000, **ALAJUELA** is Costa Rica's second largest city; it's also close to the airport and only thirty minutes from downtown San José. Although there's not much to see here, it has a certain relaxed, low-key charm. Most travellers use the city as a jumping-off point for departure and arrival into the rest of the country, as well as a base for visiting the surrounding sights. The

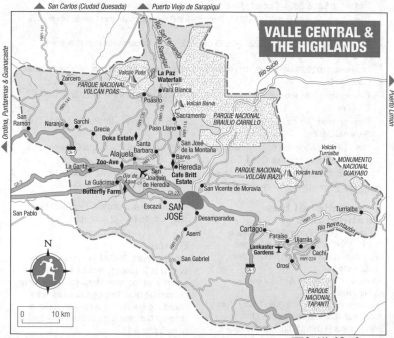

city's few attractions are close to the Parque Central.

What to see and do

The most impressive sight is the sturdy-looking, whitewashed former jail, Av 3, C 0/2, which houses the **Juan Santamaría Cultural-Historical Museum** (Tues–Sat 10am–5.30pm; ☎2441-4775). Dedicated to Alajuela's most cherished historical figure – drummer-boy-cum-martyr Juan Santamaría, who sacrificed his life to save the country from American adventurer William Walker in 1856 – the museum's curiously monastic atmosphere is almost more interesting than the small collection itself, which runs the gamut from mid-nineteenth-century maps to crumbly portraits of figures involved in the battle of 1856. Three blocks south of the museum is a small **plaza** also named after Santamaría, on the north side of which is the **municipal theatre** (☎2436-2362). The restored, Art Deco-inspired facade houses an auditorium, gallery and café, although they are only open to the public when there are performances or events.

Arrival and information

By air Juan Santamaría International Airport is less than 3km from the city. Many hotels and hostels will arrange a free pick-up with prior notice; otherwise take a bus from outside the airport or a taxi (US$5–6).

By bus Tuasa buses (red and black) from San José arrive at the Tuasa station, C 8/10, Av 0/1, three blocks west of the Parque Central. Station Wagon buses (beige and orange) from San José drop you off on Av 4, C 2/4, 50m southwest of Parque Juan Santamaría.

By car Take the *pista* towards the airport (General Cañas highway), then the turn-off to Alajuela, 17km from San José – don't use the underpass or you'll end up at the airport.

Tourist information There's no official information source in town. Goodlight Books, Av 3, C 1/3, is the best place to go with questions.

Accommodation

Alajuela Campground and Hostel Next to *Quinta San Angel* on the road to Tuetal (north of Alajuela) ☎2398-9024. Excellent hostel with basic dorms, private rooms, camping facilities, kitchen and TV lounge, plus a huge garden with fruit trees and a soccer pitch. Spanish lessons are available and staff can help organize volunteering opportunities. Camping US$5, dorms US$10, doubles US$30

Coconut House Across from Parque Loma, 10m south and 350m west of La Trinidad supermarket ☎2441-1249, ⓦ www.coconuthouse.info. Great hotel with cosy rooms – most with private baths and all with safes – and a good buffet breakfast included. Tours and car rental can be organized. US$32

Cortez Azul Av 5, C 2/4 ☎2443-6145, ⓔ hotelcortezazul@gmail.com. This artist-run establishment has simple rooms and two dorms, with lovely wooden floors, sculptures and mosaics, as well as a kitchen at the back. Dorms US$10, doubles US$30

Hotel Pacande Av 5, C 2/4 ☎2443-8481, ⓦ www.hotelpacande.com. Next to *Cortez Azul*, this is a step up in comfort, with compact private rooms with shared bath, as well as more stylish ones with private facilities, TV and dark wood furnishings (though most lack natural light). Staff are welcoming and rates include breakfast. US$30

Maleku Hostel 50m west of the main entrance of the new hospital ☎2430-4304, ⓦ www.maleku hostel.com. This small and cheerful family home is the best budget option in town: dorms and private rooms (shared baths) are immaculate, and there's lots of useful travel advice on offer, as well as free breakfast, internet and airport transfers. Dorms US$12, doubles US$35

Mango Verde Hostel Av 3, C 2/4 ☎2441-6330, ⓔ mirafloresbb@hotmail.com. A solid, economical choice offering clean, though somewhat stark rooms with private bath, set around a small courtyard. Guests can use the kitchen and there's a TV room and table football. US$25

Eating

Ambrosia Av 5, C 2. It may not serve the food of the gods, but *Ambrosia* is worth a try for its mix of hearty Tican and Italian-inspired food, which includes a good-value *plato del dia* (2200c including a juice) and a decent lasagne (2500c).

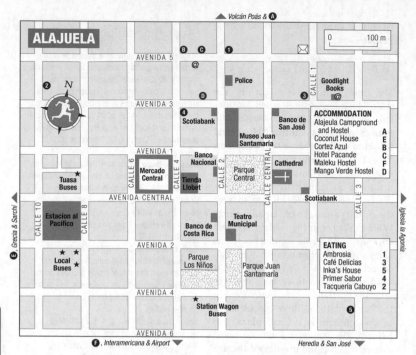

ALAJUELA

Volcán Poás & Ⓐ

0   100 m

ACCOMMODATION
Alajeula Campground and Hostel	A
Coconut House	E
Cortez Azul	B
Hotel Pacande	C
Maleku Hostel	F
Mango Verde Hostel	D

EATING
Ambrosia	1
Café Delicias	3
Inka's House	5
Primer Sabor	4
Tacquería Cabuyo	2

Ⓔ, Grecia & Sarchí

Iglesia la Agonia

Ⓕ, Interamericana & Airport ▼   Heredia & San José ▼

Café Delicias Corner Av 3 and C 1. An easy place to while away an afternoon, *Delicias* has Café Britt coffee (700–1350c), tempting cakes (650–1250c), sandwiches and light meals. There's another branch on the corner of C Ancha (C 9) and Av 6.

Primer Sabor Av 3, C 2/4. Decked out with leather booths and floral wallpaper, this Chinese restaurant serves enormous portions of fried rice, chop suey and stir-fries – one portion is enough for two – as well as a low-cost lunch-time *casado* (2200c).

TREAT YOURSELF

Inka's House C 3, Av 6/4. If you're hankering after a little more spice than the typical Tico meal provides, try this Peruvian restaurant, which serves excellent *ceviche* and seafood, as well as Andean classics like *lomito saltado* (strips of beef with onions, tomatoes, rice and fries) and Inca Kola. Their chilli sauce is fiery and the decor's smart, though no Peruvian cliché is left unturned – expect paintings of Machu Picchu, llama-wool wall hangings and pan-pipe music. Mains 3500–7500c.

Tacquería Cabuyo C 10, Av 3/5. Tiny taco joint with a loyal local following for its excellent, inexpensive snacks, which can be eaten at the counter or taken away. Tacos 450c.

Directory

Books Goodlight Books, Av 3, C 1/3 (daily 9am–6pm), has one of the country's best collections of English-language fiction and nonfiction, as well as numerous books in Spanish, French, German and Italian, plus maps, phrase books and travel guides. It also offers internet access, coffee and cakes.

Exchange Banco Nacional, C 2, Av 0/1; Banco de San José, C 0, Av 3; and Scotiabank, C 2, Av 3, have ATMs and change dollars and travellers' cheques.

Internet Electromega, Av 5, C 2/4, charges 350c/hr; Goodlight Books (see above) has access for 500c/hr.

Post office Av 5, C 1 (Mon–Fri 8am–5.30pm, Sat 7.30am–noon).

Moving on

By bus Buses moving on from San José (towards the Pacific) pass through Alajuela, but only stop depending on vacancy. Hotels should be able to pre-arrange for a bus to stop and pick you up. Services to Jacó (3 daily; 3hr 30min), La Fortuna/Arenal (3 daily; 3hr 30min), Monteverde (2 daily; 3hr), Liberia (hourly; 4hr 30min) and Puntarenas (hourly; 2hr 30min) all depart from La Radial bus stop, 75m south of the Shell petrol station (or *bomba*) at C 4, C Ancha (Av 10). The daily bus to Poás (9.15am; 1hr 30min) stops at the Tuasa terminal (C 8, Av Central/1). Services to Grecia (frequent; 1hr) and Sarchí (frequent; 1hr 15min) depart from C 8, Av 0/1. Services to nearby attractions – La Guácima Butterfly Farm (hourly; 30min), Zoo-Ave (frequent; 15min) and Sabanilla (for Doka Coffee Farm; frequent; 40min) – depart from the El Pacífico station, half a block south of the Tuasa terminal at C 8/10, Av 0/2.

AROUND ALAJUELA

Heading **north** from Alajuela, the road begins to climb, the terrain becomes greener and the air considerably cooler. Along this ascent you'll find numerous cabinas and chalets in rural settings with great vistas and access to the nearby volcano, as well as several bars and restaurants with excellent views of the Valle Central. Travelling **south** to destinations such as the Butterfly Farm, you'll pass rural stretches of land and forest; if you carry on south you'll eventually hit the urban sprawl of San José.

Doka Estate Coffee Farm

Some 15km north of Alajuela, between the towns of San Isidro and Sabanilla, is the **Doka Estate Coffee Farm** (tours daily 9am, 10am, 11am, 1.30pm & 2.30pm, also Mon–Fri 3.30pm; US$18; ☎2449-5152, ⓦwww.dokaestate.com), which produces Café Tres Generaciones. Knowledgeable guides lead tours, explaining the entire coffee-making process, from germinated seed to sun-dried bean. To see the coffee-pickers in action, visit at harvest time (Nov–Feb).

Many tour companies in San José (see p.495) include the farm on their itineraries. To arrive **independently**, take a bus from Alajuela to Sabanilla Parque and find a local taxi (about 1000c) to the estate. At the end of the tour, try to hitch a lift back to Alajuela with a returning

tour group; alternatively, the farm can arrange a taxi pick-up.

La Guácima Butterfly Farm

Some 12km southwest of Alajuela, **La Guácima Butterfly Farm** (daily 8.30am–5pm; tours 8.45am, 11am, 1pm & 3pm; US$15; ⓦwww.butterflyfarm.co.cr) breeds valuable pupae for zoos and botanical gardens all over the world. The farm also has beautiful views over the Valle Central. In the wet season, arrive early, as the rain forces the butterflies to hide and clouds obscure the view; on a sunny day, however, when the butterflies are active, it's a glorious sight; there are thousands of them fluttering about like colourful tornados.

From Alajuela, **buses** (marked "La Guácima Abajo") leave every hour from the El Pacífico station at C 8/10, Av 0/2; the Butterfly Farm is practically the last stop. Buses from San José (40min) leave every hour from C 8, Av 2/4. On the return journey, buses depart every hour for Alajuela and at 8.25am, 12.25pm, 3.25pm and 5.25pm for San José.

Zoo-Ave

Central America's largest aviary, **Zoo-Ave** (daily 9am–5pm; US$15), at Dulce Nombre, 5km northeast of La Garita, a small town near Alajulea, is just about the best place in the country to see the fabulous and many-coloured birds – especially macaws – that inhabit Costa Rica.

The La Garita **bus** from Alajuela (15min) passes right by, leaving from the El Pacífico station at C 8/10, Av 0/2; on your return, you can flag down an Alajuela bus on the main road where you arrived.

SARCHÍ

Touted as the centre of Costa Rican arts and crafts, the commercialized village of **SARCHÍ**, 30km northwest of Alajuela, has a pretty setting, but don't expect picturesque scenes of craftsmen in small historic shops: the work is done in factories. The most famous item produced here is the **Sarchí ox-cart**, a kaleidoscopically painted, square cart of Moorish origin; other crafts include tables, bedsteads and leather rocking chairs (about US$100).

Large *fábricas* (workshops) line the main road from **Sarchí Sur**, leading up to the residential area of **Sarchí Norte**. The best **hotel** is *Cabinas Daniel Zamora* (☎2454-4596; US$80), opposite the football pitch in Sarchí Norte, which has clean rooms with fans and private baths. For **food**, try *La Cafetería*, next to the I.C.E. in Sarchí Norte, which serves tortillas, *pupusas* and *casados* (1000–3000c).

Local **buses** from Alajuela run approximately every thirty minutes (6am–10pm; 1hr). Buses back (via Grecia) can be hailed on the main road. From **San José**, there's a 12.15pm service Monday–Friday and a noon service on Saturday (1hr 30min) from C 18, Av 5/7. **Taxis** between Sarchí Sur and Sarchí Norte, or to Alajeula or Zarcero, can be called on ☎2454-4028. The Banco Nacional on the main road beyond the church (in Sarchí Norte) changes dollars and cheques, as does a smaller branch in the Mercado de Artesanía, Sarchí Sur.

PARQUE NACIONAL VOLCÁN POÁS

PARQUE NACIONAL VOLCÁN POÁS (daily 8am–4pm; US$10), 55km from San José and 37km north of Alajuela, is one of the most easily accessible active volcanoes in the world. Its history of eruptions dates back eleven million years – the last gigantic blowout was on January 25, 1910, when it dumped 640,000 tonnes of ash on the surrounding area – but at the moment it is comparatively quiet. The weather is make-or-break for viewing the volcano, as mists arise from nowhere and can cover the crater within minutes; an early arrival gives you a much better chance of seeing the sights.

You need to get to the volcano before the clouds roll in, which they inevitably do, sometimes as early as 10am, even in the dry season (Dec–April). Poás has blasted out three craters in its lifetime, and due to more or less constant activity, the appearance of the **main crater** is subject to change – it's 1500m wide and filled with milky turquoise water from which sulphurous gases waft and broil. Although it's an impressive sight, you only need about fifteen minutes for viewing and picture-snapping.

Walks

The park has a few well-maintained, short and unchallenging **trails**, which take you through an otherworldly landscape, dotted with smoking fumaroles and tough ferns and trees trying valiantly to hold up against regular sulphurous scaldings. Advice and a general map can be found at the **visitors' centre**, next to the car park/bus stop, and all the trails are clearly marked.

The **Crater Overlook** trail (750m; 15min) winds its way from the visitors' centre to the main crater, along a paved road. Side-trail **Sandero Botos** (1.4km; 30min) heads up through the forest to the pretty, emerald Botos Lake, which fills an extinct crater and makes a good spot for a picnic. Named for the pagoda-like tree commonly seen along its way, the **Escalonia** trail (about 1km; 30min) starts at the picnic area (follow the signs), then takes you through the forest, where the ground cover is less stunted compared to that at the crater.

Wildlife-watching

A wide variety of **birds** ply this temperate forest, among them the ostentatiously colourful quetzal, robins and several species of hummingbird. Although a number of large mammals live in the park, including coyotes and wildcats, you're unlikely to spot them.

The small, green-yellow **Poás squirrel**, endemic to the area, is far more common.

Poás is also home to a rare version of cloudforest called dwarf or **stunted cloudforest**, a combination of pine-needle-like ferns, miniature bonsai-type trees and bromeliad-encrusted cover, all of which has been stunted by an onslaught of cold (temperatures up here can drop to below freezing), continual cloud cover and acid rain from the mouth of the volcano.

Arrival and information

By bus A daily Tuasa bus leaves San José at 8.30am from Av 2, C 12/14, calling at Alajuela at 9.15am (1hr 30min–2hr). It returns at 2pm.
By car To reach Poás before both buses and clouds, drive or take a taxi from Alajuela (roughly US$40) or San José (around US$60).
Tourist information The visitors' centre, next to the car park at the entrance, has a museum, gallery, souvenir shop, bathrooms and cafeteria.
Tours Most visitors come on tours from San José – (approximately US$50 per person for a 4–5hr trip; see box, p.495, for details of tour operators). The full-day "combo" tour organized by Expediciones Tropicales (T 2257-4171, W www.costaricainfo .com) is very popular, and also takes in the La Paz Waterfall Gardens and the Doka Coffee Estate (US$89).

Accommodation and eating

There are plenty of places to stay in the vicinity of the volcano, including mountain lodges on working dairy farms (you'll need a car to get to them) and other, more simple and inexpensive places that can be reached on the daily bus to Poás. No camping is allowed in the park.
Lo Que tu Quieras 4km before the park entrance T 2482-2092 or 8814-9150, E lomasdeper severancia@yahoo.com. A good budget option, offering a trio of rustic cabins with private baths (one also has a fireplace for the chilly mountain nights). The on-site restaurant has huge picture windows that show off the stunning views. Camping is also permitted. Camping US$5, cabins US$25
Cabinas Quetzal Just before *Lo Que tu Quieras* T 2482-2090, E restmiradorquetzal@latinmail .com. These spartan cabins with private baths are decent value for those on a tight budget, while the

attached restaurant, serving economical *comida típica*, is a good place to enjoy the vistas. Rates include breakfast. US$25

LA PAZ WATERFALL GARDENS

A fifteen-kilometre drive east of Poás is one of Costa Rica's most popular attractions, the **La Paz Waterfall Gardens** (daily 8am–5pm; US$35; W www.water fallgardens.com), an immaculate series of self-guided riverside trails linking five waterfalls on the Río La Paz. The trails are all set in a large colourful garden, and there's also a butterfly observatory, aviary, trout lake, frog exhibit and serpentarium. Viewing platforms at various points along the trails allow you to get both above and underneath the waterfalls, the highest of which, **Magia Blanca**, crashes deafeningly down some 40 metres. The marked trails conclude at the top of the **La Paz Waterfall**, Costa Rica's most photographed cascade (it can also be seen from the public highway below).

There's no public transport to the gardens, and most people visit them as part of a tour from San José (see p.495). If you're **driving**, turn right at the junction in Poasito towards Vara Blanca; at the village, turn left at the petrol station and follow the well-marked signs for 5km.

HEREDIA

Just 11km northeast of San José is the lively town of **HEREDIA**, boosted by the student population of the Universidad Nacional (UNA) at the eastern end of town. The town centre, though a bit run-down, is prettier than most, with a few historical buildings. Lacking any major tourist draws, however, Heredia is used mainly as a base for trips to Volcán Barva and Braulio Carrillo national park.

What to see and do

Heredia's layout conforms to the usual grid system, centred on the quiet **Parque Central**, draped with huge mango trees and overlooked by the plain **Basílica de la Inmaculada Concepción**, whose unexcitingly squat design – "seismic Baroque" – has kept it standing since 1797, despite several earthquakes. North

of the plaza, the old colonial tower of **El Fortín**, "the Fortress", features odd gun slats which fan out and widen from the inside to the exterior, giving it a medieval look; you cannot enter or climb it.

East of the tower on Avenida Central, the **Casa de la Cultura**, an old colonial house with a large, breezy veranda, displays local artwork, including sculpture and painting by local schoolchildren (generally open Mon–Fri 10am–5pm, occasionally at weekends). The **Mercado Central**, Av 6/8, C 2/4 (daily 5am–6pm), has the usual mess of aisles lined with rows of fruit and veg, dangling sausages and plump prawns.

Arrival

By bus Buses arrive along Av 6, C 3.
Internet There are dozens of internet cafés; the one on Av 2, between C 5 and 7, is one of the cheapest (300c/hr).

Accommodation

Accommodation in downtown Heredia is pretty sparse, though few people stay here, since San José is within easy reach. The following all have hot water.

Hotel Ceos C 4, Av 1 ☎2262-2628. A Canadian flag marks the entrance to this small hotel, which has a restaurant and walls covered with photos of Heredia a hundred years ago. Aside from the strange army-green-and-khaki colour scheme, the rooms are comfortable and have private baths, TVs, phones and fans. US$30

Hotel Las Flores Av 12, C 12/14 ☎2261-8147, ⓦwww.hotel-lasflores.com. A ten-minute walk from the centre, *Las Flores* is Heredia's best option, offering green-hued doubles with private baths, TV and small balconies (though no views). Staff are cheerful and there's a small *soda* downstairs. US$30

Hotel Heredia C 6, Av 3/5 ☎2238-0880. A decent fall-back if the other hotels are full. The slightly scruffy and dark rooms here have clean baths and TV. US$30

Eating

Café Espigas C 2, Av 2, southwest corner of the Parque Central. Though serving meal combos that include *pintos* (2800c), *casados* (3150c), sandwiches and burgers, this café specializes in Britt Finca coffee (from 650c).

Manjares Corner of Av 2 and C 3. Indulge your sweet tooth with one of the home-made pastries, cakes (the apple tart is particularly good) and sundaes (1650–3250c).

Vishnu's Mango Verde C 7, Av Central/1. Bright and bustling vegetarian *soda* with inexpensive salads, sandwiches and pastas (1300–2950c), as well as juices and smoothies.

Drinking

Nightlife is student-driven, restricted to a few local spots, generally in the four blocks immediately west of the university.

Miraflores Av 2, C 2, upstairs from *Café Espigas*. Popular nightspot, especially Mon, Tues and Thurs, when there's live music; otherwise, Latin and reggae beats dominate the dancefloor.

Océano C 4, Av 2/4. Nautically themed café-bar decorated with fishing paraphernalia and surfboards. Popular with students for its cheap drinks (beer from 850c) and *bocas*.

Rancho de Fofo C 7, Av 0. Close to the university campus, this bar and seafood restaurant is hugely popular for its banging music (the Tues reggae night, with 2-for-1 cocktails, is worth checking out) and drinks promotions. Beer from 800c, bar snacks 1500–2000c.

Directory

Exchange Banco Nacional, C 2, Av 2/4, and Scotiabank, Av 2, C 0, have ATMs and change dollars and travellers' cheques.

Post office On the northwest corner of the Parque Central (Mon–Fri 8am–5.30pm, Sat 7.30am–noon).

Taxis Available taxis line up on the east side of the Mercado Central, between Av 6 and 8, and on the southern side of the Parque Central.

Moving on

By bus The town has no central bus terminal, but a variety of well-signed stops are scattered across town, mainly around the Mercado Central, from where most local buses leave. Buses to San José leave from Av 8, a block southeast of the Mercado Central (frequent; 45min). Services to Paso Llano and Sacramento, for Volcán Barva and P.N. Braulio Carrillo (3 daily; 1hr 45min), leave from the southern side of the Mercado Central and drop you within 5km of the park's entrance.

By train A handful of services depart to San José (30–45min) during the morning and evening rush hours from the train station next to the Mercado Central.

AROUND HEREDIA

North and east of Heredia the terrain climbs to higher altitudes, reaching its highest point at **Volcán Barva**, at the western entrance of wild and rugged **Parque Nacional Braulio Carrillo**. The towns around here – **Barva**, **Santa Bárbara de Heredia** and **San Joaquín de Heredia** – are the favoured residences of expats, but there's little to detain the visitor.

Café Britt finca

Just north of Heredia is the **Café Britt finca** (☎2277-1600, ⓦwww.coffeetour .com), where you can gain an insight into Costa Rica's coffee industry. One of the country's best-known brands, Café Britt offers tours (daily 9.30am & 11am, also 3pm Dec 15–April 30; 1hr 30min; US$20), involving visits to its coffee bush nursery, plantation and "roastery", a multimedia presentation on the coffee-producing process, and tastings, as well as – of course – a stop off at the shop.

The *finca* can organize **transport** (US$15–20) from many hotels in San José, or you can drive: heading out of Heredia, take the road to Barva and follow the signs off the highway directing you to the *finca*. Alternatively, a taxi from Heredia costs around US$5.

Museo de la Cultura Popular

In a large house in landscaped coffee fields two kilometres beyond the Café Britt *finca*, the **Museo de la Cultura Popular** (Tues–Sat 8.30am–4.30pm, Sun 9am–4.30pm; US$7, students US$4; ☎2260-1619) tries to give an authentic portrayal of nineteenth- and early twentieth-century *campesino* life. The kitchen has been preserved, and you can sample authentic food of the period, although apart from this there's little to do other than to wander around the house and gardens. Frequent **buses** depart Heredia from Av 1, C 1/3, and can be flagged down on the road for the return journey.

Parque Nacional Braulio Carrillo and Volcán Barva

The **PARQUE NACIONAL BRAULIO CARRILLO** (daily 7am–4pm; US$10), 35km northeast of San José, covers 325 square kilometres of virgin rain- and cloudforest. The growth here gives you a good idea of what much of Costa Rica used to look like fifty years ago, when approximately three-quarters of the country was virgin rainforest.

The park has five staffed **ranger stations**, or *puestos*. There are picnic facilities and several marked trails leading from the *puestos* into the forest. If you want to **stay** near the volcano, basic huts and **camping** facilities are available at the Barva *puesto* (☎2261-2619); this is the most commonly used

entry point, and also marks the entry point for trails up the dormant **Volcán Barva** (separate entry US$7). The **main trail** (3km; about 1hr) up Barva's slopes begins at the western edge of Braulio Carrillo, and ascends through dense deciduous cover before reaching the cloudforest at the top. Along the way you'll get panoramic views over the Valle Central. Many travellers wander off the trails and get lost; take a compass, water, food, a jumper and rain gear, just in case. **Security** has become a growing problem; leave nothing in parked vehicles, and find a guide for longer hikes. Try to get to the park early in the morning to enjoy the clearest views at the top, and be prepared for serious mud in the rainy season.

You can get to the village of **Sacramento**, 3km from the entrance, by bus from Heredia, but there's no public transport beyond here. If driving you'll have to cope with a bad stretch of road just before the volcano – a 4WD is necessary.

CARTAGO

CARTAGO, meaning "Carthage", was Costa Rica's capital for three hundred years before the centre of power was moved to San José in 1823. Founded in 1563 by Juan Vázquez de Coronado, the city, like its ancient namesake, has been razed a number of times, although in this case by **earthquakes** rather than Romans – two, in 1823 and 1910, practically demolished the place. Most travellers don't actually stay here, but pass through to visit the basilica and ruins on trips to Volcán Irazú.

What to see and do

Cartago's highlight is the **Iglesia de la Parroquía** (known as "Las Ruinas"), which sits on the eastern end of the concrete Parque Central. Originally built in 1575, the church was repeatedly destroyed by earthquakes, but

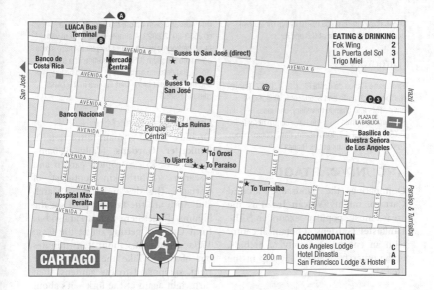

stubbornly rebuilt by the Cartagoans each time, until the giant earthquake of 1910 finally vanquished it. Only the elegantly tumbling walls remain, enclosing pretty subtropical gardens. The ruins are not open to the public, but can be viewed from the Parque Central.

From the ruins it's a five-minute walk east to Cartago's only other attraction: the cathedral, properly called the **Basílica de Nuestra Señora de Los Angeles**, at C 16 and Av 2, which was rebuilt in a decorative Byzantine style after the original was destroyed in an earthquake in 1926. Millions of Costa Ricans make an annual pilgrimage here on August 2 to honour the statue of **La Negrita** (or the Black Virgin), the nation's patron saint.

Arrival

By bus Buses arrive at Av 4/6, C 2/4, or at the bus station just north of the Mercado Central.
Internet Café la Linea, Av 4, C 8/10 (400c/hr).

Accommodation

Los Angeles Lodge Av 4, C 18, on the square by the basilica ☎ 2551-0957. The comfortable *Lodge* offers simple en-suite rooms and breakfast, as well as the *Puerta del Sol* restaurant downstairs. Ask at the bar if there's no one at reception. US$50
Hotel Dinastia C 3, Av 6/8, 100m north of the central market ☎ 2551-7057. A friendly hotel offering clean, spartan rooms with private baths; look at a few, as not all have natural light. US$30
San Francisco Lodge & Hostel C 3, Av 6/8, near the central market ☎ 2551-4804, @ hotelsan franciscolodge@costariccense.com. Vast, though gloomy rooms with private baths, kitchenettes and TVs; prices are per room, so groups do better here. The reception is in the DVD store next door. US$30

Eating

Fok Wing Av 4, C 4/6. Small, subdued Chinese diner, which does a brisk trade in fried rice, noodles, chop suey and stir-fries. Mains 3000–5000c.
La Puerta Del Sol Av 4, C 18, across from the basilica. Popular restaurant with cosy booths and the usual range of breakfast options (around 2000c), burgers and sandwiches (1400–2600c), and *casados* (from 3000c). Service can be slow, especially on Sundays.
Trigo Miel Av 4, C 16. A busy bakery with seating at the back. On the menu are pastries, cream cakes, *empanadas* and sandwiches (400–2000c).

Moving on

By bus to: San José (every 10min 5am–midnight, then every hour; 45min), leave from the bus station just north of the central market and from Av 4/6,

C 2/4. Buses to Turrialba (9–10 daily; 1hr 20min) depart from the corner of C 8 and Av 3.

Directory

Exchange Banco de Costa Rica, Av 4, C 5/7; Banco Nacional, C 3, Av 2; and Scotiabank, Av 2, C 2/4 have ATMs and change travellers' cheques.
Post office 10min from the town centre at Av 2, C 15/17 (Mon–Fri 7.30am–6pm, Sat 7.30am–noon).
Taxis There is a rank at Las Ruinas.

AROUND CARTAGO

Dominating the landscape around Cartago, mighty **Volcán Irazú** is the area's most popular excursion. The **Lankaster Gardens**, a botanical centre with an enormous variety of orchids, is the other frequented day-trip in the area.

Parque Nacional Volcán Irazú

Some 32km north of Cartago, **Parque Nacional Volcán Irazú** (daily 8am–4pm; US$10) makes for a long, but scenic, trip from the city. The park's blasted-out lunar landscape is dramatic, reaching a height of 3432m and giving fantastic views to the Caribbean on clear days, while the inactive Diego de la Haya crater is creepily impressive, its deep depression filled with a strange green lake. Two marked **trails** lead from the entrance, where you'll find the ranger's booth, to the crater.

A daily **bus** runs to the park from the *Gran Hotel Costa Rica* in San José (daily at 8am) – be there early in high season to get a seat – picking up passengers at Las Ruinas in Cartago at 8.45am; it returns to San José at 12.30pm. The park has a **visitors' centre** with information, toilets and a snack bar.

Accommodation

If you want to spend more time than the bus allows, the Ricardo Jiménez Oreamuno recreational area southwest of the volcano has several trails and camping facilities; contact the ranger station (☏ 2551-9398) for information.

Nochebuena 5km before the park entrance ☏ 2530-8013/8023. A simple cabin for rent with three bedrooms and a sweet fireplace. There's also a volcano museum (US$4) consisting of a short video, and detailed accounts of volcano history and the flora and fauna that survive in the harsh climate. US$65

Lankaster Gardens

Orchids are the main attraction at **Lankaster Gardens** (daily 8.30am–4.30pm; US$5), a tropical garden and research station 6km southeast of Cartago. The dry months of March and April are the best time to see the blooms. To get here, take a Paraíso bus from Cartago, getting off at the *Casa Vieja* restaurant, about ten minutes out of town. Take the road to your right, signposted to the gardens, then turn right again at the fork – it's about a ten-minute walk. Alternatively, a taxi from Cartago costs about US$25.

TURRIALBA

The pleasant agricultural town of **TURRIALBA**, 45km east of Cartago on the eastern slopes of the Cordillera Central, has sweeping views over the rugged eastern Talamancas, though there's little to keep visitors here – most see it as part of a trip to the **Monumento Nacional Guayabo** or en route to a **whitewater rafting** or **kayaking** trip on the Reventazón or Pacuaré rivers. Costa Rica Expeditions and Expediciones Tropicales (see box, p.495) offer rafting day-trips for US$80–100, and many of the mountain-lodge-type hotels in the area have guided walks or horseback rides up **Volcán Turrialba**. San José–Turrialba buses (2hr 30min) leave every hour 8am to 8pm Monday to Friday (weekends 8am–7pm) from C 13, Av 6. There are also buses from Cartago (9–10 daily; 1hr 20min).

Monumento Nacional Guayabo

Costa Rica's most important archeological site, the **Monumento Nacional**

Guayabo (daily 8am–4pm; US$7) lies 19km northeast of Turrialba. Though interesting, in truth there's not a great deal to see (really just some stone heaps), as the site's importance has more to do with the dearth of any other surviving contemporary structures in Costa Rica. Guayabo belongs to the archeological-cultural area known as **Intermedio**, which begins roughly in the province of Alajuela and extends to Venezuela, Colombia and parts of Ecuador. Archeologists believe that Guayabo was inhabited from about 1000 BC to 1400 AD; most of the heaps of stones and basic structures now exposed were erected between 300 and 700 AD.

Buses run to Guayabo from Turrialba from 100m south of the main bus terminal (Mon–Sat 3 daily at 11.15am, 3.10pm & 5.20pm, returning at 5.15am, 7am, 12.30pm & 4pm; Sun 3 daily at 9am, 3pm & 6.30pm, returning at 7am, 12.30pm & 4pm; 1hr), though the inconvenient timetable means you either have not enough or too much time at the site. **Driving** from Turrialba takes about thirty minutes; the last 4km is on a bad gravel road – passable with a regular car, but watch your clearance. **Taxis** charge around US$35 from Turrialba.

Limón Province and the Caribbean coast

Sparsely populated **Limón Province** sweeps south in an arc from Nicaragua down to Panama. Hemmed in to the north by dense jungles and swampy waterways, to the west by the mighty Cordillera Central and to the south by the even wider girth of the Cordillera

Talamanca, the region has a lost, end-of-the-world feel.

Limón holds much appeal for ecotourists, having the highest proportion of protected land in the country. At **Tortuguero** you can watch giant sea turtles lay their eggs, while at **Cahuita** and **Manzanillo** you can snorkel coral reefs and surf at **Puerto Viejo**. In addition, more than anywhere else in Costa Rica, the Caribbean coast exudes a sense of **cultural diversity**. The largest city, **Puerto Limón**, is a port with a large (mostly Jamaican-descended) Afro-Caribbean population; Caribbean **English** or patois is spoken widely along the coast. Near the Panamanian border you'll find communities of indigenous peoples from the **Bribrí** and **Cabécar** groups.

Getting around Limón Province requires patience. From San José to Puerto Limón there are just two roads, and from Puerto Limón to the Panama border at Sixaola there is one narrow and badly maintained route. North of Puerto Limón there is no public land transport at all: instead, private *lanchas* ply the coastal canals connecting

Moín, 8km north of Puerto Limón, to Tortuguero and Río Colorado near the Nicaraguan border. There are also daily flights from San José to Tortuguero. Travel in northern Limón Province is not as cheap as in other parts of the country due to a scarcity of options; even cheaper boat routes add up when you take connecting bus or taxi trips into account.

Note that **dengue fever** is an increasing problem across Costa Rica, particularly on the Caribbean coast, so take extra care to avoid mosquito bites.

PUERTO LIMÓN

PUERTO LIMÓN, 165km east of San José, is Costa Rica's main port, with a neglected air and a reputation as Central America's prime drug-trafficking gateway. Security has deteriorated in recent years, and while some of the stories highland Ticos tell of the place are exaggerated, you should watch your back – much of the town is not safe for solo exploration, especially at night. Generally speaking, tourists come to Limón for one of three reasons: to get a **boat** to Tortuguero from Moín, to get a **bus** south to Cahuita and Puerto Viejo or to join the annual Carnaval-like celebration of **El Día de la Raza** (Columbus Day) in October (see box, p.413).

What to see and do

Unlike other Costa Rican towns, Limón's avenidas generally run east–west in numerical order, starting at the docks. Calles run north–south, beginning with Calle 1 on the western boundary of **Parque Vargas**, by the *malecón* (sea wall). Although most of Limón is not quite the gangland paradise it's made out to be, try not to stand around looking lost. Walking around the centre, or along Avenida 1 between Parque Vargas and the stadium, is not recommended at night.

The Town

The partly pedestrianized **Avenida 2**, known locally as the "market street", is the main drag, touching the north edge of Parque Vargas, at the easternmost end of C 1 and Av 1/2, and the south side of the **Mercado Central**. There's a mildly diverting display of **marine life** housed within the arcade at C 2, Av 1/2, including some rehabilitating sea turtles; the owner of *Eskimo* ice cream next door can help with translations of the exhibit. Shops in Limón close between noon and 2pm, when everyone drifts towards Parque Vargas and the *malecón* to sit under the shady palms. Forget swimming here, no matter how hot it gets; one look at the water at the tiny spit of sand next to the *Hotel Park* is enough discouragement.

Arrival and information

By boat Some *lanchas* arriving from Tortuguero dock at Moín, just north of town; there are buses, or a taxi into town costs around US$5.
By bus Transportes Caribeños services from San José arrive at the Gran Terminal del Caribe at Av 1, C 7/8. Arrivals from the south – Cahuita, Puerto Viejo and Panama (via Sixaola) – terminate at the Transportes Mepe stop at Av 4, C 3/4, just north of the Mercado.
Tourist information Contact the San José ICT (☎2299-5800) – there's no official tourist office in Limón Province.

Accommodation

The downtown area is noisy, especially at night, and accommodation is basic, though secure enough. There's a group of more expensive hotels outside town, about 4km up the road to Moín at Portete and Playa Bonita. A taxi here costs about 1000c, and the bus to and from Moín also runs along the road. Car theft is rife, so if driving, stay at a hotel with private parking or store your car in a guarded 24hr car park. Hotel prices rise by as much as fifty percent for Carnaval week, and to a lesser extent during Semana Santa at Easter.
Apartotel Cocori Playa Bonita ☎2795-2930. Clean, simple rooms, all with TV and a/c, some facing the sea, and a small restaurant with waterfront views. Can be noisy at weekends. Rates include breakfast. US$40

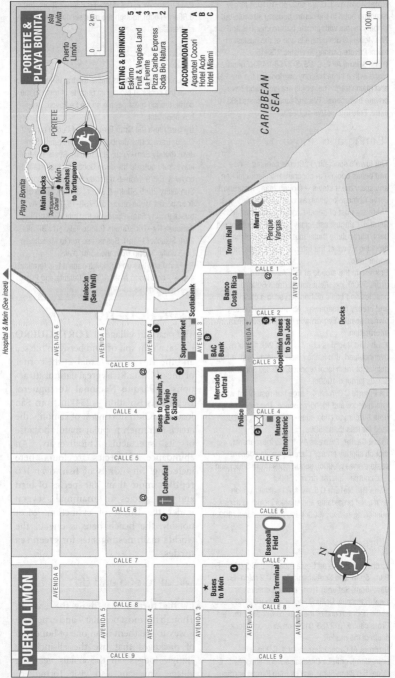

PUERTO LIMÓN

PORTETE & PLAYA BONITA

EATING & DRINKING
Eskimo ... 5
Fruit & Veggies Land ... 4
La Fuente ... 3
Pizza Caribe Express ... 1
Soda Bio Natura ... 2

ACCOMMODATION
Apartotel Cocori ... A
Hotel Acón ... B
Hotel Miami ... C

Playa Bonita

Main Docks

Moín

Tortuguero Canal

Lanchas to Tortuguero

PORTETE

Isla Uvita

Puerto Limón

0 — 2 km

N

Hospital & Moín (See inset)

CARIBBEAN SEA

Malecón (Sea Wall)

Scotiabank

Supermarket

AVENIDA 6

AVENIDA 5

AVENIDA 4

AVENIDA 3

AVENIDA 2

AVENIDA 1

CALLE 1

CALLE 2

CALLE 3

CALLE 4

CALLE 5

CALLE 6

CALLE 7

CALLE 8

CALLE 9

Town Hall

Mural

Parque Vargas

Banco Costa Rica

BAC Bank

Mercado Central

Police

Museo Ethnohistoric

Cathedral

Baseball Field

Buses to Moín

Bus Terminal

Docks

Buses to Cahuita, Puerto Viejo & Sixaola

Coopelimón Buses to San José

N

0 — 100 m

Cahuita, Puerto Viejo & San José ▼

Buses to San José & Main ▼

Hotel Acón Av 3, C 2/3 ☎2758-1010. A large, rambling hotel in the centre housing sizeable but gloomy rooms with private bathrooms, TVs and a/c. The *Aquarius* disco here is one of the busiest in town. Private parking available. US$45

Hotel Miami Av 2, C 4/5 ☎2758-0490. Friendly place with a large balcony overlooking the market and main street. The rooms are clean and have private bathrooms, TVs and fans; a/c costs US$10 extra. Free internet/wi-fi. US$30

Eating and drinking

The town's speciality is Creole cooking – rice and beans cooked in coconut milk, jerk chicken and spicy meat stews – though many restaurants serve Chinese options, as well as *comida típica*. There's a host of decent *sodas* inside the Mercado Central. Gringos, especially women, should avoid bars, particularly those that have large placards blocking views of the interior. Don't drink the tap water here.

Eskimo In the arcade at C 2, Av 1/2. Ice cream (from 500c), excellent coffee (from 600c) and pastries and basic dishes served in a clean and breezy passageway. Abraham, the friendly owner, speaks English and is a good source of information.

Fruit and Veggies Land C 7, Av 2/3. If you've overindulged, this is the place to detox, with a huge display of fresh local produce, *batidos* and fruit salads (around 1000c).

La Fuente C 3, Av 3/4. Large bar-restaurant with kitsch decor and friendly service. The menu ranges from burgers to chop suey – you can get a decent feed for less than 2500c.

Pizza Caribe Express Av 4, C 2. Inexpensive, though slightly greasy pizzeria, serving decent pasta dishes (2000c), sandwiches (from 800c) and – of course – pizzas (from 2500c).

Soda Bio Natura C 6, Av 4. A healthier option with good breakfasts and snacks including thirst-quenching *batidos* (600c) and avocado toast (800c).

Directory

Exchange Banco de Costa Rica, Av 2, C 1 (Mon–Fri 9am–5pm), and Scotiabank, Av 3, C 2 (Mon–Fri 9am–5pm, Sat until 1pm), change dollars.

Health Hospital Dr Tony Facio Castro (☎2758-0580), at the northern end of the *malecón*, or the 24hr Red Cross centre (☎2758-0125) on Av 1, one block south of the market.

Internet At Cyber Internet, Av 4, C 3 (daily 9am–8pm), or in La Casona souvenir shop, Av 2, C 1 (Mon–Sat 8am–5pm), across from Parque Vargas.

Post office Av 2, C 4 (Mon–Fri 8am–5.30pm, Sat 8.30am–noon), though the mail service from Limón is dreadful.

Moving on

By boat Irregular boats make the trip to Tortuguero from the docks at Moín, just outside of town to the north, though most people go via La Pavona (see box opposite).

By bus From the Gran Terminal del Caribe on Av 1, C 7/8, Transportes Caribeños services run to San José (hourly 5am–7pm; 2hr 30min). Buses to Moín leave from outside the Juan Goban football stadium on Av 3, C 8/9 (Mon–Sat hourly 5.30am–6.30pm, Sun every 2hr 5.30am–6.30pm; 30min). From the Transportes Mepe office (☎2758-1572), C 3, Av 4, buses (hourly 5am–6pm) run to: Bribrí (3–4hr); Cahuita (1hr–1hr 30min); Puerto Viejo (1hr 30min–2hr); Sixaola (3–4hr). Buses also run to Manzanillo (4–5 daily; 2–3hr) from the same place.

By taxi Taxis line up outside the main bus terminal, and will do trips to Moín (US$5), Cahuita and Puerto Viejo (around US$40–50).

TORTUGUERO

The peaceful village of **TORTUGUERO** lies on a thin spit of land between the sea and the Tortuguero Canal, at the corner of one of Costa Rica's great natural attractions – **Parque Nacional Tortuguero**. Despite its isolation – 254km from San José and 83km northwest of Limón – the area is extremely popular, mainly because of its spectacular biodiversity. An abundance of species are found here including: fifty kinds of **fish**, over 100 **reptiles**, more than 300 species of **bird** and 60 species of **mammal**, several under the threat of extinction. Most notably, the beach here is one of the world's main nesting sites for **green sea turtles**.

What to see and do

It's the **turtles** that draw the crowds. Though the most popular – and expensive – way to see them is on one of hundreds of **packages** that use the all-inclusive "jungle lodges" in the canals near the village, you can also visit Tortuguero

GETTING TO TORTUGUERO

Getting to Tortuguero independently can be tricky – you can either do a combination bus/boat route, or you can fly. Touts are often on the bus/boat routes from San José - ignore their overtures, and keep your eyes peeled for pickpockets. Transport to Tortuguero is particularly prone to change, so check before you head off.

If you don't want the hassle of getting there independently, numerous companies offer **transfers** (from US$40) from San José, La Fortuna, Cahuita and Puerto Viejo de Talamanca.

By bus In San José, buses depart for the town of Cariari from the Gran Terminal del Caribe – catch one at 6.30am, 9am, 10.30am or 1pm to make the onward connections from Cariari to Tortuguero (on the return journey, buses depart Cariari at 7.30am, 8.30am, 11.30am, 1pm, 3pm and 5.30pm). Purchase bus tickets in advance from the Guápiles counter (Ⓣ2222-0610) in the terminal; despite what you may be told, it is not necessary to buy boat tickets at this stage.

Upon arrival in Cariari, walk to the old bus station (*estación viejo*), about five blocks north of the arrival terminal, and buy a bus ticket to Rancho La Suerte/ Antigua Pavona (for the La Pavona dock, where the boats launch) from the counter; again it is not necessary to buy a boat ticket yet. Buses (1hr–1hr 30min; 1000c) depart at 6am, 11.30am and 3pm, returning when the boats from Tortuguero arrive in La Pavona.

By boat Two companies, Coopetraca (Ⓣ2767-7590 or 8368-1275) and Clic Clic (Ⓣ2709-8155 or 8844-0463), run daily boats (they alternate each day) from the La Pavona dock at 7am, 12.30pm and 4pm, returning at 6am, 11.30am and 3pm. A one-way ticket costs 1600c. Services from Moín (a US$5 taxi ride from Limón) are less frequent: Rubén Bananero (Ⓣ2709-8005, Ⓔviajesbananero@yahoo.com) generally has a 3pm service to Tortuguero; on the return leg, his boat leaves at 10am. A return ticket costs around US$60. Independent boat operators in Moín also run shared water-taxis to Tortuguero at 10am. In addition, Rubén Bananero occasionally operates boats from La Pavona.

By air Sansa (Ⓣ2229-4100, Ⓦwww.flysansa.com) and Nature Air (Ⓣ2299-6000, Ⓦwww.natureair.com) have daily flights from San José to Tortuguero (departing 6–7am; 20–30min).

and the park **independently**, staying in cabinas in the village and arranging trips with local guides.

The Town

Covered in wisteria, oleander and bougainvillea, Tortuguero village looks like a dilapidated tropical garden. It is centred on the main **dock**, or *muelle*, where all the *lanchas* arrive. The main signpost here has a village map to help you orient yourself. Two dirt paths run north–south through the village – the "main street" and "Avenida 2", or secondary street – from which narrow paths go off to the sea and the canal. At the north end of the village, beyond *Miss Junie's* hotel, there's a **Natural History Visitors' Centre** (daily 10am–12 & 2–5pm; 1200c) run by the Sea Turtle Conservancy (formerly the Caribbean Conservation Corporation; Ⓦwww.conserveturtles.org), which has a small but informative exhibition on the life cycle of sea turtles and a video explaining the history of turtle conservation in the area.

Parque Nacional Tortuguero

Entrance to the park (5.30am–4pm; US$10; Ⓣ2710-2929) is at the **Cuatro Esquinas Station**, just south of the village and reached by the main path (right from the main dock). Due to damage to the path, the self-guided **El Gavilán trail** (1km), which starts at the entrance and skirts a small swamp, covering the width of the land from lagoon to sea, is currently only partially open. However, it is possible to cover the better-maintained routes used on the evening turtle tours (see below), and there is talk of setting up an elevated walkway trail along the **El Gavilán route**. Exploring the park can be a muddy experience; fortunately numerous places around town rent out rubber boots (US$2/day).

You can also amble for up to 30km south along the **beach**, enjoying a bit of crab-spotting or birdwatching as you go, as well as looking for turtle tracks, which resemble the two thick parallel lines trucks leave in their wakes. Check with local information sources before swimming, though – currents can be strong, and sharks present.

Turtle tours

You can watch the turtles lay their eggs by taking part in a guided **turtle tour** (US$20 for two hours), which leave nightly at 8pm and 10pm from the village. There are more than a hundred certified guides in Tortuguero (see box opposite). Make sure you get a Turtle Spotter Program sticker when you book: this ensures a proportion of your money goes towards supporting turtle conservation projects. (If you take a tour with an unscrupulous guide charging less than US$20, this is where the saving will come from.) Visitor permits are allocated to guides via a daily lottery at 4.45pm; to guarantee yourself a place on a tour, make sure you reserve before 4.30pm on the day in question. There are five different turtle tour **routes**, two of which go through the national park, meaning you will have to pay the US$10 entrance fee as well (unless you already have one from earlier in the day). Visitors must wear dark clothing, refrain from smoking and are not allowed to bring cameras (still or video) or torches. Everyone must be off the beach by midnight.

Boat trips

Almost as popular as the turtle tours are the **boat trips** through the area's canals and *caños*, or lagoons, to spot animals including monkeys, caiman and Jesus Christ lizards, and birds including herons, cranes and kingfishers. Most operators run boat (or canoe) trips, as well as fishing excursions (all around US$20, plus park entry fees).

Cerro Tortuguero

As a result of damage to its footpaths, **Cerro Tortuguero**, an ancient volcanic deposit looming above the flat coastal plain 6km north of the village, is officially closed. However, many travellers still climb up the pretty steep, but manageable side, on either the **La Ceiba** or **La Bomba trails** (1hr 30min return), which lead you to the "peak", from where there are good views of flat jungle and inland waterways. Although you can do it on your own, paying a guide (US$20) means you are more likely to actually see snakes

---

TURTLE TIME

Every year Tortuguero is overrun with visitors who come for one reason – to see marine turtles lay their eggs (an event called the **desove**). Although Tortuguero is by no means the only place in Costa Rica to see marine turtles nesting, three of the largest kinds of endangered sea turtle regularly nest here in large numbers. Along with the **green** (verde) turtle, named for the colour of soup made from its flesh, you might see the **hawksbill** (carey), with its distinctive hooked beak, and the ridged **leatherback** (baula), the largest turtle in the world, which can easily weigh 300kg – some are as heavy as 400kg and reach 3m in length. The green turtles and hawksbills nest in the greatest numbers from July to October (August is the peak month); the leatherbacks come ashore (in far smaller numbers) from March to May.

TOUR OPERATORS IN TORTUGUERO

There are many **tour operators** in Tortuguero offering competitively-priced excursions. Avoid the beach boys who accost you at the dock or around town. If you're paying less than US$20 per person for a tour (exclusive of park entry fees), your guide is unlikely to be qualified or overly concerned with environmental and sustainability issues. In addition to those below, *Casa Marbella* (see below) organizes excellent tours.

Ballard Excursions Contact through *Casa Marbella* ☎8320-5232, ✆srossballard @gmail.com. Canadian botanist Ross Ballard runs informative trips to Cerro Tortuguero (US$20), night tours and overnight stays in the nearby biological station.

Caribeño Fishing Tours ☎2709-8026 or 8881-6656. Rod fishing (US$65/hr, minimum 2hr, for up to 3 people) and a range of other tours.

Tinamon Tours ☎2709-8004, ✆www.tinamontours.com. Run by biologist Barbara Hartung, Tinamon provides quality canoe, hiking, village and several other tours.

(before stepping on them) and other camouflaged wildlife along the way.

Arrival and information

By air Flights land at the airstrip some 4km north of the village; water-taxis (US$5 per person) will drop you off in the village; if you haven't already pre-arranged for one with your hotel, ask someone at the airport to call one for you.

By boat All *lanchas* pull into the dock, or *muelle*, in the centre of Tortuguero Town. Guides wait here to scavenge independent travellers.

Tourist information See the excellent ✆www .tortuguerovillage.com for maps, tour information and business listings.

Accommodation

Staying in Tortuguero on a budget entails bedding down in one of the independent cabinas in the village. Camping on the beach is not allowed.

Cabinas Aracari South of the football pitch ☎2709-8006. These clean and comfortable cabinas come with private baths and fans, and are set in a beautiful tree-filled garden that is ideal for taking a breather. US$16

Cabinas Balcon del Mar On the beachfront, just south of *Cabinas Icaco* ☎2709-8124 or 8870-6247. A good-value choice, *Balcon del Mar* has simple rooms with private bath (some also have their own balconies), as well as larger apartments with kitchenettes. Doubles US$16, apartments US$24

Cabinas Meriscar South of *Cabinas Aracari*, 100m before the beach ☎2709-8132 or 8876-2263. A low-cost option with slightly gloomy but acceptable cabinas with shared or private bathrooms and a

kitchen (an extra US$1 a day). If colones are really tight, you can camp. Camping US$2, cabinas US$10

Cabinas Princesa del Rio On the main street, between the dock and park entrance ☎2709-0131. The best value of the three *Princesa* locations in town, this lodge is right on the riverside and has basic but clean cabinas, sleeping one to three people; the nicest ones at the end look out onto the lagoon. US$30

Cabinas Tortuguero Across from the *Taberna* ☎2709-8114 or 8839-1200, ✆cabinas_tortuguero @yahoo.com. Comfortable rooms, with shared or private baths, plus fans and hammocks on the veranda, are set in a lovely garden. Decent food is available at the restaurant. US$16

🏃 **Casa Marbella** On the main street, opposite the old church, 100m north of the dock ☎8833-0827, ✆casamarbella.tripod.com. Edging ahead of the competition, this professionally run B&B boasts informative staff and sparkling rooms with private baths and fans; those at the back have river views. Rates include breakfast and there are excellent tours on offer. US$40

El Icaco On the beachfront, east of the village centre ☎2709-8044, ✆www.hotelelicaco.com. Renovations have smartened up this popular place, which has lime-green rooms, all en suite with hot water and fan, a communal kitchen, TV lounge and wonderfully relaxing hammock area. Rates include breakfast. US$40

Miss Junie's At the northern end of the main street ☎2709-8102, ✆www.iguanaverdetours.com. Offering a touch more comfort (and higher prices) than many other lodges nearby, *Miss Junie's* has airy wood-panelled rooms with private bathroom, security boxes and fans; those on the first floor at the front are the best of the bunch. Rates include breakfast. US$50

Eating

Tortuguero village offers good, homely food, typically Caribbean, with wonderful fresh fish. Prices, however, tend to be higher than elsewhere in Costa Rica.

Buddha Café Next to the I.C.E. building. A swanky riverfront café with an authentic Italian menu (pizzas from 4200c, pastas from 3500c), as well as great coffee and desserts (crêpes, brownies and cheesecake 2000–2700c). Closed Wed.

Dorling Bakery Across from The Jungle souvenir shop. Grab a seat out back in the riverside garden and tuck into a slice of home-made cake – chocolate, carrot, banana and lemon are just a few of the options (1000c a slice). Sandwiches and thin-crust pizzas are also on offer.

La Lapa Verde Just past *Cabinas Aracari*. If you feel as though you're eating in someone's living room, that's because you are – the TV blares and family members hang around on the sofa. There's no menu as such, just ask Doña Florentina, who runs the kitchen, what's good. Meat or seafood, rice, beans and salad, and a drink costs 3000–3500c.

Miss Miriam's Next to the football pitch. Run by the daughter of the eponymous Miss Miriam, this place is hit and miss – catch it on a good day and you'll be treated to some excellent Nicaraguan–Caribbean food (mains from 3000c). The giant river shrimp is well worth a try, as is the red snapper. Not to be confused with *Miss Miriam's II*, run by another daughter, next to the church.

El Muellecito Next to the Super Nicarao, near the dock. Scruffy but good-value place, with a *soda*-style menu: *pintos* (1700c), *arroz cons* (2500–3000c) and a few traveller favourites like hash browns and eggs (both 2000c).

Soda La Fe Near the entrance to the park. Ideal for pre- or post-park refreshments, this tiny *soda* has filling *pintos* (from 1400c) and *casados* (from 2500c), as well as *empanadas* (500c) if you're just looking for a snack.

Drinking and nightlife

La Culebra Next to the main dock. Innocuous-looking during the day, the riverfront *La Culebra* perks up considerably at night to become the town's most popular watering-hole: expect a boisterous local crowd and deafening tunes. Beer 1000c.

Restaurante Princesa On the beachfront, behind Souvenir Pura Vida. While the mainly seafood menu is expensive, the beachside location and booming tropical rhythms make it a good spot for a beer (1000c). Happy hour (50 percent off) daily 5–6pm.

Taberna Punto de Encuentro Riverside, 100m east of the main dock. An alternative to *La Culebra*, with pool tables and a large dancefloor by the river – great for sunset views, although the music volume (notably the karaoke sessions) can detract from the surroundings. Beer 1000c.

Directory

Exchange There is no bank, but in the high season supermarkets will offer cash advances for a fee.
Health Ebais, across from the dock, serves as a clinic, but the doctor only visits once a week.
Internet Try the café near *El Muellecito* (1500c/hr).
Laundry *Dorling Bakery* charges a whopping US$10 for a big bag, but your lodge might offer a cheaper service.
Post office In the middle of the village.

Moving on

By air Nature Air and Sansa both have daily flights back to San José.
By boat Coopertraca and Clic Clic (3 boats daily between them) offer transport to La Pavona, and onwards to Cariari and San José, while Rubén Bananero often offers a daily boat to Moín (for contact details, see box, p.517).

CAHUITA

The tiny coastal village of **CAHUITA**, 43km southeast of Limón, comprises just two puddle-dotted, gravel-and-sand roads running parallel to the sea, intersected by a few cross-streets. Few locals drive (bicycles are popular), so most of the vehicles you see kicking up the dust belong to visitors. Though the principal daylight activity in Cahuita is taking a boat trip out to **Parque Nacional Cahuita**'s coral reef to **snorkel** (see p.523), the fairly empty stretches of sand along the water make the beaches here perfect for relaxing and sun-bathing as well.

What to see and do

Cahuita's main street runs from the national park entrance at **Kelly Creek** to the northern end of the village, marked roughly by the football pitch. Beyond here it continues two or three kilometres

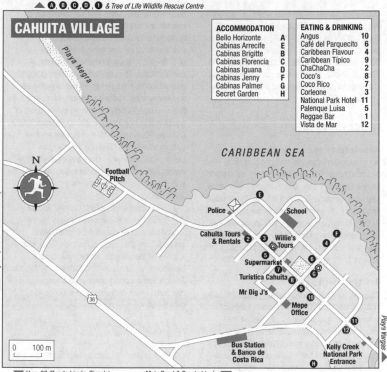

CAHUITA VILLAGE

ACCOMMODATION
Bello Horizonte	A
Cabinas Arrecife	E
Cabinas Brigitte	B
Cabinas Florencia	C
Cabinas Iguana	D
Cabinas Jenny	F
Cabinas Palmer	G
Secret Garden	H

EATING & DRINKING
Angus	10
Café del Parquecito	6
Caribbean Flavour	4
Caribbean Típico	9
ChaChaCha	2
Coco's	8
Coco Rico	7
Corleone	3
National Park Hotel	11
Palenque Luisa	5
Reggae Bar	1
Vista de Mar	12

CARIBBEAN SEA

Playa Negra

N

Football Pitch

Hwy-36 (Puerto Limón-Sixaola)

Police

Cahuita Tours & Rentals

School

Willie's @Tours

Supermarket

Turistica Cahuita

Mr Big J's

Mepe Office

Playa Vargas

0   100 m

Bus Station & Banco de Costa Rica

Kelly Creek National Park Entrance

▼ Hwy-36 (Puerto Limón-Sixaola)   Main Road & Puerto Limón ▼

north along Playa Negra (Black-Sand Beach). The small **park** at the central crossroads downtown is the focal point of the village, where locals catch up on recent gossip. The **Tree of Life Wildlife Rescue Centre** (Tues–Sun: Nov–April 15 9.30am–3pm; July & Aug 11am guided tour only; US$12; ☎8723-5616, Ⓦwww.treeoflifecostarica.com), 2km out of town on the Playa Negra road, runs breeding programmes for turtles and iguanas, shelters rescued animals and has 12 acres of botanical gardens.

The beaches

It's possible to swim on either of the village's two **beaches**, though they are generally better for paddling and sunbathing. The first 400m or so of the pretty Playa Blanca just inside the national park is dangerous on account of riptides, while **Playa Negra**, northwest of town, is littered with driftwood, although you can swim in some places. Sometimes called **Playa Vargas**, the beach south of Punta Cahuita in Parque Nacional Cahuita is better for swimming than those in the village; however, it's slightly awkward to get to (see p.523). You can also **surf** at Cahuita; boards are available to rent (US$5/hr) from *Cabinas Brigitte*. If you don't fancy snorkelling, *Cabinas Brigitte* and Mr Big J's organize **horse rides** along the beach and jungle hikes (US$45), as well as excursions to nearby waterfalls, villages and beaches.

Arrival and information

By bus Buses pull in at the station just southwest of the centre.

Tourist information The website Ⓦwww .cahuita.cr is useful; otherwise, the only sources of information in the village itself are the tour companies: Mr Big J's (☎ 8887-4695), a road back from the main street, also has a book exchange; Turística Cahuita (☎ 2755-0071), on the main street, sells the *Tico Times*. Both agencies, plus Willie's Tours (☎ 2843-4700), also on the main street, and *Cabinas Brigitte*, near Playa Negra, offer local trips and national park, kayaking and snorkelling tours (around US$25).

Accommodation

As well as in the centre of the village, there's also accommodation along the road that runs along Playa Negra; although fine during the day, it's not advisable to walk back after dark. Solo women travellers may feel more comfortable staying in town. It is possible to camp (US$5) near the Puerto Vargas ranger station in the national park (along the trail and around the point from the Kelly Creek station; see p.521). Note that you must enter through the Puerto Vargas *puesto* in order to camp there.

In the village

Cabinas Arrecife On the seafront, just north of the police station ☎ 2775-0081, ⓦ www.cabinas arrecife.com. In a pleasant spot, right on the seafront, this relaxed place is aimed firmly at backpackers, offering straightforward, economical rooms with private bath, hammocks slung on the porch and snorkelling gear for hire. US$30

Cabinas Jenny On the beach, 50m beyond *Caribbean Flavour* ☎ 2755-0256, ⓦ www .cabinasjenny.com. The beautiful top-floor rooms have high wooden ceilings, mosquito nets, fans and kitchenettes, plus thoughtful touches like filtered drinking water and sink plugs. Each one comes with a private balcony overlooking the sea. The ground-floor rooms are simpler and cheaper, but still comfortable. US$35

Cabinas Palmer Across from *Café Del Parquecito* ☎ 2755-0435, ✉ cabinaspalmer@gmail.com. A solid choice, with spick-and-span rooms featuring private facilities, fans, hammocks and planetary motifs, plus perks like an internet café out front, and free wi-fi and coffee. US$25

Secret Garden Down the side street just before Kelly Creek ☎ 2755-0581, ✉ koosiecosta@live.nl. Behind the lush, jungle-style garden strewn with kitsch statuettes are a handful of simple rooms with private bathroom, plus a dorm. The hostel also has a communal kitchen, laundry service and plenty of books to flick through. Dorms US$7, doubles US$18

Playa Negra

Bello Horizonte ☎ 2755-0206. The best budget lodging along the Playa Negra stretch, with ten large and simple cabins with kitchen, fridge, bath and fan; the nicest ones are seaside, next to the upmarket *Blue Spirit Cabinas*. US$30

Cabinas Brigitte Just behind *Reggae Bar* ☎ 2755-0053, ⓦ www.brigittecahuita.com. A well-run lodge, in a cosy location, offering brightly painted rooms and cabinas, all with private bath and kitchenettes. Rates include breakfast, and there's a laundry service, internet café and lots of equipment to hire. Doubles US$30, cabinas US$40

Cabinas Florencia A 15-minute walk north of Cahuita Village ☎ 8332-1960. Friendly and secure place with large, clean but slightly barren rooms, with beds, fans, private bathrooms and little else. There's also an (intermittently open) on-site *soda*. US$25

Cabinas Iguana Past *Cabinas Brigitte* ☎ 2755-0005, ⓦ www.cabinas-iguana .com. Lovely wood-panelled cabins on stilts, set back from the beach, and a main lodge with a screened veranda; the former have private bathrooms, while rooms in the latter share facilities. There's also a laundry service, book exchange, bike hire and a small, curvaceous pool. Lodge US$25, cabins US$40

Eating

Cahuita has plenty of places to eat fresh local food, with a surprisingly cosmopolitan selection. Prices are not low – a basic evening meal starts at around 3000c – and service tends to be laidback.

Angus On the main street, near *Coco's*. Surprisingly affordable Argentine-style steak house: a steak with sides and *chimichurri* sauce costs from 5000c, while a burger will set you back just 800c.

Café Del Parquecito By the village park. A good place for breakfast (2200–4000c), with fresh juices, pancakes and French toast, plus superb crêpes and iced coffee. Happy hour with two-for-one cocktails daily 6–8pm.

Caribbean Flavour Next to *Café Del Parquecito*. Cheap eats in a central location, with friendly, laidback service. The bar here also sells alcohol to take away. Breakfast 1600c, burger 1600c, *casado* 2200c.

ChaChaCha Diagonal to *Corleone*. To soak up the ambience at this charming restaurant and stick to a budget, steer clear of the pricey mains (from 6000c) and go for a well-prepared pasta dish (from 4300c), snack (like tapenade or bruschetta; around 3500c) or dessert like flambéed banana (2850c).

Coco Rico Near *Coco's* bar. A popular joint, filled with movie posters, huge cushions and easy chairs, that screens a film each night: the Italian dishes (2500–6200c), seafood (from 5000c) and sandwiches (1700–2800c) are all good accompaniments.

Palenque Luisa Opposite Willie's Tours. Bamboo-walled restaurant providing tasty *comida típica*, with a distinctly Caribbean taste, at fair prices. Strong on seafood, the *casados* and *arroz cons* are also good options. Mains 3800–5000c.

Vista de Mar By the park entrance at Kelly Creek. Known to locals as "El Chines", this barn-sized restaurant has a vast menu featuring inexpensive Chinese dishes (try the blue crab with hot sauce) and *comida típica*. Mains from 3000c.

Drinking and nightlife

Caribbean Tipico Across from *Coco's*. The less popular of the two main bar/discos in town (though it has the nicer balcony), with equally loud music and erratic opening hours.

Coco's At the main junction in the town centre. You'll hear *Coco's* before you see it: this unavoidable bar/disco is *the* place to go after dark in Cahuita, with frequent live music, cold beer (1000c) and a potent rum punch (2900c).

National Park Hotel By the park entrance at Kelly Creek. In a great location overlooking the national park, this hotel stages a pumping nightly disco in the high season. Beer 1000c.

Reggae Bar Attached to the *Reggae Cabinas*, Playa Negra. The location just opposite the beach makes this a great place to grab a cold beer (1000c) and enjoy the sea breeze.

Directory

Bicycle rental Bikes and scooters can be rented from *Cabinas Brigitte*, *Cabinas Iguana* (US$5/day) or Mr Big J's (3000–5000c/day).

Exchange Banco de Costa Rica, next to the bus station, has an ATM.

Health Ebais medical clinic, across from the Centro Comercial Safari, south of the bus station (closed Tues, Sat & Sun).

Internet At *Cabinas Palmer*, Willie's Tours or at *Cabinas Brigitte* (1000c/hr).

Laundry Mr Big J's, a road back from the main street, has laundry facilities (3500c/bag).

Police The *guardía rural* is on the last beach-bound road at the north end of the village.

Post office Next door to the police station, the *correo* (technically Mon–Fri 7.30am–5pm) keeps erratic hours.

Moving on

By bus to: Limón (hourly; 1hr–1hr 30min); San José (4 daily; 4hr); Puerto Viejo (14–15 daily; 30–40min); Manzanillo (4–5 daily; 1hr–1hr 15min). There are also regular services to Bribrí, Sixaola and the Panamanian border. All services leave from the bus station.

PARQUE NACIONAL CAHUITA

PARQUE NACIONAL CAHUITA (daily 6am–5pm; a donation of your choosing, if entering at Kelly Creek, or US$10 if entering at Puerto Vargas) is one of the country's smallest protected areas, covering the wedge-shaped piece of land from Punta Cahuita back to the main highway and, crucially, the **coral reef** about 500m offshore. Every tour operator in the area offers exploratory **snorkelling trips** – with guided assistance you will see the best of the reef and the animals that live here. Officially you're not allowed to snorkel in the park without a guide, though some people do. On land, Cahuita shelters the litoral, or coastal, rainforest, a lowland habitat of semi-mangroves and tall canopy cover which backs the white-sand beaches of Playa Vargas and Playa Cahuita. **Birds**, including ibis and kingfishers, are in residence, along with white-faced (*carablanca*) and howler monkeys, coati, raccoons, sloths and snakes.

The park has two **entrances**, at Kelly Creek, at the southern end of Cahuita Village, and at Puerto Vargas, 4km south of Cahuita. The park's one **trail** (7km), skirting the beach, is an easy walk, with a path so wide it feels like a road. The Río Perezoso, about 2km from the Kelly Creek entrance, or 5km from the Puerto Vargas trailhead, is not always fordable. Similarly, at high tide the beach, Playa Vargas, is impassable in places: ask at the ranger station about *marea*, or tide, schedules. Many snorkellers swim the 200 to 500m from Puerto Vargas out to the reef; again, ask about currents before diving in.

PUERTO VIEJO DE TALAMANCA

It's **surfing** that really pulls the crowds to the languorous hamlet of **PUERTO VIEJO DE TALAMANCA**, which offers some of the most challenging waves in the country, including the famous "**Salsa Brava**". The **village** itself lies between the thickly forested hills of the Talamanca mountains and the sea, where locals bathe and kids frolic with surfboards. The main drag is crisscrossed by a few dirt streets and an offshoot road that follows the shore. As in Cahuita, many expats have been drawn to Puerto Viejo and have set up their own businesses (you'll find places offering health foods and New Age remedies); and like Cahuita, most locals are of Afro-Caribbean descent. The village's backpacker and surf-party culture has created a **drugs scene**, and **crime**, particularly theft, can be a problem: never take valuables to the beach (and stay off it at night), make sure your accommodation is secure and take care after dark. If you're staying out of town, get a taxi back at night.

What to see and do

It is hard to spend time here without hitting the waves; the best **surf** is from December to March and July to August. There are plenty of places to **rent boards** and book lessons (see p.526) and the surf ranges from beginner waves on Playa Negra to the advanced, reef-side break of Salsa Brava; group lessons are the cheapest way to go. The surf crowds ensure a hot, young nightlife. Although the shopping here consists mainly of expensive, touristy boutiques, there is a run of **market stalls** along El Parquecito Cove offering jewellery and crafts.

Arrival and information

By bus Buses from San José (via Limón and Cahuita) arrive across from *Bar Maritza* in the

PUERTO VIEJO DE TALAMANCA

ACCOMMODATION
Cabinas Jacaranda	E
Cabinas Lika	F
Casa de Rolando	D
Crocodile Surf Camp	A
Hotel Puerto Viejo	C
Kaya's Place	G
Rocking J's	B

N

CARIBBEAN SEA

Buses to Cahuita, Limón, Sixaola, Manzanillo & San José

Playa Negra

Cahuita & Bribri

village centre. The roads around Puerto Viejo are covered with potholes.

Tourist information No official source, but the tour operators can give you advice and maps. The most helpful is ATEC (see box, p.526).

Accommodation

There is a wide range of hotels and cabinas, the cheapest of which have cold showers and no internet access. In addition to the options below, there are also two rooms at *Café Rico* (see p.526; ☎2750-0510, ✉caférico_puertoviejo @yahoo.com; US$40). If you're staying at or close to *Kaya's Place* and *Rocking J's*, always take a taxi back from town after dark, as muggings do occur.

Cabinas Jacaranda 25m northwest of the football pitch ☎2750-0069, ⓦwww.cabinasjacaranda.net. Follow the mosaic-tiled floor from the front gate and you discover a mini Eden: rooms feature colourful murals, wooden furniture, fans and safes, and most have private baths; there are also verdant gardens, where you can have a massage or take a yoga class, plus a kitchen and free internet. US$32

Cabinas Lika On the street behind the bank ☎2750-0209. A simple, hammock-strewn option with a garden kitchen, secure parking and clean rooms with private bath, fan and TV. Staff, however, can be brusque. US$20

Casa de Rolando 25m southeast of *Soda Miss Sam's* ☎2750-0339, ⓦwww.lacasaderolando .com. Slightly chaotic, but staff are friendly and the cabins clean and decent value, with private bath, fans and outdoor seating areas; the more expensive ones come with extra space and kitchenettes. US$20

Crocodile Surf Camp On the main road, by the *De Paso* restaurant ☎8722-2113. A similar ethos to *Rocking J's*, but on a much smaller scale, *Crocodile Surf Camp* offers basic cabinas, dorms, tents and hammocks. There's a kitchen, and surfboards can be rented next door. Hammocks US$5, camping US$6, dorms US$8, cabinas US$20

Hotel Puerto Viejo Next to *Baba Yaga* ☎2750-0620. Long-running hostel with rows of tiny wooden cabinas, most with shared bath, and a large communal kitchen. Always full of surfers and young people; owner Kurt speaks English and rents out surfboards. US$20

Kaya's Place Playa Negra, 200m north of town ☎2750-0690, ⓦwww.kayasplace.com. Arty murals, thatched roofs and carved driftwood give *Kaya's Place* a distinct rustic-chic character; each room is unique, but all are good choices. US$27

Rocking J's On the main road, 100m past Tuanis Bikes ☎2750-0657, ⓦwww.rockingjs.com. The epicentre of backpacker life in Puerto Viejo, *Rocking J's* has a bewildering array of options, including hammocks, tents, dorms, cabinas, a treehouse, suites and the blowout "J's Palace" (a whopping US$350). The beachside compound also has a big garden, chill-out areas, a restaurant and bar with live music every Friday and frequent parties. Not for the shy and retiring. Hammocks US$5, camping US$6, dorms US$7, cabinas US$20, treehouse US$25

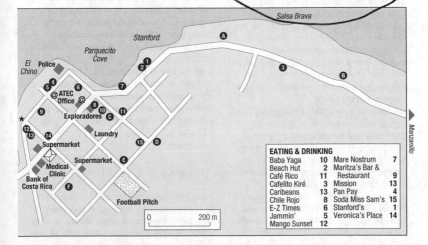

Salsa Brava

Stanford

Parquecito Cove

El Chino · Police

ATEC Office

Exploradores

Laundry

Supermarket

Supermarket

Medical Clinic

Bank of Costa Rica

Football Pitch

0   200 m

Manzanillo

EATING & DRINKING			
Baba Yaga	10	Mare Nostrum	7
Beach Hut	2	Maritza's Bar &	
Café Rico	11	Restaurant	9
Cafelito Kiré	3	Mission	13
Caribeans	13	Pan Pay	4
Chile Rojo	8	Soda Miss Sam's	15
E-Z Times	6	Stanford's	1
Jammin'	5	Veronica's Place	14
Mango Sunset	12		

Eating

Puerto Viejo has a cosmopolitan range of places to eat: traditional Creole, vegetarian, Italian and Thai cooking, as well as the obvious seafood options, can be found alongside cheaper *sodas* and bakeries; expect to pay upwards of 1500c for meals.

Beach Hut On the main road just before *Stanford's*. A beachside bar and restaurant serving English-style fry-up breakfasts, burgers and stuffed baguettes (from 1600c). There's a BBQ every Sunday.

Cafelito Kiré On the main road, 100m before Tuanis Bikes. German bakery with great muesli and fresh pastries for breakfast and a keenly-priced lunchtime *casado* (3000c, with a drink).

Café Rico Opposite *Cabinas Casa Verde*. Shady garden café with the best coffee in town (1000c), plus breakfast options (1500–3000c), sandwiches and crêpes. Book exchange, bike and snorkel rental, and wi-fi are also available.

Caribeans Next to *Mango Sunset* bar. Boost your karma – and your waistline – with a visit to this delightfully-run organic and fair-trade café. They brew a killer coffee (600–1500c), and the 80 percent cocoa chocolate is outstanding: try it in one of the muffins, cupcakes, brownies or ice-cream sundaes (1800c).

Chile Rojo On the first floor of the shopping arcade opposite ATEC. The best way to approach this otherwise budget-busting pan-Asian restaurant/ bar is to come with an empty stomach on Monday for the all-you-can-eat buffet (6000c). Get there between 6 & 8pm and you can also take advantage of the 2-for-1 happy hour. Closed Wed.

Jammin' 100m east of the bus stop. A "Juice and Jerk Joint" decked out in Rasta colours, serving tasty jerk chicken (2000c for a piece, 4800c with the works), fine smoothies (1500c) and johnny cakes (850c), and spicy veggie options (try the coconut curry; 4500c).

Mare Nostrum On the main road, not far from *Chile Rojo*. The best budget seafood spot in town, with an overwhelmingly large menu; the fresh fish (4200–4900c), paellas (3500–4200c) and sangría are all specialities.

The Mission Next to *Caribeans*. This tiny *soda* produces authentic Caribbean fare – *casados*, curries, chicken and seafood dishes – at affordable prices (a good feed costs 2500–4500c). There's ocean-front seating available across the road.

Pan Pay On the seafront across from the police station. A popular breakfast spot that has the best croissants in town (400c), plus delicious Spanish omelettes (1200c for a hefty slice with bread), low-cost coffee (450–600c) and takeaway sandwiches (1500–2300c).

Soda Miss Sam's Three blocks back from the seafront, past *Baba Yaga*. What this place lacks in ambience, it makes up for in price and quality, serving good Caribbean dishes at reasonable prices; go for a *casado* or a rice-and-bean combo (2400–5000c).

Veronica's Place 50m southeast of the bus stop. The only strictly vegetarian place in town, offering reasonably-priced Caribbean food (dishes 2500–3500c). There's plenty of vegan options too, as well as "magic" revitalizing juices, home-made ice cream, and traditional remedies if you're feeling poorly.

Drinking and nightlife

Puerto Viejo has the best backpacker nightlife on the east coast, particularly in the high season. Essentially, there's a designated popular hangout for each night of the week. A beer at any of them will set you back around 1000–1200c, though there are regular promotions. In recent years local institution *Johnny's Place* has become synonymous with robberies and aggro – one to avoid.

Baba Yaga 50m north of *Hotel Puerto Viejo*. A Rasta joint offering plenty of drink promotions and a massive sound system – on reggae (Sun) and ladies' (Tues) nights the crowds spill out onto the street.

E-Z Times One block south of the police station. Although it's not the cheapest, the treehouse setting, ambient music, good drinks menu, wood-fired pizzas and board games for rainy days ensure *E-Z Times* lives up to its name.

Mango Sunset Opposite the bus stop. Welcoming bar, with great live rock, reggae and Latin music (notably on Wed) and lots of drinks promotions to get you in the mood (think US$1 tequila shots). There are also dartboards and Sky TV for sports events.

Maritza's Bar & Restaurant 50m east of the bus stop. Across from the beach, with indoor and outdoor seating, this place has a DJ or live music most nights (including salsa on Sat and calypso on Sun).

Stanford's Just east of the main street. Restaurant and bar with a large disco – you can dance to the sound of reggae and waves crashing against the shore. The food is overpriced, but the pool table and sea views make it a worthy spot for a beer. Happy hour 4–6pm.

Directory

Bicycle rental Tuanis Bicycles on the road to Manzanillo, just before *Rocking J's* (2000c/day), or *Café Rico* (3000c/day).

Exchange Bank of Costa Rica (Mon–Fri 9am–4pm; Visa only), across from the Super Puerto Viejo, has an ATM.

Health There are two clinics in the area: Sunimedica (☎52750-0079), next to the post office, and the larger Hone Creek Clinic (☎2756-8022), 5km north of town at El Cruce. Treatment can also be sought at the Farmacia Amiga, in the small commercial centre next to the post office and Sunimedica clinic.

Internet At the ATEC office on the main road (see box opposite) or in the *Jungle Café*, across from *Jammin'* restaurant (1700c/hr).

Laundry There's a laundry service at *Café Rico* (see opposite).

Post office In the small commercial centre two blocks back from the seafront (Mon–Fri 8am–noon & 1–5.30pm).

Moving on

By bus to: Cahuita (14–15 daily; 30–40min); Manzanillo (4–5 daily; 30–45min); Puerto Limón (15 daily; 2hr 30min–3hr); San José (4 daily; 4hr 30min–5hr). There are also regular services to Bribrí, Sixaola and the Panamanian border.

SOUTH TO MANZANILLO

The 12km of coast between Puerto Viejo and **MANZANILLO** village – dotted by the tiny hamlets of **Playa Cocles**, **Playa Chiquita**, **Punta Uva** and **Punta Mona** – is one of the most beautiful stretches in the country. Though not spectacular for swimming, the **beaches** are exceedingly picturesque. If you don't want to pay to stay in the area, the whole stretch can be reached by bicycle from Puerto Viejo (1–2hr); a cycle tour of the beaches can easily be done as a day-trip. The little-visited but fascinating **Refugio Nacional de Vida Silvestre Gandoca–Manzanillo**, bordering the Río Sixaola and the Panamanian border, incorporates the small hamlets of Gandoca and Manzanillo and covers fifty square kilometres

---

ATEC AND THE KÉKÖLDI RESERVE

Skirted by the **Kéköldi Reserve** (🌐www.kekoldi.org), inhabited by about two hundred Bribrí and Cabécar peoples, Puerto Viejo retains strong links with indigenous culture. The Asociación Talamanqueña de Ecoturismo y Conservación, or **ATEC**, is a grassroots organization set up by members of the local community. As well as being able to tell you where to buy locally-made products, the group arranges some of the most interesting tours in Costa Rica. Day-trips to the reserve cost US$20–35, and include a guided hike and lunch; these can also be extended for overnight stays. Other activities include Caribbean cooking (US$25–30/2hr) and dance (US$25/2hr) classes, and tours of an organic chocolate farm (US$35/4hr). If you're spending a few days in the region, an ATEC-arranged trip is a must – contact the Puerto Viejo office (☎2750-0191; on the main street) at least one day in advance.

of land and a similar area of sea. It was established to protect some of Costa Rica's last few **coral reefs**, of which **Punta Uva** is the most accessible. You can **snorkel** here, or **dive**. **Playa Manzanillo** also has a large shelf of coral reef just offshore, which teems with marine life and offers some of the best snorkelling in Costa Rica. The village itself is small and charming, with stunning beaches, laidback locals and a couple of great places to eat and hang out.

Arrival and information

By bus Four to five daily buses run from Puerto Limón, via Cahuita and Puerto Viejo.
By bike Cycling is also an option, and takes about an hour and a half from Puerto Viejo; the road runs alongside the beaches.
Internet Try *Oh La La* café (1500c/hr).
Tour operators Aquamor, opposite the *Soda Rinconcito Alegre* (☎2759-9012, ⊛www .greencoast.com/aquamor.htm), offers diving, snorkelling and kayaking trips (the latter can be combined with dolphin-spotting trips; US$85; 5–6hr), PADI courses and equipment rental (kayak US$6/hr, snorkelling gear US$4/hr). It also has a small book exchange. The Talamanca Dolphin Foundation (☎2759-9118, ⊛www.dolphinlink .org) offers boat tours as part of their research and protection programmes (from US$35 per person; minimum two people).

Accommodation

Prices are a little higher than in Puerto Viejo, but there are several good places to kick back and enjoy the tranquillity without busting your budget.
Cabinas Bucus On the road behind *Cabinas Faya Lobi*, Manzanillo ☎2759-9143, ⓔmeltema1981 @yahoo.de. In a lovely spot backing on to jungle are four pristine doubles with wooden shutters, balconies and private stone bathrooms. This place is run by local guide Omar and his German wife Melte, who lead informative tours and rent snorkelling gear and rubber boots. US$30
Cabinas Faya Lobi 50m beyond Aquamor, Manzanillo ☎2759-9167, ⊛www.cabinasfayalobi .com. Designed with considerable flair, the rooms in this large stucco house close to the jungle are a great choice. There's also a kitchen, a lounge with TV and books, and porches and hammocks to take advantage of. US$30

Cabinas Manzanillo On the northern edge of Manzanillo ☎2759-9033, ⓔcabimanzasologood @yahoo.com. Reliable, low-key hotel, with eight clean concrete rooms, all with fan, private bath and TV; those upstairs have better jungle views. Laundry service, bike rental and tours also available. US$30
Miraflores Playa Chiquita, halfway between Puerto Viejo and Manzanillo ☎2750-0038, ⊛www .mirafloreslodge.com. Comfortable, rustic lodge opposite the beach. The upstairs rooms are brighter, with high bamboo ceilings, and there's a café, library and beautiful gardens. The owner has excellent contacts with local Kéköldi Bribrí communities and runs imaginative tours. US$50

Eating and drinking

🏃 **Oh La La** 150m north of *Maxi's*, on the beach road, Manzanillo. A little taste of France, this bamboo-walled café serves top coffee (550–1100c), *croques monsieurs* and *madames*, filled croissants and crêpes (all 2800–3500c) with a certain Gallic flair.
Maxi's Near the beach in central Manzanillo. Manzanillo's – generally thumping – heartbeat, *Maxi's* has an upstairs restaurant with great views, superlative seafood (pricey, but portions are huge), a cheaper *soda* downstairs, and a bar and reggae soundtrack. Mains 3500–12,000c.
Soda La Playa Diagonal to *Maxi's*, Manzanillo. Lime green *soda*, with low-cost *pintos* (2000c), *casados* and *arroz cons* (2300–4000c), burgers and sandwiches (1000–2300c), as well as a radio tuned into the 1980s.
Soda El Rinconcito Alegre Just beyond Aquamor, Manzanillo. The "happy little corner" has the cheapest food in town, with a handy takeaway service. Sandwiches from 900c, pancakes 1100–1400c.
Vida Sana Across from *Playa Chiquita Lodge*. Handy if you're staying at Playa Chiquita or on a day-trip, this great soda serves hearty breakfasts, tasty *bocas* and ice cream (1000–45000c).

Moving on

By bus to: Puerto Limón (4 daily at 5am, 8.30am, 12.45pm & 5.15pm; Mon–Fri also 9.45am; 1hr 40min); San José (1 daily at 7am; 4hr 30min).

BRIBRÍ

From a few kilometres north of Puerto Viejo the paved road (Hwy-36) continues inland to **BRIBRÍ**, about 10km southwest, arching over the Talamancan

INTO PANAMA: SIXAOLA

The Sixaola–Guabito border is open daily from 8am to 6pm Panama time (one hour ahead of Costa Rica). Citizens of some nationalities (for example US and Canada) may require a tourist card (US$5) to enter Panama (valid for 30 days); the Panamanian consulate in San José issues them, as does the San José office of Copa, the Panamanian airline. Immigration requirements often change; check with the Panamanian consulate. When entering Costa Rica, you will need a copy of your onward or return ticket to prove you are eventually leaving.

In Panama there's nowhere decent to stay until Bocas del Toro (see p.659) – leave time to look for a hotel once you're there, and be aware that bus and boat connections can be tricky. Water connections to Bocas can be made at Changuinola (20km) or Almirante (35km; 1hr 30min).

foothills with views of the green valleys stretching ahead to Panama. This is banana country, with little to see even in Bribrí itself, which is largely devoted to administering the affairs of indigenous reserves in the Talamanca mountains. Bribrí does, however, have a Banco Nacional (Mon–Fri 8.30am–4pm), which has an ATM and changes money and travellers' cheques. Carrying on south from here leads you to the Sixaola–Guabito border crossing, 34km along a stretch of pot-holed road.

The Central Pacific

From cool, undulating forests to rolling waves and scorching sands, the physical attributes of the **Central Pacific** region are some of the most varied and impressive in the country. Every year thousands of travellers make the rugged, 170km trek northwest from San José to the **Monteverde** and **Santa Elena** reserves, to meander on foot through some of the Americas' last remaining pristine cloudforest or to take part in a high-adrenaline canopy tour, for which the area is famous. Meanwhile, only a hundred or so kilometres away, facing out onto the Pacific, **Jacó** is perhaps the most popular **surf destination** in

Costa Rica. With consistent, mid-sized waves, it's a great place for beginners. Further south, still on the coast, **Parque Nacional Manuel Antonio** draws visitors eager to walk its trails in search of monkeys and rare birds, and discover the park's exceptional secluded beaches.

Buses to the region from San José are reliable, and, with a bit of organization, it is easy to travel without doubling back to the capital. Be prepared, though, for some "roads" of startlingly poor quality. In particular, the final 35km stretch to Monteverde will astound, although as much for the scenery as the off-roading. Even in the dry season anything but a 4WD will struggle if you're driving.

SANTA ELENA

The hub of the Monteverde region, and the base for most trips and tours into the surrounding cloudforest, **SANTA ELENA** is one of the most visited settlements in Costa Rica, with all the practical facilities a weary traveller could hope for. Once sleepy, the little town has grown rapidly, despite the best efforts of the local community, but remains an appealing base from which to explore the area's many attractions.

What to see and do

You'll soon have Santa Elena staked out: the centre of town is basically three streets in a triangle, among which sit a plethora of hostels, cafés and tour

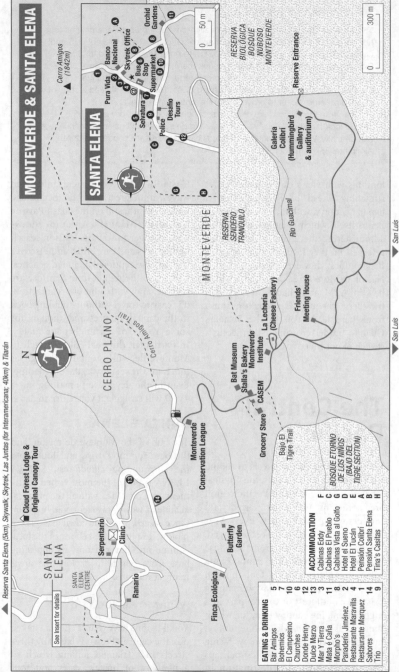

MONTEVERDE & SANTA ELENA

▲ Reserva Santa Elena (5km); Skywalk, Skytrek, Las Juntas (for Interamericana; 40km) & Tilarán

◇ Cloud Forest Lodge & Original Canopy Tour

SANTA ELENA

Orchid Gardens

Banco Nacional
Skytrek Office
Pura Vida
Bus Stop
Supermarket
Selvatura
Police
Desafío Tours

0   50 m

Cerro Amigos (1842m) ▲

MONTEVERDE

RESERVA BIOLÓGICA BOSQUE NUBOSO MONTEVERDE

RESERVA SENDERO TRANQUILO

Río Guacimal

Galería Colibri (Hummingbird Gallery) & auditorium

Reserve Entrance ⊠

0   300 m

▶ San Luis
▶ San Luis

La Lechería (Cheese Factory)

Friends' Meeting House

Bat Museum
Stalla's Bakery
Monteverde Institute
CASEM

CERRO PLANO

Cerro Amigos Trail

Grocery Store

Bajo El Tigre Trail

Monteverde Conservation League

BOSQUE ETERNO DE LOS NIÑOS (BAJO DEL TIGRE SECTION)

Serpentario
Clinic

Butterfly Garden

SANTA ELENA

SANTA ELENA CENTRE

See insert for details

Ranario

Finca Ecologica

◀ San José &

ACCOMMODATION
Cabinas Eddy	F
Cabinas El Pueblo	C
Cabinas Vista al Golfo	D
Hotel el Sueño	E
Hotel El Tucán	A
Pensión Colibrí	B
Pensión Santa Elena	G
Tina's Casitas	H

EATING & DRINKING
Bar Amigos	5
Bohemios	7
El Campesino	10
Churches	6
Donde Henry	12
Dulce Marzo	13
Mar Y Tierra	3
Mata é Caña	8
Morpho's	11
Panadería Jiménez	2
Restaurante Maravilla	4
Restaurante Marquez	1
Sabores	14
Trío	9

530

agencies. The real action is outside the town, in the form of forest tours, wildlife adventures and Reserva Santa Elena itself. Entry fees for attractions in this area are priced in US dollars, though you can pay in colones.

Orchid Gardens

The **Orchid Gardens** (daily 9am–5pm; US$8), in the centre of Santa Elena, boast more than four hundred different species of the flower, including the world's smallest. February is the best month to see them in bloom; otherwise, it's probably only worth the money for real enthusiasts.

Reserva Santa Elena

Reserva Santa Elena (daily 7am–4pm; US$14, students US$7; ☎2645-5390, ⓦwww.reservasantaelena.org), 6km northeast of the village of Santa Elena, is an area of exceptional natural beauty, and offers a glimpse of the rich biodiversity of the cloudforest. Established in 1992, the park strives to be self-funding, assisted by donations and revenue from entrance fees, and gives a percentage of its profits to local schools. Many of the maintenance and building projects depend on volunteers, usually foreign students. The trails within are highly rewarding for the keen-sighted walker, especially early in the morning, before visitors really start to pile in. You can hike with or without a guide, though the guided nature walks (7.30am; US$15) are highly recommended. There are boots and rain gear for rent, information about the trails and a small café and gift shop at the **visitors' centre** at the park entrance.

Canopy tours

Although Monteverde and Santa Elena reserves still pull in the region's biggest crowds, many people visit the region purely to experience an adrenaline-inducing **canopy tour**. Several agencies organize tours (see box, p.532), taking travellers into the parks to swing from zip lines hundreds of feet in the air, amid the canopy layers. These are undoubtedly thrilling, though if you've come to appreciate the area's wonderful wildlife, your best options are still the guided walks and trails in the parks.

Wildlife exhibits

Just outside Santa Elena, on the road to the Monteverde reserve, the **Serpentario** (daily 8.30am–8pm; US$9, students US$7, tickets valid for multiple entries; ☎2645-5238) has a number of unnerving snakes and a few other reptiles in residence, all well displayed with information panels. If you go, visit late in the afternoon, when the serpents tend to be a little more active. The **Ranario** (9am–8.30pm; US$10, students US$7, tickets valid for multiple entries; ☎2645-6320), signposted off the other side of the road, showcases a fascinating array of frogs and amphibians. It's well worth making a couple of visits – one during the day and one at night – as species emerge at different times of day. Both facilities include a guided tour in the price of admission.

Don Juan Coffee Tour

The Monteverde area is one of Costa Rica's important coffee-producing regions, and you can learn all about the process with the **Don Juan Coffee Tour**

TRAVEL IN THE MONTEVERDE REGION

Getting to the Santa Elena/Monteverde region independently from San José, especially in the dry season, entails some pre-planning. Demand for the two daily buses is high, and you should buy your ticket a few days in advance. Once you arrive, buy your return ticket immediately. There's less demand for bus seats travelling from Puntarenas, and you should be able to get away without booking.

TOUR OPERATORS IN SANTA ELENA

Operators in town offer a variety of excursions; with student ID you can save around US$10. Note that most of the hotels and lodges are able to get you slightly cheaper rates than the ones listed below.

Canopy tours
Skytrek Next to the bus stop ☎2645-5238, ⓦwww.skytrek.com. One of the most popular canopy tours (7.30am, 9.30am, 11.30am & 1.30pm; US$60), with eleven cables, including one that's an incredible 770m. It also operates aerial walkways and the SkyTram cable car.
Selvatura Opposite the bus stop ☎2645-5929, ⓦwww.selvatura.com. Reliable operator with 3km of trails and 14 cable runs (8.30am, 11am, 1pm & 2.30pm; US$45).

Other
Desafio/Monteverde Tours Opposite the Super Compro supermarket ☎2645-5874, ⓦwww.monteverdetours.com. Specializes in horseback tours, including a 2 hour 30 minutes ride through forest and farmland (US$32), a day-trip to the San Luís waterfalls (US$62) and an all-day "cowboy" ride (US$75). They can also organize canyoning trips and transfers to La Fortuna (3hr; see p.565). The basic transfer costs around US$25, but for US$85 you can add in some scenic horseriding.

(8am, 10am, 1pm & 3pm; 2hr; adults US$25, students US$18, including transfers; ☎2645-7100, ⓦwww.donjuan coffeetour.com), on the road out to Tilarán. You get to see – and participate in – each phase of the production of the country's highly profitable export crop on this well-managed organic farm.

Arrival and information

By bus Buses arrive in Santa Elena opposite the Banco Nacional at the northern apex of the triangle. The bus station itself is within five steps of the stop, round the corner in the direction of the Jiménez Bakery.
By car Driving from San José to Santa Elena takes about four hours via the Interamericana – this, the Sardinal route, takes the Interamericana north from Puntarenas towards Liberia, branching off at the Rancho Grande turning to Monteverde. From Tilarán, near Laguna de Arenal, the road (40km) is often very rough, but provides spectacular views over Laguna de Arenal and Volcán Arenal (see p.565). Whichever route you take, you'll need a 4WD in the rainy season, when some agencies refuse to rent regular cars for the trip. Check your hotel has parking as it is impossible to park in the street once you arrive.
Tourist information Although there are plenty of tour operators in town (see box above), it is definitely worth visiting *Pensión Santa Elena*, next

to Banco Nacional, whose staff offer excellent impartial advice to everyone, not just guests, and may be able to help you save a few dollars by booking things for you.

Accommodation

All the region's cheapest accommodation is in Santa Elena. Most places offer tourist information and can book tours (for which they will receive commission). In the dry months, book rooms in advance; in the wet season you can just turn up. All places have hot water.
Cabinas Eddy Along the main road into town from San José, just before the town entrance ☎2645-6635, ⓦwww.cabinas-eddy.com. Despite its rather aggressive marketing approach – stationing pushy girls at the bus stop – this hotel is a reasonable choice. Rooms are clean and functional; the more expensive ones come with private baths and in some cases TVs. There's a kitchen, laundry service and free internet. The only downsides are the walk to get there, and the unattractive concrete lot out front. US$20
Cabinas and Hotel Vista al Golfo A 15min walk from the town centre, up the hill behind the Super Compro supermarket ☎2645-6321, ⓦwww .cabinasvistaalgolfo.com. One of the best-value hotels in town offering spick-and-span rooms with shared or private baths; pay extra to get one with a TV and fridge. As well as a kitchen, hammocks and free internet, there's an upstairs terrace with stunning views of the Gulf of Nicoya. Rates include breakfast. US$20

Cabinas El Pueblo Down a dirt track beyond the Super Compro supermarket ☎ 2645-5273/6192, ⊛ www.cabinaselpueblo.com. Attractive little hostel just far away enough from the centre to miss the traffic noise. The rooms with shared bathroom are small and pared down; those with private baths have more character, as well as small TVs, fridges and towels cutely fashioned into the shape of an elephant. Breakfast is included, and there's free internet. US$18

Hotel El Sueno Down the hill from Desafío/ Monteverde Tours, towards Cerro Plano ☎ 2645-6695, ⊛ www.hotelelsuenocr.com. The all-wood rooms have a cosy, faintly Scandinavian feel to them; each has a private bathroom and some also have decent views. There's plenty of communal space, magazines and books to flick through, plus free internet and a restaurant. US$40

Hotel El Tucán At the bottom of the triangle on the way to Cerro Plano ☎ 2645-5017. One of Santa Elena's longest-standing budget hostels, *El Tucán* definitely has a certain charm, though beware the traffic noise. Very small but cosy wooden rooms come with shared baths; classier rooms are in cabins with private baths and balconies. US$20

Tina's Casitas Along the dirt road behind the Super Compro supermarket ☎ 2645-6801 or 2645-6849, ⊛ www.tinascasitas.de. These simple cabinas are a good budget option. Surrounding a shared kitchen and with views of the Gulf of Nicoya, all rooms make fine use of attractive natural woods (check out the cool bathroom mirrors), and some have private baths. Note that the rooms away from the office are of distinctly worse quality. Rates include breakfast. US$14

Pensión Colibri 50m back from the main road behind *Pensión Santa Elena* ☎ 2645-5682. A charming Tico family built and run this pretty, rather chintzy little hotel. Rooms are clean and well maintained, and the building's location helps dull the relentless noise of the motorbikes. Watch your step on the staircase. US$20

Pensión Santa Elena Next to the Banco Nacional ☎ 2645-5051, ⊛ www.pension santaelena.com. The best place to stay in town, offering a wide range of accommodation including camping spots, clean dorms and stylish private rooms with their own baths (try to get one of the nifty split-level ones). There's a kitchen, free internet and extremely knowledgeable employees. It also has an inexpensive taco counter next door. Camping US$4, dorms US$6, doubles US$17

Eating

El Campesino Near *Hotel El Sueno*. Homely little restaurant with quirky decor – nautical murals, religious iconography, cookery books and stuffed toys hanging from the ceiling – and a vast menu. The *comida típica* (*pintos* 2000c, *arroz cons* from 3000c) is much better value than the overpriced steaks and seafood (7000–10,000c). Portions are big, so come with an appetite.

Churches Opposite *Pensión Santa Elena*. Popular with local expats, this mellow café is perfect for taking a breather. The short menu features sandwiches and salads (1100–2100c), the odd pasta or Mexican dish (2200c), daily specials, and sumptuous banana bread and chocolate brownies (450–800c). The teas and coffees are also top-notch. Local artwork covers the wall, and as you'd expect from a bookshop café, there's plenty of reading material available.

Donde Henry Near *Cabinas Eddy*. Although it doesn't look like much from the outside, this Tico-run canteen has a bright and airy dining room with expansive views (on clear days). A hearty plate of rice and beans, salad, sausages, eggs, cheese and much more besides, plus a drink, costs less than 2500c.

Mar Y Tierra Opposite the bus station. The attractive view of the square and the tasty food (the seafood linguine is excellent) are just about enough to compensate for the staff's superior attitude. Main courses fall between 4000c and 5000c; sandwiches and burgers from 2600c.

Panadería Jiménez Opposite the bus station. This bakery and coffee shop offers economical, if unexciting, sandwiches, pastries and cakes (350–2000c) if you just can't face any more rice and beans.

Restaurante Maravilla Near the bus station. A typical *soda*-style menu, at slightly higher than average prices: there's *gallo pinto* (from 1800c) or

TREAT YOURSELF

Morpho's Near *Pensión Santa Elena*. A huge forest mural, chairs fashioned from tree branches, and lamps and candles shaped like butterflies, help to create a serene ambience at *Morpho's*. Although not all the dishes hit the spot, those that do – like sea bass in avocado sauce – make for a memorable meal. Finish off with the unbelievably rich frozen peanut butter pie, a dessert best shared with a friend. Mains cost 5700–8900c. Save your bill – it gets you a US$2 discount at the Orchid Gardens.

omelettes, toast and pancakes for breakfast, and *casados* (3200–3700c), tacos, quesadillas and tortilla wraps for lunch and dinner.

Restaurante Marquez At the northern point of the triangle. This pretty seafood restaurant is welcoming and fairly priced, with some very tasty dishes, in particular the excellent octopus *ceviche*. The staff are as charming as the views at the back. Mains 4000–7000c. Closed between lunch and dinner.

Trio Near the Super Compro supermarket, on the path to *Cabinas El Pueblo*. A cool, minimalist restaurant with subdued lighting, black leather seats, huge windows and an inventive menu. While main courses are a little expensive (5000–7500c), the soups (such as carrot, sweet potato, coconut and tamarind), starters, and burgers, sandwiches and wraps are good value at 2000–4000c.

Drinking and nightlife

Bar Amigos Behind the *Camino Verde* hotel. If you embrace the disco balls, thumping reggaeton and vast dancefloor, this Tico nightlclub can be good fun. The drunken brawls that occasionally occur at the end of the night just add to the flavour. Beers from 1000c.

Bohemios In the Tree House complex opposite the bus station. Atmospheric restaurant-bar, built around a living tree, with regular live music. Good nachos (2000c), though the beer is pricey (around 1750c). The health-conscious can opt for the imported Norwegian "artesian" sparkling water (2000c).

Mata é Caña 40m beyond *Morpho's*, towards Cerro Plano. Run by the folks behind *Pensión Santa Elena*, this bar has a friendly, relaxed vibe, with live music, DJs and screenings of sports events. The grill turns out excellent burgers (3000–4000c), as well as *quesadillas* and baskets of French fries (1200c). Beers from 1000c.

Directory

Books *Churches* (see p.533) has a decent selection of new and secondhand English-language books, as well as magazines and newspapers, plus a coffee shop with free wi-fi. *Dulce Marzo* (see p.535) also has a good book exchange.

Exchange Banco Nacional, at the northern apex of the triangle, has an ATM.

Internet The café next door to *Maravilla* restaurant offers access for 1200c/hr.

Laundry *Hotel El Tucán*'s travel company charges around 1250c/kg. It costs a similar amount at *Churches* (see p.533).

Moving on

By bus to: Monteverde (5 daily; 30min); Puntarenas (3 daily; 3hr); San José (2 daily; 5hr); Tilarán (2 daily; 2.30hr). Travelling to all other destinations is difficult – you get a bus to the Interamericana and hitch from there. From Tilarán there are buses to La Fortuna and Arenal (although a much quicker and more pleasant option is the boat–jeep–boat transfer – see box, p.567). It is quicker and easier to travel into Nicoya and Guanacaste from Puntarenas.

By shuttle A *colectivo* travels from Santa Elena (departing from outside *Panadería Jiménez*) to Monteverde (30min) at 6.15am, 7.30am (not Sun), 1.20pm and 3pm. Schedules change frequently, however, so check the latest times with your hostel. Another *colectivo* goes to Reserva Santa Elena (15min) at 6.30am, 8.30am, 10.30am, 12.30pm & 3pm (returning at 11am, 1pm & 4pm).

By taxi Taxis are easy to get hold of en route or through your hotel. Trips from Santa Elena to Monteverde cost around 3500c.

CERRO PLANO

The **CERRO PLANO** effectively encompasses the five-kilometre stretch between Santa Elena and Monteverde. Leaving Santa Elena, the road twists and turns all the way to the Monteverde reserve entrance, offering unforgettable views en route, as well as some natural diversions and excellent restaurants. Although the distance is easily walkable, the quantity of traffic can result in a mudbath or dustbath depending on the season, and the road's steep incline can be off-putting year-round. Hitching on the road is easy, and the frequent buses to and from Santa Elena and the reserve are an easy way to save your legs.

What to see and do

The Monteverde region offers an impressive array of activities. The stretch between Santa Elena and Monteverde towns alone are home to a butterfly garden, another smaller forest reserve and a surprisingly interesting museum devoted to bats.

Butterfly Garden

The **Butterfly Garden** (daily 9.30am–4pm; US$9, students US$7, including guided tour; ☎2645-5512, ⓦwww.monteverdebutterflygarden.com) provides an opportunity to walk among the butterfly species from Costa Rica's varying climatic regions, though it's really only likely to inspire the most devoted butterfly fans. If you visit, try to arrive between 10am and 2pm, when the butterflies are most active. It's a 10-minute taxi ride off the main road.

Children's Eternal Rain Forest

A small private reserve, the **Children's Eternal Rain Forest**, or **Bosque Eterño de los Niños** (☎2645-5554, ⓦwww.acmcr.org), close to the Monteverde settlement, offers a smaller-scale opportunity to see the landscape for which the region is famous. During the day, visitors are only permitted along the **Bajo El Tigre trail** (daily 8am–4pm; US$8, students US$5; guided tours US$30; book a day in advance), which is physically separated from the rest of the reserve. It is a short, easy trek at lower elevations than in the cloudforest reserves with great views out to the Golfo de Nicoya: sunsets here can be spectacular.

For a slightly different experience, take one of the reserve's **twilight walks** (daily 5.30pm; 2hr; US$30, including transfers). Although the route never strays too far from civilization, the informative guided tour gives you a good chance of seeing a variety of nocturnal animals, including porcupines, tarantulas, armadillos, agoutis, sloths and a marvellous variety of insects and roosting birds. The trail begins just before the cheese factory (see p.536).

The Bat Museum

The **Bat Museum** (daily 9am–7.30pm; US$10, students US$7; ☎2645 6566), next to *Stella's Bakery*, fifteen minutes from Santa Elena along the road to Monteverde, has interesting natural exhibits, multimedia presentations, and a viewing gallery in which the lighting has been changed to ensure that the nocturnal beings are up and about for day-time visitors. It also houses the excellent *Café Caburé*, serving typical Tican and Argentine lunches (around 4000c).

Eating

You will definitely have deserved your delicious meal if you choose to walk – although not a great distance, the road is an impressive uphill climb.

Dulce Marzo 15min walk from Santa Elena. Run by an engaging New Yorker, this delightful little café has a tempting array of sandwiches, salads, wraps, soups, pastas and curries (all 2500–4500c), as well as great coffee and freshly baked pastries, scones and cookies. It also offers a wonderful Sunday brunch with French toast, bacon and eggs, and breakfast burritos. Mon–Sat 11am–7pm, Sun 10am–2pm.

Sabores 20min walk from Santa Elena, just off the main road, along the turn-off to the Butterfly Garden ⓦwww.monteverdeicecream.com. Benchmark-setting ice-cream parlour that makes use of local milk to produce 17 delicious flavours: treat yourself to a fudge, caramel or strawberry sundae (small 1550c, medium 2000c or "jumbo" 4500c). There are also enticing milkshakes, iced coffees and "monkey bananas" (frozen bananas dipped in hot fudge; 400c). Not to be missed.

MONTEVERDE

Mountainous, tropical **MONTEVERDE** is one of the most visited parts of Costa Rica, thanks to its astounding natural beauty. Home to several private nature reserves, including the famous **Reserva Biológica Bosque Nuboso Monteverde**, the district's terrain – from semi-dwarf stunted forest to thick, bearded cloudforest – rarely fails to impress. Meanwhile, the area is of cultural interest as well – its namesake village, the settlement of Monteverde, was established in the 1950s by Quakers who had left their homes in Alabama to avoid military service. Although integrated into Costa Rican society, many of the Quakers still make a living from dairy farming, producing the region's distinctive **cheese**.

What to see and do

Roaming Monteverde's cloudforest is the highlight for most visitors, though there are a handful of other attractions in the area as well, including some smaller forest reserves, a cheese factory and, of course, canopy tours (see box, p.532).

Reserva Biológica Bosque Nuboso Monteverde

The world-renowned **Reserva Biológica Bosque Nuboso Monteverde**, or Monteverde Cloudforest Reserve (daily 7am–4pm; US$17, students US$9; ☎2645-5122, ⊛www.cct.or.cr), protects the last sizeable pockets of primary cloudforest in Mesoamerica. Stretching over 105 square kilometres, it supports six different **ecocommunities**, hosting an estimated 2500 plant species, more than 100 species of mammal, some 490 butterfly species and over 400 species of bird, among them the resplendent **quetzal**. Though the cloudforest cover – dense, low-lit and heavy – can make it difficult to see the animals, the park is nonetheless a mecca for nature-lovers and an essential stop during any trip to Costa Rica.

The reserve runs excellent **guided walks** during the day (7.30am, 11.30am and 1pm; 2hr 30min; US$17) and in the evening (6.15pm; 2hr 30min; US$20, including transport), as well as longer ones aimed at birdwatchers (6am, departing from *Stella's Bakery* in Monteverde; US$64); you have to pay the entry fee on top. Book through your hotel, *Pensión Santa Elena* (see p.533) or directly (☎2645-5122, Ⓔmontever@cct .or.cr); the reserve sometimes puts on extra daytime walks during the high season, but it's worth booking a day in advance, as groups are limited to 10 people.

Seemingly rather pricey, the guided walks are actually good value for money, and the experience is educational. You can also walk the trails without a guide – they are clearly marked, and you can get maps and interpretive booklets at the reserve office – but you're almost certain to see less. **Temperatures** are cool (15° or 16°C). Be sure to carry an umbrella, light rain gear, binoculars and insect repellent. It's just about possible to get away without **rubber boots** in the dry season, but you will definitely need them in the wet. The reserve office rents both boots and binoculars (US$1.50), as do some hotels.

In an attempt to limit human impact and conga-line hiking, a number of **rules** govern entrance to Monteverde, including a quota of 160 visitors at any one time. In high season, consider booking tickets a day in advance (note that bookings aren't available more than 24 hours in advance). Things get noisy and crowded between 8 and 11am, when the tour groups arrive.

Reserva Sendero Tranquilo

The **Reserva Sendero Tranquilo**, a private reserve in the grounds of a local farm behind the cheese factory in Monteverde, offers informative guided tours (book on ☎2645-5010; US$35) through primary- and secondary-growth forest. It's relatively unknown, and so offers a much more tranquil walking experience, although the number of animals you might spot is relative to its size.

La Lechería

Still using the traditional methods undertaken by their forefathers, the cheesemakers at **La Lechería**, or the Quaker Cheese Factory (tours Mon–Sat 9am & 2pm; US$10; ☎2546-7090) offer informative tours on the process used to make the unique cheese of the region, plus an interesting slide-show of the history of the region.

Arrival

By shuttle Shuttles from Santa Elena drop off right outside the Monteverde reserve after passing through Cerro Plano.

Accommodation

Budget travellers will find little in the way of inexpensive accommodation in this area, but it's easy to travel to and from Santa Elena. At the time of research, the three basic shelters in the reserve were closed to visitors. It is, however, possible to stay at the reserve's *La Casona* hostel, close to the main entrance (℡ 2645-5122; US$53), which has several big dorms. Rates include the park entry fee and full board.

Moving on

By shuttle The *colectivo* returns to Santa Elena at 6.45am (Mon–Sat), 11.30am, 2pm & 4pm. Times fluctuate, so double check at the reserve. For travel beyond Santa Elena, see "Moving on", p.534.

PUNTARENAS

Built on a sand spit only a few blocks wide, heat-stunned **PUNTARENAS**, 110km west of San José, has the look of raffish abandonment that haunts so many tropical port cities. The town's cracked, potholed streets are shaded by mop-headed mango trees and lined with wooden buildings painted in sun-bleached tutti-frutti colours. There's little for visitors to see or do – the town is of most use for its transport connections between the southern Nicoya Peninsula and the mainland. Despite being almost entirely surrounded by water, there is no surf and the water is not really considered clean enough to swim in. Nevertheless, Puntarenas has something of a rustic charm by day, and you can spend a relaxing few hours here soaking up the sun and local atmosphere, admiring the quaint little church (Av Central, C 5/7) and checking out the vibrant food market (in the northeast corner of town, off Av 3). At night, however, the town has a rather seedier feel, so avoid wandering about alone after dark.

Arrival and information

By boat The dock for the main *lanchas* from Paquera and Naranjo, on the Nicoya Peninsula, is on the northwestern point of town. The smaller passenger ferry from Paquera comes in further east along the coast behind the Mercado Central on Av 3.
By bus The main bus station is on the corner of C 2 and Paseo de los Turistas, near the old train tracks and the old dock that juts out into the gulf. Services from Manuel Antonio and Quepos arrive at the petrol station two blocks north.
Internet Internet Café Puntarenas (daily 8.30am–5pm; 500c/hr) is just east of the church in the pedestrian centre.
Tourist information The regional ICT office (Mon–Fri 8am–4pm; ℡ 2661-0407) is a block west of the bus station on Paseo de los Turistas.

Accommodation

There are several reasonable, inexpensive hotels: make sure your room has a working fan or a/c. All have cold-water showers.
Gran Hotel Chorotega C 1, Av 1/3 ℡ 2661-0998, ✉ granhotelchorotega@hotmail.com. A good-value option, with surgically clean rooms (which are tiled all over); the cheaper ones have fans and shared bathrooms, the more expensive come with a/c, cable TV and their own bathrooms. US$25
Gran Hotel Imperial Paseo de los Turistas, C 0/2 ℡ 2661-0579. This faded, wooden-boarded hotel is something of an oddity: the peeling paint in the basic rooms (all with private bathrooms, fans and TVs, some with balconies) is electric pink, while the lobby and hallways are strewn with fashion magazines and pot plants. It's handy for the bus station, and proximity to the police station ensures its security. US$35
Hotel Cabezas Av 1, C 2/4 ℡ 2661-1045. The best budget option in town, this bright and sunny hotel offers clean and compact rooms (with private or shared bathrooms and TVs) and excellent security. The *dueña* is quite the matriarch, but it adds to the familial ambience. US$15
Hotel Cayuga C 4, Av 0/1 ℡ 2661-0244/0344. This spartan flophouse is acceptable for a night, if all the other options are full up. Rooms with private bathrooms and either fans or a/c are plain and decidedly gloomy. There is a laundry service, however, and the attached restaurant is good for *gallo pinto* (1600c) and evening meals. US$20

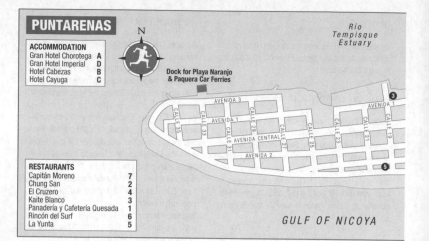

PUNTARENAS

ACCOMMODATION
Gran Hotel Chorotega	A
Gran Hotel Imperial	D
Hotel Cabezas	B
Hotel Cayuga	C

N

Río
Tempisque
Estuary

Dock for Playa Naranjo
& Paquera Car Ferries

AVENIDA 3
AVENIDA 1
AVENIDA CENTRAL
AVENIDA 2

AVENIDA 1

CALLE 35
CALLE 33
CALLE 31
CALLE 29
CALLE 27
CALLE 25
CALLE 23
CALLE 21
CALLE 19

RESTAURANTS
Capitán Moreno	7
Chung San	2
El Cruzero	4
Kaite Blanco	3
Panadería y Cafetería Quesada	1
Rincón del Surf	6
La Yunta	5

GULF OF NICOYA

Eating

Chung San Av 1, C 1/3. Red paper lanterns hang from the ceiling and holiday snaps cover the walls of *Chung San*, the best of the string of Chinese restaurants on this strip. The fried rice, noodles, chop suey and stir-fries (all from 2900c) are tasty, and there's an economical lunch special (2750c).

El Cruzero Paseo de los Turistas, opposite the bus station. This appealing open-walled *soda*, decked out in vibrant green-turquoise shades and boasting views of the sea (and the bus station), is great for low-cost *pintos* (1500c), *casados*, ice creams, milkshakes and cold drinks.

Kaite Blanco Av 1, C 17/19 ☎2661-4842. Delicious typical Tican and fresh fish dishes (from 2500c) and a dynamic atmosphere (especially at weekends, when there's live music). Also an excellent bar for cocktail lovers.

Panadería y Cafetería Quesada C 2, Av 1/3. Close to the market, this is a real local joint – it's always full of families and Tico couples. *Gallo pinto* for less than 1600c, *casados* from 2000c.

La Yunta Paseo de los Turistas, C 19/21 ☎2661-3216. As the mounted bull heads and cattle prints on the walls suggest, steaks (from 4000c) are the focus here – and are produced well. The seafood is equally appealing, but more expensive (from 5000c).

Drinking and nightlife

The nightlife along the Paseo de los Turistas takes off at weekends. The bars generally have a good-natured vibe, but get a taxi back to your hotel at the end of the night, as the area gets dodgy later on.

Capitán Moreno On the beach. This open-walled bar/club, split over two storeys, offers inexpensive beers and live music. It's hugely popular with Ticos, who come to show off their karaoke talents (or lack of them) and dance moves.

Rincón del Surf Next to *Capitán Moreno*. *Rincón del Surf* is on a smaller scale to its neighbour, but

TRANSPORT TO THE NICOYA PENINSULA

Ferries from Puntarenas go to two destinations on the **Nicoya Peninsula: Paquera** and **Naranjo**. There is nothing in Naranjo, apart from a *soda* by the ferry dock and the reasonable *Hotel El Ancla* (☎2661-3887; US$50). Buses run to Nicoya from here four times daily (7.30am, 12.15pm, 3.45pm and 8.50pm), although it is advisable to check these times before you set off from Puntarenas. **Buses** to the beaches along the southern tip only run from Paquera. Be warned that Paquera can be downright threatening at night. If you have to stop over, *Cabinas Ginana* (☎2641-0119; US$35) is clean, secure and has a restaurant. Buses depart daily from Paquera (7am, 8am, 10am, noon, 2pm and 4pm) to Montezuma, via Cóbano.

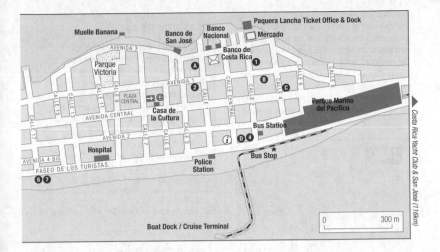

just as loud. Regular drinks promotions can take the price of a beer down to 700c, which helps to generate a lively atmosphere.

Directory

Exchange There are three banks with ATMs and currency exchanges along Av 3.
Taxis Available taxis line up along the beach road in front of Banco Costa Rica by the bus station. Journeys from here to anywhere in town should cost a maximum of 2500c.

Moving on

By boat to: Naranjo (from the Northwestern Dock; for links to Nicoya and the western peninsula; 4 daily at 6.30am, 10am, 2.30pm, 7.30pm); Paquera (from the Northwestern Dock; for links to Montezuma, Santa Teresa and Mal País; every 2hr 4.30am–8.30pm). Boats also leave for Paquera from behind the Mercado Central, but times vary; check at the tourist office (see p.537).
By bus to: Jacó (7 daily at 4.15am, 5am, 8am, 11am, 12.30pm, 2.30pm & 4.30pm; 1hr 30min); Quepos (6 daily at 5am, 8am, 11am, 12.30pm, 2.30pm & 4.30pm; 3hr); Liberia (9 daily; 3hr); San José (hourly 4am–7pm; 2hr 20min); Santa Elena/ Monteverde (3 daily at 7.50am, 1.50pm & 2.15pm; 3hr 30min).

JACÓ

The thriving resort of **JACÓ** can make no claim to either class or exclusivity:

stretching three kilometres along a main road parallel to the **beach**, it's little more than a brash strip of souvenir shops, bars, restaurants and hotels. As the closest beach to the capital, it's long been a very popular weekend destination for *Josefinos* during the summer months, and now foreign investment is allowing for almost unrestrained (and generally unattractive) development. This said, the long sandy beach remains reasonably clean, and the **surf** is good year-round – indeed, surfing is pretty much the only thing to do here, and the town is built around the industry. Dozens of places rent **boards** and give lessons (see below). Alternatively there's also some nice snorkelling around **Isla Tortuga**, off the coast of the Nicoya Peninsula. A number of operators can arrange trips (see "Tour operators", below).

Arrival and information

By bus Buses from Quepos stop in front of the Banco Nacional in the town centre, and those from San José at the bus station at the *Pizza Hut* complex at the northern end of town. The walk into town from the bus station will take roughly 10min, but there are plenty of taxis around.
Tour operators King Tours (☎ 2643-2441, ⓦ www.kingtours.com) offer a range of activities

including kayaking (US$85), canopy tours (US$89) and day-trips to Isla Tortuga (US$120). Prices are pretty much the same across the board in Jacó, and similar throughout this part of the country. For surfboard rental, try Chuck's WOW Surf, Av Pastor Díaz at C Ancha (☎2643-3844, ⓦwww .wowsurf.com; board rental US$15–20/day, lessons US$65). Experienced local surfer Gustavo Castillo (☎2643-3574 or 8829-4697), based on

> ### SAFETY IN JACÓ
>
> Jacó has a reputation for being **unsafe**, and a hive of prostitution and drugs. Make sure that your hostel has good security, and avoid wandering around by yourself at night. Don't take taxis that aren't the typical yellow and black, as they are likely to be unlicensed. However, privately booked taxis may be all black: check when you call. The **beach** is notoriously dangerous at night – stay away.

the beach in front of *Bohío Grill*, offers lessons for a similar price.

Accommodation

Reserve in advance during the high season (Dec–April), especially at weekends. Most places are on or near the main strip.

Cabinas Antonio North of the *Pizza Hut* and bus station ☎2643-3043. Friendly, peaceful place that, although slightly more expensive than the hostels, boasts a lovely pool, neat little rooms and private parking. There is a laundry next door and you're only a few yards from the beach. US$30

Camping El Hicaco On C Hicaco. Big, attractive campsite (bring your own tent), with showers, lockers and parking available for a small fee. Good central location, though it is next to a high-rise hotel. US$3

Hotel De Haan On C El Bohío ☎2643-1795, ⓦwww.hoteldehaan.com. Just off the main strip, *Hotel De Haan* has a great pool area and a relaxed vibe. The dorms are cavernous and pretty rustic; the private rooms are essentially the same – you're just paying more for privacy. There's a kitchen, free internet and laundry service, and surf lessons are available. Dorms US$16, doubles US$36

Hotel Kangaroo ☎2643-3351. About a kilometre south of the main strip. This hostel is superficially attractive if you're looking to escape the bustle of town. They offer board rental and there is a nice pool, but the security is a bit lax and staff can be standoffish. Take a taxi at night. US$30

Rutan Surf Cabinas On C Anita ☎2643-3328 or 8858-5029. Popular with surfers, this unpretentious place offers rather dark but clean, well-ventilated dorms and cold-water showers. Guests also get free internet and a 10 percent discount at Chuck's WOW Surf. US$15

EATING & DRINKING			
Bohío Grill	4	Soda Rustica	7
Marea Alta	9	Sunrise	1
Monkey Bar	3	Tsunami Sushi	5
Pachi's Pan	6	Wahoos	2
Los Sabores Ticos	8		
ACCOMMODATION			
		Hotel de Haan	C
Cabinas Antonio	A	Hotel Kangaroo	E
Camping El Hicaco	D	Rutan Surf Cabinas	B

Eating

Marea Alta Av Pastor Díaz, just south of the Red Cross. Open 24hr for end-of-the-night munchies, but by no means a fast-food joint. Tasty breakfasts and *casados* 1500–3000c.

Pachi's Pan Opposite Banco Nacional. A bakery and café with everything you need for picnics and continental breakfasts, including good pastries and cappuccinos. Most items cost 300–2000c.

Los Sabores Ticos At the southernmost end of town. Also known as *Tico Flavours*, *Sabores Ticos* is a simple place that does the basics well: tasty *empanadas* and *pupusas* (500c), filling *pintos* (less than 1400c) and fresh fruit and muesli (1500c). Well worth a look.

Soda Rustica On C Hicaco. The pick of Jacó's *sodas*: an enormous *casado* and a fruit juice or soft drink will leave with you with change from 2500c.

Sunrise Av Díaz, on the left just before Chuck's. Specializes in truly vast American-style breakfasts – the owner's motto is "no one leaves hungry" – though it's a bit overpriced (3000–5000c). Decent pizza is also on offer until the early hours.

Tsunami Sushi Av Pastor Díaz. Excellent super-fresh sushi – everything served has been caught the same day – as well as *gyoza*, spring rolls, noodles and teriyaki. Expect to pay around 5000–7000c for a good meal – a little pricey for backpackers, but worth stretching the budget for.

Drinking and nightlife

Jacó's nightlife is hedonistic and sleazy, with holiday-makers jostling for bar space with prostitutes and their clientele.

Bohío Grill On C de Bohío. This trendy spot on the beach strikes a balance between swanky cocktail bar and friendly hangout, with live music most nights. Try the *caipirioskas*, which taste especially good at 2-for-1. The fish tacos are also great.

Monkey Bar Av Pastor Díaz, opposite C las Palmeras. Entices tourists in with 2-for-1 offers and lively ladies' nights (Tues & Thurs), but is more often than not just a hangout for cigar-smoking expats and their lady friends. Solo female travellers may not feel comfortable here.

Wahoos Av Pastor Díaz, just before Chuck's and *Sunrise*. The hefty cocktail list (including 2-for-1 margaritas) helps to generate a friendly, relaxed atmosphere at *Wahoos*, which has bilingual karaoke on Fri and Sat, plus rock and reggae nights, and screens all the big (and many minor) US sports events. They also serve a good Bloody Mary.

Directory

Bike rental Condor Biker rents out mountain bikes (US$10–15/day), but widespread theft has left them insisting on a US$100 deposit and a copy of your passport. You can rent a moped (about US$50/day from Condor Bikes) and head out onto the Costañera Sur highway to explore Playa Hermosa (see below).

Books Books and Stuff, on the main drag just opposite C El Bohío, sells postcards, stamps and secondhand books.

Exchange There are several banks along the main strip. Banco Nacional (Mon–Fri 8am–5pm, Sat 8am–noon) has an ATM and currency exchange.

Health The Red Cross (☎ 2643-3090) maintains a clinic on the southern end of the strip between C El Hicaco and C Las Brisas.

Internet Café Internet, next to Mas X Menos, charges 500c/hr. Mexican Joe's, further north along the main road, has cheap international calls.

Laundry Aquamatic, just north of *Toucan Jam* on the main drag, charges 4000c/5kg.

Taxis Karen Ruz (☎ 8835-9385 or 2643-2323/ 5353) provides excellent, reliable service at any time of day. 24-hour taxis also available on ☎ 2643-2020/1919.

Moving on

By boat to: Jet-boats to Montezuma (US$40; 1hr), departing at 10.45am from Herradura beach, are run by Zuma Tours in Montezuma (see p.547).

By bus to: Puntarenas (from outside the Banco Nacional; 7 daily at 6am, 9am, noon, 2pm, 4.30pm, 5pm & 7pm; 1hr 30min); Quepos (from outside the Banco Nacional; 6 daily at 6.30am, 9.30am, 12.30pm, 2pm, 4pm & 6pm; 1hr 30min–2hr); San José (from the bus station on Av Pastor Díaz, northwest of the centre; 7 daily at 5am, 7am, 9am, 11am, 1pm, 3pm & 5pm; 2hr 30min).

PLAYA HERMOSA

If Jacó has worn you out, peaceful **Playa Hermosa** is only 7km away. Offering a long stretch of darkish sand that has a challenging, often fierce, break, the beach town is pricier than Jacó, but makes a nice break from the crowds. *Cabinas Las Arenas* (☎ 2643-7013, ⓦ www.cabinaslasarenas.com; US$49) is an ideal place for surfers with its familial atmosphere, rustic wooden cabins with private bathrooms and fans, and *Dos Gringos*, which as well as serving hearty fare (mains 5500–8000c), screens surf videos and has a Nintendo Wii. The **bus** from Jacó to Quepos runs through here – ask the driver for the right stop – or you can take a taxi (around 4000c).

QUEPOS

Arriving in **QUEPOS** from points north, it's immediately apparent that you've crossed into the lush, wetter southern-Pacific region: the vegetation is much thicker and greener. The town itself, backed against a hill and fronted by a muddy beach, can look pretty ramshackle, but it's friendly and has plenty of hotels, bars and restaurants. Of all the **sport-fishing** grounds in Costa Rica, the Quepos area has the most variety; many small tour agencies cater more or less exclusively to sport-fishers spending several hundred dollars (or more). There are also opportunities for all sorts of more budget-friendly **outdoor activities**, from horseriding to rafting and kayaking to dolphin-watching. For most visitors, however, the town's biggest draw is its proximity to Parque Nacional Manuel Antonio and its beaches, 7km south.

Arrival and information

By bus All buses arrive at and depart from the bus station in the town centre. A taxi rank is located opposite. Many travellers have had their bags stolen from the bus station, so be alert.
Tourist information Lynch Travel, one block west of the northern side of the shopping centre (☎ 2777-1170, ⓦ www.lynchtravel.com), offers friendly, bilingual and impartial advice on the area.

Accommodation

Cabinas Estefan At the beginning of the road to Manuel Antonio ☎ 2777-4452, ⓦ www.cabinas estefan.com. Popular with Tico tourists, these simple cabins have private baths and fans (the owner plans to add a/c and TVs) and there's a small pool to cool off in. Location is everything, with a bus stop to Manuel Antonio 20 seconds up the hill, and a supermarket on the corner. US$26

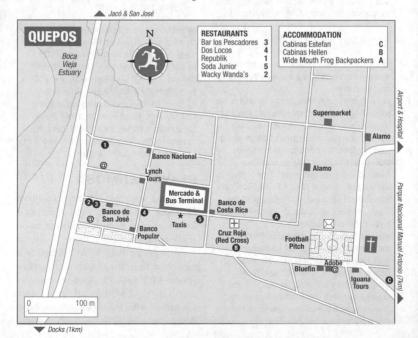

QUEPOS TOUR OPERATORS

Tour operators in the Quepos/Manuel Antonio area offer a wide range of activities – from rafting to horseriding.

Los Amigos del Río Between Quepos and Manuel Antonio (look for a large orange building on the left with inflatable rafts outside; ☎2777-0082, ⓦwww.amigosdelrio.net). Rafting outfitters.

Equus Stables On the road to Manuel Antonio (☎2777-0001, ⓔhavefun@racsa.co.cr). Organizes horseriding tours.

Iguana Tours By the football pitch (☎2777-1262, ⓦwww.iguanatours.com). Runs a variety of jungle tours.

Lynch Travel A block west of the northern side of the shopping centre (☎2777-1170, ⓦwww.lynchtravel.com). Offers horseriding trips on the beach and up into the mountains (US$55), sea kayaking (US$60) and canopy tours (US$65), among other activities.

Sunset Sails Central Manuel Antonio (☎2777-1170, ⓦwww.sunsetsailstours.com). Sunset cruises around the Manuel Antonio beaches are recommended; this company also runs dolphin-watching excursions (US$75).

Cabinas Hellen A block south of the Mercado and two east of the football pitch ☎2777-0504. Clean, secure cabinas at the back of a family home, with private bath, fridge, fans, small patio, parking and laundry service. US$25

🏃 **Wide Mouth Frog Backpackers** Two blocks west of the bus station ☎2777-2798/0093, ⓦwww.widemouthfrog.org. Behind the high security gate is a veritable oasis. Cheerful rooms – both dorms and private options – form a quad around the pool. Staff are informative, and there's free internet, a big kitchen, TV lounge, book exchange and DVD library. Rates include breakfast. Dorms US$11, doubles US$30

Eating and drinking

Bar los Pescadores Next door to *Wanda's*. This fisherman-themed bar serves up – as you'd expect – fine seafood, as well as economical *bocas*, burgers, chicken wings and sandwiches (from 2000c), and there's a/c and wi-fi too.

Dos Locos 50m west of the taxi rank. The decor in this cantina leaves no Mexican cliché unturned, but the food – such as grilled red snapper (4500c) – is good quality, and staff are attentive. Lunch from 2500c.

Republik On the road north of *Wanda's*. Swish bar/club with a long list of potent cocktails (2000–3500c; the mojitos are particularly good) and a chic retro decor. The party often lasts till 4am.

Soda Junior This tiny, Tico-run *soda* just north of the bus station is the best place in town for inexpensive fried chicken and lip-smacking *casados*. Breakfast from 1500c, mains from 2300c.

Wacky Wandas 100m west of the taxi rank. A rowdy, all-American bar serving cheap beer, cocktails and snacks like sandwiches, burgers and grilled fish (3000–3500c). "Albert's wiener schnitzel" (3500c) is on offer every Wednesday, and there's free food for those drinking at the bar on Sundays.

Directory

Exchange The Banco Nacional just northwest of the bus terminal does currency exchange. They change travellers' cheques, as will Lynch Travel.
Health Hospital Dr Max Teran (☎2777-0200), near the airport, has an excellent reputation.
Internet K.I.T. Internet café, on the second floor of the shopping centre, charges 1000c/hr.
Post office The post office (Mon–Fri 8am–5pm) is at the eastern end of town.

Moving on

By bus to: Jacó (6 daily at 4.30am, 7.30am, 10.30am, 12.30pm, 3pm & 5.30pm; 1hr 30min–2hr); Manuel Antonio (every 20–30min; 30min); Puntarenas (same times as for Jacó; 3hr); San Isidro, via Dominical (3 daily at 5.30am, 11.30am & 1.30pm; 3–4hr); San José (4 daily at 6am, 9.30am, noon & 5pm, plus Mon–Sat 4am & 2.30pm, Sun 3pm; 3hr).

MANUEL ANTONIO

The little community of **MANUEL ANTONIO**, 7km southeast of Quepos and the gateway to popular **Parque Nacional Manuel Antonio**, enjoys a truly stunning setting: spectacular white-grey sand beaches fringed by thickly forested green hills. Watching a lavish sunset over the Pacific from high up here, it seems this is one of the most charming places on earth. However, the area – especially the corridor between Quepos and the village – has experienced one of the country's most dramatic tourism booms. Along the road is an unbroken line of hotels and construction sites, which, together with the influx of people, has tainted some of the area's pristine magic. It's not cheap, either, but with a little effort you can find budget accommodation. And though crowded at times, the park remains one of Costa Rica's loveliest destinations.

What to see and do

Tiny Manuel Antonio village is booming, with an ever-increasing stream of visitors heading to the park and taking in the breathtaking sunset. It is the park and not the village, however, that is the main attraction. One word to the wise: take precautions against **theft** here even more so than in other areas – never leave anything on the beach when swimming, and don't let people handle your luggage on the bus. The town beach is also a no-go area after dark, as muggers wielding machetes are known to prowl its lengths.

Parque Nacional Manuel Antonio

Parque Nacional Manuel Antonio (Tues–Sun 7am–4pm; US$10; ☏2777-0644) is one of Costa Rica's most popular national parks, despite being the smallest. It preserves lovely **beaches**, **mangroves** and humid tropical **forest**. You can also see the unique *tómbolo* of **Punta Catedral**: a rare geophysical formation, a *tómbolo* is created when an island becomes slowly joined to the mainland through accumulated sand deposits. **Wildlife** – including sloths,

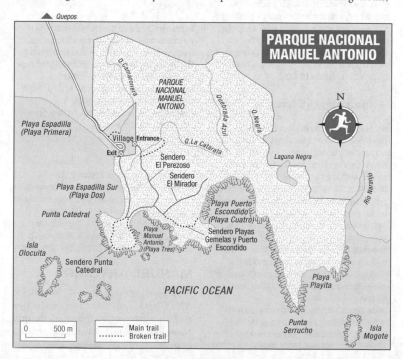

snakes, green kingfishers, laughing falcons and capuchin monkeys – is in abundance. The **climate** is humid and hot, averaging around 27°C, and although drier in the rainy season than other parts of the country, showers are nonetheless a constant threat.

A complex **trail** network allows visitors to explore deep into the park. You can swim at **Playa Espadilla Sur** (or Playa Dos), which is long and usually very calm, or at **Playa Manuel Antonio** (also called Playa Tres or Playa Blanca), which is immediately south of Punta Catedral and more sheltered than the other beaches. Dangerous riptides plague otherwise beautiful **Playa Espadilla** (Playa Primera), so only swim here with extreme caution. **Guides** are available for hire at the park (around US$20), and can be quite helpful, as untrained eyes may find it difficult to pick out wildlife among the dense foliage (this is one of those places where snakes could be mistaken for vines). Ring the park office to reserve a guide, or ask at your lodge.

Arrival and information

By bus Services from San José arrive at Quepos bus station, from where frequent buses (every 20–30min; 30min) travel through Manuel Antonio proper and drop passengers off 200m before the park entrance at the mini-roundabout. There are stops in both directions all along the 7km route and the buses run in a continuous loop all day.
By taxi A taxi from Quepos costs 2500–3000c, or you could take a *colectivo* for around 300–500c.
Exchange There's an ATM next to *Café del Mar*.
Internet Available next to the *Marlin Restaurant* along the boulevard, although the connection is slow.
Tour operators Apache Tours, in front of *Las Gemelas* bar on the boulevard (☎ 8868-7468), offers a full range of activities (most US$55–100), including dolphin-watching, horseriding, jet-skiing, whitewater rafting and ATV hire. Ask for Christi, who is bilingual and knowledgeable about the area. Kayaks del Amor, on the beach in front of *Marlin Restaurant* (☎ 2777-5125), have been around for a while, with great-value snorkel and kayak rental (US$10–15/hr, US$20–30 with guide).

Accommodation

The budget accommodation in Manuel Antonio is of decidedly variable quality, and you may prefer to stay in Quepos. Book in advance during the high season or you'll have to settle for one of the not-so-good places. Staying in the park overnight is forbidden (and wardens come round in the evenings to check).
Los Almendros From the *Marlin Restaurant*, follow the hill away from the beach for 100m ☎ 2777-0225, ☒ www.almendroshotel.com. A comfortable – if slightly overpriced – lodge whose green-roofed cabins come with TVs and private bathrooms with hot water, and there's a lovely pool, gardens and restaurant. Rates include breakfast. US$65
Backpackers Costa Linda Close to *Los Almendros* ☎ 2777-0304, ☒ www.costalinda -backpackers.com. This hostel is a hive of activity, with a sociable bar/restaurant and a great 1800c breakfast (fresh fruit, pancakes and *gallo pinto*) that draws diners from far and wide. The cell-like private rooms, however, are not for the claustrophobic, though the dorms are a bit more airy. Dorms US$10, doubles US$20
Backpackers Manuel Antonio On the main road, halfway between Quepos and Manuel Antonio ☎ 8820-4621, ☒ www.backpackersmanuelantonio .com. This hostel boasts hot-water showers, spotless dorms, private rooms (shared baths), a splash pool and a good location (handy for the bus, *Angel* restaurant, the supermarket and laundry). Dorms US$12, doubles US$35
Cabinas El Gordo At the top of the right-angled road to the beach ☎ 2777-5333. Popular with Tico families, this lodge is right on the edge of the park. The little blue cabins are cheap, but a bit dilapidated. US$20
Cabinas Picis A 10min walk from Manuel Antonio back towards Quepos ☎ 2777-0046. In a secluded spot surrounded by coconut palms, the friendly *Cabinas Picis* has simple rooms and private beach access. US$30
Cabinas Ramirez At the entrance to the village ☎ 2777-5333. These cabins are rather dark and pokey, but always full. The camping area is essentially excellent, with electricity and good *servicios*, but thieves are known to walk the beach in front, and security isn't watertight. Better for groups than individuals or couples. Camping US$5, cabins US$20
Tico Lodge 200m up the road up from the beach ☎ 2777-5085. Just beyond *Los Almendros* is this appealing little place, which boasts excellent

security, good tour advice and a laundry service. The cosy rooms have terracotta decor, TVs, fridges and cold-water bathrooms. A/c costs US$5 extra. **US$30**

Eating and drinking

Eating in Manuel Antonio village can get expensive. Perhaps more than elsewhere, prices should be taken as a rough guide, as they will inevitably increase. There's no real nightlife scene, so evenings are pretty quiet.

Angel 3km from Quepos ☎2777-2282. Unquestionably the best place in the area for relaxed Tico hospitality and cuisine, with great *casados*. It's quite hard to find – it's tucked away between the laundry and the football pitch. Meals costs from 2500c.

Café del Mar At the far end of the main strip, on the beach, this spacious restaurant/bar bears only a passing resemblance to its Ibiza namesake, although it does feature chill-out music throughout the day. A good place for a sundowner (beer from 1350c, cocktails from 3450c).

Las Gemelas On the main strip. Cheerful *Las Gemelas* has a beach-bar feel with thumping music and decorative white sombreros. Happy hour is 4–6.30pm; the cocktails (around 4200c) are tasty, the staff friendly and the *casados* delicious.

Marlin Restaurant In the centre of the village. A great spot to watch the sunset and soak up the atmosphere over a beer, this long-running institution also offers an extensive menu of Tico, seafood, Tex-Mex and American dishes (mains from 3200c). Cocktails 2500–3200c.

Vela Bar Close to *Backpackers Costa Linda* ☎2777-0413. The pick of the village restaurants, with expertly prepared *mariscos*, including ceviche and Creole shrimp (5000–6000c),

---

as well as less expensive *casados* (3500–4500c) and a fine banana split. The service, meanwhile, is as polished as the dark-wood tables, which are set in a peaceful garden terrace.

Moving on

By bus Moving on from Manuel Antonio requires heading back to Quepos on one of the shuttle buses (every 20–30min; 20–30min). From Quepos, buses run along the Pacific coast and to San José.

The Nicoya Peninsula

The Nicoya Peninsula is one of the most popular tourist destinations in Costa Rica. The majority of people come for the beaches: although places like surf-crazy **Tamarindo** have long been popular with foreigners, quieter spaces like **playas Nosara and Sámara** offer more space for contemplation of the beautiful coastline. Some of the beaches in the northern section of the peninsula (officially Guanacaste Province) can be a bit difficult to reach on public transport, but the rewards are great for those who brave the challenge. Meanwhile, much of the southern peninsula (officially Puntarenas Province) has been cleared for farming, cattle-grazing or, in the case of some areas, **golf courses**. Friendly **Cóbano**, 6km inland, is the largest (although still tiny) town in the southwest of the peninsula, with good amenities including a petrol station, post office, supermarket and *guardia rural*. There's also a Banco Nacional, with an ATM – the only reliable one in the area. There is little else of interest for travellers here, and most pass right through on the way to **Montezuma** or Santa Teresa, two of the most popular beach hangouts in the country, both only accessible by rough and rugged dirt roads.

MONTEZUMA

The colourful beach resort of **MONTEZUMA** lies near the south-western tip of the Nicoya Peninsula, about 40km south of Paquera, where the ferry from Puntarenas arrives. Some three decades ago a handful of foreigners fell in love with the place – it is astoundingly beautiful – and settled here. Then it was just a fishing village, largely cut off from the rest of the country; nowadays it's totally devoted to tourism, with virtually every building offering gringo-friendly food, accommodation or tours. This said, there's somehow been little large-scale development – Montezuma remains essentially a village, and the coastline is relatively unspoilt. Heading in either direction are some of the loveliest beaches in the country: grey-white sands, dotted with jutting rocks and leaning palms and backed by lush greenery, including rare Pacific lowland tropical forest.

What to see and do

Other than hanging out, there's not much to do in the village itself: the single most popular activity around town is probably an excursion south to the **Cabo Blanco** reserve (see p.549). Despite the inviting coastline, **swimming** isn't very good on the beaches immediately north of Montezuma – there are lots of rocky outcroppings, the waves are rough and the currents strong. It's better to continue north towards Playa Grande along an attractive, winding **nature trail** (1.5km; 30min), which dips in and out of several coves. There's reasonable swimming here, and decent surfing, as well as a small waterfall at its eastern edge; you may see some people sunbathing nude, though this isn't particularly appreciated by locals.

Montezuma's environs are laced with a number of **waterfalls**, the closest of which is about a one-kilometre walk towards Cabo Blanco, and then another 800m on a signed path through dense forest growth. Always take care with waterfalls, especially in the wet season, on account of **flash floods**, and under no circumstances try to climb them. It is possible to take a **horse ride** (around US$50) to places that are otherwise difficult to reach on foot; contact Zuma Tours (see "Tour operators", below) in town.

You can also visit **Isla Tortuga** from here – it is far cheaper a trip than from Jacó (see p.539). The island is a popular place to **snorkel** or swim in calm, warm and shallow waters, and sunbathe: a one-day trip, including lunch, guide and transport, costs about US$50. **Diving** is also popular; a full-day, two-tank dive costs around US$200.

Arrival and information

By bus Services arrive and depart from just beyond the turning down into the village.

Tour operators Zuma Tours, next to the supermarket on the road towards the beach (☎2642-0024, ⊛www.zumatours.net), is the most reputable tour operator in town, with all the necessary qualifications for snorkelling, diving and canopy tours. For anything they don't offer, they can point you in the direction of good neighbouring operators.

Accommodation

Montezuma is a popular destination and places can fill up, so consider reserving in advance. Camping on the beach is illegal.

Hotel Lucy 500m south of the centre ☎ 2642-0273. A Montezuma stalwart and one of the village's best cheapies: it has a nice upstairs veranda, and clean and simple rooms, some with private cold-water bathrooms and sea views; make sure your door locks properly, however, as not all are as secure as they should be. The owner also offers a laundry service and has an inexpensive eatery next door. US$10

Hotel Lys Just south of the centre ☎ 2642-0642. Bustling but basic Italian-run place, right on the beach, popular with budget travellers who spend more time outside than indoors. Ask to see a few rooms, as they're not all as clean as they might be. You can also camp in the grounds. Camping US$5, doubles US$15

Hotel El Parque Just north of *Pensión Arenas*. This beach-side hotel is an unexciting but acceptable choice, with rudimentary dorms and private rooms aimed at shoestring travellers. While the rooms are musty and the mattresses foamy, it's manageable for a night or two, and the beach is right on the doorstep. Dorms US$10, doubles US$20

The Mochila Inn 150m down the road to Cóbano ☎ 2642-0030. This secluded hostel is a sanctuary for wildlife, especially monkeys, who come by for lunch. Reggae plays gently in the communal area, and the mood is supremely relaxed. Accommodation is pretty basic and back-to-nature – there are even alfresco lavatories. Dorms US$9, doubles US$20, cabins US$30

Pensión Arenas Just north of *Hotel Lys* ☎ 2642-0306. Another hotel right by the beach, the *Arenas* is pretty run-down but has a certain faded charm, with pink-and-white decor and cramped – to say the least – rooms with shared baths. The beach garden is pretty inviting. US$20

Eating and drinking

Bakery Café Opposite Librería Topsy. Pretty murals lend a relaxed vibe to this open-walled café, which is particularly good for breakfast: great eggs, French toast, yoghurt and granola, and pancakes

MONTEZUMA

Cóbano & Paquera

Playa Grande

Librería Topsy

Abastecedor Montezuma

Bus Stop

Sun Trails

Mini-market

Super Montezuma

Chico's Shop

Football Field

Laundry

Bus Stop

PACIFIC OCEAN

N

0   100 m

EATING & DRINKING		ACCOMMODATION	
Bakery Café	1	Hotel Aurora	B
Chico's	5	Hotel Lucy	F
Cocolores	4	Hotel Lys	E
Montesol	6	Hotel El Parque	C
Orgánico	2	The Mochila Inn	A
Soda Naranja	3	Pensión Arenas	D

▼ Cabo Blanco, Cabuya & Mal País

Hotel Aurora In the centre of the village, at the intersection of the road to Cóbano and the road to the beach ☎2642-0051, ⊛www.playamontezuma.net/aurora.htm. This delightfully peaceful all-wooden hotel boasts sea views through the trees and a collection of rooms with private facilities, TVs, fridges, air conditioning and orthopedic mattresses. Hammocks swing in a communal balcony area, which is complete with a bubbling fountain. The German owners are extremely welcoming, and there's a fully equipped kitchen and dining area. US$45

(all around 2000c) are on offer. For those nursing a hangover, the restorative smoothies can work wonders. Service, however, can be slack.

Chico's At the bottom of the road down to the beach. The boisterous *Chico's* attracts a mix of local kids and tourists, who all guzzle from a well-stocked bar and shout to be heard above the music.

Cocolores A popular restaurant in a garden by the beach offering a varied international menu with European, Middle Eastern and Latino dishes including a great coconut fish curry. Good value considering the quality (mains from 4000c), though service is not a strong point. Closed Mon.

Montesol Next door to Zuma Tours. Run by a bubbly group of local ladies who specialize in classic Tican dishes – big, hearty *pintos* for around 1500c and all the other usuals are good value. You can't go wrong with anything on the menu.

Orgánico Next to *Soda Naranjo*, before the *Bakery Café*. This health-conscious café entices you in with its excellent range of healthy (and extremely tasty) falafels, salads, sandwiches (try the Thai-spiced burger) and other dishes. The smoothies and milkshakes are not to be missed either. As at home, you pay more to eat healthy – expect lunch to be around 4500c.

Soda Naranja Opposite *Cocolores*. Hidden behind a wall of leafy foliage, this low-key *soda* serves up delicious *casados* and fresh fish dishes at some of the best prices in town (mains around 3000c). Check out the daily specials.

Directory

Books Librería Topsy, along the beach road with a small library service, sells foreign newspapers, books and maps, and will post stamped mail for you. The charming American owner can offer advice on the area.

Internet Sun Trails central tour office, along the beach road towards Librería Topsy, has an internet café (daily 8am–9pm; 1000c/hr).

Moving on

By boat to: Jacó (1 daily at 9.30am; 1hr; US$40), run by Zuma Tours (see "Tour operators", p.547).

By bus to: Cabo Blanco (departs from the car park on the road towards Mal País; 4 daily at 8.15am, 10.15am, 2.15pm & 6.15pm; 45min–1hr); Cóbano (10–12 daily; 30min); Mal País (3 daily; times change frequently; 1hr 30min); Paquera (7 daily at 6am, 8am, 10am, noon, 2pm, 5pm & 7pm; 2hr); San José (2 daily at 6am & 2.30pm; 5hr).

RESERVA NATURAL ABSOLUTA CABO BLANCO

Some 7km southwest of Montezuma, the **RESERVA NATURAL ABSOLUTA CABO BLANCO** (Wed–Sun 8am–4pm; US$10; ☎2642-0093) is Costa Rica's oldest protected piece of land, covering the entire southwestern tip of the peninsula. The natural beauty of the area is complemented by the array of wildlife found here, including howler monkeys, sloths and snakes.

Hiking and wildlife-watching are the main activities, and visitors can enjoy stunning, if strenuous, **trails** through the evergreen forest while soaking up the sounds of the jungle. The pristine white beaches within the reserve offer a great chance to spot an array of sea birds, including the brown booby, which nests in the islands dotted off the coastline. One particularly attractive trail (5km; 2hr) leads from the ranger centre through the forest to **Playa Cabo Blanco** and **Playa Balsitas** – two very lovely, deserted (depending on the season) spots, though they're not great for swimming. The ranger hut, where you pay your entrance fee, also has trail maps.

Tours are available, but the reserve is easy enough to reach by public transport. An old **bus** rattles between Montezuma and Cabo Blanco four times daily, although it does not always run in the rainy season. A **taxi** from Montezuma costs around US$15. Alternatively, you can **cycle** the 9km down to Cabo Blanco (on a mountain bike; for rentals try Zuma Tours in Montezuma – see "Tour operators", p.547), though mind the height of the two creeks en route, as you might not get through them at high tide. You can't stay in the park, so have return transport planned. Check that you've got enough sunblock and water: the sun is stronger than you might think.

MAL PAÍS AND PLAYA SANTA TERESA

The long beach of **PLAYA SANTA TERESA**, at the tip of the peninsula on the Pacific side, is luring increasing numbers of travellers with its picturesque setting and excellent surf. By contrast, the tranquil muddle of houses, restaurants and breathtaking coastline of neighbouring **MAL PAÍS** remain virtually untouched. Despite the development in the area as a whole – a surf community has fast established itself here – the atmosphere is still chilled and friendly. Everything from daytime activities to nightlife revolves around the beach: try to time your stay for one of the full-moon parties.

Arrival and information

By bus Services from Cóbano (10.30am & 2.30pm; returning 7am & noon; around 30min) and San José (7am & 3.30pm; returning 7.30am & 3.30pm; 5hr 15min) arrive at and depart from Playa Carmen (the intersection at which the right fork takes you to Santa Teresa, and the left to Mal País); services sometimes continue into Mal País and/or Santa Teresa themselves. Santa Teresa is all of one (very) dusty track; a good landmark is *El Pulpo* restaurant, on the right-hand side about 1km from Playa Carmen – it marks the beginning of the village centre. Mal País is far less developed, so ask the bus driver to drop you off at your destination.

By taxi Taxis from Cóbano cost around 12,000c. There are no taxi ranks in Santa Teresa or Mal País but hotels can book for you.
Tour operators Tropical Tours, opposite the Banco Nacional in Playa Carmen (☎2640-1900, ⚙www .tropicaltours-malpais.com), offers everything from canopy tours to horseriding.

Accommodation

Cuesta Arriba 300m north of the football pitch in Santa Teresa ☎2640-0607. In a peaceful spot, this seems like more of a luxury villa than a hostel, with whitewashed walls, attractive arches and spacious communal areas. Dorms are equipped with sturdy bunks and proper mattresses, and there are plenty of hammocks. US$12
Tranquilo Backpackers Just off the main street in Santa Teresa ☎2640-0589, ⚙www.tranquilo backpackers.com. Matching the high standards of its sister hotel in San José (see p.496), the friendly *Tranquilo* provides simple four- to six-bed dorms and a few private doubles, plus a sociable atmosphere, board and bike rentals, and its famous pancake breakfasts. Dorms US$10, doubles US$28
🏃 **Wave Trotter Surf Hostel** Up the hill behind *El Pulpo* in Santa Teresa ☎2640-0805, ⚙www.wavetrotterhostel.com. Run by two Italian guys (and Coco the dog), this is a surfer's paradise, complete with boards lining the walls and chilled beats echoing through the communal area. The only thing that tops the hot-water showers and clean, comfortable dorms and private rooms is the welcoming, familial atmosphere. Dorms US$12, doubles US$30

Eating and drinking

🏃 **Baraka Café** Santa Teresa. This chilled-out café serves tremendous breakfasts: creamy lattes come in huge, comforting mugs, there are fabulous *tostadas* with real raspberry jam and even the *pinto* tastes like a delicacy. Expect to pay 1500–2800c.
Burger Rancho Santa Teresa. The burgers here (2000–4000c) are the real deal – unlike in so many places in Costa Rica – and can be washed down with a delicious milkshake or smoothie.
El Pulpo Santa Teresa ☎2640-0685. Though prices are a little higher than you might expect (mains 3500–6000c), the pizzas and *empanadas* are well worth it. If you're too relaxed to leave your hammock to go for dinner, they'll even deliver.

Directory

Exchange Playa Carmen (at the intersection of the roads from Cóbano, Mal País and Santa Teresa) is home to a Banco Nacional with a temperamental ATM.
Internet Tropical Tours (see "Tour operators", opposite) has a slow internet connection (1000c/hr).
Surf schools Most hostels offer lessons and board rental, but Pura Vida (☎ 2640-0118), on the beach 200m north of the Playa Carmen intersection, is a reputable store that offers lessons and boards.

Moving on

By bus to: Cóbano (4 daily; 45min); Montezuma (2 daily; 45min); San José (2 daily at 7.30am & 3.30pm; 5hr 15min).

NICOYA

Busy **NICOYA** is one of the largest settlements on the peninsula. Though it has little to offer travellers, it's a perfectly good place to spend the night if you're waiting for a bus transfer between the southern areas of the peninsula and Playa Tamarindo. The **Parque Central**, centring on a ramshackle but beautiful white adobe church, is nice to meander through, but there's little else to see.

Arrival and information

By bus The bus station is at Nicoya's southernmost point, just before the road bridge leading out of town. Services from Liberia pull into a stand 300m north of the main bus station.

Accommodation and eating

Cafetería Daniela 100m east of the *parque*. Keenly-priced café with great fajitas (3200c), *casados* (from 2300c) and *pintos* (from 1600c). You can peruse the local art on the walls while you eat. Closed Sun.
Hotel Jenny 100m northwest of the bus station ☎ 2685-5050. Although the decor doesn't appear to have changed since the 1970s, *Jenny* remains the best bet in town, with musty but clean rooms with a/c, TVs, phones and private baths. US$20
Soda Yadira 200m north and 25m east of *Hotel Jenny*. This bustling self-service place promises that you'll be eating within two minutes of walking in,

though you may have to wait for a table. Breakfast costs roughly 1500c, with *casados* around 3000c.

Directory

Exchange Banco Costa Rica, by the park, has an ATM.
Internet Available directly opposite *Hotel Jenny* (daily 9am–8pm; 400c/hr).
Post office On the southwestern point of the Parque Central.

Moving on

By bus to: Liberia (every 30min 3.50am–8.20pm; 2hr); Sámara (roughly hourly; 1hr); San José (10 daily 3am–5pm; 5hr).

PLAYA SÁMARA

SÁMARA, one of the more peaceful, though increasingly upmarket, beach resorts on the Nicoya Peninsula, lies 30km southwest of Nicoya. Compared to other Pacific beach towns, it's quite remote and relatively inaccessible, which makes for a pleasantly relaxing atmosphere. The long, clean beach here is one of the country's calmest for swimming – there's a reef about a kilometre out that takes the brunt of the Pacific's power. The moderate waves also make Sámara a great place to learn to surf.

Arrival and information

By bus Buses arrive along the main road to the beach (Calle Principal), stopping almost at the shore by the football pitch.
Tour operators Tío Tigre (follow the beachfront road towards *Hotel Casa del Mar*, and take the first left; ☎ 8885-3416 or 2656-2161) offers dolphin-watching cruises (US$45), sea kayaking (US$35) and other excursions. Matteo Caretti at the Marea Surf Shop on Calle Principal (☎ 8887-3059 or 2656-1181, ✉ mareasurf@hotmail.com) is a kind, reassuring and professional instructor (private class US$35/hr). Choco's Surf School (☎ 8937-5246 or 8349-7124, ⊕ www.chocossurfschool.com), on the beach, in front of *Soda Sherriff Rustic*, is another good option (private class US$30/hr). Skynet Tours (☎ 2656-0920) hire out motorbikes (US$35/day), scooters (US$30/day) and bicycles (US$10/day).

Accommodation

Staying in Sámara is getting pricier all the time, although during the low season most hotels can offer better rates than those listed here. On high-season weekends you should reserve regardless of how much you're looking to spend.

El Ancla Beachfront road, 200m south of the centre ☎2656-0284. Although a fresh lick of paint is well overdue, rooms are not bad for the price, and come with (cold-water) bathrooms, fans and TVs. Try to get one upstairs – those downstairs are dark. Friendly owner and good restaurant. US$30

Camping Coco Beyond *El Ancla* ☎2656-0496. In a fabulous palm-dotted beach location, this campsite has basic *servicios* and provides electricity until 10pm. Keep an eye on your stuff, as the beach is notorious for thieves at night. US$5

Hotel Belvedere 100m down the road to Carrillo ☎2656-0213, ⊛www .belvederesamara.net. This German-run hotel has stylish rooms with private bathrooms (featuring solar-heated water), fridges and nice touches like tea/coffee makers, plus a couple of apartments with kitchens. It's surrounded by verdant gardens with a good-sized pool and jacuzzi. Rates include a hearty breakfast. Doubles US$55, apartments US$80

Hotel Playa Sámara Behind the football pitch ☎2656-0190 or 8825-5757. One of the more affordable options, whose rudimentary rooms have clean beds, tiled floors and miniscule private showers and toilets, and little else. Note that the music from the club next door pounds late into the night. US$20

Hotel Casa del Mar Beach road, on the left-hand side if coming from the football pitch ☎2656-0264, ⊛www.casadel marsamara.net. Small but perfectly formed hotel boasting whitewashed rooms – with wood fittings, proper mattresses, hot-water bathrooms, air conditioning and personal hammocks – set around a small pool; there are also some cheaper economy rooms with shared facilities. Rates include breakfast, there's private beach access and you even get the company of the hotel's resident parrot, Bella. US$50

Posada Matilori First left along the beach road, then first right ☎2656-0291 or 8817-8042, ⓔposadamatilori@racsa.co.cr. Welcoming guest-house with a collection of spotless (though small) rooms, each with orthopedic mattresses, TV, safe, fan or a/c and shared baths. There's a well-equipped kitchen and free boogie boards, laundry service, internet/wi-fi, and tea and coffee. US$50

Eating

El Ancla At *El Ancla* hotel. With a long menu of fish dishes (4000–7000c) and a pretty setting close to the water, this spot attracts plenty of holidaying Ticos, who know good seafood when they smell it. The fish soup is particularly good.

El Dorado 150m past the Banco Nacional. For outstanding Italian food (3000–8000c), wine and hospitality, look no further. In true Mediterranean style, the Italian owners run things exactly as they would back home. This is one of the finest restaurants in the region. Closed during the low season.

Jardín Marino On C Principal opposite the football pitch. Although the staff could be friendlier, this low-key café/restaurant is worth a look for its reasonably priced *casados* (3200c), rice dishes (from 3000c), burgers (2500c) and grilled fish and chicken (both from 3500c).

Pizza and Pasta a Go-go On C Principal, beyond *Jardín Marino*. Don't let the cheesy name put you off: the pizzas (from 4200c) and pastas (from 39000c) are well prepared, if slightly overpriced. Finish off with a *tiramisù* or mint and chocolate *panna cotta* (both 2500c).

Soda Sheriff Rustic On the beach at the bottom of C Principal. One of the few real *sodas* left in town, with solid wooden tables and chairs shaded by a huge *nigueron* tree. Breakfast 1600c, lunch 1800–2500c.

Drinking and nightlife

Shake Joe's On the beach, 25m south of C Principal. This stunning beach spot is the ideal place for a sunset beer (1200c) or cocktail (from 2500c), though the food is overpriced.

Tutti Frutti On the beach. This distinctive yellow-and-blue bar draws Ticos and tourists alike at the weekend, when the volume, if perhaps not the quality, of the music keeps the party going until 3am. Entry 1000c.

La Vela Latina Near *El Ancla* hotel, on the beach. Sit in rocking-chairs as the friendly staff mix you one of their cracking daiquiris (2000c).

Directory

Books There's a small book exchange at Skynet Tours on C Principal.

Exchange There is a Banco Nacional with ATM and the facilities to exchange dollars on the road to the church.

Internet Skynet Tours on C Principal charge 1000c/hr.

Moving on

By bus to: Nicoya (10–11 daily; 1hr); San José (2 daily at 5.15am & 9.15am; 5hr).

By car The road to Nosara from Sámara is more of a jungle expedition, including two river crossings, so be sure you're in a 4WD.

PLAYAS NOSARA

The stimulating 25km drive from Sámara north to the **PLAYAS NOSARA** runs along shady, secluded dirt and gravel roads punctuated by a few creeks – a 4WD is essential year-round. Generally referred to collectively, there are three rugged beaches in the area – Nosara, Guiones and Pelada – of which **Playa Guiones** is the most impressive, and most popular with surfers. All three, however, are great places for sunbathing and casual exploration. The beach settlement itself is spread over a large area; the main village of Nosara is 3km inland, home to an airstrip and the only (seriously primitive) "petrol station" in the area. Some attempts have been made to limit development in the area – a good deal of the land around the Río Nosara has been designated a wildlife refuge – and the vast majority of people who come to Nosara are North Americans and Europeans in search of quiet and natural surroundings. Unfortunately, budget accommodation is increasingly hard to find.

Arrival and information

By bus Buses arrive at the Abastecedor general store in Nosara proper, via the settlement next to Playa Guiones.

Tourist information Two useful websites are Ⓦ www.nosara.com and www.surfingnosara.com.

Accommodation

Accommodation around the Playas Nosara is of high quality, but there's little for smaller budgets here.

Casa Tucan On the beach road in Playa Guiones, 100m from Banco Costa Rica ℡ 2682-0113, Ⓦ www.casatucanhotel.com. Prices are higher than you'd like, but this place has everything: spacious rooms, relaxing pool area, ping-pong tables and in-house bar and restaurant, all in a lush garden just a stone's throw from the beach. Good for groups. US$80

Gilded Iguana Behind Playa Guiones ℡ 2682-0450, Ⓦ www.thegildediguana.com. Scores highly thanks to its large rooms with high ceilings, private baths, fridges and colourful paintings, as well as its curvy pool, hammocks, bar/restaurant and free wi-fi. US$50

Kaya Sol Back from Playa Guiones ℡ 2682-0000, Ⓦ www.kayasolsurfhotel.com. With a mix of clean and airy dorms, private rooms in bungalows with their own baths, and longer-stay accommodation with kitchens, *Kaya Sol* is justifiably popular. A lovely pool with mini-waterfall, hummingbirds in the garden and an excellent restaurant complete the package. Dorms US$12, doubles US$40

Solo Bueno On the road to Playa Guiones ℡ 2682-1284, Ⓦ www.solobuenohostel.net. The owners of this place are surf addicts, and it shows in the ambience and decor – dorms are basic and the reception area packed with hammocks. You can camp in the grounds (tents for rent) and there are boards and bikes for hire, as well as yoga and surf classes, and regular Twister sessions. Camping US$5, dorms US$15

Eating and drinking

The Nosara area has a decent range of restaurants – many are very good, and prices are not as high as you might expect. There are a number of places in Nosara village, though most of the better restaurants are huddled together near Playa Guiones. The Super Nosara supermarket, in Nosara proper to the south of the football field, is good for self-caterers.

La Casona At the entrance to Nosara proper. This family-run place is a great spot for a tasty and relaxed evening meal; all the *comida típica* is in the 2000c–4000c range, and there's great pizza too.

Gilded Iguana *Gilded Iguana* hotel. Upmarket gringo bar with Mexican food, and well-priced lunch specials, including fish and chips. Mains from 3000c. Live music Tues & Fri.

Rising Sun *Kaya Sol* hotel. An array of vegetarian and vegan dishes are on offer, including tasty salads and dairy-free ice cream, as well as plenty for carnivores (try the burgers). Mains cost from 2500c. Local folk, rock, blues and reggae acts perform regularly. Closed Thurs.

Robin's Café 50m beyond Banco Costa Rica. Enjoy delicious organic sandwiches and wraps (2000–3000c), crêpes, pastries, ice creams and sorbets in the little garden in front of this café. Free wi-fi.

Soda Vanessa In Nosara village. A typical *soda* with filling and well-prepared *casados* for under 1500c, as well as other snacky fare.

Directory

Internet Nosara Office Center has access for US1000c/hr.

Post office Next to the airstrip in Nosara (Mon–Fri 7.30am–6pm).

Moving on

By bus to: Nicoya (3 daily at 7am, noon & 3pm, also Mon–Fri 5am; 2hr); San José (1 daily at 2.45pm; 5–6hr). For Sámara take the bus to Nicoya and stop at Bomba de Sámara (ask the driver). From here you can jump on buses passing through to Sámara from Nicoya.

REFUGIO NACIONAL DE FAUNA SILVESTRE OSTIONAL

Some 8km northwest of Nosara, Ostional and its chocolate-sand beach make up the **REFUGIO NACIONAL DE FAUNA SILVESTRE OSTIONAL**, one of the most important nesting grounds in the country for **Olive Ridley turtles**, which come ashore here to lay their eggs between May and November. If you're in town during the first few days of the *arribadas* – the mass arrival of turtles to lay eggs – you'll see local villagers carefully stuffing bags full of eggs and slinging them over their shoulders. This is quite legal: villagers of Ostional and Nosara are allowed to harvest eggs, for sale or consumption, during the first three days of the season only. Note that you can't swim here – the water's too rough and there are sharks.

It takes about fifteen minutes to drive the gravel-and-stone road from Nosara to the refuge; alternatively you can bike it or take a taxi (around 1500c). No buses run from Nosara, although you may be able to hitch.

PLAYA TAMARINDO

Stretching for a couple of kilometres over a series of rocky headlands, **PLAYA TAMARINDO** is one of the most popular Pacific-coast beaches, though it couldn't be any less Costa Rican in character – rampant development and swarms of tourists are its dominant features. Nonetheless, there is a decent selection of restaurants, a lively beach culture and, during the high season, a strong party vibe.

Tamarindo is also the perfect beach for beginner surfers: gentle waves push against the grey-white sands on a daily basis, all year round. Numerous places **rent surfboards** – typically US$10–15 for a day's rental of a longboard, US$60–90 for a week. Another excellent surf beach, Playa Langosta, lies a few kilometres south of town. You can also take river estuary **tours** through the mangroves of nearby Parque Nacional

---

PLAYA TAMARINDO ACTIVITIES

There are several good operators in town for surfing lessons, which should cost US$40–50: try Iguana Surf, 500m along the road to Playa Langosta (☎2653-0148, Ⓦwww.iguanasurf.net), or local institution Tamarindo Aventuras (☎2653-0108, Ⓦwww.tamarindoaventuras.com). For river estuary and turtle tours, plus canopy, snorkelling, horseriding and kayaking trips, Papagayo Excursions (☎2653-0254, Ⓦwww.tamarindo.com/papagayo), a friendly and professional outfit based 1km north of the town centre on the road to Liberia, offers the best rates.

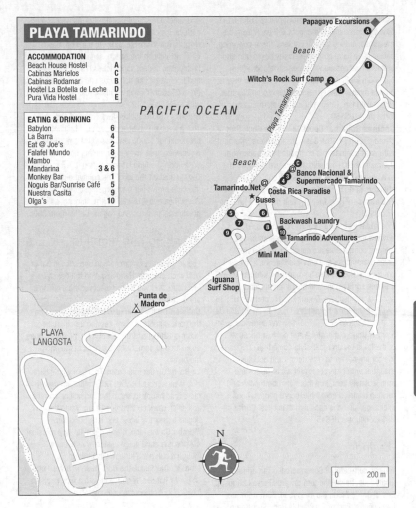

PLAYA TAMARINDO

ACCOMMODATION

Beach House Hostel	A
Cabinas Marielos	C
Cabinas Rodamar	B
Hostel La Botella de Leche	D
Pura Vida Hostel	E

EATING & DRINKING

Babylon	6
La Barra	4
Eat @ Joe's	2
Falafel Mundo	8
Mambo	7
Mandarina	3 & 6
Monkey Bar	1
Noguis Bar/Sunrise Café	5
Nuestra Casita	9
Olga's	10

PACIFIC OCEAN

Papagayo Excursions

Beach

Witch's Rock Surf Camp

Playa Tamarindo

Beach

Banco Nacional &
Supermercado Tamarindo

Tamarindo.Net   Costa Rica Paradise
Buses

Backwash Laundry

Tamarindo Adventures

Mini Mall

Iguana
Surf Shop

Punta de
Madero

PLAYA
LANGOSTA

N

0   200 m

Las Baulas (see p.557) and moonlight turtle tours to the same park (Nov to mid-Feb), as well as windsurfing and snorkelling elsewhere.

Arrival and information

By bus There is no terminal but all buses arrive by the village loop at the southern tip of the high street.

Tourist information There's no tourist office in Playa Tamarindo, but the town's tourist agencies are a good source of information (see box opposite).

Accommodation

Expect to shell out for accommodation in Tamarindo: even the budget stuff here costs more than virtually everywhere else. Book in advance during high season.

Beach House Hostel On the road towards Liberia, roughly 1km from the centre ☎ 2653-0938. Staying at this laidback hostel is a bit like having your very own beach villa – there's a great communal terrace, a/c, proper mattresses and wonderful beach views. Totally chilled surf vibe – so peaceful, in fact, that monkeys swing by in the mornings. Dorms US$13

Cabinas Marielos On the main road ☏ 2653-0141, Ⓦ www.cabinasmarieloscr.com. Set back from the main road, among tropical gardens, these charming cabins have floral curtains, security boxes, a/c and bathrooms accessed via saloon-style doors (the bathroom walls don't reach to the ceiling, so they're not the most private). There are also some cheaper rooms with fan. The owner is well informed and runs turtle tours. US$60

Cabinas Rodamar Opposite Witch's Rock Surf Camp ☏ 2653-0109. Basic backpackers' hangout, with dark cabinas in a compound set back from the main road. That said, rooms are decorated in a cheerful blue, with big beds, cold-water showers and TVs, and aren't bad for the price. The atmosphere is friendly, and there's a kitchen too. US$30

Hostel La Botella de Leche ☏ 2653-2061, Ⓦ www.labotelladeleche.com. Excellent hostel offering comfortable a/c doubles with private baths, hammocks and cow-motif decor, and clean a/c dorms. There's also a small pool, kitchen, free internet, surf lessons and board rentals, and a sociable atmosphere. Dorms US$10, doubles US$36

🏃 **Pura Vida Hostel** Next door to *La Botella de Leche* ☏ 8747-8780, Ⓦ www.puravidahostel .com. A stand-out hostel – and not just because of the huge banana-leaf-style dome that shades the communal areas. The dorms and doubles – the latter with bathrooms and a/c or fans – are immaculately kept, and there are hammocks and rocking chairs, a pool table, board games, book exchange, kitchens and internet access. Dorms US$15, doubles US$45

Eating

You can self-cater at Supermercado Tamarindo, located just before the turn towards Playa Langosta.

Eat @ Joe's Along the main road, 50m from the town centre. Part of the Witch's Rock Surf Camp, this North American hangout serves up rather expensive sushi (from 2500c), plus mains like chicken fajitas (3500–5000c) and vast servings of nachos. Beers cost from 1500c and there's often live music in the evenings.

Falafel Mundo Just off the loop. Tiny joint, with only two tables and a handful of wooden stools at the counter. The menu is similarly small: falafel or shawarma kebabs in pita bread (2500–3000c), with hummus an optional (and highly recommended) extra. Both hit the spot.

Mandarina Two branches: one on the main street, the other near *Falafel Mundo*. It may be part of a (small) chain, but *Mandarina* delivers the goods: thirst-quenching – and hangover-soothing – fruit

and vegetable smoothies (1500c), as well as iced coffees, ice cream and fruit salads.

Noguis Bar/Sunrise Café On the loop. Casual café, virtually on the beach, serving excellent breakfasts, decent sandwiches (1500c), snacks and fine meals like fish tacos and barbecued meats (from 6000c). It's a great place to enjoy the sunset with a cold beer (1200c).

Nuestra Casita Tucked away beyond *Babylon*. This adorable Tico spot dishes up a brilliant *típico* breakfast for 1500c, and *casados* from 2000c in a secluded area away from the mad buzz of town. Well worth the time it takes to find it.

Olga's Just off the loop. The eponymous owner of this café grows her own (organic) coffee in central Costa Rica and it is well worth sampling, as are the breakfasts, pastries and bagels. Coffee from 800c.

Drinking and nightlife

People generally congregate in one chosen bar or club each evening. Hang about on the beach for a few hours and you'll soon discover the evening's bar of choice.

Babylon Off the main road behind the loop. One of the hottest spots in town, serving up cheap beers (around 1200c) and the latest hits. The music goes on till around 4am. Get a taxi back at the end of the night.

La Barra On the main road. This funky little bar/club is most popular with Ticos, although they're more than happy to share the dancefloor. Merengue and salsa carry on till around 1am, when the DJ begins to mix the latest pop hits. Good fun.

Mambo On the loop. Blasting out hip-hop classics, *Mambo* is a good place to start your evening, though it can get a little rowdy later on.

Monkey Bar Inside the *Best Western* hotel. Popular on Friday (Ladies' Night), and with a nice poolside location, but otherwise unmemorable.

Directory

Exchange ATMs are dotted all over town, notably on the main road.
Internet Interlink High Speed café, 10m from *Cabinas Marielos* towards the loop, has quick connections (1000c/hr).
Laundry Lavandería Backwash (1500c/kg) is left as you turn up towards Playa Langosta from the main beach road.

Moving on

By bus to: Liberia (9–12 daily 4.30am–5.30pm; 1hr 30min–2hr); San José (3 daily at 3am, 5.30am &

7am; 5hr 30min); Santa Cruz, for points south (3 daily at 6am, 8.30am & noon; 1hr 30min).

PARQUE NACIONAL MARINO LAS BAULAS

On the Río Matapalo estuary between Conchal and Tamarindo, **PARQUE NACIONAL MARINO LAS BAULAS** (daily 8am–5pm; open for guided night tours in season; US$10, US$25 including tour; ☎2653-0470) is less a national park than a reserve, created to protect the nesting grounds of endangered **leatherback turtles**. These creatures, which come ashore to nest from October to mid-February, have laid their eggs at **Playa Grande** for possibly millions of years, and it's now one of the few remaining such nesting sites in the world. However, developers appear to have been given carte blanche in the area, the effects of which remain to be seen. The beach itself offers a beautiful sweep of light-coloured sand, and outside laying season you can surf, though the swimming is rough.

Around 200m from the park entrance, the impressive **El Mundo de la Tortuga** exhibition (daily 2–6pm, later when turtles are nesting; US$5) includes an audio-guided tour in English and some stunning turtle photographs. You'll learn about the leatherback's habitats and reproductive cycles, along with the threats they face and current conservation efforts. There's also a souvenir shop and a café.

There are two official entrances to Playa Grande, though **tickets** can only be bought at the southern entrance, where the road enters the park near the *Villa Baulas*. Booking your tickets in advance (on the park number) is highly recommended, as numbers are strictly limited. There is no public transport to the park. Most people visit by **boat** from Tamarindo, a service that usually comes as part of tour packages, or can be booked when you call to reserve your entrance ticket.

PLAYA DEL COCO

Thirty-five kilometres west of Liberia, **PLAYA DEL COCO** was the first Pacific beach to hit the big time with weekending Costa Ricans from the Valle Central. It's turned out to be something of a nightmare: a cross between an upmarket resort filled with imposing hotels, casinos and restaurants, and a hot spot for budget travellers in search of Jaegermeister and a dancefloor. Playa del Coco is fine for a couple of days: surfers use it as a jumping-off point for nearby Witch's Rock and playas Hermosa and Panamá, the nightlife is lively, and there are some good diving operators. But beyond this, it is of limited appeal.

What to see and do

The main track down to the beach is a noisy, dirty melange of roaring 4WDs and souvenir markets, while the area nearer the beach is a little quieter, with the football pitch, the budget accommodation and some funky cocktail bars that are packed out most nights. The water in the bay is rather polluted, and not very appealing for swimming. Diving, however, is a popular activity in the region, although there is no beach diving – dive centres take you to the islands off the coast, such as **Isla Santa Catalina**, 20km off shore.

Arrival and information

By bus Buses stop at the *parque* at the bottom of the main road, virtually on the beach – ask in the *sodas* on the beach if you need to check schedules.
Tour operators Rich Coast Diving, on the main road about 300m from the beach (☎2670-0176, Ⓦwww.richcoastdiving.com), organizes snorkelling (US$45) and scuba trips (from US$65), and rents out mountain bikes. Summer Salt Dive Centre, next to *Jardín Tropical* (☎2670-0308, Ⓦwww.summer-salt.com), is another reputable outfit, and also offers dolphin- and whale-watching excursions.

Accommodation

Coco has lots of basic cabinas. Reserve in advance for high-season weekends, but you can probably get away with turning up on spec midweek.

Cabinas Chale 500m north of the football pitch ☎2670-0036, 🅦www.cabinaschaleplayasdelcoco .com. Plain but acceptable doubles come with private baths, fans and fridges. The apartments sleeping up to six are a good choice if you're in a group. There's also a small pool and free wi-fi. Doubles US$48, apartments US$110

Cabinas Coco Azul Behind the church ☎2670-0431, 🅔cabinascocoazul_cr@yahoo.com. A reliable, good-value choice, offering clean and pleasant cabins with hot-water private bathrooms and fans or a/c set around a garden with mango trees. The owners are a good source of information too. US$35

Cabinas Jivao Near *Coco Alegre* ☎2670-0769. Although they're a bit tatty, the rooms aren't bad for the price, featuring bunks, clean cold-water showers and fans; some also have kitchenettes. Book in advance, particularly at weekends. US$10

🏃 **Ruby's** On the road leading to Mapache ☎2389-6746. Quiet, comfortable and friendly, this hotel boasts bright rooms with firm mattresses, hot-water baths, a/c and an attractive courtyard complete with barbecue and shaded tables. Security is tight, and the American owner is relaxed and unobtrusive. Although on the main road, it is quiet and only a 10-minute walk to the town's best bars. US$35

Eating and drinking

Coco Coffee Company Beneath *Papagayo Seafood*. Slick café selling top cappuccinos, lattes and espressos, but overpriced sandwiches and snacks (2000–3500c).

Coco Mar Right on the beach to the right of the *parque*, this is where it all kicks off after the bars close, with cocktails aplenty and a young, enthusiastic crowd.

Jardín Tropical The best breakfast in town is served overlooking the *parque* at the far end of town. A hearty *gallo pinto* will set you back 2200–2800c.

Lizard Lounge At the corner of the right turn to *Ruby's* hotel. The most popular bar on the strip serves great cocktails (around 3000c) to a dance and pop soundtrack.

Papagayo Seafood On the main road, opposite the casino on the second floor. Upmarket restaurant decked out in nautical artefacts and fairy lights. The seafood-orientated menu is quite expensive but good value – the sea bass, in particular, is superb, and you definitely won't leave hungry. Mains around 7500c.

Soda Papagayo On the main drag, opposite the casino hotel. A colourful *soda* in the centre of the strip that plays chilled beats and serves Tico snacks and meals (from 1500c).

Directory

Exchange Banco Nacional (Mon–Fri 8.30am–3.45pm), 500m up the main road from the beach next to the supermarket Luperón, will change dollars and travellers' cheques and has an ATM.

Health The Coco Medical Centre (☎2670-1557, 🅦www.crsalud.com) is in the Centro Comercial El Pueblito, signposted from *Lizard Lounge* on the road to *Ruby's*.

Internet Café Pillis (daily 8am–9pm; 1000c/hr), opposite the football pitch on the main road, above the souvenir shop on the second floor.

Post office In front of the bus station, opposite the *parque* at the bottom of the main road (Mon–Fri 7.30am–5pm).

Moving on

By bus to: Liberia (hourly 5.30am–11am & 1–6pm; 45min–1hr); San José (3 daily at 4am, 8am & 2pm; 5hr).

PLAYA PANAMÁ AND PLAYA HERMOSA

Sheltered from the full force of the Pacific, the clear blue waters and volcanic sands at **PLAYA PANAMÁ** and **PLAYA HERMOSA**, just up the road to the north of Playa del Coco, provide the perfect environment for a couple of days' relaxation, or even as a day-trip from Coco. **Diving** is the highlight of the area; jet-skis and horseriding tours are also available, but for far higher prices than in other parts of the country.

Arrival and information

By bus 8 daily buses run between Liberia and Playa Hermosa (1hr 20min).

By taxi A taxi from Playa del Coco costs around 2500c.

Tour operators Diving Safaris de Costa Rica, in Playa Hermosa just beyond the supermarket on the main road to the beach (☎2672-1259, ⊛www .costaricadiving.net), is the diving authority in the region: a one-day session costs from US$80.

Accommodation

Unfortunately, budget accommodation at Playa Panamá is nonexistent, and is restricted to only a few options at Playa Hermosa.

Ecotel On the beach 500m north of the main road ☎2672-0175. This place has a lovely relaxed atmosphere, though you should be prepared for virtually no privacy – the walls are wooden, the floors are sandy and there's a soundtrack of howler monkeys and birdcalls. Guests can use the kitchen and borrow snorkelling gear. US$20

Iguana Inn 25m from the beach on the left side of the main road ☎2672-0065. Easily the best low-cost lodge in town, offering comfortable rooms with private hot-water baths, TVs, a/c and small balconies overlooking a lovely pool and secluded garden. US$30

Guanacaste

Guanacaste Province, bordered to the north by Nicaragua and the Pacific Ocean to the west, is distinctly different from the rest of Costa Rica. While little remains of the **sabanero** (cowboy) culture, music and folklore for which the region is famous, there is undeniably something special about the place. The **landscape** is certainly beautiful, even though much of it has come about essentially through the slaughter of tropical dry forest: the wide, rolling plains and the brooding humps of volcanoes are washed in muted earthy tones. Its **history**, too, is distinct: if not for a very close vote in 1824, Guanacaste might have been part of Nicaragua. While it is the province's beaches (roughly two-thirds of the Nicoya Peninsula is in Guanacaste) that attract the most visitors, the mud pots and stewing sulphur waters of **Parque Nacional Rincón de la Vieja**,

and the tropical dry forest cover of **Parque Nacional Santa Rosa**, draw scores of nature aficionados to the interior every year.

LIBERIA

Despite the busloads of visitors arriving via the nearby international airport every day, the provincial capital of **LIBERIA** happily remains unchanged: it's still the epitome of dignified (if somewhat static) rural life. Most travellers use the town as a jumping-off point for the national parks of **Rincón de la Vieja** and **Santa Rosa**, an overnight stop to or from the **beaches** of the Nicoya Peninsula (see p.546) or a break on the way to Nicaragua. It is no hardship, however, to while away a little longer in the "**ciudad blanca**" (white city, on account of its whitewashed houses). Everything you need for a relaxing stay of a day or two is here – limited but well-priced accommodation, and a few good places to eat.

Liberia also boasts several lively **festivals**, one of which is in early March, when there's ten days of parades, bands, fireworks and bull-running. On July 25, **El Día de la Independencia** celebrates Guanacaste's independence from Nicaragua with parades, rodeos, fiestas and roving marimba bands.

What to see and do

The town is arranged around its large **Parque Central**, properly called Parque Mario Cañas Ruiz. It's dedicated to *el mes del anexión*, the month of the annexation (July), celebrating the all-important fact that Guanacaste is not in Nicaragua. This is one of the loveliest central plazas in the country, ringed by benches and tall palms that shade gossiping locals. Its **church** is startlingly modern and somewhat out of place.

About 600m away at the eastern end of town, the colonial **Iglesia de**

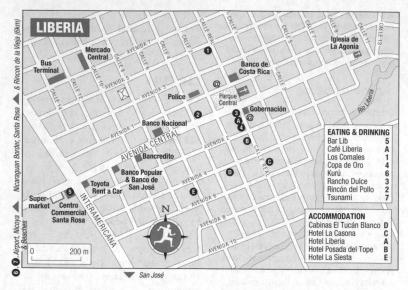

EATING & DRINKING

Bar Lib	5
Café Liberia	A
Los Comales	1
Copa de Oro	4
Kurú	6
Rancho Dulce	3
Rincón del Pollo	2
Tsunami	7

ACCOMMODATION

Cabinas El Tucán Blanco	D
Hotel La Casona	C
Hotel Liberia	A
Hotel Posada del Tope	B
Hotel La Siesta	E

la Agonía is more arresting, with a mottled yellow facade. On the verge of perpetual collapse – it has had a hard time with earthquakes – it's almost never open, but you could try shoving the heavy wooden door and hope the place doesn't collapse around you. The town's most interesting street is **Calle Real** (also known as Calle Central). In the nineteenth century this was the entrance to Liberia, and practically the entire thoroughfare has been restored to its original – and strikingly beautiful – colonial simplicity.

Arrival and information

By air Liberia's international airport is 12km west of the town. Flights arrive largely from North America, although there are also seasonal charters from Europe. A taxi into Liberia costs around US$15, or there are frequent buses.

By bus All buses except those arriving from and leaving to San José and Peñas Blancas will arrive at the Terminal Liberia, at the northwestern edge of town. The Pulmitan Terminal, for San José and Peñas Blancas services, is one block southeast of Terminal Liberia.

By car From the northbound Interamericana, turn right into town at the major intersection (large enough for traffic lights). This brings you to the town centre and the park. Make note of the petrol station on the corner too – it is often used as a landmark. The left-forking road at this intersection takes you to the beaches.

Tourist information Staff at *Hotel Liberia* and *Hotel Posada del Tope* can answer questions on the local area and provide information on a shuttle service to Rincón de la Vieja (US$20).

Accommodation

Cabinas El Tucán Blanco Av 4, C 4/6 ☎ 2666-7740, ✉ tucanblanco@yahoo.com. Although they're not much to look at, these cabinas are a fine choice. Set back off the road, with parking in front, they have plenty of space, a/c, clean bathrooms, kitchenettes and TVs. The owners are lovely and security is top notch. US$30

Hotel La Casona Av 6, C 0 ☎ 2666-2971, ✉ casona@rasca.co.cr. This sleepy guesthouse has a collection of old-fashioned doubles with private showers, TVs and ancient a/c units – they're basic and a bit gloomy, but fine for a night. Staff are friendly, and there's a handy laundry next door. US$20

Hotel Liberia C 0, 75m south of the Parque Central ☎ 2666-0161, ⊕ hotelliberia.net/about. In a historic home, this hostel has a great setup for backpackers: hammocks in the sunny courtyard, wi-fi, laundry service, book exchange and informative staff. The simple rooms and dorms have brightly painted walls or cheerful murals. Rates include a free cocktail. Reservations and deposits are required in high season. Dorms US$10, doubles US$26

Hotel Posada del Tope C 0, 150m south of the municipal government building ☎&℻ 2666-3876. Another popular place in a beautiful old house: the bare-bones rooms in the main building are clean but stuffy, so opt for the brighter and only slightly more expensive ones across the street in the annexe, which are set around a charming courtyard. All have fans and shared bathrooms. US$20

🏃 **Hotel La Siesta** C 6, Av 4/6 ☎ 2666-0878, Ⓔ lasiestaliberia@hotmail.com. This attractive hotel has comfortable a/c doubles with private bathrooms and cable TV, set around a courtyard with a fountain and small pool. There are also simpler fan rooms, with TV and private showers and toilets (though bizarrely no sinks), in a nearby annexe. In addition, there's a restaurant, laundry service, free internet and a good restaurant. US$20

Eating

Local treats include *natilla* (sour cream) eaten with eggs or *gallo pinto* and tortillas. For a real feast, try the various *desayunos guanacastecos* (Guanacastecan breakfasts). For rock-bottom-cheap lunches, head for the stalls in the bus terminal. Closed at the time of research, though likely to reopen, *Las Tinajas*, on the west side of the Parque Central, is a great spot for an inexpensive beer and burger.

Café Liberia C 0, next to *Hotel Liberia*. In a stunning nineteenth-century property, with grand wooden doors and a frescoed ceiling, *Café Liberia* has perfectly brewed cappuccinos and lattes (600–1400c), plus crêpes, bagels and sandwiches. Closed Sun.

🏃 **Los Comales** C 0, Av 3/5. Run by a women's co-operative, this *soda* has a wonderfully homely atmosphere. As well as economical *pintos* (from 1400c), they serve filling *casados* (from 2250c) – if you have an adventurous palate, try the one with cow tongue.

Copa de Oro C 0, Av 2. An unassuming joint, with sport on the TV, quick service and an intriguing mural on the far wall (an ode to a broken heart). The menu features hearty *casados* (3300c), *arroz cons* (from 2800c) and tapas (from 2000c).

Rancho Dulce C 0, Av Central. With its bamboo walls, tiny stools and laidback air, *Rancho Dulce* feels like more like a beach bar than a *soda*. Throughout the day it does a roaring trade in *casados* (from 1500c), sandwiches and *refrescos*.

Rincón del Pollo Av Central, 50m west of the Parque Central. A simple place where just 1500c will get you half a roast chicken, tortillas and salad.

Drinking and nightlife

Bar Lib On the Interamericana, in the Plaza Santa Rosa Centro Comercial. The swankiest bar in town, with a pumping sound system (mainly dance music) and a pricey cocktail list. During the daily 5–9pm happy hour, a beer costs 900c.

Kurú 200m west of the Interamericana down the road to the beaches. The town's main disco gets lively at weekends, with salsa, merengue and other Latin sounds.

Tsunami Across the road from *Kurú* and down a side street. This smaller disco is dead apart from Saturday nights, when it's great fun, serving international beers (1500c).

Entertainment

Liberia's main Saturday-evening activities involve locals parading around the Parque Central in their finery, having an ice cream and maybe going to the cinema at the Cine Liberia, in the shopping mall a kilometre south of the main Interamericana intersection.

Directory

Exchange Av Central is littered with banks, including Banco Nacional and Banco Costa Rica, both across from the Parque Central. Both have ATMs and change dollars and travellers' cheques.

Internet Cybermania (daily 8am–10pm), in a small business centre on the north side of the Parque Central, is air conditioned and cheap, as is Planet Internet (Mon–Sat 8am–10pm, Sun 9am–9pm), on C Real just off the Parque Central. Both charge around 600c/hr.

Post office Between Av 3 and Av 5 in the white house across from the empty square field bordered by mango trees (Mon–Fri 7.30am–6pm, Sat 7.30am–noon).

Moving on

By air Both Sansa and Nature Air operate daily flights from Liberia airport to the main international airport near Alajuela.

By bus to: La Cruz/Peñas Blancas and Nicaragua (5am, 5.30am, then hourly 6am–6pm; 1hr 45min); Nicoya (Mon–Sat every 20–30min 4.30am–8.30pm, Sun hourly 8am–6pm; 2hr); Playa Panamá via Playa Hermosa (8 daily 4.30am–5.30pm; 1hr 20min); Playa Tamarindo (hourly 3.50am–6pm; 1hr 30min–2hr); Playa del Coco (hourly 5am–11am, then 12.30pm, 2.30pm & 6.30pm; 1hr); Puntarenas

(8 daily 5am–3.30pm; 3hr); San José (hourly 3am–10am, every two hours noon–8pm; 4hr 30min); Santa Rosa (take the bus for the Nicaraguan border and ask to be dropped at the park; 40min).

PARQUE NACIONAL RINCÓN DE LA VIEJA

The earth around **PARQUE NACIONAL RINCÓN DE LA VIEJA** (daily 7am–5pm; US$10; ☎2661-8139), northeast of Liberia, is actually alive and breathing: **Volcán Rincón de la Vieja**, the park's namesake, is still active. Though it last erupted in 1991, rivers of lava continue to boil beneath the thin epidermis of ground, while **mud pots** (*pilas de barro*) bubble, and puffs of steam rise out of lush foliage, signalling sulphurous subterranean springs. The dramatically dry surrounding landscape, meanwhile, varies from rock-strewn savanna to patches of tropical dry forest and deciduous trees, culminating in the blasted-out vistas of the volcano crater itself. This is great terrain for **camping**, **riding** and **hiking**, with a comfortable, fairly dry heat – although it can get damp and cloudy at the higher elevations around the crater. **Birders**, too, will enjoy Rincón de la Vieja, as there are more than two hundred species in residence.

What to see and do

The park has **hiking trails** for all enegry levels, which begin from one of the two *puestos* (ranger stations) – Santa María to the east, and Las Pailas to the west. Most start from Las Pailas, although the main one – the demanding uphill track to the volcano's **crater**, which can be tackled on foot, horseback or a combination of the two – can be embarked on from both. This is one of the best hikes, if not *the* best hike, in the country. A variety of elevations and habitats reveals hot springs, sulphur pools, bubbling mud pots and fields of purple orchids, plus of course the great smoking volcano

at the top. It is possible to hike without a **guide**, but should you wish to organize a guided trek ask at Las Pailas (☎2661-8139). Alternatively, many hotels In Liberia offer treks. Ring ahead before you start out, as the trail is often closed due to low visibility or high winds.

There are more **gentle walks** in the Las Pailas sector, and one in the Santa María sector, that take you to fumaroles and mud pots, and you can also hike to two waterfalls, the *cataratas escondidas*. From the Las Pailas entrance, a very satisfying 6km circular trail takes you around some unusual natural features, with bubbling mud pots and a mini-volcano as well as steaming sulphurous vents that make for a highly atmospheric experience. The *puesto* Santa María is an old colonial house, rumoured to once be the country retreat of US President Lyndon Johnson, and has some rustic sleeping arrangements (see below).

Arrival and information

There is no public transport to the park. A 4WD taxi from Liberia costs US$25–30.

For Sector Pailas Travel through the hamlet of Curubandé, 6km north of Liberia along the Interamericana. The 20km road (1000c to pass through a private section) is a dirt track and the signpost modest, so keep your eyes peeled. Hitching may be feasible along this road; if you're driving, a 4WD is recommended year-round, and compulsory in the wet season. Transfers from *Hotel Posada del Tope* and *Hotel Liberia* (see p.560) are available for US$20.

For Santa María Go through Liberia's Barrio La Victoria in the northeast of the town (ask for the *estadio* – the football stadium – from where it's a signed 24km drive to the park). Transfers are available from Liberia hotels and the *Rinconcito Lodge* (see opposite).

Accommodation

Most budget travellers stay in Liberia: reasonably priced accommodation around the park is scarce, and there are no restaurants. There are campsites (US$2) at both ranger stations – Santa María is better equipped – with pit toilets, showers and grills, but you must bring your own food and drinking water. Be prepared for cold nights, strong winds and fog.

Rinconcito Lodge On the road to Santa María ☎2666-2764, ⓦwww.rinconcitolodge.com. The cheapest option close to the park, this eco-farm has simple, good-value cabinas with hot-water private baths. Horseriding and trekking tours are also on offer (US$35–50), and the owners are friendly and helpful. Meals and packed lunches are available, and you can camp. Camping US$3, cabinas US$35

PARQUE NACIONAL SANTA ROSA

PARQUE NACIONAL SANTA ROSA (daily 8am–4pm; US$10; ☎2666-5051), 35km north of Liberia, is hugely popular, thanks to its good trails, great surfing (though poor swimming) and turtle-spotting opportunities.

Santa Rosa has an amazingly diverse topography for its size, ranging from mangrove swamp to rare tropical dry forest and savanna. With a staggering biodiversity of mammals, birds, amphibians and reptiles, Santa Rosa is also of prime interest to anyone keen to do some wildlife-spotting. Jaguars and pumas prowl the park, but you're unlikely to see them. Coati, coyotes and peccaries, on the other hand, are often found snuffling around watering holes. Between July and November (peaking in September and October), the sight of hundreds of **Olive Ridley turtles** (*lloras*) nesting on Playa Nancite puts all other animal sightings into obscurity; a maximum of twenty visitors are allowed access to the nesting area each day (call ahead to reserve your place). Though too rough for swimming, the picturesque **beaches** of Naranjo and Nancite, about 12km down a bad road from the administration centre, are popular with serious **surfers**.

Arrival and information

By bus Buses from Liberia (use the Peñas Blancas/La Cruz service) run past the entrance. Tell the driver well in advance that you want to stop at the park. The entrance hut is signed from the Interamericana; it is a 7km walk from here to the campsite and administration/visitors' centre.
By car Go north from Liberia on the Interamericana (roughly 35km).
Tourist information The visitors' centre, a 7km walk from the Interamericana, is effectively the main reception (☎2666-5051), where you pay your entrance fee and pick up information.

Accommodation and eating

The camping facilities (pay at visitors' centre) are some of the best in the country. Watch your fires (the area is a tinderbox in the dry season), take plastic bags for your food, do not leave anything edible in your tent (it will be stolen by scavenging coati) and carry plenty of water. Buy food before entering the park. Drinks are sold at the visitors' centre, but little else.
La Casona Near the visitors' centre. This campground has bathrooms and grill pits. US$2
Playa Naranjo On the beach. Camping with picnic tables and grill pits, a ranger's hut with outhouses and showers – and from time to time, a boa constrictor in the roof. Only open outside the turtle-nesting season. US$2

INTO NICARAGUA: PEÑAS BLANCAS

Peñas Blancas (daily 6am–8pm), the main crossing point into Nicaragua, is emphatically a border post, and not a town. Arrive as early as possible – you'll be lucky to get through the procedures in less than ninety minutes. Things run most smoothly if you come with Tica Bus – all passengers are processed together. Costa Rican and Nicaraguan border officials are quite strict. Few travellers will need a visa for Nicaragua, but it's worth checking the current situation before leaving San José. **Exit stamps** are given on the Costa Rican side, where there's a restaurant. For travellers entering Nicaragua from Costa Rica, there is a fee of US$10. Most nationalities pay nothing to enter Costa Rica. Moneychangers are always on hand and have colones, córdobas and dollars. After getting your Costa Rican exit stamp, it's a short walk north to the barrier. If you're coming from Nicaragua, the last San José bus leaves at 7pm and the last Liberia bus at 6.30pm.

The Zona Norte

Costa Rica's **Zona Norte** ("northern zone") spans the hundred-odd kilometres from the base of the Cordillera Central to just short of the mauve-blue mountains of southern Nicaragua. Cut off from the rest of the country by a lack of roads, the Zona Norte has developed a unique character, with independent-minded farmers and Nicaraguan refugees making up large segments of the population. Many people from the north hold a special allegiance to, and pride in, their area. Less obviously picturesque than many parts of the country, the entire region nonetheless has a distinctive appeal, with lazy rivers snaking across steaming plains and flop-eared cattle languishing beneath the trees.

Most travellers only venture here to see **Volcán Arenal**. To the east is the humid **Sarapiquí** area, with its tropical forest **ecolodges** and research stations of **La Selva** and **Rara Avis**. Further

north, the remote flatlands are home to the increasingly accessible **Refugio Nacional de Vida Silvestre Caño Negro**, which harbours an extraordinary amount of birdlife. There's a serviceable **bus** network, though if you're travelling outside the La Fortuna or Sarapiquí areas, consider renting a car. The area around Arenal is best equipped for visitors; between Boca de Arenal and Los Chiles in the far north, there is a real shortage of accommodation, though fuel and food are in good supply.

LA FORTUNA

That the north attracts the numbers of visitors it does is mainly due to majestic **Volcán Arenal**, one of the most active volcanoes in the Western Hemisphere. Just 6km away, **LA FORTUNA DE SAN CARLOS**, or **La Fortuna**, as it is more often called, was once a simple agricultural town but has boomed beyond recognition due to its perfect location as a jumping-off point for volcano-based activities. There's little to do in the town itself except book tours, eat, sleep and look at views of the volcano – when you can see it; the summit is often shrouded

ACCOMMODATION
Arenal Backpackers	E
Cabinas Sissy	I
Cabinas Las Tinajas	A
La Choza Inn	B
Essence Arenal	F
Gringo Pete's	D
Gringo Pete's Too	G
Hotel Dorothy	J
La Posada Inn	C
Sleep Inn Guesthouse	H

LA FORTUNA

AVENIDA VOLCÁN

Banco Nacional

AVENIDA FORTUNA

School

Mercado Artesanía

Parque Central

Taxi Rank
Banco Popular

Police

Eagle Tours

Laundry

Desafío

Pura Vida Tours

AVENIDA CENTRAL

Supermarket

Aventuras Arenal

Laundry

Jacamar Naturalist Tours

Bus Terminal

AVENIDA ARENAL

N

EATING & DRINKING
Choza de Laurel	4
Gecko Gourmet	1
Lava Lounge Bar and Grill	2
Lava Rocks	5
La Parada	3
Saltamar	6

0   150 m

Baldi Hot Springs, Los Lagos, Volcán Arenal & Tilarán

San Carlos, San José, Caño Negro & Puerto Viejo

J, Cataratas La Fortuna & San Ramón

TOURS AND ACTIVITIES IN LA FORTUNA

Competition between tour agencies in La Fortuna is fierce: you may save a few dollars by going with the cheapest agency, but could end up on a badly organized tour with under-qualified guides. You should go with an established tour operator, rather than the freelance "guides" who may approach you, some of whom have been involved in serious incidents over the years.

Aventuras Arenal 150m east of Parque Central (☎2479-9133, ⓦwww.arenal adventures.com). Professionally-run trips by a reliable operator, plus transport to just about anywhere in the country.

Desafío Tours West of the church ☎2479-9464, ⓦwww.desafiocostarica .com. Friendly, efficient and community-aware rafting specialists who run trips on the Río Toro (US$85) and guided hikes up Cerro Chato (US$75). Their Monteverde transfer includes a horseriding excursion (US$85), and they can arrange flights, tours and accommodation anywhere in the country.

Eagle Tours In *La Choza Inn* ☎2479-9091, ⓦwww.eagletours.net. Recommended trips with well-qualified guides. Volcano tours (US$50) include the entrance fee to the Baldi hot springs (Tabacón costs US$100); if you don't see lava, they'll take you to the viewpoint the next day for free. They also have trips to Caño Negro (see p.568; US$55), and jeep–boat–jeep transfers to Monteverde (US$25).

Jacamar Next to *Lava Rocks* ☎2479-9767, ⓦwww.arenaltours.com. Runs volcano tours (US$70), trips to Caño Negro (US$73) and rafting on the Río Peñas Blancas (US$65–85).

Pura Vida Tours Opposite the Parque Central ☎2479-9045, ⓦwww.puravidatours .com. In addition to the usual tours, this company runs a shuttle and boat service to Tortuguero (see p.516; US$40).

in clouds for days at a time, and glimpses of rolling lava from the town are rare. La Fortuna also has excellent bus connections, and is something of a transport hub for the region.

Beware of opportunistic **theft** in La Fortuna: you're not likely to experience anything too malicious, but don't walk around alone late at night, and avoid "guides" offering their services on the street.

What to see and do

The natural wonders of the region lend themselves to both active and relaxing pursuits; from tough hikes to relaxing in hot springs, there is something for everyone.

Volcán Arenal

Volcán Arenal is spectacular, whether admired from La Fortuna, where its slopes are still a lush green, or from the barren and desolate western face, where the foliage has been gradually scorched by the ash and lava that tumble down the side every day. You can get a bit closer by heading to the **Parque Nacional Volcán Arenal** (daily 8am–4pm; US$10); though fences are in place to keep you from tackling the volcano's slopes, the park does have some good **trails**, including the four-kilometre "Tucanes" trail that passes through the section of forest flattened by the 1968 eruption. You can't visit the park after dark except by taking one of the **night tours** that leave La Fortuna every evening at about 3 or 4pm (see above for operators). Although most tours run even when it's cloudy, few offer refunds if you don't see anything, so you might want to wait for a clear evening before signing up.

Travelling to the park independently, the 12km **taxi ride** from La Fortuna to the west side of the volcano costs roughly US$35, so unless you're in a group, it's cheaper to take a tour. Alternatively, the **bus** to Tilarán can drop off at the park entrance, though the return journey can be a bit tricky – unless you manage to connect with the infrequent return bus, your only option is to hitch back with other park visitors.

Hot springs

Three lodges, all approximately 13km west of La Fortuna, offer visitors the opportunity to watch the volcano's pyrotechnics while soaking in **hot springs**. **El Tabacón** (daily 10am–10pm; US$70 for a morning or evening session, including a meal, US$90 for an all-day pass with two meals; ☎2391-1900, ⓦwww.tabacon.com) is the most expensive, and a bit pretentious. **Baldi Hot Springs** is cheaper and more relaxed (daily 10am–10pm; US$25; ⓦwww.baldi hotsprings.cr). Agencies in town (see box, p.565) can often get you a slightly cheaper price.

Cataratas La Fortuna

You can make an excursion to La Fortuna's stunning **waterfalls** (Cataratas La Fortuna), which sit amid some beautiful jungle terrain just 6km from the south side of the church in town. A taxi (3500–4000c) can take you right to the entrance office, or it's a good uphill trek on foot. Once in, it is a steep climb down a winding overgrown path and a gruelling return journey, but the waterfalls are well worth the effort. At the entrance to the *cataratas* you'll also find the start of a hardcore 5km hike up **Cerro Chato**, a smaller volcanic peak that clings to Arenal's skirts, and offers views of its big brother.

Arrival

By bus The bus station is 100m south of the church.

Accommodation

Budget accommodation is everywhere in La Fortuna, though the lodges around the periphery are, almost without exception, for the moneyed traveller. For those with their own tents, there's also a small campsite (US$5) close to the entrance of Parque Nacional Volcán Arenal.

🏃 **Arenal Backpackers** 500m west of the town centre ☎2479-7000, ⓦwww .arenalbackpackersresort.com. With its neatly tended lawns, pool lined with palm trees, and wet bar, *Arenal Backpackers* feels more like a mini-resort than a hostel – something reflected in its prices. Dorms and rooms are spacious, clean and bright (the latter have private baths, a/c and TVs). There's free internet, excellent security and camping, too. Service sometimes fails to match these high standards, but it's still arguably the best hostel in the country. Camping US$14, dorms US$14, doubles US$56

Cabinas Sissy 100m south and 125m west of the central park ☎2479-9256, ⓔhotelreyarenal @hotmail.com. Friendly budget-traveller hangout with a variety of rooms with fans and private or shared hot-water baths; some have TVs. There's also a simple shared kitchen, and you can camp too. Camping US$5, doubles US$20

Cabinas Las Tinajas 100m north and 25m west of the central park ☎2479-9308, ⓔcbtinajas@gmail .com. Just four cabinas, each sparklingly clean, with private bathroom, TV, fan and the odd homely touch like pot plants and bowls of potpourri. There are rocking chairs on the terrace, and the owners are very friendly. A good deal all round. US$20

La Choza Inn 300m east of Parque Central ☎2479-9361, ⓦwww.lachozainnhostel.com. In a quiet part of the town, this efficiently run hotel has clean dorms and comfortable doubles with bathrooms, fans and coffee makers; a/c, TVs and fridges cost a little extra. There's free internet and wi-fi and a communal kitchen. Guests get a discount at Eagle Tours (see box, p.565). Dorms US$8, doubles US$35

Gringo Pete's 300m southeast of the central park ☎2479-8521, ⓔgringopetes2003@yahoo.com. The most popular place for real shoestring travellers, whose boxy dorms and private rooms have little natural light but fantastically low prices, as well as sociable communal areas, kitchen and free coffee. The newer *Gringo Pete's Too*, near *Cabinas Sissy*, is a touch more comfortable. Dorms US$5, doubles US$10

Hotel Dorothy 500m south of the town centre, just past the bullring ☎2479-8068. A welcoming, well-run place with simple, clean rooms with private baths, and a first-floor terrace from which to enjoy views of the volcano. Guests can use the kitchen and have access to free internet and wi-fi. US$20

La Posada Inn 300m east of the central park ☎2479-9793. No-frills rooms with either shared or private bathrooms, owned by a charming and

Essence Arenal In the village of El Castillo, around 16km west of La Fortuna ☎2479-1131, ⓦwww.essencearenal.com. In a secluded location, *Essence Arenal* touts itself as a "boutique hostel" and largely succeeds: it has smart rooms with private or shared facilities, a pool with superlative volcano views, a TV lounge, free internet, movie nights, a great vegetarian café and a travel desk. Ideal if you have your own wheels, as there's no public transport here, though the amiable staff will arrange pick-ups from La Fortuna (US$6). US$28

hospitable family. There's also a communal garden and parking. US$10

Sleep Inn Guesthouse 350m southwest of the central park ☎2394-7033, ⓔcarlossleepinn@hotmail.com. Renowned for larger-than-life owner Carlos, aka "Mr Lava-Lava", who offers inexpensive volcano tours, you can't help feel like part of the family as soon as you arrive, even if the living quarters are decidedly basic. US$10

Eating and drinking

Although there are numerous decent restaurants, La Fortuna's nightlife is underwhelming.

Choza de Laurel 200m west of Parque Central on the main road. Despite being a little touristy, and far from the cheapest option in town, *Choza de Laurel* produces quality, well-presented rice and pasta dishes, tortillas and rotisserie chicken (all 3600–4900c), as well as more expensive steaks and seafood (6550–9950c) if you fancy a treat.

Gecko Gourmet Just west of the church. Catering to homesick gringos, this café has breakfast

burritos (3000c), salmon and cream-cheese bagels (3000c), meatloaf sandwiches (3500c) and BLTs (3500c), as well as fine coffee and smoothies.

Lava Lounge Bar and Grill On the main road 50m before the church. By day a restaurant with well-prepared and reasonably priced wraps, salads and light meals (2500–4500c), this is also a trendy evening spot.

Lava Rocks Opposite the church. Not to be confused with *Lava Bar and Grill*, this rather bland-looking place has heartbreakingly nice staff and well-executed *comida típica* (*casados* and *arroz cons* from 3250c), though the meat and seafood dishes are overpriced.

La Parada Opposite Parque Central. Perfect for an early breakfast, or quick economical feed. There's a self-service buffet (1800c) featuring all the usual Tico dishes, as well as big breakfasts, *casados*, burgers, pizzas and pastas.

Saltamar Opposite *Arenal Backpackers*. Dinner might be a touch over budget, but there's a good-value lunch special (Mon–Fri 11am–4pm; 2500–3500c for a main meal and drink) and wonderful smoothies.

Directory

Internet At the café next to Jacamar Tours, opposite the church (650c/hr).

Laundry There's a laundry service a block before *La Choza Inn* (US$3/kg).

Taxis There's a rank on the east side of the Parque Central. They rarely (if ever) use their meters, so agree on a price before getting in and beware of overcharging.

Moving on

By bus to: Monteverde (take the 8am bus to Tilarán, changing there for the 12.30pm bus to Monteverde; 6–8hr); Puerto Viejo de Sarapiquí (take the bus to San Carlos/Ciudad Quesada – 12 daily

LA FORTUNA TO MONTEVERDE: JEEP–BOAT–JEEP TRANSFERS

The most interesting way to travel between La Fortuna and Monteverde (see p.535) is by a **"jeep–boat–jeep" transfer**, a time-saving and spectacularly pretty connection taking two to three hours. It shows off both the breathtaking mountain pastures of Monteverde, and your first (or last, depending on the direction) glimpse of majestic Volcán Arenal. Prices range from US$18 to US$25, so shop around – many hotels and agencies can arrange them. The least expensive trips are generally available via *Arenal Backpackers* and Eagle Tours in La Fortuna and *Pensión Santa Elena* in Santa Elena/Monteverde.

5.40am–9.30pm; 1hr 30min – and change there for Sarapiquí – 8 daily 4.40am–6.30pm; 2–3hr); San José (2 daily at 12.45pm & 2.45pm; 4hr), via San Carlos (1hr 30min); Tilarán (2 daily at 8am & 4.30pm; 3hr 30min).

LOS CHILES

Few tourists make it to **LOS CHILES**, a border settlement 3km from Nicaragua. Those that do come en route to **Caño Negro**, 25km downstream on the Río Frío (see below), or to cross the Nicaraguan border, though the majority of travellers still cross at Peñas Blancas (see p.563).

Arrival and information

By bus Buses from C 12, Av 7/9 in San José (2 daily at 5.30am & 3.30pm, returning 5am & 3pm; 5hr) stop at Los Chiles' small bus station, as do almost hourly services from San Carlos (Ciudad Quesada). **Exchange** You can change dollars and travellers' cheques at the Banco Nacional on the north side of the football pitch (Mon–Fri 8am–3.30pm); it also has an ATM.
Tourist information Although Los Chiles has no official information office, everyone in town knows the current bus schedules and the times of the boat to the Nicaraguan border, though few speak English. Servicios Turísticos Caño Negro (☎2471-1438), at *Cabinas Jabirú*, can provide general tourist information.

Accommodation and eating

Cabinas Jabirú One block west and north of the bus station ☎2471-1211. The economical rooms here, each with private bath, TV, fridge and a/c, may lack character, but they're fine for a day or two. Staff, however, can be brusque. US$20
Rancho Tulipan 100m from the dock ☎2471-1414, ⊛www.ranchotulipan.com. A more comfortable option, *Rancho Tulipan* has comfortable singles, doubles, triples and quads with private bathrooms, TVs and a/c set amid a garden filled with medicinal plants. It also has a decent restaurant serving Tico and continental fare (mains from 2500c). US$50
Soda Pamela Opposite the bus station. A slightly cheaper option than *Rancho Tulipan*, offering *pintos* and *casados* from 2000c.

REFUGIO NACIONAL DE VIDA SILVESTRE CAÑO NEGRO

The largely pristine **REFUGIO NACIONAL DE VIDA SILVESTRE CAÑO NEGRO** (daily 8am–4pm; US$10; ☎2471-1309), 25km west of Los Chiles, is one of the best places in the Americas to view huge concentrations of both migratory and indigenous birds, along with mammalian and reptilian river wildlife. Until recently its isolation – it's 192km from San José – kept it well off the beaten track, though nowadays more and more tours are visiting the area (you can visit on an excursion from La Fortuna (see box, p.565), Los Chiles (see below) or any of the larger hotels in the Zona Norte; getting there independently is still fairly complicated. Even if you do get here under your own steam, hiring an experienced **guide** (from US$20) is well worth the money; the ranger station and *Rancho Tulipan*

INTO NICARAGUA: LOS CHILES

Currently, the only way to reach Nicaragua from the Los Chiles crossing is by **boat** (1hr) on the Río Frío: one to three daily services leave the docks in Los Chiles for San Carlos de Nicaragua (see p.460), depending on demand and tides. You need to get an exit stamp from the Costa Rican immigration office, opposite *Rancho Tulipan*, first. Most nationalities don't need visas for Nicaragua; for those that do, visa issues must be taken care of in San José. Make sure the **Nicaraguan border patrol**, 3km upriver from Los Chiles, stamps your passport, as you will need proof of entry when leaving Nicaragua. You'll also need some cash upon arrival in San Carlos; change a few colones for córdobas at the Los Chiles bank. From San Carlos it's also possible to cross the lake to **Granada** and on to **Managua**. There is a US$10 charge to enter Nicaragua. Note that the border crossing closes at 5pm.

in Los Chiles (see opposite) can help to put you in contact with one.

Arrival and information

By boat It's possible to rent a boat for travel down the Río Frío from Los Chiles (US$50–75). While the skippers may not be trained guides, they are often good at spotting wildlife.

By bus Buses leave from Los Chiles at 5am & 2pm (1hr), but it is worth confirming hours back as times are liable to change. The ranger station will have information on this, and can book a taxi for you.

Tourist information The entrance fee (US$10) is payable at the ranger station. They have information on the refuge and can advise on transport (☎ 2471-1309).

Tour operators *Rancho Tulipan* runs guided boat tours of Caño Negro (US$85, including entry fees), as well as fishing trips. Several agencies in La Fortuna (see box, p.565) also offer day-trips, including Eagle Tours (US$55) and Jacamar (US$73). Tours generally involve a 4–5hr boat trip up the Río Frío with guides pointing out birds, caimans, monkeys, iguanas, sloths and other wildlife.

Accommodation

It's possible to stay in the ranger station (☎ 2471-1309; US$6). Camping (US$5) is permitted, but there are no formal facilities. There is also some very basic accommodation in the village of Caño Negro, but most budget travellers stay in Los Chiles (see opposite).

PUERTO VIEJO DE SARAPIQUÍ

Steamy, tropical and carpeted with fruit plantations, the eastern part of the Zona Norte bears more resemblance to the hot and dense Caribbean lowlands than the plains of the north and, despite the toll of deforestation, still shelters some of the country's best-preserved premontane rainforest. The largest settlement, **PUERTO VIEJO DE SARAPIQUÍ**, is principally a river transport hub and a place for the region's banana, coconut and pineapple plantation workers to stock up on supplies. You will find most of the area's budget accommodation here, as well as some excellent river-based activities and hiking trails.

There are two options when it comes to getting here from the Valle Central. The western route, taking just over three hours, goes via Varablanca and the La Paz waterfall, passing the hump of Volcán Barva. This route offers great views of velvety green hills clad with coffee plantations, which turn, eventually, into rainforest. It's faster (1hr–1hr 30min), but marginally less scenic, to travel via the **Guápiles Highway**. The region receives a lot of **rain** – as much as 4500mm annually – so wet-weather gear is essential.

Arrival and information

By bus The bus station is in the centre of town on the main road by the football pitch.

Tour operators The owner of Souvenir Río Sarapiquí, opposite the Banco Nacional on the main road (☎ 2766-6727, ✉ luisalbertosm@racsa.co.cr), is a reliable source of information on the region and offers good rates on rafting, kayaking, hiking and canopy tours. Aguas Bravas (☎ 2292-2072 or 2776 6621, ✉ www.aguas-bravas.co.cr), 100m down from Banco Nacional towards the river, is great for rafting trips (though activities have been affected by the ongoing effects of the 2009 Cinchona earthquake).

Accommodation and eating

Hotel Bambú Above the bus station opposite the football pitch ☎ 2766-6005, ✉ www.elbambu.com. This central hotel has a wonderful pool, reasonable restaurant and comfortable rooms with private baths, a/c, TVs and phones. However, the noise from the main road can be overpowering. US$65

Mi Lindo Sarapiquí On the corner of the football pitch as you enter town ☎ 2766-6281/6074. A good budget option, with clean, spacious rooms, private hot showers and a friendly atmosphere. The restaurant is very popular too. If you arrive at the hotel before 10am, however, you will not be able to get in as the reception is generally closed. US$30

🏃 **Posada Andrea Cristina** 1km west of town on the road to Chilamate ☎ 2766-6265, ✉ www.andreacristina.com. A veritable tropical haven, with lovely, quirky cabins, bungalows and a wonderful room in a treehouse set among the jungle plants. The hospitable owner has a wealth of information on conservation projects, runs river and trekking tours, offers Spanish classes and serves excellent (mainly vegetarian) food. US$48

La Quinta Lodge 7km west of Sarapiquí, and 5km east of La Virgen, 1.5km up a side road served by the occasional bus (☎2761-1052, 🌐www.quinta sarapiqui.com). On the banks of the Río Sardinal, this comfortable lodge has great rooms in bungalows equipped with balconies and rocking chairs. Activities include swimming in the pool or river and exploring the lodge's cultivated lands, butterfly garden and on-site rainforest exhibition. There's a pleasant, pricey restaurant (around 8000c for dinner), and biking, horseriding and birdwatching can be arranged by the cheerful staff. US$110

Soda Llyxi On the road into town 10m before the football pitch. Most hotels have restaurants, but of the other eating-out options, this place stands out: a clean and bright open-fronted *soda* complete with wooden benches and a TV, dishing up delicious *pintos* (from 1200c) and rocket-fuel coffee (500c).

Directory

Exchange Banco Nacional (Mon–Fri 8.30am–3pm), at the far northern end of C Principal, changes travellers' cheques and dollars.
Internet Internet La Viña (600c/hr), in the bookstore adjacent to La Viña supermarket; the sign is visible across the football pitch from the bus station. There's also internet access at *Mi Lindo Sarapiquí* (500c/hr).

Moving on

By bus to: San Carlos/Ciudad Quesada, for buses to La Fortuna, Monteverde and points west (9 daily 4.40am–7pm; 2–3hr); San José (8 daily 5am–5.30pm; 1hr 30min–2hr).

AROUND PUERTO VIEJO DE SARAPIQUÍ

The lush Caribbean climate and vegetation in the area around Sarapiquí make for a striking environment, with plenty of scope for outdoor activities.

Rara Avis

The incredible and completely isolated private rainforest reserve of **Rara Avis** (☎2253-0844 or 2764-3131, 🌐www.rara -avis.com), 17km south of Puerto Viejo, also acts as an expensive tourist lodge and a **research station**, accommodating student groups and volunteers from around the world whose aim is to develop rainforest products – orchids, palms and so forth – as crops for the use of local communities. It offers one of the most thrilling and authentic eco-experiences in Costa Rica, featuring both primary rainforest and some secondary cover. The rich array of **wildlife** can't fail to impress, and you could meander the excellent trail network for days.

Visiting the park is usually a premeditated venture, requiring at least one night's stay in one of the lodges, and recommended perhaps only to the true nature enthusiast, or someone with deep pockets. Most people organize their trip here before arriving in Costa Rica as it takes a great deal of planning: the route alone up to Rara Avis involves getting to the village Las Horquetes, either by taxi (roughly US$30) or bus from Puerto Viejo, where you will meet a pre-booked **tractor** for the rest of the 15km journey. Advance bookings are required, as space is limited and costly: lodges in the park (the only option) cost from US$55 per person per night (rates include all meals, transport to and from Las Horquetas, and guided walks).

Estación Biológica La Selva

A fully equipped research station, **Estación Biológica La Selva**, 93km northeast of San José and 4km southwest of Puerto Viejo de Sarapiquí (☎2766-6565, in San José ☎2240-6696, 🌐www .ots.ac.cr), is probably the best place to visit in the Sarapiquí region, especially if you are a botany student or have a special interest in the scientific life of a rainforest. Like Rara Avis, it is also a superb birder's spot, with more than four hundred species of indigenous and migratory **bird**.

However, you will find yourself paying roughly US$100 a night for very basic living quarters, though visiting on half-day guided **treks** (US$30) through the extensive trails is a worthy option if you can't afford the fees. Call or reserve online in advance.

Río Sarapiquí

The roaring **Río Sarapiquí** used to be the most important trade route in northern Costa Rica, ferrying coffee and bananas between Nicaragua, southern Costa Rica and overseas. Now, however, it is a prime location for some of the most invigorating **whitewater rafting** and **kayaking** in the country. Visit Souvenir Río Sarapiquí or Aguas Bravas (see "Tour operators", p.569) to arrange a trip.

The Zona Sur

Costa Rica's **Zona Sur** ("southern zone") is the country's least-known region, both for Ticos and international travellers, although tourism has started to increase. Geographically, it's a diverse area, ranging from the agricultural heartland of the Valle de El General to the high peaks of the Cordillera de Talamanca. South of Cerro el Chirripó, one of the highest peaks in Central America, the cordillera falls away into the lowlands of the Valle de Diquis and the coffee-growing Valle de Coto Brus, near the Panama border. Climatically, the Osa Peninsula, Golfito and Golfo Dulce experience rain even during the dry season, and during the wettest part of the year (Oct–Dec), spectacular thunderstorms canter in from the Pacific.

The region's chief draw is the **Osa Peninsula**, home to **Parque Nacional Corcovado**, one of the country's prime rainforest hiking destinations, and the remote and picturesque **Bahía Drake**. More accessible, the **Playa Dominical** area of the Pacific coast is a surfing destination of tremendous tropical beauty. **Golfito**, the only town of any size, isn't particularly exciting, though it has improved since being made a tax-free zone for goods from Panama.

DOMINICAL

DOMINICAL, 44km south of Quepos (see p.542), probably represents the face of things to come along this stretch of the Pacific coast. Once a secluded fishing village, it has begun to expand dramatically. The coastal areas to the south, mainly unspoilt stretches of beach and rainforest, are rapidly being bought up by property developers and hotel chains. The fear expressed by many locals, that the area is destined to become the country's next Manuel Antonio – a once pristine area, now massively overdeveloped – seems about to be realized. Despite this, the town remains relatively small scale, with just a few dirt-track roads. **Surfing** is the big draw; thousands of (mainly American) visitors flock in every year to ride the beach break and hit the numerous beachfront bars. Swimming is ill-advised in the area due to strong riptides.

Arrival and information

By bus Buses travel the length of the strip before turning at the end and coming back the same way in order to leave town. The bus stop is opposite the telecommunications building at the southern end of town.

Internet There's access at the *Arena y Sol* hotel and restaurant on the main street (1000c/hr).

Tour operators Jungle Jive Surf Camp (☎2316-0651, ✉junglejivesurfcamp@hotmail.com), in *Domilocos* hotel, has surf lessons (US$40/2hr). Dominical Surf and Adventures (☎8839-8542, ⓦwww.dominicalsurfadventures.com) also runs classes (US$40–50/2hr), rents boards and has information on tours in the area, including rappelling, paragliding, kayaking and rafting.

THE ZONA SUR

Map features:
- San José
- Cartago
- RESERVA BIOLÓGICA HITOY CERERE
- Cahuita
- Bribrí
- Santa María de Dota
- PARQUE NACIONAL CHIRRIPÓ
- Cerro de la Muerte (3491 m)
- Cerro Chirripó (3819 m)
- CA-1
- San Gerardo de Rivas
- Savegre
- San Isidro de El General
- PANAMA
- PARQUE INTERNACIONAL LA AMISTAD
- Dominical
- RESERVA BIOLÓGICA DURIKÁ
- Parque Nacional Manuel Antonio & Quepos
- Uvita
- Buenos Aires
- PARQUE NACIONAL MARINO BALLENA
- RESERVA INDÍGENA BORUCA
- PACIFIC OCEAN
- Cortés
- Palmar
- Río Grande de Térraba
- CA-1
- Valle de Coto Brus
- Santa Elena
- Progreso
- Sierpe
- REFUGIO NACIONAL DE FAUNA SILVESTRE GOLFITO
- San Vito
- RESERVA BIOLÓGICA ISLA DEL CAÑO
- Bahía Drake
- Río Sierpe
- Drake
- Agujitas
- Marenco
- Rincón
- PARQUE NACIONAL CORCOVADO
- La Palma
- Golfito
- Neily
- CA-1
- San Pedrillo
- PARQUE NACIONAL CORCOVADO
- Los Patos
- Puerto Jiménez
- Zancudo
- Paso Canoas
- Sirena
- Carate
- Golfo Dulce
- David & Panama City
- Osa Peninsula
- La Leona
- Pavones
- Punta Banco
- N
- 0   25 km

Tourist information Southern Expeditions (☎2787-0110, ⓦwww.southernexpeditionscr .com), at the northern end of town, gives good, impartial advice on the area.

Accommodation

Dominical is full of hotels, but those geared towards budget travellers and surfers are not of a high standard, so spend a few extra colones if you can.

Arena y Sol Along the main drag just before the right turn down to the beach ☎2787-0140, ⓦwww.arenaysol.com. Plain, modern cabins with private bathrooms, TV and fans or a/c. Internet and breakfast are free, and the pool provides blessed relief from the heat. US$45

Cabinas San Climente On the main road just before the right turn down to the beach ☎2787-0026. The wooden cabins here are simple, clean and secure. You pay more for private bathrooms, hot water, a/c and sea views. US$20

Camping Antorchas Just off the beach road ☎2771-0459, ⓦwww.campingantorchas.com. As well as camping spots, there are a few basic cabins with private or shared bathrooms. The campsite has a kitchen, parking and lockers. Camping US$8, cabins US$20

Piramys On the beach road ☎2787-0196, ⓔpiramys@hotmail.com. Feels like a hippy commune, with a jumble of attractive but basic rooms, airy mezzanines and an alfresco kitchen. Some rooms have hot water. Two minor downsides: the staff can be a little too laidback, and while very peaceful, the bucolic location makes it prone to uncomfortably large spiders. US$25

Tortilla Flats On the beach ☎ 2787-0033. Popular surfers' hotel whose brightly decorated rooms come with attached baths and their own hammocks. There's also a beachfront restaurant/bar where crowds gather every evening to watch the sun set. US$30

Eating and drinking

The Back Porch In a little cluster of huts at the entrance to the village. This café serves up real lattes and cappuccino (1000c), with either regular or soy milk, and delicious bagels (1500–2500c). The lovely American owner makes you feel right at home.

Maracatú Funky restaurant in the middle of the drag opposite *Cabinas San Climente* offering mouthwatering vegan, vegetarian and fish dishes (3000–6000c), and surf videos on loop. Wed is reggae night, and on Tues there's an open jam session. Daily happy hour 4–5.30pm.

Soda Nanyoya Tucked away behind the town's fruit stand. At this breezy, open-walled bar/restaurant you may have to queue for a table, but it's probably the freshest orange juice you'll ever taste, and the best breakfast in town at blissfully low prices (*pinto* 1400c).

Tortilla Flats *Tortilla Flats* hotel. The prime spot in town to watch the sun set while nursing a cool beer (happy hour 4–6pm). A tasty menu offers typical dishes, fresh seafood and American options like foot-long subs (from 2500c). Thurs is Ladies' Night.

Moving on

By bus to: Palmar (2 daily at 4.30am & 10.30am; 2hr); Quepos (6 daily at 7.30am, 8am, 10.30am, 1.45pm, 4pm & 5pm; 2hr); San Isidro (2 daily at 6am & 1.45pm; 1hr 30min); San José (2 daily at 5am & 1pm; 6hr). Buses run from Palmar to Bahía Drake and Puerto Jiménez.

GOLFITO

A former banana port, just 33km north of the Panamanian border, **GOLFITO** stretches along the water at the cusp of the glorious Golfo Dulce. The shadow of the Osa Peninsula shimmers in the distance, and the vegetation has the soft muted look of the tropics. Golfito's history is inextricably intertwined with the giant **United Brands** company, which first set up here in 1938. When it

pulled out in a hurry in 1985, it created a social vacuum, and the town became known as one of the most unsavoury places in Costa Rica. These days the area is steadily improving, thanks primarily to Golfito's establishment as a tax-free zone (*depósito libre*) for imports from Panama. South of the *depósito libre*, and the more affluent part of town, is the **pueblo civil**, where you'll find good-value hotels, as well as the *lancha* across the Golfo Dulce to Puerto Jiménez and the Osa Peninsula. There isn't much to do in Golfito, but it is a pleasant enough place to stay while you're waiting to cross to Puerto Jiménez or into Panama.

Arrival and information

By boat A *lancha* arrives twice daily from Puerto Jiménez to the tiny *muellecito* (little dock) behind *Hotel Golfito*.

By bus Services stop by the Banco Nacional. Buy your return ticket as soon as you arrive.

Tour operators Land Sea Tours (☎ 2775-1614, ✉ landsea@racsa.co.cr), on the waterfront at the southern end of the *pueblo civil*, organizes a wide range of tours, has a book exchange and is an excellent source of information.

Accommodation

Accommodation in Golfito comes in two varieties: swish places catering to business travellers and shoppers at the *depósito* in the *zona americana*, originally the wealthier part of town and now home to the bank and bus station, and cheaper rooms in the *pueblo civil*.

Happy Daze On the road up towards the post office, beyond *8° Latitude* ☎ 2775-0058. The Californian owner has allowed his surfer attitude to flow into this little hostel, which has a kitchen, TV room and rather shambolic dorms. He offers waterfall and fishing trips, and surf lessons for US$20. US$8

Hotel Golfito Next to the petrol station on the way into town ☎ 2775-0047. Worthy budget hotel in front of the *muellecito*: rooms are simple and clean with private cold-water bathrooms and sturdy fans (a/c costs extra). The communal balcony sits virtually on the water, and has beautiful views. US$20

Mar Y Luna 500m before the *pueblo civil* on the main road ☎ 2775-0901, ⊛ www.hotelmaryluna andsuites.com. The bright doubles are very comfortable, with private baths, a/c, TVs and sea views; they

also have larger rooms with kitchenettes for longer stays. It also boasts a renowned seafood restaurant with decking almost on the sea. US$30

Samoa del Sur On the main road between the *zona americana* and the *pueblo civil* ☎ 2775-0233, Ⓦ www.samoadelsur.com. A range of decent, though slightly dowdy rooms with private baths, a/c and TVs, plus a large and rather raucous bar/restaurant – a favourite for US marines on leave. US$30

Eating and drinking

8º Latitude North of the football pitch. Run by an eccentric and charming American couple, this is the perfect place for a weary traveller to enjoy a cold beer (around 1000c) in friendly surroundings.

Buenos Días In front of the petrol station. Cheerful café with something of the feel of an American diner: *gallo pintos* (from 1500c) and *casados* (from 2500c) are dished up, while Disney paraphernalia covers the walls.

Hai Pin Behind *Buenos Días* ☎ 2775-0032. This Chinese restaurant entices locals and tourists with a solid menu of fried rice, noodles and stir-fries (dishes 1500–3500c).

Directory

Exchange Banco Nacional in the *zona americana* changes travellers' cheques and gives cash advances on credit cards, but it's a tediously slow process.

Internet Access is available at the café on the main street next to the petrol station (1000c/hr).

Post office Right in the centre of the *pueblo civil* (Mon–Fri 8.30am–4pm).

Moving on

By boat to: Puerto Jiménez (2 daily at 6am & 10am; 1hr 30min). Confirm times at your hotel beforehand.

By bus to: San José (2 daily at 5am & 1.30pm; 8hr). Buy your ticket in advance, particularly if you want to catch the 5am service.

PUERTO JIMÉNEZ

In the extreme southwest of the country, the **Osa Peninsula** is home to an area of immense biological diversity, much of it protected by Parque Nacional Corcovado. Most visitors base themselves in the tiny town of **PUERTO JIMÉNEZ**. From here, you could feasibly "do" the whole peninsula in four days, but this would be rushing it, especially if you want to spend time walking the trails and wildlife-spotting at Corcovado – better to allot five to seven days or more.

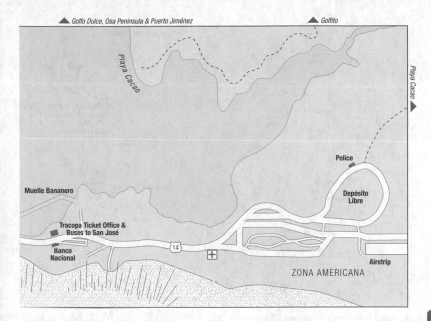

Playa Cacao

Playa Cacao

Playa Cacao ▶

Police

Muelle Bananero

Depósito
Libre

Tracopa Ticket Office &
Buses to San José

Banco
Nacional

14

Airstrip

ZONA AMERICANA

You can pick up the *colectivo* from here to Carate, 43km southwest, or to Bahía Drake, from where you can enter Corcovado (see p.578). If you're driving yourself, don't use anything other than a 4WD at any time of year. The roads have "improved" in recent years, but it's still a horrendously bumpy ride. Puerto Jiménez has the only petrol station on the peninsula, so fill up before you head out.

Arrival and information

By bus There's only one daily bus from San José's Transporte Blanco terminal; it arrives at the bus station on the western side of town in the evening. If you don't want to arrive in the dark you could take the early bus to Golfito and the *lancha* from there to Puerto Jiménez.

Exchange Banco Nacional (Mon–Fri 8.30am–3.45pm), on the main road two blocks north of the centre, has an ATM and currency exchange.

Internet Café Internet Osa Corcovado, near *Hotel Oro Verde*, has access for 1000c/hr.

Tour operators Escondido Trex (☎2735-5210) offers excellent-value kayak (from US$40), snorkelling (US$45), dolphin-spotting (US$50) and mangrove tours (US$67), all with very knowledgeable

guides. For those with a head for heights, try the waterfall rappelling (US$100) or climbing a giant *areno* tree (US$100).

Tourist information Corcovado Information Centre (MINAI; ☎2735-5036, ✉pncorcovado@gmail.com) is the government body in charge of Corcovado National Park. You need to come here to reserve your time in the park (max 5 days/4 nights) if you want to trek independently.

Accommodation

Reserve ahead in the dry season.

Cabinas Marcelina Along the main road, 200m before the Banco Nacional ☎2735-5286, ✉cabmarce@hotmail.com. This comfortable hotel is an idyllic hideaway from the dusty streets: all the rooms come with private hot-water baths and a/c or fans. Most look onto the sweet breakfast garden comprising a long wooden table under a trellis and tropical flowers. US$45

The Corner On a quiet corner, just off the main road ☎2735-5328. Alongside the plain fan-cooled four- and five-bed dorms are a couple of rudimentary doubles with private baths. It's a good place to meet other travellers and the *dueña* is a keen – and vocal – conservationist. Dorms US$5, doubles US$12

Hotel Oro Verde Just off the main road ☎2735-5241. Rooms are reasonable, if a little dark, with optional hot water and a/c. Bring

Jetty for Lancha to Golfito

Golfo
Dulce

N

0   200 m

San José & Colectivo stop

Football
Field

Police

Supermarket

★
Bus stop
La Palma

Escondido
Trex Office

Sansa
Office

Banco
Nacional

Puerto
Jiménez
Airport

EATING & DRINKING
Restaurante Carolina   3
Soda Deya   2
Soda El Ranchito   1

ACCOMMODATION
Cabinas Jiménez   A
Cabinas Marcelina   E
The Corner   C
Hotel Oro Verde   D
Iguana Iguana   B

PUERTO JIMÉNEZ

▼ Carate & Corcovado

earplugs, as it can be noisy. In-house tour guide
Josh is bubbling with enthusiasm for the national
park (day-trips around US$55). US$30
Iguana Iguana Northwest of the *parque*
☎2735-5258. In a tree-filled compound on the
edge of town, these cabinas are clean and have

private baths, but are also a bit gloomy and – at
times – noisy. The on-site bar is a local hotspot,
and has pool tables. US$40

Eating and drinking

Restaurante Carolina In the centre of town. A hub
of activity throughout the day, this restaurant serves
up fine local dishes (such as black bean soup and
arroz con mariscos) for 1500–5000c.
Soda Deya Around the corner from the supermarket. A tiny joint, popular with locals for its
delicious *pintos* (1500c) and fresh juices.
Soda El Ranchito Overlooking the football pitch.
This low-key place has a welcoming vibe and
hearty breakfasts (1400c).

Moving on

By bus to: San Isidro (2 daily at 5am & 1pm;
5–6hr); San José (1 daily at 5am; 8hr).
By colectivo to: Carate (2 daily at 6am & 1pm; 1hr
30min–2hr).

TREAT YOURSELF

Cabinas Jiménez North of the
parque ☎2735-5090, ⊛www
.cabinasjimenez.com. In a great
spot overlooking the Golfo
Dulce, this charming place has
attractive rooms with all mod
cons, including nice touches
like tea/coffee makers; it's worth
spending a little extra to get one
with views of the water. There's
a pleasant garden, pool, free wi-fi
and bikes and kayaks for guests to
use. Staff can organize boat, fishing,
snorkelling and dolphin-watching
trips too. US$50

BAHÍA DRAKE

The **BAHÍA DRAKE** (pronounced "Dra-kay") is one of the most stunning – and remote – areas in Costa Rica, with the blue wedge of **Isla del Caño**, a prime snorkelling destination, floating just off the coast and fiery-orange Pacific sunsets. The tiny hamlet of **Agujitas**, 10km south of Bahía Drake Town, is a wonderful base for the majority of travellers who come to the area to explore **Parque Nacional Corcovado**, which sits on the southwest corner of the Osa Peninsula – the park's San Pedrillo entrance is within walking distance, and hikers can combine serious trekking with serious comfort at either end of their trip by staying at one of the upscale rainforest **ecolodges** that have sprung up around the park in recent years.

Brave is the person who tackles the **buses** in this area; they run very infrequently and without any real schedule; having your own car makes things a lot easier, even though the roads are frightful and littered with river crossings: be careful and ask local advice, especially if there's been a lot of rain.

Arrrival and information

By bus From the north, take a Puerto Jiménez-bound bus to Rincón, from where a morning bus (Mon–Sat) heads to Bahía Drake; check the latest times with Corcovado Expeditions or the Fondación Corcovado (see below) beforehand, otherwise you could end up stranded in Rincón, a hostel-free intersection. Alternatively, a taxi to Sierpe from San Isidro costs around US$20 and from there you can take a river taxi (1hr 30min–2hr) to Bahía Drake for around US$15. From the south, *colectivos* run from Puerto Jiménez to La Palma, from where there are morning and afternoon buses to Drake; check the latest times first in Puerto Jiménez.

Tourist information and tours Most hotels offer tours, from snorkelling to horseriding, for US$75–100. Corcovado Expeditions, set back from the beach just next to the Corcovado Foundation (☎8818-9962, ⓦwww.corcovadoexpeditions.net), has trips to Isla del Caño and Corcovado (both US$75), and mangrove and canopy tours. The Fondación Corcovado (☎2297-3013, ⓦwww.corcovadofoundation.org), a volunteer organization set up to maintain the park, improve local amenities and rally against encroaching developers, maintains a beachfront office that doubles as an unofficial tourist information office and has a wealth of information about park etiquette and practicalities.

Accommodation

Camping on the beach is frowned upon, though many people do it; don't leave any litter if you do. Unless otherwise specified, all the places listed here are in the settlement of Agujitas. All have hot water.

Cabinas Jade Mar 200m up from the beach ☎2384-6681, ⓦwww.jademarcr.com. This pretty lodge boasts a range of rooms from cabins with private bathrooms, kitchens and sea views to simple doubles with shared facilities. It also has hammocks and a nice communal deck. Doubles US$30, cabins US$55

Cabinas Manolo At the bottom of the last hill coming into Agujitas ☎2885-9114, ⓦwww.cabinasmanolo.com. Rooms at this friendly Tico-run hostel are good value: though small and a bit musty, they are clean and bright, and most have a balcony with hammock. Private bathrooms cost US$5 extra. There's a good restaurant too (mains 1500–3500c). US$30

Hotel Finca Maresia 2km outside Agujitas ☎2775-0279, ⓦwww.fincamaresia.com. On undulating land surrounded by tropical forest is a delightful collection of bungalows with private baths and balconies, plus some simpler rooms with shared baths. There's a wonderfully serene vibe and staff can arrange pick-ups and excellent tours. Rates include breakfast. Doubles US$40, bungalows US$60

Eating

Mar y Bosque In Agujitas. This lovely, open-air *soda* overlooks a butterfly-filled garden, with the sea lying just beyond the trees. It's a great option throughout the day: for breakfast go for a delicious juice or smoothie to wash down your pancakes or *pinto* (1500c); the more substantial lunch and dinner options (3000c plus) are equally good. Esteban, the son of the owner, offers very informative trips into the Corcovado reserve (☎2311-7402).

Restaurante Jade Mar In Agujitas ☎2822-8595. This open-sided strip-lit place is always busy with locals and visitors. The big menu offers steaks, seafood, pizza and pastas – if you feel like pushing the boat out, go for the lobster (around 10,000c). Mains from 4000c.

Moving on

By boat Most hotels can organize private transfers to Sierpe.
By bus Leaving the village of Agujitas, there are buses (4.30am & 12.30pm; note that times change frequently) to Rincón, where connections run to San Isidro and San José. The Rincón service also goes on to La Palma, where you can pick up connections to Puerto Jiménez.

PARQUE NACIONAL CORCOVADO

Created in 1975, **PARQUE NACIONAL CORCOVADO** ("hunchback"), 368km southwest of San José (daily 8am–4pm; US$10; ☎2735-5036), houses 2.5 percent of the world's total biodiversity, protecting a fascinating and complex area of land. It's a beautiful park, with deserted beaches, waterfalls, high canopy trees and good **wildlife-spotting**. Exploring Corcovado, however, is not for the faint-hearted. The **terrain** includes sand, riverways, mangroves, *holillo* (palm) swamps and dense forest, although most of it is at lowland elevations; hikers can expect to spend most of their time on the beach trails that ring the outer perimeters of the park. The coastal areas of the park receive around 3800mm of rain a year, with precipitation rising to about 5000mm in the higher elevations of the interior. There is a dry season (December–March), but the inland lowland areas, especially those around the lagoon, can be amazingly **hot** during this period.

What to see and do

The *pulpería* in the village of **Carate**, about 43km from Jiménez, sells basic foodstuffs; you can also camp here for a nominal fee. From here it's a nearly two-hour walk along the beach to the park entrance at **La Leona** *puesto*, although you can stop off for refreshment en route at the Corcovado and La Leona tent camps. It's then a sixteen-kilometre hike – allow six hours, as you have to wind along the beach, where it's slow going – to **Sirena**, the biggest *puesto* in the park, where you can stay in the simple lodge, exploring the local trails around the Río Sirena. If you're walking from Bahía Drake, you'll enter the park at **San Pedrillo** *puesto* and walk the 25km to Sirena from there.

The small hamlet of **La Palma**, 24km north of Puerto Jiménez, is the starting point for the walk to the Los Patos

---

PLANNING A TRIP TO CORCOVADO

You have to **reserve a space** in Corcovado in advance – this will include meals and either camping space or lodging at the *puesto* of your choice. To reserve, contact the park's Puerto Jiménez office (see "Tourist information", p.575) at least two weeks in advance, or go through a tour agency. Within the park, all *puestos* have camping areas, drinking water, information, toilets and telephone or radio. Wherever you enter, jot down the details of the **marea** (tide tables), which are posted in prominent positions. You'll need to cross most of the rivers at low tide; to do otherwise is dangerous. Rangers can advise on conditions.

Plan to hike early – though not before dawn, due to snakes – and shelter during the hottest part of the day. Rangers at each *puesto* always know how many people are on a given trail, and how long those hikers are expected to be. If you are late getting back, they'll go looking for you. Brush up on your **Spanish** before coming to Corcovado. You'll need to ask the rangers for a lot of information, and few, if any, speak English. If you're not fluent, bring a phrase book. If you hike with a guide, all these details will be dealt with for you. All reputable tour operators use bilingual tour guides.

INTO PANAMA: PASO CANOAS

The only reason to come to **PASO CANOAS** is to cross the border into Panama; you will not want to stay here longer than you have to. As you arrive, either driving or on the Tracopa or international Tica Bus service, you'll pass the Costa Rican customs checkpoint. The border is open 24 hours a day, but if you're waiting overnight for an early bus, *Cabinas Romy* (☎2732-2873; US$30), along the road past the station for buses to Neily, is an acceptable place to bed down for the night. There is a Banco Nacional on the Costa Rican side (Mon–Sat 9am–4pm, Sun 9am–1pm), with an ATM and currency exchange.

For travel into Panama you need to pick up a **tourist card** (not necessary for some European travellers, including those from Ireland and the UK, but required for Australia, Canada, New Zealand and the US, among many others; US$5). You may have a long wait, so arrive early. From here you pass over to the Panama immigration post southwest of town. If you get on a San José–David–Panama City Tica Bus in San José you get pushed to the front of the queue, as all international bus passengers are processed together. You may be required to produce proof of onward travel from Panama of a date within three months.

David, the first city of any size in Panama, is about ninety minutes beyond the border. Buses run from the Panamanian border bus terminal hourly until 5pm. From David it's easy to pick up local services, including the Tica Bus to Panama City. Alternatively, buses pass through the bus station just before the *migración* on the Interamericana into Bocas del Toro and Panama City.

puesto, a twelve-kilometre hike, much of it through hot lowland terrain. You need to arrive at Los Patos soon after dawn. The **El Tigre** *puesto*, at the eastern inland entrance to the park, is a good place to have breakfast or lunch with the rangers before setting off on the local trails. To get there from Jiménez, drive 10km north and take the second left, a dirt track, signed to El Tigre and Dos Brazos. Taxis cost in the region of US$15.

The El Tigre area is gradually becoming more developed, with short walking trails being laid out around the *puesto*. These provide an introduction to Corcovado without making you slog it out on the marathon trails, and it can easily be covered in a morning or afternoon.

The trails

The sixteen-kilometre trail from **La Leona to Sirena** runs just inland from the beach. If you can avoid anything untoward, you should be able to do the walk in five to six hours, taking time to look out for birds. En route you

may be able to spot a flock of **scarlet macaws**, which roost in the coastal trees, and perhaps **monkeys**, particularly white-faced capuchins, the most confident and inquisitive of the park's four breeds of monkey. Take lots of sunscreen, a big hat and at least five litres of water per person – the trail gets very hot.

The really heroic walk in Corcovado, all 25km of it, is from **Sirena to San Pedrillo** – the stretch along which you'll see the most impressive trees. It's a two-day trek, so take a tent, sleeping bag and mosquito net, and you must be able to set up camp in the jungle. Fording the **Río Sirena**, just 1km beyond the Sirena *puesto*, is the biggest obstacle. The deepest of all the rivers on the peninsula, it has to be crossed with care and at low tide only: not only does it have the strongest out-tow current, but sharks come in and out in search of food at high tide. Get the latest information from the Sirena rangers before you set out.

The trail across the peninsula from **Los Patos to Sirena** is 20km long.

You may want to rest at the entrance, as this is an immediately demanding walk, continuing uphill for about 6–8km and taking you into high, wet and dense rainforest – and after that you've still got 14km or so of incredibly hot lowland walking to go. This is a trail for experienced rainforest hikers and hopeful **mammal**-spotters: taking you through the interior, it gives you a reasonable chance of coming across, for example, margays, peccaries, or the tracks of tapirs and jaguars. It's a gruelling trek, especially with the hot inland temperatures (at least 26°C, with 100-percent humidity) and the lack of sea breezes.

Information

Tour operators To increase your chances of seeing some of the park's wildlife, it's well worth investing in the services of a guide: a twelve-hour trek should cost from US$50. Hotels and tour operators in Puerto Jiménez – such as Escondido Trex (see "Tour operators", p.575) – can help arrange guides and trips to the park.

Accommodation and eating

You can camp in the *puestos* (US$4) or sleep in the accommodation block at Sirena (US$12). Bring your own tent, mosquito net, sleeping bag, food and water. You can either take expensive meals with the rangers (US$15–20; pay in colones at the *puesto*) or bring your own utensils and use their stove.

Panama

HIGHLIGHTS ✪

BOCAS DEL TORO:
dive into the aquamarine
Caribbean from your own
private stretch of sand

SAN BLAS ARCHIPELAGO:
witness the traditional
culture of the Kuna

PANAMA CANAL:
take in this incredible feat of
engineering by boat or train

CASCO VIEJO:
the most captivating
part of the city, full of
faded grandeur

CHIRIQUÍ HIGHLANDS:
breathe cool mountain air,
sip coffee and explore
untouched cloudforest

ISLA CAÑAS:
one of the few places in the
world to host a sea turtle "arribada"

ROUGH COSTS

DAILY BUDGET Basic US$35/
occasional treat US$50

DRINK Beer (355ml) US$1,
coffee US$0.75

FOOD *Arroz con pollo* US$3

CAMPING/HOSTEL/BUDGET HOTEL
US$5/US$12/US$30

TRAVEL Panama City–Bocas
del Toro by bus (600km): 9hr,
US$23

FACT FILE

POPULATION 3.24 million

AREA 75,990 sq km

LANGUAGE Spanish

CURRENCY US dollar (US$)

CAPITAL Panama City
(population: 814,000)

INTERNATIONAL PHONE CODE
☎507

TIME ZONE GMT -5hr

Introduction

A narrow, snake-shaped stretch of land that divides oceans and continents, Panama has long been one of the world's greatest crossroads – far before the construction of its famous canal. Though its historical ties to the US have led to an exaggerated perception of the country as a de facto American colony, Spanish, African, West Indian, Chinese, Indian, European, and several of the least assimilated indigenous communities in the region have all played a role in the creation of the most sophisticated, open-minded and outward-looking society in Central America. The comparatively high level of economic development and use of the US dollar also make it one of the more expensive countries in the region, but the wildlife-viewing and adventure-travel options are excellent, and the polished nightlife of Panama City is a diamond in the rough.

Cosmopolitan and contradictory, **Panama City** is the most striking capital city in Central America, its multiple personalities reflected in the frenzied energy of its international banking centre, the laidback street-life of its old colonial quarter and the antiseptic order of the US-built Canal Zone. Located in the centre of the country, it is also a natural base from which to explore many of Panama's most popular destinations, including its best-known attraction, the monumental **Panama Canal**. The colonial ruins and Caribbean coastline of **Colón Province** are also within reach of the capital. Southeast of Panama City stretches **Darién**, the infamously wild expanse of rainforest between Central and South

America, while to the north, along the Caribbean coastline, **Kuna Yala** is the autonomous homeland of the Kuna, who live in beautiful isolation on the coral atolls of the **San Blas Archipelago**. West of Panama City, the Carretera Interamericana runs through the Pacific coastal plain, Panama's agricultural heartland. This region lures travellers intrigued by the folkloric traditions and nature reserves of the **Azuero Peninsula**, also a major surf destination, and the protected cloudforests of the **Chiriquí Highlands** on the Costa Rican border. The mostly uninhabited Caribbean coast west of the canal meets Costa Rica near the remote archipelago of **Bocas del Toro**, a popular holiday destination thanks to its largely unspoiled

WHEN TO VISIT

Panama is well within the tropics, with temperatures hovering at 25–32°C throughout the year, and varying only with altitude (the Chiriquí Highlands are generally 15–26°C). Visiting Panama during the dry season (mid-Dec to April; known as *verano*, or summer) maximizes your chance of finding sunny days. However, seasonal climatic variation is really only evident on the Pacific side of the country's mountainous spine. The average annual rainfall here is about 1500mm; on the Caribbean, about 2500mm falls, spread more evenly throughout the year. From May to December, the storms of the Pacific's winter (*invierno*) rainy season are intense but rarely extended.

rainforests, beaches, coral reefs, surfing hotspots and easygoing vibe.

CHRONOLOGY

1501–02 Spanish explorers Rodrigo de Bastidas and Christopher Columbus visit modern-day Panama.

1510 Conquistador Diego de Nicuesa establishes Nombre de Dios, one of the earliest Spanish settlements in the New World.

1513 Vasco Núñez de Balboa crosses Panama, becoming the first European to see the Pacific Ocean.

1519 Panama City is founded on August 15 by conquistador Pedro Arias de Ávila (known as Pedrarias).

1596–1739 Spanish colonies and ships, loaded with treasure from indigenous Central and South American empires, are attacked several times by British privateers. Henry Morgan sacks Panamá Viejo in 1671.

1746 Spain re-routes treasure fleet around Cape Horn, but trade remains Panama's dominant economic activity.

1821 Panama declares independence from Spain, and joins the confederacy of Gran Colombia (Bolivia, Peru, Ecuador, Venezuela, Colombia and Panama).

1830 Panama becomes a province of Colombia after the dissolution of Gran Colombia.

1851 US company begins building railroad across Panamanian isthmus; project is completed in 1855.

1881 French architect Ferdinand de Lesseps begins excavations for the Panama Canal, which turns out to be an unmitigated disaster. Some 20,000 workers die before the venture is abandoned in 1889.

1903 Backed by the US, Panama declares independence from Colombia. French engineer Philippe Bunau-Varilla signs a treaty with the US, essentially selling rights to the canal, and giving the US control of the Canal Zone "in perpetuity".

1914 The canal is completed. Over 75,000 people have a hand in its construction.

1939 Panama ceases to be US protectorate, but tensions continue to build between Panama and the US territory of the Canal Zone.

1964 "Martyrs' Day" riots, precipitated by a student protest, leave 21 Panamanians dead and over 500 injured in the Canal Zone.

1968 General Omar Torrijos Herrera, Chief of the National Guard, overthrows president Arnulfo Arias and imposes a dictatorship.

1977 Torrijos signs new canal treaty with US President Jimmy Carter, who agrees to transfer the canal to Panamanian control by December 31, 1999.

1983 Colonel Manuel Noriega becomes de facto military ruler. He is initially supported by the US, but also cultivates drug-cartel connections.

1988 US charges Noriega with rigging elections, drug smuggling and murder; Noriega declares state of emergency, dodging a coup and repressing opposition.

1989 Guillermo Endara wins the presidential election, but Noriega declares the results invalid and seizes presidency. US troops invade Panama and oust Noriega, but also kill and leave homeless thousands of civilians.

1992 US court finds Noriega guilty of drug charges, sentencing him to 40 years in prison.

1999 Mireya Moscoso, the widow of former president Arnulfo Arias, is elected as Panama's first female president. US closes military bases and hands full control of the canal to Panama in December.

2003 A country-wide strike over mismanagement of the nation's social-security fund shuts down public services and turns violent.

2004 Martin Torrijos, son of former dictator Omar Torrijos, is elected president.

2004 The canal, under Panamanian management, earns record revenues of one billion US dollars.

2006 Referendum on a US$5.2 billion plan to expand the Panama Canal is passed by an overwhelming majority. Panama and the US sign a free-trade agreement.

2007 Work begins on the Panama Canal expansion project.

2008 A US judge rules that Manuel Noriega, released from prison, cannot be extradited to France until his appeals in the US are exhausted.

2010 Manuel Noriega receives a seven-year sentence from a French court for money-laundering crimes.

Basics

ARRIVAL

International **flights** arrive at **Tocumen International Airport (PTY)** in Panama City. Services arrive daily from the US (most are routed through Atlanta, Dallas/Fort Worth, Houston or Miami) and other Central and South American cities; KLM and Iberia fly from Amsterdam and Madrid, respectively. Flights from San José, in neighbouring Costa Rica, often stop in David before continuing on to Bocas del Toro or Panama City.

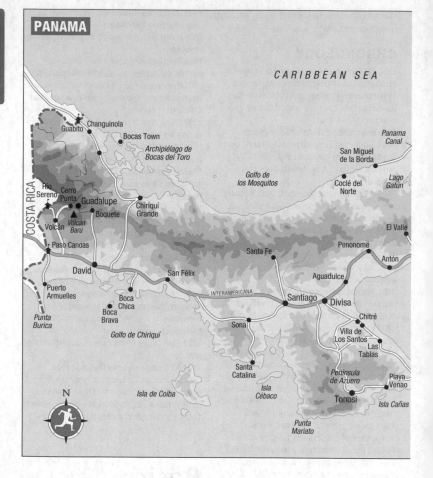

Crossing by **land** from Costa Rica is a possibility (see box, p.586), though due to security concerns crossing from Colombia is not an option. Though you can take local transport and switch **buses** at the border, the slightly costlier fares on international services run by Tica Bus (ⓦwww.ticabus.com) and Panaline give you a better shot at an efficient and hassle-free passage. To avoid undue trouble, keep your documents, stamps, and tourist visas in order. In addition to official documents, travellers at the border crossing will often be asked to show an onward or return ticket to provide proof of eventual departure from Panama. If travelling on a one-way ticket, *migración* is likely to require advance purchase of your bus fare back to San José.

There are a growing number of regular **boat** services between Panama and its neighbours, and backpackers are increasingly booking passages by boat to and from Colombia (see box, p.586).

VISAS

Travellers from Australia, Canada, New Zealand and the US do not require a **visa** to enter Panama. Visitors from

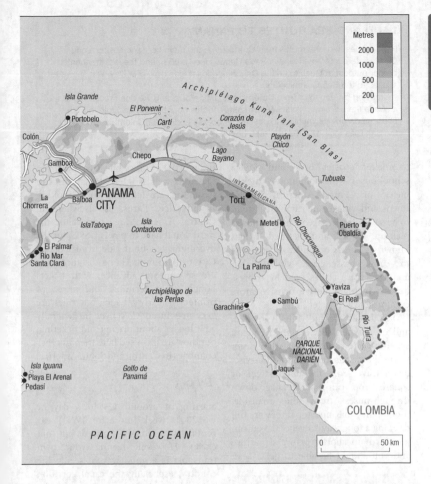

Ireland and the UK can also enter Panama without a **tourist card**; those from Australia, Canada, New Zealand and the US must pay for a US$30 tourist card upon arrival. Passports are generally stamped for ninety-day visits; extending your stay beyond this requires a trip to immigration, which can be costly and time consuming.

GETTING AROUND

Ease of travel within Panama varies according to geography. Although the canal corridor and the western Pacific region are covered by a comprehensive road network served by regular public transport, both eastern Panama and Bocas del Toro are linked to the rest of the country by just a single road.

By bus

Where there are roads, **buses** are the cheapest and most popular way to travel. Panama City is the hub of the network, with regular buses to Colón, Metetí in Darién, Almirante (for Bocas del Toro) and all the western cities and towns. Buses vary in comfort and size, from modern, air-conditioned Pullmans to smaller "coaster" buses and old US school buses – the ubiquitous "chicken buses" of Central America. Smaller towns and villages in rural areas tend to be served by less frequent minibuses, pick-up trucks and flat-bed trucks known as *chivas* or *chivitas*, converted to carry passengers, while Colón and David are also served by express buses, which are more expensive, more comfortable and faster.

Most buses are individually owned, and even when services are frequent, **schedules** are variable. Cities and larger towns have bus terminals; otherwise, buses leave from the main street or square. You can usually flag down through-buses from the roadside, though they may not stop if they are full or going a long way. In general, you can just turn up shortly before departure and you should be able to get a seat,

though the express buses to and from David as well as international buses to Costa Rica are definitely worth **booking in advance**. **Fares**, as elsewhere in Central America, are good value: the most you'll have to pay is US$23 for the overnight, ten-hour ride from Panama City to Almirante. Long-distance fares are set out in advance, with tickets bought in a terminal and a receipt printed – nearly all such bus rides are very structured. *Colectivos* are generally a bit looser about pricing and ticketing, but they are less used here than in other countries in Central and South America.

By car

Starting at around US$40 a day or US$200 a week (more for 4WD), **car rental** is reasonably priced but not cheap. However, having your own transport is a good way of seeing the country, especially the canal corridor, areas close to Panama City and the Azuero Peninsula. All of the main rental companies are based in Panama City airport, but some also have offices at the regional airports and in David; National Panama (Ⓦ www.nationalpanama.com) is preferred by locals as it offers some of the cheapest rentals in the country.

Driving in Panama is pretty straightforward, though even the paved roads in the canal corridor and the west can be badly maintained. The main roads on the Azuero Peninsula are in good condition, however, as are the secondary roads to Cerro Punta, Boquete, El Valle and Almirante. **4WD** is rarely necessary except during the rainy season and in more remote rural areas, particularly Darién. Police **checkpoints** appear throughout the country, mainly on provincial borders, and normally you are only required to slow down. If the police ask you to stop, in most cases they will just want to know your destination and see your licence.

Hitching is possible, but carries all the obvious risks. Private cars are unlikely to stop for you on main roads, though in more remote areas, hitching is often the only motor transport available, and there is little distinction between private vehicles and public transport – drivers will pick you up, but you should expect to pay the same kind of fares you would for the bus.

In larger cities, like Panama City and David, **taxis** are plentiful and inexpensive. Most intra-city rides will cost US$1–2 and none should cost more than US$5. There are many unlicensed cab drivers patrolling the streets who are willing to negotiate on prices, but who may engage in unscrupulous practices. Even licensed cab drivers won't hesitate to exploit an obviously unsavvy, lost or needy tourist. Specifically, be wary of price hikes on the Panama City Causeway.

By boat

Scheduled **ferries** run from Panama City to Isla Taboga as well as between Bocas del Toro and Almirante and Changuinola. Motorized **water-taxis** and **dugout canoes** are important means of transport in Bocas del Toro, Darién and Kuna Yala, though the only scheduled small-boat services are the water-taxis in Darién (between Puerto Quimba and La Palma). Otherwise, you'll have to either wait for somebody going your way, or hire a boat. The latter can be expensive, but becomes increasingly economical with more people sharing. Hiring a dugout canoe also opens up possibilities for wilderness adventure – up jungle rivers to isolated villages or out to uninhabited islands.

By air

Cities and larger towns are served by regular **flights** through Aeroperlas (☎315 7500, Ⓦwww.aeroperlas.com), the principal domestic carrier, which also has regular flights to parts of Darién and Kuna Yala, and Air Panama (☎315 0439, Ⓦwww.flyairpanama.com), which also flies to parts of Darién as well as the Las Perlas islands. With the exception of these more isolated areas, though, most destinations are so close to Panama City that it's scarcely worth flying, especially because flight prices are on the rise (at the time of writing, high-season return flights between Panama City and Bocas cost around US$180).

By bike

Cycling is a popular way to get around in western Panama, where roads are generally paved and traffic scarce (away from the Carretera Interamericana and other major routes), and towns usually have a shop offering parts and simple repairs. The stretch from the continental divide to Chiriquí Grande on the road from David to Almirante, in particular, is a cyclist's dream – some 40km downhill on a well-surfaced, less-driven main road through rainforest-covered mountains. Other good roads for cycling include all those on the Azuero Peninsula and the roads to Cerro Punta and El Valle off the Interamericana.

By rail

The **Panama Canal Railway** (Ⓦwww .panarail.com; US$22), which runs alongside the canal between Panama City and Colón, offers an excellent way of seeing the canal and the surrounding rainforest.

ACCOMMODATION

Most areas in Panama offer a wide choice of places to stay. In general, the cheapest **hotel** rooms, normally doubles with private baths and air conditioning, cost US$30–40 a night, although **hostels** – most common in well-travelled spots like Bocas Town, Boquete, David, Isla Taboga and Panama City – will often put you up for around US$12. In **Panama City**, where many hotels target business travellers, prices tend to be slightly higher, while at the very low end of the market some hotels – euphemistically termed drive-in motels and auto-hotels – cater largely to Panamanian couples, with hourly rates. Locally referred to as a Push, the units are accessed by a push-button garage door to provide couples with privacy. These operations are often the least expensive lodgings but are not recommended for a solid night's sleep or those looking for hygienic conditions.

For popular hostels, particularly in the city, you are better off **booking in advance**, especially for weekends and during public holidays, fiestas and Carnaval. During these times prices can double, and many places are booked out months in advance, so be prepared for slim pickings if you turn up without a reservation. The ten percent **tourist tax** charged on hotel accommodation is usually included in the quoted price and has been factored into the prices given throughout the chapter.

There are no official **campsites** in Panama, but you will find several hostels, particularly within San Blas and along the Azuero Peninsula coast, that allow you to pitch your tent for around US$5. That said, camping is never really necessary – even in the smallest villages there's almost always somewhere you can bed down for the night. If you do camp, either a **mosquito net** or mosquito coils (known as *mechitas*) are essentials. Almost all the national parks have ANAM (see p.593) **refuges** where you can spend the night for US$5–10,

though this fee is not always charged. They are usually pretty basic, but they do have bunk beds, cooking facilities and running water.

FOOD AND DRINK

Street vendors are less common in Panama than elsewhere in Central America. The cheapest places to eat are the ubiquitous canteen-like **self-service restaurants** (sometimes called *cafeterías*), which serve a limited but filling range of Panamanian meals for a few dollars; these usually open for lunch and stay open late. Larger towns generally have several upmarket **restaurants** with waiter service, where a main dish may cost upwards of US$5, as well as US-style fast-food places. There is often a five percent **tax** to pay on meals. Large **supermarkets** in the major cities offer a good range of cold and hot snacks to eat in or take out.

Known as *comida típica*, traditional Panamanian cooking is similar to what you find elsewhere in Central America. Rice and beans or lentils served with a little chicken, meat or fish form the mainstay, and *yuca* (cassava) and plantains are often served as sides. The national dish is **sancocho**, a chicken soup with *yuca*, plantains and other root vegetables flavoured with coriander. **Seafood** is plentiful, excellent and generally cheap, particularly *corvina* (sea bass), *pargo rojo* (red snapper), lobster and prawns; there is an excellent fresh fish market at the entrance of Panama's old city centre (see p.597). Fresh tropical **fruit** is also abundant, but rarely on the menu at restaurants – you're better off buying it in local markets. Popular **snacks** include *carimañolas* or *enyucados* (fried balls of manioc dough filled with meat), *empanadas*, *tamales* and *patacones* (fried, mashed and refried plantains). Toasted sandwiches called *emparedados* or *derretidos* are also very popular, appearing on most menus, from humble cafeterias to high-end cafés.

The diverse **cultural influences** that have passed through Panama have left their mark on its cuisine, especially in Panama City, where there are scores of international restaurants – Italian, Greek and Chinese being the most numerous. Almost every town has at least one Chinese restaurant, often the best option for **vegetarians**. Perhaps the strongest outside influence on Panamanian food, though, is the distinctive **Caribbean** culture of the West Indian populations of Panama City, Colón Province and Bocas del Toro. Speciality dishes involve seafood and rice cooked with lime juice, coconut milk and spices.

Drink

Coffee is excellent where grown locally (in the Chiriquí Highlands) and generally good throughout Panama, made espresso-style and served black or with milk as *café americano*. The **drinking water** of Panama City is so good that it is known as the "Champagne of the Chagres". Iced water, served free in restaurants, along with tap water in all towns and cities except Bocas del Toro and remote areas, is perfectly safe. **Chichas**, delicious blends of ice, water and tropical-fruit juices, are sometimes served in restaurants and by street vendors (except in Kuna Yala, where *chicha* is a ceremonial drink made from fermented sugar-cane juice flavoured with coffee or cacao). **Batidos**, delicious when prepared with fresh fruit, are thick milkshakes. Also popular are **pipas**, sweet water from green coconuts served either ice-cold or freshly hacked from the palm tree. Said to cleanse the system, these can also have diuretic properties when consumed in large quantities. Although Panama is rich in fruit varieties, the nation mysteriously seems to prefer canned beverages to fresh-fruit drinks, and in many towns you will not be able to find fresh juices for sale even if the trees are bursting

with ripe fruit, so be prepared to buy fruit and make your own juice.

Beer is extremely popular in Panama. Locally brewed brands include Panama, Atlas, Soberana and Balboa; imported beers such as Budweiser, Heineken and Guinness are available in Panama City. For a quicker buzz, many Panamanians turn to locally produced **rum** – Seco Herrerano (known as *seco*), Carta Vieja and Abuelo are the most common brands; imported whiskies and other spirits are widely available. You can get **wine** in most towns.

CULTURE AND ETIQUETTE

Panama, like much of the rest of Latin America, is **socially conservative**, with a vast majority of the population reported as Roman Catholic. Thanks to the country's rather international history more religions are present than in other parts of the region, but the combination of a largely Catholic cultural identity, economic stratification and other ingrained colonial legacies has produced a country and people who appreciate rules and accept established social castes. This is not to say, however, that Panamanian society is stagnant. The history of a US presence, widespread access to global media and entertainment, and relatively diverse demographics as well as recent economic expansion, have all contributed to making Panama a country familiar with change.

A **macho** attitude is nonetheless prevalent throughout Panama. Objectification of the female body is common, though generally not blatant outside of Panama City. For women travelling in Panama, unsolicited attention in the form of whistles and cat-calls is almost inevitable, though easily ignored. In personalized settings, more respect is typically accorded, though intimate advances are often very direct. Overall, the Caribbean and indigenous areas of Panama hold more relaxed and less macho attitudes, though revealing clothing is not tolerated (except on the beach) in Bocas del Toro, where even men are required, by law, to wear shirts in public. Attitudes toward homosexuality are, by and large, intolerant.

Tipping is only expected in more expensive places, where a tip is sometimes included on the final bill, or where service has been particularly good.

SPORTS AND OUTDOOR ACTIVITIES

With every important match being televised and broadcast on radio, both European and Latin American **football** leagues have a broad fan base and are closely followed in Panama, but

baseball (*beisbol*) is Panama's official national sport. The baseball season in Panama is short, starting up in January and continuing through the northern hemisphere's winter months (Panama's dry season). There are ten teams in the national league, each representing one of Panama's provinces, and home teams are sacred to their impassioned fans, making the experience of attending a game lively and culturally rich. The baseball stadium in Panama City, Estadio Rod Carew is named after Major League Baseball Hall-of-Fame player and Panamanian native Rod Carew. This modern complex holds 26,000 and is nestled in the hillside of Cerro Patacon between Avenida de la Paz and Autopista Panamá–Colón, just north of the city. You can get tickets to a game for less than US$5, and, other than during the play-offs, the stadium is never full. **Boxing** is also popular in Panama, with Panamanian Roberto Durán arguably one of the best competitors the sport has ever seen.

Hiking, rafting, surfing and diving are probably the most common and easily accessible of the outdoor activities. Boquete, in the Chiriquí Highlands, provides an ideal departure point for **hikes** up the Volcán Barú (see p.658), Panama's highest point, as well as for **rafting** trips down the formidable Río Chiriquí and Río Chiriquí Viejo (see p.655). Bocas del Toro is a world-renowned **dive** site (see p.659), with trips ranging from all-day snorkel tours to underwater exploration of shipwrecks and spectacular reef walls. Even experienced divers should make an effort to dive in the Panama Canal, where huge amounts of machinery and entire villages submerged by the rising waters of Lago Gatún make for unusual underwater attractions. Bocas can also have excellent **surf**, though it is seasonal and less consistent than on the Pacific coast, where Santa Catalina has the most popular break. Ancon Expeditions (see p.664) is a good place to ask for information on arranging trips, and ⓦwww.wannasurf.com lists the best breaks.

COMMUNICATIONS

Other than in remote areas, Panama's **communications** network is good. **Letters** posted with the Correo Nacional (COTEL) cost US$0.35 to both the US and Europe, and should reach their destination within a week or two. Even though **post offices**, generally open Monday to Friday from 8am to 5pm, Saturday 8am to noon, can be found in most small towns, it's best to post mail in Panama City.

Panama's privatized telephone company is owned by Cable & Wireless. **Local calls** are cheap, and there's a wide network of payphones that take phone-cards sold in shops and street stalls in denominations of US$3, US$5, US$10 and US$20. Local numbers should have seven digits; local mobile numbers have eight digits and begin with a "6" or a "5". Many internet cafés also provide international phone calls for about US$1.50 for the first minute and US$0.25 per minute thereafter. You can make inter-national collect calls from payphones via the international operator (☎106), and both AT&T (☎109) and MCI (☎108) can place collect or credit-card calls to the US. **Mobile phone** coverage is growing, and even covers remote stretches of the Darién and Kuna Yala, with Movil and Digicel having the best coverage outside of the capital. It's easy to buy a local SIM card in Panama City and replace the card in your own phone with it, although you may need a "hacker" to unlock your phone for use of the Panamanian networks.

You should be able to find an **internet** café almost anywhere you go; rates are normally US$1–2 per hour in more remote towns. Wi-fi is becoming more common, especially in Panama City where it is available in many of the city's public parks.

CRIME AND SAFETY

Panama has something of an unjust reputation as a dangerous place to travel. Although **violent crime** does occasionally occur, Panama is far safer than most other countries in Central America. Nonetheless, you should take

---

PANAMA ON THE NET

ⓦ**www.almanaqueazul.com** A green portal, promoting ecological and sustainable tourism within Panama.

ⓦ**www.ancon.org** National Conservation Association website. Panama's most influential environmental group has general information (in Spanish) on national parks, ecology, voluntary work and endangered species.

ⓦ**www.extremepanama.com** A great portal, with links to independent tour operators, organized by region and activity.

ⓦ**www.focuspublicationsint.com/New_Site/index.html** Website of *El Visitante/ The Visitor*, a dual-language, bi-monthly publication.

ⓦ**www.panamainfo.com** A comprehensive portal providing listings of hotels, restaurants and tourist activities across the country.

ⓦ**www.thepanamanews.com** Panama's frequently updated online newspaper is a good place to keep up with the latest events.

ⓦ**www.pancanal.com** The official site of the Panama Canal Authority, offering plenty of information and news, a history of the canal and photographs, as well as live webcams at two locks.

ⓦ**www.visitpanamav2.com** Panamanian Tourist Institute site, with information on attractions and links to hotels, airlines and tour agencies.

special care in **Colón**, as well as in the El Chorillo and Santa Ana districts of **Panama City**. Late at night or when carrying luggage, take a taxi. Outside these two cities, the only other area where there is any particular danger is near the **Colombian border** in Darién and Kuna Yala. This frontier has long been frequented by guerrillas, bandits and cocaine traffickers, and several travellers attempting to cross overland to Colombia have been kidnapped or killed – or have simply disappeared. It is possible to visit some areas of Darién safely, including parts of the national park, but we recommend that you travel here as part of an organized tour group, with a pre-arranged local guide, or after having taken expert advice – see p.628 for more information about the region. Note, too, that many of the boats that ply the coast are involved in smuggling.

If you become the victim of a crime, report it immediately to the local **police** station, particularly if you will later be making an insurance claim. If treated respectfully, Panamanian police are generally honest and helpful, though it is not uncommon for travellers to be asked to present identification when walking in the city at night. In Panama City the **tourist police** (*policia de turismo*) are better prepared to deal with foreign travellers and more likely to speak English – they wear white armbands and are often mounted on bicycles or mopeds.

Although by law you are required to carry your **passport** at all times, you will rarely be asked to present it except when in transit; the tourist police recommend that when walking around the towns and cities it's better to carry a copy of your passport (including the page with the entry stamp). When caught without identification, a "fine" may be levied on the spot, usually about US$20, or you could be taken to the immigration office (*migración*), and held until your identity is verified.

> **EMERGENCY NUMBERS**
> Ambulance ☎225 1436 or 228 2187 or 269 9778
> Cruz Roja (Red Cross) ☎228 2187
> Fire ☎103
> Police ☎104
> Seguro Social ☎229 1133
> Tourist Police ☎270 2467

HEALTH

Medical care in Panama is best sought in the two largest cities: Panama City and David. Panama City has a handful of top-notch **hospitals** with many US- and European-trained doctors and English-speaking staff; see p.608 for listings. As most doctors and hospitals expect payment up front, frequently in cash, check your health insurance plan or buy supplementary travel insurance before you leave home.

Pharmacies are numerous; Farmacias Arrocha is the largest national chain, and its stores stay open until 11pm. Pharmacies in Supermercado Rey grocery stores are open 24 hours. Hospitals and occasionally health clinics have pharmacies on site, and many types of medicines are available over the counter, without a prescription.

MONEY AND BANKS

Panama adopted **US dollars** (referred to interchangeably as *dólares* or *balboas*) as its currency in 1904, and has not printed any paper currency since. The country does, however, mint its own coinage: 1, 5, 10, 25 and 50 **centavo** pieces, which are used alongside US coins. Both US$100 and US$50 bills are often difficult to spend, so try to have US$20 as the largest bills you carry. It is difficult to **change foreign currency** in Panama – change any cash into US dollars as soon as you can. In Panama City there are Banco Nacional branches at the airport and on Via España in the El Cangrejo district, or you could try Panacambios, a *casa de cambio* also on Via España. Foreign banks will generally change their own currencies.

Travellers' cheques are impossible to change, so you're better off with a debit card. The three major **banks** in Panama – Banco Nacional, Banistmo and Banco General – are generally open from 8am to 3pm Monday to Friday, and from 9am to noon on Saturday; almost all branches have **ATMs**, as do many large supermarkets. Major **credit cards** are accepted in most hotels and restaurants in Panama City and the larger provincial towns, though hardly anywhere in Bocas del Toro. Visa is the most widely accepted, followed by MasterCard.

INFORMATION AND MAPS

Good, impartial information about Panama is hard to come by once you're in the country. The biggest network of information is the Panamanian Tourist Institute (ⓦwww.visitpanamav2.com) or the Autoridad de Turismo Panama (ATP), which has its main office in Panama City (see p.603) and many provincial branches; their IPAT offices generally offer flyers and pamphlets, while the CEFATI branches display information on boards. You can get some useful information at these offices – advice, free maps, leaflets – but unless you go there with some fairly specific questions you may end up with little more than glossy brochures. The provincial offices vary, but even in the most rudimentary you should be able to find someone who speaks English. *The Visitor/El Visitante* (ⓦwww.thevisitorpanama.com), a free, twice-monthly **tourist promotion magazine** in English and Spanish, is available at IPAT offices and tourist venues throughout Panama, and lists attractions and upcoming events. Several **tour operators** based in Panama City (see p.603) can give you advice on the rest of the country, in the hope of selling you a tour.

Panama's **national parks** and other protected areas are administered by the National Environment Agency, **ANAM** (ⓦwww.anam.gob.pa). The main office in Panama City (see p.603) is, in theory, keen to promote ecotourism, though they offer almost no information. The ANAM regional offices are generally more helpful (though still unaccustomed to the idea of travellers visiting the parks independently), and are an essential stop before visiting areas where permission is needed or if you want to spend the night in a refuge.

The best **map** of Panama (1:480,000) is produced by International Travel Maps. In the country, large-scale maps are available at the Instituto Geográfico Nacional Tommy Guardia (Mon–Fri 8.30am–4pm) on Via Simón Bolívar, opposite the entrance to the university in Panama City. Good-quality maps of Panama City are available throughout the city for US$5–10.

OPENING HOURS AND PUBLIC HOLIDAYS

Opening hours vary, but generally businesses and government **offices** are open Monday to Saturday from 8 or

PUBLIC HOLIDAYS

Jan 1 New Year's Day

Jan 9 Martyrs' Day (in remembrance of those killed by US troops in the 1964 riots)

Feb/March (date varies) Carnaval

March/April Good Friday

May 1 Labor Day

Aug 15 Foundation of Panama City (Panama City only)

Nov 2 All Souls' Day

Nov 3 Independence Day (from Colombia, 1903)

Nov 4 Flag Day (government holiday only)

Nov 5 National Day (Colón only)

Nov 10 First Cry of Independence

Nov 28 Emancipation Day (independence from Spain)

Dec 8 Mother's Day

Dec 25 Christmas Day

9am to 4 or 5pm. **Museums** generally open the same hours from Tuesday to Saturday, with some also opening on Sunday morning and some closing for lunch at around 12.30 or 1pm. **Shops** are usually open from Monday to Saturday from 9am to 6pm.

Panama has several national **public holidays** (see box, p.593), when most government offices, businesses and shops close. Panama City and Colón also each have their own public holiday, and there is one public holiday for government employees only. When the public holidays fall near a weekend many Panamanians take a long weekend (known as a *puente*) and head to the beach or the countryside, so it can be difficult to find hotel rooms during these times. Several of these public holidays also coincide with **national fiestas** that continue for several days.

FESTIVALS

For festivals in the Península de Azuero, see the box on p.643.

January Feria de las Flores y del Café in Boquete (date varies).

February Comarca de Kuna Yala (Feb 25) celebrates the Kuna Revolution of 1925, their independence day; Carnaval (Feb/March) celebrated all over the country, but especially in Las Tablas and Panama City.

March Semana Santa (March/April) celebrated everywhere, but most colourfully in La Villa de Los Santos, Pesé and Guararé, on the Azuero Peninsula.

April Feria de las Orquídeas in Boquete (date varies); Feria International del Azuero in La Villa de Los Santos (date varies).

June Corpus Christi (date varies) in La Villa de Los Santos.

July Nuestra Señora del Carmen (July 16) on Isla Taboga; Patronales de La Santa Librada and Festival de la Pollera in Las Tablas (July 20–22).

August Festival del Manito Ocueno (date varies) in Ocú.

October Festival of Nogagope (Oct 10–12) on Isla Tigre, Comarca de Kuna Yala; Feria Kuna (Oct 13–16) on Isla Tigre; Festival de la Mejorana (Oct 21) in Guararé; Fiesta de Cristo Negro (Oct 21) in Portobelo.

November The "First Cry of Independence" (Nov 10), Independence Day, celebrated as part of "El Mes de la Patria". Cities and town across the nation put on parades featuring school drumming troupes and majorettes, which the whole population comes out to watch.

Panama City

Few cities in Latin America can match the diversity and cosmopolitanism of **PANAMA CITY**: polyglot and postmodern before its time, its atmosphere is surprisingly more similar to the mighty trading cities of Asia than to anywhere else in the region. The city has always thrived on commerce; its unique position on the world's trade routes and the economic opportunity this presents has attracted immigrants and businesses from all over the globe. With nearly a third of the country's population living in the urbanized corridor between Panama City and Colón, the capital's metropolitan melting pot is a study in contrasts. East and West, ancient and modern, wealth and poverty: they all have a place in Panama City.

The city's layout, too, encompasses some startling incongruities. On a small peninsula at the southwest end of the Bay of Panama stands the old city centre of **Casco Viejo**, a breezy jumble of ruins and restored colonial buildings; 4km or so to the northeast rise the shimmering skyscrapers of **El Cangrejo**, the modern banking and commercial district. West of the old centre, the former US Canal Zone town of **Balboa** retains a distinctly North American character, while eastward from El Cangrejo, amid sprawling suburban slums, stand the ruins of **Panamá Viejo**, the first European city on the Pacific coast of the Americas. Isles of tranquillity far from the frenetic squalor of the city include **Isla Taboga**, the "Island of Flowers", some 20km off the coast; the islets of the Amador Causeway alongside the Pacific entrance to the canal; and the **Parque Nacional Metropolitano**, an island of tropical rainforest within the capital. Panama City is also a good base for day-trips to the canal and the Caribbean coast as far as Portobelo.

What to see and do

The old city centre of **Casco Viejo** (also known as Casco Antiguo or San Felipe) is the most picturesque and historically interesting part of Panama City and houses many of its most important buildings and several museums. Declared a UNESCO World Heritage Site in 1997, it is gradually being restored to its former glory after decades of neglect, though it can still be a dangerous neighbourhood at night, as it borders **El Chorillo**, the city's most notorious slum. For views of the modern city and ships waiting to cross the canal, head for the bougainvillea-shaded **Paseo Las Bóvedas**, running some 400m along the top of the old city's defensive wall between the Plaza de Francia and the corner of Calle 1 and Avenida A.

To the west, the **Amador Causeway** marks the entrance to the canal and the Canal Zone, comprised of the Causeway, Fort Amador and the town of Balboa. East along the bay from the old city centre, the pulsing and chaotic commercial heart of the capital lies in the neighbouring districts of **Bella Vista**, **El Cangrejo** and **Punta Paitilla**, where the majority of banks, hotels, restaurants, shops and luxurious private residences can be found.

ORIENTATION IN PANAMA CITY

Getting around Panama City can be disconcerting, so it's often best to take a taxi to your accommodation. Confusingly, many streets in Panama City have at least two names: Avenida Cuba, for instance, is also Avenida 2 Sur, and the road commonly known as Calle 50 is also Avenida 4 Sur or Avenida Nicanor de Obarrio. We have used the most common names throughout this account.

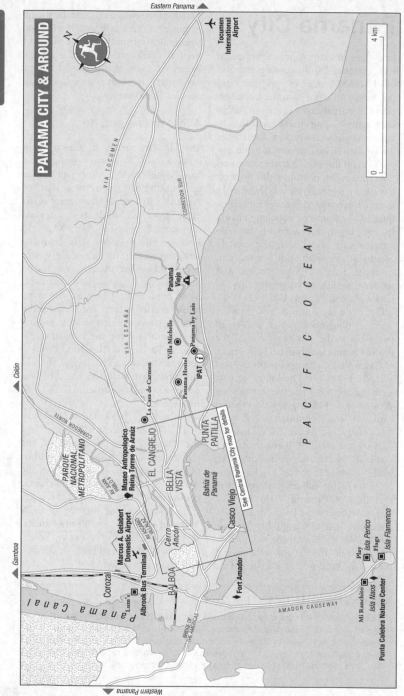

PANAMA CITY & AROUND

N

Eastern Panama ▲

Tocumen International Airport

VIA TOCUMEN

CORREDOR SUR

Colón ◀

CORREDOR NORTE

PARQUE NACIONAL METROPOLITANO

VIA ESPAÑA

Panamá Viejo

Villa Michelle

Panama by Luis

Panama Hostel

IPAT ℹ

La Casa de Carmen

Museo Antropológico Reina Torres de Araúz

VIA JUAN PABLO II

EL CANGREJO

PUNTA PAITILLA

BELLA VISTA

Bahía de Panamá

See Central Panama City map for details

P A C I F I C   O C E A N

Gamboa ▲

Marcus A. Gelabert Domestic Airport

VIA ISRAEL

Cerro Ancón

Casco Viejo

Corozal

Albrook Bus Terminal

BALBOA

Fort Amador

BRIDGE OF THE AMERICAS

AMADOR CAUSEWAY

Punta Calebra Nature Center

Mi Ranchito

Isla Naos

Isla Perico

Flags

Play

Isla Flamenco

P a n a m a   C a n a l

Lim

Western Panama ▲

0   4 km

Casco Viejo and El Cangrejo are joined by **Avenida Central**, the city's main thoroughfare. Running north of the old centre, its name changes to **Via España** as it continues through the downtown districts of Calidonia and La Exposición and the residential neighbourhood of Bella Vista. Several other main avenues run parallel to Avenida Central: Avenida Perú, Avenida Cuba, Avenida Justo Arosemena and, along the seafront, Avenida Balboa.

Plaza Catedral

Elderly men dressed sharply in pressed linen suits chat amiably among the shaded benches and gazebos of cobblestoned **Plaza Catedral**, which sits at the heart of Casco Viejo and the old city. Also known as Plaza de la Independencia, in honour of the proclamations of independence from both Spain and Colombia that were issued here, the western side of the plaza is dominated by the classical facade of the **cathedral** (daily 8am–2pm). Built between 1688 and 1796, it was constructed using stones from the ruined cathedral of Panamá Viejo (see p.609). Three of its bells were also recovered from its predecessor; reputedly, they owe their distinctive tone to a ring thrown by Empress Isabella of Spain into the molten metal from which they were cast. They ring throughout the day to announce Mass.

Across the square from the cathedral is the bare concrete skeleton of the **Hotel Central**, built to replace the Grand Hotel, which was, in its time, the plushest hotel in Central America. It was here that jubilant crowds gathered in 1903 to celebrate Panamanian independence by pouring champagne over the head of General Huertas, the defecting garrison commander, for over an hour.

Southeast of the cathedral is the Neoclassical Palacio Municipal, whose small **Museo de Historia Panameña**

(Mon–Fri 8am–4pm; US$1) offers a cursory introduction to Panamanian history.

Mercado del Mariscos

Even if you don't smell the **fish market** from a mile away, the buzzards circling outside are a sure indication that you've reached the city's seafood hub, on Avenida Balboa at the entrance to Casco Viejo. Inside you'll find a fantastic selection of Panama's marine life on ice, with lime, and ready to consume. Upstairs is the popular *Restaurante Mercado de Mariscos* (daily 11am–7pm; ☎212–3898), serving what many locals call the best *ceviche* in the city (US$3–4), and all things fresh and fishy.

Museo del Canal Interoceánico

The excellent **Museo del Canal Interoceánico** (Tues–Sun 9am–5pm; US$2; ⓦwww.museodelcanal.com), on the south side of the Plaza Catedral, explains in great detail the history of the country's transisthmian waterway. Photographs, video footage and historic exhibits – including the original canal treaties – document everything from the first Spanish attempt to find a passage to Asia to the contemporary management of the canal. All displays are in Spanish, but most of the guides (US$5 per person for groups of 3–10) speak English; book **tours** in advance (☎221–1649).

Palacio Presidencial

On the seafront two blocks north of the Plaza Catedral along Calle 6, the **Palacio Presidencial**, originally built in 1673, was home to several successive colonial and Colombian governors. In 1922 it was rebuilt in grandiose neo-Moorish style under the orders of President Belisario Porras, who also introduced white Darién herons to the grounds, giving the palace the nickname of "Palacio de las Garzas". The birds and their descendants have

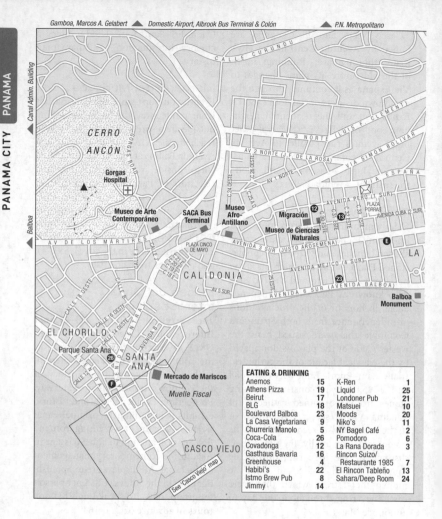

EATING & DRINKING			
Anemos	15	K-Ren	1
Athens Pizza	19	Liquid	25
Beirut	17	Londoner Pub	21
BLG	18	Matsuei	10
Boulevard Balboa	23	Moods	20
La Casa Vegetariana	9	Niko's	11
Churreria Manolo	5	NY Bagel Café	2
Coca-Cola	26	Pomodoro	6
Covadonga	12	La Rana Dorada	3
Gasthaus Bavaria	16	Rincon Suizo/	
Greenhouse	4	Restaurante 1985	7
Habibi's	22	El Rincon Tableño	13
Istmo Brew Pub	8	Sahara/Deep Room	24
Jimmy	14		

lived freely around the patio fountain ever since, although rumour has it that when US President Jimmy Carter visited the palace in 1977 for the signing of the new canal treaty his security team sprayed the building with a disinfectant that proved fatal to the herons, and replacements had to be rushed in under cover of darkness. The streets around the palace are closed to traffic and pedestrians, but the presidential guards allow visitors to view the exterior of the palace between 8am and 5pm daily via a checkpoint on Calle 4.

Plaza Bolívar

A block back down Calle 6 and two blocks east along Avenida B is **Plaza Bolívar**, an elegant square dedicated in 1883 to Simón Bolívar, whose statue, crowned by a condor, stands in its centre. Bolívar came here in 1826 for the first Panamerican Congress, held in the chapter-room of the old **monastery** on the northeast corner of the square. The building has been beautifully restored but now houses government offices and non-official visitors are not permitted. Next door stands the church

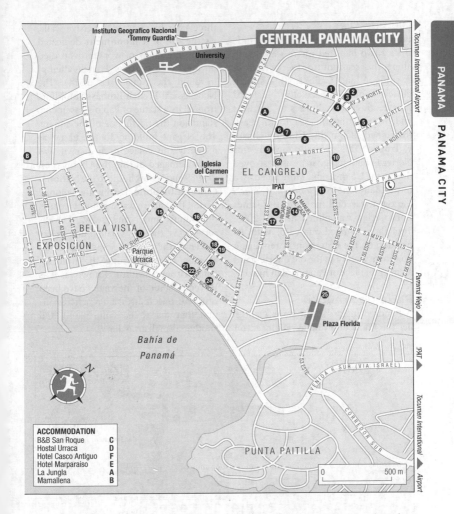

CENTRAL PANAMA CITY

Instituto Geografico Nacional 'Tommy Guardia'

University

VIA SIMÓN BOLIVAR

EL CANGREJO

Iglesia del Carmen

IPAT

BELLA VISTA

EXPOSICIÓN

Parque Urraca

Bahía de Panamá

Plaza Florida

PUNTA PAITILLA

| 0 | 500 m |

Tocumen International Airport

Panamá Viejo ▶

IPAT ▶

Tocumen International Airport ▶

ACCOMMODATION

B&B San Roque	C
Hostal Urraca	D
Hotel Casco Antiguo	F
Hotel Marparaiso	E
La Jungla	A
Mamallena	B

and monastery of **San Francisco**, built in the seventeenth century but extensively modified since. The church is usually closed, but if you ask in the parish office on Avenida B someone may be willing to open it up and show you around. Other than the carved wooden confessional dating to 1736 the interior is unspectacular, but the tower offers fine views across the city.

Teatro Nacional

Just south of Plaza Bolívar on Avenida B is the **Teatro Nacional** (☎262 3525),

designed by Genaro Ruggieri, the Italian architect responsible for La Scala in Milan. Extensively restored in the early 1970s and built to the most exacting acoustic standards, the splendid Neoclassical interior is richly furnished and decorated in red and gold, with French crystal chandeliers, busts of famous dramatists and a vaulted ceiling painted with scenes depicting the birth of the nation by Panamanian artist Roberto Lewis. When the theatre is open there is usually a docent on hand to give tours of the building.

Club de Clases y Tropas

From the car park at the end of Avenida B it's a two hundred-metre walk south along the seafront to the corner of Avenida A and Calle 1. This stretch passes some immaculately restored nineteenth-century houses to the west and, overlooking the sea to the east, the ruined shell of the **Club de Clases y Tropas**. This recreation centre for Noriega's national guard was destroyed during the US invasion. More recently, a formal ball scene for *Quantum of Solace*, the twenty-second movie in the James Bond series, was filmed here in 2008. Though a bombed-out ruin, with its position on the waterfront it remains a dominant feature of the old quarter, and an integral piece of Panamanian history.

Plaza de Francia

A hundred metres south along Calle 1 lies the **Plaza de Francia**. Enclosed on three sides by seaward defensive walls, it's the site of a **monument** dedicated to the thousands of workers who died during the disastrous French attempt to build the canal (see p.614). The Neoclassical **French Embassy** building, fronted by a statue of Pablo Arosemena, stands on the north side of the square. The elegant building to the east was formerly the Palace of Justice; it was badly damaged during the US invasion in 1989 and is now home to the **National Cultural Institute**. During the colonial period the square was a military centre, the vaults under the seaward walls serving as the city's jail; built below sea level, they would sometimes flood at high tide, drowning the unfortunate prisoners within. Known as **Las Bóvedas**, some of the vaults have been restored: one houses a French restaurant that shares the same name, and another a small art gallery.

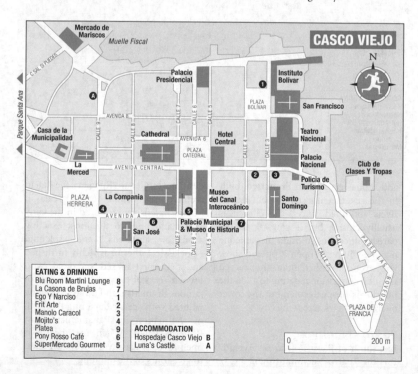

CASCO VIEJO

EATING & DRINKING
Blu Room Martini Lounge 8
La Casona de Brujas 7
Ego Y Narciso 1
Frit Arte 2
Manolo Caracol 3
Mojito's 4
Platea 9
Pony Rosso Café 6
SuperMercado Gourmet 5

ACCOMMODATION
Hospedaje Casco Viejo B
Luna's Castle A

0   200 m

Church and Convent of Santo Domingo

Two blocks west along Avenida A from the corner with Calle 1 stands the ruined **Church and Convent of Santo Domingo**, completed in 1678 and famous for the **Arco Chato** (flat arch). Only 10.6m high but spanning some 15m with no external support, the Arco Chato was reputedly cited as evidence of Panama's seismic stability when the US Senate was debating where to build an interoceanic canal. Unfortunately, the arch collapsed just after the centenary celebrations of Panama's independence in 2003. Although the reason for the collapse is unclear, some say it was due to the estimated twenty thousand people who descended on Casco Viejo for the celebrations.

Church of San José and Plaza Herrera

West along Avenida A at the corner with Calle 8 is the **Church of San José**. Built in 1673 and since remodelled, the church is exceptional only as the home of the legendary Baroque Golden Altar, one of the few treasures to survive Henry Morgan's ransacking of Panamá Viejo in 1671 – it was apparently painted or covered in mud to disguise its real value.

One block west of San José, Avenida A emerges onto **Plaza Herrera**, a pleasant square lined with nineteenth-century houses. This was originally the Plaza de Triunfo, where bullfights were held, but was renamed in 1922 in honour of General Tomás Herrera, whose statue stands at its centre. Herrera was the military leader of the short-lived independence attempt in 1840; he went on to be elected president of Colombia, but was assassinated in 1854. The area can be dodgy at night, so is best avoided after dark.

Avenida Central

Avenida Central runs north all the way from the waterfront in the old city centre, through the scary, off-limits barrios of Santa Ana and El Chorillo, towards the more modern portion of the city. The pedestrianized, ten-block stretch between **Parque Santa Ana**, a small park and busy transport hub, and Plaza Cinco de Mayo is the liveliest and most popular **shopping** district in the city. Blasts of air conditioning and loud music pour from the huge superstores that line the avenue, while hawkers with megaphones attempt to entice shoppers inside with deals on clothing, electronics and household goods. Nowhere is the diversity and vitality of the city more evident. Because the avenue runs through some of the poorer areas of town, it's best not to venture down any side streets.

Plaza Cinco de Mayo

As Avenida Central emerges onto **Plaza Cinco de Mayo**, the pedestrianized section ends and the maelstrom of traffic takes over again. The plaza is actually two squares rolled into one. The first has a small monument to the volunteer firemen killed while fighting an exploded gunpowder magazine in 1914; *bomberos* occupy a revered position in a city that has so often been devastated by fire. The second square, Plaza Cinco de Mayo proper, borders the legislative palace compound and has a black, monolithic monument emblazoned with the nationalist slogan: "Ni limosnas, ni millones, queremos justicia" ("Neither alms, nor millions, we want justice"). Heading north from here, Avenida Central splits, with the north fork called Avenida Central and the south called Avenida Justo Arosemena (Av 3 Sur).

Museo Afro-Antillano

At the corner of Avenida Justo Arosemena and Calle 24 is a wooden former church, now the **Museo Afro-Antillano** (Tues–Sun 9am–4pm; US$1; ☎262–5348), dedicated to preserving

THE AFRO-ANTILLANOS

Some five percent of Panama's population are Afro-Antillanos – descendants of the black workers from the English- and French-speaking West Indies who began migrating to Panama in the mid-nineteenth century to help build the railroad and canal. Widely considered second-class citizens or undesirable aliens, Afro-Antillanos worked and lived in appalling conditions under French and American control. Most of the twenty thousand workers who died during the French canal attempt were West Indians, and the mortality rate was four times higher among black workers than white during US construction.

Panamanian treatment of Afro-Antillanos during the first half of the twentieth century was little better than French or American. Consequently, though they are somewhat less discriminated against than other black populations in Central America, Afro-Antillanos remain among the most marginalized segments of the population.

In spite of these obstacles, more than a century after their arrival in Panama, the Afro-Antillanos maintain a vibrant and distinct culture whose influence is widely felt in contemporary Panamanian society. Many second- and third-generation Afro-Antillanos still speak the melodic patois of the West Indies, and the street Spanish of Panama City and Colón is peppered with Jamaican slang. Unique Protestant beliefs imported from the West Indies continue to thrive, heavily spiced Caribbean dishes permeate Panamanian cuisine, and the music, from jazz in the 1950s to "reggaespañol" in the 1990s, has made an indelible mark on the region.

the history and culture of Panama's large West Indian population. It is very small, but its exhibits – photographs, tools and furniture – give a good idea of the working and living conditions of black canal-workers. The venue also has a small library and occasionally hosts events, including Afro-Antillano cookery courses and jazz festivals.

Museo de Ciencias Naturales

Northeast of Plaza Cinco de Mayo, Avenida Central remains the city's main thoroughfare and a busy shopping street as it runs through the barrios of Calidonia and La Exposición. Two blocks east of Avenida Central on Avenida Cuba between Calle 29 and Calle 30, the **Museo de Ciencias Naturales** (Tues–Sat 9am–4pm; US$1) offers a basic introduction to Panama's geology and ecology, with many stuffed animals – look out for the pickled fer-de-lance, the venomous snake that killed the director of Panama's old zoo in 1931.

Balboa Monument

A short walk south down Calle 30 from the science museum brings you to waterside Avenida Balboa, and, several blocks to the north in a small, shady park, the glorious **Balboa Monument**. Erected in 1913 with Spanish help, the likeness of Vasco Núñez de Balboa, the sixteenth-century explorer, stands atop a globe with a sword in one hand and a flag in the other, looking out in perpetual triumph on the southern ocean he "discovered".

Arrival

By air International flights arrive at Tocumen International Airport (☎ 238 4322), about 26km northeast of Panama City. Domestic flights arrive at Marcos A. Gelabert Airport (☎ 315 0241), better known as Albrook airport, roughly a 15-minute taxi ride from the centre. Taxis from the international airport to the city cost from US$25 per person, with prices dropping depending on the number of people with whom you share. Taxis from Albrook to the city should cost from US$10.
By bus International buses from Costa Rica and domestic buses from almost everywhere in the interior of Panama arrive at and depart from the

Albrook terminal, just north of the city and very close to the domestic airport. Taxis can take you into town from US$10, and local city-bound buses (departing regularly from the terminal) make the run for about a dollar.

Information

Tour operators ANCON Expeditions, Edificio El Dorado, C Elvira Méndez (T 269 9415, W www.anconexpeditions.com), the commercial arm of the National Conservation Association, provides Panama's best ecotours. Scuba Panamá, Av 6 Norte at C 62A (T 261 3841, W www .scubapanama.com), offers countrywide diving excursions, equipment sale and rental, and diving instruction.

Tourist information For simple queries, ask at the international or domestic airport booths. The main IPAT office (Mon–Fri 8.30am–4.30pm; T 526 7000, W www.visitpanamav2.com) is just off Via España in the Central Building, at Av Samuel Lewis and C Gerardo Ortega. The city's hostels are generally where you will find the best information on budget travel options within the country, and can book travel and accommodation for trips including San Blas, the canal and beyond, with boat trips to Colombia. Panama's national parks and other protected natural areas are managed by the National Environment Agency (ANAM; T 315 0855, W www.anam.gob.pa), in Edificio 804 at the former US military base of Albrook.

City transport

Buses Panama City's public buses – known as *diablos rojos*, or red devils – are the cheapest way to get around. They cost just US$0.25 per ride, payable on exit, and operate 6am–midnight. There are no fixed routes or schedules: destinations are painted on the windscreen. Buses head almost everywhere in the city from Plaza Santa Ana and Albrook bus terminal.

Taxis Taxis are plentiful and cheap, if prone to hiking prices for tourists. Fares are based on a zone system; most intra-city rides will cost about US$2 for one person, US$0.50 per extra person, US$0.50 per zone change, and US$0.50 extra at night. No trip should cost more than US$5, except those to Tocumen international Airport (from US$25). Be aware that taxis in Panama City are legally obliged to accept passengers; if a driver doesn't want to go your way you'll be quoted a vastly inflated price, which is meant to either put you off or make it a worthwhile trip for the driver.

Bikes The safest place to ride a bicycle in Panama City is on Amador Causeway. For rentals head to the as yet unopened Museo de la Biodiversidad (see p.611) where Bicicletas Moses (Sat & Sun daylight hours) and Tony's Bike Rentals (Tues–Sun 10am–6pm in high season) will kit you out for US$3–4/hr. Rali-Carretero, Via España at Av Argentina (T 263 4136, W www.rali-carretero.com), has spare parts and a maintenance centre.

Accommodation

A growing number of budget travellers bed down in Casco Viejo, the city's old colonial centre. The restoration of many of the area's historic buildings makes it a pleasant retreat from the congestion and the pollution of the rest of the city. A number of lively bars and restaurants as well as some new backpacker-friendly hostels have also made it a popular nightlife destination. Immediately north and east of Casco Viejo lies the notoriously unsafe neighbourhood of El Chorillo, to be pointedly avoided at all times. Crossing east in a taxi, the Calidonia/La Exposición area offers unexceptional but affordable modern hotels and *residenciales*. Further east along Via España, the districts of Bella Vista and El Cangrejo, the hub of the city's nightlife and commercial activity, have the densest concentration of hostels, plus a few mid-range options.

Considering Panama's booming tourist economy, it's a good idea to book in advance no matter where you're staying. It's also best to exercise caution in all neighbourhoods after dark.

Casco Viejo

Hospedaje Casco Viejo C 8A, nos. 8–31 T 211 2127, W www.hospedajecascoviejo.com. A well-kept and surprisingly spacious hostel just off Av A and around the corner from the Iglesia de San José, this *hospedaje* may be lacking in colonial charm but is a calmer alternative in the old town. Shared kitchen, free wi-fi and rooftop access. Dorms US$10, doubles US$20

Hotel Casco Antiguo C 12 Oeste at Av B T 228 8510. This creaky, run-down property is the picture of wasted potential. Beautiful tilework in the lobbies, wide staircases, old-fashioned lifts and a wonderful view from the third-floor balcony are its redeeming features, though they don't make up for the dark, musty rooms with lumpy mattresses, and total lack of vibe. US$16

Luna's Castle C 9A Este between Av B & Av Alfaro T 262 1540, W www.lunas castlehostel.com. A colonial maze of high-ceilinged rooms, a busy kitchen, loads of chill-out spaces with wi-fi, and a cinema, framed by a kaleidoscope of vibrant artwork. Experienced gringo owners and friendly young staff who will arrange your onward travel (including boats to Colombia) complete the circus. Downstairs houses the *Relic* bar with crypt-style interior and breezy courtyard, which heaves until the wee hours with a healthy mix of locals and travellers (Wed–Sun) – perfect for partying 'packers, but not the best option for a weary traveller in need of sleep. Dorms US$13, doubles US$30

Bella Vista and El Cangrejo

B&B San Roque C Ricardo Arias off Via España ☎ 264 3566, ⓦ www.sanroquepanama.com. A small hotel with clean and icy-cold en-suite rooms, whose downtown location is a great base for exploring the city. Rooms come with hot water, wi-fi and a/c, and groups of up to six can rent the apartment suite for US$77/night. US$44

Hostal La Casa de Carmen Calle Primera El Carmen, Casa 32 ☎ 263 4366, ⓦ www.lacasadecarmen.net. *Carmen* attracts a wide age range with serene and colourful surroundings and a long list of free services including breakfast, internet, shared kitchen, laundry, hot water and barbecue area. Strongly recommended by travellers and usually full, so book ahead. Dorms US$15, doubles US$30

Hostal Urraca C 44, No. 2–112, Parque Urraca ☎ 391 3972, ⓦ www.hostalurraca.com. A newer hostel in a very central location, where tidy little dorms and rooms share bright communal spaces. Internet, communal kitchen, laundry services, free basic breakfast, and tourist information are also at your disposal. Dorms US$15, doubles US$40

La Jungla Hostel ☎ 6497 5672, ⓦ www.miradoradventures.com. This urban venture by the owner of the well-known *Hostel Nomba* in Boquete is spotlessly clean, spacious and well laid out. Set in a high-rise, there's a huge kitchen, internet, laundry facilities, balconies with urban views, free buffet breakfast, and a mix of upmarket dorms and private rooms. Best of all, you couldn't be any closer to the hip nightlife on Via Argentina. Dorms US$10, doubles US$28

Rest of Panama City

Hostel Mamallena C Primera, Casa de la Junta Comunal por el Colegio Javier, Perejil ☎ 6676 6163. Popular with a more "conscious" traveller (read hippy), although you may not be greeted with the warmest welcome, *Mamallena* has clean dorms and small private rooms, as well as a communal kitchen where you can make breakfast pancakes, an

outdoor courtyard and wi-fi. A good option for those who want a decent night's sleep, or need help with planning and booking onward travel. Dorms US$12, doubles US$30

Hotel Marparaiso C 34 at Av Justo Arosemena, La Exposición ☎ 227 6767, ⓦ www.marparaisopma.com. A stay of two nights, booked in advance, includes transport from the airport. Guests enjoy discounted breakfasts in the restaurant downstairs, and there's free wi-fi throughout. Rooms sleeping up to six people are homey rather than modern, and the street noise can be bothersome, but it's one of the best budget options in this sketchy area. US$40

Panama by Luis C Benito Reyes Testa por el condominio Davinci, San Francisco ☎ 393 6275 or 6726 6031, ⓦ panamabyluis.com. A small house with clean dorms and private rooms, tucked away on a quiet downtown street. Though the exterior is not so inviting, inside is a pleasant surprise, with funky modern touches; they're often full so phone ahead to check availability. Arrange tours and onward travel here, including trips to Kuna Yala. Dorms US$14, doubles US$33

Panama Hostel C 68 Este Casa 114, San Francisco ☎ 226 6687, ⓦ thepanamahostel.com. An ecofriendly setup in a safe, welcoming house, only a few minutes' walk from the central MultiPlaza Mall. Graffitied walls, a luxurious pool set in a large patio garden, and the funky *Karma Bar* create a fun vibe, although it can be noisy at weekends. Uncrowded dorms and cosy private rooms share a clean kitchen and living room as well as the fantastic outdoor space, overlooked by the pretty balcony of the upstairs dorm. Dorms US$15, doubles US$30

Villa Michelle C 2 ½ Sur at C 82 Este, Pueblo Nuevo ☎ 221 2310, ⓦ www.villamichellepanama.com. A gorgeous home of 9 private rooms – all with a/c, TV and wi-fi, some en suite – sleeping up to four guests. You can also cook in one of two kitchens, hang out in the numerous living rooms, or laze on the terrace by the pool. Owners Michelle and Ivonne run tours, and can arrange onward travel. US$45

Eating

Panama City's cosmopolitan nature is reflected in its restaurants: anything from US fast food to Greek, Italian, Chinese, Japanese and French can easily be found, and excellent seafood is widely available. Colombian snacks like *arepas* – corn tortillas fried and filled with meat or seafood, tomatoes, eggs and cheese – are a favoured street-food; the most popular vendor is at Calle Asia el Santuario Nacional on Via España. Cheap takeaway meals are also available from the Rey supermarket (open 24hr) on Via España.

Casco Viejo and Amador

Lum's Carretera Diablo, Building 340, Ancon. Near the canal in Ancon, this enormous building has gringo honky-tonk atmosphere, complete with billiards, foosball and good beer selection, and filling American-style meals. US$5–10 for starters and main courses.

Mi Ranchito Calzador de Amador, near the Nature Center (see p.611). This place is extremely popular with locals for its cocktails, seafood and sunset city views. That said, the pricey mains (from US$8) and round-trip taxi fare can be a blow to the budget.

Pony Rosso Cafe Av A and C 7. Also home to the Diablo Rosso Art Gallery, this trendy boutique café has an eclectic, Mediterranean-influenced menu of large and delicious paninis and salads (US$5–10). Displaying a collection of quirky furniture and art, *Pony*'s adds to the bohemian vibe of this colonial neighbourhood. One-off designer clothing and accessories, and all the artwork adorning the walls, are for sale; the venue also hosts film screenings every Tues. Closed Sun.

SuperMercado Gourmet Av A at C 6. A café and deli serving good sandwiches and excellent set lunches for US$4–10, and the best coffees in the

old town. Also has a decent selection of hard-to-find gourmet and imported goods, from British jams to bulgur wheat. Closed Sun.

Calidonia and Santa Ana

Boulevard Balboa Av Balboa at C 31 Este. The spartan 1970s interior here is livened up by a smart lunchtime crowd of local politicians and office workers. Although specializing in toasted sandwiches (US$3), the lengthy menu also includes a number of filling Panamanian dishes (from US$5), such as a chicken and rice platter (*pollo y arroz*) or *ceviche de corvina*.

Coca-Cola On Plaza Santa Ana, C 12 at Av Central. The self-proclaimed "oldest restaurant in Panama" and something of an institution among the city's older residents, who gather to drink coffee, read the paper and discuss the news. Filling Panamanian staples (*ceviche*, chicken with rice, soups) from US$3.50, and generous breakfasts cooked to order.

Covadonga C 29 at Av Perú. A 24hr restaurant on the bottom storey of a hotel by the same name, *Covadonga* has reasonably priced (US$5–10) Panamanian and international dishes. Hints of Colombian, Greek and Spanish influences abound, from the Colombian flag on the wall to the Greek salads and flan.

El Rincón Tableño Av Cuba at C 31. Another example of the city's ubiquitous cafeteria-style eateries, *Tableño* serves up *comida típica* with relish and at economical prices, under US$5. Try the *sancocho*, Panama's favourite meat-and-veg soup, here.

Bella Vista and El Cangrejo

Athens Pizza (Pano's Kretan House) C 48 Este at C 50, behind the Delta petrol station. Near the party spots on C Uruguay, this joint serves up a tasty and filling meal for around US$5. The Greek dishes are abundant and the pizza is the best comfort food you'll find in Panama. Closed Wed. There's another branch on C 57 (closed Tues).

Beirut C 49A Este at Av 3 Sur, opposite the *Marriott*. A largely Lebanese menu (from US$4) with bowls of tasty hummus and *baba ganoush* for US$5, and halal shawarma and kofta plates for US$12. Popular with wealthy locals for its good service, hookah pipes and occasional belly-dancing at weekends.

Caffé Pomodoro C 49B Oeste in *ApartHotel Las Vegas*. Extremely popular Italian restaurant, with outdoor seating in an enclosed tropical garden. One of several venues owned by local celebrated chef Willy Diggleman (see box below), with a menu of antipasti, salads and pastas from US$6.

La Casa Vegetariana Via Veneta at the Edificio Veneto. Popular Chinese vegetarian buffet, where a plate piled high with tasty tofu stir-fry, steamed vegetables and noodles will set you back about US$3.

Churrería Manolo Via Argentina no. 12. Café specializing in the sweet, cigar-shaped *churro* pastries (US$0.50), as well as serving coffees and *emparedados*. US$4–10.

K-Ren Via Argentina at C Felipe Motta. The Panamanian equivalent to a "greasy spoon", this cafeteria serves a popular mix of *comida típica* and Chinese for US$3–6.

Matsuei C Eusebio A. Morales, near *Hotel El Parador*. A Japanese restaurant with friendly service and a large menu that offers sushi, tempura, curries and teriyaki. Prices range from US$9 to US$30 for a large sushi tray (which can be shared). Closed Sun lunch.

TREAT YOURSELF

Rincon Suizo/Restaurante 1985 C Eusebio A. Morales ☎263 8571 or 263 8310, ⓦwww.1985.com. The crown jewel of famed chef Willy Diggelmann's Panama City restaurant empire, these stylish Swiss and French restaurants sit side by side in El Cangrejo. Extensive menus of mouth-watering steak (try one with the bacon and mushroom sauce) and seafood dishes (the trout and sea bass are excellent), polished and creative daily specials and the impeccable wine list all give credence to the restaurants' reputation as two of the city's finest eateries. It's possible to eat for less than US$20, but not likely once you've had your first bite of an appetizer.

Niko's Just off Via España, opposite Plaza Regency. Extremely popular 24hr cafeteria with branches all over the city, serving a wide choice of Panamanian and international fast food. Much of the large menu, from grilled meat and fish to sandwiches, pizza and strong coffee, can be tasted for under US$5. Takeaway available.

NY Bagel Café On Plaza de Einstein, C Felipe Motta at Via Argentina. The exposed brick walls and large open kitchen lend a touch of the Big Apple to this popular hangout for travellers, expats and wealthy locals. One of the only bagel joints in Panama, *NY* serves a wide variety of bagels with home-made cream-cheese flavours (US$3), breakfasts and burgers, fruit smoothies, good coffee and more.

Drinking and nightlife

Panama City is very much a 24hr metropolis, and its residents like nothing better than to drink and dance into the early hours. At one end of the great range of places to go are the cantinas and bars around Avenida Central: hard-drinking dives where women are scarce. Most of the upmarket places are found around El Cangrejo, Amador and Casco Viejo. Once in a particular neighbourhood, it's easy and relatively safe to walk between venues at night. Cover charges are more often levied on weekends and tend to be high, but often include several free drinks. Most clubs are closed on Mondays and Tuesdays. See ⓦwww.panama1.com for a list of clubs and bars in the city.

Casco Viejo and Amador

Blu Room Martini Lounge C 1. A popular first stop for people making a night of it in Amador. Latin music dominates and the club can be selective over its clientele, so dress smart.

La Casona de las Brujas Av 8A. Artsy, laidback and hip, *La Casona* or "the witches' lair" provides a casual venue for live music and art displays, with beer and cocktails for under US$5.

Ego y Narciso Plaza Bolívar. There are plenty of places to go for tapas and a drink, but these Peruvian and Italian sister restaurants, on the relaxed and picturesque Plaza Bolívar, will give you a glamorous glimpse of colonial-era Panama City. Incredibly fancy cocktails from US$5.50.

Flags Calzador de Amador. A vast, modern, open-fronted complex with four restaurants, a bar area and great views of Panama City across the bay. It's particularly popular at weekends, when the central stage plays host to live music, including salsa bands.

Mojito's Opposite Plaza Herrera in the old city centre. Small, cheap and buzzing with expats,

If you haven't yet had your fill of bus trips, the Party Bus Panama (T 301 0010, W www.partybuspanama.net), a self-contained, moving party, is an easy, gimmicky night out. Call or email for reservations; the basic 2hr tour costs US$25 per person and includes an open bar.

locals and travellers, this mini-bar is a must for a night out in Casco Viejo.

Platea C 1, in front of the old *Club Union* T 228 4011. Upscale jazz bar underneath the pricey *Scena* restaurant – if you crave jazz, this is the place to go.

Play Isla Perico, Brisas de Amador. An ocean-view venue re-creating a trendy Miami-style beach club, where diners and drinkers lounge around looking fabulous. Expect a strict dress code and stiff prices.

Bella Vista and El Cangrejo

Anemos C 47. This chatty club gets going late and is a budget fave, offering a wealth of drink promotions and no cover charge, though there's not much of a crowd before midnight.

BLG C Uruguay between C 50 and Av 4A Sur. *BLG* serves the gay community and everyone else unlimited drinks with the US$25 cover charge. It's quickly becoming a well-known party spot, and the excellent DJs spinning seriously good groves will only make it more popular.

Gasthaus Bavaria C 50, Building 25. As the name implies, this hip yet bare-bones dive is fashioned after a German alehouse. Paulaner and Warsteiner on tap US$3.

Greenhouse Via Argentina near Plaza de Einstein. The *Greenhouse* is a popular choice to get the night started for a posh crowd. Fancy cocktails (US$5–7) and upmarket bar food, including sea bass fingers (US$8) and Greek chicken wrap (US$8), hit the spot while leaving a hole in your wallet.

Habibi's Off C Uruguay. Right in the thick of things, *Habibi's* has seemingly limitless indoor and outdoor seating perfect for enjoying hookahs, cocktails (from US$5) and Lebanese snacks.

Istmo Brew Pub Av Eusebio A. Morales. If you're craving something other than the standard local *cerveza*, *Istmo* is sure to refresh your tired palate – all of the beer is brewed on site (US$3–5) in beautiful copper kegs. Its open-air atmosphere, pool table and televised football matches are further pluses. Food is good if somewhat pricey (US$3–10).

Liquid Discothèque C 50 at C José de la Cruz. *Liquid* plays a range of music, from Europop to house, to the well-dressed crowd on its huge dancefloor. In keeping with the chic image, the cover charge is pricey: US$15 at weekends.

Londoner Pub C Uruguay. A slightly over-modernized take on the British pub, the *Londoner* has beers on tap (from US$3), darts and flat-screen TVs showing football matches. It's missing the warm woods and cosy corners of a true pub, but its location draws a crowd on busy nights (Thurs–Sat).

Moods C Uruguay. This popular spot brings in a slightly older clientele on weekdays, when there's no cover, but its prime location and live tropical beats draw all kinds at weekends (cover around US$10).

La Rana Dorada Via Argentina at Einstein's Head. Brasserie Bar popular with young expats and wealthy Panamanians, serving beer, cocktails (from US$3) and food (from US$5). The excellent location halfway down trendy Via Argentina has the crowds spilling out onto the street, to see and be seen.

Sahara/Deep Room C Uruguay. A popular after-hours gathering spot, *Sahara* is an oasis of energy in the wee hours. Cover charges (around US$5) are selectively enforced, and mixed drinks can get expensive.

Entertainment

Check the papers, as well as W www.thepanama news.com and W www.prensa.com, for entertainment listings, including live music and theatre.

Cinema There are lots of cinemas in the city showing current, subtitled Hollywood blockbusters. Prices range from US$3–6; W www.cinespanama .com and W www.prensa.com list show times. Try the Alhambra, on Via España in El Cangrejo; the Cinemark, in the Albrook Mall, across from the bus terminal, which shows a wide selection of current movies; or Extreme Planet and Kinomaxx, which are within 100m of each other on Av Balboa, near Av Israel and Via Italia in Punta Paitilla.

Cockfighting This exceptionally bloody betting game and spectacle is immensely popular throughout the country. If you've the stomach for it, it can be seen at Club Gallístico, Via España at Via Cincuentenario (Mon, Sat & Sun; US$1; T 221 5652).

Dance Venues for traditional Panamanian dancing include: *Las Brisas de Amador*, Calzador de Amador; *Las Tinajas*, C 51 Este at Av Federico Boyd (Tues & Thurs–Sat from 9pm; reservations recommended; US$8 cover charge; T 269 3840); and Mi Pueblito, Av 4 de Julio, Cerro Ancon (Fri and Sat evenings).

Theatre Most theatre productions are in Spanish, and can be found advertised outside theatre buildings and in local papers like *La Prensa*. The Teatro Balboa, Stevens' Circle, Balboa (☎ 228 0327), hosts jazz, folk dancing and theatre productions sponsored by the National Cultural Institute. The Teatro Nacional, Av B, Plaza Bolívar (☎ 262 3525), hosts theatre and ballet productions.

Shopping

Books Exedra Book, on Via Brazil at Via España, is a large, modern bookshop with café and internet (Mon–Sat 9.30am–9.30pm, Sun 11am–8.30pm). Librería Argosy, on Via Argentina at Via España, sells mostly used books, with titles in Spanish and English. Gran Morrison, on Via España in El Cangrejo, sells English-language books on Panama.

Crafts and souvenirs Mercado de Buhonerías y Artesanías is on Plaza Cinco de Mayo behind the old railway building, and Mercado Nacional de Artesanías is next to the ruins of Panamá Viejo; shopping areas are split into stalls and you can get a good representation of the country's different ethnic groups and their wares. There is also Gran Morrison on Via España in El Cangrejo, Mi Pueblito on Av 4 de Julio on the way out to Amador and several souvenir shops lining Via Veneto, the centre of the banking district in El Cangrejo. A handful of shops catering to tourists are also clustered along C 1 in Casco Viejo, at the foot of the peninsula near Plaza de Francia.

Malls Albrook Mall across from the Albrook bus terminal; El Dorado on Av Ricardo J. Alfaro; MultiPlaza Mall at Via Israel and C 50; Multicentro on Av Balboa at Plaza Paitilla. Av Central, the pedestrian zone running between Plaza Cinco de Mayo and Casco Viejo, is the place to go for low prices on any type of goods.

Directory

Car rental Most major rental companies have desks at the airport; National Panama (ⓦ www .nationalpanama.com) is a local company with branches at both airports.

Embassies Australia (in Mexico; ☎ 52/55 1101 2200); Canada, Edificio Banco Central Hispano, 4th floor, Av Samuel Lewis, Balboa (☎ 264 9731); Costa Rica, Av Samuel Lewis (☎ 264 2980); Mexico, C 58 at Av Samuel Lewis (☎ 263 4900); UK, Torre Swiss Bank, C 53 (Mon–Thurs 7.30am–3.30pm, Fri 7.30am–12.30pm; ☎ 269 0866); US, Torre Miramar Building, Av Balboa and C 39 (Mon–Fri 8am–5pm; ☎ 207 7000).

Exchange Branches of Banco Nacional de Panamá (BNP; Mon–Fri 8am–3pm, Sat 9am–noon) and Banistmo (Mon–Fri 8am–3.30pm, Sat 9am–noon) allow cash withdrawals on credit cards; most have ATMs. Foreign currency is more difficult to change – foreign banks will generally change foreign currencies, especially their own, and there is a licensed exchange house, Panacambios (Mon–Fri 8am–4pm; ☎ 223 1800), in the Plaza Regency Building on Via España, opposite the El Rey supermarket. American Express is in Torre BBVA, 9th Floor, Av Balboa (Mon–Fri 9am–noon; ☎ 225 5858).

Health Hospitals include: Hospital Nacional, Av Cuba, C 38/39 (☎ 207-8100; emergencies ☎ 207-8110); Centro Médico Paitilla, C 53 and Av Balboa (☎ 265 8800); Clínica Hospital San Fernando, Via España (☎ 229 3800; emergencies ☎ 229 2004); and Hospital Punta Pacífica, C 53 in Bella Vista (☎ 263 5287). Pharmacies are found all over the city and often have a big green sign with a cross; Farmacia Arrocha is popular – the largest branch is on Via España in front of *El Panamá* hotel, and there are others on Via Argentina and one in Punta Paitilla. City-wide branches of El Rey super-market (24hr) will also fill prescriptions at their pharmacy counter.

Immigration Av Cuba at C 29 (Mon–Fri 8am–3pm). Come here to extend your visa or to get permission to leave the country if you have been in Panama for over three months – for the latter you will also have to visit the office of Paz y Salvo (Mon–Fri 8.30am–4pm) in the Ministerio de Hacienda y Tesoro on Av Cuba at C 35. At both offices it's best to arrive early; take a ticket and be prepared to wait.

Internet There's a large number of internet cafés throughout the city, especially in El Cangrejo on Via Veneto, C 49B Oeste, a block up from Via España. Rates are typically around US$0.50/hr.

Language schools Berlitz, C 47, Edificio Marbella ☎ 265 4800, ⓦ www.berlitz.com; ILERI, Via La Amistad, El Dorado ☎ 260 4424; Spanish Panama, off Via Argentina, El Cangrejo ☎ 213 3121, ⓦ www .spanishpanama.com.

Police Emergencies ☎ 104; tourist police ☎ 270 2467.

Post office The most central post office is on Av Central at C 34, opposite the Don Bosco church; there's another in El Cangrejo in the Plaza de la Concordia shopping centre on Via España. Both Mon–Fri 7am–6pm, Sat 7am–5pm.

Telephones Public phone booths throughout the city take US$5, US$10 and US$20 phonecards; some take coins. The main Cable & Wireless office (Mon–Fri 7.15am–6.30pm, Sat 7.30am–2pm) is in the Banco Nacional building on Via España. Calls cost US$0.10, US$0.25 and US$0.35/min for local, long distance and mobile calls, respectively. Most internet cafés offer cheap international calls for about US$0.25/min (US$1.50 for the first minute).

Moving on

There are many daily flights to destinations all around the country, but buses are cheaper and go to nearly all the same places.

By air

All domestic flights leave from Marcos A. Gelabert domestic airport in Albrook. The only operators are Aeroperlas (☎315 7500, ⓦwww.aeroperlas.com) and Air Panama (☎316 9000, ⓦwww.flyairpanama.com). Flights to: Bocas del Toro (with Aeroperlas and Air Panama 4–5 daily; 1hr); Contadora (with Acroperlas and Air Panama 2 daily; 20min); Kuna Yala (daily flights on Aeroperlas and Air Panama to Achutupo, Ailigandi, Cartí, Corazón de Jesús, El Porvenir, Mulatupo, Playon Chico, Puerto Obaldía, Río Sidra, Tupile and Ustupo; 30min–1hr 15min); Sambú (with Air Panama 3 weekly; 1hr 50min).

By bus

Domestic bus terminal

Terminal de Buses All domestic buses – with the exception of those to Ancon, Balboa, Gamboa, Paraíso and the Canal Zone (all of which are served by several city buses daily from the terminal at Plaza Cinco de Mayo) – depart from the modern Terminal de Buses in Albrook. Destinations include: Almirante and Changuinola (2 daily; 10hr); Chitré (hourly; 4hr); Colón (local departures every 20min, 2hr; express departures every 20min, 1hr); David (local departures hourly, 7hr; 2 express departures daily, 5hr); El Valle (every 30min; 2hr 30min); Gamboa (8 daily; 45min); Las Tablas (every 2hr; 4hr 30min); Metetí (7 daily; 7–8hr); Ocú (8 daily; 4hr); Paso Canoas (9 local departures daily, 9hr; 2 express departures daily, 7hr); Penonomé (every 30min; 2hr 30min); Santiago (every 30min; 3hr 30 min); Soná (for Santa Catalina; every 30min; 5hr).

International bus terminal

Tica Bus Terminal International services with Tica Bus (☎314 6385, ⓦwww.ticabus.com) depart from their terminal in Albrook. Two buses daily run to San José (Costa Rica): 11am (executive class; 14–15hr) & 11pm (economy class; 16–17hr). Panaline also covers this route but currently do not have offices or booking facilities apart from a booth at Albrook terminal.

AROUND PANAMA CITY

From the ruins of Panamá Viejo, to the Amador Causeway, to the urban jungle of the Metropolitan National Park, Panama's sights incorporate man-made and natural, old and new, and everything in between.

Panamá Viejo

On the coast about 6km east of El Cangrejo stand the ruins of **Panamá Viejo**, the original colonial city founded by Pedro Arias de Ávila in 1519. Abandoned in 1671 after being sacked by Henry Morgan and his band of pirates, many of its buildings were later dismantled to provide stones for the construction of Casco Viejo, and in recent decades much of the site has been built over as the modern city has spread eastward. Despite this encroachment, a surprising number of the original buildings still stand.

The best place to start a visit is the **museum** (Tues–Sun 9am–5pm; US$3, US$6 with entrance to ruins; ☎224 2155, ⓦwww.panamaviejo.org) on Via Cincuentenario near the ruins, where exhibits explain the changes that have taken place since this was a tiny Indian village around 500 BC. Only one section of the ruins, the former **Plaza Mayor**, requires an entry fee. The major draw here is the three-storey square stone tower of the cathedral, built between 1619 and 1629. It has a modern stairway with a lookout at the top and is flanked by the square **cabildo** (town hall) to the right and the bishop's house to the left. Nearby and free to the public is the site of La Merced, the church and monastery where Francisco Pizarro took communion before embarking on the conquest of Peru in 1531. La Merced was once considered Panama City's most beautiful church, and survived Morgan's burning of the city by his use of it as a headquarters.

To **get to** Panamá Viejo, either take a taxi (US$3–4) or catch any bus marked

"Panamá Viejo" or "Vía Cincuentenario". If you're short on time and leaving Panama by air, you can see quite a lot of the ruins by asking your taxi driver to take the slow route to the airport via Panamá Viejo.

Balboa

To the southwest of Calidonia and El Chorrillo, Panama City encompasses the former Canal Zone town of **Balboa**, administered by the US as de facto sovereign territory from 1903 to 1979. Balboa retains many of the characteristics of a US provincial town: clean and well ordered, it stands in stark contrast to the chaotic vitality of the rest of the city. However, it conceals a troubled past.

Along the border of the former Canal Zone runs **Avenida de Los Mártires**. An extension of Avenida 4 de Julio and often called by the same name, Avenida de Los Mártires was named in honour of the young Panamanians, mostly students, killed by the US military during the riots of 1964. A sculpture by González Palomino, depicting three people climbing a flagpole, was erected here in 2004 as a tribute to the fallen; above it rises **Cerro Ancón**, crowned by a huge Panamanian flag that is visible throughout the city.

Just off the entrance to Cerro Ancón from Avenida de Los Mártires is **Mi Pueblito** (Tues–Sun 9am–9pm; US$1, free on holidays), a theme-park–style replica of the traditional villages of four of Panama's ethnic groups. Although aimed primarily at Panamanian tourists, it's worth visiting if you are not going to see the real thing. Folk dances are performed on Friday and Saturday evenings and restaurants serve traditional food.

Museo de Arte Contemporáneo

Some 200m east of the entrance to Cerro Ancón, on Avenida de Los Mártires, is a turn-off that leads to Gorgas Road. This winds around the side of Cerro Ancón to the Canal Authority Building in Balboa Heights (see below), about twenty minutes away on foot. Just off Gorgas Road to the right, the **Museo de Arte Contemporáneo** (Tues–Sun 9am–5pm; free; ☎262 3380, ⓦwww .macpanama.org), housed in a former Masonic temple, has a small collection of modern paintings and engravings by Panamanian and Latin American artists, as well as temporary international exhibitions.

Canal Authority Administration Building

Continuing around Cerro Ancón, passing the Palace of Justice and several beautiful estates on Heights Road, Gorgas Road reappears to the right (heading left will take you to the summit of Cerro Ancón) and winds down to the three-storey **Panama Canal Authority Administration Building** (daily 8am–11pm; free), built during the canal construction and still home to the principal administration offices. Inside, four dramatic murals by US artist William Van Ingen depict the story of the canal's construction under a domed ceiling supported by marble pillars.

At the rear of the building, where a Panamanian flag now flutters, a broad stairway runs down to the **Goethals monument**, a white megalith with stepped fountains that represent the canal's different locks, erected in honour of George Goethals, chief engineer from 1907 to 1914 and first governor of the Canal Zone. Beside the monument is **Balboa High School**, whose ordinary appearance belies the dramatic events it has witnessed. It was here in 1964 that Zonians attacked students attempting to raise the Panamanian flag, triggering the **flag riots** that left a group of young Panamanians dead. During the 1989 invasion, the school was used as a detention camp for Panamanian prisoners, some of whom were allegedly executed by US soldiers.

Fort Amador

From Balboa, Calle Amador runs towards the Causeway through **Fort Amador**, a former US military base that was returned to Panama in 1996 and is now being redeveloped as the centre-piece of the country's plans to promote tourism in the former Canal Zone. The complex includes luxury bars, restaurants and hotels, and a marina, as well as the **Museo de la Biodiversidad** (🌐www .biomuseopanama.com), a "biodiversity exhibition centre" designed by architect Frank Gehry. Construction of the centre started in February 2004; while the first phase is complete, an opening date has yet to be set, with construction due to continue until at least 2012.

Amador Causeway

The **Amador Causeway** (**Calzada de Amador**) runs 6km out into the bay, linking the mainland with the tiny islands of **Naos**, **Perico** and **Flamenco**. The Causeway is a popular weekend escape for the city's residents, who come here to jog, swim, stroll, rollerblade or cycle (you can rent bicycles at the entrance at Bicicletas Moses and just before the bridge to Perico at Tony's Bike Rentals; see p.603) and to enjoy the sea air and the views of the city and the canal.

On Punta Culebra, accessible from the end of Naos, 4km along the Causeway, the **Punta Culebra Nature Center** (Tues–Thurs & Sun 10am–6pm, Fri & Sat 10am–8pm; US$2; 🌐www.stri .org), run by the Smithsonian Tropical Research Institute, offers an introduction to Panama's marine ecology, including an aquarium where you can stroke sea urchins, starfish and sea cucumbers. There is a small **beach** and **swimming pool** (daily 10am–5pm; US$5) just outside the entrance. On the opposite side of Punta Culebra is the departure point for passenger ferries to Isla Taboga and for some ships embarking on canal transit tours. The second island, tiny

Perico, hosts **Las Brisas de Amador**, a strip mall almost entirely made up of restaurants where city folk enjoy cocktails and snacks before a night out. Finally, Flamenco is home to a marina and shopping centre (🌐www.fuerteamador .com) and is another popular nocturnal hangout, thanks to its abundant bars and restaurants.

Parque Natural Metropolitano and Museo Antropólogico Reina Torres de Araúz

A couple of kilometres north of central Panama City, the 2.65-square-kilometre **Parque Natural Metropolitano** (daily 6am–6pm; 🌐www.parquemetropolitano .org) is an unspoilt tract of tropical rainforest that is home to more than two hundred species of birds and mammals, such as titi monkeys, white-tailed deer, sloths and agoutis. In a slice of the former Canal Zone that reverted to Panamanian control in 1983, the park provides an excellent introduction to the rainforest environment. It's possible to complete the four main trails in just a few hours; the best of these is the combined La Ciena-guita and MonoTiti trail (3km), which leads to a *mirador* with fantastic views across the forest to the city. As elsewhere, the best time to see wildlife, particularly birds, is early in the morning – there is nothing to stop you from coming in earlier than the official opening time to take advantage of this. The **park office** (Mon–Fri 8am–4pm, Sat 8am–1pm; US$2 – you need only pay if entering the park during official hours) and main entrance is on Avenida Juan Pablo II; some buses can drop you nearby, and a taxi from El Cangrejo should cost about US$2. There is a small exhibition centre and library here, and three-hour **guided tours** can be arranged (US$2; book in advance at the office).

Nearby, the **Museo Antropólogico Reina Torres de Araúz** (Tues–Sun 10am–4pm; US$2) is a worthy stop, with

PANAMA

PANAMA CITY

611

displays including the Salón de Oro, an exhibit of pre-Columbian gold objects, as well as carved stone statues from the ancient Barriles culture of Chiriquí.

Isla Taboga

Some 20km off the coast and about an hour away by boat, tiny **Isla Taboga** is one of the most popular retreats for Panama City residents, who come here to enjoy the island's clear waters, peaceful atmosphere and verdant beauty. Known as the "Island of Flowers" for the innumerable fragrant blooms that decorate its village and forested slopes, Taboga gets very busy at weekends, particularly during the summer, but is usually quiet during the week. Passenger ferries (US$12) leave for the island from the Flamenco Marina at the end of the Amador Causeway; see ⓦ www.taboga .panamanow.com for schedules.

Taboga's one **fishing village** is very picturesque, with narrow streets, white-washed houses and dozens of gardens filled with bougainvillea and hibiscus. Most visitors head straight for one of the sections of **beach**, either right in front of the village or in front of the defunct *Hotel Taboga*, to the right of the pier as you disembark. The water is calmer here and the view of Panama City is magnificent, though the rubbish on the beach is unsightly.

Behind the village, forested slopes rise to the 300-metre peak of **Cerro Vigia**, where a viewing platform on top of an old US military bunker offers spectacular 360-degree views. It's about an hour's climb through the forest to the *mirador* – follow the path some 100m up behind the church until you find a sign marked Sendero de los Tres Cruces, beyond which the trail is easy to follow. The other side of the island is home to one of the biggest brown pelican breeding colonies in the world and, together with the neighbouring island of Urabá, forms a protected wildlife refuge.

Thanks to the abundance of marine life, particularly around El Morro, a rocky island off the coast, accessible by a sandbar at low tide, **snorkelling and diving** are popular activities on Taboga, though you're better off organizing a diving trip with one of the dive companies in Panama City (see "Tour operators", p.603).

There are several restaurants, two of which are locted in hotels: the *Chu* serves reasonable Chinese dishes and good seafood on a broad wooden balcony over the beach, while *Vereda Tropical Hotel* offers more varied and expensive international and Panamanian cuisine in a breezy, Caribbean-coloured and Spanish-tiled hillside location. Opposite the church, *Aquario* serves good seafood (from US$5).

The Panama Canal and Colón Province

Stretching eighty kilometres, from Panama City in the south to Colón in the north, the **Panama Canal** is a work of mesmerizing engineering brilliance. One of the largest and most ambitious endeavours ever undertaken by man, the waterway allows massive vessels – which otherwise would have to travel all the way south around Cape Horn – to traverse the isthmus in less than one day. East of the canal spreads the rainforest of **Parque Nacional Soberanía**, the greatest possible contrast to its mechanical might. Delve into the park's humming, humid atmosphere on one of its many accessible pathways, and you'll discover unparalleled biodiversity. **Colón**, at the Atlantic entrance to the canal, and only a boat or train or bus ride away from Panama City, seems like a different world from the capital –

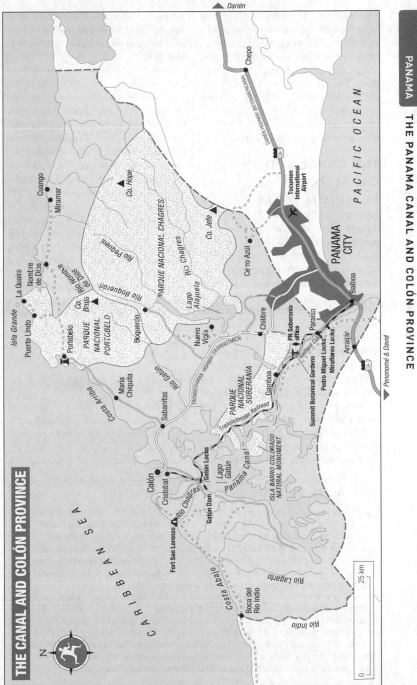

THE CANAL AND COLÓN PROVINCE

N

CARIBBEAN SEA

PACIFIC OCEAN

Darién

Chepo

DARIÉN HIGHWAY (INTERAMERICANA)

CA-1

Tocumen International Airport

PANAMA CITY

Balboa

Penonomé & David

CA-1

Arraiján

Miraflores Locks

Pedro Miguel Locks

Gaillard Cut

Paraíso

PN Soberanía office

Summit Botanical Gardens

Chilibre

Cerro Azul

Co. Jefe

Lago Alajuela

Río Chagres

PARQUE NACIONAL: CHAGRES

Co. Hope

Río Pequení

Río Boquerón

Cuango

Miramar

Nombre de Dios

La Guaira

Isla Grande

Puerto Lindo

Portobelo

PARQUE NACIONAL PORTOBELO

Co. Bruja

Río Nombre de Dios

Boquerón

Nuevo Vigía

TRANSISTHMIAN HIGHWAY (TRANSÍSTMICA)

Río Gatún

Sabanitas

María Chiquita

Costa Arriba

Colón

Cristóbal

Río Chagres

Gatún Dam

Gatún Locks

Fort San Lorenzo

Costa Abajo

Lago Gatún

Panamá Cana

Transisthmian Railroad

Gamboa

PARQUE NACIONAL SOBERANÍA

ISLA BARRO COLORADO NATURAL MONUMENT

Río Lagarto

Río Indio

Boca del Río Indio

0   25 km

613

a brief tour of the poverty-stricken city from the safety of a taxi leaves no doubt as to the canal's socioeconomic importance. Some 45km northeast of Colón lies another port – **Portobelo** – whose glory days are even more distant. Its riches once proved irresistible to such pirates as Sir Francis Drake and Henry Morgan, and its once-mighty fortifications are now atmospheric ruins.

THE CANAL AND THE CANAL ZONE

The **PANAMA CANAL** really is amazing, both physically and in concept. The basis of the country's modern economy, it's also the key to much of its history: were it not for the US government's determination to build the waterway, Panama might never have come into existence as an independent republic. Construction on the project began in the late nineteenth century, initiated by the French, but their efforts were abandoned in 1893, having taken the lives of nearly twenty-two thousand workers through disease. The US took up the construction ten years later, aided by more powerful machinery than the French had been using and improved understanding of malaria and yellow fever. The job was finally finished in 1914, the isthmus having been breached by the 77-kilometre-long canal, with vessels raised from and lowered to sea level by three sets of locks totalling 5km in length.

From 1903 to 1977, the strip of land that extends 8km on either side of the canal was de facto US territory, an area known as the **Canal Zone**. After more than ninety years the waterway was finally handed over to Panamanian jurisdiction at midnight on December 31, 1999, to be managed thereafter by the Autoridad del Canal de Panamá (ACP). In 2006 a proposal for a US$5 billion expansion of the canal, due to be completed in 2015, was approved first by President Torrijos and then by an overwhelming majority in a public referendum. The ACP claims that the expansion will directly benefit Panama's people, though critics contend that the country will be crippled by debt – the project will be paid for by increased tolls, supplemented by US$2.3 billion in loans – and that only the elite of society will benefit.

What to see and do

A striking mix of man's mastery of nature and nature magnificently untamed, the canal region has an eclectic range of attractions. A day-trip from Panama City could see you scanning

---

CANAL GEOGRAPHY

From the Bahía de Panamá on the country's Pacific coast, the canal runs at sea level approximately 6km inland to the **Miraflores Locks**, where ships are raised some 16.5m to Lago de Miraflores. About two kilometres further on, ships are raised another 10m to the canal's maximum elevation of 26.5m above sea level, after which they enter the **Gaillard Cut**. This 14km slice through the shifting shale of the continental divide was the deepest and most difficult section of the canal's construction and was plagued by devastating landslides.

The canal channel continues for 38km across the broad expanse of **Lago Gatún**, once the largest artificial lake in the world. Covering 420 square kilometres, it is tranquil and stunningly beautiful; until you see an ocean-going ship appear from behind one of the densely forested headlands, it's difficult to believe that this is part of one of the busiest waterways in the world. At the lake's far end ships are brought back down to sea level in three stages by the **Gatún Locks**, after which they run 3km through a narrow cut into the calm Caribbean waters of Bahía Limón.

EXPLORING THE CANAL AND CANAL ZONE

The most interesting way to explore the canal and its surroundings is by boat, though this can be pricey, as vessels are charged around US$17,000 to make the trip. Buses also serve the roads along the canal, or you can take a ride on one of Central America's only passenger trains.

By boat Canal & Bay Tours in Panama City (℡209 2009 or 2010, ⓦwww.canaland baytours.com) offers half-day partial transit (Sat only) of the canal through Miraflores and Pedro Miguel locks and into the Gaillard Cut (US$115). Full transit, including Lago Gatún and Gatún Locks, is offered once a month (US$165). Alternatively, Panama City hostels, including *Luna's Castle* and *Mamallena* (see p.603 & p.604) offer day-trips to the canal and reserve from US$30 per person. A much more affordable option, although unreliable, is to get taken on as a linehandler aboard one of the private yachts that transit the canal. Law requires four linehandlers on each boat. It's a straightforward role, but be aware that it carries genuine responsibility. You will not be paid, although food and drink are usually supplied. Your best chance of getting linehandling work is either to ask the staff at the Panama City hostels or the Colón yacht club (see "Moving on", p.620) if they can advise you as to the yacht owners' current favourite hangout.

By bus Eight daily buses from the SACA terminal near Plaza Cinco de Mayo take the road running 26km along the side of the canal, past the Miraflores and Pedro Miguel locks (15–20min to either), to the town of Gamboa near Lago Gatún (1hr). It passes the Parque Nacional Soberanía office (p.617) and the entrances to Summit Botanical Gardens and Zoo (see p.616). If time is short, you can easily find a taxi in Panama City to take you to Miraflores, wait for an hour or so and take you back for US$20–25. The Gatún Locks, on the Caribbean side, can be visited via Colón (see p.616).

By rail The Panama Canal Railway (7.15am from Corozal, 5.15pm from Colón; US$22 one way; ℡317 6070, ⓦwww.panarail.com) runs along the east side of the canal. Primarily for moving freight, once a day a passenger train makes the one-hour journey from Panama City to Colón and back. An observation carriage with oversized windows gives a widescreen version of whatever the view is offering – canal, rainforest or lake – and there are open-sided sections between carriages throughout the train. A taxi to the train station at Corozal, 2km north of Albrook bus terminal (see p.609), costs US$4–6 (agree the price in advance), or you could take a bus to the terminal and a shorter taxi ride from there. Arrive at the terminal thirty minutes in advance to secure a ticket.

the rainforest canopy for harpy eagles from the top of a former radar station, taking in the engineering masterpiece of the **Miraflores Locks**, or visiting an indigenous Emberá community in **Parque Nacional Chagres**. If you're in the mood for hiking, try out the celebrated routes of Camino de Cruces and the Pipeline Road in **Parque Nacional Soberanía**. The first takes you along the crumbling cobblestones laid by the Spanish to transport treasure across the isthmus, while the latter is a pathway legendary among globetrotters for its abundance of birdlife. A cool and comfortable early-morning train ride on the **Panama Canal Railway** to **Colón** gives wonderful panoramic views of the canal and the rainforest, and from the city it's a hot and bumpy bus ride northeast along the coast to **Portobelo**. Note that if you take the bus from Panama City towards the Atlantic coast you can cut Colón out entirely by changing at Sabanitas for a Portobelo-bound bus coming from Colón.

Miraflores Locks

Heading north out of Panama City along the canal, the first sight of note is the **Miraflores Locks**. The first lock gates here are the biggest in the whole canal system. Even so, they open in just two minutes, guiding ships through by electric locomotives known as mules. The **visitor complex** (daily 9am–5pm; US$5–8; ☎276 8325, ⓦwww.pancanal .com) is a ten-minute walk from the point on the main road where any Gamboa-bound **bus** from Panama City can drop you off – just indicate to the driver where you are going. The US$5 ticket allows access to the observation decks only; for US$8 you can also check out the exhibitions and watch a short movie about the canal, but they don't merit parting with the extra cash. The best time to see ships passing through is 8am to 10.30am, when they come up from the Pacific side, and after 3pm, when they complete their descent from the Atlantic side. There is an overpriced café here, as well as an expensive restaurant and a souvenir shop.

Summit Botanical Gardens

At a fork in the road 9km on from the Miraflores Locks is the office for Parque Nacional Soberanía (see opposite). The left fork, heading towards Gamboa, brings you to **Summit Botanical Gardens and Zoo** (daily 9am–6pm; US$1; ☎232 4854). Any Gamboa-bound **bus** from Panama City can drop you off at the entrance.

Established by the US in 1923, the gardens house more than fifteen thousand plant species spread throughout the landscaped grounds, as well as a popular zoo. The wonderful harpy eagles, patriarchs of the rainforest canopy food-chain, perch high in their huge enclosure and peer down disdainfully at visitors, while a nearby crocodile in a murky pond and a group of tapirs – granted a more spacious enclosure than many of the other animals – are also highlights.

Gamboa

Some 8km north of the botanical gardens lies the curious town of **Gamboa**, built by the US in the 1930s.

With its wooden buildings, "No Necking" sign at the half-empty swimming pool and McGrath Field, a grassy expanse with a baseball diamond and wooden bleachers, it feels like an abandoned, small American town. The Smithsonian Tropical Research Institute occupies a number of properties in the town, and their small dock is the jumping-off point for trips to Isla Barro Colorado (BCI), the principal site for their research. Several hundred metres north of Gamboa is the entrance to Pipeline Road (Camino del Oleoducto), a 24-kilometre trail through the Parque Nacional Soberanía and one of the world's premier birding sites. There's a small grocery shop (daily 8am–7pm) in town, a snack van, an HSBC with ATM and a post office (Mon–Fri 8am–3pm). To get here take one of the eight **buses** that run daily from Panama City.

Isla Barro Colorado

As the waters of Lago Gatún began to rise after the damming of the Chagres in 1913, much of the wildlife in the surrounding forest was forced to take refuge on points of high ground, which eventually became islands. One of these, **Isla Barro Colorado** (BCI), administered by the Smithsonian Tropical Research Institute, is among the most intensively studied areas of tropical rainforest in the world. Though the primary aims of the reserve are conservation and research, you can arrange visits through the STRI (one tour daily Tues, Wed & Fri–Sun; US$70, students US$40; ☎212 8951/8026, ⊛www.stri.org) – contact them well in advance. The tour lasts between four and six hours and most guides speak English (double-check when booking). The cost covers the boat from Gamboa pier, the tour and lunch at the island.

Parque Nacional Soberanía

Stretching along the eastern flank of the canal, the 220-square-kilometre **Parque Nacional Soberanía** (daily 6am–5pm; US$5; ⊛www.anam.gob.pa) provides essential protection for the rainforest-covered watershed that is vital for the canal's continued operation. Just thirty minutes from Panama City by road, Soberanía is the most easily accessible national park in Panama and is popular with both locals and visitors. Most spend just a few hours exploring one of the trails, all of which are well marked and pass over rugged terrain cloaked in pristine rainforest, offering reasonable odds of seeing monkeys, innumerable birds and, if you're really lucky, large mammals such as deer or tapir.

You can collect **trail** information and pay the entrance fee at the **park office** (Mon–Fri 7.30am–4pm), where the road to Gamboa branches off the main road from Panama City. Indicate to the bus driver that you want to go to the park office. There may be rangers on hand at the trailheads who you can pay if you don't make it to the office.

All of the trails have something to recommend them, but a few stand out. The **Pipeline Road**, which borders the park, is world famous for its birding opportunities; visit the Rainforest Discovery Centre (US$15 10am–4pm, US$20 6am–4pm; ⊛www.pipelineroad.org) for easy access to the trails and observation platform. **Plantation Road**, which begins at a right-hand turn-off

1.5km past the Summit Botanical Gardens and Zoo, runs some 4km to an intersection with **Camino de las Cruces**. Plantation Road itself follows a stream (Río Chico Masambi) and offers great birdwatching. Camino de las Cruces is a remnant of the cobbled track that the Spanish colonizers used to transport their goods and treasures to Portobelo on the Caribbean coast. To get to the Plantation Road turn-off either walk the 1.5km from the zoo or take the Gamboa-bound bus directly there from Panama City, indicating to the driver that you want to get off at Plantation Road.

Parque Nacional Chagres

East of the highway that connects Panama City with Colón – the Transistmica – lies **Parque Nacional Chagres**, 1290 square kilometres of mountainous rainforest comprising four different life zones that are home to more than three hundred bird species and several Emberá communities displaced by the flooding of Lago Bayano, further east.

The park is a bit tricky to get to independently, but *La Casa de Carmen* in Panama City (see p.604) offers a trip to visit an **Emberá–Drúa** community in the park (US$80 per person; often cheaper with larger groups). The price includes transport, a traditional meal and the opportunity to purchase handicrafts direct from their creators.

COLÓN

COLÓN, situated at the Atlantic entrance to the Panama Canal, is all rubble and attitude. The city is dangerously poor, with a bad record of violent crime, set in a crumbling colonial shell that begs for a renovation it is unlikely to ever see. For many, Colón's edginess will not appeal in the slightest, and will only be a necessary evil in finding linehandling work (see box, p.615), boats to various destinations, and visiting the nearby Gatún Locks,

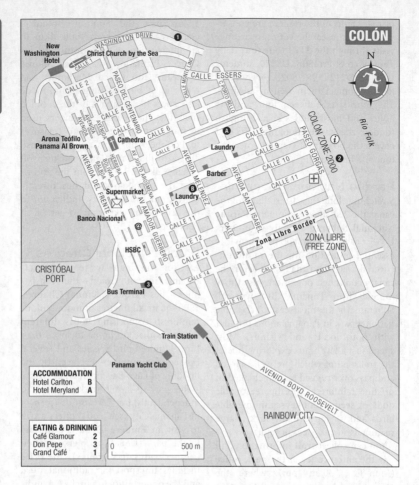

COLÓN

N

New Washington Hotel
Christ Church by the Sea
WASHINGTON DRIVE ❶
CALLE 1
CALLE 2
CALLE 3
CALLE 4
PASEO DEL CENTENARIO
AVENIDA
AVENIDA
AVENIDA
CALLE
5
CALLE 6
CALLE 7
CALLE MONTE LIMO
CALLE ESSERS
C PORTO BELLO
Arena Teófilo Panama Al Brown
Cathedral
Ⓐ
CALLE 8
CALLE 9
Laundry
COLÓN ZONE 2000
PASEO GORGAS
Río Folk
ⓘ
❷
AV JUSTO AROSEMENA
AVENIDA BOLIVAR
AVENIDA HERRERA
AVENIDA BALBOA
AVENIDA DEL FRENTE
AVENIDA MELÉNDEZ
Barber
Laundry
Ⓑ
CALLE 10
CALLE 11
Supermarket
Banco Nacional
CALLE 10
Ⓐ
AV AMADOR GUERRERO
CALLE 11
CALLE 12
CALLE 13
AVENIDA SANTA ISABEL
CALLE
CALLE 12
CALLE 13
CALLE 14
Zona Libre Border
CALLE 13
CALLE 15
CALLE 16
ZONA LIBRE (FREE ZONE)
HSBC
CRISTÓBAL PORT
Bus Terminal
❸
Train Station
Panama Yacht Club
AVENIDA BOYD ROOSEVELT
RAINBOW CITY

ACCOMMODATION
Hotel Carlton   B
Hotel Meryland   A

EATING & DRINKING
Café Glamour   2
Don Pepe   3
Grand Café   1

0   500 m

Fort San Lorenzo or the Costa Arriba (although in this case the city could be avoided entirely by changing buses at Sabanitas). Many visitors come solely to shop at the **Colón Free Zone** – a walled enclave where goods from all over the world can be bought at very low prices – and assiduously avoid the rest of the city. However, the combination of a luxurious rail trip from Panama City followed by a taxi tour of this unique and decaying town is fascinating, and can give powerful insights into what the canal has meant physically and economically to the country.

Founded in 1852 as the Caribbean terminal of the Panama Canal Railway, conceived to speed up the journey of US gold prospectors whose preferred route to the west exploited the narrowness of the isthmus, it initially enjoyed a degree of prosperity. In 1869, however, the completion of the transcontinental railroad in the US reduced traffic across the isthmus, and the town began to slip into decline. Its fortunes revived somewhat with the early stages of the French canal construction in 1879, though it suffered another setback in 1885, when Pedro Prestan, a Haitian rebel, burned it to the ground. Rebuilt by the French, it prospered again when the US took up the canal construction effort. By the 1950s, Colón was Panama's main port. Despite this, and the success of the Free Zone (founded in 1949), the rest of the city was slowly eroding – the employment that had vanished when the canal was completed in 1914 profoundly undermined the city. The situation today remains much the same: although the port and Free Zone continue to thrive, little of the money they generate stays in Colón – indeed many of the workers in these areas live in Panama City. In the face of extreme poverty and unemployment levels, the crime rate – particularly drug-related crime – has rocketed.

What to see and do

From the bus terminal, a left turn takes you north up **Avenida del Frente**. Running along the waterfront of Bahía Limón, it was once the city's main commercial road but is now crumbling. Just off it on Calle 6 is the boxing **Arena Teófilo Panama Al Brown**, named in honour of the country's most famous boxer. The arena was built in the 1970s to nurture the mass of local talent, including "Panama Al" Brown, one of the greatest boxers of all time, but today there's little to see other than a wall full of photographs. The **New Washington Hotel** (☎441 7133), at the northernmost end of Av del Frente, was built in 1913 and has clung onto its chandeliers and marble stairs, doing its best to live in the past. The rooms are overpriced (from US$60) but you could always come for a drink on the seafront veranda and watch the ships in the bay.

Cristóbal

Behind the bus terminal is the port enclave of **Cristóbal**, formerly part of the Canal Zone and still one of Latin America's busiest ports, handling more than two million tonnes of cargo a year. Apart from the yacht club (see p.620) there's not much of interest here, and most of the port is off-limits to visitors.

Colón Free Zone

The southeast corner of Colón is occupied by the **Zona Libre**, or Free Zone (✪www.colonfreezone.com). Covering more than a square kilometre, this is the second biggest duty-free zone in the world after Hong Kong, with an annual turnover of more than US$10 billion. Colón's residents are not allowed in unless they work there, but you and your wallet are free to enter if you present your passport at the gate. Once inside you'll find that the streets (as potholed as everywhere else in Colón) are lined with nothing but shops, big and small, and brand names of all shapes and sizes clinging to every patch of grimy wall. Most of the trade is in bulk orders, but you can sometimes buy individual items at low prices – shop around. You may be approached by someone asking what you are here to buy – they aim to act as your personal haggler but it is better to go it alone. Officially, goods bought here must be sent to the international airport for you to pick up as you leave the country.

SAFETY IN COLÓN

Colón's reputation throughout the rest of the country for violent crime is not undeserved, and if you come here you should exercise extreme caution – mugging, even on the main streets in broad daylight, does happen. Don't carry anything that may attract attention or that you can't afford to lose, try to stay in sight of the police on the main streets and take taxis rather than walk. Many drivers will give tours of the city (about US$10/hr); consider hiring one if you want to explore.

Although the shop workers and checkpoint guards will not always enforce this, be prepared for it to happen.

Near the Free Zone, an enclave known as **Colón Zone 2000** has been set up in the hopes of luring passengers from the many cruise ships that pass through the canal, but it has little to offer besides souvenir shops and a fairly hopeless IPAT office.

Arrival and information

By boat Yachts coming through the canal dock outside the Panama Canal Yacht Club in Cristóbal, behind the bus station, and you can usually pick up taxis in the vicinity.

By bus The bus terminal is on the corner of Av del Frente & C 13. Buses arrive from Panama City every 20–30min, 4am–10pm. Don't linger – jump into one of the many taxis that cluster in the nearby streets.

Tourist information There's an IPAT in Colón Zone 2000 (Mon–Fri 8.30am–4.30pm; ☎ 475 2300), but it's not overburdened with useful information.

City transport

Taxis Most trips in the city will cost US$1. You can also hire drivers for around US$10/hr, plus a bit more for stopping and starting, to take you around the city.

Accommodation

If you are going to stay overnight, it's worth splashing out on a more expensive hotel with armed security and a restaurant so you won't have to go out at night.

Hotel Carlton Av Meléndez and C 10 ☎ 447 0111/0112. A weary but proud place, with photographs of the canal, a display of flags and an impressive central staircase in the lobby. The rooms (en suite and a/c) are a bit shabby considering the price, but they have a good selection of in-house services, including a restaurant (mains US$6–8), laundry and pharmacy. US$44

🏃 **Hotel Meryland** C 7, opposite Parque Sucre ☎ 441 7055/7127, ⊛ www.hotelmeryland .com. Little atmosphere, but it's tucked away in a leafy and relatively safe patch of the city and is a cut above all other options. Smartly tiled, spacious and professionally staffed, with en-suite, a/c rooms and large, firm beds. The restaurant serves filling soups and a good selection of mains (from US$7). US$50

Eating

Though Colón's kitchens are known for their Caribbean influence and heavy reliance on seafood, spices and coconut milk, the most authentic places are too riskily situated to visit safely. If you're feeling brave and can find a willing cab driver, ask to be escorted to the little streetside grill opposite *Hotel Carlton*. Its fresh and cheap pepper-stuffed fish (US$2) is a favourite and comes with *patacones*. *García Panadería*, a bakery at the corner of Paseo del Centenario and C 12, is also worth a visit, but again, only by taxi.

Café Glamour Colón Zone 2000. This place lies in wait for cruise-ship passengers missing their fancy coffees; grab a latte for US$2.50.

Don Pepe In the bus terminal. A tiny kiosk to one side of the food counter's seating area, it has a green sign with yellow writing and sells excellent sticky buns (US$0.60) for your journey.

🏃 **Grand Café** At the northeast end of town near Washington Drive ☎ 433 2092. Sporting a vaguely Middle-Eastern decor, Lebanese menu and hookah pipes, this venue also offers pretty views of the boats bobbing off shore. Buzzy atmosphere and professional attitude; the menu includes falafel (US$5), meat and fish dishes (US$8–12) and pizza (US$3–9). The only restaurant open late in Colón (until 11pm daily).

Directory

Exchange There's a branch of Banco Nacional in the Free Zone on C 14 and another on Av Bolívar near C 10 (Mon–Fri 8am–3pm).

Hospital Manuel Amador Guerrero (☎ 441 5060) lies between Calle 10 and 11 at Paseo Gorgas, by Colón Zone 2000.

Internet Bit's International (daily 8am–6pm; US$1/hr) is on C11 at Av Amador Guerrero. There are also several cafés with computers and wi-fi in the Colón Zone 2000, although these charge US$3/hr when cruise ships are in town.

Laundry Victor's, on the corner of Av Santa Isabel and C 9, is in a relatively safe part of town.

Pharmacy In the Super 99 supermarket on Av Bolívar.

Post office On C 9 near Av Balboa (Mon–Fri 7am–6pm, Sat 7am–5pm).

Moving on

By boat To enquire about linehandling opportunities along the canal go to the Panama Canal Yacht Club, behind the bus station, and speak to the yacht

INTO COLOMBIA BY BOAT

Private yachts and freight boats carry passengers between Colón and the Colombian city of Cartagena. This adventurous trip – costing about the same as a flight to Cartagena (US$300 per person, meals extra) – takes around four days and passes through the San Blas Archipelago. Hostels in Panama City (see p.603) usually have up-to-date information on which yachts are plying this route, and you can always ask at the yacht club in Colón. You are strongly advised to get a sense of a captain's reputation before signing on – there are nightmare tales of drunken captains, vastly overcrowded boats, poor seamanship and, worst of all, drug-running. Hostels should be able to advise you.

owners. Though theoretically possible, the chances of getting a ride from one of the freight ships that leave Colón for Kuna Yala and Colombia are extremely slim; this is also not a particularly safe way to travel, as it's impossible to tell which ships are drug-running.

By bus to: Gatún Locks (every 20min until 5pm; 15min); La Guaira (6 daily; 2hr–2hr 30min); Miramar (6 daily; 3hr); Nombre de Dios (6 daily; 2hr–2hr 30min); Portobelo (4 daily; 1hr 30min); Panama City (local every 30min until 10pm, 2hr 30min; express every 45min until 8.30pm, 2hr).

By taxi A taxi to Fort San Lorenzo (no bus service) costs from US$30 return, plus waiting time.

AROUND COLÓN

If you don't fancy a taxi tour of Colón, then get straight onto a bus to the mighty Gatún Locks or splash out on a taxi to the beautiful and atmospheric Fort San Lorenzo.

Gatún Locks

From Colón, a road runs 10km southwest to the **Gatún Locks** (daily 8am–3.45pm), where ships transit between Lago Gatún and Bahía Limón. The nearly two-kilometre-long locks, which raise and lower ships the 26.5m between the lake and sea level in three stages, are among the canal's most monumental engineering features. The

If you plan to visit Portobelo or points further east, be aware that there are no ATMs past Colón and nearby Sabanitas – make sure to take money out before making your way to the coast.

observation platform at the visitors' centre is so close to the canal that you could speak quite easily to anyone on deck of the ships – your best chance of having a chat is between 9am and 11am, and after 3pm. The locks can also be visited as part of a tour; *Luna's Castle* in Panama City (see p.603) offers day-trips that include a guide, kayak rental and lunch, at US$50 per person.

Buses from Colón terminal will drop you just before a swing bridge by a road branching off to the left; the **visitors' centre** and entrance to the observation deck is a five- to ten-minute walk down this road. You will see an HSBC ATM and a gift shop (daily 8am–3.45pm) where you buy your US$5 entrance ticket. A **taxi** from Colón costs about US$5 each way, plus more for waiting time.

Fort San Lorenzo

With a spectacular setting on a promontory above the Caribbean and overlooking the mouth of the Río Chagres, **Fort San Lorenzo** is the most impressive Spanish fortification still standing in Panama. Until the construction of the railway, the Chagres was the main cargo route across the isthmus to Panama City, and thus of enormous strategic importance to Spain. The first fortifications to protect the entrance to the river were built here in 1595, but the fort was taken by Francis Drake in 1596 and, though heavily reinforced, fell again to Henry Morgan's pirates in December 1670. Morgan then proceeded up the Chagres and across the isthmus to ransack Panama City. The fortifications that remain today were built in the mid-eighteenth century. The site as a whole is imposing, with a moat surrounding stout stone walls and great cannons looking out from the embrasures, all of it kept in isolation by the dense rainforest all around.

Fort San Lorenzo can only be reached by car or **taxi**. With waiting time it is a US$35–40 return trip from Colón, one hour each way, passing through rainforest and the former US training base of **Fort Sherman**, which until 1999 was home to the 17,000-acre US Army Jungle Warfare Training Center. If a vessel is passing through Gatún Locks you may be stuck on either side for around an hour.

PORTOBELO

The Costa Arriba, stretching northeast of Colón, features lovely beaches, excellent diving and snorkelling, and the historic towns of Nombre de Dios and **PORTOBELO** ("beautiful harbour"). After the former was destroyed by Francis Drake in 1597, Portobelo was founded to replace it as the Atlantic terminus of the Camino Real – the route across the isthmus along which the Spanish hauled their plundered treasures. Portobelo's setting on a deep-water bay was supposed to make it easier to defend from the ravages of pirates, and for 150 years it played host to the famous *ferias*, grand trading events held when the Spanish treasure fleet came to collect the riches that arrived on mule trains from Panama City. Unsurprisingly, the pirates who scoured the Spanish Main – most famously Henry Morgan – could not resist the wealth concentrated in the royal warehouses here. Eventually the Spanish decided enough was enough: the treasure fleet was rerouted around Cape Horn and Portobelo's star began to fade. Even though the town today has a somewhat stagnant atmosphere, the remnants and ruins of its former glories retain an evocative power. More powerful still – at least to the thousands of pilgrims who come to gaze on it – is the agonized face of the small Black Christ statue in the Church of San Felipe. As an outsider to the traditions, it is fascinating to consider what enormous significance can be projected onto one small object (see box below).

What to see and do

Most of the town is pretty down-at-heel, with the **ruins** being the main attraction. Walking into Portobelo along the road from Colón brings you to the well-preserved **Santiago Battery**, which still features fourteen rusting but menacing cannons. The road then leads to the main tree-shaded plaza, just off which stands the **Casa Real de**

THE BLACK CHRIST OF PORTOBELO

Without question the most revered religious figure in Panama is the Black Christ or *Cristo Negro* in Portobelo, which draws tens of thousands of pilgrims to the town every October. A small effigy carved from black cocobolo wood with an agonized face and eyes raised to heaven, the Black Christ is reputed to possess miraculous powers. The origins of the icon still remain something of a mystery. Some say that it was found floating in the sea during a cholera epidemic, which ended after the Christ was brought into the town; others maintain it was on a ship bound for Colombia that stopped at Portobelo for supplies and was repeatedly prevented from leaving the bay by bad weather, sailing successfully only when the statue was left ashore. Every year on October 21 up to fifty thousand devotees, known as Nazareños and dressed in purple robes, come to Portobelo for a huge procession that is followed by festivities throughout the night.

la **Aduana** (daily 8am–4pm; US$1), the royal customs house, which has been restored with Spanish help and now houses a small museum. It was the biggest civil building in colonial Panama and stored the Camino Real treasure awaiting transport to Spain. As well as a brief exhibition outlining the history of Portobelo, the museum has a display of the purple robes donated each year to the revered Black Christ (see box opposite). The icon itself can be found in the large, white **Church of San Felipe**, on the square a further one hundred metres along the road. Outside the church is the tiny Mercado San Felipe, a small cluster of stalls selling religious (often quite kitsch) paraphernalia, most of which depicts the image of *El Cristo*, and a variety of Panamanian *artesanía*. Looking out onto the bay behind the church are the ruins of the **San Geronimo Battery** – creep to its outermost edge and peep out through the arrow slats.

Arrival and information

By bus Buses for Portobelo leave from Colón; if you're coming from Panama City and want to avoid Colón, change at the Rey supermarket in Sabanitas, 14km before Colón. Buses from Colón arrive near the Church of San Felipe in the centre of town, within a few minutes' walk of the main sights and accommodation.
Internet Internet Enilda, on the square near the church, has two computers (Mon–Fri 9am–5pm; US$1.25/hr).
Tour operators Panama Divers (☎6613 4405, ⓦwww.panamadivers.com) works with *Coco Plum* (see below) and offers a package for US$125 that includes transport from your Panama City accommodation, two day-dives in Portobelo (with a Divemaster) and tours of the ruins there. Portobelo Tours, ☎448 2504, ⓦwww.piratescovepanama .com, has a good selection of trips to local beaches and sites. *Hostel Wunderbar* (see below) can arrange trips to Isla Grande, as well as visits to other nearby islands, yacht tours of San Blas, and passage by yacht to Colombia.
Tourist information There's a CEFATI office (Mon–Fri 8.30am–4.30pm; ☎448 2200) on the main street opposite the Mayor's office.

Accommodation

Hospedaje Sangui Leaving Portobelo, on the road to Isla Grande ☎448 2204 or 6651 8972. The helpful English-speaking owner offers basic, clean rooms with fan and shared bath. Prices are often negotiable. US$12

🏃 **Hostel Wunderbar** On the mainland in Puerto Lindo, close to La Guaira ☎448 2426 or 6626 8455, ⓦwww.hostelwunderbar.com. A notable new addition, this place makes a characterful alternative to staying in Portobelo or on Isla Grande. Internet access and use of a kitchen are available; there's also a basic grocery, restaurant and bar nearby. Accommodation is in a large, Kuna-style house. The hostel also arranges tours (see above), rents bikes and can arrange horse-riding excursions. Buses coming from Sabanitas and Colón pass in front of the hostel, just before the Puerto Lindo Yacht Club. Hammocks US$8, dorms US$11, doubles US$25
Ofluras Hostal On the road to Portobelo ☎448 2400 or 6444 6998. A small family-run business set on the water's edge, with two clean and simple rooms with fans, and an upstairs apartment that sleeps up to six; the friendly owners also run local boat tours. Doubles US$20, apartment US$40

Eating

Las Anglas At *Coco Plum* ☎264 1338. The most charming restaurant in the area specializes in fish dishes (US$8–12), with alternatives including burgers (US$6) and breakfast (from US$4). Closes 9.30pm.

🏃 **Panadería Nazareño** On the main street. This bargain bakery is open all day and sells juices for a dollar, tasty sandwiches from US$2 and a delicious variety of fresh bread. With purple walls and colourful plastic chairs, this spot adds a cheerful shot of adrenaline to the town. Closed Mon.

TREAT YOURSELF

Coco Plum On the road towards Colón ☎448 2102, ⓦwww.cocoplum-panama .com. This place, a few minutes' drive from the town centre, has luxurious cabins (with TV and a/c) that sleep up to four people. The cute wooden pier has a little dining area and the bar looks out onto the ocean. US$60

Restaurante Ida On the square near the church. Offers meat stews and fried fish dishes (from US$4), and can rustle up a veggie-friendly plate of rice, beans and plantain for US$3.

Moving on

By bus to: Colón (every 30min until 6pm; 1hr 30min); La Guaira (6 daily; 30min–1hr); Miramar (6 daily; 1hr 30min–2hr); Nombre de Dios (6 daily; 30min–1hr).

AROUND PORTOBELO

Exploring this area means exploring the coast. Isla Grande is a well-established getaway for Panamanians and tourists alike, while a more adventurous trip may be possible from the village of Miramar, where you might catch a ride on a trading boat all the way to Kuna Yala.

Parque Nacional Portobelo

The **Parque Nacional Portobelo** encompasses the town and surrounding coast, although the area receives little protection or responsible management and you don't need permission from ANAM to enter. It does have good **beaches** and some of the best diving and snorkelling on the Caribbean coast, including coral reefs, shipwrecks and, somewhere in front of Isla de Drake, the as-yet-undiscovered grave of Francis Drake, buried at sea in a lead coffin after he died of dysentery in 1596. Most of this area can be reached only by sea; you can either hire a boatman in town or join an excursion; Portobelo Tours and PADI-certified Panama Divers run trips within the park (see "Tour operators", p.623).

Miramar

Around six buses daily go from Colón all the way to **Miramar**, passing through Portobelo on the way. The second-to-last stop along this stretch of coastline, the town is mainly of use as a possible jumping-off point for Kuna Yala, the frontier of which is about 25km further east along the coast. **Kuna trading boats** travel between Miramar and the *comarca* (territory) – you may be able to catch a lift with one of these. You will need to be at the village's dock no later than 10am. Expect to pay around US$10–15, though this may be negotiable. The journey can take anywhere from four to seven hours: boats head first to El Porvenir and then on to other points on the coast. Note that between January and April the seas are often too rough for this journey.

ISLA GRANDE

Some 12km northeast along the coast from Portobelo, a side road branches off the badly potholed pavement and runs a few kilometres to the tiny village of **La Guaira**, from where *lanchas* provide transport to **ISLA GRANDE**, a hugely popular weekend resort for residents of Colón and Panama City.

Though undeniably beautiful, friendly and relaxed, with some good beaches, Isla Grande is no more spectacular than other parts of Costa Arriba. It does, however, have better facilities. On the hill in front of the surf break is a path leading to the **lighthouse**, El Faro, a thoroughly rusted structure over 200 years old that sways gently in the wind; how long it will be before it collapses or gets closed down remains to be seen. For those not suffering from vertigo or a logical fear of the construction falling down, it affords fine 360-degree views of the island and surroundings. The only real sand **beach**, known as "La Punta", is around the island to the right (southwest) as you face the mainland; around to the left by *Sister Moon* you'll find a reef break that's good for **surfing**. For snorkellers, there's plenty to see around the Christ statue in front of the village, though beware of the current beyond the reef and of passing boats. **Scuba diving** is also available with Isla Grande Dive Center (☎232 5942, ⓦgeo .ya.com/dive_islagrande/home.htm; US$70 for two immersions). The island is quiet during the week, fills up at weekends, and peaks during national holidays; plan your trip accordingly.

Arrival

By boat *Lanchas* (US$2) to Isla Grande leave from La Guaira. There are usually six buses daily from Colón to La Guaira (US$3), via Portobelo. Check with locals for a current timetable.

Accommodation and eating

Although Isla Grande is a major holiday destination for many Panamanians, there is little in the way of reasonably priced accommodation on the island, and thus the suntanned, drunken partygoers who create a buzz during the day generally disappear with the light at sunset. Locals living on the island may rent out rooms or whole houses during busier periods; ask around in the restaurants to try your luck.

Cabañas Candy Rose ☎ 448 2947. This waterfront restaurant – with pricey cabins set behind, on the main path – is strong on seafood, with plates from US$5. Try the spicy coconut octopus (US$7), a delicious example of local flavours. Cabins US$60

Cabañas Cholita On the main path next to *Ensueños* ☎ 232 4561. Another waterfront restaurant with rooms, rather threadbare and uninteresting, set across the main path. A good deal for larger groups, with an 8-person room for US$85/night; rates vary, so ring ahead. US$66.

Restaurant Teleton On the seafront main stretch, next to the Rasta-coloured reggae bar. A BYOB barbecue dining experience that feels somewhat like you've crashed a local dinner party

– in a good way. Shrimp with coco-rice, fried fish and *patacones*, plus a variety of brochettes, go for US$6–7.

Villas Ensueños On the seafront main path ☎ 448 2964. Charmless but comfortable place on the main drag, with a/c rooms and a mediocre restaurant (dishes US$4–10) looking out over the water; camping and the use of the facilities may be an option; phone ahead to confirm. US$50

Moving on

By boat *Lanchas* are readily available for the short hop back to La Guaira (US$2), from where you catch one of five daily buses on to Portobelo and Colón; the last bus to Colón, via Portobelo, leaves at 1pm (Mon–Fri) or 4pm (Sat) – confirm times in advance with boat drivers and local hotel owners, as schedules are erratic.

Darién

The sparsely populated 17,000 square kilometres that make up **Darién** are one of the last great, untamed **wildernesses** in America. The beginning of an immense forest that continues almost unbroken across the border into the Chocó region of Colombia and down the Pacific coast to Ecuador, this was the first region on the American mainland to be settled by the Spanish. Although they extracted great wealth from **gold mines** deep in the forest at Cana, they were never able to establish effective control over the region, hampered by the almost impassable terrain, the fierce resistance put up by its inhabitants and European pirates and bands of renegade African slaves known as *cimarrones*.

The **Interamericana** is the only road that takes the plunge and enters the region, but it goes no further than the settlement of **Yaviza**, 276km east of Panama City. Along the border with Colombia, the **Parque Nacional Darién**, the largest and most important protected area in Panama, safeguards vast swathes of forest that support one

THE PEOPLE OF DARIÉN

Darién's population is made up of three main groups: black, indigenous and colonist.

Other than a few Kuna communities, the indigenous population of Darién is composed of two closely related but distinct peoples, the Wounaan and the more numerous Emberá, both semi-nomadic South American rainforest societies. Recognizable by the black geometric designs with which they decorate their bodies, the Emberá-Wounaan, as they are collectively known, have been migrating across the border from Colombia for the past two centuries. Only since the 1960s have they begun to settle in permanent villages and establish official recognition of their territorial rights in the form of a *comarca*, divided into two districts: the Comarca Emberá Cemaco, in the north, and the Comarca Emberá Sambú, in the southwest.

The black people of Darién, descended from *cimarrones* and released slaves, are known as Dariénitas or libres (the free) and are culturally distinct from the Afro-Antillano populations of Colón and Panama City (see p.602).

The colonists, meanwhile, are the most recent arrivals, poor peasants driven off their lands in western Panama by expanding cattle ranches and encouraged to settle in Darién during the construction of the Darién Highway. Many colonists still wear their distinctive straw sombreros as a badge of identity and maintain the folk traditions of the regions they abandoned.

of the most pristine and biologically diverse ecosystems in the world, as well as a large indigenous population.

Until quite recently, the combination of drug trafficking and the decades-long Colombian **civil war** spilling over into Panama has made the border area utterly treacherous. The Marxist guerrillas of the Colombian Revolutionary Armed Forces (FARC) have long maintained bases close to the border in Darién, but right-wing paramilitary groups backed by powerful landowners and drug traffickers have taken to pursuing them, terrorizing isolated Panamanian communities they accuse of harbouring the guerrillas. Given the **security concerns** affecting the border area, including parts of the national park and the Comarca Emberá Cemaco, a visit to southwestern Darién is the safest way to experience the ecology and culture of the region independently. Once in Darién, you can ask for news of recent incidents or developments.

THE DARIÉN HIGHWAY

East of Panama City the **DARIÉN HIGHWAY** (the Interamericana) is well paved as far as Lago Bayano, after which the pace slows down considerably and the road becomes gravelly for long stretches. Just before the lake, the highway passes through the quiet village of El Llano, where a side road leads up towards **Kuna Yala** (see p.633). From the lake the highway rolls on for 196km through a desolate, deforested landscape, passing Emberá-Wounaan hamlets, with their characteristic open-walled houses raised on stilts, and half-hearted roadside settlements. The highway ends on the banks of the Río Chucunaque at **Yaviza**, the start of the Darién Gap, though most buses only go as far as **Metetí**, 50km before Yaviza and 25km beyond **Santa Fe**.

Metetí and Puerto Quimba

Some 50km before the highway ends in jungle it passes through **Metetí**, a small roadside settlement that leads on to Yaviza or west to jumping-off point **Puerto Quimba**. For most buses, the town's miniature **Terminal de Transporte de Darién** is the end of the road. The *chiva* (daily 6am–5pm; 20min; US$1.50) that shuttles back and forth between Metetí and Puerto Quimba departs from this terminal.

The scheduled **boat** (daily 7.30am–5.30pm; 30min; US$3) or a **water-taxi** (US$15) to La Palma depart from Puerto Quimba's dock area – a dirt road with space for vehicles to park, a pier, a police hut (where you present your passport to register your details) and a tiny bar. At the time of research, a new dock was under construction here to accommodate a **ferry**, which should eventually shuttle passengers and cargo between Puerto Quimba and La Palma.

If you miss your onward connection you can **stay** at one of the basic hotels in town; try US-army favourite *Hotel Felicidad* (☎299 6544; air-conditioned rooms from US$18), with on-site restaurant, or the *Hospedaje 2 Hermanos Morenos* (☎299 6512; US$9), whose basic rooms come with fan, both on the main drag. There are also several basic **restaurants** serving *comida típica* on this strip, of which *Johana #2* is the nicest. Metetí is one of the last stops for cash before entering the jungle, with a branch of the Banco Nacional and a 24hr **ATM** on the main street. If you're lacking supplies, visit the well-stocked Ventas Metetí **supermarket**, also on the main drag.

Yaviza

Yaviza marks the end of the Inter-americana and the beginning of the

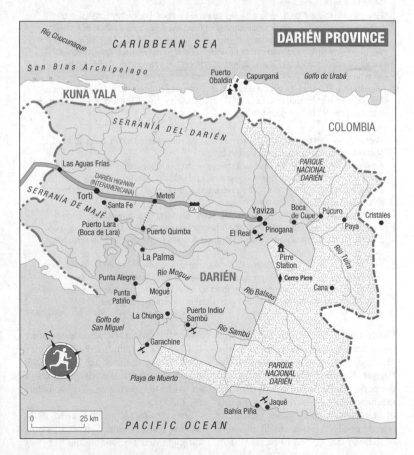

DARIÉN PRACTICALITIES

Most people who travel to Darién go with a **tour**. However, taking everything into your own hands and going **independently** is entirely feasible (see box opposite, for information on travel to and within the region). This course of action does require a certain leap of faith – you can't plan every last detail before you leave – and some knowledge of Spanish, but the very fact that it is not a simple undertaking is what makes it so special. Before making the journey to Darién it's a good idea to check with ANAM in Panama City (see "Tourist information", p.603) and the Darién National Park office at El Real (☏299 6965) regarding the current safety situation in the region. The office in Panama City will likely be more discouraging than the staff at the El Real office, who are more in tune with the day-to-day developments.

Supplies

Whether you go with a tour operator or on your own, there are a few items you should take with you.

Clothing You will need trousers and long-sleeved shirts, partly to keep the huge variety of insect life at bay, but also because it can get quite cool during the night. Do not take or wear anything that resembles army fatigues or has a camouflage pattern.

Equipment You will be able to pick up basic provisions (including bottled water), but it is advisable to pack a small supply of food even so, plus a ration of bottled water, and water-purifying tablets. If you are sleeping on a floor in a village you will need something to sleep on, in or under, and a mosquito net. Bring a cover for your pack for boat travel and damp conditions. A large stash of US$1 bills is recommended.

Medication You should start taking anti-malaria medication well before you arrive. Be aware that chloroquine is not sufficient in Darién – check the exact requirements with your doctor before your trip.

Tour operators

There are several operators in Panama City that run trips to Darién, ranging from short stays to two-week, trans-Darién treks.

Advantage Panama ⊛www.advantagepanama.com/darienadventure. A good-value "Darién Adventure" tour (4 days/3 nights; US$217), setting off from Tortí, on the Interamericana around 50km beyond Lago Bayano. This company is also involved in important conservation work.

Exotic Adventures ☏223 9283 or 6673 5381, ⊛www.panamaexoticadventures .com. A French-owned outfit that offers pricier packages (from US$500 for 3 days/2 nights) and also runs some beautiful jungle lodges for those willing to splash out even more.

Panamaniac ☏6718 2826, ⊛www.panamaniac.net. This consultancy agency is great for those avoiding package tours. Director Vincent is an excellent source of information and an experienced traveller in the region, can advise on itineraries, and will put you in touch with local businesses and guides.

Darién Gap. If the police on the highway deem that it is safe to visit, then the town can be used as a gateway into the **Parque Nacional Darién**. To get to the park, head down to the port in the morning, when there are likely to be lots of motorized dugout canoes (*piraguas*) trading goods. You can usually hire one of these to take you to **El Real** (US$5), where the Parque Nacional Darién office is (daily 8am–4pm; ☏299 6965). You'll need to pay the park fee here (US$5) before entering. It is advisable to check in with the police in Yaviza before moving on.

Seven **buses** serve the town daily, leaving from Panama City and passing through Metetí before pulling in beside the dock at the entrance to the town. Buses return from Yaviza to Panama City from 4am (8hr 30min).

PARQUE NACIONAL DARIÉN

Covering almost 5800 square kilometres of pristine rainforest along the border with Colombia, **PARQUE NACIONAL DARIÉN** is possibly the most biologically diverse region on earth – over five hundred bird species have been reported here. Inhabited by scattered indigenous communities, the park contains the largest expanse of forest in Central America that has not been affected by logging and provides a home for countless rare and endangered species, including jaguars, harpy eagles and several types of macaw. Parts of the park are safe to visit, but the security situation can change rapidly, so phone ahead to the park office in El Real (see opposite) to confirm safe entry points into the park, or visit the ANAM office in Panama City (see "Tourist information", p.603) to check on the current status.

To **enter** the park you need permission from the **ANAM Parque Nacional Darién office** (daily 8am–4pm; US$5/day; ☎299 6965) in El Real. (Note that most of the rangers speak only Spanish.) Check here, too, about the relative safety and accessibility of the park's **ranger stations**, all of which have basic lodges.

Given the extreme wilderness and lack of infrastructure, this park is only recommended for visitors with a wealth of jungle survival knowledge, or those travelling with a tour (see box opposite). Necessary **supplies** include food, mosquito repellent and nets or coils, bedding, and a water bottle and purifiers, even if you plan on staying at one of the ranger stations.

LA PALMA

LA PALMA's spectacular setting, overlooking the broad mouth of the Río Tiura, surrounded by densely

---

DARIÉN TRAVEL

To get to Darién independently, you can either fly or take the bus. Once you've arrived, boats are the best way to get around.

Getting there

By air Both Aeroperlas (☎315 7500, ⊛www.aeroperlas.com) and Air Panama (☎316 9000, ⊛www.flyairpanama.com) offer flights to Darién (US$100 return), although the former currently only serves routes to Bahía Piña and Jaqué in the far south of the region. Air Panama flies to Sambú and Garachiné, both of which lie near the Gulf of San Miguel and are good starting points for boat-based exploration of the more accessible – and safer – parts of Darién; other destinations include El Real, the jumping-off point for the Parque Nacional Darién (see above).

By bus Buses run from Panama City to Metetí (hourly 4am–6am, every 1hr 30min 7.15am–4.15pm; 6hr 30min) and to Yaviza (2 daily at 4am & 5am; 8hr 30min). Both of these small towns lie to the north of – and make good gateways to – the parts of the region that are accessible to (and usually safe for) visitors.

Getting around

By boat The inhabitants of Darién use *piraguas* – motorized dug-out canoes – as well as slightly more modern boats. Fuel prices were rising steadily at the time of writing; in general, you will find trips far cheaper if you can latch onto someone who is already heading in the direction you want to go (trading or fishing boats), so you are simply hitching a ride, rather than chartering a boat and crew. A ride from La Palma to Mogué, for instance, could be as little as US$10 if you find someone who is already going there, or upwards of US$100 (return) if you have to hire someone's services.

INTO COLOMBIA: THE DARIÉN GAP

The Darién Gap is a band of dense and entirely untamed rainforest, just 100km or so in length, that keeps the northern strand of the Interamericana (Panamerican Highway) from joining up with the southern strand, thus rendering land travel from Panama to Colombia truly hazardous. Because of this, crossing the Gap has always been one of the most celebrated adventures in Latin America. However, given the present security situation we do not recommend you attempt this trip. Even if you can find guides willing to take you (no easy task in itself, given that many of the villages in the region have been attacked or overrun by bandits and the inhabitants have fled), travel in this region comes with a risk of robbery and/or kidnapping; many travellers have disappeared or been killed attempting this trip. It's also worth remembering that there is a war raging across the border in Colombia.

Currently the Panamanian authorities are not allowing civilians to travel east of Boca de Cupe. Should the security situation in Darién improve, however, then before crossing you must first get permission from ANAM (see p.603) as well as the Colombian consulate in Panama City. (If you have been in Panama for more than three months, make sure you have your exit permission from *migración*.) In Colombia you must register on arrival with DAS, the immigration agency.

forested mountains and with ruined colonial forts for neighbours, makes it a worthy capital of Darién Province, however small. Brightly painted houses are cake-layered down a steep slope to the waterfront and the town's only **street**, a narrow strip of concrete. Scenic it may be, but there's not a whole lot to do other than soak in the views before moving on.

Although you can easily work out how much transport to La Palma will cost, it's far less easy to estimate what any onward travel is likely to set you back – it will be by boat, and the price of fuel is steadily rising. The opportunities to come into contact with indigenous communities are greater in the Sambú area, but to get there you need to fly (although a one-way boat ride from La Palma would be around the US$150 mark), which cranks up the expense of your Darién trip from the outset. While you're here it's worth telling the **police** in town where you are going next, even if it is back on yourself, and checking on any developments or incidents in the region.

Arrival and information

By air At the time of going to press, there were no flights to or from La Palma. Check Air Panama

(ⓦ www.flyairpanama.com) for up-to-date information.

By boat Boats and water-taxis from Puerto Quimba arrive at the passenger dock below the main street, opposite mini-mercado La Virgen del Carmen.

Exchange There is a branch of Banco Nacional (Mon–Fri 8am–3pm) with a 24hr ATM at the far end of town (take a right from the taxi dock).

Hospital There is a small hospital behind the main street, to the left of the passenger dock.

Tourist information IPAT is in the MICI office (Ministerio de Comercio e Industrias; Mon–Fri 8.30am–4.30pm; ☎ 292 5337) opposite the Banco Nacional.

Accommodation

Hospedaje Pablo & Benita 100m to the right from the passenger dock ☎ 299 6490. This waterfront building has very basic rooms, with a fan and worn mattresses. Rooms with a/c cost double. US$12

Hotel Biaquiru Bagara ☎ 299 6224. This family-run place is extremely handsome. Rooms are wood-panelled with bamboo ceilings, and there's a huge terrace upstairs with hammocks and breezy views of the water, with a general store downstairs. The owner, Profesora Lesbia Alarcon, can help you arrange boat trips but speaks only a little English. Come out of the passenger dock, turn left, keep going past the commercial dock and it is on the left in a green-painted building with a sign that says, confusingly, "Casa Ramada". US$10

Eating

A nameless food stand opposite *Hotel Biaquiru Bagara* does delicious *hojaldres*, pan-fried bread, for US$0.20.

Restaurante Aura On the main street next to mini-mercado La Virgen. This tiny peach-and-white building serves cheap and filling seafood and fast food (US$3–4); located opposite the passenger dock, it's the best place to grab a bite while waiting for a boat.

Restaurante Nayelis About 100m right of the passenger dock. This place is said to serve the best seafood specials in town, with a plate of *concha negra* going for US$3.50.

Moving on

By boat to: Puerto Quimba (6am–6pm; 30min; US$3). There is a small "port office" next door to La Virgen where you can pay for your passage before embarking. These boats are met by the *chiva* back up to Metetí (see p.626). Get to the dock at least 30min before the first or last boat leaves; buy tickets from the booth next to the dock.

AROUND LA PALMA

Exploring La Palma's **surroundings** requires a bit of preparation and can be accomplished in a number of different ways. Local fishermen are used to being approached for transport, and may be willing to show you isolated beaches and the uninhabited islands dotting the gulf. Sometimes a cargo boat delivering and collecting goods in Darién's villages will be heading in a convenient direction, in which case you may be able to jump aboard for a fee of US$5–10.

You might also pay someone to take you to your destination directly, though this would mean adding a zero to the price above. If you're travelling solo, taking a boat from here to Sambú could be costlier than flying from Panama City. Hitching rides with fishermen is the cheapest way to visit nearby communities, beaches and islands – just be sure to confirm your pick-up before disembarking. Ask at the MICI office (see "Tourist information", p.603) for boat travel information.

Punta Alegre

You may be able to find a boat from La Palma headed towards **Punta Alegre**. The trip is a fantastic two hours through the Golfo de San Miguel, passing forested islands and a wild coastline fringed with mangroves and deserted beaches. You can **stay** the night with a local guide for US$15, which is organized as a homestay, although cabinas were under construction at the time of writing. To arrange your visit, contact Pili, a local fisherman and entrepreneur, on ☎6509 9616. He and his wife are very attentive and will ensure you sample the gargantuan shrimp, *pargo* and *corvina*, oysters, mussels, clams, crab and more, all caught by Pili and prepared by Jeni. There's not a whole lot to do apart from visiting the shell-strewn, jungle-fringed beaches, learning how to fish or cultivate rice, and eating endless amounts of incredible seafood. A ride with Pili costs from US$45, or you can

---

ARTESANÍA AND SEAFOOD, RICHES OF DARIÉN

Darién's **Golfo de San Miguel**, where the flow of jungle rivers meets the abundant Pacific Ocean, is a nutrient-rich, predator-safe environment in which **seafood** flourishes. Calamari, giant shrimp, sea bass, snapper, black conch, oysters and lobsters are only a few of the marine treats you'll find in every fisherman's catch.

The other speciality of the region is the artisanal **weavings** made by Emberá and Wounaan communities; delicately intricate baskets, plates and masks are hand-woven with dyed and natural grasses to create stunning works of art. You can visit indigenous communities, meet with the artists and directly support the communities by buying local pieces. Many of the finer items take several years to create, with prices starting at about US$150.

THE SETTLING OF NEW EDINBURGH

In the late 1600s, the Scots gambled half the country's wealth on a colony in Darién in the hopes of transforming Scotland into a trading power to rival England. A fleet of five ships and 1200 men set sail in July 1698 and, arriving in the Caribbean, attempted to trade goods and restock the ships, though their wigs, shoes, stockings, thick cloth and Bibles found few takers in the tropics. The fleet finally anchored in Caledonia Bay, and for five months the Scots worked hard to build New Edinburgh, hindered by low rations and disease. The only help they received came from the local Kuna. When, after ten months, the promised supply ships failed to materialize, the Scots set sail for home. Only one ship, the *Caledonia*, made it back to Scotland. A second fleet, however, set sail just two months after this first group abandoned the settlement, but shortly after their arrival in 1700 they drew the attention of the Spanish based in Portobelo. Small battles soon broke out – with the Kuna lending their military muscle to the Scots – but within six months the Scots finally surrendered to the Spanish. They were allowed to evacuate with full military honours, but none of the ships made it back to Scotland. The venture crippled Scotland financially, leaving the kingdom at the mercy of rival England. Several years later, in 1707, England agreed to compensate all those who had subscribed to the venture in return for the creation of a joint kingdom of England and Scotland.

wait for a local fisherman who's heading your way.

SAMBÚ

The small town of **SAMBÚ** is the best place to base yourself for affordable exploration in Darién. Although there's little to do in the town itself, a day spent among the locals lends valuable insight into the simple and tough livelihoods of those inhabiting this culturally diverse and isolated community.

What to see and do

Exploring the area around Sambú, the last outpost of civilization in this part of the jungle, is most rewarding if you are not restrictive about where you want to go. When arranging river trips, as wise as it is to be courteous and affable, it's equally important to be on the ball regarding **costs**. Agree on everything very clearly before you accept – this is where having some Spanish is very important. Prices are based on the predicted amount of petrol required and the services of the boatmen. Find out about the current cost of petrol and

you'll be less likely to be hoodwinked – but you should remain wary of extra costs slipping in.

A rickety suspension bridge on the edge of the town leads to **Puerto Indio**, part of the **Comarca Emberá–Wounan**. This indigenous territory resides under its own legal jurisdiction, separate from Panamanian law. Locals are deeply protective of their culture and serious about the formalities of receiving visitors. Upon crossing the bridge, the architecture visibly shifts from Sambú's concrete constructions to traditional stilted huts with single-log ladders. Visitors should immediately ask to be presented to the Nokó (village leader), or a member of the tourism committee, in order to pay the US$10 entry fee. The tourism committee can organize tours of Puerto Indio, trips to more remote communities, presentations of local artisans, and exhibitions of traditional dance.

Arrival and information

All arriving tourists must register their passports with the *migración*, currently housed in a lean-to next to the police office at the airstrip.

By air Air Panama (@www.flyairpanama.com) flights arrive from Panama City three times a week (Mon, Wed & Fri) at the airstrip just outside of the town.

Health A small hospital opposite the police station is the only place for hundreds of miles where you can receive medical treatment.

Phone The community payphone (☎ 333 2512) is at the end of the airstrip.

Tourist information Ask for Juan Morillo, who can be reached by calling one of his children on ☎ 254 8146, 6656 7815 or 6767 2586. A spritely old man with bags of energy, Juan knows everyone and everything to do in the area, but speaks almost no English.

Accommodation and eating

Juan Morillo (see "Tourist information", above) offers accommodation in thatched cabinas next to the airstrip (US$12), as well as a central "apartment" for up to three people (US$10 per person). You could also ask the people who live in Sambú if anyone there could put you up for the night – this will almost certainly be possible. It will cost around US$5–10 per night for lodging and a little more for food. Be aware that most restaurants shut at 4pm so you need to pre-arrange your dinner, at a set time, with the owner.

Bar Kolashin At the far end of the riverside path. For drinks or supplies, head to this huge canteen, a popular party spot with massive speakers blaring

TREAT YOURSELF

Heave your trembling river legs to the brightly painted **Sambú Hause** (☎ 6766 5102, @www .sambuhausedarienpanama .com), about 500m from the Sambú airstrip. Rooms are clean and surprisingly comfortable, with luxuries such as hot water and air conditioning, and there's a sitting room, kitchen and porch with an outdoor grill. María, the housekeeper, can show you around the village and arrange river trips (from US$40) and jungle treks to interior villages (US$20/hr), and will also cook meals on request. This is one of the few "upscale" accommodation options in Darién: prices start at US$20.

a mash-up of music, serving icy cold beers at US$0.70. You'll also find the best-stocked general store in town here.

Hotel & Restaurante Mi Sueño At the end of the airstrip. Offers cheap meals and simple rooms with camp beds and fan. US$20

Restaurante Marantha On the main path before the bridge. There are several basic restaurants in town, most without names, which serve basic portions of lentils or beans with beef or fish; this is the most organized, with plates from US$2–3.

Villa Fiesta At the end of the airstrip. The fanciest place in town, offering air-conditioned lodging which can accommodate 2–4 guests, with firm mattresses and a mini-fridge. US$25

Moving on

By air Air Panama flights depart three times a week for Panama City (Mon, Wed & Fri). You should confirm your flight at least an hour before your scheduled departure at the hut by the airstrip.

Kuna Yala

Stretching nearly four hundred kilometres, **Kuna Yala** – the autonomous *comarca* (territory) of the Kuna people – takes in the narrow band of mainland Panama north of the Serranía de San Blas and the sweep of nearly four hundred tropical islands that is the **San Blas Archipelago**. Only about forty of the minute islands are inhabited, with some straining to contain towns, while others are little more than sandbanks that a lone family has made their home. Changes in recent years, including a direct road from Panama City and mobile phone reception for many of the islands, may have opened up travel in the region, but the carefully preserved Kuna culture set in this Caribbean utopia is no less impressive.

The Kuna have gradually made their way here over the centuries, migrating first from Colombia to the Darién region sometime in the sixteenth century. Abandoning that area after

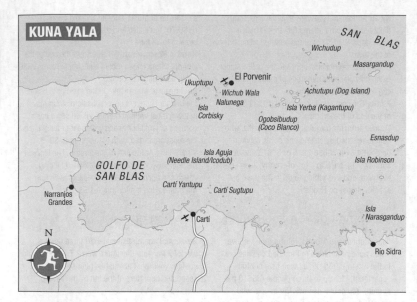

years of struggles with the Spanish and the Emberá tribe, they settled afresh along the coast and on the San Blas islands in the nineteenth century, but it took what they call "the Revolution" in 1925 to have the territory recognized as

VISITING KUNA YALA

Budget-wise, the best way to experience the San Blas Archipelago is to book a package visit through one of the Panama City hostels (see p.603). However, it is also possible to visit independently. The prices given here are generally per person per night, and include three meals.

With a tour

Tours to the region usually comprise transport by 4WD to the Cartí River (US$20–25 each way), pick-up from here by the owners of the accommodation you have been booked into, and transport to the designated island. A night's stay as part of a package starts at US$21, which includes three meals and unlimited use of basic snorkelling equipment.

On your own

By air Aeroperlas (☎315 7500, ⓦwww.aeroperlas.com) and Air Panama (☎316 9000, ⓦwww.flyairpanama.com) together service the islands daily. Flights (US$50–55) leave from Marcos A. Gelabert domestic airport in Albrook, Panama City. In the Archipelago, the principal airstrip for visitors is on El Porvenir. Flights are frequently delayed or cancelled, but there are sometimes flights not listed on the website, so phone in advance. Luggage exceeding 12kg incurs a surcharge of US$0.50/kg.

By road A 4WD can whisk you from Panama City to the Cartí River in 3 hours. From the drop-off it's a short boat transfer to the nearby islands. This is the preferred package-tour mode of transport that most hostels will arrange for you, but you can also book your own ride for US$25 each way by calling Rigoberto González (☎6527 3367), his partner Boyd (☎6719 9889) or Alexis Lam (☎6634 9384 or 6528 5862).

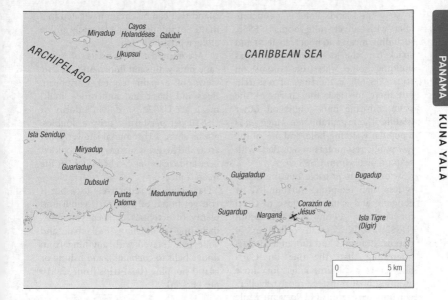

theirs alone. To this day, no non-Kuna may live in the *comarca*; it's a privilege just to hop among the islands, soaking up their beauty, and to spend the night in the community, perhaps sleeping in the same room as a Kuna family. Learning a little about their cultural heritage and how it informs their world view (particularly among the younger Kuna) and observing the fascinating ins and outs of island life are excellent reasons to come here – even if you can't stand idyllic beaches.

What to see and do

Day-trips include visits to picturesque, uninhabited islands such as the tiny **Dog Island** (Achutupo/Isla Perro)– a cargo ship was wrecked in the shallows here in the 1940s, making for great snorkelling. Other trips are sometimes made to **Kuna cemeteries** on the mainland; ask at your accommodation for the rundown of possible destinations. All of the islands are privately "owned" by the Kuna, and when your

hotel drops you off for an afternoon of sun-drenched laziness you will be approached for your payment of a visitor tax, usually US$1–2 – check with your guide beforehand, as it may be included in the price of the trip. When going on an excursion, be sure to bring **water** and something to do, whether it's a book or snorkelling gear.

If you're heading here on your own, most lodgings accept independent bookings and will pick you up from the airstrip or river dock (where you'll pay a US$2 "river tax"). With more expensive lodging there's no charge for this ride – just confirm in advance. For individual accommodation **listings**, see the island accounts that follow. Unless otherwise stated, prices – both packages and independently arranged – include three basic meals a day. Bring a torch, as electricity is usually switched off around 10pm, if there is any at all.

El Porvenir
The landing strip here, which serves as an airport, brings a lot of traffic to the area, but it's not the prettiest place

to stay. The island's hotel is a concrete affair with bare en-suite rooms (US$55, including meals and boat transfers) and snack bar; the local government was building some waterfront rooms on stilts (US$60) at the time of research, but these too lack the charm of the palm-and-cane huts found on other islands. The restaurant *Nan Magiryai* is a popular watering-hole, and one of the few public restaurants in San Blas, with seafood plates from US$5.

Swimming is possible but the beach is less than tempting, surrounded by concrete and a little to close to Cartí for comfort. A tiny Kuna museum (US$2), with a small collection of photos, drawings and dioramas, is less interesting than the one on Cartí but serves as a time-killer for those awaiting boat transfers; most travellers will only see or stop at El Porvenir while in transit.

Isla Senidup

Offering some of the cheapest and most popular lodging in San Blas is *Franklin's Place* (☎299 29058, or book through hostels in Panama City – see p.603), set on a stamp-sized and postcard-perfect island that can be circumnavigated in a matter of minutes – at a leisurely amble along a pristine beach.

Accommodation consists of small cane huts with sand floors, and dreamy views of a palm-framed Caribbean. Beds and (basic and sometimes small) meals are US$22 per day in a dorm, or US$30 per person for private doubles; guests share a communal shower/toilet area, and luxuries such as juice, cookies, beer and cigarettes can be bought at the main "office".

Days here are seductively lazy, but if you get bored of the beach you'll find plenty of activities to keep you busy, including snorkelling, basketball and volleyball (played with anything from dodge balls to coconuts), and fishing or island-hopping (boat trips from US$10 per person).

Isla Narasgandup

Isla Narasgandup, or **Little Orange Island**, is the other backpacker favourite, with several options for bedding down; Ina or her cousin Robinson have the most economical cabins at US$25 per person per night. Book through Panama City hostels (p.603).

KUNA CULTURE

Kuna society is regulated by a system of highly participative democracy: every community has a *casa de congreso* where the *onmakket*, or congress, meets regularly. Each community also elects a *sahila*, usually a respected elder, who attends the Kuna General Congress twice a year. The General Congress is the supreme political authority in Kuna Yala, and in turn appoints three *cacique* to represent the Kuna in the national government.

Colonial missionaries struggled in vain to Christianize the Kuna, who cling to their own religious beliefs, based above all on the sanctity of Nan Dummad, the Great Mother, and on respect for the environment they inhabit. Though Kuna men wear standard Western clothes, Kuna women wear gold rings in their ears and noses and blue vertical lines painted on their foreheads; they don headscarves and bright bolts of trade cloth round their waists, their forearms and calves are bound in coloured beads and their blouses are sewn with beautiful reverse-appliqué designs known as *molas*.

Given that no non-Kuna is permitted to live on the islands and that tourism is a prickly issue, your status as an outsider is symbolic and your behaviour will probably be scrutinized. Cover up unless it is clearly fine to do otherwise, and cut out public displays of affection. You must ask permission to visit the islands – ask the advice of people you meet to find a contact – and to take photographs.

INTO COLOMBIA: PUERTO OBALDÍA

You can enter **Colombia** by boat via **Puerto Obaldía**, a remote border outpost at the far southeastern edge of Kuna Yala, served by light aircraft from Panama City. Aeroperlas runs one flight from Wednesday to Sunday (US$53 one way). After going through customs and providing the Colombian consulate with proof of onward travel, you can take a **boat** (about US$10) to Capurganá, a small fishing village and holiday resort on the Colombian coast, where DAS (℗00574 824 3838, Ⓦwww.das.gov.co) will stamp your passport. From Capurganá, ADA (℗00574 444 42 32, Ⓦwww.ada-aero.com) flies to Medellín and other destinations in Colombia. There are also boats from Capurganá across the Gulf of Urabá to Turbo. From Turbo you can catch one of the regular light aircraft flights to Medellín and Cartagena, or continue your journey by bus. There are places to change money around the border, but they charge around twenty percent commission, so it is best to change only a small amount and wait until you reach a town with an ATM.

Cartí

Cartí refers to a group of islands and an area on the mainland roughly 10km south of El Porvenir. **Cartí Sugtupu** (Sugdup is also frequently used) is the most populated island in the isthmus, with a health centre, school, library and small, rough-hewn restaurant – *La Pampa* – that does fried chicken, rice, salad and good lentils for US$3. You can observe the community meetings that take place every evening, and from February 1 to 25 there's a daily dramatization of the 1925 revolution, when a number of the islanders dress, disconcertingly, as policemen.

Overall the island is crowded, with little to do aside from visit the small but interesting **museum** (US$2). Fascinatingly cluttered, it's covered floor-to-ceiling with drawings and paintings in various styles – some by children – representing different aspects of Kuna culture, myth and history.

Swimming is not an option on this island, as sewage systems spew waste directly into the surrounding waters. There are several *hospedajes* here, but given the wealth of uncrowded *islitas* nearby – where you can loll on empty beaches and snorkel in crystal-line waters – you are unlikely to find a reason to spend the night here.

Isla Icodub

Also known as **Isla Aguja** (or Needle Island), Isla Icodub harbours *Hotel Icodub* (US$60, including meals; ℗6909 1873), with a lovely beach. The hotel provides a "shipwrecked" experience, offering only a few well-separated cabins with communal bathrooms. Fish, lobster and octopus are usually on the menu for dinner; if you're not sleeping here, the restaurant is also open to the public for simple seafood dishes from US$5.

Central Panama and the Azuero Peninsula

Central Panama is a strikingly diverse region that rewards exploration. Head west from Panama City and your bus will barely have hit top speed before you can hop off and spend some time sprawled on one of the abundant **beaches** just south of the Interamericana. It's worth spending a night in the relative cool of **El Valle**, a popular weekend getaway for

Panama City residents, before heading down into the **Península de Azuero**. Here you can visit some of the towns founded by the colonial Spanish and explore two islands – Isla Iguana and Isla Cañas – that are both wonderful, but in very different ways.

INTERAMERICANA BEACHES

West of Panama City, the **Interamericana Highway** runs along a narrow plain squeezed between the Pacific and the slopes of the Cordillera Central. At the border of Coclé Province, 193km from Panama City, the road forks at **Divisa**; the Interamericana continues west to Santiago, the capital of Veraguas Province, while the Carretera Nacional turns south into the Península de Azuero.

For 50km beyond the village of Bejuco (around 60km west of Panama City and 120km east of Divisa), the coast is lined with some of the most beautiful and popular **Pacific beaches** in Panama, all just a few kilometres from the highway and accessible by taxi or local bus. Infrequent public transport calls for patience, so those with time constraints should consider hiring a car in Panama City (see p.608). Beaches close to the city – such as Playa Gorgona and Punta Barco – have seen price-hikes in recent years, as weekend getaways owned by wealthy city folk take over, but heading further west you'll still find plenty of options for camping and budget accommodation.

Playa Río Mar

Two exits past the El Rey supermarket (which is the turn-off for Playa Gorgona) is the entrance to **Playa Río Mar**, which draws backpackers and surfers alike with its lovely beach and popular break. The *Río Mar Hotel* (☎345 3010, ⊛www.riomarsurf.com) has air-conditioned rooms from US$39 and may allow camping during the week. Located at the entrance to the beach, the hotel also has a pool, small bar and restaurant, and a half pipe for skaters.

To get here, take any westbound **bus** from Panama City along the Interamericana, and ask to be let off at Río Mar (after Playa Gorgona).

Playa El Palmar

El Palmar can be visited as a day-trip from the city, but beach-goers and surfers who want an early start have a good selection of budget accommodation to choose from – especially during the week when there are fewer visitors. *El Palmar Surf Camp* (☎6615 6564 or 240 8004), is a hostel and hotel on the beach with a campsite (US$5), dorm beds from US$15, and pricey air-conditioned rooms (US$65). Surf lessons, and board and kayak rental are also available. The beach bar and restaurant offers expensive seafood and beer, so stock up on supplies before arriving. *Carlito's Pizza*, at the turn-off on the highway, is a popular and slightly more reasonable alternative, with cheesy pizzas from US$5.

Those travelling on westbound **buses** should ask to stop at the pueblo of San Carlos, just beyond the entrances of Gorgona and Río Mar beaches. From here it's a long hike, or you can find a local taxi to ferry you to the beach; if staying at the camp (see above) you may be able to arrange a lift with the owner in advance.

Playa Santa Clara

Some 30km east of Penonomé (see p.640), **Playa Santa Clara** is probably the area's loveliest beach, with white, dust-fine sand as far as the eye can see. If you're staying the night, bar and restaurant *El Balneario* (☎993 2123) allows camping for US$3, which also buys you use of their bathroom, shower and changing rooms. The restaurant closes at 6pm, so get there early for their fresh fish and plantain dishes (US$7–9).

Taxis usually hang around by the beach to take you back to the highway (US$3). Moving on from Santa Clara, **Penonomé** (see p.640) is a thirty- to forty-minute bus ride west; several buses should pass this route every hour.

EL VALLE

About 100km west of Panama City, a twisty road climbs up into the cordillera to **EL VALLE**, a small village in a fertile valley that was once the crater of a volcano. At 600m above sea level, El Valle is comparatively cool, and the surrounding countryside is good for walking or horseriding. Renowned for its flowers – particularly orchids, which appreciate the slightly lower temperatures – the area is a popular retreat for wealthy Panama City residents at weekends.

What to see and do

Most of the village's amenities can be found on **Avenida Central**, along with signposts pointing the way to local attractions, mostly located on the outskirts of the village. In the centre, the daily **market** draws the biggest crowds, especially on Sundays, when locals sell fruit, flowers and crafts. A small **museum** (Sun 10am–2pm; US$0.50), run by nuns, houses exhibits on local history and folklore and stands next to the church of San José. Beyond the church by the Río Anton, a side road leads to the enjoyably quirky **thermal baths** (daily 8am–5pm; US$2), or *pozos termales*, reputed to have medicinal powers.

One of the most worthwhile sights nearby, **El Chorro Macho** is a 35-metre waterfall in a private reserve (daily 6am–5pm; US$4), with **ziplines** (US$12 or US$45) fitted around it. To get here, take a local bus headed for La Mesa from Av Central, or you could walk here in half an hour (take the right-hand fork at the western end of town). As far as the zipline goes, the budget version is not worth the money – if you're intent on doing it, splash out on the more expensive ride, which passes among the platforms and over the waterfall.

Head 1km up a signposted side road off Av Principal to visit the **El Nispero zoo and orchid nursery** (daily 7am–5pm; US$2). It's home to not the happiest looking animals, but a great spot to view the many orchids that grow here, as well as Panama's endangered golden frog. Further afield, innumerable trails climb up into the **cloudforests** of the surrounding mountains. Best known here is the trail that peaks at **La India Dormida**, a mountain ridge looming west of the valley, whose silhouette quite strikingly resembles a woman lying on her back. The passage to the **Piedra Pintada**, an ancient rock with petroglyphs, is somewhat less visited, with a series of waterfalls to cool you down on the way.

Arrival and information

By bus Buses pull in at the covered market on Av Principal. Direct buses from Panama City arrive 7.30am–6.30pm.

Exchange Banco Nacional has an ATM on Av Principal, near the turn-off for El Nispero.

Internet There are computers in the public library (Mon–Sat 8.30am–3.30pm; US$1/hr).

Tourist information There's a small IPAT office in a kiosk next to the market, but your hostel owner will probably have as much (if not more) knowledge about tourist activities in the area.

Accommodation

Accommodation prices in El Valle reflect its popularity among Panamanians, who flock here for Carnaval, public holidays and weekends. That said, there are still several options catering to travellers on a tighter budget; these generally do not accept credit cards.

Cabañas Potosí West 150m past the church, take the road to the right, then the fork to the left and continue for 1.5km ☎ 983 6181. Comfortable, good-looking rooms in a series of smart concrete cabañas. Offers camping (bring your own tent) plus an extra US$1 to use the facilities, including an outdoor grill. Camping US$10, doubles US$45

La Casa de Juan Roughly 1.5km before the town centre, look for a sign pointing left; it's 200m down this road ☎6453 9775, @ lacasadejuan@hotmail .com. Laidback Señor Juan provides private en-suite rooms and one dorm, set in a sprawling home packed with odd and interesting artefacts. An open-air kitchen and hammock-strewn living spaces connect with a large garden, where you can pitch a tent. Bikes are loaned for local exploration, and discounts can be negotiated. Camping US$5, dorms US$10, doubles US$25

La Casita de Don Daniel At the foot of La India Dormida ☎6615 5511, @ www.lacasitadedon daniel.com. This place offers camping with use of bathrooms and communal kitchen. Local crafts are sold on site, while the weekends offer live music and snacks. US$5

El Gaital Av Central ☎6956 4561. Homely rooms with private bathrooms in a handy central location; the attached restaurant serves decent pizzas from US$5–7. US$35

Eating

Two stalls on Av Central open in the early evening and sell good fried chicken; another nearby sells very fine *batidos* (ask them to hold the sugar). The *abarrotería* next to the library deals in lovely little ice-cream cones (try the *guanabana*) for US$0.50, while the *panadería* opposite has great fresh bread.

Anton Valley Hotel Av Central ☎983 6097, @ www.antonvalleyhotel.com. The breakfast at this hotel, open to the public, is naughtily good. Choose from walnut-and-cinnamon waffles, platters of fresh fruit or proper Panamanian breakfasts, from US$5.

Bambusillo Av Central. A new vegetarian café with snacks from US$3 and wi-fi, where you can also browse local *artesanía*. Guided tours to the orchid farm, canopy and trails can also be arranged. Closed Mon & Tues.

Restaurante Bruschetta Av Central. Small but in demand among locals, this place serves large portions, including enormous bruschettas (US$4) and tasty salads. Closed Tues.

Restaurante Mar de Plata Av Central ☎6478 4138. Neat and airy with pink tablecloths and a mountain view from the window seats. The menu has an interesting mix of Panamanian fare, seafood, Chinese and Creole flavours, with dishes for US$3–6.

Restaurante Massiel Av Central. Come for the *comida típica* and fast food – chicken with rice is US$3 and hamburger combos go for US$3.50.

Moving on

By bus You can either take a direct bus to Panama City (every 30 min until 6pm; around 2hr; US$3.50) or a minibus to San Carlos (every 30min; 40min; US$1.80), where you can flag down buses heading in either direction along the Interamericana.

PENONOMÉ

Founded in 1581 as a *reducción de Indios* – a place where conquered indigenous groups were forcibly resettled so as to be available for labour service – and briefly the capital of the isthmus after the destruction of Panamá Viejo, **PENONOMÉ** was named after Nomé, a local chieftain cruelly betrayed and executed here by the Spaniards after years of successful resistance. Now the capital of Coclé Province, Penonomé doesn't have much to see apart from a small museum, though it makes a good enough base for exploring the surrounding area.

What to see and do

From the makeshift bus terminal – really just the point on the Interamericana where buses pick up and drop off – Penonomé's busy commercial **main street**, referred to as either Via Central or Avenida J.D. Arosemena, runs a few hundred metres to the **Plaza 8 de Diciembre**. Featuring a statue of Simón Bolívar and the inevitable bandstand, the square is flanked by government buildings and the San Juan Bautista church. From here, head two blocks down Calle Damián Carles, take a right and continue for two blocks and you'll arrive at the **Museo de Penonomé** (Tues–Sat 9am–5pm; US$1), near Parque Rubén Darío Carles. Here you'll find pre-Columbian ceramics decorated with abstract designs and colonial religious art. Upstairs in a creaking attic are artefacts arranged to evoke what a local residence may have looked like a century ago.

Arrival

By bus Buses that travel the Interamericana pick up and drop off opposite the *Hotel Dos Continentes* at the intersection of Av J.D. Arosemena (Via Central) and the Interamericana. Buses from Panama City arrive every 30min.

Accommodation and eating

Hostal Villa Esperanza Off the Interamericana, 5 minutes from the central drag ☎ 997 8055. Comfortable private rooms set, US motel-style, in a compound complete with pool and restaurant. A better deal for groups, with a four-person room at US$65/night, while the secure parking comes in handy for those with a car. US$50.

Hotel Dos Continentes Av J.D. Arosemena (Via Central), opposite the bus terminal ☎ 997 9325/9326, ⊛ www.hoteldoscontinentes .net. This is a big place, where a/c rooms with private baths are un-ironically retro in decor. Rooms, cheaper during weekdays, sleep up to four guests. The hotel's very popular restaurant may lack views, but the food's good: try the shrimp omelette and *patacones* (US$5) and steak and fish dishes (US$5–10). They also serve *bollo* – plantain mashed and then compacted into chunks (tastier than it sounds). US$35

Panadería El Paisa Via Central, just before the church. Busy bakery with a large selection of bread (from US$0.30), pastries and sandwiches (US$1–3), plus outdoor seating where you can soak up the town's atmosphere.

Restaurante Gallo Pinto #1 A block south of the church. Cheery chequered tablecloths and a bustling central location make this branch more alluring than its other locations. The kitchen whips up *comida típica* staples like beef *guisado* (stew) for US$2.50, and full breakfasts with popular bean-and-rice combo *gallo pinto* for US$3.

Restaurante Gran China C Hector Conte Bermudez, just west of the bus terminal. Tasty Chinese food in huge portions, with wonton soup for US$3, and a meal of garlic shrimp, fried rice and salad for US$7.

Directory

Exchange There is a Banco Nacional with ATM on Av J.D. Arosemena/Via Central.
Internet @Cybers on Av J.D. Arosemena/Via Central has computers and wi-fi for US$1/US$0.50.
Laundry The Lavamat is two blocks north of *Hotel Dos Continentes*.

Pharmacy There are three pharmacies in the immediate vicinity of *Hotel Dos Continentes*.
Post office Near Plaza 8 de Diciembre.

Moving on

By bus Services to Chitré (every 30min; 1hr 30min) leave from the Shell station, as do buses to Panama City (every 30min; approx 2hr).

AROUND PENONOMÉ

From the market area in Penonomé, *chivas* and *busitos* (minibuses) head off to villages scattered in the folds of the cool, forested mountains that rise to the north.

Chiguirí Arriba

Of the potential destinations in the mountains, **Chiguirí Arriba**, 29km to the northeast, makes an easy day-trip with plenty of good hiking trails, spectacular views, plump red chickens running about and a thirty-metre waterfall nearby – local children may guide you there for a small tip. There's a shop and local hangout that sells coffee, multicoloured popcorn, Quaker Oats and a curiously wide range of artist's materials.

The first **bus** to Chiguirí Arriba from Penonomé is at 6am, the next at 9am and then they run approximately every

TREAT YOURSELF

Buses from Penonomé depart every 30 minutes (6am–9pm) to the Churuquita Grande community, some 14km away, where **La Iguana Resort** (☎ 991 0879 or 6785 7550, ⊛ www.laiguanaresort.com), a small ecofriendly hotel, is set amid lush gardens and a private forest reserve. Rooms are en suite with a fan (a/c is an extra US$5), and amenities include a jungle pool, ping-pong tables and a volleyball pitch. Meals at the restaurant are reasonably priced, if not delicious, from US$4 a plate. There are several hiking trails; the longest leads to the Zaratí River, which is safe for swimming – very refreshing after a long walk. US$25 hour to hour and a half until the late afternoon; arrive at least fifteen minutes before the bus leaves. The last bus back to Penonomé from Chiguirí Arriba leaves at 3.30pm from in front of the shop.

CHITRÉ

The capital of Herrera Province and the largest town on the Azuero Peninsula, **CHITRÉ** is a slow-paced market centre studded with colourful discount stores. Other than the market there's not much to see here, but Chitré is the peninsula's main transport hub and as such it is a good base for exploration.

What to see and do

Chitré centres on the bandstand, trees and benches of **Parque Unión**. The square is flanked on one side by the gleaming white **cathedral**, with its impressive, vaulted wooden roof and extensive wooden panelling decorated with gold. The seemingly immovable glass windows are hinged at the centre so that they can swivel, allowing breezes into the cathedral – a curious sight. The cathedral faces down Avenida Herrera – walk down a block and turn left on Calle Manuel Correa and you'll reach the **Museo de Herrera** (Tues–Sat 8am–noon & 1–4pm, Sun 8–11am; US$1), three blocks away. Set in an elegant colonial mansion, the museum has a collection of pre-Columbian pottery from the surrounding area and a good display on local folklore and customs, featuring traditional masks, costumes and musical instruments.

A ten-minute drive north of Chitré lies the village of **La Arena,** famous for its pottery, which is sold by the potters on the roadside.

Arrival and information

By bus Buses from Panama City pull in at the terminal on the southern outskirts of town. Local buses run to the town centre from the terminal, or it's a 10min walk.

Tourist information There's a CEFATI office in the Parque Industrial La Arena, on the road into town (☎974 4532).

Accommodation

Book accommodation well in advance for Carnaval.

Hotel Bali Av Herrera, north of the cathedral ☎996 4620, ⊛www.hotelbalipanama.com. Despite the seedy-looking entrance, the *Bali* is one of the best options in town. The clean rooms, sleeping up to six, all have cable TV and en-suite bathrooms with hot water, and secure parking. The lobby has a nice balcony where you can use wi-fi while eating breakfast (US$2–4) or Indonesian snacks like chicken satay (US$5). US$32

Hotel Rex Opposite Parque Unión ☎996 2391. The fanciest spot in Chitré, where a/c rooms come with breakfast in the on-site restaurant. Rooms are not available during Carnaval. US$45

Hotel Santa Rita Av Herrera, north of the cathedral ☎996 4610. Run by the same family for over a hundred years, this hotel has lost its period charm but is still a good-value option in a central location. US$20

Miami Mike's Av Herrera, north of the cathedral ☎910 0628, ⊛www.miamimikeshostel.com. *Mike's* is the only real hostel in town and shows plenty of potential, with a massive roof terrace that is set to become the hostel's best feature. The rudimentary dorms are the cheapest beds in town that are not rented by the hour, and you can cook your own meals in the communal kitchen. The English-speaking owner will be more than happy to advise you on exploring the area, or help arrange onward travel, including booking boat trips from Panama City to Colombia. Dorms US$10, doubles US$13

Eating

El Anzuelo Paseo Enrique Geenzier. With a rambling outdoor eating area, this place is full of contented diners and plates that are empty but for fish heads. Fish dishes (including croaker, dorado and mahi, not just the ubiquitous *corvina*) from US$7.
Panadería Chiquita Av Herrera. Popular with local taxi drivers, this spot serves simple rice-with-meat or rice-with-fish dishes (from US$4).
Pizzería Treri One block south of the church. Service is not a forte here, but the pizzas (US$3–8) pastas and salads (US$3–5) are decent and filling.
Restaurante La Estrella Av Herrera, on the corner opposite the church. A large fast-food canteen, often overflowing at lunchtime, with plates of mixed rice or chow mein for US$3–4.

Directory

Exchange There's a branch of HSBC (Mon–Fri 9am–1pm) with 24hr ATM on Av Herrera a block north of the cathedral, and a branch of Banco Nacional (Mon–Sat 9am–1pm) on Paseo Enrique Geenzier, northwest of the town centre.
Internet There are several cafés on Av Herrera, charging US$1/hr.
Pharmacy On Av Herrera opposite the cathedral.

Moving on

By bus Services to Panama City (hourly; 4hr), Santiago (every 30min; 1hr 20min), Las Tablas (every 15min; 45min) and villages in the interior of the peninsula leave from the terminal (see "Arrival", opposite). You can catch a bus to the terminal from the stop next to the fountain by the museum.

LAS TABLAS

LAS TABLAS, south along the peninsula's coast from Chitré, was founded in the seventeenth century by refugees fleeing by sea from Panamá Viejo after Henry Morgan and his band of pirates sacked it. The settlers dismantled their ships to build the first houses, hence the town's name, which means "the planks".

Though you wouldn't believe it if you turned up at any other time of year, this quiet, colonial market town hosts the wildest **Carnaval** celebrations in Panama (see box below). For five days in February the place is overwhelmed by visitors from all over the country, who come here to join in the festivities. The town divides into two halves – **Calle Arriba** and **Calle Abajo** – to fight a pitched battle with water, paint and soot on streets awash with *seco*, Panama's vicious firewater. Less raucous but just as colourful is the fiesta of **Santa Librada** in July, which includes the **pollera fiesta**, celebrating the peninsula's embroidered, colonial-style dresses.

RELIGIOUS FESTIVALS IN THE PENÍNSULA DE AZUERO

Jutting out into the Pacific Ocean, the **Península de Azuero** was one of the first regions of Panama to be settled by Spanish colonists. The towns and villages you come across – the main recommended bases include Chitré, Las Tablas and Pedasí – in this dry, scrubby landscape hum with their colonial heritage, visually manifested in the traditional handicrafts and folk costumes of the region, but the real giveaway is the gusto with which the people throw themselves into their **religious fiestas**. Usually honouring a particular patron saint, many of these date back almost unchanged to the days of the early settlers. Religious processions are accompanied by traditional music, fireworks and costumed folk dances which are as pagan as they are Catholic. Listed below are just a few of the major events; every village and hamlet has its own fiesta, and there's almost always one going on somewhere.

Jan 6 Fiesta de los Reyes and Encuentro del Canajagua in Macarcas.
Jan 19–22 Fiesta de San Sebastián in Ocú.
Feb (date varies) Carnaval in Las Tablas (and everywhere else in the country).
March/April (date varies) Semana Santa, celebrated most colourfully in La Villa de Los Santos, Pesé and Guararé.
Late April Feria International del Azuero in La Villa de Los Santos.
June (date varies) Corpus Christi in La Villa de Los Santos.
June 24 Patronales de San Juan in Chitré.
June 29–30 Patronales de San Pedro y San Pablo in La Arena.
July 20–22 Patronales de La Santa Librada and Festival de la Pollera in Las Tablas.
Aug 15 Festival del Manito in Ocú.
Sept 24 Festival de la Mejorana in Guararé.
Oct 19 Foundation of the District of Chitré, in Chitré.
Nov 10 The "First Cry of Independence" in La Villa de Los Santos.

Produced in the town, they are something of a national symbol.

What to see and do

The most popular sight in Las Tablas is the church, **Iglesia Santa Librada**, opposite the main square known as **Parque Porras**. With the doors on both sides usually kept wide open, the town's balconies and bright colours seem to crowd in from outside. Locals wander in one side and out the other, too, almost as if the church were just part of the street furniture.

Also sitting on the main square in a lovely colonial building is the tiny **Museo Belisario Porras** (Tues–Sun 9.30am–4pm), an array of belongings and articles pertaining to the former president who was born here in 1856. For US$1, an enthusiastic guide will proudly explain (in Spanish only) the significance of the items on display, including presidential correspondence and several splendid outfits worn by the man himself – a lovingly assembled collection, best suited to history buffs.

Arrival

By bus Buses from Panama City pull up on Av Laureano Lopez, at the terminal near the Shell station a few blocks from the square, while those from Chitré arrive at Parque Porras.

Accommodation

If you want to come for Carnaval, you'll have to book several months in advance, at least.
Hotel Piamonte Av Belisario Porras ☎923 1903/ 1603. If you don't like one room, ask to see – or smell – another, as the quality is not consistent. This place also offers rooms – without hot water or wi-fi – across the street, with negotiable prices. There's also a restaurant, with toasted sandwiches for US$2.50. US$26
Hotel Sol del Pacífico C Augustin Cano ☎994 1280. An uninspiring, green concrete bunker, with large rooms good for groups and an apartment (US$120 for nine guests); all come equipped with microwave and mini-fridge, making this handy for longer stays. US$25

Eating and drinking

Bambú Parque Porras. Nearing completion at the time of research, this new venue offers upmarket drinks and snacks on an upstairs balcony, with atmospheric views of the park and town below – this spot will be overflowing come Carnaval time.
El Mesón Parque Porras. Frequently clogged with people hungry for pizza (US$3–4) and deliciously good value chicken or beef stews (US$1.50).
Los Portales Av Belisario Porras. This place has a small terrace for dining right on the pavement, offering fine people-watching, though too close for comfort during Carnaval. A little overpriced, but the cooking is good quality. Dishes US$4–8.
Portofino Parque Porras, next door to *El Mesón*. The menu's uncannily similar to its neighbour's, but it's anyone's guess which one's the copycat. *Portofino* does a fine line in *batidos* (guanabana, papaya, etc), all for around US$1.
Restaurante El Caserón C Augustin Bautista. The fancy joint in town, this restaurant is situated on its own down a dusty, gravelly side-road, with checked tablecloths and pink server uniforms to brighten things up. Their mixed meat grills (US$4–8), the house speciality, are highly recommended.

Directory

Exchange Banco Nacional is near the bus station on Av Laureano Lopez (Mon–Fri 8am–3pm & Sat 9am–noon).
Laundry Lavandería Taty's is one block from the Shell station at the entrance to town.
Pharmacy There are two on Parque Porras.
Post office Down the side road opposite the Banco Nacional on Av Laureano Lopez (Mon–Fri 7am–6pm, Sat 7am–5pm).

Moving on

By bus to: Chitré (every 20min 6am–7pm; 45min), from Banco Nacional de Panamá on Av Laureano Lopez; Panama City (hourly 6am–8pm, Fri & Sun until 5.30pm; 4hr 30min) from the terminal (see above); Pedasí (hourly 6am–7pm; 45min) from outside the supermarket on Av Belisario Porras; Tonosí (hourly; 1hr 30min), from outside the same supermarket. To go west from Las Tablas, take a Panama City bus and get off at Divisa. Cross over the highway to catch westbound buses for either Santiago (30min from Divisa), the main way-point between here and David, or David itself.

PEDASÍ

It's 42km south through cattle country from Las Tablas to **PEDASÍ**, a friendly little village that is fast becoming a surf destination, best known as a jumping-off point for Isla Iguana, Isla Cañas and a wealth of beaches in the surrounding area.

What to see and do

Other than a visit to the **church** on the town square, which features chandeliers and a cheerful blue-sky-and-green-fields mural behind the altar, activities in Pedasí involve day-trips to the **islands and the nearby surf breaks**. Dive-N-Fish Pedasí (daily 7–11am & 1–5pm; ☎995 2405, ⓦwww.dive-n-fish panama.com), near the Accel petrol station at the north end of town, offers a range of good-value **activities** in the area, including trips to Isla Iguana (US$45, plus US$3.50 park fee); ask about camping. Night trips are organized to try and catch a glimpse of turtles laying their eggs on the beach at Isla Cañas (US$45), leaving at 10pm and returning at 4am. Whale-watching trips, typically most successful between April and November, combined with snorkelling or an Isla Iguana visit, go for US$45.

Arrival and information

By bus Buses pull up on the one main street that runs through the town.
Exchange The Banco Nacional and Caja de Ahorros, both on the main street, have ATMs.
Internet Cyber@ opposite the main square, charges US$1/hr; there's also free wi-fi at *Maudy's* (see below).
Tour operators Shokogi, an Israeli-run outfit, offers trips in the area as well as kitesurfing and S.U.P. (Stand Up Paddle, a cross between surfing and kayaking) lessons and rentals (☎6921 1532, ⓦwww.surfpedasi.com).
Tourist information The IPAT office (Mon–Fri 9am–noon & 1–4pm; ☎995 2339) is on the second left as you enter the village from the north, near Dive-N-Fish Pedasí.

Accommodation

🏃 **Dim's Hostal** ☎995 2303. This long-established option has pretty, cosy rooms with dainty curtains at the windows and comfortable beds. There's a hammock-slung patio in the lush garden out back with a large, palm-thatched roof anchored to the trunk of a mango tree – a nice place for a beer and a snooze. Prices include breakfast, a/c, private bathroom and TV. US$50
Residencial Moscoso ☎995 2203. Well acquainted with backpackers, the *Moscoso* is clean and friendly – the reception is in the owner's living room. Rooms come with a/c and private bathroom. US$28

Eating

Dulceria Yely Opposite *Residencial Moscoso*. With a cabinet full of delicious cakes at just US$0.60 a slice, you could get through a whole one yourself very quickly.
Koko's On the main street. Sit on the front porch and enjoy the simple, freshly cooked food, with plates like delicious breaded-chicken pieces (*deditos*) with beans, rice and salad for US$4. Closed Tues & Wed.
Maudy's On the main street. The breakfast spot in town, with locally made yoghurt, granola and fruit plates for US$4, as well as smoothies and toasties from US$2.50. Good coffee and wi-fi are further reasons to stop here.
Restaurante El Ejecutivo C Las Tablas, across from the square. The cheap choice, with *típica* breakfasts for US$2.50 and greasy Chinese dishes for US$3–5.
Tiesto On the square behind the main road. An airy place with a high roof and a stone arch that does good-quality brick-oven pizzas from US$4–8.

Moving on

By bus Three daily services for Cañas (3 daily; 45min) leave from the main street in town, as do buses back to Chitré (hourly 6am–5pm; 45min). For Playa Venao, hop on one of the Cañas-bound buses (7am, noon & 3pm; 30min), departing from the main street. Bus timetables are subject to change, so check with locals for current schedules.
By taxi A taxi to Cañas costs from US$20; you can pick one up on the main street.

AROUND PEDASÍ

Pedasí is a great base for exploration of this area's fascinating marine identity.

You can set off in search of whales, iguanas and sea turtles safe in the knowledge that you can come back and lay your head somewhere cosy.

Playa El Arenal

Playa El Arenal, a very long, very empty and very flat beach, is a thirty-minute walk from Pedasí or a few dollars in a taxi. It's roundly recommended by locals for its tranquil waters. Keeping a low profile on the edge of the beach is *Coco's*, a restaurant owned by a local co-operative. When local fishermen bring in their catch, the restaurant gets first pick at rock-bottom prices, which they pass on to customers. The fried fish (US$3.50 with *patacones*) is truly delicious, which must be down to its freshness – not to mention the view, the beer and the sense of calm.

Playa Venao

Surfer's beach **Playa Venao** lies thirty minutes by car or *chiva* from Pedasí. The beautiful bay is still relatively undeveloped, although it has recently become home to two designer rancho-restaurants, which serve overpriced food and drink; both businesses also rent surfboards and sell wax. There are also several choices for bedding down here; see the box below or try *La Choza* (☎832 1010; dorms US$15, doubles US$35), 200m from the beach break: a new venture by the owners of *Hotel El Sitio*, with compact yet comfortable rooms, breezy balcony and intimate garden-rancho kitchen.

Isla Iguana

Some 7km off the coast of Pedasí lies **Isla Iguana**, an uninhabited wildlife reserve managed by the state and surrounded by the most extensive **coral reefs** in the Bahía de Panamá, making it one of the best sites for **snorkelling** and **diving** in the country. The island has white-sand beaches, crystalline waters and a colony of magnificent frigate birds, and between April and November you may see **whales**. Despite the island's name, iguanas have become scarce due to the locals' fondness for their meat – though since the island was declared a national park their numbers have been creeping back up.

You can hire a **boat** to take you here from **Playa El Arenal** (see above). Fishermen charge about US$40 for a return trip (20min each way); at weekends you may find other visitors to share the cost. Take all the food and drink you need. If you want to **camp** on the island, arrange a pick-up time with your boatman.

ISLA CAÑAS

Archeological evidence suggests that people have been coming to the area now designated as the **ISLA CAÑAS WILDLIFE RESERVE** to hunt turtles and harvest their eggs for many centuries, although the island was only settled in the 1960s. Since 1988, the hunting of turtles here has been prohibited and a co-operative has been established to control the harvest.

TREAT YOURSELF

Harmonize with your surroundings and support sustainable ecological development of the area with a stay at the **Hostel Eco-Venao** (☎832 5030, ⓦwww.eco venao.com), halfway between Pedasí and Cañas. Set across from the beach on the main road between Pedasí and Cañas, the property encompasses a large patch of wild jungle mountainside with great views. Accommodation ranges from an eco-campsite and dorms to private rooms and cabinas. Food, cooked in a large communal kitchen, must be purchased in advance; arrive prepared with plenty of supplies. Camping US$6, dorms US$12, doubles US$25, cabinas US$40

THE ISLA CAÑAS ARRIBADA

Isla Cañas has one of the few beaches in the world that sees the phenomenon known as the **arribada**, when thousands of female sea turtles simultaneously come ashore to lay their eggs. It's still not entirely understood what triggers this mass exodus from the sea at one particular moment, though smaller numbers emerge at other times, too, within a roughly ten-day period on either side of a full moon (when tides are highest, allowing the turtles to lay their eggs further up the beach). Whether or not your visit coincides with an *arribada* (usually Aug–Nov), if you come between May and January you'll almost certainly see green, hawksbill or Olive Ridley turtles laying their eggs at night. From December to March there's a good chance of seeing leviathan-like leatherbacks, which can weigh over 800kg.

Members watch over the beaches at night and collect the eggs as soon as they are laid, keeping eighty percent for sale and consumption and moving the rest to a nursery where the turtles can hatch and return to the sea in safety. A night-time **turtle walk**, at least half an hour in each direction along the beach, will set you back about US$10. Torch use is stringently rationed, as the turtles are frightened by the piercing beams. The long, near-silent walk along soft sand, the lapping water and the incredible number of stars may just lull you to sleep on your feet.

The functional but unmemorable **main village** on Isla Cañas is prepared for visitors, as are the mosquitoes and sandflies.

Accommodation and eating

One accommodation option is to arrange a homestay; try the lovely Enie, whose rooms (US$5) do not include board, though she's a fine cook. There's a small restaurant near the dock where you can eat for around US$4, although the food does not seem especially fresh.

Turtle co-operative The co-operative has set aside a building where guests can stay. The larger room has a/c, but don't expect much for your money. Windowless cabañas are a cheaper option, but if you take this route be prepared for serious battle with mosquitoes. Cabañas US$10, doubles US$40

GETTING TO ISLA CAÑAS

If you're not setting out with a tour, getting to and from **Isla Cañas** is not as straightforward as you might hope. To reach the island, you'll need to start out from Pedasí. Here, flag down a **bus** on the main road heading for Tonosí, or wait outside *Koko's* restaurant (see p.645). The buses (hourly 7am–4pm) look like vans and should display their destination on the windscreen; tell the driver you want to go to the "dock", the jumping-off point for the island. You could also take a **taxi** for around US$25, but make sure the driver takes you past Cañas Town to the jumping-off point, which they're often loath to do because of the poor road. When you arrive at the dock – essentially the point where the road ends and the mangrove swamp begins – there will often be **boats** waiting. If there are none smack loudly on the metal wheel rim that is hung up in a tree near the edge of the swamp. This will alert people on the island (it is very close) and someone will come to get you in due course.

Moving on, one scheduled boat leaves the island daily at 7am to make the 7.30am bus that runs from the dock to Las Tablas. Another bus leaves at 8am for Tonosí (35min), from where you can connect for Las Tablas (hourly: Mon–Thurs & Sat 6am–4pm, Fri 6am–5pm, Sun 7.30am–4pm; 1hr 30min). There are no taxis in Cañas Town; you'll have to arrange pick-up by a Pedasí-based driver.

Veraguas Province

Although many travellers only see Veraguas while en-route between David and Panama City, there are a growing number of reasons to stop here, from the marine life in Coiba National Park and the mountains of Santa Fe to the pounding surf of Santa Catalina. Travel in the area is relatively simple as most destinations are accessed from the Interamericana, with the majority of attractions within easy reach of provincial capital Santiago.

SANTIAGO

The halfway point between Panama City and David, **Santiago** has few sights apart from its main square and the pretty Santiago Apostal cathedral, but is a handy stopover and jumping-off point for travel to nearby towns; you might find yourself spending the night here or grabbing a quick meal before carrying on to your next destination. The **Museo Regional** (Tues–Sat 9am–4pm; US$1) on the main square has changing art exhibitions and an archeology room with locally excavated fossils and ceramics. *Hostal Veraguas* (☎958 9021 or 6669 6126; dorms US$10) is the only real budget lodging in town, but stays must be arranged in advance or you may find it closed.

Buses arrive from and depart to David or the Azuero Peninsula by *Restaurante Los Túcanes*, a roadside pit-stop with bathrooms, a café and pharmacy. Buses depart roughly every thirty minutes for Santa Fe (1hr 30min; US$2.50) and Soná (frequent; 45min; US$2) – where you catch Santa Catalina-bound buses (3–4 daily; 1hr 45min; US$3) – from C 10 by Av Central.

SANTA FE

The laidback mountain village of **Santa Fe** has become popular as a retreat from the "backpacker trail" – which ironically has put Santa Fe firmly on the must-do list. The area is cheaper than El Valle, but shares similar lush hillsides and a cool microclimate. There's a wealth of outdoor activities here, including hiking, river rafting, horseriding and waterfall trips; to organize these, contact staff at *La Qhia* (see below), who will put you in touch with a local guide.

The best way to enjoy the environment is staying in a lodge, such as *Hostal La Qhia* (☎954 0903, ⓦwww .panamamountainhouse.com; dorms US$12, doubles US$28). Dorms and private rooms come with use of the large hammock-strewn rancho, where you can take in the views of surrounding hills even if you don't want to hike them.

SANTA CATALINA

Boasting world-class surf and beautiful beaches, **Santa Catalina** (ⓦwww.santa catalinabeach.com) is considered by many to have the most impressive waves in Panama. Catalina's popularity has skyrocketed in the last decade, through surf tourism and as the jumping-off

SANTA CATALINA ACTIVITIES

Surfboards can be rented at most camps (see "Accommodation", opposite) or with Surf and Shake (ⓦsurfandshake.com) from US$10/day; both businesses offer lessons from US$25 per hour. Trips to Coiba (see opposite) and nearby **dive sites** can be arranged through Scuba Coiba (ⓦwww.scubacoiba.com) or Coiba Dive Center (ⓦscuba-charters.com), while **kayak rentals** and **Coiba tours** are offered by Fluid Adventures (☎832 2368, ⓦwww.fluidadventurespanama.com) from US$20 a head. Fishermen on the beach may also give you a lift to Coiba, from around US$10 per person one-way, but there's no way to guarantee a return journey.

COIBA NATIONAL PARK

Blessed with a striking abundance of marine biodiversity, the group of 38 islands that make up **Coiba National Park** (including the namesake) has become one of Panama's most popular national parks, although strict conservation laws and relatively little access means that tourism here is still relatively underdeveloped. For information on travel to the islands, see Ⓦwww.coibanationalpark.com.

For those travelling independently, Santa Catalina is the closest destination from which you can **access** the island. So far, the only **accommodation** on the island is at the ANAM ranger station (☏998 0615; US$40), which offers a/c cabinas. **Moving on**, one scheduled boat leaves the island daily at 7am to make the 7.30am bus to Las Tablas.

point for Isla Coiba (see box above), but the distance from major cities and airports has left this small fishing village well preserved. The village and most of its businesses are based around one main street, the road from Soná, which ends where the concrete meets Santa Catalina beach.

Arrival

By bus Catalina is accessed by Soná-bound buses; direct from Panama City's Albrook bus terminal (every 30min; 5hr; US$9), or from Santiago's main terminal (departing every 30min; 45min; US$2), before changing in Soná for onward buses to Santa Catalina (3–4 daily; 1hr 45min; US$4).
By car Many visitors opt to hire cars in Panama City (see p.608) or David (see p.653), as this saves time waiting for public transport and guarantees access to nearby beaches and surf.
By taxi Taxis will make the run from US$25 if you miss your bus in Soná – travel with cash or withdraw funds here, as there are no banks or ATMs beyond this point.

Accommodation

A large number of surf camps and budget hostels have kept prices low and availability likely, although the best lodgings have views of and easy access to the break and need to be booked in advance.
Blue Zone Beachfront Ⓦwww.bluezonepanama .com. A small and tidy hotel with a great waterfront location. Surf and scuba lessons and rentals can be organized here. US$24
Oasis Beachfront Ⓦwww.oasissurfcamp.com. A more luxurious option. Clean, cheerfully painted bungalows within spitting distance of the sandy beach. Camping is possible too. Camping US$6, bungalows US$45

Rolo's ☏6494 3916, Ⓦwww.rolocabins.net. Spotless cabins, complete with balconies and hammocks, house dorms, doubles and triples. Boat trips, surf lessons and rentals can be arranged here too. Dorms US$10, doubles US$40

Moving on

By bus to: Soná (3 daily; 1hr 45min; US$4), from the main street.
By taxi Taxis to Soná cost from US$30 and depart in the main street.

Chiriquí Province

Striking out west along the Interamericana from the Península de Azuero brings you to the rich agricultural province of **Chiriquí** and ultimately to **David**, Panama's second city and a crossroads for travellers heading through Central America. Until you enter the region, the 120km or so from Divisa is pretty dull. But soon the beautiful **Chiriquí Highlands** appear to the north, and at the roadside you'll occasionally see stalls set up by the Ngöbe-Buglé to display their wares, such as traditional dresses and necklaces. By the time the bus reaches the Tabasará River, there are hills in all directions. The real treat of this westward slog is the opportunity to visit the visually arresting and gloriously chilly highlands, where you can sniff orchids, drink amazing coffee and get a good night's sleep in cosy accommodation. If you want to break the long journey west and see some sea before heading for the hills, a visit to **Isla Boca Brava** is highly recommended.

ISLA BOCA BRAVA

This attractive Pacific island has two **beaches** – both quite plain – and is crisscrossed by paths that are nice to ramble around on. The island's small size ensures that you're not in any danger of getting lost. If you're bored of lolling on the sand you can hire **kayaks** (US$25/4hr), and arrange trips to nearby beaches (from US$5).

Arrival

By bus and boat Get off the bus at the Horconcitos turn-off, a six- to seven-hour journey from Panama City, or three- to four-hour journey from Divisa. During the day there are always taxis waiting here to take people down to the village of Boca Chica (40min; US$15), which is the departure point for the island. You'll be dropped at the dock near *Wahoo Willy's*, a bar, restaurant and hotel; the boat ride across to Boca Brava costs US$2 a head.

Accommodation

Hotel y Restaurante Boca Brava ☎ 700 0017, ⓦ www.hotelbocabrava.com. Accommodation is offered in hammocks and dorms, with prices rising for the private rooms and cabinas. The rooms are fine but a little shabby. Hammocks US$7, dorms US$10, cabinas US$42, doubles US$45

DAVID

Three Spanish settlements were founded in this area in 1602; **DAVID** was the only one to survive repeated attacks from indigenous groups. It developed slowly as a marginal outpost of the Spanish Empire, but in 1732 it was overrun and destroyed by British-backed Miskito groups raiding from Nicaragua. As settlement of Chiriquí increased in the nineteenth century, David began to thrive once again. Today, despite being a busy commercial city – the third largest in Panama after Panama City and Colón – it retains a sedate provincial atmosphere. Hot and dusty, its unexceptional modern architecture spreads out on a grid, with recent attempts to restore original colonial structures in the east side. While it is not so much a destination in itself, plenty of travellers stop here en route to or from Panama City, Costa Rica, Boquete or Bocas del Toro, and find they enjoy the visit. At Carnaval, of course, things spice up considerably, and David also has a festival all of its own: the **Feria de San José** thunders its way through ten raucous days every March.

What to see and do

David centres on **Parque Cervantes**, a fine, tree-shaded place to people-watch with a cup of freshly squeezed sugar-cane juice (*caña*) perked up with tropical lemon, or a dose of coconut water (*agua de pipa*). Three blocks southeast of the park lies the **Museo de Historia y Arte José de Obaldía** (Mon–Sat 8.30am–4.30pm; US$1). The building is a beautiful colonial mansion that was home to successive generations of the distinguished Obaldía family, but was closed for renovation at the time

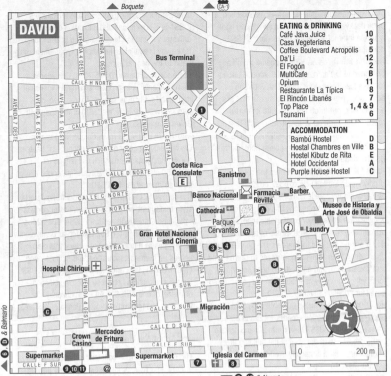

Map labels:

DAVID

▲ Boquete ▲ (CA-1)

Bus Terminal

CALLE H NORTE
CALLE G NORTE
CALLE F NORTE
CALLE E NORTE
CALLE D NORTE

AVENIDA OBALDÍA
PASEO ESTUDIANTE
AVENIDA CENTRAL

AVENIDA 4 OESTE
AVENIDA 3 OESTE
AVENIDA 7 OESTE
AVENIDA 6 OESTE
AVENIDA 5 OESTE
AVENIDA 2 OESTE
AVENIDA 1 OESTE

Costa Rica
Consulate [E]

Banistmo

CALLE C NORTE
CALLE B NORTE
CALLE A NORTE
CALLE CENTRAL

Banco Nacional   Farmacia   Barber
Revilla
Cathedral ✛
Parque
Cervantes @   [i]   Laundry

Museo de Historia y
Arte José de Obaldia

Gran Hotel Nacional
and Cinema

Hospital Chiriqui ✛

CALLE A SUR
CALLE B SUR
CALLE C SUR
CALLE D SUR
CALLE E SUR
CALLE F SUR

AVENIDA CINCUENTENARIO
AVENIDA 1 ESTE
AVENIDA 2 ESTE
AVENIDA 3 ESTE
AVENIDA 4 ESTE
AVENIDA 5 ESTE
AVENIDA 6 ESTE
AVENIDA 7 ESTE
AVENIDA 8 ESTE

AVENIDA 2 OESTE
AVENIDA 3 OESTE
AVENIDA 4 OESTE

Migración

Crown
Casino   Mercados
de Fritura

Supermarket   Supermarket   Iglesia del Carmen

⬤ D & Balneario
⬤ 6

0 — 200 m

▼ ⬤ E, ⑫ & Airport

EATING & DRINKING

Café Java Juice	10
Casa Vegeteriana	3
Coffee Boulevard Acropolis	5
Da'Li	12
El Fogón	2
MultiCafe	B
Opium	11
Restaurante La Típica	8
El Rincón Libanés	7
Top Place	1, 4 & 9
Tsunami	6

ACCOMMODATION

Bambú Hostel	D
Hostal Chambres en Ville	B
Hostel Kibutz de Rita	E
Hotel Occidental	A
Purple House Hostel	C

of going to press with no confirmed reopening date.

Arrival and information

By air Flights from Panama City and Bocas del Toro arrive at the airport, about 5km out of town and a US$4 taxi ride away.

By bus Buses from Panama City, Almirante, Boquete, Cerro Punta and Paso Canoas, as well as Tracopa international buses from San José, all pull in at the terminal on Paseo Estudiante.

Tourist information The IPAT office (Mon–Fri 9am–4pm; ☎775 4120/2839), opposite Importadores Ropa Americana between C 5 and C 6, is full of friendly faces. Staff will gladly (although not so usefully) hand you brochures. Hostel-owners who are tapped into the traveller network have the most practical experience in local tourism, with *Rita's Kibutz* (see p.652) offering extensive tours of Chiriquí at budget prices.

Accommodation

Bambú Hostel In the San Mateo Abajo neighbourhood, C de la Virgencita ☎730 2961, ⓦwww.bambuhostel.com. Southwest of the centre, a five-minute taxi ride from the bus station, is the funky *Bambú*. Owned by a fun-loving former rock star, this place has a variety

---

GETTING AROUND DAVID

Navigating David can be confusing, despite the grid layout. Although most people refer to the streets in the town by using their alphabetical or numerical designation – Calle B Sur, Avenida 3 Oeste, etc – many streets have an "official" name (often honouring a famous person or date) that appears on the posted street signs. State names of businesses rather than street addresses, and hope for recognition.

of accommodation options, as well as a kitchen, a huge backyard with fruit trees, a swimming pool and free internet. Camping US$5, dorms US$9, doubles US$28

Hostal Chambres en Ville Diagonal from La Universidad Latina ☎ 6404 0203. A good choice for couples and mature travellers, with one dorm and cosy en-suite private rooms that are a little dark, but brightened up with colourful murals. The large open-air kitchen leads to a fruit-filled garden, complete with hammocks and a swimming pool. French is spoken here. Dorms US$10, doubles US$20

Hostel Kibutz de Rita 5min from the centre, Urbanisación Santa Lucia ☎ 6677 6622, ℮ info@panatourguide.com. Run by a friendly Panamanian–Israeli couple with a passion for wildlife, *Rita's* has a few comfortable rooms and a makeshift zoo, with a large variety of rescued birds and monkeys living in the garden. The couple also offer rafting trips, canyon tours, visits to Cerro Punta and Volcán Barú, and more. If you book several tours your room may be included in the package, so email for prices in advance. US$20

Hotel Occidental Parque Cervantes ☎ 730 5451. Good-value and spacious rooms, including a 5-person room at US$39 – all with a/c and private bathroom. Those at the front of the building are brighter and share a balcony overlooking the square. US$28

The Purple House Hostel C Sur at Av 6 Oeste ☎ 774 4059, ⓦ www.purplehousehostel.com. The original hostel in David, where every square inch is somewhat obsessively decorated in shades of lavender. The small dorms and private rooms are clean and well kept, with internet, wi-fi and coffee on the house, but be prepared for extra charges for TV and a/c. Dorms US$8, doubles US$20

Eating

Calle F Sur has a collection of street-food stalls known as the Mercados de Fritura. They open up around 6pm and keep on frying tasty bits and pieces (such as *hojaldres*, or pan-fried bread, stuffed *yuca*, beef and pork) until the early hours.

🏃 **Café Java Juice** C F Sur. Delicious *batidos* and a general feeling of healthiness. Try a banana smoothie (US$2) or a salmon burger (US$4) for a healthy change from *arroz con pollo*.

Casa Vegetariana C Central. A buzzing Chinese veggie buffet with portions for US$0.40 each. Closed Sun.

Coffee Bouelvard Acropolis C A Sur. Despite the name, this is less of a coffee shop and more of a snack bar, with a cheap menu of burgers (US$1.50),

sandwiches, nachos (US$2.50) and milkshakes (US$1.50). Low prices and a location opposite the university mean the limited seating is often full, but takeaway is available; just pick up your lunch and head to the central park.

El Fogón Av 2 Oeste ☎ 775 7091. Considered a treat by locals, with an extensive (and expensive) menu and lively atmosphere. Try the *filete de pescado a la parmesana* (US$8) or the spaghetti Bolognese (US$5).

MultiCafe Under the *Hotel Occidental*, Parque Cervantes. A huge and deservedly popular canteen serving tasty standards such as lasagne for US$2.50 and a range of Mexican-influenced dishes such as *quesadillas* for US$0.85.

Restaurante La Típica C F Sur. Central cafeteria-style restaurant, serving large portions of *comida típica* and Chinese dishes from US$4. Open 24hr.

El Rincón Libanés C F Sur. Looking as benevolently on veggies as it does on meat-eaters, this place serves up hummus, moussaka and *kibbe*, among other treats. Falafel and pita will set you back US$5, as will a refreshing Lebanese salad. A selection of *meze* for one is US$13.50 – not cheap, but a welcome change from the usual Panamanian fare.

Drinking and nightlife

The nightlife scene is constantly changing so ask around on arrival, or just listen for music playing – open-air public parties sometimes take place. Wednesdays are generally Ladies' Nights, with free or cheap entry and drinks promotions for women. There are no established gay nights in the city.

🏃 **Da'Li** Av 4 Este and C H Sur. Offering something a bit different, this is a multifaceted café gallery space with changing exhibitions of local art, a variety of classes including tai chi and salsa, fresh coffee (US$1–3) and designer nibbles (US$2–3). With aspirations to morph into a wine bar, this may become the coolest venue in town.

Opium Next to the Crown Casino, opposite the Super 99 on C F Sur. This place is currently in favour with David's in-crowd. It doesn't usually get going until around 11pm and the preferred music is the Panamanian brand of reggae. Men need to dress smartly. Entry around US$5.

Top Place Three locations – one on C F Sur, opposite Super 99 supermarket, one on C Central and Av Cincuentenario and one on Av Obaldía, near the bus terminal. Good spots for a beer and a game of pool, although women travelling alone may be overwhelmed by all the testosterone.

Tsunami In the Chiriquí Mall. Very similar to *Opium*, though this will cost you a US$2–2.50 taxi ride too.

Directory

Car rental Budget (☎721 0845) and Thrifty (☎721 2477), both at the airport.
Cinema The screen at the *Gran Hotel Nacional* (C Central) shows all the new flicks.
Consulate Costa Rica, Calle C Norte (☎774 1923).
Exchange Banco Nacional (Mon–Fri 8am–3pm, Sat 9am–noon) is on Parque Cervantes; Banistmo (Mon–Fri 8am–3.30pm, Sat 9am–noon) is a block away from Parque Cervantes on C Norte. Both have 24hr ATMs.
Health There are two well-regarded hospitals: Hospital Chiriquí on C Central at Av 3 Oeste, and Mae Lewis Hospital, which is on the Interamericana. The Romero supermarket on C F Sur has a 24hr pharmacy; Farmacia Revilla is on Parque Cervantes.
Immigration On C Sur (Mon–Fri 8am–3pm; ☎775 4515).
Internet There are plenty of internet cafés here; there's a 24hr one next to *Java Juice* on C F Sur.
Laundry Opposite the IPAT office on C Central at Av 6 Este (daily 8am–6pm).
Post office A block away from Parque Cervantes on C Norte (Mon–Fri 7am–6pm, Sat 7am–5pm).

Moving on

By air Flights to Panama City and Bocas del Toro leave from the airport, which is about 5km out of town and a US$4 taxi ride away. Both Aeroperlas (☎315 7500, ⊛www.aeroperlas.com) and Air

---

INTO COSTA RICA: PASO CANOAS

You can cross the border into Costa Rica at the Paso Canoas crossing, 56km west of David along the Interamericana. After passing through *migración* (24hr) and customs (a formality unless you have anything to declare), you simply walk across the border, though queues for both can be long if international buses are passing through. The banks in David can be reluctant to change dollars to colones so it's best to change them at the border. There are banks (Banco Nacional de Panama and Banco Nacional de Costa Rica) on both sides of the border that will usually change currency, as well as individual money changers.

THE CHIRIQUÍ HIGHLANDS

North of David, you can escape the flat heat of the city and take refuge up in the cool of the **Chiriquí Highlands**, a region of cloudforests, fertile valleys and charming settlements. The varied landscapes all share the same basic characteristics of head-clearing air, cold nights and a deep, relentless green. Parks here – including Volcán Barú and La Amistad – are well protected, offering wonderful natural encounters and endless hiking opportunities. The substantial town of **Boquete** has many attractions of its own – particularly coffee-related – but it's also a great base for activities, from rafting to hot-spring soaks.

Panama (☎316 9000, ⊛www.flyairpanama.com) run flights every day from David to Panama City. Aeroperlas sometimes operates a flight between David and Bocas del Toro; check online for current routes.
By bus to: Almirante (take Changuinola-bound buses and ask to be let off at the entrance to Almirante); Boquete (every 30min 5.15am–9.45pm; 1hr); Cerro Punta (every 15min 5am–8pm; 2hr); Changuinola (every 30min until 7pm; 4hr 30min); Panama City (roughly hourly 6.30am–8.15pm; 7–8hr; express at 10.45pm, midnight & 3am; 6hr); Paso Canoas (every 10min 4.30am–9.30pm; 1hr 20min).

BOQUETE

BOQUETE is set in the tranquil Caldera Valley, 1000m above sea level. Some 37km north of David, it is the biggest town in the Chiriquí Highlands, and sits smack in the middle of Panama's two coasts. The road to Boquete ends in the highlands, so those wishing to travel on to Bocas del Toro from here must go back to David before catching a bus onwards. The slopes surrounding the town are dotted with coffee planta-tions, flower gardens and orange groves, and rise to rugged peaks that are usually obscured by thick clouds. When those clouds clear, however – most often in the morning – you can see the imperious peak of **Volcán Barú**, which dominates

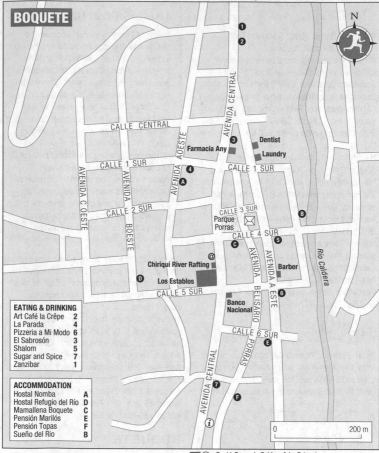

BOQUETE

N

❶
❷

CALLE CENTRAL

AVENIDA CENTRAL

Dentist

Farmacia Any ❸

Laundry

CALLE 1 SUR

AVENIDA A OESTE

AVENIDA C OESTE

AVENIDA B OESTE

❹ A

CALLE 1 SUR

CALLE 2 SUR

CALLE 3 SUR

Parque
Porras ✉

B

CALLE 4 SUR

C ❺

AVENIDA A ESTE

AVENIDA BELISARIO PORRAS

Río Caldera

@
Chiriquí River Rafting

Los Establos

Barber

D

CALLE 5 SUR

❻

Banco
Nacional

CALLE 6 SUR

E

AVENIDA CENTRAL

❼

F

ⓘ

0   200 m

EATING & DRINKING
Art Café la Crêpe   2
La Parada   4
Pizzeria a Mi Modo   6
El Sabrosón   3
Shalom   5
Sugar and Spice   7
Zanzibar   1

ACCOMMODATION
Hostal Nomba   A
Hostal Refugio del Río   D
Mamallena Boquete   C
Pensión Marilós   E
Pensión Topas   F
Sueño del Río   B

ⓘ , David, Pozos de Caldera & La Estancia

the town to the northwest. Foreign investment targeting retirees from the US has flooded the area in recent years, seeing the construction of an all-inclusive luxury condo and the clearing of cloudforest to make way for golf courses.

What to see and do

The big attraction of Boquete is the opportunities it affords for exploring the surrounding **countryside**. As well as the climb to the summit of the volcano – a strenuous day's walk or a couple of hours' drive – there are plenty of less demanding walks you can make along the narrow country lanes.

Café Ruiz

One of these walks, heading out of town to the north towards the hamlet of Alto Lino, takes you past the **Café Ruiz factory** (☎720 1000, ⓦwww.caferuiz .com). Tours (Mon–Sat 9am & 1pm; 3hr; US$25) explore every step of the coffee-making process, from the farm to the roasting plant. A 45-minute tour (Mon–Sat 8am; US$7) visits only the roasting plant.

Mi Jardín es Su Jardín

Mi Jardín es Su Jardín (daily 9am–6pm) is a bountiful, landscaped garden with a slender metal tower that affords nice views as well as access to a mysterious slide that drops directly into a flowerbed. It's worth wandering up here, particularly if you're visiting the nearby Café Ruiz factory, which is just before it.

Los Pozos de Caldera

At the hot springs known as **Los Pozos de Caldera** (US$1 paid to caretaker; no official hours), just outside the nearby town of Caldera, you can alternate between dips in the scalding hot water and pulse quickening splashes in the frigid river. Boquete Mountains Safari Tours (see "Tour operators", p.656) runs half-day tours to the springs (US$45, without horses US$35), which include an optional hour's horseriding.

To get here on foot it's about 12km south of town, starting on Av Central; turn left at the blue "Caldera" sign, pass the town of Caldera, take a right at the next sign, heading down a gravel road, cross the cable bridge and turn left, go through the (unmarked) red metal gate and find the caretaker's house on your right. Alternatively you can take a taxi (US$7) or bus (US$1.50) from central Boquete to the town of Caldera, and walk from there.

Watersports

Over thirty-five rivers in Chiriquí Province are used for **kayaking** and **rafting**, including the Río Caldera, Río Gariché, Río Chiriquí and Río Chiriquí Viejo, with whitewater of every classification. Tour operators in town (see box, p.656) can arrange day-trips and courses for all experience levels, for around US$60–80.

La Estancia (daily 10am–6pm; US$2), 3.5km from the town centre, is a bar and restaurant with outdoor swimming pools and three waterslides. It's a US$2 taxi ride from town. Up in the hills and with some great views just outside the entrance, it's a nice place to relax and soak up some rays.

Arrival and information

By bus Buses from David arrive at the main square (Parque Porras), and minibuses head up to the surrounding hamlets from the streets around this same square – taking one of these and then walking back to town is a good way to see the nearby countryside.

Tourist office There is a fairly useless CEFATI office on the road from David; much more helpful is the Boquete Visitors' Centre (daily 8am–5pm; ☎720 2545) on the same road, located just before the main drag. Staff members speak English and can provide you with maps, listings and basic information on country walks.

Accommodation

Accommodation prices often increase on weekends and holidays, so check ahead of time.

Hostal Nomba Av A Oeste ☎6401 6278, ⊛www.nombapanama.com. Very popular with backpackers, this place has two kitchens and the staff speak English. They can help you arrange a camping trip on the mountain or near the hot

---

FESTIVAL DE LAS FLORES

January's **Festival de las Flores y del Café** sees Boquete's otherwise tasteful and discreet appreciation of coffee and flowers give way to lusty rejoicing. Throughout the ten-day celebrations the local fairgrounds explode with flower fireworks – you'll never see so many orchids – to coincide with the coffee harvest that ensures the next money-spinning batch of the region's most famous export. The locals adjust their own gardens accordingly, and stalls spring up selling food, handicrafts and plentiful coffee to the thousands of visitors wandering around, followed everywhere by loud, live music. In the evenings the rum is cracked open and people dance around the fairgrounds until dawn. Book accommodation far in advance.

BOQUETE TOURS AND ACTIVITIES

There's a wealth of nature-themed trips and tours to keep you occupied in Boquete; the operators listed below offer some of the most economical and interesting packages in town.

Boquete Mountains Safari Tours On Avenida Central, south of the main square (℡6627 8829 or 6742 6614, ⓦwww.boquetesafari.com). Trips to the Pozos de Caldera, as well as horseback trips, coffee-tasting tours and cloudforest visits, all costing around US$35 per person.

Boquete Outdoor Adventures In the Los Establos complex (℡720 2284 or 6474 0274, ⓦwww.boqueteoutdooradventures.com). The founder of this outfit has been running white water trips since 1997.

Boquete Tree Trek At the Los Establos complex on the corner of Av Central and C 5 Sur (℡720 1635, ⓦwww.aventurist.com). A zipline tour (Mon–Sat 7.30am–12.15pm & 1.15–4.30pm) through the canopy of the forest near Volcán Barú. You can also rent bikes here (US$3/hr or US$15/day).

springs, and have equipment for hire. Dorms US$10, doubles US$25

Hostal Refugio del Río Av B Oeste ℡720 2088 or 6613 1179, ⓦwww.refugiodelrio.com. This place is so handsome you may think there's been some mistake as they lead you to the dorm. But there isn't, and even the bedding, seemingly of crushed velvet, exceeds expectations. There's also space for camping, a flash kitchen and lovely gazebo with a barbecue pit, and a treehouse room for two. Dorms US$11, doubles US$20

Hostal Sueños del Río On the riverfront, just left of the bridge ℡66601 7771, ⓦboquetesuenos delrio.com. A cosy little house with en-suite dorms and private rooms. The patio garden, positioned directly over the river, has hammocks – great for catching mountain breezes. Dorms US$12, rooms US$28

Mamallena Boquete Parque Porras ℡720 1260, ⓦwww.mamallenaboquete.com. The Boquete branch of *Mamallena* caters to a strong backpacker crowd, with tidy dorms and private rooms in the most central location possible. Dorms US$11, doubles US$28

Pensión Marilós Av A Este at C 6 Sur ℡720 1380, ⓔmarilos66@hotmail.com. This place feels like a home, with a pleasant dining area, intriguing paintings on the walls and tiled corridors. Rooms with shared bath are airy, and sheets are crisp. The owner is helpful and speaks English. US$16

Pensión Topas Av B. Porras ℡720 1005. The private rooms are very reasonable at this Tintin-themed hotel, and there are two smaller, budget rooms with solar-powered shared bath. Camping in the garden is permitted, and you can hire bikes too. The owner speaks English. Camping US$6, doubles US$11

Eating and drinking

La Parada C 1 Sur. A hole-in-the-wall snack spot, with pittas, toasties (US$2), tea and fresh *batidos* (US$2). Takeaway available. Closed Sun.

Pizzeria a Mi Modo Av A Este. Small restaurant dishing up good-value pizza (US$4–9) and pastas (US$3–5), as well as fresh fruit *batidos* for US$2. The brightly painted walls outside make it hard to miss this spot.

El Sabrosón Av Central. Plain and airy canteen with good Panamanian food and fish cooked to order. Rice, beans, salad and something meaty from US$3.

Shalom C 4A Sur. A rare purveyor of bagels and other savouries. Coffee and wi-fi complete the coffeehouse vibe and make it a strong contender for breakfast.

TREAT YOURSELF

Art Café La Crêpe ℡720 1821 or 6769 6090. A wee gem, with brightly painted walls covered in Art Deco posters, offering authentic French cuisine. Brioche breakfasts (US$2), goat's cheese salad and pâté are just some of the savouries on offer, while desserts include the namesake in a variety of flavours, and a heavenly *crème brûlée* (US$4). Owner Jean-Marie has over twenty years' experience and a passion for local ingredients (aside from the imported goodies such as snails and pastis). Reservations are recommended for dinner, especially at weekends. Closed Mon.

Sugar and Spice Av Central. International bakery with posh breads, such as sourdough, 9-grain and rye for US$3 per loaf, plus a host of sweet snacks including butterscotch bars and blueberry muffins. Closed Wed.

Zanzibar Av Central. African-flavoured bar covered in animal prints and tribal artwork, where partying travellers come for cocktails (US$4) and hookahs (US$10). Open late at weekends, when the place gets packed.

Directory

Bookshops There's a great bookshop (Tues–Sat 9am–5pm) in Dolega on the road from David. The Book Mark carries a huge selection of largely English literature, offered at decent prices, considering you're in the Panamanian highlands (US$3–10). Trades of new or quality books may also be accepted.

Exchange There's a Banco Nacional (Mon–Fri 8am–3pm, Sat 9am–noon) on the main road a block south of the main square, and a Banco General ATM in the Los Establos complex.

Internet Hastor Computers Internet Café (daily 8am–11pm; US$1/hr) is on the second floor of the building opposite *Pizza La Volcánica* on Av Central.

Post office On the main square (Mon–Fri 7am–6pm, Sat 7am–5pm).

Moving on

By bus to: David (every 30min 5.30am–7pm; 1hr), from the main square (Parque Porras).

CERRO PUNTA AND AROUND

Almost 2000m above sea level in a bowl-shaped valley surrounded by densely forested mountains, **CERRO PUNTA** is the highest village in Panama. In the eighty or so years since it was settled, the town's fertile soil has produced some eighty percent of all the vegetables consumed in Panama – there are little patches of cultivated land everywhere you look – although this agricultural boom has not done the surrounding forests any good. The town's altitude gives it a very special atmosphere – it seems incredibly crisp, and the taste of the food and the smell of the orchids seem all the better for it.

What to see and do

Everything in tiny Cerro Punta is spread out along the main road from David and a side road leading towards Parque Internacional La Amistad (see p.658). The scenery, together with the cool, crisp mountain air, makes Cerro Punta a perfect base for **hiking** – the pristine cloudforests of Parque Internacional La Amistad and Parque Nacional Volcán Barú are both within easy reach. These parks are perhaps the best places in all of Central America to catch a glimpse of the elusive quetzal, particularly in the dry season between January and April.

Local busus run from the centre of Cerro Punta to the nearby village of **Guadalupe**, famous for its jam, orchids and neat little gardens. The jam is made from the strawberries that grow in the area, small enough that you'll find some whole ones as you spread it on your bread. Buy it in the local shop or at the stalls that arc sometimes set up in the road. You can admire the orchids at **Finca Dracula Orchid Farm** (daily 8am–5pm; US$3; ☎771 2070), a ten- to fifteen-minute walk from *Los Quetzales Lodge and Spa* (see below). With the lodge on your left, head up the road until the wooden "Dracula" sign pointing left; the farm is a further five minutes in this direction.

Arrival

By bus Services from David stop on the one main street running through the town.

Accommodation and eating

Hotel Cerro Punta On the main street ☎771 2020. Chalet-style lodging whose appealing rooms have pretty curtains and ivy growing past the windows. The windows, however, face the back and not towards the mountains and fantastic views. US$35

Hotel Los Quetzales Lodge and Spa In Guadalupe ☎771 2182/2291, ⊛www .losquetzales.com. This hotel accommodates backpackers, honeymooners, families and retirees, and makes it look easy. Budget travellers will find only the dorms affordable – chunky wood, quality bedding – though there are also plush rooms, suites and cabins on offer. There are several activities to enjoy, including cycling and horseriding, and long or short walks through the surrounding cloudforest. In the restaurant, pizza and pasta go for around US$5. Dorms US$18, doubles US$75

Eating

🏃 **Hotel Cerro Punta** On the main road. This excellent restaurant has floor-to-ceiling windows, so you can gaze at the view as you munch on carefully prepared meals; the flavourful grilled fish with chips and broccoli salad (US$8) is worth every cent. A breakfast of pancakes, local strawberries, syrup and a big mug of coffee is only US$5.
Restaurante Anthony On the road to La Amistad. Clean and friendly, this place deals in your basic but nicely done *comida corriente* such as US$2 portions of *arroz de guandú* (Panamanian dish of rice and beans) with chicken, pork or beef.

Moving on

By bus to: David (every 15min 5am–6pm; 2hr), from the main street; Guadalupe (local buses run regularly throughout the day).

PARQUE INTERNACIONAL LA AMISTAD

PARQUE INTERNACIONAL LA AMISTAD covers four thousand square kilometres of rugged, forested mountains teeming with wildlife (including five cat species), on either side of the border with Costa Rica. Although most of Panama's share technically falls in Bocas del Toro, the sliver that is in Chiriquí is best prepared for visitors, with three well-marked **trails**, including a four-kilometre round-trip to a 55-metre waterfall.

To get to the park from Cerro Punta, take a local **bus** to Las Nubes. There's a permanently staffed **park office** here, where you pay the US$5 admission charge; they also have a refuge (US$6 per person) – bring your own food, warm clothes and, ideally, a sleeping bag, as it gets cold at night.

PARQUE NACIONAL VOLCÁN BARÚ

Covering an area of 140 square kilometres, **PARQUE NACIONAL VOLCÁN BARÚ** (daily 9am–4pm) runs from Cerro Punta across the northern flank of Volcán Barú, Panama's highest peak, to Boquete. Hiking the well-known **Quetzales** trail in this direction will lead you downhill, an easier journey than the reverse. On reaching Boquete you'll have the satisfaction of having travelled on foot between the Highlands' two principal towns, a journey which otherwise requires a bus down from the mountain to David and back up again. There is no head office, so entry fees are paid at ranger stations within the park.

Sendero Los Quetzales

Due to the large numbers of visitors and several tricky patches – particularly during the rainy season – the **Sendero Los Quetzales** trail has been closed several times, including at the time of research. If you do attempt it, a guide is highly recommended. To reach the trailhead, take a **taxi** from Cerro Punta to the El Respingo ranger station (US$10–15) and pay your US$5 park entry fee. From here – the start of the trail – to the Alto Chiquero ranger station near Boquete – the end – should take you between four and six hours. From **Alto Chiquero** it's another 8km (downhill) to Boquete but the walk is enjoyable, continuing along the Río Caldera and affording direct access to a pretty little waterfall and a scenic hike through coffee *fincas* and rural communities. You might also be able to hitch a ride or catch a taxi into town for a few dollars.

Volcán Barú

Boquete's most majestic attraction is **Volcán Barú**, Panama's tallest mountain (3475m) and an extinct volcano that dares all visitors to take it

On the road from David to Changuinola is a wonderful ecofriendly setup in the cloudforest. **The Lost and Found** (☎6432 8182 or 6920 3036, ⓦwww .lostandfoundlodge.com; dorms US$12, doubles US$30) – the only accommodation within the Fortuna reserve – has been constructed with such care that it feels like the jungle hasn't even noticed it's there yet. Guests hang out on the deck, where meals are taken – the coffee you drink at breakfast is processed from berries growing a few metres away – and the observation platform sees nightly visits from local animals. Chilly weather is countered with fleece blankets, luxurious hot-water showers with serene views of the forest, and beer-and-foosball sessions in the bar. Wild, mostly unmarked trails offer phenomenal wildlife encounters and hiking opportunities, and can be explored at your leisure or with one of the lodge's tours.

To get here from David, take a **bus** towards Changuinola. After about an hour you'll reach a tollbooth, shortly after which you'll see three yellow boulders painted with "Lost and Found". Coming from Bocas del Toro by bus, after about three hours you'll reach a dam; from here it's only ten or fifteen minutes to the hostel, on your left. If you can't arrive during daylight hours, try to arrange a pick-up in David with the owner.

on. A 22-kilometre road winds up to the cloud-shrouded peak through spectacular scenery. From the top, the cloud cover breaks every so often to reveal the sight of at least one of the oceans. Outside of the mid-December-to-April dry season, your best chance of enjoying the view is to be on the peak at dawn. To manage this, you'll need to camp out or walk all night; *Mamallena Boquete* (see p.656) has sleeping bags and sweaters for the trip, for a fee.

Tours can be arranged through several operators, including Boquete Mountains Safari (see p.656) and *Rita's* in David (see p.652). If you'd prefer to go it alone you will need to take a minibus or a taxi (US$5–6 during the day, up to US$20 at night) from Boquete. This will bring you 6km to the end of the paved road, after which it becomes a rough track passable only with a customized 4WD. Beyond this point it's a steep and strenuous four- to eight-hour hike and another six hours or so back to Boquete. Take waterproof clothing, dress in layers and wear good hiking shoes. You will also need plenty of **food and water**. If you wish to **camp** (US$6), there is an area near the ANAM ranger station close to the summit where you can set up your tent.

Bocas del Toro

Isolated on the Costa Rican border between the Caribbean and the forested slopes of the Cordillera Talamanca, **Bocas del Toro** ("mouths of the bull") is one of the most beautiful areas in Panama. It's also one of the most remote – the mainland portion of the province is connected to the rest of Panama by a single road, and the island chain offshore requires a ferry ride to reach.

Christopher Columbus first explored the coast of Bocas del Toro in 1502 in the search for a route to Asia; later, during the colonial era, European pirates often sheltered in the calm waters of the archipelago. By the nineteenth century, English ships from Jamaica were visiting the coast frequently, but it wasn't until 1826 that West Indian immigrants founded the town of Bocas del Toro, still the province's largest settlement. The arrival of the United Fruit **banana plantations** in the late 1800s gave the islands a measure of prosperity; by 1895 bananas from Bocas accounted for more than half of Panama's export earnings, and Bocas Town boasted five foreign consulates and three English-language newspapers. Early in the

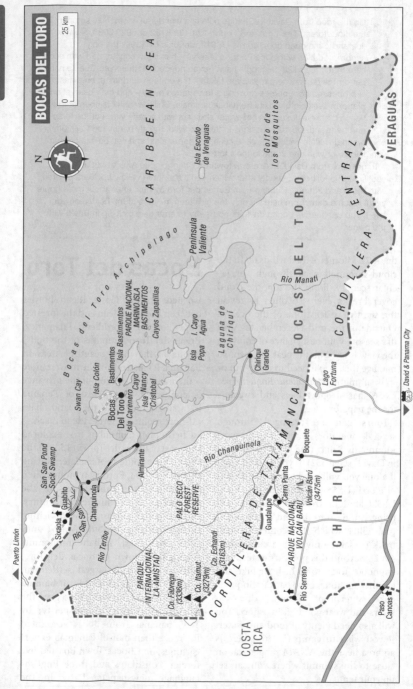

BOCAS DEL TORO

0 _____ 25 km

N

CARIBBEAN SEA

Bocas del Toro Archipelago

Swan Cay

Isla Colón

Bastimentos
Isla Bastimentos
PARQUE NACIONAL
MARINO ISLA
BASTIMENTOS
Cayos Zapatillas

Bocas
Del Toro
Isla Carenero
Cayo
Cristóbal
Isla Nancy

Isla
Popa

I. Cayo
Agua

Laguna de
Chiriquí

Isla Escudo
de Veraguas

Península
Valiente

Golfo de
los Mosquitos

Río Manatí

VERAGUAS

Chiriquí
Grande

BOCAS DEL TORO

CORDILLERA CENTRAL

San San Pond
Sock Swamp

Guabito

Changuinola

Almirante

Río Changuinola

PALO SECO
FOREST
RESERVE

CORDILLERA DE TALAMANCA

Lago
Fortuna

(A4) David & Panama City

Puerto Limón

Sixaola

Río San San

Río Teribe

PARQUE
INTERNACIONAL
LA AMISTAD

Co. Fábrega
(3336m)

Co. Itamut
(3279m)

Co. Echandi
(3163m)

COSTA
RICA

Guadalupe

Cerro Punta

Volcán Barú
(3475m)

PARQUE NACIONAL
VOLCÁN BARÚ

Río Sereno

Paso
Canoas

Boquete

CHIRIQUÍ

twentieth century, however, banana crops were repeatedly devastated by disease, causing the archipelago's economy to suffer.

In recent years, **tourism** and real estate speculation have come to the economic forefront in Bocas. Foreign investors have purchased huge portions of the archipelago for luxury resorts and holiday homes. While this boom has enhanced the region's wealth, generating employment and income for local residents, much concern still exists over how economically and environmentally sustainable it really is.

Despite the development, the archipelago remains home to an **ecosystem** so complex and well preserved that it has been described by biologists as "the Galapagos of the twenty-first century". This, and the equally unusual diversity of the human population – Ngöbe-Buglé, Naso and Bribrí populate the mainland, while the islands are dominated by the descendants of **West Indian** migrants who still speak Guari-Guari, an English patois embellished with Spanish and Ngobere – make Bocas Province one of the country's most fascinating.

ALMIRANTE

From the village of Chiriquí, 14km east of David on the Interamericana, a spectacular road crosses the continental divide, passes over the Fortuna hydroelectric dam, through the pristine forests that protect its watershed and the small town of **Chiriquí Grande**, then, 50km on, into **ALMIRANTE**. This ramshackle port town of rusting tin-roofed houses, propped up on stilts over the calm waters of the Caribbean, is the best place for those coming via David to catch a water-taxi to the Bocas del Toro archipelago.

Arriving by bus, passengers are dropped off and picked up at the town's small bus station or beside the main road; in either case, it's a short taxi ride (US$0.50) or about a ten-minute walk to the port. Touts from the water-taxi companies will lead you to one of the two docks – the services are exactly the same, though you should check which company is leaving first before you buy a ticket.

Moving on

By bus Buses for Changuinola (US$1), where you can get connections to the border, are frequent. There are also buses and *colectivos*, or minibuses, between Almirante and David (frequent; 4hr; US$7) as well as an "express" bus to Panama City (3 daily at 8am, 7pm & 8pm; 10hr; US$23).

By ferry The Palanga, or car ferry, runs to the islands four days a week and takes two hours (US$15).

By water-taxi Water-taxis to Bocas (US$5) leave every thirty minutes until about 6.30pm; the trip takes half an hour.

CHANGUINOLA

Some 16km from the border and 29km west of Almirante through

TRAVEL BETWEEN BOCAS DEL TORO AND PANAMA CITY

The overnight bus route from Changuinola to Almirante and Panama City is served by one company, TRANCEIBOSA (☎303-6326). The daily bus, leaving at 8pm, is frequently overbooked, and to take on the additional passenger load, TRANCEIBOSA contracts with local minibuses, charging passengers the same fee they would pay for a larger bus. However, the company does not always inform passengers that they will be travelling in minibuses, which lack the facilities of larger buses. To avoid this and save a bit of money, take one of the frequent minibuses from Almirante to David and switch to a full-size bus for the longer trip to Panama City. Purchase tickets as early as possible and check that you have been assigned a seat on the full-size bus.

seemingly endless banana plantations, **CHANGUINOLA** is a typically hot and uninteresting banana town where almost everyone works for the Chiriquí Land Company ("the Company", successor to United Fruit). **Buses** from Almirante and the border at Guabito arrive at the town terminal.

Moving on

By bus to: Guabito and the border (every 30min; 20min); San Jose (1 daily at 10am; 8hr).
By water-taxi to: Bocas del Toro (every 45min until 5.30pm; 45min; US$4), from the dock near Finca 60, on the outskirts of town.

BOCAS TOWN

On the southeastern tip of Isla Colón, the provincial capital of **BOCAS DEL TORO**, otherwise known as Bocas Town, is the easiest base from which to explore the islands, beaches and reefs of the archipelago. The town, connected to the rest of the island by a narrow causeway, is busy and bustling, especially during the high season from December to April, when it explodes with tourists and backpackers. Rickety wooden buildings painted in cheerful colours and a friendly and laidback, mostly English-speaking population welcome you to the island's casual mêlée. The palm-fringed Caribbean beaches, decent waves, and a buzzing young nightlife have made these islands a must-see for partying backpackers.

What to see and do

Bocas Town offers a variety of aquatic activities, starting with **surfing** – now the most popular activity in the area, with an abundance of spots for both beginners and experts (see box, p.664). Endless possibilities exist for **boat excursions** further afield as well: east around the Península Valiente to the Isla Escudo de Veraguas, which aficionados consider one of the best diving spots in the whole of the Caribbean, or up one of the rivers into the rainforests of the mainland to visit isolated Ngöbe-Buglé communities. These excursions may or may not involve **snorkelling**, the cheapest way to explore local marine life. Alternatively, you can head to Dolphin Bay, where you have a good chance of seeing the rather shy **bottle-nosed dolphins** that live here year-round. When booking a tour, be aware that bad weather may result in a change of itinerary or even cancellation, and that beyond the main islands the sea can get very rough.

Arrival and information

By air All flights arrive at Bocas airport, four blocks from the main street. Aeroperlas (☎757 9341) and Air Panama (☎757 9841) both offer multiple daily flights from Panama City and David, while Air Nature (☎757 9963) operates flights to and from San José, Costa Rica.
By boat The ferry from Almirante pulls in at the southern end of the main street, while scheduled

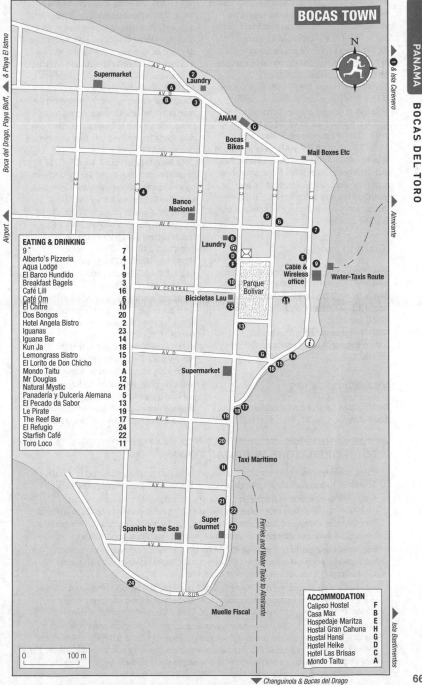

BOCAS TOWN

N

Boca del Drago, Playa Bluff, & Playa El Istmo

Airport

1 & Isla Carenero

Almirante

Isla Bastimentos

Changuinola & Bocas del Drago

Supermarket

AV H

2 Laundry

A

AV G

B

3

ANAM

C

Bocas Bikes

Mail Boxes Etc

AV F

C6

C5

4

C4

Banco Nacional

C3

C2

5

6

7

AV E

Laundry

8

@

D

F

Parque Bolivar

E

Cable & Wireless office

9

Water-Taxis Route

AV CENTRAL

10

Bicicletas Lau

12

11

13

i

AV D

G

14

15

16

Supermarket

AV C

19

18

17

20

H

Taxi Marítimo

AV B

21

22

Spanish by the Sea

Super Gourmet

23

AV A

24

AV SUR

Muelle Fiscal

Ferries and Water Taxis to Almirante

EATING & DRINKING

9 °	7
Alberto's Pizzeria	4
Aqua Lodge	1
El Barco Hundido	9
Breakfast Bagels	3
Café Lili	16
Café Om	6
El Chitre	10
Dos Bongos	20
Hotel Angela Bistro	2
Iguanas	23
Iguana Bar	14
Kun Ja	18
Lemongrass Bistro	15
El Lorito de Don Chicho	8
Mondo Taitu	A
Mr Douglas	12
Natural Mystic	21
Panadería y Dulcería Alemana	5
El Pecado da Sabor	13
Le Pirate	19
The Reef Bar	17
El Refugio	24
Starfish Café	22
Toro Loco	11

ACCOMMODATION

Calipso Hostel	F
Casa Max	B
Hospedaje Maritza	E
Hostal Gran Cahuna	H
Hostal Hansi	G
Hostel Heike	D
Hotel Las Brisas	C
Mondo Taitu	A

0   100 m

water-taxis arrive and depart from the Taxi Marítimo dock next door. Unscheduled water-taxis to the various islands and beaches also dock here, or they can be hailed from anywhere on the seafront.

By bus Buses from David and the border arrive at Almirante, where taxi drivers hover to take passengers to the Taxi Marítimo dock (US$1).

Tourist information The IPAT office, on C 1 next to the police station (℡ 757 9642, ✉ bocas deltoro@atp.gob.pa), provides information, toilet facilities, internet, and an exhibit on the history and ecology of the archipelago. ANAM's local office, C 3 & Av H (℡ 757 9442), gives permission to camp within the Isla Bastimentos Marine Park and can organize visits to see turtles laying their eggs (May–Sept). Detailed maps of the area are available from most shops for US$2, and ✺ www .bocas.com is a good resource for hotel and tour operator information.

Getting around

Bikes Bicycles are available for rent all over town; try Bocas Bikes, Av G at C 3 (US$2/hr or US$10/day), or for mopeds go to Bicicletas Lau, C 3 at Parque Bolívar (US$20/hr or US$90/day, with US$50 deposit).

Taxis Though everything in town is within easy walking distance, taxis are available (US$1 per person).

Accommodation

There's a good range of accommodation in Bocas, though it can be difficult to find a room during high season, and nearly impossible for groups of two or more without reservations. Things also fill up quickly on weekends and holidays, so it's a good idea to book in advance. Many budget places don't accept reservations, so it's best to arrive mid-morning. Hot water is not usually provided.

Calipso Hostel C 3 between Av Central & Av E ℡ 757 9848, ✺ www.calipsobocas.com. Caribbean colours and a bustling balcony overlooking the main drag mark this perennially busy, central hostel. There's little to distinguish it from *Heike* next door, although the dorms here are reputedly cleaner. US$10

Casa Max Av G between C 4 & C 5 ℡ 757 9120, ✉ casa1max@hotmail.com. The clean, cheerfully painted rooms with balconies and comfortable beds give this place a homey feel, though the international cast of characters adds a bit of excitement. There's a pleasant patio area, a restaurant and good advice from the Dutch owners. US$30

Hospedaje Maritza C 1 between Av Central and Av E ℡ 6654 3771. Across from the *Barco Hundido*, this small and pleasant inn has a few clean, basic rooms and apartments at a good price. There's hot water but no a/c. The only real drawback to staying here is the disco across the way that thumps well into the night. US$20

Hostal Gran Kahuna C 3 at Av B ℡ 757 9038, ✺ www.grankahunabocas.com. Handily located on the main drag, just steps from the water-taxis waiting to whisk you to a nearby surf spot, *Kahuna* is a solid budget option with large dorms and great mattresses. No a/c, but the traditional, open-shuttered and large-windowed rooms are

TOUR OPERATORS IN BOCAS TOWN

There are many tour operators in town – below is just a small selection of what's available. Tours cost US$20–30, depending on destinations and gear rental.

ANCON Expeditions at *Bocas Inn*, Av G at C 3 ℡ 269 9451, ✺ www.ancon expeditions.com. Excursions into the marine park and the forests on the mainland. Slightly more expensive than other operators but the most organized, with good boats. The only tour company in town with experienced naturalist guides.

Bocas Water Sports C 3 at Av A ℡ 757 9541, ✺ www.bocaswatersports.com. Professional and well-established US-run outfit offering diving, kayaking and snorkelling outings as well as equipment rental.

J&J and Transparente Tours C 3 ℡ 757 9915, ✉ transparentetours@hotmail .com. Run by experienced locals, this long-established company offers regular trips into the marine park and more. They also rent out snorkel gear.

Starfleet C 1 ℡ 757 9630, ✺ www.starfleetscuba.com. Canadian company with a friendly, professional team focusing on diving excursions and full PADI open-water diving courses (about US$225). Starfleet also offers the only spa in Bocas Town, with treatments such as pedicures and massages (high season only).

breezy enough. The upstairs balcony is perfect for socializing and people-watching, while the private dock in front is a great chill-out spot. US$10

Hostal Hansi C 2 at Av D ☎757 9932. A tight ship run by fastidious German owners, *Hansi* is named after the large and friendly feline who's really the one in charge. Shared kitchen and simple, immaculate double and single rooms with private and shared baths are spotlessly clean and good value. US$25

Hostel Heike C 3 between Av Central & Av E ☎757 9708, ⓦwww.hostelheike.com. *Heike* offers dorms that share clean, hot-water bathrooms, and small private rooms. There's also a communal kitchen, a balcony overlooking the main street, and free wi-fi. Dorms US$10, doubles US$22

Hotel Las Brisas C 3 at Av H ☎757 9549, ⓦwwwbrisasbocas.com. On the water, recently renovated *Las Brisas* has a range of rooms, many with sea views, all equipped with TV, a/c, wi-fi and hot water. US$30

Mondo Taitu Av G between C 4 & C 5 ☎757 9425, ⓦwww.mondotaitu.com. The most original surfer hostel/party bar on Bocas, *Mondo Taitu* is full of youthful exuberance. It has a rainwater filtration system that provides fresh drinking water and is also working to promote awareness of an underutilized recycling centre on Bocas. All rooms and dorms share hot-water bathrooms, plus there's a communal kitchen and a small cocktail bar. Dorms US$12, doubles US$22

Eating

Bocas has an excellent range of restaurants, with several international and budget options. Lobster, conch, octopus and other locally caught specialities taste particularly delicious in local coconut milk and Caribbean spice preparations. Be aware that restaurant opening hours can be erratic, and that tap water is not drinkable, so don't expect free iced water. A large range of groceries is available at supermarkets (see p.667), though prices are higher than on the mainland.

Cafés

Breakfast Bagels Av G between C 4 & C 5, next to *Casa Max*. Bocas bagel joint, with a large variety, plus wi-fi and outdoor seating. Bagels from US$3, pizzas US$5. Daily 8am–noon.

Café Lili C 1 at Av D. The Caribbean fare here includes delicious home-made bread and good breakfasts (US$4–6). The waterfront location is priceless.

TREAT YOURSELF

9 ° C 1 in the Tropical Market. Sushi bar meets seafood grill, overlooking the water, where you'll find some of the poshest food on the island. Try the speciality "panko" (deep fried) roll, like the jalapeño-octopus-coconut, from US$6. Caribbean-style mains are extortionate, from US$15, but those on a budget can splash out on seafood starters and sushi for less than US$20.

Lemongrass Bistro C 1. A creative Asian-influenced menu, which changes daily but usually includes delectable seafood delights, is refreshing after endless days of rice and beans. Plates start at US$10, and there's a good set lunch for about US$8.

Panadería y Dulceria Alemana Av E at C 2. The place to go for a European style bakery breakfast. The combination of a Nutella-filled croissant and delicious cup of coffee will make your mouth water (US$2.50).

Starfish Café C 3. A good stop if you just can't live without that speciality coffee drink (US$2–4), *Starfish* also serves breakfast (US$3–5), sandwiches, salads and pastries. Comfy couches, board games and magazines to flick through make this a good spot for rainy days. Closed Sun.

Restaurants

Alberto's Pizzeria C 5 Av E–F at *Hotel Kala Luna*. This spacious, open-fronted restaurant serves "the best pizza in Bocas" and spaghetti dishes (US$4–10). Mon–Sat 5–11pm.

Café Om Av E at C 2. The Canadian–Indian owner draws from traditional family recipes, dishing up excellent curries with rice, naan and home-made chutney (from US$7), as well as juices, wraps, and lighter morning munchies. Breakfast & dinner Mon, Tues & Thurs–Sun.

El Chitre C 3 & Av Central. Locals trust this place, serving enormous portions of *comida típica* at low prices (from US$3), and so should you.

Dos Bongos C 3 at Av C. An open-air eatery on the main drag serving *comida típica* and other offerings to a mixed clientele, at slightly inflated prices (from US$5).

Kun Ja C 3 at Av C. This Chinese restaurant, with indoor and waterfront seating, is one of the friendliest budget spots in town. It serves large portions of tasty meat and seafood dishes with fried rice, chow mein or chop suey (US$4). Takeaway is available. Closed Tues.

🏃 **Hotel Angela Bistro** C 1. Brand new, *Angela Bistro*'s modern-eclectic menu and talented young chef set this venue apart from others in Bocas Town. The menu changes weekly, according to supplies of mostly local produce, with treats like mahi-mahi *ceviche* with home-made chips (US$6) and a heavenly passionfruit *crème brûlée* (US$4) sure to lure you back for more.

El Lorito de Don Chicho C 3 at Av E, across from Parque Bolívar. *Lorito* serves tasty, inexpensive, self-service Panamanian food – locals seldom eat anywhere else. *Don Chicho*'s conglomerate also includes an internet café and a laundry next door; there's an accurate bus schedule to Boca del Drago out front. Breakfast and lunch for under US$5.

Mr Douglas C 3 at Av Central, across from Parque Bolívar. Apparently inspired by well-known US fast-food chains, *Mr Douglas* has just about every kind of greasy food you can imagine at rock-bottom prices. Burger and fries US$3.

🏃 **Natural Mystic** C 3, opposite *Iguana's*. Portions are small, but the flavours are large and the prices kept low, with most of the items on the vegetarian menu at US$3–4; dips and coconut bread, veggie burgers and salads are fresh and tasty. Hang out, use the free wi-fi or smoke a hookah (US$5). This is also a good spot to warm up for the night, with happy-hour beers at US$0.75, and a well-positioned balcony from which you can observe the flow of partygoers on the main street below.

El Pecado de Sabor C 3. A menu comprised of delicious Thai, Lebanese and Mexican dishes, made with the finest local and imported ingredients (US$3–10). The best tables are on the rickety balcony overlooking the main street. Closed Sun & Mon.

El Ultimo Refugio Just off C 3 at Av Sur. The building is rather flimsy, but it houses the only restaurant in town where you can watch the sun set over the mainland from the water's edge. Run by experienced gringos, this spot offers good seafood from US$7.

Drinking and nightlife

Several restaurants double as music and drinking venues in the evening, plus there are a few good bars where you can relax with a cold Balboa Ice or cocktail.

Bars

🏃 **Mondo Taitu** Av G. These guys take their dressing up almost as seriously as their commitment to sustainable travel. With all kinds of creative cocktails and drink specials, there's a frat-house-style theme party here most nights of the week.

Le Pirate C 3. Seafront restaurant serving unremarkable fish and seafood – it's more popular as a bar, especially for sundowners.

The Reef Bar C 3. At the southern tip of the street, come here for a local experience, with cheap drinks and dancing at weekends.

Toro Loco C 3. The newest expat hotspot is an American sports bar and grill: all gringo memorabilia, dart boards, a bar bedecked with dancing poles for wilder nights, and loud rock/alternative music. It often showcases live music and is filled beyond maximum capacity, with crowds spilling out onto the street.

Clubs

🏃 **Aqua Lodge** Isla Carenero. Just across the water from Bocas Town, a US$1 boat ride away, *Aqua Lodge* really gets going on ladies' nights (Wed & Sat), with free drinks until midnight for the girls, a big, starlit dancefloor and a water trampoline and diving board on which to cool your heels. This Peter Pan playground hosts legendary parties, where the sandflies and mosquitoes are the only unwanted guests – come prepared with plenty of repellent.

El Barco Hundido C 1, beside the Cable & Wireless office. Locally known as the "Wreck Deck", this spot used to be the most popular hangout for locals, tourists and surfers, who came here to drink cold beer (US$2) until the early hours. Though no longer the hottest joint in town, it's still a good venue for a night on the town, with regular DJs playing a mix of modern r'n'b, '80s pop and the ubiquitous Bob Marley. Opens at 7pm and gets lively after 9pm.

Iguana's C 3, opposite *Natural Mystic*. The sister bar to buzzing hostel *Gran Kahuna*, *Iguana's* always seems to have promotions on offer, especially on Ladies' Night. The large dancefloor packs out with partiers, while the dock out back provides a cool-down space with ambient seating overlooking the water.

Directory

Books Bocas Bookstore, below *Café Om* on Ave E and C 2, has a good selection of English books

SURFER'S PARADISE

In the past few years, Bocas has garnered a lot of attention as an international **surfing** destination. The best waves hit between December and March, and there are many excellent and varied surfing spots in the area. Although none are within walking distance of Bocas, the town remains the best base for catching water-taxis that will take you on to your wave of choice. The main hotspots include **Carenero**, off the northeastern tip of Isla Carenero; **Dumpers**, just north of Boca del Drago; **Paunch**, on the northeastern tip of Isla Colón; **Red Frog Beach**, on Bastimentos; and **Silverbacks**, between Bastimentos and Carenero. These break over reef, some of which is fire coral, so wear booties or be careful.

You can **rent surfboards** for US$10–20/day, but prices vary with size, quality and availability. One option is Tropix, C 3 (closed Sun); there's also the *Gran Kahuna* on C3 and *Hostal Heike* and *Mondo Taitu*, C 3 at Av G.

(US$2–10) and magazines, and will also buy used books.

Exchange Banco Nacional, C 4 (Mon–Fri 8am–2pm, Sat 9am–noon), has a 24hr ATM.

Internet Don Chicho Internet is on C 3 (daily 7am–11pm; US$2/hr).

Health There is one hospital on the island at Av G & C 10 (☎757 9201). It has 24hr emergency services. Rosa Blanca Pharmacy is on C 3 near Av A (Mon–Sat 9am–5pm).

Language schools Spanish by the Sea, Av A at C 4 (☎757 9518, ⒲www.spanishbythesea.com), is one of three lively and relaxed schools for travellers run by a hip Dutch/Tico family. Affordable lesson plans for extended stays, as well as a 6hr crash course for US$60.

Laundry The best place in town is behind Don Chicho's – a slim alley behind the internet spot leads you back to the laundry (US$5/bag).

Post office The main post office is on Av E (Mon–Fri 8am–4pm, Sat 8am–noon). There's also Mail Boxes Etc, Av F (Mon–Fri 8am–5pm, Sat & Sun noon–5pm).

Supermarkets Isla Supermercado, C 3 and Av D, is the main grocery. Super Gourmet, Av A and C 3, carries hard-to-find items and is a good option for vegetarians; it also has a decent lunch counter. Supermercado Hawaii, Av G, has a small selection but cheaper prices for basic items.

Moving on

By air to: Changuinola (4–5 daily; 15min); Panama City (4–5 daily; 1hr); Puerto Limón (1 daily; 30min); San José (3 weekly; 1hr). All flights leave from the airport on Av E, a few blocks from town. The operators are Aeroperlas (☎757 9341, ⒲www.aeroperlas.com), Air Panama (☎757 9841, ⒲www.flyairpanama.com) and Nature Air (☎757 9963, ⒲www.natureair.com).

By boat to: Almirante (every 30min; 30min); Changuinola (8 daily; 1hr).

AROUND BOCAS TOWN

The islands, cays and mainland waterways surrounding Bocas Town offer wide-ranging opportunities for relaxing on pristine beaches, visiting Ngöbe-Buglé villages and diving near unspoilt coral reefs. A quick bus or taxi ride away are the beaches of the rest of **Isla Colón**, while nearby islas Carenero and Bastimentos are favoured by visiting surfers. Most visitors make a point of exploring the **Parque Nacional Marino Isla Bastimentos**, a renowned marine park that stretches across a series of islands in the archipelago.

Playa El Bluff

Some 20 minutes from Bocas Town by taxi, **Bluff Beach** sees some of the

TREAT YOURSELF

Tesoro Escondido ☎674 97435, ⒲www.bocas tesoroescondido.com. A great escape from the party atmosphere in town, this hotel is set on land which slopes from the bluff to the beach, offering excellent views and a choice of accommodation including rooms (US$35) and charming cabinas (US$65).

heaviest action at the height of the Bocas surf season. There are several choices for staying and eating here, and the distance from town results in a more tranquil pace that is often preferred by couples and more mature travellers.

As taxis aren't plentiful and car rental is not possible, the easiest way to get around is to rent a bicycle in Bocas Town (see "Getting around", p.664).

Isla Carenero

Just 200m across the water from Bocas Town, tiny **Isla Carenero** is beginning to receive more visitors thanks to hostel and adult playground *Aqua Lodge* (see p.666), and the most accessible and consistent surf break in the archipelago at Punta Carenero. On the westward side of the island, a narrow concrete path goes as far as the small marina; the island is rather dingy here, and wooden houses on stilts stand over the partially water-logged and heavily littered ground. Quieter than Bocas Town, the island has its charms, but these may be outweighed by the hefty populations of sandflies and mosquitoes that plague beachgoers here.

For great **seafood** (US$4–10), head to *Bibi's in the Beach,* which looks out over the water at a popular beginners' surf spot; the large balcony provides the perfect refuge from the pestering insects on shore. *Bibi's* also houses the Escuela del Mar (☎757 9137 or 6785 7984), offering **snorkel and kayak hire**, surfboard and S.U.P. (Stand Up Paddle board) rentals and lessons, and surfboard repairs. To get to the island, catch a **water-taxi** (US$1) from Bocas.

Bastimentos

Outside the national marine park on the western tip of Isla Bastimentos, the small fishing community of **Basti-**

mentos is not really set up for mass tourism, making it a great place to stay if you're seeking more relaxation than Bocas Town offers. Be sure to bring cash, though, as there's no bank or ATM on the island.

An undulating concrete path acts as the community's main thoroughfare, snaking its way between the coastline and a steep, green hillside dotted with wooden stilt houses. A jungle path, occasionally impassable after heavy rains, leads to several pristine **beaches** twenty minutes away on the other side of the island.

The future of this spectacular area remains shaky, as locals and environmental enthusiasts continue to fight with potential developers – building projects, unless very carefully planned and executed, will almost certainly cause irreparable damage to the fragile ecosystem.

Arrival

By boat Regular boats run from the water-taxi terminal in Bocas Town (US$3 per person), and arrive at the main dock; for another dollar you can be dropped off at Red Frog Beach across the island – but you'll probably have to wade in from the sea.

Accommodation and eating

Beverly's Hill Left from the main dock ☎757 9923, ✉beverleyshill@gmail.com. A gem on the hillside, with cabaña rooms set in a lush tropical garden that's home to the elusive red frog. Try to book the room at the top for stunning Caribbean views (US$40). US$22

Hospedaje El Jaguar ☎757 9383, ✉hosp _jaguar@hotmail.es. This purple, hammock-strewn spot over the water is clean, comfortable and run by the Archibalds, one of the best-known families on the island. The breezy rooms are cheap and cheerful. US$20

Hostal Bastimentos ☎757 9053, ⊛gianhostalbastimentos.com. This sprawling maze of a backpackers' hostel gives a choice of accommodation, from dorms to posh bedrooms with a/c and hot water. There's a communal kitchen and vibe here, and it's just a

VISITING THE MARINE PARK

The easiest way to visit the marine park and other spots around Bocas Town is with one of the area's **tour companies** (see box, p.664). A large number of agencies offer day-trips to beaches and snorkelling spots in and around the park, typically costing US$20–30 per person and including a stop at a restaurant for lunch (US$6–10). The more expensive tours often provide free cold drinks and snorkelling equipment. Alternatively, you can **hire a boat** in Bocas Town or Bastimentos: with a group of four or more people this could be cheaper than an agency tour and lets you decide exactly where you want to go. A typical day's excursion might include a visit to the Cayos Zapatillas in the morning, lunch and snorkelling at Crawl Cay and an afternoon on Red Frog Beach.

20min jungle hike to a pristine, undeveloped beach. Dorms US$6, doubles US$40

Island Time On the path towards *Up in the Hill* ☎ 6844 7704. Although frequently lacking key ingredients, this small restaurant has decent Thai-style food, from curries and soups to pad Thai at US$8, served on a little balcony with great views of the Caribbean. One of the few places on the island to offer wi-fi, which is free for guests. Closed Sun. Jungle cabins are also available to rent (from US$25).

Pantai Pizza Just over the bridge from *Roots* restaurant. A sandwich and pizza joint, with tasty breakfasts from US$3–5, large sandwiches from US$4, and crispy pizzas from US$5. Closed at lunchtime, but takeaway is available if you order before noon.

Roots 200m right of the main dock. The most popular eatery in town, *Roots* serves up dynamite Caribbean dishes of fresh seafood and coconut rice for under US$10. Closed Tues.

Tio Tom's Just left of the main dock ☎ 757 9831, ⊛ www.tiotom.com. A thatched-roof inn, built over water with five cosy en-suite rooms. Food, including great breakfasts, is cooked by the German owners, who also rent out kayaks at US$10/half-day, and snorkel equipment for US$4. An avid naturalist, the man of the house also offers customized tours exploring the islands' natural wonders, and plans are afoot to open an on-site dive shop. US$22

Up in the Hill Follow the path near the police station and continue up through the jungle, keeping watch for markers along the way. Holistic café and shop set in a private *finca*, producing organic cocoa and coconut-based products. Treats include icy lemonade, delectable fresh truffles and strong fresh coffee. Making the most of their natural resources, the owners have also created a range of natural creams and balms, sold here (from US$2; cash only).

Parque Nacional Marino Isla Bastimentos

Most visitors to Bocas come to explore the pristine beauty of **Parque Nacional Marino Isla Bastimentos**, a 130-square-kilometre reserve encompassing several virtually undisturbed ecosystems that include rainforest, mangrove and coral reef supporting an immense diversity of marine life, including dolphins, sea turtles and a kaleidoscopic variety of fish.

Some of the best **beaches** in the archipelago are also in the park, on the eastern side of the island facing the open sea. Due to their powerful surf and currents, swimming here is dangerous, but they are huge, uncrowded and undeveloped. The most popular is **Red Frog Beach**, an idyllic stretch of sand that takes its name from the tiny bright-red poison-dart frogs (don't touch!) that inhabit the forest behind the beach and are found nowhere else in the world.

Much further east, the fourteen-kilometre stretch of **Playa Larga** is an important nesting site for **sea turtles** between May and September. There's an ANAM ranger station here, where you may be charged a US$10 park entrance fee, and a basic refuge where you can **camp** for another US$10; you'll need to stay overnight if you want to see the turtles lay their eggs. Request permission from the ANAM office in Bocas Town (see p.664) to come here.

Southeast of Isla Bastimentos, but still within the park, are the **Cayos Zapatillas**. Two dreamy, coral-fringed islands, the Zapatillas are excellent for snorkelling, but you must pay the park admission fee at the ANAM station on the southern island. On the prettier northern island, **camping** is also possible with permission from ANAM in Bocas Town.

Language

Language

There's a bewildering collection of languages across the Central American isthmus, numbering well above thirty in all; fortunately for the traveller, there are two that dominate – English, primarily in Belize, the Bay Islands of Honduras, and the Atlantic coast and Corn Islands of Nicaragua, but spoken to some extent all along the Caribbean coast; and Spanish everywhere else.

ENGLISH

Belizean English may sound familiar from a distance and, if you listen to a few words, you may think that its meaning is clear. Listen a little further, however, and you'll realize that complete comprehension is just out of reach. What you're hearing is, in fact, **Creole**, a beautifully warm and relaxed language, typically Caribbean and loosely based on English, with elements of Spanish and indigenous languages. A similar dialect, Guari Guari, is spoken in the Panamanian province of Bocas del Toro. Written Creole, which you'll come across in Belizean newspapers, is a little easier to get to grips with. There's an active movement in Belize to formalize the language, which led to the publication of the *Kriol-Inglish Dikshineri* in 2007. Luckily, almost anyone who can speak Creole can also speak English.

In the Bay Islands of Honduras things are much simpler. English is English rather than Creole, and immediately understandable, albeit spoken with a unique, broad accent. Influenced by Caribbean, English and Scots migrants over the years, local inflexions turn even the most commonplace of remarks into an attractive statement. English, however, is slowly being supplanted by Spanish as the language heard on the street, as growing numbers of mainlanders make the islands their home.

SPANISH

Those new to the region can take heart – **Spanish**, as spoken across Latin America, is one of the easier languages there is to learn and even the most faltering of attempts to speak it is greatly appreciated. Apart from the major tourist areas in Guatemala, Nicaragua, Costa Rica and in some parts of Panama, English is not widely spoken; taking the trouble to get to know at least the basics of Spanish will both make your travels considerably easier and reap countless rewards in terms of reception, appreciation and understanding of people and places.

Overall, Latin American Spanish is clearer and slower than that of Spain – gone are the lisps and bewilderingly rapid, slurred, soft consonants of the old country. There are, however, quite strong variations in accent across Central America: Guatemalan Spanish has the reputation of being clear, precise and eminently understandable even to the worst of linguists, while the language as spoken in Honduras – thick and fast – can initially bewilder even those who believed themselves to be reasonably fluent. Nicaraguans in particular take great pleasure in fooling around with language, creating new words, pronouncing certain letters differently and employing different grammar. There are enough Nicaraguanismos – words and sayings particular to Nicaragua – to fill a 275-page dictionary. As far as pronunciation goes, the "s" is often dropped from word endings and the "v" and "b" sounds are fairly interchangeable.

Pronunciation

For the most part, the rules of **pronunciation** are straightforward and strictly observed. Unless there's an accent, words ending in d, l, r and z are **stressed** on the last syllable, all others on the second last. All **vowels** are pure and short.

A somewhere between the "A" sound of back and that of father.

E as in get.

I as in police.

O as in hot.

U as in rule.

C is soft before E and I, otherwise hard; cerca is pronounced "serka".

G works the same way – a guttural "H" sound (like the ch in loch) before E or I, a hard G elsewhere; gigante is pronounced "higante".

H is always silent.

J is the same sound as a guttural G; jamón is pronounced "hamon".

LL sounds like an English Y; tortilla is pronounced torteeya.

N is as in English, unless there is a tilde (accent) over it, when it becomes like the N in "onion"; mañana is pronounced "manyana".

QU is pronounced like an English K.

R is rolled, RR doubly so.

V sounds like a cross with B, vino becoming beano.

X is slightly softer than in English, sometimes almost like SH, so that Xela becomes "sheyla"; between vowels in place names it has an H sound – México is pronounced "May-hee-ko".

Z is the same as a soft C; cerveza is pronounced "servesa".

Formal and informal address

For English speakers one of the most difficult things to get to grips with is the distinction between formal and informal address – when to use it and to whom and how to avoid causing offence. Generally speaking, the third-person "**usted**" indicates respect and/or a non-familiar relationship and is used in business, for people you don't know and for those older than you. Second-person "**tú**" is for children, friends and contemporaries in less formal settings. (Remember also that in Latin America the second-person **plural** – "vosotros" –

is never used, so "you" plural will always be "ustedes".) In day-to-day exchanges, genuine mistakes on the part of an obviously non-native speaker will be well received and corrected with good humour.

One idiosyncrasy is the widespread use of "**vos**" in Central America. Now archaic in Spain, it is frequently used in place of *tú*, as an intimate form of address between friends of the same age. In most tenses, conjugation is exactly the same as for *tú*. In the present indicative, however, the last syllable is stressed with an accent (*tú comes/vos comés*); in "-ir" verbs in this tense, the final "i" is kept instead of changing to an "e" (*tú escribes/vos escribís*). In commands, the "vos" form drops the final "r" of the infinitive, replacing it with an accented vowel (*tú come/vos comé*). Take your lead from those around you – if you are addressed in the "vos" form it is a sign of friendship and should be reciprocated; on the other hand it is sometimes seen as patronizing to use it with someone you don't know well.

Nicknames and turns of speech

Nicknames are very common in Central America, used in both speech and writing and for any situation from addressing a casual acquaintance to referring to political candidates. Often they centre on obvious physical characteristics – *flaco/a* (thin), *gordo/a* (fat), *rubio/a* (blond).

Often, these nicknames will be further softened by **diminution** – the addition of the suffix -*ito* or -*ita* at the end of nouns and adjectives, a trend used sometimes with a passion in everyday speech. You are quite likely to hear someone talk about their *hermanito* for example, which translates as "little brother" regardless of respective ages, while *mi hijita* ("my little daughter") can as easily mean a grown woman as a child.

Also very common are **endearments**, used lightly in brief encounters and to soothe transactions. Heard in virtually every country are *(mi) amor* – used in much the same way as "love" in England and also between friends – as is *jóven* or *jovencito/a*, young one. More specific to each country (often but not always between men) are terms used to make casual questions or remarks less intrusive. *Papa* (literally "father") is used daily in Honduras, for example as in "*¿Qué hora tiene, papa?*" (What time is it?), while the Nicaraguans use *primo* (cousin). Panamanians address one another as *joven* (youth), regardless of age, and refer to friends as "mis panas" (my panas or Panamanians). In Nicaragua light-skinned or fair-haired visitors will be referred to or addressed as *chele/a*; the syllables of leche (milk) in reverse.

Politesse

Verbal courtesy is an integral part of speech in Spanish and one that – once you're accustomed to the pace and flow of life in Central America – should become instinctive. Saying *buenos días/buenas tardes* and waiting for the appropriate response is usual when asking for something at a shop or ticket office for example, as is adding *señor* or *señora* (in this instance similar to the US "sir" or "ma'am"). The "you're welcome" response is more likely to be *para servirle* (literally "here to serve you") rather than the casual *de nada* ("you're welcome"). The *tss tss* sound is commonly employed to attract attention, particularly in restaurants. In this very polite culture shouting is frowned upon.

On meeting, or being introduced to someone, Central Americans will say *con mucho gusto*, "it's a pleasure", and you should do the same. On departure you will more often than not be told *¡que le vaya bien!* ("may all go well"), a simple phrase that nonetheless

invariably sounds sincere and rounds off transactions nicely. In rural areas, especially, it is usual to leave even complete strangers met on the path with *!Adiós, que le vaya bien!* Note that the Castilian term **coger** (to take/grab) has a very different meaning in Central and South America; here this refers to the act of sex, while the verb **tomar** is used for take/grab. Make sure you therefore say "tomar un autobus" (get the bus), instead of the Castilian "coger un autobus"!

WORDS AND PHRASES

Basic words

a lot	mucho
afternoon	tarde
and	y
bad	mal(o)/a
big	gran(de)
boy	chico
closed	cerrado/a
cold	frío/a
day	día
entrance	entrada
exit	salida
girl	chica
good	bien/buen(o)/a
he	él
her	ella
here	aquí
his	suyo
hot	calor/caliente
how much	cuánto
if	si
information	información
later	más tarde/después
less	menos
ma'am/missus	señora
man	señor/hombre
miss	señorita
more	más
morning	mañana
night	noche
no	no
now	ahora
open	abierto/a
or	o
please	por favor
she	ella
small	pequeño/a

sir/mister	señor
thank you	gracias
that	eso/a
their	suyo/de ellos
there	allí
they	ellos
this	este/a
today	hoy
tomorrow	mañana
what	qué
when	cuándo
where	dónde
with	con
without	sin
woman	mujer/hembra
yes	sí
yesterday	ayer

Basic phrases

Hello	¡Hola!
Goodbye	Adiós
See you later	Hasta luego
Good morning	Buenos días
Good afternoon	Buenas tardes
Good night	Buenas noches
Sorry	Lo siento/Discúlpame
Excuse me	Con permiso/perdón
How are you?	¿Cómo está (usted)?/ ¿Qué tal?
Nice to meet you	Mucho gusto
Not at all/ You're welcome	De nada
I (don't) understand	(No) Entiendo
Do you speak English?	¿Habla (usted) inglés?
I (don't) speak Spanish	(No) Hablo español
What?/How?	¿Cómo?
Could you ..., please?	¿Podría ... por favor?
... repeat that	... repetirlo
... speak slowly	... hablar más despacio
... write that down	... escribirlo
My name is ...	Me llamo ...
What's your name?	¿Cómo se llama usted?
I'm from	Soy de ...
... America	... Estados Unidos
... Australia	... Australia
... Canada	... Canadá
... England	... Inglaterra
... Ireland	... Irlanda
... New Zealand	... Nueva Zelanda
... Scotland	... Escocia
... South Africa	... Sudáfrica
... Wales	... Gales
Where are you from?	De dónde es usted?

How old are you?	¿Cuántos años tiene? (usted)
I am ... years old	Tengo ... años
I don't know	No sé
Do you know ...?	¿Sabe ...?
I want	Quiero
I'd like ...	Quisiera ... por favor
What's that?	¿Qué es eso?
What is this called in Spanish?	¿Cómo se llama este en español?
There is (is there)?	Hay (?)
Do you have ...?	¿Tiene ...?
What time is it?	¿Qué hora es?
May I take a photograph?	¿Puedo sacar una foto?

Basic needs, services and places

ATM	cajero automático
bank	banco
bathroom/toilet	baño/sanitario
beach	playa
bookstore	librería
border crossing	frontera
cheap hotel	un hotel barato
church	iglesia
embassy	embajada
highway	carretera
immigration office	Migración
internet café	cibercafé
lake	lago
laundry	lavandería
library	biblioteca
main street	calle principál
map	mapa
market	mercado
museum	museo
national park	parque nacional
pharmacy	farmacia
(main) post office	correo (central)
restaurant	restaurante
supermarket	supermercado
telephone office	cabina de teléfono
telephones	teléfonos
tourist office	oficina de turismo

Numbers, months and days

Numbers (números)

1	un/uno/una
2	dos
3	tres
4	cuatro
5	cinco

6	seis
7	siete
8	ocho
9	nueve
10	diez
11	once
12	doce
13	trece
14	catorce
15	quince
16	dieciséis
17	diecisiete
18	dieciocho
19	diecinueve
20	veinte
21	veintiuno
22	veintidos
30	treinta
40	cuarenta
50	cincuenta
60	sesenta
70	setenta
80	ochenta
90	noventa
100	cien
101	ciento uno
200	doscientos
201	doscientosuno
500	quinientos
1000	mil
1999	mil novecientos noventa y nueve
2000	dos mil
100,000	cien mil
1,000,000	un millón
first	primero/a
second	segundo/a
third	tercero/a
fourth	cuarto/a
fifth	quinto/a
tenth	décimo/a

Months (meses)

January	enero
February	febrero
March	marzo
April	abril
May	mayo
June	junio
July	julio
August	agosto
September	septiembre
October	octubre
November	noviembre
December	diciembre

Days (días)

Monday	lunes
Tuesday	martes
Wednesday	miércoles
Thursday	jueves
Friday	viernes
Saturday	sábado
Sunday	domingo

Colours

red	rojo/a
orange	naranja
yellow	amarillo/a
green	verde
blue	azul
indigo	índigo/a
violet/purple	violeta
white	blanco/a
black	negro/a
brown	marrón or café
grey	gris

Getting around

Transport

bus	autobús/camión
bus station	estación de autobuses
bus stop	parada de autobús
boat	barco/lancha
ferry	transbordador
dock/pier	muelle
airplane	avión
airport	aeropuerto
car	carro
4WD	tracción integral
taxi	taxi
truck	camión
pick-up	camioneta
hitchhike	hacer autostop (to hitchhike) or pedir un ride (to ask for a ride)
train	tren
train station	estación de trenes
bicycle	bicicleta (abb. bici)
motorcycle	moto
ticket	boleto
ticket office	taquilla/ boletería
I'd like a ticket to ...	(Necesito) un boleto para ...
How much is a ... ticket from...to...?	¿Cuanto cuesta un ... boleto de ...a...?
... first-class	... primera clase
... second-class	... segunda clase
... one-way	... sólo ida
... return/round-trip	... ida y vuelta

I would like to rent a ...	Me gustaría alquilar un/una ...
Where does ... to leave from?	¿De dónde sale ...para ...?
What time does the ... leave for ...?	¿A qué hora sale ...para ...?
What time does the ... arrive in ...?	¿A qué hora llega ... en ...?

Directions

Where is ...?	¿Dónde está ...?
How do I get to ...?	¿Como llego a ...?
I'm looking for ...	Estoy buscando ...
Is this the way to ...?	¿Es esta la carretera hacia ...?
I'm lost	Estoy perdido/a
Is it far?	¿Está lejos?
left	izquierda
right	derecha
straight ahead	derecho/recto
north	norte
south	sur
east	este
west	oeste
street	calle
avenue	avenida
block	cuadra

Money (dinero)

How much is it?	¿Cuánto es/cuesta?
It's too expensive	Es demasiado caro
Do you have anything cheaper?	¿No tiene algo más barato?
Do you accept ...?	Aceptan ...?
... credit cards	... tarjetas de crédito
...travellers' cheques	... cheques de viajero
... US dollars	... dólares americanos
I would like to change some dollars	Me gustaría cambiar unos dólares
Can you change dollars?	¿Se puede cambiar dólares?
What is the exchange rate?	¿Cuál es el tipo de cambio?

Shopping

I would like to buy ...	Me gustaría comprar ...
... a bag	... una bolsa
... a book	... un libro
... clothes	... ropas
... film	... una película
... a hammock	... una hamaca
... a hat	... un sombrero
... a jacket	... una chaqueta
... a mobile phone	... un celular
... a painting	... una cuadra
... a shirt	... una camisa
... shoes	... unos zapatos
... a skirt	... una falda
... a sleeping bag	... un saco de dormir
... socks	... unos calcetines
... a tent	... una carpa
... trousers	... pantalónes
... underwear	... ropa interior
I'm just looking	Estoy mirando
Could I look at it/that?	¿Puedo ver eso/aquello?
Please give me ...	Por favor deme
... one like that	... uno asi

Accommodation

Is there a ... nearby?	¿Hay ... aquí cerca?
... guesthouse	... una casa de huéspedes
... hotel	... un hotel
... hostel	... un hostal
... campground	... un camping
Do you have ...?	¿Tiene ...?
... a room	... un cuarto
... with two beds	... con dos camas
... a double bed	... con cama matrimonial
... a dorm room	... dormitorio compartido
... a tent	... una carpa
... a cabin	... una cabina
It's for	Es para
... one person	... una persona
... two people	... dos personas
... for one night	... una noche
... one week	... una semana
Does it have ...	¿Tiene ...?
... a shared bath	... baño compartido
... a private bath	... baño privado
... hot water	... agua caliente
... air conditioning	Aire acondicionado
Can one ...?	¿Se puede ...?
... camp (near) here	...acampar aquí (cerca)
... sling a hammock here?	... poner una hamaca aquí
... swim here?	... nadar aquí
How much is it ...?	¿Cuánto es/cuesta ...?
... per night	... por noche
... per person	... por persona
... per room	... por cuarto
Does the price include breakfast?	¿El precio incluye el desayuno?
May I see a room?	¿Puedo ver un cuarto?
May I see another room?	¿Puedo ver otro cuarto?

Yes, it's fine	Sí, está bien
I'd like to reserve a …	Me gustaría reservar un/una …

Health and safety

I'm ill	Estoy enfermo/a
He/she is ill	Él/Ella está enfermo/a
I'm allergic to …	Soy alérgica a …
He/she is allergic to …	Él/Ella es alérgica a …
I need to see a doctor	Tengo que ver un doctor
He/she needs to see a doctor	Él/ella tiene que ver un doctor
I need to go to …	Tengo que ir …
… the hospital	… al hospital
… a health clinic	… a una clínica
… a pharmacy	… a una farmacia
He/she needs to go to…	Él/ella tiene que ir a …
I have a …	Me duele …
… headache	… la cabeza
… stomach ache	… el estómago
I have a fever	Tengo fiebre
I have hurt my…	Me hice daño …
… arm	… al brazo
… back	… a la espalda
… foot	… al pie
… head	… a la cabeza
… hand	… a la mano
… knee	… a la rodilla
… leg	… a la pierna
… neck	… al cuello
He/she has hurt	Él/ella se hizo daño …
I was bitten/ scratched by …	Me mordió/arañó …
… a dog	… un perro
… a cat	… un gato
… a snake	… una serpiente
… a mosquito	… un mosquito
… a spider	… una araña
… a jellyfish	… una medusa
He/she was bitten/ scratched by …	Le mordío/arañó un/una …
I am dehydrated	Estoy deshidratado/a
medicine	medicina
dose/dosage	dosis
sunscreen/sunblock	crema solar/filtro solar
bug repellent	repelente para insectos
antibiotics	antibióticos
It's an emergency	Es una emergencia
police	policía
policeman	un policía
police station	comisaría
tourist police	policía turística

ambulance	ambulancia
fire brigade	bomberos
Red Cross	Cruz Roja
Help!	¡Ayuda!
Fire!	¡Fuego!
Go away!	¡Váyase!
Leave me alone!	¡Déjeme en paz!
I've been robbed	Me han robado
He/she has been robbed	Le han robado
I need to fill out an insurance report	Tengo que rellenar una reclamación de seguro
I need help	Necesito ayuda
Please can you help me?	¿Me podría ayudar por favor?

MENU READER

While dishes vary by country and region, these words and terms will help negotiate most menus.

Basic dining vocabulary

almuerzo	lunch
carta (la)	menu
cena	dinner
cocina	kitchen
comida corriente	cheap set menu, usually served at lunch time
comida típica	typical cuisine
cuchara	spoon
cuchillo	knife
desayuno	breakfast
merienda	afternoon tea
mesa	table
plato	plate
plato del día	dish of the day
plato fuerte	main course
plato vegetariano	vegetarian dish
servilleta	napkin
silla	chair
taza	mug/cup
tenedor	fork
vaso	glass
La cuenta, por favor	The bill, please
¿Contiene …?	Does this contain …? (for food allergies, vegetarians, etc)
Soy vegetariano/a	I'm a vegetarian
No como carne	I don't eat meat

Basics

aceite	oil
ajillo	garlic butter

ajo	garlic
arroz	rice
azúcar	sugar
chile	chilli
galletas	biscuits
hielo	ice
huevos	eggs
mantequilla	butter
mermelada	jam
miel	honey
mixto	mixed seafood/meats/ salad
mostaza	mustard
pan (integral)	bread (wholemeal)
pan de coco	coconut bread
pimienta	pepper
queso	cheese
sal	salt
salsa de tomate	tomato sauce

Frutas (fruit)

banano	banana
cereza	cherry
ciruela	plum
coco	coconut
durazno	peach
fresa	strawberry
guayaba	guava
higo	fig
lima	lime
limón	lemon
manzana	apple
maracuyá	passion fruit
melón	melon
mora	blackberry
naranja	orange
papaya	papaya
pera	pear
piña	pineapple
pithaya	dragon fruit
plátano	plantain
sandía	watermelon
tamarindo	tamarind
tomate	tomato
toronja	grapefruit
uva	grapes

Legumbres/verduras (vegetables)

aguacate	avocado
alcachofa	artichoke
apio	celery
arvejas	peas
berenjena	aubergine/eggplant
brécol	broccoli

calabaza	pumpkin
calabazín	courgette/zucchini
cebolla	onion
champiñón/hongo	mushroom
coliflor	cauliflower
curtida	pickled cabbage, beetroot and carrots
ensalada	salad
espinaca	spinach
frijoles	beans
frijoles volteados	refried beans
gallo pinto	mixed rice and beans
lechuga	lettuce
lentejas	lentils
maíz	sweetcorn/maize
menestra	bean/lentil stew
palmito	palm heart
papa	potato
papas fritas	French fries
pepinillo	gherkin
pepino	cucumber
tomate	tomato
zanahoria	carrot

Carne (meat) and aves (poultry)

bistec	steak
búfalo	buffalo
carne	beef
carne de chancho	pork
cerdo	pork
chicharrones	pork scratchings, crackling
chuleta	pork chop
conejo	rabbit
cordero	lamb
filete	steak
gallina	hen
jamón	ham
lechón	roasted pig
lomo	steak
pato	duck
pavo	turkey
pollo	chicken
res	beef
ternera	veal
tocino	bacon
venado	venison

Menudos (offal)

chunchules	intestines
corazón	heart
guatita	tripe
hígado	liver
lengua	tongue
patas	trotters

Mariscos (seafood) and pescado (fish)

almejas	clams
anchoa	anchovy
atún	tuna
bacalao	cod
calamares	squid
camarón	shrimp
cangrejo	crab
ceviche	raw seafood marinated in lime juice with onions
corvina	sea bass
erizo	sea urchin
gambas	prawns
langosta	lobster/crayfish
langostina	king prawn
lenguado	sole
mejillónes	mussels
ostión	oyster
pargo rojo/blanco	red/white snapper
pulpo	octopus
trucha	trout

Soups (sopas)

caldo	broth
caldo de gallina	chicken broth
crema de espárragos	cream of asparagus
sopa de caracol	spicy conch stew
sopa de frijoles	bean soup
sopa del día	soup of the day
tapado	a seafood soup, served on the Caribbean coast of several countries in the isthmus

Bocados (snacks)

bocadillo	little snack
casado	meal of rice, beans, salad and meat or fish (phrase mainly seen in Costa Rica, translating to "married")
chuchito	corn-dough parcels made with beans and eggs (sometimes also pork), popular in Guatemala and El Salvador
empanada	cheese/meat pastry
hamburguesa	hamburger
nacatamales	Nicaraguan corn-dough parcels filled with vegetables, pork, beef or chicken
patacones	fried green plantains

pupusa	small, thick Salvadorean tortilla filled with cheese, beans or pork and topped with salad
salchichas	sausages
tamale	ground maize with meat/cheese wrapped in leaf
tortilla	toasted maize pancake
tortilla de huevos	omelette
tostada	toast

Postres (desserts)

ensalada de frutas	fruit salad
flan	crème caramel
helado	ice cream
pastel	cake
piñonate	candied papaya
torta	tart
tres leches	cake made with three varieties of milk

Bebidas (drinks)

agua (mineral)	mineral water
… con gas	… sparkling
… sin gas	… still
… con/sin hielo	… with/without ice
… con limón	… with lemon
aguardiente	raw alcohol made from sugar cane
café	coffee
café con leche	milk with a little coffee
cerveza	beer
gaseosa	fizzy drink
horchata	milky, cereal-based drink sweetened with cinnamon
jugo	juice
leche	milk
licuado	fresh fruit milkshake
limonada	fresh lemonade
raspados	ice shavings with sweet topping
refresco	generic term for cold drink
ron	rum
licor	spirits
té	tea
té aromática	herbal tea
hierba luisa	lemon verbena
manzanilla	camomile
menta	mint
vino blanco	white wine
vino tinto	red wine

Cooking terms

a la parrilla	barbecued
a la plancha	grilled
ahumado	smoked
al ajillo	in garlic sauce
al horno	oven-baked
al vapor	steamed
apanado	breaded
asado	roast
asado al palo	spit roast
crudo	raw
duro	hard boiled
encebollado	cooked with onions
frito	fried
picante	hot, spicy
puré	mashed
revuelto	scrambled
saltado	sautéed
secado	dried

USEFUL VOCABULARY

aguacero downpour

ahorita right now (any time within the coming hour)

alcalde mayor

aldea village

algodón cotton

almohada pillow

artesanía arts and crafts

bahía bay

balneario resort or spa

barranca steep-sided ravine

barrio neighbourhood, or area within a town or city; suburb

biotopo protected area of national ecological importance, usually with limited tourist access

bomba pump at a petrol station

caballo horse

cabaña literally a cabin, but can mean anything from a palm-thatched beach hut to a room; usually applies to tourist accommodation

cabina cubicle/booth/cabin

cacique chief (originally a colonial term, now used for elected leaders/figureheads of indigenous *comarcas* in Panama)

cafetería café

calzada road/carriageway

cama bed

camioneta small truck or van (in Guatemala, a chicken bus)

campesino peasant/farmer

campo countryside

cantina local, hard-drinking bar, usually men-only

carro car, equivalent of the Castilian *coche*

casa de cambio currency exchange bureau

cascada waterfall

caseta telefónica phone booth

catedral cathedral

cepillo de dientes toothbrush

chabola shack

chapín slang term for someone from Guatemala

chicle chewing gum

chorreador sack-and-metal coffee-filter contraption, still widely used

Churrigueresque highly elaborate, decorative form of Baroque architecture (usually found in churches)

cigarrillo cigarette

ciudad city

Clásico period during which ancient Maya civilization was at its height, usually given as 300–900 AD

colchón mattress

colectivo shared taxi/minibus, usually following fixed route (can also be applied to a boat – *lancho colectivo*)

colina hill (also *el cerro*)

colonia city suburb or neighbourhood, often seen in addresses as "Col"

comedor basic restaurant, usually with just one or two things on the menu, always the cheapest place to eat; literally "dining room"

conquistador "one who conquers": member of early Spanish expeditions to the Americas in the sixteenth century

convento convent or monastery

cordillera mountain range

correo aéreo air mail

corriente second-class bus

cuadra street block

cuevas caves

descompuesto out of order

Dios God

discoteca club/disco

Don/Doña courtesy titles (sir/madam), mostly used in letters, for professional people or for a boss

dolor pain/ache

edificio building

efectivo cash

ejido communal farmland

encendedor lighter (for cigarettes)

encomienda package/parcel

entrada entry/entry fee

estatua statue

extranjero foreigner

fecha date

feria fair (market); also a town fête

fiesta party

finca ranch, farm or plantation

fósforos matches

gambas buttresses; the giant above-ground roots that some rainforest trees put out

gasolina petrol

gasolinera petrol station

golfo gulf

gringo/gringa specifically American, but used widely for any white-skinned foreigner; not necessarily a term of abuse, it does nonetheless have a slightly pessimistic connotation

gruta cave

guaca pre-Columbian burial ground or tomb

hacienda big farm, ranch or estate, or big house on it

henequén fibre from the *agave* (sisal) plant, used to make rope

hospedaje very basic pensión or small hotel

huipil Maya woman's traditional dress or blouse, usually woven or embroidered

huracán hurricane

I.V.A. sales tax

indígena an indigenous person; preferred term among indigenous groups, rather than the more racially offensive *índio*

invierno winter (May–Oct)

isla island

jardín garden

juego de pelota ball-game/ball-court

ladino a vague term – applied to people it means Spanish-influenced as opposed to indigenous, and at its most specific defines someone of mixed Spanish and indigenous blood; it's more commonly used simply to describe a person of "Western" culture, or one who dresses in "Western" style, be they of indigenous or mixed blood

lanterna torch

lavabo sink

litera bunk bed

llave key

malecón seafront promenade

mar sea

mestizo person of mixed indigenous and Spanish blood, though like the term *ladino* it has more cultural than racial significance

metate Pre-Columbian stone table used for grinding corn

milpa maize field, usually cleared by slash-and-burn farming

mirador look-out point

mochila backpack

mochilero backpacker

moneda coins

montar a caballo to go horseriding

neotrópicos "neotropics": tropics of the New World

noreste northeast; often seen in addresses as "NE"

noroeste northwest

nublado cloudy

occidente west

oriente east; often seen in addresses as "Ote"

otoño autumn

paisaje landscape

palacio mansion, but not necessarily royal

palacio de gobierno headquarters of state/federal authorities

palacio municipal headquarters of local government

palapa palm thatch (used to describe any thatched/palm-roofed hut)

panadería bakery

parque park

paseo a broad avenue; also a walk, especially the traditional evening walk around the plaza

pasta de dientes toothpaste

pelota ball, or ball-court

peón farm labourer, usually landless

personaje someone of importance, a VIP, although usually used pejoratively to indicate someone who is putting on airs

piscina swimming pool

planta baja ground floor – abbreviated PB in elevators

plaza square

Plateresque elaborately decorative Renaissance architectural style

poniente west; often seen in addresses as "Pte"

Postclásico period between the decline of Maya civilization and the arrival of the Spanish, 900–1530 AD

Preclásico archeological era preceding the blooming of Maya civilization, usually given as 1500 BC–300 AD

primavera spring

propina tip

pueblo town/village

puente bridge

puerta door

pulpería general store or corner store; also sometimes serves cooked food and drinks

quetzal quetzal (bird), and also the currency of Guatemala

rancho palm-thatched roof; can also mean a smallholding

recibo receipt

redondel de toros bullring, used for local rodeos

río river

ruinas ruins

sábana sheet

sacbé Maya road, or ceremonial causeway

saco de dormir sleeping bag

santo saint

seda silk

sendero path

sierra mountain range

sincretismo syncretism, the attempted amalgamation of different religions, cultures or schools of thought; mainly applied to religion and in Central America usually refers to the merging of Maya and Catholic beliefs soda Costa Rican cafeteria or diner; in the rest of Central America it's usually called a *comedor*

sol sun

sótano basement

stela freestanding carved monument; most are of Maya origin

sudeste southeast (also sureste)

sudoeste southwest (also suroeste)

temblor tremor

temporada season: *la temporada de lluvia* is the rainy season

terremoto earthquake

terreno land; small farm

tiempo weather (can also mean time)

tienda shop

tierra land/earth

típico/típica literally "typical"; used to anything pertaining to a specific culture, from food to dress to art.

traje traditional costume (also means suit)

vaquero cowboy

vela candle/sail (of a boat); also means "wake" or funeral gathering in Nicaragua

ventana window

verano summer (Nov–April)

vista view

volcán volcano

Small print and
Index

A Rough Guide to Rough Guides

Published in 1982, the first Rough Guide – to Greece – was a student scheme that became a publishing phenomenon. Mark Ellingham, a recent graduate in English from Bristol University, had been travelling in Greece the previous summer and couldn't find the right guidebook. With a small group of friends he wrote his own guide, combining a highly contemporary, journalistic style with a thoroughly practical approach to travellers' needs.

The immediate success of the book spawned a series that rapidly covered dozens of destinations. And, in addition to impecunious backpackers, Rough Guides soon acquired a much broader and older readership that relished the guides' wit and inquisitiveness as much as their enthusiastic, critical approach and value-for-money ethos.

These days, Rough Guides include recommendations from shoestring to luxury and cover more than 200 destinations around the globe, including almost every country in the Americas and Europe, more than half of Africa and most of Asia and Australasia. Our ever-growing team of authors and photographers is spread all over the world, particularly in Europe, the US and Australia.

In the early 1990s, Rough Guides branched out of travel, with the publication of Rough Guides to World Music, Classical Music and the Internet. All three have become benchmark titles in their fields, spearheading the publication of a wide range of books under the Rough Guide name.

Including the travel series, Rough Guides now number more than 350 titles, covering: phrasebooks, music guides from Opera to Heavy Metal, reference works as diverse as Conspiracy Theories and Shakespeare, and popular culture books from iPods to Poker. Rough Guides also produce a series of more than 120 World Music CDs in partnership with World Music Network.

Visit www.roughguides.com to see our latest publications.

Rough Guide credits

Text editor: Natasha Foges
Layout: Nikhil Agarwal
Cartography: Lokamata Sahu, Swati Handoo
Picture editor: Mark Thomas
Production: Rebecca Short
Proofreader: Diane Margolis
Cover design: Nicole Newman, Dan May
Editorial: **London** Andy Turner, Keith Drew, Edward Aves, Alice Park, Lucy White, James Smart, James Rice, Emma Beatson, Emma Gibbs, Kathryn Lane, Monica Woods, Mani Ramaswamy, Harry Wilson, Alison Roberts, Lara Kavanagh, Eleanor Aldridge, Ian Blenkinsop, Charlotte Melville, Lorna North, Joe Staines, Matthew Milton, Tracy Hopkins; **Delhi** Madhavi Singh, Jalpreen Kaur Chhatwal, Dipika Dasgupta, Prema Dutta
Design & Pictures: **London** Dan May, Diana Jarvis, Nicole Newman, Rhiannon Furbear; **Delhi** Umesh Aggarwal, Ajay Verma,

Jessica Subramanian, Ankur Guha, Pradeep Thapliyal, Sachin Tanwar, Anita Singh, Sachin Gupta
Production: Liz Cherry, Louise Minihane, Erika Pepe
Cartography: **London** Ed Wright, Katie Lloyd-Jones; **Delhi** Rajesh Chhibber, Ashutosh Bharti, Rajesh Mishra, Animesh Pathak, Jasbir Sandhu, Deshpal Dabas
Marketing, Publicity & roughguides.com: Liz Statham
Design Director: Scott Stickland
Rough Guides Publisher: Jo Kirby
Digital Travel Publisher: Peter Buckley
Reference Director: Andrew Lockett
Operations Coordinator: Becky Doyle
Operations Assistant: Johanna Wurm
Publishing Director (Travel): Clare Currie
Commercial Manager: Gino Magnotta
Managing Director: John Duhigg

Publishing information

This second edition published November 2011 by
Rough Guides Ltd,
80 Strand, London WC2R 0RL
11 Community Centre, Panchsheel Park, New Delhi 110017, India

Distributed by the Penguin Group

Penguin Books Ltd,
80 Strand, London WC2R 0RL

Penguin Group (USA)
375 Hudson Street, NY 10014, USA

Penguin Group (Australia)
250 Camberwell Road, Camberwell, Victoria 3124, Australia

Penguin Group (NZ)
67 Apollo Drive, Mairangi Bay, Auckland 1310, New Zealand

Rough Guides is represented in Canada by Tourmaline Editions Inc. 662 King Street West, Suite 304, Toronto, Ontario M5V 1M7

Cover concept by Peter Dyer.

Typeset in Bembo and Helvetica to an original design by Henry Iles.

Printed in Singapore
© Rough Guides, 2011
Maps © Rough Guides

No part of this book may be reproduced in any form without permission from the publisher except for the quotation of brief passages in reviews.
696pp includes index
A catalogue record for this book is available from the British Library
ISBN: 978-1-40538-227-4

The publishers and authors have done their best to ensure the accuracy and currency of all the information in **The Rough Guide to Central America on a Budget**, however, they can accept no responsibility for any loss, injury, or inconvenience sustained by any traveller as a result of information or advice contained in the guide.

11 12 13 14 8   7   6   5   4   3   2   1

Help us update

We've gone to a lot of effort to ensure that the second edition of **The Rough Guide to Central America on a Budget** is accurate and up-to-date. However, things change – places get "discovered", opening hours are notoriously fickle, restaurants and rooms raise prices or lower standards. If you feel we've got it wrong or left something out, we'd like to know, and if you can remember the address, the price, the hours, the phone number, so much the better.

Please send your comments with the subject line "**Rough Guide Central America on a Budget Update**" to ©mail@uk.roughguides.com. We'll credit all contributions and send a copy of the next edition (or any other Rough Guide if you prefer) for the very best emails.

Find more travel information, connect with fellow travellers and book your trip on ® www .roughguides.com

Acknowledgements

Huw Hennessy Thanks to Cristina Cunchillos (Central America Travel Association), Maria José Rendón & Ricardo Ayala (CorsaTur), René Barbón (Suchitoto Adventure Outfitters), Manolo González (El Imposible Tours), Julio & Gabi Vega (Akwaterra), Alex Novoa (Esencia Nativa), César & Janne (*Hotel Anahuac*), Ron Brenneman (*Hotel Perkin Lenca*/ Amun Shea School). I couldn't have got around and seen so many amazing places without your help, not to mention your prompt response to all my pesky questions after returning home.

Shafik Meghji Muchas gracias to all the travellers and Ticos who helped out along the way. In addition, a special thank you must go out to: Keith Drew and Natasha Foges at Rough Guides in London; Randall and all the staff at *Pension Santa Elena*; Daryl and Isabella at *Casa Marbella* in Tortuguero; Ross Ballard, also in Tortuguero; Natalie Ewing of Costa Rica Expeditions; Jean, Nizar and Nina Meghji; and Sioned Jones for all her love and support.

James Smart Thanks to Natasha Foges, Mani Ramaswamy and the rest of the fine Rough Guides team, Mum n' Dad, Andreas Beer, Jessyca Molina, Paul Isherwood, Ian Ball, Brendon Griffin, Tim Abrahams, Juanita Boyd, Gerry at *Casa del Agua*, Kimmo Lehtonen, Nuria Dixon, Tomasz Gucio, Connor at Quetzal Trekkers, Mika Pols (seriously, careful with the snakes), the Thanksgiving crew, Paola's non-rabid dog, Flor de Caña and all the many other exceedingly helpful and charming tourists and Nicaraguans I met on the way. I promise to put those pictures up some time.

Iain Stewart Thanks to Inguat (especially Marlon Laz); Lorena, Hank and José in Guatemala City; Mike in Antigua; all the crew at the lake (Dave, Deedle, Anna, Phil and Roberta); Don David and Billy in El Remate; Lucas and Tom in Xela; the Zephyr boys in Lanquin and Rusty in Livingston.

Index

Map entries are in colour.

D

E

F

INDEX

W

X

Y

Z

T

U

V

Map symbols

maps are listed in the full index using coloured text

··——	International boundary		♦	Border crossing
·———	Chapter division boundary		♦	Place of interest
(CA-1)	Carretera Interamericana		⚘	Gardens
	Major road		⊙	Statue
	Minor road		★	Transport stop
====	Unpaved road		@	Internet access
	Pedestrianized street		ⓘ	Information centre
::::::	Steps		⊠	Post office
------	Path		©	Phone office
▬|▬	Railway		⊞	Hospital
— —	Ferry route		⛽	Fuel station
	River		♛	Castle
⌃⌃	Mountain range		◉	Accommodation
▲	Mountain peak		▣	Restaurant
/⋀\	Volcano		⚠	Campsite
⚘	Waterfall		🏑	Sports field
◠	Cave		◯	Stadium
⋎	Viewpoint		▬	Building
⚓	Ruin		⊞	Church
ⵀ	Lighthouse		▭	Market
✈	Airport		▨	Park
✗	Airstrip		�	Marshland/swamp
🏛	Monument		▨	Beach
♦	Museum		⊞	Cemetery

So now we've told you about the things not to miss, the best places to stay, the top restaurants, the liveliest bars and the most spectacular sights, it only seems fair to tell you about the best travel insurance around

WorldNomads.com
keep travelling safely

Recommended by Rough Guides